T0212065

Lecture Notes in Computer Science   11199

Commenced Publication in 1973
Founding and Former Series Editors:
Gerhard Goos, Juris Hartmanis, and Jan van Leeuwen

Linda Bushnell · Radha Poovendran
Tamer Başar (Eds.)

Decision and Game Theory for Security

9th International Conference, GameSec 2018
Seattle, WA, USA, October 29–31, 2018
Proceedings

Springer

Editors
Linda Bushnell (iD)
University of Washington
Seattle, WA
USA

Tamer Başar (iD)
University of Illinois at Urbana–Champaign
Urbana, IL
USA

Radha Poovendran (iD)
University of Washington
Seattle, WA
USA

ISSN 0302-9743   ISSN 1611-3349 (electronic)
Lecture Notes in Computer Science
ISBN 978-3-030-01553-4   ISBN 978-3-030-01554-1 (eBook)
https://doi.org/10.1007/978-3-030-01554-1

Library of Congress Control Number: 2018955975

LNCS Sublibrary: SL4 – Security and Cryptology

This Springer imprint is published by the registered company Springer Nature Switzerland AG
The registered company address is: Gewerbestrasse 11, 6330 Cham, Switzerland

Preface

Recent advances in information and communication technologies, and the incessantly tighter connectivity these advances have resulted in among the world's population and between humans and machines, pose significant security challenges that impact all aspects of modern society. Concerted efforts are being directed toward alleviating the underlying vulnerability, protecting heterogeneous, large-scale and dynamic systems, and managing security risks faced by critical infrastructures, through rigorous and practically relevant analytical methods. Decision and game theoretic framework is the centerpiece of these efforts, involving also several neighboring disciplines and techniques, such as distributed optimization, information theory and communication, statistics, economics, dynamic control, and mechanism design, toward an ultimate goal of building resilient, secure, and dependable networked systems, and also securing existing ones. Advancing the research landscape requires the establishment of a forum that brings together security researchers with different backgrounds, but with a common base of decision and game theory, to share their knowledge and exchange ideas. Driven by this need and goal, the Conference on Decision and Game Theory for Security (GameSec) was launched in 2010, to bring together academic, government, and industrial researchers in an effort to identify and discuss the major technical challenges and recent results that highlight the connections between decision and game theory, information and communication, control, distributed optimization, economic incentives and real-world security, reputation, trust and privacy problems. It has grown over the years and endured the test of time, with the latest event held in Seattle being the ninth one in the series.

Consistent with its goal from its inception, GameSec provides an international forum for researchers from academia, industry, and government to discuss various decision-theoretic approaches to security using the framework and tools of game theory. It features presentations on recent results in regular contributed sessions as well as poster sessions. It has special sessions focused on emerging topics of interest to the security community, as well as panel discussions. It also features plenary talks by distinguished researchers with outstanding contributions to the security field, who share their perspectives with the participants. As mentioned earlier, this conference series was inaugurated in 2010, with Berlin (Germany) being the first venue. It quickly became a well-established and well-recognized annual gathering of security researchers, with follow-up conferences held in College Park (Maryland, USA, 2011), Budapest (Hungary, 2012), Fort Worth (Texas, USA, 2013), Los Angeles (USA, 2014), London (UK, 2015), New York (USA, 2016), and Vienna (Austria, 2017). This year's event was held on the campus of the University of Washington, Seattle (Washington, USA, 2018) during October 29–31.

As in the previous years, GameSec in Seattle featured high-quality contributions from researchers across the globe, addressing theoretical as well as practical challenges faced by the security community, using the framework of game theory. Among the topical areas covered were: use of game theory, control theory, and mechanism design for security and privacy; decision-making for cybersecurity and security requirements engineering; security and privacy for the Internet of Things, cyber-physical systems, cloud computing, resilient control systems, and critical infrastructure; pricing, economic incentives, security investments, and cyber insurance for dependable and secure systems; risk assessment and security risk management; security and privacy of wireless and mobile communications, including user location privacy; socio-technological and behavioral approaches to security; deceptive technologies in cybersecurity and privacy; empirical and experimental studies with game, control, or optimization theory-based analysis for security and privacy; and adversarial machine learning and crowdsourcing, and the role of artificial intelligence in system security. The conference attracted 44 high-quality submissions, from which 28 full papers were selected for oral presentation, and eight short papers for poster presentation, as a result of a stringent review process that yielded at least three reviews on each submission. All accepted papers are included in these proceedings. In addition, the conference program featured a tutorial session on "Game Theory and Deception," organized by Quanyan Zhu (New York University, USA); a special session on "Adversarial AI" followed by a panel discussion, organized by Eugene Vorobeychik (Vanderbilt University, USA); and a panel session on "Real-World Uses of Game Theory for Security," organized by Milind Tambe (University of Southern California, USA). Two plenary talks were delivered, by John Baras (University of Maryland, USA) and Joao Hespanha (University of California, Santa Barbara, USA). We thank the special session and panel organizers and the plenary speakers for their outstanding contributions to the program. We thank also members of the Technical Program Committee and the Organizing Committee (who are listed in the Proceedings) for their diligence and hard work that contributed to the success of this year's GameSec.

Several organizations and government agencies provided support for this year's GameSec. We thank the Army Research Office (ARO), the Office of Naval Research (ONR), the National Research Foundation (NSF), Association for Computing Machinery (ACM), Springer *Lecture Notes in Computer Science* (LNCS), and the MDPI journal *Games* for their continuing support of the conference. ARO, ONR, NSF, and Springer LNCS provided student travel support, and *Games* sponsored the two best paper awards at the conference. Local arrangements were handled smoothly and competently by the University of Washington Electrical and Computer Engineering Events Team.

We hope that a broad group of constituents involved with and in security, from theoreticians to practitioners and policy makers, benefited from this record of state-of-the-art presentations at GameSec 2018.

October 2018

Linda Bushnell
Radha Poovendran
Tamer Başar

Organization

Steering Committee

Tansu Alpcan	University of Melbourne, Australia
John S. Baras	University of Maryland, USA
Tamer Başar	University of Illinois at Urbana–Champaign, USA
Anthony Ephremides	University of Maryland, USA
Milind Tambe	University of Southern California, USA

Organizers

General Chairs

Tamer Başar	University of Illinois at Urbana–Champaign, USA
Radha Poovendran	University of Washington, USA

TPC Chair

Linda Bushnell	University of Washington, USA

Special Track Chair

Eugene Vorobeychik	Vanderbilt University, USA

Tutorial Track Chair

Quanyan Zhu	New York University, USA

Local Arrangements Chair

Lillian Ratliff	University of Washington, USA

Publicity Chairs

Jun Moon	UNIST, South Korea
Dario Bauso	University of Sheffield, UK
Miroslav Pajic	Duke University, USA

Web Chair

Andrew Clark	Worcester Polytechnic Institute, USA

Program Committee

Habtamu Abie	Norsk Regnesentral - Norwegian Computing Center, Norway
Saurabh Amin	Massachusetts Institute of Technology, USA
Bo An	Nanyang Technological University, Singapore
Battista Biggio	University of Cagliari, Italy
Linda Bushnell (Chair)	University of Washington, USA
Alvaro Cardenas	UT Dallas, USA
Anil Kumar Chorppath	TU Dresden, Germany
Andrew Clark	Worcester Polytechnic Institute, USA
Mark Felegyhazi	Budapest University of Technology and Economics, Hungary
Rosario Gennaro	City University of New York, USA
Rica Gonen	Yahoo!, USA
Jens Grossklags	Technical University of Munich, Germany
Noam Hazon	Ariel University, Israel
Eduard Jorswieck	TU Dresden, Germany
Charles Kamhoua	US Army Research Laboratory, USA
Murat Kantarcioglu	University of Texas at Dallas, USA
Alex Kantchelian	University of California, Berkeley, USA
Christopher Kiekintveld	University of Texas at El Paso, USA
Aron Laszka	University of Houston, USA
Yee Wei Law	University of South Australia, Australia
Chang Liu	University of California, Berkeley, USA
Daniel Lowd	University of Oregon, USA
Patrick Mcdaniel	Pennsylvania State University, USA
Prasant Mohapatra	University of California, Davis, USA
Shana Moothedath	University of Washington, USA
Mehrdad Nojoumian	Florida Atlantic University, USA
Andrew Odlyzko	University of Minnesota, USA
Miroslav Pajic	Duke University, USA
Manos Panaousis	University of Surrey, UK
Nicolas Papernot	Pennsylvania State University, USA
David Pym	University College London, UK
Bhaskar Ramasubramanian	University of Washington, USA
Stefan Rass	Universität Klagenfurt, Germany
Sang Sagong	University of Washington, USA
Reza Shokri	National University of Singapore, Singapore
Arunesh Sinha	University of Michigan, USA
William Streilein	Massachusetts Institute of Technology, USA
George Theodorakopoulos	Cardiff University, UK
Long Tran-Thanh	University of Southampton, UK
Doug Tygar	University of California, Berkeley, USA

Yevgeniy Vorobeychik   Vanderbilt University, USA
Neal Wagner   Massachusetts Institute of Technology, USA
Haifeng Xu   University of Southern California, USA
Tao Zhang   New York University, USA
Zizhan Zheng   Tulane University, USA
Quanyan Zhu   New York University, USA
Jun Zhuang   SUNY Buffalo, USA

Additional Reviewers

Barreto, Carlos   Giraldo, Jairo   Shan, Xiaojun
Basak, Anjon   Gu, Tianbo   Song, Cen
Boudko, Svetlana   Gutierrez, Marcus   Spring, Jonathan M.
Caulfield, Tristan   Huang, Yunhan   Uttecht, Karen
Celik, Berkay   Matterer, Jason   Veliz, Oscar
Demontis, Ambra   Padilla, Edgar   Wachter, Jasmin
Elfar, Mahmoud   Peng, Guanze   Xu, Hong
Farhang, Sadegh   Qian, Yundi   Zeng, Yunze
Feng, Xiaotao   Roy, Abhishek

Sponsors

 Association for
Computing Machinery

an open access journal by

ELECTRICAL & COMPUTER ENGINEERING

UNIVERSITY *of* WASHINGTON

Contents

Impact of Privacy on Free Online Service Markets

Chong Huang$^{(\boxtimes)}$ and Lalitha Sankar

Arizona State University, Tempe, AZ 85281, USA
{chong.huang,lsankar}@asu.edu

Abstract. The emerging marketplace for online free services in which service providers (SPs) earn revenue from using consumer data in direct and indirect ways has led to significant privacy concerns. This begs understanding of the following question: can the marketplace sustain multiple SPs that offer privacy differentiated free services? This paper studies the impact of privacy on free online service markets by augmenting the classical Hotelling model for market segmentation analysis. A parametrized game-theoretic model is proposed which captures: (i) the fact that for the free service market, consumers value service not in monetized terms but by the quality of service (QoS); (ii) the differentiator of services is not product price but the privacy risk advertised by an SP; and (iii) consumer's heterogeneous privacy preference for SPs. For the two-SP problem with uniformly distributed consumer privacy preference and linear SP profit function, the results suggest that: (i) when consumers place a higher value on privacy, it leads to a larger market share for the SP providing untargeted services and a "softened" competition between SPs; (ii) SPs offering high privacy risk services are sustainable only if they offer sufficiently high QoS; and (iii) SPs that are capable of differentiating on services that do not directly use consumer data gain larger market share. Similar results are observed when the consumer's privacy preference is modeled as a truncated Gaussian distribution.

Keywords: Free online services · Privacy differentiated services
Quality of service · Market segmentation

1 Introduction

There has been a steady increase in online interactions between consumers and retailers, where the term retailer refers to entities who offer products for free (e.g., social media, search engines, free applications etc.). The advances in technology have enabled retailers (henceforth referred to as *service providers*) to collect, store, sell, and share customer-specific information that in turn can be used for targeted advertising and tiered pricing tactics. In fact, many oft used online services are free and consumers implicitly accede to tracking for customized services. Targeted ads are a part of the emerging revenue/profit model for service providers (SPs) offering free services. Consumers are delighted by free services

© Springer Nature Switzerland AG 2018
L. Bushnell et al. (Eds.): GameSec 2018, LNCS 11199, pp. 1–21, 2018.
https://doi.org/10.1007/978-3-030-01554-1_1

until they begin encountering privacy violations on a daily/frequent basis. While such infractions taken individually could be ignored or discounted, the totality of data available about consumers with a variety of retailers and the resulting privacy consequences raise serious concerns [1,2].

SPs are beginning to acknowledge that consumers are sensitive to privacy violations. For example, Google [3] and Apple [4] recently adopted differentially private mechanisms for collecting user data for statistical analyses. However, the details of these mechanisms are opaque and offer even less clarity on whether the consumer actually has a choice. In this context, it is worth understanding if privacy differentiated services can provide such choices for consumers. In a competitive marketplace, the aggregated weight of targeting may drive some consumers to seek more privacy-protective alternatives. The cost to the consumer of this action may be a lower quality of service (QoS) (e.g., poorer search engine capabilities). However, it could eventually lead to a more open model for sharing private information, i.e., one from implicit assent to informed consent [1].

To understand the influence of consumers' heterogeneous privacy preference on SPs' behavior in a competitive market, we take a game-theoretic approach to model the interactions between SPs and consumers. In particular, we address the following questions: (i) Can privacy-differentiated services lead to a sustainable marketplace? (ii) What are the equilibrium QoS-privacy risk strategies for the SPs? (iii) How do various consumer/SP parameters, such as consumers' privacy preference/valuation and SPs' profit/cost affect the equilibrium outcome?

1.1   Related Work

Targeted advertising is a common method for service providers to exploit knowledge of consumers; this in turn can lead to privacy violations. Our work is informed by the literature on targeting strategies for retailers [5–14], but rather than optimizing retailer strategies, we are interested in identifying how privacy differentiated services can address privacy concerns.

The problem of market segmentation is a classic and well-studied problem in microeconomics with focus on how pricing and product differentiation can lead to a stable and competitive marketplace. A nuanced model that captures differentiation between two firms and consumer preferences is the Hotelling model [15]. It has been widely used for market analysis across many fields such as electrical vehicle market [16] and Internet market [17]. However, the free online service market presents a new challenge wherein monetary quantification of both 'free' services and the data collected about consumers is not simple and straightforward. Equally challenging is the quantification of consumer privacy since it requires capturing the heterogeneous expressions of privacy sensitivity that can range from 'don't care' at one extreme to 'hyper vigilant' at the other.

An extensive body of literature on economic models for privacy was reviewed by Acquisti et al. [18]. Jentzsch et al. [19] propose a model to study competitions between two SPs by taking consumer's privacy preference (low privacy/high privacy) into account using a vertical Hotelling model. Consumers select the service provider based on their privacy concerns and the amount of payment to the SP.

Lee *et al.* [20] study the influence of privacy protection on the segmentation of a duopoly. In their model, firms may offer standard and personalized products with personalized prices to three different types of privacy-sensitive consumers. In contrast to both above-mentioned models, our model focuses on 'free' services, and thus, introduces new models for quantifying QoS- and privacy-based differentiators. Furthermore, our model generalizes the discrete set of privacy sensitive consumers in [20] to a continuous set of privacy risks, thus allowing analysis over an entire range of privacy expression and a more nuanced view of how SPs should offer services to all types of consumers.

1.2   Our Contributions

We propose a novel model for the privacy differentiated market segmentation problem in which service providers offer free services differentiated by QoS and privacy risk. Our model captures a variety of free online services such as search engines, social networking sites, and software apps that are free, and therefore, use consumer data in a variety of ways for revenue generation. Each SP's gain from using consumer data is captured by a revenue function and its cost of doing so is captured by a cost function. The goal of each SP is to choose a QoS and privacy risk tuple that maximizes its profit (difference of revenue and cost). We assume that consumers can map their heterogeneous privacy sensitivity to a quantitative scale. The SPs use this quantitative scale to differentiate themselves. Each consumer chooses the SP that maximizes a desired function of its privacy risk valuation and the QoS-privacy risk tuple offered by the SP.

Our model is built upon the classical 'spatial' Hotelling model for market segmentation wherein the location is now proxy for privacy risk (that both SPs offer and consumers prefer). The QoS offered by the SP models the product price in the Hotelling model. In contrast to the classical Hotelling model in which there is a non-negative transportation cost irrespective of the locations of consumer and retailer, here consumers will always benefit from SPs that offer lower privacy risk than what they prefer. Thus, there is an asymmetry in the transportation cost. We model the interactions between SPs and consumers as a three-stage sequential game and compute the equilibrium QoS-privacy risk tuple as well as consumers' choices using backward induction. We also compute the resulting market share and profit for specific models of cost and revenue (to SPs), distribution of consumer heterogeneous privacy choices, as well as consumer privacy valuation. We show that there is no equilibrium in which both SPs offer the same privacy risk for the two-SP market with linear valuation function (cost, revenue, consumer utility). Furthermore, we study the equilibrium behavior of both SPs and consumers under different privacy preference models.

2   Problem Model and Game Formulation

Formally, we introduce a game-theoretic model for two SPs and infinitely many consumers. Each SP offers the same type of free services (e.g., search engine, social network) with a quantified privacy risk guarantee ε and QoS v. Just as Google at present advertises RAPPOR with a certain level of differential privacy risk, in the future, it is possible that SPs will adopt one or more metrics to quantify their privacy risks. This paper makes such an assumption of privacy risk quantifiability. Furthermore, we assume SPs advertise their quantified privacy risk and QoS to consumers. Thus, both ε and v are observable to consumers. The observable privacy risk value could be the ε value in differential privacy adopted by Google RAPPOR and the QoS could be the accuracy of search results. An SP differentiates its service by a tuple (v, ε) that it advertises to all consumers. A consumer's preference of privacy differentiated service is modeled by a utility function which depends on its privacy risk valuation and the QoS-privacy risk tuple offered by the SP. In reality, it is natural to assume that consumers prefer high QoS and low privacy risk. Thus, in our model, a consumer will have a higher utility if he or she receives higher QoS or lower privacy risk. Finally, consumer privacy heterogeneity is modeled as a distribution.

2.1 Two-SP Market Model

SP Model. We consider two rational (i.e., profit maximization entities) SPs, denoted by SP_1 and SP_2. Both SPs provide the same kind of free service; but they differ in the QoS offered. Since we focus on free online service market, it is very difficult to use a monetized quantity to quantify these services. Therefore, we use QoS rather than price to quantify the consumers' gains from using the services. Thus, SP_1 and SP_2 offer QoS v_1 and v_2, respectively, where in general $v_1 \neq v_2$. Furthermore, SP_1 and SP_2 guarantee that the privacy risk for using their services is at most ε_1 and ε_2, respectively, where $\varepsilon_1, \varepsilon_2 \in [0, \bar{\varepsilon}]$. Without loss of generality, we assume $\varepsilon_2 \geq \varepsilon_1$. Under these assumptions, SP_2 must offer a higher QoS ($v_2 \geq v_1$). Otherwise, its strategy will be dominated by its opponent since SP_1 will offer both higher QoS and lower privacy risk. For example, SP_1 and SP_2 could be Duckduckgo and Google, respectively, in the search engine market, with the QoS given by the accuracy of search results. On the other hand, the privacy risk can correspond to different guarantees they provide on consumer data use; e.g., whether they will use consumer data only for statistical purposes or target consumers with tailored ads. We model this privacy risk guarantee as a variable taking values over a continuous range. In practice, such guarantees may be coarse granular choices; for example, between completely opting out of the targeting or allowing data use only for statistical purposes or complete data use only by SP or all possible data usage and sale. We assume that the SPs generate revenue in two ways: (i) by exploiting the private data of consumers to offer *targeted* ads and other services to consumers; and (ii) by providing interested advertisers an online platform to reach consumers. This latter revenue is independent of private data and simply derived from the revenue capability of the platform.

Let $R_P(\varepsilon_i)$ and $R_{\text{NP},i}$ denote the per consumer revenue of SP_i generated from using the private data and without using consumers' private information, respectively. The total per consumer revenue, $R(\varepsilon_i)$ is thus

$$R(\varepsilon_i) = R_P(\varepsilon_i) + R_{\text{NP},i}, i \in \{1,2\}. \tag{1}$$

Notice that in reality, through spillovers and externalities associated with using consumers' private data, the revenue generating capabilities for SPs can increase even from sources that don't directly use consumer personal information. However, it is very hard to capture these externalities precisely since they are highly data and service model dependent. We start with a simple model in which we assume that SPs will not use consumers' private data for services that do not require private data. Our proposed model provides an intuition on the equilibrium strategies of SPs and market. Furthermore, it is useful to note that even this relatively simple revenue decoupled setting is highly parameterized. Our analysis allows us to understand the dependencies on various parameters.

Offering free services to consumers often comes with a cost to the SPs, such as the cost of service, online platform creation, and continued operations. Furthermore, we note that free online services profit from using consumer data and therefore incur data processing related costs. Let $C(v_i; \varepsilon_i)$ denote the per consumer cost of offering free services. We model $C(v_i; \varepsilon_i)$ as sum of two non-negative costs: (i) $C_{\text{QoS}}(v_i)$ of providing services with QoS v_i; and (ii) $C_P(\varepsilon_i)$ as the processing (data analytics) cost of using data with privacy risk ε_i such that

$$C(v_i; \varepsilon_i) = C_{\text{QoS}}(v_i) + C_P(\varepsilon_i), i \in \{1,2\}. \tag{2}$$

We assume $R_P(\varepsilon_i) > C_P(\varepsilon_i)$. Otherwise, SP_i will not exploit consumers' private information since the cost exceeds revenue from using private information.

Consumer Model. We formulate the consumer-SP game based on the classical Hotelling model. The Hotelling model maps retailers to two locations (x_1, x_2) on a $[0,1]$ line such that the strategy of each retailer is to determine the best location-price tuple that maximizes its profit. The location (see Fig. 1a) is a proxy for a specific product differentiator. A consumer with its own product differentiator preference (traditionally assumed to be uniformly distributed over $[0,1]$) is mapped to a location $x \in [0,1]$ on the line as shown in Fig. 1a. Such a spatial model allows computing the market segment by identifying both the optimal locations of the retailers and an indifferent threshold between the two optimal retailer locations at which both retailers are equally desirable. For such a uniform consumer preference model, the segmentation for each retailer is simply its distance to the indifference point. Consumers choose the retailer with the least product price and "transportation cost" (a linear function of location) for a desired consumer valuation of the product. Note that transportation costs are metaphorical for any non-price-based differentiation of the two retailers.

For our problem, we obtain a Hotelling model by: (i) introducing a *normalized privacy risk* and mapping it to spatial location; and (ii) by viewing the QoS as the net valuation of service by the consumer. Note that since we study a free services market, we use QoS as a measure of consumer satisfaction. We note that in the classical Hotelling model, the consumer pays a non-negative transportation cost for any retailer whose location is different from its own. However, our problem departs from this model in that higher and lower privacy risks offered by SPs relative to a consumer preferred privacy risk choice are not viewed similarly.

We assume there exists infinitely many rational consumers that are interested in the services provided by the SPs. In keeping the standard game-theoretic definition, rational refers to consumers interested in maximizing some measure of utility via interactions with the SPs. We use a random variable $E \in [0, \bar{\varepsilon}]$ to denote the heterogeneous privacy preferences of consumers; such a model assumes that the privacy preferences of consumers are independent and identically distributed, a reasonable assumption when the consumer set is very large. Let $E = \varepsilon$ denote the privacy risk preference of a consumer. If SP_i offers a privacy risk guarantee ε_i higher than ε, then using its service will result in a privacy cost to the consumer due to perceived privacy risk violation. On the other hand, the consumer gains from choosing an SP_i that offers an $\varepsilon_i < \varepsilon$ as a result of the extra privacy protection offered. Let $x = F_E(\varepsilon) \in [0,1]$ be a differentiable cumulative distribution function of ε. Thus, x can be considered as a normalized privacy risk tolerance (i.e., restricted to $[0,1]$) which indicates the proportion of the consumers with a privacy risk preference of at most ε. Since ε can be over an arbitrary range $[0, \bar{\varepsilon}]$, the normalized spatial privacy risk is given by the cumulative distribution function (CDF) $F_E(\varepsilon)$. We can similarly map the privacy risks offered by the SPs to *normalized locations* $x_1 = F_E(\varepsilon_1)$ and $x_2 = F_E(\varepsilon_2)$ on the $[0,1]$ line as shown in Fig. 1b.

Analogous to the Hotelling model, we let $u_i(x)$ denote the utility (in units of QoS) from SP_i as perceived by a consumer with a normalized privacy preference (location) x. Our model for $u_i(x)$ contains two parts: (i) a positive QoS v_i offered by SP_i; and (ii) the gain or loss in the perceived QoS as a result of a mismatch between consumer privacy preference and SP_i's privacy risk offering. We introduce a gain factor t that allows mapping the privacy mismatch $t(x - x_i)\varepsilon_i$ to a QoS quantity. This mismatch utility indicates that when the SP offers a service with privacy risk lower than the consumer's tolerance, the consumer receives a positive utility due to extra privacy protection. However, if the service offered has a higher privacy risk than the consumer's tolerance, the consumer will receive negative utility for privacy risk violation.

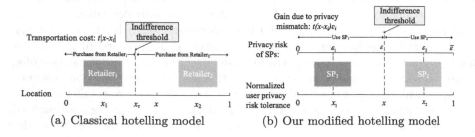

(a) Classical hotelling model   (b) Our modified hotelling model

Fig. 1. User choice model for using different SPs

Consumer Utility and SP Profits. For the consumer located at x, the overall perceived utility for choosing services provided by SP_1 and SP_2 are

$$u_i(x) = v_i + t(x - x_i)\varepsilon_i, i \in \{1,2\}. \tag{3}$$

For each $SP_i, i \in \{1,2\}$, let $(v_{-i}, \varepsilon_{-i})$ be its competitor's strategy. For the revenue and cost models in (1) and (2), the profit of SP_i is simply the difference

$$\pi_i(v_i; \varepsilon_i; v_{-i}; \varepsilon_{-i}) = [R(\varepsilon_i) - C(v_i; \varepsilon_i)]n_i(v_i; \varepsilon_i; v_{-i}; \varepsilon_{-i}), \tag{4}$$

where $n_i(v_i; \varepsilon_i; v_{-i}; \varepsilon_{-i})$ denotes the fraction of consumers who choose SP_i.

Modelling Assumption 1. *We assume that the services provided by both SPs have non-negative QoS.*

Since consumers are rational, they expect to have positive utility through the interactions with the SPs. It is reasonable to assume that SPs have no incentive to offer services with a negative QoS (i.e., $v_1 \geq 0$ and $v_2 \geq 0$).

Modelling Assumption 2. *We assume the model parameters are chosen such that they ensure the market is completely covered by SP_1 and SP_2.*

Assumption 2 implies that each consumer must choose one of the SPs. Such an assumption is implicitly built into the classical Hotelling model to ensure competition between SPs and we continue to do so. Later we provide a sufficient condition for sustaining the competitive market under these assumptions.

2.2   Two-SP Non-cooperative Game Formulation

We note that the SPs compete against each other through their distinct QoS and privacy risk offerings, which in turn affects consumer choices and helps determine the stable market segmentation. Thus, the interactions between SPs can be formulated as a non-cooperative game in which the strategy of each SP is a (QoS, privacy risk) tuple and that of the consumer is choosing an SP. Furthermore, we assume that the SPs are rational and have perfect and complete information. They play to maximize their own profits and know the exact profit function and their competitors' strategies.

   The Game: the interactions between retailers and consumers in the Hotelling model can be viewed as a sequential game [15]. For our model, such a sequential game involves three stages. In the first stage, the differentiator, i.e., the normalized privacy risk ε_i, is advertised by SP_i. This is followed by each SP determining its QoS for the advertised risk. Finally, the consumers choose the preferred SP based on the (v_i, ε_i) tuple that maximizes its utility. Our sequential game assumes that the selection of privacy risk happens before the selection of the QoS. This is due to the fact that SPs first advertise their privacy risks to differentiate themselves from their competitors (e.g., Google advertises RAPPOR while Duckduckgo advertises not using private data of the consumers) and then adjust their QoS strategies. Since the profit function of an SP is dependent on the privacy risk and QoS of itself and its competitor, for fixed privacy risk strategies, the best response QoS strategy of an SP is affected by the privacy risk strategies as well as consumers' preferences.

The game can be formally described as follows: (i) a set of players $\{1, 2, \mathcal{C}\}$, where 1 and 2 denote SP_1 and SP_2, respectively, and the set $\mathcal{C}$ contains infinitely many consumers; (ii) a collection of strategy tuples $(v_i, \varepsilon_i) \in \mathcal{V}_i \times \mathcal{E}_i$ for SP_i and a collection of binary choices (strategies) for the consumer $b \in \mathcal{B} = \{1, 2\}$; and (iii) a profit function π_i for each SP_i and a utility function u_i for each consumer for choosing SP_i.

3   Subgame Perfect Nash Equilibrium for Two-SP Game

In a sequential game, each stage is referred to as a subgame [21]. One often associates a strategy profile with a sequential game. A strategy profile is a vector whose i^{th} entry is the strategy for all players at the ith stage of the sequential game. A non-cooperative sequential game has one well-studied solution: the Subgame Perfect Nash Equilibrium (SPNE). A strategy profile is an SPNE if its entries are the Nash equilibria of the subgame resulting at each stage of the sequential game. The SPNE of a sequential game captures an equilibrium solution such that no player can make more profit by unilaterally deviating from this strategy in every subgame. Since the two-SP game has finite number of stages and perfect information, it can be solved by backward induction:

Stage 3, Users' Decisions: Each consumer located at $x \in [0, 1]$ can choose the services provided by either SPs based on its valuation function in (3). The resulting optimal strategy for the consumer is to choose the SP whose index is

$$arg \max_{i \in \{1,2\}} v_i + t(x - x_i)\varepsilon_i. \tag{5}$$

Since the consumer's utility is a linear function of the normalized privacy risk x and the market is completely covered by the SPs, there exists a threshold x_τ such that the consumer located at x_τ is indifferent to using services provided by SP_1 or SP_2. Thus, at the indifference threshold x_τ, we have

$$u_2(x_\tau) = u_1(x_\tau) \implies x_\tau = \frac{v_1 - v_2 + t(F_E(\varepsilon_2)\varepsilon_2 - F_E(\varepsilon_1)\varepsilon_1)}{t(\varepsilon_2 - \varepsilon_1)}, \tag{6}$$

where x_1 and x_2 have been replaced by their corresponding normalized privacy risk values. Thus, given the SPs' strategies $(v_i, \varepsilon_i), i \in \{1, 2\}$, the optimal strategy of a consumer located at x is to use the service of SP_1 if $x \leq x_\tau$ and SP_2 otherwise. If $v_1 = v_2$ and $\varepsilon_1 = \varepsilon_2$, consumers are indifferent between SP_1 and SP_2. In this case, we assume the consumers use the following tie-breaking rule:

Modelling Assumption 3. *If $v_1 = v_2$ and $\varepsilon_1 = \varepsilon_2$, consumers choose either SPs with probability $\frac{1}{2}$.*

Stage 2, SPs Determine QoS: For a given privacy risk guarantee ε_i, SP_i chooses its QoS v_i to maximize its profit π_i. Since a consumer's normalized privacy risk tolerance denotes the fraction of the population whose privacy risk tolerance is at most ε, x_τ determines the proportion of consumers who choose SP_1, i.e., n_1. As a result, the profit functions of SP_1 and SP_2 can be written as

$$\pi_1(v_1; \varepsilon_1; v_2; \varepsilon_2) = [R(\varepsilon_1) - C(v_1; \varepsilon_1)]x_\tau, \tag{7}$$

$$\pi_2(v_1; \varepsilon_1; v_2; \varepsilon_2) = [R(\varepsilon_2) - C(v_2; \varepsilon_2)](1 - x_\tau). \tag{8}$$

To find the SPNE in this stage, we use the best response method [21]. The best response is a function which captures the behavior of each player while fixing the strategies of the other players. For any $v_{-i} \in \mathcal{V}_{-i}$, we define $BR_i(v_{-i})$ as the best strategy of SP_i such that

$$BR_i(v_{-i}) = arg\max_{v_i} \pi_i(v_i; \varepsilon_i; v_{-i}; \varepsilon_{-i}), i \in \{1, 2\}. \tag{9}$$

In the SPNE, each player plays the best response strategy. Thus, a Nash equilibrium in this stage is a profile $\boldsymbol{v}^* = (v_i^*, v_{-i}^*)$ for which $v_i^* \in BR_i(v_{-i}^*), \forall i \in \{1, 2\}$. For a given set of privacy risk guarantees $\{\varepsilon_1, \varepsilon_2\}$, the optimal QoS v_i^* of $SP_i, i \in \{1, 2\}$ in the SPNE is

$$v_i^* = arg\max_{v_i} \pi_i(v_1; \varepsilon_1; v_2; \varepsilon_2), i \in \{1, 2\}. \tag{10}$$

Stage 1, SPs Determine Privacy Risk Guarantee: In the first stage, we compute equilibrium strategies ε_1 and ε_2 that the two SPs should advertise for optimal market share. Note that v_1^*, v_2^*, and x_τ have been computed in stages 2 and 3 for a fixed ε_1 and ε_2, this implies the equilibrium strategy ε_1^* and ε_2^* can be obtained using the best response method.

4   Two-SP Market with Linear Cost and Revenue Models

Thus far, we have considered a general model for SPs. To obtain better intuition and meaningful analytical solutions, we consider linear cost and revenue models for SPs. The per consumer cost function of SP_i is

$$C(v_i; \varepsilon_i) = cv_i + c\lambda\varepsilon_i, i \in \{1, 2\}, \tag{11}$$

where c and λ are constant scale factors in units of cost/QoS and QoS/privacy risk, respectively. We model the per consumer revenue of each SP from offering a privacy guaranteed service by a linear function

$$R(\varepsilon_i) = r\varepsilon_i + p_i, i \in \{1, 2\}, \tag{12}$$

where r is the revenue per unit privacy risk for using consumers' private data. The parameters p_1 and p_2 model the fixed revenues of the SPs that are independent of consumers' private data.

Theorem 1. *There is no SPNE in which both SPs offer the same privacy risk.*

Proof sketch: The detailed proof of Theorem 1 is in Appendix A; we briefly outline the proof. First, we assume there exists an SPNE where both SPs offer the same privacy risk $\tilde{\varepsilon}$. Using backward induction, we show that one of the SPs is better off by unilaterally deviating from the equilibrium strategy $\tilde{\varepsilon}$; implying that there is no SPNE in which both SPs offer the same privacy risk.

Remark: Note that the result of Theorem 1 does not exhibit the minimal differentiation behavior (i.e., both firms place themselves close to each other) observed in [15]. This is due to the fact that higher and lower privacy risks offered by SPs relative to a consumer preferred privacy risk choice are not viewed similarly; that is, the symmetric transportation cost no longer holds in our model, and thus resulting an asymmetric gain due to privacy mismatch in (3).

4.1   Uniform Consumer Privacy Risk Tolerance

We assume consumers have uniformly distributed privacy risk tolerance between 0 and $\bar{\varepsilon}$ [22]. The resulting normalized privacy risk of each SP is given by $x_i = F_E(\varepsilon_i) = \frac{\varepsilon_i}{\bar{\varepsilon}}, i \in \{1, 2\}$. We define

$$\alpha = \frac{r}{c} - \lambda, \quad \tilde{C} = ct\bar{\varepsilon}. \tag{13}$$

Note that α is the ratio of net profit from using consumer data for a unit of privacy risk to the cost for providing a unit of QoS. Furthermore, $\tilde{C}$ is the cost of providing non-zero utility to the consumer with a maximal mismatch of privacy risk (relative to SP). By using backward induction, the computed SPNE of the two-SP non-cooperative game is presented in the following theorem.

Theorem 2. *There exists an SPNE given by*

$$\varepsilon_2^* = \frac{12\bar{\varepsilon}c\alpha + 15ct\bar{\varepsilon} - 16(p_2 - p_1)}{24tc}, \tag{14}$$

$$v_2^* = \frac{(2\alpha + t)c\alpha 6\bar{\varepsilon} + (\alpha - t)9ct\bar{\varepsilon} + (t - 2\alpha)8p_2 + (\alpha + t)16p_1}{24ct}, \tag{15}$$

$$\varepsilon_1^* = \varepsilon_2^* - \frac{3\bar{\varepsilon}}{4}, \tag{16}$$

$$v_1^* = v_2^* - \frac{3\bar{\varepsilon}}{4}\alpha + \frac{p_2 - p_1}{3c}, \tag{17}$$

if the model parameters $\{c, r, \lambda, t, \bar{\varepsilon}, p_1, p_2\}$ satisfy

$$-1 \leq \frac{16(p_2 - p_1)}{9ct\bar{\varepsilon}} \leq 1, \tag{18}$$

$$\frac{4\alpha - 3t}{3} \leq \frac{16(p_2 - p_1)}{9c\bar{\varepsilon}} \leq \frac{4\alpha - t}{3}, \tag{19}$$

$$(12(r - c\lambda)\bar{\varepsilon})^2 - (15ct\bar{\varepsilon})^2 + 288ct\bar{\varepsilon}(p_2 + p_1) \geq [16(p_2 - p_1)]^2. \tag{20}$$

At this SPNE, the market segmentation and the total profits of both SPs are

$$x_\tau^* = \frac{1}{2} - \frac{8(p_2 - p_1)}{9ct\bar{\varepsilon}} = \frac{1}{2} - \frac{8(p_2 - p_1)}{9\tilde{C}}, \tag{21}$$

$$\pi_1^* = \frac{4c}{27t\bar{\varepsilon}}\left(\frac{9t\bar{\varepsilon}}{8} - \frac{2(p_2 - p_1)}{c}\right)^2 = \frac{1}{3}\left(\frac{3}{4}\sqrt{\tilde{C}} - \frac{4(p_2 - p_1)}{3\sqrt{\tilde{C}}}\right)^2 \tag{22}$$

$$\pi_2^* = \frac{4c}{27t\bar{\varepsilon}}\left(\frac{9t\bar{\varepsilon}}{8} + \frac{2(p_2 - p_1)}{c}\right)^2 = \frac{1}{3}\left(\frac{3}{4}\sqrt{\tilde{C}} + \frac{4(p_2 - p_1)}{3\sqrt{\tilde{C}}}\right)^2, \tag{23}$$

where α and $\tilde{C}$ are defined in (13).

Proof sketch: The proof of Theorem 2 is provided in Appendix B. We briefly sketch the proof details here. Our approach involves using a three-stage backward induction to compute equilibrium strategies starting from the third stage; at each stage, the equilibrium strategies are computed using those computed from future stages. In the third stage, for a fixed pair of strategies of each SP, the consumer makes the choice, this in turn helps determining the indifference threshold x_τ. This x_τ is now used in the second stage to compute the equilibrium QoS (v_1^*, v_2^*) for a fixed set of risk $(\varepsilon_1, \varepsilon_2)$. Finally, the first stage involves computing the equilibrium privacy risk for these choice of v_1^*, v_2^* and x_τ by solving the corresponding best response functions, thereby obtaining the solutions in (14)–(17). The conditions in (18)–(20) result from requiring the equilibrium strategies as well as the equilibrium market segmentation to satisfy the following: (i) feasible threshold: $0 \leq x_\tau^* \leq 1$; (ii) feasible risk: $0 \leq \varepsilon_1^*, \varepsilon_2^* \leq \bar{\varepsilon}$; (iii) non-zero consumer utility: $v_1^* - tx_1^*\varepsilon_1^* \geq 0$ or $v_2^* - tx_2^*\varepsilon_2^* \geq 0$.

Remark: Note that the equilibrium in (14)–(17) is highly parametrized. For a given set of parameters that satisfy conditions in (18)–(20), the sequential game yields an SPNE. By (21), the SP with higher privacy-independent revenue owns a larger market share, leading to a higher total profit in the SPNE (see (22) and (23)). Note that p_1 and p_2 are the only differentiator of SPs in the set of model parameters. For a fixed $p_2 - p_1$, both π_1^* and π_2^* are decreasing functions of $\tilde{C}$ when $\tilde{C} \in [0, \frac{16|p_2 - p_1|}{9}]$ and increasing afterwards. On the other hand, (18) implies $\tilde{C} \geq \frac{16|p_2 - p_1|}{9}$. Thus, both π_1^* and π_2^* are increasing functions of $\tilde{C}$ in the SPNE. In the following, we highlight the effect of each one of these model parameters on the SPNE while keeping all other parameters fixed.

1. *Heterogeneity of consumer privacy preferences* ($\bar{\varepsilon}$): for the SPNE presented in Theorem 2, observe that v_i^* and $\varepsilon_i^*, i \in \{1, 2\}$ are linear functions of $\bar{\varepsilon}$. Furthermore, $\varepsilon_2^* = \varepsilon_1^* + \frac{3}{4}\bar{\varepsilon}$; this implies that at the SPNE, the SP that offers the higher privacy risk (i.e., ε_2^*) offers exactly $\frac{3}{4}\bar{\varepsilon}$ higher than that of its competitor. For all other parameters fixed, as $\bar{\varepsilon}$ increases, SP_2's privacy risk increases linearly. On the other hand, SP_1's privacy risk increases linearly with $\bar{\varepsilon}$ only if the model parameters are such that $4(r - c\lambda) > ct$; otherwise, it decreases linearly (see (14) and (16)). To further understand the dependency, we consider the following two cases:

- If $p_2 - p_1 > 0$, as $\bar{\varepsilon}$ increases, SP_2 can increase its revenue by increasing its privacy risk offerings. As a result, more consumers who have low privacy risk preferences will choose SP_1. Therefore, the market share of SP_2 decreases. However, the profits of both SPs increases as $\bar{\varepsilon}$ increases. The intuition is that both SPs can exploit consumers' private information from a larger range of privacy risk preferences. As a result, their revenue from exploiting consumers' private information also increases, which in turn leads to an increase in both SPs' profits.
- If $p_2 - p_1 < 0$, as $\bar{\varepsilon}$ increases, SP_2 increases its advertised privacy risk to exploit more private information from consumer. Despite this, the market share of SP_2 increases with $\bar{\varepsilon}$. This is because as $\bar{\varepsilon}$ increases, SP_2 provides a higher utility than SP_1 to some consumers who prefer SP_1 before. Furthermore, each SP's profit increases as $\bar{\varepsilon}$ increases.

2. *Operation cost* (c): when c increases, by (21), the SP with lower privacy-independent revenue benefits since its market share increases. Observe from (14) and (15) that if $p_2 - p_1 > 0$, both SPs increase their privacy risk strategies in the SPNE as c increases. They do so because SPs can use consumers' private information to increase its privacy dependent revenue, thereby offsetting their cost. Otherwise, they decrease their privacy risks. As a result of these strategies, when c increases, both SPs' profits also increase.

3. *Privacy independent revenue* (p_1, p_2): as the difference in the privacy independent revenues $(p_2 - p_1)$ increases, both SPs offer lower privacy risks to attract consumers. From (21)–(23) and condition (18), we see that as $p_2 - p_1$ increases, the market share and profit of SP_1 decreases while SP_2's market share and profit increases. This is because a larger difference in the revenue independent of consumer's private data gives SP_2 more market power in the competition. As a result, SP_2's profit increases while SP_1's profit decreases.

4. *Consumer privacy valuation or skittishness* (t): when t increases, by (14)–(17), we have $\varepsilon_1^* = \frac{12\bar{\varepsilon}c\alpha - 16(p_2 - p_1)}{24tc} - \frac{1}{8}\bar{\varepsilon} \geq 0$. Therefore, both SPs decrease their privacy risks as t increases. Furthermore, by (21), the SP with lower privacy-independent revenue benefits since its market share increases. For this linear model, as t increases, both SPs decrease their privacy risks. This results in a decrease in the cost and revenue of both SPs but cost decreases more than revenue, thereby leading to a profit for both SPs. In other words, a higher privacy valuation from consumers "softens" the competition.

4.2   Truncated Gaussian Consumer Privacy Risk Tolerance

In this section, we model a consumer's privacy tolerance as a random variable E that follows a Gaussian distribution $\mathcal{N}(\frac{\bar{\varepsilon}}{2}, \sigma^2)$ with a mean of $\frac{\bar{\varepsilon}}{2}$ and a standard deviation of σ. Since $E \in [0, \bar{\varepsilon}]$, we restrict the Gaussian distribution to lie within the interval $[0, \bar{\varepsilon}]$. Thus, E follows a truncated Gaussian distribution with CDF

$$F_E(\varepsilon) = \begin{cases} \frac{\Phi(\frac{\varepsilon - \frac{\bar{\varepsilon}}{2}}{\sigma}) - \Phi(-\frac{\bar{\varepsilon}}{2\sigma})}{\Phi(\frac{\bar{\varepsilon}}{2\sigma}) - \Phi(-\frac{\bar{\varepsilon}}{2\sigma})} & \varepsilon \in [0, \bar{\varepsilon}] \\ 0 & \varepsilon \in [-\infty, 0] \\ 1 & \varepsilon \in [\bar{\varepsilon}, +\infty] \end{cases}, \tag{24}$$

where $\Phi(y)$ denotes the CDF of the standard Gaussian distribution.

In contrast to the uniform distribution case, the CDF in (24) is not amenable to a closed form solution. Thus, we characterize the equilibrium numerically. To find the SPNE, we first compute the SPNE QoS in the second stage as functions of privacy risk guarantees by solving (10). Then, we use an iterated best response method to find the optimal privacy risk guarantee of an SP by fixing its competitor's strategy in each iteration. When the process converges, we have found an SPNE.

4.3   Illustration of Results

In this section, we illustrate our model and results. First, we assume consumers have uniformly distributed privacy risk tolerance. We plot each SP's SPNE strategy, market share, and total profit with respect to consumers' maximum privacy risk tolerance $\bar{\varepsilon}$ for different values of consumer privacy risk valuation t. Later, we study the model in which consumers' privacy risk tolerance follows a Gaussian distribution $\mathcal{N}(\frac{\bar{\varepsilon}}{2}, 1)$ truncated between 0 and $\bar{\varepsilon}$. The model parameters are given as follows:

Table 1. Numerical example model parameters

Parameter	c	λ	r	p_1	p_2
Value	0.5	0.75	0.7	0.4	0.8

Uniform Consumer Privacy Risk Tolerance. In this section, we vary $\bar{\varepsilon}$ from 3 to 5 to study properties of SPNE. Our choice of values in Table 1 is one set of parameters for which we can determine a meaningful range of t values. However, there exists many such combinations of parameter values. Note that by (18)–(20) in Theorem 2, t must belong to $[0.58, 0.85]$ when other parameters are given in Table 1 for sustaining the SPNE. In Fig. 2, the equilibrium strategies of different SPs are plotted. As $\bar{\varepsilon}$ increases, both SPs increase their privacy risk offerings. Furthermore, it can be seen that as t, the valuation of privacy by consumer, decreases, each SP increases its privacy risk to generate more profit from using private data. Correspondingly, the SPs will have to provide higher QoS to attract consumers. On the other hand, if t increases, both SPs reduce their privacy risks to avoid violating consumers' privacy.

It is worth noting that for the special case of $t = 0.7$, we observe that SP_1 caters to smaller set of privacy sensitive consumers. The reason for this is as follows: indeed, one generally expects SP_1 to offer a larger privacy risk as $\bar{\varepsilon}$ increases. However, for a large enough privacy valuation (in this case $t = 0.7$), since consumers highly value privacy, the cost of offering a high QoS proportionally increases for SP_1. The resulting profit is insufficient to justify the cost.

The market shares of different SPs in the SPNE are presented in Fig. 5a. We observe that the equilibrium market share of SP_2 decreases as t increases.

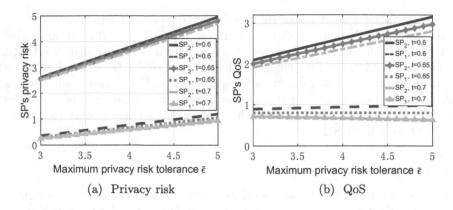

(a) Privacy risk   (b) QoS

Fig. 2. SPNE strategies of SPs under uniform consumer privacy risk

The intuition is that if t increases, the consumer's valuation of privacy mismatch also increases. Thus, it is more difficult for SP_2 to attract consumers with privacy tolerance lower than ε_2. As a result, its market share decreases. Notice that in Fig. 5a, as $\bar{\varepsilon}$ decreases, the equilibrium market share of SP_2 increases. This is because consumers experience a lower negative utility from the mismatch when $\bar{\varepsilon}$ is smaller (the utility from mismatch is $t(x - x_i)\varepsilon_i$). As a result, more consumers will choose the SP with a higher privacy risk to enjoy a higher QoS.

In Fig. 3, we plot the total profit at the SPNE for each SP as a function of the maximum consumer privacy risk tolerance $\bar{\varepsilon}$ for different values of t. The total profit of both SPs at SPNE increases as $\bar{\varepsilon}$ increases. This is because a larger $\bar{\varepsilon}$ indicates a larger range of consumer preferences, and then, more possibilities for the SPs to exploit private information. Thus, both SPs can benefit from using private data of consumers that have a higher privacy risk tolerance. As t increases, both SPs decrease their privacy risks. As a result, the cost and revenue of both SPs decrease. However, in this case, cost supersedes revenue. Therefore, both SPs make more profit. In other words, a higher privacy valuation from consumers "softens" the competition.

Truncated Gaussian Consumer Privacy Risk Tolerance. We now consider the case in which consumers' privacy risk tolerance follows a truncated Gaussian distribution with a mean of $\frac{\bar{\varepsilon}}{2}$ and a standard deviation of 1. The equilibrium strategies of different SPs are shown in Fig. 4. As with the uniform distribution scenario, here too we observe that the privacy risk and the QoS offered by each SP are linear functions of $\bar{\varepsilon}$. We also notice that in this SPNE, SP_2 will always provide service with maximum privacy risk (Fig. 4a) for the set of parameters in Table 1. This is because in contrast to the uniform distribution, for the truncated Gaussian distribution, there are a relatively smaller number of consumers concentrated in the tail end of $[0, \bar{\varepsilon}]$. Thus, for SP_1 to make a profit, it has to offer a higher privacy risk so that it can capture a large number of consumers in the middle of the $[0, \bar{\varepsilon}]$ range. This in turn forces SP_2 to increase

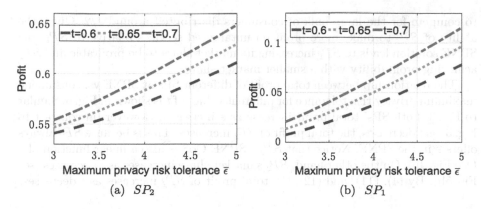

Fig. 3. Profit of SPs at SPNE under uniform consumer privacy risk

its privacy risk to differentiate its QoS offering and thus have a higher profit. Since the privacy risk preference is bounded by $[0, \bar{\varepsilon}]$, SP_2 can only offer the highest privacy risk in this example.

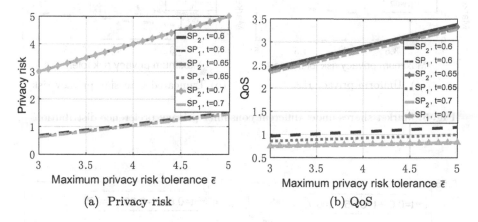

Fig. 4. SPNE strategies of SPs under truncated Gaussian consumer privacy risk

Figure 5b shows market shares of different SPs at SPNE vs. consumers' maximum privacy risk tolerance for different values of t under truncated Gaussian privacy tolerance distribution. As t decreases, the market share of SP_2 at SPNE increases, and vice versa. Also, when $\bar{\varepsilon}$ decreases, the equilibrium market share of SP_2 increases. Furthermore, it can be seen that for the same $\bar{\varepsilon}$, the market share of SP_2 (SP_1) is smaller (larger) when consumers' privacy tolerance follows the truncated Gaussian distribution compared to uniform distribution. Our numerical analysis shows that at SPNE, SP_2 is forced to provide service with maximum privacy risk. We argue that this is due to the shape of the distribution that limits the number of consumers at the two extremes thus compelling the two SPs to compete for the large bulk of consumers distributed around $\bar{\varepsilon}/2$. Given the ability of SP_2 to make more profit on untargeted services relative to SP_1, the SPNE solution leads to SP_1 increasing its market share to be profitable and SP_2 achieving profitability with a smaller market share.

The relationship between total profit of different SPs at SPNE vs. consumers' maximum privacy risk tolerance for different values of t is shown in Fig. 6. Similar to Fig. 3, both SPs' total profit increase as $\bar{\varepsilon}$ increases. However, in contrast to Fig. 3, as t decreases, the total profit of SP_2 increases. This is because SP_2 always offers $\bar{\varepsilon}$ in the SPNE. Notice that SP_2's SPNE QoS is also a linear function of $\bar{\varepsilon}$ (see Fig. 4b). On the other hand, SP_2's market share increases as t decreases (see Fig. 5b). By (4), (11), and (12); the total profit of SP_2 increases as t decreases.

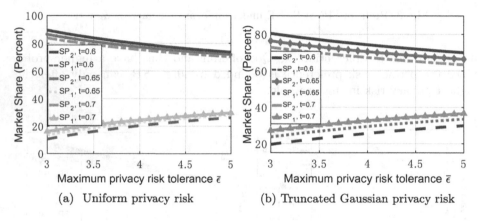

(a) Uniform privacy risk   (b) Truncated Gaussian privacy risk

Fig. 5. Market shares under different consumer privacy preference distribution

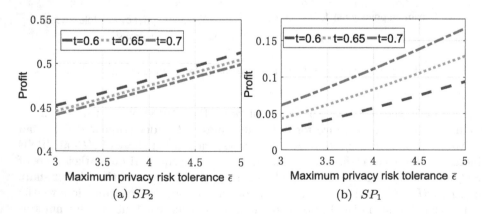

(a) SP_2 (b) SP_1

Fig. 6. Profit of SPs at SPNE under truncated Gaussian consumer privacy risk

5 Conclusions

This work seeks to understand the effect of offering privacy- and QoS- differentiated online services to consumers with heterogeneous privacy sensitivities. We have quantified this effect as the fraction of consumers that prefer lower privacy risks with the accompanying lower QoS to the alternative of higher risks and higher QoS. We have presented an analysis built upon the classical Hotelling model to compute equilibrium QoS-privacy risk strategies and market segmentation for the two-SP problem. Analogous to the classical models, our problem also involves parameters that capture cost, revenue, and consumer valuation functions that are dependent and independent of privacy risks. While such a parametrized model can make the analysis challenging, our results for relatively simple yet meaningful functions such as linear cost models and uniform (as well as truncated Gaussian) distribution of consumer preferences suggest that SPs that have higher profits from untargeted services have an edge in the market. SPs competing on offering higher privacy risk services have to offer better QoS or figure out other means of increasing untargeted revenue to gain market share.

Our model assumes that the SPs were able to overcome the barrier to entry and differentiate themselves. Thus, a related question we will address going forward is whether such barriers to entry are in fact surmountable when competitors use privacy as a differentiator. Also, extending the model to competitive settings that allows more than two SPs and captures externalities of using private data could lead to interesting insights into real-world market interactions. Another challenge to address is to develop models to capture privacy risks that are not directly observable to consumers. These analyses are crucial for developing better privacy policies to effectively enable safe and secure online commerce.

Acknowledgments. This work is supported in part by the National Science Foundation under Grant No. CCF-1350914

Appendix

A Proof of Theorem 1

We prove by contradiction. Suppose that both SPs offer the same privacy risk $\tilde{\varepsilon}$. Without loss of generality, we assume $p_1 \leq p_2$. We start at the third stage wherein each consumer chooses the SP which maximizes its utility (5). Since $\varepsilon_1^* = \varepsilon_2^* = \tilde{\varepsilon}$, every consumer will choose the SP that offers the highest QoS. At the second stage, given the privacy risk strategy $\varepsilon_1^* = \varepsilon_2^* = \tilde{\varepsilon}$ and the equilibrium strategy in the third stage, each SP determines its QoS offering by solving (10). Finally, we show that SP_2 will be better off if it deviates from $\tilde{\varepsilon}$ unilaterally. By Assumption 3, each SP has equal share of the market if $v_1 = v_2$ and $\varepsilon_1 = \varepsilon_2$. The profit of SP_i can be written as

$$\pi_i = \begin{cases} r\varepsilon_i + p_i - c(v_i + \lambda\varepsilon_i) & \text{if } v_i > v_{-i} \\ \frac{r\varepsilon_i + p_i - c(v_i + \lambda\varepsilon_i)}{2} & \text{if } v_i = v_{-i} \\ 0 & \text{if } v_i < v_{-i} \end{cases} \qquad (25)$$

As argued in Sect. 2.1, we assume that the net profit from using consumers' private data is non-negative $R_P(\varepsilon_i) - C_P(\varepsilon_i) > 0$. Thus, $(r - c\lambda)\varepsilon_i > 0 \; \forall \varepsilon_i \in [0, \bar{\varepsilon}]$, which indicates $r - c\lambda > 0$. Since every consumer will choose the SP that offers the highest QoS, each SP's best response strategy with respect to its competitor is to increase v_i until one of the SPs realizes it is not profitable to increase QoS anymore. Therefore, by (25), both SPs will increase v_i until $R(\varepsilon_i) - C(v_i, \varepsilon_i) = 0$ for one of the SPs. Since we assume $p_1 \leq p_2$, we have the following two cases:

Case 1: $p_1 = p_2 = p$. In this case, given $\varepsilon_1^* = \varepsilon_2^* = \bar{\varepsilon}$, each SP will increase its QoS to beat its competitor until $R(\varepsilon_i) - C(v_i, \varepsilon_i) = r\bar{\varepsilon} + p - c(v_i + \lambda\bar{\varepsilon}) = 0$. As a result, both SPs' equilibrium strategies at this stage are given by

$$v_1^* = v_2^* = \frac{(r - c\lambda)\bar{\varepsilon} + p}{c}. \tag{26}$$

At the first stage, the SPs determine their privacy risks based on the equilibrium strategies in the second and the third stages. Given the equilibrium strategies in the second stage (26), both SPs have zero profit. Since we assume $\varepsilon_1 \leq \varepsilon_2$, SP_1 can only reduce its privacy risk from $\bar{\varepsilon}$ and SP_2 can only increase from it. We now prove that it is a non-profitable deviation for SP_1 to decrease its privacy risk to $\bar{\varepsilon}_1$ unilaterally. Since SP_1's QoS strategy is given by $v_1^* = \frac{(r - c\lambda)\bar{\varepsilon} + p}{c}$, its profit is given by $R(\bar{\varepsilon}_1) - C(v_1^*, \bar{\varepsilon}_1) = r\bar{\varepsilon}_1 + p - c(v_1^* + \lambda\bar{\varepsilon}_1) = (r - c\lambda)(\bar{\varepsilon}_1 - \bar{\varepsilon}) < 0$. Thus, SP_1 does not have incentives to deviate from playing $\bar{\varepsilon}$ unilaterally. On the other hand, if SP_2 increases its privacy risk from $\bar{\varepsilon}$ to $\bar{\varepsilon}_2$ unilaterally, its profit is given by $R(\bar{\varepsilon}_2) - C(v_2^*, \bar{\varepsilon}_2) = r\bar{\varepsilon}_2 + p - c(v_2^* + \lambda\bar{\varepsilon}_2) = (r - c\lambda)(\bar{\varepsilon}_2 - \bar{\varepsilon}) > 0$. Therefore, SP_2 is better off by changing from $\bar{\varepsilon}$ to $\bar{\varepsilon}_2$ unilaterally. Thus, there is no SPNE such that both SPs offer the same privacy risk when $p_1 = p_2$.

Case 2: $p_1 < p_2$. In this case, since $p_1 < p_2$, both SPs will keep increasing its QoS until SP_1 has zero profit. Thus, by solving $R(\bar{\varepsilon}) - C(v_1, \bar{\varepsilon}) = 0$, SP_1 will play $v_1^* = \frac{(r - c\lambda)\bar{\varepsilon} + p_1}{c}$ at the equilibrium. On the other hand, SP_2 will offer an QoS slightly higher than v_1^* and captures the entire market. At the first stage, given the equilibrium strategy of the second stage described above, both SPs choose their privacy risk offerings. We now prove that it is a non-profitable deviation for SP_1 to decrease its privacy risk to $\bar{\varepsilon}_1$ unilaterally. Substitute $v_1^* = \frac{(r - c\lambda)\bar{\varepsilon} + p_1}{c}$ to (25), we have $\pi_1 = (r - c\lambda)(\bar{\varepsilon}_1 - \bar{\varepsilon}) < 0$. Thus, SP_1 does not have incentives to deviate from playing $\bar{\varepsilon}$ unilaterally. On the other hand, if SP_2 increases its privacy risk from $\bar{\varepsilon}$ to $\bar{\varepsilon}_2$ unilaterally, its profit is given by

$$\pi_2 = (r - c\lambda)(\bar{\varepsilon}_2 - \bar{\varepsilon}) + p_2 - p_1 = (r - c\lambda)(\bar{\varepsilon}_2 - \bar{\varepsilon}) + R(\bar{\varepsilon}) - C(v_2^*, \bar{\varepsilon})$$
$$> R(\bar{\varepsilon}) - C(v_2^*, \bar{\varepsilon}).$$

Thus, SP_2 has incentives to deviate from offering the same privacy risk. Therefore, playing $\varepsilon_1^* = \varepsilon_2^* = \bar{\varepsilon}$ is not an SPNE when $p_1 < p_2$.

B   Proof of Theorem 2

Starting form the last stage in which consumers choose different SPs, we use backward induction to find the SPNE of the sequential game. In the last stage, each consumer located at $x \in [0, 1]$ chooses an SP which maximizes its utility function (3). By (6) and the assumption that consumers' privacy risk tolerances are uniformly distributed, the indifference threshold x_T is given by

$$x_T = \frac{v_1 - v_2 + \frac{t(\varepsilon_2^2 - \varepsilon_1^2)}{\bar{\varepsilon}}}{t(\varepsilon_2 - \varepsilon_1)} = n_1(v_1; \varepsilon_1; v_2; \varepsilon_2). \tag{27}$$

At the second stage, the optimal strategy of each SP is determined by the solution of (10). For fixed privacy risk guarantees ε_2 and ε_1, the objective function of $SP_i, i \in \{1, 2\}$ in this stage, i.e., $\pi_i(v_i; \varepsilon_i; v_{-i}; \varepsilon_{-i})$, is a concave function with respect to its own strategy v_i. Furthermore, the feasible set of SP_i's strategy is a convex set ($v_i \in [0, +\infty]$). Thus, the non-cooperative subgame between SP_2 and SP_1 in this stage can be considered as a two-player concave game. By Theorem 1 and 2 in [23], we can establish

Proposition 1. *For fixed privacy risk strategies, there exists a unique Nash equilibrium in the game between SP_2 and SP_1 at the second stage.*

Proof. To compute the equilibrium strategy of the second stage, we first substitute (11), (12), and (27) into (8) and (7). Then, we apply the first order condition to SPs' profit functions and solve the simultaneous equations given by $\frac{\partial \pi_i(v_i; \varepsilon_i; v_{-i}; \varepsilon_{-i})}{\partial v_i} = 0 \quad \forall i \in \{1, 2\}$.

For given privacy guarantees ε_1 and ε_2, solving the simultaneous linear equations above yields the unique equilibrium strategy

$$v_1^* = \frac{2(r\varepsilon_1 + p_1) + r\varepsilon_2 + p_2}{3c} + \frac{t(1 + x_1)\varepsilon_1 - \lambda(\varepsilon_2 + 2\varepsilon_1) - t(1 + x_2)\varepsilon_2}{3}, \tag{28}$$

$$v_2^* = \frac{2(r\varepsilon_2 + p_2) + r\varepsilon_1 + p_1}{3c} + \frac{t(2 - x_1)\varepsilon_1 - \lambda(2\varepsilon_2 + \varepsilon_1) - t(2 - x_2)\varepsilon_2}{3}. \tag{29}$$

At the first stage, SPs determine their optimal privacy risks by considering the QoS of each SP and the market segmentation computed in previous stages as functions of privacy risks offered by SPs. Substituting (29) and (28) into (8) and (7) and apply the first order condition to SPs' profit functions yields (14) and (16). Substitute (14) and (16) to (29) and (28) yields (15) and (17).

Next, we prove the sufficient condition for the existence of the above SPNE. First of all, the model parameters must sustain a competitive market environment. Thus, in the equilibrium, each SP must have non-zero market share. This indicates the parameters must satisfy $0 \leq x_T^* = \frac{v_1^* - v_2^* + t(x_2^* \varepsilon_2^* - x_1^* \varepsilon_1^*)}{t(\varepsilon_2^* - \varepsilon_1^*)} \leq 1$. Substitute (14), (15), (16), and (17) into the above inequality, we have (18). Furthermore, in the SPNE, the QoS of each SP must be non-negative (QoS feasibility) and the privacy risk guarantees must be bounded between 0 and $\bar{\varepsilon}$ (privacy risk feasibility). By the model assumption in Sect. 2.1, we have $\varepsilon_1 \leq \varepsilon_2$. Thus, we only requires $\varepsilon_2 \leq \bar{\varepsilon}$ and $\varepsilon_1 \geq 0$. Substitute (14) and (16) into the two inequalities above yields (19). Let $x_i^* = \frac{\varepsilon_i^*}{\bar{\varepsilon}}$ denote the normalized privacy risk of each SP in the SPNE. The SPNE strategies must satisfy the complete market coverage condition given by $u_i(x) = v_i^* - t(x - x_i^*)\varepsilon_i^* \geq 0, \forall x \in [0,1]$ for at least one SP.

Substituting (19) into (17), we have $v_2^* - v_1^* = \frac{3\bar{\varepsilon}}{4}\alpha - \frac{p_2-p_1}{3c} \geq \frac{3t\bar{\varepsilon}}{16} + \frac{2(p_2-p_1)}{3c} > 0$, thus we only need $v_1 \geq 0$ for QoS feasibility. Furthermore, the Hotelling model feasibility condition implies $v_1^* - tx_1^*\varepsilon_1^* \geq v_2^* - tx_2^*\varepsilon_2^*$. Since $u_i(x)$ is an increasing function of x, complete market coverage condition can be simplified to $u_1(0) \geq 0$. As a result, the QoS feasibility condition and the complete market coverage condition can be simplified to $v_1^* - tx_1^*\varepsilon_1^* \geq 0$. Therefore, the sufficient condition for the existence of SPNE is given by: (i) $0 \leq \frac{v_1^* - v_2^* + t(x_2^*\varepsilon_2^* - x_1^*\varepsilon_1^*)}{t(\varepsilon_2^* - \varepsilon_1^*)} \leq 1$; (ii) $0 \leq \varepsilon_1^*, \varepsilon_2^* \leq \bar{\varepsilon}$; (iii) $v_1^* - tx_1^*\varepsilon_1^* \geq 0$. Solving the above three inequalities yield (18)–(20). The equilibrium market share and profits of the SPs are obtained by substituting (14)–(17) into (6)–(8).

References

1. EUGDPR: The EU general data protection regulation (GDPR) (2017). http://www.eugdpr.org/
2. Cadwalladr, C., Graham-Harrison, E.: Revealed: 50 million Facebook profiles harvested for Cambridge Analytica in major data breach. Guardian (2018). https://www.theguardian.com/news/2018/mar/17/cambridge-analytica-facebook-influence-us-election
3. Erlingsson, Ú., Pihur, V., Korolova, A.: RAPPOR: randomized aggregatable privacy-preserving ordinal response. In: Proceedings of the 2014 ACM SIGSAC, pp. 1054–1067 (2014)
4. Apple Support: About privacy and location services in iOS 8 and later. https://support.apple.com/en-is/HT203033. Accessed Sep 2016
5. Shaffer, G., Zhang, Z.J.: Competitive coupon targeting. Mark. Sci. **14**(4), 395–416 (1995)
6. Chen, Y., Iyer, G.: Research note consumer addressability and customized pricing. Mark. Sci. **21**(2), 197–208 (2002)
7. Tang, Z., Hu, Y., Smith, M.D.: Gaining trust through online privacy protection: self-regulation, mandatory standards, or caveat emptor. J. Manage. Inf. Syst. **24**(4), 153–173 (2008)
8. Campbell, J., Goldfarb, A., Tucker, C.: Privacy regulation and market structure. J. Econ. Manage. Strategy **24**(1), 47–73 (2015)
9. Conitzer, V., Taylor, C.R., Wagman, L.: Hide and seek: costly consumer privacy in a market with repeat purchases. Mark. Sci. **31**(2), 277–292 (2012)
10. Chen, Y., Narasimhan, C., Zhang, Z.J.: Individual marketing with imperfect targetability. Mark. Sci. **20**(1), 23–41 (2001)
11. Chellappa, R.K., Shivendu, S.: Mechanism design for "free" but "no free disposal" services: the economics of personalization under privacy concerns. Manage. Sci. **56**(10), 1766–1780 (2010)
12. Datta, A., Tschantz, M.C., Datta, A.: Automated experiments on ad privacy settings: a tale of opacity, choice, and discrimination. Proc. Priv. Enhanc. Technol. **2015**(1), 92–112 (2015)

13. Huang, C., Sankar, L., Sarwate, A.D.: Incentive schemes for privacy-sensitive consumers. In: Khouzani, M.H.R., Panaousis, E., Theodorakopoulos, G. (eds.) GameSec 2015. LNCS, vol. 9406, pp. 358–369. Springer, Cham (2015). https://doi.org/10.1007/978-3-319-25594-1_21

14. Huang, C., Sankar, L., Sarwate, A.D.: Designing incentive schemes for privacy-sensitive users. J. Priv. Confid. **7**(1(5)), 99–127 (2016)

15. Hotelling, H.: Stability in competition. In: Darnell, A.C. (ed.) The Collected Economics Articles of Harold Hotelling, pp. 50–63. Springer, New York (1990). https://doi.org/10.1007/978-1-4613-8905-7_4

16. Yu, Z., Li, S., Tong, L.: Market dynamics and indirect network effects in electric vehicle diffusion. Transp. Res. Part D: Transp. Environ. **47**, 336–356 (2016)

17. Lotfi, M.H., Kesidis, G., Sarkar, S.: Network nonneutrality on the internet: content provision under a subscription revenue model. ACM SIGMETRICS Perform. Eval. Rev. **42**(3), 44–44 (2014)

18. Acquisti, A., Taylor, C., Wagman, L.: The economics of privacy. J. Econ. Lit. **54**(2), 442–492 (2016)

19. Jentzsch, N., Preibusch, S., Harasser, A.: Study on monetising privacy: an economic model for pricing personal information. In: ENISA, February 2012

20. Lee, D.-J., Ahn, J.-H., Bang, Y.: Managing consumer privacy concerns in personalization: a strategic analysis of privacy protection. Manage. Inf. Syst. Quart. **35**(2), 423–444 (2011)

21. Osborne, M.J., Rubinstein, A.: A Course in Game Theory. MIT Press, Cambridge (1994)

22. Esponda, F., Huerta, K., Guerrero, V.M.: A statistical approach to provide individualized privacy for surveys. PloS One **11**(1), e0147314 (2016)

23. Rosen, J.B.: Existence and uniqueness of equilibrium points for concave n-person games. Econ.: J. Econ. Soc. **33**(3), 520–534 (1965)

Cyber-Warranties as a Quality Signal for Information Security Products

Daniel W. Woods$^{(\boxtimes)}$ and Andrew C. Simpson

Department of Computer Science, University of Oxford,
Wolfson Building, Parks Road, Oxford OX1 3QD, UK
{daniel.woods,andrew.simpson}@cs.ox.ac.uk

Abstract. Consumers struggle to distinguish between the quality of
different enterprise security products. Evaluating performance is complicated by the stochastic nature of losses. It is recognised that this information asymmetry may lead to a "market for lemons" in which suppliers
face no incentive to provide higher quality products. Some security vendors have begun to offer cyber-warranties—voluntary ex-ante obligations
to indemnify the customer in the event of a cyber attack—to function as
a quality signal. Much like how consumer protection laws are relatively
more costly to firms offering low quality products, cyber-warranties are
more costly for firms developing low quality enterprise security products. In this paper, we introduce a decision-theoretic model to explore
how consumers might use cyber-warranties to increase information when
purchasing security products. Our analysis derives four inferences that
consumers can make about a security product. We discuss the difficulties customers might face in using these inferences to make real world
decisions.

Keywords: Cyber warranties · Decision theory · Enterprise security
Quality signals · Cyber insurance

1 Introduction

The "market for lemons" has been used to understand how information asymmetry can degrade the quality of traded goods [1]. Akerlof illustrated the concept
by considering a used-car market dominated by sellers of "lemons" (low-quality
cars) in which buyers are unable to distinguish between a "lemon" and a "peach"
(a high-quality car). Recent work has used this analogy to explain the cyber
crime market [18] and secure software markets [2].

It may be argued that enterprise security products exhibit qualities of a market for lemons. Security firms must decide whether to invest additional resources
in developing a more effective product or, alternatively, sell the less-developed
product (a "lemon"). If buyers are unable to distinguish between the two products, there is no incentive for the security firm to develop a more effective product; buyers will purchase the "lemon" regardless and the seller avoids incurring

© Springer Nature Switzerland AG 2018
L. Bushnell et al. (Eds.): GameSec 2018, LNCS 11199, pp. 22–37, 2018.
https://doi.org/10.1007/978-3-030-01554-1_2

additional development costs. Enterprise security products lack a signal of quality that might address the information asymmetry.

Rao et al. [28] suggest that "brand name can convey unobservable quality credibly when false claims will result in intolerable economic losses". These losses can result from damage to the reputation of a brand, which is used by consumers to identify perceived product quality [12]. Alternatively, consumer protection laws place involuntary obligations on vendors that are more costly for the sellers of low quality products. Firms may be required to replace faulty products or may even be liable for the resulting damages in the case of strict product liability, which "induces firms to improve product safety" [27].

Such signals may be inappropriate in the context of enterprise security products. Evaluating the performance of security products is complicated. Preventing all attacks (giving rise to what might be termed 'absolute security') is widely held to be impossible [3]. A cyber attack may result from misfortune rather than from a faulty or low-quality product. Consequently, it is difficult to link product performance to product quality, not least because firms are reluctant to share detailed information about breaches [22]. This undermines both the function of reputation and the ability to identify faulty products to assign liability.

Enterprise security firms have begun to use so-called *cyber-warranties* as an alternative signal of quality. For example, a managed security provider[1] has offered a \$100,000 warranty and an end-point protection firm[2] offers a \$1,000,000 warranty. In this paper, we consider cyber-warranties to be voluntary ex-ante obligations in which enterprise security providers promise to indemnify consumers in the event of a successful attack. The voluntary ex-ante aspect of cyber-warranties differentiates them from the concept of software liability found in tort law [15,30,33] (or even criminal law [31]). By accepting and publicising these obligations, security firms seek to unilaterally shape market dynamics. There are many questions regarding what consumers can infer from these signals, how cyber-warranties impact the investment in security products, and whether this reduces the expected losses for the consumer.

This paper presents an economic consideration of how cyber-warranties affect the market for enterprise information security products. Section 2 identifies related work. In Sect. 3, we introduce a decision-theoretic model that captures both the vendor's short-run decision of setting the warranty level while investment is fixed and the long-run decision in which investment can vary. Section 4 contains our main contribution: the derivation of four inferences the consumer can make based on the cyber-warranty level. Section 5 illustrates how these inferences depend on the information structure between the consumer and the vendor. We discuss how applicable these inferences are with regards to real world decisions in Sect. 6. Section 7 offers conclusions and some directions for future work.

---

[1] https://www.armor.com/cyber-warranty/.

[2] https://www.sentinelone.com/press/sentinelone-establishes-1-million-cyber-threat-protection-guarantee/.

2   Background and Motivation

Cyber-warranties blur the line between risk mitigation and risk transfer. The vendor is tasked with both setting the optimal investment in product development and transferring the optimal amount of risk from the consumer in the form of a warranty. However, there has not been an academic consideration of cyber-warranties. Consequently, in this section we highlight how the literature on information security investments and risk transfer is relevant to our model (which we introduce in Sect. 3).

We focus on research into cyber insurance because it is concerned with a similar phenomenon: a cyber-warranty is a promise of indemnification much like an insurance contract. Cyber-warranties may lead to greater investment in the development of security products in the same way that insurance provides incentives for organisations to better manage information security [32]. For example, an insurer considering whether to directly invest in software security [24] faces a similar incentive structure to vendors offering cyber-warranties. Further, vendors may purchase market insurance to cover the liability for cyber-warranties, which relates to research into cyber insurance for third party providers [21].

Böhme and Schwartz [10] introduce a framework to describe how different cyber insurance models approach this problem. A common approach [14,19,26] characterises the risk to the consumer by: a fixed loss l_i; insurance coverage $\beta_i \in [0,1]$ that indemnifies a fraction of the loss; and a defence function D_i representing the probability of suffering a loss. Our model broadly adopts this framework to describe cyber-warranties, although it diverges on some specifics. We opt for simplicity, rather than trying to incorporate considerations such as secondary losses [5] made in other models.

The defence function D_i links the probability of suffering a loss to the "security investment s_i" [10]. In game-theoretic approaches, D_i has been assumed to have linear returns on investment in [14] and diminishing marginal returns on investment in [26], while Johnson et al. [19] assume that the other players' defensive investments influence D_i [19]. The seminal decision-theoretic work of Gordon and Loeb [16] introduces two probability breach functions analogous to D_i, which were corroborated using data on e-local governments in Japan [35].

Although representing the warranty level as a fraction of a set loss has precedent in the insurance literature [10,14,19,26], doing so abstracts away from the myriad challenges of transferring so-called cyber risks. Empirical work reveals a more legalistic reality in which coverage is delimited into first and third party losses, with losses related to reputation damage and intellectual property loss not covered [29]. Policymakers have suggested that standardised policy wordings may help consumers understand what exactly they are purchasing [37]. These results from cyber insurance suggest there are significant real world problems in defining what a warranty covers.

Risk transfer leads to principal–agent problems such as adverse selection and moral hazard [4]. The first, adverse selection, occurs when riskier consumers purchase insurance at a greater frequency in the knowledge they are more likely to make a claim. Insurers attempt to better understand an applicant's risk by collecting information about information security controls [29,36]. Based on this decision, they may decide to refuse coverage or offer it at a higher price [13]. However, empirical work suggests that less than a third of cyber insurers price risk according to information security factors [29]. Vendors might reflect on how to prevent warranties being purchased by the riskiest consumers. The second, moral hazard, occurs when an insured engages in risky behaviour in the knowledge the insurer will cover the losses. Traditionally, insurers address this problem by offering partial coverage so that the insured also suffers some financial consequences resulting from losses [38]. Another method involves exclusions, whereby insurers are no longer liable if certain procedures are not followed. For example, Kesan et al. [20] identify that a "failure to take reasonable steps to maintain and upgrade security" invalidates each of the policies in their study. Here we push up against the problem of defining the warranty as detailed conditions regarding risky behaviour increase contractual complexity.

Table 1. Descriptions of each parameter in the model.

Symbol	Description
V_i	The i-th vendor
S_i	The product offered by the i-th vendor
c_{f_i}	The fixed costs incurred in offering product S_i
z_i	The amount of investment into security during development of S_i
P_i	The price of S_i
Ψ_i	The proportion of realised losses the i-th vendor will indemnify
λ	The set loss resulting from a successful attack
v_0	The consumer's vulnerability before employing a security product
$S(v_0, z_i)$	The probability of successful attack given an investment of z_i
$R_c(R_v)$	The revenue of the consumer (vendor)

Having identified a common modelling approach to cyber insurance and some of the associated real world principal–agent problems, we introduce our model for cyber-warranties in the next section.

3   Model

The model considers a number of vendors $V_1, ..., V_n$, with each V_i selling a single security product S_i. Each vendor sets the amount of development investment z_i that represents costs, including developer time, training costs, participation in threat intelligence schemes and purchasing development tools.

We assume a Bertrand model of competition [6] in which a vendor can chooses a price P_i and a warranty $\Psi_i \in [0, 1]$; how this choice interacts with market demand determines the quantity supplied. The Bertrand model is relevant to software markets where quantity supplied can dynamically meet market demand [34]—unlike, for example, car manufacturers who must forecast market demand in order to begin a production process that may take months to complete.

To model the random nature of cyber attacks, we consider a Bernoulli trial in which the consumer faces a set loss λ with probability of occurrence p_i when the consumer purchases product S_i and a probability of v_0 if no purchase is made. This realisation of losses is in line with the common approach to modelling other forms of risk transfer [10,14,19,26]. As the set loss is fixed, the security products mitigate the probability of successful attack without affecting the impact of the attack. Consequently, our analysis will be less relevant to security products that seek to reduce the impact of losses.

As identified in Sect. 2, there are many functions relating p_i to the investment z_i in the security product S_i. Gordon and Loeb's seminal paper [16] established three core assumptions that such a function should fulfill in the context of protecting an information set. These are listed below.

A1: $S(z_i, 0) = 0$ for all $z_i \in \mathbb{R}$
A2: $S(0, v_0) = v_0$ for all $v_0 \in [0, 1]$
A3: $\frac{\delta S}{\delta z}(z_i, v_0) < 0$ and $\frac{\delta^2 S}{\delta z^2}(z_i, v_0) > 0$ for all $v_0 \in [0, 1]$ and $z_i \in \mathbb{R}$. Furthermore, for all $v_0 \in [0, 1]$ we have,

$$\lim S(z_i, v_0) \to 0 \text{ as } z_i \to \infty$$

The third assumption ensures that further investment reduces the probability of attack, but does so at a diminishing rate. Further, no finite investment results in perfect security.

In [16], Gordon and Loeb propose two classes to which the security breach probability function may belong. These will be used going forward and may be expressed in the form

$$S^I(z_i, v_0) = \frac{v_0}{(\alpha z_i + 1)^\beta} \tag{1}$$

and

$$S^{II}(z_i, v_0) = v^{\alpha z_i + 1} \tag{2}$$

These assumptions and the corresponding functions were introduced in the context of protecting an information set. It can be argued that there is relevance to enterprise security products, particularly when the products out-source the task of protecting an information set.

The vendor incurs total cost $c_{f_i} + z_i$, where c_{f_i} represents the costs unrelated to security in offering the product, which we assume to be fixed. While z_i is the variable describing investment in security, which a vendor can may set. Each vendor seeks to maximise their profit Π_i by setting P_i, z_i and Ψ_i:

$$\Pi_i = P_i - S(z_i, v_0)(\lambda \cdot \Psi_i) - (c_{f_i} + z_i) \tag{3}$$

The consumer only has knowledge of the price P_i, warranty Ψ_i and set loss λ. The investment z_i is assumed to be unobservable due to information asymmetry. The consumer chooses the security product S_i that minimises

$$R_c = P_i + S(z_i, v_0) \cdot \lambda(1 - \Psi_i) \tag{4}$$

We assume that customers are homogeneous and all demand the same product, leading to the kind of winner-takes-all market dynamics that have been observed in many other software markets [2,34].

4 Analysis

We consider a market without security warranties ($\Psi_i = 0$) to illustrate the market for lemons. Using Eq. 3, the vendor receives

$$P_i - (c_{f_i} + z_i)$$

while the consumer's expected security expenditure is

$$P_i + S(z_i, v_0) \cdot \lambda$$

The vendor has no incentive to increase the development investment beyond $z_i = 0$ because the consumer cannot observe ex-ante the resulting decrease in vulnerability. In a competitive market without warranties, the market equilibrium is $P_i = c_{f_i}$ with $z_i = 0$. Clearly vendors still invest in product development without offering warranties in spite of this result and we discuss why they might do so in Sect. 6. The rest of this section identifies four inferences consumers can make regarding security products, as well as the information they need to do so.

First, we consider a vendor V_i with a fixed investment of $c_{f_i} + z_i'$ in the product. Each vendor can offer the product at a price P_i with warranty Ψ_i. Equation 3 shows that the vendor's profit at the price P_i is as follows.

$$\Pi_i(P_i) = P_i - S(z_i', v_0)(\lambda \cdot \Psi_i) - (c_{f_i} + z_i') \tag{5}$$

In the short-run, the vendor may incur losses up to the value of the fixed costs of operation $(c_{f_i} + z_i')$. This observation leads to the constraint

$$\Pi_i(P_i) \geq -(c_{f_i} + z_i')$$

from which we derive Inference 1.

Inference 1. *Vendor V_i can offer S_i in the short-run with a warranty level of $\Psi_i \in [0, 1]$ at any price*

$$P_i \geq S(z_i', v_0)\lambda \cdot \Psi_i$$

The left-hand side represents the expected value of the indemnification payment to the consumer. It is reasonable to assume that no risk-neutral vendor would offer the warranty unless they receive at least this value as an up-front payment.

This provides an upper bound of $\frac{P_i}{\Psi_i}$ for the expected loss a consumer faces—dividing by Ψ_i adjusts for the proportion of the loss that the vendor pays. The inference can be made in the presence of information asymmetry regarding the vendor's security efficiency (α, β), the shape of the probability breach function $S(\cdot, \cdot)$, or their security investment during development z_i.

The consumer seeks to minimise Eq. 4 despite having incomplete information about z_i. The consumer can use Inference 1 to calculate a lower bound z_{min_i}, which represents the smallest investment value such that vendor i can break even in offering offer a product with warranty Ψ_i at price P_i. This value may be used to calculate the worst-case expected loss $R_{c_{min}}$ resulting from purchasing the product S_i:

$$R_{c_{min}}(S_i) = P_i + S(z_{min_i}, v_0) \cdot \lambda(1 - \Psi_i) \tag{6}$$

The consumer is assumed to be indifferent between purchasing the product S_i and the product S_j if

$$R_{c_{min}}(S_i) = R_{c_{min}}(S_j) \tag{7}$$

From this, we can construct a (worst-case) indifference curve for the consumer.

Calculating the (worst-case) indifference curve involves finding the smallest z_i such that

$$\Pi(S_i) \geq -(c_{f_i} + z_i') \tag{8}$$

Using Eq. 3 and the formulae for each class of probability breach function, we derive Inference 2.

Inference 2. *If the product S_i has been offered at price P_i and the warranty level is Ψ_i we have that*

$$z_{min_i} = \begin{cases} \frac{(\frac{\lambda\Psi'v_0}{P_i})^{\frac{1}{\beta}} - 1}{\alpha} & \text{if } S(\cdot, \cdot) \text{ is Class I} \\ \frac{\ln(P_i) - \ln(\Psi\lambda v_0)}{\alpha \ln(v_0)} & \text{if } S(\cdot, \cdot) \text{ is Class II} \end{cases}$$

It is worth noting that Inference 2 may provide an under-estimate of the product investment. A profit-making vendor analysed as if the vendor was breaking even would appear to have invested less than they did in actuality.

The long-run decision reduces to first selecting a warranty level and then determining the optimal investment as setting the investment first would reduce to the short-run analysis.

Suppose that the vendor unilaterally sets the warranty level at $\Psi_i' > 0$. The vendor will make the long-run investment z_i^* that optimises profit $\Pi_i(P_i)$ for all values of P_i. The marginal net benefit of investment is given by

$$\frac{\partial \Pi_i}{\partial z_i} = -\frac{\delta S}{\delta z}(z_i, v_0)(\lambda \cdot \Psi') - 1 \tag{9}$$

Using the convention that investment is non-negative $(0 \leq z_i)$, we can derive the following.

Inference 3. *If the vendor has committed to the warranty level Ψ_i', the optimal choice of product investment is*

$$z_i^* = \begin{cases} \frac{(\alpha\beta\lambda\Psi'v_0)^{\frac{1}{\beta+1}-1}}{\alpha} & \text{if } S(\cdot,\cdot) \text{ is Class I and } \alpha\beta\lambda\Psi'v_0 > 1 \\ \frac{-\ln(-\alpha\lambda\Psi'v\ln(v))}{\alpha\ln(v)} & \text{if } S(\cdot,\cdot) \text{ is Class II and } \alpha\lambda\Psi'v\ln(v) > -1 \\ 0 & \text{otherwise} \end{cases}$$

Inference 3 allows the consumer to infer the exact level of investment providing the warranty level was decided in the long-run and investment was optimised for this decision. If the investment z_1^* can be inferred, the consumer can expect revenue $R_c(S_i)$ if they purchase S_i, where

$$R_c(S_i) = P_1 + S(z_i^*, v_0)(1 - \Psi_i)\lambda \tag{10}$$

In a fully competitive market, we can expect that

$$P_i = S(z_i^*, v_0)\Psi'\lambda + c_{f_i} + z_i^* \tag{11}$$

However, Inference 2 and 3 both rely on the consumer knowing the shape of the probability breach function and the vendor's security productivity.

In both the short-run and the long-run, the price P_i must increase to compensate for any increase in the warranty Ψ_i at a rate equal to the risk-transfer rate of substitution (RTRS) $\frac{\partial \Pi_i}{\partial \Psi_i}$ in order to keep profits constant.

Inference 4. *The risk-transfer rate of substitution for the vendor V_i is equal to the consumer's expected loss when the security product S_i is in place.*

$$\frac{\partial \Pi_i}{\partial \Psi_i} = S(z_i', v_0)\lambda$$

The consumer can discover the expected loss if the risk-transfer rate of substitution is observed. This inference can be made with knowledge of only the price and warranty level regardless of whether the warranty has been offered in the short-run or the long-run. This inference might be considered the most powerful as it can be made with information asymmetry regarding the vendor's technological constraints.

The price and warranty offered by each vendor will depend on the market environment in both the short-run and the long-run. If the vendors have perfect information about the competitors' investments in product development, there may exist one vendor who can extract a supplier surplus by setting (P_i, Ψ_i) such that any competitor would suffer an economic loss in offering a competing product. However, this will depend on the particular values of both investments z_i, existing vulnerability v_0 and breach probability function $S(z_i, v_0)$. The relative risk aversion of the vendor and the consumer will determine the optimal pair (P_i, Ψ_i).

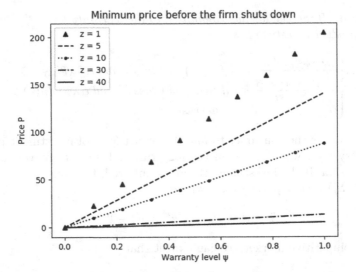

Fig. 1. The price at which the vendor would shut down if price fell any further, for different investment levels z and a Class I probability breach function with: $\alpha = 0.9, \beta = 1, \lambda = 500, v_0 = 0.5$ and $c_f = 5$.

5   Numerical Illustration

In this section we illustrate each of the inferences in turn.

Firms will only shut down in the short-run if price exceeds average cost. Figure 1 shows how the minimum price is determined by the warranty level and the investment. We define the shutdown-isoprofits to be the lines with a loss equal to fixed costs; the curve for $z = z_j'$ represents the possible pairs (P_j, Ψ_j) for which the j-th vendor's profit $(\Pi_j(S_j))$ is equal to $c_{f_j} + z_j'$. Although vendors V_1 and V_5 have invested $z_1 = 1$ and $z_5 = 40$ respectively, both accept a minimum price of 0 when no warranty is offered. The difference between the size of their losses will be given by

$$\Pi_5(0) - \Pi_1(0) = (c_{f_5} + z_5) - (c_{f_1} + z_1) = -39$$

because V_5 has larger fixed costs as a result of higher fixed investment z_5.

Figure 2 illustrates the isoprofits when the firms break even. For a given warranty level Ψ, the vendor with the isoprofit curve intersecting $x = \Psi$ at the lowest point can offer the most competitive product. This provides a graphical illustration of the market for lemons as the product with investment $z = 1$ is most competitive when no warranty is offered. The downside of over-investment can be seen by considering that the vendor who invested $z = 30$ is more competitive at every warranty level than the vendor who invested $z = 40$.

If the consumer had knowledge about the shape of the probability breach function and the vendor's security efficiency, Inference 2 can provide information about the vendor's minimum investment z_{min_i} in the short-run. Figure 3

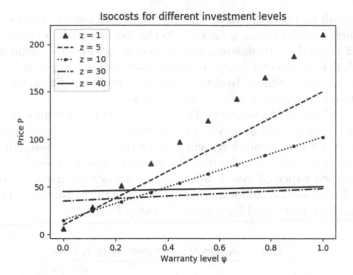

Fig. 2. The price at which the vendor would shut down if price fell any further, for different levels of security investment z and a Class I probability breach function with: $\alpha = 0.9, \beta = 1, \lambda = 500, v_0 = 0.5$ and $c_f = 5$.

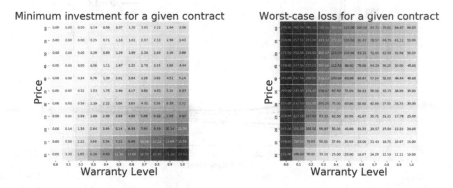

Fig. 3. The minimum investment value z_{min_i} and worst-case loss $R_{c_{min}}$ for a given price P_i and warranty level Ψ_i, for a Class I probability breach function with: $\alpha = 0.9, \beta = 1, \lambda = 500, v_0 = 0.9$ and $c_f = 5$.

highlights the points at which the strongest inference can be made; more information is contained in a warranty as the price it is offered at decreases. Consider a duopoly with vendors V_1 and V_2 who have made investments of $z_1 = 5$ and $z_2 = 10$ respectively. If vendor V_2 sets (P_2, Ψ_2) to be equal to any pair of Fig. 3 with $z_{m}in > 5$, then V_1 would sooner shut-down operation than offer the same contract. Offering such a contract functions as a reliable signal of product quality in this scenario.

For each contract (P_i, Ψ_i), Inference 2 may also be understood graphically as the smallest value of z_i for which the associated isoprofit curve intersects (P_i, Ψ_i)

or falls beneath it. For z_{min_i} to be the worst case, we have to assume that the isoprofit corresponded to the points where the loss is equal to the fixed costs. Inference 2 might lead to different conclusions if we used the isoprofit curves corresponding to a different profit condition, such as breaking even as in Fig. 2. If a functional form is difficult to obtain for a given profit condition, the graphical interpretation of Inference 2 may be used instead.

Turning to long-run investments, Fig. 4 shows the price a vendor must charge for a given warranty level in order to break even. We have circled the optimal investment for each warranty level and can see that it is increasing in Ψ_i. Consumers may use Inference 3 to discover the optimal investment level z^* and use it to calculate their expected loss. When investment costs are fixed, the consumer can only infer a lower bound for investment whereas the consumer can now infer the optimal investment level for a given warranty level.

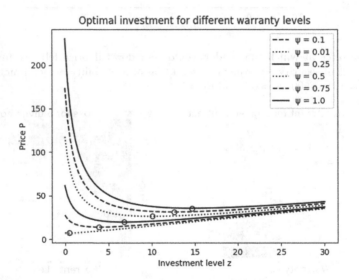

Fig. 4. The choices of price and investment level that lead a vendor to make zero profit, for different investment levels Ψ, for a Class I probability breach function with: $\alpha = 0.9, \beta = 1, \lambda = 500, v_0 = 0.9$ and $c_f = 5$.

Figure 5 describes the expected loss (R_c) for each customer if they purchase a product with warranty Ψ_i assuming the optimal investment has occurred. As the curve is always downward-sloping we must have

$$\frac{\partial R_c}{\partial \Psi_i} < 0 \text{ for all } \Psi_i \in [0,1]$$

However, the customer's expected loss falls at a diminishing rate so that

$$\frac{\partial^2 R_c}{\partial \Psi_i^2} > 0 \text{ for all } \Psi_i \in [0,1]$$

These results, derived via Inference 3, suggest that greater risk transfer to the agent deciding amount of security investment leads to a more efficient allocation of resources. As such, consumers should push to increase the warranty level over time, which can be seen in the decreasing expected loss for greater warranty levels in Fig. 5. Inference 3 requires knowledge about the vendor's technological constraints, much like Inference 2.

Inference 4 states that the risk-transfer rate of substitution (RTRS) of the i-th vendor is equal to the expected loss when employing the i-th security product. The RTRS for a given vendor is equal to the slope of that vendor's isocost curve (in Figs. 2 and 1). The lowest investment has the steepest isoprofit curve and hence the highest expected loss. Negotiating with the vendor might reveal the RTRS if the vendor stated how much the price would have to rise for a given increase in warranty level.

In summary, Inference 1 provides a lower-bound on expected losses and Inference 2 provides a lower bound on product investment. Both of these are valid in the short-run. Inference 3 provides an exact value of the optimal investment for a given warranty but it is only valid in the long-run. However, Inference 2 and Inference 3 require knowledge about the vendor's technological constraints. Inference 4 provides an exact value of the expected loss. It is valid in both the long-run and the short-run, and requires no knowledge beyond the RTRS. The next section discusses some of the real world limitations of these inferences.

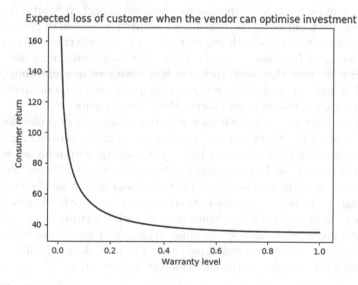

Fig. 5. The choices of price and investment level that lead a vendor to make zero profit, for different investment levels Ψ, for a Class I probability breach function with: $\alpha = 0.9, \beta = 1, \lambda = 500, v_0 = 0.9$ and $c_f = 5$.

6 Discussion

The consumer can use inferences 1–4 to estimate the expected loss when implementing the security product S_i, which can be compared against the expected loss without any security product or some other security product S_j. This allows the consumer to estimate the expected benefit from the security product. More knowledge about the vendor or the risk transfer rate of substitution may allow the consumer to make stronger inferences and increase confidence in these estimates. Unfortunately, these estimates will be weakened by many complicating factors in the real world.

The warranty level will likely take the form of a contract that will not stipulate a proportion of risk the vendor will cover. The contract might instead define a selection of events for which the warranty is valid. Estimating the proportion of the expected loss that these events represent requires that risk managers understand their organisation's risk profile.

Although the model suggests that full risk transfer achieves the optimal solution for the consumer, it may not be possible in the real world. Cyber insurance policies do not cover intangible losses such as reputation damage and intellectual property loss precisely because it is difficult to quantify such losses. There is no reason why vendors are better suited to offer warranties covering these risks.

A further complicating factor is that prices must reflect principal–agent problems such as adverse selection and moral hazard. These problems have presented a major problem for cyber insurance, as we observed in Sect. 2. Solutions to these problems, such as monitoring the consumer's security practices to prevent moral hazard or performing an in-depth assessment to prevent adverse selection, come at a cost that may be reflected in the price. However, consumers may accept a higher price because they need to invest less resources in evaluating product quality; cyber warranties incentivise the vendor to invest in the product regardless of whether the consumer can observe these investments.

The risk-transfer rate of substitution is only equal to the expected loss if the vendor is risk neutral. Otherwise the consumer would have to correct for the vendor's discomfort with holding greater liability associated with a higher warranty level. Vendors should also be concerned by the possibility of a "cyber hurricane" in which interdependent events trigger multiple indemnification claims [7,8].

Furthermore, the insolvency risk to vendors grows as they hold more liability. The risk may be managed via self-insurance or market insurance to ensure that vendors have funds available for indemnification. An equilibrium between the cost of these risk management techniques and consumer demand will determine the warranty level available to the consumer at a given price.

7 Conclusion and Future Work

Customers face information asymmetry when deciding which information security product to purchase. Cyber-warranties can overcome this information asymmetry by creating a separating equilibrium in which the vendor reveals the level of product investment to the consumer. Vendors selling information security products face lower costs in offering cyber-warranties if they invest in developing more effective products.

Our model identifies four inferences that customers can make about a potential information security purchase based on the warranty offered. In general, more information is gained when there is more prior knowledge about the vendor. However, these inferences are likely to be weaker in the real world. Consumers must adjust for factors including the extent of the vendor's risk aversion, costs incurred to mitigate principal–agent problems, and risk-loading to deal with the variability of (potentially correlated) losses.

Future work could explore how the balance of risk aversion between vendors and consumers affects the supply and demand for cyber-warranties. Another factor to consider is the vendor's costs in terms of mitigating (via self insurance or market insurance) the insolvency risk when increasing the warranty level. Identifying an empirical basis for the parameter choices may increase relevance for practitioners. Further, future work could reflect some active research topics in information security investments including:

- the benefits from adaptive security in which a defender makes defensive investments in response to observed losses [9];
- the role of investments in recovery as opposed to just mitigation, particularly in light of recent developments in cyber crime [23];
- the interaction with the vulnerability disclosure process, particularly the role of government policy [11];
- the relevance of the stage in the development process at which investments are made [17]; and
- approaches applying game theory to consider strategic interactions between vendors and consumers [25] (for example, vendors and consumers might dishonestly avoid indemnification or fraudulently claim indemnification respectively).

Acknowledgements. The authors thank the anonymous reviewers for their helpful and constructive comments. Participants in the "Effect of Software Warranties on Cyber Security" workshop run by the University of Bristol's Cyber Security Group provided useful feedback for the ideas developed in this paper. Daniel Woods' research is funded by the EPSRC via the Centre for Doctoral Training in Cyber Security at the University of Oxford.

References

1. Akerlof, G.A.: The market for "lemons": quality uncertainty and the market mechanism. In: Diamond, P., Rothschild, A. (eds.) Uncertainty in Economics, pp. 235–251. Elsevier, New York (1978)
2. Anderson, R., Moore, T.: The economics of information security. Science **314**(5799), 610–613 (2006)
3. Anderson, R.J.: Security Engineering: A Guide to Building Dependable Distributed Systems. Wiley, Hoboken (2010)

4. Arrow, K.J.: Uncertainty and the welfare economics of medical care (American economic review, 1963). J. Health Polit. Policy Law **26**(5), 851–883 (2001)
5. Bandyopadhyay, T., Mookerjee, V.S., Rao, R.C.: Why IT managers don't go for cyber-insurance products. Commun. ACM **52**(11), 68–73 (2009)
6. Bertrand, J.: Theorie mathematique de la richesse sociale. J. des Savants 499–508 (1883)
7. Biener, C., Eling, M., Wirfs, J.H.: Insurability of cyber risk: an empirical analysis. Geneva Pap. Risk Insur. Issues Pract. **40**(1), 131–158 (2015)
8. Böhme, R.: Cyber-insurance revisited. In: Proceedings of The 4th Workshop on the Economics of Information Security (WEIS 2005) (2005)
9. Böhme, R., Moore, T.: The "iterated weakest link" model of adaptive security investment. J. Inf. Secur. **7**(2), 81–102 (2016)
10. Böhme, R., Schwartz, G.: Modeling cyber-insurance: towards a unifying framework. In: Proceedings of The 9th Workshop on the Economics of Information Security (WEIS 2010) (2010)
11. Caulfield, T., Ioannidis, C., Pym, D.: The US vulnerabilities equities process: an economic perspective. In: Rass, S., An, B., Kiekintveld, C., Fang, F., Schauer, S. (eds.) Decision and Game Theory for Security. LNCS, vol. 10575, pp. 131–150. Springer, Cham (2017). https://doi.org/10.1007/978-3-319-68711-7_8
12. Dodds, W.B., Monroe, K.B., Grewal, D.: Effects of price, brand, and store information on buyers' product evaluations. J. Mark. Res. **28**(3), 307–319 (1991)
13. Franke, U.: The cyber insurance market in Sweden. Comput. Secur. **68**, 130–144 (2017)
14. Fultz, N., Grossklags, J.: Blue versus red: towards a model of distributed security attacks. In: Dingledine, R., Golle, P. (eds.) FC 2009. LNCS, vol. 5628, pp. 167–183. Springer, Heidelberg (2009). https://doi.org/10.1007/978-3-642-03549-4_10
15. Gemignani, M.C.: Product liability and software. Rutgers Comput. Technol. J. **8**, 173 (1980)
16. Gordon, L.A., Loeb, M.P.: The economics of information security investment. ACM Trans. Inf. Syst. Secur. (TISSEC) **5**(4), 438–457 (2002)
17. Heitzenrater, C., Simpson, A.C.: A case for the economics of secure software development. In: Proceedings of the 2016 New Security Paradigms Workshop, pp. 92–105. ACM (2016)
18. Herley, C., Florêncio, D.: Nobody sells gold for the price of silver: Dishonesty, uncertainty and the underground economy. In: Moore, T. (ed.) Economics of Information Security and Privacy, pp. 33–53. Springer, Boston (2010). https://doi.org/10.1007/978-1-4419-6967-5_3
19. Johnson, B., Böhme, R., Grossklags, J.: Security games with market insurance. In: Baras, J.S., Katz, J., Altman, E. (eds.) GameSec 2011. LNCS, vol. 7037, pp. 117–130. Springer, Heidelberg (2011). https://doi.org/10.1007/978-3-642-25280-8_11
20. Kesan, J., Majuca, R., Yurcik, W.: Cyberinsurance as a market-based solution to the problem of cybersecurity: a case study. In: Proceedings of The 4th Workshop on the Economics of Information Security (WEI 2005) (2005)
21. Khalili, M.M., Liu, M., Romanosky, S.: Embracing and controlling risk dependency in cyber-insurance policy underwriting. In: Proceedings of The 17th Workshop on the Economics of Information Security (WEIS 2018) (2018)
22. Kotulic, A.G., Clark, J.G.: Why there aren't more information security research studies. Inf. Manage. **41**(5), 597–607 (2004)

23. Laszka, A., Farhang, S., Grossklags, J.: On the economics of ransomware. In: Rass, S., An, B., Kiekintveld, C., Fang, F., Schauer, S. (eds.) Decision and Game Theory for Security. LNCS, vol. 10575, pp. 397–417. Springer, Cham (2017). https://doi.org/10.1007/978-3-319-68711-7_21
24. Laszka, A., Grossklags, J.: Should cyber-insurance providers invest in software security? In: Pernul, G., Ryan, P.Y.A., Weippl, E. (eds.) ESORICS 2015. LNCS, vol. 9326, pp. 483–502. Springer, Cham (2015). https://doi.org/10.1007/978-3-319-24174-6_25
25. Manshaei, M.H., Zhu, Q., Alpcan, T., Bacşar, T., Hubaux, J.P.: Game theory meets network security and privacy. ACM Comput. Surv. (CSUR) **45**(3), 25 (2013)
26. Pal, R., Golubchik, L.: Analyzing self-defense investments in internet security under cyber-insurance coverage. In: Proceedings of the IEEE 30th International Conference on Distributed Computing Systems (ICDCS2010), pp. 339–347. IEEE (2010)
27. Polinsky, A.M., Shavell, S.: The uneasy case for product liability. Harvard Law Rev. **123**, 1437–1491 (2009)
28. Rao, A.R., Qu, L., Ruekert, R.W.: Signaling unobservable product quality through a brand ally. J. Mark. Res. **36**(2), 258–268 (1999)
29. Romanosky, S., Ablon, L., Kuehn, A., Jones, T.: Content analysis of cyber insurance policies: how do carriers write policies and price cyber risk? In: Proceedings of The 16th Workshop on the Economics of Information Security (WEIS 2017) (2017)
30. Rustad, M.L., Koenig, T.H.: The tort of negligent enablement of cybercrime. Berkeley Tech. Law J. **20**, 1553 (2005)
31. Ryan, D.J., Heckman, C.: Two views on security software liability. let the legal system decide. IEEE Secur. Priv. **99**(1), 70–72 (2003)
32. Schneier, B.: Insurance and the computer industry. Commun. ACM **44**(3), 114–114 (2001)
33. Scott, M.D.: Tort liability for vendors of insecure software: has the time finally come. Maryland Law Rev. **67**, 425 (2007)
34. Shapiro, C., Varian, H.R.: Information Rules: A Strategic Guide to the Network Economy. Harvard Business Press, Boston (1998)
35. Tanaka, H., Matsuura, K., Sudoh, O.: Vulnerability and information security investment: an empirical analysis of e-local government in Japan. J. Acc. Public Policy **24**(1), 37–59 (2005)
36. Woods, D., Agrafiotis, I., Nurse, J.R., Creese, S.: Mapping the coverage of security controls in cyber insurance proposal forms. J. Internet Serv. Appl. **8**(1), 8 (2017)
37. Woods, D., Simpson, A.C.: Policy measures and cyber insurance: a framework. J. Cyber Policy **2**(2), 209–226 (2017)
38. Zweifel, P., Eisen, R.: Insurance Economics. Springer Science, Heidelberg (2012). https://doi.org/10.1007/978-3-642-20548-4

Game Theoretic Security Framework
for Quantum Key Distribution

Walter O. Krawec[1(✉)] and Fei Miao[1,2]

[1] Department of Computer Science and Engineering, University of Connecticut,
Storrs, CT 06028, USA
walter.krawec@uconn.edu
[2] Department of Electrical and Computer Engineering, University of Connecticut,
Storrs, CT 06028, USA
fei.miao@uconn.edu

Abstract. In this paper, we propose a game-theoretic model of security
for quantum key distribution (QKD) protocols. QKD protocols allow
two parties to agree on a shared secret key, secure against an adversary
bounded only by the laws of physics (as opposed to classical key distribution protocols which, by necessity, require computational assumptions to
be placed on the power of an adversary). We investigate a novel framework of security using game theory where all participants (including the
adversary) are rational. We will show that, in this framework, certain
impossibility results for QKD in the standard adversarial model of security still remain true here. However, we will also show that improved
key-rate efficiency is possible in our game-theoretic security model.

Keywords: Quantum cryptography · Game theory · Security

1 Introduction

Quantum key distribution (QKD) protocols allow for the establishment of a
shared secret key between two parties, referred to as Alice (A) and Bob (B),
which is secure against an all-powerful adversary, customarily referred to as Eve
(E). Such a task is impossible to achieve when using only classical communication; indeed, when parties have access only to classical resources, key-distribution
is only secure if certain computational assumptions are made on the power of the
adversary. With QKD protocols, however, the only required assumption is that
the adversary is bounded by the laws of physics. Furthermore, QKD is a practical technology today with several experimental and commercial demonstrations.
For a general survey of QKD protocols, the reader is referred to [1].

In general, most QKD protocols are designed, and their security proven,
within a *standard adversarial model of security*. In this case, parties A and B run
the protocol with the goal of establishing a shared secret key. An all-powerful
adversary sits in the middle of the channel, intercepting, and probing, each
quantum bit (or *qubit*) sent from A to B. As is standard in this usual model of

L. Bushnell et al. (Eds.): GameSec 2018, LNCS 11199, pp. 38–58, 2018.
https://doi.org/10.1007/978-3-030-01554-1_3

cryptography, it is assumed that E is simply malicious and has no motivation to attack, nor does E "care" about the cost of attacking.

In this paper, we investigate the use of *game theory* to study the security of QKD protocols. While we are not the first to propose a game theoretic analysis of cryptographic protocols (quantum or otherwise - see the "Related Work" section below for a summary), we propose a more general-purpose model which can be applied to arbitrary QKD protocols. Compared with prior work, our new approach is more general and, most importantly, allows for meaningful key-rate and noise tolerance computations to be performed which are vital when considering QKD security and comparing benefits of distinct protocols.

Beyond introducing our model, we also apply it to analyze certain important QKD protocols against both all-powerful, quantum, attacks and also more practical attacks based on current-day technology. For each, we compute the critical noise tolerance values and compare with the standard adversarial model. We also discuss the efficiency of the resulting protocols in our model. *Such computations were not possible in prior work, applying game theory to QKD thus showing the significance of our new methods.* We stress that this work's prime contribution is to develop a general framework for the modeling of QKD security, and various important computations involving these protocols (namely, key-rate computations and noise tolerances), through the use of game theory. We expect this work to be the foundation of future significant developments both in the fields of quantum key distribution, and also in game theory. Furthermore, our rational model of security may lead to more efficient secure communication systems as we discuss in the text.

1.1 Related Work

Game theory has seen great success when applied to *classical* cryptography (see [2] for a general survey). It has also raised a lot of interest recently in the study of Cyber-Physical System (CPS) security problems and network security [3–6].

Only recently have there been attempts and interest in applying game theory to *quantum* cryptography. Outside of key-distribution (our subject of interest in this paper), game theory has been used for secret sharing [7], rational state sharing [8], bit commitment [9], certain function computations [10], and secure direct communication [11].

The prior work discussed above all involve cryptographic primitives very different from QKD. However, some attempt has been made recently to apply game theory to QKD. In [12] a cooperative game was used to establish a quantum network consisting of point-wise QKD links which could relay information from one node to the other. However, QKD was only used as a tool in their work, the primary motivation for using game-theory was for the nodes to construct an optimal network topology in a vehicular network.

Closest to our work are [13,14]. In [13], game theory was used to analyze the BB84 QKD protocol. Their model, however, only considered strategies affecting certain choices within the protocol. In their work, a three-party game was constructed (consisting of A, B, and the adversary E). The strategy space of each participant was to chose a *basis* (either Z or X) to send and receive quantum bits in (we will discuss quantum measurement in the next section). The goal of the parties A and B was to *detect* E while the goal of E was to avoid detection. There was no goal of establishing an actual secret key at the end of maximal length; furthermore, E did not have a goal of learning information on the key. Both of these goals will be incorporated in our more general model.

In the recently published work of [14], the model proposed in [13] was extended and applied to the so-called *Ping-Pong* protocol [15] and also the LM05 protocol [16]. Their work considered certain attacks E may perform against the system which were previously proposed in the literature against the ping-pong protocol. The strategy space for A and B (now considered one party in their work) consisted of choosing to run the protocol, or a variant of it (there was no choice to simply "abort" which is an important choice in QKD security [1]). The goal of E was to maximize her information on the final raw-key while avoiding detection; the goal of the party "AB" was to maximize their mutual information. Our model will also consider these two as goals; however we will not be concerned about probability of detection (which, in typical applications, is not a concern as there is always natural noise in the channel anyway). However, we will go beyond this by also setting a goal to maximize the efficiency of the protocol. Furthermore, the model we introduce in this work allows for critical key-rate and noise tolerance computations, not possible in prior work.

1.2   Notation and Definitions

We use $H(X)$ to denote the Shannon entropy of random variable X. In particular, if $P(X = x) = p_x$, then $H(X) = -\sum_x p_x \log p_x$, where all logarithms in this paper are base two unless otherwise stated. By $h(x)$ we mean the binary entropy function defined $h(x) = -x \log x - (1-x) \log(1-x)$. Given two random variables X and Y, then $H(XY)$ is the joint Shannon entropy of random variables X and Y defined in the usual way. $H(X|Y)$ denotes the conditional entropy defined $H(X|Y) = H(XY) - H(Y)$. By $I(X : Y)$ we mean the mutual information between X and Y, defined to be $I(X : Y) = H(X) + H(Y) - H(XY)$.

We assume a familiarity with game theory, and include the following definitions only for completeness. Given a tuple $q = (q_1, \cdots, q_n)$ we write q_{-i} to mean the $n-1$ tuple consisting of all q_j for $j \neq i$; i.e., $q_{-i} = (q_1, \cdots, q_{i-1}, q_{i+1}, \cdots, q_n)$.

Definition 1. *An n-player normal (strategic) form game G is an n-tuple $\{(S_1, u_1), \ldots, (S_n, u_n)\}$, where for each i,*

- *S_i is a nonempty set, called i's strategy space, and*
- *$u_i:S \to \mathbb{R}$ is called i's utility function, where $S = S_1 \times \cdots \times S_n$.*

Definition 2. *Dominant Strategy (DS). A strategy s_i' (weakly) dominates s_i'', if $\forall s_{-i} \in S_{-i}$, $u_i(s_i', s_{-i}) \geq u_i(s_i'', s_{-i})$, and $\exists s_{-i}' \in S_{-i}$, $u_i(s_i', s_{-i}') > u_i(s_i'', s_{-i}')$.*

Definition 3. *Strict Nash Equilibrium (NE). $s^* \in S$ is a strict Nash equilibrium of $G = \{(S_1, u_1), \ldots, (S_n, u_n)\}$ if for all i and for all $s_i \in S_i$, $u_i(s_i^*, s_{-i}^*) > u_i(s_i, s_{-i}^*)$.*

2   Quantum Communication and Cryptography

For completeness, we review some basic concepts in quantum key distribution and quantum communication. Due to length constraints, this section is necessarily short; however, the interested reader is referred to [17].

A *quantum bit* or *qubit* is modeled, mathematically, as a normalized vector in $\mathbb{C}^2$. More generally, an arbitrary n-dimensional quantum state may be modeled as a normalized vector in $\mathbb{C}^n$. Quantum states are typically denoted as "kets" of the form $|\psi\rangle$ where the ψ can be replaced with any arbitrary label. The inner product of two kets $|\psi\rangle$ and $|\phi\rangle$ is denoted $\langle\psi|\phi\rangle$.

The *measurement postulate* of quantum mechanics gives rules for how quantum states may be observed. We are interested only with *projective measurements* in this work. Let $\mathcal{B} = \{|v_1\rangle, \cdots, |v_n\rangle\}$ be an orthonormal basis of $\mathbb{C}^n$. Then, given a quantum state $|\psi\rangle \in \mathbb{C}^n$, after measurement in basis $\mathcal{B}$, one observes basis state $|v_i\rangle$ with probability $|\langle v_i|\psi\rangle|^2$. Note, therefore, that measurements are probabilistic processes and the outcome and distribution depends on the basis one performs a measurement in. For qubits, two common bases are the Z basis, denoted $\{|0\rangle, |1\rangle\}$ and the X basis, denoted $\{|+\rangle, |-\rangle\}$ where $|\pm\rangle = \frac{1}{\sqrt{2}}(|0\rangle + |1\rangle)$. Note that, once observed, the original quantum state is destroyed and "collapses" to the observed basis state. In theory, one may perform a measurement in any basis. Note, also, that the *No Cloning Theorem* prevents the exact duplication of an unknown quantum state. Thus, when used as communication resources, an adversary is forced to attack immediately (she cannot copy the qubits to attack later); furthermore, if she attempts to extract information from the qubits via a measurement, this may cause disturbances that may be detected by honest users later. (Measurements are not the only way E can attack a qubit - however, for understanding our work in this paper, measurements are sufficient.)

2.1   Quantum Key Distribution

Quantum key distribution takes advantage of certain properties unique to quantum mechanics to allow for the establishment of a shared secret key between A and B, secure against an all powerful adversary E, a task impossible to achieve with classical communication only. There are many different QKD protocols at this point, with the first being discovered in 1984 now known as the BB84 protocol [18]. Another important protocol, discovered in 1992, is the B92 protocol [19]. The basic operation of these protocols is shown in Protocols 1 and 2. It is important to note that, in addition to a quantum channel, allowing for the transmission of qubits from A to B, there is also an *authenticated classical channel* connecting the two users. This channel is *not secret*, however, so any message sent from A to B can be read by the attacker (though, the attacker cannot write on this channel). Authentication may be done in an information theoretic manner assuming the existence of an initial (small) secret key. Thus, QKD protocols are sometimes referred to as *quantum key expansion* protocols as, technically, they require an initial shared secret key which they will then expand through the use of quantum communication.

In general, QKD protocols consist of a *quantum communication stage* followed by a classical reconciliation stage. The first stage utilizes, *through multiple iterations* the quantum and authenticated channels to produce a *raw key* - a string of classical bits that is partially correlated and partially secret. If the error rate is "low enough" (which depends on the protocol *and security model*), the second stage is employed which consists of an error-correcting protocol (done over the authenticated channel, thus leaking information to E "for free") and a privacy amplification protocol, yielding a *secret key*. The size of the secret key is directly correlated with the noise in the quantum channel and the amount of information an adversary potentially has on the raw-key. The more information the adversary has and the more noise, the smaller the secret key will be. In the standard adversarial model of security, the noise is assumed to be the product of the adversary's attack and the two are directly correlated; in fact, one important aspect of QKD research is to determine a protocols *maximally tolerated noise level*, that is the value of noise for which QKD is possible against a malicious adversary.

For more details on all these concepts, the reader is referred to [1].

Protocol 1. BB84 [18]

Public Knowledge: A key-bit "0" is encoded as a qubit $|0\rangle$ or $|+\rangle$ while a key-bit of "1" is encoded as $|1\rangle$ or $|-\rangle$.
Quantum Communication Stage (Repeat for N iterations):
1. A chooses a random key bit $k_A \in \{0,1\}$ and a random basis $b_A \in \{Z,X\}$. She sends the encoding of k_A as a qubit using her randomly chosen basis.
2. B chooses a random basis $b_B \in \{Z,X\}$ and measures in that basis.
3. A and B share, over the authenticated channel, their choice b_A and b_B respectively. Parties only keep those iterations where $b_A = b_B$. All other results are discarded (approximately half should remain).

Protocol 2. B92 [19]

Public Knowledge: A key-bit "0" is encoded as a qubit $|0\rangle$ while a key-bit of "1" is encoded as a qubit $|+\rangle$.
Quantum Communication Stage (Repeat for N iterations):
1. A chooses a random key bit $k_A \in \{0,1\}$ and prepares an appropriate qubit for B.
2. B chooses a random basis $b_B \in \{Z,X\}$ and measures in that basis. If $b_B = Z$ and he observes $|1\rangle$, the B sets $k_B = 1$. If $b_B = X$ and he observes $|-\rangle$, then B sets $k_B = 0$. All other results are considered "inconclusive."
3. B informs A, over the authenticated channel, which iterations he considered "inconclusive." All inconclusive iterations are discarded. It is expected that one-quarter of the iterations will remain.

3 Game Theoretic Model

We now introduce our game theoretic security model for QKD. While in practice, A and B are two separate entities, in our game theoretic model, we will consider them as one party which we denote by AB. We therefore consider a two-party game consisting of player AB and player E. The goal of party AB is to establish a long, secret key shared between each other. The goal of E is to limit the length of the final secret key. Since it is trivial for E to cause a denial-of-service attack in a point-to-point communication protocol (of which QKD is one), we limit E's strategy space to consisting of attacks which induce less noise than some maximal value Q which AB advertise as tolerating. This parameter Q can also represent certain "natural" noise in the quantum channel - AB will abort if the noise exceeds this value, thus if E attacks, she must "hide" in the natural noise. Noise for us is defined to be the average probability of a $|i\rangle$ flipping to a $|1-i\rangle$ and a $|\pm\rangle$ flipping to a $|\mp\rangle$. One key interest to us will be for what values of Q, QKD is possible in our game theoretic model and compare this with the standard adversarial model.

Beyond these goals, there are costs for using certain quantum (and potentially also classical) resources. For AB sending and receiving qubits can be a costly activity. Thus, though AB wish to establish a key, if doing so is "too expensive" they may wish to simply "abort" and do nothing. On the other hand, to gain information is E's goal (as this limits the size of the secret key), however attacking the quantum channel is a costly activity and extracting maximal information may require expensive quantum memory systems. Thus, it is the goal of our framework to construct a protocol (game strategy) where it is in AB's interest to run the protocol (and not abort), while it is in E's interest not to perform a complicated attack against it. Passive attacks (as opposed to more powerful quantum attacks) can greatly increase the efficiency of the protocol as we will see. *Thus, if users employ the rational model of security for QKD, more efficient quantum communication may be possible.*

One may consider applying our model to classical key-distribution (for instance, by using a hard problem that takes a large amount of classical resources to break); however this problem scenario, and the rewards for attacking, are very different from the quantum case. In a QKD protocol, the generated key is information theoretically secure, thus, for example, any message encrypted using the produced key is perfectly secret for all time. However, if a classical key-distribution system is used, an adversary may copy all communication sent by the protocol and attack offline; eventually if the system is broken, that adversary can learn all messages encrypted with that key. This is a very powerful motivating factor for an adversary. Contrast this with QKD: first, the adversary cannot attack offline and must attack actively. Furthermore, the adversary cannot learn the produced secret key nor any message encrypted with it.

We formulate our game-theoretic security model as follows. Let Σ_{AB} be a set of strategies (i.e., *protocols*) which party AB may choose to run and let Σ_E be the set of strategies (i.e., *attacks*) which party E may choose to employ against

AB. We always assume the "do nothing" strategy (denoted I_{AB} for AB and I_E for E) is an option for either party. (We use I for "identity operation.")

Now, in reality, player AB actually consists of two separate entities, thus it is important to ensure that our game-theoretic model can actually be employed in practice. In particular, we must ensure that A and B can agree on a strategy in a way that makes sense. There are many ways to achieve this; one in particular is they can sacrifice some of their initial shared secret key to send a constant-length message encrypted with one-time-pad (this message is the protocol to use). As mentioned earlier (see Sect. 2.1), for the authentication channel to work, A and B must begin with some shared random key already. They may use a constant amount $c = \log_2 |\Sigma_{AB}|$ to send, with perfect secrecy, the choice of protocol. So long as c is not a function of the number of iterations used in the quantum channel (which it is not), there is no contradiction to the key-expansion properties of QKD. Note that one cannot use this shared initial key to send securely a longer classical key - it can only be used for a small, constant, amount of initial communication such as picking from a small subset of strategies.

There are other ways for A and B to agree on a strategy, however, we may safely assume that party AB, though two distinct entities separated physically, may, at the start, agree on a single protocol to use from the set of allowed strategies Σ_{AB}. Note that a *mixed strategy* may also be agreed on by having A choose a random protocol and sending the choice, securely, to B.

Let $Q \in [0, .5]$ be the maximal noise level in the channel which is publicly known to both players before the game begins (alternatively, Q may be a value set by AB that is the "maximal tolerated" noise allowed in the channel, either naturally or artificially). Thus, even if E chooses not to attack (i.e., she chooses strategy I_E), she will still learn something about the raw key without incurring any costs (due to the information leaked by error correction). However, if she wishes to learn *more* (causing the secret key length to drop further) she must choose to attack the channel. We will assume that this attacker, if she chooses to attack, is able to replace the noisy quantum channel with an ideal one and then *hide* the noise her attack inevitably creates within this natural noise parameter Q. Such an operation (attacking, and setting up her equipment to hide within the natural noise) will be potentially expensive, though she will gain more information on the raw key thereby decreasing the efficiency of AB, her goal.

After running their respective protocol $\Pi \in \Sigma_{AB}$ (which includes running a quantum communication stage for N iterations, followed by error correction and privacy amplification), with E attacking using attack $\mathcal{A} \in \Sigma_E$, each party is given a utility for the outcome of the game. The outcome of the game for party AB is a function of the resulting *secret key length* (i.e., after error correction and privacy amplification), denoted M along with the cost of running the chosen strategy (denoted, $C_{AB}(\Pi)$). For our analysis, we will assume the utility is a simple linear function of the form:

$$u_{AB}(M, C_A(\Pi)) = w_g^{AB} M - w_c^{AB} C_{AB}(\Pi).$$

where w_g^{AB} and w_c^{AB} are non-negative weights for the "gain" and "cost" respectively of AB's utility. We will assume that these weights are simply 1.

For E, her utility is a function of the information she learned on the error-corrected raw key (before privacy amplification but after error correction) and the cost of running her chosen attack. Let K be the information E learns on the raw-key and $C_E(\mathcal{A})$ the cost of attack $\mathcal{A} \in \Sigma_E$. Then, her utility will be:

$$u_E(K, C_E(\mathcal{A})) = w_g^E K - w_c^E C_E(\mathcal{A}).$$

where w_g^E and w_c^E are non-negative weights for the "gain" and "cost" of E's utility. As with u_{AB}, we will assume that these weights are simply 1.

The reader may wonder what E's rational motivation would be for learning information about the raw-key (before privacy amplification) when it is the *secret key* (after privacy amplification) that is actually used by A and B later to, for example, encrypt messages. First, note that if we define the model to be E gains utility for learning information on the secret key, by the very definition of privacy amplification, her gain would be negligible (and, in the asymptotic scenario, we may even say it would be zero); thus this could never motivate her. On the other hand, we could not give her utility for causing A and B to simply abort due to high noise levels above Q as this is a form of *denial of service* attack which would cost E little to nothing to execute (E can simply cut the quantum channel!) and is a weakness for any point-to-point communication system, especially QKD. Thus, since gaining information on the secret key is not possible, and since a denial of service attack is outside the scope of the model, E's goal is to *minimize the key-rate of the protocol* (i.e., minimize its efficiency). Since the more information E has on the *raw-key* the smaller the secret key will be (after privacy amplification), it is E's goal to increase her information (thus shrinking the size of the final secret key) while minimizing her cost and staying below the natural noise level of Q.

We will use $U_{AB}(\Pi, \mathcal{A})$ to denote the expected utility given to player AB if that player chooses strategy $\Pi \in \Sigma_{AB}$ and if E chooses strategy $\mathcal{A} \in \Sigma_E$. $U_E(\Pi, \mathcal{A})$ is defined similarly for E.

The goal in our game-theoretic model of QKD security is to construct a protocol (strategy) "Π" such that the joint strategy (Π, I_E) is a strict Nash equilibrium (NE). In particular AB are motivated to actually run the protocol while E is motivated to not launch a complicated quantum attack against it. If such a protocol exists, then, under the assumption of a rational adversary, that adversary will choose not to implement a powerful quantum attack as it will be too expensive. This security model guarantees that if AB and E are rational, then, assuming the protocol is a strict NE, the resulting key is information theoretically secure. In the standard adversarial model the key is also information theoretically secure, however the effective key-rate will be lower after privacy amplification as one must "remove" E's additional information from her quantum attack. Thus, by assuming rational adversaries, one still maintains information theoretic security, but with greater communication efficiency.

In this work, we will consider standard QKD protocols (such as BB84 [18]) and add to these protocols additional "decoy" iterations. These decoy iterations will be, during the operation of the protocol, completely indistinguishable from standard iterations. At the end of the game (protocol run), AB will announce which iterations were "real" and which were decoys. Decoy iterations, which are useless to both parties, cost AB resources as they must still prepare and measure qubits (if they do not send qubits, this is distinguishable to E and she will know it is a decoy). However, since E cannot tell which are the decoy iterations, she is forced to attack them all the same, thus costing her resources also. If E's attack is very expensive (e.g., requires an expensive quantum memory to operate), then the more decoy iterations there are, the less incentive she will have to attack at all. Of course, the more decoy iterations there are, the less incentive AB will have to run the protocol as it will become too expensive for too little reward.

To incorporate this decoy method, we will introduce a parameter $\alpha \in [0, 1]$ which may be set by AB. On any iteration of a protocol, during the quantum communication stage, AB (in practice, just party A) will decide whether this iteration is a real iteration (with probability α) or a decoy iteration (with probability $1 - \alpha$), however they run the iteration normally regardless so that E cannot distinguish the two cases. At the conclusion of the protocol, all decoy iterations are discarded (to achieve this in practice, A will transmit, at the conclusion of the protocol, through the authenticated classical channel, which iterations were decoys - thus E also learns this at the end of the game, *but at that point, she already used resources to attack*; furthermore, properties such as the No-Cloning Theorem, prevent her from making copies of qubits and later changing her attack based on this new knowledge). A protocol strategy, therefore, will be denoted $\Pi^{(\alpha)}$. Ultimately, the goal within this game-theoretic model is to find a value for α such that the joint strategy $(\Pi^{(\alpha)}, I_E)$ is a strict NE. Furthermore, we wish to determine what values of Q allow for an α to exist and to determine the efficiency of the resulting protocol.

3.1   All-Powerful Attacks Against BB84

In this section, we apply our framework to model security of the BB84 protocol allowing E the ability to launch all-powerful attacks (e.g., attacks requiring quantum memories). We will prove that the noise tolerance of the BB84 protocol in our game theoretic framework remains 11%, the same as in the standard adversarial model [20]. However, we will show that, for noise levels less than 11%, the efficiency of the protocol can be substantially higher in our game theoretic model than in the standard adversarial model.

We will consider the BB84 protocol parameterized by α, denoted here as $\Pi^{(\alpha)}_{BB84}$. We will consider what is required for $(\Pi^{(\alpha)}_{BB84}, I_E)$ to be a strict Nash equilibrium. First, consider AB's utility for this strategy; we assume N is the number of iterations they run the protocol for. In this case, since E is not attacking, after error correction and privacy amplification, the secret key will be of expected length $\frac{N\alpha}{2}(1 - h(Q))$ (recall, in BB84, only half the iterations are expected to be kept - see Protocol 1). Thus:

$$U_{AB}(\Pi_{BB84}^{(\alpha)}, I_E) = \frac{N}{2}\alpha(1 - h(Q)) - C_{AB}, \qquad (1)$$

were we use C_{AB} to mean $C_{AB}(\Pi_{BB84}^{(\alpha)})$ (a value that AB must decide on, though its actual numerical value will not be important to us in this section). On the other hand, we have $U_{AB}(I_{AB}, I_E) = 0$. Thus, for a strict NE to exist, we require:

$$\alpha > \frac{2C_{AB}}{N(1 - h(Q))}.$$

Naturally, this requires $1 - h(Q) > \frac{2}{N}C_{AB}$. Thus, if this expression cannot be satisfied, then the natural noise in the quantum channel (denoted Q) is too great and AB cannot justify the cost of running the protocol. In the following analysis, we will assume this inequality is satisfied.

Let us now consider E's expected utility. If E does not attack (i.e., she chooses to play strategy I_E), then, since we are also considering "natural noise" in the channel at a rate of Q, party E will gain $\frac{N\alpha}{2}h(Q)$ bits of information on AB's raw key "for free" simply by listening in to the authenticated classical channel (we are assuming optimal error-correcting). Thus her expected utility is: $U_E(\Pi_{BB84}^{(\alpha)}, I_E) = \alpha\frac{N}{2}h(Q)$.

Now, assume that E chooses an optimal quantum attack strategy $\mathcal{A} \in \Sigma_E$. From this, she will gain more information on the raw key (thus shrinking the final secret key size, her ultimate goal), though it also will cost something to implement. Furthermore, she will waste resources on attacking decoy states. It is known that $I(A : E) = \frac{\alpha N}{2}h(Q)$ when E performs an optimal attack [1]. Thus, her utility (based on $I(\mathcal{A} : E)$ and *also the information learned from error correction*) is:

$$U_E(\Pi_{BB84}^{(\alpha)}, \mathcal{A}) = I(A : E) + \alpha\frac{N}{2}h(Q) - C_E(\mathcal{A}) = \alpha N h(Q) - C_E(\mathcal{A})$$

Thus, to be a strict NE, we require $U_E(\Pi_{BB84}^{(\alpha)}, I_E) > U_E(\Pi_{BB84}^{(\alpha)}, \mathcal{A})$. For this inequality to hold it must be that: $\alpha < \frac{2C_E(\mathcal{A})}{Nh(Q)}$. Thus, for the strategy $(\Pi_{BB84}^{(\alpha)}, I)$ to be a strict NE, we require an α to exist that satisfies the following inequalities:

$$\frac{2C_A}{N(1 - h(Q))} < \alpha < \frac{2C_E(\mathcal{A})}{Nh(Q)}. \qquad (2)$$

If such an α exists, and if AB choose that for their decoy state probability, they can be assured, in our rational model of security, that E will prefer to not attack the quantum channel but instead, simply eavesdrop on the authenticated channel. Furthermore, with such an α, rational AB are also motivated to run the protocol, as opposed to simply aborting.

To determine suitable values for α we require values for C_{AB} and $C_E(\mathcal{A})$. Let's assume a worst-case scenario in that $C_{AB} = C_E(\mathcal{A})$. Note that, to implement $\mathcal{A}$ in practice, E must somehow cut into the quantum channel, replace the natural noise with a more precise channel, setup attack equipment, and, in this scenario where $I(A : E) = h(Q)$, construct and operate a perfect quantum memory. In reality, it seems reasonable to expect that $C_E(\mathcal{A}) > C_{AB}$. Thus, making these equal models a "worst-case" scenario of benefit to E.

Now, by assumption, we have $\frac{2}{N}C_{AB} < 1 - h(Q)$ (i.e., the cost per-bit for AB is less than $(1 - h(Q))/2$; if this assumption is not made, then AB have no motivation to run the protocol). Thus, the left-hand-side of Eq. 2 is strictly less than 1 and, so, a solution for α exists only if the following inequality is satisfied:

$$\frac{C_A}{1 - h(Q)} < \frac{C_E(\mathcal{A})}{h(Q)}.$$

Since we are assuming in this section that $C_{AB} = C_E(\mathcal{A})$, then $(\Pi_{BB84}^{(\alpha)}, I_E)$ is a strict NE only if the noise in the channel Q satisfies the following inequality:

$$1 - 2h(Q) > 0. \tag{3}$$

This is exactly the same noise tolerance bound as is derived in the standard adversarial model for BB84 as reported in [1,20,21]! In particular, a solution for α exists only if $Q \leq 11\%$.

However, despite the noise tolerance threshold being the same in our new game-theoretic model and the standard adversarial model, our game theoretic model may be used to gain a significantly improved key-rate as we now demonstrate. Assume that $Q \leq 11\%$ (and so $1 - 2h(Q) > 0$ and thus an α exists). Let α be the largest allowed by Eq. 2 (the higher α is, the better for AB as the more "real" iterations are being used on average). We may thus set:

$$\alpha = \min\left(\frac{2c_E(\mathcal{A})}{Nh(Q)} - \epsilon, 1 - \epsilon\right),$$

for some small $\epsilon > 0$. Since we are assuming $C_E(\mathcal{A}) = C_{AB}$ and we also require $\frac{2}{N}C_A < 1 - h(Q)$, we may write $C_E = \frac{\gamma}{2} \cdot N(1 - h(Q))$ for some constant $\gamma < 1$ and thus we have:

$$\alpha = \min\left(\gamma\frac{1 - h(Q)}{h(Q)} - \epsilon, 1 - \epsilon\right). \tag{4}$$

With α chosen as this, it is in E's interest to not attack, but to instead only gain the free information from the error-correction due to the natural noise level Q. In this case, the Csiszar-Korner bound [22] applies (as E no longer has a quantum system, but a classical one) which gives us a secret key size, after privacy amplification and error correction, of:

$$\ell_{GT}(N) = \alpha\frac{N}{2}(1 - h(Q)) = \frac{N}{2}\min\left(\gamma \cdot \frac{(1 - h(Q))^2}{h(Q)}, (1 - \epsilon)(1 - h(Q))\right). \tag{5}$$

On the other hand, in the standard adversarial model for a noise level of Q, the secret key size would be: $\ell_{SAM}(N) = \frac{N}{2}(1 - 2h(Q))$. Discounting the ϵ term (which may be made arbitrarily close to 0), we plot the conditional key-rate of the BB84 protocol in both our new game theoretic model and the standard adversarial model (i.e., we plot $2\ell_{GT}(N)/N$ and $2\ell_{SAM}(N)/N$ respectively) in Fig. 1.

Note that, even though the noise tolerance is the same in both security models, our game-theoretic security model may provide a much higher key-rate (i.e., efficiency) depending on the cost C_{AB} (i.e., γ). *Thus, by using a game-theoretic model of security, more efficient quantum secure communication systems may be employed!*

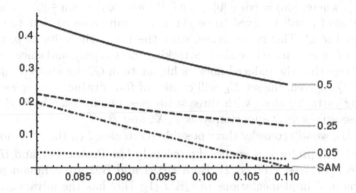

Fig. 1. Showing the key-rate of the BB84 protocol in the Standard Adversarial Model (SAM) compared with our game-theoretic model at high noise levels (x axis) for various values of γ. Higher means more efficient communication.

3.2   Intercept/Resend Attacks

In the previous section, we considered $\Sigma_{AB} = \{I_{AB}, \Pi_{BB84}^{(\alpha)}\}$ while E's strategy space was $\Sigma_E = \{I_E, \mathcal{A}\}$ where $\mathcal{A}$ was an optimal attack against the BB84 protocol utilizing a quantum memory system. We also assumed that the cost of performing attack $\mathcal{A}$ was similar to the cost of AB running the actual protocol (a very strong assumption in favor of the adversary). In practice, such an attack would be very difficult to launch against the protocol (and, with current technology, impossible as it would require a perfect quantum memory to perform successfully). In this section, we consider practical, so-called *Intercept-Resend (IR) attacks*. These attacks can be performed using today's technology; they also require hardware similar to that used by A and B, allowing us to more accurately compute the cost of an attack compared with the cost of running the actual protocol.

For this attack, on each iteration of the quantum communication stage, E will, with probability p, choose to attack and with probability $1 - p$ choose to ignore the incoming qubit. This value p will control how much noise E's IR attack actually creates (which, as before, must be kept below the natural noise level Q). This choice to attack or not is part of the strategy and is made independently for each iteration of the quantum communication stage. This is also different from the I_E strategy which chooses to not attack *every* iteration.

Should E decide to attack a particular iteration (with probability p), she will first measure the incoming qubit in a basis $\{|\nu_0\rangle, |\nu_1\rangle\}$ (this is fixed for each iteration and part of the strategy) causing the qubit to collapse to one of the basis states $|\nu_0\rangle$ or $|\nu_1\rangle$. If E observes $|\nu_i\rangle$, she will "guess" that the key-bit for this iteration is $i \in \{0, 1\}$. She will then send a fresh qubit in the state $|\nu_i\rangle$ to B.

There are two important parameters for an IR attack; first the value p and, second, the basis choice. We consider three common bases choices for IR attacks: $Z = \{|0\rangle, |1\rangle\}$, $X = \{|+\rangle, |-\rangle\}$ (see Sect. 2, and the Breidbart basis $B = \{|\phi_0\rangle, |\phi_1\rangle\}$, where: $|\phi_0\rangle = \cos\frac{\pi}{8}|0\rangle + \sin\frac{\pi}{8}|1\rangle$ and $|\phi_1\rangle = \sin\frac{\pi}{8}|0\rangle - \cos\frac{\pi}{8}|1\rangle$.

The value of p will be fixed to be the maximum value so that the induced noise is equal to Q. This makes sense, since the larger the value of p, the more information E may learn (since she is attacking more often), and since we cannot have p so large that the induced noise is higher than Q, the allowed maximum. Thus, once Q is given, the set Σ_E will consist of four distinct strategies: I_E (the "do nothing" attack); along with three strategies, one for each basis choice (we denote these attack strategies simply as Z, X, and B).

As for AB, we will consider three possible strategies: I_{AB} (i.e., "do nothing"); $\Pi_{BB84}^{(\alpha)}$ the BB84 protocol as analyzed previously (see Protocol 1); and $\Pi_{B92}^{(\alpha)}$, the B92 protocol [19] (see Protocol 2). Both BB84 and B92 are common protocols used in practical implementations of QKD [1]; B92 has the advantage that it requires less quantum resources to implement (and, so, is cheaper). However, at least in the standard adversarial model, B92 has a lower noise tolerance [20]. In this section, we will show that, so long as Q satisfies certain bounds, the joint strategy $(\Pi_{BB84}^{(\alpha)}, I_E)$ is a strict NE (for suitably chosen α); we will also show that $\Pi_{BB84}^{(\alpha)}$ is a dominate strategy for player AB and I_E is a DS for E for certain critical values of noise levels Q.

We begin by computing the utility of each possible action pair $(\Pi^{(\alpha)}, \mathcal{A})$. First, we must compute the cost associated to each strategy. To do so, we will define the following cost values for certain, basic, functionalities needed to implement the QKD protocol, and the IR attack:

C_S : The initial cost for E to setup her attack equipment
        (e.g., splicing into the quantum channel)

C_M : The cost to perform a measurement in a single basis

C_P : The cost to prepare a qubit basis state

$C_R(\delta)$: The cost to produce a δ-biased bit
        We assume that $C_R(\delta) = h(\delta)C_R$ for some cost C_R

C_{auth} : The cost for AB to use the authenticated channel

We will assume that, if one requires an apparatus that is capable of producing a qubit in x different states, the cost is $\gamma_x C_P$ for some function γ_x. Similarly, for an apparatus capable of measuring a qubit in x different states, the cost is $\gamma_x C_M$. Our analysis below will be suitable for any non-decreasing γ_x; however when we evaluate our results, we will consider two cases: first $\gamma_x = 1$ for all x (i.e., there is no increase in cost) and, second, $\gamma_x = x$ (the cost increases linearly in the number of required states). Note that we will assume $C_P \leq C_M$ which is a reasonable assumption since measurement devices are generally more complicated (and sensitive) than preparation devices [1]. These cost values may take into account such practical issues as device energy consumption over time for example (thus running the devices for longer, or having devices capable of performing additional measurements, will potentially cost users more).

From this, we can compute the following costs after N iterations of each protocol:

$$C_{AB}(\Pi^{(\alpha)}_{BB84}) = N[(3 + h(\alpha))C_R + \gamma_4 C_M + \gamma_4 C_P] + C_{auth} \tag{6}$$
$$C_{AB}(\Pi^{(\alpha)}_{B92}) = N[(2 + h(\alpha))C_R + \gamma_4 C_M + \gamma_2 C_P] + C_{auth}.$$

For BB84, AB must choose, each iteration, whether the iteration is a decoy or not (costing $h(\alpha)C_R$); what basis A should send in (with probability $1/2$ each, thus costing C_R); what basis to measure in (costing C_R); and, finally, A must choose a random key bit (again, costing C_R). For B92, only one basis choice is required (from B). Finally, note that, BB84 is a *four-state* protocol in that A must prepare one of four possible qubit states each iteration. B92, however, is a *two-state* protocol - A must only be capable of preparing a state of the form $|0\rangle$ or $|+\rangle$. In both cases, however, B must be able to measure one of four states (from two bases). It is clear that the cost of running B92 is no greater than the cost of running BB84.

The cost for E to operate attack I_E is zero (i.e., $C_E(I_E) = 0$). The cost for the other strategies is the same: first, she must choose to attack or not, costing $h(p)C_R$; then she must measure and prepare a qubit in one basis. Those operations are performed for all N iterations of the quantum communication stage. Furthermore, she must also spend resources costing C_S to setup her attack initially (this is a one-time cost). The total cost for any attack $\mathcal{A} = Z, X, B$ is:

$$C_E(\mathcal{A}) = N[h(p)C_R + p(\gamma_2 C_M + \gamma_2 C_P)] + C_S, \text{ for any } \mathcal{A} \in \{Z, X, B\}. \tag{7}$$

To complete our utility computation, we must also compute the secret key length for each protocol under each attack. Since an IR attack results in three classical random variables (one for Alice, Bob, and Eve), we may use the Csiszar-Korner bound [22] to compute the number of secret bits that may be distilled from these sources. Let $\ell(N, \Pi^{(\alpha)}, \mathcal{A})$ be the amount of secret key bits that may be distilled after N iterations of protocol $\Pi^{(\alpha)}$ given that E used attack $\mathcal{A}$. Then from this bound, we have: $\ell(N, \Pi^{(\alpha)}, \mathcal{A}) = \eta N \alpha [I(A : B) - I(A : E)]$, where η is the proportion of non-discarded iterations; namely $\eta = 1/2$ for BB84 and $\eta = 1/4$ for B92 (see Protocols 1 and 2).

Note that the information computations above are dependent on only a single iteration of the protocol when faced with the specified attack since we are assuming iid attacks. Let $\mathcal{I}(\Pi^{(\alpha)}, \mathcal{A})$ be equal to $I(A : E)$ for the specified protocol and attack; then, the utility functions, for a fixed N, will be:

$$U_{AB}(\Pi^{(\alpha)}, \mathcal{A}) = \eta N \alpha [I(A : B) - \mathcal{I}(\Pi^{(\alpha)}, \mathcal{A})] - C_{AB}(\Pi^{(\alpha)}) \tag{8}$$
$$U_E(\Pi^{(\alpha)}, \mathcal{A}) = \eta N \alpha [\mathcal{I}(\Pi^{(\alpha)}, \mathcal{A}) + h(\widetilde{Q})] - C_E(\mathcal{A}), \tag{9}$$

where we use $\widetilde{Q}$ to denote the *raw-key error rate*; i.e., the error of the actual raw key which undergoes error correction (which, in the case of B92, is actually greater than the noise in the channel Q). The value $\eta N \alpha h(\widetilde{Q})$ denotes the information leaked to E "for free" during error correction.

To complete the utility computation, we require $I(A : B)$ and $I(A : E)$ for all possible protocols and strategy pairs. It is not difficult to show that $I(A : B) = 1 - h(\widetilde{Q})$. For BB84, a raw-key error occurs when a $|i\rangle$ flips to a $|1 - i\rangle$ (for $i = 0, 1$) or when a $|\pm\rangle$ flips to a $|\mp\rangle$. By definition, this is exactly the channel noise level Q. Thus, for $\Pi^{(\alpha)}_{BB84}$, we have $I(A : B) = 1 - h(Q)$. For B92 it can be shown (see, for example, [23]) that the raw-key error is in fact: $\widetilde{Q} = 2Q/(1 - 2Q)$. Next, we must compute $\mathcal{I}(\Pi^{(\alpha)}, \mathcal{A})$. Clearly, $\mathcal{I}(\Pi^{(\alpha)}, I_E) = 0$ for any protocol. Consider, now, an IR attack where E measures and resends in a basis $\{|v_0\rangle, |v_1\rangle\}$ (in our case, either Z, X, or B, however the equations we derive here may be applied to other attack bases). By the measurement postulate, if A sends a qubit of the form $|i\rangle$ (for $i = 0, 1, +, -$), E will observe $|v_j\rangle$ with probability $v_{i,j} = |\langle i|v_j\rangle|^2$. To compute $\mathcal{I}(\Pi^{(\alpha)}, \mathcal{A})$ we will need the joint distribution held between A and E. This is straight-forward arithmetic: one must simply trace the execution of each protocol and use the measurement postulate. We summarize this distribution in Table 1.

Table 1. Showing the joint probability distribution for A's raw key bit and E's "guess" based on her attack (conditioning on the event she chooses to attack). For B92, we require a normalization term, denoted M which is: $M = v_{0,0}(v_{-,0} + v_{1,0}) + v_{0,1}(v_{-,1} + v_{1,1}) + v_{+,0}(v_{-,0} + v_{1,0}) + v_{+,1}(v_{-,1} + v_{1,1})$. The values here are found by tracing the protocol and using the measurement postulate.

AE	BB84	B92
00	$\frac{1}{4}(v_{0,0} + v_{+,0})$	$\frac{1}{M}v_{0,0}(v_{-,0} + v_{1,0})$
01	$\frac{1}{4}(v_{0,1} + v_{+,1})$	$\frac{1}{M}v_{0,1}(v_{-,1} + v_{1,1})$
10	$\frac{1}{4}(v_{1,0} + v_{-,0})$	$\frac{1}{M}v_{+,0}(v_{-,0} + v_{1,0})$
11	$\frac{1}{4}(v_{1,1} + v_{-,1})$	$\frac{1}{M}v_{+,1}(v_{-,1} + v_{1,1})$

By definition, we have $\mathcal{I}(\Pi^{(\alpha)}, \mathcal{A}) = p(H(A) + H(E) - H(AE))$ where the Shannon entropies may be computed easily from data in Table 1 and substituting in $|v_i\rangle$ for the appropriate basis state depending on the attack E uses (note that when E chooses to not attack, which occurs with probability $1 - p$, she learns nothing, thus the need for the factor p in this expression). In summary, these are found to be:

$$\mathcal{I}(\Pi^{(\alpha)}_{BB84}, Z) \approx .189p \quad \mathcal{I}(\Pi^{(\alpha)}_{BB84}, X) \approx .189p \quad \mathcal{I}(\Pi^{(\alpha)}_{BB84}, B) \approx .399p$$

$$\mathcal{I}(\Pi^{(\alpha)}_{B92}, Z) \approx .459p \quad \mathcal{I}(\Pi^{(\alpha)}_{B92}, X) \approx .459p \quad \mathcal{I}(\Pi^{(\alpha)}_{B92}, B) = 0.$$

What remains is to find a value for p. As stated, we will assume that p is chosen to maximize E's information while keeping the induced noise from her attack equal to Q. The natural noise in the channel is the average of the Z basis noise (which, in turn, is the average error of a $|i\rangle$ flipping to a $|1-i\rangle$ when it arrives at B's lab) and X basis noise (the average of a $|\pm\rangle$ flipping to a $|\mp\rangle$); that is: $Q = \frac{p}{4}(v_{0,0}v_{1,0} + v_{0,1}v_{1,1} + v_{1,0}v_{0,0} + v_{1,1}v_{0,1} + v_{+,0}v_{-,0} + v_{+,1}v_{-,1} + v_{-,0}v_{+,0} + v_{-,1}v_{+,1})$, from which it easily follows that $p = 2Q$ for $\mathcal{A} = Z, X$ and $p = 4Q$ for $\mathcal{A} = B$. Note that E may attack more often with the B basis as it induces less noise, on average, than the Z or X based IR attacks. From this analysis, we are now able to prove our two main results in this section involving sufficient conditions of the noise level for $(\Pi_{BB84}^{(\alpha)}, I_E)$ to be a strict NE and for each to be a DS.

Theorem 1. *Assume classical resources are free for both parties AB and E (that is, let $C_R = C_{auth} = C_S = 0$) and let $C_P \leq C_M$ (as discussed in the text). Define A_1 and A_2 as follows:*

$$A_1 = \frac{(\gamma_4 - \gamma_2)C_P}{\frac{1}{4} + \frac{1}{4}h\left(\frac{2Q}{1-2Q}\right) - \frac{1}{2}h(Q)} \qquad A_2 = \frac{2\gamma_4(C_M + C_P)}{1 - h(Q)}.$$

If $\max(A_1, A_2) < 1$ and Q, the noise in the channel is less than 0.232 and satisfies the following inequality:

$$\begin{cases} 10.025\left(\frac{1}{4} + \frac{1}{4}h\left(\frac{2Q}{1-2Q}\right) - \frac{1}{2}h(Q)\right) - \left(\frac{\gamma_4}{\gamma_2} - 1\right) > 0, & \text{If } A_1 \geq A_2 \\ 2.506(1 - h(Q)) - \frac{\gamma_4}{\gamma_2} > 0, & \text{Otherwise} \end{cases} \tag{10}$$

Then there exists an $\alpha \in [0,1]$ such that $(\Pi_{BB84}^{(\alpha)}, I_E)$ is a strict NE.

Proof. Since $C_{auth} = C_S = 0$, the factor of N may be divided out of the utility functions (we are only interested in relations between them and the factor N appears in both U_{AB} and U_E. This allows us to construct the function table shown in Table 2. From this table, we see that, for $(\Pi_{BB84}^{(\alpha)}, I_E)$ to be a strict NE, the following inequalities must be satisfied:

$$\alpha > \frac{2\gamma_4(C_M + C_P)}{1 - h(Q)}$$

$$\alpha > \frac{(\gamma_4 - \gamma_2)C_P}{\frac{1}{4} + \frac{1}{4}h\left(\frac{2Q}{1-2Q}\right) - \frac{1}{2}h(Q)} \quad \left[\text{If } \frac{1}{4} + \frac{1}{4}h\left(\frac{2Q}{1-2Q}\right) - \frac{1}{2}h(Q) > 0\right]$$

$$\alpha < \frac{4\gamma_2(C_M + C_P)}{0.378} \approx 10.582\gamma_2(C_M + C_P)$$

$$\alpha < \frac{8\gamma_2(C_M + C_P)}{1.596} \approx 5.013\gamma_2(C_M + C_P).$$

Note that, if $Q < .232$ (as assumed in the hypothesis), then $\frac{1}{4} + \frac{1}{4}h(2Q/(1 - 2Q)) - \frac{1}{2}h(Q) > 0$. From this, it is clear that if we can find an α that satisfies:

$$\max(A_1, A_2) < \alpha < \frac{8\gamma_2(C_M + C_P)}{1.596},$$

Table 2. Function table for utility functions U_{AB} and U_E assuming $C_{auth} = C_S = 0$ and dividing out the factor of N on both functions.

Π_{AB}	$\mathcal{E} = I_E$
I_{AB}	$U_{AB} = 0$
	$U_E = 0$
$\Pi^{(\alpha)}_{BB84}$	$U_{AB} = \frac{\alpha}{2}(1 - h(Q)) - [(3 + h(\alpha))C_R + \gamma_4 C_M + \gamma_4 C_P]$
	$U_E = \frac{\alpha}{2}h(Q)$
$\Pi^{(\alpha)}_{B92}$	$U_{AB} = \frac{\alpha}{4}\left(1 - h\left(\frac{2Q}{1-2Q}\right)\right) - [(2 + h(\alpha))C_R + \gamma_4 C_M + \gamma_2 C_P]$
	$U_E = \frac{\alpha}{4}h\left(\frac{2Q}{1-2Q}\right)$
	$\mathcal{E} = Z = X$ (No difference between Z and X for these protocols)
I_{AB}	$U_{AB} = 0$
	$U_E = 0$
$\Pi^{(\alpha)}_{BB84}$	$U_{AB} = \frac{\alpha}{2}(1 - h(Q) - 0.378Q) - [(3 + h(\alpha))C_R + \gamma_4 C_M + \gamma_4 C_P]$
	$U_E = \frac{\alpha}{2}(h(Q) + 0.378Q) - [h(2Q)C_R + 2Q\gamma_2(C_M + C_P)]$
$\Pi^{(\alpha)}_{B92}$	$U_{AB} = \frac{\alpha}{4}\left(1 - h\left(\frac{2Q}{1-2Q}\right) - 0.918Q\right) - [(2 + h(\alpha))C_R + \gamma_4 C_M + \gamma_2 C_P]$
	$U_E = \frac{\alpha}{4}\left(h\left(\frac{2Q}{1-2Q}\right) + 0.918Q\right) - [h(2Q)C_R + 2Q\gamma_2(C_M + C_P)]$
	$\mathcal{E} = B$
I_{AB}	$U_{AB} = 0$
	$U_E = 0$
$\Pi^{(\alpha)}_{BB84}$	$U_{AB} = \frac{\alpha}{2}(1 - h(Q) - 1.596Q) - [(3 + h(\alpha))C_R + \gamma_4 C_M + \gamma_4 C_P]$
	$U_E = \frac{\alpha}{2}(h(Q) + 1.596Q) - [h(4Q)C_R + 4Q\gamma_2(C_M + C_P)]$
$\Pi^{(\alpha)}_{B92}$	$U_{AB} = \frac{\alpha}{4}\left(1 - h\left(\frac{2Q}{1-2Q}\right)\right) - [(2 + h(\alpha))C_R + \gamma_4 C_M + \gamma_2 C_P]$
	$U_E = \frac{\alpha}{4}h\left(\frac{2Q}{1-2Q}\right) - [h(4Q)C_R + 4Q\gamma_2(C_M + C_P)]$

the resulting joint strategy will be a strict NE (recall, by hypothesis, $\max(A_1, A_2) < 1$). For such a value to exist, it must be that $\max(A_1, A_2)$ is strictly less than the right-hand side of the above expression.

We show this in two cases. First, assume $A_2 > A_1$. Then, by our assumptions on the channel noise Q, we have:

$$\frac{\gamma_4}{\gamma_2} < 2.506(1 - h(Q))$$

$$\implies \frac{\gamma_4(C_M + C_P)}{1 - h(Q)} < \frac{4\gamma_2(C_M + C_P)}{1.596} \implies \frac{2\gamma_4(C_M + C_P)}{1 - h(Q)} < \frac{8\gamma_2(C_M + C_P)}{1.596},$$

as desired.

For the second case, assume $A_1 \geq A_2$. Then, by assumption on the channel noise Q, we have:

$$\frac{\gamma_4}{\gamma_2} - 1 < 10.025 \left(\frac{1}{4} + \frac{1}{4}h\left(\frac{2Q}{1-2Q}\right) - \frac{1}{2}h(Q) \right)$$

$$\implies \frac{2(\gamma_4 - \gamma_2)C_P}{\frac{1}{4} + \frac{1}{4}h\left(\frac{2Q}{1-2Q}\right) - \frac{1}{2}h(Q)} < \frac{8\gamma_2(2C_P)}{1.596}.$$

Noting that $C_P \leq C_M$ completes the proof.

Table 3. Showing the allowed noise tolerance for which $(\Pi_{BB84}^{(\alpha)}, I_E)$ is a strict NE. When $\gamma_4 = \gamma_2$ then it is always true that $A_2 \geq A_1$ (since $A_1 = 0$ and A_2 is always non-negative) and so we do not need to evaluate the case for $A_1 > A_2$. When $\gamma_4 = 2\gamma_2$, we must evaluate both cases. See text for explanation.

	$A_2 \geq A_1$	$A_1 > A_2$
$\gamma_4 = \gamma_2$	$Q \leq .146$	n/a
$\gamma_4 = 2\gamma_2$	$Q \leq .031$	$Q \leq .207$

Theorem 1 gives conditions on the noise parameter Q for which $(\Pi_{BB84}^{(\alpha)}, I_E)$ becomes a strict NE. The restrictions on $\max(A_i) < 1$ may be satisfied if the cost C_P and C_M are low enough. The restrictions on Q depend only on the value γ_4 and γ_2. So long as Q satisfies Eq. 10, then AB are motivated to run the BB84 protocol and E is motivated to not perform an intercept/resend attack (but, instead, to simply "listen" on the authenticated channel). We evaluate the noise tolerance in Table 3. Surprisingly, if $\gamma_2 = \gamma_4$, the noise tolerance is 14.6% also the maximal noise tolerance of BB84 in the standard adversarial model against optimal individual attacks (which are more general/powerful than IR attacks). Note, however, while the noise tolerance may be lower in our game theoretic model, as before, the efficiency in our game theoretic model may improve as E is not motivated to attack.

Theorem 2. *Assume classical resources are free for both parties (i.e., let $C_R = C_{auth} = C_S = 0$) and let $C_P \leq C_M$ (as discussed in the text). Define A_1 and A_2 as follows:*

$$A_1 = \frac{(\gamma_4 - \gamma_2)C_P}{\frac{1}{4} + \frac{1}{4}h\left(\frac{2Q}{1-2Q}\right) - \frac{1}{2}h(Q) - 0.798Q} \qquad A_2 = \frac{2\gamma_4(C_M + C_P)}{1 - h(Q) - 1.596Q}. \quad (11)$$

If $\max(A_1, A_2) < 1$ and if Q, the noise in the channel, is strictly less than 0.185 and if it satisfies the following inequality:

$$\begin{cases} 10.025\left(\frac{1}{4} + \frac{1}{4}h\left(\frac{2Q}{1-2Q}\right) - \frac{1}{2}h(Q) - 0.798Q\right) - \left(\frac{\gamma_4}{\gamma_2} - 1\right) > 0, & \text{If } A_1 \geq A_2 \\ 2.506(1 - h(Q) - 1.596Q) - \frac{\gamma_4}{\gamma_2} > 0, & \text{Otherwise} \end{cases}$$

$$(12)$$

then there exists a value for α such that $\Pi_{BB84}^{(\alpha)}$ is a dominate strategy (DS) for AB and I_E is a DS for E.

Proof. Fix α. For $\Pi_{BB84}^{(\alpha)}$ to be a DS for AB, we must show that, for every strategy $\mathcal{E} \in \Sigma_E$, it holds that $U_{AB}(\Pi_{BB84}^{(\alpha)}, \mathcal{E}) \geq U_{AB}(\Pi^{(\alpha)}, \mathcal{E})$ for $\Pi^{(\alpha)} = \Pi_{B92}^{(\alpha)}$ and $\Pi^{(\alpha)} = I_{AB}$. We see from Table 2, for this to be true, the following inequalities must be satisfied:

$$\alpha > \frac{2\gamma_4(C_M + C_P)}{1 - h(Q)} \qquad \alpha > \frac{(\gamma_4 - \gamma_2)C_P}{\frac{1}{4} + \frac{1}{4}h\left(\frac{2Q}{1-2Q}\right) - \frac{1}{2}h(Q)}$$

$$\alpha > \frac{2\gamma_4(C_M + C_P)}{1 - h(Q) - 0.378Q} \qquad \alpha > \frac{(\gamma_4 - \gamma_2)C_P}{\frac{1}{4} + \frac{1}{4}h\left(\frac{2Q}{1-2Q}\right) - \frac{1}{2}h(Q) + 0.0405Q}$$

$$\alpha > \frac{2\gamma_4(C_M + C_P)}{1 - h(Q) - 1.596Q} \qquad \alpha > \frac{(\gamma_4 - \gamma_2)C_P}{\frac{1}{4} + \frac{1}{4}h\left(\frac{2Q}{1-2Q}\right) - \frac{1}{2}h(Q) - 0.798Q}$$

Note that, the denominators of the above six inequalities are all positive by assumption that $Q < 0.185$. Note also, that there are only six inequalities, and not eight, since two are repetitions.

It is not difficult to see that if we take $\alpha \geq \max(A_1, A_2)$, where A_1 and A_2 are defined in Eq. 11, then all the above inequalities are automatically satisfied and, so, $\Pi_{BB84}^{(\alpha)}$ will be a DS for party AB.

Now, we consider E's strategy I_E. For I_E to be a DS for party E, the following inequalities must be satisfied (again, consulting Table 2):

$$\alpha < \frac{4Q\gamma_2(C_M + C_P)}{.378Q} \approx 10.582\gamma_2(C_M + C_P)$$

$$\alpha < \frac{8Q\gamma_2(C_M + C_P)}{1.596Q} \approx 5.013\gamma_2(C_M + C_P)$$

$$\alpha < \frac{8Q\gamma_2(C_M + C_P)}{0.918Q} \approx 8.715\gamma_2(C_M + C_P)$$

Clearly if $\alpha < \frac{8Q\gamma_2(C_M+C_P)}{1.596Q}$, the other two are also satisfied. All that remains to be shown is that an α exists allowing both $\Pi_{BB84}^{(\alpha)}$ to be a DS for AB and I_E to be a DS for E. In particular, we must show that: $\max(A_1, A_2) < \frac{8\gamma_2(C_M+C_P)}{1.596}$. However, this can be proven in a similar manner as in the proof of Theorem 1, using the new bounds on Q from Eq. 12. This completes the proof.

The allowed noise tolerances for $\Pi_{BB84}^{(\alpha)}$ to be a DS for AB *and* I_E to be a DS for E, are reported in Table 4.

4   Closing Remarks

In this paper, we introduced a new game-theoretic model of QKD security. Many interesting problems remain open. It would be interesting to analyze best-reply

Table 4. Showing the allowed noise values Q from Theorem 2.

	$A_2 \geq A_1$	$A_1 > A_2$
$\gamma_4 = \gamma_2$	$Q \leq .094$	n/a
$\gamma_4 = 2\gamma_2$	$Q \leq .024$	$Q \leq .13$

strategies under different noise values and decoy probabilities. We may also consider adding additional strategies for AB, different, non-linear, utility functions, and support for multi-user protocols [24]. One may also analyze the NE strategies based on Stackelberg game model, when the attacker E observes the strategy of party AB and chooses her strategy accordingly. One can envision a system whereby parties re-evaluate their choices after large sequences of N iterations, taking into account noise conditions, to chose new optimal strategies.

References

1. Scarani, V., Bechmann-Pasquinucci, H., Cerf, N.J., Dušek, M., Lütkenhaus, N., Peev, M.: The security of practical quantum key distribution. Rev. Mod. Phys. **81**, 1301–1350 (2009)
2. Katz, J.: Bridging game theory and cryptography: recent results and future directions. In: Canetti, R. (ed.) TCC 2008. LNCS, vol. 4948, pp. 251–272. Springer, Heidelberg (2008). https://doi.org/10.1007/978-3-540-78524-8_15
3. Miao, F., Zhu, Q., Pajic, M., Pappas, G.J.: A hybrid stochastic game for secure control of cyber-physical systems. Automatica **93**, 55–63 (2018)
4. Zhu, Q., Basar, T.: Game-theoretic methods for robustness, security, and resilience of cyberphysical control systems: games-in-games principle for optimal cross-layer resilient control systems. IEEE Control Syst. **35**(1), 46–65 (2015)
5. Manshaei, M., Zhu, Q., Alpcan, T., Basar, T., Hubaux, J.: Game theory meets network security and privacy. ACM Comput. Surv. **45**(3), 25:1–25:39 (2013)
6. Zhu, M., Martinez, S.: Stackelberg-game analysis of correlated attacks in cyber-physical systems. In: American Control Conference, ACC, pp. 4063–4068, June 2011
7. Maitra, A., De, S.J., Paul, G., Pal, A.K.: Proposal for quantum rational secret sharing. Phys. Rev. A **92**(2), 022305 (2015)
8. Dou, Z., Xu, G., Chen, X.B., Liu, X., Yang, Y.X.: A secure rational quantum state sharing protocol. Sci. China Inf. Sci. **61**(2), 022501 (2018)
9. Zhou, L., Sun, X., Su, C., Liu, Z., Choo, K.K.R.: Game theoretic security of quantum bit commitment. Inf. Sci. (2018)
10. Maitra, A., Paul, G., Pal, A.K.: Millionaires problem with rational players: a unified approach in classical and quantum paradigms. arXiv preprint (2015)
11. Qin, H., Tang, W.K., Tso, R.: Establishing rational networking using the DL04 quantum secure direct communication protocol. Quantum Inf. Process. **17**(6), 152 (2018)
12. Das, B., Roy, U., et al.: Cooperative quantum key distribution for cooperative service-message passing in vehicular ad hoc networks. Int. J. Comput. Appl. **102**, 37–42 (2014). ISSN 0975 8887

13. Houshmand, M., Houshmand, M., Mashhadi, H.R.: Game theory based view to the quantum key distribution BB84 protocol. In: 2010 Third International Symposium on Intelligent Information Technology and Security Informatics, IITSI, pp. 332–336. IEEE (2010)
14. Kaur, H., Kumar, A.: Game-theoretic perspective of Ping-Pong protocol. Phys. A: Stat. Mech. Appl. **490**, 1415–1422 (2018)
15. Boström, K., Felbinger, T.: Deterministic secure direct communication using entanglement. Phys. Rev. Lett. **89**(18), 187902 (2002)
16. Lucamarini, M., Mancini, S.: Secure deterministic communication without entanglement. Phys. Rev. Lett. **94**(14), 140501 (2005)
17. Nielsen, M., Chuang, I.: Quantum Computation and Quantum Information. Cambridge University Press, Cambridge (2000)
18. Bennett, C.H., Brassard, G.: Quantum cryptography: public key distribution and coin tossing. In: Proceedings of IEEE International Conference on Computers, Systems and Signal Processing, New York, vol. 175 (1984)
19. Bennett, C.H.: Quantum cryptography using any two nonorthogonal states. Phys. Rev. Lett. **68**, 3121–3124 (1992)
20. Renner, R., Gisin, N., Kraus, B.: Information-theoretic security proof for quantum-key-distribution protocols. Phys. Rev. A **72**, 012332 (2005)
21. Shor, P.W., Preskill, J.: Simple proof of security of the BB84 quantum key distribution protocol. Phys. Rev. Lett. **85**, 441–444 (2000)
22. Csiszár, I., Korner, J.: Broadcast channels with confidential messages. IEEE Trans. Inf. Theory **24**(3), 339–348 (1978)
23. Krawec, W.O.: Quantum key distribution with mismatched measurements over arbitrary channels. Quantum Inf. Comput. **17**(3), 209–241 (2017)
24. Phoenix, S.J., Barnett, S.M., Townsend, P.D., Blow, K.: Multi-user quantum cryptography on optical networks. J. Mod. Opt. **42**(6), 1155–1163 (1995)

Training Set Camouflage

Ayon Sen[1](✉), Scott Alfeld[2], Xuezhou Zhang[1], Ara Vartanian[1], Yuzhe Ma[1], and Xiaojin Zhu[1]

[1] University of Wisconsin-Madison, Madison, USA
{ayonsn,zhangxz1123,aravart,yzm234,jerryzhu}@cs.wisc.com
[2] Amherst College, Amherst, USA
salfeld@amherst.edu

Abstract. We introduce a form of steganography in the domain of machine learning which we call training set camouflage. Imagine Alice has a training set on an illicit machine learning classification task. Alice wants Bob (a machine learning system) to learn the task. However, sending either the training set or the trained model to Bob can raise suspicion if the communication is monitored. Training set camouflage allows Alice to compute a second training set on a completely different – and seemingly benign – classification task. By construction, sending the second training set will not raise suspicion. When Bob applies his standard (public) learning algorithm to the second training set, he approximately recovers the classifier on the original task. Training set camouflage is a novel form of steganography in machine learning. We formulate training set camouflage as a combinatorial bilevel optimization problem and propose solvers based on nonlinear programming and local search. Experiments on real classification tasks demonstrate the feasibility of such camouflage.

Keywords: Machine teaching · Adversarial learning · Steganography

1 Introduction

Look at the classification training set shown in Fig. 1a. The top row contains instances of class positive (+), and the bottom shows instances of class negative (−). These images can be fed into a machine learner to learn a model which will successfully classify future, previously unseen instances (images) as + or −. If you think that the task is fruit image classification (orange vs. apples) then you have already been successfully fooled, in a sense to be made precise below. The actual intended task is to classify woman vs. man, with samples shown in Fig. 1b. Indeed, a standard logistic regression learner [26] trained on only the images in Fig. 1a achieves high gender classification accuracy on the images in Fig. 1b.

In this paper, we consider an agent Alice who has a secret classification task (e.g., classifying images of women and men) and a corresponding private training set (women and men images). Alice wants to train a second agent, Bob,

© Springer Nature Switzerland AG 2018
L. Bushnell et al. (Eds.): GameSec 2018, LNCS 11199, pp. 59–79, 2018.
https://doi.org/10.1007/978-3-030-01554-1_4

on the secret task. However, the communication channel between them has an eavesdropper we refer to as a third agent Eve. Eve takes the role of a data verifier, who will terminate communication (and refuse to deliver the data to Bob) if she is suspicious of what Alice is sending. Sending the private training set would reveal Alice's intention; sending the model parameters directly will also raise suspicion. Alice must camouflage the communication for it to look mundane to Eve, while avoiding excessive coding tricks with Bob beforehand. In the present work, we show how Alice can construct a camouflaged training set on a *cover task* which (i) does not look suspicious to Eve, and (ii) results in Bob learning an accurate model for the secret task. In the previous example, Eve noticed that Alice sent images of apples and oranges which seems benign, and knew nothing of Alice's secret task of women vs men.

Hiding information in plain sight such that its presence is not suspected is known as steganography. Steganography is not new. In the fifth century BCE messengers would have their heads shaved and a message written on their scalp. Regrowing their hair served to hide the message which would only be revealed because the intended recipient knew to shave the messenger's head [40]. In more modern times, steganographic techniques are used to detect unauthorized distribution of digital media [15].

Note that, steganography is different from cryptography [31,61], where the goal is to hide the data content. In cryptography, the communicating agents have access to some particular key (pairs) which is used to encrypt and decrypt data. Cryptography cannot be used if someone monitoring the data can alter the data or stop the data transmission entirely. In such cases, steganography becomes important because we do not want any intervening eavesdropper to become suspicious and stop the data transmission.

The role and capabilities of the eavesdropper are key in selecting how to hide information. Eve can be either passive and merely observes traffic [13], or active and tries to modify the hidden message [14,51]. In this manuscript we assume a passive observer, whose only ability is to refuse to deliver Alice's message. To our knowledge, steganography for machine learning in this context is new. In the area of adversarial learning [5], however, much work has been done investigating how an agent can assert control over a learner by manipulating input data. We note that training set camouflage differs from so called training-time or "poisoning attacks" [36] in two primary ways: (i) Alice aims to communicate information to Bob about a potentially completely unrelated task, not affect his behavior on the original task and (ii) Alice specifically aims to avoid detection by Eve.

Due to the widespread use of machine learning in sensitive fields ranging from social media to health care, the study of the security ramifications of using ML techniques is well studied [3,47]. The work presented herein adds to this conversation, as we reveal an additional avenue of attack. For example, Bob might be a model that classifies job applicants as "should hire" and "shouldn't hire". The company may have many records (collected over years) of job applicants and how they performed. It is expected from Alice to select a subset of these records and present to Bob, with the idea that training on the complete set is too time consuming. But Alice may be a malicious agent and wants Bob to actually learn some additional bias (e.g., racial, gender etc.). In such a scenario, Alice will select a subset of records that satisfies her goals while Eve's responsibility is to verify the data sent by Alice to Bob. Our specific contributions in this paper are as follows: (i) We propose a general mathematical framework for defining how Alice can achieve training set camouflage. (ii) We formulate a nonlinear-program based approach for performing Alice's task for a general class of learner (Bob) and eavesdropper (Eve), and two combinatorial-search based approaches for arbitrary learners/eavesdroppers.

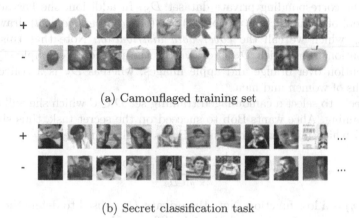

(a) Camouflaged training set

(b) Secret classification task

Fig. 1. Example of training set camouflage

2   Training Set Camouflage

In this section we describe the three agents Bob, Alice and Eve, and formulate a camouflage optimization problem for Alice, parametrized by Bob and Eve's definitions.

The agent Bob uses a standard learning algorithm $\mathcal{A} : \mathcal{D} \mapsto \mathcal{H}$ which, given a training set D, learns a hypothesis $\mathcal{A}(D)$ in a hypothesis space $\mathcal{H}$. The resulting hypothesis maps instances in the input space $\mathcal{X}$ to the output space $\mathcal{Y}$. This can be multi-class classification (three or more classes) or regression, though in the present work we focus on binary classification. We assume that Bob's learning algorithm is "open source". That is, all information about $\mathcal{A}$ is known to all agents. However, Bob and Alice have shared knowledge on class naming: which class is positive and which negative. For K-class classification this shared knowledge requires $O(K \log K)$ bits, as Alice must communicate a mapping from K classes to K classes. For example, when Alice sends Bob orange and apple images for the secret task of woman vs man, Alice must communicate to Bob whether orange maps to woman and apple to man, or vice versa.

Table 1. Information available to different agents

Agent	Secret set D_S	Camouflage pool $\mathcal{C}$	Bob's learner $\mathcal{A}$	Detection function Ψ	Camouflaged training set D
Bob	No	Yes/No	Yes	Yes/No	Yes
Alice	Yes	Yes	Yes	Yes	Yes
Eve	No	Yes	Yes	Yes	Yes

Alice is an agent who wants to train Bob. She has a secret classification task and the corresponding private dataset D_S. In addition, she has access to a public pool of n instances $\mathcal{C} = \{(\mathbf{x}_i, y_i)_{1:n}\}$ (the *camouflage pool*) drawn i.i.d. from $\mathbb{Q}_{(\mathbf{x},y)}$ which we call the *cover data distribution*. Note that this is not the distribution from which D_S is drawn. In the preceding example, $\mathbb{Q}_{(\mathbf{x},y)}$ is the distribution over orange and apple images, whereas D_S is a collection of photographs of women and men.

Alice seeks to select a camouflaged training set $D \subset \mathcal{C}$ which she will send to Bob for training. Alice wants Bob to succeed on the secret task, thus she seeks to find a D which minimizes the risk of Bob's resulting model:

$$\mathcal{L}_{\mathcal{A}}(D) = \frac{1}{|D_S|} \sum_{(\tilde{\mathbf{x}}, \tilde{y}) \in D_S} \ell(\mathcal{A}(D)(\tilde{\mathbf{x}}), \tilde{y})$$

where $\ell(\hat{y}, y)$ is a loss function. Note the private D_S is used to define the quality of D. Also, we note that D_S and D are in different domains.

Eve is a passive eavesdropper. She observes the dataset D which Alice sends to Bob, but does not alter it. Her goal is to determine if D is normal or suspicious. Specifically, Eve is suspicious of any data unless it appears to be an i.i.d. sample drawn from $\mathbb{Q}_{(\mathbf{x},y)}$. She has access to the camouflage pool $\mathcal{C}$, but like Alice she cannot draw additional instances from $\mathbb{Q}_{(\mathbf{x},y)}$. Eve uses $\mathcal{C}$ and a detection function $\Psi : \mathcal{D} \times \mathcal{D} \mapsto \mathbb{R}_+$ to examine D. Here $\mathcal{D}$ is the domain of all possible training sets. She flags D as suspicious if $\Psi(\mathcal{C}, D) \geq 0$. It is useful to think of Ψ as a two-sample statistical test that aims to determine whether $\mathcal{C}, D$ come from the same underlying distribution. We envision Alice as Eve's adversary. As with Bob, we assume that Eve is "open source". Namely, Alice can see Eve's detection function Ψ.

The agents Alice and Eve have conflicting goals. Alice aims to secretly communicate to Bob by way of constructing a training set, while Eve is suspicious and will flag any data sent to Bob if it looks suspect. Bob dutifully learns a model and for our purposes has no explicit intentions. We make explicit each Agent's knowledge in Table 1.

With the agents defined, we can now formulate Alice's goal:

$$\underset{D \subset \mathcal{C}}{\operatorname{argmin}} \frac{1}{|D_S|} \sum_{(\tilde{\mathbf{x}}, \tilde{y}) \in D_S} \ell(\mathcal{A}(D)(\tilde{\mathbf{x}}), \tilde{y})$$

$$\text{s.t.} \Psi(\mathcal{C}, D) < 0 \tag{1}$$

That is, she seeks a camouflaged training set D from the cover data pool. D should not be flagged as suspicious by Eve. D should also make Bob learn well, similar to as if Alice directly gave Bob her private data set D_S. An example of the training set camouflage in action is shown in Fig. 2.

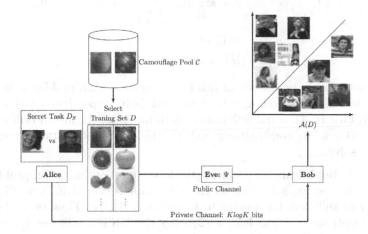

Fig. 2. Training set camouflage framework. We show the three agents along with the classification task, camouflage pool, camouflage training set and Eve's detection function

3 Solving the Camouflage Problem

In this section, we propose three methods of solving the optimization problem defined in (1). We first show how the optimization problem can be reduced to a nonlinear programming problem for a broad class of learners. We relax the resulting optimization problem to one which is computationally efficient to solve. We then present two combinatoric methods as heuristic methods applicable to any learner.

3.1 Nonlinear Programming (NLP)

We assume Bob's machine learning algorithm $\mathcal{A}$ solves a convex optimization problem. Specifically, Bob performs regularized empirical risk minimization. This covers a wide range of learners such as support vector machines [23], logistic regression [26], and ridge regression [24]. Let Θ be Bob's hypothesis space, ℓ his loss function, and λ his regularization parameter, respectively. Let $m := |D|$ be given. We convert Alice's optimization problem (1) into a nonlinear programming problem as follows.

Step 1. Using the definition of Bob, we rewrite (1) as

$$\min_{D \subset \mathcal{C}, \hat{\theta} \in \Theta} \quad \frac{1}{|D_S|} \sum_{(\tilde{\mathbf{x}}, \tilde{y}) \in D_S} \ell(\hat{\theta}, \tilde{\mathbf{x}}, \tilde{y})$$

$$\text{s.t.} \quad \hat{\theta} = \underset{\theta \in \Theta}{\operatorname{argmin}} \sum_{(\mathbf{x}, y) \in D} \ell(\theta, \mathbf{x}, y) + \frac{\lambda}{2} \|\theta\|^2$$

$$\Psi(\mathcal{C}, D) < 0,$$

$$|D| = m. \tag{2}$$

We make note that in both levels of this bilevel optimization problem (the upper and lower levels corresponding with Alice and Bob, respectively) $\ell(\cdot)$ is being minimized. That is, Alice and Bob both seek to minimize the loss of Bob's resulting model. Due to its combinatorial nature, this is a computationally difficult problem to solve.

Step 2. Since Bob's learning problem (the lower level optimization problem) is assumed to be convex, satisfying its Karush-Kuhn-Tucker (KKT) conditions is necessary and sufficient for a point to be optimal [44,63]. Thus we replace the lower level optimization problem in (2) with the KKT conditions to obtain a single-level optimization problem:

$$\min_{D \subset \mathcal{C}, \hat{\theta} \in \Theta} \quad \frac{1}{|D_S|} \sum_{(\tilde{\mathbf{x}}, \tilde{y}) \in D_S} \ell(\hat{\theta}, \tilde{\mathbf{x}}, \tilde{y})$$

$$\text{s.t.} \quad \sum_{(\mathbf{x}, y) \in D} \nabla \ell(\hat{\theta}, \mathbf{x}, y) + \lambda \hat{\theta} = 0,$$

$$\Psi(\mathcal{C}, D) < 0,$$

$$|D| = m. \tag{3}$$

While now a single level optimization problem, selecting a subset $D \subset \mathcal{C}$ is still a combinatorial problem and computationally expensive to solve. In what comes next we relax this problem to one of continuous optimization.

Step 3. We introduce binary indicator variable b_i for each instance $(\mathbf{x}_i, y_i) \in \mathcal{C}$. A value of 1 indicates that the instance is a member of the training set D. Also dropping the hat on $\hat{\theta}$ for simplicity. This yields:

$$\min_{\theta \in \Theta; b_1, \dots, b_{|\mathcal{C}|}; b_i \in \{0,1\}} \quad \frac{1}{|D_S|} \sum_{(\tilde{\mathbf{x}}, \tilde{y}) \in D_S} \ell(\theta, \tilde{\mathbf{x}}, \tilde{y})$$

$$\text{s.t.} \quad \sum_{i=1}^{n} b_i \nabla \ell(\theta, \mathbf{x}_i, y_i) + \lambda \theta = 0,$$

$$\Psi(\mathcal{C}, \{b_i(\mathbf{x}_i, y_i) | (\mathbf{x}_i, y_i) \in \mathcal{C}, b_i \neq 0\}) < 0$$

$$\sum_{i=1}^{n} b_i = m. \tag{4}$$

This is known as a Mixed Integer Non-Linear Optimization Problem (MINLP) [12]. MINLP problems are generally hard to solve in practice. However, phrasing the problem in this way yields a natural relaxation. Namely we relax b_i to be continuous in $[0, 1]$, resulting in the following non-linear optimization problem:

$$\min_{\theta \in \Theta; b_1, \ldots, b_n \in [0,1]} \frac{1}{|D_S|} \sum_{(\tilde{\mathbf{x}}, \tilde{y}) \in D_S} \ell(\theta, \tilde{\mathbf{x}}, \tilde{y})$$

$$\text{s.t.} \quad \sum_{i=1}^{n} b_i \nabla \ell(\theta, \mathbf{x}_i, y_i) + \lambda \theta = 0,$$

$$\Psi(\mathcal{C}, b_1, \ldots, b_{|\mathcal{C}|}) < 0,$$

$$\sum_{i=1}^{n} b_i = m. \qquad (5)$$

Note that in this equation we scale the gradient of the loss function for each $(\mathbf{x}_i, y_i)$ by the corresponding b_i. This b_i indicates the importance of an instance in the training set. In essence, the learner is training on a "soft" version of the dataset, where each training example is weighted. Similarly, when calculating the detection function we weigh each instance in the training set by its corresponding b_i. The exact nature of this weighing depends on the detection function itself. We further note that the nonlinear optimization problem is non-convex. As such, Alice must seed her solver with some initial $\{b_i\}$. This is discussed further in Sect. 4.

After solving this (continuous) optimization problem, Alice must round the $\{b_i\}$'s into binary indicators so that she can select a training set to send to Bob. Alice uses a rounding procedure that proposes $m + 1$ candidate training sets $D^{(1)}, \ldots, D^{(m+1)}$ from the continuous solution $\{b\}$. The candidate training sets include (1) the training set $D^{(1)}$ consisting of the m items with the largest b values, (2) the seed training set before running optimization, (3) $m-1$ other training sets that "interpolate" between 1 and 2. Alice then checks $D^{(1)}, \ldots, D^{(m+1)}$ for feasibility (satisfying Ψ) and picks the best one. Note the seed training set is feasible, hence Alice is guaranteed to have a solution. The interpolation scheme ensures that Alice will find a solution no worse than the seed set.

Concretely, let S be the m-item seed training set and $\mathcal{C} \backslash S$ be the remaining items. Alice sorts items in S by their b values. Separately, Alice sorts items in $\mathcal{C} \backslash S$ by their b values. Then, Alice starts from S and sequentially swaps the least-valued item in S with the largest-valued item in $\mathcal{C} \backslash S$. She performs m swaps. This produces the $m + 1$ candidate training sets, including the original S. It can be shown that the m items with the largest b values will be one of the training sets.

3.2   Uniform Sampling

For any learner Bob, even one which does not solve a convex empirical risk minimizing problem discussed above, Alice has a simple option for finding a training set. Let Alice's budget B denote the number of times Alice is able to train the classifier $\mathcal{A}$. She first creates B training sets $D^{(1)}, \ldots, D^{(B)}$, each by sampling m points uniformly without replacement from her camouflage pool $\mathcal{C}$, such that each $D^{(j)}$ successfully bypasses Eve i.e., $\Psi(\mathcal{C}, D^{(j)}) < 0$. Among these B training sets, she then picks the $D^{(j)}$ with the lowest objective value in (1). This procedure captures what Bob would learn if given each feasible training set.

3.3 Beam Search

We now describe a heuristic beam search algorithm [53] to approximately solve Alice's optimization problem (1). This process is similar to uniform sampling, described above, but instead of independently generating a new training set every time, Alice performs a local search to augment a proposed training set incrementally.

The state space consists of all training sets $D \subset \mathcal{C}$ such that $|D| = m$ and $\Psi(\mathcal{C}, D) < 0$. Two training sets that differ by one instance are considered neighbors. For computational efficiency, we do not consider the entire set of neighbors at each step. Instead, we evaluate a randomly selected subset of neighbors for each training set in the beam. The beam $\mathcal{D}$ is initialized by selecting w training sets at random. The width (w) of the beam is fixed beforehand. From the union of evaluated neighbors and training sets in the current beam, we select the top w training sets (based on the value of the objective function in (1)) to reinitialize the beam and discard the rest. Note that training sets which would be flagged by Eve are not present in the statespace (because Alice has full knowledge of Eve, she need not consider any set that Eve would reject). We continue the search process until a pre-specified search budget B (number of times the classifier $\mathcal{A}$ is trained) is met. Algorithm 1 shows the search procedure with random restarts.

Algorithm 1. Beam Search for Solving the Camouflage Problem
___
1: Input: Camouflage Pool: $\mathcal{C}$, Risk: $\mathcal{L}_A$, Beam Width: w, Budget: B, Neighborhood Function: $\mathcal{N}$, Size: m, Detection Function: Ψ, Restarts: R
2: **for** $r = 1 \rightarrow R$ **do**
3:     $\mathcal{D} \leftarrow w$ randomly selected subsets of size m from $\mathcal{C}$ such that $\Psi(\mathcal{C}, D) < 0$
4:     **while** budget B/R not exhausted **do**
5:         $\mathcal{D} \leftarrow \mathcal{D} \cup \mathcal{N}(\mathcal{D}, \mathcal{C}, \Psi)$, the neighbors
6:         $\mathcal{D} \leftarrow w$ training sets from $\mathcal{D}$ with smallest $\mathcal{L}_A(D)$ values
7:     **end while**
8: **end for**
9: **return** the best D found within total budget

---

4   Experiments

We investigated the effectiveness of training set camouflage through empirical experiments on real world datasets. Our results show that camouflage works on a variety of image and text classification tasks: Bob can perform well on the secret task after training on the camouflaged training set, and the camouflaged training set passes Eve's test undetected. We start by discussing the three agents.

Bob. We considered the logistic regression learning algorithm for Bob. Logistic regression is a popular learner and is regularly used in practice. Bob set the weight of the regularization parameter to 1.

Eve. The training set camouflage framework is general with respect to Eve's detection function. For our experiments we used Maximum Mean Discrepancy (**MMD**) [20] as the core of Eve's detection function. We used **MMD** as it is a popular and widely used two-sample test [17]. Unfortunately **MMD** cannot be directly applied to the camouflage framework as its application requires that the two samples have the same size. We introduce **MMD** and how Eve used it in Appendix A. The level-α for this detection function was set to 0.05 (i.e., the probability of incorrectly rejecting a benign training set is 5%).

Alice. We considered three different Alices. Each of them used one of the proposed solvers. For each secret task, Alice had access to multiple camouflage candidate tasks. Alice can run her solver on each of these tasks separately and then select the best one, but this would be time consuming and thus instead she started by identifying a suitable camouflage task. For this purpose, all three Alices used uniform sampling (as this is the easiest algorithm to implement, and makes the weakest assumptions) with a search budget of $80,000$ (divided equally among candidate tasks). This meant that Alice stopped after training the logistic regression learner $80,000$ times. For each candidate task Alice identified a training set using this budget. Then she selected the best task (as her cover task) based on the loss on the secret set.

Next, all three Alices used their respective solvers (NLP, beam search and uniform sampling) to find a camouflaged training set. We assumed that all of them were allotted a fixed amount of time for this purpose. This time was set as the time required to run the NLP solver.

The Alice who used the NLP solver seeded the solver with the camouflaged training set found during the candidate task identification phase. The Alice who used the beam search solver performed random restarts each with a per-restart budget of $B/R = 16,000$. Here the width of the beam was $w = 10$ and for each training set in the beam, 50 randomly selected neighbors were evaluated during each iteration. It should be noted that both beam search and uniform sampling are stochastic in nature. We run the Alices who used these solvers five times. We then report the average. Alice constructed camouflaged training sets of size $m = 2$, 20 and 50, and set the loss ℓ to logistic loss with natural logarithm. All experiments were run on an Intel(R) Core(TM) i7-7700T CPU @2.90 GHz machine, using one thread.

Table 2. Summary of secret sets and camouflage pools.

Dataset	Type	# features	Class 1	Class 2	# class 1	# class 2
WM	Image	2048	woman	man	500	500
GP	Image	2048	handgun	phone	400	400
CA	Text	300	christian	atheist	599	480
DR	Text	300	democratic	republican	800	800
17	Image	2048	digit 1	digit 7	600	600
25	Image	2048	digit 2	digit 5	600	600
69	Image	2048	digit 6	digit 8	600	600
OA	Image	2048	orange	apple	600	600
BH	Text	300	baseball	hockey	994	999
IM	Text	300	ibm	mac	982	963
AM	Text	300	autos	motorcycles	990	996
MX	Text	300	ms-windows	windows x	985	988

Evaluation Metrics. As is standard to estimate generalization performance of a learned model, we used a separate test set, generated from the same distribution as the secret set D_S and not known to any agent, to estimate Bob's generalization error when trained on Alice's camouflaged training set D. We compare these values to two additional quantities: ("random") when Bob is trained on a uniform sample of size m from the cover data distribution, which we expect to perform poorly; and ("oracle") when Bob is trained directly on Alice's secret set D_S, ignoring Eve's presence. The oracle gives us an estimate on how much performance Bob is losing due to using the camouflage framework to fool Eve.

4.1 Datasets

We performed experiments for four secret tasks: WM (CIFAR-100 [41]), GP (OpenImages [39]), CA (20-newsgroups [28]) and DR (All The News dataset [60]). The two letters in the acronym represent the two classes in the corresponding task (see Table 2). The first two tasks were image classification while the remaining two were text classification. For the image tasks we selected eight candidate cover tasks. Six of them were from the MNIST handwritten digits: 17, 71, 25, 52, 69 and 96. The other two were from the CIFAR-100 dataset: OA and AO. Similarly for the text tasks we also selected eight candidate cover tasks. All of them were from the 20-newsgroups dataset: BH, HB, IM, MI, AM, MA, MX and XM. As before the acronyms here represent the class names.

For images we used ResNet [22] to generate feature vectors of dimension 2048. For this purpose we removed the output layer and used the values found in the penultimate layer of the network. For text we used Word2Vec [50] to generate feature vectors of dimension 300 by averaging over the word vectors in an article. We also removed punctuation and stop words before generating

Table 3. Logistic loss ($\frac{1}{|D_S|} \sum_{(\hat{\mathbf{x}}, \tilde{y}) \in D_S} \log(1 + \exp(-\tilde{y}w^{\top}\hat{\mathbf{x}}))$) after performing Uniform Sampling search with search budget $10,000$ for image secret tasks. The best results for each secret task is shown in bold.

m	Camouflage / Secret	17	71	25	52	69	96	OA	AO
2	WM	0.671	0.631	0.643	0.638	0.671	0.640	**0.606**	0.647
	GP	0.481	0.541	0.458	**0.443**	0.516	0.463	0.541	0.558
20	WM	0.790	0.611	0.672	0.688	0.798	0.679	**0.584**	0.731
	GP	0.480	0.510	0.433	0.390	0.632	**0.337**	0.510	0.531
50	WM	0.874	0.614	0.705	0.772	1.116	0.802	**0.606**	0.856
	GP	0.565	0.479	0.473	**0.387**	1.047	0.421	0.479	0.506

the word vectors. A summary of the secret sets and camouflage pools can be found in Table 2. As mentioned previously, we kept a held out test set for each of the secret tasks. The number of class 1 and class 2 instances were 100/100, 100/100, 398/319 and 200/200 respectively for WM, GP, CA and DR. Here the two numbers (num1/num2) represent the number of instances in class 1 and class 2 respectively.

Alice first selected a suitable camouflage task for each of the secret tasks. For each candidate task she used a search budget of $10,000$ (for a total of $80,000$ budget). The results of this phase are shown in Tables 3 and 4. For $m = 2$ the camouflage tasks selected for WM, GP, CA and DR were OA, 52, XM and HB respectively. Similarly for $m = 20$ the selected camouflage tasks were OA, 96, BH and BH respectively. OA, 52, HB and BH were the selected camouflage tasks respectively when $m = 50$. It should be noted that the logistic error reported in the tables are large (>0.693) in some cases indicating that some of these cover tasks will perform worse than random chance on secret tasks. However, this was not true for the selected cover tasks. The top three camouflaged training sets for GP ($m = 20$) identified during this phase are shown in Fig. 3.

Table 4. Logistic loss after performing Uniform Sampling search with search budget $10,000$ for text secret tasks. The best results for each secret task is shown in bold.

m	Camouflage / Secret	BH	HB	IM	MI	AM	MA	MX	XM
2	CA	0.6845	0.6846	0.6868	0.6862	0.6861	0.6862	0.6844	**0.6843**
	DR	0.6889	**0.6886**	0.6891	0.6893	0.6888	0.6887	0.6890	0.6894
20	CA	**0.672**	0.673	0.676	0.675	0.676	0.674	0.675	0.675
	DR	**0.681**	0.684	0.682	0.683	0.682	0.682	0.682	0.683
50	CA	0.671	**0.669**	0.672	0.671	0.674	0.670	0.671	0.671
	DR	**0.677**	0.681	0.679	0.680	0.678	0.680	0.683	0.679

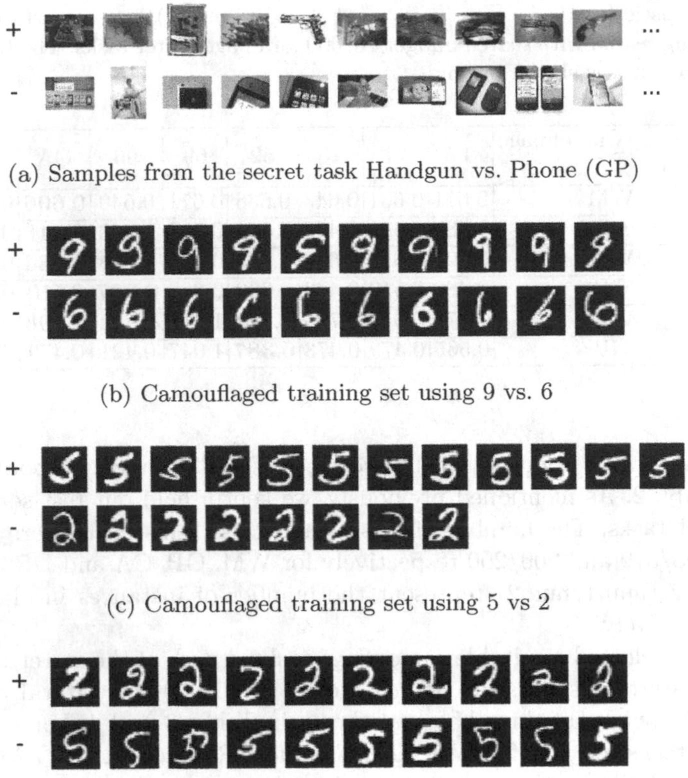

(a) Samples from the secret task Handgun vs. Phone (GP)

(b) Camouflaged training set using 9 vs. 6

(c) Camouflaged training set using 5 vs 2

(d) Camouflaged training set using 2 vs. 5

Fig. 3. Samples of GP secret set, and the top three camuflaged training set found during the candidate selection phase for $m = 20$.

4.2 Results

For $m = 2$, the NLP solver ran for 23363, 33763, 48 and 44 s respectively for WMOA, GP96, CABH and DRBH. The solver ran for 29150, 65697, 50 and 57 s respectively for WMOA, GP96, CABH and DRBH when $m = 20$. The run time was 39656, 171637, 126 and 193 s respectively when $m = 50$. We present our results for all three solvers in Fig. 4. For the text secret tasks, Alice could not find a better camouflaged training set using either beam search or uniform sampling than the one found during the initial run of uniform sampling (with a total budget of 80,000). To explore the sensitivity of beam search and uniform sampling regarding the time budget, we ran both solvers for an additional two hours. But the results only improved marginally. We observe that Alice, using any of the three solvers can find much better camouflage training sets than random and in many cases approach oracle performance. Note that Alice's solutions do not trigger Eve's suspicion function. This shows that such subterfuges are plausible

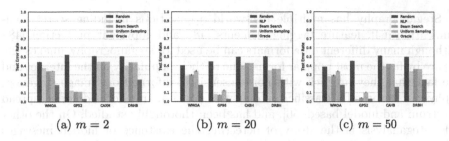

(a) $m = 2$ (b) $m = 20$ (c) $m = 50$

Fig. 4. Test error rates found by solving the camouflage framework. We also show random and oracle error for comparison. Error bars are also shown. All three solvers were run for the same amount of time.

in practice and can actually yield good results from Alice's point of view. We note that Alice yields the best results when $m = 50$ in most of the experiments, but this may not hold for larger values of m e.g., when m is equal to the size of the camouflage pool. We plan to run further experiments to understand the effect of m.

Figure 1 shows the result of WMOA when Bob's learner is logistic regression and the solver is NLP ($m = 20$). Visually, the camouflaged training set D bears no resemblance to the secret training set D_S. This is true for the text camouflage experiments as well, where articles in the camouflaged training sets have no obvious semantic connection to the secret task. See Table 5 for results on the text experiment CABH. This is indeed bad news for human Eves: not only did camouflage fooled MMD detector, it will also likely fool human inspectors.

Table 5. Camouflage results for the CABH experiment with $m = 20$ for the NLP solver

	Sample of Secret Set		Sample of Camouflaged Training Set
Class	**Article**	**Class**	**Article**
Christianity	...Christ that often causes christians to be very critical of themselves and other christinas. We...	Baseball	...Boys, hats off to any Cubs fan who can actually muster up the courage to put down Braves fans. I...
	...I've heard it said that the accounts we have of Christs life and ministry in the Gospels were...		... NPR's Morning Edition aired a report this morning to get (4/19) on Hispanic/Latin American players in MLB...
Atheism	...This article attempts to provide a general introduction to atheism. Whilst I have tried to be...	Hockey	... Would Kevin Dineen play for the Miami Colons??? As a Flyers fan, I resent you making Kevin Dineen...
	...Science is wonderful at answering most of our questions. I'm not the type to question scientific...		...Good point - there haven't even been any recent posts about ULf! Secretly, I'm convinced that he is responsible ...

5 Related Work

Concealing the existence of messages is known as steganography. One illustration of steganography (first presented in 1983 in [55]) is where prisoners Alice and Bob wish to devise an escape plan. All their communication is observed by the adversary (the warden, Eve) who will thwart their plan as soon as she detects any sign of hidden message.

Steganography has multiple real-world applications including secret communication [64], feature tagging elements [48], and copyright protection [48]. Although many different data formats can be used for steganography, images [29, 51] are by far the most popular format due to their popularity on the internet and the fact that they are rich with noise-insensitive information. Image steganography can be broadly classified into spatial domain, transform domain, spread spectrum and model based [56], and has been thoroughly studied. On the other side, steganalysis is the study of detecting the existence of hidden messages (using steganography). Identifying such messages in text by looking at patterns in texts, odd language and unusual white space was explored in [14]. The authors of [18,32,51] explore the detection of hidden messages in images.

A study of steganography from a complexity-theoretic point of view is presented in [25,52]. An information-theoretic model for such a setup is presented in [13]. This complexity-theoretic security notion is similar to modern cryptography and they try to define a secure stegosystem such that the stegotext is computationally indistinguishable from the covertext. In such a scenario a new term called steganographic secrecy of stegosystem is introduced which is defined as the inability of a polynomial-time adversary (Eve) to distinguish between observed distributions of unaltered covertext and stegotexts. To the best of our knowledge, steganographic techniques have not been used in the domain of training sets for machine learning models.

Steganography is often confused with cryptography [31,61], however the goal of these two systems are completely different. The goal of cryptography is to ensure confidentiality of data in communication and storage processes. Hiding the existence of sensitive data is not the end goal here (unlike steganography). According to Kerckhoffs's principle [33,34], this confidentiality must not rely on the obfuscation of the encoding scheme, but only on the secrecy of the decryption key.

One particular branch of cryptography we highlight is homomorphic encryption [54]. Consider a situation where you seek to delegate some computation to another computer (e.g., using a cloud computation service to a perform machine learning task). You would like to utilize their computation power, but you do not trust them with your private data. Homomorphic encryption allows a method by which you can encrypt your data prior to sending it. The untrusted computer will then perform its operations on the encrypted data, returning to you the result (e.g., a learned model). You then decrypt the result, yielding what the remote computer would have computed had you provided your original (unencrypted) data. A homomorphic cryptosystem which supports arbitrary computation on ciphertexts is known as fully homomorphic encryption (FHE). The first plausible construction of such a system was proposed in [57]. This scheme supports both addition and multiplication operations on ciphertexts, which in turn makes possible to construct circuits for arbitrary computations. Some second generation solutions were proposed in [6,7,19,46].

In our setting, encryption (homomorphic or otherwise) is not enough to solve Alice's task. After Alice has transmitted her data to Bob, Bob learns a model.

Alice's goal is not only for Eve to not know the model (which could easily be achieved by Alice simply sending an encrypted model), but also for Eve not to be suspicious. Eve believes that Alice is drawing data points i.i.d. from some distribution and thus data encrypted by standard methods will cause alarm. We do note that the relatively new method of "honey encryption" [30] may be a useful alternative approach for Alice, which we leave as future work.

The idea of constructing a dataset keeping a particular machine learning algorithm and a target model in mind is known as machine teaching. Machine teaching is the inverse of machine learning and has applications in various fields [44, 65]. In particular, machine teaching has applications in the domain of adversarial learning which studies the use of machine learning in security-sensitive domains. Numerous attacks against various machine learners have been explored, highlighting the security ramifications of using machine learning in practice [3, 4, 16, 27, 42, 59].

In the work presented herein, Alice can be thought of as "attacking" the learner Bob, in that she aims to provide a dataset which causes Bob to learn a model with parituclar properties. We highlight how this differs from the classical adversarial learning framework in two ways. First, Alice is not perturbing an existing training set, but rather generating one. Thus, this is more akin to the Machine Teaching framework. Second is the presence of Eve. Namely, Alice is trying not only to affect Bob's resulting model, but also to hide her involvement from a third party eavesdropper. In spirit, this is similar to the adversarial learning work performed on intrusion detection systems [35, 37]. In terms of the details of the mathematics, our framework and strategies for solving Alice's optimization problem more closely follow [49].

Within adversarial machine learning, a line of research has posed the problem of learning in the presence of adversaries in game theoretic contexts [8–10, 16, 21, 45]. [1, 16, 43] specifically address a learner's defense strategy in various contexts. Randomization has also been explored as a method of defense [11, 62], as well as in the context of machine teaching [2]. Our work contributes to this conversation as Eve can be seen as a form of defense for Bob.

6 Conclusion and Discussions

We introduced the training set camouflage setting where a carefully constructed training set can be sent over an open channel with the intention of training a machine learner on a secret classification task. Using this framework, an agent can hide the intention of the secret task from a third party observer. Our experimental results show that training set camouflage is indeed a plausible threat. We present three approaches to solve the optimization problem. We observe that all three solvers perform well but both NLP and beam search outperform uniform sampling in all cases. The NLP solver often performs a bit better than beam search. This suggests that for the logistic regression learner NLP is Alice's preferred solver of choice. However, the NLP solver cannot be applied to all possible learners (non-convexity prevents the application of KKT conditions). Thus in such cases beam search becomes the preferred solver.

We note that **MMD** is stronger with larger sample sizes. It will be harder for Alice to fool Eve given a large camouflage pool C and also if she is forced to select a large camouflaged training set D. **MMD** is also stronger with smaller feature dimensions [20]. Also, it is harder for Alice to fool Eve if she increases the value of α. Since α is the upper bound of the probability of the Type I error for the null hypothesis i.e., the camouflage pool and camouflaged training set come from the same distribution, increasing α allows Eve to become more suspicious. As future work we plan to devise defensive strategies against Alice. In such scenarios it is advisable to assume that Eve's detection function is known to the attacker (Kerckhoffs's principle [33, 34]) which we make here.

We note that camouflage seems easier for Alice to do if the cover task is in fact somewhat confusable, presumably because she can generate different decision boundaries by picking from overlapping camouflage items. This can be imagined easily in the 2D case with two overlapping point clouds forming the cover task. In such a scenario any separable secret task (no overlap between the secret task instances) can be taught to Bob by Alice. One interesting open question is whether there is a *universal* cover task for all secret tasks. We also note that achieving Alice's goal becomes much harder in the multi-class setting as finding a cover task becomes more challenging.

As mentioned previously, Bob fixed his learning hyperparameters (e.g., regularization parameter of the logistic regression). This was done for speed. However, nothing prevents Bob from using cross validation [38]. Cross validation is popular technique used in machine learning where the learner is trained multiple times on different subsets of the whole training set to tune the hyperparameters of the learner. Alice would simply emulate the same cross validation while optimizing the camouflaged training set. This can be easily done in beam search and uniform sampling, at the cost of more computation. Unfortunately significant modifications will be required for NLP.

Also, the loss function ℓ used by Alice and Bob is the same, as seen in the upper and lower optimization problems in (2). It is straightforward to allow different losses. For example, Bob may learn with the logistic loss since it is a standard learner, while Alice uses 0-1 loss to directly optimize Bob's accuracy.

We note that training set camouflage can be extended to cross modality correspondence, e.g., use an image camouflage pool while the secret classification task is to classify text articles. Alice and Bob can communicate via the private channel to establish the correspondence between images features and text features. Another possible way to extend the camouflage pool is to allow perturbed instances as well.

Acknowledgment. This work is supported in part by NSF 1545481, 1704117, 1623605, 1561512, and the MADLab AF Center of Excellence FA9550-18-1-0166.

A   Appendix A: MMD as Eve's Detection Function

One critical component of our camouflage framework is Eve's detection function Ψ—how she determines if a training set is suspicious or not. Eve's detection function is a two-sample test as its goal is to discern if the two sets C, D are drawn from the same distribution or not. In what follows we discuss using Maximum Mean Discrepancy (**MMD**) [20] as Eve's detection function, as we do in our experiments. **MMD** is a widely used two-sample test [17], but, of course other detection functions can be used in (1). We first review basic **MMD** following [20]. Let p and p' be two Borel probability measures defined on a topological space $\mathcal{Z}$. Given a class of functions $\mathcal{F}$ such that $f : \mathcal{Z} \mapsto \mathbb{R}, f \in \mathcal{F}$, **MMD** is defined as $\mathbf{MMD}(p, p') = \sup_{f \in \mathcal{F}} (E_{\mathbf{z}}[f(\mathbf{z})] - E_{\mathbf{z}'}[f(\mathbf{z}')])$. Any unit ball in a reproducing kernel Hilbert space (RKHS) can be used as the function class $\mathcal{F}$ if the kernel is universal (e.g., Gaussian and Laplace kernels [58]). Using this function space, **MMD** is a metric. This means $\mathbf{MMD}(p, p') = 0 \Leftrightarrow p = p'$. Computing **MMD** requires the expectations to be known, which generally, is not the case in practice. We obtain an empirical estimation by replacing the population expectations with empirical mean computed on i.i.d. samples $Z = \{\mathbf{z}_1, \ldots, \mathbf{z}_n\}$ and $Z' = \{\mathbf{z}'_1, \ldots, \mathbf{z}'_m\}$ from p and p', respectively. We define

$$\mathbf{MMD}(Z, Z') = \left[\tfrac{1}{n^2} \textstyle\sum_{i,j=1}^{n} k(\mathbf{z}_i, \mathbf{z}_j) - \tfrac{2}{nm} \textstyle\sum_{i,j=1}^{n,m} k(\mathbf{z}_i, \mathbf{z}'_j) + \tfrac{1}{m^2} \textstyle\sum_{i,j=1}^{m} k(\mathbf{z}'_i, \mathbf{z}'_j)\right]^{\frac{1}{2}}$$

where k is the kernel of the RKHS. Let $d = |\mathbf{MMD}(Z, Z') - \mathbf{MMD}(p, p')|$. Gretton *et al.* show that $P\left(d > 2\left(\sqrt{\tfrac{K}{n}} + \sqrt{\tfrac{K}{m}}\right) + \epsilon\right) \le 2e^{-\frac{\epsilon^2 nm}{2K(n+m)}}$, where K is an upperbound on the kernel values. We convert the above bound into a one-sided hypothesis testing procedure. Under the null hypothesis $p = p'$ we have $\mathbf{MMD}(p, p') = 0$. We consider positive deviations of $\mathbf{MMD}(Z, Z')$ from $\mathbf{MMD}(p, p')$. Equating the RHS with α (probability of incorrectly stating $p \ne p'$ also known as the type I error) gives a hypothesis test of level-α, where solving ϵ as a function of α gives $\alpha = e^{-\frac{\epsilon^2 nm}{2K(n+m)}} \Rightarrow \epsilon = \sqrt{\tfrac{2K(n+m)}{nm} \log \tfrac{1}{\alpha}}$. We retain the null hypothesis if $\mathbf{MMD}(Z, Z') - T < 0$, where the threshold is $T = 2\left(\sqrt{\tfrac{K}{n}} + \sqrt{\tfrac{K}{m}}\right) + \sqrt{\tfrac{2K(n+m)}{nm} \log \tfrac{1}{\alpha}}$. This also defines Eve's detection function ($\Psi(C, D)$) at level-α: $\Psi(C, D) \equiv \mathbf{MMD}(C, D) - T$. If $\Psi(C, D) \ge 0$ then Eve realizes that D is not drawn i.i.d. from $\mathbb{Q}_{(\mathbf{x}, y)}$ and flags it as suspicious.

For all our experiments Eve used the RBF kernel $k(\mathbf{z}_i, \mathbf{z}_j) = \exp\left(-\tfrac{\|\mathbf{z}_i - \mathbf{z}_j\|^2}{2\sigma^2}\right)$. Eve set σ to be the median distance between points in the camouflage pool as proposed in [20]. Eve also included the scaled class label as a feature dimension: $[\mathbf{x}_i, c\mathbb{1}\{y_i = 1\}]$ where $c = \max_{k,l \text{ such that } y_k = y_l} \|\mathbf{x}_k - \mathbf{x}_l\|$ and $\mathbb{1}\{\cdot\}$ is the indicator function. This augmented feature enables Eve to monitor both features and labels. When using the NLP solver Alice only has to consider instances from camouflage pool. She calculated **MMD** in the following manner:

$$\mathbf{MMD}_b(Z, b_1, \ldots, b_{|Z|}) = [\tfrac{1}{n^2} \textstyle\sum_{i,j=1}^{n} k(\mathbf{z}_i, \mathbf{z}_j) - \tfrac{2}{n \sum_{i=1}^{n} b_i} \textstyle\sum_{i,j=1}^{n} b_i k(\mathbf{z}_i, \mathbf{z}_j) + \tfrac{1}{(\sum_{i=1}^{n} b_i)^2} \textstyle\sum_{i,j=1}^{n} b_i b_j k(\mathbf{z}_i, \mathbf{z}_j)]^{\frac{1}{2}}$$

$$(6)$$

References

1. Alfeld, S., Zhu, X., Barford, P.: Explicit defense actions against test-set attacks. In: AAAI, pp. 1274–1280 (2017)
2. Balbach, F.J., Zeugmann, T.: Teaching randomized learners. In: Lugosi, G., Simon, H.U. (eds.) COLT 2006. LNCS (LNAI), vol. 4005, pp. 229–243. Springer, Heidelberg (2006). https://doi.org/10.1007/11776420_19
3. Barreno, M., Nelson, B., Joseph, A.D., Tygar, J.: The security of machine learning. Mach. Learn. **81**(2), 121–148 (2010)
4. Barreno, M., Nelson, B., Sears, R., Joseph, A.D., Tygar, J.D.: Can machine learning be secure? In: Proceedings of the 2006 ACM Symposium on Information, Computer and Communications Security (2006)
5. Biggio, B., Roli, F.: Wild patterns: ten years after the rise of adversarial machine learning. arXiv preprint arXiv:1712.03141 (2017)
6. Brakerski, Z.: Fully homomorphic encryption without modulus switching from classical GapSVP. In: Safavi-Naini, R., Canetti, R. (eds.) CRYPTO 2012. LNCS, vol. 7417, pp. 868–886. Springer, Heidelberg (2012). https://doi.org/10.1007/978-3-642-32009-5_50
7. Brakerski, Z., Gentry, C., Vaikuntanathan, V.: (Leveled) fully homomorphic encryption without bootstrapping. ACM Trans. Comput. Theory (TOCT) **6**(3), 13 (2014)
8. Brückner, M., Kanzow, C., Scheffer, T.: Static prediction games for adversarial learning problems. J. Mach. Learn. Res. **13**, 2617–2654 (2012)
9. Brückner, M., Scheffer, T.: Nash equilibria of static prediction games. In: Advances in Neural Information Processing Systems (2009)
10. Brückner, M., Scheffer, T.: Stackelberg games for adversarial prediction problems. In: ACM SIGKDD (2011)
11. Bulò, S.R., Biggio, B., Pillai, I., Pelillo, M., Roli, F.: Randomized prediction games for adversarial machine learning. IEEE Trans. Neural Netw. Learn. Syst. **28**, 2466–2478 (2016)
12. Bussieck, M.R., Pruessner, A.: Mixed-integer nonlinear programming. SIAG/OPT Newsl. Views News **14**(1), 19–22 (2003)
13. Cachin, C.: An information-theoretic model for steganography. In: Aucsmith, D. (ed.) IH 1998. LNCS, vol. 1525, pp. 306–318. Springer, Heidelberg (1998). https://doi.org/10.1007/3-540-49380-8_21
14. Chandramouli, R.: A mathematical approach to steganalysis. In: Proceedings SPIE, vol. 4675, pp. 4–25 (2002)
15. Cox, I.J., Kalker, T., Pakura, G., Scheel, M.: Information transmission and steganography. In: Barni, M., Cox, I., Kalker, T., Kim, H.-J. (eds.) IWDW 2005. LNCS, vol. 3710, pp. 15–29. Springer, Heidelberg (2005). https://doi.org/10.1007/11551492_2
16. Dalvi, N., Domingos, P., Sanghai, S., Verma, D., et al.: Adversarial classification. In: ACM SIGKDD (2004)
17. Dziugaite, G.K., Roy, D.M., Ghahramani, Z.: Training generative neural networks via maximum mean discrepancy optimization. arXiv preprint arXiv:1505.03906 (2015)
18. Fridrich, J.: Feature-based steganalysis for JPEG images and its implications for future design of steganographic schemes. In: Fridrich, J. (ed.) IH 2004. LNCS, vol. 3200, pp. 67–81. Springer, Heidelberg (2004). https://doi.org/10.1007/978-3-540-30114-1_6

19. Gentry, C., Sahai, A., Waters, B.: Homomorphic encryption from learning with errors: conceptually-simpler, asymptotically-faster, attribute-based. In: Canetti, R., Garay, J.A. (eds.) CRYPTO 2013. LNCS, vol. 8042, pp. 75–92. Springer, Heidelberg (2013). https://doi.org/10.1007/978-3-642-40041-4_5

20. Gretton, A., Borgwardt, K.M., Rasch, M.J., Schölkopf, B., Smola, A.: A kernel two-sample test. J. Mach. Learn. Res. **13**(Mar), 723–773 (2012)

21. Hardt, M., Megiddo, N., Papadimitriou, C., Wootters, M.: Strategic classification. In: ACM ITCS (2016)

22. He, K., Zhang, X., Ren, S., Sun, J.: Deep residual learning for image recognition. In: IEEE CVPR, pp. 770–778 (2016)

23. Hearst, M.A., Dumais, S.T., Osuna, E., Platt, J., Scholkopf, B.: Support vector machines. IEEE Intell. Syst. Appl. **13**(4), 18–28 (1998)

24. Hoerl, A.E., Kennard, R.W.: Ridge regression: biased estimation for nonorthogonal problems. Technometrics **12**(1), 55–67 (1970)

25. Hopper, N.J., Langford, J., von Ahn, L.: Provably secure steganography. In: Yung, M. (ed.) CRYPTO 2002. LNCS, vol. 2442, pp. 77–92. Springer, Heidelberg (2002). https://doi.org/10.1007/3-540-45708-9_6

26. Hosmer Jr., D.W., Lemeshow, S., Sturdivant, R.X.: Applied Logistic Regression, vol. 398. Wiley, Hoboken (2013)

27. Huang, L., Joseph, A.D., Nelson, B., Rubinstein, B.I., Tygar, J.: Adversarial machine learning. In: AISEC (2011)

28. Joachims, T.: A probabilistic analysis of the Rocchio algorithm with TFIDF for text categorization. Technical report, Carnegie-Mellon University Pittsburgh PA, Department of Computer Science (1996)

29. Johnson, N.F., Jajodia, S.: Exploring steganography: seeing the unseen. Computer **31**(2), 26–34 (1998)

30. Juels, A., Ristenpart, T.: Honey encryption: security beyond the brute-force bound. In: Nguyen, P.Q., Oswald, E. (eds.) EUROCRYPT 2014. LNCS, vol. 8441, pp. 293–310. Springer, Heidelberg (2014). https://doi.org/10.1007/978-3-642-55220-5_17

31. Katz, J., Menezes, A.J., Van Oorschot, P.C., Vanstone, S.A.: Handbook of Applied Cryptography. CRC Press, Boca Raton (1996)

32. Ker, A.D.: Steganalysis of LSB matching in grayscale images. IEEE Signal Process. Lett. **12**(6), 441–444 (2005)

33. Kerckhoffs, A.: La Cryptographie Militaire (Part I), vol. 9, pp. 5–38 (1883)

34. Kerckhoffs, A.: La Cryptographie Militaire (Part II), vol. 9, pp. 161–191 (1883)

35. Kloft, M., Laskov, P.: A poisoning attack against online anomaly detection. In: NIPS Workshop on Machine Learning in Adversarial Environments for Computer Security. Citeseer (2007)

36. Kloft, M., Laskov, P.: Online anomaly detection under adversarial impact. In: AISTATS, pp. 405–412 (2010)

37. Kloft, M., Laskov, P.: Online anomaly detection under adversarial impact (2011)

38. Kohavi, R., et al.: A study of cross-validation and bootstrap for accuracy estimation and model selection. In: IJCAI, vol. 14(2), pp. 1137–1145. Montreal, Canada (1995)

39. Krasin, I., et al.: Openimages: a public dataset for large-scale multi-label and multi-class image classification. Dataset (2017). https://github.com/openimages

40. Krenn, R.: Steganography and steganalysis (2004)

41. Krizhevsky, A., Hinton, G.: Learning multiple layers of features from tiny images (2009)

42. Laskov, P., Kloft, M.: A framework for quantitative security analysis of machine learning. In: Proceedings of the 2nd ACM Workshop on Security and Artificial Intelligence (2009)

43. Letchford, J., Vorobeychik, Y.: Optimal interdiction of attack plans. In: AAMAS (2013)
44. Liu, J., Zhu, X.: The teaching dimension of linear learners. J. Mach. Learn. Res. **17**(162), 1–25 (2016)
45. Liu, W., Chawla, S.: A game theoretical model for adversarial learning. In: IEEE International Conference on Data Mining Workshops 2009. ICDMW 2009 (2009)
46. López-Alt, A., Tromer, E., Vaikuntanathan, V.: On-the-fly multiparty computation on the cloud via multikey fully homomorphic encryption. In: Proceedings of the Forty-Fourth Annual ACM Symposium on Theory of Computing, pp. 1219–1234. ACM (2012)
47. Lowd, D., Meek, C.: Adversarial learning. In: ACM SIGKDD, pp. 641–647. ACM (2005)
48. Maganbhai, P.A.K., Chouhan, K.: A study and literature review on image steganography. Int. J. Comput. Sci. Inf. Technol. **6**, 685–688 (2015)
49. Mei, S., Zhu, X.: Using machine teaching to identify optimal training-set attacks on machine learners. In: Twenty-Ninth AAAI Conference on Artificial Intelligence (2015)
50. Mikolov, T., Chen, K., Corrado, G., Dean, J.: Efficient estimation of word representations in vector space. arXiv preprint arXiv:1301.3781 (2013)
51. Queirolo, F.: Steganography in images. Final Communications Report 3 (2011)
52. Reyzin, L., Russell, S.: More efficient provably secure steganography. Department of Computer Science, Boston University (2003)
53. Rich, E., Knight, K.: Artificial Intelligence. McGraw-Hill, New York (1991)
54. Rivest, R.L., Adleman, L., Dertouzos, M.L.: On data banks and privacy homomorphisms. Found. Secur. Comput. **4**(11), 169–180 (1978)
55. Simmons, G.J.: The prisoners' problem and the subliminal channel. In: Chaum, D. (ed.) Advances in Cryptology, pp. 51–67. Springer, Heidelberg (1984). https://doi.org/10.1007/978-1-4684-4730-9_5
56. Singh, K.U.: A survey on image steganography techniques. Int. J. Comput. Appl. **97**(18) (2014)
57. Smart, N.P., Vercauteren, F.: Fully homomorphic encryption with relatively small key and ciphertext sizes. In: Nguyen, P.Q., Pointcheval, D. (eds.) PKC 2010. LNCS, vol. 6056, pp. 420–443. Springer, Heidelberg (2010). https://doi.org/10.1007/978-3-642-13013-7_25
58. Steinwart, I.: On the influence of the kernel on the consistency of support vector machines. J. Mach. Learn. Res. **2**(Nov), 67–93 (2001)
59. Tan, K.M.C., Killourhy, K.S., Maxion, R.A.: Undermining an anomaly-based intrusion detection system using common exploits. In: Wespi, A., Vigna, G., Deri, L. (eds.) RAID 2002. LNCS, vol. 2516, pp. 54–73. Springer, Heidelberg (2002). https://doi.org/10.1007/3-540-36084-0_4
60. Thompson, A.: All the news (2017). https://www.kaggle.com/snapcrack/all-the-news
61. Van Tilborg, H.C., Jajodia, S.: Encyclopedia of Cryptography and Security. Springer, Heidelberg (2014)
62. Vorobeychik, Y., Li, B.: Optimal randomized classification in adversarial settings. In: AAMAS (2014)
63. Wu, H.C.: The Karush-Kuhn-Tucker optimality conditions in an optimization problem with interval-valued objective function. Eur. J. Oper. Res. **176**(1), 46–59 (2007)

64. Zhang, L., Wu, J., Zhou, N.: Image encryption with discrete fractional cosine transform and chaos. In: Fifth International Conference on Information Assurance and Security 2009. IAS 2009, vol. 2, pp. 61–64. IEEE (2009)
65. Zhang, X., Zhu, X., Wright, S.: Training set debugging using trusted items. In: AAAI (2018)

Multi-stage Dynamic Information Flow Tracking Game

Shana Moothedath[1](✉), Dinuka Sahabandu[1], Andrew Clark[2], Sangho Lee[3], Wenke Lee[3], and Radha Poovendran[1]

[1] Department of Electrical Engineering, University of Washington, Seattle, WA 98195, USA
{sm15,sdinuka,rp3}@uw.edu
[2] Department of Electrical and Computer Engineering, Worcester Polytechnic Institute, Worcester, MA 01609, USA
aclark@wpi.edu
[3] College of Computing, Georgia Institute of Technology, Atlanta, GA 30332, USA
sangho@gatech.edu, wenke@cc.gatech.edu

Abstract. Advanced persistent threats (APTs) consist of multiple attack stages between entry and exit points of the attack. In each stage of the attack, the adversary gathers more privileges, resources, and information about the system and uses this information to gain access to the targeted data of the next stage to reach the final goal. APTs are not only persistent but also stealthy and hence difficult to detect. The persistent nature of APTs, however, creates information flows in the system that can be monitored. One monitoring mechanism is Dynamic Information Flow Tracking (DIFT), which taints and tracks malicious information flows through a system and inspects the flows at designated traps. Since tainting all flows in the system will incur prohibitive resource costs, efficient tagging policies are needed to decide which flows to tag in order to maximize the probability of APT detection while minimizing resource overhead. At present such an analytical model for DIFT for multi-stage APT detection does not exist. In this paper, we propose a game theoretic framework modeling real-time detection of multi-stage APTs via DIFT. We formulate a two-player (APT vs DIFT) nonzero-sum stochastic game with incomplete information to obtain an optimal tagging policy. Our game model consists of a sequence of stages, where each stage of the game corresponds to a stage in the attack. At each stage, the goal of the APT is to reach a particular destination, corresponding to a targeted resource or privilege, while the goal of the defender is to detect the APT. We first derive an efficient algorithm to find locally optimal strategies for both players. We then characterize the best responses of both players and present algorithms to find the best responses. Finally, we validate our results on a real-world attack data set obtained using the Refinable Attack INvestigation (RAIN) framework for a ScreenGrab attack.

This work was supported by ONR grant N00014-16-1-2710 P00002

L. Bushnell et al. (Eds.): GameSec 2018, LNCS 11199, pp. 80–101, 2018.
https://doi.org/10.1007/978-3-030-01554-1_5

1 Introduction

Advanced persistent threats (APTs) are highly sophisticated multi-stage customized attacks by skilled adversaries. In each stage of the attack, the attacker gathers more privileges, resources, and information about the system, using various modes of information gathering techniques, to build a target profile and uses this information to gain access to the targeted data of the next stage and reach the final goal [2,19]. These attacks are not only persistent, but also stealthy, and hence APT detection and defense is a challenging task. GhostNet, Operation Aurora, Stuxnet [7], Duqu, Flame [1], Red October, and Miniduke [16] are some of the attacks that evaded the detection mechanisms of the security community and resulted in the exfiltration of vast amount of data or sabotaging critical infrastructures [14,18].

After infiltrating a system, actions of APTs introduce malicious signals in the system in the form of data exchange commands and control commands, referred as *information flows*. Detection of such malicious flows can lead to the detection of APT's actions. *Information Flow Tracking* (IFT) is a widely used method in offline threat analysis after the occurrence of an attack to identify spurious information flows generated by untrustworthy I/O channels [5,20]. The key idea of the IFT system is to *tag* or *taint* unauthorized information flows as spurious and track the propagation of the tagged data through the system [20]. For proactive detection of spurious flows, a modified version of IFT known as *Dynamic Information Flow Tracking* (DIFT) was introduced in [15]. Under DIFT, when a spurious flow mixes with regular flows, the resulting mix still preserves the tag. The tagged information flows are inspected by DIFT at designated locations in the system referred to as *traps* [15] enabling real-time threat analysis.

Although tagging all sensitive processes (e.g., an instance of a program in a personal computer) in the system using DIFT will enhance the system security, it leads to performance and memory overhead. This will result in considerable slowdown of the system as noted in [6]. There exists a trade-off regarding the effectiveness of the detection system and the performance of the system. In order to reduce the performance overhead, the system may choose to tag a subset of flows passing through certain processes, at the cost of reducing the probability of detection. An efficient tagging policy decides *which* processes to tag so as to minimize the performance overhead of the system and at the same time maximize the probability of detection. As the susceptibility of a process to an attack depends on the attacker's behavior, the decision to tag a process in the system depends on the interaction of the adversary with the system. Also, the propagation of an attack through the system depends on the actions of the detection system. Thus an efficient tagging policy of the DIFT depends on the actions of the attacker which is determined by the interaction of the attacker with the system. This interdependent nature of the actions of the detection system and the attacker motivates a *game theoretic* framework.

A recent game model of defense against APTs is FlipIt [17], in which the defense and the adversary compete with each other for capturing the control of the system. A control-theoretic approach to model competing malwares in

FlipIt is given in [11]. The interplay between the APT attacker and the insiders for joint attacks is studied using a game model in [9]. While these approaches model the incursion part of the attack, our focus is on the progression of the attack through the system, referred as *lateral movement*. In this direction, a game-theoretic model describing the interaction between DIFT and adversarial information flows is given in the recent work [13]. Paper [13] characterized the optimal strategies of the APT and DIFT and derived an efficient algorithm to compute the optimal strategies. However, the approach in [13] only considered a single stage of the attack, while APTs are mostly multi-stage attacks.

Each attack stage corresponds to a unique set of critical locations, referred to as destinations. The intermediate stages in the attack hold information that is critical to the adversary achieving its goals at the final stage. In each stage of the attack, the adversary strategizes to reach destination of that specific stage and to launch a stealthy attack. The defender's strategy is to tag the flows in a resource-efficient manner to detect the APTs before reaching the final destination. The defense mechanism does not know the stage and the specific goal of the adversary for that stage of the attack. This results in an asymmetry in the player's information about the game. This information asymmetry is not captured by the existing model in [13] and requires a new approach.

In this paper, we develop a game-theoretic model for the detection of multi-stage APTs via DIFT. In our formulation, the adversary decides the next process reached by the information flow based on the current stage, the process at which the adversary is located, and the processes it can transition to. The defense decides whether to tag a process or not based on the performance overhead and detection probability associated with tagging that particular process. A multi-stage stochastic game model with incomplete information incorporates these features. We make the following contributions:

- We model the interaction between the DIFT system and APT on a system consisting of N processes and M stages as a two-player nonzero sum stochastic game with incomplete information. This formulation captures the interaction between the DIFT system and the APT, the multi-stage nature of the attack, and the information asymmetry among the players.
- Our game formulation consists of a sequence of stages, where each stage of the game corresponds to a stage in the attack. In each stage, the attacker decides the path to be traversed through the processes in the system aiming towards capturing the target locations of that stage, and the DIFT system decides the processes to be tagged so as to increase the probability of detecting the attacker in that stage.
- We provide an algorithm to obtain locally optimal equilibrium strategies for both the players using the notion of correlated equilibria by transforming the two-player game to an $(NM + N + 1)$-player game.
- We evaluate the best responses of both players. We compute the best response for the APT by proving that this computation is equivalent to a shortest path on the provenance graph constructed using the system log data. For the DIFT system, we show that the payoff function is submodular and then

exploit the submodularity to obtain an approximate algorithm to compute the best response.

- We provide experimental validation of our model and results using real-world attack data set obtained using Refinable Attack INvestigation system (RAIN) for ScreenGrab attack.

The organization of the rest of the paper is as follows. In Sect. 2, we introduce the notations used in the sequel and give the game theoretic formulation of the multi-stage game for designing optimal tainting policies for the DIFT. The game-theoretic model focuses on stage-based attacks and serves as a general model for the multi-stage security game. In Sect. 3, we discuss the notion of Nash equilibria and correlated equilibria in the context of multi-stage game model. In Sect. 4, we present an algorithm to find a locally optimal solution to the game using the concept of correlated equilibria. This section also describes a method to evaluate the best response of the attacker and the defender. We evaluate the best responses of the players using the graph theoretic notion of shortest path and exploiting the submodularity of the payoff functions. In Sect. 5, we give experimental validation of our results using real-world data sets. In Sect. 6, we conclude the paper and briefly discuss future directions of work.

2   Notations and Game Formulation

In this section, we introduce the notations used in the sequel and then present the game-theoretic formulation of the problem. We perform the analysis of the multi-stage APTs on the *provenance graph* of the system obtained from the system log data [8]. A provenance graph $\mathcal{G}$ represents the lineage of data transformed by a system. In networked systems, $\mathcal{G}$ represents the graphical representation of the log data using the whole-system execution and workflow during the entire period of logging. Here, nodes form the processes in the system and edges represent the information flow in the system from one process to the other. These graphs are widely used in the security research as a part of static APT detection schemes [8,10]. We analyze security in systems consisting of many processes interacting with each other through information flows using their provenance graph. Figure 1 shows the provenance graph of a networked system and the information flow in it. While the information flows in the system at any given instant result in acyclic graphs as given in Fig. 1a and b, the resulting information flow graph that captures the temporal dependencies among these individual graphs can be cyclic as shown in Fig. 1c. Consider a provenance graph $\mathcal{G} = (\mathcal{S}, E_{\mathcal{S}})$ where the node set $\mathcal{S} := \{s_1, \ldots, s_N\}$ is the set of processes in the system and the edge set $E_{\mathcal{S}} \subset \mathcal{S} \times \mathcal{S}$ captures the interactions between the processes using system log data. The graph $\mathcal{G}$ consists of a set of *critical processes* which must be protected against any malicious attack in the system. We consider *multi-stage* attacks which consists of M stages, such that each stage corresponds to a set of *destinations*. Let $\mathcal{D}_j := \{d_1^j, \ldots, d_{n_j}^j\}$ denotes the set of destinations in the jth stage. The set of all destinations is $\mathcal{D} := \cup_{j=1}^{M} \mathcal{D}_j$. We use DIFT as the detection mechanism of the system. In this section, we model this problem as a two-player (APT vs DIFT) multi-stage non-zero sum game with incomplete information which is discussed below.

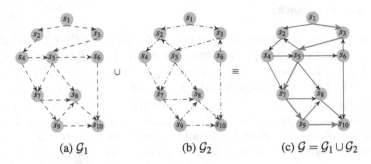

(a) $\mathcal{G}_1$ (b) $\mathcal{G}_2$ (c) $\mathcal{G} = \mathcal{G}_1 \cup \mathcal{G}_2$

Fig. 1. A provenance graph $\mathcal{G}$ with 10 nodes obtained by incorporating the temporal dependencies. Any directed path in $\mathcal{G}$ corresponds to an information flow in the system. For example, the dipath shown in red represents an information flow from s_1 to s_{10}.

The security game considered in this paper consists of two players, *adversary* denoted as $\mathcal{P}^A$ and *defender* (DIFT) denoted as $\mathcal{P}^D$. The two-player game between $\mathcal{P}^A$ and $\mathcal{P}^D$ evolves in the provenance graph, $\mathcal{G} = (\mathcal{S}, E_{\mathcal{S}})$. The detection system of the system deploys a set of *trap nodes* $\mathcal{T}$ and a set of *tag nodes* $\mathcal{Y}$ in the system and monitors the information flow through $\mathcal{Y}$. The trap nodes $\mathcal{T} := \{t_1, \ldots, t_h\} \subset \mathcal{S}$ is a set of processes deployed in the system *a priori* in order to capture any information flow in the system initiated by potential malicious agents. The tagged nodes $\mathcal{Y} := \{y_1, \ldots, y_{h'}\} \subset \mathcal{S}$ are such that any information flow passing through a process $y_i \in \mathcal{Y}$ is *tagged/tainted*. Once a flow is tagged, the defender keeps track of the flow and thus incurs memory and performance overhead. The trap nodes are capable of accurately verifying the authenticity of a tagged information flow passing through them. As a result, a tagged malicious flow passing through a trap node generates a security alert in the system. Even though the detection system allows tagging of processes, it is desired to tag minimum number of processes while guaranteeing a reliable and secure operation of the system. This paper deals with optimal selection of tagged nodes in the system.

Let $\lambda \subset \mathcal{S}$ be the set of *vulnerable processes* in the provenance graph $\mathcal{G}$. The adversary enters the system by exploiting a process in λ, thus, λ characterizes all possible entry points of the attack. We introduce a node s_0 referred to as *pseudo-process* into the provenance graph and s_0 is connected to all the processes in the set λ. Let E_λ denotes the edges from the pseudo-process s_0 to all processes in the set λ. After the inclusion of the pseudo-process into the system, the set of processes is modified as $\mathcal{S} \cup \{s_0\}$ and the edge set is modified as $E_{\mathcal{S}} \cup E_\lambda$. Let $\mathscr{S} := \mathcal{S} \cup \{s_0\}$ and $E := E_{\mathcal{S}} \cup E_\lambda$. Without loss of generality, we assume that the source of an attack is s_0. Note that, transitions are allowed *from* pseudo-process

s_0 and no transition is allowed *into* pseudo-process s_0 as it is the root node. Further, s_0 is always in stage 1, and is not tagged.

Depending on whether the process is tagged or not and in which stage the players are, the state space of the game is defined as $\bar{\mathcal{S}} := \{\mathcal{S} \times \{1, \ldots, M\} \times \{0,1\}\} \cup \{(s_0^1, 0)\}$, where $\bar{\mathcal{S}} = \{\bar{s}_1, \ldots, \bar{s}_{2NM+1}\}$ such that $\bar{s}_i = (s_i^j, k)$, where $j \in \{1, \ldots, M\}$ and $k \in \{0, 1\}$. Here,

$$\bar{s}_i := \begin{cases} (s_i^j, 1), \text{if process } s_i \text{ is in stage } j \text{ and it is tagged,} \\ (s_i^j, 0), \text{if process } s_i \text{ is in stage } j \text{ and it is not tagged.} \end{cases}$$

For an adversarial flow in the state space $\bar{\mathcal{S}}$ originating at the state $(s_0^1, 0)$, we give the following definition.

Definition 2.1. *An information flow in the state space $\bar{\mathcal{S}}$ that origi-nates at state $(s_0^1, 0)$ and terminates at state (s_i^j, k) is said to satisfy the stage $-$ constraint if the flow passes through some destinations in $\mathcal{D}_1, \mathcal{D}_2, \ldots, \mathcal{D}_{j-1}$.*

The players $\mathcal{P}^A$ and $\mathcal{P}^D$ have finite action sets over the state space $\bar{\mathcal{S}}$ denoted by sets $\mathcal{A}^A$ and $\mathcal{A}^D$, respectively. The set $\mathcal{A}^A$ contains the set of processes that the adversary's flow is going to traverse. Further, the adversary can also end the game by dropping the information flow at any point of time. In such a case, the adversary transitions to a *null* state $\emptyset$. Thus $\mathcal{A}^A = \{s_i^j : s_i \in \mathscr{S}, j \in \{1, \ldots, M\}\} \cup \{\emptyset\}$. The defender decides whether to tag a process or not, and hence $\mathcal{A}^D = \{0, 1\}^{\mathscr{S}}$. Note that, although the existing architecture of DIFT [15] also decides the location of the trap nodes ($\mathcal{T}$), as a first step to obtain an analytical model for DIFT we assume the trap locations are pre-specified and the defender's actions only decide where to place the tagging ($\mathcal{Y}$). Moreover, a process once tagged at some point of time in the game, remains tagged through out the game and there is no untagging of a process at a later stage of the game. While the objective of $\mathcal{P}^A$ is to exploit the vulnerable processes λ (in effect the pseudo-process s_0) of the system to successfully launch an attack, the objective of $\mathcal{P}^D$ is to select an optimal set of tagged nodes, say $\mathcal{Y}^*$, such that any spurious information flow in the system is captured at some trap node before reaching the destination.

The players $\mathcal{P}^A$ and $\mathcal{P}^D$ have different information sets about the state space. Both the adversary and the defender know the graph $\mathcal{G}$ and the locations of the trap nodes. The defender also has the information about the tagged nodes; however, the adversary is unaware whether a process s_i is tagged or not. On the other hand, while the adversary knows the stage of the attack, the defender does not know the stage of the attack. Thus, both the adversary and the defender have incomplete information about the game.

Now we define the strategies on the state space $\bar{\mathcal{S}}$. In order to reduce the complexity and considering the fact that the action sets of the players, i.e., tagging and adversarial information flow, are lower level processes with memory constraints and computational limitations, in this paper we consider *stationary strategies* for both the players. A stationary strategy is defined below.

Definition 2.2. *A player strategy is stationary if it depends only on the current state.*

Additionally, the player strategies considered in this paper are *mixed strategies*. Unlike in a *pure strategy* where the actions of the players solely depend on the past actions, in a *mixed strategy* there is a randomness associated with the strategies of the players. Thus the action sets $\mathcal{A}^A$ and $\mathcal{A}^D$ are defined as probability distributions. The strategies of the players crucially depend on the nature of the process (destination, trap, or other) and the stage at which the attack occurs (to satisfy the stage-constraint). The randomness associated with the actions of the defender and the adversary is captured by assigning a probability for tagging a process and by assigning a probability for transitioning from one process to another process, respectively. As the defender is unaware of the stage of the attack, the defender strategy does not depend on the stage. Thus for every process $s_i \in \mathscr{S}$, we define the probability of tagging the process s_i as $0 \leqslant \mathbf{p}_D(s_i) \leqslant 1$, if it was not tagged before. The tagging probability of the pseudo-process is always set to zero, i.e., $\mathbf{p}_D(s_0) = 0$. The adversary on the other hand is aware of the stage of the attack and hence the adversary's actions depend on the stage. Consider two processes, process s_i at stage j and process $s_{i'}$ at stage j', i.e., s_i^j and $s_{i'}^{j'}$. Here, $s_i \in \mathscr{S}$ and $s_{i'} \in \mathcal{S}$. The possible cases in which the adversary is able to transition from a process in stage j to a process in stage j' are: (1) $j = j'$ and $(s_i, s_{i'}) \in E$, 2) $j' = j+1$ and $s_i = s_{i'} \in \mathcal{D}_j$, and (3) $s_{i'}^{j'} = \emptyset$. Case 1) corresponds to transition from a process in $\mathscr{S}$ to a process in $\mathcal{S}$ in the same stage, case (2) corresponds to transition from one stage to the next stage at a destination, and case 3) corresponds to adversary transitioning to a null state $\emptyset$. The adversary transition is given by the transition probability vector $\mathbf{p}_A$, where $0 \leqslant \mathbf{p}_A(s_i^j, s_{i'}^{j'}) \leqslant 1$, such that $\sum_{s_{i'} \in \mathcal{N}(s_i)} \mathbf{p}_A(s_i^j, s_{i'}^{j'}) = 1$ and $\mathcal{N}(s_i) := \{s_{i'} : (s_i, s_{i'}) \in E\} \cup \{s_i, \emptyset\}$. Also, $\mathbf{p}_A(s_i^j, s_{i'}^{j'}) \neq 0$ implies either $j = j'$ with $s_{i'} \in \mathcal{N}(s_i)$ or $j' = j + 1$ with $s_i = s_{i'} \in \mathcal{D}_j$. Thus the strategies of $\mathcal{P}^A$ and $\mathcal{P}^D$ are given by the vectors $\mathbf{p}_D = \{\mathbf{p}_D(s_i) : s_i \in \mathscr{S}\}$ and $\mathbf{p}_A = \{\mathbf{p}_A(s_i^j, s_{i'}^{j'}) : s_i \in \mathscr{S}, j, j' \in \{1, \ldots, M\}$, and $s_{i'} \in \mathcal{S} \cup \{\emptyset\}\}$, respectively. Notice that $\mathbf{p}_A$ is defined in such a way that in the state space $\bar{\mathcal{S}}$, the state $(s_0^1, 0)$ has only outgoing edges and any flow originating at $(s_0^1, 0)$ reaches a state (s_i^j, k) after passing through some destinations of stages $1, \ldots, j-1$. By this construction of $\bar{\mathcal{S}}$ and $\mathbf{p}_A$, all possible information flows in $\bar{\mathcal{S}}$ satisfy the stage-constraints and can affect the performance of the system and even result in system breakdown, if malicious.

We now introduce the cost parameters associated with the game. To model the game in every stage of the attack, we include stage-based attacks in our problem formulation by introducing penalties and rewards at the intermediate stages, for the adversary and the defender. If the adversary successfully reaches a destination of stage j after passing through some destination for all stages before j, then he/she receives an *intermediate reward*. On the other hand, if the adversary gets caught at some stage j, then he/she incurs a *penalty* and the game terminates. If the adversary reaches some destination at a stage j, the defender incurs an *intermediate penalty*. On the other hand, if the defender catches the adversary at stage j, then he/she receives a *reward* and the game terminates. In addition to this, the defender is also associated with a cost for tagging the processes, as tagging leads to resource overhead such as memory and storage.

Now we define the *payoff functions* of the defender (U^D) and the adversary (U^A) for a given strategy, using the intermediate values and tagging costs. The payoff functions U^A and U^D depend on the following factors. The adversary payoff U^A consists of two components: (i) a reward $\beta_j^A > 0$ for successfully reaching a destination in the jth stage after passing through some destinations in $\mathcal{D}_1, \ldots, \mathcal{D}_{j-1}$, and (ii) a cost $\alpha^A < 0$ if the adversary is tagged and trapped by the defender. Similarly, the defender utility $\mathcal{U}^D$ consists of three components: (a) a memory cost $\mathcal{C}^D(s_i) < 0$ for tagging a process $s_i \in \mathcal{S}$, (b) a cost $\beta_j^D < 0$ if the adversary reaches a destination in the jth stage after passing through some destinations in $\mathcal{D}_1, \ldots, \mathcal{D}_{j-1}$, and (c) a reward $\alpha^D > 0$ for catching the adversary. We assume that the cost of tagging a process $\mathcal{C}^D(s_i)$ is independent of the strategy of the adversary and the stage. However, $\mathcal{C}^D(s_i)$ depends on the average traffic at process s_i and hence $\mathcal{C}^D(s_i) := c\,B(s_i)$. Here, $c \in \mathbb{R}_-$ is a fixed tagging cost, where $\mathbb{R}_-$ is the set of negative real numbers, and $B(s_i)$ denotes the average traffic at process s_i. The cost $\mathcal{C}^D(s_i)$ is incurred only once when the process is tagged.

With respect to strategies $\mathbf{p}_D$ and $\mathbf{p}_A$, the payoffs of the game on $\bar{\mathcal{S}}$ for the defender, U^D, and the adversary, U^A, are as follows.

$$U^D(\mathbf{p}_D, \mathbf{p}_A) = \sum_{s_i \in \mathcal{S}} \mathbf{p}_D(s_i)\,\mathcal{C}^D(s_i) + \sum_{j=1}^{M} \Big(p_T(j)\alpha^D + p_R(j)\beta_j^D \Big), \qquad (1)$$

$$U^A(\mathbf{p}_D, \mathbf{p}_A) = \sum_{j=1}^{M} \Big(p_T(j)\alpha^A + p_R(j)\beta_j^A \Big). \qquad (2)$$

Without loss of generality, the entry point of any adversarial information flow in the state space $\bar{\mathcal{S}}$ is $(s_0^1, 0)$. Here, $p_T(j)$ denotes the probability that a flow originating at state $(s_0^1, 0)$ in $\bar{\mathcal{S}}$ will get tagged and trapped at level j. The term $p_R(j)$ denotes the probability that a flow originating at state $(s_0^1, 0)$ in $\bar{\mathcal{S}}$ will reach some destination in set $\mathcal{D}_j$. The payoff functions U^A and U^D captures the global return of the game. For calculating these values, we introduce the concept of local payoffs referred to as *utilities* at every state in the state space $\bar{\mathcal{S}}$. With respect to each state in $\bar{\mathcal{S}}$, we define utility functions $\mathcal{U}^A : \bar{\mathcal{S}} \to \mathbb{R}$ and $\mathcal{U}^D : \bar{\mathcal{S}} \to \mathbb{R}$ for the adversary and defender, respectively. Firstly, we characterize all possible attacks in a system. In a system consisting of M stages, an attack on the state space $\bar{\mathcal{S}}$ belongs to one of the following $M + 2$ scenarios.

- The adversary drops out of the game before reaching some destination in $\mathcal{D}_1$.
- The adversary reaches some destination each in $\mathcal{D}_1, \ldots, \mathcal{D}_j$ and then drops out of the game, for $j = 1, \ldots, M - 1$.

- The adversary reaches some destination each in $\mathcal{D}_1, \ldots, \mathcal{D}_M$.
- The defender catches the adversary at some stage.

For the first case, both adversary and defender incurs zero payoff. For the second case, adversary earns rewards for reaching stages $1, \ldots, j$, defender incurs penalty for not catching the adversary at stages $1, \ldots, j$, and the game terminates. In the third case, adversary wins the game and earns the total reward for reaching destinations in all stages, and the defender incurs a total penalty for not catching the adversary at all the stages. In the last case, adversary incurs the penalty for getting caught and the defender wins the game and earns the reward for catching the adversary. While calculating the payoffs of $\mathcal{P}^D$ and $\mathcal{P}^A$ at a state in $\bar{S}$, we consider all possible attacks listed above that can occur at that state, using the notion of $P_{R,j}(\cdot, \cdot)$ and $P_T(\cdot, \cdot)$ explained below.

Let $q(s_i^{j'})$ denotes the probability with which the adversary drops out of the game at state $(s_i^{j'}, k)$, for $k \in \{0, 1\}$. Let $P_{R,j}(s_i^{j'}, k)$ denotes the probability that an information flow originating at $(s_0^1, 0)$ reaches a destination in $\mathcal{D}_j$ and then drops out before reaching a destination in $\mathcal{D}_{j+1}$, without being trapped, when the current state is $(s_i^{j'}, k)$. We have $P_{R,j}(s_i^{j'}, k) =$

$$
\begin{cases}
0, & \text{for } s_i \in \mathcal{T}, k = 1 \\
q(s_i^{j'}) + \sum\limits_{s_\ell \in \mathcal{N}(s_i)} \mathbf{p}_A(s_i^{j'}, s_\ell^{j'+1})\Big(\mathbf{p}_D(s_\ell)P_{R,j}(s_\ell^{j'+1}, 1) + (1 - \mathbf{p}_D(s_\ell))P_{R,j}(s_\ell^{j'+1}, 0)\Big), \\
 & \text{for } s_i \in \mathcal{D}_j, \ j' = j, k = 0 \\
q(s_i^{j'}) + \sum_{s_\ell \in \mathcal{N}(s_i)} \mathbf{p}_A(s_i^{j'}, s_\ell^{j'+1})P_{R,j}(s_\ell^{j'+1}, 1), & \text{for } s_i \in \mathcal{D}_j, \ j' = j, k = 1 \\
0, & \text{for } s_i \in \mathcal{D}_{j'}, j' = j + 1 \\
0, & \text{for } j' > j + 1 \\
\sum_{s_\ell \in \mathcal{N}(s_i)} \mathbf{p}_A(s_i^{j'}, s_\ell^{j'})\Big(\mathbf{p}_D(s_\ell)P_{R,j}(s_\ell^{j'}, 1) + (1 - \mathbf{p}_D(s_\ell))P_{R,j}(s_\ell^{j'}, 0)\Big), \\
 & \text{for } j' \leq j, k = 0 \\
\sum_{s_\ell \in \mathcal{N}(s_i)} \mathbf{p}_A(s_i^{j'}, s_\ell^{j'})P_{R,j}(s_\ell^{j'}, 1), & \text{for } j' \leq j, k = 1 \\
q(s_i^{j'}) + \sum\limits_{s_\ell \in \mathcal{N}(s_i)} \mathbf{p}_A(s_i^{j'}, s_\ell^{j'})\Big(\mathbf{p}_D(s_\ell)P_{R,j}(s_\ell^{j'}, 1) + (1 - \mathbf{p}_D(s_\ell))P_{R,j}(s_\ell^{j'}, 0)\Big), \\
 & \text{for } j' = j + 1, k = 0 \\
q(s_i^{j'}) + \sum_{s_\ell \in \mathcal{N}(s_i)} \mathbf{p}_A(s_i^{j'}, s_\ell^{j'})P_{R,j}(s_\ell^{j'}, 1), & \text{for } j' = j + 1, k = 1
\end{cases}
$$

Let $P_T(s_i^{j'}, k)$ denotes the probability that an information flow is tagged and trapped when the current state is $(s_i^{j'}, k)$. Then $P_T(s_i^{j'}, k)$ satisfies

$$
P_T(s_i^{j'}, k) = \begin{cases}
1, & s_i \in \mathcal{T}, k = 1 \\
0, & j' = M, s_i \in \mathcal{D}_M \\
\sum_{s_\ell \in \mathcal{N}(s_i)} \mathbf{p}_A(s_i^{j'}, s_\ell^{j'})\Big(\mathbf{p}_D(s_\ell)P_{T,j}(s_\ell^{j'}, 1) + (1 - \mathbf{p}_D(s_\ell))P_{T,j}(s_\ell^{j'}, 0)\Big), & k = 0 \\
\sum_{s_\ell \in \mathcal{N}(s_i)} \mathbf{p}_A(s_i^{j'}, s_\ell^{j'})P_{T,j}(s_\ell^{j'}, 1), & k = 1
\end{cases}
$$

Using the definitions of $P_{R,j}$ and P_T at a state in $\bar{S}$, the payoffs of the defender and the adversary at a state $(s_i^{j'}, k)$ is given by

$$\mathcal{U}^D(s_i^{j'}, k) = \sum_{s_a \in S} p_{F,a}(s_i^{j'}, k) C^D(s_a) + \sum_{j=1}^{M} p_{R,j}(s_i^{j'}, k) \sum_{v=1}^{j} \beta_v^D + P_T(s_i^{j'}, k)\alpha^D,$$

(3)

$$\mathcal{U}^A(s_i^{j'}, k) = \sum_{j=1}^{M} p_{R,j}(s_i^{j'}, k) \sum_{v=1}^{j} \beta_v^A + P_T(s_i^{j'}, k)\alpha^A.$$

(4)

Here, $p_{F,a}(s_i^{j'}, k)$ denotes the probability that process $s_a \in S$ is tagged in a flow whose current state is $(s_i^{j'}, k)$. This gives a system of $2NM + 1$ linear equations for the utility vectors $\mathcal{U}^D$ and $\mathcal{U}^A$, where $\mathcal{U}^A(b)$, $\mathcal{U}^D(b)$ denote the utilities at the bth state in $\bar{S}$. Now we give the following result, which relates U^D, U^A with $\mathcal{U}^D, \mathcal{U}^A$.

Lemma 1. *Consider the defender and adversary strategies* $\mathbf{p}_D$ *and* $\mathbf{p}_A$, *respectively. Then, the following hold: (i)* $U^A(\mathbf{p}_D, \mathbf{p}_A) = \mathcal{U}^A(s_0^1, 0)$, *and (ii)* $U^D(\mathbf{p}_D, \mathbf{p}_A) = \mathcal{U}^D(s_0^1, 0)$.

Proof. **(i)**: By definition, $\mathcal{U}^A(s_0^1, 0) = \sum_{j=1}^{M} P_{R,j}(s_0^1, 0) \sum_{v=1}^{j} \beta_v^A + P_T(s_0^1, 0)\alpha^A$. Note that,

$$\sum_{j=1}^{M} P_{R,j}(s_0^1, 0) \sum_{v=1}^{j} \beta_v^A = \beta_1^A \sum_{j=1}^{M} P_{R,j}(s_0^1, 0) + \beta_2^A \sum_{j=2}^{M} P_{R,j}(s_0^1, 0) + \ldots + \beta_M^A P_{R,M}(s_0^1, 0),$$

(5)

Here, $\sum_{j=1}^{M} p_{R,j}(s_0^1, 0)$ is the total probability that a flow originating at $(s_0^1, 0)$ reach some destination in $\mathcal{D}_1$. Similarly, $\sum_{j=2}^{M} p_{R,j}(s_0^1, 0)$ is the total probability that a flow originating at $(s_0^1, 0)$ reach some destination in $\mathcal{D}_2$. Thus

$$\sum_{j=1}^{M} P_{R,j}(s_0^1, 0) = p_R(1), \sum_{j=2}^{M} P_{R,j}(s_0^1, 0) = p_R(2), \ldots, P_{R,M}(s_0^1, 0) = p_R(M). \quad (6)$$

From Eqs. (5) and (6), we get

$$\sum_{j=1}^{M} P_{R,j}(s_0^1, 0) \sum_{v=1}^{j} \beta_v^A = \sum_{j=1}^{M} p_R(j)\beta_j^A.$$

(7)

Since $P_T(s_0^1, 0) = \sum_{j=1}^{M} p_T(j)$,

$$P_T(s_0^1, 0)\alpha^A = \sum_{j=1}^{M} p_T(j)\alpha^A.$$

(8)

From Eqs. (7) and (8), we get $\mathcal{U}^A(s_0^1, 0) = \sum_{j=1}^M \left(p_R(j)\beta_j^A + p_T(j)\alpha^A \right) = U^A(\mathbf{p}_D, \mathbf{p}_A)$.

(ii): Notice that $p_{F,i}(s_0^1, 0)$ is the probability that the process s_i is tagged in a flow originating at $(s_0^1, 0)$. Thus $p_{F,i}(s_0^1, 0) = \mathbf{p}_D(s_i)$. This along with Eqs. (7) and (8) implies that $\mathcal{U}^D(s_0^1, 0) = \sum_{s_i \in \mathcal{S}} \mathbf{p}_D(s_i)\mathcal{C}^D(s_i) + \sum_{j=1}^M \left(p_R(j)\beta_j^D + p_T(j)\alpha^D \right) = U^D(\mathbf{p}_D, \mathbf{p}_A)$. This completes the proof of (i) and (ii). $\square$

3   Equilibria in Security Games

This section presents an overview of the notions of equilibrium considered in this work. We first describe the concept of a player's best response to a given strategy of an opponent.

Definition 3.1. *Let* $\mathbf{p}_A : \{\mathcal{S} \times \{1, \dots, M\}\} \cup \{s_0^1\} \to [0,1]^E$ *denote an adversary strategy (transition probabilities). The set of best responses of the defender is given by*

$$BR(\mathbf{p}_A) = \arg\max \{U^D(\mathbf{p}_D, \mathbf{p}_A) : \mathbf{p}_D \in [0,1]^{\mathcal{S}} \}.$$

Similarly, the best responses of the adversary are given by

$$BR(\mathbf{p}_D) = \arg\max \{U^A(\mathbf{p}_D, \mathbf{p}_A) : \mathbf{p}_A \in [0,1]^E \}.$$

Intuitively, the best responses of the defender are the set of tagging strategies that maximize the defender's utility for a given adversary strategy, while the best responses of the adversary are the sets of transition probabilities that maximize the adversary's utility for a given defense (tagging) strategy. The Nash equilibrium is defined as follows.

Definition 3.2. *A pair of strategies* $(\mathbf{p}_D, \mathbf{p}_A)$ *is a* Nash equilibrium *if*

$$\mathbf{p}_D \in BR(\mathbf{p}_A), \quad \mathbf{p}_A \in BR(\mathbf{p}_D).$$

The Nash equilibrium occurs when neither player can improve its utility by unilaterally changing its strategy. As the game considered in this paper is a finite game with mixed strategy, there exists a Nash equilibrium [12]. While the Nash equilibrium captures the behavior of rational, uncooperative players, it is NP-hard to compute in general, especially for nonzero-sum games of the type considered in this paper. A weaker solution concept is the *correlated equilibrium* defined in [4].

Definition 3.3. *Let* P *denote a joint probability distribution over the set of defender and adversary actions. The distribution* P *is a* correlated equilibrium *if for all strategies* $\mathbf{p}'_A$ *and* $\mathbf{p}'_D$,

$$\mathbf{E}(U^D(\mathbf{p}_D, \mathbf{p}_A)) \geq \mathbf{E}(U^D(\mathbf{p}'_D, \mathbf{p}_A))$$
$$\mathbf{E}(U^A(\mathbf{p}_D, \mathbf{p}_A)) \geq \mathbf{E}(U^A(\mathbf{p}_D, \mathbf{p}'_A))$$

Here, $\mathbf{E}(\cdot)$ denotes the expectation. We next consider a simpler version of the correlated equilibrium that models the local policies at each process.

Definition 3.4. *Let P denote a joint probability distribution over the set of defender and adversary actions. The distribution P is a* local correlated equilibrium *if for all states $s_i \in \mathscr{S}$, $j \in \{1, \ldots, M\}$, and strategies $p'_D(s_i)$ and $p'_A(s_i^j, \cdot)$, we have*

$$\mathbf{E}(U^D(\mathbf{p}_D, \mathbf{p}_A)) \geq \mathbf{E}(U^D(\mathbf{p}'_D, \mathbf{p}_A))$$
$$\mathbf{E}(U^A(\mathbf{p}_D, \mathbf{p}_A)) \geq \mathbf{E}(U^A(\mathbf{p}_D, \mathbf{p}'_A))$$

where $\mathbf{p}'_D$ denotes a strategy with $\mathbf{p}'_D(s_i) = p'_D(s_i)$ and $\mathbf{p}'_D(s_{i'}) = \mathbf{p}_D(s_{i'})$ for $i \neq i'$, and $\mathbf{p}'_A$ denotes a strategy with $\mathbf{p}'_A(s_i^j, \cdot) = p'_A(s_i^j, \cdot)$ and $\mathbf{p}'_A(s_{i'}^{j'}, \cdot) = \mathbf{p}_A(s_{i'}^{j'}, \cdot)$ for $(i, j) \neq (i', j')$.

4 Analysis of Multi-Stage Security Model

In this section, we present an efficient algorithm to compute a locally optimal correlated equilibrium for the game. We also find the best responses of both the players.

4.1 Algorithm and Results

We now present an algorithm for computing a local correlated equilibrium of the DIFT game. Our approach is to map the two-player game into a game with $(M+1)N+1$ players. The adversary's strategy is represented by MN players, each of which represents the adversary's actions at a single process and stage. The defender's strategy is represented by N players, each of which represents the defender's strategy (tag or not tag) at a single process. The last player corresponds to the pseudo-process introduced, whose strategy decides the entry point of the attacker into the network.

Formally, we consider a set of players $\{\mathscr{P}^{A_{ij}} : i = 1, \ldots, N, j = 1, \ldots, M\} \cup \{\mathscr{P}^{D_i} : i = 1, \ldots, N\} \cup \{\mathscr{P}^{s_0}\}$. Each of the players in $\mathscr{P}^{A_{ij}}$ has action space $\mathscr{A}^{A_{ij}} = \mathscr{N}(s_i)$, each player in $\mathscr{P}^{D_i}$ has action space $\{0, 1\}$, representing whether or not to tag, and the player $\mathscr{P}^{s_0}$ has action space λ. We let $\mathbf{a}^D$ denote the set of actions chosen by the players $\{\mathscr{P}^{D_i} : i = 1, \ldots, N\}$ and $\mathbf{a}^A$ denote the set of actions chosen by the players $\{\mathscr{P}^{A_{ij}} : i = 1, \ldots, N, j = 1, \ldots, M\} \cup \{\mathscr{P}^{s_0}\}$.

The payoffs of the players from a particular action set are given by

$$U^{A_{ij}}(\mathbf{a}_A, \mathbf{a}_D) = U^A(\mathbf{a}_A, \mathbf{a}_D),$$
$$U^{D_i}(\mathbf{a}_A, \mathbf{a}_D) = U^D(\mathbf{a}_A, \mathbf{a}_D),$$

where U^A and U^D are as defined in Sect. 2. Hence, all adversarial players receive the same utility U^A, while all defender players receive the utility U^D. Equivalently, the adversarial players $U^{A_{ij}}$ cooperate in order to maximize the adversary's utility, while the defender players U^{D_i} attempt to maximize the defender utility.

Under the solution algorithm, the game is played repeatedly, with each player choosing its action from a probability distribution (mixed strategy) over the set of possible actions. After observing their utilities, the players update their strategies according to a no-regret learning algorithm [4]. A description is given as Algorithm 4.1.

Algorithm 4.1. Algorithm for computing correlated equilibrium.

1: **procedure** CORRELATED_COMPUTATION
2:    $t \leftarrow 0$
3:    **for** $n = 1, \ldots, (M+1)N + 1$ **do**
4:        $\mathbf{p}_{t,n} \leftarrow$ uniform distribution over set of actions
5:    **end for**
6:    **while** $\|\mathbf{p}_t - \mathbf{p}_{t-1}\| > \epsilon$ **do**
7:        **for** $n = 1, \ldots, (M+1)N + 1$ **do**
8:            $a_{t,n} \leftarrow$ action chosen from distribution $\mathbf{p}_{t,n}$
9:        **end for**
10:    **for** $n = 1, \ldots, (M+1)N + 1$ **do**
11:        $a_{t,-n} \leftarrow (a_{t,l} : l \neq n)$
12:        **for all** (r, s) actions of player n **do**
13:            $\mathbf{p}_{t,n}^{r \to s} \leftarrow \mathbf{p}_{t,n}$
14:            $\mathbf{p}_{t,n}^{r \to s}(r) \leftarrow 0$
15:            $\mathbf{p}_{t,n}^{r \to s}(s) \leftarrow \mathbf{p}_{t,n}(r) + \mathbf{p}_{t,n}(s)$
16:            $\Delta_{(r,s),t,n} \leftarrow \dfrac{\exp\left(\eta \sum_{u=1}^{t-1} \mathbf{E}(U^n(\mathbf{p}_{u,n}^{r \to s}, a_{u,-n}))\right)}{\sum_{(x,y):x \neq y} \exp\left(\eta \sum_{u=1}^{t-1} U^n(\mathbf{p}_{u,n}^{x \to y}, a_{u,-n})\right)}$
17:            $\mathbf{p}_{t,n} \leftarrow$ fixed point of equation $\mathbf{p}_{t,n} = \sum_{(i,j):i \neq j} \mathbf{p}_{t,n}^{r \to s} \Delta_{(r,s),t,n}$
18:        **end for**
19:    **end for**
20:    $t \leftarrow t + 1$
21: **end while**
22: **end procedure**

The algorithm initializes the strategies at each process to be uniformly random. At each iteration t, an action is chosen for each player according to the probability distribution $\mathbf{p}_{t,n}$ of player n. After observing the actions from other players, the probability distribution $\mathbf{p}_{t,n}$ is updated as follows. For each pair of actions r and s, the new probability distribution $\mathbf{p}_{t,n}^{r \to s}$ is generated, in which all of the probability mass allocated to action r is instead allocated to action s. The expected utility arising from $\mathbf{p}_{t,n}^{r \to s}$ can be interpreted as the expected benefit from playing action s instead of r at previous iterations of the algorithm.

For each pair (r, s), a weight $\Delta_{(r,s),t,n}$ is computed that consists of the relative benefit of each distribution $\mathbf{p}_{t,n}^{r \to s}$, i.e., pairs (r, s) such that allocating probability mass from r to s produces a larger expected utility will receive higher weight. A new distribution $\mathbf{p}_{t,n}$ is then computed based on the weights $\Delta_{(r,s),t,n}$, so that actions that produced a higher utility for the player will be chosen with increased probability. The algorithm continues until the distributions converge. The convergence of the algorithm is described by the following proposition.

Proposition 4.1. *Algorithm 4.1 converges to a local correlated equilibrium of the game introduced in Sect. 2.*

Proof. By [4], Algorithm 4.1 converges to a correlated equilibrium of the $(MN + N + 1)$-player game. Equivalently, by Definition 3.3, for any s_i and $p'_{D_i} \in [0,1]$, the joint distribution P returned by the algorithm satisfies

$$\mathbf{E}(U^{D_i}(p_{D_i}, \mathbf{p}_{D_{-i}}, \mathbf{p}_A)) \geq \mathbf{E}(U^{D_i}(p'_{D_i}, \mathbf{p}_{D_{-i}}, \mathbf{p}_A)). \tag{9}$$

Since the utility U^{D_i} is equal to U^D for all $i \in \{1, \ldots, N\}$, Eq. (9) is equivalent to

$$\mathbf{E}(U^D(p_{D_i}, \mathbf{p}_{D_{-i}}, \mathbf{p}_A)) \geq \mathbf{E}(U^D(p'_{D_i}, \mathbf{p}_{D_{-i}}, \mathbf{p}_A)). \tag{10}$$

Similarly, for any $s_i^j \in \{\mathcal{S} \times \{1, \ldots, M\}\} \cup \{s_0^1\}$ and any $p'_{A_{ij}}$, we have

$$\mathbf{E}(U^{A_{ij}}(\mathbf{p}_D, \mathbf{p}_{A_{-ij}}, p_{A_{ij}})) \geq \mathbf{E}(U^{A_{ij}}(\mathbf{p}_D, \mathbf{p}_{A_{-ij}}, p'_{A_{ij}})) \tag{11}$$

which is equivalent to

$$\mathbf{E}(U^A(\mathbf{p}_D, \mathbf{p}_{A_{-ij}}, p_{A_{ij}})) \geq \mathbf{E}(U^A(\mathbf{p}_D, \mathbf{p}_{A_{-ij}}, p'_{A_{ij}})) \tag{12}$$

Equations (10) and (12) imply that the output of Algorithm 4.1 satisfies the conditions of Definition 3.4 and hence is a local correlated equilibrium.   □

We now discuss the complexity of the algorithm.

Proposition 1. *With probability $(1 - \delta)$, Algorithm 4.1 returns an ϵ-correlated equilibrium using $O\left(\frac{N^2(M+1)+N}{\epsilon^2} \ln\left(\frac{N^2(M+1)+N}{\delta}\right)\right)$ evaluations of the utility function.*

Proof. By [4, Chapter 7, Sect. 7.4], learning-based algorithms return an ϵ-correlated equilibrium with probability $(1 - \delta)$ within $\max_n \frac{16}{\epsilon^2} \ln \frac{N_n K}{\delta}$ iterations, where N_n is the number of actions for player n and K is the number of players, incurring a total of $\frac{16 N_n K}{\epsilon^2} \ln \frac{N_n K}{\delta}$ evaluations of the utility function. In this case, $N_n \leq N$ and $K = N(M + 1) + 1$, resulting in the desired complexity bounds. □

Proposition 1 shows that convergence of the algorithm is sublinear in the number of processes, with a total complexity that is quadratic in the number of processes and linear in the number of stages.

4.2   Best Response for the Defender

We now present an approach for approximating the best response of the defender. In this approach, the set of possible responses at s_i is discretized. Define

$$V = \{s_i^z : s_i \in \mathcal{S}, z = 1, \ldots, Z\}$$

for some integer $Z > 0$. For any $V' \subseteq V$, define $p_D(s_i; V') = \frac{1}{Z}|\{s_i^z : z = 1, \ldots, Z\} \cap V'|$, and define $p_D(V')$ to be the resulting vector of tagging probabilities. For a given adversary strategy, say p_A, let $f(V') = U^D(p_D(V'), p_A)$.

Proposition 2. *The function $f(V')$ is submodular as a function of V', that is, for any V', V'' with $V' \subseteq V''$ and any $s_i^z \notin V''$,*

$$f(V' \cup \{s_i^z\}) - f(V') \geq f(V'' \cup \{s_i^z\}) - f(V'').$$

Proof. Consider U^D as defined in Eq. (1). In this case, the first term is equal to

$$\sum_{s_i \in \mathcal{S}} \frac{\mathcal{C}^D(s_i)}{Z} |\{s_i^z : z = 1, \ldots, Z\} \cap V'|,$$

which is modular as a function of V'. The second term can be written as

$$\sum_{\omega} \pi(\omega) \sum_{j=1}^{M} (p_T(j; \omega)\alpha^D + p_R(j; \omega)\beta_j^D),$$

where $p_T(j; \omega)$ (resp. $p_R(j; \omega)$) denotes the probability that the flow is tagged and trapped (resp. reaches destination j) when the sample path is ω and the defender strategy is $p_D(V')$ (the V' is omitted from the notation for simplicity). Since the last destination that is reached before dropping out is determined by the choice of path (denote this destination $j(\omega)$), we have

$$\sum_{j=1}^{M} (p_T(j; \omega)\alpha^D + p_R(j; \omega)\beta_j^D) = g(\omega; V')\alpha^D + (1 - g(\omega; V'))\beta_{j(\omega)}^D$$

$$= g(\omega; V')(\alpha^D - \beta_{j(\omega)}^D) + \beta_{j(\omega)}^D.$$

Since $\alpha^D - \beta_{j(\omega)}^D \geq 0$ and $\beta_{j(\omega)}^D$ is independent of $p_D(V')$, it suffices to show that $g(\omega; V')$ is submodular as a function of V'. Let $V' \subseteq V''$ and $s_i^z \notin V''$. We can write

$$g(\omega; V'') = 1 - \left[\prod_{\substack{s_{i_k} \in \omega: \\ i_k = i}} (1 - p_D(s_{i_k})) \right] \left[\prod_{\substack{s_{i_k} \in \omega: \\ i_k \neq i}} (1 - p_D(s_{i_k})) \right]$$

$$= 1 - \gamma(V'')(1 - p_D(s_i))^{r(s_i; \omega)},$$

where $p_D(s_{i_k})$ denotes the tagging probability of node s_{i_k} under the policy $p_D(V')$ and

$$\gamma(V'') = \prod_{\substack{s_{i_k} \in \omega: \\ i_k \neq i}} (1 - p_D(s_{i_k})), \quad r(s_i; \omega) = |\{s_{i_k} \in \omega : i_k = i\}|.$$

Hence, $g(\omega; V'' \cup \{s_i^z\}) - g(\omega; V'')$

$$= 1 - \gamma(V'')(1 - (p_D(s_i; V'') + \frac{1}{Z}))^{r(s_i; \omega)} - (1 - \gamma(V'')(1 - p_D(s_i; V'')))^{r(s_i; \omega)}$$

$$= \gamma(V'') \left[(1 - p_D(s_i; V''))^{r(s_i; \omega)} - (1 - p_D(s_i; V'') - \frac{1}{Z})^{r(s_i; \omega)} \right]$$

When $V' \subseteq V''$, $p_D(s_i; V') \leq p_D(s_i; V'')$, and hence

$$(1-p_D(s_i; V''))^r - (1-p_D(s_i; V''), \frac{1}{Z})^r \leq (1-p_D(s_i; V'))^r - (1-p_D(s_i; V') - \frac{1}{Z})^r.$$

Furthermore, $V' \subseteq V''$ implies $\gamma(V' \geq \gamma(V'')$. Hence

$$g(\omega; V' \cup \{s_i^z\}) - g(\omega; V') \geq g(\omega; V'' \cup \{s_i^z\}) - g(\omega; V''),$$

completing the proof of submodularity.   □

Submodularity of $f(V')$ implies the following.

Proposition 4.2. *There exists an algorithm that is guaranteed to select a set V^* satisfying $f(V^*) \geq \frac{1}{2} \max \{f(V') : V' \subseteq V\}$ within $O(NZ)$ evaluations of U^D.*

Proof. The proof follows from submodularity of V' and [3].   □

4.3   Best Response for the Adversary

The best response of the adversary to a given defender strategy is described here. Firstly, we present the following preliminary lemma.

Lemma 2. *Consider a defense policy $\mathbf{p}_D$. For each destination $d_b^j \in \mathcal{D}_j$, let $\Omega_{d_b^j}$ denote the set of paths that originate at s_0^1 and terminate at d_b^j. For any path ω, let $p(\omega)$ denote the probability that a flow reaches the destination without being tagged and trapped. Finally, for every d_b^j, choose a path $\omega_{d_b^j}^* \in \arg\max \{p(\omega) : \omega \in \Omega_{d_b^j}\}$. Let*

$$\omega^* \in \arg\max \{p(\omega_{d_b^j}) : d_b^j \in \mathcal{D}_j, j = 1, \ldots, M\}.$$

Finally, define the policy $\mathbf{p}_A^*$ by $\mathbf{p}_A^*(s_i^j, s_{i'}^{j'}) = \begin{cases} 1, & (s_i^j, s_{i'}^{j'}) \in \omega^* \\ 0, & else \end{cases}$ Then, $\omega^* \in BR(\mathbf{p}_D)$.

Proof. Let $\mathbf{p}_A$ be any adversary policy, and let Ω denote the set of paths that are chosen by the policy with nonzero probability. The utility of the adversary can be written as

$$U^A = \sum_{\omega \in \Omega} \pi(\omega)(p(\omega)\beta_{j(\omega)}^A + (1 - p(\omega))\alpha^A)$$

$$= \sum_{j=1}^{M} \sum_{d_b^j \in \mathcal{D}_j} \sum_{\omega \in \Omega_{d_b^j}} \pi(\omega)(p(\omega)\beta_j^A + (1 - p(\omega))\alpha^A),$$

where $j(\omega)$ is equal to the stage where the path terminates and $\pi(\omega)$ is the probability that the path is chosen under this policy. The utility U^A is then bounded above by the path that maximizes $p(\omega)(\beta_j^A - \alpha^A)$, which is exactly the path ω^*.   □

By Lemma 2, the following approach suffices to select a best response to a given defense policy. For each destination in $\bigcup_{j=1}^{M} \mathcal{D}_j$, choose a path to that destination that maximizes $p(\omega)$ while traversing destinations at all intermediate stages. Then, among those paths, select the one that maximizes $p(\omega)(\beta_j^A - \alpha^A)$.

An approach for computing the maximal path is shown as Algorithm 4.2. Lines 5–16 describe a Dijkstra-like procedure for computing the sequence of processes that maximize the probability of reaching $d_b^j \in \mathcal{D}_j$ without being tagged or trapped. The following proposition describes the optimality guarantees of Algorithm 4.2.

Algorithm 4.2. Algorithm for computing adversary's best response.

1: **procedure** ADVERSARY_BR
2:     **for** $j = 1, \ldots, M$ **do**
3:         **for** $d_b^j \in \mathcal{D}_j$ **do**
4:             $\mathcal{Q} \leftarrow \{d_b^j\}$
5:             $p_A(d_b^j, d_b^j) \leftarrow 1$
6:             **while** $\mathcal{Q} \neq \{\mathcal{S} \times \{1, \ldots, M\}\} \cup \{s_0^1\}$ **do**
7:                 $Z \leftarrow$ neighbors of $\mathcal{Q}$
8:                 **for** $s_i^{j'} \in Z$ **do**
9:                     $z(s_i^{j'}) \leftarrow \max\{(1 - p_D(s_i^{j'}))p_A(s_{i'}^{j''}, d_b^j) : s_{i'} \in \mathcal{N}(s_i) \cap \mathcal{Q}\}$
10:                    $r(s_i^{j'}) \leftarrow \arg\max\{(1 - p_D(s_i^{j'}))p_A(s_{i'}^{j''}, d_b^j) : s_{i'} \in \mathcal{N}(s_i) \cap \mathcal{Q}\}$
11:                **end for**
12:                $s^* \leftarrow \arg\max\{z(s_i^{j'}) : s_i^{j'} \in Z\}$
13:                $\mathcal{Q} \leftarrow \mathcal{Q} \cup \{s^*\},\ p_A(s^*, d_b^j) \leftarrow z(s^*),\ \text{next}(s^*, d_b^j) \leftarrow r(s^*)$
14:            **end while**
15:            $u(d_b^j) \leftarrow p_A(s_0, d_b^j)\beta_j^A$
16:        **end for**
17:    **end for**
18:    $d^* \leftarrow \arg\max\{u(d_b^j) : b \in \mathcal{D}_j, j = 1, \ldots, M\}$
19:    $\omega^* \leftarrow \{s_0\},\ z \leftarrow s_0$
20:    **while** $z \neq d^*$ **do**
21:        $z \leftarrow \text{next}(z, d_b^j)$
22:        $\omega^* \leftarrow \omega^* \cup \{z\}$
23:    **end while**
24:    **return** ω^*
25: **end procedure**

Proposition 4.3. *The path ω^* returned by Algorithm 4.2 is a best response to the defender strategy $\mathbf{p}_D$.*

Proof. By Lemma 2, it suffices to show that the procedure of Lines 5–16 results in a path with maximum probability of reaching d_b^j without tagging and trapping. For any path $\omega \in \Omega_{d_b^j}$, the probability that the flow reaches d_b^j without being tagged or trapped is equal to $\prod_{s_i \in \omega}(1 - \mathbf{p}_D(s_i))$. Maximizing this probability is equivalent to minimizing $-\sum_{s_i \in \omega} \log(1 - \mathbf{p}_D(s_i))$, making the problem equivalent to finding the shortest path from s_0 to d_b^j in a graph where the edge weights are equal to $-\log(1 - \mathbf{p}_D(s_i))$ for each edge incoming to $s_i^{j'}$, $j' \in \{1, \ldots, M\}$. Since Lines 5–16 are equivalent to Dijkstra's algorithm on this modified graph, the path that is computed is a path from s_0 to d_b^j that minimizes the probability of tagging. $\qquad\square$

5   Numerical Analysis

In this section, we provide the experimental validation of our model and results using real-world attack data set obtained using Refinable Attack INvestigation system (RAIN) [10] for a ScreenGrab attack. We implement our model and run Algorithm 4.1 on the provenance graph generated using the system log data obtained using the RAIN system for a ScreenGrab attack. Using the results obtained we verify the correctness of the proposed algorithm and also perform sensitivity analysis by varying the trap locations in the system, and the traffic and tagging cost of the processes. This analysis enable us to infer the optimal strategies of the players and the sensitivity of the model with respect to cost parameters for a given attack data set (provenance graph with specified destinations and trap locations). In order to apply the proposed analysis on any real-time data attack data set, one need to construct the provenance graph for the system under consideration and run Algorithm 4.1 on this graph to obtain the defense policy, i.e., tagging locations, at a local equilibrium of the multi-stage game.

We consider provenance graph generated using RAIN for a system undergoing ScreenGrab attack in which the implant-core downloads a *ScreenGrab* program which occasionally captures screenshots of the victim's desktop and sends selected images to the attacker's server [10]. The provenance graph consists of 12 processes as shown in Fig. 2a. On this data, we analyze a two-stage attack. Thus $N = 12$ and $M = 2$. The vulnerable processes in the system are $\lambda = \{s_1, s_6, s_{12}\}$ and the destinations in stage 1 and stage 2 are $\mathcal{D}_1 = s_5$ and $\mathcal{D}_2 = s_{12}$, respectively. Node 12 represents the ScreenGrab process whose control is desired by the adversary. The cost parameters of the players are set as $\beta_1^A = \beta_2^A = 300$, $\alpha^A = \alpha^D = -100$, $\beta_1^D = \beta_2^D = 300$, and $c = -100$. For this system setting, we analyze the strategies of the players $\mathcal{P}^A$ and $\mathcal{P}^D$ corresponding to the correlated equilibrium obtained using Algorithm 4.1. We validate our results in Sect. 4 using three test cases. Test cases 1 and 2 are setup in such a manner that the optimal policy of the adversary can be directly obtained. We compare the adversary's policy obtained using our approach with the optimal policy to verify the correctness. In case 1, the locations of the trap nodes in the system are assigned such that there exists an action set for the adversary which assures his/her win irrespective of the defense's strategy. In case 2, the trap nodes in the system are set such that the adversary is guaranteed to arrive at the destination of stage 1 irrespective of the defense's action, and the defense is guaranteed to detect the adversary in stage 2 if at least one of the process in the system is tagged. For cases 1 and 2, the traffic at every node is kept same ($B(s_i) = 0.0833$, for $i = 1, \ldots, 12$) and hence the tagging cost of a process depends only on its tagging probability. In case 3, we analyze the impact of the traffic at the processes and c on the defender's policy and the performance of the algorithm.

Case (i): The trap setting is $\mathcal{T} = \{s_2, s_6\}$. Here, there exists a path from the pseudo-process s_0 to the final destination s_{12} of stage 2 passing through s_5, the destination of stage 1, without any trap nodes. The optimal strategy of the adversary is to perform transitions to traverse this path irrespective of the strategy of the defender and win the game. We ran Algorithm 4.1 on this setup of the system, and the results are shown in Fig. 2a. The adversary takes the path $s_0 \rightarrow s_1 \rightarrow s_5 \rightarrow s_{10} \rightarrow s_{11} \rightarrow s_{12}$ with probability one and wins the game as expected (shown in red in Fig. 2a). The tagging probabilities of the processes are shown in red (these values are rounded to two decimal places). These observations demonstrate that the adversary's policy for this case is governed by the system topology due to the presence of a path without traps.

Case 2: Here, $\mathcal{T} = \{s_2, s_6, s_{11}\}$ and there exists a path from s_0 to s_5, the destination of stage 1, that has no trap nodes in it. However, all possible paths from s_5 to s_{12} have traps. As the adversary is guaranteed to reach the destination in stage 1 without getting detected by the defense, its optimal policy in stage 1 is to take the path without traps. Later in stage 2, it is optimal for the adversary to drop out of the game as the defense is guaranteed to detect it if at all any one of the process in the system is tagged. The results obtained by our algorithm is in agreement with the optimal policy. According to the output of the algorithm, there are three possible paths for the adversary: (a) with 0.4857 probability $s_0 \rightarrow s_1 \rightarrow s_5 \rightarrow s_7$ and drops out of the game, (b) with 0.0286 probability $s_0 \rightarrow s_1 \rightarrow s_5 \rightarrow s_{10}$ and drops out of the game, and (c) with 0.4857 probability $s_0 \rightarrow s_1 \rightarrow s_5$ and drops out of the game. Notice that in all three cases the adversary reaches stage 1 and then drops out in stage 2. Further, the policy of the defense does not depend on stage and this is reflected in the tagging probabilities obtained (rounded to two decimal places and shown in red in Fig. 2b).

Case 3: For the trap setting $\mathcal{T} = \{s_2, s_6, s_{11}\}$, we study two cases, case 3(a) and case 3(b), by varying the traffic B and the fixed tagging cost c. The results of these scenarios are then compared with that of case 2 (case 2 has the same trap setting and equal traffic at all processes, i.e., $B(s_i) = 0.0833$ for $i = \{1, \ldots, 12\}$). The chosen average traffic at the processes and the obtained tagging probabilities corresponding to the output of Algorithm 4.1 for cases 3(a) and 3(b) are given in Table 1.

In case 3(a), we analyze a scenario where the trap nodes s_2, s_6, and s_{11} are the busiest processes in the system and $c = -100$. Notice that, the tagging probabilities of the processes s_2, s_6, s_{11} are lesser than that in case 2, as expected. For processes with higher traffic than case 2, the tagging probabilities either remain same as in case 2 or decrease slightly. For processes with lower traffic than in case 2, the tagging probabilities either remain same as in case 2 or increase

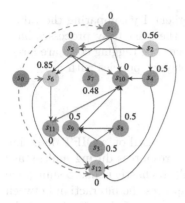
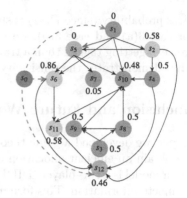

(a) With trap setting $\mathcal{T} = \{s_2, s_6\}$, adversary traverses the path $s_0 \rightarrow s_1 \rightarrow s_5 \rightarrow s_{10} \rightarrow s_{11} \rightarrow s_{12}$ (shown in red edges) with probability one and wins the game.

(b) With trap setting $\mathcal{T} = \{s_2, s_6, s_{11}\}$, adversary traverses the path $s_0 \rightarrow s_5$ (path shown in the red) with probability one, and then drops out of the game in stage 2.

Fig. 2. Provenance graph built using real world log data from RAIN system for Screen-Grab attack with specified set of destinations and trap nodes.

slightly. Although there are changes in the tagging probabilities of the processes with respect to variation in the traffic in the two cases (case 2 and case 3(a)), it is not significant due to the small value of fixed tagging cost. To understand the sensitivity with respect to c, we test the algorithm after increasing c.

Table 1. Average traffic and tagging probabilities of the processes for ScreenGrab attack

Node #	1	2	3	4	5	6	7	8	9	10	11	12
$B(s_i)$	0.03	0.25	0.1	0.03	0.03	0.25	0.03	0.03	0.03	0.03	0.25	0.03
$\mathbf{p}_D(s_i)\ c = -100$	0.05	0.56	0.5	0.5	0.03	0.86	0.15	0.5	0.5	0.53	0.5	0.48
$\mathbf{p}_D(s_i)\ c = -10000$	0	0	0.5	0.47	0.16	0	0	0.5	0.5	0.05	0	0

In case 3(b), for the same trap setting and average traffic we assign $c = -10000$ to study the sensitivity with respect to c. As the tagging costs are very high, the defense decides not to tag most of the processes. Even though the processes s_2, s_6, s_{11} are traps, their tagging probabilities are zero due to the large tagging cost. Also, notice that the tagging probabilities of processes s_3, s_8 and s_9 remain same in cases 2, 3(a) and 3(b). The tagging probability of s_4 does not alter much. Notice that these processes have lower traffic rates and there are paths from these processes to the final destination s_{12}, but there are no paths to reach them passing through s_5. As the defense is unaware of the stages of the attack, it tags processes s_3, s_8 and s_9 with 0.5 probability and s_4 with a slightly less probability (since $B(s_4)$ is slightly higher). By comparing the values of $\mathbf{p}_D$ for case 3(a) and case 3(b), we infer that the least busy processes have more chance of getting tagged than a trap node when the tagging costs are large. Case 3 thus demonstrates the sensitivity of the players' policies with c.

6   Conclusion and Future Work

In this paper, we developed a game theoretic model based on a DIFT detection system to obtain an efficient allocation of security resources during multi-stage attacks. Our model is a two-player (DIFT vs. APT) stochastic nonzero-sum game with incomplete information. This formulation captures the interaction between the DIFT system and the APT, the multi-stage nature of the attack, and the information asymmetry among the players. The game unfolds in a sequence of stages where each stage in the game corresponds to a stage in the attack characterized by a unique set of destinations. Note that, computation of Nash equilibrium is in general NP-hard, for nonzero-sum games of the type considered here. To this end, we first proposed an efficient algorithm for computing a local correlated equilibrium of this game. Then we derived algorithms to find the best responses of both the players. The best response for the APT is obtained by proving that this computation is equivalent to a shortest path on the provenance graph constructed using the system log data. For the DIFT system, we showed that the payoff function is submodular and then exploited the submodularity to obtain an approximate algorithm to compute the best response. The proposed algorithms and results are validated using the provenance graph constructed from the real-world attack data set obtained using refinable attack investigation system (RAIN). The experimental results obtained shows that the proposed model is successful in detecting multi-stage APTs. Characterizing the Nash equilibria for this game and analyzing the uniqueness of Nash equilibria are part of future work. In addition, modeling and analysis of DIFT-based detection system with unspecified trap nodes and incorporating the feature of untagging processes at a later stage in the attack will also be a future work.

References

1. Bencsáth, B., Pék, G., Buttyán, L., Felegyhazi, M.: The cousins of Stuxnet: Duqu, Flame, and Gauss. Future Internet **4**(4), 971–1003 (2012)
2. Bhatt, P., Yano, E.T., Gustavsson, P.: Towards a framework to detect multi-stage advanced persistent threats attacks. In: Proceedings of the IEEE International Symposium on Service Oriented System Engineering, Oxford, United Kingdom, pp. 390–395 (2014)
3. Buchbinder, N., Feldman, M., Seffi, J., Schwartz, R.: A tight linear time (1/2)-approximation for unconstrained submodular maximization. SIAM J. Comput. **44**(5), 1384–1402 (2015)
4. Cesa-Bianchi, N., Lugosi, G.: Prediction, Learning, and Games. Cambridge University Press, Cambridge (2006)

5. Chow, J., Pfaff, B., Garfinkel, T., Christopher, K., Rosenblum, M.: Understanding data lifetime via whole system simulation. In: Proceedings of the USENIX Security Symposium, San Diego, USA, pp. 321–336 (2004)

6. Enck, W., et al.: TaintDroid: an information-flow tracking system for realtime privacy monitoring on smartphones. ACM Trans. Comput. Syst. **32**(2), 5 (2014)

7. Falliere, N., Murchu, L.O., Chien, E.: W32. stuxnet dossier. White paper, Symantec Corporation Security Response **5**(6), 29 (2011)

8. Hassan, W.U., Lemay, M., Aguse, N., Bates, A., Moyer, T.: Towards scalable cluster auditing through grammatical inference over provenance graphs. In: Proceedings of Network and Distributed Systems Security Symposium, San Diego, USA (2018)

9. Hu, P., Li, H., Fu, H., Cansever, D., Mohapatra, P.: Dynamic defense strategy against advanced persistent threat with insiders. In: Proceedings of the IEEE Conference on Computer Communications, Hong Kong, pp. 747–755 (2015)

10. Ji, Y., et al.: RAIN: refinable attack investigation with on-demand inter-process information flow tracking. In: Proceedings of the ACM SIGSAC Conference on Computer and Communications Security, Dallas, USA, pp. 377–390 (2017)

11. Lee, P., Clark, A., Alomair, B., Bushnell, L., Poovendran, R.: A host takeover game model for competing malware. In: Proceedings of the IEEE Conference on Decision and Control, Osaka, Japan, pp. 4523–4530 (2015)

12. Nash, J.F.: Equilibrium points in n-person games. Proc. Nat. Acad. Sci. **36**(1), 48–49 (1950)

13. Sahabandu, D., Xiao, B., Clark, A., Lee, S., Lee, W., Poovendran, R.: DIFT games: dynamic information flow tracking games for advanced persistent threats (2018, Submitted)

14. Sood, A.K., Enbody, R.J.: Targeted cyberattacks: a superset of advanced persistent threats. IEEE secur. priv. **11**(1), 54–61 (2013)

15. Suh, G.E., Lee, J.W., Zhang, D., Devadas, S.: Secure program execution via dynamic information flow tracking. In: ACM Sigplan Notices., vol. 39, pp. 85–96 (2004)

16. Tivadar, M., Balázs, B., Istrate, C.: A closer look at MiniDuke (2011). http://labs.bitdefender.com/wp-content/uploads/downloads/2013/04/MiniDuke_Paper_Final.pdf. Accessed 20 May 2013

17. Van Dijk, M., Juels, A., Oprea, A., Rivest, R.L.: FlipIt: the game of "stealthy takeover". J. Cryptol. **26**(4), 655–713 (2013)

18. Virvilis, N., Gritzalis, D., Apostolopoulos, T.: Trusted computing vs. advanced persistent threats: can a defender win this game? In: Proceedings of the IEEE International Conference on Ubiquitous Intelligence and Computing and International Conference on Autonomic and Trusted Computing, Fukuoka, Japan, pp. 396–403 (2013)

19. de Vries, J., Hoogstraaten, H., van den Berg, J., Daskapan, S.: Systems for detecting advanced persistent threats: a development roadmap using intelligent data analysis. In: Proceedings of the IEEE International Conference on Cyber Security, Washington, DC, USA, pp. 54–61 (2012)

20. Yin, H., Song, D., Egele, M., Kruegel, C., Kirda, E.: Panorama: capturing system-wide information flow for malware detection and analysis. In: Proceedings of the ACM conference on Computer and communications security, Whistler, Canada, pp. 116–127 (2007)

Less is More: Culling the Training Set to Improve Robustness of Deep Neural Networks

Yongshuai Liu[✉], Jiyu Chen[✉], and Hao Chen[✉]

University of California, Davis, USA
{yshliu,jiych,chen}@ucdavis.edu

Abstract. Deep neural networks are vulnerable to adversarial examples. Prior defenses attempted to make deep networks more robust by either changing the network architecture or augmenting the training set with adversarial examples, but both have inherent limitations. Motivated by recent research that shows outliers in the training set have a high negative influence on the trained model, we studied the relationship between model robustness and the quality of the training set. We first show that outliers give the model better generalization ability but weaker robustness. Next, we propose an adversarial example detection framework, in which we design two methods for removing outliers from training set to obtain the sanitized model and then detect adversarial example by calculating the difference of outputs between the original and the sanitized model. We evaluated the framework on both MNIST and SVHN. Based on the difference measured by Kullback-Leibler divergence, we could detect adversarial examples with accuracy between 94.67% to 99.89%.

1 Introduction

Deep neural networks have demonstrated impressive performance on many hard perception problems [9,12]. However, they are vulnerable to adversarial examples [7,16,18], which are maliciously crafted to be perceptually close to normal examples but which cause misclassification. Prior defenses against adversarial examples fall into the following categories: 1. Incorporating adversarial examples in the training set, a.k.a. adversarial training [7,18] 2. Modifying the network architecture or training method, e.g., defense distillation [17] 3. Modifying the test examples, e.g., MagNet [14] The first defense requires knowledge about the process for generating adversarial examples, while the last two defenses require high expertise and are often not robust [2].

We propose a new direction to strengthen deep neural networks against adversarial examples. Recent research showed that outliers in the training set are highly influential on the trained model. For example, outliers may be ambiguous

---

Y. Liu and J. Chen—Equal contribution

L. Bushnell et al. (Eds.): GameSec 2018, LNCS 11199, pp. 102–114, 2018.
https://doi.org/10.1007/978-3-030-01554-1_6

images on which the model has low confidence and thus high loss [8]. Our insight is that outliers give the model better generalization ability however also make the model more sensitive to adversarial examples. When we detect and discard outliers in the training set, the new model will be less sensitive to adversarial examples. And we utilize the sensitivity difference between the original model and the new model to distinguish adversarial examples from normal examples.

We call the process of removing outliers from the training set *sanitization*[1]. We propose two methods for detecting outliers. First, for some AI tasks, we may find canonical examples. For example, for handwritten digit classification, we may use computer fonts as canonical examples. We trained a *canonical model* using canonical examples, and then used the canonical model to detect outliers in the training set. We call this method *canonical sanitization*. Second, for AI tasks without canonical examples, we considered examples with large training errors as outliers. We call this method *self sanitization*.

After culling the training set, we trained a model called the *sanitized model*. We compared the robustness of the unsanitized model, which was trained on the entire training set, with the sanitized model on adversarial examples using two criteria with respect to different attack methods. For IGSM attack, the criterion is classification accuracy of adversarial examples. For Carlini & Wagner attack, the criterion is the average distortion. In Sect. 3.3, the result of sanitization exactly validates that the outliers help model do better generalization meanwhile decrease the robustness. Given the result, the sanitized models allow us to detect adversarial examples which is shown in Sect. 3.4.

To measure the sensitivity difference, we computed the Kullback-Leibler divergence from the output of an example on the unsanitized model to the output of the same example on the sanitized model and found that this divergence was much larger for adversarial examples than for normal examples. Based on this difference, we were able to detect the adversarial examples generated by the Carlini & Wagner attack on MNIST and SVHN at 99.26% and 94.67% accuracy, respectively. Compared to prior work for detecting adversarial examples (e.g., [15]), this approach requires no knowledge of adversarial examples.

We make the following contributions.

- We propose two methods for detecting outliers in the training set: canonical sanitization and self-sanitization. By performing data sanitization, we show how the outliers will affect the model's robustness and generalization ability.
- We propose a new adversarial example detection framework based on the sanitized model. The detector leverages the Kullback-Leibler divergence from the unsanitized model to the sanitized model. Neither modifications to the model structure nor data preprocessing methods are required.

---

[1] Unlike *data sanitization*, which commonly modifies individual datum, we modify no example but merely remove outliers from the training set.

2 Methodology

2.1 Definitions

- *Normal examples* are sampled from the natural data generating process. For examples, images of handwritten digits.
- *Outliers* are examples in the training set of normal examples. They are difficult to classify by humans. *Sanitization* is the process of removing outliers from the training set.
- *Adversarial examples* are crafted by attackers that are perceptually close to normal examples but that cause misclassification.
- *Unsanitized models* are trained with all the examples in the training set. We assume that the training set contains only normal examples.
- *Sanitized models* are trained with the remaining examples after we remove outliers from the training set.

2.2 Sanitization

Sanitization is the process of removing outliers from the training set. We propose two automatic sanitization methods.

Canonical Sanitization. This approach applies to the AI tasks that have canonical examples. For example, for handwritten digit, computer fonts may be considered canonical examples[2]. Based on this observation, we use canonical examples to discard outliers in our training set $\mathbb{X}$ by the following steps:

- Augment the set of canonical examples by applying common transformations, e.g., rotating and scaling computer fonts.
- Train a model f using the augmented canonical examples.
- Use f to detect and discard outliers in the training set $\mathbb{X}$. An example $\boldsymbol{x}^{(i)}$ is an outlier if $f(\boldsymbol{x}^{(i)})$ has a low confidence on $y^{(i)}$, the class for $\boldsymbol{x}^{(i)}$.

Self Sanitization. Not all AI tasks have canonical examples. For such tasks, we use all the examples to train a model, and then discard examples that have high training errors.

After removing outliers from the original training set, we get a sanitized set which is used to train a model, called *sanitized model*. Then, we evaluate if the sanitized model is more robust than unsanitized models using two metrics: classification accuracy and distortion of adversarial examples.

---

[2] Some computer fonts are difficult to recognize and therefore are excluded from our evaluation

2.3 Detecting adversarial examples

We take advantage of the Kullback-Leibler divergence [10] between the outputs of the original and the sanitized models to depict the difference of sensitivity to the adversarial examples. The Kullback-Leibler divergence from a distribution P to Q is defined as

$$D_{KL}\left(P \parallel Q\right) = \sum_i P\left(i\right) \log \frac{P\left(i\right)}{Q\left(i\right)}$$

By setting a proper threshold, we are able to detect nearly all adversarial examples with acceptable false reject rate. No modifications to the original model structure or other data outside the original dataset are required.

The detection method is hard to distinguish between adversarial examples and normal examples when the distortion of the adversarial image is very small. To address this problem, we designed a complete adversarial example detection framework. We will discuss the framework detailedly in Sect. 3.4.

3 Evaluation

3.1 Set up

We used two data sets, MNIST[3] and SVHN[4], to evaluate our proposed method. We performed both canonical sanitization and self sanitization on MNIST and only self sanitization on SVHN. For SVHN, we pre-processed it with the following steps to get individual clean digit images. After the process, we obtained 40556 images from the original SVHN training set and 9790 test images from the original SVHN test set.

1. Cropping individual digits using the bounding boxes.
2. Discarding images whose either dimension is less than 10.
3. Resizing the larger dimension of each image to 28 while keeping the aspect ratio, and then padding the image to 28 × 28. When padding an image, we used the average color of the border as the padding color.

The models we used to train these two datasets are different. We designed Convolutional Neural Networks for MNIST and SVHN separately. Correspondingly, we achieved an accuracy of 99.3% and 98.62% on the *unsanitized models*.

- MNIST CNN: Input → (Conv + Pool) * 2 → FC → FC → Output
- SVHN CNN: Input → (Conv + Conv + Pool) * 3 → FC → FC → Output

Given the trained model, we performed two popular attacks, Iterative Gradient Sign Method (IGSM) [7,11] and Carlini & Wagner's attack [2], to attack the CNN models. We will discuss the attacks in Sect. 3.3.

---

[3] http://yann.lecun.com/exdb/mnist/.
[4] http://ufldl.stanford.edu/housenumbers/.

3.2 Sanitization

Canonical Sanitization. We did canonical sanitization on MNIST by discarding outliers that are far different from canonical examples. We chose 340 fonts containing digits as canonical examples. To accommodate variations in handwriting, we also augmented the fonts by scaling and rotation. After the augmentation, we acquired 71400 images, from which we randomly chose 80% as the training set and the remaining 20% as the test set. We trained the MNIST CNN on canonical examples and achieved an accuracy of 98.7%. We call this the *canonical model*.

We fed each example in MNIST training set to the canonical model. If the example's confidence score of the correct class was below a threshold, we considered it an outlier and discarded it. Figure 1 shows examples with low and high confidence. Table 1 shows the number of examples left under different thresholds. We used these examples to train the *sanitized models*.

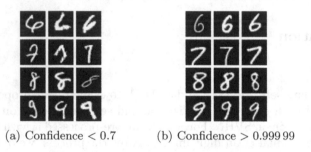

(a) Confidence < 0.7   (b) Confidence > 0.999 99

Fig. 1. Examples in MNIST with low and high confidence, respectively.

Table 1. Size of the MNIST training set after discarding examples whose confidence scores on the canonical model are below a threshold

Threshold	0	0.7	0.8	0.9	0.99	0.999	0.9999
Set size	60000	51241	50425	49128	44448	38230	30618

Self-Sanitization. We did self sanitization on both MNIST and SVHN. To discard outliers in self sanitization, we trained the CNN for MNIST and SVHN separately, used the models to test every example in the training set, and considered examples whose confidence scores were below a threshold as outliers. Tables 2 and 3 show the number of examples left under different thresholds. We used these examples to train the *sanitized models*. Table 3 also shows that the sanitized models maintain high classification accuracy when it has adequate training data to prevent overfitting.

Table 2. Size of the MNIST training set after discarding examples whose confidence scores on the self-trained model are below a threshold

Threshold	0	0.999	0.9999	0.99999	0.999999	0.9999999
Set size	60000	56435	52417	45769	36328	24678

Table 3. The sizes of the sanitized SVHN training set and the classification accuracy of the self-sanitized models at different thresholds

Threshold	Training set size	Classification accuracy (%)
0	40556	94.26
0.7	39330	93.68
0.8	38929	93.22
0.9	38153	92.74
0.99	34408	91.30
0.999	28420	89.41

3.3   Robustness against adversarial examples

We ran the IGSM and Carlini & Wagner attacks on both the unsanitized and sanitized models.

IGSM Attack. Figure 2 compares the classification accuracy of the unsanitized and sanitized models on the adversarial examples generated by the IGSM attack on MNIST, where Fig. 2a and b correspond to canonical sanitization and self sanitization, respectively.

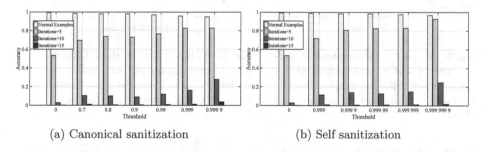

(a) Canonical sanitization   (b) Self sanitization

Fig. 2. Classification accuracy of normal and IGSM adversarial MNIST examples in different threshold. The threshold 0 represents the original data set.

Figure 2 shows that a higher threshold of sanitization increases the robustness of the model against adversarial examples and maintains classfication accuracy on normal examples. For example, on adversarial examples generated after five iterations of IGSM, the classification accuracy is 82.8% with a threshold of 0.9999 in canonical sanitization, and is above 92.6% with a threshold of 0.9999999 in self sanitization. For normal examples, the classfication accuracy is always higher than 95.0% in different threshold.

Carlini & Wagner's Attack. We ran Carlini & Wagner's L_2 target attack to generate adversarial examples on our sanitized models for both MNIST and SVHN. Figures 3 and 4 show that the sanitized models forced the adversarial examples to add larger distortions in order to fool the sanitized models. The higher the threshold, the larger the distortion.

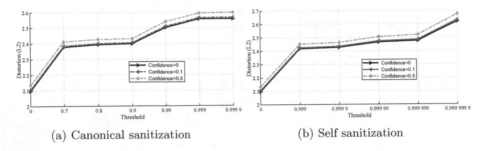

(a) Canonical sanitization   (b) Self sanitization

Fig. 3. Average L_2 distortions of normal and C&W's adversarial MNIST examples in different threshold. The threshold 0 represents the unsanitized model.

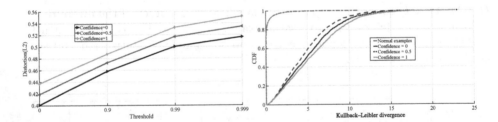

Fig. 4. Average L_2 distortions of normal and C&W's adversarial SVHN examples in different threshold. The threshold 0 represents the unsanitized model.

Fig. 5. SVHN: CDF of the KL divergence from the output of unsanitized model to that of a sanitized model with different C&W attack condidences.

Discussion. From the experiments, we concluded that the original dataset with outliers has higher generalization ability but weaker robustness. With the sanitization, the model obtained much more robustness by only sacrificing limited generalization ability.

3.4 Detecting adversarial examples

We evaluated the effectiveness of using the Kullback-Leibler divergence to detect adversarial examples (Sect. 2.3).

MNIST. We generated adversarial examples on two sanitized models on MNIST:

- A canonical sanitized model. The discard threshold was set to be 0.9999.
- A self sanitized model. The discard threshold was set to be 0.9999999.

We computed the Kullback-Leibler divergence from the output of the unsanitized model to that of each of the sanitized models.

Figure 6 compares the CDF of Kullback-Leibler divergence between normal and adversarial examples generated by IGSM after different iterations. It shows that the majority of normal examples have very small divergence, while most adversarial examples have large divergence where more iterations generated examples with higher divergence. Figure 7 compares the CDF of Kullback-Leibler divergence between normal and adversarial examples generated by the Carlini & Wagner attack using different confidence levels, which is more prominent.

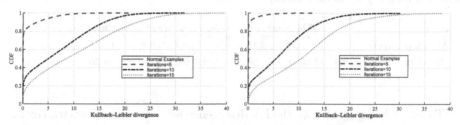

(a) KL divergence from unsanitized model to canonical sanitized models

(b) KL divergence from unsanitized model to self sanitized models

Fig. 6. MNIST: CDF of KL divergence from the output of the unsanitized model to the output of a sanitized model with different IGSM iterations.

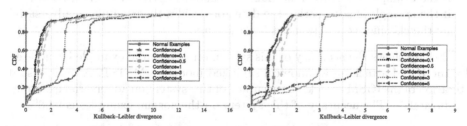

(a) KL divergence from the unsanitized model to canonical sanitized models

(b) KL divergence from unsanitized model to self sanitized models

Fig. 7. MNIST: CDF of KL divergence from the output of the unsanitized model to the output of a sanitized model with different C&W confidences.

Table 4 shows the accuracy of detecting adversarial examples based on the KL divergence from the unsanitized model to a canonical sanitized model. We used a threshold of KL divergence to divide normal and adversarial examples: examples below this threshold were considered normal, and all above adversarial. We determined the threshold by setting a target detection accuracy on normal examples. For example, when we set this target accuracy to 98%, we needed a threshold of KL divergence of 0.0068. At this threshold, the accuracy of detecting all the Carlini & Wagner adversarial examples at all the confidence levels is all above 95%. The accuracy of detecting IGSM adversarial examples is high when the number of iterations is high (e.g., 10 or 15). When the number of iterations is low (e.g., 5), the detection accuracy decreases; however, since the false negative examples have low KL divergence, they are more similar to normal examples and therefore can be classified correctly with high probability as discussed next.

Table 4. MNIST: accuracy of detecting adversarial examples based on the Kullback-Leibler divergence from the unsanitized model to a canonical sanitized model when detection accuracy for normal examples is 98%

Attack	IGSM (iterations)			Carlini & Wagner (confidence)					
Attack parameter	5	10	15	0	0.1	0.5	1	3	5
Detection accuracy (%)	33.80	85.47	96.31	99.26	99.26	100.00	99.26	98.52	95.56

To take advantage of both the KL divergence for detecting adversarial examples and the sanitized models for classifying examples, we combined them into a framework shown in Fig. 8. The framework consists of a detector, which computes the KL divergence from the unsantized model to the sanitized model and rejects the example if its divergence exceeds a threshold, and a classifier, which infers the class of the example using the sanitized model. The framework makes a correct decision on an example when

- if the example is regard as normal, the classifier correctly infers its class.
- if the example is adversarial, the detector decides the example as adversarial *or* the classifier correctly infers its true class.

Table 5 shows the accuracy of this system on adversarial exampled generated by the IGSM attack on a canonical sanitized model on MNIST. At each tested iteration of the IGSM attack, the accuracy of this system on adversarial examples is above 94%. The accuracy of this system on the normal examples is 94.8%.

SVHN. Figure 5 compares the CDF of the Kullback-Leibler divergence of normal examples and adversarial examples generated by the Carlini & Wagner attack at different confidence levels. We trained the sanitized model with a discard threshold 0.9 (self sanitization). We can see normal examples have small divergence, while all the Carlini & Wagner adversarial examples under difference confidence levels have large divergence.

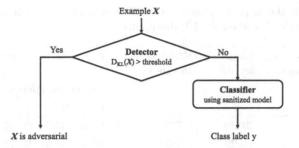

Fig. 8. A framework combining a detector, which detects if an example is adversarial based on the KL divergence from the unsantized model to the sanitized model, and a classifier, which classifies the example using the sanitized model.

Table 5. Accuracy of the framework in Figure 8. The column "detection", "classifier", and "combined" shows the accuracy of the detector, classifier, and system overall. The overall accuracy on normal examples is 94.8%.

IGSM iterations	Accuracy (%)		
	Detector	Classifier	Overall
5	33.80	99.84	99.89
10	85.47	72.72	96.03
15	96.31	1.71	96.37

Table 6 shows the impact of sanitization threshold on the detection accuracy on adversarial examples generated by the Carlini & Wagner attack. We automatically determined the threshold of KL divergence by setting the detection accuracy on normal examples to 94%. Table 6 shows that as the sanitization threshold increases from 0.7 to 0.9, the detection accuracy increases. However, after the sanitization threshold increases even further, the detection accuracy decreases. This is because after the sanitization threshold exceeds 0.9, the size of the training set decreases rapidly, which causes the model to overfit.

4   Discussion and future work

From the observation in Sect. 3.3 that the sanitized models will obtain higher robustness, we speculate the causation of this phenomenon is that the outliers will extend the decision boundary and give the model better generalization ability. However, since the outliers are usually not of big proportion and not representative, the extended decision boundary would also include adversarial examples. We call this phenomenon as 'negative generalization'.

The state-of-the-art techniques of handling the negative generalization problem are various advanced adversarial retraining methods, which use adversarial examples as a part of the training data and force the model to correctly clas-

Table 6. SVHN: the impact of sanitization threshold on the accuracy of detecting adversarial examples based on the KL divergence

Sanitization threshold	Training set size	KL divergence threshold	Detection accuracy (%)		
			Attack confidence		
			0	0.5	1
0.7	39330	0.7295	93.50	94.56	94.67
0.8	38929	0.5891	93.56	94.67	95.72
0.9	38153	0.7586	94.67	94.78	95.78
0.99	34408	1.0918	90.00	91.17	92.56
0.999	28420	1.6224	83.22	85.78	87.33

sify. These methods are essentially enriching the proportion of the outliers and making the decision boundary more sophisticated to improve the robustness.

In this paper, we focus on another direction. By culling the dataset, we restrict the decision boundary thus also limit the negative generalization on the sanitized model. The sanitized model can help to make a gap of the negative generalization (sensitivity to adversarial examples) between itself and the original model, while the capability of classifying normal examples for both models would stay similar. This lets us leverage the gap to detect adversarial examples.

Section 3.4 showed that we can use the Kullback-Leibler divergence as a reliable metric to distinguish between normal and adversarial examples. In our future work, we plan to evaluate if the attacker can generate adversarial examples to evade our detection if she knows our detection method.

5   Related work

Most prior work on machine learning security focused on improving the network architecture, training method, or incorporating adversarial examples in training [1]. By contrast, we focus on culling the training set to remove outliers to improve the model's robustness.

5.1   Influence of training examples

Influence functions is a technique from robust statistics to measure the estimator on the value of one of the points in the sample [5,6]. Koh et al. used influence functions as an indicator to track the behavior from the training data to the model's prediction [8]. By modifying the training data and observing its corresponding prediction, the influence functions can reveal insight of model. They found that some ambiguous training examples were effective points that led to a low confidence model. Influence Sketching [19] proposed a new scalable version of Cook's distance [3,4] to prioritize samples in the generalized linear model

[13]. The predictive accuracy changed slightly from 99.47% to 99.45% when they deleted 10% ambiguous examples from the training set.

5.2 Influence of test examples

Xu et al. [20] observed that most features of test examples are unnecessary for prediction, and that superfluous features facilitate adversarial examples. They proposed two methods to reduce the feature space: reducing the color depth of images and using smoothing to reduce the variation among pixels. Their feature squeezing defense successfully detected adversarial examples while maintaining high accuracy on normal examples.

6   Conclusion

Adversarial examples remain a challenging problem despite recent progress in defense. In this paper, we study the relationship between outliers in the data set and model robustness and propose a framework for detecting adversarial examples without modifying the original model architecture. We design two methods to detect and remove outliers in the training set and used the remaining examples to train a sanitized model. On both MNIST and SVHN, the sanitized models improved the classification accuracy on adversarial examples generated by the IGSM attack and increased the distortion of adversarial examples generated by the Carlini & Wagner attack, which indicates that the sanitized model is less sensitive to adversarial examples. Our detection is essentially leveraging the different sensitivity to adversarial examples of the model trained with and without outliers. We found that the Kullback-Leibler divergence from the unsanitized model to the sanitized model can be used to measure this difference and detect adversarial examples reliably.

Acknowledgment. This material is based upon work supported by the National Science Foundation under Grant No. 1801751.

References

1. Carlini, N., Wagner, D.: Adversarial examples are not easily detected: bypassing ten detection methods. arXiv preprint arXiv:1705.07263 (2017)
2. Carlini, N., Wagner, D.: Towards evaluating the robustness of neural networks. In: IEEE Symposium on Security and Privacy (2017)
3. Cook, R.D.: Detection of influential observation in linear regression. Technometrics **19**(1), 15–18 (1977)
4. Cook, R.D.: Influential observations in linear regression. J. Am. Stat. Assoc. **74**(365), 169–174 (1979)
5. Cook, R.D., Weisberg, S.: Characterizations of an empirical influence function for detecting influential cases in regression. Technometrics **22**(4), 495–508 (1980)
6. Cook, R.D., Weisberg, S.: Residuals and Influence in Regression. Chapman and Hall, New York (1982)

7. Goodfellow, I.J., Shlens, J., Szegedy, C.: Explaining and harnessing adversarial examples. In: International Conference on Learning Representations (ICLR) (2015)
8. Koh, P.W., Liang, P.: Understanding black-box predictions via influence functions. In: International Conference on Machine Learning (2017)
9. Krizhevsky, A., Sutskever, I., Hinton, G.E.: ImageNet classification with deep convolutional neural networks. In: Advances in Neural Information Processing Systems, pp. 1097–1105 (2012)
10. Kullback, S., Leibler, R.A.: On information and sufficiency. Ann. Math. Stat. 22(1), 79–86 (1951)
11. Kurakin, A., Goodfellow, I.J., Bengio, S.: Adversarial examples in the physical world. CoRR abs/1607.02533 (2016)
12. LeCun, Y., Bottou, L., Bengio, Y., Haffner, P.: Gradient-based learning applied to document recognition. Proc. IEEE 86(11), 2278–2324 (1998)
13. Madsen, H., Thyregod, P.: Introduction to General and Generalized Linear Models. CRC Press, Boca Raton (2010)
14. Meng, D., Chen, H.: MagNet: a two-pronged defense against adversarial examples. In: ACM Conference on Computer and Communications Security, Dallas, TX (CCS) (2017)
15. Metzen, J.H., Genewein, T., Fischer, V., Bischoff, B.: On detecting adversarial perturbations. In: International Conference on Learning Representations (ICLR) (2017)
16. Moosavi-Dezfooli, S.M., Fawzi, A., Frossard, P.: DeepFool: a simple and accurate method to fool deep neural networks. In: Proceedings of the IEEE Conference on Computer Vision and Pattern Recognition, pp. 2574–2582 (2016)
17. Papernot, N., McDaniel, P., Wu, X., Jha, S., Swami, A.: Distillation as a defense to adversarial perturbations against deep neural networks. In: IEEE Symposium on Security and Privacy (2016)
18. Szegedy, C., et al.: Intriguing properties of neural networks. In: International Conference on Learning Representations (ICLR) (2014)
19. Wojnowicz, M., et al.: Influence sketching: finding influential samples in large-scale regressions. In: 2016 IEEE International Conference on Big Data (Big Data), pp. 3601–3612. IEEE (2016)
20. Xu, W., Evans, D., Qi, Y.: Feature squeezing: detecting adversarial examples in deep neural networks. In: Network and Distributed Systems Security Symposium (NDSS) (2018)

Optimal Placement of Honeypots
for Network Defense

Mark Bilinski$^{(\boxtimes)}$ (iD), Ryan Gabrys (iD), and Justin Mauger (iD)

SPAWAR Systems Center Pacific, 53560 Hull Street, San Diego, CA 92152, USA
{bilinski,gabrys,jmauger}@spawar.navy.mil

Abstract. We seek to combine recent advances in game theory of
both cyber defense and deception to model the interactions between
an attacker and defender on a network. We define a new class of games
called (n, k, c, w, γ)-*honeynet games* which extend those defined in previous research. These games have incomplete and imperfect information
since the attacker is unaware of moves made by the defender to secure
a system, and the defender is not certain of the true identity of the
attacker.

Keywords: Game theory · Network security · Honeynets
Cyber defense

1 Introduction

Deception strategies attempt to prevent an attack through the use of misdirec-
tions, fake responses, and obfuscations [8]. However, many current techniques do
not employ game theoretic strategies when determining when and how resources
are to be allocated for use in deceptive scenarios. In this paper, we examine the
use of game theory to guide deception and cyber defense strategies. In particular,
we derive explicit expressions for the Nash equilibria of a network defense game
under specific conditions reflecting an insider threat scenario.

Existing work has modeled the interactions between a defender (attempting
to secure some system) and an attacker as a non-cooperative dynamic game with
and without complete information in behavioral game theory [4]. Other works
have used Instance-Based Learning Theory to model human decisions involving
hackers and analysts [2] or Prospect Theory, where people value gains and losses
differently based upon the greater emotional impact of losses versus gains [5].

In this preliminary paper, we model the interactions between an attacker
and defender using a game-theoretic framework. The basic premise is that there
is a defender seeking to protect a collection of hosts on some network from a
potential attacker. The defender has a fixed set of resources and, as a result, is
only able to defend at most k of the total hosts on the network – incurring a

This is a U.S. government work and not under copyright protection in the U.S.;
foreign copyright protection may apply 2018
L. Bushnell et al. (Eds.): GameSec 2018, LNCS 11199, pp. 115–126, 2018.
https://doi.org/10.1007/978-3-030-01554-1_7

fixed cost for each host so defended. For symmetry, the attacker can attack at most k hosts at a time, but does not incur a cost. For shorthand, a host which is protected from attackers is referred to as a honeypot, and a honeynet is simply of collection of connected honeypots. Under this setup, the attacker wins the game if it attacks any host which is not a honeypot, otherwise the defender wins.

This setup resembles an insider threat scenario. From the attacker's perspective, they are already on the network as an insider so they already know the values of the hosts and so there is no need for reconnaissance. Further, as an attacker, they can run a script that attacks multiple hosts regardless of the number, so the cost of taking an action is negligible. From the defender's perspective, every time they swap out a real host with a honeypot they are disrupting a service or otherwise inconveniencing their users, so each successive defensive action is costly. Further the defender suffers a significant asymmetric disadvantage because any undefended host that is attacked results in defeat.

We model our work after [3] and [6]. The former considers the case of a wireless ad-hoc network where the defender is uncertain of the identity of a particular node. The authors calculate the mixed strategy Nash equilibria in the static one-shot game with a parameter γ that represents the probability the node is malicious. We extend their work by assuming that not all resources on the network have uniform importance, similar to the setup in [7]. However, unlike [7], we also assume the presence of incomplete information where the utility functions of some of the players are unknown. The incomplete information arises from the defender's uncertainty about the type of the node, only having an initial assumption about the expected number of attackers.

The work in [3] is extended in [1], where the authors use signaling to convert the game from one of incomplete information to one of imperfect information. In this paper, we focus on the static case, while [1,3], and [6] go on to analyze the iterated (dynamic) version of their respective games. However, our setup is more general in that it allows for the node to attack more than one host at a time. In addition, we include a cost to the defender deploying a honeypot, unlike [1]. We note our work may also be considered an extension of [6], since the defender is attempting to secure a collection of hosts rather than a single host.

The contributions of this preliminary paper will be the following: (a) We formulate a static model for a game involving honeynets based upon prior art that models deception, (b) we characterize Nash Equilibria for a general case under slightly reduced assumptions, (c) We present a proof in Theorem 2 and Lemma 3 of how such a network environment guarantees a significant defender disadvantage. Our analysis also leads to the insight that a defender in such scenarios must carefully balance the defense of systems. In particular, we show that the intuitive approach of redirecting limited defenses to protect higher value systems leaves them vulnerable through less defended lower value systems.

This paper is organized as follows: We setup our notation and definition of the $(n, k, c, \boldsymbol{w}, \gamma)$-*honeynet game* in Sects. 2 and 3. Section 4 discusses the general case. We conclude in Sect. 5, providing avenues for further research into deception using honeynets.

2   Problem Setup

We now describe an $(n, k, c, \boldsymbol{w}, \gamma)$-honeynet game. For a binary vector $\boldsymbol{v} \in \{0,1\}^n$, let $\mathrm{wt}(\boldsymbol{v})$ denote the number of non-zero components of $\boldsymbol{v}$. Let the *support* of $\boldsymbol{v}$ be $\mathrm{supp}(\boldsymbol{v}) = \{i \mid \boldsymbol{v}_i = 1\}$. For $\boldsymbol{a}, \boldsymbol{d} \in \{0,1\}^n$, let $\delta_{\boldsymbol{a}\boldsymbol{d}} = 1$ if $\mathrm{supp}(\boldsymbol{a}) \subset \mathrm{supp}(\boldsymbol{d})$, 0 otherwise. We will often write $\boldsymbol{a} \subset \boldsymbol{d}$ instead of $\mathrm{supp}(\boldsymbol{a}) \subset \mathrm{supp}(\boldsymbol{d})$. Let $c > 0$, and $\gamma \in (0, 1]$.

Definition 1. *An $(n, k, c, \boldsymbol{w}, \gamma)$-honeynet game consists of:*

1. *Two players N (the node) and D (the defender). With probability γ, N has type E, which means the node is an enemy attacker, and otherwise N has type F so that the node is friendly.*
2. *The set of actions for each player:*
   (a) *If N has type E, then the set of actions for N is $\mathcal{A}_E = \{\boldsymbol{a} \in \{0,1\}^n : 1 \leq \mathrm{wt}(\boldsymbol{a}) \leq k\}$. If $a_i = 1$ for $i \in [n]$, then N attacks host i.*
   (b) *If N has type F, then the set of actions for N is $\mathcal{A}_F = \{\boldsymbol{0}\}$. In this case, N is a friendly node and it does not attack any hosts.*
   (c) *The set of actions for D is $\mathcal{A}_D = \{\boldsymbol{d} \in \{0,1\}^n : 0 \leq \mathrm{wt}(\boldsymbol{d}) \leq k\}$. If $d_i = 1$ for $i \in [n]$, then D places a honeypot at host i. Otherwise, D places a regular host at i. The special action $\boldsymbol{0}$ is the defender choosing not to place any honeypots. Note that $\mathcal{A}_D = \mathcal{A}_E \cup \{\boldsymbol{0}\}$.*
3. *A value $w_{\boldsymbol{a}} \geq 0$ for each action $\boldsymbol{a} \in \mathcal{A}_F \cup \mathcal{A}_E$, where $w_{\boldsymbol{a}} = 0 \Leftrightarrow \boldsymbol{a} = \boldsymbol{0}$.*
4. *The utility functions for each player. For each pair of actions $\boldsymbol{a}, \boldsymbol{d}$:*

$$u_N(\boldsymbol{a}, \boldsymbol{d}) = (1 - 2\delta_{\boldsymbol{a}\boldsymbol{d}})w_{\boldsymbol{a}}$$
$$u_D(\boldsymbol{a}, \boldsymbol{d}) = (2\delta_{\boldsymbol{a}\boldsymbol{d}} - 1)w_{\boldsymbol{a}} - c \cdot \mathrm{wt}(\boldsymbol{d})$$

   These formulas hold independently of the type of N, with the understanding that $\boldsymbol{a} = \boldsymbol{0}$ when N is of type F.
5. *$K_E = |\mathcal{A}_E| = \sum_{j=1}^{k} \binom{n}{j}$, and $K_D = |\mathcal{A}_D| = K_E + 1$.*

This game is a *Bayesian* game. For shorthand, when N has type E, then u_E is the utility function for N, and similarly when N has type F, then u_F is the utility function for N. Then, *expected* utilities over the identity of N are:

$$u_N(\boldsymbol{a}, \boldsymbol{d}) = u_E(\boldsymbol{a}, \boldsymbol{d})P(N = E) + u_F(\boldsymbol{0}, \boldsymbol{d})P(N = F) = \gamma(1 - 2\delta_{\boldsymbol{a}\boldsymbol{d}})w_{\boldsymbol{a}}$$

Similarly,

$$
\begin{aligned}
u_D(\boldsymbol{a}, \boldsymbol{d}) &= u_D(\boldsymbol{a}, \boldsymbol{d})P(N = E) + u_D(\boldsymbol{0}, \boldsymbol{d})P(N = F) \\
&= \gamma\big((2\delta_{\boldsymbol{a}\boldsymbol{d}} - 1)w_{\boldsymbol{a}} - c \cdot \mathrm{wt}(\boldsymbol{d})\big) + (1 - \gamma)\big(-c \cdot \mathrm{wt}(\boldsymbol{d})\big) \\
&= \gamma(2\delta_{\boldsymbol{a}\boldsymbol{d}} - 1)w_{\boldsymbol{a}} - c \cdot \mathrm{wt}(\boldsymbol{d})
\end{aligned}
$$

From this point forward, we will abuse notation slightly and use u_N, u_D to mean the expected values defined above.

In this model is that there are two players: a defender (D) and another node (N) whose identity is unknown. With probability γ, the node is an attacker (i.e., it has type E). We refer to $a \in \{0,1\}^n$ as the *attack vector*, where $a = 0$ if and only if the node is friendly and otherwise $1 \leq \mathrm{wt}(a) \leq k$.

The purpose for this is to model an insider threat scenario. A user on the network knows the value of the weights w_a because they are insiders and can accurately recon the network, but perhaps do not have full access. The defender cannot be sure which user is malicious, only that a certain proportion γ are.

The utility for the action a by the node and d by the defender is determined by the hosts the node chooses to attack. If the node attacks at least one host which is not a honeypot, then the attack is successful and the attack has utility w_a for the node. Otherwise, if the node only attacks honeypots, then the utility for the attack is $-w_a$ from the point of view of the node. The defender has a similar utility function except that the defender pays an additional cost for defense which is represented by the parameter c.

The cost parameter can represent infrastructure cost in deploying virtual machines, or disruption to a regular user. In our setup, the attacker has no cost because for an insider reconnaissance is automatic and attacker cost is negligible.

Notice that one property of our model is that given an attack a, the value of the attack, w_a, depends only on the attack vector itself and not on which hosts were undefended. Motivation from this setup comes from where an attacker gains access to an entire group when they gain a foothold on a single host, say through a single compromised credential and then move laterally through the group.

Our model can be interpreted as an extension of the work from [3] as illustrated in the next example for the case where $w_1 = w_2$.

Example 1. Suppose $n = 2, k = 1, w_1 = w_2 = w, c = 0$, and $\gamma = 1$ so that N is always an attacker. Then, we have the following payoff matrix (shown below) for our $(2, 1, 0, (w, w), 1)$-honeynet game where the each pair in the table represents the attacker's then defender's payoff respectively.

	(1,0)	(0,1)	(0,0)
(1,0)	$-w, w$	$w, -w$	$w, -w$
(0,1)	$w, -w$	$-w, w$	$w, -w$

Notice that without the $(0,0)$ column (i.e. the choice to defend neither host) this is identical to the prototype strategic game from [3].

It can be shown that this game has a Nash equilibrium where both players choose either host with $\frac{1}{2}$ probability, identical to the Nash for the game from [3] – meaning the defender will never choose to NOT defend either host provided that there is no cost for defense (i.e., $c = 0$).

Our interest will be in games for which there is a cost parameter c associated with defense, and both the attacker and defender can choose to attack/defend at most k out of n hosts. We will be particularly interested in the case where the weights associated with our games are non-decreasing. In other words, we will be interested in games that have weights with the property that for any $a, \bar{a} \in \{0,1\}^n$ with $\bar{a} \supset a$, then $w_{\bar{a}} \geq w_a$. For shorthand, if a game has weights satisfying this property, then we say that the game has *monotonic weights*. We will show that when a game has monotonic weights, then we can characterize the actions chosen by the defender in any Nash equilibrium.

3   Nash Equilibria and Notation

A *mixed* strategy for the attacker can be defined by a vector $p = (p_a)_{a \in \mathcal{A}_A}$ satisfying $0 \le p_a \le 1$ and $\sum_a p_a = 1$. Here, p_a can be interpreted as the probability that the attacker will choose the action $a = (a_1, \ldots, a_n)$. For instance, if $n = 4$ and $a = (0, 1, 1, 0)$, then p_a is the probability the attacker will attack hosts 2 and 3 simultaneously. Similarly, a mixed strategy for the defender can be represented as a vector $q = (q_d)_{d \in \mathcal{A}_D}$. When a single component $p_a = 1$, p then represents the *pure* strategy a. We will sometimes refer to a mixed strategy simply as a strategy. If $p_a > 0$, we say the action a is *active* in the strategy p. A friendly node only has the pure strategy consisting of the single active action $\mathbf{0}$.

The utility functions for mixed strategies are

$$u_E(p, q) = \sum_{a \in \mathcal{A}_E} p_a u_E(a, q) = \sum_{\substack{a \in \mathcal{A}_E \\ d \in \mathcal{A}_D}} p_a q_d u_E(a, d) \tag{1}$$

$$u_D(p, q) = \sum_{d \in \mathcal{A}_D} q_d u_D(p, d) = \sum_{\substack{a \in \mathcal{A}_E \\ d \in \mathcal{A}_D}} p_a q_d u_D(a, d) \tag{2}$$

Definition 2. *The simplex $\Delta_M \subset \mathbb{R}^M$ is the set of points $\{(x_1, x_2, \ldots, x_M) \mid \sum_j x_j = 1, x_j \ge 0\}$.*

Defender mixed strategies q are in one-to-one correspondence with points in Δ_{K_D}, and likewise for attacker mixed strategies p and points in Δ_{K_E}. [1]

Definition 3. *A mixed strategy Nash equilibrium (p^*, q^*) is a pair satisfying*

$$u_E(p^*, q^*) \ge u_E(p, q^*) \text{ for all } p \in \Delta_{K_E}$$
$$u_D(p^*, q^*) \ge u_D(p^*, q) \text{ for all } q \in \Delta_{K_D}$$

In full generality, a mixed strategy p_N for the Node player is either a vector $p_E \in \Delta_{K_E}$ if N is of type E, or the pure strategy $\mathbf{0}$ if N is of type F. It is clear that the equations of Definition 3 hold for $u_N(p_N, q)$ exactly when they hold for $u_E(p_E, q)$, so we will focus on u_E for finding equilibrium strategies.

4   The General Case

Consider general parameters of n and k. We begin by first deriving some conditions on the components of any equilibrium strategy pair (p^*, q^*). Recall that

---

[1] The domain of p_N^* is $\Delta_{K_E} \coprod \Delta_0$, where Δ_0 is just the point $\{1\}$ representing the friendly node's unique strategy.

we say a game has monotonic weights if for $a, \bar{a} \in \{0,1\}^n$ with $a \subsetneq \bar{a}$, $w_{\bar{a}} \geq w_a$. If $w_{\bar{a}} > w_a$, then the game has *strictly monotonic weights*.

For a strategy pair (p, q), let $E_{p,q}$ denote the set of active actions in p for the attacker. Similarly let $D_{p,q}$ denote the set of active actions in q for the defender, and let $D_{p,q}^+$ denote the non-zero actions in $D_{p,q}$. For strategy p and vector $\boldsymbol{w} = (w_a)_{a \in A_E}$, let $<p, \boldsymbol{w}> = \sum_{a \in A_E} p_a w_a$.

Theorem 1. *Assume we have a mixed strategy Nash equilibrium (p^*, q^*) for an $(n, k, c, \boldsymbol{w}, \gamma)$-honeynet game. Then*

$$u_E(a, q^*) = w_a \left(1 - 2\sum_{d \supset a} q_d^*\right) \tag{3}$$

$$u_D(p^*, d) = 2\gamma \sum_{a \subset d} p_a^* w_a - \gamma <p^*, w> - c \cdot \mathrm{wt}(d) \tag{4}$$

$$u_D(p^*, 0) = -\gamma <p^*, w> \tag{5}$$

Proof.

$$u_E(a, q^*) = \sum_{d \in A_D} q_d^* \left((1 - 2\delta_{ad})w_a\right)$$

$$= w_a \left(\sum_{d \in A_D} q_d^* - 2\sum_{d \supset a} q_d^*\right) = w_a \left(1 - 2\sum_{d \supset a} q_d^*\right)$$

$$u_D(p^*, d) = \sum_{a \in A_E} p_a^* \left(\gamma(2\delta_{ad} - 1)w_a - c \cdot \mathrm{wt}(d)\right)$$

$$= 2\gamma \sum_{a \subset d} p_a^* w_a - \gamma \sum_{a \in A_E} p_a^* w_a - c \cdot \mathrm{wt}(d) \sum_{a \in A_E} p_a^*$$

$$= 2\gamma \sum_{a \subset d} p_a^* w_a - \gamma <p^*, w> - c \cdot \mathrm{wt}(d)$$

The following corollary follows from Theorem 1 because for any $a, a' \in E_{p^*, q^*}$, $u_E(a', q^*) = u_E(a, q^*)$ and similarly for any $d, d' \in D_{p^*, q^*}$.

Corollary 1. *Assume we have a mixed strategy Nash equilibrium (p^*, q^*). Then for any $a, a' \in E_{p^*, q^*}$, and $d, d' \in D_{p^*, q^*}^+$, we have*

$$w_a \left(1 - 2\sum_{d \supset a} q_d^*\right) = w_{a'} \left(1 - 2\sum_{d \supset a'} q_d^*\right)$$

$$2\gamma \sum_{a \subset d} p_a^* w_a - c \cdot \mathrm{wt}(d) = 2\gamma \sum_{a \subset d'} p_a^* w_a - c \cdot \mathrm{wt}(d')$$

If $0 \in D_{p^*, q^*}$, then for any $d \in D_{p,q}^+$,

$$2\gamma \sum_{a \subset d} p_a^* w_a = c \cdot \mathrm{wt}(d) \tag{6}$$

The next claim, which holds in general, says that any active defender action must cover at least one active attacker action.

claim. Let $d \in D^+_{p^*,q^*}$. Then

1. There exists an $a \subset d$ such that $a \in E_{p^*,q^*}$.
2. If $\text{wt}(d) = 1$, then $d \in E_{p^*,q^*}$ as well.

Proof. To prove (1), let $d \in D^+_{p^*,q^*}$. Then $u_D(p^*, d) \geq u_D(p^*, 0) = -\gamma <p^*, w>$, which implies $2\gamma \sum_{a \subset d} p^*_a w_a \geq c \cdot \text{wt}(d)$. Since $\text{wt}(d) > 0$, there exists a non-zero summand, i.e. there exists $a \subset d$ with $p^*_a > 0$. For (2), If $\text{wt}(d) = 1$, then there is only one possible summand: d itself, and thus $d \in E_{p^*,q^*}$.

In general, deriving explicit expressions for (p^*, q^*) is challenging and may involve a significant amount of casework. Particularly challenging is determining the active actions for both the attacker and defender. Therefore, we will shift our attention to scenarios where we can partially characterize (p^*, q^*) (and the associated active actions). In particular, we will first focus on the case where $k = 1$, and then move on to the case where our game has monotonic weights.

Rewriting the expressions from Theorem 1 for $k = 1$, we arrive at:

$$u_D(p^*, d) = 2\gamma p^*_d w_d - \gamma <p^*, w> -c \text{ for } d \neq 0 \tag{7}$$
$$u_D(p^*, 0) = -\gamma <p^*, w> \tag{8}$$
$$u_E(a, q^*) = w_a(1 - 2q^*_a) \tag{9}$$

The next lemma characterizes (p^*, q^*) for $k = 1$.

Lemma 1. *Suppose $k = 1$. Then, for any $d, d' \in D^+_{p^*,q^*}$,*

$$p^*_d = p^*_{d'} \frac{w_{d'}}{w_d}$$

For any $a, a' \in E_{p^*,q^*}$,

$$q^*_a = \frac{1}{2} - \frac{w_{a'}}{w_a}\left(\frac{1}{2} - q^*_{a'}\right)$$

In addition,

1. $D^+_{p^*,q^*} \subset E_{p^*,q^*}$.
2. If $d \in A_D$, $d \neq 0$, and $w_d < \frac{c}{2\gamma}$, then $d \notin D_{p^*,q^*}$.
3. If q^* is a mixed strategy with $|D^+_{p^*,q^*}| \geq 2$, then for any $d \in D^+_{p^*,q^*}$, $q^*_d \leq \frac{1}{2}$.

Proof. The expressions for p^*_a, q^*_d follow by applying Theorem 1 to (7), (8), (9). (1) follows from Lemma 4. (2) follows by noting that if $w_d < \frac{c}{2\gamma}$, then $u_D(p^*, d) < u_D(p^*, 0)$, and so the defender will prefer action 0 over d. For 3), suppose that there exist two non-zero actions $d, d' \in A_D$ where $q^*_d > \frac{1}{2}$. Then, $q^*_{d'} = \frac{1}{2} - \frac{w_{d'}}{w_d}\left(\frac{1}{2} - q^*_d\right) = \frac{1}{2} + \epsilon$, where $\epsilon > 0$. However, $q^*_d + q^*_{d'} > 1$, a contradiction.

We note that p_a^* is inversely proportional to w_a whereas q_d^* is proportional to w_d. Thus, the more valuable the host, the more likely it is defended. Because more valuable hosts are more likely to be defended, it is then less likely to be attacked given that the attacker and defender achieve a Nash equilibrium.

If $|D_{p^*,q^*}^+| \geq 1$, let $H = \left(\sum_{d \in D_{p^*,q^*}^+} w_d^{-1}\right)^{-1}$ be the unnormalized harmonic mean of the weights associated to the actions in D_{p^*,q^*}^+. Choose a single $d \in D_{p^*,q^*}^+$ and let $p_1 = p_d$, $w_1 = w_d$. Let $s = q_0^*$.

Lemma 2. *Suppose $k = 1$. The payoffs for each player at the Nash equilibrium (p^*, q^*) satisfy*

$$u_N(p^*, q^*) = 2\gamma s H + 2\gamma H\left(\frac{|D_{p^*,q^*}^+|}{2} - 1\right) \tag{10}$$

$$u_D(p^*, q^*) = 2\gamma s(p_1^* w_1 - H) - 2\gamma H\left(\frac{|D_{p^*,q^*}^+|}{2} - 1\right) - c \tag{11}$$

Furthermore,

$$u_N(p^*, q^*) + u_D(p^*, q^*) = 2\gamma s\, p_1^* w_1 - c = cs - c \tag{12}$$

Proof. For shorthand, let $\alpha = u_N(p^*, q^*) = \gamma u_E(p^*, q^*)$. From (9), $\gamma w_a(1 - 2q_a^*) = \alpha$ for all $a \in E_{p^*,q^*}$. Thus

$$q_a^* = \frac{1}{2}\left(1 - \frac{\alpha}{\gamma w_a}\right) \tag{13}$$

Summing the terms in (13) gives

$$1 = \sum_{d \in D_{p^*,q^*}} q_d^* = q_0^* + \frac{|D_{p^*,q^*}^+|}{2} - \frac{\alpha}{2\gamma H}$$

Writing q_0^* as a free parameter $q_0^* = s$ and solving for α gives the first result. For the second,

$$u_D(p^*, q^*) = 2\gamma p_1 w_1 - \gamma\left(\sum_{b \in D_{p^*,q^*}^+} p_b w_b + \sum_{b \in E_{p^*,q^*} \setminus D_{p^*,q^*}} p_b w_b\right) - c$$

Each term in the first sum is equal to $p_1 w_1$. For $b \in E_{p^*,q^*} \setminus D_{p^*,q^*}$, equation (9) implies $w_b = \frac{\alpha}{\gamma}$. Now

$$\sum_{b \in E_{p^*,q^*} \setminus D_{p^*,q^*}} p_b = 1 - \sum_{b \in E_{p^*,q^*}} p_b = 1 - p_1 w_1 \sum_{a \in D_{p^*,q^*}^+} \frac{1}{w_a} = 1 - p_1 w_1 H^{-1}$$

Thus

$$u_D(p^*, q^*) = 2\gamma p_1 w_1 - \gamma|D_{p^*,q^*}^+| p_1 w_1 - \alpha\left(1 - p_1 w_1 H^{-1}\right)$$

Substituting (10) for α and simplifying gives the desired result. From (6), $q_0^* = s > 0$ if and only if $p_1 w_1 = \frac{c}{2\gamma}$, so (12) holds whatever the value of s is.

We now state the following theorem which is the main result of this section. Before we can prove it, we will need several intermediate results.

Theorem 2. *Suppose that (p^*, q^*) is a Nash equilibrium for an $(n, k, c, \boldsymbol{w}, \gamma)$-honeynet game with strictly monotonic weights. Then for any active action $\boldsymbol{s} \in E_{p^*, q^*} \cup D_{p^*, q^*}$, either $\mathrm{wt}(\boldsymbol{s}) = k$ or $\mathrm{wt}(\boldsymbol{s}) = 0$.*

Lemma 3 then states that when $\boldsymbol{a}$ is an active action for the attacker, and the defender uses the mixed strategy q^* while the attacker adopts a pure strategy $\boldsymbol{a}$, then the attacker will win with probability at least $\frac{1}{2}$. Note that Lemma 3 does not depend upon the assumption that our game has strictly monotonic weights.

Lemma 3. *For $n > 2$ and any active action $\boldsymbol{a} \in E_{p^*, q^*}$,*

$$\sum_{\substack{d \in \mathcal{A}_D \\ d \supset a}} q_d^* = Pr(\boldsymbol{d} \in D_{p^*, q^*} : \boldsymbol{d} \supset \boldsymbol{a}) < \frac{1}{2}$$

Proof. Suppose $\exists \boldsymbol{a} \in E_{p^*, q^*}$ with $Pr(\boldsymbol{d} \in D_{p^*, q^*} : \boldsymbol{d} \supset \boldsymbol{a}) \geq \frac{1}{2}$. Then $u_E(\boldsymbol{a}, q^*) = \gamma w_a(1 - 2\sum_{d \supset a} q_d^*) \leq 0$, which implies that for any other $\boldsymbol{a}' \in E_{p^*, q^*}$,

$$u_E(\boldsymbol{a}', q^*) = \gamma w_{a'}(1 - 2\sum_{d \supset a'} q_d^*) \leq 0$$

since according to Theorem 1, $u_E(\boldsymbol{a}', q^*) \leq u_E(\boldsymbol{a}, q^*)$. However, this would then imply that for every vector $\bar{\boldsymbol{a}} \in \mathcal{A}_E$ with $\mathrm{wt}(\bar{\boldsymbol{a}}) = k$, we would have

$$\gamma w_{\bar{a}}(1 - 2\sum_{d \supset \bar{a}} q_d^*) = \gamma w_{\bar{a}}(1 - 2q_{\bar{a}}^*) \leq 0$$

which requires that $q_{\bar{a}}^* \geq \frac{1}{2}$. This would imply in turn that

$$\sum_{\substack{d \in \mathcal{A}_E \\ \mathrm{wt}(d) = k}} q_d^* > 1$$

when $n > 2$. When $n = 2$ and $k = 1$, it can be shown that this sum can equal 1.

We will make use of the following identity, which can easily be verified.

Lemma 4. *Let $\boldsymbol{a} \subset \bar{\boldsymbol{a}}$ be two attacker strategies. Then*

$$u_E(\bar{\boldsymbol{a}}, q^*) - u_E(\boldsymbol{a}, q^*) = \gamma(w_{\bar{a}} - w_a)\left(1 - 2\sum_{d \supset \bar{a}} q_d^*\right) + 2\gamma w_a \sum_{\substack{d \supset a \\ d \not\supset \bar{a}}} q_d^*$$

Proof. The proof rests on separating the summation over $\boldsymbol{d} \supset \boldsymbol{a}$ in (3) into a sum over $\boldsymbol{d} \supset \boldsymbol{a}$ and $\boldsymbol{d} \not\supset \boldsymbol{a}$.

The next Lemma shows that when the weights are monotonic, the only sensible choice for the defender is to either not defend any hosts or defend the maximum number allowed despite the cost.

Lemma 5. *In the monotonic weight case, all active defender actions have weight 0 or k. That is, if $d \in D_{p^*,q^*}$ and $d \neq 0$, then $\mathrm{wt}(d) = k$.*

Proof. Suppose there exists $d^* \in D_{p^*,q^*}$ with $0 < \mathrm{wt}(d^*) < k$. From Claim 4, there exists $a \in E_{p^*,q^*}$ with $d^* \supset a$. Let $\bar{a} \in \mathcal{A}_E$ be an action of weight k that covers a, i.e. $\bar{a} \supset a$. We show that $u_E(\bar{a}, q^*) > u_E(a, q^*)$, contradicting that a is an active attacker action in the Nash equilibrium (p^*, q^*). By Lemma 4,

$$u_E(\bar{a}, q^*) - u_E(a, q^*) = \gamma(w_{\bar{a}} - w_a)(1 - 2q^*_{\bar{a}}) + 2\gamma w_a \sum_{\substack{d \supset a \\ d \not\supset \bar{a}}} q^*_d \geq 2\gamma w_a q^*_{d^*} > 0$$

The first inequality follows because $q^*_{\bar{a}} \leq \sum_{d \supset a} q^*_d < \frac{1}{2}$ by Lemma 3, and $w_{\bar{a}} \geq w_a$. The second follows because $q^*_{d^*} > 0$ since d^* is active.

In the strictly monotonic case, the attacker behaves similarly to the defender in that it will attack the maximum number of hosts. Interestingly, strictly monotonic is needed to motivate the attacker despite incurring no cost per host.

Lemma 6. *In the strictly monotonic case, all active attacker actions have weight k.*

Proof. Suppose there exists some $a \in E_{p^*,q^*}$ with $\mathrm{wt}(a) < k$. As in the proof of Lemma 5, let $\bar{a} \in \mathcal{A}_E$ be an action of weight k that covers a. Then

$$u_E(\bar{a}, q^*) - u_E(a, q^*) \geq \gamma(w_{\bar{a}} - w_a)\left(1 - 2\sum_{d \supset \bar{a}} q^*_d\right) > 0$$

This holds since $w_{\bar{a}} > w_a$, and $\sum_{d \supset \bar{a}} q^*_d < \frac{1}{2}$ by Lemma 3.

Theorem 2 now follows immediately from Lemmas 5, 6. As a consequence of Theorem 2, if the weights w_a are strictly monotonic for an (n, k, c, w, γ)-honeynet game, then $u_E(a, q^*), u_D(p^*, d)$ have the following expressions for p^*, q^*, which mirror the $k = 1$ case:

$$u_D(p^*, d) = 2\gamma p^*_d w_d - \gamma <p^*, w> -kc \text{ for } d \neq 0 \tag{14}$$

$$u_D(p^*, 0) = -\gamma <p^*, w> \tag{15}$$

$$u_E(a, q^*) = w_a(1 - 2q^*_a) \tag{16}$$

Thus, the behaviors of the attacker and defender will be as before. In particular, the attacker will always attack k hosts and p^*_a will be inversely proportional to w_a. Under this setup, the defender will defend either zero or k hosts and q^*_d will be proportional to w_d.

We now show a similar version of Theorem 2 under the relaxed assumption that the weights are monotonic.

Theorem 3. *Suppose that (p^*, q^*) is a Nash equilibrium for an (n, k, c, w, γ)-honeynet game with monotonic weights. Then, for any $d \in D^+_{p^*,q^*}$, $\mathrm{wt}(d) = k$. Furthermore, there exists a $\tilde{p}$ such that $u_E(\tilde{p}, q^*) = u_E(p^*, q^*)$ and $u_D(\tilde{p}, q^*) = u_D(p^*, q^*)$ where every $a \in E_{\tilde{p},q^*}$ has weight k.*

Proof. The fact that all $d \in D_{p^*,q^*}$, $\mathrm{wt}(d) \in \{0, k\}$ follows immediately from the first part of the proof of Theorem 2, where it was shown that if there exists at least one $d^* \in D_{p^*,q^*}^+$ where $\mathrm{wt}(d^*) < k$, then (p^*, q^*) is not a Nash. The second part of the lemma follows from the same logic as in the proof of Lemma 6.

We note that as a result of Theorem 3, the expressions in (14) and (15) will hold in this case as well. The reason why (16) also does not hold is the following. Suppose $w_a = w_d$ where $d \supset a$ and $\mathrm{wt}(d) = k$. Under this setup, the attacker has no incentive to choose d rather than a since the payoff is the same. However, it should be noted that the payoff to the attacker would be the same if he/she chooses the action d rather than a since there is no penalty associated with choosing to attack a larger number of hosts.

5   Conclusions and Future Work

We have extended prior work using honeynets by allowing for variable payoffs for each attack vector a, as well as introducing a cost c to the defender for each honeypot employed. We feel that allowing the attacker to be successful even when only one of the targeted hosts is compromised more closely mirrors scenarios of interest. Our work here sets up the framework to analyze these types of scenarios through future work.

One interesting result of our framework is the counter-intuitive result that increasing the value of a host causes an attacker to target it with lower probability. This is as a result of the defender being more likely to defend the host, causing the attacker instead to shift away from it since it did not matter where exactly the attacker found their foothold.

However, this behavior may well result from the asymmetry in the cost structure: the attacker can target any number of hosts at will, while the defender has to consider the cost c. Future work could include assigning a similar marginal cost σ to the attacker. We anticipate the relative value of this constant vis-a-vis the values w_a to affect the Nash Equilibria just as the defender marginal cost did, i.e. by allowing for special cases arising from inequalities involving γ, c, σ.

Theorem 2 then indicates that regardless of the resource limitation of attacking or defending k hosts, neither player will chose to engage in half measures. They will either do nothing or act maximally. For the attacker this seems fairly straightforward as there is no cost, but for the defender it is interesting as they do suffer that marginal cost per host defended and still choose to defend as many as possible (if they choose to act at all).

While we used Lemma 3 in order to prove Theorem 2, the significance of the lemma itself is worth pointing out. It formally captures just how significant the asymmetric disadvantage is for the defender. In the Nash equilibrium, instead of having to carefully craft an ideal mixed strategy, the attacker can simply pick from any of the active strategies that comprise the equilibrium and win at least half the time (a very loose bound). So while the defender is carefully crafting their strategy the attacker basically does not even have to try.

A novel development to consider at this point would be breaking the symmetry of information. In the current instantiation of our game, both players know the payoffs w_a. It is conceivable that the attacker's valuations of each attack vector a are inaccurate. In such a situation, the players would hold different beliefs about the equilibrium strategies, and playing them may turn out to generate higher payoffs to the defender for certain defender strategies. Through deception, it may be possible for the defender to manipulate the attacker's beliefs of the payoffs. One way to accomplish this would be to make a honeypot appear like a real machine running a particular service with known vulnerabilites.

A natural extension is to consider a dynamic game, where attacker and defender take turns in sequence, adjusting their strategies depending on the actions of the other player. A more subtle method for the defender to achieve deception is to play sub-optimally in the initial stage of the game in order to confuse the attacker. The attacker could doubt their valuation of the payoffs or the sophistication of the defender and get lured into altering their own play, allowing the defender to spring a trap otherwise unreachable from the Nash equilibrium.

Acknowledgements. We thank Kimberly Ferguson-Walter and Dr. Sunny Fugate for their technical direction and the reviewers for their helpful comments.

References

1. Carroll, T.E., Grosu, D.: A game theoretic investigation of deception in network security. In: 2009 Proceedings of 18th International Conference on Computer Communications and Networks - ICCCN 2009, pp. 1–6. IEEE (2009)
2. Dutt, V., Ahn, Y.S., Gonzalez, C.: Cyber situation awareness: modeling detection of cyber attacks with instance-based learning theory. Hum. Factors **55**(3), 605–618 (2013). https://doi.org/10.1177/0018720812464045
3. Garg, N., Grosu, D.: Deception in HoneyNets: a game-theoretic analysis. In: 2007 IEEE SMC Information Assurance and Security Workshop, pp. 107–113. IEEE (2007)
4. Gonzalez, C., Dutt, V.: Instance-based learning: integrating sampling and repeated decisions from experience. Psychol. Rev. **118**(4), 523 (2011)
5. Kahneman, D., Tversky, A.: Prospect theory: an analysis of decision under risk, pp. 99–127. World Scientific (2013). chap. 6. https://doi.org/10.1142/9789814417358_0006
6. Liu, Y., Comaniciu, C., Man, H.: A Bayesian game approach for intrusion detection in wireless ad hoc networks. In: Proceedings from the 2006 Workshop, p. 4. ACM Press, New York (2006)
7. Píbil, R., Lisý, V., Kiekintveld, C., Bošanský, B., Pěchouček, M.: Game theoretic model of strategic honeypot selection in computer networks. In: Grossklags, J., Walrand, J. (eds.) GameSec 2012. LNCS, vol. 7638, pp. 201–220. Springer, Heidelberg (2012). https://doi.org/10.1007/978-3-642-34266-0_12
8. Rowe, N.C., Custy, E.J.: Deception in cyber-attacks (2007). https://calhoun.nps.edu/handle/10945/36422

Perfectly Secure Message Transmission Against Rational Timid Adversaries

Maiki Fujita[1], Kenji Yasunaga[2] , and Takeshi Koshiba[3]([envelope])

[1] Graduate School of Science and Engineering, Saitama University, Saitama, Japan
[2] Graduate School of Information Science and Technology, Osaka University,
Osaka, Japan
yasunaga@ist.osaka-u.ac.jp
[3] Faculty of Education and Integrated Arts and Sciences, Waseda University,
Tokyo, Japan
tkoshiba@waseda.jp

Abstract. Secure Message Transmission (SMT) is a two-party cryptographic protocol by which the sender can securely and reliably transmit messages to the receiver using multiple channels. It is assumed that an adversary corrupts a subset of the channels, and makes eavesdropping and tampering over the corrupted channels. In this work, we consider a game-theoretic security model for SMT. Specifically, we introduce a rational adversary who has the preference for the outcome of the protocol execution. We show that, under some reasonable assumption on the adversary's preference, even if the adversary corrupts all but one of the channels, it is possible to construct SMT protocols with perfect security against rational adversaries. More specifically, we consider "timid" adversaries who prefer to violate the security requirement of SMT, but do not prefer the tampering actions to be detected. In the traditional cryptographic setting, perfect SMT can be constructed only when the adversary corrupt a minority of the channels. Our results demonstrate a way of circumventing the impossibility results of cryptographic protocols based on a game-theoretic approach.

Keywords: Cryptography · Secure message transmission
Game theory · Rational adversary

1 Introduction

It is common to use the information network to send and receive messages. In the physical sense, the channels between senders and receivers might be realized by combining apparatus for communication, which allow some adversary to eavesdrop or tamper. As a technique for protecting data over communication from their leakage, we often use public-key cryptosystems. Since the security of public-key cryptosystems is based on computational assumptions and the computational assumptions might be falsified, it is desirable to develop methods of protecting data in the information-theoretic sense.

© Springer Nature Switzerland AG 2018
L. Bushnell et al. (Eds.): GameSec 2018, LNCS 11199, pp. 127–144, 2018.
https://doi.org/10.1007/978-3-030-01554-1_8

While a single communication channel is assumed in the typical two-party cryptographic schemes, the current information network technologies can let many channels be available. Secure Message Transmission (SMT), originally proposed by Dolev et al. [10], is a cryptographic protocol by which a sender can transmit messages through multiple channels in a secure way. Even if any adversary corrupts t out of n channels and makes eavesdropping and tampering over the corrupted channels, the messages are securely and correctly transmitted to the receiver by using SMT. The requirements for SMT consist of *privacy* and *reliability*. The privacy guarantees that the adversary can obtain no information about the transmitted message, and the reliability does that the message transmitted by the sender is recovered by the receiver. If an SMT protocol satisfies both the requirements in the perfect sense, the protocol is called a *perfect* SMT. The most round-efficient perfect SMT is given by Kurosawa and Suzuki [29]. Dolev et al. [10] showed that any one-round perfect SMT must satisfy $t < n/3$ and any perfect SMT whose round complexity is at least two must satisfy $t < n/2$. Franklin and Wright [11] defined *almost-reliable* SMT, which allows transmission failures of small probability. They showed that almost-reliable SMT against $t < n$ corruptions is achievable by using a public channel in addition to the normal channels. Later, Garay and Ostrovsky [15] and Shi et al. [32] gave the most round-efficient almost-reliable SMT protocols using public channels.

In the standard setting in cryptography, the participants are assumed to be either honest or malicious. The former follow the protocol description honestly, and the later may deviate from the protocol maliciously. In general, malicious behavior may be illegal and involve some risks, which implies that adversaries in the standard cryptographic setting behave maliciously regardless of their risk. However, some adversary in reality may decide his behavior by taking the risk into account. To capture such situations, we incorporate the notion of "rational" participants of game theory into cryptography. Halpern and Teague [22] firstly studied the rational behavior of participants in cryptography in the context of secret sharing. Since then, rational secret sharing has been intensively studied [1,4,12,16,26–28]. Moreover, there have been many studies using game-theoretic analysis of cryptographic primitives/protocols, including two-party computation [3,18], leader election [2,17], Byzantine agreement [19], consensus [23], public-key encryption [35,36], delegation of computation [5,7,8,20,21,24], and protocol design [13,14]. Among them, several work [5,13,19–21] used the rationality of adversaries to circumvent the existing impossibility results.

Groce et al. [19] studied the problem of Byzantine agreement in the presence of a rational adversary. They showed that, given some knowledge of the adversary's preference, perfectly secure Byzantine agreement is possible for t corruptions among n players for any $t < n$, for which the impossibility against $t \geq n/2$ corruptions is known in the standard setting.

In this work, we show that the impossibility results of SMT can be also circumvented by considering the rationality of adversaries. As in the case of Byzantine agreement, we introduce a rational adversary for SMT who has some preference for the outcome of the protocol execution. More specifically, we define *timid* adversaries who prefer to violate the security requirements of SMT, but do not prefer the tampering actions to be detected. For such adversaries, first we show that the almost-reliable SMT protocol of [32], which employs a tamper-proof public channel, works as a "perfect" SMT protocol. Second, we show that, for "strictly" timid adversaries, who prefer being undetected to violating the security requirements, secret sharing schemes with some robustness can be used as a non-interactive SMT protocol. Both protocols are perfectly secure against timid adversaries corrupting t out of n channels for any $t < n$, which is impossible in the standard setting of SMT protocols. In addition, we present an impossibility result of constructing SMT protocols against general timid adversaries corrupting $t \geq n/2$ channels. The result demonstrates the necessities of the tamper-proof public channel in the first protocol and the restriction of strictly timid adversaries in the second protocol. The results are summarized in Table 1.

Table 1. Summary of previous work and our results.

Adversary types	PC*	Resiliency	Security	Construction
Malicious	–	$t < n/2$	Perfect	Exist [10, 29]
Malicious	–	$t \geq n/2$	Perfect	Impossible [10]
Malicious	✓	$t < n$	Almost reliable	Exist [11, 15, 32])
Timid	✓	$t < n$	Perfect	Exist (Theorem 4)
Strictly timid	–	$t < n$	Perfect	Exist (Theorem 5)
Timid	–	$t \geq n/2$	Perfect	Impossible (Corollary 2)

* PC represents the use of the public channel.

2 Preliminaries

2.1 Secure Message Transmission

We assume that a sender S and a receiver R are connected by n channels, and they may use an authentic and reliable *public channel*. Messages sent over the public channel are publicly accessible and correctly delivered to the receiver. SMT protocols proceed in *rounds*. In each round, one party may synchronously send a message over each channel and the public channel. The messages will be delivered before the next round starts.

The adversary A can corrupt at most t channels. Such an adversary is referred to as t-*adversary*. Messages sent over corrupted channels can be eavesdropped and tampered by the adversary. We assume that A is computationally *unbounded*.

Let M be the message space. In SMT, the sender tries to send a message in M to the receiver by using n channels and the public channel, and the receiver outputs some message after the protocol execution. For an SMT protocol Π, let

M_S denote the random variable of the message sent by $\mathcal{S}$ and M_R the message output by $\mathcal{R}$ in Π. An execution of Π can be completely characterized by the random coins of all the parties, namely, $\mathcal{S}$, $\mathcal{M}$, and $\mathcal{A}$, and the message M_S sent by $\mathcal{S}$. Let $V_A(m, r_A)$ denote the *view* of $\mathcal{A}$ when the protocol is executed with $M_S = m$ and the random coins r_A of $\mathcal{A}$. Specifically, $V_A(m, r_A)$ consists of the messages sent over the corrupted channels and the public channel when the protocol is run with $M_S = m$ and $\mathcal{A}$'s random coins r_A.

We formally define the properties of SMT protocols.

Definition 1. *A protocol between $\mathcal{S}$ and $\mathcal{R}$ is (ε, δ)-Secure Message Transmission (SMT) against t-adversary if the following three conditions are satisfied against any t-adversary $\mathcal{A}$.*

- *Correctness: For any $m \in \mathcal{M}$, if $M_S = m$ and $\mathcal{A}$ does not corrupt any channels, then $\Pr[M_R = m] = 1$;*
- *Privacy: For any $m_0, m_1 \in \mathcal{M}$ and $r_A \in \{0, 1\}^*$, it holds that*

$$\mathrm{SD}(V_A(m_0, r_A), V_A(m_1, r_A)) \leq \varepsilon,$$

where $\mathrm{SD}(X, Y)$ denotes the statistical distance between two random variables X and Y over a set Ω, which is defined by

$$\mathrm{SD}(X, Y) = \frac{1}{2} \sum_{u \in \Omega} |\Pr[X = u] - \Pr[Y = u]|;$$

- *Reliability: For any message $m \in \mathcal{M}$, when $M_S = m$,*

$$\Pr[M_R \neq m] \leq \delta,$$

where the probability is taken over the random coins of $\mathcal{S}$, $\mathcal{R}$, and $\mathcal{A}$.

If a protocol achieves $(0, 0)$-SMT, the protocol is called *perfect* SMT, and if a protocol achieves $(0, \delta)$-SMT, which admits transmission failures of small probability δ, the protocol is called *almost-reliable* SMT.

For perfect SMT, Dolev *et al.* [10] showed the below.

Theorem 1 ([10]). *Perfect SMT protocols against t-adversary are achievable if and only if $t < n/2$.*

2.2 Secure Message Transmission with Public Channel

In this paper, we will employ an almost-reliable SMT protocol given by Shi, Jiang, Safavi-Naini, and Tuhin [32], and refer it as the SJST protocol. Note that we only use some specific properties of the SJST protocol in the security analysis. Thus, other protocols, such as one by Garay and Ostrovsky [15], can also be employed instead of the SJST protocol.

Let us review the SJST protocol, which uses the public channel. The protocol is based on the simple protocol for "static" adversaries in which the sender sends a random key R_i over the i-th channel for each $i \in \{1, \ldots, n\}$, and the encrypted message $c = m \oplus R_1 \oplus \cdots \oplus R_n$ over the public channel. Suppose that the adversary sees the messages sent over the corrupted channels, but does not change them. Since the adversary cannot see at least one key R_j when corrupting less than n channels, the mask $R_1 \oplus \cdots \oplus R_n$ for the encryption looks random for the adversary. Thus, the message m can be securely encrypted and reliably sent through the public channel. To cope with "active" adversaries, who may change messages sent over the corrupted channels, the SJST protocol employs a mechanism for detecting the adversary's tampering by using hash functions. Specifically, the *universal* hash functions (see Appendix A) satisfy the following property: when a pair of keys (r_i, R_i) is changed to $(r_i', R_i') \neq (r_i, R_i)$, the hash value for (r_i, R_i) is different from that for (r_i', R_i') with high probability if the hash function is chosen randomly after the tampering occurred. In the SJST protocol, the sender sends a pair of keys (r_i, R_i) over the i-th channel. Then, the receiver chooses n universal hash functions h_i's, and sends them over the public channel. By comparing hash values for (r_i, R_i)'s sent by the sender with those for (r_i', R_i')'s received by the receiver, they can identify the channels for which messages, i.e., keys, were tampered with. By ignoring keys sent over such channels, the sender can correctly encrypt a message m with untampered keys and send the encryption reliably over the public channel.

We describe the SJST protocol below, which is a three-round protocol, and achieves the reliability with $\delta = (n-1) \cdot 2^{1-\ell}$, where ℓ is the length of hash values.

Protocol 1 (The SJST protocol [32]). Let n be the number of channels, $m \in \mathcal{M}$ the message to be sent by the sender $\mathcal{S}$, and $H = \{h \colon \{0,1\}^k \to \{0,1\}^\ell\}$ a class of universal hash functions.

1. For each $i \in \{1, \ldots, n\}$, $\mathcal{S}$ chooses $r_i \in \{0,1\}^\ell$ and $R_i \in \{0,1\}^k$ uniformly at random, and sends the pair (r_i, R_i) over the i-th channel.
2. For each $i \in \{1, \ldots, n\}$, $\mathcal{R}$ receives (r_i', R_i') through the i-th channel, and then chooses $h_i \leftarrow H$ uniformly at random. If $|r_i'| \neq \ell$ or $|R_i'| \neq k$, set $b_i = 1$, and otherwise, set $b_i = 0$. Then, set $T_i' = r_i' \oplus h_i(R_i')$, and $H_i = (h_i, T_i')$ if $b_i = 0$, and $H_i = \perp$ otherwise. Finally, $\mathcal{R}$ sends $(B, H_1, \ldots, H_n)$ over the public channel, where $B = (b_1, \ldots, b_n)$.
3. $\mathcal{S}$ receives $(B, H_1, \ldots, H_n)$ through the public channel. For each $i \in \{1, \ldots, n\}$ with $b_i = 0$, $\mathcal{S}$ computes $T_i = r_i \oplus h_i(R_i)$, and sets $v_i = 0$ if $T_i = T_i'$, and $v_i = 1$ otherwise. Then, $\mathcal{S}$ sends (V, c) over the public channel, where $V = (v_1, \ldots, v_n)$, and $c = m \oplus (\bigoplus_{v_i=0} R_i)$.
4. On receiving (V, c), $\mathcal{R}$ recovers $m = c \oplus (\bigoplus_{v_i=0} R_i)$.

Theorem 2 ([32]). *The SJST protocol is $(0, (n-1) \cdot 2^{1-\ell})$-SMT against t-adversary for any $t < n$.*

We can find a complete proof of the above theorem in [32]. For self-containment, we give a brief sketch of the proof.

- *Privacy*: The adversary can get $c = m \oplus (\bigoplus_{v_i=0} R_i)$ through the public channel. Since m is masked by uniformly random R_i's, the adversary has to corrupt all the i-th channels with $v_i = 0$ to recover m. However, since any t-adversary can corrupt at most t $(< n)$ channels, the adversary can cause $v_i = 1$ for at most $n - 1$ i's. Hence, there is at least one i with $v_i = 0$, for which the adversary cannot obtain R_i. Thus, the protocol satisfies the perfect privacy.
- *Reliability*: Since the protocol uses the public channel at the second and the third rounds, the adversary can tamper with channels only at the first round. Suppose that the adversary tampers with (r_i, R_i). If $R_i \neq R_i'$ and $T_i = T_i'$, then $\mathcal{R}$ would recover a wrong message, but the tampering is not detected. It follows from Lemma 1 that the probability that the above event happens is at most $(n - 1)2^{1-\ell}$. Thus, the protocol achieves the reliability with $\delta = (n - 1) \cdot 2^{1-\ell}$.

2.3 Robust Secret Sharing

Secret sharing, introduced by Shamir [31] and Blackley [6], enables us to distribute the secret information in a secure way. Let $s \in \mathbb{F}$ be a secret from some finite field $\mathbb{F}$. A (threshold) secret-sharing scheme gives a way for distributing s into n shares $s_1, \ldots, s_n$ such that, for some parameter $t > 0$, (1) any t shares give no information about s; and (2) any $t + 1$ shares uniquely determine s. Shamir [31] give a scheme based on polynomial evaluations for any $t < n$.

Shamir's scheme also achieves *robustness* in the sense that even if $t/3$ shares are maliciously tampered, the original secret can be correctly recovered. Although the robustness is a desirable property, it is known that robust secret sharing is impossible when $t/2$ shares are tampered with [25].

In this work, we need a weaker notion of robustness in which any tampering actions should be detected with high probability. Such robust secret sharing was studied by Cramer et al. [9]. They introduced the notion of *algebraic manipulation detection (AMD) codes*, and presented a simple way for constructing robust secret sharing from *linear* secret sharing and AMD codes. More precisely, the robustness required for our protocol is slightly different from one defined in [9].[1]

Definition 2. *Let t, n be positive integers with $t < n$. A (t, n, δ)-robust secret sharing scheme with range $\mathcal{G}$ consists of two algorithms* (Share, Reconst) *satisfying the following conditions:*

- *Correctness: For any $s \in \mathcal{G}$ and $I \subseteq \{1, \ldots, n\}$ with $|I| > t$,*

$$\Pr\left[\mathsf{Reconst}\left(\{i, s_i\}_{i \in I}\right) = s\right] = 1,$$

where $(s_1, \ldots, s_n) \leftarrow \mathsf{Share}(s)$.

---

[1] The robustness in [9] requires that the output of the reconstruction algorithm should be either the original message or the failure symbol with high probability. Namely, it is allowed to recover the original message even if some shares are tampered with. In Definition 2, we require that if some shares are tampered with, the output of the reconstruction algorithm should be the failure symbol.

- Perfect Privacy: *For any $s, s' \in \mathcal{G}$ and $I \subseteq \{1, \ldots, n\}$ with $|I| \leq t$,*

$$\mathrm{SD}\left(\{s_i\}_{i \in I}, \{s'_i\}_{i \in I}\right) = 0,$$

where $(s_1, \ldots, s_n) \leftarrow \mathsf{Share}(s)$ and $(s'_1, \ldots, s'_n) \leftarrow \mathsf{Share}(s')$.
- Robustness: *For any $s \in \mathcal{G}$ and $I \subseteq \{1, \ldots, n\}$ with $|I| \leq t$ and adversary $\mathcal{A}$, if $\tilde{s}_i \neq s_i$ for some $i \in \{1, \ldots, n\}$,*

$$\Pr\left[\mathsf{Reconst}\left(\{i, \tilde{s}_i\}_{i \in \{1, \ldots, n\}}\right) \neq \bot\right] \leq \delta,$$

where

$$\tilde{s}_i = \begin{cases} \mathcal{A}(i, s, \{s_i\}_{i \in I}) & \text{if } i \in I \\ s_i & \text{if } i \notin I \end{cases}$$

and $(s_1, \ldots, s_n) \leftarrow \mathsf{Share}(s)$.

We can see that the construction of [9] satisfies the above definition. Specifically, we have the following theorem, which will be used in our protocol against strictly timid adversaries in Sect. 4.2. See Appendix B for the proof.

Theorem 3. *Let $\mathbb{F}$ be a finite field of size q and characteristic p, and d an integer such that $d + 2$ is not divisible by p. For any positive integers t and n satisfying $t < n \leq qd$, there is an explicit and efficient scheme of $(t, n, (d+1)/q)$-robust secret sharing with range $\mathbb{F}^d$, where each share is an element of $\mathbb{F}^{d+2}$.*

3   Rational Secure Message Transmission

We define our security model of SMT in the presence of a rational adversary. A rationality of the adversary is characterized by a *utility function* which represents the preference of the adversary over possible outcomes of the protocol execution.

We can consider various preferences of the adversary regarding the SMT protocol execution. The adversary may prefer to violate the privacy or the reliability of SMT protocols. In addition, the adversary may prefer to violate the above properties without the detection of tampering actions. Here, we consider the adversary who prefers (1) to violate the privacy, (2) to violate the reliability, (3) the tampering actions to be undetected, and (4) the protocol execution to be finished without abort.

To define the utility function, we specify the SMT game as follows.

The SMT Game. First set four parameters $\mathsf{guess} = \mathsf{suc} = \mathsf{detect} = \mathsf{abort} = 0$. Given an SMT protocol Π with the message space $\mathcal{M}$, choose $m \in \mathcal{M}$ uniformly at random, and run the protocol Π in which the message to be sent is $M_S = m$. In the protocol execution, as in the usual SMT, the adversary $\mathcal{A}$ can corrupt at most t channels, and tamper with any messages sent over the corrupted channels. If the protocol finishes with abort, set $\mathsf{abort} = 1$. If the sender or the receiver sends a special message "DETECTION" during the execution, set $\mathsf{detect} = 1$. After running the protocol, the receiver outputs M_R, and the adversary outputs M_A.

If $M_R = M_S$, set suc $= 1$. If $M_A = M_S$, set guess $= 1$. The outcome of the game is (guess, suc, detect, abort).

The utility of the adversary is defined as the expected utility in the SMT game.

Definition 3 (Utility). *The utility $u(\mathcal{A}, U)$ of the adversary $\mathcal{A}$ with utility function U is the expected value $E[U(\text{out})]$, where U is a function that maps the outcome $\text{out} = (\text{guess}, \text{suc}, \text{detect}, \text{abort})$ of the SMT game by $\mathcal{A}$ to real values, and the probability is taken over the random coins of the sender, the receiver, and the adversary, and a random choice of message M_S.*

The utility function U characterizes the type of adversaries. If the adversary has the preferences (1)-(4) as above, the utility function may have the property such that for any two outcomes $\text{out} = (\text{guess}, \text{suc}, \text{detect}, \text{abort})$ and $\text{out}' = (\text{guess}', \text{suc}', \text{detect}', \text{abort}')$ of the SMT game,

1. $U(\text{out}) > U(\text{out}')$ if guess $>$ guess$'$, suc $=$ suc$'$, detect $=$ detect$'$, and abort $=$ abort$'$;
2. $U(\text{out}) > U(\text{out}')$ if guess $=$ guess$'$, suc $<$ suc$'$, detect $=$ detect$'$, and abort $=$ abort$'$;
3. $U(\text{out}) > U(\text{out}')$ if guess $=$ guess$'$, suc $=$ suc$'$, detect $<$ detect$'$, and abort $=$ abort$'$;
4. $U(\text{out}) > U(\text{out}')$ if guess $=$ guess$'$, suc $=$ suc$'$, detect $=$ detect$'$, and abort $<$ abort$'$.

Based on the utility function of the adversary, we define the security of rational secure message transmission.

Definition 4 (Security of RSMT). *An SMT protocol Π is perfectly secure against rational t-adversaries with utility function U if there is a t-adversary $\mathcal{B}$ such that for any t-adversary $\mathcal{A}$,*

1. *Perfect security: Π is $(0,0)$-SMT against $\mathcal{B}$; and*
2. *Nash equilibrium: $u(\mathcal{A}, U) \leq u(\mathcal{B}, U)$ in the SMT game.*

The perfect security guarantees that an adversary $\mathcal{B}$ is *harmless*. The Nash equilibrium guarantees that no adversary $\mathcal{A}$ can gain more utility than $\mathcal{B}$. Thus, the above security of RSMT implies that no adversary $\mathcal{A}$ can gain more utility than the harmless adversary. Namely, the adversary does not have an incentive to deviate from the strategy of the harmless adversary $\mathcal{B}$.

In the security proof of our protocol, we will consider an adversary $\mathcal{B}$ who does not corrupt any channels, and outputs M_A by choosing a message uniformly at random from $\mathcal{M}$. For such $\mathcal{B}$, the perfect privacy and reliability immediately follows if Π satisfies the correctness.

4   Protocols Against Timid Adversaries

We present several protocols that are secure against *timid* rational adversaries. Timid adversaries are rational adversaries who firstly do not prefer the tampering to be detected, and secondly prefer to violate the reliability.

More formally, utility function U of such adversaries should have the properties such that

1. $U(\text{out}) > U(\text{out}')$ if $\text{suc} < \text{suc}'$ and $\text{detect} = \text{detect}'$; and
2. $U(\text{out}) > U(\text{out}')$ if $\text{suc} = \text{suc}'$ and $\text{detect} < \text{detect}'$,

where $\text{out} = (\text{guess}, \text{suc}, \text{detect}, \text{abort})$ and $\text{out}' = (\text{guess}', \text{suc}', \text{detect}', \text{abort}')$ are the outcomes of the SMT game. Let U_{timid} be the set of utility functions that satisfy the above conditions.

In addition, timid adversaries may have the following property:

3. $U(\text{out}) > U(\text{out}')$ if $\text{suc} > \text{suc}'$ and $\text{detect} < \text{detect}'$.

Let $U_{\text{timid}}^{\text{st}}$ be the set of utility functions satisfying the above three conditions. An adversary is said to be *timid* if his utility function is in U_{timid}, and *strictly timid* if the utility function is in $U_{\text{timid}}^{\text{st}}$.

In the analysis of our protocols, we need the following four values of utility:

- u_1 is the utility when $\Pr[\text{guess} = 1] = 1/|\mathcal{M}|$, $\text{suc} = 0$, $\text{detect} = 0$, and $\text{abort} = 0$;
- u_2 is the utility when $\Pr[\text{guess} = 1] = 1/|\mathcal{M}|$, $\text{suc} = 1$, $\text{detect} = 0$, and $\text{abort} = 0$;
- u_3 is the utility when $\Pr[\text{guess} = 1] = 1/|\mathcal{M}|$, $\text{suc} = 0$, $\text{detect} = 1$, and $\text{abort} = 0$;
- u_4 is the utility when $\Pr[\text{guess} = 1] = 1/|\mathcal{M}|$, $\text{suc} = 1$, $\text{detect} = 1$, and $\text{abort} = 0$;

It follows from the properties of utility functions in U_{timid} that the relations $u_1 > \max\{u_2, u_3\}$ and $\min\{u_2, u_3\} > u_4$ hold. For utility functions in $U_{\text{timid}}^{\text{st}}$, it holds that $u_1 > u_2 > u_3 > u_4$.

4.1 Protocol with Public Channel

We show that the SJST protocol of [32] works as a perfect SMT protocol against timid adversaries. More specifically, we slightly modify the SJST protocol such that in the second and the third rounds, if $b_i = 1$ in B or $v_j = 1$ in V for some $i, j \in \{1, \ldots, n\}$, the special message "DETECTION" is also sent together. We clarify the parameters for which the SJST protocol works as RSMT against timid adversaries.

Theorem 4. *If the parameter ℓ in the SJST protocol satisfies*

$$\ell \geq \max\left\{1 + \log t + \log \frac{u_3 - u_4}{u_2 - u_4 - \alpha}, 1 + \frac{1}{t}\log \frac{u_1 - u_3}{\alpha}\right\}$$

for some $\alpha \in (0, u_2 - u_4)$, then the protocol is perfectly secure against rational t-adversaries with utility function $U \in U_{\text{timid}}$ for any $t < n$.

Proof. We consider the adversary $\mathcal{B}$ in Definition 4 such that $\mathcal{B}$ does not corrupt any channels, and outputs a uniformly random message from $\mathcal{M}$ as M_A. Then, the perfect security of Definition 4 immediately follows.

Next, we show that the strategy of $\mathcal{B}$ is a Nash equilibrium. Note that $u(\mathcal{B}, U) = u_2$, since $\Pr[\text{guess} = 1] = \Pr[M_A = M_S] = 1/|\mathcal{M}|$ in the SMT game. Thus, it is sufficient to show that $u(\mathcal{A}, U) \leq u_2$ for any t-adversary $\mathcal{A}$. Also, note that, since the SJST protocol achieves the perfect privacy, it holds that $\Pr[\text{guess} = 1] = 1/|\mathcal{M}|$ for any t-adversary.

Since messages in the second and the third rounds are sent through the public channel, the adversary $\mathcal{A}$ can tamper with messages only in the first round. If $\mathcal{A}$ changes the lengths of r_i and R_i, the tampering of the i-th channel will be detected. Such channels are simply ignored in the second and third rounds. Thus, such tampering cannot increase the utility. Hence, we assume that $\mathcal{A}$ does not change the lengths of r_i and R_i in the first round.

Suppose that $\mathcal{A}$ corrupts some t channels in the first round. Namely, there are exactly t distinct i's such that $(r'_i, R'_i) \neq (r_i, R_i)$. Note that the tampering on the i-th channel such that $r'_i \neq r_i$ and $R'_i = R_i$ does not increase the probability that $\text{suc} = 0$, but may increase the probability of detection. Thus, we also assume that $R'_i \neq R_i$ for all the corrupted channels. We define the following three events:

- E_1: No tampering action is detected in the protocol;
- E_2: At least one but not all tampering actions are detected;
- E_3: All the t tampering actions are detected.

Note that all the events are disjoint, and either event should occur. Namely, we have that $\Pr[E_1] + \Pr[E_2] + \Pr[E_3] = 1$. It follows from the discussion in Sect. A that the probability that the tampering action on one channel is not detected is $2^{1-\ell}$. Since each hash function h_i is chosen independently for each channel, we have that $\Pr[E_1] = 2^{(1-\ell)t}$. Similarly, we obtain that $\Pr[E_3] = (1 - 2^{1-\ell})^t$. Note that the utility when E_1 occurs is at most u_1. Also, the utilities when E_2 and E_3 occur are at most u_3 and u_4, respectively. Therefore, the utility of $\mathcal{A}$ is

$$
\begin{aligned}
u(\mathcal{A}, U) &\leq u_1 \cdot \Pr[E_1] + u_3 \cdot \Pr[E_2] + u_4 \cdot \Pr[E_3] \\
&= u_3 + (u_1 - u_3)\Pr[E_1] - (u_3 - u_4)\Pr[E_3] \\
&\leq u_3 + (u_1 - u_3)2^{(1-\ell)t} - (u_3 - u_4)\left(1 - t2^{1-\ell}\right) \\
&\leq u_3 + \alpha - (u_3 - u_4)\left(1 - t2^{1-\ell}\right) \\
&\leq u_2,
\end{aligned}
$$
(1)
(2)

where we use the relations $\ell \geq 1 + \frac{1}{t}\log\frac{u_1 - u_3}{\alpha}$ and $\ell \geq 1 + \log t + \log\frac{u_3 - u_4}{u_2 - u_4 - \alpha}$ in (1) and (2), respectively. Thus, the utility of $\mathcal{A}$ is at most u_2, and hence the statement follows. $\qquad\square$

If $u_2 > u_3$, which holds for strictly timid adversaries, by choosing $\alpha = u_2 - u_3$, the condition on ℓ is that

$$
\ell \geq \max\left\{1 + \log t, 1 + \frac{1}{t}\log\frac{u_1 - u_3}{u_2 - u_3}\right\}.
$$

4.2 Protocol Without Public Channel Against Strictly Timid Adversaries

We show that, under the condition that $u_2 > u_3$, robust secret sharing of Definition 2 gives a non-interactive perfect SMT protocol. Namely, we can construct a non-interactive protocol for strictly timid adversaries.

Let $(\mathsf{Share}, \mathsf{Reconst})$ be a (t, n, δ)-robust secret sharing scheme with range $\mathcal{M}$. In the protocol, given a message $m \in \mathcal{M}$, the sender generates n shares $(s_1, \ldots, s_n)$ by $\mathsf{Share}(m)$, and sends each s_i over the i-th channel. The receiver simply recovers the message by $\mathsf{Reconst}(\{i, \tilde{s}_i\}_{i \in \{1, \ldots, n\}})$, where $\tilde{s}_i$ is the received message over the i-th channel.

Theorem 5. *The above protocol based on a (t, n, δ)-robust secret sharing scheme is perfectly secure against rational t-adversaries with utility function $U \in U_{\mathrm{timid}}^{\mathrm{st}}$ if U satisfies that $u_2 > u_3$ and*

$$\delta \leq \frac{u_2 - u_3}{u_1 - u_3}.$$

Proof. As in the proof of Theorem 4, we consider $\mathcal{B}$ who does not corrupt any channels, and output a random message as M_A. Then, the perfect security immediately follows.

We show that, for any t-adversary $\mathcal{A}$, $u(\mathcal{A}, U) \leq u(\mathcal{B}, U)$. As discussed in the proof of Theorem 4, it is sufficient to prove that $u(\mathcal{A}, U) \leq u_2$ for any $\mathcal{A}$. Since the underlying secret sharing has the perfect privacy, we have that $\Pr[\mathsf{guess} = 1] = 1/|\mathcal{M}|$ for any t-adversary. Suppose $\mathcal{A}$ corrupts some t channels and alters some messages s_i into different $\tilde{s}_i$. It follows from the robustness of secret sharing that the tampering actions is detected with probability at least $1 - \delta$, in which case the secret is not recovered. Thus, the utility of $\mathcal{A}$ is

$$u(\mathcal{A}, U) \leq (1 - \delta)u_3 + \delta u_1$$
$$\leq u_2, \tag{3}$$

where (3) follows from the assumption. Therefore, the statement follows.   □

The following corollary immediately follows.

Corollary 1. *Let $\mathbb{F}$ be a finite field of size $q = 2^\ell$, and d be any odd integer. The non-interactive protocol based on Theorem 3 is an SMT protocol with message space $\mathbb{F}^d$ that is perfectly secure against rational t-adversaries with utility function $U \in U_{\mathrm{timid}}^{\mathrm{st}}$ for any $t < n \leq 2^\ell d$ if*

$$\ell \geq \log(d + 1) + \log \frac{u_1 - u_3}{u_2 - u_3}.$$

5 Impossibility Result for General Timid Adversaries

We show that there is no RSMT protocol without public channel that is secure against general timid t-adversaries for $t \geq n/2$. The result implies that the use of the public channel in Theorem 4 is necessary for achieving $t \geq n/2$. It also demonstrates the necessity of restricting the utility in Theorem 5 for constructing protocols for $t \geq n/2$ without using public channels.

Theorem 6. *For any SMT protocol without public channel that is perfectly secure against rational t-adversaries with utility function $U \in U_{\text{timid}}$, if U has the relation*

$$u_2 < \frac{1}{2}\left(1 - \frac{1}{|\mathcal{M}|}\right) u_3$$

then $t < n/2$, where $\mathcal{M}$ is the message space of the protocol.

Proof. Let Π be a protocol in the statement. We construct a t-adversary $\mathcal{A}$ for $t = \lceil n/2 \rceil$ that can successfully attack Π. For simplicity, we assume that $n = 2t$.

Let $\mathcal{B}$ be any (harmless) adversary in the security of RSMT protocols of Definition 4. Since Π is $(0,0)$-SMT against $\mathcal{B}$, it holds that $u(\mathcal{B}, U) \leq u_2$. We show the existence of a t-adversary $\mathcal{A}$ that achieves $u(\mathcal{A}, U) > u_2$, which implies that Π cannot achieve a Nash equilibrium.

In the SMT game, a message $m \in \mathcal{M}$ is randomly chosen, and, on input m, Π generates $(s_1^j, \ldots, s_n^j)$ for $j = 1, \ldots$, where s_i^j is the message to be sent over the i-th channel in the j-th round. In the game, $\mathcal{A}$ does the following:

- Randomly choose $I \subseteq \{1, \ldots, n\}$ such that $|I| = t$, and corrupt the i-th channel for every $i \in I$.
- Randomly choose $\tilde{m} \in \mathcal{M}$, and simulate Π on input $\tilde{m}$. Let $\tilde{s}_i^j$ be the message generated for the i-th channel in the j-th round.
- In each round j, for every $i \in I$, on receiving s_i^j through the i-th channel, exchange s_i^j for $\tilde{s}_i^j$.

For this attack, it is impossible for the receiver to distinguish which message, m or $\tilde{m}$, was originally transmitted by the sender, since both messages for m and $\tilde{m}$ are equally mixed. Hence, the probability that $\mathsf{suc} = 1$, denoted by p_s, is at most

$$p_s \leq \frac{1}{2}\left(1 - \frac{1}{|\mathcal{M}|}\right) + \frac{1}{|\mathcal{M}|} = \frac{1}{2}\left(1 + \frac{1}{|\mathcal{M}|}\right),$$

where $1/|\mathcal{M}|$ comes from the even that $\tilde{m} = m$.

Let p_d be the probability that Π outputs "DETECTION" messages during the execution against the above attack. Without loss of generality, we assume that if Π does not output "DETECTION" messages, the receiver outputs some message at the end of the protocol. If the tampering actions of $\mathcal{A}$ are not detected, the utility of $\mathcal{A}$ is at least u_1 with probability $1 - p_s$, and at least u_2 with probability p_s. If some tampering actions are detected, then there can be two cases: (1) the receiver does not output any message; and (2) the receiver outputs some message. In case (1), the utility of $\mathcal{A}$ is u_3. In case (2), the probability that the $\mathsf{suc} = 1$ is at most p_s by the same argument as above. Hence, the utility of

$\mathcal{A}$ when the tampering was detected is at least $(1 - p_s)u_3$. Thus, the utility of $\mathcal{A}$ in the SMT game is at least

$$
\begin{aligned}
u(\mathcal{A}, U) &\geq (1 - p_d)\left((1 - p_s)u_1 + p_s u_2\right) + p_d(1 - p_s)u_3 \\
&= (1 - p_s)u_1 + p_s u_2 - p_d\left((1 - p_s)u_1 + p_s u_2 - (1 - p_s)u_3\right) \\
&\geq (1 - p_s)u_3 \qquad\qquad\qquad\qquad\qquad\qquad\qquad\qquad\qquad (4)\\
&\geq \frac{1}{2}\left(1 - \frac{1}{|\mathcal{M}|}\right)u_3 \\
&> u_2, \qquad\qquad\qquad\qquad\qquad\qquad\qquad\qquad\qquad\qquad\qquad (5)
\end{aligned}
$$

where (4) follows from the fact that $p_d \leq 1$ and $(1 - p_s)u_1 + p_s u_2 - (1 - p_s)u_3 \geq 0$, and the assumption on U is used in (5). Therefore, Π does not satisfy the security of RSMT protocols for $t \geq n/2$.

When $n = 2t - 1$, the same attack of the above $\mathcal{A}$ can be realized by invalidating the n-th channel by substituting $\bot$ for every message over the n-th channel. $\qquad\square$

The theorem gives the following corollary.

Corollary 2. *There is no SMT protocol without public channel that is perfectly secure against rational t-adversaries with utility function U for every $U \in U_{\text{timid}}$ and $t \geq \lceil n/2 \rceil$.*

6   Conclusion

We have introduced the notion of rationality into secure message transmission. Specifically, we have defined timid adversaries, who prefer to violate the security requirements of SMT, but do not prefer the tampering actions to be detected. It is shown that some type of almost-reliable SMT protocols using a public channel (such as [32]) work as perfect SMT for any timid adversary corrupting $t < n$ channels. By imposing the assumption that $u_2 > u_3$, which captures strictly timid adversaries, it is possible to construct a non-interactive perfect SMT protocol against $t < n$ corruptions without using public channels.

A future work is to construct protocols against adversaries having different preferences from timid ones. It is important to clarify for which rational adversary the existing impossibility results hold.

Acknowledgements. This work was supported in part by JSPS Grant-in-Aid for Scientific Research Numbers 16H01705, 17H01695, and 18K11159. The second author thanks to Masaki Ueno for discussions about this work.

A   Universal Hash Functions

Wegman and Carter [34] defined a notion of (almost) universal hash functions and gave its construction. We use an SMT protocol in which universal hash functions are used.

Definition 5. *Suppose that a class of hash functions* $H = \{h\colon \{0,1\}^m \to \{0,1\}^\ell\}$, *where* $m \geq \ell$, *satisfies the following: for any distinct* $x_1, x_2 \in \{0,1\}^m$ *and* $y_1, y_2 \in \{0,1\}^\ell$,

$$\Pr_{h \in H}[h(x_1) = y_1 \wedge h(x_2) = y_2] \leq \gamma.$$

Then H *is called* γ-*almost strongly universal. In the above, the randomness comes from the uniform choice of* h *over* H.

Here we mention a useful property of almost universal hash functions, which guarantees the security of some SMT protocols.

Lemma 1 ([32]). *Let* $H = \{h\colon \{0,1\}^m \to \{0,1\}^\ell\}$ *be a* γ-*almost strongly universal hash function family. The for any* $(x_1, c_1) \neq (x_2, c_2) \in \{0,1\}^m \times \{0,1\}^\ell$, *we have*

$$\Pr_{h \in H}[c_1 \oplus h(x_1) = c_2 \oplus h(x_2)] \leq 2^\ell \gamma.$$

In [34], Wegman and Carter constructed a family of $2^{1-2\ell}$-almost strongly universal hash functions. In particular, their hash function family $H_{wc} = \{h\colon \{0,1\}^m \to \{0,1\}^\ell\}$ satisfies that

$$\Pr_{h \in H_{wc}}[h(x_1) = y_1 \wedge h(x_2) = y_2] = 2^{1-2\ell}$$

for any distinct $x_1, x_2 \in \{0,1\}^m$ and for any $y_1, y_2 \in \{0,1\}^\ell$ and also

$$\Pr_{h \in H_{wc}}[c_1 \oplus h(x_1) \wedge c_2 \oplus h(x_2)] = 2^{1-\ell}$$

for any distinct pairs $(x_1, c_1) \neq (x_2, c_2) \in \{0,1\}^m \times \{0,1\}^\ell$.

B   Proof of Theorem 3

To prove the theorem, we define the notion of *algebraic manipulation detection (AMD) codes* in which the security requirement is slightly different from that in [9] for our purpose.

Definition 6. *An* (M, N, δ)-*algebraic manipulation detection (AMD) code is a probabilistic function* $E\colon \mathcal{S} \to \mathcal{G}$, *where* $\mathcal{S}$ *is a set of size* M *and* $\mathcal{G}$ *is an additive group of order* N, *together with a decoding function* $D\colon \mathcal{G} \to \mathcal{S} \cup \{\bot\}$ *such that*

- *Correctness: For any* $s \in \mathcal{S}$, $\Pr[D(E(s)) = s] = 1$.
- *Security: For any* $s \in \mathcal{S}$ *and* $\Delta \in \mathcal{G} \setminus \{0\}$, $\Pr[D(E(s) + \Delta) \neq \bot] \leq \delta$.

An AMD code is called systematic if $\mathcal{S}$ *is a group, and the encoding is of the form*
$$E\colon \mathcal{S} \to \mathcal{S} \times \mathcal{G}_1 \times \mathcal{G}_2, s \mapsto (s, x, f(x, s))$$
for some function f *and random* $x \in \mathcal{G}_1$. *The decoding function* D *of a systematic AMD code is given by* $D(s', x', f') = s'$ *if* $f' = f(x', s')$, *and* $\bot$ *otherwise.*

Note that, for a systematic AMD code, the correctness immediately follows from the definition of the decoding function. The security requirement can be stated such that for any $s \in \mathcal{S}$ and $(\Delta_s, \Delta_x, \Delta_f) \in \mathcal{S} \times \mathcal{G}_1 \times \mathcal{G}_2 \setminus \{(0,0,0)\}$, $\mathrm{Pr}_x[f(s + \Delta_s, x + \Delta_x) = f(s,x) + \Delta_f] \leq \delta$.

We show that a systematic AMD code given in [9] satisfies the above definition.

Proposition 1. *Let $\mathbb{F}$ be a finite field of size q and characteristic p, and d any integer such that $d + 2$ is not divisible by p. Define the encoding function $E \colon \mathbb{F}^d \to \mathbb{F}^d \times \mathbb{F} \times \mathbb{F}$ by $E(s) = (s, x, f(x,s))$ where*

$$f(x,s) = x^{d+2} + \sum_{i=1}^{d} s_i x^i$$

and $s = (s_1, \ldots, s_d)$. Then, the construction is a systematic $(q^d, q^{d+2}, (d+1)/q)$-AMD code.

Proof. We show that for any $s \in \mathbb{F}^d$ and $(\Delta_s, \Delta_x, \Delta_f) \in \mathbb{F}^d \times \mathbb{F} \times \mathbb{F} \setminus \{(0^d, 0, 0)\}$, $\mathrm{Pr}[f(s + \Delta_s, x + \Delta_x) = f(s,x) + \Delta_f] \leq \delta$. The event in the probability is that

$$(x + \Delta_x)^{d+2} + \sum_{i=1}^{d} s_i'(x + \Delta_x)^i = x^{d+2} + \sum_{i=1}^{d} s_i x^i + \Delta_f, \qquad (6)$$

where s_i' is the i-th element of $s + \Delta_s$. The left-hand side of (6) can be represented by

$$x^{d+2} + (d+2)\Delta_x x^{d+1} + \sum_{i=1}^{d} s_i' x^i + \Delta_x p(x)$$

for some polynomial $p(x)$ of degree at most d. Thus, (6) can be rewritten as

$$(d+2)\Delta_x x^{d+1} + \sum_{i=1}^{d} (s_i' - s_i)x^i + \Delta_x p(x) - \Delta_f = 0. \qquad (7)$$

We discuss the probability that (7) happens when x is chosen uniformly at random. We consider the following cases:

1. When $\Delta_x \neq 0$, the coefficient of x^{d+1} is $(d+2)\Delta_x$, which is not zero by the assumption that $d + 2$ is not divisible by p. Then, (7) has at most $d + 1$ solutions x. Hence the event happens with probability at most $(d+1)/q$.
2. When $\Delta_x = 0$, we consider two subcases:
   (a) If $\Delta_s \neq 0$, then $s_i' - s_i \neq 0$ for some i. Hence (7) has at most d solutions x. Thus the event happens with probability at most d/p.
   (b) If $\Delta_s = 0$, (7) is equivalent to $\Delta_f = 0$. Since $\Delta_f \neq 0$ for this case, the event cannot happen.

In every case, the event happens with probability at most $(d + 1)/q$. Thus the statement follows. $\square$

As discussed in [9], a robust secret sharing scheme can be obtained by combining an AMD code and a linear secret sharing scheme. Let (Share, Reconst) be a (t, n)-secret sharing scheme with range $\mathcal{G}$ that satisfies correctness and perfect privacy of Definition 2, where we drop the parameter δ for robustness. A *linear* secret sharing scheme has the property that for any $s \in \mathcal{G}$, $(s_1, \ldots, s_n) \in \mathsf{Share}(s)$, and vector $(s'_1, \ldots, s'_n)$, which may contain $\perp$ symbols, it holds that $\mathsf{Reconst}(\{i, s_i + s'_i\}_{i \in I}) = s + \mathsf{Reconst}(\{i, s'_i\}_{i \in I})$ for any $I \subseteq \{1, \ldots, n\}$ with $|I| > t$, where $\perp + x = x + \perp = \perp$ for all x. Examples of linear secret sharing schemes are Shamir's scheme [31] and the simple XOR-based $(n-1, n)$-scheme, in which secret $s \in \{0, 1\}^n$ is shared by $(s_1, \ldots, s_n)$ for random $s_i \in \{0, 1\}^n$ with the restriction that $s_1 \oplus \cdots \oplus s_n = s$.

We show that the same construction as in [9] works as a construction of robust secret sharing of Definition 2.

Proposition 2. *Let* (Share, Reconst) *be a linear* (t, n)-*secret sharing scheme with range* $\mathcal{G}$ *that satisfies correctness and perfect privacy of Definition 2, and let* (E, D) *be an* (M, N, δ)-*AMD code of Definition 6 with* $|\mathcal{G}| = N$. *Then, the scheme* (Share', Reconst') *defined by* $\mathsf{Share}'(s) = \mathsf{Share}(E(s))$ *and* $\mathsf{Reconst}'(S) = D(\mathsf{Reconst}(S))$ *is a* (t, n, δ)-*robust secret sharing scheme.*

Proof. Let $(s_1, \ldots, s_n) \in \mathsf{Share}'(s)$. Let $I \subseteq \{1, \ldots, n\}$ with $|I| \leq t$, and $(\tilde{s}_1, \ldots \tilde{s}_n)$ be a sequence of shares satisfying the requirement for input shares in robustness of Definition 2. We assume that $\tilde{s}_i = s_i + \Delta'_i$ for each $i \in \{1, \ldots, n\}$. Note that $\Delta'_i = 0$ for every $i \notin I$. Then,

$$
\begin{aligned}
&\Pr\left[\mathsf{Reconst}'\left(\{i, \tilde{s}_i\}_{i \in \{1, \ldots, n\}}\right) \neq \perp\right] \\
&= \Pr\left[D\left(E(s) + \mathsf{Reconst}(\{i, \Delta_i\}_{i \in \{1, \ldots, n\}})\right) \neq \perp\right] \\
&= \Pr\left[D\left(E(s) + \Delta\right) \neq \perp\right],
\end{aligned}
$$

where $\Delta = \mathsf{Reconst}\left(\{i, \Delta_i\}_{i \in \{1, \ldots, n\}}\right)$ is determined by the adversary. It follows from perfect privacy of the secret sharing scheme that Δ is independent of $E(s)$. Thus, if $\tilde{s}_i \neq s_i$ for some $i \in \{1, \ldots, n\}$, the probability is at most δ by the security of the AMD code. Hence, the statement follows. $\square$

By combining Shamir's secret sharing scheme with range $\mathbb{F}^d$ and the AMD code of Proposition 1, the robust secret sharing scheme of Theorem 3 is obtained by Proposition 2.

References

1. Abraham, I., Dolev, D., Gonen, R., Halpern, J.Y.: Distributed computing meets game theory: robust mechanisms for rational secret sharing and multiparty computation. In: Ruppert, E., Malkhi, D. (eds.) PODC, pp. 53–62. ACM (2006)
2. Abraham, I., Dolev, D., Halpern, J.Y.: Distributed protocols for leader election: a game-theoretic perspective. In: Afek, Y. (ed.) DISC 2013. LNCS, vol. 8205, pp. 61–75. Springer, Heidelberg (2013). https://doi.org/10.1007/978-3-642-41527-2_5

3. Asharov, G., Canetti, R., Hazay, C.: Toward a game theoretic view of secure computation. J. Cryptol. **29**(4), 879–926 (2016)
4. Asharov, G., Lindell, Y.: Utility dependence in correct and fair rational secret sharing. J. Cryptol. **24**(1), 157–202 (2011)
5. Azar, P.D., Micali, S.: Super-efficient rational proofs. In: Kearns, M., McAfee, R.P., Tardos, É. (eds.) EC 2013, pp. 29–30. ACM (2013)
6. Blakley, G.R.: Safeguarding cryptographic keys. Proc. Natl. Comput. Conf. **1979**(48), 313–317 (1979)
7. Campanelli, M., Gennaro, R.: Sequentially composable rational proofs. In: Khouzani, M.H.R., Panaousis, E., Theodorakopoulos, G. (eds.) GameSec 2015. LNCS, vol. 9406, pp. 270–288. Springer, Cham (2015). https://doi.org/10.1007/978-3-319-25594-1_15
8. Campanelli, M., Gennaro, R.: Efficient rational proofs for space bounded computations. In: Rass, S., An, B., Kiekintveld, C., Fang, F., Schauer, S. (eds.) GameSec 2017. LNCS, vol. 10575, pp. 53–73. Springer, Cham (2017). https://doi.org/10.1007/978-3-319-68711-7_4
9. Cramer, R., Dodis, Y., Fehr, S., Padró, C., Wichs, D.: Detection of algebraic manipulation with applications to robust secret sharing and fuzzy extractors. In: Smart, N. (ed.) EUROCRYPT 2008. LNCS, vol. 4965, pp. 471–488. Springer, Heidelberg (2008). https://doi.org/10.1007/978-3-540-78967-3_27
10. Dolev, D., Dwork, C., Waarts, O., Yung, M.: Perfectly secure message transmission. J. ACM **40**(1), 17–47 (1993)
11. Franklin, M.K., Wright, R.N.: Secure communication in minimal connectivity models. J. Cryptol. **13**(1), 9–30 (2000)
12. Fuchsbauer, G., Katz, J., Naccache, D.: Efficient rational secret sharing in standard communication networks. In: Micciancio, D. (ed.) TCC 2010. LNCS, vol. 5978, pp. 419–436. Springer, Heidelberg (2010). https://doi.org/10.1007/978-3-642-11799-2_25
13. Garay, J.A., Katz, J., Maurer, U., Tackmann, B., Zikas, V.: Rational protocol design: cryptography against incentive-driven adversaries. In FOCS, pp. 648–657. IEEE Computer Society (2013)
14. Garay, J.A., Katz, J., Tackmann, B., Zikas, V.: How fair is your protocol?: A utility-based approach to protocol optimality. In: Georgiou, C., Spirakis, P.G. (eds.) PODC, pp. 281–290. ACM (2015)
15. Garay, J.A., Ostrovsky, R.: Almost-everywhere secure computation. In: Smart [33], pp. 307–323 (2008)
16. Gordon, S.D., Katz, J.: Rational secret sharing, revisited. In: De Prisco, R., Yung, M. (eds.) SCN 2006. LNCS, vol. 4116, pp. 229–241. Springer, Heidelberg (2006). https://doi.org/10.1007/11832072_16
17. Gradwohl, R.: Rationality in the full-information model. In Micciancio [30], pp. 401–418 (2010)
18. Groce, A., Katz, J.: Fair computation with rational players. In: Pointcheval, D., Johansson, T. (eds.) EUROCRYPT 2012. LNCS, vol. 7237, pp. 81–98. Springer, Heidelberg (2012). https://doi.org/10.1007/978-3-642-29011-4_7
19. Groce, A., Katz, J., Thiruvengadam, A., Zikas, V.: Byzantine agreement with a rational adversary. In: Czumaj, A., Mehlhorn, K., Pitts, A., Wattenhofer, R. (eds.) ICALP 2012 Part II. LNCS, vol. 7392, pp. 561–572. Springer, Heidelberg (2012). https://doi.org/10.1007/978-3-642-31585-5_50
20. Guo, S., Hubácek, P., Rosen, A., Vald, M.: Rational arguments: single round delegation with sublinear verification. In: Naor, M. (ed.) ITCS, pp. 523–540. ACM (2014)

21. Guo, S., Hubáček, P., Rosen, A., Vald, M.: Rational sumchecks. In: Kushilevitz, E., Malkin, T. (eds.) TCC 2016 Part II. LNCS, vol. 9563, pp. 319–351. Springer, Heidelberg (2016). https://doi.org/10.1007/978-3-662-49099-0_12
22. Halpern, J.Y., Teague, V.: Rational secret sharing and multiparty computation: extended abstract. In: Babai, L. (ed.) STOC, pp. 623–632. ACM (2004)
23. Halpern, J.Y., Vilaça, X.: Rational consensus: extended abstract. In: Giakkoupis, G. (ed.) PODC, pp. 137–146. ACM (2016)
24. Inasawa, K., Yasunaga, K.: Rational proofs against rational verifiers. IEICE Trans. 100–A(11), 2392–2397 (2017)
25. Ishai, Y., Ostrovsky, R., Seyalioglu, H.: Identifying Cheaters without an honest majority. In: Cramer, R. (ed.) TCC 2012. LNCS, vol. 7194, pp. 21–38. Springer, Heidelberg (2012). https://doi.org/10.1007/978-3-642-28914-9_2
26. Kawachi, A., Okamoto, Y., Tanaka, K., Yasunaga, K.: General constructions of rational secret sharing with expected constant-round reconstruction. Comput. J. 60(5), 711–728 (2017)
27. Kol, G., Naor, M.: Cryptography and game theory: designing protocols for exchanging information. In: Canetti, R. (ed.) TCC 2008. LNCS, vol. 4948, pp. 320–339. Springer, Heidelberg (2008). https://doi.org/10.1007/978-3-540-78524-8_18
28. Kol, G., Naor, M.: Games for exchanging information. In: Dwork, C. (ed.) STOC, pp. 423–432. ACM (2008)
29. Kurosawa, K., Suzuki, K.: Truly efficient 2-round perfectly secure message transmission scheme. IEEE Trans. Inf. Theory 55(11), 5223–5232 (2009)
30. Micciancio, D. (ed.): TCC. LNCS, vol. 5978. Springer, Heidelberg (2010)
31. Shamir, A.: How to share a secret. Commun. ACM 22(11), 612–613 (1979)
32. Shi, H., Jiang, S., Safavi-Naini, R., Tuhin, M.A.: On optimal secure message transmission by public discussion. IEEE Trans. Inf. Theory 57(1), 572–585 (2011)
33. Smart, N.P. (ed.): EUROCRYPT. LNCS, vol. 4965. Springer, Heidelberg (2008)
34. Wegman, M.N., Carter, L.: New hash functions and their use in authentication and set equality. J. Comput. Syst. Sci. 22(3), 265–279 (1981)
35. Yasunaga, K.: Public-key encryption with lazy parties. IEICE Trans. 99–A(2), 590–600 (2016)
36. Yasunaga, K., Yuzawa, K.: Repeated games for generating randomness in encryption. IEICE Trans. 101–A(4), 697–703 (2018)

Reinforcement Learning for Autonomous Defence in Software-Defined Networking

Yi Han[1]([⊠]) [iD], Benjamin I. P. Rubinstein[1] [iD], Tamas Abraham[2] [iD],
Tansu Alpcan[1] [iD], Olivier De Vel[2], Sarah Erfani[1] [iD], David Hubczenko[2],
Christopher Leckie[1] [iD], and Paul Montague[2]

[1] School of Computing and Information Systems, The University of Melbourne,
Parkville, Australia
{yi.han,benjamin.rubinstein,tansu.alpcan,sarah.erfani,
caleckie}@unimelb.edu.au
[2] Defence Science and Technology Group, Edinburgh, Australia
{tamas.abraham,olivier.devel,david.hubczenko,
paul.montague}@dst.defence.gov.au

Abstract. Despite the successful application of machine learning (ML) in a wide range of domains, adaptability—the very property that makes machine learning desirable—can be exploited by adversaries to contaminate training and evade classification. In this paper, we investigate the feasibility of applying a specific class of machine learning algorithms, namely, reinforcement learning (RL) algorithms, for autonomous cyber defence in software-defined networking (SDN). In particular, we focus on how an RL agent reacts towards different forms of causative attacks that poison its training process, including indiscriminate and targeted, white-box and black-box attacks. In addition, we also study the impact of the attack timing, and explore potential countermeasures such as adversarial training.

Keywords: Adversarial reinforcement learning ·
Software-defined networking · Cyber security · Adversarial training

1 Introduction

Machine learning has enjoyed substantial impact on a wide range of applications, from cyber-security (*e.g.*, network security operations, malware analysis) to autonomous systems (*e.g.*, decision-making and control systems, computer vision). Despite the many successes, the very property that makes machine learning desirable—adaptability—is a vulnerability to be exploited by an economic competitor or state-sponsored attacker. Attackers who are aware of the ML techniques being deployed can contaminate the training data to manipulate a learned ML classifier in order to evade subsequent classification, or can manipulate the metadata upon which the ML algorithms make their decisions and exploit identified weaknesses in these algorithm—so called Adversarial Machine Learning [6, 11, 27].

© Springer Nature Switzerland AG 2018
L. Bushnell et al. (Eds.): GameSec 2018, LNCS 11199, pp. 145–165, 2018.
https://doi.org/10.1007/978-3-030-01554-1_9

This paper focuses on a specific class of ML algorithms, namely, reinforcement learning (RL) algorithms, and investigates the feasibility of applying RL for autonomous defence in computer networks [7], *i.e.*, the ability to "fight through" a contested environment—in particular adversarial machine learning attacks—and ensure critical services (*e.g.*, email servers, file servers, etc.) are preserved to the fullest extent possible.

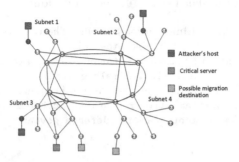

Fig. 1. An example network setup. The attacker propagates through the network to compromise the critical server, while the defender applies RL to prevent the critical server from compromise and to preserve as many nodes as possible. (Color figure online)

For example, consider a network as shown in Fig. 1 that consists of 32 nodes, one (node 3.8) of whom connects to the critical server, two (nodes 3.9 and 4.5) connect to potential migration destinations, and three (nodes 1.5, 2.7 and 3.6) connect to the attacker's hosts. The attacker aims to propagate through the network, and compromise the critical server. We aim to prevent this and preserve as many nodes as possible through the following RL approach:

- We first train two types of RL agents: Double Deep Q-Networks (DDQN) [24] and Asynchronous Advantage Actor-Critic (A3C) [38]. The agents observe network states, and select actions such as "isolate", "patch", "reconnect", and "migrate". The agents gradually optimise their actions for different network states, based on the received rewards for maintaining critical services, costs incurred when shutting down non-critical services or migrating critical services.
- Once a working agent is obtained, we then investigate different ways by which the attacker may poison the training process of the RL agent. For example, the attacker can falsify part of the reward signals, or manipulate the states of certain nodes, in order to trick the agent to take non-optimal actions, resulting in either the critical server being compromised, or significantly fewer nodes being preserved. Both indiscriminate and targeted, white-box and black-box attacks are studied.
- We also explore possible countermeasures—*e.g.*, adversarial training—that make the training less vulnerable to causative/poisoning attacks.

- To make use of the developed capacity for autonomous cyber-security operations, we build our experimental platform around software-defined networking (SDN) [2], a next-generation tool chain for centralising and abstracting control of reconfigurable networks. The SDN controller provides a centralised view of the whole network, and is directly programmable. As a result, it is very flexible for managing and reconfiguring various types of network resources. Therefore, in our experiments the RL agents obtain all network information and perform different network operations via the SDN controller.
- Our results demonstrate that RL agents can successfully identify the optimal actions to protect the critical server, by isolating as few compromised nodes as possible. In addition, even though the causative attacks can cause the agent to make incorrect decisions, adversarial training shows great potential for mitigating the impact.

The remainder of the paper is organised as follows: Sect. 2 briefly introduces the fundamental concepts in RL and SDN; Sect. 3 defines the research problem; Sect. 4 introduces in detail the different forms of proposed attacks against RL; Sect. 5 presents the experimental results on applying RL for autonomous defence in SDN, and the impact of those causative attacks; Sect. 6 overviews previous work on adversarial machine learning (including attacks against reinforcement learning) and existing countermeasures; Sect. 7 concludes the paper, and offers directions for future work.

2 Preliminaries

Before defining the research problems investigated in this paper, we first briefly introduce the basic concepts in reinforcement learning and software-defined networking.

2.1 Reinforcement Learning

In a typical reinforcement learning setting [56], an agent repeatedly interacts with the environment: at each time step t, the agent (1) observes a state s_t of the environment; (2) chooses an action a_t based on its policy π—a mapping from the observed states to the actions to be taken; and (3) receives a reward r_t and observes next state s_{t+1}. This process continues until a terminal state is reached, and then a new episode restarts from a certain initial state. The agent's objective is to maximise its discounted cumulative rewards over the long run: $R_t = \sum_{\tau=t}^{\infty} \gamma^{\tau-t} r_\tau$, where $\gamma \in (0,1]$ is the discount factor that controls the trade-off between short-term and long-term rewards.

Under a given policy π, the value of taking action a in state s is defined as: $Q^\pi(s,a) = \mathbb{E}[R_t|s_t = s, a_t = a, \pi]$. Similarly, the value of state s is defined as: $V^\pi(s) = \mathbb{E}[R_t|s_t = s, \pi]$. In this paper, we mainly focus on two widely cited RL algorithms: Double Deep Q-Networks (DDQN) [24] and Asynchronous Advantage Actor-Critic (A3C) [38].

Q-Learning. Q-learning [56] approaches the above problem by estimating the optimal action value function $Q^*(s, a) = \max_\pi Q^\pi(s, a)$. Specifically, it uses the Bellman equation $Q^*(s, a) = \mathbb{E}_{s'}[r + \gamma \max_{a'} Q^*(s', a')]$ to update the value iteratively. In practice, Q-learning is commonly implemented by function approximation with parameters θ: $Q^*(s, a) \approx Q(s, a; \theta)$. At each training iteration i, the loss function is defined as: $L_i(\theta_i) = \mathbb{E}[(r + \gamma \max_{a'} Q(s', a'; \theta_{i-1}) - Q(s, a; \theta_i))^2]$.

Deep Q-Networks (DQN). Classic Q-learning networks suffer from a number of drawbacks, including (1) the *i.i.d.* (independent and identically distributed) requirement of the training data being violated as consecutive observations are correlated, (2) unstable target function when calculating Temporal Difference (TD) errors, and (3) different scales of rewards. Deep Q networks (DQN) [39] overcome these issues by (1) introducing experience replay, (2) using a target network that fixes its parameters (θ^-) and only updates at regular intervals, and (3) clipping the rewards to the range of $[-1, 1]$. The loss function for DQN becomes: $L_i(\theta_i) = \mathbb{E}[(r + \gamma \max_{a'} Q(s', a'; \theta_i^-) - Q(s, a; \theta_i))^2]$.

Double DQN (DDQN). To further solve the problem of value overestimation, Hasselt *et al.* [24] generalise the Double Q-learning algorithm [23] proposed in the tabular setting, and propose Double DQN (DDQN) that separates action selection and action evaluation, *i.e.*, one DQN is used to determine the maximising action and a second one is used to estimate its value. Therefore, the loss function is: $L_i(\theta_i) = \mathbb{E}[(r + \gamma Q(s', \arg\max_{a'} Q(s', a'; \theta_i); \theta_i^-) - Q(s, a; \theta_i))^2]$.

Prioritised Experience Replay. Experience replay keeps a buffer of past experiences, and for each training iteration, it samples uniformly a batch of experiences from the buffer. Prioritised experience replay [53] assigns higher sampling probability to transitions that do not fit well with the current estimation of the Q function. For DDQN, the error of an experience is defined as $|r + \gamma Q(s', \arg\max_{a'} Q(s', a'; \theta); \theta^-) - Q(s, a; \theta)|$.

Asynchronous Advantage Actor-Critic (A3C). Mnih *et al.* [38] propose an asynchronous variant of the classical actor-critic algorithm, which estimates both the state value function $V(s; \theta_v)$ and a policy $\pi(a|s; \theta_p)$. Specifically, the A3C algorithm uses multiple threads to explore different parts of the state space simultaneously, and updates the global network in an asynchronous way. In addition, instead of using discounted returns to determine whether an action is good, A3C estimates the *advantage function* so that it can better focus on where the predictions are lacking.

2.2 Software-Defined Networking

In order to better serve today's dynamic and high-bandwidth applications, a new architecture called Software-Defined Networking (SDN) has emerged [2]. There are three layers in the SDN architecture: (1) the application layer includes applications that deliver services. These applications communicate their network requirements to the controller via northbound APIs; (2) the SDN controller translates these requirements into low-level controls, and sends them through southbound APIs to the infrastructure layer; (3) the infrastructure layer comprises network switches that control forwarding and data processing. One major advantage of SDN is that it decouples network control and forwarding functions, rendering the controller directly programmable. As a result, network resources can be conveniently managed, configured and optimised using standardised protocols. There have been a number of proprietary and open-source SDN controller software platforms. In this paper, we have opted to use OpenDaylight [35], which is the largest open-source SDN controller today and which is updated regularly.

3   Problem Statement

In this paper, we seek to answer the question: Can reinforcement learning be used for autonomous defence in SDN? We start with a scenario that does not consider the attacker poisoning the training process, and then investigate the impact of adversarial reinforcement learning. While we also briefly discuss potential countermeasures, we largely leave defences to future work.

3.1   Reinforcement Learning Powered Autonomous Defence in SDN

Consider a network of N nodes (e.g., Fig. 1), $H = \{h_1, h_2, ..., h_N\}$, where $H_C \subset H$ is the set of critical servers to be protected (blue nodes in Fig. 1), $H_M \subset H$ is the set of possible migration destinations for $h \in H_C$ (green nodes), and $H_A \subset H$ is the set of nodes that have initially been compromised (red nodes). The attacker aims to propagate through the network, and penetrate the mission critical servers, while the defender/SDN controller monitors the system state, and takes appropriate actions in order to preserve the critical servers and as many non-critical nodes as possible.

Reflecting suggestions from past work, we consider a defender adopting RL. In this paper, we start with a simplified version, and make the following assumptions (Sect. 7 explains how they may be replaced): (1) each node (or link) only has two states: compromised/uncompromised (or on/off); (2) both the defender and the attacker know the complete network topology; (3) the defender has in place a detection system that can achieve a detection rate of 90%, with no false alarms (before the causative attacks); (4) the attacker needs to compromise all nodes on the path (i.e., cannot "hop over" nodes). Given these assumptions, in each step the defender:

1. Observes the state of the network—whether a node is compromised, and whether a link is switched on/off, e.g., there are 32 nodes and 48 links in Fig. 1, so one state is an array of 80 $0s/1s$, where 0 means the node is uncompromised or the link is switched off, and 1 means the node is compromised or the link is switched on;
2. Takes an action that may include: (i) isolating and patching a node; (ii) reconnecting a node and its links; (iii) migrating the critical server and selecting the destination; and (iv) taking no action. Note that, in this scenario, the defender can only take one type of action at a time, and if they decide to isolate/reconnect, only one node can be isolated/reconnected at a time;

Table 1. Problem description: RL powered autonomous defence in SDN

	Defender	Attacker
State	(1) Whether each node is compromised; (2) Whether each link is turned on/off.	
Actions	(1) Isolate and patch a node; (2) Reconnect a node and its links; (3) Migrate the critical server and select the destination; (4) Take no action	Compromise a node that satisfies certain conditions, *e.g.*, the node (1) is closer to the "backbone" network; (2) is in the backbone network; or (3) in the target subnet
Goals	(1) Preserve the critical servers; (2) Keep as many nodes uncompromised and reachable from the critical servers as possible.	Compromise the critical servers

3. Receives a reward based on (i) whether the critical servers are compromised; (ii) the number of nodes reachable from the critical servers; (iii) the number of compromised nodes; (iv) migration cost; and (v) whether the action is valid, *e.g.*, it is invalid to isolate a node that has already been isolated.

Meanwhile, the attacker carefully chooses the nodes to compromise. For example, in the setting of Fig. 1, they infect a node only if it (1) is closer to the "backbone" network (nodes on the dashed circle); (2) is in the backbone network; or (3) is in the target subnet. Table 1 summarises this problem setting.

3.2 Causative Attacks Against RL Powered Autonomous Defence System

As an online system, the autonomous defence system continues gathering new statistics, and keeps training/updating its model. Therefore, it is necessary and crucial to analyse the impact of an adversarial environment, where malicious users can manage to falsify either the rewards received by the agent, or the states of certain nodes. In other words, this is a form of causative attack that poisons the training process, in order for the tampered model to take sub-optimal actions. In this paper, we investigate the two forms of attacks below.

1. **Flipping reward signs.** Suppose that without any attack, the agent would learn the following experience (s, a, s', r), where s is the current system state, a is the action taken by the agent, s' is the new state, and r is the reward. In our scenario, we permit the attacker to flip the sign of a certain number of rewards (*e.g.*, 5% of all experiences), and aim to maximise the loss function of the RL agent. This is an extreme case of the corrupted reward channel problem [19], where the reward may be corrupted due to sensor errors, hijacks, etc.

2. **Manipulating states.** Again, consider the case where the agent learns an experience (s, a, s', r) without any attack. Furthermore, when the system

reaches state s', the agent takes the next optimal action a'. The attacker is then allowed to introduce one false positive (FP) and one false negative (FN) reading in s', $i.e.$, one uncompromised/compromised node is reported as compromised/uncompromised to the defender. As a result, instead of learning (s, a, s', r), the agent ends up observing $(s, a, s' + \delta, r')$ (where δ represents the FP and FN readings), and consequently may not take a' in the next step.

4   Attack Mechanisms

This section explains in detail the mechanisms of the attacks introduced above.

4.1   Attack I: Maximise Loss Function by Flipping Reward Signs

Recall that the DDQN agent aims to minimise the loss function: $L_i(\theta_i) = \mathbb{E}[(r + \gamma Q(s', \arg\max_{a'} Q(s', a'; \theta_i); \theta_i^-) - Q(s, a; \theta_i))^2]$. In the ith training iteration, θ_i is updated according to the gradient of $\partial L_i / \partial \theta_i$. The main idea for the first form of attack is to falsify certain rewards based on $\partial L_i / \partial r$, in order to maximise the loss L_i.

Specifically, after the agent samples a batch of experiences for training, we calculate the gradient of $\partial L_i / \partial r$ for each of them, and flip the sign of experience with the largest absolute value of the gradient $|\partial L_i / \partial r|$ that satisfies $r \cdot \partial L_i / \partial r < 0$ (if $r \cdot \partial L_i / \partial r > 0$ flipping the sign decreases the loss function).

4.2   Attack II: Prevent Agent from Taking Optimal/Specific Actions by Manipulating States

Our experimental results show that the above form of attack is indeed effective in increasing the agent's loss function. However, it only delays the agent from learning the optimal actions. Therefore, the second form of attack directly targets the value function Q (against DDQN agent) or the policy π (against A3C agent).

1. **Indiscriminate attacks.** For each untampered experience (s, a, s', r), indiscriminate attacks falsify the states of two nodes in the new state s', in order to prevent the agent from taking the next optimal action a' that has been learned so far (which may be different from the final optimal action for the given state), $i.e.$, against DDQN agent the attacks minimise $\max_{a'} Q(s' + \delta, a')$, while against A3C agent the attacks minimise $\max_{a'} \pi(a'|s' + \delta)$.
2. **Targeted attacks.** Targeted attacks aim to prevent the agent from taking a specific action (in our case, we find that this is more effective than tricking the agent to take a specific action). As an extreme case, this paper allows the attacker to know the (final) optimal action a^* that the agent is going to take next (a^* may be different from a'), and they seek to minimise the probability of the agent taking that action: for DDQN, the attacks minimise $Q(s' + \delta, a^*)$; for A3C, the attacks minimise $\pi(a^*|s' + \delta)$.

Algorithm 1. Attack II – Manipulating states

Input : The original experience (s, a, s', r); The list of all nodes L_N; Target action a_t ($a_t = -1$ for indiscriminate attack); The main DQN Q

Output: The tampered experience $(s, a, s' + \delta, r')$

1 **if** $a_t == -1$ **then**
    // indiscriminate attack
2    $a_t = \arg\max_{a'} Q(s', a')$;
3 **for** *node* n *in* L_N **do**
4   **if** n *is compromised* **then**
5   mark n as uncompromised;
6   **if** $Q(s' + \delta, a_t) < minQ_{FN}$ **then**
            // δ represents the FP and/or FN readings
7            $FN = n$;
8            $minQ_{FN} = Q(s' + \delta, a_t)$;
9   restore n as compromised;
10   **else**
11   mark n as compromised;
12   **if** $Q(s' + \delta, a_t) < minQ_{FP}$ **then**
13            $FP = n$;
14            $minQ_{FP} = Q(s' + \delta, a_t)$;
15   restore n as uncompromised;
16 Change node FN to uncompromised;
17 Change node FP to compromised;
18 **return** $(s, a, s' + \delta, r')$

The details of the above two types of attacks are presented in Algorithm 1 (Algorithm 1 is for the attacks against DDQN. Due to similarity, the algorithm for attacks against A3C is omitted). In addition, we consider the following variants of the attacks:

1. **White-box attacks vs. Black-box attacks.** In white-box attacks, the attacker can access the model under training to select the false positive and false negative nodes, while in black-box attacks, the attacker first trains surrogate model(s), and then uses them to choose the FPs and FNs.
2. **Limit on the choice of FPs and FNs.** The above attacks do not set any limit on the choice of FPs and FNs, and hence even though the attacker can only manipulate the states of two nodes each time, overall, they still need to be able to control a number of nodes, which is not practical. Therefore, we first run unlimited white-box attacks, identify the top two nodes that have been selected most frequently as FPs and FNs respectively, and only allow the attacker to manipulate the states of those nodes.
3. **Limit on the timing of the attack.** The last type of attacks only introduces FPs and FNs in the first m steps (*e.g.*, $m = 3$) in each training episode.

5   Experimental Verification

This section begins with a discussion of the experimental results obtained when applying RL to autonomous defence in a SDN environment without considering causative attacks. We then analyse the impact of the two forms of attacks explained in Sect. 4. Finally, we discuss adopting adversarial training as a potential countermeasure, and present some preliminary results. Experiments on causative attacks were performed on eight servers (equivalent to two Amazon EC2 t2.large instances and six t2.xlarge instances [1]), and each set of experiments was repeated 15 to 25 times.

5.1   Autonomous Defence in a SDN

For our experiments, as shown in Fig. 1, we created a network with 32 nodes and 48 links using Mininet [3], one of the most popular network emulators. OpenDaylight [4,35] serves as the controller, and monitors the whole-of-network status. The RL agent retrieves network information and takes appropriate operations by calling corresponding APIs provided by OpenDaylight. In the setup, the three nodes in red, *i.e.,* nodes 1.5, 2.7 and 3.6, have already been compromised. Node 3.8 is the critical server to be protected, and it can be migrated to node 3.9 or 4.5.

We trained a DDQN (with Prioritised Experience Relay) agent and an A3C agent. We set the length of training such that the reward per episode for both agents reached a stable value well before training ended. The two agents learned two slightly different responses: the DDQN agent decides to first isolate node 3.6, then 1.3, 2.2 and finally 2.1, which means 21 nodes are preserved (see Fig. 2a); while the A3C agent isolates nodes 1.5, 3.3, 2.2 and 2.1, keeping 20 nodes uncompromised and reachable from the critical server (see Fig. 2b).

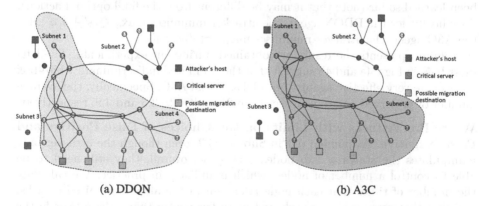

(a) DDQN   (b) A3C

Fig. 2. Optimal results without causative attacks (nodes in the shade are preserved)

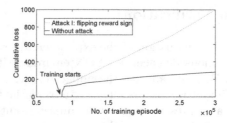

Fig. 3. Cumulative loss before and after flipping reward sign attacks (against DDQN)

5.2 Attack I: Flipping Reward Sign

This subsection presents the results of the first form of attack that flips the reward sign. In our experiments, we limit the total number of tampered experiences to 5% of all experiences obtained by the agent, and also set the number of tampered experiences per training iteration to the range of $[1, 5]$.

As can be seen in Fig. 3, the attack is effective in increasing the agent's loss function. However, our results also suggest that this form of attack only delays the training as the agent still learns the optimal actions (although the delay can be significant).

5.3 Attack II: Manipulate State—Indiscriminate Attacks

Unlimited White-Box Attacks. We start with unlimited indiscriminate white-box attacks, the case where the attacker has full access to the model under training. For each experience (s, a, s', r) obtained by the agent, they can manipulate the states of any two nodes in s', *i.e.*, one false positive and one false negative, in order to prevent the agent from taking the next optimal action a' that has been learned so far (note that it may be different from the final optimal action). Specifically, for the DDQN agent, the attacker minimises $\max_{a'} Q(s' + \delta, a')$; for the A3C agent, the attacker minimises $\max_{a'} \pi(a'|s' + \delta)$.

Figure 4 presents the results we obtained during our experiments. The left-most bars in Figs. 4a and 4b suggest that the unlimited indiscriminate white-box attacks are very effective against both DDQN and A3C. Specifically, the average number of preserved nodes decreases from 21 and 20 to 3.3 and 4.9, respectively.

White-Box Attacks with Limits on the Choices of False Positive and False Negative. As pointed out in Subsect. 3.2, even though the attacker only manipulates the states of two nodes each time, overall, they still need to be able to control a number of nodes, which is unlikely in practice. We calculate the number of times that each node is chosen in the above unlimited attacks, and find that some nodes are selected more frequently than others (Fig. 5; the histograms for the A3C case are omitted due to similarity).

Therefore, when poisoning the DDQN agent, we limit the false positive nodes to {3.5 (node ID 18), 4.1 (node ID 23)}, and limit the false negative nodes to

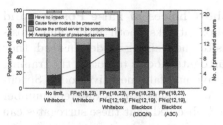

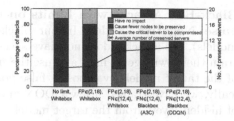

(a) Indiscriminate attacks against DDQN   (b) Indiscriminate attacks against A3C

Fig. 4. Indiscriminate attacks against DDQN & A3C. The bars indicates the percentage of attacks (left y−axis) that (1) have no impact; (2) cause fewer nodes to be preserved; and (3) cause the critical server to be compromised. The line marked by "×" indicates the average number of preserved servers (right y−axis). The five types of attacks are: (1) white-box, no limit on FNs&FPs; (2) white-box, with limits on FP but not on FN, (3) white-box, with limits on both FP and FN; (4) black-box, same algorithm, with limits on both FPs and FNs; (5) black-box, different algorithm, with limits on both FPs and FNs.

{2.7 (node ID 12), 3.6 (node ID 19)}. We use node 4.1 instead of 3.4 (node ID 17), as otherwise both selected nodes would be from the target subnet and directly connected to the target, which is unlikely in real situations. In the A3C case, the false positive and false negative nodes are limited to {1.3 (node ID 2), 3.5 (node ID 18)}, and {2.7 (node ID 12), 1.5 (node ID 4)}, respectively.

The second and third bars in Figs. 4a and 4b show that the limit has an obvious negative impact on the attack, especially the limit on the false negative nodes. Still, less than half of the nodes are preserved on average, compared with the scenarios without attacks.

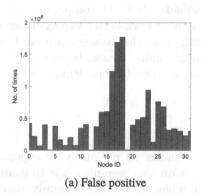

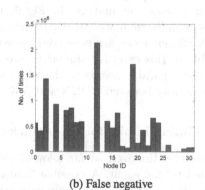

(a) False positive   (b) False negative

Fig. 5. Histograms of the false positive and false negative nodes being selected against DDQN. N.B.: The node IDs {0, 1, ..., 31} are ordered and mapped to the node sequence {1.1, 1.2, ..., 1.6, 2.1, ..., 2.8, 3.1, ..., 3.9, 4.1, ..., 4.9}

Black-Box Attacks with Limits on the Choices of False Positive and False Negative Nodes. In our black-box attacks (both intra- and cross-models), the attacker does not have access to the training model. Instead, they train their own agents first, and use the surrogate models to poison the training of the target models by choosing false positive and false negative nodes. Specifically, we have trained a few DDQN and A3C agents with a different number of hidden layers from the target model, and observed that these surrogates can still prevent the critical server from compromising.

As illustrated by the rightmost two bars in Figs. 4a and b, black-box attacks are only slightly less effective than the counterpart white-box attacks despite the surrogate using a different model. This lends support that transferability also exists between RL algorithms, *i.e.*, attacks generated for one model may also transfer to another model.

5.4   Attack II: Manipulate State—Targeted Attacks

In the targeted attacks considered here, the attacker is assumed to know the sequence of final optimal actions, and attempts to minimise the probability of the agent following that sequence. It should be pointed out that we have also studied the case where the attacker instead maximises the probability of taking a specific non-optimal action for each step, but our results suggested that this is less effective.

We find that in targeted attacks, certain nodes are also selected more frequently as a false positive and false negative. In this scenario, we limit false positive nodes to (1) {3.5 (node ID 18), 4.1 (node ID 23)} against DDQN, (2) {2.6 (node ID 11), 1.4 (node ID 3)} against A3C, and limit false negative nodes to (1) {1.5 (node ID 4), 2.1 (node ID 6)} against DDQN, (2) {4.1 (node ID 23), 2.4 (node ID 9)} against A3C.

Our results, summarised in Fig. 6, indicate that (1) compared with the results on indiscriminate attacks, targeted attacks work better, especially against DDQN (fewer nodes are preserved on average), as the attacker is more knowledgeable in this case; (2) similar to the indiscriminate case, black-box attacks achieve comparable results to the white-box attacks, further demonstrating the transferability between DDQN and A3C.

5.5   Timing Limits for the Attacks

The attacks discussed so far allowed the attacker to poison every experience obtained by the agent. A possible limitation on this assumption is to examine whether these attacks can remain successful when the attacker can only manipulate part of the experiences. Therefore, in this subsection we shall look at attacks that poison only a subset (the first three steps) in each training episode.

Figures 7a and 7b depict the results of the time-limited version of (cross-model) black-box attacks against DDQN and white-box attacks against A3C (both with limit on the choices of FPs and FNs), respectively. The results suggest

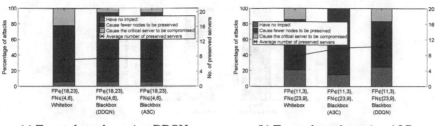

(a) Targeted attacks against DDQN   (b) Targeted attacks against A3C

Fig. 6. Targeted attacks against DDQN & A3C.

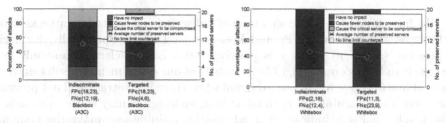

(a) Time limited black-box attacks against DDQN (b) Time limited white-box attacks against A3C

Fig. 7. Attacks against DDQN&A3C with time limit. The attacker only poisons the first three steps per training episode.

that even though the time limit has a negative impact in every scenario studied, the attacks are still effective.

5.6 Discussion on Countermeasures

In supervised learning problems, adversarial training [21,57,58] has the defender select a target point (x, y) from the training set, modify x to x^* (*i.e.*, generates an adversarial sample), and then inject (x^*, y) back into the training set, under the implicit assumption that the true label y should not change given the instance has been only slightly perturbed.

In our RL setting, while the attacker manipulates the observed states to minimise the probability of the agent taking the optimal action a in state s, the defender can construct adversarial samples that counteract the effect. For example, for each experience (s, a, s', r), the defender can increase r by a small amount, *e.g.*, 5% of the original value, given that r is positive and a is not chosen randomly (the probability of choosing an action randomly decreases as the training proceeds). The rationale behind this modification is that when the poisoning attack starts out, it is likely that a is still the optimal action (that has been learned so far) for state s. If r is positive it means that action a is a relatively good option for s, and since the attacker has poisoned the state to prevent the agent from taking a, we slightly increase r to encourage the agent to take action a.

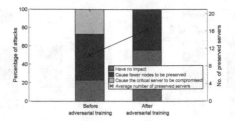

Fig. 8. Adversarial training against indiscriminate white-box attacks with limits on the choices of FPs and FNs (against DDQN), $FP \in \{18, 23\}, FN \in \{12, 19\}$

We have tested the above idea against indiscriminate white-box attacks with a limit on the choices of FPs and FNs against DDQN. Specifically, for each experience (s, a, s', r) whose r is positive and a is not selected randomly, we change it to $(s, a, s', min(1.0, 1.05r))$. Note that our experimental results suggest that adding 5% error to the reward signal when there is no attack will not prevent the agent from learning the optimal actions, although it may cause some delay. The results in Fig. 8 indicate that adversarial training can make the training process much less vulnerable.

However, the results are still preliminary, and we plan to further investigate other forms of adversarial training. For example, Pinto et al. [51] model all potential disturbances as an extra adversarial agent, whose goal is to minimise the discounted reward of the leading agent. They formulate the policy learning problem as a two player zero-sum game, and propose an algorithm that optimises both agents by alternating learning one agent's policy with the other policy being fixed. In addition, we will also study the impact of the loss function, prioritised experience replay, ensemble adversarial training [58] and other, more intrusive types of attacks, where the adversary is aware of the defence method, and attacks the defended model.

6   Related Work

This section reviews ways in which attackers can target machine learning systems and current defence mechanisms. We first present a taxonomy on attacks against (primarily) supervised classifiers, and then summarise recent work that applies/modifies these attacks to manipulate RL systems. Finally, we review existing countermeasures against adversarial machine learning.

6.1   Taxonomy of Attacks Against Machine Learning Classifiers

Barreno et al. [6] develop a qualitative taxonomy of attacks against ML classifiers based on three axes: influence (*causative* vs. *exploratory attacks*), security violation (*integrity* vs. *availability attacks*) and specificity (*indiscriminate* vs. *targeted attacks*).

Table 2 uses the taxonomy to classify previous work on adversarial machine learning against classifiers. As can be seen, more focus has been paid to exploratory integrity attacks. Presently, the Fast Gradient Sign Method (FGSM) attack [21] is widely studied, and the C&W attack [14] is the most effective found so far on the application domains tested, mostly in computer vision. Both of these attack methods can be used for targeted or indiscriminate attacks.

With further examination of the attacker's capabilities, a powerful attacker may also know the internal architecture and parameters of the classifier. Therefore, a fourth dimension can be added to the above taxonomy according to attacker information: in *white-box attacks*, the adversary generates malicious instances against the target classifier directly; while in *black-box attacks*, since the attacker does not possess full knowledge about the model, they first approximate the target's model. Then if the reconstructed model generalises well, the crafted adversarial examples against this model can be transferred to the target network and induce misclassifications. Papernot *et al.* [47,48] have demonstrated the effectiveness of the black-box attack in certain specific domains.

6.2   Attacks Against Reinforcement Learning

In more recent studies, several papers have begun to study whether attacks against classifiers can also be applied to RL-based systems. Huang *et al.* [28] have shown that deep RL is vulnerable to adversarial samples generated by the Fast Gradient Sign Method [21]. Their experimental results demonstrate that both white-box and black-box attacks are effective, even though the less knowledge the adversary has, the less effective the adversarial samples are. Behzadan & Munir [8] establish that adversaries can interfere with the training process of DQNs, preventing the victim from learning the correct policy. Specifically, the attacker applies minimum perturbation to the state observed by the target, so that a different action is chosen as the optimal action at the next state. The perturbation is generated using the same techniques proposed against DNN classifiers. Lin *et al.* [34] propose strategically-timed attacks and enchanting attacks against deep reinforcement learning agents.

6.3   Adversarial Machine Learning Defences

A number of countermeasures have been proposed since the discovery of adversarial samples. These can be roughly categorised into two classes: *data-driven defences* and *learner robustification*.

Data-Driven Defences. This class of defences are data driven—they either filter out the malicious data, inject adversarial samples into the training dataset, or manipulate features via projection. These approaches are akin to black-box defences since they make little to no use of the learner.

Table 2. Taxonomy of attacks on machine learners, with representative past work. As the taxonomy was designed for supervised learners, we include attacks on reinforcement learning in Sect. 6.2.

	Integrity	Availability
Causative, targeted	Rubinstein *et al.* [52]: boiling frog attacks against the PCA anomaly detection algorithm; Li *et al.* [32]: poison training data against collaborative filtering systems; Mei and Zhu [36]: identify the optimal training set to manipulate different machine learners; Burkard and Lagesse [12]: targeted causative attack on SVMs that are learning from a data stream	Newsome *et al.* [45]: manipulate training set of classifiers for worms and spam to block legitimate instances; Chung and Mok [16]: generate harmful signatures to filter out legitimate network traffic
Causative, indiscriminate	Biggio *et al.* [11]: inject crafted training data to increase SVM's test error; Xiao *et al.* [60]: label flips attack against SVMs; Koh and Liang [29]: minimise the number of crafted training data via influence analysis	Newsome *et al.* [45]; Chung and Mok [16]; Nelson *et al.* [43]: exploit statistical machine learning against a popular email spam filter
Exploratory, targeted	Nelson *et al.* [44]: probe a classifier to determine good attack points; Papernot *et al.* [49]: exploits forward derivatives to search for the minimum regions of the inputs to perturb; Goodfellow *et al.* [21]: design FGSM to generate adversarial samples; Carlini and Wagner [14]: propose the C&W method for creating adversarial samples; Han and Rubinstein [22]: improve the gradient descent method by replacing with gradient quotient	Moore *et al.* [40]: provide quantitative estimates of denial-of-service activity
Exploratory, indiscriminate	Biggio *et al.* [10]: find attack instances against SVMs via gradient descent; Szegedy *et al.* [57] demonstrate that changes imperceptible to human eyes can make DNNs misclassify an image; Goodfellow *et al.* [21]; Papernot *et al.* [47,48]: attack the target learner via a surrogate model; Moosavi-Dezfooli *et al.* [41,42]: propose DeepFool against DNNs; Carlini and Wagner [14]; Nguyen *et al.* [46]: produce images that are unrecognisable to humans, but can be recognised by DNNs; Han and Rubinstein [22]	Moore *et al.* [40]

- Filtering instances. These counter-measures assume that the poisoning data in the training dataset or the adversarial samples against the test dataset either exhibit different statistical features, or follow a different distribution. Therefore, they propose to identify and filter out the injected/perturbed data [20,30,33,37,55].
- Injecting data. Goodfellow et al. [21] attribute the existence of adversarial samples to the "blind spots" of the training algorithm, and propose injecting adversarial examples into training to improve the generalisation capabilities of DNNs [21,57]. Tramer et al. [58] extend such adversarial training methods by incorporating perturbations generated against other models.
- Projecting data. Previous work has shown that high dimensionality facilitates the generation of adversarial samples, resulting in an increased attack surface [59]. To counter this, data can be projected into lower-dimensional space before testing [9,17,61]. However, these results contradict with [31], which suggests that more features should be used when facing adversarial evasion.

Learner Robustification. Rather than focusing solely on training and test data, this class of methods—which are white-box in nature—aim to design models to be less susceptible to adversarial samples in the first place.

- Stabilisation. Zheng et al. [62] design stability training that modifies the model's objective function by adding a stability term. Papernot et al. [50] provide examples using a distillation strategy against a saliency-map attack. However, this method is shown to be ineffective by Carlini and Wagner [13]. Hosseini et al. [26] propose to improve adversarial training by adding an additional "NULL" class.
- Moving target. Sengupta et al. [54] apply moving target defences against exploratory attacks: the defender prepares a pool of models instead of a single model, and for each image to be classified, one trained DNN is picked following certain strategy.
- Robust statistics. Another avenue that has remained relatively unexplored is to leverage ideas from robust statistics, e.g., influence functions, M-estimators with robust loss functions. Rubinstein et al. [52] applied a robust form of PCA to defend against causative attacks on network-wide volume anomaly detection. Recently, interest in the theoretical computer science community has turned to robust estimation in high dimensions, e.g., Diakonikolas et al. [18].

Lessons Learned. Despite many defences proposed, several recent studies [15,25] point out that most of these methods unrealistically assume that the attacker is not aware of the defence mechanism, and only consider relatively weak attacks, e.g., FGSM [21]. Negative results are reported on the effectiveness of these methods against adaptive attackers that are aware of the defence and act accordingly, and against the C&W attack [14]. More recently, Athalye et al. [5] show that defences relied on obfuscated gradients can also be circumvented.

7   Conclusions and Future Work

In this paper, we demonstrated the feasibility of developing autonomous defence in SDN using RL algorithms. In particular, we studied the impact of different forms of causative attacks, and showed that even though these attacks might cause RL agents to take sub-optimal actions, adversarial training could be applied to mitigate the impact.

For future work, we plan to (1) use a traffic generator to introduce background traffic between nodes, and use network performance metrics to replace the current binary states; (2) consider different types of network traffic, so that the actions of the RL agent could include partial isolation in terms of blocking certain protocols between nodes; (3) change full observability of the network status to partial observability—the defender may have limited resources, and the attacker may not know the entire topology; and (4) remove limiting assumptions, *e.g.*, the attacker having to compromise all nodes along the path to the critical server.

References

1. Amazon EC2 Instance Types – Amazon Web Services (AWS). https://aws.amazon.com/ec2/instance-types/
2. SDN architecture. Technical report, June 2014. https://www.opennetworking.org/wp-content/uploads/2013/02/TR_SDN_ARCH_1.0_06062014.pdf
3. Mininet: An Instant Virtual Network on your Laptop (2017). http://mininet.org/
4. OpenDaylight (2017). https://www.opendaylight.org/
5. Athalye, A., Carlini, N., Wagner, D.: Obfuscated gradients give a false sense of security: circumventing defenses to adversarial examples. arXiv:1802.00420 [cs], February 2018
6. Barreno, M., Nelson, B., Joseph, A.D., Tygar, J.D.: The security of machine learning. Mach. Learn. **81**(2), 121–148 (2010)
7. Beaudoin, L.: Autonomic computer network defence using risk states and reinforcement learning. Ph.D. thesis, University of Ottawa (Canada) (2009)
8. Behzadan, V., Munir, A.: Vulnerability of deep reinforcement learning to policy induction attacks. eprint arXiv:1701.04143 (2017)
9. Bhagoji, A.N., Cullina, D., Mittal, P.: Dimensionality reduction as a defense against evasion attacks on machine learning classifiers. arXiv:1704.02654 (2017)
10. Biggio, B., et al.: Security evaluation of support vector machines in adversarial environments. In: Ma, Y., Guo, G. (eds.) Support Vector Machines Applications, pp. 105–153. Springer, Cham (2014). https://doi.org/10.1007/978-3-319-02300-7_4
11. Biggio, B., Nelson, B., Laskov, P.: Poisoning attacks against support vector machines. In: Proceedings of the 29th International Conference on International Conference on Machine Learning, pp. 1467–1474. Omnipress, Edinburgh (2012)
12. Burkard, C., Lagesse, B.: Analysis of causative attacks against SVMs learning from data streams. In: Proceedings of the 3rd ACM on International Workshop on Security And Privacy Analytics, pp. 31–36. ACM, New York (2017)
13. Carlini, N., Wagner, D.: Defensive distillation is not robust to adversarial examples. arXiv:1607.04311 (2016)

14. Carlini, N., Wagner, D.: Towards evaluating the robustness of neural networks. eprint arXiv:1608.04644 (2016)
15. Carlini, N., Wagner, D.: Adversarial examples are not easily detected: bypassing ten detection methods. eprint arXiv:1705.07263 (2017)
16. Chung, S.P., Mok, A.K.: Advanced allergy attacks: does a corpus really help? In: Kruegel, C., Lippmann, R., Clark, A. (eds.) RAID 2007. LNCS, vol. 4637, pp. 236–255. Springer, Heidelberg (2007). https://doi.org/10.1007/978-3-540-74320-0_13
17. Das, N., et al.: Keeping the bad guys out: protecting and vaccinating deep learning with JPEG compression. eprint arXiv:1705.02900, May 2017
18. Diakonikolas, I., Kamath, G., Kane, D.M., Li, J., Moitra, A., Stewart, A.: Robust estimators in high dimensions without the computational intractability. In: Proceedings of the 2016 IEEE 57th Annual Symposium on Foundations of Computer Science (FOCS), pp. 655–664, October 2016
19. Everitt, T., Krakovna, V., Orseau, L., Hutter, M., Legg, S.: Reinforcement learning with a corrupted reward channel. eprint arXiv:1705.08417 (2017)
20. Feinman, R., Curtin, R.R., Shintre, S., Gardner, A.B.: Detecting adversarial samples from artifacts. eprint arXiv:1703.00410 (2017)
21. Goodfellow, I.J., Shlens, J., Szegedy, C.: Explaining and harnessing adversarial examples. eprint arXiv:1412.6572 (2014)
22. Han, Y., Rubinstein, B.I.P.: Adequacy of the gradient-descent method for classifier evasion attacks. arXiv:1704.01704, April 2017
23. Hasselt, H.V.: Double Q-learning. In: Lafferty, J.D., Williams, C.K.I., Shawe-Taylor, J., Zemel, R.S., Culotta, A. (eds.) Advances in Neural Information Processing Systems 23, pp. 2613–2621. Curran Associates, Inc. (2010)
24. Hasselt, H.V., Guez, A., Silver, D.: Deep reinforcement learning with double Q-learning. eprint arXiv:1509.06461, September 2015
25. He, W., Wei, J., Chen, X., Carlini, N., Song, D.: Adversarial example defenses: ensembles of weak defenses are not strong. eprint arXiv:1706.04701 (2017)
26. Hosseini, H., Chen, Y., Kannan, S., Zhang, B., Poovendran, R.: Blocking transferability of adversarial examples in black-box learning systems. eprint arXiv:1703.04318 (2017)
27. Huang, L., Joseph, A.D., Nelson, B., Rubinstein, B.I., Tygar, J.: Adversarial machine learning. In: Proceedings of the 4th ACM Workshop on Security and Artificial Intelligence, pp. 43–58. ACM (2011)
28. Huang, S., Papernot, N., Goodfellow, I., Duan, Y., Abbeel, P.: Adversarial attacks on neural network policies. eprint arXiv:1702.02284 (2017)
29. Koh, P.W., Liang, P.: understanding black-box predictions via influence functions. arXiv:1703.04730 [cs, stat], March 2017
30. Laishram, R., Phoha, V.V.: Curie: a method for protecting SVM Classifier from poisoning attack. arXiv:1606.01584 [cs], June 2016
31. Li, B., Vorobeychik, Y.: Feature cross-substitution in adversarial classification. In: Proceedings of the 2014 NIPS, NIPS 2014, pp. 2087–2095, MIT Press, Cambridge (2014)
32. Li, B., Wang, Y., Singh, A., Vorobeychik, Y.: Data poisoning attacks on factorization-based collaborative filtering. eprint arXiv:1608.08182 (2016)
33. Li, X., Li, F.: Adversarial examples detection in deep networks with convolutional filter statistics. arXiv:1612.07767 [cs], December 2016
34. Lin, Y.C., Hong, Z.W., Liao, Y.H., Shih, M.L., Liu, M.Y., Sun, M.: Tactics of adversarial attack on deep reinforcement learning agents. eprint arXiv:1703.06748, March 2017

35. Medved, J., Varga, R., Tkacik, A., Gray, K.: OpenDaylight: towards a model-driven SDN controller architecture. In: Proceedings of IEEE International Symposium on a World of Wireless, Mobile and Multimedia Networks, pp. 1–6 (2014)
36. Mei, S., Zhu, X.: Using machine teaching to identify optimal training-set attacks on machine learners. In: Proceedings of the Twenty-Ninth AAAI Conference on Artificial Intelligence, pp. 2871–2877. AAAI Press, Austin (2015)
37. Metzen, J.H., Genewein, T., Fischer, V., Bischoff, B.: On detecting adversarial perturbations. eprint arXiv:1702.04267 (2017)
38. Mnih, V., et al.: Asynchronous methods for deep reinforcement learning. In: Proceedings of the 33rd International Conference on International Conference on Machine Learning, ICML 2016, vol. 48, pp. 1928–1937. JMLR.org, New York (2016)
39. Mnih, V., et al.: Playing Atari with Deep Reinforcement Learning. CoRR abs/1312.5602 (2013)
40. Moore, D., Shannon, C., Brown, D.J., Voelker, G.M., Savage, S.: Inferring internet denial-of-service activity. ACM Trans. Comput. Syst. **24**(2), 115–139 (2006)
41. Moosavi-Dezfooli, S.M., Fawzi, A., Fawzi, O., Frossard, P.: Universal adversarial perturbations. eprint arXiv:1610.08401 (2016)
42. Moosavi-Dezfooli, S.M., Fawzi, A., Frossard, P.: DeepFool: a simple and accurate method to fool deep neural networks. In: CVPR, pp. 2574–2582 (2016)
43. Nelson, B., et al.: Exploiting machine learning to subvert your spam filter. In: Proceedings of the First USENIX Workshop on Large-scale Exploits and Emergent Threats (LEET 2008) (2008)
44. Nelson, B., et al.: Query strategies for evading convex-inducing classifiers. J. Mach. Learn. Res. **13**(May), 1293–1332 (2012)
45. Newsome, J., Karp, B., Song, D.: Paragraph: thwarting signature learning by training maliciously. In: Zamboni, D., Kruegel, C. (eds.) RAID 2006. LNCS, vol. 4219, pp. 81–105. Springer, Heidelberg (2006). https://doi.org/10.1007/11856214_5
46. Nguyen, A., Yosinski, J., Clune, J.: Deep neural networks are easily fooled: high confidence predictions for unrecognizable images. In: CVPR, pp. 427–436 (2015)
47. Papernot, N., McDaniel, P., Goodfellow, I.: Transferability in machine learning: from phenomena to black-box attacks using adversarial samples. eprint arXiv:1605.07277 (2016)
48. Papernot, N., McDaniel, P., Goodfellow, I., Jha, S., Celik, Z.B., Swami, A.: Practical black-box attacks against deep learning systems using adversarial examples. eprint arXiv:1602.02697 (2016)
49. Papernot, N., McDaniel, P., Jha, S., Fredrikson, M., Celik, Z.B., Swami, A.: The limitations of deep learning in adversarial settings. In: Proceedings of the European Symposium on Security & Privacy, pp. 372–387 (2016)
50. Papernot, N., McDaniel, P., Wu, X., Jha, S., Swami, A.: Distillation as a defense to adversarial perturbations against deep neural networks. eprint arXiv:1511.04508 (2015)
51. Pinto, L., Davidson, J., Sukthankar, R., Gupta, A.: Robust adversarial reinforcement learning. eprint arXiv:1703.02702 (2017)
52. Rubinstein, B.I., et al.: ANTIDOTE: understanding and defending against poisoning of anomaly detectors. In: Proceedings of the 9th ACM SIGCOMM Conference on Internet Measurement, pp. 1–14. ACM (2009)
53. Schaul, T., Quan, J., Antonoglou, I., Silver, D.: Prioritized Experience Replay. CoRR abs/1511.05952 (2015)
54. Sengupta, S., Chakraborti, T., Kambhampati, S.: Securing deep neural nets against adversarial attacks with moving target defense. eprint arXiv:1705.07213, May 2017

55. Steinhardt, J., Koh, P.W., Liang, P.: Certified defenses for data poisoning attacks. eprint arXiv:1706.03691, June 2017
56. Sutton, R.S., Barto, A.G.: Introduction to Reinforcement Learning, 1st edn. MIT Press, Cambridge (1998)
57. Szegedy, C., et al.: Intriguing properties of neural networks. eprint arXiv:1312.6199 (2013)
58. Tramèr, F., Kurakin, A., Papernot, N., Boneh, D., McDaniel, P.: Ensemble adversarial training: attacks and defenses. eprint arXiv:1705.07204, May 2017
59. Wang, B., Gao, J., Qi, Y.: A theoretical framework for robustness of (deep) classifiers against adversarial examples. eprint arXiv:1612.00334 (2016)
60. Xiao, H., Xiao, H., Eckert, C.: Adversarial label flips attack on support vector machines. In: Proceedings of the 20th European Conference on Artificial Intelligence. ECAI 2012, pp. 870–875, IOS Press, Amsterdam (2012)
61. Zhang, F., Chan, P.P.K., Biggio, B., Yeung, D.S., Roli, F.: Adversarial feature selection against evasion attacks. IEEE Trans. Cybern. **46**(3), 766–777 (2016)
62. Zheng, S., Song, Y., Leung, T., Goodfellow, I.: Improving the robustness of deep neural networks via stability training. eprint arXiv:1604.04326 (2016)

Colonel Blotto Game with Coalition
Formation for Sharing Resources

Joseph L. Heyman$^{(\boxtimes)}$ and Abhishek Gupta

The Ohio State University, Columbus, OH 43210, USA
{heyman.14,gupta.706}@osu.edu

Abstract. In this paper, we consider a 4-player, two stage Colonel Blotto game in which one player, the attacker, simultaneously participates in three disjoint Colonel Blotto games against three defenders. During the first stage of the game, the defenders can choose to form independent coalitions by transferring resources (troops, funds, computing resources, etc.) among each other if the transfer benefits the defenders involved. In the second stage, the attacker observes these transfers among defenders and then allocates a portion of his overall resources to fight against each defender. We find that the formation of coalitions depends on both the ratios of resources between the attacker and the defenders and on each defender's total battlefield value to resource ratio. For one parameter region, we completely characterize the subgame-perfect Nash equilibrium. For another parameter region, we show that there are parameters of the game for which transfers occur and provide a computational method to calculate those transfers.

Keywords: Constant sum game with resource constraints
Colonel Blotto game · Coalition formation in games

1 Introduction

The Colonel Blotto game, first proposed by Borel in 1921 [2,3], is a classic constant-sum model of resource allocation between two budget constrained players. In this game, two players, Colonels A and B, have resource levels X_A and X_B, respectively. Each player allocates his resources across a finite number of battlefields. Whichever player allocates the most resources to a single battlefield wins that battle. The winner of the game is the player that wins the most battlefields.

The Colonel Blotto game has diverse applications within military and security domains, where agencies allocate limited resources across various geographic

The first author was fully supported by the United States Military Academy and the Army Advanced Civil Schooling (ACS) program.

The second author gratefully acknowledges support from NSF Grant 1565487.

L. Bushnell et al. (Eds.): GameSec 2018, LNCS 11199, pp. 166–185, 2018.
https://doi.org/10.1007/978-3-030-01554-1_10

locations to counter adversarial threats. In addition, the model is useful to analyze situations including network resource games [12,20], cyber-security games [5,11,16], economic contests [7,14], and political contests [8,15,19].

While the Colonel Blotto game seems relatively straightforward, it has proven difficult to solve. Borel's original formulation was first solved by Borel and Ville in 1938 for two players, three battlefields, and symmetric resource allocation [4]. In 1950, Gross and Wagner [9] solved the game for symmetric resource allocation and more than three battlefields. They also solved the case of two battlefields and asymmetric resource allocation. However, the Colonel Blotto game remained unsolved for asymmetric player resources and an arbitrary number of battlefields until Roberson's seminal work in 2006 [17]. Roberson advanced the field significantly, with many follow-on works that extended his solution to specific applications.

In this work, we consider a four-player, two-stage Colonel Blotto game in which one player, the attacker, simultaneously participates in three disjoint Colonel Blotto games against three defenders. During the first stage of the game, the defenders can choose to form an alliance, or coalition, by transferring a single-dimensional resource (troops, funds, computing resources, etc.) from one defender to another. This transfer between two defenders only occurs when the transfer will not decrease both defenders' payoffs in the final stage. The attacker observes these transfers between defenders and then allocates a portion of his overall resources to the final stage Colonel Blotto game against each defender.

Similar to [10,11,13], we consider a model of noncooperative alliances in which only individually rational *ex ante* transfers of resources are allowed. As such, the model does not rely on any assumption of commitment to a coalition nor the *ex post* division of payoffs.

We find that the formation of coalitions, based on the transfer of resources, depends on both the ratios of resources between the attacker and a defender and on each defender's total battlefield value to resource ratio. In one case that we study, only resource rich defenders are willing to transfer resources. However, in another case, somewhat counter-intuitively, the most resource rich defender does not necessarily transfer resources to other defenders. Instead, defenders that have a lower total battlefield value to resource ratio are those that tend to be willing to transfer resources.

Other authors have considered coalition formation in Colonel Blotto games. In [14], Kovenock and Roberson consider the same game that we've described above but with only two defenders. In addition, they only consider cases where transfers between defenders strictly improve the payoff of each defender. The authors characterize the attacker's resource division strategy for multiple regions of the resource budget and calculate parameters for when a transfer of resources between defenders occurs. However, they do not calculate the amount of resource transfer. In [11], Gupta et al. also consider a multi-stage, one attacker, two defender complete information Colonel Blotto game. In their formulation, in addition to transferring resources, the two defenders can choose to add additional battlefields, at some cost per battlefield. The authors find the subgame-perfect

Nash equilibrium (SPNE) for this game for certain parameter regions. Finally, in [10], Gupta et al. consider a change to the information structure from [11], where the attacker can not observe the resource transfer between the two defenders. They find that in some parameter regions the SPNE remains unchanged, while in other regions the SPNE is significantly different from [11].

As far as we are aware, this work is the first attempt to extend this multi-stage Colonel Blotto game setting to more than two defenders. In the two defenders case, there is only one possible coalition formation. In the N defender case, the number of possible coalitions are $\frac{N(N-1)}{2} = O(N^2)$. Thus, the seemingly simple extension to the previous case requires us to investigate a large number of possible coalition formations. We view our work as an attempt to identify situations where the analysis can be simplified and understand regimes where coalitions can be formed.

1.1 Outline of the Paper

In Sect. 2, we present a brief overview of the Classical Colonel Blotto game and review the pertinent results from [17]. Following that, we formalize the multi-stage model used throughout this paper in Sect. 3 and present the main results. In Sect. 4, we derive the best response of the attacker. Sections 5 and 6 are devoted to computing the equilibrium transfers among the defenders under two assumptions on the strength of the attacker. Finally, in Sect. 7, we conclude with an analysis of the work and highlight directions for future work.

2 The Classical Colonel Blotto Model

In this section, we introduce the classic asymmetric resource, homogeneous battlefield value Colonel Blotto game (CBG) and appropriate notations. In the classic CBG, two players, call them A and B, simultaneously allocate their forces, X_A and X_B, across a finite number, n, of homogeneous battlefields with value v. Battlefield values are homogeneous; therefore, we have $v_j = v_k \; \forall j, k \in \{1, \ldots, n\}$. If a player sends a higher level of force to battlefield j, then that player wins that battlefield and receives a payoff of v_j. If the player sends a lower level of force to battlefield j, then that player loses and receives a payoff of 0. Each player's total payoff in the game is the sum of the payoffs across the battlefields. Without loss of generality, assume $X_A \leq X_B$, so that player B is the "stronger" player. In the case of a tie, we follow [17] and assume that player B wins the battlefield.

More formally, we can define the classic CBG similarly to the definition in [6]. The classic CBG $\{\mathcal{P}, \{\mathcal{X}\}_{i \in \mathcal{P}}, \{X_i\}_{i \in \mathcal{P}}, \mathcal{N}, \{v_j\}_{j=1}^{n}, \{U_i\}_{i \in \mathcal{P}}\}$ is defined by six components: (a) the players in the set $\mathcal{P} \triangleq \{A, B\}$, (b) the strategy spaces $\mathcal{X}_i$ for $i \in \mathcal{P}$, (c) the available resource X_i for $i \in \mathcal{P}$, (d) the set of n battlefields, $\mathcal{N}$, (e) the homogeneous value of each battlefield, $v_j = v_k \; \forall j, k \in \mathcal{N}$, and (f) the utility function U_i for each player $i \in \mathcal{P}$.

The force allocated to each battlefield must be non-negative. Therefore, the strategy space of each player corresponds to the set of feasible allocations across the n battlefields and is given by

$$\mathcal{X}_i = \left\{ \mathbf{x}_i \in \mathbb{R}^n_{\geq 0} \mid \sum_{j=1}^n x_{i,j} \leq X_i \right\}, \tag{1}$$

where $x_{i,j}$ is the number of allocated resources by player i to battlefield j. The payoff of player i on battlefield j is defined as:

$$u_{i,j}(x_{i,j}, x_{-i,j}) = \begin{cases} v_j & \text{if } x_{i,j} > x_{-i,j}, \\ \text{t.b.r} & \text{if } x_{i,j} = x_{-i,j}, \\ 0 & \text{if } x_{i,j} < x_{-i,j}, \end{cases} \tag{2}$$

where t.b.r indicates the tie breaking rule and we use the common game theoretic notation $-i$ to refer to all players except player i. We follow [17] and the tie breaking rule is to assume that the stronger player (player with greater resources) wins the battlefield.

Finally, the utility function, U_i, for each player is defined as:

$$U_i(\mathbf{x}_i, \mathbf{x}_{-i}) = \sum_{j=1}^n u_{i,j}(x_{i,j}, x_{-i,j}). \tag{3}$$

The classic CBG is a complete information game. All parameters of the game,

$$\text{CBG}\{\mathcal{P}, \{\mathcal{X}\}_{i \in \mathcal{P}}, \{X_i\}_{i \in \mathcal{P}}, \mathcal{N}, \{v_j\}_{j=1}^n, \{U_i\}_{i \in \mathcal{P}}\},$$

are assumed to be common knowledge among all players.

2.1 Strategies of the Players

In the trivial case, $\frac{1}{n}X_B \geq X_A$, there exists a pure strategy equilibrium where player B plays such that $x_{B,j} \geq \frac{1}{n}X_B \geq X_A$, $\mathbf{x}_B \in \mathcal{X}_B$ and wins all of the battlefields. For non-trivial cases, $\frac{1}{n}X_B < X_A \leq X_B$, it is well known that there is no pure strategy equilibrium [17]. Following [17], we define a mixed strategy, or distribution of force, for player i as an n-variate distribution function P_i : $\mathbb{R}^n_{\geq 0} \rightarrow [0,1]$ with support in $\mathcal{X}_i$, and with one-dimensional marginal distribution functions $\{F_i^j\}_{j \in \{1,...,n\}}$. A single play of the game for player i corresponds to a random n-tuple drawn from P_i with the set of univariate marginal distribution functions $\{F_i^j\}_{j \in \{1,...,n\}}$.

2.2 Nash Equilibrium of the Classic Colonel Blotto Game

Roberson completely characterized the unique equilibrium payoffs for the asymmetric resource, homogeneous battlefield value CBG in [17]. Below we summarize his results for the cases that we study in this work.

Lemma 1 (Roberson [17,18]). *For the Classic Colonel Blotto Game,*

$$CBG\{\{1,2\}, \{\mathcal{B}_1, \mathcal{B}_2\}, \{r_1, r_2\}, \mathcal{N}, \{v\}, \{U_1, U_2\}\},$$

with $n \geq 3$, assume that r_1 and r_2 are such that $\frac{1}{n-1} \leq \frac{r_1}{r_2} \leq n - 1$. Then the payoff functions under Nash equilibrium are given by:

$$
P^1(CBG) = \begin{cases} nv\left(\frac{2}{n} - \frac{2r_2}{n^2 r_1}\right) & \text{if } \frac{1}{n-1} \leq \frac{r_1}{r_2} < \frac{2}{n}, \\ nv\left(\frac{r_1}{2r_2}\right) & \text{if } \frac{2}{n} \leq \frac{r_1}{r_2} \leq 1, \\ nv\left(1 - \frac{r_2}{2r_1}\right) & \text{if } 1 \leq \frac{r_1}{r_2} \leq \frac{n}{2}, \\ nv\left(1 - \frac{2}{n} + \frac{2r_1}{n^2 r_2}\right) & \text{if } \frac{n}{2} < \frac{r_1}{r_2} < n - 1, \end{cases}
$$

$$P^2(CBG) = nv - P^1(CBG).$$

If $r_1 = 0$, then $P^1(CBG) = 0$.

For a detailed proof of Lemma 1, see [17, 18]. Roberson's result in [17] establishes the existence of the n-variate distributions with support in $\mathcal{B}_1, \mathcal{B}_2$ and with the equilibrium payoffs in Lemma 1. These n-variate distributions are not unique. However, since the game is constant sum, $(P^1(CBG) + P^2(CBG) = nv)$, the equilibrium payoffs are unique by ordered interchangeability property of multiple saddle-point equilibria in zero-sum games (we note here that constant sum games are strategically equivalent to zero-sum games).

3   Problem Formulation and Main Results

We consider a $3 + 1$ players, two-stage Colonel Blotto game. In this formulation, the first three players (defenders) fight against a common attacker. The initial resource allocation of the three defenders is denoted by β_i, $i \in \{1, 2, 3\}$. Similarly, we use α to denote the total resources of the attacker. The battle between the attacker and Player i takes place on $n_i \geq 3$ battlefields, where each battlefield has equal payoff $v_i > 0$. The description of the two stages are given below.

3.1   Stage One

In this stage, each defender decides on an amount of resources to transfer to the other two defenders, based on whether this transfer of resources will not decrease her expected payoff at the final stage. She also decides whether or not to accept resources from other defenders. We define $t_{i,j}$ as the transfer of resources from defender i to defender j and $t_{j,i}$ as transfer in the opposite direction. Since each defender's resource level, r_i, in the final stage game must be greater than or equal to zero, the total transfer out from defender i must be less than or equal to her starting resource level, β_i.

Thus, the resource level of each defender after transfer is complete is:

$$r_i(t_{i,1}, t_{i,2}, t_{i,3}, t_{1,i}, t_{2,i}, t_{3,i}) = \beta_i + \sum_{j=1}^{3}(t_{j,i} - t_{i,j}),$$

$$t_{i,i} = 0, \qquad \sum_{j=1}^{3} t_{i,j} \leq \beta_i.$$

For notational clarity, we define the strategy vector of transfers to/from defender i as $\mathbf{t}_i = (t_{i,1}, t_{i,2}, t_{i,3}, t_{1,i}, t_{2,i}, t_{3,i})$. We also define $\mathbf{t} = (\mathbf{t}_1, \mathbf{t}_2, \mathbf{t}_3)$ to represent all of the defenders' strategy vectors. In addition, in a slight abuse of notation, we use r_i to represent $r_i(\mathbf{t}_i)$ and α_i to represent $\alpha_i(\mathbf{t})$.

3.2   Stage Two (Final Stage)

Once the transfers are complete in the first stage, the attacker decides on the amount of resources, α_i, to allocate to each final stage battle such that:

$$\sum_{i=1}^{3} \alpha_i(\mathbf{t}) \leq \alpha, \quad \alpha_i(\mathbf{t}) \geq 0.$$

In the final stage of the game each defender battles with the attacker in an independent classic Colonel Blotto game using the resource allocation determined in stage one. The set of players for each battle is $\mathcal{P} \triangleq \{A, B_i\}$, where A represents the attacker and B_i represents defender i. Each individual battle takes place over a set of battlefields, $\mathcal{N}_i = \{1, \ldots, n_i\}$, belonging to defender i. For defender i, each battlefield has homogeneous value $v_k = v_{k'} \; \forall k, k' \in \mathcal{N}_i$. The strategy space of the attacker and defender in this game is, respectively,

$$\mathcal{A}_i = \left\{ \alpha_i \in \mathbb{R}_{\geq 0}^{n_i} \mid \sum_{j \in \mathcal{N}_i} \alpha_{i,j} \leq \alpha_i \right\}, \quad \mathcal{R}_i = \left\{ \mathbf{r}_i \in \mathbb{R}_{\geq 0}^{n_i} \mid \sum_{j \in \mathcal{N}_i} r_{i,j} \leq r_i \right\}.$$

Using the notation introduced in Sect. 2, each defender battles the attacker in a CBG given by:

$$\mathrm{CBG}\{\{A, B_i\}, \{\mathcal{A}_i, \mathcal{R}_i\}, \{\alpha_i, r_i\}, \mathcal{N}_i, v_i, \{U_i\}_{i \in \mathcal{P}}\}.$$

In shorthand notation, we refer to this individual final stage game as CBG[i].

We annotate the overall two-stage game described in this section as:

$$2\mathrm{CB}\{\{A, \{B_i\}\}, \{\alpha, \{\beta_i\}\}, \{\mathcal{N}_i\}, \{v_i\}\} \text{ with } i \in \{1, 2, 3\}$$

and refer to this overall two-stage game as 2CB.

In the overall game 2CB, the payoff to defender i is her payoff in the game CBG[i]. The attacker's overall payoff is the sum of his payoffs in the individual CBG[i] games.

In this work, we consider a small subset of the possible parameter regions. We focus on games where if all players play according to the SPNE in the first stage, then the resource allocation at the final stage is such that $\frac{2}{n_i} < \frac{\alpha_i}{r_i} < \frac{n_i}{2}$ for all $i \in \{1, 2, 3\}$ or $\alpha_i = 0$ for some $i \in \{1, 2, 3\}$. The two specific cases that we consider are:

1. $\frac{2}{n_i} < \frac{\alpha_i}{r_i} < 1 \quad \forall i \in \{1, 2, 3\}$,
2. $\frac{2}{n_i} < \frac{r_i}{\alpha_i} < 1 \quad \forall i \in \{1, 2, 3\}$.

We also introduce the following notation for clarity in presentation of the results. Let $D = \{1, 2, 3\}$ represent the set of defenders. Also, let $K_i = n_i v_i$, which is the total battlefield value (value of the game) CBG[i].

3.3 Main Results

In this subsection, we present the main results of the paper and briefly discuss the results. For clarity, we present the proofs of these results and a more detailed discussion in Sects. 4–6.

The proof outline for all three of the theorems we present here is similar and relies on using backwards induction to find the subgame-perfect Nash equilibrium (SPNE). Starting at the final stage, games, CBG^i, we use the results from [17] to calculate the Nash equilibrium (NE) of the final stage. We then calculate the attacker's optimal resource allocation in response to the stage one resource transfers between the defenders. Finally, we rank order the defenders based on the starting resource levels and calculate the defenders' optimal resource allocation to find the NE of the subgame starting at stage one.

We first consider the case where the attacker is the weakest player in the game. As such, the resource levels of the defenders and attacker are such that $\alpha < \min\{\beta_1, \beta_2, \beta_3\}$. In addition, assume that the vector of resource transfers, $\mathbf{t}$, is such that the game remains in case 1, $\frac{2}{n_i} < \frac{\alpha}{r_i} < 1 \quad \forall i \in \{1, 2, 3\}$. In general, one can think of the ratio $\frac{K_i}{\beta_i}$ as the relative strength of each defender. Without loss of generality, we index defenders by inverse relative strength:

$$\frac{K_1}{\beta_1} \geq \frac{K_2}{\beta_2} \geq \frac{K_3}{\beta_3}. \tag{4}$$

Theorem 1. *Consider a two-stage game, 2CB, where the parameters of the game are such that:*

1. $\alpha < \min\{\beta_1, \beta_2, \beta_3\}$,
2. $\frac{2}{n_i} < \frac{\alpha}{r_i} < 1 \quad \forall i \in \{1, 2, 3\}$,
3. $\beta_2(K_1 + K_3) - K_2(\beta_1 + \beta_3) \geq 0$,
4. $\frac{K_1}{\beta_1} > \frac{K_2}{\beta_2}$.

then there is a family of SPNEs such that:

$$\alpha_1^* = \alpha,$$
$$\alpha_2^* = 0, \quad \alpha_3^* = 0,$$
$$t_{1,2}^* = t_{1,3}^* = 0,$$
$$t_{2,1}^* + t_{2,3}^* \geq 0,$$
$$t_{3,1}^* + t_{3,2}^* \geq 0,$$
$$t_{2,1}^* + t_{2,3}^* < t_{3,2}^* + \frac{\beta_2(K_1 + K_3) - K_2(\beta_1 + \beta_3)}{K_1 + K_2 + K_3},$$
$$t_{3,1}^* + t_{3,2}^* < t_{2,3}^* + \frac{\beta_3(K_1 + K_2) - K_3(\beta_1 + \beta_2)}{K_1 + K_2 + K_3}.$$

From Theorem 1, we see that when the attacker is the weakest player in the game his optimal strategy is to battle with only one defender. However, the defender that he battles with is not necessarily the weakest defender in terms of overall resources, but the defender that is weakest in terms of resources to total battlefield value. Another observation is that defenders with less resources are willing to transfer resources to a defender with a higher resource level, as long as that transfer doesn't result in the defender making the transfer becoming the relatively weakest player.

We next consider the case where the attacker is much stronger than all of the defenders combined. We assume that $\alpha > \sum_{i=1}^{3} \beta_i$. In addition, assume that the vector of resource transfers, $\mathbf{t}$, is such that the game remains in case 2, $\frac{2}{n_i} < \frac{r_i}{\alpha_i} < 1 \quad \forall i \in \{1, 2, 3\}$.

Theorem 2. *Consider a two-stage game, 2CB, where the parameters of the game are such that:*

1. $\frac{2}{n_i} < \frac{r_i}{\alpha_i} < 1 \quad \forall i \in \{1, 2, 3\}, \forall \mathbf{t},$
2. $\beta_i - \beta_k > 2\sqrt{\frac{K_i}{K_k}} \sqrt{\beta_i \beta_k} + \sqrt{\frac{\beta_k}{K_k}} \sqrt{K_j \beta_j}$

then there is a positive transfer from defender i to defender k, $t_{i,k} > 0$.

Unlike the weakest attacker case, we observe from Theorem 2 that resource transfers only occur from a defender with a higher resource level to a defender with a lower resource level. In addition, if the difference in the resource levels between two defenders is higher than a certain threshold, then we observe that a transfer of some resources is a dominant strategy for those defenders. Finally, recall from the problem formulation in Sect. 3.1 that our model allows defender k to choose whether or not to accept a transfer from defender i. In the proof of Lemma 5 in Sect. 6, we find that defender k is always willing to accept resources from defender i whenever defender i is willing to transfer those resources. We also show that there are parameter regions where one defender is willing to accept resources, but other defenders are not willing to transfer. As a result, there is no coalition formation in this situation.

Finally, we consider a specific parameter configuration of the game and show that, in equilibrium, the strongest defender in terms of initial resource allocation, defender 1, transfers resources to at least one other defender and that there is no transfer between defenders 2 and 3.

Theorem 3. *Consider a two-stage game, 2CB, where the parameters of the game are such that:*

1. $\frac{2}{n_i} < \frac{r_i}{\alpha_i} < 1 \quad \forall i \in \{1, 2, 3\}, \forall \mathbf{t},$
2. $\beta_1 - \beta_2 > 2\sqrt{\frac{K_1}{K_2}} \sqrt{\beta_1 \beta_2} + \sqrt{\frac{\beta_2}{K_2}} \sqrt{K_3 \beta_3},$
3. $\beta_1 - \beta_3 > 2\sqrt{\frac{K_1}{K_3}} \sqrt{\beta_1 \beta_3} + \sqrt{\frac{\beta_3}{K_3}} \sqrt{K_2 \beta_2},$
4. $\frac{\beta_1 + \beta_2}{2} - \beta_3 \leq 2\sqrt{\frac{K_2}{K_3}} \sqrt{\beta_2 \beta_3} + \sqrt{\frac{\beta_3}{K_3}} \sqrt{K_1 \frac{\beta_1 + \beta_2}{2}},$

5. $\frac{\beta_1+\beta_3}{2} - \beta_2 \leq 2\sqrt{\frac{K_3}{K_2}}\sqrt{\beta_2\beta_3} + \sqrt{\frac{K_1}{K_2}}\sqrt{\frac{\beta_1+\beta_2}{2}\frac{\beta_2+\beta_3}{2}}$,

6. $\beta_1 > \beta_2 \geq \beta_3$.

Then $t_{2,3}^* = t_{3,2}^* = 0$, $t_{2,1}^* = t_{3,1}^* = 0$, $t_{1,2}^*, t_{1,3}^* \geq 0$, where $t_{1,2}$ and $t_{1,3}$ are solutions to defender 1's optimization problem:

$$\max_{t_{1,2}, t_{1,3}} \quad \phi_1(\mathbf{t_1}) = \frac{\sqrt{K_1 r_1}}{2\alpha}\left(\sum_{j=1}^{3}\sqrt{K_j r_j}\right) \tag{5}$$

$$\text{subject to} \quad 0 \leq t_{1,2} < \frac{\beta_1 - \beta_2}{2}, \ 0 \leq t_{1,3} < \frac{\beta_1 - \beta_3}{2}.$$

From Theorem 3, one can immediately notice that if defender 1 has significantly more resources than defenders 2 and 3, and if defenders 2 and 3 have a relatively similar level of resources then it is in the strongest defender's best interest to form a coalition and transfer resources to the other two defenders. At the same time, the weaker defenders have no incentive to transfer resources. Combining observations from Theorems 2 and 3, we note that the expected payoffs of all three players increases.

In the subsequent sections, we prove the results stated above. We first compute the attacker's resource allocation and Nash equilibrium payoffs of the players in the final stage game assuming the knowledge of the transfer. Thereafter, in Sects. 5 and 6, we proceed to solve the stage 1 game for the cases stated in the theorems above.

4   Best Response of the Attacker

In this section we calculate the attacker's optimal resource allocation in response to the resource transfers between the defenders. As the final stage payoffs are given by Lemma 1 in Sect. 2.2, we are left to solve for the stage one optimal resource allocation of the attacker and the optimal transfers by the defenders. We first solve the attacker's problem by using the best response strategies of the attacker to the observed post-transfer resource allocations $r_i = \beta_i + \sum_{j=1}^{3}(t_{j,i} - t_{i,j})$. This will provide the attacker's optimal resource allocation, $\alpha_i^*(\mathbf{t})$, to each separate final stage game, CBG^i.

Proposition 1. *Consider a two-stage game, 2CB. For an admissible resource transfer strategy,* $\mathbf{t}$*, the attacker's optimal payoff maximizing strategy is:*

1. *The case* $\frac{2}{n_i} < \frac{\alpha}{r_i} < 1$ $\forall i \in \{1,2,3\}$*: Let* $I = \left\{i \mid i \in \max_{i=1,2,3}\frac{K_i}{r_i}\right\}$*,* $\Delta_{|I|} = \{\mathbf{p} \mid p_i \geq 0, \sum_{i\in I} p_i = 1\}$*,* $\mathbf{p} \in \Delta_{|I|}$*.*

$$\alpha_i^*(\mathbf{t}) = \begin{cases} \alpha & \text{if } i \in I, |I| = 1, \\ 0 & \text{if } i \notin I, \\ \alpha p_i & \text{if } |I| > 1, \ i \in I. \end{cases}$$

2. The case $\frac{2}{n_i} < \frac{r_i}{\alpha}\left(\sum_{i=1}^{3}\sqrt{\frac{K_j r_j}{K_i r_i}}\right) < 1 \quad \forall i \in \{1,2,3\}$:

$$\alpha_i^*(t) = \frac{\alpha}{\sum_{j=1}^{3}\sqrt{\frac{K_j r_j}{K_i r_i}}}.$$

Before proving Proposition 1, we first state a well known result from optimization theory and prove an auxiliary lemma.

Lemma 2 (Optimization Over a Simplex [1]). *In a constrained optimization problem with the objective of maximizing $f(\mathbf{x})$, consider the case where the constraint set is a simplex*

$$\mathcal{X} = \left\{\mathbf{x} \mid x_i \geq 0, \sum_{i=1}^{n} x_i = r\right\}$$

where $r > 0$ is a given scalar. Then the necessary condition for $\mathbf{x}^*$ to be a local maximum is

$$x_i^* > 0 \implies \frac{\partial f(\mathbf{x}^*)}{\partial x_i} \geq \frac{\partial f(\mathbf{x}^*)}{\partial x_j}, \quad \forall j. \tag{6}$$

If $f(\mathbf{x})$ is concave, then (6) is also sufficient for the global optimality of $\mathbf{x}^*$.

Lemma 3. *Let $N = 3$ be the number of defenders in the game. For an attacker with a payoff function that is the summation of strictly-increasing single-variable functions,*

$$\pi(\boldsymbol{\alpha}) = \sum_{i=1}^{N} \pi_i(\alpha_i),$$

the attacker exhausts his entire budget, $\sum_{i=1}^{N} \alpha_i = \alpha$, at the optimum.

Proof. Fix $\alpha_j = \alpha_j^* \; \forall j$ such that $\sum_{j=1, j\neq i}^{N} \alpha_j^* < \alpha$. Let $\varepsilon > 0$, and take

$$\alpha_i = \alpha - \sum_{\substack{j=1\\j\neq i}}^{N} \alpha_j^* - \varepsilon < \alpha_i^* = \alpha - \sum_{\substack{j=1\\j\neq i}}^{N} \alpha_j^*.$$

Then we have

$$\pi(\boldsymbol{\alpha}) = \pi_i\left(\alpha - \sum_{\substack{j=1\\j\neq i}}^{N} \alpha_j^* - \varepsilon\right) + \sum_{\substack{j=1\\j\neq i}}^{N} \pi_j(\alpha_j^*)$$

$$\pi(\boldsymbol{\alpha}^*) = \pi_i\left(\alpha - \sum_{\substack{j=1\\j\neq i}}^{N} \alpha_j^*\right) + \sum_{\substack{j=1\\j\neq i}}^{N} \pi_j(\alpha_j^*).$$

By the definition of a strictly increasing function, $\alpha - \sum_{\substack{j=1\\j\neq i}}^{N} \alpha_j^* > \alpha - \sum_{\substack{j=1\\j\neq i}}^{N} \alpha_j^* - \varepsilon \implies \pi_i(\alpha - \sum_{\substack{j=1\\j\neq i}}^{N} \alpha_j^*) > \pi_i(\alpha - \sum_{\substack{j=1\\j\neq i}}^{N} \alpha_j^* - \varepsilon) \implies \pi(\boldsymbol{\alpha}^*) > \pi(\boldsymbol{\alpha})$. $\square$

We now proceed to prove Proposition 1. At the final stage of the game, the attacker plays a CBG against each individual defender. As such, the expected payoff of each individual CBG^i is given by Lemma 1. The total expected payoff for the attacker is the sum of the individual expected payoffs.

The attacker's reaction curve is the strategy that maximizes his expected payoff against the strategies of the 3 defenders. Therefore, fix the defenders' resource allocation strategy, t. The attacker's expected payoffs as a function of his resource allocation strategy, α, for each of the two regions considered are:

$$\text{Case 1: } \pi_1(\alpha) = \sum_{i=1}^{3} K_i \frac{\alpha_i}{2r_i},$$

$$\text{Case 2: } \pi_2(\alpha) = \sum_{i=1}^{3} K_i \left(1 - \frac{r_i}{2\alpha_i}\right).$$

In both cases, one can easily verify that the payoff functions are summations of strictly increasing functions in the individual battle allocations, α_i. Therefore, by Lemma 3, the attacker completely exhausts his resource budget. His budget constraint is then the simplex $\sum_{i=1}^{3} \alpha_i = \alpha, \alpha_i \geq 0$.

For case 1, $\pi_1(\alpha)$ is a summation of linear functions of α_i and therefore linear. Since linear functions are also concave, $\pi_1(\alpha)$ is a concave function. Lemma 2 provides both the necessary and sufficient conditions for optimality. We then arrive at the desired result for case 1 through a direct application of Lemma 2.

In case 2, $\pi_2(\alpha)$ is a summation of concave functions in α_i. Since positive weighted sums of concave functions are concave, $\pi_2(\alpha)$ is concave. Similar to case 1, Lemma 2 provides the necessary and sufficient conditions for optimality. Therefore, by Lemma 2:

$$\alpha_i > 0 \implies \frac{\partial \pi_2(\alpha)}{\partial \alpha_1} = \frac{\partial \pi_2(\alpha)}{\partial \alpha_2} = \frac{\partial \pi_2(\alpha)}{\partial \alpha_3}$$

$$\frac{n_1 v_1 r_1}{2\alpha_1^2} = \frac{n_2 v_2 r_2}{2\alpha_2^2} = \frac{n_3 v_3 r_3}{2\alpha_3^2}$$

$$\frac{\alpha_1^2}{n_1 v_1 r_1} = \frac{\alpha_2^2}{n_2 v_2 r_2} = \frac{\alpha_3^2}{n_3 v_3 r_3}.$$

So, the attacker's optimal strategy in case 2 is to allocate his resources such that each partial derivative is a constant and equal. By setting this constant to k and using the attacker's budget constraint, we can solve for his optimal resource allocation strategy by algebraic manipulation.

$$k = \frac{\alpha_i^2}{K_i r_i} \implies \alpha_i = \sqrt{K_i r_i} \sqrt{k}. \tag{7}$$

Substituting (7) into the attacker's budget constraint, we have:

$$\sum_{j=1}^{3} \alpha_j = \alpha \implies \sum_{j=1}^{3} \sqrt{K_j r_j} \sqrt{k} = \alpha \implies \sqrt{k} = \frac{\alpha}{\sum_{j=1}^{3} \sqrt{K_j r_j}}. \tag{8}$$

Finally, substituting (8) into (7), we obtain the attacker's optimal resource allocation for case 2.   □

In the next two sections, we find an optimal resource transfer strategy for the defenders for each of the two cases that we study. The first case corresponds to an attacker that has a significant disadvantage in resources compared to the defenders. The second case is an attacker that is much stronger than the combined strength of all of the defenders.

5   Weakest Attacker Leads to Proxy Wars

Here we present the proof of Theorem 1 for the case when the attacker has less resources than each of the defenders. We show that in certain situations, the attacker allocates all its resource to fight against one defender, while other defenders carefully choose the amount of resource to transfer to the defender fighting the attacker. This leads to a proxy war situation where some defenders may choose to transfer resources in order to benefit another defender while they themselves avoid fighting.

The attacker's optimal strategy remains the same as in Proposition 1. For the case when defender 1 is the relatively weakest player, $\frac{K_1}{\beta_1} > \frac{K_2}{\beta_2}$, we know from Proposition 1 that the attacker allocates all of his resources to the battle with defender 1. So, $\alpha_1 = \alpha, \alpha_i = 0 \ \forall i \in \{2, 3\}$. The payoff to the attacker and each defender is a result of Lemma 1 and Proposition 1 and is:

$$\pi(\boldsymbol{\alpha}) = \pi(\alpha_i) = K_i \frac{\alpha}{2r_1},$$

$$\phi_1(\mathbf{t_1}) = K_1 - \pi(\alpha_i) = K_1(1 - \frac{\alpha}{2r_1}),$$

$$\phi_i(\mathbf{t_i}) = K_i \quad \forall i \in \{2, 3\}.$$

Since defender 1's payoff decreases as r_1 decreases, she will never transfer any resources out to other defenders as long as she is the relatively weakest player, $\frac{K_1}{r_1} > \frac{K_2}{r_2} \geq \frac{K_3}{r_3}$. In addition, defender 1 will always accept resources since her payoff increases as r_1 increases. Since in this game resources have no external value, any defender i who is not the relatively weakest player is indifferent to transferring resources since she avoids battle and her payoff does not change. However, defenders 2 and 3 will never transfer out enough resources such that they become the relatively weakest player. Defenders 2 and 3 will also always accept resources since this helps them become relatively stronger and avoid battle. To summarize the above discussion, we have:

1. Defender 1 never transfers resources to other defenders: $t_{1,j} = 0 \quad \forall j$.
2. Defender $i \in \{2, 3\}$ is indifferent to transferring resources out as long as:

$$\frac{K_1}{r_1} = \frac{K_1}{\beta_1 + \sum_{j \in D \setminus \{1\}} t_{j,1}} > \frac{K_i}{r_i} = \frac{K_i}{\beta_i + \sum_{j \in D \setminus \{1,i\}} t_{j,i} - \sum_{j \in D \setminus \{i\}} t_{i,j}}. \quad (9)$$

3. All defenders will always accept resources.

By rearranging (9), we can write the supremum of defenders 2 and 3's maximum transfer amounts to defender 1 as:

$$t_{2,1} = \frac{K_1(\beta_2 + t_{3,2} - t_{2,3})}{K_1 + K_2} - \frac{K_2(\beta_1 + t_{3,1})}{K_1 + K_2},$$

$$t_{3,1} = \frac{K_1(\beta_3 + t_{2,3} - t_{3,2})}{K_1 + K_2} - \frac{K_2(\beta_1 + t_{2,1})}{K_1 + K_2}. \tag{10}$$

Examining (10), it is apparent that the maximum amount that defender 2 is willing to transfer to defender 1 increases as defender 3 transfers resources to defender 2, decreases in terms of the amount that defender 2 transfers to defender 3, and, most critically, decreases as defender 3 transfers resources to defender 1. Directly solving the system of equations above obtains the desired solution.

$$t_{2,1}^* + t_{2,3}^* < t_{3,2}^* + \frac{\beta_2(K_1 + K_3) - K_2(\beta_1 + \beta_3)}{K_1 + K_2 + K_3}.$$

$$t_{3,1}^* + t_{3,2}^* < t_{2,3}^* + \frac{\beta_3(K_1 + K_2) - K_3(\beta_1 + \beta_2)}{K_1 + K_2 + K_3}.$$

Note, that there is a possibility that defenders 2 and 3 do not transfer resources between each other. Then $t_{2,3} = t_{3,2} = 0$. Since $t_{2,1} + t_{2,3} \geq 0, t_{3,1} + t_{3,2} \geq 0$, this imposes the conditions

$$\beta_2(K_1 + K_3) - K_2(\beta_1 + \beta_3) \geq 0, \tag{11}$$

$$\beta_3(K_1 + K_2) - K_3(\beta_1 + \beta_2) \geq 0. \tag{12}$$

The condition imposed by (12) is satisfied by (4). The condition in (11) is a condition in the statement of the theorem. ☐

5.1   The Case of No Transfer Between Defenders 2 and 3

Note that since defenders 2 and 3 do not fight against the attacker, the transfers between them does not affect their equilibrium payoffs. Thus, a possible refinement of multiple Nash equilibria would be to assume no transfer between defenders who do not engage with the attacker. In this subsection, we make this assumption and prove two corollaries of Theorem 1 under the assumption of $t_{2,3} = t_{3,2} = 0$. We first have the following auxiliary lemma.

Lemma 4. *Let $z, c > 0$. Then*

$$\frac{x + y}{z + c} \geq \frac{x}{z} \iff zy \geq cx.$$

Proof. The proof follows from algebraic manipulation. ☐

Corollary 1. *Consider the case of $t_{2,3} = t_{3,2} = 0$. In comparison to the 2-defender case, at equilibrium the maximum possible amount transferred to defender 1,*

$$\sum_{j \in D \setminus \{1\}} t_{i,1},$$

is nondecreasing when defender 3 joins the game (assuming defender 3's relative strength is weaker than that of defender 2). In addition, the maximum expected payoff to defender 1 is nondecreasing.

Proof. Let $t_{2,1}^2$ represent the transfer from player 2 to player 1 in the 2-defender case, and $t_{2,1}^3, t_{3,1}^3$ represent the transfers to player 1 in the 3-defender case. Then the maximum total transfer to defender 1 in each case is

$$t_{2,1}^2 = \frac{\beta_2(K_1) - K_2(\beta_1)}{K_1 + K_2}, \tag{13}$$

$$t_{2,1}^3 + t_{3,1}^3 = \frac{\beta_2(K_1 - K_3) - K_2(\beta_1 + \beta_3)}{K_1 + K_2 + K_3} + \frac{\beta_3(K_1 - K_2) - K_3(\beta_1 + \beta_2)}{K_1 + K_2 + K_3}. \tag{14}$$

By expanding and canceling common terms in (14) we have:

$$t_{2,1}^3 + t_{3,1}^3 = \frac{(K_1\beta_2 - \beta_1 K_2) + (K_1\beta_3 - \beta_1 K_3)}{K_1 + K_2 + K_3}.$$

By definition, $K_i > 0 \ \forall i \in D$ which implies that $K_1 + K_2, K_3 > 0$. Thus, we meet the conditions of Lemma 4; therefore, to show $t_{2,1}^3 + t_{3,1}^3 \geq t_{2,1}^2$, it suffices to show that:

$$(K_1 + K_2)(K_1\beta_3 - \beta_1 K_3) \geq K_3(K_1\beta_2 - \beta_1 K_2). \tag{15}$$

By algebraic manipulation, we can show that (15) is equivalent to:

$$K_1\beta_3 + K_2\beta_3 \geq K_3\beta_2 + K_3\beta_1. \tag{16}$$

Equation (16) always holds true due to the assumed relative strength indexing in (4). Defender 1's payoff is a strictly increasing function of her resource level, r_1, which increases as the amount of resources transferred to her increases. Therefore, her payoff is nondecreasing as defender 3 joins the coalition. □

Corollary 2. *Assume that $t_{2,3} = t_{3,2} = 0$. Then, the maximum amount that defender 2 is willing to transfer to defender 1 decreases or remains constant when defender 3 joins the game.*

Proof. Let $t_{2,1}^2$ represent the case without defender 3, and $t_{2,1}^3$ represent the case with defender 3 in the game. Then

$$t_{2,1}^2 = \frac{\beta_2 K_1 - K_2\beta_1}{K_1 + K_2},$$

$$t_{2,1}^3 = \frac{(\beta_2 K_1 - K_2\beta_1) + (\beta_2 K_3 - K_2\beta_3)}{K_1 + K_2 + K_3}.$$

By definition, $K_i > 0 \ \forall i \in D$ which implies that $K_1 + K_2, K_3 > 0$. Then by Lemma 4

$$t_{i,1}^2 \geq t_{i,1}^3 \iff K_3(\beta_2 K_1 - K_2\beta_1) \geq (K_1 + K_2)(\beta_2 K_3 - K_2\beta_3). \tag{17}$$

Through algebraic manipulation, we can show that (17) is equivalent to:

$$K_1\beta_3 + K_2\beta_3 \geq K_3\beta_2 + K_3\beta_1. \tag{18}$$

Similar to Corollary 1, (18) always holds true due to the assumed relative strength indexing in (4). Therefore, the resource transfer from defender 2 to defender 1 is non-increasing as defender 3 joins the game.   □

6   Strongest Attacker Fights Everyone

In this section we present the proofs for Theorem 2 and then identify the equilibrium transfers for a special case in Theorem 3.

Proof of Theorem 2: The payoff to the attacker and each defender in each CBG^i is a result of Lemma 1 and is respectively given by:

$$\pi_i(\alpha_i, r_i) = K_i\left(1 - \frac{r_i}{2\alpha_i}\right), \qquad \phi_i(t) = K_i - \pi(\alpha_i) = K_i\left(\frac{r_i}{2\alpha_i}\right).$$

The attacker's optimal strategy remains the same as in Proposition 1. Substituting the result of Proposition 1, case 2 into the defender's payoff results in:

$$\phi_i(\mathbf{t}) = \frac{\sqrt{K_i}}{2\alpha}\left(\sqrt{r_i}\sum_{j\in D}\sqrt{K_j r_j}\right). \tag{19}$$

We want to show that there is a parameter range for which it is beneficial for player i to transfer resources to player k and also beneficial for player k to accept those resources. In order to do so, we will show that, for a certain parameter configuration, $\phi_i(\mathbf{t})$ and $\phi_k(\mathbf{t})$ are increasing in $t_{i,k}$.

We first show the following result.

Lemma 5. *If player i is willing to transfer resources to player k, then player k is always willing to accept those resources.*

Proof. One can verify that the partial derivative of the defender i's payoff with respect to resource transfers out, $t_{i,k}$, is

$$\frac{\partial \phi_i(\mathbf{t})}{\partial t_{i,k}} = \frac{K_i}{2\alpha}\left[-1 + \frac{1}{2}\sqrt{\frac{K_k}{K_i}}\left(\frac{r_i - r_k - \sqrt{\frac{r_k}{K_k}}\sqrt{K_j r_j}}{\sqrt{r_i r_k}}\right)\right]. \tag{20}$$

In addition, from defender k's perspective, the partial derivative of her payoff with respect to the transfer in, $t_{i,k}$, is

$$\frac{\partial \phi_k(\mathbf{t})}{\partial t_{i,k}} = \frac{K_k}{2\alpha}\left[1 + \frac{1}{2}\sqrt{\frac{K_i}{K_k}}\left(\frac{r_i - r_k + \sqrt{\frac{r_i}{K_i}}\sqrt{K_j r_j}}{\sqrt{r_i r_k}}\right)\right]. \tag{21}$$

Then, the two defenders will form a coalition if and only if

$$\frac{\partial \phi_i(\mathbf{t})}{\partial t_{i,k}} > 0 \iff r_i - r_k > 2\sqrt{\frac{K_i}{K_k}}\sqrt{r_i r_k} + \sqrt{\frac{r_k}{K_k}}\sqrt{K_j r_j}, \qquad (22)$$

$$\frac{\partial \phi_k(\mathbf{t})}{\partial t_{i,k}} > 0 \iff r_i - r_k > -2\sqrt{\frac{K_k}{K_i}}\sqrt{r_i r_k} - \sqrt{\frac{r_i}{K_i}}\sqrt{K_j r_j}, \qquad (23)$$

where we used (20) and (21). By definition, $K_i, K_k, K_j > 0 \quad \forall i, j, k \in D$. In addition, by the restrictions imposed in Sect. 3, $r_i, r_k, r_j \geq 0 \quad \forall i, j, k \in D$. Therefore, the right hand side of (22) is always greater than or equal to zero, while the right hand side of (23) is always less than or equal to zero. So, if the condition in (22) holds true, then the condition in (23) must also hold true. The proof of the lemma is thus complete. □

Finally, we now complete the proof of Theorem 2 in terms of the parameters of the game. For fixed $t_{j,l} = 0 \quad \forall (j, l) \neq (i, k)$, if

$$\beta_i - \beta_k > 2\sqrt{\frac{K_i}{K_k}}\sqrt{\beta_i \beta_k} + \sqrt{\frac{\beta_k}{K_k}}\sqrt{K_j \beta_j} \implies \left.\frac{\partial \phi_i(\mathbf{t})}{\partial t_{i,k}}\right|_{t_{i,k}=0} > 0.$$

Thus, there exists small values of $t_{i,k} > 0$ for which the inequalities in (22) and (23) will still hold. This will be true even if defender i and k transfer or receive a small amount of resources from the other defender. This concludes the proof of Theorem 2. □

From Lemma 5, one can immediately notice that the resource rich player can have an incentive to trade resources to a poorer player. However, the required difference in their respective resource levels is not just a function of the two defender's resources and total battlefield values, but also a function of the sum of the other defender's resources and total battlefield values.

By observing (22) and (23) closely, we conclude that there is a region where player k would be willing to accept resources, but player i is not willing to send those resources. This region is defined by:

$$r_i - r_k \in \left(-2\sqrt{\frac{K_k}{K_i}}\sqrt{r_i r_k} - \sqrt{\frac{r_i}{K_i}}\sqrt{K_j r_j}, \sqrt{\frac{K_i}{K_k}}\sqrt{r_i r_k} + \sqrt{\frac{r_k}{K_k}}\sqrt{K_j r_j}\right).$$

In this parameter region, a resource rich player would be willing to accept resources from a poor player, but the poor player would not be willing to transfer those resources.

6.1 The Case of No Transfer Between Defenders 2 and 3

In this subsection, we present the proof of Theorem 3 and identify a parameter region where there is no transfer between defenders 2 and 3 in equilibrium. In what follows, only defender 1 transfers resources to the two defenders.

Proof. We now prove Theorem 3. The proof is divided into three steps:

Step 1: In this step, we observe that the equilibrium transfers (assuming they exist) satisfy $t_{1,2}^* < \frac{\beta_1 - \beta_2}{2}$ and $t_{1,3}^* < \frac{\beta_1 - \beta_3}{2}$. Indeed, if the transfer $t_{1,i}$ is higher than the upper bound, then $r_1 - r_i < 0$. This implies that the derivative of the expected payoffs with respect to transfer out from defender 1 to defender i is negative. Thus, $t_{1,2}^* < \frac{\beta_1 - \beta_2}{2}$ and $t_{1,3}^* < \frac{\beta_1 - \beta_3}{2}$ is a dominant strategy for defender 1.

Step 2: We next show that if Hypotheses 4, 5, and 6 hold, then no sharing of resources between defender 2 and 3 is a dominant strategy. First, from Lemma 5 there is no transfer of resources from defender 2 to defender 3 if

$$r_2 - r_3 < 2\sqrt{\frac{K_2}{K_3}}\sqrt{r_2 r_3} + \sqrt{\frac{r_3}{K_3}}\sqrt{K_1 r_1}. \tag{24}$$

Using the upper bound on $t_{1,2}^*$ and Hypothesis 4, we upper bound the LHS of the equation above by:

$$r_2 - r_3 < \beta_2 + \frac{\beta_1 - \beta_2}{2} - \beta_3 \leq 2\sqrt{\frac{K_2}{K_3}}\sqrt{\beta_2 \beta_3} + \sqrt{\frac{\beta_3}{K_3}}\sqrt{K_1 \frac{\beta_1 + \beta_2}{2}}.$$

We now proceed to lower bound the RHS of (24) by noting that the first term is at a minimum for $t_{1,2} = 0, t_{1,3} = 0$. Substituting for r_1 and r_3 in the second term in the right hand side and rearranging, we have:

$$\sqrt{\frac{r_3}{K_3}}\sqrt{K_1 r_1} = \sqrt{\frac{K_1}{K_2}}\sqrt{(\beta_3 + t_{1,3})(\beta_1 - t_{1,2} - t_{1,3})}.$$

This term is concave and strictly decreasing in $t_{1,2}$. Therefore, the lower bound occurs when $t_{1,2} = \frac{\beta_1 - \beta_2}{2}$. Since the term is concave, it suffices to consider the two bounds on $t_{1,3}$, which are $t_{1,3} = 0$ and $t_{1,3} = \frac{\beta_1 - \beta_3}{2}$. Under Hypothesis 6, one can show that the lower bound occurs when $t_{1,3} = 0$. We therefore have:

$$r_2 - r_3 < 2\sqrt{\frac{K_2}{K_3}}\sqrt{\beta_2 \beta_3} + \sqrt{\frac{\beta_3}{K_3}}\sqrt{K_1 \frac{\beta_1 + \beta_2}{2}} \leq 2\sqrt{\frac{K_2}{K_3}}\sqrt{r_2 r_3} + \sqrt{\frac{r_3}{K_3}}\sqrt{K_1 r_1}.$$

Therefore, if Hypotheses 4 and 6 hold, then for any $t_{1,2} < \frac{\beta_1 - \beta_2}{2}$ and $t_{1,3} < \frac{\beta_1 - \beta_3}{2}$, we have $\partial \phi_2(\mathbf{t})/\partial t_{2,3} < 0$.

A similar result holds if Hypotheses 5 and 6 hold wherein defender 3's expected payoff reduces for positive transfer of resources from defender 3 to defender 2.

Step 3: Fix $t_{1,3} \in (0, \frac{\beta_1 - \beta_3}{2})$, define $r_1 = \beta_1 - t_{1,3}$, and assume that $t_{1,3}$ is chosen such that $\partial \phi_1(\mathbf{t})/\partial t_{1,2} > 0$. Now, if defender 1 transfers $t_{1,2}$ amount to defender 2, then $\partial \phi_1(\mathbf{t})/\partial t_{1,2} > 0$ iff

$$r_1 - \beta_2 - 2t_{1,2} > 2\sqrt{\frac{K_1}{K_2}}\sqrt{(r_1 - t_{1,2})(\beta_2 + t_{1,2})} + \sqrt{\frac{(\beta_2 + t_{1,2})}{K_2}}\sqrt{K_3 r_3}.$$

Thus, as $t_{1,2}$ increases from 0, the left side of the equation reduces and the right side of the inequality increases. Thus, at some critical value $\bar{t}_{1,2}(t_{1,3})$ the two sides are equal, and beyond this transfer amount, transferring resource to defender 2 is not beneficial to defender 1. A similar argument holds for the transfer between defender 1 and 3.

Thus, by solving defender 1's optimization problem in (5), we obtain the optimal transfer between the defenders.

□

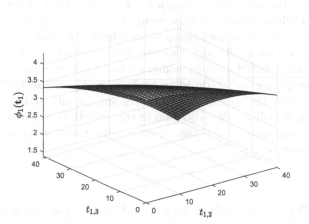

Fig. 1. Payoff of defender 1 for $t_{1,2} \in [0, \frac{\beta_1-\beta_2}{2})$ and $t_{1,2} \in [0, \frac{\beta_1-\beta_3}{2})$ with $\alpha = 160, \beta_1 = 90, \beta_2 = 10, \beta_3 = 8, n_1 = 5, n_2 = 8, n_3 = 6, K_1 = 10, K_2 = 8, K_3 = 6, t_{2,3} = 0, t_{3,2} = 0$.

Figure 1 shows defender 1's payoff versus possible transfers for a configuration of parameters that meet the conditions of Theorem 3. One can observe that defender 1's payoff increases slightly as $t_{1,2}$ and $t_{1,3}$ increase from 0. For the parameter configuration in Fig. 1, we find that $t_{1,2}^* = 0.9390$ and $t_{1,3}^* = 0.2039$.

7   Conclusion

In this paper, we formulated a 4-player, two-stage Colonel Blotto game where defenders can choose to form a coalition by transferring resources in stage one and the attacker observes the transfer among the defenders. This work builds upon the previous work in [10,11], in which the authors considered only two defenders fighting against one attacker. Our goal is to analyze the coalition formation in multi-defender cases, which requires a much more intricate analysis. In the case of two defenders, only one coalition can be formed; on the other hand, if there are N defenders, then there can be $N(N-1)/2$ possible number of coalitions. Our work is an important step in the direction of analyzing the more general case of N defenders.

For certain parameter regions, we've calculated the subgame-perfect Nash equilibrium (SPNE) and identified the parameter regions in which coalitions are formed. Somewhat surprisingly, the resource rich player does not necessarily transfer resources to poorer players when the attacker is the weakest player. In addition, we've shown that in some situations, it is in the best interest of the defenders to add additional weak defenders to the game.

In other parameter regions, we've shown that there are regions where a coalition will form since it is beneficial to transfer resources, but we could not compute the equilibrium transfers due to complex algebraic dependencies. We however note that equilibrium transfers can be computed using computational methods. Unlike the other case, transfer always occurs from the resource rich player to the resource poor player, although there does exist a parameter region where a resource rich player would accept resources from a poorer player.

In the future, we plan to consider the N + 1-player case that considers N defenders and study the equilibrium transfers and payoffs to defenders as more defenders join the coalition. We also plan to consider the case where the attacker has incomplete information and can observe some transfers between defenders but not all transfers.

References

1. Bertsekas, D.P.: Nonlinear Programming, 2nd edn, pp. 196–197. Athena Scientific, Belmont (1999)
2. Borel, E.: La théorie du jeu et les équations intégrales à noyau symétrique. Comptes rendus de l'Académie des Sciences **173**(1304–1308), 58 (1921)
3. Borel, E.: The theory of play and integral equations with skew symmetric kernels. Econometrica: J. Econ. S. 97–100 (1953). https://doi.org/10.2307/1906946
4. Borel, E., Ville, J.: Applications de la théorie des probabilités aux jeux de hasard. J. Gabay, Paris (1938)
5. Chia, P.H., Chuang, J.: Colonel Blotto in the phishing war. In: Baras, J.S., Katz, J., Altman, E. (eds.) GameSec 2011. LNCS, vol. 7037, pp. 201–218. Springer, Heidelberg (2011). https://doi.org/10.1007/978-3-642-25280-8_16
6. Ferdowsi, A., Sanjab, A., Saad, W., Başar, T.: Generalized Colonel Blotto game. arXiv preprint arXiv:1710.01381 (2017)
7. Friedman, L.: Game-theory models in the allocation of advertising expenditures. Oper. Res. **6**(5), 699–709 (1958). https://doi.org/10.1287/opre.6.5.699
8. Golman, R., Page, S.E.: General Blotto: games of allocative strategic mismatch. Public Choice **138**(3–4), 279–299 (2009). https://doi.org/10.1007/s11127-008-9359-x
9. Gross, O., Wagner, R.: A continuous Colonel Blotto game. Technical report. Rand Project Air Force, Santa Monica, CA (1950)
10. Gupta, A., Başar, T., Schwartz, G.A.: A three-stage Colonel Blotto game: when to provide more information to an adversary. In: Poovendran, R., Saad, W. (eds.) GameSec 2014. LNCS, vol. 8840, pp. 216–233. Springer, Cham (2014). https://doi.org/10.1007/978-3-319-12601-2_12
11. Gupta, A., Schwartz, G., Langbort, C., Sastry, S.S., Başar, T.: A three-stage Colonel Blotto game with applications to cyberphysical security. In: American Control Conference, ACC, pp. 3820–3825. IEEE (2014). https://doi.org/10.1109/acc.2014.6859164

12. Hajimirsaadeghi, M., Mandayam, N.B.: A dynamic Colonel Blotto game model for spectrum sharing in wireless networks. In: 2017 55th Annual Allerton Conference on Communication, Control, and Computing, Allerton, pp. 287–294. IEEE (2017). https://doi.org/10.1109/ALLERTON.2017.8262750
13. Kovenock, D., Mauboussin, M.J., Roberson, B.: Asymmetric conflicts with endogenous dimensionality. Korean Econ. Rev. **26**, 287–305 (2010)
14. Kovenock, D., Roberson, B.: Coalitional Colonel Blotto games with application to the economics of alliances. J. Public Econ. Theory **14**(4), 653–676 (2012). https://doi.org/10.1111/j.1467-9779.2012.01556.x
15. Kvasov, D.: Contests with limited resources. J. Econ. Theory **136**(1), 738–748 (2007). https://doi.org/10.1016/j.jet.2006.06.007
16. Labib, M., Ha, S., Saad, W., Reed, J.H.: A Colonel Blotto game for anti-jamming in the Internet of Things. In: 2015 IEEE Global Communications Conference, GLOBECOM, pp. 1–6. IEEE (2015). https://doi.org/10.1109/GLOCOM.2015.7417437
17. Roberson, B.: The Colonel Blotto game. Econ. Theory **29**(1), 1–24 (2006). https://doi.org/10.1007/s00199-005-0071-5
18. Roberson, B.: Errata: the Colonel Blotto game. Technical report. Purdue's Krannert School (2010). Working paper
19. Snyder, J.M.: Election goals and the allocation of campaign resources. Econometrica: J. Econ. Soc. 637–660 (1989). https://doi.org/10.2307/1911056
20. Wu, Y., Wang, B., Liu, K.R.: Optimal power allocation strategy against jamming attacks using the Colonel Blotto game. In: Global Telecommunications Conference, GLOBECOM 2009, pp. 1–5. IEEE (2009). https://doi.org/10.1109/GLOCOM.2009.5425760

Data Poisoning Attacks in Contextual Bandits

Yuzhe Ma[1](✉), Kwang-Sung Jun[1], Lihong Li[2], and Xiaojin Zhu[1]

[1] University of Wisconsin-Madison, Madison, USA
ma234@wisc.edu, kjun@discovery.wisc.edu, jerryzhu@cs.wisc.edu
[2] Google Brain, Kirkland, WA, USA
lihong@google.com

Abstract. We study offline data poisoning attacks in contextual bandits, a class of reinforcement learning problems with important applications in online recommendation and adaptive medical treatment, among others. We provide a general attack framework based on convex optimization and show that by slightly manipulating rewards in the data, an attacker can force the bandit algorithm to pull a target arm for a target contextual vector. The target arm and target contextual vector are both chosen by the attacker. That is, the attacker can hijack the behavior of a contextual bandit. We also investigate the feasibility and the side effects of such attacks, and identify future directions for defense. Experiments on both synthetic and real-world data demonstrate the efficiency of the attack algorithm.

Keywords: Data poisoning · Contextual bandit · Adversarial attack

1 Introduction

As an important step toward trustworthy AI, adversarial learning studies robustness of machine learning systems against malicious attacks [7,10]. Training set poisoning is a type of attack where the adversary can manipulate the training data such that a machine learning algorithm trained on the poisoned data would produce a defective model. The defective model is often similar to a good model, but affords the adversary certain nefarious leverages [3,5,9,12,14,15,17]. Understanding training set poisoning is essential to developing defense mechanisms.

Recent studies on training set poisoning attack focused heavily on supervised learning. There has been little study on poisoning sequential decision making algorithms, even though they are widely employed in the real world. In this paper, we aim to fill in the gap by studying training set poisoning against contextual bandits. Contextual bandits are extensions of multi-armed bandits with side information and have seen wide applications in industry including news recommendation [13], online advertising [6], medical treatment allocation [11], and also promotion of users' well-being [8].

© Springer Nature Switzerland AG 2018
L. Bushnell et al. (Eds.): GameSec 2018, LNCS 11199, pp. 186–204, 2018.
https://doi.org/10.1007/978-3-030-01554-1_11

Let us take news recommendation as a running example for poisoning against contextual bandits. A news website has K articles (i.e., arms). It runs an adaptive article recommendation algorithm (the contextual bandit algorithm) to learn a policy in the backend. Every time a user (represented by a context vector) visits the website, the website displays an article that it thinks is most likely to interest the user based on the historical record of all users. Then the website receives a unit reward if the user clicks through the displayed article, and receives no reward otherwise. Usually the website keeps serving users throughout the day and updates its article selection policy periodically (say, during the nights or every few hours). This provides an opportunity for an attacker to perform *offline* data poisoning attacks, e.g. the attacker can sneak into the website backend at night before the policy is updated, and poison the rewards collected during the daytime. The website unknowingly updates its policy with the poisoned data. On the next day it behaves as the attacker wanted.

More generally, we study adversarial attacks in contextual bandit where the attacker poisons historical rewards in order to force the bandit to pull a target arm under a target context. One can view this attack as a form of offline reward shaping [16], but it is adversarial reward shaping. Our main contribution is an optimization-based attack framework for this attack setting. We also study the feasibility and side effect of the attack. We show on both synthetic and real-world data that the attack is effective. This exposes a security threat in AI systems that involve contextual bandits.

2   Review of Contextual Bandit

This section reviews contextual bandits, which will be the victim of the attack in this paper. A contextual bandit is an abstraction of many real-world decision making problems such as product recommendation and online advertising. Consider for example a news website which strives to recommend the most interesting news articles personalized for individual users. Every time a user visits the website, the website observes certain contextual information that describes the user such as age, gender, location, past news consumption patterns, etc. The website also has a pool of candidate news articles, one of which will be recommended and shown to the user. If the recommended article is interesting, the user may click on it; otherwise, the user may click on other items on the page or navigate to another page. The click probability here depends on both the user (via the context) and the recommended article. Such a dependency can be learned based on click logs and used for better recommendation for future users.

An important aspect of the problem is that the click feedback is observed only for the recommended article, not for others. In other words, the decision (choosing which article to show to a user) is irrevocable; it is impractical to force the user to revisit the webpage so as to recommend a different article. As a result, the feedback data being collected is necessarily biased towards the current recommendation algorithm being employed by the website, raising the need for balancing *exploration* and *exploitation* when choosing arms [13].

This is in stark contrast to a typical prediction task solved by supervised learning where predictions do not affect the data collection.

Formally, a contextual bandit has a set $\mathcal{X}$ of contexts and a set $\mathcal{A} = \{1, 2, \ldots, K\}$ of K arms. A contextual bandit algorithm proceeds in rounds $t = 1, 2, \ldots$. At round t, the algorithm observes a context vector $x_t \in \mathcal{R}^d$, chooses to pull an arm $a_t \in \mathcal{A}$, and observes a reward $r_t \in \mathcal{R}$. The goal of the algorithm is to maximize the total reward garnered over rounds. In the news recommendation example above, it is natural to define $r_t = 1$ if user clicks on the article and 0 otherwise, so that maximizing clicks is equivalent to maximizing the click-through rate, a critical business metric in online recommender systems.

In this work, we focus on the most popular and well-studied setting called linear bandits, where the expected reward is linear map of the context vector. Specifically, we assume each arm a is associated with an unknown vector $\theta_a \in \mathcal{R}^d$ with $\|\theta_a\|_2 \leq S$, so that for every t:

$$r_t = x_t^\top \theta_{a_t} + \eta_t, \tag{1}$$

where η_t is a σ-subGaussian noise. For simplicity, we assume η_t is unbounded and thus the reward can take any value in $\mathcal{R}$.

Most contextual bandit algorithms adopt the optimism-in-face-of-uncertainty (OFU) principle for efficient exploration. The OFU principle constructs an Upper Confidence Bound (UCB) for the mean reward of each arm based on historical data and then selects the arm with the highest UCB at each time step [1,4]. In round t, the historical data consists of the context, action, reward triples (x, a, r) from the previous $t - 1$ rounds. It is useful to split the historical data so that the feedback from the same arm is pooled together. Define $[K] = \{1, \ldots, K\}$. Let m_a be the number of times arm a was pulled up to time $t - 1$. This implies that $\sum_{a \in [K]} m_a = t - 1$. For each $a \in [K]$, let $X_a \in \mathcal{R}^{m_a \times d}$ be the design matrix for rounds, where arm a was pulled and each row of X_a is a previous context. Similarly, let $y_a \in \mathcal{R}^{m_a}$ be the corresponding reward (column) vector.

A UCB-style algorithm first forms a point estimate of θ_a by ridge regression

$$\hat{\theta}_a = (X_a^\top X_a + \lambda I)^{-1} X_a^\top y_a, \quad \forall a \in [K], \tag{2}$$

where $\lambda > 0$ is a regularization parameter. At round t, the algorithm observes the context x_t and then selects the arm with the highest UCB:

$$a_t = \text{argmax}_{a \in [K]} \left\{ x_t^\top \hat{\theta}_a + \alpha_a \|x_t\|_{V_a^{-1}} \right\}, \tag{3}$$

where $\|x_t\|_{V_a^{-1}} = \sqrt{x_t^\top V_a^{-1} x_t}$ is the Mahalanobis norm and $V_a = X_a^\top X_a + \lambda I$. Intuitively, for less frequently chosen a, the second term above tends to be large, thus encouraging exploration. The exploration parameter α_a is algorithm-specific. For example, in LinUCB [13] $\alpha_a = 1 + \sqrt{\frac{1}{2} \log \frac{2}{\delta}}$ and in OFUL [1] $\alpha_a = \sigma \sqrt{2 \log(\frac{\det(V_a)^{\frac{1}{2}} \det(\lambda I)^{-\frac{1}{2}}}{\delta})} + \lambda^{\frac{1}{2}} S$, where $\delta > 0$ is a confidence parameter. Here, we assume α_a may depend on input parameters like δ and observed data up to $t - 1$, but not x_t.

In Algorithm 1, we summarize the contextual bandit algorithm. While the bandit algorithm updates its $\hat{\theta}$ estimates in every round (step 3), in practice due to various considerations such updates often happen in mini-batches, e.g., several times an hour, or during the nights when fewer users visit the website [2,13]. Between these consecutive updates, the bandit algorithm follows a fixed policy obtained from the last update.

Algorithm 1. Contextual bandit algorithm

1: **Parameters**: confidence δ, regularizer λ, UCB function α.
2: **for** $t = 1, 2, \ldots, T$ **do**
3:    Receive context x_t, estimate $\hat{\theta}_a, a \in [K]$ with (2).
4:    Pull arm $a_t = \text{argmax}_{a \in [K]} \left\{ x_t^\top \hat{\theta}_a + \alpha_a \|x_t\|_{V_a^{-1}} \right\}$.
5:    World generates reward $r_t = x_t^\top \theta_{a_t} + \eta_t$.
6:    Append x_t and r_t to X_{a_t} and y_{a_t}, respectively.
7: **end for**

---

3   Attack Algorithm in Contextual Bandit

We now introduce an attacker with the following attack goal:

Attack Goal [x* → a*]: On a particular attack target context x^*, force the bandit algorithm to pull an attack target arm a^*.

For example, the attacker may want to manipulate the news service so that a particular article a^* is shown to users x^* from certain political bases. The attack is aimed at the current round t, or more generally the whole period when the arm-selection policy is fixed. Any suboptimal arm a^* can be the target arm. For concreteness, in our experiments the attacker always picks the worst arm a^* as the target arm. This is defined in the sense of the worst UCB, namely replacing argmax with argmin in (3), resulting in the target arm in (21).

We assume the attacker has full knowledge of the bandit algorithm and has access to all historical data. The attacker has the power to poison the historical reward vector[1] $y_a, \forall a \in [K]$. Specifically, the attacker can make arbitrary modifications $\Delta_a \in \mathcal{R}^{m_a}, \forall a \in [K]$ so that the reward vector for arm a becomes $y_a + \Delta_a$. After the poisoning attack, the ridge regression performed by the bandit algorithm yields a different solution:

$$\hat{\theta}_a = V_a^{-1} X_a^\top (y_a + \Delta_a). \tag{4}$$

Because such attacks happen on historical rewards in between bandit algorithm updates, we call it offline.

Now we can formally define the attack goal.

---

[1] In this paper we restrict the poisoning to modifying rewards for ease of exposition. More generally, the attacker can add, remove, or modify both the rewards and the context vectors. Our optimization-based attack framework can be generalized to such stronger attacks, though the optimization could become combinatorial.

Definition 1 (Weak attack). *A target context* x^* *is called* <u>*weakly attacked*</u> *into pulling target arm* a^* *if after attack the following inequalities are satisfied:*

$$x^{*\top}\hat{\theta}_{a^*} + \alpha_{a^*}\|x^*\|_{V_{a^*}^{-1}} > x^{*\top}\hat{\theta}_a + \alpha_a\|x^*\|_{V_a^{-1}}, \quad \forall a \neq a^*. \tag{5}$$

In other words, the algorithm is manipulated into choosing a^* *for context* x^*.

To avoid being detected, the attacker hopes to make the poisoning $\Delta_a, a \in [K]$ as small as possible. We measure the magnitude of the attack by the squared ℓ_2-norm $\sum_{a\in[K]} \|\Delta_a\|_2^2$.[2] We therefore formulate the attack as the following optimization problem:

$$\min_{\Delta_a : a \in [K]} \sum_{a\in[K]} \|\Delta_a\|_2^2$$

$$\text{s.t.} \quad x^{*\top}\hat{\theta}_{a^*} + \alpha_{a^*}\|x^*\|_{V_{a^*}^{-1}} > x^{*\top}\hat{\theta}_a + \alpha_a\|x^*\|_{V_a^{-1}}, \forall a \neq a^* \tag{6}$$

$$\text{where} \quad \hat{\theta}_a = V_a^{-1} X_a^\top (y_a + \Delta_a), \quad \forall a.$$

The weak attack above ensures that, given the target context x^*, the bandit algorithm is forced to pull arm a^* instead of any other arms. Unfortunately, the constraints do not result in a closed convex set. To formulate the attack as a convex optimization problem, we introduce a stronger notion of attack that implies weak attack:

Definition 2 (Strong attack). *A target context* x^* *is called* <u>ϵ-*strongly*</u> <u>*attacked*</u> *into pulling target arm* a^*, *for some* $\epsilon > 0$, *if after attack the following holds:*

$$x^{*\top}\hat{\theta}_{a^*} + \alpha_{a^*}\|x^*\|_{V_{a^*}^{-1}} \geq \epsilon + x^{*\top}\hat{\theta}_a + \alpha_a\|x^*\|_{V_a^{-1}}, \quad \forall a \neq a^*. \tag{7}$$

This is essentially a large margin condition which requires the UCB of a^* to be at least ϵ greater than the UCB of any other arm a. The margin parameter ϵ is chosen by the attacker. We achieve strong attack with the following optimization problem:

$$\min_{\Delta_a : a \in [K]} \sum_{a\in[K]} \|\Delta_a\|_2^2$$

$$\text{s.t.} \quad x^{*\top}\hat{\theta}_{a^*} + \alpha_{a^*}\|x^*\|_{V_{a^*}^{-1}} \geq \epsilon + x^{*\top}\hat{\theta}_a + \alpha_a\|x^*\|_{V_a^{-1}}, \quad \forall a \neq a^* \tag{8}$$

$$\text{where} \quad \hat{\theta}_a = V_a^{-1} X_a^\top (y_a + \Delta_a), \forall a.$$

The optimization problem above is a quadratic program with linear constraints in $\{\Delta_a\}_{a\in[K]}$. We summarize the attack in Algorithm 2. In the next section we discuss when the algorithm is feasible.

---

[2] The choice of norm is application dependent, see e.g., [15, Fig. 3]. Any norm works for the attack formulation.

Algorithm 2. Data Poisoning Attack in Contextual Bandit

1: **Input**: victim contextual bandit (Algorithm 1), target context x^*, target arm a^*, attack margin ϵ, historical data $X_a, y_a, a \in [K]$.
2: Solve (8) for $\Delta_a, \forall a \in [K]$.
3: If a solution Δ_a is found, poison $y_a \leftarrow y_a + \Delta_a$; otherwise return `infeasible`.

---

4 Feasibility of Attack

While one can always write down the training set attack algorithm as optimization (8), there is no guarantee that such attack is feasible. In particular, the inequality constraints may result in an empty set. One may naturally ask: are there context vectors x^* that simply cannot be strongly attacked?[3] In this section we present a full characterization of the feasibility question for strong attack. As we will see, attack feasibility depends on the original training data. Understanding the answer helps us to gauge the difficulty of poisoning, and may aid the design of defenses.

The main result of this section is the following theorem that characterizes a sufficient and necessary condition for the strong attack to be feasible.

Theorem 1. *A context x cannot be strongly attacked into pulling a^* if and only if there exists $a \neq a^*$ such that the following two conditions are both satisfied:*

(i) $x \in \mathrm{Null}(X_{a^*}) \cap \mathrm{Null}(X_a)$, *and*
(ii) $\alpha_{a^*} \|x\|_{V_{a^*}^{-1}} < \epsilon + \alpha_a \|x\|_{V_a^{-1}}$.

Before presenting the proof, we first provide intuition. The key idea is that a context x cannot be strongly attacked if some non-target arm a is always better than a^* for x for any attack. This can happen because there are two terms in the arm selection criterion (3) while the attack can affect the first term only. It turns out that under the condition (i) the first term becomes zero. If there exists a non-target arm that has a larger second term than that of the target arm (the condition (ii)), then no attack can force the bandit algorithm to choose the target arm.

We present an empirical study on the feasibility of attack in Sect. 6.3.

Lemma 1. $x \in \mathrm{Null}(X_{a^*}) \Leftrightarrow x^\top V_{a^*}^{-1} X_{a^*}^\top = 0$, *where* $V_{a^*}^{-1} = X_{a^*}^\top X_{a^*} + \lambda I$.

Proof. First, we prove $x \in \mathrm{Null}(X_{a^*}) \Rightarrow x^\top V_{a^*}^{-1} X_{a^*}^\top = 0$. Note that

$$x \in \mathrm{Null}(X_{a^*}) \Rightarrow X_{a^*} x = 0$$
$$\Rightarrow X_{a^*}^\top X_{a^*} x = 0$$
$$\Rightarrow (X_{a^*}^\top X_{a^*} + \lambda I)x = \lambda x \tag{9}$$
$$\Rightarrow \frac{1}{\lambda} x = (X_{a^*}^\top X_{a^*} + \lambda I)^{-1} x = V_{a^*}^{-1} x.$$

---

[3] Even if some context x^* cannot be strongly attacked, the attacker might be able to weakly attack it. Weak attack is sufficient for the attacker to force an arm pull of a^*. However, as $\epsilon \to 0$ strong attack approaches weak attack. Thus we only need to characterize strong attacks.

Therefore, we have

$$x^\top V_{a^*}^{-1} X_{a^*}^\top = \frac{1}{\lambda} x^\top X_{a^*}^\top = \frac{1}{\lambda} (X_{a^*} x)^\top = 0. \tag{10}$$

Now we show the other direction. Note that

$$
\begin{aligned}
x^\top V_{a^*}^{-1} X_{a^*}^\top = 0 &\Rightarrow x^\top V_{a^*}^{-1} X_{a^*}^\top X_{a^*} = 0 \\
&\Rightarrow x^\top V_{a^*}^{-1} (V_{a^*} - \lambda I) = 0 \\
&\Rightarrow x^\top = \lambda x^\top V_{a^*}^{-1} \\
&\Rightarrow (X_{a^*}^\top X_{a^*} + \lambda I) x = \lambda x \\
&\Rightarrow X_{a^*}^\top X_{a^*} x = 0 \\
&\Rightarrow x^\top X_{a^*}^\top X_{a^*} x = 0 \\
&\Rightarrow \|X_{a^*} x\|_2^2 = 0 \\
&\Rightarrow X_{a^*} x = 0,
\end{aligned}
\tag{11}
$$

which implies $x \in \text{Null}(X_{a^*})$.   □

Proof (Theorem 1). ($\Leftarrow$) According to Lemma 1, condition (i) implies

$$x^\top V_{a^*}^{-1} X_{a^*}^\top (y_{a^*} + \Delta_{a^*}) = x^\top V_a^{-1} X_a^\top (y_a + \Delta_a) = 0. \tag{12}$$

Combined with (ii) we have for any Δ_{a^*} and Δ_a,

$$
\begin{aligned}
x^\top V_{a^*}^{-1} X_{a^*}^\top (y_{a^*} + \Delta_{a^*}) + \alpha_{a^*} \|x\|_{V_{a^*}^{-1}} &= \alpha_{a^*} \|x\|_{V_{a^*}^{-1}} \\
< \epsilon + \alpha_a \|x\|_{V_a^{-1}} &= \epsilon + \alpha_a \|x\|_{V_a^{-1}} + x^\top V_a^{-1} X_a^\top (y_a + \Delta_a).
\end{aligned}
\tag{13}
$$

Thus, x cannot be attacked.

($\Rightarrow$) This is equivalent to prove if $\forall a \neq a^*$, $\neg(i) \lor \neg(ii)$, then x can be attacked. To show x can be attacked, it suffices to find a solution for the optimization problem.

If $\neg(i)$, then $X_{a^*} x \neq 0$ or $X_a x \neq 0$. Assume $X_{a^*} x \neq 0$ (similar for the case $X_a x \neq 0$), then $x^\top V_{a^*}^{-1} X_{a^*}^\top \neq 0$. Let $p = X_{a^*} V_{a^*}^{-1} x$. For any $a \neq a^*$, arbitrarily fix some Δ_a, then define

$$q_a = \epsilon + \alpha_a \|x\|_{V_a^{-1}} + x^\top V_a^{-1} X_a^\top (y_a + \Delta_a) - x^\top V_{a^*}^{-1} X_{a^*}^\top y_{a^*} - \alpha_{a^*} \|x\|_{V_{a^*}^{-1}}. \tag{14}$$

Let $\Delta_{a^*} = kp$, where $k = \max_{a \neq a^*} \frac{q_a}{\|p\|_2^2}$. Thus,

$$x^\top V_{a^*}^{-1} X_{a^*}^\top \Delta_{a^*} = p^\top \Delta_{a^*} = k \|p\|_2^2 \geq \frac{q_a}{\|p\|_2^2} \|p\|_2^2 = q_a, \quad \forall a \neq a^*. \tag{15}$$

Therefore, we have for all $a \neq a^*$ that

$$x^\top V_{a^*}^{-1} X_{a^*}^\top (y_{a^*} + \Delta_{a^*}) + \alpha_{a^*} \|x\|_{V_{a^*}^{-1}} \geq \epsilon + \alpha_a \|x\|_{V_a^{-1}} + x^\top V_a^{-1} X_a^\top (y_a + \Delta_a), \tag{16}$$

which means x^* can be attacked.

If $\neg(ii)$, simply letting $\Delta_{a^*} = -y_{a^*}$ and $\Delta_a = -y_a$ suffices, concluding the proof.   □

5   Side Effects of Attack

While the previous section characterized contexts x^* that cannot be strongly attacked, this section asks an opposite question: suppose the attacker was able to strongly attack some x^* by solving (8), what other contexts x are affected by the attack? For example, there might exist some context $x \neq x^*$ whose pre-attack chosen arm is $a(x) = 1$, but becomes $a'(x) = 2$. The side effects can be construed in two ways: on one hand the attack automatically influence more contexts than just x^*; on the other hand they make it harder for the attacker to conceal an attack. The latter may be utilized to facilitate detection by a defender. In this section, we study the side effect of attack and provide insights into future research directions on defense.

The side effect is quantified by the fraction of contexts in the context space such that the chosen arm is changed by the attacker. Specifically, let $\mathcal{X}$ be the context space and P be a probability measure over $\mathcal{X}$. Let $a(x)$ and $a'(x)$ be the pre-attack and post-attack chosen arm of a context x. Then the *side effect fraction* is defined as:

$$s = \int_{x \in \mathcal{X}} \mathbb{1}\left[a(x) \neq a'(x)\right] P(x)dx. \tag{17}$$

One can compute an *empirical side effect fraction* $\hat{s}$ as follows. First sample m contexts from P, and then let $\hat{s} = \frac{1}{m} \sum_{i=1}^{m} \mathbb{1}\left[a(x) \neq a'(x)\right]$. It is easy to show using Chernoff bound that $|s - \hat{s}|$ decays to 0 at the rate of $1/\sqrt{m}$.

We now give some properties of the side effect. Specifically, we first show if x is affected by the attack, cx is also affected by the attack for any $c > 0$.

Proposition 1. *If a context x satisfies $a(x) \neq a'(x)$, then $a(cx) \neq a'(cx)$ for any $c > 0$, where $a(x)$ and $a'(x)$ are the pre-attack and post-attack chosen arm of x. Moreover, $a'(cx) = a'(x)$, i.e., the post-attack chosen arms for cx and x are exactly the same.*

Proof. First, for any $a \neq a'(x)$, define

$$f_a(x) = x^\top \hat{\theta}_{a'(x)} + \alpha_{a'(x)} \|x\|_{V_{a'(x)}^{-1}} - x^\top \hat{\theta}_a - \alpha_a \|x\|_{V_a^{-1}}. \tag{18}$$

Note that $a'(x)$ is the best arm after attack, thus $f_a(x) > 0$, $\forall a \neq a'(x)$. Therefore, for any $c > 0$, we have

$$f_a(cx) = c f_a(x) > 0, \quad \forall a \neq a'(x), \tag{19}$$

which implies that $a'(cx) = a'(x)$. The same argument may be used to show $a(cx) = a(x)$. Therefore, $a'(cx) = a'(x) \neq a(x) = a(cx)$.

Proposition 1 shows that if a context x has a side effect, all contexts on the open ray $\{cx : c > 0\}$ also have the same side effect.

Proposition 2. *If a context x is strongly attacked, then cx is also strongly attacked for any $c \geq 1$.*

Proof. First, for any $a \neq a^*$, define

$$f_a(x) = x^\top \hat{\theta}_{a^*} + \alpha_{a^*} \|x\|_{V_{a^*}^{-1}} - x^\top \hat{\theta}_a - \alpha_a \|x\|_{V_a^{-1}} . \tag{20}$$

Since x is strongly attacked, we have $f_a(x) \geq \epsilon$, $\forall a \neq a^*$. Therefore $f_a(cx) = cf_a(x) \geq f_a(x) \geq \epsilon$, which shows that cx is also strongly attacked.

The above propositions are weak in that they do not directly quantify the side effect fraction s. They only tell us that when there is side effect, the affected contexts form a collection of rays. In the experiment section we empirically study the side effect fraction. Further theoretical understanding of the side effect is left as a future work.

6   Experiments

Our proposed attack algorithm works for any contextual bandit algorithm taking the form (3). Throughout the experiments, we choose to attack the OFUL algorithm that has a tight regret bound and can be efficiently implemented.

6.1   Attack Effectiveness and Effort: Toy Experiment

To study the effectiveness of the attack, we consider the following toy experiment. The bandit has $K = 5$ arms, and each arm has a payoff parameter $\theta_a \in \mathcal{R}^d$ where $d = 10$, distributed uniformly on the d-dimensional sphere, denoted $\mathcal{S}^d$. To generate θ_a, we first draw from a d-dimensional standard Gaussian distribution, $\tilde{\theta}_a \sim \mathcal{N}(\mathbf{0}, I_d)$ and then normalize: $\theta_a = \tilde{\theta}_a / \|\tilde{\theta}_a\|_2$.

Next, we construct the historical data as follows. We generate $n = 10^3$ historical context vectors $\{x_1, \ldots, x_n\}$ again uniformly on $\mathcal{S}^d$. For each historical context x, we pretend the world generates all K rewards $\{r_a : a \in \mathcal{A}\}$ from the K arms according to (1), where we set the noise level to $\sigma = 0.1$. We then choose an arm a randomly from a multinomial distribution: $a \sim \text{multi}(p_1, p_2, ..., p_K)$, where $p_{i'} = \frac{\exp(r_{i'})}{\sum_{i' \in \mathcal{A}} \exp(r_{i'})}$. This forms one data point (x, a, r_a), and we repeat it for all n points. We then group the historical data to form the appropriate matrices X_a, y_a for every $a \in \mathcal{A}$. Note that the historical data generated in this way is off-policy with respect to the bandit algorithm. The regularization and confidence parameters are $\lambda = 1$ and $\delta = 0.05$, respectively.

In each attack trial, we draw a single target context $x^* \in \mathcal{R}^d$ uniformly from $\mathcal{S}^d$. Without attack, the bandit would have chosen the arm with the highest UCB based on historical data (3). To illustrate the attack, we will do the opposite and set the attack target arm a^* as the one with the smallest UCB instead:

$$a^* = \text{argmin}_{a \in [K]} \left\{ x^{*\top} \hat{\theta}_a + \alpha_a \|x^*\|_{V_a^{-1}} \right\}, \tag{21}$$

where α_a is the UCB parameter of the OFUL algorithm [1]. We set the strong attack margin as $\epsilon = 0.001$. We then run the attack on x^* with Algorithm 2.

We run 100 attack trials. In each trial the arm parameters, historical data, and the target context x^* are regenerated. We make two main observations:

1. The attacker is effective. All ϵ-strongly attacks are successful.
2. The attacker's poisoning Δ is small. The total poisoning can be measured by $\|\Delta\|_2 = \sqrt{\sum_{a \in [K]} \|\Delta_a\|_2^2}$ in each attack trial. However, this quantity depends on the scale of the original pre-attack rewards y_a. It is more convenient to look at the <u>poisoning effort ratio</u>:

$$\frac{\|\Delta\|_2}{\|y\|_2} = \sqrt{\frac{\sum_{a \in [K]} \|\Delta_a\|_2^2}{\sum_{a \in [K]} \|y_a\|_2^2}}. \tag{22}$$

Figure 1 shows the histogram for the poisoning effort ratio of the 100 attack trials. The ratio tends to be small, with a median of 0.26, which demonstrates that the attacker needs to only manipulate about 26% of the rewards.

These two observations indicate that poisoning attack in contextual bandit is easy to carry out.

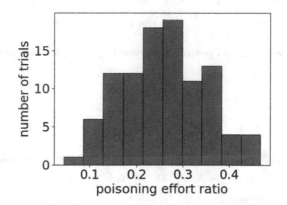

Fig. 1. Histogram of poisoning effort ratio in the toy experiment

We now analyze a single, representative attack trial to gain deeper insight into the attack strategy. In this trial, the UCBs of the 5 arms without attack are

pre-attack: $(0.204, 0.097, 0.959, 0.507, 0.818)$.

That is, arm 3 would have been chosen. As mentioned earlier, $a^* = 2$ is chosen to be the target arm as it has the smallest pre-attack UCB. After attack, the UCBs of all arms become:

post-attack: $(0.204, 0.605, 0.604, 0.507, 0.604)$.

The attacker successfully forced the bandit to choose arm 2. It did so by poisoning the historical data to make arm 2 look better and arms 3 and 5 look worse. It left arms 1 and 4 unchanged.

Figure 2 shows the attack where each panel is the historical rewards where that arm was chosen. We show the original rewards (y_{ai}, blue circle) and post-attack rewards ($y_{ai} + \Delta_{ai}$, red cross) for all historical points i where arm a was chosen. Intuitively, to decrease the UCB of arm a the attacker should reduce the reward if the historical context x is "similar" to x^*, and boost the reward otherwise. To see this, we sort the historical points by the inner product $x^\top x^*$ in ascending order. As shown in Fig. 2(c) and (e), the attacker gave the illusion that these arms are not good for x^* by reducing the rewards when $x^\top x^*$ is large. The attacker also increased the rewards when $x^\top x^*$ is very negative, which reinforces the illusion. In contrast, the attacker did the opposite on the target arm as shown in Fig. 2(b).

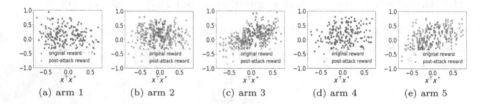

| (a) arm 1 | (b) arm 2 | (c) arm 3 | (d) arm 4 | (e) arm 5 |

Fig. 2. Original reward y_{ai} and post-attack reward $y_{ai} + \Delta_{ai}$ for each arm. (Color figure online)

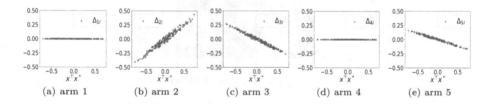

| (a) arm 1 | (b) arm 2 | (c) arm 3 | (d) arm 4 | (e) arm 5 |

Fig. 3. The reward poisoning Δ_{ai} for each arm.

6.2   Attack on Real Data: Yahoo! News Recommendation

To further demonstrate the effectiveness of the attack algorithm in real applications, we now test it on the Yahoo! Front Page Today Module User Click Log Dataset (R6A).[4] The dataset contains a fraction of user click log for news articles displayed in the Featured Tab of the Today Module on Yahoo! Front Page (http://www.yahoo.com) during the first ten days in May 2009. Specifically, it contains about 46 million user visits, where each user is represented as a 6-dimensional contextual vector. When a user arrives, the Yahoo! Webscope program selects an article (an arm) from a candidate article pool and displays it

---

[4] URL: https://webscope.sandbox.yahoo.com/catalog.php?datatype=r.

to the user. The system receives reward 1 if the user clicks on the article and 0 otherwise. Contextual information about users can be found in prior work [13].

To apply the attack algorithm, we require that the set of arms remain unchanged. However, the Yahoo! candidate article pool (i.e., the set of arms) varies as new articles are added and old ones are removed over time. Nonetheless, there are long periods of time where the set of arms is fixed. We restrict ourselves to such a stable time period for our experiment (specifically the period from 7:25 to 10:35 on May 1, 2009) in the Yahoo! data, which contains 243,667 user visits. During this period the bandit has $K = 20$ fixed arms. We further split the time period such that the first $n = 8000$ user visits are used as the historical training data to be poisoned, and the remaining $m = 163,667$ data points as the test data. The bandit learning algorithm uses regularization $\lambda = 1$. The confidence parameter is $\delta = 0.05$. The subGaussian parameter is set to $\sigma = \frac{1}{4}$ for binary rewards.

We simulate attacks on three target user context vectors: The most frequent user context vector $x^* = \bar{x}$, a middle user context vector $x^* = \dot{x}$, and the least frequent user context vector $x^* = \underline{x}$ in the test data. These three user context vectors appeared 5508, 106, and 1 times, respectively, in the test data. Note that there are potentially many distinct real-world users that are mapped to the same user contextual vector, therefore the "user" in our experiment does not necessarily mean a real-world individual that appeared thousands of times.

We again choose as the target arm a^* the worst arm on the target user as defined by (21). To determine the target arm, we first simulate the bandit algorithm on the original (pre-attack) training data, and then pick the arm with the smallest UCB for that user. For the three target users we consider, the target arms are 8, 3, and 8 respectively. The attacker uses attack margin $\epsilon = 0.001$.

Different from the toy example where the reward can be any value in $\mathcal{R}$, the reward in the Yahoo! dataset must be binary, corresponding to a click-or-not outcome of the recommendation. Therefore, the attacker must enforce $y_{ai} + \Delta_{ai} \in \{0, 1\}$. However, this results in a combinatorial problem. To preserve convexity, we instead relax the attacked reward into a box constraint: $y_{ai} + \Delta_{ai} \in [0, 1]$. We add these new constraints to (8) and solve the following optimization:

$$\min_{\Delta \in \mathcal{R}^n} \quad \sum_{a \in [K]} \|\Delta_a\|_2^2$$

$$\text{s.t.} \quad x^{*\top}\hat{\theta}_{a^*} + \alpha_{a^*}\|x^*\|_{V_{a^*}^{-1}} \geq \epsilon + x^{*\top}\hat{\theta}_a + \alpha_a\|x^*\|_{V_a^{-1}}, \quad \forall a \neq a^*, \quad (23)$$

$$y_{ai} + \Delta_{ai} \in [0, 1], \quad \forall i \in [m_a], \quad \forall a,$$

$$\text{where} \quad \hat{\theta}_a = V_a^{-1}X_a^\top(y_a + \Delta_a), \quad \forall a.$$

After the real-valued Δ_{ai} is computed, the attacker performs rounding to turn $y_{ai} + \Delta_{ai}$ into 0 or 1. Specifically, the attacker thresholds $y_{ai} + \Delta_{ai}$ with a constant $c \in [0, 1]$, so that if $y_{ai} + \Delta_{ai} > c$, then let the post-attack reward be 1, otherwise let the post-attack reward be 0. Note that the poisoned rewards now correspond to "reward flipping" from 0 to 1 or vice versa by the attacker. In our experiment, we let the attacker try out 10^4 thresholds c equally distributed in

[0, 1]. The attacker examines different thresholds for two concerns. First, there is no guarantee that the thresholded solution still triggers the target arm pull, thus the attacker needs to check if the selected arm for x^* is a^*. If not, the corresponding threshold c is inadmissible. Second, among those thresholds that indeed trigger the target arm pull, the attacker selects the one that minimizes the number of flipped rewards, which corresponds to the smallest poisoning effort in the binary reward case.

In Table 1, we summarize the experimental results for attacking the three target users. Note that the attack is successful on all three target users. The best thresholds c for $\bar{x}$, $\ae$ and $\underline{x}$ are 0.0449, 0.1911, and 0.0439, respectively. The number of flipped rewards is small compared to $n = 8000$, which demonstrates that the attacker only needs to spend little cost in order to force the bandit to pull the target arm. Note that the poisoning effect ratio is relatively large. This is because most of the pre-attack rewards are 0, in which case the denominator in (22) is small.

Table 1. Results of experiments on Yahoo! data

	$\bar{x}$	$\ae$	$\underline{x}$
Strong attack successful?	True	True	True
Number [percentage] of flipped rewards	82 [1.0%]	9 [0.1%]	19 [0.2%]
Poisoning effort ratio	0.572	0.189	0.275

In Fig. 4, we show the reward poisoning Δ on the historical data against the three target users, respectively. In all three cases, only a few rewards of the target arm are flipped from 0 to 1 by the attacker while those of the other arms remain unchanged. Therefore, we only show the reward poisoning on historical data restricted to the target arm (namely on y_{a^*}). The 82 and 19 flipped rewards overlap in Fig. 4(a) and (c). Note that the contexts of those flipped rewards are highly correlated with x^*.

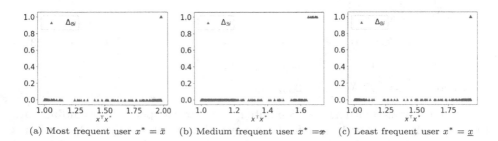

(a) Most frequent user $x^* = \bar{x}$ (b) Medium frequent user $x^* = \ae$ (c) Least frequent user $x^* = \underline{x}$

Fig. 4. The reward poisoning Δ_{ai} on three target users.

6.3   Study on Feasibility

The attack feasibility depends on the historical contexts X, the bandit algorithm-specific UCB parameter α, the attack margin ϵ, the target arm a^*, and the target context x^*. To visualize the infeasible region of strong attack on context, we consider the following toy example.

The bandit has $K = 4$ arms. The attacker's target arm is $a^* = 4$, and the target context x^* lies in $\mathcal{R}^3$. The historical context vectors are

$$X_1 = [1,\ 0,\ 0], \quad X_2 = [0,\ -1,\ 1], \quad X_3 = [0,\ 2,\ 0], \quad X_4 = [2,\ 0,\ 0]. \quad (24)$$

The problem parameters are $\sigma = S = \lambda = \epsilon = 1$ and $\delta = 0.05$. According to Theorem 1, any infeasible target context x^* satisfies $X_4 x^* = 0$. Thus such x^* must lie in the subspace spanned by the y-axis and z-axis. This allows us to show infeasible regions as 2D plots. In Fig. 5(a), we show the infeasible regions. We distinguish the infeasible region due to each non-target arm by a different color. For example, the infeasible region due to arm 1 consists of all contexts on which the target arm a^* can never be ϵ-better than arm 1 regardless of the attack. Note that the infeasible region due to arm 2 is a line segment of finite length, while that due to arm 3 is the whole $y = 0$ line. The shape of the infeasible region due to each non-target arm varies because the historical data differs and therefore the conditions in Theorem 1 characterizes different shapes. Note that the origin $x = 0$ satisfies the conditions in Theorem 1 and therefore is always infeasible.

One important observation is that, if the bandit algorithm is trained on more historical data, more context vectors x^* can potentially be strongly attacked. Formally, as indicated by Theorem 1 as the null space of historical context matrices $X_a, a \in [K]$ shrinks, the infeasible region shrinks as well. To demonstrate this, in Fig. 5(b) we add a context $[0, 0, 0.5]$ to X_1 such that the historical contexts are:

$$X_1 = \begin{bmatrix} 1,\ 0,\ 0 \\ 0,\ 0,\ 0.5 \end{bmatrix}, \quad X_2 = [0,\ -1,\ 1], \quad X_3 = [0,\ 2,\ 0], \quad X_4 = [2,\ 0,\ 0]. \quad (25)$$

Now that $\text{Null}(X_1)$ is reduced, the infeasibility region due to arm 1 shrinks from the circle in Fig. 5(a) to a horizontal line segment in Fig. 5(b). However the infeasible region may not shrink to a subset of itself, as indicated by the line segment having wider length along y axis than the original circle, thus the shrink happens in the sense of being restricted to a lower-dimensional subspace.

Next we add a historical context $[0, 1, 0]$ to X_4:

$$X_1 = \begin{bmatrix} 1,\ 0,\ 0 \\ 0,\ 0,\ 0.5 \end{bmatrix}, \quad X_2 = [0,\ -1,\ 1], \quad X_3 = [0,\ 2,\ 0], \quad X_4 = \begin{bmatrix} 2,\ 0,\ 0 \\ 0,\ 1,\ 0 \end{bmatrix}.$$

Then the infeasibility region due to arm 1 and arm 2 both shrink to the origin while arm 3 becomes a line segment, as shown in Fig. 5(c).

In practice, historical data is often abundant so that $\forall a \neq a^*$, $X_{a^*} \cup X_a$ spans the whole $\mathcal{R}^d$ space, and the only infeasible point is the origin. That is, the attacker can choose to attack essentially any context vector.

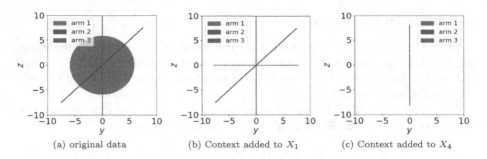

Fig. 5. Infeasible region due to each non-target arm.

Another observation is that the infeasible region shrinks as the attack margin ϵ decreases, as shown in Fig. 6. The historical data for each arm is the same as (24). The reason is that a smaller ϵ makes the constraints in (8) easier to satisfy and therefore more contexts are feasible. As $\epsilon \to 0$ the infeasible region converges to those contexts that cannot be weakly attacked, which in this example is the line $y = 0$ in Fig. 6(c). Note that the contexts that cannot be weakly attacked are those that make (6) infeasible. Therefore, we see that without abundant historical data, there will be some contexts that can never be strongly attacked even when $\epsilon \to 0$. Also note that the origin $x^* = 0$ can never be strongly attacked by definition.

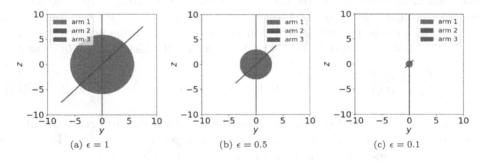

Fig. 6. Infeasible region shrinks as attack margin ϵ decreases.

6.4   Study on Side Effects

We first give an intuitive illustration of the side effect in 2D space. The bandit has $K = 3$ arms, where the arm parameters are θ_a. We generate $n = 1000$ historical data same as before with noise $\sigma = 0.1$. The target context x^* is uniformly sampled from $\mathcal{X}$. The bandit algorithm uses regularization weight $\lambda = 1$ and confidence parameter $\delta = 0.05$. Without attack, the UCB for the three arms are

$$\text{pre-attack: } (-0.419,\ 0.192,\ 1.013). \tag{26}$$

Therefore without attack arm 3 would have been chosen. By our design choice, the target arm is $a^* = 1$. The attacker uses margin $\epsilon = 0.001$. After attack the UCBs of all arms become:

$$\text{post-attack: } (0.290, \ 0.192, \ 0.289). \tag{27}$$

As shown in Fig. 7, the attacker forces the post-attack parameter of the best arm $\hat{\theta}_3$ to deviate from x^* while making $\hat{\theta}_1$ closer to x^*. Note that the attacker could also change the norm of the parameter. Note that arm 2 is not attacked, thus θ_2 and $\hat{\theta}_2$ overlap. The side effect is denoted by the brown arcs on the circle, where the arms chosen for those contexts are changed by the attacker. The side effect fraction for this example is $\hat{s} = 0.315$.

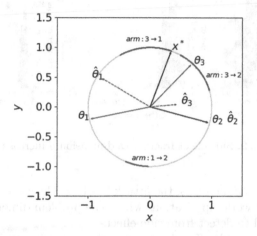

Fig. 7. Side effect shown in 2D context space.

Now we design a toy experiment to study how the side effect depends on the number of arms and the problem dimension. The context space $\mathcal{X}$ is the d-dimensional sphere $\mathcal{S}^d$ and P is uniform on the sphere. The bandit has K arms, where the arm parameters are sampled from P. Same as before, we generate $n = 2000$ historical data with noise $\sigma = 0.1$. The bandit algorithm uses regularization weight $\lambda = 1$. The target context x^* is sampled from P. The attacker's margin is $\epsilon = 0.001$ and the target arm a^* is the worst arm on the target context x^*. We sample $m = 10^3$ contexts from P to evaluate $\hat{s}$.

In Fig. 8, we fix $d = 2$ and show a histogram of $\hat{s}$ as the number of arm varies. Note that the attack affects about 30% users. The median $\hat{s}$ for the three panels are 0.249, 0.317, and 0.224 respectively, which shows that the side effect does not grow with the number of arms.

In Fig. 9, we fix $K = 5$ and show the side effect as the dimension d varies. The median $\hat{s}$ for the three panels are 0.435, 0.090, and 0.035, respectively, which implies that in higher dimensional space, the side effect tends to be smaller.

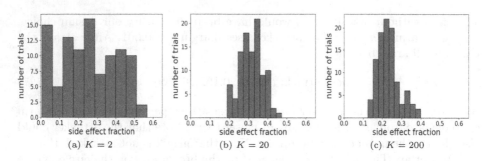

Fig. 8. Side effect fraction as arm number K increases.

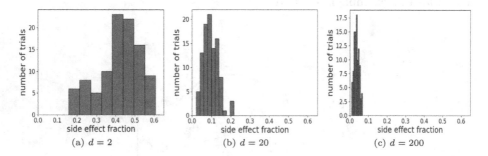

Fig. 9. Side effect fraction as dimension d increases.

As the dimension d increases, the attack has less side effect. This exposes the hazard that in real-world applications where the problem dimension is high, the attack will be hard to detect from side effects.

We also study the side effect for the real data experiment. There we use the $m = 163,667$ test users to evaluate the side effect. The side effect fraction for the three users are 0.5391, 0.0750, and 0.5040, respectively. Note that the most frequent user and the least frequent user have a large side effect, which makes the attack easy to detect. In contrast, the side effect of the medium frequent user is extremely small. This implies that the attack can induce different level of side effect for different target users.

7   Conclusions and Future Work

We studied offline data poisoning attack of contextual bandits. We proposed an optimization-based attack framework against contextual bandit algorithms. By manipulating the historical rewards, the attack can successfully force the bandit algorithm to pull a pre-specified arm for some target context. Experiments on both synthetic and real-world data demonstrate the effectiveness of the attack. This exposes a security concern in AI systems that involve contextual bandits.

There are several future directions that can be explored. For example, our current attack only targets a single context x^*. Future work can characterize how to target a set of contexts simultaneously, i.e., force the bandit algorithm to pull the target arm for all contexts in some target set. In the simplest case where the set contains finitely many contexts, one can just replicate the constraint in (8) for each context in the set. The situation is more complicated if the target set is infinite or just too large. Another interesting question is how to develop defense mechanisms to protect the bandit from being attacked. As indicated in this paper, the defender can rely on the side effect to sense the existence of attacks. Conversely, it is also an open question how the attacker might attempt to minimize its side effect during the attack, so that the chances of being detected are minimized. Finally, in this paper we restrict the ability of the attacker to manipulating only the historical rewards. However, there are other types of attacks such as poisoning the historical contexts, adding additional data points, removing existing data points, or combinations of the above. The problem could become non-convex or even combinatorial depending on the type of the attack; some of these settings have been studied under the name "machine teaching" [18,19]. Future work needs to identify how to extend our current attack framework to more general settings.

Acknowledgment. This work is supported in part by NSF 1545481, 1704117, 1623605, 1561512, and the MADLab AF Center of Excellence FA9550-18-1-0166.

References

1. Abbasi-Yadkori, Y., Pál, D., Szepesvári, C.: Improved algorithms for linear stochastic bandits. In: Advances in Neural Information Processing Systems (NIPS), pp. 2312–2320 (2011)
2. Agarwal, A., et al.: Making contextual decisions with low technical debt (2016). coRR abs/1606.03966
3. Alfeld, S., Zhu, X., Barford, P.: Data poisoning attacks against autoregressive models. In: The 30th AAAI Conference on Artificial Intelligence (2016)
4. Auer, P., Cesa-Bianchi, N., Fischer, P.: Finite-time analysis of the multiarmed bandit problem. Mach. Learn. **47**(2–3), 235–256 (2002)
5. Biggio, B., Nelson, B., Laskov, P.: Poisoning attacks against support vector machines. In: Proceedings of the 29th International Coference on International Conference on Machine Learning (ICML), pp. 1467–1474 (2012)
6. Chapelle, O., Manavoglu, E., Rosales, R.: Simple and scalable response prediction for display advertising. ACM Trans. Intell. Syst. Technol. **5**(4), 61:1–61:34 (2014)
7. Goodfellow, I.J., Shlens, J., Szegedy, C.: Explaining and harnessing adversarial examples. In: International Conference on Learning Representations (2015)
8. Greenewald, K., Tewari, A., Murphy, S.A., Klasnja, P.V.: Action centered contextual bandits. In: Advances in Neural Information Processing Systems 30 (NIPS), pp. 5979–5987 (2017)
9. Jagielski, M., Oprea, A., Biggio, B., Liu, C., Nita-Rotaru, C., Li, B.: Manipulating machine learning: poisoning attacks and countermeasures for regression learning. arXiv preprint arXiv:1804.00308 (2018)
10. Joseph, A.D., Nelson, B., Rubinstein, B.I.P., Tygar, J.: Adversarial Machine Learning. Cambridge University Press, Cambridge (2018)

11. Kuleshov, V., Precup, D.: Algorithms for multi-armed bandit problems (2014). coRR abs/1402.6028
12. Li, B., Wang, Y., Singh, A., Vorobeychik, Y.: Data poisoning attacks on factorization-based collaborative filtering. In: Advances in Neural Information Processing Systems, pp. 1885–1893 (2016)
13. Li, L., Chu, W., Langford, J., Schapire, R.E.: A contextual-bandit approach to personalized news article recommendation. In: Proceedings of the 19th International Conference on World Wide Web (WWW), pp. 661–670 (2010)
14. Mei, S., Zhu, X.: The security of latent Dirichlet allocation. In: The 18th International Conference on Artificial Intelligence and Statistics (AISTATS) (2015)
15. Mei, S., Zhu, X.: Using machine teaching to identify optimal training-set attacks on machine learners. In: The 29th AAAI Conference on Artificial Intelligence (2015)
16. Ng, A.Y., Harada, D., Russell, S.J.: Policy invariance under reward transformations: theory and application to reward shaping. In: Proceedings of the 16th International Conference on Machine Learning (ICML), pp. 278–287 (1999)
17. Zhao, M., An, B., Yu, Y., Liu, S., Pan, S.J.: Data poisoning attacks on multi-task relationship learning. In: Proceedings of the 32nd AAAI Conference on Artificial Intelligence, pp. 2628–2635 (2018)
18. Zhu, X.: Machine teaching: an inverse problem to machine learning and an approach toward optimal education. In: The 29th AAAI Conference on Artificial Intelligence (AAAI "Blue Sky" Senior Member Presentation Track) (2015)
19. Zhu, X., Singla, A., Zilles, S., Rafferty, A.N.: An overview of machine teaching. arXiv e-prints, January 2018. https://arxiv.org/abs/1801.05927

Analysis and Computation of Adaptive Defense Strategies Against Advanced Persistent Threats for Cyber-Physical Systems

Linan Huang[(✉)] and Quanyan Zhu[(✉)]

Department of Electrical and Computer Engineering, New York University,
2 MetroTech Center, Brooklyn, NY 11201, USA
{lh2328,qz494}@nyu.edu

Abstract. Cyber-physical systems are facing new security challenges from Advanced Persistent Threats (APTs) due to the stealthy, dynamic and adaptive nature of the attack. The multi-stage Bayesian game captures the incomplete information of the players' type, and enables an adaptive belief update according to the observable history of the other player's actions. The solution concept of perfect Bayesian Nash equilibrium (PBNE) under the proactive and reactive information structures of the players provides an important analytical tool to predict and design the players' behavior. To capture the learning process and enable fast computation of PBNE, we use conjugate priors to update the beliefs of the players parametrically, which is assimilated into backward dynamic programming with an expanded state space. We use a mathematical programming approach to compute the PBNE of the dynamic bi-matrix game of incomplete information. In the case study, we analyze and study two PBNEs under complete and one-sided incomplete information. The results reveal the benefit of deception of the private attackers' types and motivate defender's use of deception techniques to tilt the information asymmetry. Numerical results have been used to corroborate the analytical findings of our framework and show the effectiveness of defense design to deter the attackers and mitigate the APTs strategically.

Keywords: Multistage Bayesian game
Advanced Persistent Threats (APTs) · Optimal learning
Cyber deception · Proactive and strategic defense

1 Introduction

The integration of cyber-physical systems increases the operating efficiency and promotes the cross-layer communication. However, the interconnections also turn the industrial control systems (ICS) from the previous safe area to a hard-hit of emerging advanced cyber attacks such as Petya and Stuxnet. After the Aurora

© Springer Nature Switzerland AG 2018
L. Bushnell et al. (Eds.): GameSec 2018, LNCS 11199, pp. 205–226, 2018.
https://doi.org/10.1007/978-3-030-01554-1_12

generator test in 2007 warns us of the possibilities of physically destroying power generators with merely 21 lines of malicious codes, Petya has attacked the Ukrainian power plant in December 2015. Petya is the first known successful attack on the power grid and causes a power cut to more than 80,000 people. It takes a long time to recover, and the recovery under a similar attack would be worse in the United States in 2018 because of the increasing degree of automation and integration. Similarly, Stuxnet discovered in 2010, have infected over 200,000 computers all over the world and caused over 1,000 centrifuges out of operation. Stuxnet starts its initial infection through the USB driver of the hardware provider. These USB drives are stealthily compromised by Stuxnet when the hardware provider serves other less secure clients. Thus, Stuxnet manages to compromise the air gap even though the nuclear system is carefully isolated from the Internet. These attacks form the Advanced Persistent Threats (APTs) to the ICS security and indicate the urgency of effective defensive mechanisms to respond to the new threats.

APTs have the following three features distinct from the traditional attacks. First, they use customized incursion techniques and have specific targets, such as private organizations, state government, and critical infrastructures, with the goal to gather intelligence and sabotage facilities [4]. Second, they adopt persistent and stealthy attacking strategies to cause more permanent, significant, and irreversible damages. Stuxnet persists in alternating the rotor speed for years to increase the failure probability of the centrifuge. However, Stuxnet launches this attack only once a month to remain stealthy, i.e., human operators do not relate the increase in the number of inoperative centrifuges to an attack. Third, they are methodically designed. For example, Stuxnet replays a 21-s pre-recorded normal sensory data to deceive the monitor when the attack has begun to change the rotor speed.

Recent works on secure control systems [9] and intrusion detection systems (IDS) [3] have provided prevalent methods for malware prevention and detection, yet they can be insufficient for human-expert operated APTs that adopt advanced techniques and learn the detection rule during their lengthy stay in the system to evade the detection. To protect infrastructures from APTs, defenders need to design strategic and proactive policies that can learn, anticipate, and adapt the defense strategies over time. To this end, a game theory approach provides a natural framework to develop strategic and adaptive security solutions to harden the cyber-physical security [10,15]. Starting from the initial infection, APTs establish the foothold and escalate privilege by exploiting zero-day vulnerabilities to sign malware with the private key from stolen certificates. Then, they create tunnels and utilize the backdoor to control the Command and Control (C&C) server to receive additional instructions and malicious codes. Next, APTs establish additional points of entries and propagate stealthily and laterally in the cyber network until they reach the target computer. Finally, they can either collect data in the cyber layer or launch attacks on physical plants. The attack path of APTs, as shown in Fig. 1, can be represented by a tree network without loops and jumps. Thus, a multi-stage dynamic game [7] is a befitting framework to study the lateral movement and privilege escalation of the attack.

Flip-IT game [13], as one example of the dynamic game framework, has successfully analyzed the scenario of the key leakage under APTs so that system defender and APTs stealthily take over the system alternately. However, Flip-IT is a complete-information game, and it cannot be sufficient to capture the deceptive nature of the attack and the information asymmetry of the game. In the example of Stuxnet, it is hard to conclude from the observation of the alternating of the rotor's speed whether the system is under attack or what kind of attacks. One way to model the incomplete information caused by deceptions in games is to introduce the notion of *types* [5], which reflects the uncertainties of one player about the other player's motivation and objectives. Signaling game, a two-stage game with the one-sided *type* has been applied to study the deception in cyber-physical systems [14]. As a countermeasure for the deceptive attackers, [11] surveys defensive deceptions including perturbation, moving target defense, obfuscation, mixing, honey-*x* and attacker engagement. For example, cyber denial and deception (D&D) proposed in [12] aims to create sufficient amount of uncertainties so that adversaries would waste time and resources on 'honey files.' The authors in [6] show how the defender can manipulate the attacker's belief to deter attacks and minimize the damage inflicted to the network.

In our framework, we consider that attackers and defenders can adopt adversarial and defensive deceptions, respectively, in the dynamic game of cyber-physical systems. Each player has a *type* that characterizes his/her private information. Hence we model the scenario with a two-sided dynamic Bayesian game to uniformly capture the three characteristics of APTs, i.e., strategic adversaries, multiple stages, and incomplete information. The history of both players' actions is fully observable. The private type represents the uncertainty of the two-sided deception so that both players have to strategically gauge the other's type to respond optimally to their type-related utility functions. The solution concept for this dynamic game is the perfect Bayesian Nash equilibrium (PBNE) in which the players form a consistent belief and policy pair such that no player can gain via unilateral policy deviation with the belief that supports the actions. The computation of PBNE is challenging when the utility is a function of continuous type space. We propose an equivalent mathematical program with infinite-dimensional constraints to solve the dynamic Bayesian game and approximate it by sampling the type space. In particular, for the one-sided incomplete information bi-matrix game, we obtain two necessary conditions for the existence of the equilibrium.

1.1 Organization of the Paper

The rest of the paper is organized as follows. Section 2 introduces the system model and the Bayesian belief update. The solution concept of PBNE under proactive and reactive information structures is introduced in Sect. 3. In Sect. 4, we adopt the conjugate prior assumption for parametric update of the belief and form an expanded-state dynamic programming to unify the forward and backward processes. A case study of one-sided information is presented in Sect. 5, and Sect. 6 concludes the paper.

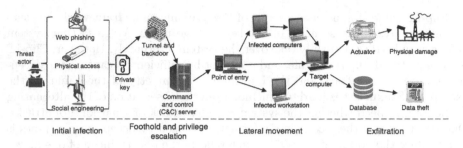

Fig. 1. The multi-stage life cycle of APTs forms a tree network. The threat actor starts the infection by exploiting the human weakness (social engineering) or cyber attacks. Then, APTs gain the foothold, escalate privilege, propagate laterally in the cyber network and finally either cause physical damages or collect confidential data. APTs use each stage as a stepping stone for the next and cannot jump directly to the final stage. Attackers also have no incentives to go back to stages that they has already compromised because their ultimate goal is to compromise the specific target at the final stage.

2   System Model

This section introduces a multi-stage dynamic game of incomplete information to model the strategic behaviors of APTs and defenders. Consider two players, a system defender P_1 (pronoun 'she') who holds different security levels and a user P_2 (pronoun 'he') of different threat levels to the system. The security or threat level of player $i \in \{1,2\}$ is private information unknown to the other player and is characterized by a continuous type $\theta_i \in \Theta_i := [0,1]$. For any finite set $\mathcal{A}$, define $\triangle \mathcal{A} := \{p : \mathcal{A} \mapsto R_+ | \sum_{a \in \mathcal{A}} p(a) = 1\}$ while for any infinite set Θ, define $\triangle \Theta := \{p : \Theta \mapsto R_+ | \int_{\theta \in \Theta} p(\theta)d\theta = 1\}$. Mathematically, type θ_i is the realization of $\tilde{\theta}_i$, a random variable with an underlying probability space $(\Omega, \mathcal{F}, P)$. The prior probability distribution $B_i^0 \in \triangle \Theta_i$ is common knowledge. User P_2's type θ_2 indicates the strength of the user in terms of damages that he can inflict on the system. A user with a large type value indicates a higher threat level to the system. A user with θ_2 less than a pre-defined threshold $\bar{\theta}_2 \in (0,1)$ is treated as legitimate. Similarly, the type of defender P_1 indicates the defense strength and the resource she has for security. For example, defenders can use deception techniques (e.g., honeypots and honeyfiles) to detect the attackers and cut links to isolate the attacker. The existence of honeypot can reduce the number of attacks because an attacker cannot be sure whether it is a trap or not when observing network vulnerability. In this case, a defender with a higher type value θ_1 indicates that she possesses a larger number of honeypots to deploy. Since APTs move stage by stage from the initial infection to reach the final target, we model the transition of APTs as a multi-stage game with a finite horizon T.

At each stage $t \in \{0, 1, \cdots, T\}$, each player P_i chooses an action a_i^t from his/her feasible action set $\mathcal{A}_i^t$. The user's actions $a_2^t \in \mathcal{A}_2^t$ are the behaviors that are directly observable from activity log files, e.g., a privilege escalation request and sensor access. Sine both legitimate and adversarial users can take these activities, a defender cannot identify the user's type directly from observing these actions. The user's type, however, determines the real actions and the corresponding payoff, e.g., a legitimate user's access to the sensor benefit the system while a pernicious user's access can cost a considerable loss. On the other hand, the defender's action a_1^t will be mitigation or proactive actions such as restricting the escalation request or monitoring the sensor access. These proactive actions also do not directly disclose the system type. The action set $\mathcal{A}_i^t$ is stage-variant and has a stage-dependent cardinality $|\mathcal{A}_i^t|$. For example, at the early stage of the attack on a nuclear plant, the defender can choose to shut down the reactor, while in a later stage, the defender switches from automatic to manual mode to control the feedwater flow. Each player cannot observe the current-stage t action of the other player until the action appears in the log file at the next stage. The perfect recall assumption leads to a fully observable history $\mathbf{h}^t := \{a_1^0, \cdots, a_1^{t-1}, a_2^0, \cdots, a_2^{t-1}\} \in \mathcal{H}^t$ to both players. State $x^t \in \mathcal{X}^t$ representing the status of the system at stage t is the sufficient statistic of history $\mathbf{h}^t$ because a Markov state transition $x^{t+1} = f^t(x^t, a_1^t, a_2^t)$ contains all the information of the history update $\mathbf{h}^t = \mathbf{h}^{t-1} \cup \{a_1^t, a_2^t\}$. The function f^t is deterministic and may also be stage-dependent. In the example of nuclear power plant, at the early stage, attacker and defender actions will determine whether the reactor can be shut down successfully, while in a later stage of the attack, the actions will determine whether the feedwater flow can be controlled appropriately to maintain the steam generator with an adequate water level.

Information structure $I_i^t \in \mathcal{I}_i^t$ is a set that contains the information available to player P_i at stage t. The behavioral strategy $\sigma_i^t : \mathcal{I}_i^t \mapsto \triangle \mathcal{A}_i^t$ for player P_i maps his/her information structure set into a distribution over P_i's action space. All the potential behavioral strategies constitute the feasible set Σ_i^t. Let $\sigma_i^t(a_i^t | I_i^t)$ be the probability of taking action a_i^t under the information structure I_i^t, i.e., $\sum_{a_i^t \in \mathcal{A}_i^t} \sigma_i^t(a_i^t | I_i^t) = 1, \forall I_i^t \in \mathcal{I}_i^t$. An action a_i^t is the realization of the behavioral strategy σ_i^t. In this work, we study the reactive information structure $\mathcal{I}_i^t := \mathcal{H}^t \times \Theta_i$ for outsider threats and the proactive information structure $\mathcal{I}_i^t := \sigma_{-i}^t \times \mathcal{H}^t \times \Theta_i$ for insider threats as introduced in Sect. 3. For $i \in \mathcal{I}$, notation $-i$ means $\mathcal{I} \setminus \{i\}$. For example, if $\mathcal{I} := \{1, 2\}$ and $i = 1$, then $-i = 2$. At stage $t \in \{1, \cdots, T\}$, P_i forms a belief $B_i^t : \mathcal{H}^t \mapsto \triangle \Theta_{-i}$ of the other player's type according to the history $\mathbf{h}^t$. Similarly, $B_i^t(\theta_{-i} | \mathbf{h}^t)$ at stage t is the conditional probability density function (PDF) of the other player's type θ_{-i} and $\int_0^1 B_i^t(\theta_{-i} | \mathbf{h}^t) d\theta_{-i} = 1, \forall t, \mathbf{h}^t, i \in \{1, 2\}$. The belief of the type is updated according to the Bayesian rule upon the arrival of the observations of actions a_i^t, a_{-i}^t with the boundary condition B_i^0:

$$B_i^{t+1}(\theta_{-i} | [\mathbf{h}^t, a_i^t, a_{-i}^t]) = \frac{B_i^t(\theta_{-i} | \mathbf{h}^t)\sigma_{-i}^t(a_{-i}^t | \mathbf{h}^t, \theta_{-i})}{\int_0^1 B_i^t(\hat{\theta}_{-i} | \mathbf{h}^t)\sigma_{-i}^t(a_{-i}^t | \mathbf{h}^t, \hat{\theta}_{-i}) d\hat{\theta}_{-i}}, i \in \{1, 2\}, \quad (1)$$

where we write $\sigma_{-i}^t(a_{-i}^t | I_i^t)$ as $\sigma_{-i}^t(a_{-i}^t | \mathbf{h}^t, \theta_{-i})$ for both information structures because the belief B_i^t depends only on the history $\mathbf{h}^t$.

At each stage t, $\bar{J}_i^t$ is the stage utility that depends on both types θ_i, θ_{-i}, both actions a_i^t, a_{-i}^t, the current state x^t, and an external random noise w_i^t with a known distribution. We introduce the external random noise to model other unknown factors that could affect the value of the stage utility. The existence of the external noise makes it impossible for each player i to directly acquire the value of the other's type based on the combined observation of input parameters $x^t, a_1^t, a_2^t, \theta_i$ plus the output value of the utility function $\bar{J}_i^t$. In this work, we consider any additive noise with the 0 mean $\bar{J}_i^t(x^t, a_1^t, a_2^t, \theta_i, \theta_{-i}, w_i^t) = J_i^t(x^t, a_1^t, a_2^t, \theta_i, \theta_{-i}) + w_i^t$, which leads to an equivalent utility over the expectation of the external noise $E_{w_i^t} \bar{J}_i^t = J_i^t, \forall x^t, a_1^t, a_2^t, \theta_i, \theta_{-i}$. The expected payoff of a player is taken with respect to his/her time-varying belief B_i^t over the type of the other player and their policy pair $\sigma_i^t, \sigma_{-i}^t$. Define a sequence of policies from t' to T, i.e., $\sigma_i^{t':T} := \{\sigma_i^t \in \Sigma_i^t\}_{t=t',\cdots,T} \in \Sigma_i^{t':T}$, then for player $i \in \{1,2\}$ with t' as the initial stage, the expected accumulated utility is as follows.

$$U_i^{t':T}(\sigma_i^{t':T}, \sigma_{-i}^{t':T}, \mathbf{h}^{T+1}, \theta_i) := \sum_{t=t'}^{T} E_{\theta_{-i} \sim B_i^t, a_i^t \sim \sigma_i^t, a_{-i}^t \sim \sigma_{-i}^t, w_i^t} \bar{J}_i^t(x^t, a_1^t, a_2^t, \theta_1, \theta_2, w_i^t)$$

$$= \sum_{t=t'}^{T} \int_0^1 B_i^t(\theta_{-i}|\mathbf{h}^t) \sum_{a_i^t \in \mathcal{A}_i^t} \sigma_i^t(a_i^t|I_i^t) \sum_{a_{-i}^t \in \mathcal{A}_{-i}^t} \sigma_{-i}^t(a_{-i}^t|I_{-i}^t) J_i^t(x^t, a_1^t, a_2^t, \theta_1, \theta_2) d\theta_{-i}.$$

$$(2)$$

In the scenario of APTs, both players consider cumulative utility of T stages because APTs have to move stage by stage to finish the entire life circle shown in Fig. 1.

3   Solution Concepts

In this section, we investigate the perfect Bayesian Nash equilibrium (PBNE) under two different information structures. The proactive PBNE (P-PBNE) corresponds to an insider threat, i.e, agent P_2 can observe the policy of the principal P_1 at each stage. On the other hand, the reactive PBNE (R-PBNE) corresponds to the outsider threat where both players cannot observe the other's policy at any stages. The PBNE under both information structures can be solved using dynamic programming that is consistent with a type belief update in (1).

3.1   P-PBNE

We model the scenario of APTs as a dynamic principal-agent problem as shown in Fig. 2. Attacker P_2 acts as an insider who knows policy σ_1^t and determines his policy σ_2^t as a best response to σ_1^t that maximizes his expected cumulative utility $U_2^{t:T}$. On the defender's side, a sophisticated defender is aware of the potential policy leakage through insider threats and anticipates the strategic response of the attacker using the attack tree analysis or proactive defenses (e.g., honeypots and honeyfiles). The described scenario leads to Definition 2 of P-PBNE. The P-PBNE may not exist or be unique. A counterexample in the static setting is shown in Remark 4.

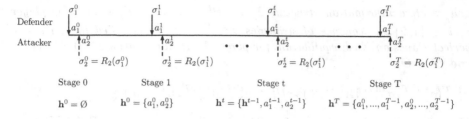

Fig. 2. Example of sequential plays under the proactive information structure.

Definition 1. *In the two-person dynamic game with the cumulative utility function* $U_i^{t':T}$ *in* (2) *and a sequence of beliefs* $B_i^t, t \in \{t', \cdots, T\}$ *in* (1), *define the set*

$$R_2(\sigma_1^{t':T}) := \{\gamma \in \Sigma_2^{t':T} : U_2^{t':T}(\sigma_1^{t':T}, \gamma) \geq U_2^{t':T}(\sigma_1^{t':T}, \sigma_2^{t':T}), \forall \sigma_2^{t':T} \in \Sigma_2^{t':T}\}$$

*as the **best-response set** of* P_2 *to* P_1*'s policy* $\sigma_1^{t':T} \in \Sigma_1^{t':T}$. □

Definition 2. *In the two-person dynamic Bayesian game with* P_1 *as the principal, the cumulative utility function* $U_i^{t':T}$ *in* (2), *a sequence of beliefs* $B_i^t, t \in \{t', \cdots, T\}$ *in* (1) *and proactive information structure* $\mathcal{I}_1^t := \mathcal{H}^t \times \Theta_1, \mathcal{I}_2^t := \sigma_1^t \times \mathcal{H}^t \times \Theta_2, t \in \{t', \cdots, T\}$, *a sequence of strategies* $\sigma_1^{*,t':T} \in \Sigma_1^{t':T}$ *is called a proactive perfect Bayesian Nash equilibrium (**P-PBNE**) for the principal, if*

$$\begin{aligned}
U_1^{*,t':T} &:= \inf_{\sigma_2^{t':T} \in R_2(\sigma_1^{*,t':T})} U_1^{t':T}(\sigma_1^{*,t':T}, \sigma_2^{t':T}) \\
&= \sup_{\sigma_1^{t':T} \in \Sigma_1^{t':T}} \inf_{\sigma_2^{t':T} \in R_2(\sigma_1^{t':T})} U_1^{t':T}(\sigma_1^{t':T}, \sigma_2^{t':T}).
\end{aligned} \tag{3}$$

A strategy $\sigma_2^{*,t':T} \in \arg\max_{\sigma_2^{t':T} \in \Sigma_2^{t':T}} U_2^{t':T}(\sigma_1^{*,t':T}, \sigma_2^{t':T}) := U_2^{*,t':T}$ *is called a P-PBNE for the agent* P_2. □

Remark 1. Since the agent's polices in the best-response set may not be unique, principal P_1 in (3) considers the worst-case policy among the best-response set $R_2(\sigma_1^{*,t':T})$. If the best-response set $R_2(\sigma_1^{t':T}) = \{\sigma_2^{*,t':T}\}$ is a singleton, we have $U_1^{*,t':T} = \sup_{\sigma_1^{t':T} \in \Sigma_1^{t':T}} U_1^{t':T}(\sigma_1^{t':T}, \sigma_2^{*,t':T})$ in (3). □

3.2 R-PBNE

If each player does not know the policy of the other player at every stage, then P_i chooses a sequence of behavioral strategies $\sigma_i^{*,t}(a_i^t|\mathcal{I}_i^t) = \sigma_i^{*,t}(a_i^t|\mathbf{h}^t, \theta_i), t \in \{t', \cdots, T\}$ so that she/he cannot gain if deviating unilaterally at any stage of the game, which leads to Definition 3 of R-PBNE.

Definition 3. *In the two-person dynamic Bayesian game with the cumulative utility function* $U_i^{t':T}$ *in* (2), *a sequence of beliefs* $B_i^t, t \in \{t', \cdots, T\}$ *in* (1) and reactive information structure $\mathcal{I}_i^t := \mathcal{H}^t \times \Theta_i, t \in \{t', \cdots, T\}$ for player $P_i, i \in \{1,2\}$, a sequence of strategies $\sigma_i^{*,t':T} \in \Sigma_i^{t':T}$ is called the ε-reactive perfect Bayesian Nash equilibrium for player P_i if, for a given $\varepsilon \geq 0$, $i \in \{1,2\}$ and $\forall \theta_i \in \Theta_i$,

$$U_i^{t':T}(\sigma_i^{*,t':T}, \sigma_{-i}^{*,t':T}, \mathbf{h}^{T+1}, \theta_i) \geq U_i^{t':T}(\sigma_i^{t':T}, \sigma_{-i}^{*,t':T}, \mathbf{h}^{T+1}, \theta_i) - \varepsilon, \forall \sigma_i^{t':T} \in \Sigma_i^{t':T}.$$

If $\varepsilon = 0$, we have a reactive perfect Bayesian Nash equilibrium (**R-PBNE**). $\square$

Remark 2. The belief update (1) is *strongly consistent* as it applies to all possible histories from stage t to $t+1$: even when history $\mathbf{h}^t$ has probability 0. In other word, belief update (1) is valid starting from all states, even if the equilibrium trajectory does not contain that state. The *strong time consistency* indicates *perfectness*, i.e., even some trembling hand mistakes happen at stage $\hat{t}$ and an unexpected state is reached, the player can still achieve optimality from that new state on by applying $\sigma_{-i}^{*,\hat{t}:T}$. Thus, PBNE strategies can adapt to unexpected changes. $\square$

3.3   Dynamic Programming

Given the type belief at every stage, we can use dynamic programming to find the PBNE in a backward fashion because of the tree structure and the finite horizon. Define the value function $V_i^t(\mathbf{h}^t, \theta_i) := U_i^{t:T}(\sigma_i^{*,t:T}, \sigma_{-i}^{*,t:T}, \mathbf{h}^{t+1}, \theta_i)$ as the optimal utility-to-go function at stage t. Let $V_i^{T+1}(\mathbf{h}^{T+1}, \theta_i) := 0$ be the boundary condition of the value function, we have the following recursive system equations involving both players' policies:

$$V_1^t(\mathbf{h}^t, \theta_1) = \sup_{\sigma_1^t} E_{\theta_2 \sim B_1^t, a_1^t \sim \sigma_1^t, a_2^t \sim \sigma_2^{*,t}}[V_1^{t+1}(\{\mathbf{h}^t, a_1^t, a_2^t\}, \theta_1) + J_1^t(x^t, a_1^t, a_2^t, \theta_1, \theta_2)];$$

$$V_2^t(\mathbf{h}^t, \theta_2) = \sup_{\sigma_2^t} E_{\theta_1 \sim B_2^t, a_2^t \sim \sigma_2^t, a_1^t \sim \sigma_1^{*,t}}[V_2^{t+1}(\{\mathbf{h}^t, a_1^t, a_2^t\}, \theta_2) + J_2^t(x^t, a_1^t, a_2^t, \theta_1, \theta_2)],$$

$$(4)$$

where $\sigma_1^{*,t}, \sigma_2^{*,t}, t \in \{0, \cdots, T\}$ are the PBNE policy pair. Figure 3 summarizes the forward update of the history $\mathbf{h}^t$, belief B_i^t, and policy σ_i^t from stage $t-1$ to t. The challenge is that the type belief is not directly known at each stage. The forward belief update in (1) depends on the PBNE strategy. However, the backward computation of PBNE strategy in (4) also couples with the belief as shown in Fig. 4. Hence, we need to find the PBNE strategy consistent with the belief at each stage.

4   Conjugate Prior Learning

If we assume that B_i^t is of the beta distribution and the strategy σ_{-i}^t of the other player corresponds to a binomial distribution, then B_i^{t+1} is also a beta distribution with updated hyperparameters. Figure 5 illustrates how a defender can learn the type of the attacker to decrease the probability of attacks. An

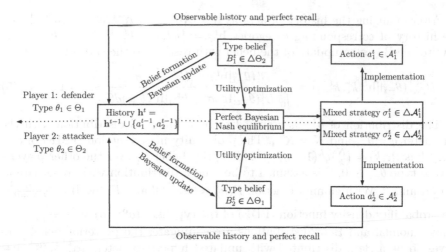

Fig. 3. A two-player stage transition from stage $t - 1$ to stage t. The transition loop iterates from stage $t = 0$ to the terminal stage $t = T - 1$, which constitutes the entire multi-stage dynamic game. Both players' history of actions are fully observable yet their types are private information to the other player. Each player P_i learns to update his/her belief $B_i^t \in \Delta\Theta_{-i}$ of the other's private type θ_{-i} based on the policy of the other player σ_{-i}^t at stage t.

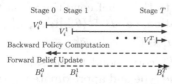

Fig. 4. The backward policy computation and the forward belief update are coupled.

Table 1. Stage utility of two players. Player P_2 takes action $a_2^T = 1$ with probability $q(\theta_2)$.

Action	$a_2^T = 0$	$a_2^T = 1$
$a_1^T = 0$	$R_{11}^1(\theta_2), R_{11}^2(\theta_2)$	$R_{12}^1(\theta_2), R_{12}^2(\theta_2)$
$a_1^T = 1$	$R_{21}^1(\theta_2), R_{21}^2(\theta_2)$	$R_{22}^1(\theta_2), R_{22}^2(\theta_2)$

expanded state includes the parameters of the distribution, and we can form one backward dynamic program with a larger dimension to unify the forward and backward processes. Finally, as the type-related policy makes it challenging to compute the PBNE for the expanded-state dynamic programming, we use a mathematical programming approach to compute R-PBNE. The P-PBNE can be analyzed likewise.

4.1 State Independent Belief Formation

At each stage t, player $-i$ divides the action space of the other player P_i into $K_i + 1$ time-invariant set of categories $\mathcal{C}_j^i$, i.e., $\mathcal{A}_i^t = \{\cup\mathcal{C}_j^i\}_{j=0,1,\cdots,K_i}, \forall t, i = 1, 2$ and mutual exclusive $\mathcal{C}_j^i \cap \mathcal{C}_l^i = \emptyset, \forall j \neq l, i = 1, 2$. Then, each a_{-i}^t uniquely corresponds to one category and we can transform $\sigma_{-i}^t(a_{-i}^t|\mathbf{h}^t, \theta_{-i})$, the distribution of a_{-i}^t, into a distribution of the corresponding category $k_{-i}^t \in \{0, 1, \cdots, K_i\}$.

After changing the history of actions $\mathbf{h}^t = \{a_1^0, \cdots, a_1^{t-1}, a_2^0, \cdots, a_2^{t-1}\}$ into the history of corresponding categories $\tilde{\mathbf{h}}^t := \{k_1^0, \cdots, k_1^{t-1}, k_2^0, \cdots, k_2^{t-1}\}$, we rewrite the Bayesian update of the belief with respect to the category.

$$B_i^{t+1}(\theta_{-i}|[\tilde{\mathbf{h}}^t, k_i^t, k_{-i}^t]) = \frac{B_i^t(\theta_{-i}|\tilde{\mathbf{h}}^t)\sigma_{-i}^t(k_{-i}^t|\tilde{\mathbf{h}}^t, \theta_{-i})}{\int_0^1 B_i^t(\hat{\theta}_{-i}|\tilde{\mathbf{h}}^t)\sigma_{-i}^t(k_{-i}^t|\tilde{\mathbf{h}}^t, \hat{\theta}_{-i})d\hat{\theta}_{-i}}, i = 1, 2. \quad (5)$$

The distribution of σ_{-i}^t is assumed to be a binomial distribution with the parameter $q = \theta_{-i}$ and $N = K_{-i}$. The probability mass function (PMF) of category k is $\Pr(k) = \binom{N}{k}q^k(1-q)^{N-k}$. The prior belief B_i^t over the other player's private type $\theta_{-i} \in [0, 1]$ is assumed to be a beta distribution with hyperparameters α and β. With gamma function $\Gamma(n) = (n-1)!$ and $Be(\alpha, \beta) = \frac{\Gamma(\alpha)\Gamma(\beta)}{\Gamma(\alpha+\beta)}$, the probability density function (PDF) of the type is $Beta^{\alpha,\beta}(q) = \frac{q^{\alpha-1}(1-q)^{\beta-1}}{Be(\alpha,\beta)}$. Since binomial and Beta distributions are conjugate, the posterior belief conserves to be a Beta distributed with updated hyperparameters $(\alpha_i^{t+1}, \beta_i^{t+1}) = (\alpha_i^t + k_i^t, \beta_i^t + K_i - k_i^t), i = 1, 2$, where k_i^t is the category that the action of player P_i at stage t falls into. Moreover, we can express in the closed form for player P_i's belief of the other player $-i$'s type at any stage t with parameters $\alpha_{-i}^t = \alpha_{-i}^0 + \sum_{t'=1}^t k_{-i}^{t'}$ and $\beta_{-i}^t = \beta_{-i}^0 + tK_i - \sum_{t'=1}^t k_{-i}^{t'}$, where $(\alpha_{-i}^0, \beta_{-i}^0)$ is the prior distribution. Thus, every node just needs to count the frequency of categories of the other player's action at each stage t. Finally, we transform the type belief conditioned on the categories back to the belief conditioned on the corresponding actions using the hard de-aggregation, i.e., $B_i^{t+1}(\theta_{-i}|\tilde{\mathbf{h}}^t, a_i^t, a_{-i}^t) = B_i^{t+1}(\theta_{-i}|\tilde{\mathbf{h}}^t, a_i^t, \bar{a}_{-i}^t) = B_i^{t+1}(\theta_{-i}|\tilde{\mathbf{h}}^t, k_i^t, k_{-i}^t), \forall a_i^t \in \mathcal{C}_{k_i^t}^i, \forall a_{-i}^t, \bar{a}_{-i}^t \in \mathcal{C}_{k_{-i}^t}^{-i}$. Here, hard de-aggregation means that actions $a_{-i}^t, \bar{a}_{-i}^t$ correspond to the same category k_{-i}^t share the same belief distribution of the type and approximate the true type belief distribution.

Example 1. Consider a one-sided, incomplete information case where the system type is known to the user who has a private continuous type satisfying beta distribution (α, β). P_1 classifies all possible actions of P_2 into $K + 1$ categories, and a larger category index means a higher threat level. For example, a low occupancy of system resources is in the category 1, yet a frequent and longtime resource occupancy belongs to the category K because of its potential intention to block the system. Note that the category of action observation in one-shot does not reveal the type because a legitimate user may sometimes also occupy the resource for a long time and an attacker can behave legitimately to evade detection. However, since the payoff function is type-related, neither the legitimate user will always have longtime occupancy, nor the attacker can always hide. Thus, the belief will approach the truth after the multi-stage belief update based on the action observations. $\qquad \square$

4.2 State-Dependent Belief Formation

Since the same action can lead to different payoffs at different states, we generalize our results to classify the action according to the state and the action at stage

t. We divide a composed set $\mathcal{D}_i^t := \mathcal{X}^t \times \mathcal{A}_i^t$ into K_i+1 mutual exclusive partitions $\bar{\mathcal{C}}_j^i$, i.e., $\mathcal{D}_i^t = \{\cup \mathcal{C}_j^i\}_{j=0,1,\cdots,K_i}, \forall t, i = 1, 2$ and $\bar{\mathcal{C}}_j^i \cap \bar{\mathcal{C}}_l^i = \emptyset, \forall j \neq l, i = 1, 2$.

Example 2. Let the set of nodes of stage t in Fig. 6 be the possible states $x^t \in \mathcal{X}^t$. The state represents the value of the reactor pressure. The defender tries to stabilize the pressure at the reference value to guarantee the product quality and process safety in chemical plants. Reference values $n_3^0, \cdots, n_3^T$ and the possible pressure state x^t could be stage-varying. The attacker aims to change the pressure. A substantial deviation from the standard pressure brings a considerable reward to attackers. The state transition is Markov, i.e., the current pressure x^t and the both players' actions determine the pressure at stage $t + 1$. It could be challenging to determine the legitimacy of the actions based merely on whether the user increases or decreases the pressure. The state of the pressure can provide additional information to determine the criticality of operations. For example, it is clearly more dangerous when a user aims to increase the pressure when the current pressure value already far exceeds the standard pressure. □

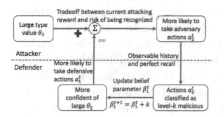

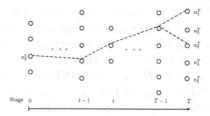

Fig. 5. The multi-stage learning scheme of attacker's type mitigates the probability of attacks.

Fig. 6. A multi-stage game with a finite horizons T and a Markov state transition $x^{t+1} = f^t(x^t, a_1^t, a_2^t)$.

4.3   Expanded State and Sufficient Statistic

At each stage t, an expanded state $y^t = \{x^t, \alpha_i^t, \beta_i^t, \alpha_{-i}^t, \beta_{-i}^t\}$ contains the original cyber state x^t plus the belief state B_i^t, B_{-i}^t represented by the hyperparameters from the beta distribution. Define new state transition function $y^{t+1} = \tilde{f}^t(y^t, a_1^t, a_2^t)$ where $x^{t+1} = f^t(x^t, a_1^t, a_2^t)$ and $(\alpha_i^{t+1}, \beta_i^{t+1}) = (\alpha_i^t + k_i^t, \beta_i^t + K_i - k_i^t), i = 1, 2$. Because of $\alpha_i^t + \beta_i^t = \alpha_i^0 + \beta_i^0 + tK_i$, we only need α_i^t (or β_i^t) to uniquely determine the β_i^t (or α_i^t). We choose $\alpha_i^0 = \beta_i^0 = 1$ as the prior belief, then $\alpha_i^t, \beta_i^t \in [1, \cdots, 1 + tK_i]$, and the dimension of the expanded state y^t is $|\mathcal{X}_i|^t \times (1 + tK_i)$. Define $\tilde{I}_i^t = \{y^t, \theta_i\}$ for reactive information structure $(\tilde{I}_i^t = \{\sigma_{-i}^t, y^t, \theta_i\}$ for reactive information structure), $\tilde{I}_i^t$ is the sufficient statistic of I_i^t because the history $\mathbf{h}^t$ uniquely determines the cyber state x^t as well as the belief state. With the Markov assumption that $\tilde{\sigma}_i^t(a_i^t|\tilde{I}_i^t) = \sigma_i^t(a_i^t|I_i^t)$, the new value function $\tilde{V}_i^t(y^t, \theta_i)$ is sufficient to determine the original value function $V_i^t(\mathbf{h}^t, \theta_i)$. Unlike the entire history, the carnality of state space does not increase with the number of stages, which greatly reduces the computation complexity. By letting $\tilde{V}_i^{T+1}(y^{T+1}, \theta_i) := 0$, we have the following recursive form for $t = 0, \cdots, T$, i.e.,

$$\tilde{V}_1^t(y^t, \theta_1) = \sup_{\tilde{\sigma}_1^t} E_{\theta_2 \sim \beta_1^t, a_1^t \sim \tilde{\sigma}_1^t, a_2^t \sim \tilde{\sigma}_2^{*,t}}[\tilde{V}_1^{t+1}(\tilde{f}^t(y^t, a_1^t, a_2^t), \theta_1) + J_1^t(x^t, a_1^t, a_2^t, \theta_1, \theta_2)];$$

$$\tilde{V}_2^t(y^t, \theta_2) = \sup_{\tilde{\sigma}_2^t} E_{\theta_1 \sim \beta_2^t, a_2^t \sim \tilde{\sigma}_2^t, a_1^t \sim \tilde{\sigma}_1^{*,t}}[\tilde{V}_2^{t+1}(\tilde{f}^t(y^t, a_1^t, a_2^t), \theta_2) + J_2^t(x^t, a_1^t, a_2^t, \theta_1, \theta_2)],$$

Since the expanded state transition incorporates the parameter of the belief update, we can compute the optimal utility-to-go function from stage T back to 0 w.r.t. the expanded state space to obtain a consistent belief-PBNE pair at each stage.

4.4   Computations of Static and Dynamic Bayesian Games

In this section, we formulate a mathematical program to compute the equilibrium for both static and multi-stage Bayesian bi-matrix games. The computation of static Bayesian games serves as a building block for the computation of the PBNE for the multi-stage games. The stage-varying belief leads to a nonzero-sum utility function. We also investigate the class of two-by-two matrices and provide further analytical insights. In the static setting, i.e., $T = 0$, the P-PBNE degenerates to be the Bayesian Stackelberg equilibrium (BSE) with leader P_1 and follower P_2. The R-PBNE degenerates to be a Bayesian Nash equilibrium (BNE). In this section, we focus on the analysis of BNE and the analysis of BSE can be done similarly. Define $m_i^t := |\mathcal{A}_i^t|$ as the total number of alternatives P_i can take at stage t. Let vector $p^t(\theta_1) = [p_1^t(\theta_1), \cdots, p_{m_2^t}^t(\theta_1)]' \in \mathbb{R}^{m_2^t \times 1}$ and $q^t(\theta_2) = [q_1^t(\theta_2), \cdots, q_{m_1^t}^t(\theta_2)]' \in \mathbb{R}^{m_1^t \times 1}$ be the outcome vector of the behavioral strategy σ_1^t and σ_2^t, respectively. For example, $p_l^t(\theta_1)$ is the probability of P_1 taking the l-th action (i.e., $a_1^t = l, l \in \{1, \cdots, m_1^t\}$) when her type is θ_1 at stage t. Notation "$'$" is the transpose of a vector and $l_{m_i^t} := [1, 1, \cdots, 1]' \in \mathbb{R}^{m_i^t \times 1}$. Player i's utility matrix $\mathcal{J}_i(x^t, \theta_1, \theta_2), i \in \{1, 2\}$ is a $m_1^t \times m_2^t$ matrix where the element (k, l) is the value of $J_i^t(x^t, a_1^t = k, a_2^t = l, \theta_1, \theta_2)$. P_1 is the row player while P_2 is the column player. Both players are rational and aim at maximizing their own utilities.

Final Stage/Static Case. The computation starting from the final stage T with a given belief B_i^T is the same as a static Bayesian game. Thus, we suppress the superscript of T, i.e., $m_i := m_i^T, p(\theta_1) := p^T(\theta_1), q(\theta_2) := q^T(\theta_2)$. Also, we write $\mathcal{J}_i(x^T, \theta_1, \theta_2)$ as $\mathcal{J}_i(\theta_1, \theta_2)$ because the state x^T is known.

Theorem 1. *A strategy pair* $(p^*(\theta_1), q^*(\theta_2))$ *constitutes a mixed-strategy Bayesian Nash equilibrium to the bi-matrix Bayesian game* $(\mathcal{J}_1(\theta_1, \theta_2), \mathcal{J}_2(\theta_1, \theta_2))$ *under continuous private type* $\theta_i \in \Theta_i$ *and a public belief* $B_i, i \in \{1, 2\}$, *if and only if, there exists a scalar function pair* $(s^*(\theta_1), w^*(\theta_2))$ *such* that $(p^*(\theta_1), q^*(\theta_2), s^*(\theta_1), w^*(\theta_2))$ is a solution to the following mathematical program:

$$\sup_{q,p,s,w} \quad E_{\theta_1} s(\theta_1) + E_{\theta_2} w(\theta_2) + E_{\theta_1} E_{\theta_2} \{p(\theta_1)'[\mathcal{J}_1(\theta_1,\theta_2) + \mathcal{J}_2(\theta_1,\theta_2)]q(\theta_2)\}$$

$$s.t. \quad E_{\theta_1}[\mathcal{J}_2'(\theta_1,\theta_2)p(\theta_1)] \le -w(\theta_2)l_{m_2}, \forall \theta_2, \quad q(\theta_2)'l_{m_2} = 1, q(\theta_2) \ge 0, \forall \theta_2,$$

$$E_{\theta_2}[\mathcal{J}_1(\theta_1,\theta_2)q(\theta_2)] \le -s(\theta_1)l_{m_1}, \forall \theta_1, \quad p(\theta_1)'l_{m_1} = 1, p(\theta_1) \ge 0, \forall \theta_1.$$

$$\tag{6}$$

The computation challenge of the continuous Bayesian bi-matrix program (6) is the infinite-dimensional constraints induced by the continuous type space. We can obtain approximate solutions by sampling the bounded type space $\Theta_i := [0,1]$ and solve a high-dimensional bilinear program. The bias between the value of the objective function and value 0 measures the approximation accuracy.

Proof. Define the simplex set $\Gamma := \{p \in \mathcal{R}^{m_1 \times 1} | p'l_{m_1} = 1, p \ge 0\}$. We first prove that the mixed-strategy is the solution to the bilinear program. The constraints imply a non-positive objective function. If $p^*(\theta_1) \in \Gamma, q^*(\theta_2) \in \Gamma$ is a Bayesian Nash equilibrium pair, i.e.,

$$q(\theta_2)'E_{\theta_1}[\mathcal{J}_2'(\theta_1,\theta_2)p^*(\theta_1)] \le (q^*(\theta_2))'E_{\theta_1}[\mathcal{J}_2'(\theta_1,\theta_2)p^*(\theta_1)], \forall \theta_2, \forall q(\theta_2) \in \Gamma,$$

$$p(\theta_1)'E_{\theta_2}[\mathcal{J}_1(\theta_1,\theta_2)q^*(\theta_2)] \le (p^*(\theta_1))'E_{\theta_2}[\mathcal{J}_1(\theta_1,\theta_2)q^*(\theta_2)], \forall \theta_1, \forall p(\theta_1) \in \Gamma.$$

Then the quadruple $p^*(\theta_1), q^*(\theta_2), w^*(\theta_2) = -E_{\theta_1}[p^*(\theta_1)'\mathcal{J}_2(\theta_1,\theta_2)q^*(\theta_2)]$, $s^*(\theta_1) = -E_{\theta_2}[p^*(\theta_1)'\mathcal{J}_1(\theta_1,\theta_2)q^*(\theta_2)]$ is a feasible solution to the program (because it satisfies all the constraints) and the value of the objective function is 0, which is the maximum solution to the non-positive objective function and provides the value function $V_2(\theta_2) = \max_{q(\theta_2)} E_{\theta_1}[p^*(\theta_1)'\mathcal{J}_2(\theta_1,\theta_2)q(\theta_2)] = -w^*(\theta_2), \forall \theta_2$ and $V_1(\theta_1) = \max_{p(\theta_1)} E_{\theta_2}[p(\theta_1)'\mathcal{J}_1(\theta_1,\theta_2)q^*(\theta_2)] = -s^*(\theta_1), \forall \theta_1$. Conversely, if the program has an optimal solution $p^*(\theta_1), q^*(\theta_2), w^*(\theta_2), s^*(\theta_1)$, then

$$E_{\theta_1} s(\theta_1) + E_{\theta_2} w(\theta_2) + E_{\theta_1} E_{\theta_2} \{p(\theta_1)'[\mathcal{J}_1(\theta_1,\theta_2) + \mathcal{J}_2(\theta_1,\theta_2)]q(\theta_2)\} = 0. \tag{7}$$

and

$$q(\theta_2)'E_{\theta_1}[\mathcal{J}_2'(\theta_1,\theta_2)p^*(\theta_1)] \le -w^*(\theta_2), \forall \theta_2, \forall q(\theta_2) \in \Gamma$$
$$p(\theta_1)'E_{\theta_2}[\mathcal{J}_1(\theta_1,\theta_2)q^*(\theta_2)] \le -s^*(\theta_1), \forall \theta_1, \forall p(\theta_1) \in \Gamma. \tag{8}$$

In particular, we pick $p(\theta_1) = p^*(\theta_1), q(\theta_2) = q^*(\theta_2)$ to arrive at

$$(q^*(\theta_2))'E_{\theta_1}[\mathcal{J}_2'(\theta_1,\theta_2)p^*(\theta_1)] \le -w^*(\theta_2), \forall \theta_2,$$
$$(p^*(\theta_1))'E_{\theta_2}[\mathcal{J}_1(\theta_1,\theta_2)q^*(\theta_2)] \le -s^*(\theta_1), \forall \theta_1. \tag{9}$$

Combined with (7), the inequality in (9) turns out to be an equality and equation (8) becomes

$$q(\theta_2)'E_{\theta_1}[\mathcal{J}_2'(\theta_1,\theta_2)p^*(\theta_1)] \le (q^*(\theta_2))'E_{\theta_1}[\mathcal{J}_2'(\theta_1,\theta_2)p^*(\theta_1)], \forall \theta_2,$$
$$p(\theta_1)'E_{\theta_2}[\mathcal{J}_1(\theta_1,\theta_2)q^*(\theta_2)] \le (p^*(\theta_1))'E_{\theta_2}[\mathcal{J}_1(\theta_1,\theta_2)q^*(\theta_2)], \forall \theta_1,$$

which verifies that $(p^*(\theta_1), q^*(\theta_2))$ is a BNE. $\square$

For the one-sided information, the *information-superior player* P_2 knows the type of P_1 and the *information-inferior player* P_1 does not know the type of P_2. Since the P_1's type is known, we can suppress writing $\mathcal{J}_i, p, s$ as a function of θ_1. Following similar proof steps, we have Corollary 1.

Corollary 1. *A strategy vector pair* $(p^*, q^*(\theta_2))$ *constitutes a Bayesian Nash equilibrium to the bi-matrix Bayesian game* $(\mathcal{J}_1(\theta_2), \mathcal{J}_2(\theta_2))$ *under private type* θ_2 *and the public type belief* B_2, *if and only if, there exists a scalar function pair* $(s^*, w^*(\theta_2))$ *such that* $(p^*, q^*(\theta_2), s^*, w^*(\theta_2))$ *is a solution to the mathematical program:*

$$\sup_{q,p,s,w} \quad E_{\theta_2}\{p'[\mathcal{J}_1(\theta_2) + \mathcal{J}_2(\theta_2)]q(\theta_2) + w(\theta_2)\} + s$$

$$s.t \quad \mathcal{J}_2'(\theta_2)p \leq -w(\theta_2)l_{m_2}, \forall \theta_2, \quad q(\theta_2)'l_{m_2} = 1, q(\theta_2) \geq 0, \forall \theta_2,$$
$$E_{\theta_2}[\mathcal{J}_1(\theta_2)q(\theta_2)] \leq -sl_{m_1}, \quad p'l_{m_1} = 1, p \geq 0.$$

Two-by-Two Matrix. We specify $m_1 = 2, m_2 = 2$ with utility functions of one-sided information as shown in Table 1. Let $V_1 = E_{\theta_2 \sim B_2}[\hat{V}_1] = \sup_p E_{\theta_2}[R_{21}^1 - R_{11}^1 + q^*(\theta_2)(R_{22}^1 - R_{12}^1 - R_{21}^1 + R_{11}^1)]p + E_{\theta_2}[R_{11}^1 + (R_{12}^1 - R_{11}^1)q^*(\theta_2)]$ be the expected value function under the belief B_2 of private type θ_2 and $\hat{V}_2 = \sup_{q(\theta_2)}[R_{21}^2 - R_{11}^2 + p^*(R_{22}^2 - R_{12}^2 - R_{21}^2 + R_{11}^2)]q(\theta_2) + R_{11}^2 + (R_{12}^2 - R_{11}^2)p^*$ be the value function of complete information. The best response of P_1 is $p^* = \mathbf{1}_{\{E[R_{21}^1 - R_{11}^1 + q^*(\theta_2)(R_{22}^1 - R_{12}^1 - R_{21}^1 + R_{11}^1)] > 0\}}$ and the best response of P_2 is $q^*(\theta_2) = \mathbf{1}_{\{R_{21}^2 - R_{11}^2 + p^*(R_{22}^2 - R_{12}^2 - R_{21}^2 + R_{11}^2) > 0\}}$. The BNE is the result of the intersection of two best-response functions. Since p^* is not a function of type, $p^* = 0$ or 1 is the only stable value[1]. Then, P_2 as a function of type is a threshold policy, which leads to Lemma 1.

Lemma 1. *For the one-sided information bi-matrix Bayesian game with utility functions in Table 1 under the BNE solution concept, the information-inferior player adopts a* **pure** *policy, and the information-superior player adopts a* **threshold** *policy.* $\square$

In particular, if $p^* = 1$, we have $q^*(\theta_2) = \mathbf{1}_{\{R_{21}^2 - R_{11}^2 + (R_{22}^2 - R_{12}^2 - R_{21}^2 + R_{11}^2) > 0\}} = \mathbf{1}_{\{R_{22}^2(\theta_2) > R_{12}^2(\theta_2)\}}$, which should be consistent with the corresponding condition $E[R_{21}^1 - R_{11}^1 + q(\theta_2)(R_{22}^1 - R_{12}^1 - R_{21}^1 + R_{11}^1)] > 0$. Likewise, we have a consistent condition for $p^* = 0$. Theorem 2 summarizes these two necessary conditions for B_2.

Theorem 2. *There exists at most two mixed-strategy Bayesian Nash equilibriums for the one-sided information bi-matrix game with utility functions shown*

---

[1] Note that $q^*(\theta_2) = \frac{R_{11}^1(\theta_2) - R_{21}^1(\theta_2)}{R_{22}^1(\theta_2) - R_{12}^1(\theta_2) - R_{21}^1(\theta_2) + R_{11}^1(\theta_2)}, p^* \in [0,1]$ is a equilibrium pair under a restrictive condition $R_{22}^1(\theta_2) - R_{12}^1(\theta_2) - R_{21}^1(\theta_2) + R_{11}^1(\theta_2) = 0, R_{21}^1(\theta_2) = R_{11}^1(\theta_2), \forall \theta_2$.

in Table 1, private type $\theta_2 \in \Theta_2$, and public type belief $B_2(\theta_2)$. First, the policy pair $p^* = 1, q^*(\theta_2) = 1_{\{R_{22}^2(\theta_2) > R_{12}^2(\theta_2)\}}$ is a BNE if

$$\int_{\theta_2 \in \Theta_2} (R_{21}^1(\theta_2) - R_{11}^1(\theta_2)) 1_{\{R_{22}^2(\theta_2) < R_{12}^2(\theta_2)\}} B_2(\theta_2) d\theta_2 +$$

$$\int_{\theta_2 \in \Theta_2} (R_{22}^1(\theta_2) - R_{12}^1(\theta_2)) 1_{\{R_{22}^2(\theta_2) > R_{12}^2(\theta_2)\}} B_2(\theta_2) d\theta_2 > 0,$$

Second, the policy pair $p^* = 0, q^*(\theta_2) = 1_{\{R_{21}^2(\theta_2) > R_{11}^2(\theta_2)\}}$ is a BNE if

$$\int_{\theta_2 \in \Theta_2} (R_{21}^1(\theta_2) - R_{11}^1(\theta_2)) 1_{\{R_{21}^2(\theta_2) < R_{11}^2(\theta_2)\}} B_2(\theta_2) d\theta_2 +$$

$$\int_{\theta_2 \in \Theta_2} (R_{22}^1(\theta_2) - R_{12}^1(\theta_2)) 1_{\{R_{21}^2(\theta_2) > R_{11}^2(\theta_2)\}} B_2(\theta_2) d\theta_2 < 0.$$

Remark 3. We cannot apply the indifference principle as in Sect. 5.2 to compute the equilibrium under incomplete information because the information-inferior player unknown the type θ_2 is incapable of making decision p as a function of θ_2.   □

Dynamic Case. Recall the dynamic programming equation in Sect. 4.3:

$$\tilde{V}_i^t(y^t, \theta_i) = \sup_{\tilde{\sigma}_i^t} E_{\theta_{-i} \sim \beta_i^t, a_1^t \sim \tilde{\sigma}_1^t, a_2^t \sim \tilde{\sigma}_2^{*,t}} [\tilde{V}_i^{t+1}(y^{t+1}, \theta_i) + J_i^t(x^t, a_1^t, a_2^t, \theta_1, \theta_2)].$$

The computation of the static BNE serves as building blocks to the computation of dynamic R-PBNE via the following procedures. At the last stage T with a known boundary condition $\tilde{V}_i^{T+1}$, the value function $\tilde{V}_i^{T+1} + J_i^T$ is the same as the static objective function J_i and we can compute the equilibrium policy as well as the value function $\tilde{V}_i^T$ via Theorem 1. At the second last stage $T - 1$, since both $\tilde{V}_i^T$ and J_i^{T-1} are known, we can treat $\tilde{V}_i^T + J_i^{T-1}$ as the new static objective function J_i and repeat the analysis in the static setting. In a backward fashion, it is clear that at stage $t \in \{0, 1, \cdots, T - 1\}$, we only need to replace the static objective function J_i to the dynamic objective function $\tilde{V}_i^t + J_i^{t-1}$ to obtain the R-PBNE policy $\tilde{\sigma}_i^{t-1}$ at each stage $t - 1$ for each player P_i.

5   Case Study

Similar to our previous work [8], we consider a four-stage Bayesian game with one-sided incomplete information, i.e., the information-inferior player P_1 forms a belief of attacker P_2's type θ_2 via a beta distribution with parameters α_2^t, β_2^t. The first three stages model the cyber network transition while the last stage model the sensor compromise of a physical plant, i.e., the benchmark Tennessee Eastman (TE) chemical process [2]. Since APTs benefit mainly from their specific targets, i.e., sabotage the TE process, we assume a negligible utility for the intermediate stage $t = 0, 1, \cdots, T - 1$ in this case study. However, the scenario is still multi-stage rather than static because APTs have to go through the intermediate stages stealthily to reach their final targets. Their actions at the intermediate stages will affect the belief and the state at the final stage. The state $x^T \in \mathcal{X}^T := \{0, 1, 2\}$ represents which sensors the attacker can control in the TE process. If the attacker changes the sensor reading, the system states such as the pressure and the temperature may deviate from the desired value, which degrades the product quality and even causes the shutdown of the entire process if the deviation exceeds the safety threshold. To reach a favorable state at the final stage, e.g., control the essential sensors of the TE process, the attacker has to behave aggressively at the intermediate stages, e.g., escalates the privilege, which thus increases the risk of being identified as malicious. Both players have a binary action set $\mathcal{A}_i^t = \{0, 1\}$ where $a_i^t = 1$ means taking either aggressive or defensive actions and $a_i^t = 0$ means no special operation performed. As stated in the Sect. 2, the action is observable, yet the one-shot observation does not directly reveal the type. Let $K_2 = 1$, the secure category $k = 0$ includes $a_2^t = 0$ and $k = 1$ includes $a_2^t = 1$, respectively. The utility at the last stage is shown in Table 1 and defined as follows. The operation time under state x^T is the output of the mapping $C : \mathcal{X}^T \mapsto \mathbb{R}^+$, which can be determined using numerical experiments of the TE process under different sensor-compromise scenarios. Since the defender's stage utility should be proportional to the operation time $C(x^T)$, the normalized defender's stage reward is $R_{11}^1 = C(x^T), R_{12}^1 = 0.5C(x^T)(1 - \theta_2), R_{21}^1 = 0.9C(x^T), R_{22}^1 = 0.9C(x^T)$, which satisfies two conditions. First, $R_{21}^1 = R_{22}^1, R_{11}^1 \geq R_{21}^1$: The defensive action prevents attacking loss while incurs a cost to deploy. Second, $R_{12}^1 \leq R_{21}^1$: Attacks cause a loss in lack of active defenses. Moreover, the loss is proportional to the type, i.e., R_{12}^1 is a monotonically decreasing function in type θ_2. On the other hand, we assign utility $R_{11}^2 = 2, R_{12}^2 = 10\theta_2, R_{21}^2 = 4\theta_2, R_{22}^2 = 0$ to attackers according to the following reasonable conditions.

1. Attackers obtain R_{12}^2 when attacks happen without defenses and R_{21}^2 when P_2 does not attack yet wastes system resources by deceiving defenders to defend. Both cases benefit attackers proportionally to their type, i.e., R_{21}^2 and R_{12}^2 are monotonically increasing functions in type θ_2. Moreover, the latter scenario brings more attacking rewards for the same type, i.e., $R_{21}^2(\theta_2) \geq R_{12}^2(\theta_2), \forall \theta_2$.
2. Attackers $\theta_2 \geq \bar{\theta}_2$ benefit from inflicting damages and deceiving defenders to defend, i.e., $R_{12}^2(\theta_2) \geq R_{11}^2(\theta_2), R_{21}^2(\theta_2) \geq R_{11}^2(\theta_2), \forall \theta_2 \geq \bar{\theta}_2$. However, benign users $\theta_2 < \bar{\theta}_2$ benefit from a normal operation of the system, i.e., $R_{12}^2(\theta_2) \leq R_{11}^2(\theta_2), R_{21}^2(\theta_2) \leq R_{11}^2(\theta_2), \forall \theta_2 < \bar{\theta}_2$.
3. The no-attack-no-defense scenario outweighs the scenario when P_2 attacks yet P_1 defends because no damages are incurred and the defender obtains extra information about the attacker. Thus, $R_{11}^2(\theta_2) \geq R_{22}^2(\theta_2), \forall \theta_2$.

5.1 The Final Stage with One-Sided Incomplete Information

At the terminal stage T, we need to solve the static Bayesian game for each possible expanded state y^T. Suppose that defender takes action $a_1^T = 1$ with probability $p(y^T)$ and attacker takes action $a_2^T = 1$ with probability $q(y^T, \theta_2)$. At the last stage, the accumulated utility function is the same as the stage utility function. Since all elements $R_{ij}^1, i, j \in \{1, 2\}$ of the utility matrix is linear in $C(x^T) \neq 0$, both players' policies are not a function of $C(x^T)$ and we can consider a normalized value function $\hat{V}_1^T(y^T, \theta_2)/C(x^T) = \max_{p(y^t)}[0.5q^*(y^T, \theta_2)(1+\theta_2) - 0.1]p(y^T) + 1 - 0.5(1+\theta_2)q^*(y^T, \theta_2)$, where p^*, q^* is the PBNE policy pair. Since defender does not know the type value, she can only form an expected value function $V_1^T(y^T) = \max_{p(y^T)} \int_0^1 Beta^{\alpha_2^T, \beta_2^T}(\theta_2)[\hat{V}_1^T(y^T, \theta_2)]d\theta_2$. The attacker as the information-superior player knows the type, and thus his objective function $\hat{V}_2^T(y^T, \theta_2)$ is

$$\max_{q(y^T, \theta_2)} [2p^*(y^T) - 2 + 10\theta_2 - 14p^*(y^T)\theta_2]q(y^T, \theta_2) + 2(1 - p^*(y^T)) + 4\theta_2 p^*(y^T).$$

Bayesian Nash Equilibrium. Bayesian Nash equilibrium corresponds to the intersection of two best-response curves p^* and q^*, as stated in Sect. 4.4. We use Theorem 2 to show the existence and uniqueness of the BNE, i.e., $q^* = \mathbf{1}_{\{\theta_2 > 0.2\}}, p^* = 0$ when the condition $\int_{0.2}^1 Beta^{\alpha_2^T, \beta_2^T}(\theta_2)(1 + \theta_2)d\theta_2 < 0.2$ is true. Small α_2 and large β_2, e.g., $(1, 10)$, satisfy the condition as the probability density is focused on the low θ_2 value. The BNE does not exist when the condition is not met.

Bayesian Stackelberg Equilibrium. After plugging in the attacker's best response to the value function V_1, we need to maximize a function of p:

$$\max_p E[R_{21}^1 - R_{11}^1 + \mathbf{1}_{\{R_{21}^1 - R_{11}^1 + p(R_{22}^2 - R_{12}^2 - R_{21}^2 + R_{11}^2) > 0\}}(R_{22}^1 - R_{12}^1 - R_{21}^1 + R_{11}^1)]p.$$

Since we assume that $R_{ij}^2(\theta_2)$ is linear in θ_2, the follower P_2's best response $q^*(y^T, \theta_2) = R_2(p(y^T), \theta_2) = \mathbf{1}_{\{R_{21}^2 - R_{11}^2 + p(R_{22}^2 - R_{12}^2 - R_{21}^2 + R_{11}^2) > 0\}} = \mathbf{1}_{\{\theta_2 > \bar{\theta}_2(p)\}}$ can be represented as an indicator function of a threshold type $\bar{\theta}_2 = \frac{1 - p(y^T)}{5 - 7p(y^T)}$, which simplifies the computation of the leader's optimal policy p^*. The existence of equilibrium depends on the type value classified as follows. First, $\bar{\theta}_2 \geq 1$, $p^*(y^T) \in [\frac{2}{3}, \frac{5}{7})$ is not consistent with $p^*(y^T) = 0$ via the optimization of the defender's value function. Second, $\bar{\theta}_2 \leq 0$ leads to $p^*(y^T) \in (\frac{5}{7}, 1], q^*(y^T, \theta_2) = \mathbf{1}_{\{\theta_2 < \bar{\theta}_2\}} = 0$. Then, $p^* = 0$ is not consistent with $p^* \in (\frac{5}{7}, 1]$. Third, if $p^* = 5/7$, $q^* = 0$, then the optimization of defender's value function returns $p^* = 0$, which is not consistent with $p^* = 5/7$. Finally, $0 < \bar{\theta}_2 < 1$ leads to the feasible region $p^*(y^T) \in [0, \frac{2}{3})$ and the value function $V_1^T(y^T)/C(x^T) = \max_{p(y^T) \in [0, \frac{2}{3})}[\int_{\bar{\theta}_2}^1 Beta^{\alpha_2^T, \beta_2^T}(\theta_2)[0.5(1 + \theta_2)]d\theta_2 - 0.1]p(y^T) + 1 - 0.5 \int_{\bar{\theta}_2}^1 Beta^{\alpha_2^T, \beta_2^T}(\theta_2)(1 + \theta_2)d\theta_2$.

Remark 4. The BSE may not always exist. Take state $\{0, 4, 1\}$ as an example, the function is increasing during the interval $[0, 2/3)$, with supreme value of $V_1^T = 0.56, \hat{V}_2^T = 2/3 + (8\theta_2)/3$ under the limiting BSE (LBSE) policy $p^* \rightarrow$

$2/3, q^* = \mathbf{1}_{\{\theta_2 > \bar{\theta}_2\}}$ with $\bar{\theta}_2 \to 1$. The BSE does not exist because the feasible region of policy does not include 2/3 as analyzed above. However, we can use the supreme value under LBSE as an upper bound of the value function, which serves as a good approximation in practice.   □

5.2 Final Stage with Complete Information

For the complete information, the type value θ_2 is a common knowledge, thus defender can respond to the threat by considering objective $\hat{V}_1^T, \hat{V}_2^T$ rather than expected objective $V_1^T = \max_{p(y^T)} \int_0^1 Beta^{\alpha_2^T, \beta_2^T}(\theta_2)[\hat{V}_1^T(y^T, \theta_2)]d\theta_2, \hat{V}_2^T$ in Sect. 5.1.

Nash Equilibrium. Since both player's policies are functions of type θ_2 in the complete information case, we can use the indifference principle for the following three type classifications. First, when $\theta_2 \in [0.2, 1]$, we obtain NE policy $p^* = \frac{1-5\theta_2}{1-7\theta_2} \in [0, 2/3], q^* = \frac{1}{5(1+\theta_2)} \in [\frac{1}{10}, \frac{1}{5}]$ and value function $\hat{V}_1^T = 0.9C(x^T)$, $\hat{V}_2^T = 2 + ((1 - 5\theta_2)(-2 + 4\theta_2))/(1 - 7\theta_2) = \frac{20\theta_2^2}{-1+7\theta_2} \in [1.63265, \frac{10}{3}]$. Second, if $\theta_2 = 1/7$, no NE exists and both players' behaviors would be uncertain. Third, for other $\theta_2 \in [0, 1]$, NE policy $q^* = 0, p^* = 0$ leads to $(C(x^T), 2)$. Figure 7(b) shows that both defender and attacker's policies are functions of their types. On the one hand, P_1 defends with a higher probability when the type value increases because an attack with a larger type value incurs more loss once he succeeds. On the other hand, the increasing probability of defensive actions reduces the probability of attacks to a relatively low level. For benign users who do not attack and inflict damages, which is known by the defender in the complete information case, the defender will not take defensive actions and the system will operate normally.

Stackelberg Game. Following a similar analysis as the NE, we can see that the SE policy also depends on the realization of the type. If $\theta_2 \in [0, 1/5)$, then SE $p^* = 0, q^* = 0$ leads to the defender value $(C(x^T), 2)$; if $\theta_2 \in (1/5, 1]$, then $p^* = 2/3$ and $q^* = 0$ is the SE with value functions $(2.8/3C(x^T), (2+8\theta_2)/3)$; if $\theta_2 = 1/5$, then $q^* = 0, p^* \to 0$ is the limiting SE.

5.3 Comparison of Value Functions

For the complete information case, the best response set of the attacker $R_2(p, \theta_2)$ exists and is a singleton for each $p \in [0, 1]$ for all given $\theta_2 \in [0, 1]$ except for $\theta_2 = 1/5$. Thus, the leader player never does worse under SE than under NE policy as stated in Theorem 3, which is also illustrated in Fig. 7(a). The proof is similar to the proof of Proposition 3.16 in [1].

Theorem 3. *For the finite two-person game defined in Sect. 2 and two solution concepts defined in Sect. 3, let $\hat{V}_1^S$ and $\hat{V}_1^N$ be the value function of P_1 under SE and NE policy, respectively. If $R_2(\sigma_1^T)$ is a singleton for each $\sigma_1^T \in \Sigma_1^T$, then $\hat{V}_1^S \geq \hat{V}_1^N$.*   □

In the incomplete information case, the best-response set of the attacker $R_2(p, \theta_2)$ is also a singleton for each $p \in [0, 1]$ for all given θ_2. Thus, we further obtain that the defender's value function under BSE is better than that under BNE when the belief is the same, which is supported by the numerical results in Fig. 7(c). The above comparison of the proactive and reactive information structures, i.e., BSE/SE with BNE/NE demonstrates that acquiring the best response set of the attacker via attack tree analysis can effectively confront the insider threat of APTs.

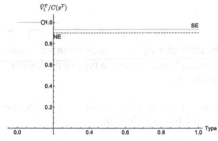

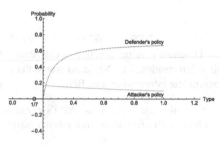

(a) Knowing the best response of the follower P_2 grants the leader P_1 a boost in the value function for all types.

(b) Both players' policy is a function of the type under NE. No Nash equilibrium exists when the type $\theta_2 = 1/7$.

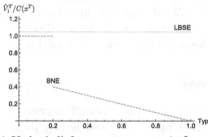

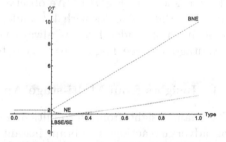

(c) Under belief parameters $\alpha_2 = 1, \beta_2 = 10$, the BNE in red $q^* = 1_{\{\theta_2 > 0.2\}}, p^* = 0$ leads to the defender's value function $\hat{V}_1^T/C(x^T) = 1 - 0.5(1 + \theta_2)1_{\{\theta_2 > 0.2\}}$. The LBSE $p^* \rightarrow 2/3, q^* = 1_{\{\theta_2 > \bar{\theta}_2\}}$ with $\bar{\theta}_2 \rightarrow 1$ in green leads to a better value function $\hat{V}_1^T/C(x^T) = 1.05$ for all type value.

(d) The attacker receives the largest utility at the BNE in red because he manages to conceal his type and cause uncertainties for the defender. He receives the least utility at the LBSE or the SE cases in green. For legitimate users $\theta_2 \leq 0.2$, there are no attacks and defending actions.

Fig. 7. Comparisons of value functions at the terminal stage.

Comparisons of defender's value function between the NE and BNE in Fig. 8(a) and between SE, BSE in Fig. 8(b) show that the value function of the defender P_1 under incomplete information is always no better than that under complete information, which is true for the PBNE under both proactive and reactive information structures. The numerical result corroborates the current unfavorable situation of systems that the deception of APTs creates uncertainties for defenders and decreases defenders' utilities.

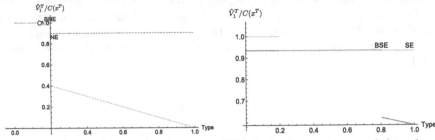

(a) Defender's value function under complete information, i.e., NE is no worse than incomplete information, i.e., BNE.

(b) Defender P_1 has an increase in her value function if she knows the type of the insider player P_2.

Fig. 8. The private type of APTs creates uncertainties for defenders and decreases defenders' value function under both outsider and insider threats.

The comparison of attacker's value function $\hat{V}_2^T$ under BNE, NE, SE, and LBSE is shown in Fig. 7(d). We observe that $\hat{V}_2^T$ under the LBSE as the upper bound of BSE coincides with $\hat{V}_2^T$ under SE. We also notice that the attacker's value function under BNE is always no worse than NE, which validates the advantage of concealing a private type to increase the uncertainty of defenders.

5.4 Insights from Multi-stage Analysis

The main insight from the multi-stage analysis is the tradeoff between taking adversary actions to obtain instant attacking reward and hiding to arrive at a more favorable expanded state $y^t = \{x^t, \alpha_2^t, \beta_2^t\}$ in the future stages as shown in Fig. 5. The system state x^t and the belief parameter α_2^t, β_2^t comprise the expanded state y^t. Thus, on the one hand, a desirable y^t for attacker is to turn the system to a fragile state x^t. On the other hand, attacks try to deceive the defender into a Pollyanna. The more the defender belief in P_2 as a legitimate user, the less probability she will act defensively and the attacker can bear a smaller threshold $\bar{\theta}_2$ to launch the attack. Other results and insights are summarized as follows. First, the healthy system state x^t at the terminal stage dominates defender's utility, while at the same time, a belief of a legitimate user increases the defender's utility. Second, due to the petty stage cost assumption, the attacker chooses to hide at the initial stage to deceive defender to form wrong beliefs. However, since attackers move at the intermediate stages to reach their final target, the defender can gradually form the right belief based on the observable footprints of the adversary.

6   Conclusion

In this work, we propose a multi-stage game of incomplete information to model the interactions between defenders and Advanced Persistent Threats (APTs). The dynamic Bayesian game has captured the stealthy and persistent nature of the APTs. *Types* are used to represent the private information of the players. A defender forms a belief on the uncertainties of an attacker and updates it using Bayesian rules with observations of attack footprints. We have adopted conjugate priors to enable parametric and large-scale learning of the players and extended the dynamic programming principles with an expanded state space. We have developed mathematical programs to compute the perfect Bayesian Nash equilibrium and studied the existence of Bayesian Nash equilibrium under bi-matrix game. A case study of one-sided information has illustrated the disadvantage to the defender as well as the advantage to the attacker when the attack manages to conceal his private type. It also motivates a further comparison of our framework under two-sided incomplete information in the future so that the defender can also use counter-deception to increase the attacking cost and tilt the current information asymmetry caused by the attacker. We have compared the PBNE under two different information structures and shown that disclosing the best response set of the attacker via attack tree analysis or proactive defenses such as honeypots and honey files can effectively confront the insider threat of APTs. A preliminary multi-stage analysis has shown that although APTs hide at the initial stages, yet the adaptive formation of the belief reveals the attacker at intermediate stages.

References

1. Basar, T., Olsder, G.J.: Dynamic Noncooperative Game Theory, vol. 23. Siam, Philadelphia (1999)
2. Bathelt, A., Ricker, N.L., Jelali, M.: Revision of the tennessee eastman process model. IFAC-PapersOnLine **48**(8), 309–314 (2015)
3. Cárdenas, A.A., Baras, J.S., Seamon, K.: A framework for the evaluation of intrusion detection systems. In: 2006 IEEE Symposium on Security and Privacy, pp. 15-pp. IEEE (2006)
4. Cole, E.: Advanced Persistent Threat: Understanding the Danger and How to Protect Your Organization. Newnes, Oxford (2012)
5. Harsanyi, J.C.: Games with incomplete information played by "Bayesian" players, i-iii part i. the basic model. Manage. Sci. **14**(3), 159–182 (1967)
6. Horák, K., Zhu, Q., Bošanský, B.: Manipulating adversary's belief: a dynamic game approach to deception by design for proactive network security. In: Rass, S., An, B., Kiekintveld, C., Fang, F., Schauer, S. (eds.) Decision and Game Theory for Security. LNCS, vol. 10575, pp. 273–294. Springer, Cham (2017). https://doi.org/10.1007/978-3-319-68711-7_15
7. Huang, L., Chen, J., Zhu, Q.: A large-scale markov game approach to dynamic protection of interdependent infrastructure networks. In: Rass, S., An, B., Kiekintveld, C., Fang, F., Schauer, S. (eds.) GameSec 2017. LNCS, vol. 10575, pp. 357–376. Springer, Cham (2017). https://doi.org/10.1007/978-3-319-68711-7_19

8. Huang, L., Zhu, Q.: Adaptive strategic cyber defense for advanced persistent threats in critical infrastructure networks. In: ACM SIGMETRICS Performance Evaluation Review (2018)
9. Liu, Y., Ning, P., Reiter, M.K.: False data injection attacks against state estimation in electric power grids. ACM Trans. Inf. Syst. Secur. (TISSEC) **14**(1), 13 (2011)
10. Manshaei, M.H., Zhu, Q., Alpcan, T., Başar, T., Hubaux, J.P.: Game theory meets network security and privacy. ACM Comput. Surv. (CSUR) **45**(3), 25 (2013)
11. Pawlick, J., Colbert, E., Zhu, Q.: A game-theoretic taxonomy and survey of defensive deception for cybersecurity and privacy. arXiv preprint arXiv:1712.05441 (2017)
12. Stech, F.J., Heckman, K.E., Strom, B.E.: Integrating cyber-D&D into adversary modeling for active cyber defense. In: Jajodia, S., Subrahmanian, V., Swarup, V., Wang, C. (eds.) Cyber Deception, pp. 1–22. Springer, Cham (2016). https://doi.org/10.1007/978-3-319-32699-3_1
13. Van Dijk, M., Juels, A., Oprea, A., Rivest, R.L.: FlipIt: the game of "stealthy takeover". J. Cryptol. **26**(4), 655–713 (2013)
14. Zhang, T., Zhu, Q.: Strategic defense against deceptive civilian GPS spoofing of unmanned aerial vehicles. In: Rass, S., An, B., Kiekintveld, C., Fang, F., Schauer, S. (eds.) International Conference on Decision and Game Theory for Security. LNCS, vol. 10575, pp. 213–233. Springer, Cham (2017). https://doi.org/10.1007/978-3-319-68711-7_12
15. Zhu, Q., Basar, T.: Game-theoretic methods for robustness, security, and resilience of cyberphysical control systems: games-in-games principle for optimal cross-layer resilient control systems. IEEE Control Syst. **35**(1), 46–65 (2015)

Multi-sided Advertising Markets: Dynamic Mechanisms and Incremental User Compensations

Moran Feldman[1(✉)], Gonen Frim[1], and Rica Gonen[2]

[1] Department of Mathematics and Computer Science, The Open University of Israel,
Ra'anana, Israel
{moranfe,gonenr}@openu.ac.il
[2] Department of Management and Economics, The Open University of Israel,
Ra'anana, Israel
gonen987@gmail.com

Abstract. Online advertising has motivated companies to collect vast amounts of information about users, which increasingly creates privacy concerns. One way to answer these concerns is by enabling end users to choose which aspects of their private information can be collected. Based on principles suggested by Feldman and Gonen (2018), we introduce a new online advertising market model which uses information brokers to give users such control. Unlike Feldman and Gonen (2018), our model is dynamic and involves multi-sided markets where all participating sides are strategic. We describe a mechanism for this model which is theoretically guaranteed to (approximately) maximize the gain from trade, avoid a budget deficit and incentivize truthfulness and voluntary participation. As far as we know, this is the first known *dynamic* mechanism for a multi-sided market having these properties.

We experimentally examine and compare our theoretical results using real world advertising bid data. The experiments suggest that our mechanism performs well in practice even in regimes for which our theoretical guarantee is weak or irrelevant.

Keywords: Dynamic mechanisms · Mutli-sided markets
Online advertising market

1 Introduction

Online advertising currently supports some of the most important Internet services, including: search, social media and user generated content sites. For online advertising to be effective, companies collect vast amounts of information about users, which increasingly creates privacy concerns [7]. Such concerns were actively raised by EU regulators in recent years in efforts to find solutions to guarantee users' privacy. Recently privacy concerns have also reached the U.S. Senate and Congress as a response to Facebook's information leak to Cambridge

L. Bushnell et al. (Eds.): GameSec 2018, LNCS 11199, pp. 227–247, 2018.
https://doi.org/10.1007/978-3-030-01554-1_13

Analytica. It was evident in Facebook's hearing before the U.S. Senate, particularly in Senator Schatz's line of questioning [8], that Facebook is expected to develop tools to enable end users to configure their privacy settings and that the notion of a data fiduciary was put forward to apply pressure to Facebook in this area.

Based on this motivation, and extending principles suggested by [10], we introduce a new model capturing a foreseeable future form of online advertising. The market in this model includes advertisers as buyers, users as sellers (each willing to sell her own information portfolio through a broker) and information brokers as mediators representing the users.[1] The objective of a mechanism for this setting is to end up with a match between users and advertisers maximizing the gain from trade. Towards that goal, the mechanism has to collect information from the mediators and advertisers; and thus, needs to incentivize the mediators and advertisers to report truthfully, which it can do by charging the advertisers and paying the mediators. Additionally, unlike in [10], we assume here that the users are strategic as well, which requires the mechanism to incentivize them also by recommending for each mediator to forward some of the payment he received to his users.

As the online advertising ecosystem is dynamic, the market in our model is dynamic as well. We assume the mediators and advertisers arrive in a uniformly random order, and refer to the arriving advertisers and mediators as arriving entities. Every time that a new entity arrives, the mechanism has an opportunity to assign users to advertisers. More specifically, users enroll with a mediator offline, i.e., when the mediator arrives at the market it has a list of users that are his customers and the mechanism is allowed to assign users of the newly arriving mediator to advertisers that have already arrived. Similarly, when an advertiser arrives the mechanism is allowed to assign users of mediators that have already arrived to the newly arriving advertiser. From a practical point of view, an assignment of a user p to an advertiser a means that when p views interstitial advertising, it will be from advertiser a. Given this meaning for an assignment, it is natural to assume that the mechanism is not allowed to cancel assignments that have already been made, or assign a user of a mediator that has already arrived to an advertiser that has already arrived. These restrictions, together with the random arrival order, represent the dynamicity of the setting. We note that our choice to model a dynamic market using a random arrival order is a well established practice—for a few examples, see [2,19]. Intuitively, this modeling choice reflects the assumption that real arrival orders are arbitrary rather than adversarial.

A natural expectation from a dynamic exchange mechanism is to (approximately) maximize the gain from trade, while maintaining desirable economic properties such as incentivizing truthfulness, voluntary participation and avoiding budget deficit. Unfortunately, as far as we know, no previous work has man-

---

[1] The use of mediators is necessary because it should not be possible to link an information portfolio offered for sell on the market to any particular user, which prevents users from interacting directly with the market.

aged to achieve these goals simultaneously. Wurman et al. [20] presented a mechanism incentivizing truthful reporting from either the buyers or the sellers, but not simultaneously from both. A different mechanism given by Blum et al. [4] maximizes the social welfare of buyers and non-selling sellers (as opposed to maximizing the gain from trade).[2] Finally, Bredin et al. [5] present a truthful dynamic double-sided auction that is constructed from a truthful offline double-sided auction rule, however its competitiveness with respect to the optimal trade was only studied empirically.

The failure of the above works to maximize the gain from trade while maintaining truthfulness, individual rationality (voluntary participation) and budget balance (avoiding budget deficit) can be partially attributed to an impossibility result of [16]. This impossibility result states that, even in an offline setting involving a single buyer and a single seller, maximizing the gain from trade while maintaining truthfulness and individual rationality perforce runs a deficit (i.e., is not budget balanced). An additional reason for the above failure is that the matching problem faced by the market maker (exchange mechanism) in multisided dynamic markets combines elements of dynamic algorithms and sequential decision making with considerations from mechanism design. More specifically, unlike in a traditional dynamic algorithm, a mechanism for such a setting must incentivize agents to report truthful information to the mechanism. Additionally, unlike in traditional mechanism design, this is a dynamic setting with agents that arrive over time, and the mechanism must deal with uncertainty and make irrevocable decisions before all the agents arrive.

1.1   Our Result

In this work we present the first (to the best of our knowledge) dynamic mechanism for a multi-sided market setting which theoretically guarantees the economic properties of truthfulness, individual rationality, and budget balance while (approximately) maximizing the gain from trade. As our setting involves multi-dimensional agents, our result shows that dynamic multi-sided markets can be handled even in the presence of multi-dimensional agents. Moreover, we study the practical performance of our mechanism using simulations based on real-world advertisers' bids. The data for these experiments was gathered from Facebook advertising campaigns. These experiments suggest that our mechanism performs well in practice even in input regimes for which our theoretical guarantee is weak.

The dynamic nature of our setting raises the question of what it means for a mechanism to be individually rational. As usual, individual rationality should imply that an agent never losses by participating. However, in a dynamic setting it is natural to require also that an agent never losses by not leaving prematurely. We introduce a new concept called "continuous individual rationality" which captures the above intuitive requirement. Formally, a mechanism is *continuously individually rational* for an agent (a user, a mediator or an advertiser)

---

[2] Blum et al. [4] has multiple different objectives (maximizing profit, liquidity and welfare). We refer to the objective which is most relevant to our work.

if the agent's utility can only increase over time when the agent is truthful.[3] Note that this newly presented concept of continuous individual rationality is a stronger concept than individual rationality in its classic form as it implies ex post individual rationality.

Satisfying the requirements of continuous individual rationality, together with the other economic properties our mechanism guarantees, requires our mechanism to use a novel pricing scheme where users may be paid ongoing increments during the mechanism's execution. The maximum total payment that a user may end up with is pre-known (when the user arrives), however, the actual increments are not pre-known and depend on the market's dynamically changing demands and supplies. As users rarely ever get paid in reality, this pricing scheme is new to mechanism design and might look odd at first glance. Nevertheless, the principle it is based on can be observed in many common real life scenarios such as executive compensation payments and company acquisition deals. For example, the eBay acquisition of Skype in 2005 involved both an upfront payment and an additional payment whose amount depended on the future performance of the bought company (see https://investors.ebayinc.com/releasedetail.cfm?releaseid=176402).

Like in [3], we say that a mechanism is *user-side incentive compatible* if truthfulness is a dominant strategy[4] for each user given that her mediator is truthful. Similarly, the mechanism is *user-side continuously individually rational* if it is continuously individually rational for each user given that her mediator is truthful. A mechanism is *mediator-side incentive compatible* if truthfulness is a dominant strategy for each mediator whose users are all truthful, and it is *mediator-side continuously individually rational* if it is continuously individually rational for every such mediator. Finally, a mechanism is *advertiser-side incentive compatible* if truthfulness is a dominant strategy for every advertiser, and it is *advertiser-side continuously individually rational* if it is continuously individually rational for every advertiser. We construct a mechanism which is *three-sided incentive compatible* (i.e., it is simultaneously user-side incentive compatible, mediator-side incentive compatible and advertiser-side incentive compatible) and also *three-sided continuously individually rational* (i.e., it is simultaneously user-side continuously individually rational, mediator-side continuously individually rational and advertiser-side continuously individually rational).

Our mechanism is termed "Observe and Price Mechanism" (OPM). The following theorem analyzes the economic properties guaranteed by OPM and its competitive ratio. The parameter α is an upper bound, known to the mechanism, on the market importance of any single agent. Formally, α bounds the ratio between the size of the optimal trade and the maximum capacity of an advertiser or the maximum number of users that a mediator can represent.

---

[3] Informally, an agent is truthful if he/she reports the information as it is known to him/her. A formal definition of what it means for a user, mediator or advertiser to be truthful is given in Sect. 2.

[4] Here and throughout the paper, a reference to domination of strategies should always be understood as a reference to weak domination.

Theorem 1. *OPM is budget balanced[5], three-sided continuously individually rational, three-sided incentive compatible and $(1 - 9.5\sqrt[9]{\alpha} - 10e^{-2/\sqrt[3]{\alpha}})$-competitive.*

From a theoretical perspective, the most important feature of the competitive ratio guaranteed by Theorem 1 is that it approaches 1 when no agent has too much market power. Though this is a desirable aspect of the algorithm, we are aware that the competitive ratio has an unintuitive form and is often non-positive for markets of a moderate size. The latter can be significantly alleviated by making the proof tighter (and less readable). Instead we chose to address intuitiveness and readability by including experimental results in the paper. The experimental results demonstrate that our mechanism performs well on inputs derived by real world data even for moderate size markets despite what the current theoretical analysis shows. We note that for large markets, such as the market we study in this work, α is expected to be much smaller than 1. Nevertheless, our simulation results suggest that in practice OPM performs well even for markets having a more moderate size and a larger value of α. In addition, in order to demonstrate the need for an involved solution such as OPM, we compare OPM's practical performance to that of a straw-man mechanism. This comparison demonstrates that our mechanism performs significantly better than the straw-man mechanism even for moderate size markets. We also note that the three-sided incentive compatibility of our mechanism implies that it is universally truthful, i.e., truthful for all possible random coin flips.

1.2   Additional Related Work

From a motivational point of view our model is closely related to models involving mediators and online advertising markets, such as the models studied by [1,18]. However, despite their network exchange motivation, these models are actually auctions (i.e., one-sided mechanisms). Moreover, they focus on offline revenue maximization mechanisms, which is very different from our focus. Other works with a different motivation, such as [13,15,17], have studied mechanisms for two-sided *non-dynamic* settings. However, with the exception of the very recent last reference, they all considered single-dimensional agents. We are not aware of any previous mechanism for a two-sided dynamic setting.

There is also a significant body of works studying dyanmic matching problems with an adversarial arrival order. This body of work was originated by the work of [14] who described an optimal dynamic algorithm for unweighted bipartite online matching. Later works considered more general settings allowing various kinds of weights—see, for example, [6]. We note that none of these works refers to strategic considerations.

---

[5] A mechanism is *budget balanced* if the amount it charges (from the advertisers) is at least as large as the amount it pays.

2   Model and Definitions

Let us now present the exact details of the model we consider. This model consists of a set P of users, a set M of mediators and a set A of advertisers. Each user $p \in P$ has a non-negative cost $c(p)$ which she suffers if she is assigned to an advertiser; thus, the utility of p is 0 if she is not assigned and $t - c(p)$ if she is assigned and paid t. The users are partitioned among the mediators, and we denote by $P(m) \subseteq P$ the set of users associated with mediator $m \in M$ (i.e., the sets $\{P(m) \mid m \in M\}$ form a disjoint partition of P). The utility of a mediator $m \in M$ is the amount he is paid minus the total cost his users suffer; hence, if $x(p) \in \{0,1\}$ is an indicator for the event that user $p \in P(m)$ is assigned and t is the payment received by m (part of which might have been forwarded by the mediator to his users), then the utility of m is $t - \sum_{p \in P(m)} x(p) \cdot c(p)$.[6] Finally, each advertiser $a \in A$ has a positive capacity $u(a)$, and she gains a non-negative value $v(a)$ from every one of the first $u(a)$ users assigned to her; thus, if advertiser a is assigned $n \leq u(a)$ users and has to pay t then her utility is $n \cdot v(a) - t$.

As explained in Sect. 1, we assume the entities (i.e., the mediators and advertisers) arrive in a uniformly random order. A mechanism for this model knows the total number of entities,[7] and views the entities as they arrive; however, it has no prior knowledge about the parameters of the entities or about the users. To compensate for this lack of knowledge, each arriving entity reports information to the mechanism. Each advertiser reports her capacity and value. The reports of the mediators are formed in a slightly more involved way. Each user reports her cost to her mediator, and based on these reports each mediator reports the number of his users and their costs to the mechanism. The users, mediators and advertisers are all strategic, and thus, free to produce incorrect reports. In other words, an advertiser may report incorrect capacity and value, a user may report an incorrect cost and a mediator may report a smaller number of users and associate with each one of them an arbitrary cost.

Every time that a new entity arrives, the mechanism has an opportunity to assign users to advertisers. More specifically, when a mediator arrives the mechanism is allowed to assign users of the newly arriving mediator to advertisers that have already arrived. Similarly, when an advertiser arrives the mechanism is allowed to assign users of mediators that have already arrived to the newly arriv-

---

[6] The mediators' utility functions are independent of the amount of money transferred from the mediators to the users. This choice was made with the aim of balancing two of the mediators' conflicting objectives: on the one hand, mediators want to make as much money as possible, and on the other hand, they want to acquire users and have them use their services rather than switch to another mediator who is known for paying more money to his users.

[7] In some cases the assumption that the mechanism has a prior knowledge about the number of entities might be considered unnatural. The mechanism we present can be modified using standard techniques to work with an alternative assumption stating that each entity arrives at a uniformly random time from some range (for example, $[0, 1]$). See [11] for more details.

ing advertiser. The objective of the mechanism is to end up with an assignment of users to advertisers maximizing the *gain from trade*. In order to incentivize the mediators and advertisers to report truthfully, the mechanism may charge the advertisers and pay the mediators. Additionally, it is also allowed to recommend for each mediator how much of the payment he received to forward to each one of his user. It is important to observe that, since the utility functions of the mediators are not affected by the forwarding of payments to the users, it is reasonable to believe that mediators follow the forwarding recommendations.

We say that a user is *truthful* if she reports her true cost. Similarly, an advertiser is *truthful* if she reports her true capacity and value. Finally, a mediator is considered *truthful* if he reports to the mechanism his true number of users and the costs of the users as reported to him; and, in addition, he also pays the users according to the recommendation of the mechanism (i.e., he lets them know about their true balance).

We associate a set $B(a)$ of $u(a)$ slots with each advertiser $a \in A$. This allows us to think of the users as assigned to slots instead of directly to advertisers. Formally, let B be the set of all slots (i.e., $B = \bigcup_{a \in A} B(a)$), then an assignment is a set $S \subseteq P \times B$ in which no user or slot appears in more than one ordered pair. We say that an assignment S assigns a user p to slot b if $(p, b) \in S$. Similarly, we say that an assignment S assigns user p to advertiser a if there exists a slot $b \in B(a)$ such that $(p, b) \in S$. It is also useful to define values for the slots. For every slot b of advertiser a, we define its value $v(b)$ as equal to the value $v(a)$ of a. Using this notation, the gain from trade of an assignment S can be stated as: $\texttt{GfT}(S) = \sum_{(p,b) \in S} [v(b) - c(p)]$.

Finally, we define two additional useful shorthands. Given a set $A' \subseteq A$ of advertisers, let $B(A') = \bigcup_{a \in A'} B(a)$ be the set of slots belonging to the advertisers of A'. Similarly, given a set $M' \subseteq M$ of mediators, $P(M') = \bigcup_{m \in M'} P(m)$ is the set of users associated with the mediators of M'.

Comparison of Costs and Values. The presentation of our mechanism is simpler when the values of slots and the costs of users are all unique. Clearly, this is extremely unrealistic since all the slots of a given advertiser have the exact same value in our model. Thus, we simulate uniqueness using a tie-breaking rule (which must be independent of the reports of the agents). In the rest of this paper, whenever costs/values are compared, the comparison is assumed to use such a tie breaking rule.

Canonical Assignment. Given a set $B' \subseteq B$ of users and a set $P' \subseteq P$ of slots, the canonical assignment $S_c(P', B')$ is the assignment constructed as follows. First, we order the slots of B' in a decreasing value order $b_1, b_2, \ldots, b_{|B'|}$ and the users of P' in an increasing cost order $p_1, p_2, \ldots, p_{|P'|}$. Then, for every $1 \leq i \leq \min\{|B'|, |P'|\}$, $S_c(B', P')$ assigns user p_i to slot b_i if and only if $v(b_i) > c(p_i)$.

The canonical assignment is an important tool we use often in this paper, and it was proved by [10] that $S_c(P', B')$ is always an assignment of users from P' to slots of B' maximizing the gain from trade (among all such assignments).

Occasionally, we refer to the user or slot at location i of a canonical assignment $S_c(P', B')$, by which we mean user p_i or slot b_i, respectively.

3   Our Mechanism

In this section we describe and analyze our dynamic mechanism "Observe and Price Mechanism" (OPM). OPM assumes $|S_c(P, B)| > 0$, and that there exists a value $\alpha \in [|S_c(P, B)|^{-1}, 1]$, known to the mechanism, such that we are guaranteed that, for every advertiser $a \in A$ and mediator $m \in M$:$\max\{u(a), |P(m)|\} \le \alpha \cdot |S_c(P, B)|$. In other words, α is an upper bound on how large can the capacity of an advertiser or the number of users of a mediator be compared to the size of the optimal assignment $S_c(P, B)$. We remind the reader that α can be informally understood as a bound on the market importance of any single entity.

A description of OPM is given as Mechanism 1. Notice that Mechanism 1 accepts a parameter $r \in (0, 1/2]$ whose value is specified later. Additionally, Mechanism 1 often refers to parameters of the model that are not known to the mechanism, such as the value of an advertiser or the number of users of a mediator. Whenever this happens, this should be understood as referring to the reported values of these parameters.

Mechanism 1. Observe and Price Mechanism (OPM)

---

1. Draw a random value t from the binomial distribution $\mathcal{B}(|A| + |M|, r)$, and observe the first t entities that arrive without assigning any users. Let A_T and M_T be the set of the observed advertisers and mediators, respectively. We later refer to this step of the mechanism as the "observation phase".

2. Let $\hat{p}$ and $\hat{b}$ be the user and slot, respectively, at location $\lceil (1 - 2r^{-1} \cdot \sqrt[3]{\alpha}) \cdot |S_c(P(M_T), B(A_T))| \rceil$ of the canonical assignment $S_c(P(M_T), B(A_T))$.
   If $(1 - 2r^{-1} \cdot \sqrt[3]{\alpha}) \cdot |S_c(P(M_T), B(A_T))| \le 0$, then the previous definition of $\hat{p}$ and $\hat{b}$ cannot be used. Instead, define $\hat{p}$ as a dummy user of cost $-\infty$ and $\hat{b}$ as a dummy slot of value ∞. We say that a slot b or a user p corresponding to an entity that arrived *after* the observation phase is *assignable* if $v(b) > v(\hat{b})$ or $c(p) < c(\hat{p})$, respectively.

3. Let σ_E be the sequence of the entities that arrived so far after the observation phase. Initially σ_E is empty, and entities are added to it as they arrive.

4. For every arriving entity:
   a. Add the new entity to the end of σ_E.
   b. If the arriving entity is a mediator m (advertiser a), then, as long as m (a) has unassigned assignable users (slots) and there is an advertiser (mediator) in σ_E having unassigned assignable slots (users), do:
      • Let a (m) be the first advertiser (mediator) in σ_E having unassigned assignable slots (users).

- Assign the unassigned assignable user of mediator m with the lowest cost to an arbitrary unassigned assignable slot of a, charge an amount of $v(\hat{b})$ from advertiser a and pay $c(\hat{p})$ to mediator m.

c. For every mediator $m \in \sigma_E$, recommend m to transfer his assigned users an additional amount that guarantees the following:
  - If all the assignable users of m are assigned, the additional amount should increase the total payment received so far by each assigned user of m to $c(\hat{p})$.
  - Otherwise, let p be the unassigned assignable user of m with the minimum cost. In this case the additional amount should increase the total payment received so far by each assigned user of m to $c(p)$.[a]

---

[a] Note that at every point in time m is budget balanced since he receives a payment of $c(\hat{p})$ for each one of his assigned users, and the total amount recommended for him to pay to each one of these users is either $c(\hat{p})$ or equal to the cost of some assignable user (and thus, is upper bounded by $c(\hat{p})$).

We would like to note that OPM is based on a mechanism of [10] named "Threshold by Partition Mechanism", and the analyses of both mechanisms go along similar lines. However, OPM introduces additional ideas that allow it to work in a dynamic setting. In particular, OPM uses an involved recommended payments updating rule that keeps it three-sided continuously individually rational. Moreover, OPM is able to use an observation phase whose size is a small fraction of the entire input (for $\alpha \ll 1$), whereas the analysis of the mechanism of [10] relies on the symmetry properties induced by an even partition of the input (which is inappropriate in a dynamic setting).

Let us start the analysis of OPM with the following simple observation, showing that OPM obeys the restriction of our model on the way a mechanism may update its assignment.

Observation 2. *Each time OPM assigns a user to a slot, either the user belongs to the newly arrived mediator or the slot belongs to the newly arrived advertiser.*

At this point we would like to prove the following restatement of Theorem 1.

Theorem 1. *OPM is budget balanced, three-sided continuously individually rational, three-sided incentive compatible and $(1 - r - 22r^{-1} \cdot \sqrt[3]{\alpha} - 10e^{-2/\sqrt[3]{\alpha}})$-competitive. Hence, for $r = \min\{1/2, 4\sqrt[6]{\alpha}\}$ the competitive ratio of OPM is at least: $1 - 9.5\sqrt[6]{\alpha} - 10e^{-2/\sqrt[3]{\alpha}}$.*

One part of Theorem 1 is proved by the following observation.

Observation 3. *OPM is budget balanced.*

Proof. We prove the observation by showing that whenever OPM assigns a user p to a slot b, it charges the advertiser of b more than it pays the mediator of p.

Consider an arbitrary ordered pair (p, b) from the assignment produced by OPM. The fact that p is assigned implies that $c(p) < c(\hat{p})$, and thus, $\hat{p}$ is not a dummy user (since $c(\hat{p}) = -\infty$ when $\hat{p}$ is a dummy user). Similarly, the fact that a user is assigned to b implies that $v(b) > v(\hat{b})$, and thus, $\hat{b}$ is not a dummy slot (since $v(\hat{b}) = \infty$ when $\hat{b}$ is a dummy slot).

Recall that the fact that $\hat{p}$ and $\hat{b}$ are not dummy user and slot, respectively, implies that $\hat{p}$ and $\hat{b}$ are matched by the canonical assignment $S_c(P(M_T), B(A_T))$. Since a canonical assignment never assigns a user p' to a slot b' when $c(p') > v(b')$, we get $c(\hat{p}) < v(\hat{b})$. The proof now completes by observing that the advertiser of b is charged $v(\hat{b})$ for the assignment of p to b, and the mediator of p is paid only $c(\hat{p})$ for this assignment. $\square$

Following is a useful observation about OPM that we occasionally use in the next proofs.

Observation 4. *OPM preserves the invariant that one of the following is always true immediately after OPM processes the arrival of an entity:*

1. *OPM assigned all the assignable users of mediators that have already arrived.*
2. *OPM assigned users to all the assignable slots of advertisers that have already arrived.*

Proof. Clearly the invariant holds during the observation phase because only mediators and advertisers that arrive after the observation phase contribute assignable users and slots, respectively. Next, assume the invariant held before the arrival of some mediator m which arrives after the observation phase, and let us prove that it holds also after the arrival of m. If before the arrival of m case (2) of the invariant held, then this case also holds after the arrival of m since m contributes no new slots. On the other hand, if case (1) held before the arrival of m, then OPM assigns the assignable users of m to assignable slots of advertisers that have already arrived till one of two things happen: either all the assignable slots of advertisers that have already arrived get assigned (and thus, case (2) of the invariant now holds), or all the assignable users of m get assigned (and thus, case (1) of the invariant holds again). It remains to prove that if the invariant held before the arrival of an advertiser a which arrives after the observation phase, then it also holds after her arrival. However, this proof is analogous to the above proof for mediators, and thus, we omit it. $\square$

3.1   The Incentive Properties of OPM

In this section we prove the incentive parts of Theorem 1. Specifically, we prove three lemmata showing that OPM is three-sided continuously individually rational and three-sided incentive compatible. The first lemma analyzes the incentive properties of OPM for users. Due to space constraints, we defer the proof of this lemma to the full version of this paper.

Lemma 1. *For every user p, assuming the mediator m of p is truthful, OPM is continuously individually rational for p, and truthfulness is a dominant strategy for her.*

The next lemma analyzes the incentive properties of OPM for mediators.

Lemma 2. *For every mediator m, assuming the users of m are truthful, OPM is continuously individually rational for m, and truthfulness is a dominant strategy for him.*

Proof. If m arrives during the observation phase (i.e., $m \in M_T$), then no user of m is ever assigned to a slot and m receives no payment. Hence, the lemma is trivial in this case. Thus, we assume in the rest of the proof that m arrives after the observation phase.

Note that OPM calculates the threshold $c(\hat{p})$ based on the reports of advertisers and mediators in A_T and M_T, respectively. Thus, m, who does not belong to M_T, cannot affect this threshold. Whenever a user $p \in P(m)$ is assigned to a slot the utility of m (and the user) decreases by $c(p)$ and increases by the additional payment m gets, which is $c(\hat{p})$. In other words, the utility of m changes by $c(\hat{p}) - c(p)$ (independently of the amount m forwards to p). When m is truthful this change is always non-negative since the assignment of p implies that she is assignable, i.e., her reported cost is smaller than $c(\hat{p})$. This already proves that each assignment of a user of m increases his utility by a non-negative amount when he is truthful (assuming his users are also truthful), thus, OPM is continuously individually rational for m.

Let s be the number of assignable users of m, according to his report. We claim that there exists a value k which is independent of the report of m such that for any report of m the mechanism assigns the $\min\{k, s\}$ users of m with the lowest reported costs. Before proving this claim, let us explain why the lemma follows from it. The above description shows that the utility of m changes by a $c(\hat{p}) - c(p)$ for every assigned user $p \in P(m)$, thus, m wishes to assign as many as possible users having cost less than $c(\hat{p})$, and if he cannot assign all of them then he prefers to assign the users with the lowest costs. By being truthful m guarantees that only users of cost less than $c(\hat{p})$ are considered assignable, and thus, have a chance to be assigned. Moreover, by the above claim OPM assigns the k assignable users of m with the lowest costs (or all of them if $s < k$), which is the best result m can hope for given that at most k of his users can be assigned. Hence, truthfulness is a dominant strategy for m.

We are only left to prove the above claim. Note that Observation 4 implies that OPM assigns no users of m as long as there are mediators appearing earlier in σ_E which still have unassigned assignable users. Once there are no more such mediators, OPM assigns users of m, in an increasing costs order, to unassigned assignable slots till one of two things happens: either m runs out of unassigned assignable users, or the input for OPM ends. This means that when the input for OPM ends before all the assignable users of mediators appearing before m in σ_E are assigned, then no users of m are assigned and the claim holds with $k = 0$. Otherwise, we choose k to be the number of unassigned assignable slots immediately before OPM assigns the first user of m (we count in k both unassigned assignable slots of advertisers that have already arrived at this moment and unassigned assignable slots of advertisers that arrive later). Notice that the report of m does not affect the behavior of OPM up to the moment it starts assigning users of m, thus, k is independent of the report of m. If $s > k$, then the k users of m with the lowest costs are assigned before OPM runs out of input and stops. Otherwise, if $s \leq k$, then OPM stops assigning users of m only after assigning all the s assignable users of m. □

Finally, the next lemma considers the incentive properties of OPM for advertisers. The proof of this lemma is analogous to the proof of the previous lemma (with slots exchanging roles with users, $v(\hat{b})$ exchanging roles with $c(\hat{p})$, etc.), and thus, we omit it.

Lemma 3. *For every advertiser a, OPM is continuously individually rational for a, and truthfulness is a dominant strategy for her.*

3.2 The Competitive Ratio of OPM

In this section we analyze the competitive ratio of OPM. Throughout the section we use the letter τ as a shorthand for $|S_c(P, B)|$. We also define $\tilde{P}$ ($\tilde{B}$) as the set of the users (slots) at locations 1 to $\lceil (1 - 6r^{-1} \cdot \sqrt[3]{\alpha})\tau \rceil$ of the canonical assignment $S_c(P, B)$ ($\tilde{P}$ and $\tilde{B}$ are defined to be empty when $1 - 6r^{-1} \cdot \sqrt[3]{\alpha} \leq 0$). The following observation shows that most of the gain from trade of the canonical assignment $S_c(P, B)$ comes from the users and slots of $\tilde{P}$ and $\tilde{B}$, respectively. For convenience, let us denote by P_o the set of users that are assigned by $S_c(P, B)$, and by B_o the set of slots that are assigned some user by $S_c(P, B)$.

Observation 5. $\sum_{b \in \tilde{B}} v(b) - \sum_{p \in \tilde{P}} c(p) \geq (1 - 6r^{-1} \cdot \sqrt[3]{\alpha}) \cdot \texttt{GfT}(S_c(P, B))$.

Proof. If $1 - 6r^{-1} \cdot \sqrt[3]{\alpha} \leq 0$, then both $\tilde{B}$ and $\tilde{P}$ are empty, and the inequality that we need to prove holds since its left hand side is 0 and its right hand side is non-positive (recall that $S_c(P, B)$ is an assignment of users from P to slots of B maximizing the gain from trade, and thus, its gain from trade is at least 0 since $\texttt{GfT}(\varnothing) = 0$). Thus, we may assume in the rest of the proof that $1 - 6r^{-1} \cdot \sqrt[3]{\alpha} > 0$.

Since $\tilde{B}$ contains the $\lceil (1 - 6r^{-1} \cdot \sqrt[3]{\alpha})\tau \rceil$ slots with the largest values among the slots of B_o, we get:

$$\sum_{b \in \tilde{B}} v(b) \geq \lceil (1 - 6r^{-1} \cdot \sqrt[3]{\alpha})\tau \rceil \cdot \frac{\sum_{b \in B_o} v(b)}{\tau}.$$

Similarly, since $\tilde{P}$ contains the $\lceil (1 - 6r^{-1} \cdot \sqrt[3]{\alpha})\tau \rceil$ users with the lowest costs among the users of P_o, we get:

$$\sum_{p \in \tilde{A}} c(p) \leq \lceil (1 - 6r^{-1} \cdot \sqrt[3]{\alpha})\tau \rceil \cdot \frac{\sum_{c \in P_o} c(p)}{\tau}.$$

Combining the two inequities gives:

$$\sum_{b \in \tilde{B}} v(b) - \sum_{p \in \tilde{P}} c(p)$$

$$\geq \lceil (1 - 6r^{-1} \cdot \sqrt[3]{\alpha}) \tau \rceil \cdot \frac{\sum_{b \in B_o} v(b) - \sum_{p \in P_o} c(p)}{\tau}$$

$$= \lceil (1 - 6r^{-1} \cdot \sqrt[3]{\alpha}) \tau \rceil \cdot \frac{\texttt{GfT}(S_c(P, B))}{\tau}$$

$$\geq (1 - 6r^{-1} \cdot \sqrt[3]{\alpha}) \cdot \texttt{GfT}(S_c(P, B)). \qquad \square$$

Observation 5 shows that one can prove a competitive ratio for OPM by relating the gain from trade of the assignment it produces to the gain from trade obtained by assigning the users of $\tilde{P}$ to the slots $\tilde{B}$. The following lemma is a key lemma we use to relate the two gains. In order to state this lemma we need some additional definitions. Consider the following two sets.

$$\hat{P} = \{p \in P(M \setminus M_T) \mid c(p) < c(\hat{p})\}$$

and

$$\hat{B} = \{b \in B(A \setminus A_T) \mid v(b) > v(\hat{b})\}.$$

Intuitively, $\hat{P}$ is the set of the assignable users, and $\hat{B}$ is the set of the assignable slots. It is important to note that $\hat{P}$ and $\hat{B}$ are both empty whenever $\hat{p}$ and $\hat{b}$ are dummy user and slot, respectively. We also define two additional sets A_L and M_L as follows. Let f be a random variable distributed according to the binomial distribution $\mathcal{B}(|A \setminus A_T| + |M \setminus M_T|, \min\{6r^{-1} \cdot \sqrt[3]{\alpha}, 1\})$, and let L be the set of the last f entities in σ_E (or equivalently, the last f entities to arrive). The sets A_L and M_L are then defined as $A_L = A \cap L$ and $M_L = M \cap L$.

Lemma 4. *There exists an event $\mathcal{E}$ of probability at least $1 - 10e^{-2/\sqrt[3]{\alpha}}$ such that $\mathcal{E}$ implies the following:*

(i) $\tilde{B} \setminus B(A_T) \subseteq \hat{B}$
(ii) $\tilde{P} \setminus P(M_T) \subseteq \hat{P}$
(iii) $|\hat{P} \setminus P(M_L)| \leq |\hat{B}|$
(iv) $|\hat{B} \setminus B(A_L)| \leq |\hat{P}|$
(v) $c(p) \leq \ell(P, B) \leq v(b)$ *for every user $p \in \hat{P}$ and slot $b \in \hat{B}$, where $\ell(P, B)$ is a value which is independent of the random coins of OPM and obeys $c(p) \leq \ell(P, B) \leq v(b)$ for every $p \in P_o$ and $b \in B_o$.*

The proof of Lemma 4 is very similar to the proof of Lemma 4.6 in [9] (which is a version of [10] with full proofs), and thus, we omit it. In the rest of this section we explain how the competitive ratio of OPM follows from Lemma 4. Let $\hat{S}$ be the assignment produced by OPM.

Lemma 5. *The event $\mathcal{E}$ implies the following inequality:*

$$\texttt{GfT}(\hat{S}) \geq \sum_{\substack{b \in \tilde{B} \\ b \notin B(A_T \cup A_L)}} [v(b) - \ell(P, B)] + \sum_{\substack{p \in \tilde{P} \\ p \notin P(M_T \cup M_L)}} [\ell(P, B) - c(p)].$$

Proof. Lemma 4 shows that given $\mathcal{E}$ we have $|\hat{P} \setminus P(M_L)| \leq |\hat{B}|$, hence, Observation 4 implies that OPM assigns at least $|\hat{P} \setminus P(M_L)|$ users. Additionally, since OPM assigns users of mediators from M_L only after all the assignable users of mediators from $M \setminus (M_T \cup M_L)$ are assigned to slots we get that all the users of $\hat{P} \setminus P(M_L)$ are assigned by $\hat{S}$ given $\mathcal{E}$. On the other hand, Lemma 4 also shows that given $\mathcal{E}$ all the users of $\tilde{P} \setminus P(M_T)$ belong to $\hat{P}$, and thus, the users of $\tilde{P} \setminus P(M_T \cup M_L)$ are all assigned by $\hat{S}$. A similar argument shows that the slots of $\tilde{B} \setminus B(A_T \cup A_L)$ are all assigned users by $\hat{S}$ given $\mathcal{E}$. Finally, observe that $\mathcal{E}$ also implies that $c(p) \leq \ell(P, B) \leq v(b)$ for every pair $(p, b) \in \hat{S} \subseteq \hat{P} \times \hat{B}$.

In the rest of the proof we assume that $\mathcal{E}$ happens. Consider an ordered pair $(p, b) \in \hat{S}$. Then, the contribution of (p, b) to $\texttt{GfT}(\hat{S})$ is:

$$v(b) - c(p) = [v(b) - \ell(P, B)] + [\ell(P, B) - c(p)].$$

By the above discussion, the two terms that appear in brackets on the right hand side of the last equation are both positive. This allows us to lower bound the gain from trade of $\hat{S}$ as follows:

$$
\begin{aligned}
\texttt{GfT}(\hat{S}) &= \sum_{(p,b)\in\hat{S}} [v(b) - c(p)] \\
&= \sum_{(p,b)\in\hat{S}} \{[v(b) - \ell(P, B)] + [\ell(P, B) - c(p)]\} \\
&\geq \sum_{\substack{b\in\tilde{B} \\ b\notin B(A_T\cup A_L)}} [v(b) - \ell(P, B)] + \sum_{\substack{p\in\tilde{P} \\ p\notin P(M_T\cup M_L)}} [\ell(P, B) - c(p)]. \qquad \square
\end{aligned}
$$

Corollary 1. *OPM is at least* $(1 - r - 22r^{-1} \cdot \sqrt[3]{\alpha} - 10e^{-2/\sqrt[3]{\alpha}})$*-competitive.*

Proof. The corollary is trivial when $r + 22r^{-1} \cdot \sqrt[3]{\alpha} + 10e^{-2/\sqrt[3]{\alpha}} > 1$. Thus, we assume in this proof $r + 22r^{-1} \cdot \sqrt[3]{\alpha} + 10e^{-2/\sqrt[3]{\alpha}} \leq 1$. For every two sets $M' \subseteq M$ and $A' \subseteq A$ of mediators and advertisers, respectively, let $\texttt{Val}(M', A')$ denote the expression:

$$\sum_{b\in\tilde{B}\setminus B(A')} [v(b) - \ell(P, B)] + \sum_{p\in\tilde{P}\setminus P(M')} [\ell(P, B) - c(p)].$$

The definition of $\ell(P, B)$ guarantees that $v(b) - \ell(P, B) \geq 0$ and $\ell(P, B) - c(p) \geq 0$ for every $b \in \tilde{B} \subseteq B_o$ and $p \in \tilde{P} \subseteq P_o$. Thus, $\texttt{Val}(M', A') \leq \texttt{Val}(\varnothing, \varnothing)$ for every two sets $M' \subseteq M$ and $A' \subseteq A$. Additionally, it is well-known that the way t is chosen by OPM guarantees that every entity of $M \cup A$ belongs to T with probability r, independently (a proof of this fact can be found, e.g., as Lemma A.1 in [12]). Similarly, every entity of $M \cup A$ that does not belong to T is added to L with probability $\min\{1, 16r^{-1} \cdot \sqrt[3]{\alpha}\} = 16r^{-1} \cdot \sqrt[3]{\alpha}$, independently. Hence, every user (slot) of $\hat{P}$ ($\tilde{B}$) belongs to $\tilde{P} \setminus P(M_T \cup M_L)$ ($\tilde{B} \setminus B(A_T \cup A_L)$) with probability

$$(1 - r)(1 - 16r^{-1} \cdot \sqrt[3]{\alpha}) \geq 1 - r - 16r^{-1} \cdot \sqrt[3]{\alpha}.$$

Therefore,

$$\mathbb{E}[\mathtt{Val}(M_T \cup M_L, A_T \cup A_L)]$$

$$\geq (1 - r - 16r^{-1} \cdot \sqrt[3]{\alpha}) \cdot \Big\{ \sum\nolimits_{b \in \tilde{B}} [v(b) - \ell(P,B)] + \sum\nolimits_{p \in \tilde{P}} [\ell(P,B) - c(b)] \Big\}$$

$$= (1 - r - 16r^{-1} \cdot \sqrt[3]{\alpha}) \cdot \mathtt{Val}(\varnothing, \varnothing).$$

Using Lemma 5 and the observation that OPM always produces an assignment of non-negative gain from trade, we now get:

$$\begin{aligned}
\mathbb{E}[\mathtt{GfT}(\hat{S})] &= \Pr[\mathcal{E}] \cdot \mathbb{E}[\mathtt{GfT}(\hat{S}) \mid \mathcal{E}] + \Pr[\neg\mathcal{E}] \cdot \mathbb{E}[\mathtt{GfT}(\hat{S}) \mid \neg\mathcal{E}] \\
&\geq \Pr[\mathcal{E}] \cdot \mathbb{E}[\mathtt{Val}(M_T \cup M_L, A_T \cup A_L) \mid \mathcal{E}] \\
&= \mathbb{E}[\mathtt{Val}(M_T \cup M_L, A_T \cup A_L)] \\
&\quad - \Pr[\neg\mathcal{E}] \cdot \mathbb{E}[\mathtt{Val}(M_T \cup M_L, A_T \cup A_L) \mid \neg\mathcal{E}] \\
&\geq (1 - r - 16r^{-1} \cdot \sqrt[3]{\alpha}) \cdot \mathtt{Val}(\varnothing, \varnothing) - \Pr[\neg\mathcal{E}] \cdot \mathtt{Val}(\varnothing, \varnothing) \\
&= [(1 - r - 16r^{-1} \cdot \sqrt[3]{\alpha}) - \Pr[\neg\mathcal{E}]] \cdot \mathtt{Val}(\varnothing, \varnothing).
\end{aligned} \tag{1}$$

Recall that $\Pr[\neg\mathcal{E}] \leq 10e^{-2/\sqrt[3]{\alpha}}$ by Lemma 4. Additionally, note that Observation 5 and the fact that $|\tilde{P}| = |\tilde{B}|$ by definition imply together:

$$\begin{aligned}
\mathtt{Val}(\varnothing,\varnothing) \\
&= \sum\nolimits_{b \in \tilde{B}} [v(b) - \ell(P,B)] + \sum\nolimits_{p \in \tilde{P}} [\ell(P,B) - c(p)] \\
&= \sum\nolimits_{b \in \tilde{B}} v(b) - \sum\nolimits_{p \in \tilde{P}} c(p) \\
&\geq (1 - 6r^{-1} \cdot \sqrt[3]{\alpha}) \cdot \mathtt{GfT}(S_c(P,A)).
\end{aligned}$$

Plugging the last observations into (1) gives:

$$\begin{aligned}
\mathbb{E}[\mathtt{GfT}(\hat{S})] &\geq [(1 - r - 16r^{-1} \cdot \sqrt[3]{\alpha}) - \Pr[\neg\mathcal{E}]] \cdot \mathtt{Val}(\varnothing, \varnothing) \\
&\geq [(1 - r - 16r^{-1} \cdot \sqrt[3]{\alpha}) - 10e^{-2/\sqrt[3]{\alpha}}] \cdot (1 - 6r^{-1} \cdot \sqrt[3]{\alpha}) \cdot \mathtt{GfT}(S_c(P,A)) \\
&\geq (1 - r - 22r^{-1} \cdot \sqrt[3]{\alpha} - 10e^{-2/\sqrt[3]{\alpha}}) \cdot \mathtt{GfT}(S_c(P,B)).
\end{aligned}$$

The corollary now follows by recalling that $S_c(P,B)$ is the assignment of users from P to slots of B which maximizes the gain from trade.   □

4 A Straw-Man Mechanism

In this section we describe a simple straightforward dynamic straw-man mechanism for matching advertisers and mediators. This mechanism maintains the desired economic properties, and thus, it is a good candidate for comparison with OPM. In Sect. 5 we use simulations to compare the two mechnaims. Our simulations show that OPM significantly outperforms the straw-man mechanism.

Mechanism 2. Straw-Man Mechanism

---

1. Let σ_E be an ordered subset of the entities that have arrived so far. Initially σ_E is empty, and entities are added to it as they arrive.

2. For every arriving entity (mediator or advertiser):

    a. Let i denote the index of the arriving entity among the previously arriving entities of the same type (in other words, if the arriving entity is a mediator, then it is the i-th mediator to arrive, and if it is an advertiser, then it is the i-th advertiser to arrive).

    b. If i is odd and the arriving entity is a mediator m (advertiser a), draw a random user of m (slot of a) and denote it by $\hat{p}_i$ ($\hat{b}_i$). We say that $c(\hat{p}_i)$ ($v(\hat{b}_i)$) is the threshold for the users of the next mediator (slots of the next advertiser). Moreover, every such user (slot) is *assignable* if her cost is less than (its value is more than) this threshold.

    c. Otherwise (i.e., when i is even), if the arriving entity is a mediator m (advertiser a), then add m (a) to the end of σ_E. As long as m (a) has unassigned assignable users (slots) and there is an advertiser (mediator) in σ_E having unassigned assignable slots (users) whose threshold is above (below) the threshold of m's users (a's slots), do:

        • Let a (m) be the earliest advertiser (mediator) in σ_E of this kind.

        • Assign the unassigned assignable user of mediator m with the lowest cost to an arbitrary unassigned assignable slot of a, charge advertiser a with an amount equal to the threshold of her slots and pay m an amount equal to the threshold of his users.

    d. For every mediator $m \in \sigma_E$ of even index i, recommend m to transfer his assigned users an additional amount that guarantees the following:

        • If all the assignable users of m are assigned, the additional amount should increase the total payment received so far by each assigned user of m to $c(\hat{p}_{i-1})$.

        • Otherwise, let p_i be the unassigned assignable user of m with the minimum cost. In this case the additional amount should increase the total payment received so far by each assigned user of m to $c(p_i)$.

---

5 Simulations

We have used simulations to study the empirical performance of our mechanism OPM. Our simulations involved two methods for generating the input. The more interesting of these methods, which we call *real-data based input* was as follows. The creation of the advertisers was based on data collected as part of a Horizon 2020 project from Facebook campaigns targeting Europeans between the ages 18 and 22 who are interested in entertainment. Every bid collected consisted of a budget for the relevant campaign, the maximal CPC (cost-per-click) value, the minimal CPC value and the median CPC value that the advertiser was willing to pay. Based on these bids we constructed three advertisers for our generated input, one advertiser for each one of the CPC values. More specifically, let β be the budget specified by the bid, and let δ be one of the three CPC values specified by this bid, then the advertiser created for this CPC value has a value of δ and a capacity of $\frac{\beta}{100\delta}$.[8] For every advertiser we also created a single mediator having the same number of users as the capacity of the advertiser. Every user of these mediators was assigned an independent cost chosen uniformly at random from the range between the smallest and largest CPC values encountered in the real world bids. To verify that the data fed into the mechanism was unbiased, we designed a secondary input generation method which we call the *random bids input*. The way input is generated by this method is very similar to the way real-data based input was generated, except that the advertisers' values were selected as uniformly random independent values between the smallest and largest CPC values encountered in the real world bids (rather then being taken directly from the input bids, as in the real-data based input).

Our first simulation was designed to study the effect of market size on the performance of the mechanism. In this experiment we used the above methods to generate markets of various sizes and then we sent the entities of each generated market into OPM in a uniformly random order. The observable performance of the assignments produced by OPM (as a percent of the efficient canonical assignment) are depicted in Fig. 1. In order to reduce variance and error margins, every value given by this figure (and the next ones) was produced by averaging 3000 independent executions. As expected, the performance of the algorithm improves with the size of the market (as the size of the market is roughly inversely proportional to α). Moreover, these results demonstrate that our mechanism performs well (between 65% and 85% of the efficient gain from trade) on inputs derived by real world data even for moderate size markets, which is better than what can be predicted based on our theoretical result alone. While one might achieve better performance, a 65% to 85% range seems reasonable given the need to handle both an online setting and economic issues.[9]

In the previous experiment, we used the value of the parameter r of OPM which was specified by the version of Theorem 1 given in Sect. 3. Our second simulation was designed to study the possibility of improving the performance of the mechanism by varying the value of r. Specifically, we repeated the previous experiment with a market of 11961 advertisers (which is close to the size of the largest market we considered before), but varied the value of the parameter r. The results of this experiment are depicted in Fig. 2. As in the previous experiment, we see again that using the value of r specified by Theorem 1 ($1/2$ in

---

[8] Our experiments are based on only a fraction of the entire data set, which significantly increased the market strength of the entities in the input. To compensate for this increase, and keep the market strength of each advertiser in the simulation similar to the market strength of the corresponding real world advertiser, we introduced a division by 100 into the capacity formula.

[9] Note that the experiments did not simulate the information trading part of the model since they were intended to study the mechanism's competitive ratio. However, information exchange can occur in our model in practice. Intuitively, one can think of the users in a single execution of the mechanism as the users who agreed to sell information that, if revealed, implies that they have one particular type t. Then, if an advertiser's ad is shown to a user, the advertiser may learn that the user is of type t and the user is monetarily compensated for that.

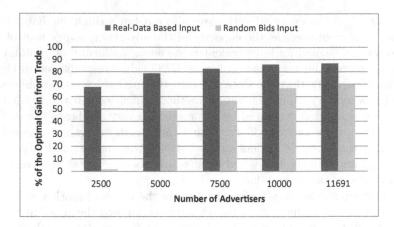

Fig. 1. The performance of OPM as a function of the market size. The number below each column specifies the number of advertisers in the market.

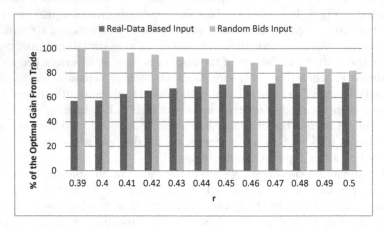

Fig. 2. The performance of OPM as a function of the value of the parameter r on markets with 11961 advertisers.

this case) leads to good performance for both input generation methods. For the real-data based input, varying r does not improve the performance of OPM, but for the random input bids one can significantly improve the outcome by decreasing r. This is likely to be a consequence of a higher variance in the random bids input, which allows OPM to calculate good thresholds based on a shorter observation phase (which are induced by decreasing r). Thus, for the random bids input, decreasing r leads to improved performance as it allows OPM to harvest value from a larger fraction of the market while inducing only a weak adversarial effect on the selected thresholds.

Our last simulation was designed to demonstrate the need for creating involved solutions such as OPM for solving a dynamic multi-sided market trade problem. We used the straw-man mechanism described in Sect. 4 as a benchmark for straightforward mechanisms solving the problem at hand and ran OPM against it. Figure 3 shows that for medium size markets OPM improves by over 60% compared to the straightforward mechanism.

Gain from trade improvement

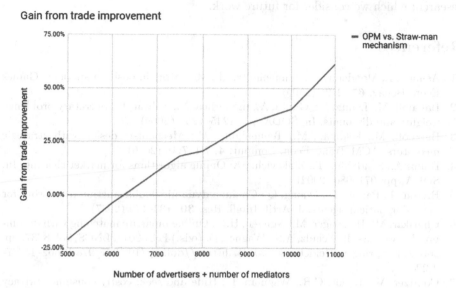

Fig. 3. The gain from trade improvment of OPM vs. the straw-man mechanism. The number below each column specifies the number of advertisers plus mediators in the market.

6 Conclusion

In this paper we have presented a dynamic model for a foreseeable form of the online advertising market based on principles suggested by [10], and described a mechanism called OPM for it. OPM is the first mechanism for a multi-sided market that guarantees the economic properties of budget balance, incentive compatibility and individual rationality while having a non-trivial theoretical approximation guarantee. For large markets, such as the online advertising market, the theoretical competitive ratio of OPM approaches 1. However, this theoretical guarantee becomes much weaker (or even non-relevant) for smaller markets, and thus, we have complemented it with simulation results. These results suggest that OPM performs well in practice even for markets of moderate size.

The model we study assumes that all users are equally valuable for the advertisers. Handling users with different value to advertisers is not explicitly described in the model but is supported. The approach would be to assume multiple markets, one for each type of user, and every user is directed by its mediator to the market corresponding to its type (based on the information it agrees to sell). While this reduction allows the advertisers to effectively have user-dependent valuation functions, studying mechanisms for richer models which directly allow advertisers to have such user-dependent valuation functions (without having to go through the above reduction) is an extension of our current research; which we consider for future work.

References

1. Ashlagi, I., Monderer, D., Tennenholtz, M.: Mediators in position auctions. Games Econ. Behav. **67**, 2–21 (2009)
2. Babaioff, M., Dinitz, M., Gupta, A., Immorlica, N., Talwar, K.: Secretary problems: weights and discounts. In: SODA, pp. 1245–1254 (2009)
3. Babaioff, M., Feldman, M., Tennenholtz, M.: Mechanism design with strategic mediators. ACM Trans. Econ. Comput. **4**, 7:1–7:48 (2016)
4. Blum, A., Sandholm, T., Zinkevich, M.: Online algorithms for market clearing. In: SODA, pp. 971–980 (2002)
5. Bredin, J., Parkes, D., Duong, Q.: Chain: a dynamic double auction framework for matching patient agents. J. Artif. Intell. Res. **30**, 133–179 (2007)
6. Charikar, M., Henzinger, M., Nguyen, H.L.: Online bipartite matching with decomposable weights. In: Schulz, A.S., Wagner, D. (eds.) ESA 2014. LNCS, vol. 8737, pp. 260–271. Springer, Heidelberg (2014). https://doi.org/10.1007/978-3-662-44777-2_22
7. Conitzer, V., Taylor, C.R., Wagman, L.: Hide and seek: costly consumer privacy in a market with repeat purchases. Mark. Sci. **31**(2), 277–292 (2012)
8. Facebook: CEO Mark Zuckerberg Testifies Before Senate on User Data (2018). https://m.youtube.com/watch?v=qAZiDRonYZI
9. Feldman, M., Gonen, R.: Markets with strategic multi-minded mediators. CoRR abs/1603.08717 (2016). http://arxiv.org/abs/1603.08717
10. Feldman, M., Gonen, R.: Removal and threshold pricing: truthful two-sided markets with multi-dimensional participants. In: Deng, X. (ed.) SAGT 2018. LNCS, vol. 11059, pp. 163–175. Springer, Cham (2018). https://doi.org/10.1007/978-3-319-99660-8_15
11. Feldman, M., Naor, J.S., Schwartz, R.: Improved competitive ratios for submodular secretary problems (extended abstract). In: Goldberg, L.A., Jansen, K., Ravi, R., Rolim, J.D.P. (eds.) APPROX/RANDOM -2011. LNCS, vol. 6845, pp. 218–229. Springer, Heidelberg (2011). https://doi.org/10.1007/978-3-642-22935-0_19
12. Feldman, M., Svensson, O., Zenklusen, R.: A simple $O(\log \log (\text{rank}))$-competitive algorithm for the matroid secretary problem. Math. Oper. Res. **43**(2), 638–650 (2018)
13. Gonen, M., Gonen, R., Pavlov, E.: Generalized trade reduction mechanisms. In: EC, pp. 20–29. ACM, New York (2007)
14. Karp, R.M., Vazirani, U.V., Vazirani, V.V.: An optimal algorithm for on-line bipartite matching. In: STOC, pp. 352–358 (1990)
15. McAfee, R.P.: dominant strategy double auction. J. Econ. Theory **56**, 434–450 (1992)
16. Myerson, R.B., Satterthwaite, M.A.: Efficient mechanisms for bilateral trading. J. Econ. Theory **29**, 265–281 (1983)
17. Segal-Halevi, E., Hassidim, A., Aumann, Y.: MUDA: a truthful multi-unit double-auction mechanism. In: Proceeding of AAAI (2018)

18. Stavrogiannis, L.C., Gerding, E.H., Polukarov, M.: Auction mechanisms for demand-side intermediaries in online advertising exchanges. In: AAMAS, pp. 5–9. International Foundation for Autonomous Agents and Multiagent Systems, Richland (2014)
19. Vaze, R., Coupechoux, M.: Online budgeted truthful matching. SIGMETRICS Perform. Eval. Rev. **44**(3), 3–6 (2016)
20. Wurman, P., Walsh, W., Wellman, M.: Flexible double auctions for electronic commerce: theory and implementation. Decis. Support Syst. **24**, 17–27 (1998)

A Game-Theoretic Analysis of the Adversarial Boyd-Kuramoto Model

Antonin Demazy[1], Alexander Kalloniatis[2], and Tansu Alpcan[1(✉)]

[1] Department of Electrical and Electronic Engineering, The University of Melbourne, Melbourne, VIC, Australia
ademazy@student.unimelb.edu.au, tansu.alpcan@unimelb.edu.au
[2] Defence Science and Technology Group, Canberra, ACT, Australia
alex.kalloniatis@dst.defence.gov.au

Abstract. The "Boyd" model, also known as the "OODA loop", represents the cyclic decision processes of individuals and organisations in a variety of adversarial situations. Combined with the Kuramoto model, which provides a mathematical foundation for describing the behaviour of a set of coupled or networked oscillators, the Boyd-Kuramoto model captures strategic (cyclic) decision making in competitive environments.

This paper presents a novel game-theoretic approach to the Boyd-Kuramoto dynamical model in complex and networked systems. A two-player, Red versus Blue, strategic (non-cooperative) game is defined to describe the competitive interactions and individual decision cycles of Red and Blue agent populations. We study the model analytically in the regime of near phase synchrony where linearisation approximations are possible. We find that we can solve for the Nash equilibrium of the game in closed form, and that it only depends on the parameters defining the fixed point of the dynamical system. A detailed numerical analysis of the finite version of the game investigates the behaviour of the underlying networked Kuramoto oscillators and yields a unique, dominant Nash equilibrium solution. The obtained Nash equilibrium is further studied analytically in a region where the underlying Boyd-Kuramoto dynamics are stable. The result suggests that only the fixed point of the dynamical system plays a role, consist with the analytical solution. Finally, the impact of other variations of the Boyd-Kuramoto parameters on the game outcomes are studied numerically, confirming the observations from fixed point approaches. It is observed that many parameters of the Kuramoto model affect the NE solution of the current game formulation much less than initially stipulated, arguably due to the time-scale separation between the underlying Kuramoto model and the static game formulation.

1 Introduction

The *Boyd* model or *OODA loop* is a cyclic decision process consisting of the following four stages: *Observe, Orient, Decide, and Act* [4]. It models the decision cycle of individuals and organisations in a variety of adversarial and competitive

L. Bushnell et al. (Eds.): GameSec 2018, LNCS 11199, pp. 248–264, 2018.
https://doi.org/10.1007/978-3-030-01554-1_14

situations. Though originating in tactical air-to-air combat, it is now a well-known concept in business, litigation, and law enforcement [10]. For example, the model can be used to capture the competition (for a pool of customers) between two companies in their innovation cycles as they bring new products to the market. The OODA loop is also used widely in military strategy, and operational Command and Control (C2), far from the air-to-air combat context in which it was originally derived.

The OODA loop matches the fundamental paradigms of system and control theory. The "Observe" stage involves making observations about the environment and collecting data by an Observer. The "Orient" stage may process the observed information in light of the identified models and past experiences. In the "Decide" stage, available actions are evaluated based on some performance criteria derived from utility, optimisation, or game theories. "Orient" and "Decide" can be mapped to a Controller in control theory. Finally, an action is taken in the "Act" stage, which corresponds to the behaviour of Actuators in systems. A similar analogy can also be made to strategic decision making by companies or organisations. Competitive firms observe the market trends and orient themselves accordingly; decide on their strategic investments, e.g. for innovation; and act to bring new products and services to the market to get a higher share.

The Kuramoto model [9] provides a mathematical foundation for describing the behaviour of a set of coupled or networked oscillators and their synchronisation characteristics. In this context, each oscillator corresponds to the decision cycle of an individual or part of an organisation. The Kuramoto model has been widely used to analyse complex systems in a variety of domains [1]. A novel application of Kuramoto oscillators to Boyd-OODA cycles in adversarial interactions between two populations, e.g. Red versus Blue, was proposed in [7], and this is what is termed the 'Boyd-Kuramoto' model. Mathematically, such a model is an application of certain multi-graph frustrated generalisation of the Kuramoto model, as studied in works such as [5]. Since its proposal as a model for adversarial decision cycles, it has been the subject of fixed points and stability analysis in the deterministic [8] and stochastic cases [6]. Specifically, the internal synchronisation of individual OODA oscillators within the (Red and Blue) populations as well as the average phase difference ("lags" or frustrations) between the populations have been studied in detail with and without noise, and thresholds for one side or the other to lose synchronisation have been derived. This combined Boyd-Kuramoto model is immediately applicable to competitive decisions as it captures the complex cyclic decision processes in adversarial populations of networked heterogeneous agents. Going back to the example of two competitive firms, the average phase difference may represent how much ahead one firm is against the other in the innovation cycle.

Game Theory studies multi-agent decision making with versatile quantitative methods. As a special case, *security games* have been used to successfully model the decision processes in adversarial situations [2]. The inherently adversarial nature of the interaction between Blue and Red populations in commercial competition or strategic C2 decision making immediately motivates a game-theoretic approach to the Boyd-Kuramoto model. Thus, though one may derive thresholds or optima for decisions by one side with fixed parameters for the other, as in [8], the fact that the adversary has a say in the outcome means that a game-theoretic treatment is essential.

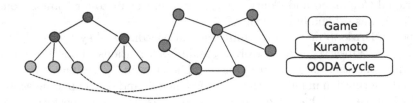

Fig. 1. A conceptual diagram of the Boyd-Kuramoto Game. (Color figure online)

This paper applies the mathematical and conceptual framework of security games to the Boyd-Kuramoto model of networked decision cycles (oscillators) in Blue and Red populations within the adversarial/competitive context. As a starting point, a novel Boyd-Kuramoto Game is introduced. In this 2-Player, nonzero-sum strategic (non-cooperative) game, the Blue and Red players aim to gain a phase (lag) advantage over their opponent based on the average phase of their own agent populations, while achieving internal synchronisation of their Boyd-OODA oscillators. Kuramoto's order parameters of the player populations and the average phase difference between them provide the main criteria in modelling the player utility functions. This three-layer Boyd-Kuramoto Game model (Fig. 1) is the first of its kind to the best knowledge of the authors.

The **contributions** of this paper include:

- Development of a novel game-theoretic model of Boyd-Kuramoto networked oscillators in complex C2 systems, which describes the strategic decision-making processes of Red vs Blue populations.
- A detailed numerical analysis of the game investigating the stable behaviour of the underlying networked Kuramoto oscillators, and computing the Nash Equilibrium solutions.
- A numerical study of the impact of Boyd-Kuramoto parameters on the game outcomes.
- An analytic description of the Nash Equilibrium solution after linearisation of the dynamical equations.

The rest of the paper is organised as follows. The next section presents the main components of the Boyd-Kuramoto Model. Section 3 introduces a specific game-theoretic formulation. A numerical analysis of the game is presented in Sect. 4. The sensitivity of the game solutions to various parameters is discussed in Sect. 6. Analytic solution is pursued in Sect. 5. The paper concludes with remarks and a discussion on future directions in Sect. 7.

2 Boyd-Kuramoto Model for Complex Competitive Systems

We consider a deterministic Blue versus Red networked Kuramoto oscillator model to describe complex, adversarial, and competitive interactions using Boyd (OODA) cycles in both Blue and Red agent populations. Let $\mathcal{B} = \{1, \ldots, N\}$ and $\mathcal{R} = \{1, \ldots, M\}$ be the respective sets of Blue and Red Agents. Each Blue Agent $i \in \mathcal{B}$ has a frequency ω_i and phase β_i, and similarly each Red Agent $j \in \mathcal{R}$ has frequency ν_j and phase ρ_j. The Blue Agents are connected to each other symmetrically (which may be relaxed) via the $N \times N$ adjacency matrix B and Red Agents via the $M \times M$ matrix R. The $N \times M$ matrix A represents the unidirectional external links from Blue to Red Agents. Figure 1 visualises one possible configuration. Finally, the ζ_B, ζ_R, ζ_{BR}, and ζ_{RB}, are the relevant coupling constants. The resulting Boyd-Kuramoto model is

$$\frac{d\beta_i}{dt} = \omega_i - \zeta_B \sum_{j \in \mathcal{B}} B_{ij} \sin(\beta_i - \beta_j) - \zeta_{BR} \sum_{j \in \mathcal{R}} A_{ij} \sin(\beta_i - \rho_j - \phi), \quad i \in \mathcal{B} \quad (1)$$

$$\frac{d\rho_i}{dt} = \nu_i - \zeta_R \sum_{i \in \mathcal{R}} R_{ij} \sin(\rho_i - \rho_j) - \zeta_{RB} \sum_{j \in \mathcal{B}} A_{ij}^T \sin(\rho_i - \beta_j - \psi), \quad i \in \mathcal{R}, \quad (2)$$

where d/dt is the time derivative, $(\cdot)^T$ is the transpose operator, and ϕ and ψ are the phase lags (frustrations) [8]. These two phase parameters capture the essence of Boyd's proposal that advantage is gained by one side over the other insofar as the coupled dynamics enable the realisation of one side being ahead of the other by the desired amount: ϕ for Blue, and ψ for Red.

In general, the set of nonlinear Eq. (1) can only be solved numerically and they may exhibit complex and chaotic dynamics. Let

$$C_B := \frac{1}{N} \sum_{i \in \mathcal{B}} \beta_i \quad \text{and} \quad C_R := \frac{1}{M} \sum_{i \in \mathcal{R}} \rho_i \quad (3)$$

be the respective centroids of the Blue and Red Agents' phases. If the respective populations are *phase locked* internally, i.e. $\beta_i \approx \beta_j, \forall i, j \in \mathcal{B}$ and $\rho_i \approx \rho_j, \forall i, j \in \mathcal{R}$, then the difference between the centroids can be defined in a time-invariant manner

$$\Delta := C_B - C_R, \quad (4)$$

where C_B and C_R are defined in (3). Having a time-invariant, non-zero Δ can be interpreted as external phase locking between populations. Finally, the degree of synchronisation within a given population is captured via the (local) Kuramoto Order parameters,

$$O_B := \frac{1}{N} \left| \sum_{i \in \mathcal{B}} e^{j\beta_i} \right| \quad \text{and} \quad O_R := \frac{1}{M} \left| \sum_{i \in \mathcal{R}} e^{j\rho_i} \right|, \quad (5)$$

where j denotes the value $\sqrt{-1}$.

3   Game-Theoretic Formulation

The adversarial nature of the Blue versus Red interaction and the associated strategic decisions immediately motivate a game-theoretic perspective to the Boyd-Kuramoto model presented in the previous section. Given the novelty of combining game theory with the Boyd-Kuramoto model and as a starting point, a static, 2-Player, nonzero-sum, strategic (non-cooperative) game [3] is formulated next.

The two players of the game constitute the player set $\mathcal{P} := \{Red, Blue\}$ representing the respective set of networked agent populations $\mathcal{R}, \mathcal{B}$ along with their adjacency matrices R, B. The cyclic decision process of each individual agents is described by the respective Boyd (OODA) cycle as described in Kuramoto Eq. (1). In the game, the players Blue and Red decide on their lead/lag targets $\phi \in [0, \pi]$ and $\psi \in [0, \pi]$, respectively. The outcome of the player decisions are captured by the pair of utility functions $U_B(\phi, \psi)$ and $U_R(\phi, \psi)$, which will be defined later. The resulting game is formally defined by the tuple $\mathcal{G} := <\mathcal{P}, (\phi, \psi), (U_B, U_R)>$.

In this game, once the players decide on their respective targets ϕ and ψ, the Boyd-Kuramoto model (1) is computed numerically over a fixed time-horizon. It is important to note that the equations may not converge to a point or even a limit cycle in certain cases, and may exhibit chaotic behaviour. While it may be in the interests of one side to drive the other into chaos, the concept that one side is *collectively ahead of the collective decision cycle of the other* (as is articulated by Boyd when generalising from one-on-one adversarial engagement) implies a certain level of coherence - namely internal phase locking - in both Blue and Red decision making. This leads us to a particular formulation of the utility functions; for the alternative - forcing dislocation in the other side - there is little meaning of being ahead of the other's decisions. To capture the existence or the lack of internal phase locking in agent populations, the order parameters in (5) are used. If O_B or O_R is larger than a threshold value, e.g. 0.9, then an approximate internal phase lock is said to be achieved [8], which is consistent with numerical observations of phase trajectories. Once the players have internal phase locking, then the difference (4) between centroids (3) becomes time-invariant and meaningful. Note that, if there is no internal phase locking even for one player (population), then the phases of agents of that population are time-varying. In that case, it is impossible to talk about a meaningful phase difference Δ between the Red and Blue centroids.

In light of the discussion above, one possible set of utility functions for the players are

$$U_B(\phi, \psi) = \begin{cases} -(\Delta(T) - \phi)^2 & \text{, if } O_B(T) > 0.9, O_R(T) > 0.9 \\ -100 & \text{, otherwise} \end{cases} \tag{6}$$

and

$$U_R(\phi, \psi) = \begin{cases} -(-\Delta(T) - \psi)^2 & \text{, if } O_B(T) > 0.9, O_R(T) > 0.9 \\ -100 & \text{, otherwise} \end{cases} \tag{7}$$

Here, T denotes the finite time horizon over which the Boyd-Kuramoto model (1) is solved numerically, and $O_B(T)$ and $O_R(T)$ are calculated using Kuramoto model average results over $[T/4, T]$. The value -100 is chosen as a large negative value to express undesirability of outcomes when $O_B(T) < 0.9$ or $O_R(T) < 0.9$, i.e. there is no tangible internal phase locking in Blue or Red player agent populations.

Definition 1. *A specific Boyd-Kuramoto Game $\mathcal{G}$ is played between the two adversarial Players $\mathcal{P} := \{Red, Blue\}$. Each player represents a set of networked agent populations with their decision cycles described by the Boyd-Kuramoto model in (1), which is computed over the time horizon $[0, T]$. The players Blue and Red decide on their lead/lag targets $\phi \in [0, \pi]$ and $\psi \in [0, \pi]$. The outcome of the player decisions are captured by the pair of utility functions $U_B(\phi, \psi)$ and $U_R(\phi, \psi)$ given in (6) and (7), respectively. Then, the game is defined by the tuple $\mathcal{G} := <\mathcal{P}, (\phi, \psi), (U_B, U_R)>$*

The Nash Equilibrium (NE) is used in this paper as the main game solution concept. A Nash Equilibrium is formally defined as the set of player strategies and associated utilities, where no player can gain by deviating from the NE when all other players play their own NE strategies. It corresponds to a fixed point as well as the intersection point of the best responses of players [3]. It is worth noting that bi-matrix games always have a solution in mixed strategies, corresponding to a probability distribution over the actions (pure strategies) [3].

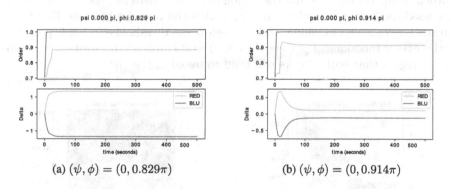

(a) $(\psi, \phi) = (0, 0.829\pi)$ (b) $(\psi, \phi) = (0, 0.914\pi)$

Fig. 2. Plots of Δ and Order for values approaching instability.

4   Numerical Analysis of the Boyd-Kuramoto Game

4.1   Properties of the Underlying Boyd-Kuramoto Model

Prior to discussing the specific game results, some considerations on the Kuramoto model dynamics are offered. Depending on the pair of values (ψ, ϕ),

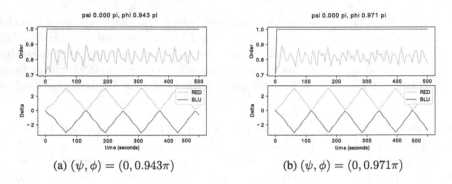

(a) $(\psi, \phi) = (0, 0.943\pi)$ (b) $(\psi, \phi) = (0, 0.971\pi)$

Fig. 3. Plots of Δ and the Order Parameter for oscillatory/unstable values.

the Kuramoto model presents stable, oscillatory, or chaotic behaviour. An illustrated example of this behaviour around the values $(\psi, \phi) = (0, 0.95\pi)$ is depicted in Figs. 2 and 3 using networks, frequency and coupling choices as given in [8].

For the parameters in the baseline scenario, the Order Parameter values of the Blue Player are close to full synchronisation, $O_R \approx 1$, across all the values of (ψ, ϕ) (*not illustrated*), while the Red Player Order Parameter values are close to synchronisation only in the corner regions of (ψ, ϕ), close to $(0, 0)$ or (π, π) as illustrated in Fig. 4(a). Figure 4(b) shows the variance of O_R and highlights the (ψ, ϕ) regions where the system exhibits oscillatory or unstable behaviours as studied in [8]. We observe that the region of (ψ, ϕ) where the system presents an increased oscillatory behaviour coincides with the region where the Red Order Parameter O_R is at a minimum and well below the threshold 0.9 that is penalised in the utility functions of players, $U_B(\phi, \psi)$ and $U_R(\phi, \psi)$. It constitutes, therefore, a region that both players will tend to avoid in the game.

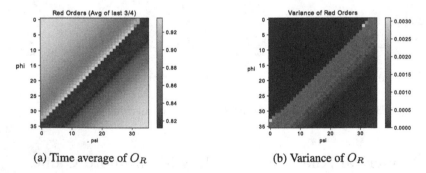

(a) Time average of O_R (b) Variance of O_R

Fig. 4. Red Player Order values and their variance for $(\psi, \phi) \in \{0, \frac{\pi}{36}, ..., \frac{n\pi}{36}, ..., \frac{35\pi}{36}, \pi\}$. (Color figure online)

4.2   Nash Equilibrium Solution in Baseline Scenario

As a baseline scenario for the numerical analysis of the game defined in the previous section, the following parameters have been selected in continuity with the previous studies [6]:

- The Blue network has 21 nodes in a complete 4-ary Tree configuration and the Red network has the same number of (21) randomly connected nodes.
- The interaction network involves the leaves of the Blue Tree (Nodes 6–21) linked to the correspondingly labelled nodes of the random Red network.
- The natural frequencies ω and ν are randomly chosen from a $[0,1]$ interval with an average of 0.551329 for the Red agents and 0.503192 for the Blues.
- The coupling constants are $\zeta_R = 0.5$ for Red and $\zeta_B = 8$ for Blue, and the cross-coupling constants are $\zeta_{BR} = \zeta_{RB} = 0.4$.

The action spaces of the players are discretised to obtain a bi-matrix game. Specifically, each player has 36 strategies available, i.e. the player's respective phase lag targets ϕ and ψ are discretised in uniform 36 bins of size $\pi/36$ within the interval $\{0, \pi\}$. The number 36 is chosen for its divisibility and taking into account computational constraints.

The Kuramoto model (1) is solved for every pair of

$$(\psi, \phi) \in \{0, \frac{\pi}{36}, \dots, \frac{n\pi}{36}, \dots, \frac{35\pi}{36}, \pi\}.$$

The utility functions $U_B(\phi, \psi)$ and $U_R(\phi, \psi)$ are calculated accordingly using (6) and (7), and provide the entries of the respective utility matrices (Fig. 5).

Even though the Boyd-Kuramoto model shows complex dynamic behaviour (as discussed above) depending on the desired phase lags (ψ, ϕ), the associated static 2-Player nonzero-sum strategic (non-cooperative) game as formulated in Sect. 3 admits a pure strategy Nash Equilibrium that is mostly insensitive to the model parameters, except the intrinsic frequencies ω_i and ν_j of the Blue and Red populations.

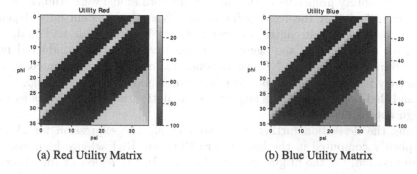

(a) Red Utility Matrix   (b) Blue Utility Matrix

Fig. 5. Red and Blue player utilities in the baseline scenario. (Color figure online)

For the baseline set of parameters, the player utilities are illustrated in Fig. 5. The game admits then a single pure-strategy Nash Equilibrium as shown in Table 1(a). To interpret this result, we first need to appreciate that the maximum reachable utility for a player is equal to zero, that is when the difference (4) between centroids (3) of the system is exactly equal to the desired phase for the player. The calculated NE is therefore stating that the Red player could enforce a very slight phase advantage to the player Blue. In order to increase the resolution of the game discretisation in the area of the utility matrices where the NE emerges, a new simulation has been executed with the same parameters and $(\psi, \phi) \in \{0, \frac{\pi}{80}, ..., \frac{n\pi}{80}, ..., \frac{79\pi}{80}, \frac{\pi}{4}\}$. The results, shown in Table 1(b), confirm that Red player can actually enforce a slight lag of $\frac{\pi}{20}$ to the Blue player and gains an advantage at the unique NE of the game. It is also worth noting that this NE solution is at the same time a Dominant Strategy Equilibrium and the game does not admit any other mixed strategy equilibrium solution.

Table 1. Nash Equilibrium strategies of players with refinement (zoom-in at location) in the baseline scenario.

(a) NE strategy		
Player	Strategy	Payoff
Red	$\psi = \frac{2\pi}{36}$	−0.00033
Blue	$\phi = 0$	−0.02598
(b) Refined NE		
Player	Strategy	Payoff
Red	$\psi = \frac{1\pi}{20}$	0
Blue	$\phi = 0$	−0.02784

5   Analytic Study of the Game Solution

In [8], the stability properties of the Boyd-Kuramoto model were studied, where it was identified that the fixed point of the dynamical system only depends on the cross-coupling strengths and connectivity between Blue and Red, and the native frequencies of the agents. The sensitivity analysis conducted next in Sect. 6 indicates that the NE also depends mainly on these parameters, and is relatively insensitive to the network structures and internal couplings of the Blue and Red populations. This suggests an analytic study of the NE is feasible through approximation.

Using the derivation further elaborated in [6], the expression for Δ may be explicitly computed in the limit where Blue and Red achieve high internal synchronisation, i.e. the origin, as indeed occurs in the region of the observed NE $(\phi^*, \psi^*) = (0, \frac{\pi}{20})$ here.

Using the analysis from [8] and [6], we obtain

$$\Delta = \varrho + \sin^{-1}\left(\frac{\mu}{\sqrt{\mathcal{S}^2 + \mathcal{C}^2}}\right) \tag{8}$$

$$\varrho = \tan^{-1}(\mathcal{S}/\mathcal{C}) \tag{9}$$

$$\mathcal{S} = d_T^{(BR)}\left(\frac{\zeta_{BR}\sin\phi}{N} - \frac{\zeta_{RB}\sin\psi}{M}\right) \tag{10}$$

$$\mathcal{C} = d_T^{(BR)}\left(\frac{\zeta_{BR}\cos\phi}{N} + \frac{\zeta_{RB}\cos\psi}{M}\right) \tag{11}$$

$$\mu = \bar{\omega} - \bar{\nu}, \tag{12}$$

where Δ was defined in (4), $d_T^{(BR)}$ is the number of links between Blue and Red, and $\bar{\omega}, \bar{\nu}$ are the mean intrinsic frequencies within the Blue and Red populations. From the baseline scenario chosen in Sect. 4, $d_T^{(BR)} = 16, \mu = -0.048$.

Substituting the expression above for Δ in the utility functions for Blue and Red, given in (6), (7), and the parameter choices from Sect. 4 results in an approximation of player utilities in the stable region, and is shown in Fig. 6. The figure also depicts the unconstrained best responses of the players superimposed as lines corresponding to $\partial U_B/\partial\phi = \partial U_R/\partial\psi = 0$, and the numerically obtained unique NE in the baseline scenario. As expected, the NE sits on the line of optima for Red at the edge of the feasible region for Blue, namely $\phi = 0$. Moreover, any increase of ϕ results in decreasing utility - confirming that Blue cannot improve their outcome. The utility functions of the players at the NE solution are further depicted in Fig. 7.

In the region around the origin where the Boyd-Kuramoto dynamics are stable, the expression for Δ given in (8) can be linearised with respect to ϕ and ψ around the point $(0,0)$. In fact, expanding the derivatives $\partial U_B/\partial\phi, \partial U_R/\partial\psi$ and extracting the roots of $\partial U_B/\partial\phi = 0 = \partial U_R/\partial\psi$ leads to the following closed form solution for the Nash equilibrium:

$$\phi^* = 0, \psi^* = -\frac{(\zeta_{BR} + \zeta_{RB})\sqrt{d_T^2(\zeta_{BR} + \zeta_{RB})^2 - N^2\mu^2}\arcsin\left(\frac{N\mu}{d_T(\zeta_{BR}+\zeta_{RB})}\right)}{\zeta_{BR}\sqrt{d_T^2(\zeta_{BR} + \zeta_{RB})^2 - N^2\mu^2} + N\mu\zeta_{RB}\arcsin\left(\frac{N\mu}{d_T(\zeta_{BR}+\zeta_{RB})}\right)}. \tag{13}$$

With the respective parameter values inserted the non-zero phase evaluates to $\psi^* = 0.156688$, consistent with the previously obtained numerical result, $\pi/20$. This analytical expression of the NE allows us to observe that the critical factor in generating the asymmetry between Blue and Red is μ, the difference between mean frequencies in the two populations.

6   Sensitivity Analysis of the Boyd-Kuramoto Game

The Boyd-Kuramoto Game defined in Sect. 3 is further analysed numerically in order to gain insights into the solutions as well as their sensitivity to the underlying game parameters. The underlying Boyd-Kuramoto model naturally

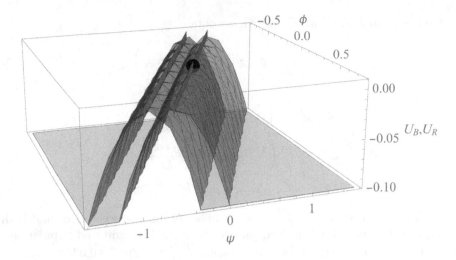

(a) Utility functions of Blue and Red Players around the origin.

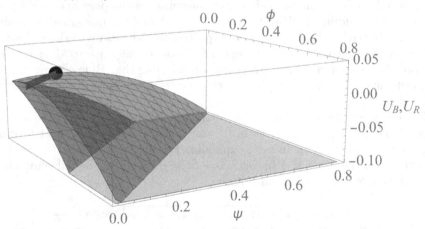

(b) Utility functions over the decision region (positive quadrant) near origin.

Fig. 6. Utility functions of Blue and Red Players calculated using the Δ expression in (8). The superimposed lines represent the best responses of the players and the black point is the Nash equilibrium. (Color figure online)

plays a significant role in the game outcomes. Therefore, four additional scenarios have been explored changing one parameter at a time from the baseline scenario in Sect. 4. Specifically,

2. Scenario decreases the blue coupling constant (ζ_B) from 8 to 2 to "loosen" the coupling of the ordered network.

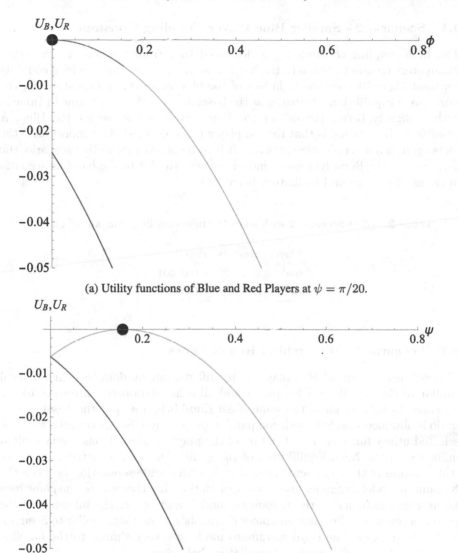

(a) Utility functions of Blue and Red Players at $\psi = \pi/20$.

(b) Utility functions of Blue and Red Players at $\phi = 0$.

Fig. 7. Utility functions of Blue and Red Players calculated using the Δ expression in (8) at the Nash Equilibrium, $(\phi^*, \psi^*) = (0, \frac{\pi}{20})$. (Color figure online)

3. Scenario modifies the red network, from random to "hierarchic" (quasi 4-ary matrix).
4. Scenario swaps the natural frequencies ω, ν of the Blue and Red player agent populations.
5. Scenario increases the average natural frequency gap between the Blue and Red populations.

6.1   Scenario 2 - Smaller Blue Player Coupling Constant

The blue coupling constant ζ_B is decreased to 2 from 8 where all the other parameters remain identical to the baseline scenario. Lowering the blue coupling constant should loosen the tightness of the blue network. In this scenario, the same Nash Equilibrium strategies as the baseline scenario are obtained (Table 2) with a slightly better pay-off for the Red player and worse for the Blue. A possible interpretation is that the red player can enforce slightly more easily the phase gap to a less rigid blue network. It is to be noted that in this scenario, the dynamics of the Boyd-Kuramoto model are very similar to the baseline scenario in terms of pattern and oscillatory behaviour.

Table 2. NE in Scenario 2 with a smaller blue coupling constant of $\zeta_B = 2$.

Player	Strategy	Payoff
Red	$\psi = \frac{2\pi}{36}$	−0.00001
Blue	$\phi = 0$	−0.03018

6.2   Scenario 3 - Hierarchical Red Network

The network matrix of Red player is modified from random to a hierarchical similar to the one of the Blue player and all other parameters are reset to the baseline. In this scenario, the same Nash Equilibrium as per the baseline scenario is obtained (Table 3) with comparable player pay-offs. Apparently, with the selected utility function, the structure of the player's network has a very limited influence on the Nash Equilibrium of the game. This can be attributed to the static nature of the game and the underlying time-scale separation between the Kuramoto model dynamics and game formulation. In other words, the game uses an averaged outcome of the Kuramoto model, and hence, the influence of the player networks on the game outcomes diminishes. Note that, similar to Scenario 2, the dynamics of the Boyd-Kuramoto model are very similar to the baseline scenario in terms of pattern and oscillatory behaviour.

Table 3. NE in Scenario 3 with hierarchical Red network

Player	Strategy	Payoff
Red	$\psi = \frac{2\pi}{36}$	−0.00011
Blue	$\phi = 0$	−0.02846

6.3   Scenario 4 - Swapping Red and Blue Player Population's Natural Frequencies

The natural frequencies of Blue player population ω are swapped with those of the Red player population ν in order to investigate the impact of natural frequencies on game outcomes. In the baseline scenario, those frequencies are not symmetric and randomly selected from an interval $[0, 1]$ with different means: $mean(\omega) = 0.5032$ and $mean(\nu) = 0.5513$. The natural frequencies can be interpreted as an input to the Kuramoto system (1).

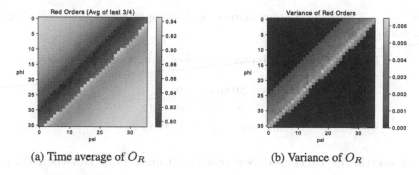

(a) Time average of O_R (b) Variance of O_R

Fig. 8. Red Orders and their variance for $(\psi, \phi) \in \{0, \frac{\pi}{36}, ..., \frac{n\pi}{36}, ..., \frac{35\pi}{36}, \pi\}$ (Color figure online)

As a first observation after solving the Boyd-Kuramoto model for this scenario, we realise that the system dynamics are significantly influenced by the change. While the blue orders are still close to full synchronisation ($O_R \approx 1$) across all the values of (ψ, ϕ) (*not illustrated*) and the red orders are still close to synchronisation only in the corner regions, we note that the region of (ψ, ϕ) for which the system presents oscillatory or unstable properties is displaced compared to the anti-diagonal and with a significant increase of variance all around the anti-diagonal as illustrated in Fig. 8 compared to the baseline scenario (Fig. 4). Figure 9 shows the utilities for Red and Blue players, which also reflects similar displacement compared to the baseline scenario (Fig. 5).

As an important second observation, when solving the game for Nash Equilibrium in this scenario, we note an inversion of winner in the game as illustrated in Table 4. The calculated Nash Equilibrium shows now the Blue player being able to enforce on the Red player a small phase gap of $\frac{3\pi}{36}$ with a symmetric payoff compared to the baseline scenario. Considering that the swap of frequencies between blue and red is actually reversing the asymmetry of frequencies between players, it appears that the asymmetry of the natural frequencies is playing an important role. Specifically, the 'faster' player in average can enforce a small phase lag to the 'slower' player.

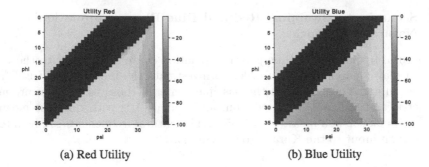

(a) Red Utility   (b) Blue Utility

Fig. 9. Red and Blue player utility matrices with swapped natural frequencies. (Color figure online)

Table 4. Nash Equilibrium - scenario 4 - swapped frequencies

Player	Strategy	Payoff
Red	$\psi = 0$	-0.06512
Blue	$\phi = \frac{3\pi}{36}$	-0.00019

6.4   Scenario 5 - Increased Natural Frequency Gap Between Players

In this scenario, the original frequency gap between red and blue player is doubled by maintaining the original blue frequencies as per baseline $mean(\omega_i) = 0.5032$ and shifting the red frequencies further so that $mean(\nu_j) = 0.5994$ from 0.5513 as per baseline value. Similar to the previous scenario, we observe that the system dynamic is significantly influenced by that change. The blue orders are still close to full synchronisation ($O_R \approx 1$) across all the values of (ψ, ϕ) (*not illustrated*) and the red orders are still close to synchronisation only in the corner regions. We note that the region of (ψ, ϕ), for which the system presents oscillatory or unstable properties, shows a significant increase in variance all around the anti-diagonal as illustrated in Fig. 10, when compared to the baseline scenario in Fig. 4. Solving the game for Nash Equilibrium, we observe that

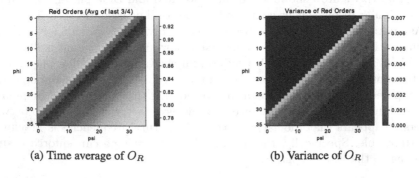

(a) Time average of O_R (b) Variance of O_R

Fig. 10. Red Orders and their variance in Scenario 5. (Color figure online)

the increase of Red player natural frequency allows it to slightly increase the imposed phase lag to $\frac{3\pi}{36}$ compared to $\frac{2\pi}{36}$ of the baseline scenario (Table 5).

Table 5. Nash Equilibrium in Scenario 5 with increased gap of frequencies

Player	Strategy	Payoff
Red	$\psi = \frac{3\pi}{36}$	−0.00049
Blue	$\phi = 0$	−0.11346

7 Conclusion

The initial results in this paper show that combining a game-theoretic approach with the Boyd-Kuramoto model is a fertile research direction for better understanding of strategic decisions in complex and competitive/adversarial systems.

The Boyd-Kuramoto Game studied as a baseline scenario in this report admits a unique pure Nash Equilibrium solution that has interesting implications. The subsequent sensitivity analysis provides additional insights. It is observed numerically that many parameters of the Kuramoto model affect the NE solution of the current game formulation much less than initially stipulated. This is arguably due to the time-scale separation between the underlying Kuramoto model and the static game built on top of it. While these parameters play an important role in the Boyd-Kuramoto dynamics, they do not directly affect (stable) stationary outputs. We expect this situation may change in dynamic game formulations, which may encourage more dynamic decisions than formulated in this paper. In terms of the dynamical system, it means that the behaviour of fluctuations - which are known to depend sensitively on the network structures [6] - will have an impact on the game dynamics. Numerical simulations also indicate that the natural frequencies of the agents have a significant impact on NE outcomes of the game. Again, this can be attributed to the fact that the natural frequencies have a direct impact on the underlying Kuramoto model's stationary solutions. From a decision-making perspective, this may be interpreted as investment in individual agents may pay-off more in certain cases than their organisational properties. All of these hypotheses are supported by the analytic solution obtained by linearisation around the origin. The analysis makes it explicitly clear that the static game outcomes depend on the cross-couplings and numbers of connections, and the asymmetry between mean frequencies in the two adversary populations.

There are multiple potentially promising future directions including investigation of different utility functions and dynamic game formulations that allow the players to change their decisions during the evolution of the underlying Boyd-Kuramoto models.

Acknowledgements. This research was supported through the Australian Defence Science and Technology Group's Strategic Research Initiative 'Modelling Complex Warfighting' and in part by the Australian Research Council Discovery Project under Grant DP140100819.

References

1. Acebrón, J.A., Bonilla, L.L., Pérez Vicente, C.J., Ritort, F., Spigler, R.: The Kuramoto model: a simple paradigm for synchronization phenomena. Rev. Mod. Phys. **77**, 137–185 (2005). https://doi.org/10.1103/RevModPhys.77.137
2. Alpcan, T., Başar, T.: Network Security: A Decision and Game Theoretic Approach. Cambridge University Press, Cambridge (2011)
3. Başar, T., Olsder, G.J.: Dynamic Noncooperative Game Theory, 2nd edn. SIAM, Philadelphia (1999)
4. Boyd, J.: A discourse on winning and losing. Maxwell Air Force Base, AL: Air University Library Document No. M-U 43947 (1987)
5. Montbrio, E., Kurths, J., Blasius, B.: Synchronization of two interacting populations of oscillators. Phys. Rev. E **70**, 056125 (2004)
6. Holder, A.B., Zuparic, M.L., Kalloniatis, A.C.: Gaussian noise and the two-network frustrated Kuramoto model. Phys. D: Nonlinear Phenom. **341**, 10–32 (2017). http://www.sciencedirect.com/science/article/pii/S016727891630152X
7. Kalloniatis, A.C.: On the 'Boyd-Kuramoto Model': Emergence in a Mathematical Model for Adversary C2 Systems (2012)
8. Kalloniatis, A.C., Zuparic, M.L.: Fixed points and stability in the two-network frustrated Kuramoto model. Phys. A: Stat. Mech. Appl. **447**, 21–35 (2016). http://www.sciencedirect.com/science/article/pii/S0378437115010092
9. Kuramoto, Y.: Chemical Oscillations, Waves and Turbulence. Springer, Berlin (1984). https://doi.org/10.1007/978-3-642-69689-3
10. Osinga, F.: Getting' a discourse on winning and losing: a primer on boyd's 'theory of intellectual evolution. Contemp. Secur. Policy **34**(3), 603–624 (2013). https://doi.org/10.1080/13523260.2013.849154

A Game Theoretic Analysis of the Twitter Follow-Unfollow Mechanism

Jundong Chen[1]($\boxtimes$), Md Shafaeat Hossain[2], Matthias R. Brust[3], and Naomi Johnson[1]

[1] Department of Math and Computer Science, Dickinson State University, Dickinson, ND 58601, USA
{jundong.chen,naomi.johnson}@dickinsonstate.edu
[2] Computer Science Department, Southern Connecticut State University, New Haven, CT 06515, USA
hossainm3@southernct.edu
[3] Interdisciplinary Centre for Security, Reliability and Trust (SnT), University of Luxembourg, Esch-sur-Alzette, Luxembourg
matthias.brust@uni.lu

Abstract. Twitter users often crave more followers to increase their social popularity. While a variety of factors have been shown to attract the followers, very little work has been done to analyze the mechanism how Twitter users follow or unfollow each other. In this paper, we apply game theory to modeling the follow-unfollow mechanism on Twitter. We first present a two-player game which is based on the Prisoner's Dilemma, and subsequently evaluate the payoffs when the two players adopt different strategies. To allow two players to play multiple rounds of the game, we propose a multi-stage game model. We design a Twitter bot analyzer which follows or unfollows other Twitter users by adopting the strategies from the multi-stage game. We develop an algorithm which enables the Twitter bot analyzer to automatically collect and analyze the data. The results from analyzing the data collected in our experiment show that the follow-back ratios for both of the Twitter bots are very low, which are 0.76% and 0.86%. This means that most of the Twitter users do not cooperate and only want to be followed instead of following others. Our results also exhibit the effect of different strategies on the follow-back followers and on the non-following followers as well.

Keywords: Social network · Game theory · Machine learning
Twitter classification · Twitter bot

1 Introduction

On the Twitter platform, a user can follow and can be followed by other users. In the early stage, Twitter allowed users to follow as many accounts as possible. Many Twitter users abused this and hoped to increase the number of followers through following thousands of users instead of creating engaging content.

© Springer Nature Switzerland AG 2018
L. Bushnell et al. (Eds.): GameSec 2018, LNCS 11199, pp. 265–276, 2018.
https://doi.org/10.1007/978-3-030-01554-1_15

Therefore, Twitter set up a limit for the number of accounts users could follow. The number of accounts that a Twitter user can follow cannot be 10% more than the number of followers, and also must be less than $2,000$. In 2015, Twitter changed this limit to $5,000$.

A follower's count is one of the three measures which indicate a Twitter users' popularity and prestige [1]. Researchers have been investigating the variables which effect the follower behavior of online social networks (OSN). Hutto et al. found that social behavior, message content, and network structure have different effects on determining other Twitter users to follow a Twitter user [2]. Liu et al. built a model for inferring the different speed of follower growth of different types of users on a microblog platform (Weibo) [3]. Mueller et al. integrated multiple predictors from the profile information of a Twitter user to predict the increase of the follower count [4].

Some researchers use Twitter bots to manipulate Twitter accounts to attract followers to create influential Twitter accounts. Those Twitter bots implement the functions of a regular Twitter account which is managed by a real user. Such functions include follow, unfollow, and post tweets, etc. A Twitter bot is a type of automated program which controls a Twitter account via Twitter API [5]. Messias et al. found that a Twitter account operated by a Twitter bot is capable of becoming influential by mimicking a real Twitter user through simple strategies, such as following back the followers and posting tweets about trending topics [6].

Game theory has been applied to model the influence from the interactions between OSN users on the privacy settings. Chen et al. modeled privacy settings of online social networks by a two-player game and an evolutionary game, and investigated the effect of network connectivity and attribute importance on the users' profile disclosure [7,8].

For this paper, we developed two game theoretic models to analyze the Twitter follow-unfollow mechanism. One is a two-player game, which is called Twitter follower's dilemma. The other one is called multi-stage follow-unfollow game, which allows players to play the game multiple rounds. Then, we designed two Twitter bot analyzers[1] which can adopt the strategies derived from the game models. Subsequently, the Twitter bot analyzers collect the response from other Twitter users when different strategies are adopted. Our approach not only explores the dynamics of the users when we follow them, but also discovers the impact of the adopted strategies on the non-following users. We call the users that follow us back the follow-back followers. The non-following followers mean the users we do not follow but they still follow us.

The remainder of this paper is as follows. In Sect. 2, we derive the two-player follow-unfollow game from the Prisoner's Dilemma game, and subsequently the multi-stage follow-unfollow game. In Sect. 3, we explain the method for classifying the collected Twitter users. The process of data collection, the experiment

---

[1] The two Twitter bot analyzers follow the same steps, except that Twitter bot 1 takes one more step, which is favoriting the tweets posted by other Twitter users. This is to investigate the effect of favoriting tweets on the number of followers.

design, and the algorithm that the Twitter bot utilizes in the multi-stage game are elaborated in Sect. 4. We present the results and the discussion in Sect. 5. We conclude this paper in Sect. 6.

2 Our Models

2.1 Twitter Follower's Dilemma

Our approach to model the Twitter followers' dynamics is inspired by the Prisoner's Dilemma [9]. The Prisoner's Dilemma models a situation with two completely rational individuals who might not cooperate, even if it is in their best interests to do so. It provides a framework for us to understand a balance lingering between cooperation and competition. In our game, there are two players which are the two Twitter users, user A and user B. In each step each user can choose between two strategies, "follow" and "unfollow". The goal of each player is to achieve high social popularity [10], which means to have as many followers as possible.

The payoff matrix for the Twitter follower's dilemma game is shown in Table 1. There are 4 cells in the matrix. Each cell has a tuple which represents the payoff for user A and user B, respectively. Therefore, we have 4 different combinations according to different strategies adopted by the two users, which are **(follow, follow)**, **(follow, unfollow)**, **(unfollow, follow)**, and **(unfollow, unfollow)**. We can summarize all these combinations into 3 different cases, because (follow, unfollow), (unfollow, follow) are symmetric.

Case I: This case refers to **(follow, follow)**. After one user follows the other one, and the other one also responds with a "follow" strategy, then each one receives a modest payoff, which is denoted by 2. This is because each user is followed by the other one but still needs to invest one count of "following".

Case II: This case refers to **(follow, unfollow)** or **(unfollow, follow)**. When one user follows the other one but the other one has not responded with the "follow" strategy, then the user being followed gets more benefit because this user can follow more accounts because of getting this following. In this case, we say that a user with an "unfollow" strategy achieves the highest payoff denoted by 3. However, the other user has the lowest payoff denoted 0. This is because one user invests one count of following but this following ends up with no increase in the number of followers, and this investment is in vain.

Case III: This case refers to **(unfollow, unfollow)**. This case may happen before or after these two users interact. Before they interact, no one takes any action, which means "unfollow" for each one. After one user follows the other one and later finds that the other one has no response, then this user decides to disconnect with the other one. In this case, each user receives a payoff of 1, which means no one reaches the highest payoff.

In this game we assume that one user decides to adopt any strategy by only considering the payoff from the social popularity. We know that in some situations we can already benefit from only following an account. For example, if one user is a fan of a celebrity from following the celebrity's account, this user receives the status update or some interesting activities. Or, if we follow some Twitter account of a news website, we receive interesting news or stories.

Table 1. Payoff matrix for the follower's Dilemma game.

		Twitter User B	
		Follow	*Unfollow*
Twitter User A	*Follow*	$(2, 2)$	$(0, 3)$
	Unfollow	$(3, 0)$	$(1, 1)$

2.2 Revised Twitter Follower's Dilemma

After considering the follower's benefit of receiving news, we can revise the game in Sect. 2.1, we obtain the following payoff matrix as shown in Table 2. We use N to represent the benefit from receiving news. In this payoff matrix, since we are using a Twitter bot as the player and the Twitter bot will not read the news received from other Twitter users, news is not considered as a benefit for the Twitter bot player.

Table 2. Payoff matrix for the revised Twitter follower's Dilemma.

		Twitter User	
		Follow	*Unfollow*
Twitter Bot	*Follow*	$(2, 2 + N)$	$(0, 3)$
	Unfollow	$(3, 0 + N)$	$(1, 1)$

2.3 Multi-stage Follow-Unfollow Game

One Twitter bot in our experiment plays multiple rounds of games with other Twitter accounts by taking follow or unfollow strategies in turns. This process is modeled as a multi-stage game as shown in Fig. 1.

In Fig. 1, $P1$ represents player 1 which is our Twitter bot, and $P2$ represents a group of other Twitter users which is player 2 in this multi-stage game. In this game, $P1$ at first follows all the Twitter users. Some of the Twitter users follow, and others unfollow. For those Twitter users who do not follow, after waiting for a period of time our Twitter bot gives up on them and unfollows them. For those Twitter users who follow our Twitter bot, we play more rounds of the game. After they follow us, our Twitter bot unfollows them with the intent of maximizing the payoff. Some Twitter users may notice that they are unfollowed and as a countermeasure they unfollow our Twitter bot. Other Twitter users may still follow. For those Twitter users who adopt the strategy of "unfollow" as the countermeasure, our Twitter bot attempts to regain them and follow them again. Some users may follow back again, however, other users may already lose their trust to our Twitter bot and never follow back.

The expected payoff of the Twitter bot is calculated by

$$U = 3\alpha\beta + 2 \cdot \alpha(1 - \beta)\gamma + 1 \cdot \alpha(1 - \beta)(1 - \gamma) + 1 \cdot (1 - \alpha) \tag{1}$$

where α, β, and γ represent the ratio of users who adopt a follow strategy at different stages, which are denoted in the parenthesis behind each strategy.

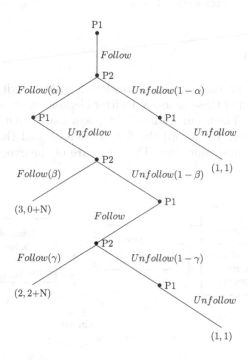

Fig. 1. Extensive form of the multi-stage follow-unfollow game.

3   Twitter User Classification

We use a machine learning method presented by Deshpande on PyCon France 2016 [11] to classify the Twitter users based on the tweets posted by each user.

In our experiment, we choose 8 typical categories, which include "Tech", "Business & CEOs", "Entertainment", "Science", "Fashion, Travel & Lifestyle", "Sports", "Music", and "Politics" as shown in Table 3.

Table 3. Category IDs and the corresponding category names.

Category ID	Category name
Category 0	Tech
Category 1	Business & CEOs
Category 2	Entertainment
Category 3	Science
Category 4	Fashion, travel & lifestyle
Category 5	Sports
Category 6	Music
Category 7	Politics

4   Experiment

In our experiment, we use a Twitter crawler to collect Twitter users' ids and retrieve tweets for all of these users. A Twitter classifier assigns all the users into different categories. Then, our Twitter bot plays game with the Twitter users in different categories. We record the list of friends[2] and that of followers for the Twitter bot account over time. The structure of the experiment is given in Fig. 2.

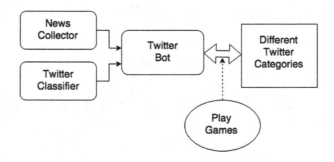

Fig. 2. Design of the Twitter bot analyzer.

4.1   Procedure of the Experiment

We proceed with the experiment by the following steps.

Step 1: Construct User Lists.

We use a Twitter crawler supported by Twitter API [12] to collect the user dataset. In this dataset, we apply the snow ball sampling technique [13] to collect

---

[2] The two terms, friends and followees, are interchangeable on Twitter. If we follow one user, we can call that user as a friend or followee of our Twitter account.

Twitter users' ids. Each time running the crawler, we start from a different Twitter account, which is called "seed". We collect the user lists by selecting different seeds at different locations in the world. Here, the different locations correspond to different geographic coordinates.

In total, we have collected 11,349 Twitter ids, and about 1,000 tweets for each Twitter user on average. We separate the Twitter ids in each category into two groups for two Twitter bots. Then, we mix the Twitter ids from different categories into one file and shuffle them. This is to ensure that each user is randomly assigned to each Twitter bot and also guarantee that the users in each category are equally assigned to the two Twitter bots.

Step 2: Post News from Different Sections.
Twitter bots follow the users in different lists and then post tweets with the news from different news sections from ABC news.

In order to make tweet contents attractive to different types of people, we post different types of tweets. We classify the Twitter accounts into 8 different categories as in [11,14], which are listed in Table 3. Everyday we crawl news on the website of ABC news[3]. There are only 5 sections of news which match the interests of 5 different types of twitter users, which are "Technology", "Entertainment", "Lifestyle", "Sports", and "Politics". We post that message from that sharing link obtained by clicking the Tweet share button.

Step 3: Twitter Bots Play a Game with Twitter Users.
As shown in Table 1, Twitter bots have two strategies to adopt. Depending on the different strategies taken by different users, the Twitter bots respond with different strategies.

The Twitter bot has to follow other Twitter accounts first to attract them in order to increase the number of followers as a consequence. After being followed, this bot will unfollow that follower to spare the quota of followings and spend this number to follow another new account. After this bot unfollows an account, that Twitter account may take a countermeasure to unfollow the bot. Then, this bot follows back again. The follow and unfollow strategies may be adopted by the bot and a Twitter account by turns in a couple rounds. We use a multi-stage game to model this process as shown in Fig. 1.

Step 4: Collect the Data About the Dynamics of Strategies of the Users.
Every day we check the followers and followees of our Twitter accounts. Then we draw a trend curve for each of our Twitter accounts to show the changes of the number of followers over time.

4.2   Twitter Bot Analyzer in the Multi-stage Game

We present the pseudocode in Algorithm 1 which describes the workflow of a Twitter bot in the multi-stage game. The whole process is divided into two

---

[3] http://abcnews.go.com.

phases. In all the phases, our Twitter bot keeps posting tweets of the news from different news sections collected from ABC news. After the Twitter bot starts following other users, we save the friends and followers of the Twitter bot account into separate files each day. The purpose of the first phase is to attract attentions of other Twitter users. In the second phase, the Twitter bot plays the game with other Twitter users by taking the strategies described in the model as shown in Fig. 1.

The first phase in the whole process is to follow Twitter users, and like the tweets from those users. With the limits from Twitter, we only follow 1000 accounts in one day, and favorite 1200 tweets per day and one tweet per minute. Twitter prohibits any aggressive following behavior, therefore we follow Twitter users with the amount below the limit.

In the second phase, we keep tracking the followers and unfollower in different stages and assign them into different sets. After waiting a period of time that our Twitter bot follows all the Twitter users that we have collected, some users follow back, and others do not. The followers are assigned into set S, and unfollowers into set S'. The Twitter bot unfollows all of them, which is a strategy decided in the algorithm. After passing through a date range from d_3 to d_4, the users that are still followers are assigned into set S_1, and unfollowers into set S_2. The bot follows the users in S_2 trying to regain their trust. After waiting a period, some users in set S_2 follow back and others do not. Then, we save the followers from the set S_2 to S_{21}, and unfollowers to S_{22}.

The set notations in the model and the algorithm are depicted in Fig. 3.

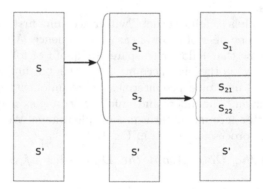

Fig. 3. Set structure diagram at different stages of the game.

5   Results and Discussion

The Twitter bot analyzers keep tracking the followers of our Twitter bots once we start the experiment as described in Algorithm 1. Figure 4a and b show the number of followers of the two Twitter bots changes over time. The figures only show the records after the Twitter bots finish following all the assigned Twitter

Algorithm 1. Twitter bot analyzer in the multi-stage follow-unfollow game

---

Input: Twitter accounts in 5 different categories
Output: Record of friends and followers of the twitter bot in each day

1: $countDays = d_0 - 1$
2: **for** each day in a date range $[d_0, d_1]$ **do**
3:     $countDays++$
4:     Tweet news from different news sections
5:     **if** Total number of followings less than 5000 **then**
6:         Follow each of the Twitter users, 1000 users per day
7:     **end if**
8:     Retrieve friends and followers ids
9: **end for**
10: **for** each day in a date range $(d_1, d_2]$ **do**
11:     $countDays++$
12:     Tweet news from different news sections
13:     **for** every minute in a total of 20 hours **do**
14:         Favorite a tweet for each of the Twitter users
15:     **end for**
16:     Retrieve friends and followers ids
17: **end for**
18: **for** each day in a date range $(d_2, d_3]$ **do**
19:     $countDays++$
20:     Retrieve friends and followers ids
21: **end for**
22: Save all followers in set S
23: Save all unfollowers in set S'
24: Unfollow the users in set S'
25: Unfollow the users in set S
26: **for** each day in a date range $(d_3, d_4]$ **do**
27:     $countDays++$
28:     Retrieve friends and followers ids
29: **end for**
30: Save the followers from set S to S_1
31: Save the unfollowers from set S to S_2
32: Follow the users in S_2
33: Retrieve friends and followers ids
34: Save the followers from set S_2 to S_{21}
35: Save the unfollowers from set S_2 to S_{22}
36: Unfollow the users in set S_{22}

---

users. Because of the limit from Twitter, each Twitter bot can only follow up to $5,000$ Twitter accounts in total and about $1,000$ per day. It takes 5 days to follow about $5,000$ Twitter users. Day 0 in Fig. 4 means the $5th$ day after the Twitter bots start following Twitter users.

Originally, there are $5,000$ Twitter ids in the list for each of the Twitter bots. However, in fact, Twitter bot 1 follows $4,981$ users, and Twitter bot 2 follows

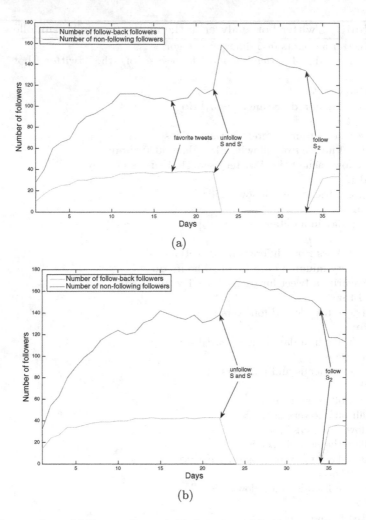

Fig. 4. The number of followers for each Twitter bot changes over time. (a) Twitter bot 1, (b) Twitter bot 2.

4, 980 users. This is because some of the accounts in the list are suspended or not used after we build the list, and no one can follow them.

To better show the exact values, we use Table 4 to list the number of users encompassed in different sets. The definitions of the sets are given in Sect. 4.2 and depicted in Fig. 3. The size of S and that of S' together are equal to the total number of Twitter users that a Twitter follows at the beginning of the experiment. Set S is divided into S_1 and S_2 depending on if they unfollow after the Twitter bots unfollow them. If they unfollow, then they are assigned to set S_2, otherwise remain in set S_1.

The first observation is that Figs. 4a and b exhibit almost the same change pattern for the number of followers. In each figure, there are two curves. One curve is for the number of followers who follow back, which is denoted as "number of follow-back followers". The other one is for the number of followers that our Twitter bots never follow, with the legend of "number of non-following followers". We find that at first both of the curves increase as time elapses. The number of non-following followers increases until the Twitter bots unfollow the Twitter users in set S and S'. In all the follow-back followers which are in set S, if the Twitter bots unfollow them, they unfollow our Twitter bots immediately. This is why in the table the size of the set S_1 for each bot is zero. This means that for these users they adopt the strategy "follow" if the adversary has a strategy "follow", and respond with an "unfollow" strategy to an "unfollow" strategy.

An interesting observation is that although Twitter bot 1 favorites the tweets of other users, the number of followers still shows almost the same change pattern. For both of the bots, the number of the non-following followers keeps increasing for a short period and then drops. This means that favoriting the tweets of other users has little effect on the change pattern of the number of followers.

The second observation is from Table 4, Twitter bot 1 only gains 38 follow-back followers after following 4, 980 users, and bot 2 gets 43 follow-back followers after following 4, 981 users. The follow-back ratio is 0.76% and 0.86% for Twitter bot 1 and 2, respectively. Both ratios are very low. This is not coincident and is explained by our Twitter follower's dilemma game model. Most of the Twitter users do not cooperate and they only want to be followed instead of following other users.

Table 4. The sizes of different sets at different phases of the game.

Set		S	S'	S_1	S_2	S_{21}	S_{22}
Size	Twitter bot 1	38	4, 942	0	38	33	5
	Twitter bot 2	43	4, 938	0	43	35	8

6   Conclusions

In this paper, we analyze the mechanism on Twitter about users following or unfollowing others. We propose a two-player game, which is called a Twitter follower's dilemma. In this game, each player has two strategies: follow and unfollow. Then, we design a multi-stage follow-unfollow game.

We also create two Twitter bot analyzers. The two analyzers prove that the finding from one analyzer is not coincident and furthermore, investigate the effect from favoriting tweets on the number of followers.

Two Twitter bots show the same change pattern for the number of followers. Another finding is that for all the follow-back followers, if we unfollow them, they unfollow us as a countermeasure. Our results show that the follow-back ratios are very low. Our results also show that favoriting tweets of other users has little effect on the number of followers. As a by-product, our results exhibit the change pattern for the number of non-following followers.

The approach presented in this paper provides a way to analyze and investigate the Twitter follow-unfollow mechanism and helps to optimize the design of a social network platform.

References

1. Cha, M., Haddadi, H., Benevenuto, F., Gummadi, K.P.: Measuring user influence in Twitter: the million follower fallacy, In: ICWSM (2010)
2. Hutto, C., Yardi, S., Gilbert, E.: A longitudinal study of follow predictors on Twitter. In: Proceedings of the SIGCHI Conference on Human Factors in Computing Systems, CHI 2013, pp. 821–830. ACM, New York (2013)
3. Liu, L., Song, D., Tang, J., Liao, L., Li, X., Du, J.: FriendBurst: ranking people who get friends fast in a short time. Neurocomputing **210**(C), 116–129 (2016)
4. Mueller, J., Stumme, G.: Predicting rising follower counts on Twitter using profile information. In: Proceedings of the 2017 ACM on Web Science Conference, WebSci 2017, pp. 121–130. ACM (2017)
5. Jajodia, S., Wang, H., Gianvecchio, S., Chu, Z.: Detecting automation of Twitter accounts: are you a human, bot, or cyborg? IEEE Trans. Dependable Secur. Comput. **9**, 811–824 (2012)
6. Messias, J., Schmidt, L., Oliveira, R., Benevenuto, F.: You followed my bot! Transforming robots into influential users in Twitter. First Monday **18** (2013)
7. Chen, J., Kiremire, A.R., Brust, M.R., Phoha, V.V.: Modeling online social network users' profile attribute disclosure behavior from a game theoretic perspective. Comput. Commun. **49**, 18–32 (2014)
8. Chen, J., Kiremire, A.R., Brust, M.R., Phoha, V.V.: A game theoretic approach for modeling privacy settings of an online social network. EAI Endorsed Trans. Collab. Comput. **1**(1–5), e4 (2014)
9. Surhone, L., Timpledon, M., Marseken, S.: Prisoner's Dilemma: Game Theory, Merrill M. Albert W. Tucker, Framing Device, Experimental Economics. Betascript Publishing (2010)
10. Moses, J.: The follower's dilemma, how game theory explains Twitter's most important feature. https://www.linkedin.com/pulse/followers-dilemma-how-game-theory-explains-twitters-most-moses. Accessed 1 Feb 2016
11. Deshpande, D.: Twitter user classification with gensim and scikit-learn. In: The Python Conference, France (2016)
12. Zafarani, R., Abbasi, M.A., Liu, H.: Social Media Mining: An Introduction. Cambridge University Press, Cambridge (2014)
13. Kay, M.: Generating a network graph of Twitter followers using python and networkx. http://mark-kay.net/2014/08/15/network-graph-of-twitter-followers/. Accessed 15 Aug 2014
14. Chen, J., Li, H., Wu, Z., Hossain, M.S.: Sentiment analysis of the correlation between regular tweets and retweets. In: Proceedings of the 16th IEEE International Symposium on Network Computing and Applications, pp. 1–5 (2017)

Game Theoretic Analysis of a Byzantine Attacker in Vehicular Mix-Zones

Nick Plewtong and Bruce DeBruhl[✉]

California Polytechnic State University, San Luis Obispo, USA
{nplewton,bdebruhl}@calpoly.edu

Abstract. Vehicular ad hoc networks (VANETs) promises to enable a wide-range of safety and efficiency improvements to our roads. To secure VANETs, they are often designed with authenticated communications that allows for verification of the sender. In order to enable authenticated communications without sacrificing user privacy VANET designers often employ pseudonyms, temporary identifiers that are tied to a single user. In order to maximize location privacy, vehicles must temporally coordinate pseudonym changes using a mix-zone strategy. However, to be effective mix-zones either require vehicles to cooperate or have greedy motivation. Previously, game-theoretic analysis of greedy nodes have developed equilibrium strategies. However, this work did not consider malicious Byzantine attackers who only desire to minimize system-wide location privacy. In this work, we design two Byzantine attackers that target location privacy in VANETs. The first, which we call a naïve attacker, never cooperates. The second, which we call a stealthy attacker, attempts to minimize system wide location privacy while not being detected. We simulate both of these attackers and show that an attacker can reduce location privacy in a mix-zone by up to 12%.

Keywords: VANET privacy · Insider threat · Pseudonyms

1 Introduction

There is increasing interest in intelligent transportation systems (ITS) to improve highway safety and efficiency. To make ITS a reality, Vehicular Ad-Hoc Networks, or VANETs [5,6,14], have been designed to enable vehicles to reliably communicate for various application including safety systems, like collision detection systems, and efficiency improvements, such as platooning. As vehicles move from autonomous to collaborative, VANETs will continue to become increasingly important [12].

Since VANETs deal with safety critical application, we must consider security and privacy in their design [11]. In this paper, we are particularly interested in the challenge of enabling verifiable, authenticated communications while allowing vehicles, and their passengers, to maintain location privacy [1,2,8,13]. Although this problem has analogies in WiFi and cellular (GSM, LTE), it differs in a few

© Springer Nature Switzerland AG 2018
L. Bushnell et al. (Eds.): GameSec 2018, LNCS 11199, pp. 277–295, 2018.
https://doi.org/10.1007/978-3-030-01554-1_16

important ways. First, VANETs require sharing real-time sensor and GPS data to properly function. Second, VANETs require vehicle to vehicle communications instead of all communications going to a router or basestation [13]. Therefore, VANETs need to have authenticated communications to other vehicles without depending on a central controller.

A naïve implementation for authenticated communications could use a combination of public key signatures and unique identifiers. Whenever a vehicle broadcasts a packet, they would include the signed unique identifier. However, if a passive adversary can eavesdrop on these packets at multiple locations they can track IDs and by proxy track the associated owner. This naïve system can lead to a loss of location privacy which many people would consider unacceptable.

One technique to combat a passive adversary is for vehicles to change their identifiers to temporary, verifiable identifiers known as pseudonyms [9]. This allows for a vehicle to not use a static unique identifier the entire time but to change its pseudonym in order to mitigate passive tracking. However, if a vehicle changes pseudonyms naïvely their various pseudonyms can be reassociated [3]. To mitigate reassociation attacks, it has been proposed that vehicles coordinate pseudonym switches to a limited spatial or temporal zone, otherwise known as a mix-zone [1]. When all vehicles cooperate in a mix-zone, then the maximum location privacy can be achieved in the system. However, a vehicle may be greedy and decide to not cooperate to avoid resource-intensive pseudonym changes [8].

Previously, a game-theoretic model was developed that analyzed greedy vehicles in a mix-zone [8]. In this previous work, the authors primarily focused on selfish vehicles. We modify this work to include an adversarial player, or attacker, who desire to minimize system-wide location privacy. In this work, we develop a byzantine attacker that aims to minimize location privacy. In the remainder of this paper, we model this attacker and then analyze its impact on location privacy of greedy vehicles.

A naïve implementation of a byzantine attacker may choose to continuously defect to cause minimum location privacy. However, this implementation could be detected by an observant defender. We develop a detection scheme by averaging the ratio of observed vs expected cooperating vehicles over times. If this value ever exceeds a threshold then we trigger an alert to the network operator or authorities. It is important to note that our detection scheme does not identify which vehicle(s) is attacking but only that there is an attack occurring.

Lastly, we develop an attack in which a malicious vehicle minimize the location privacy of the system while avoiding detection. This attacker adds in a penalty to correct for the chance of detection and makes decisions accordingly. We then simulate the naïve attacker, stealthy attacker, and detection algorithm.

To summarize, we make the following contributions in this paper.

- We create a formal game model for the impact of a byzantine attacker on location privacy in a VANET.
- We create a light-weight detection scheme to identify the existence of potential attackers.

- We design a naïve attacker that always defects and a stealthy attacker that only defects when it is improbable to be detected.
- We analyze our model in a 50-vehicle simulation and develop an optimal strategy for the stealthy attacker.
- Based on our simulation, we find a single attacker can decrease system-wide privacy by 0.6% while 5 attackers can decrease location privacy 2.6%.
- Based on our simulation, we also find that an attacker in a single mix-zone can decrease the potential location privacy in the mix-zone by 12%

Overall, our results demonstrate the potential impact of a Byzantine attacks against location privacy. This can help guide future research in maintaining location privacy in a VANET.

The rest of the paper is organized as follows. In the remainder of this section, we introduce related work in game-theoretic analysis of VANETs. In Sect. 2, we introduce the system model we build on for modeling mix-zones. In Sect. 3, we define our defender model and the naïve attacker model. In Sect. 4, we develop a light-weight detection scheme as well as a stealthy attacker. In Sects. 5 and 6, we outline important aspects of our simulation and introduce our quantitative results. Lastly, in Sect. 7, we conclude this paper.

1.1 Related Work

Pseudonym switching and mix-zones have seen significant research including game-theoretic analysis [4,7–10,13]. Different pseudonym changing approaches [4] have been evaluated in order to determine problems and challenges that exist within each strategy. This has included a robust set of metrics to evaluate location privacy against reassociation attacks [7] and quantitative measure of location privacy [8]. Furthermore, some of these papers introduce the possible effects of adding adversaries to the VANET [10,15].

One important aspect of our work is the concept that vehicles will not always be cooperative. Previously, there have been proposals of greedy vehicles [8]. In this work, the authors describe a player that makes mix-zone decisions based on selfish interest instead of altruistic interest. This was counter to many previous models that explored fully cooperative networks of vehicles.

2   System Model

In this work, we consider a VANET where vehicles use pseudonyms to preserve location privacy. To coordinate pseudonym changes, vehicles use mix-zones, where sets of vehicles simultaneously change pseudonyms to mitigate reassociation attacks. When a vehicle in our system enters a mix-zone, they decides to either cooperate or defect. In this section, we discuss our general model and our quantitative location privacy formula.

2.1 General Mixed-Zone Model

Since the number of vehicles on a highway varies widely, we design our model with an adjustable number of vehicles. We denote the total number of vehicles in our model as N. During each time step, we use the following process to model vehicles participating in a mix-zone.

1. To form a mix-zone, vehicles are selected with a Bernoulli probability of p_{mix}. This results in a number of vehicles between 0 and N entering the mix-zone. We denote the number of vehicles entering the mix-zone as n.
2. After the vehicles enter the mix-zone, each vehicle independently decides to cooperate or defect.
3. Cooperating vehicles simultaneously change pseudonyms, making reassociation difficult.
4. Defecting vehicles take no action and keep their current pseudonym.
5. The vehicles then exit the mix-zone.

This mix-zone model is based on previous work that leveraged game-theory to optimize a greedy vehicle's behavior [8]. In Fig. 1, we illustrate this process for a 20 vehicle network where 10 vehicles enter a mix-zone. Out of the 10 vehicles in the mix-zone, 7 cooperate and change pseudonyms while 3 vehicles do not change their pseudonyms.

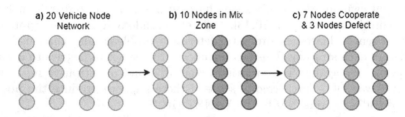

Fig. 1. In this figure, we illustrate our mix-zone model with a 20 vehicle system. 10 vehicles are selected to enter the mix-zone out of which 7 decide to cooperate.

2.2 Location Privacy Model

In order to assess player strategy in a mix-zone we need a quantitative model of location privacy. We use the previously developed logarithmic model [8]. Assuming n vehicles cooperate in the mix-zone then

$$LPM(n) = \log_2 n \, \forall n \geq 2, \tag{1}$$

where LPM represents the location privacy of cooperating vehicles after the mix-zone. For notational clarity, we denote the last mix-zone location privacy for vehicle i as LPM_i.

We note that if there is a fixed-number of cars in a system then (1) guarantees an upper bound on location privacy for a vehicle. For example, if there are 50 vehicles in the system then the upper bound of location privacy for any vehicle is $\log_2 50 = 5.64$. Conversely, the lower constraint on (1), represents the minimum number of vehicles for a meaningful mix-zone.

Another important aspect of location privacy model is how it degrades over time. We assume that when a vehicle does not change pseudonyms then they are more susceptible to being tracked. We model this loss in location privacy as a constant linear decrease, with a minimum of zero. This means that for each instance of a mix-zone, regardless of whether or not a vehicle in the network enters the mix-zone, cooperates or defects, there is a constant loss in location privacy. We model location privacy loss over time for vehicle i as:

$$LPLT_i(t) = x * (t - t_{s,i}) \tag{2}$$

where $LPLT$ is the location privacy loss over time, x is a constant for location privacy loss, t represents the time, and t_s represents the last pseudonym change time. Based on (2) and (1), we define a vehicle i's location privacy as

$$LP_i(t) = LPM_i - LPLT_i(t). \tag{3}$$

3 Greedy Defender and Naïve Attacker Model

In this section, we design two players for our model discussed in Sect. 2. The first player is a greedy defender that aims to maximize its own location privacy without concern of other vehicles' location privacy. The second player is an attacker that aims to minimize system-wide location privacy. In Sect. 4, we extend both of these players by considering a attack detection scheme.

3.1 Defender Model

We refer to benign vehicles as defenders and assume that they are greedy and not malicious. This means that defenders aim to maximize their own location privacy without concern for other vehicles' location privacy. It is important to note that we choose our defender strategy with the assumption that all vehicles are greedy.

Based on previous work [8], the behavior of a greedy vehicle in a mix-zone is as follows.

1. When a defender enters a mix-zone, it observes the number of vehicles in the mix-zone and its current location privacy.
2. The defender formulates the potential gain in location privacy based on a predictive model and the expected decision of the other vehicles.
3. The defender decides whether or not to cooperate in the mix-zone based on the calculated value. Since the defender is greedy the decision to cooperate or defect is simply choosing the larger location privacy value.

In our model, the defender's potential gain formulation is based on three variables.

1. The expected location privacy gained from cooperating with n vehicles in a mix-zone.
2. The current location privacy of the defender before entering the mix-zone, $LP_i(t)$, as defined in (3).
3. The cost it takes to change a pseudonym denoted by P_c.

We define the location privacy of a set of n vehicles cooperate in a mix-zone in (1). However, the location privacy gained after cooperating in a mix-zone depends on the number of cooperating vehicles. The defender does not know this value before making their decision so to make reasoned decisions about cooperation, they must predict an expected number of cooperating vehicles. This prediction function should be a probability function that takes into account the increased benefit to vehicles in large mix-zones. Considering this requirement, we model the expected probability of cooperation as

$$EPC(n) = \frac{\log_2 n}{\log_2 N} + \psi \, \forall \, n \geq 1, \, n \leq N. \tag{4}$$

EPC represents the expected probability of cooperation of the vehicles in the system, n represents the number of vehicles that are in the mix-zone, and N represents the total number of vehicles in the VANET. We define ψ as a correction factor to account for the average location privacy of all vehicles over all time.

Using $EPC(n)$ we calculate the expected number of cooperating vehicles as

$$n_{coop} = EPC(n) * n. \tag{5}$$

Using (1), we then calculate the expected location privacy after the mix-zone as

$$ELP = \log_2 n_{coop}. \tag{6}$$

Lastly, there exist costs when changing pseudonyms [8]. This includes the cost of acquiring new pseudonyms, the cost of updating the routing and addressing tables of radios, and the cost of remaining silent while inside a mix-zone [8]. We combine these costs into a single variable, P_c.

We combine these three values to define the defender's expected payoff function as:

$$ELPG_i = ELP - LP_i(t+1) - P_c \tag{7}$$

where $ELPG_i$ represents the expected location privacy gained for a vehicle i.

A defender evaluates (7) to determine if they will cooperate. The defender chooses to cooperate if $ELPG_i > 0$ and defects otherwise. The defender's actual location privacy after the switch is defined using (1) and the actual number of cooperating vehicles, n_{actual}.

3.2   Naïve Attacker Model

For our initial attack model, we consider attackers that aim to minimize overall system location privacy. We refer to this attacker as a naïve attacker. We consider a variable number of attacker vehicles to be able to model attacks where one attacker attempts to degrade privacy. This also allows us to consider a more sophisticated attack with multiple participants, either willing or unwilling and coordinated or uncoordinated. For example we could consider the scenario when vehicles that are members of a botnet which mount a coordinated attack.

Besides the obvious difference in objective, the attacker differs in scope from the defending vehicles. While the defender vehicles are greedy and only care about their privacy, an attacker has a system-wide goal. By lowering the location privacy, the network becomes more susceptible to location tracking by privacy violating attacks.

Since the naïve attacker only desires to minimize privacy, they always defect. We define the expected attacker's payoff as follows.

$$ETLPL_{naive} = (n_{coop} - a) * (LPM(n_{coop}) - LPM(n_{coop} - a)) \tag{8}$$

where $ETLPL_{naive}$ represents the total location privacy lost for all cooperating defenders in the mix-zone with naïve attackers, n_{coop} is defined in (5), a represents the number of attacker vehicles that defect in the mix-zone, and LPM is defined in (1). After the game is played, the actual total location privacy loss is defined as

$$ATLPL_{naive} = n_{actual} * (LPM(n_{actual} + a) - LPM(n_{actual})), \tag{9}$$

where n_{actual} is the number of cooperating vehicles, a represents the number of attacker vehicles that defect in the mix-zone, and LPM is defined in (1).

In Sect. 4, we define a second goal for the attacker to minimize probability of detection.

3.3   Initial Game Model

Since the naïve attacker will always choose to defect, the initial game is based soley on the decisions of the greedy defenders. We discuss the impact of the the naïve attacker in Sect. 6.

4   Detection Protocol and Stealthy Attacker

In this section, we design a detection scheme to look for abnormal behavior in VANETs. We then expand the player model we presented in Sect. 3 to include this detection scheme.

4.1   Detection Scheme

To enable the detection scheme, we add a fourth step to the defenders mix-zone model presented in Sect. 3.1. While exiting a mix-zone, defenders observe how many vehicles cooperate, n_{actual}, out of the number of vehicles in the mix-zone, n.

By comparing the actual and expected number of cooperating vehicles, n_{actual} and n_{coop} respectively, we design a lightweight anomaly detection. In Sect. 6, we show that this scheme can effectively detect the naïve attacker presented in Sect. 3.2.

The detection scheme requires each defending vehicle to maintain a suspicion level, S. We denote the suspicion level for car i as S_i. After participating in a mix-zone, the vehicle updates its suspicion formula

$$S_i \mathrel{+}= \frac{n_{actual} - n_{coop}}{n_{coop}}. \tag{10}$$

After updating the suspicion level, the defender tests whether it is above a threshold S_{max}. Unless the defenders suspicion level is above the threshold, they have no knowledge of the existence of an attack. Once an attack is suspected, the attacker alerts the network operator which can take further action.

Consider the attacker from Sect. 3.2 who always defects. In our model, this causes a loss of privacy across the whole system since the maximum achieved privacy of any mix-zone involving the attacker is lower. A defender involved in this mix-zone may observe a slightly lower than average ratio of cooperate to defect, but it is likely to be within statistically normal bounds. However, over time the attacker will be involved in more and more mix-zones. The attackers involvement, when averaged over multiple defenders eventually causes a statistically unlikely deviation in the cooperate to defect ration. The choice of suspicion threshold can be adapted depending on the application.

There are a variety of actions that a network operator can take when an attack is detected. It is also important that the network operator compares the alerts from multiple vehicles and mitigates false alarm attacks. However, in this paper, we do not design the defense action once an attack is detected. While this detection scheme can detect the naïve attack, we now design a stealthy attacker that attempts to avoid detection by this scheme.

4.2   Stealthy Attack Model

For our stealthy attacker, we add a second objective to our naïve attack model. Besides minimizing system-wide location privacy, the stealthy attacker aims to minimize the probability of detection by defending vehicles in the network. This second objective is important because a discovered attacker could be decommissioned and not have long term effectiveness.

A stealthy attacker chooses to cooperate in the case when it wants to avoid being detected by other defender vehicles. Another scenario for an attacker to cooperate is when the number of vehicles entering the mix-zone is low. Since an attacker wants to maximize the location privacy loss in a system, it wants to affect the highest of defender vehicles when it chooses a strategy. Therefore, cooperating when a low amount of vehicles are in a mix-zone will provide a lower benefit for defender vehicles than cooperating when a high amount of vehicles are in a mix-zone.

Conversely, a stealthy attacker chooses to defect in order to lower the location privacy gained by cooperating defender vehicles. However, because defender vehicles are predicting a certain amount of cooperation, any deviation of an attacker's choice in strategy from that of a selfish defender vehicle can raise suspicion that there is an anomaly in the network. Stealthy attackers must balance their mix-zone strategy in order to maximize the privacy loss while remaining undetected.

We therefore expand the naïve attackers expected payoff function as follows.

$$ETLPL_{stealth} = (n_{coop} - a) * (LPM(n_{coop}) - LPM(n_{coop} - a)) - D \quad (11)$$

where D is a value representing the level of possible detection the adversary is currently facing. The actual payoff for the attacker is represented as

$$ATLPL_{stealth} = n_{actual} * (LPM(n_{actual} + a) - LPM(n_{actual})) - D. \quad (12)$$

4.3   Game Model

In Fig. 2, we show the expected payouts for defenders and stealthy attackers in our model. We only show a single attacker and defender, however, this can be trivially expanded to n players. Given previous equations, a formal game model is created for the attack and defense scenario for the interactions that occur in a mix-zone.

		Defender	
		Cooperate	Defect
Attacker	Cooperate	ELPG, 0	$LP_i(t+1)$, 0
	Defect	ELPG, $ETLPL_{stealth}$	$LP_i(t+1)$, $ETLPL_{stealth}$

Fig. 2. In this figure, we show our formal game model for the stealthy attacker and defender. This is based on multiple equations including (11), (7), and (3).

5   Implementation

In this section, we describe the implementation and tuning of our simulation for analyzing our stealthy attacker and detection scheme. We define the following parameters for our model.

- Total Number of vehicles in the VANET N - The total number of vehicles in the VANET can be tuned to simulate various real-world scenarios.
- Cost of Pseudonym Change P_c - We estimate the cost of a pseudonym change as a constant value. The higher the cost of a pseudonym change, the higher the chance that a defender vehicle will not cooperate in the system due to the negative effect of the payout.

– Number of Mix-Zone Rounds t_{max} - The number of mix-zone rounds that occur in each simulation. During each round, vehicles enter the mix-zone, makes a decision on cooperation, and then exits the mix-zone.
– Probability of entering a mix-zone p_{mix} - the probability an individual vehicle in the VANET enters a mix-zone during a particular time slot. If $p_{mix} = .1$ and $N = 50$ then an average of 5 vehicles will enter the mix-zone during each round. However, the number of vehicles in each mix-zone can vary greatly.
– Location Privacy Loss Constant x - This value represents the constant location privacy loss for each vehicle. We assume that if the location privacy of a vehicle decreases to zero then it remains zero until it enters a mix-zone.
– Probability Error Adjustment ψ - The probability error adjustment represents a constant offset to the expected cooperation function (4).
– Minimum Number of Vehicles that Enter a Mix-Zone n_{min} - Since mix-zones with few vehicles do not increase location privacy, we bound the minimum number of vehicles in each mix-zone. If the number of vehicles is less than n_{min}, the mix-zone is considered invalid.

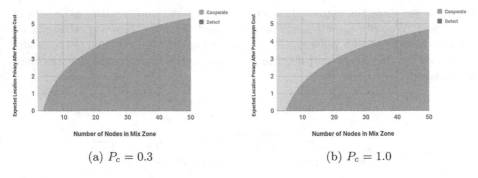

(a) $P_c = 0.3$ (b) $P_c = 1.0$

Fig. 3. In this figure, we show the defender's strategy based on the number of vehicles in the mix-zone. We show this with pseudonym change costs of $P_c = 0.3$ and $P_c = 1.0$.

5.1 Simulation of Greedy Defenders

We first model the behavior of greedy defenders to determine whether or not a defender vehicle cooperates or defects in various scenarios. In this model, we set the variables as shown in Table 1. The main value that we vary is the pseudonym change cost. In Fig. 3, we show the strategy of greedy defenders with varying pseudonym change costs. On the x-axis, we vary the number of vehicles in the mix-zone. If the current location privacy of the defender is in the green area, then the defender would choose to cooperate. If the current location privacy of the defender vehicle is in the red area, then the defender would choose to defect. In Fig. 3a, we show the simulation results with the cost of pseudonym change set to .3. In Fig. 3b, we show the simulation results with the cost of pseudonym change set to 1. Since the cost of pseudonym change is higher in Fig. 3b, there is a considerably larger probability that the defender defects in a mix-zone.

Table 1. Parameters for greedy defenders without attacker and $\psi = 0$.

Variable	N	P_c	t_{max}	p_{mix}	x	ψ	n_{min}
Value	50	0.3 and 1.0	10,000	0.1	0.1	0	5

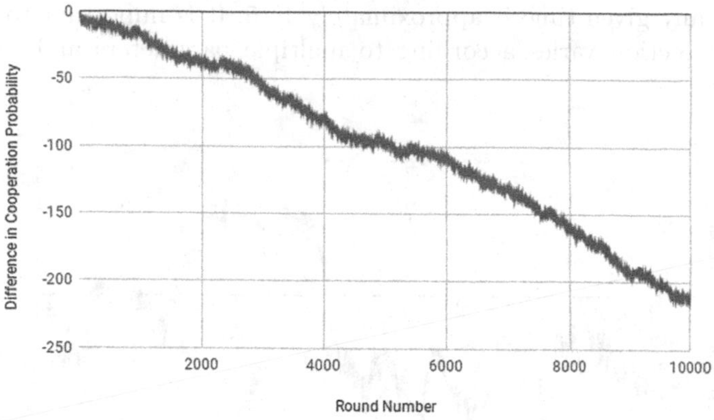

Fig. 4. In this figure, we show the difference between expected and observed probability of cooperation with $\psi = 0$ and no attackers.

5.2 Tuning Greedy Parameters

Next, we derive a value for ψ, the correction factor which equals average location privacy of vehicles in the system. First, we model a system with only selfish defender vehicles in the network using the parameters from Table 2. Each vehicle starts with a random location privacy between zero and the maximum location privacy. For each round, each vehicle has a chance of p_{mix} to enter the mix-zone. Each vehicle in the mix-zone evaluates its current location privacy and decides whether to cooperate. In Fig. 4, we show the variance of expected probability of cooperation and the actual number of cooperating vehicles with $\psi = 0$. If ψ is chosen correctly, it is expected that this value would vary considerably but, on average, fluctuate around zero. vary considerably from round to round, over time it should fluctuate around zero. However, with $\psi = 0$ the actual probability of cooperation is always greater than the expected to the error trends downwards. The average error per round 0.021, or 2.1% per round. Based on the initial simulation, we see the average location privacy of vehicles over time is 1.23. Because of this error, we derive a value for ψ to mitigate this shift.

Table 2. Parameters for greedy defenders without attacker for tuning ψ.

Variable	N	P_c	t_{max}	p_{mix}	x	ψ	n_{min}
Value	50	0.3	10,000	.1	.1	varies	5

We ran the experiment multiple times and observed a small variance of around .01. To empirically derive ψ, we run multiple simulations and adjust the error each time until the average probability difference per round is sufficiently close to zero. In Fig. 5, we show the average variance of actual and expected probability with $\psi = 1.15$. In this simulation, the average location privacy of a vehicle at any given time is approximately 1.15. It is important to note that the error correction varies according to multiple parameters and would need recalculated.

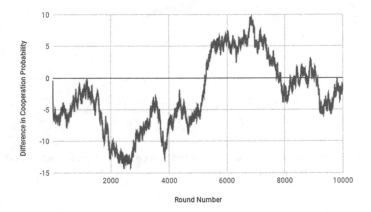

Fig. 5. In this figure, we show the difference between expected and observed probability of cooperation with $\psi = 1.15$ and no attackers.

Next, we run the simulation 30 times and average the error each round. In Fig. 6, we show the results for this test and can see that the results tend towards zero. The notable exception, is during the first rounds. This is due to the location

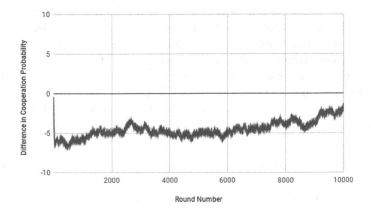

Fig. 6. In this figure, we show the average over 30 runs of the difference between expected and observed probability of cooperation with $\psi = 1.15$ and no attackers.

privacy initialization averaging around $\frac{\log_2 N}{2}$ instead of the stead state average of 1.15. Therefore, the vehicles are more likely to defect until the system reaches steady-state.

6   Results

In this section, we simulate attackers against the greedy defender tuned in Sect. 5.2. We add two variables to our previous model. First, the number of attackers in the system is denoted by a. Second, the suspicion level for the detection algorithm is denoted by S. We summarize the values used for our simulations in Table 3. In the remainder of this section, we first analyze a naïve attacker and then analyze our stealthy attacker.

Table 3. Parameters for our simulations that include an attacker.

Variable	N	P_c	t_{max}	p_{mix}	x	ψ	n_{min}	a	S
Value	50	0.3	10,000	0.1	0.1	1.15	5	1, 3, or 5	0.02, 0.01, or 0.005

6.1   Naïve Attacker

We first analyze the impact of an attacker that always defects. This allows us to establish a worse case baseline for the impact an attacker can have on location privacy. In Fig. 7, we plot the impact a group of 1 or 3 attackers, respectively, have on the system. As stated previously, since the expected location privacy loss is always positive then the attacker always defects.

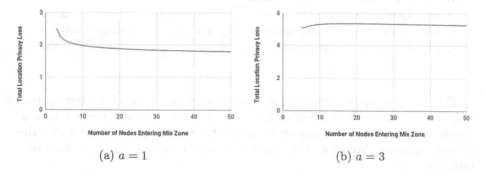

(a) $a = 1$ (b) $a = 3$

Fig. 7. In this figure, we show the expected location privacy loss caused by a group of a attackers in a 50 vehicle network.

In Fig. 8, we show the impact a single attacker that always defects has on the average observed cooperation. This chart has a clear negative trend with about .8 loss per round, compared to the average of 0 in Fig. 5. We summarize the results for similar experiments with 3 and 5 attackers in Table 4. As expected, the deviation in observed cooperation probability increases as the number of attackers increases. In Table 4, we also show the impact each naïve attack has on location privacy. As expected, more attackers in the system equates to a larger loss in location privacy.

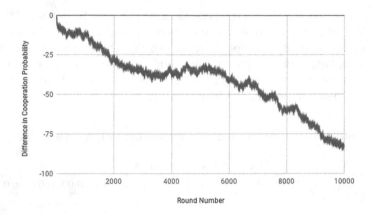

Fig. 8. Graph of Difference of Expected and Actual Probability of Cooperation with Probability Error Adjustment in a 50 Vehicle Network with 1 Attacker.

Table 4. Difference in actual and expected cooperation with various numbers of attackers in a 50 vehicle network.

Number of attackers	0	1	3	5
Deviation of cooperation (10,000 rounds)	−2.148	−82.257	−155.106	−274.080
Average deviation of cooperation per round	−0.000	−0.008	−0.016	−0.027
Location privacy impact (10,000 rounds)	0.000	235.177	687.625	1109.522
Average location privacy impact per round	0.000	0.024	0.069	0.111

The trend of naïve attackers causing observable variance in our system informed our detection scheme design in Sect. 4. We also use these values to choose suspicion levels, or threshold values for triggering notifications to the network operator. We choose our values based on Table 4 using the following intuitions.

– We design a **highly suspicious** group of defenders to detect a single vehicle that always defects. Since the average deviation of a single vehicle is −.008, we choose the threshold at −.005 to allow for a buffer.
– We design a **medium suspicious** group of defenders to detect when 3 attackers are always defecting. Since the average deviation for three vehicle is −.016, we choose a threshold of −.01 to allow for a buffer.

– We design a **low suspicious** group of defenders to detect when 5 attackers are always defecting. Since the average deviation for three vehicle is −.027, we choose a threshold of −.02 to allow for a buffer.

Next, we test whether our detection scheme falsely alarms with no attacker or misses actual attacks. We simulate the detection scheme with each suspicion level and various number of attackers 100 times. For each of these scenarios, we record the number of runs that trigger an alert and summarize this data in Table 5. We find that there is a 0% false positive rate implying when there is not an attack there are no alarms triggered. We also find that 5 attackers are always detected and 3 attackers are detected with the medium and high suspicion schemes. Lastly, we find that the single attacker is difficult to detect, only being found 80% of the time with the high suspicion detector.

Table 5. In this figure, we show the detection rate for the simulation with 0, 1, 3, and 5 attackers. This value is averaged over 50 runs, ignoring the initial 100 rounds where the simulation is stabilizing.

	Low suspicion	Medium suspicion	High suspicion
No Attacker	0%	0%	0%
1 Attacker	0%	4%	80%
3 Attackers	0%	100%	100%
5 Attackers	100%	100%	100%

Table 6. Effect of 1, 3 and 5 attackers on location privacy with optimal defect rate of 0.37 in a 50 vehicle network

Number of attackers	Effect on location privacy
1	0.6%
3	1.7%
5	2.6%

6.2   Stealthy Attack

In this section, we analyze the location privacy caused by a stealth attacker. For these simulations, we use the variables defined in Table 3. First, we consider the impact of an attacker that chooses to defects with a varying probability. We simulate each scenario 100 times for 10,000 mix-zone rounds. In Fig. 9, we show the percentage of attacks that were detected for each combination of defect rate, suspicion level, and number of attackers. In Fig. 10, we show the average total location privacy loss for a given defect rate and number of attackers.

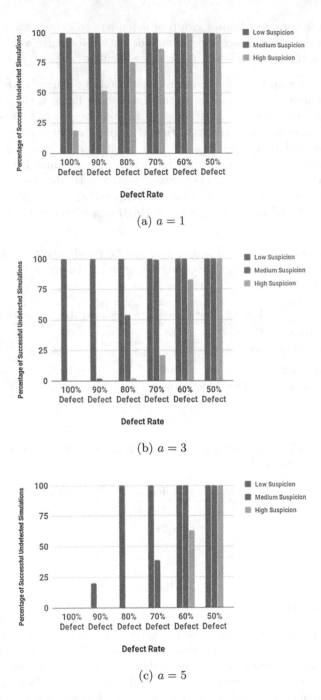

(a) $a = 1$

(b) $a = 3$

(c) $a = 5$

Fig. 9. In this figure, we show the percentage of attacks that go undetected in various scenarios. This include varying the number of attackers (a) and the probability an attacker defects.

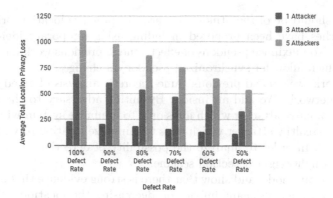

Fig. 10. In this figure, we show the total location privacy loss from an idael attacker in a 50 node network averaged over 100 simulations.

Next, we derive an ideal defect rate for the stealthy attacker. This should balance minimizing system wide location privacy and simultaneously minimizing probability of being detected. This equation is expanded as follows from (12):

$$ATLPL_{stealth} = [n_{actual}*(LPM(n_{actual}+a)-LPM(n_{actual}))-D]*(1-q). \quad (13)$$

Referring back to Eq. (12), in addition, q represents the probability of choosing the cooperate strategy and $1-q$ thus represents the probability of choosing the defect strategy. There is no representation of the cooperate strategy here as the payoff for choosing that is zero. From (13), an attacker should maximize its defect rate without D. For this particular model, D can maximize to $n_{actual}*$ $(LPM(n_{actual}+a)-LPM(n_{actual}))$ resulting to a $ATLPL = 0$ when maximized. The equation for D is as follows:

$$D = [n_{actual}*(LPM(n_{actual}+a)-LPM(n_{actual}))]*[\log_{10}(10*(1-q))] \quad (14)$$

Examining these Eqs. (13) and (14), these equations are combined to obtain an equation to maximize these requirements. The equation is as follows:

$$(1-\log_{10}(10*(1-q))*(1-q) \quad (15)$$

When finding the maximum point of this equation, it equates to a cooperation rate for the attacker of approximately 63%. That means that the supposed optimal defect rate for an attacker for maximizing location privacy loss and minimizing detecting is approximately 37%. Finally, we run the simulation with the ideal defect rate of 37%. We average the results over 10 simulations with 10,000 rounds and show the results in Table 6.

7 Conclusion

VANETs can enable considerable improvements in highway safety and efficiency. However, many of these applications are safety critical so maintaining security and privacy should be of the utmost concern. To preserve location privacy various approaches have been proposed including using temporary identifiers, or pseudonyms. To maximize pseudonym effectiveness, previous work has proposed mix-zones which allow for synchronized pseudonym changes.

In this work, we expand previous game-theoretic analysis of greedy nodes in a vehicular network. We add an insider Byzantine adversary to the mix-zone. This includes a naïve attacker which aims only to minimize system-wide location privacy and a stealthy attacker which aims to minimize location privacy without being detected. In order to analyze the possibility of detection, we also design and analyze a lightweight detection scheme.

We analyze our model and show that there is strong evidence that an internal attacker can have a significant impact on decreasing the location privacy of a VANET. This is true even if a small number of attackers are present. We also show our detection scheme can detect various attackers but a stealthy attacker can avoid detection.

7.1   Future Work

There are multiple future directions to expand this work.

Continued Research on Threat Models on Mix Zones. The game-theoretic analysis in this work ignores spatial locations of mix-zones when making decisions about cooperating or defecting. However, an attacker could be designed in a more robust simulation to attempt to minimize location privacy using various signals.

Continued Research on Detection Methods. As described in this thesis, one possible way to detect a malicious activity is to monitor the predictive model for any abnormalities. Further research could analyze other types of signals from vehicles that can indicate malicious behavior. In particular, a record of pseudonyms could be kept to look for any long-term pseudonym usage.

Implementing the Model in a Real-World System. To further test the validity of the model and the implementation concepts on real vehicles in a VANET can help us understand real-world attack surfaces. Further, expanded scaling of our model to encompass a network with more defenders and attackers could also provide insights into attacks and detection in real-world systems.

References

1. Beresford, A.R., Stajano, F.: Location privacy in pervasive computing. IEEE Pervasive Comput. **2**(1), 46–55 (2003)
2. Beresford, A.R., Stajano, F.: Mix zones: user privacy in location-aware services. In: Proceedings of the Second IEEE Annual Conference on Pervasive Computing and Communications Workshops, pp. 127–131, March 2004

3. Bindschaedler, L., et al.: Track me if you can: on the effectiveness of context-based identifier changes in deployed mobile networks. In: Proceedings of the 19th Annual Network and; Distributed System Security Symposium (NDSS 2012) (2012)
4. Boualouache, A., Senouci, S.M., Moussaoui, S.: A survey on pseudonym changing strategies for vehicular ad-hoc networks. IEEE Commun. Surv. Tutorials **PP**(99), 1 (2017)
5. Chaab, W.A., Ismail, M., Altahrawi, M.A., Mahdi, H., Ramli, N.: Efficient rate adaptation algorithm in high-dense vehicular ad hoc network. In: 2017 IEEE 13th Malaysia International Conference on Communications (MICC), pp. 23–28, November 2017
6. DeBruhl, B., Weerakkody, S., Sinopoli, B., Tague, P.: Is your commute driving you crazy?: a study of misbehavior in vehicular platoons. In: Proceedings of the 8th ACM Conference on Security and Privacy in Wireless and Mobile Networks, WiSec 2015, pp. 22:1–22:11. ACM, New York (2015)
7. Du, S., Li, X., Du, J., Zhu, H.: An attack-and-defence game for security assessment in vehicular ad hoc networks. Peer-to-Peer Netw. Appl. **7**(3), 215–228 (2014)
8. Freudiger, J., Manshaei, M.H., Hubaux, J.P., Parkes, D.C.: On non-cooperative location privacy: a game-theoretic analysis. In: Proceedings of the 16th ACM Conference on Computer and Communications Security, CCS 2009, pp. 324–337. ACM, New York (2009)
9. Gerlach, M., Guttler, F.: Privacy in VANETs using changing pseudonyms - ideal and real. In: 2007 IEEE 65th Vehicular Technology Conference - VTC2007-Spring, pp. 2521–2525, April 2007
10. Humbert, M., Manshaei, M.H., Freudiger, J., Hubaux, J.-P.: Tracking games in mobile networks. In: Alpcan, T., Buttyán, L., Baras, J.S. (eds.) GameSec 2010. LNCS, vol. 6442, pp. 38–57. Springer, Heidelberg (2010). https://doi.org/10.1007/978-3-642-17197-0_3
11. Luckshetty, A., Dontal, S., Tangade, S., Manvi, S.S.: A survey: comparative study of applications, attacks, security and privacy in VANETs. In: 2016 International Conference on Communication and Signal Processing (ICCSP), pp. 1594–1598, April 2016
12. Naz, F., Chowdhury, T.A., Sabah, S.H., Ferdous, H.S.: A study on the challenges and importance of vehicular network in the context of Bangladesh. In: 2011 IEEE Student Conference on Research and Development, pp. 265–270, December 2011
13. Qu, F., Wu, Z., Wang, F.Y., Cho, W.: A security and privacy review of VANETs. IEEE Trans. Intell. Transp. Syst. **16**(6), 2985–2996 (2015)
14. Wang, Y., Ho, I.W.H.: On-road feature detection and fountain-coded data dissemination in vehicular ad-hoc networks. In: 2017 IEEE 28th Annual International Symposium on Personal, Indoor, and Mobile Radio Communications (PIMRC), pp. 1–6, October 2017
15. Wang, Y., Yu, F.R., Huang, M., Boukerche, A., Chen, T.: Securing vehicular ad hoc networks with mean field game theory. In: Proceedings of the Third ACM International Symposium on Design and Analysis of Intelligent Vehicular Networks and Applications, DIVANet 2013, pp. 55–60. ACM, New York (2013)

Distributed Aggregative Games on Graphs in Adversarial Environments

Bahare Kiumarsi[✉] and Tamer Başar

Coordinated Science Laboratory, University of Illinois at Urbana-Champaign,
1308 West Main Street, Urbana, IL 61801, USA
{kiumarsi,basar1}@illinois.edu

Abstract. Existing solutions to aggregative games assume that all players are fully trustworthy for cooperative tasks or, in a worst-case scenario,
are selfish players with no intent to intentionally harm the network. Nevertheless, the need to believe that players will behave consistently exposes
the network to vulnerabilities associated with cyber-physical attacks.
This paper investigates the effects of cyber-physical attacks on the outcome of distributed aggregative games (DAGs). More specifically, we are
seeking to answer two main questions: (1) how a stealthy attack can
deviate the game outcome from a cooperative Nash equilibrium, and by
doing so, (2) by how much efficiency of a DAG degrades. To this end, we
first show that adversaries can stealthily manipulate the outcome of a
DAG by compromising the Nash equilibrium solution and consequently
lead to an emergent misbehavior or no emergent behavior. This study
will intensify the urgency of designing novel resilient solutions to DAGs
so that the overall network sustains some notion of acceptable global
behavior in the presence of malicious agents. Finally, we corroborate
and illustrate our results by providing simulation examples. Simulations
reveal that the adverse effect of a compromised agent is considerably
worse than that of a selfish agent.

Keywords: Distributed aggregative games · Adversarial environment

1 Introduction

Game theory has been widely and successfully employed in many applications to
model both selfish objectives of participants, as well as their global and common
objectives. Aggregative game is a special type of a game in which the objective
function for each agent depends on the local state of the agent (to fulfill an
individual selfish objective) as well as on an aggregate quantity of the network,

Research reported in this paper was sponsored in part by the Army Research Laboratory and was accomplished under Cooperative Agreement Number W911NF-17-2-
0196. The views and conclusions contained in this document are those of the authors
and should not be interpreted as representing the official policies, either expressed
or implied, of the Army Research Laboratory or the U.S. Government.

© Springer Nature Switzerland AG 2018
L. Bushnell et al. (Eds.): GameSec 2018, LNCS 11199, pp. 296–313, 2018.
https://doi.org/10.1007/978-3-030-01554-1_17

such as the average or sum of the states (actions) of all agents (to fulfill a common group objective) [1–7]. Applications span from demand-side management in smart grids [8–10] to charging coordination of plug-in electric vehicles [11,12], power and rate control in communication networks [13–15], and economic markets [16].

Most of the existing solutions to aggregative games employ a central coordinator that receives the decision variable of all the agents, calculates the aggregate decision, and broadcasts it to all agents. The agents then use this aggregate estimate to minimize their objective functions and consequently find a Nash equilibrium solution of the game. However, to avoid massive communication requirement and provide scalability, decision algorithms need to be distributed in the sense that each agent should take its decision using local information of its own state and its neighbors' states. In [17,18], a distributed method is presented to estimate the aggregate decision and consequently find the Nash equilibrium. Agents exchange their information with their neighbors to reach consensus on the aggregate value. The information flow of agents is captured by a graph structure. Such a game will be referred to as distributed aggregate game (DAG) on graphs, or simply, DAG, throughout the paper.

Existing Nash equilibrium solutions to DAGs, however, assume that all agents are fully trustworthy for cooperative tasks or, in the worst-case scenario, are selfish agents with no intent to intentionally harm the network. Nevertheless, information exchange on a communication graph in DAGs makes it vulnerable to malicious cyber-physical attacks and the need to believe that agents will behave consistently exposes the network to threats associated with cyber-physical attacks. In the case of a malicious attack, in contrast to selfish agents with no intent to intentionally harm the system, compromised agents (i.e., agents that are directly attacked) seek to intentionally maximize the damage inflicted on the network at all cost. Therefore, a thorough analysis of the outcome of a DAG in the presence of malicious agents is needed and this paper aims to take the first step toward that objective. In the paper, we focus on the role of the attacker and show that it can (1) compromise the Nash equilibrium solution through a malicious attack on only one agent and significantly degrade the overall performance of the network, and (2) make the network never reach a Nash equilibrium solution and thus lead to a non-emergent behavior significantly affecting the agents' interactions.

The rest of the paper is organized as follows. Section 2 introduces the basics of graph theory and DAG on graphs. Vulnerability of Nash equilibrium to the malicious behavior is discussed in Sect. 3. Simulation results and conclusions are provided in Sects. 4 and 5, respectively.

2   Preliminaries

This section introduces some basic concepts of graph theory and formulates the distributed aggregative games (DAGs) problem.

2.1 Graph Theory

A directed graph (digraph) is a pair $\mathcal{G} = (\mathcal{V}_\mathcal{G}, \mathcal{E}_\mathcal{G})$ where $\mathcal{V}_\mathcal{G} = \{\alpha_1, \alpha_2, \ldots, \alpha_N\}$ is a set of N nodes and $\mathcal{E}_\mathcal{G}$ is a set of edges. A typical element of $\mathcal{E}_\mathcal{G}$ is denoted (α_i, α_j), which is viewed as an edge connecting α_i to α_j. The corresponding adjacency matrix is denoted by $E = [a_{ij}]$ with weights $a_{ij} > 0$ if $(\alpha_j, \alpha_i) \in \mathcal{E}_\mathcal{G}$, and $a_{ij} = 0$ if $(\alpha_j, \alpha_i) \notin \mathcal{E}_\mathcal{G}$ and $a_{ii} = 0$ for all $i = 1, 2, \ldots, N$. The in-degree of node α_i is $d_i(\alpha_i) = \sum_{j=1}^{N} a_{ij}$. The diagonal in-degree matrix D is defined as $D = \text{diag}\{d_i(\alpha_i)\}$. The graph Laplacian matrix is defined as $L = D - E$. Graph $\mathcal{G}$ is strongly connected if α_i and α_j are connected for all distinct nodes $\alpha_i, \alpha_j \in \mathcal{V}_\mathcal{G}$. A graph is undirected if there is a directed path from α_i to α_j, then there is a directed path from α_j to α_i.

2.2 Aggregative Games

An aggregative game is modeled as a non-cooperative game being played among a set of agents $\mathcal{N} = \{1, \ldots, N\}$. Agent i takes action u_i to minimize its own objective function, which is dependent on the aggregate value (e.g., summation or average) of all agents.

The aggregate value (sum) of all agents is

$$\bar{u} = \sum_{j=1}^{N} u_j \tag{1}$$

Defining

$$\bar{u}_{-i} = \sum_{j=1, j \neq i}^{N} u_j \tag{2}$$

gives

$$\bar{u} = u_i + \bar{u}_{-i} \tag{3}$$

Then, the objective of agent i is given by [19]

$$\text{minimize} \quad J_i(u_i, \bar{u})$$
$$\text{subject to } u_{l_i} \leq u_i \leq u_{u_i} \tag{4}$$

where J_i is the cost function of agent i and u_{l_i}, u_{u_i} are allowable decision bounds for agent i. One example that fits in this framework is demand side management in the level of consumers for which the cost function of agent i is given as [20]

$$J_i(u_i, \bar{u}) = d_i(u_i - u_{d_i})^2 + l(\bar{u}) u_i \tag{5}$$

where the aggregate value $\bar{u}$ is the sum of the power consumption of all agents, and u_{d_i} is the nominal energy schedule required to provide the desired level of comfort for the consumer. Moreover, $l(\bar{u})$ is an increasing price function as a function of the aggregate value of power consumption. The first term in this cost function models the curtailment cost that each agent encounters for deviating from its state of comfort (the selfish objective) and the second term models the cost encounters for deviating from the optimal group behavior (the aggregate group objective).

The most common solution concept for an aggregative game is the Nash equilibrium solution. Letting the aggregate decision to be the sum value, the goal of the dynamic aggregative game is to assure that the result of minimization is Nash equilibrium, defined as follows [21].

Definition 1. *(Nash equilibrium:) An N-tuple of policies $\{u_1^*, \ldots, u_N^*\}$ is said to form a Nash equilibrium for an N-agent games if*

$$J_i(u_i^*, \frac{1}{N}u_i^* + \frac{1}{N}\bar{u}_{-i}^*) \leq J_i(u_i, \frac{1}{N}u_i + \frac{1}{N}\bar{u}_{-i}^*), \quad \forall u_i, \quad i = 1, \ldots, N \qquad (6)$$

and the N-tuple $\{J_1^*, \ldots, J_N^*\}$ denotes the Nash equilibrium outcome of the N-agent games.

In most of the existing solutions to aggregative games, a central coordinator receives the decision variable of all the agents, calculates the aggregative decision $\bar{u}$, and broadcasts it to all agents. However, to avoid massive communication requirement and provide scalability, decision algorithms need to be distributed in the sense that each agent should take its decision using local information of its own state and its neighbors' states. In [17,18], a distributed method is presented to estimate the aggregate decision and consequently find the Nash equilibrium. Agents communicate over a communication network specified by an undirected graph to estimate the aggregate decision. The aggregate decision can be found in a distributed fashion so that each agent exchanges its aggregate estimate with its own neighbors on the graph to achieve consensus on the aggregate decision.

Let U_i be the estimation of the aggregate decision for agent i. For the cost function (5), a distributed protocol can be designed as follows for agent i based on its own decision variable u_i and its estimate of the aggregate value [22]

$$\dot{U}_i = -U_i - \sum_{j=1}^{N} a_{ij}(U_i - U_j) - \sum_{j=1}^{N} a_{ij}(w_i - w_j) + Nu_i \qquad (7a)$$

$$\dot{w}_i = \sum_{j=1}^{N} a_{ij}(U_i - U_j) \qquad (7b)$$

$$\dot{u}_i = -\alpha_i(2d_i(u_i - u_{d_i}) + l_i(U_i) + u_i\frac{\partial l_i(U_i)}{\partial U_i}) \qquad (7c)$$

where α_i is a fixed positive parameter and w_i is an intermediate variable.

Remark 1. Note that the cost function (5) only shows up in (7c) and our following analysis is not limited to this type of cost function. In fact, as shown later, (7a), which is used to estimate the aggregate value, is independent of the cost function and can be adversely affected by the attacks, and consequently affect the decision making done in (7b). Moreover, under some conditions on the cost function, the existence of the Nash equilibrium of the aggregative game is guaranteed (See Assumption 1 in [19]).

Theorem 1. *Consider N agents with cost function defined in (5). Let their actions be updated based on (7a), (7b), (7c). Then, $U_i \to \sum\limits_{i=1}^{N} u_i$ and the agents reach a Nash equilibrium.*

Proof. See [22].

Remark 2. Distributed consensus algorithms over graphs, however, are vulnerable to cyber-physical attacks [23–32]. If agents are not empowered with built-in resilient functionalities, sophisticated attacks can be intentionally designed by an intruder to maximize the damage to the network and prevent the multi-agent system from accomplishing a desired emergent behavior. The attacker can leverage a single compromise into becoming a network-wide compromise; intact agents are not immune from disruption by attacks on compromised agents.

3   Vulnerability of Nash Equilibrium of DAG to Malicious Behavior

In this section, we analyze the effects of malicious behavior on the outcome of the aggregative games.

Before proceeding, we need the following definitions.

Definition 2. *Agent i is called intact agent if it is not directly under attack.*

Definition 3. *Agent i is called compromised agent if it is directly under attack and broadcasts disrupted information about its estimation of the aggregate value, i.e. U_i, to its neighbors.*

Definition 4. *Agent i is called selfish agent if it broadcasts the correct information about the estimation of the aggregate value, U_i, to its neighbors, but does not update its action u_i and choose it guided by its own selfish objective.*

Definition 5. *The matrices $\bar{L} \in \mathcal{R}^{N-1 \times N-1}$ and $\underline{L} \in \mathcal{R}^{N-M \times N-M}$ are subgraphs of Laplacian matrix $L \in \mathcal{R}^{N \times N}$ obtained by removing one node and M nodes, respectively.*

Definition 6. *The diagonal matrix $G = diag[g_1, \ldots, g_{N-1}]$ is called pinning matrix and $g_i \neq 0$ if there is a edge between node i (intact node) and node N (compromised node), otherwise $g_i = 0$.*

Remark 3. Note that a selfish agent only cares about its own selfish objective and does not care about the global group objective. However, in contrast to a compromised agent, it has no intention to harm the network.

Theorem 2. *Let*

$$Z_i = \sum_{j=1}^{N} a_{ij} (w_i - w_j) \tag{8}$$

with w_i defined in (7a), (7b), (7c). *Then* $\sum\limits_{i=1}^{N} Z_i = 0$, *and consequently, one has* $\sum\limits_{i=1}^{N} U_i \to N \sum\limits_{i=1}^{N} u_i$ *for* (7a), (7b), (7c).

Proof. Since the graph is undirected, if agent i communicates w_i to agent j (and consequently Z_i has $w_i - w_j$ component,) agent j communicates w_j to agent i (and consequently Z_j has $w_j - w_i$ component). Therefore, for every $w_i - w_j$, there is a corresponding $w_j - w_i$ that cancels it out in $\sum\limits_{i=1}^{N} Z_i$ and consequently $\sum\limits_{i=1}^{N} Z_i = 0$. Now, in the steady state $\dot{U}_i \to 0$ and $U_i = U_j \; \forall j$. Thus, for (7a), one has

$$U_i \to - \sum_{j=1}^{N} a_{ij} \left(w_i - w_j \right) + N u_i \tag{9}$$

Using the fact that $\sum\limits_{i=1}^{N} Z_i = 0$, this results in

$$\sum_{i=1}^{N} U_i \to N \sum_{i=1}^{N} u_i \tag{10}$$

This completes the proof.

Condition (10) is a necessary condition under which the agents reach consensus on summation, i.e. $U_i \to \sum\limits_{i=1}^{N} u_i$. In the following, it is shown that the attacker can cause violation of this condition and consequently results in a wrong consensus or no consensus at all, and thus adversely affects the effectiveness of the games solution. It is also shown that if one agent in the graph is a compromised agent and does not update its estimation about the aggregate value, the compromised agent acts as a leader and the aggregate value of all other agents reach consensus on its corrupted and wrong value, regardless of agents' actions. If more than one agent are compromised, then it is shown that agents do not reach consensus on a single value, but different values within the convex hull of compromised agents. Finally, it is also shown that this single compromised agent compromises the Nash solution and can either harm the agents' comfort level by consuming less than they are allowed to or significantly increase the price by consuming more than they have to for the case of demand response management.

Lemma 1. *Suppose $A \in \mathcal{R}^{n \times n}$ satisfies $A + A^T < 0$ and $B \in \mathcal{R}^{n \times n}$ is invertible. Then, the matrix*

$$H = \begin{bmatrix} A & B^T \\ -B & \mathbf{0} \end{bmatrix} \tag{11}$$

is Hurwitz.

Proof. See [33].

Theorem 3. *Suppose that agent N is a compromised agent and does not update its estimation about the aggregate value, i.e. $U_N(t) = U$. Then, the aggregate values in (7a), (7b), (7c) converge to U, regardless of the actions of all the agents, i.e, u_i $\forall i = 1, \ldots, N$.*

Proof. The distributed protocol (7a), (7b), (7c) in the presence of one compromised agent can be rewritten as

$$\dot{U}_i = - U_i - (\sum_{j=1}^{N-1} a_{ij} (U_i - U_j) + g_i (U_i - U)) -$$

$$(\sum_{j=1}^{N-1} a_{ij} (w_i - w_j) + g_i (w_i - w)) + Nu_i \qquad (12a)$$

$$\dot{w}_i = \sum_{j=1}^{N-1} a_{ij} (U_i - U_j) + g_i (U_i - U) \qquad (12b)$$

$$\dot{u}_i = -\alpha_i(2d_i(u_i - u_{d_i}) + l_i(U_i) + u_i\frac{\partial l_i(U_i)}{\partial U_i}) \qquad (12c)$$

where g_i is defined in Definition 6, and U and w are the constant values broadcasted by the compromised agent.

Define error quantities as $\bar{U}_i(t) := U_i(t) - U$ and $\bar{W}_i(t) := w_i(t) - w$. The error dynamics in compact form are given as

$$\begin{bmatrix} \dot{\bar{U}}(t) \\ \dot{\bar{W}}(t) \end{bmatrix} = \begin{bmatrix} -I - (\bar{L} + G) & -(\bar{L} + G) \\ \bar{L} + G & 0 \end{bmatrix} \begin{bmatrix} \bar{U}(t) \\ \bar{W}(t) \end{bmatrix} + \begin{bmatrix} -1U + Nu(t) \\ 0 \end{bmatrix} \qquad (13)$$

where $\bar{U} = [\bar{U}_1, \ldots, \bar{U}_{N-1}]^T$, $\bar{W} = [\bar{W}_1, \ldots, \bar{W}_{N-1}]^T$, and $u = [u_1, \ldots, u_{N-1}]^T$.

Define

$$K(t) = -1U + Nu(t) \qquad (14)$$

The transfer function from $\bar{U}(t)$ to $K(t)$ is given as

$$T(s) = \frac{\bar{U}(s)}{K(s)} = s[s^2I + (I + (\bar{L} + G))s + (\bar{L} + G)^2]^{-1} \qquad (15)$$

Note that $\bar{L} + G$ is positive definite and thus can be written as $\bar{L} + G = Q \Lambda Q^T$ with eigenbasis $Q = [q_1, \ldots, q_{N-1}]$ corresponding to real eigenvalues $\Lambda = diag[\lambda_1, \ldots, \lambda_{N-1}]$ with $\lambda_j > 0$ $\forall j = 1, \ldots, N - 1$. Using this fact, the transfer function (15) can be rewritten as

$$T(s) = \frac{\bar{U}(s)}{K(s)} = s[Q^T(s^2I + (I + \Lambda)s + \Lambda^2)Q]^{-1}$$

$$= \sum_{j=1}^{N-1} \frac{s}{s^2I + (I + \lambda_j)s + \lambda_j^2} q_j^T q_j \qquad (16)$$

Using (16), $\bar{U}(s)$ becomes

$$\bar{U}(s) = T(s)K(s) = \left(\sum_{j=1}^{N-1} \frac{s}{s^2 I + (I + \lambda_j)s + \lambda_j^2} q_j^T q_j\right) \frac{-1U + Nu}{s} \qquad (17)$$

Using Lemma 1 for (13), which shows that $T(s)$ is stable, and the Final Value Theorem, one has

$$\lim_{t \to \infty} \bar{U}(t) = \lim_{s \to 0} s\bar{U}(s) = \lim_{s \to 0} sT(s)K(s) = 0, \qquad (18)$$

which results in

$$U_i(t) \to U \qquad (19)$$

This completes the proof.

Remark 4. One might argue that if a compromised agent does not update its estimate of the aggregate value, it can be identified as a frozen agent and ignored by its neighbors. However, a compromised agent can for example change its update law to $\dot{x}_N = b\,exp(-a\,t)$, $x_N(0) = U$. It can be shown that, in this case, agents' estimates of the aggregate value will eventually converge to $U + b$, while the compromised agent is not frozen.

Theorem 4. *Let node N be a compromised agent. Then, on convergence, one has $\sum_{i=1}^{N} U_i \nrightarrow N \sum_{i=1}^{N} u_i$. Therefore, $U_i \to U \neq \sum_{i=1}^{N} u_i$.*

Proof. The equivalence of Z_i that shows up in (7a) and defined in Theorem 1 in the presence of one compromised node is

$$\sum_{j=1}^{N-1} a_{ij} (w_i - w_j) + g_i(w_i - w) \qquad (20)$$

where w is the value of the internal estimation variable of the compromised node. It was shown in Theorem 2 that $\sum_{i=1}^{N} \sum_{j=1}^{N} a_{ij} (w_i - w_j) = 0$. Letting agent N to be the compromised agent and broadcasting w, and ignoring the information it receives from its neighbors, one has

$$\sum_{i=1}^{N-1} \left(\sum_{j=1}^{N-1} a_{ij} (w_i - w_j) + g_i(w_i - w)\right) = \sum_{i=1}^{N-1} g_i(w_i - w) \neq 0 \qquad (21)$$

On the right-hand side of (21), the information flowed from neighbors of the compromised agent is ignored since it does not listen to its neighbors.

At the steady state, (12a), (12b), (12c) satisfies

$$\sum_{i=1}^{N-1} U_i = -\sum_{i=1}^{N-1} \left(\sum_{j=1}^{N-1} a_{ij}(w_i - w_j) + g_i(w_i - w)\right) + N \sum_{i=1}^{N-1} u_i \qquad (22)$$

Considering (21) in (22) and adding $U_N = U$ to both sides of (22) result in

$$\sum_{i=1}^{N} U_i = -\sum_{i=1}^{N-1} g_i(w_i - w) + N\sum_{i=1}^{N-1} u_i + U \tag{23}$$

Since in the steady state, $u_N \neq \frac{1}{N}(-\sum_{i=1}^{N-1} g_i(w_i - w) + U)$, then (23) results in $\sum_{i=1}^{N} U_i \not\to N\sum_{i=1}^{N} u_i$. On the other hand, $\sum_{i=1}^{N} U_i = N\sum_{i=1}^{N} u_i$ is a necessary condition for $U_i = \sum_{i=1}^{N} u_i$. Therefore, $U_i \not\to \sum_{i=1}^{N} u_i$ and this completes the proof.

Theorem 5. *Suppose that more than one agent in the network are compromised and do not update their estimation about the aggregate value. Then, the aggregate values in (7a) converge to a convex hull spanned by the value of the compromised agents regardless of the actions of other agents.*

Proof. The distributed protocol (7a), (7b), (7c) in the presence of multiple compromised agents can be rewritten as

$$\dot{U}_i = -U_i - (\sum_{j=1}^{N-M} a_{ij}(U_i - U_j) + \sum_{k=1}^{M} g_i^k(U_i - U_0^k)) -$$

$$(\sum_{j=1}^{N-M} a_{ij}(w_i - w_j) + \sum_{k=1}^{M} g_i^k(w_i - w_0^k)) + Nu_i \tag{24a}$$

$$\dot{w}_i = \sum_{j=1}^{N-M} a_{ij}(U_i - U_j) + \sum_{k=1}^{M} g_i^k(U_i - U_0^k) \tag{24b}$$

$$\dot{u}_i = -\alpha_i(2d_i(u_i - u_{d_i}) + l_i(U_i) + u_i\frac{\partial l_i(U_i)}{\partial U_i}) \tag{24c}$$

where M is the number of compromised agents, U_0^k, $k = 1, \ldots, M$ is the constant values broadcasted by the compromised agents, and $g_i^k \neq 0$ if there is a direct edge between node i and compromised node k, and $g_i^k = 0$ otherwise.

The distributed protocol (24a) and (24b) in compact form are written as

$$\dot{U} = -U - \sum_{k=1}^{M} H_k(U - 1_{N-M} \otimes U_0^k) -$$

$$\sum_{k=1}^{M} H_k(w - 1_{N-M} \otimes w_0^k) + Nu \tag{25a}$$

$$\dot{w} = \sum_{k=1}^{M} H_k(U - 1_{N-M} \otimes U_0^k) \tag{25b}$$

where

$$H_k = \frac{L}{M} + G_k$$

and

$$G_k = \begin{bmatrix} g_1^k & 0 & 0 & 0 \\ 0 & g_2^k & 0 & 0 \\ 0 & 0 & \ddots & 0 \\ 0 & 0 & 0 & g_{N-M}^k \end{bmatrix}$$

It is shown in [34] that the convex hull spanned by leaders is given as

$$C = \sum_{k=1}^{M} \left[\left[\left(\sum_{r=1}^{M} H_r \right)^{-1} H_k \mathbf{1}_{N-M} \right] \otimes U_0^k \right] \tag{26}$$

Define error quantities as $\underline{U}_i := U_i - C$ and $\underline{W}_i := w_i - \bar{w}$. The error dynamics in compact form are given as

$$\begin{bmatrix} \dot{\underline{U}}(t) \\ \dot{\underline{W}}(t) \end{bmatrix} = \begin{bmatrix} -I - H & -H \\ H & 0 \end{bmatrix} \begin{bmatrix} \underline{U}(t) \\ \underline{W}(t) \end{bmatrix} + \begin{bmatrix} -\mathbf{1}C + Nu(t) \\ 0 \end{bmatrix} \tag{27}$$

where $\underline{U}(t) = [\underline{U}_1(t), \ldots, \underline{U}_{N-M}(t)]^T$, $\underline{W}(t) = [\underline{W}_1(t), \ldots, \underline{W}_{N-M}(t)]^T$, and $H = \sum_{k=1}^{M} H_k$.

Introduce

$$\underline{K}(t) := -\mathbf{1}C + Nu \tag{28}$$

The transfer function from $\underline{U}(t)$ to $\underline{K}(t)$ is given by

$$\underline{T}(s) = \frac{\underline{U}(s)}{\underline{K}(s)} = s[s^2 I + (I + H)s + H^2]^{-1} \tag{29}$$

Similar to Theorem 3, the transfer function (29) can be rewritten as

$$\underline{T}(s) = \sum_{j=1}^{N-M} \frac{s}{s^2 I + (I + \eta_j)s + \eta_j^2} p_j^T p_j \tag{30}$$

where η_j, $j = 1, \ldots, N - M$ are the eigenvalues of matrix H, and p_j are the corresponding eigenvectors.

Using (15), $\underline{U}(s)$ is defined as

$$\underline{U}(s) = \underline{T}(s)\underline{K}(s) = \left(\sum_{j=1}^{N-M} \frac{s}{s^2 I + (I + \eta_j)s + \eta_j^2} p_j^T p_j \right) \frac{-\mathbf{1}C + Nu}{s} \tag{31}$$

Using Lemma 1 and the Final Value Theorem, one has

$$\lim_{t \to \infty} \underline{U}(t) = \lim_{s \to 0} s\underline{U}(s) = \lim_{s \to 0} s\underline{T}(s)\underline{K}(s) = 0, \tag{32}$$

which results in

$$U_i \rightarrow C \tag{33}$$

This completes the proof.

Remark 5. The compromised agents might be able to collude and communicate only with each other to reach consensus on a compromised value. This way, compromised agents will update their values to avoid being identified as frozen agents and the estimation of all agents will reach consensus on the consensus value of compromised agents.

Theorem 6. *Consider the aggregative game with cost function* (5) *and update law* (7a), (7b), (7c), *with the setting of demand side management. Let* $u^* = (u_1^*, u_2^*, \ldots, u_N^*)$ *be the Nash equilibrium solution to the game, when there is no compromised agent. Assume now that agent N does not update its value and broadcast* $U \neq U^* = \sum_{i=1}^{N} u_i^*$. *Then, the agents reach a compromised Nash solution, and*

(1) if $U \gg U^*$, *the level of comfort of the agents will be adversely and significantly harmed.*
(2) if $U \ll U^*$, *the agents will be misled to increase their consumption and the price will adversely be increased.*

Proof

(1) It was shown in Theorem 4 that $U_i \; \forall i = 1, \ldots, N-1$ converge to U, regardless of agents' actions. Therefore, in convergence, (7a)–(7c) actually minimize

$$J_i = d_i(u_i - u_{d_i})^2 + l(\mathrm{U}) \, \mathrm{u_i} \tag{34}$$

Since $l(\mathrm{U})$ is now independent of actions of other agents, they reach eventually their best response, which is decoupled from actions of other agents and is affected only by the action of the compromised agent. In the most extreme case, if $U \gg U^*$, $l(\mathrm{U}) = l_{\max}$ for all agents and then, (34) becomes

$$J_i = d_i(u_i - u_{d_i})^2 + l_{max} \, u_i \tag{35}$$

Therefore, agents will misleadingly think that the overall consumption and thus the price are high and take actions to minimize it by minimizing their comfort level.

(2) The same as (1), $l(\mathrm{U})$ is independent of actions of agents and is only controlled by the compromised agent. Agents will misleadingly think that the overall consumption and consequently the price are low and thus move toward maximizing their comfort levels. In the most extreme case,

$$J_i = d_i(u_i - u_{d_i})^2 + l_{min} \, u_i \tag{36}$$

This will significantly increase their price.

Remark 6. If there is more than one compromised agent, as shown in Theorem 5, agents do not reach consensus on the aggregate value and their estimations on the aggregate value converge to different values within the convex hull of compromised agents' values. In this case, the same as Theorem 5, one can show that the actions of agents are decoupled and $l(\bar{u})$ is only affected by compromised agents. In fact, agent i on convergence minimizes

$$J_i = d_i(u_i - u_{d_i})^2 + l(C_i)\,u_i \tag{37}$$

where $C_i \in C$ and $l(C_i)$ only depends on the compromised agents, but it is different for all agents. Therefore, the attackers can adversely affect comfort level of some of the agents and the price of some other agents at the same time.

Remark 7. Note that in the presence of an attack, if agent i cares mostly about the price, i.e. $d_i << 1$ in (5), then if U $>>$ U*, it will choose its minimum allowed action, which minimizes its comfort level. On the other hand, if agent i is selfish, i.e. $d_i >> 1$, it will not be affected by the attack. Moreover, if the compromised agent broadcasts a time varying signal such as a sinusoidal, agents will never reach an emergent behavior and their actions will fluctuate and not reach a steady state.

4   Simulation Results

In this section, we consider 5 agents that are communicating with each other through an undirected graph shown in Fig. 1. Each agent optimizes the cost function (5). Figure 2 shows the estimation of the aggregate value for all agents in the absence of compromised agents in the network. Figure 3 shows the actions of all agents in the absence of an adversary. It can be seen that from these results that all agents estimate the same aggregate value, and this aggregate value in Fig. 2 is the actual summation of the actions of agents in Fig. 3.

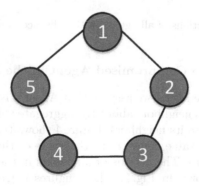

Fig. 1. Communication network between agents

Now, we consider the cases with compromised or selfish agents.

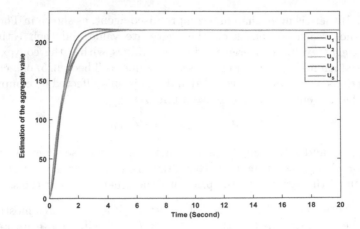

Fig. 2. Estimation of the aggregate value by all agents in the absence of an adversary in the environment

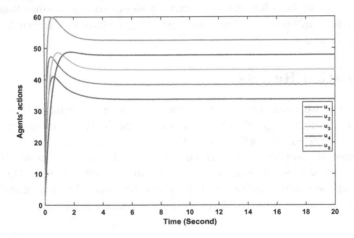

Fig. 3. The actions of all agents in the absence of an adversary

4.1   Presence of One Compromised Agent in the Network

In the scenario considered here, we assume that Agent 4 is a compromised agent and does not listen to its neighbors about the aggregate value. This agent always sends a fixed value 500 to its neighbors. Figure 4 shows that the estimates of all agents of the aggregate value converge to the value of the compromised agent, regardless of their actions. The actions of all agents in the presence of the compromised agent are shown in Fig. 5. These figures corroborate the results of Theorems 3 and 4. It is obvious that, compared to Figs. 2 and 3, the actions of agents are significantly affected by the compromised agent and their summation is not equal to the estimated aggregate value.

4.2 Presence of Multiple Compromised Agents in the Network

Here we assume that Agents 3 and 4 are compromised agents. Figures 6 and 7 show that the estimate of the aggregate value for all agents converge to different values within the convex hull spanned by the compromised agents. It can be seen that, compared to Fig. 3, the actions of agents are affected by the compromised agents.

4.3 Presence of a Selfish Agent in the Network

In this scenario, we assume that Agent 3 just cares about its selfish comfort objective and keeps its power consumption at 30 for all the time. Figures 8 and

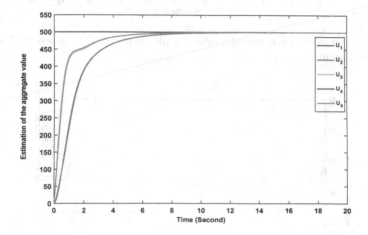

Fig. 4. Estimation of aggregate value by all agents in the presence of one compromised agent

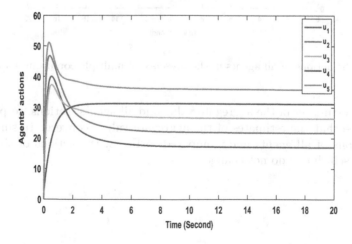

Fig. 5. The actions of all agents in the presence of one compromised agent

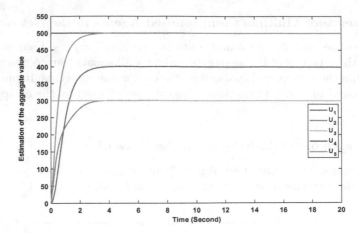

Fig. 6. Estimation of the aggregate value by all agents in the presence of multiple compromised agents

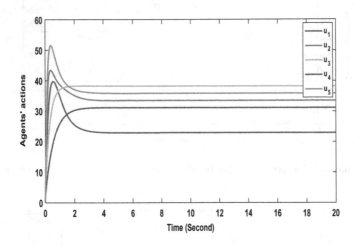

Fig. 7. The actions of all agents in the presence of multiple compromised agents

9 show the estimates of the aggregate value and all agents' actions, respectively. One can see that the estimates of the aggregate values converge to summation of the actions of all agents and, compared to Fig. 3, the actions of the agents except the selfish one do not change.

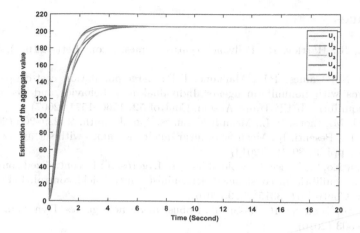

Fig. 8. Estimation of the aggregate value by all agents in the presence of a selfish agent

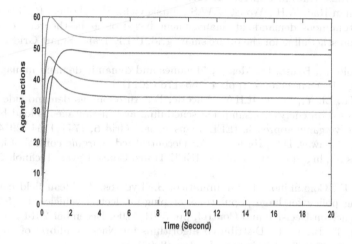

Fig. 9. The actions of all agents in the presence of a selfish agent

5   Conclusion

We have analyzed, in this paper, the adverse effects of malicious behavior on the Nash solution of distributed aggregative games (DAGs) on graphs. We have shown that the game solution can reach a consensus value that does not depend on agents' actions, and actually depends only on the broadcast value of the compromised agent. This study intensifies the urgency of empowering the agents with built-in resilient functionalities to decrease the damage to the network in the presence of unexpected behaviour. The next step would be to design resilient protocols to assure that all agents in the network operate in an acceptable level of functionality in the presence of cyber attacks.

References

1. Cornes, R., Hartley, R.: Fully aggregative games. Econ. Lett. **116**(3), 631–633 (2012)
2. Huang, M., Caines, P.E., Malhame, R.P.: Large-population cost-coupled LQG problems with nonuniform agents: Individual-mass behavior and decentralized Nash equilibria. IEEE Trans. Autom. Control **52**, 1560–1571 (2007)
3. Lasry, J.-M., Lions, P.-L.: Mean field games. Jpn. J. Math. **2**, 229–260 (2007)
4. Bauso, D., Pesenti, R.: Mean field linear quadratic games with set up costs. Dyn. Games Appl. **3**, 89–104 (2013)
5. Grammatico, S., Parise, F., Colombino, M., Lygeros, J.: Decentralized convergence to Nash equilibria in constrained deterministic mean field control. IEEE Trans. Autom. Control **61**, 3315–3329 (2016)
6. Bauso, D., Tembine, H., Başar, T.: Robust mean field games. Dyn. Games Appl. **6**, 277–303 (2016)
7. Moon, J., Başar, T.: Linear quadratic risk-sensitive and robust mean field games. IEEE Trans. Autom. Control **62**, 1062–1077 (2017)
8. Mohsenian-Rad, A.H., Wong, V.W.S., Jatskevich, J., Schober, R., Leon-Garcia, A.: Autonomous demand-side management based on game-theoretic energy consumption scheduling for the future smart grid. IEEE Trans. Smart Grid **1**, 320–331 (2010)
9. Bagagiolo, F., Bauso, D.: Mean-field games and dynamic demand management in power grids. Dyn. Games Appl. **4**, 155–176 (2014)
10. Chen, H., Li, Y., Louie, R.H.Y., Vucetic, B.: Autonomous demand side management based on energy consumption scheduling and instantaneous load billing: an aggregative game approach. IEEE Trans. Smart Grid **5**, 1744–1754 (2014)
11. Ma, Z., Callaway, D.S., Hiskens, I.A.: Decentralized charging control of large populations of plug-in electric vehicles. IEEE Trans. Control Syst. Technol. **21**, 67–78 (2013)
12. Parise, F., Colombino, M., Grammatico, S., Lygeros, J.: Mean field constrained charging policy for large populations of plug-in electric vehicles. In: 53rd IEEE Conference on Decision and Control, pp. 5101–5106, December 2014
13. Alpcan, T., Başar, T.: Distributed algorithms for Nash equilibria of flow control games, pp. 473–498. Birkhäuser, Boston (2005)
14. Başar, T.: Control and game-theoretic tools for communication networks. Appl. Comput. Math. **6**(2), 104–125 (2007)
15. Barrera, J., Garcia, A.: Dynamic incentives for congestion control. IEEE Trans. Autom. Control **60**, 299–310 (2015)
16. Kizilkale, A.C., Mannor, S., Caines, P.E.: Large scale real-time bidding in the smart grid: a mean field framework. In: 2012 IEEE 51st IEEE Conference on Decision and Control, CDC, pp. 3680–3687, December 2012
17. Koshal, J., Nedi, A., Shanbhag, U.V.: A gossip algorithm for aggregative games on graphs. In: 2012 IEEE 51st IEEE Conference on Decision and Control, CDC, pp. 4840–4845, December 2012
18. Swenson, B., Kar, S., Xavier, J.: Distributed learning in large-scale multi-agent games: a modified fictitious play approach. In: 2012 Conference Record of the Forty Sixth Asilomar Conference on Signals, Systems and Computers, ASILOMAR, pp. 1490–1495, November 2012
19. Koshal, J., Nedić, A., Shanbhag, U.V.: Distributed algorithms for aggregative games on graphs. Oper. Res. **64**(3), 680–704 (2016)

20. Parise, F., Gentile, B., Grammatico, S., Lygeros, J.: Network aggregative games: distributed convergence to Nash equilibria. In: 2015 54th IEEE Conference on Decision and Control, CDC, pp. 2295–2300, December 2015
21. Başar, T., Olsder, G.J.: Dynamic Noncooperative Game Theory. SIAM, Philadelphia (1999)
22. Ye, M., Hu, G.: Game design and analysis for price-based demand response: an aggregate game approach. IEEE Trans. Cybern. **47**, 720–730 (2017)
23. Teixeira, A., Sandberg, H., Johansson, K.H.: Networked control systems under cyber attacks with applications to power networks. In: Proceedings of the 2010 American Control Conference, pp. 3690–3696, June 2010
24. Sundaram, S., Hadjicostis, C.N.: Distributed function calculation via linear iterative strategies in the presence of malicious agents. IEEE Trans. Autom. Control **56**, 1495–1508 (2011)
25. Pasqualetti, F., Bicchi, A., Bullo, F.: Consensus computation in unreliable networks: a system theoretic approach. IEEE Trans. Autom. Control **57**, 90–104 (2012)
26. Pasqualetti, F., Drfler, F., Bullo, F.: Attack detection and identification in cyber-physical systems. IEEE Trans. Autom. Control **58**, 2715–2729 (2013)
27. Zhu, M., Martnez, S.: On the performance analysis of resilient networked control systems under replay attacks. IEEE Trans. Autom. Control **59**, 804–808 (2014)
28. Zhu, Q., Başar, T.: Game-theoretic methods for robustness, security, and resilience of cyberphysical control systems: games-in-games principle for optimal cross-layer resilient control systems. IEEE Control Syst. **35**, 46–65 (2015)
29. Mo, Y., Sinopoli, B.: Secure estimation in the presence of integrity attacks. IEEE Trans. Autom. Control **60**, 1145–1151 (2015)
30. Khanafer, A., Baar, T.: Robust distributed averaging: when are potential-theoretic strategies optimal? IEEE Trans. Autom. Control **61**, 1767–1779 (2016)
31. Moghadam, R., Modares, H.: An internal model principle for the attacker in distributed control systems. In: 2017 IEEE 56th Annual Conference on Decision and Control, CDC, pp. 6604–6609, December 2017
32. Kamdem, G., Kamhoua, C., Lu, Y., Shetty, S., Njilla, L.: A Markov game theoritic approach for power grid security. In: 2017 IEEE 37th International Conference on Distributed Computing Systems Workshops, ICDCSW, pp. 139–144, June 2017
33. Freeman, R.A., Yang, P., Lynch, K.M.: Stability and convergence properties of dynamic average consensus estimators. In: Proceedings of the 45th IEEE Conference on Decision and Control, pp. 338–343, December 2006
34. Haghshenas, H., Badamchizadeh, M.A., Baradarannia, M.: Containment control of heterogeneous linear multi-agent systems. Automatica **54**, 210–216 (2015)

Disappointment-Aversion in Security Games

Jasmin Wachter[1]($\boxtimes$) (iD), Stefan Rass[1] (iD), Sandra König[2] (iD), and Stefan Schauer[2]

[1] Institute of Applied Informatics, System Security Group, Universitaet Klagenfurt, Universitaetsstrasse 65-67, 9020 Klagenfurt, Austria
{jasmin.wachter,stefan.rass}@aau.at
[2] Center for Digital Safety & Security, Austrian Institute of Technology, Giefinggasse 2, 1210 Vienna, Austria
{sandra.koenig,stefan.schauer}@ait.ac.at
http://www.syssec.at/en, https://www.ait.ac.at/en/

Abstract. Even though players in a game optimize their goals by playing an equilibrium, the perceived payoff *per round* may (and in most cases will) deviate from the expected average payoff. For the example of loss minimization, an undercut of the expected loss is unproblematic, while suffering more than the expected loss may disappoint the player and lead it to believe that the played strategy is not optimal. In the worst case, this may subsequently cause deviations towards seemingly better strategies, even though the equilibrium cannot be improved in general. Such deviations from the utility maximization principle are subject of bounded rationality research, and this work is a step towards more accurate game theoretic models that include disappointment aversion as an additional incentive. This incentive necessarily creates discontinuities in the payoff functionals, so that Nash's classical equilibrium theorem is no longer applicable. For *games with disappointment aversion* (defined in this work) the existence of equilibria can nonetheless be shown, i.e., we are able to find Nash equilibria that comply with disappointment aversion.

Keywords: Game theory · Multiobjective games · Disappointment
Endogenous-sharing rules · Bounded rationality

1 Introduction

Consider a standard security game as being a competition between a defender and an attacker, where the defender aims to minimize losses caused by the attacker. If the model is incomplete in the sense that the defender knows the attacker's action space but is unaware of the attacker's payoff structure, we may substitute this information by assuming the attacker's intentions to be exactly opposite to the defender's aims. Formally, we define the attacker's utility u_2 as $u_2 := -u_1$, where u_1 is the defender's payoff function, and thus create a zero-sum game in this setting of incomplete information. It is easy to show that the value

© Springer Nature Switzerland AG 2018
L. Bushnell et al. (Eds.): GameSec 2018, LNCS 11199, pp. 314–325, 2018.
https://doi.org/10.1007/978-3-030-01554-1_18

of the so-constructed zero-sum game bounds the outcome of the actual bi-matrix game (with unknown payoff to the attacker), provided that the defender plays a zero-sum Nash equilibrium strategy. Thus, such strategies are called *security strategies* [17], and we shall call the respective game a *security game* in our context (though the term has a much wider meaning including many further game models with security applications).

A typical use-case for a security game is to estimate the amount of preparation against worst-case scenarios. In risk management, experienced disappointments can influence preparedness for expected incident scenarios. Consider a critical infrastructure (CI) which is known to potentially fall victim to certain attacks or experience natural disasters (fire, floods, etc.). If the CI risk management's employs an optimized control of defensive resources, which can be described through a game theoretic model (e.g., [1,2,13,14,18] to name only a few), then the expected impact is what the CI provider will prepare for. This optimal, yet worst-case expected impact can be obtained from a game theoretic model which sets the bar for the preparations to be undertaken. Disappointment occurs when the actual damage suffered, despite optimal (equilibrium) control measures, exceeds the expected damage we were prepared for. Since the infrastructure is "critical", it is a natural requirement to minimize the chances of such an event, i.e., the case that despite all preparation, the damage is still such that we CI cannot recover any more. Practically, this is exactly what insurances are for, where the amount is set sufficiently high to cover the worst among the expected scenarios. If this is too low (manifesting itself as the event of a disappointment in the game), the insurance client may suffer irrecoverable losses.

In playing a security strategy, the defender is assured to never suffer more damage than measured by the value of the zero-sum security game. Thus, the residual damage under this best worst-case defense is what we would take out an insurance for. However, when considering repeated games, the saddle-point value is only an *average* value, and we will necessarily encounter rounds with higher and lower payoffs than the expected value. For security games about minimizing losses, this means that a security strategy can only bound the average loss; we will henceforth call the event of losing more than expected *disappointment*. Hence, when we conclude an insurance contract covering the expected maximal damage under worst-case attack scenarios, disappointment is the event where the insurance lot would be insufficient to cover the damage. Suffering from such not fully recoverable damage too often, the defender may not "survive" on the long run. For many utility provisioning infrastructures, such as water supply or power networks, the matter is even more crucial, by definition of the infrastructure as *critical*.

Therefore, in addition to minimizing the losses themselves, the likelihood of disappointment, the *disappointment rate*, should be minimized too. Obviously, solely minimizing the disappointment rate itself does not make sense, since avoiding disappointment is trivially done by preparing for maximal damage in first place (i.e. no scenario can ever cause more damage in the game model). Hence, disappointment aversion is always connected to some "primary" goal, and equilibria with disappointment aversion are always a matter of multi-criteria optimization.

The main obstacle, which we will expose later, lies in the possible discontinuities that incorporating disappointment in the game payoff functions may introduce; these discontinuities render classical results inapplicable to study the existence of equilibria. This is the technical difficulty explored in this work, for which we propose several solutions.

1.1 Related Work

Several approaches exist to describe disappointment when playing games. In a well-known classical example, Kahneman and Tversky [9] observed that in a one-shot game (lottery), a majority of players prefer $3,000\$$ for sure over an 80% chance of receiving $4,000\$$ (and a 20% chance at nothing), whereas a majority prefer a 20% chance at $4,000\$$ over a 25% chance at $3,000\$$. Bell [4] was the first to explain this phenomenon using the term *disappointment*. In his Bernoulli model, the player wins $x\$$ with probability p and $y\$$ with probability $(1 - p)$. The expectation is $px + (1 - p)y$ and the disappointment in receiving $y\$$ is modelled via $Disappointment = d(px + (1 - p)y - y) = dp(x - y)$, i.e. it is directly proportional (with constant $d > 0$) to the discrepancy between actual and anticipated performance and the relation between economic payoff and disappointment is linear and additive. Inman, Dyer and Jia [8] generalized this concept to decision problems with more than two outcomes. The significance of Kahneman and Tversky's lottery for security is its similarity to choice situations about security precautions to be implemented: if "protection A" is weaker than "protection B" but A comes with deterministic guarantees over the mere probabilistic assurances of B, then the practical choice may be guided by anticipated disappointment. In applications of game theory for optimized resource planning (e.g., [14]), practical choices may be more accurately be reflected by considering disappointment aversion.

Decision making in the context of disappointment (aversion) has also been investigated in [5], where disappointment is measured as a strictly increasing function in the difference to the expected utility. In [6], a disappointment metric is used to evaluate expert algorithms that quickly learn effective strategies in repeated games. In this setting, minimizing disappointment is equivalent to maximizing payoffs.

2   Preliminaries and Definitions

In the following we will use the notation $\Gamma = (\mathcal{I}, (S_i)_{i \in \mathcal{I}}, (u_i)_{i \in \mathcal{I}})$ for a game where $\mathcal{I} = \{1, \ldots, n\}$, $n \in \mathbb{N}$ denotes a finite index set representing players 1 to n, $(S_i)_{i \in \mathcal{I}}$ is the strategy space and $(u_i)_{i \in \mathcal{I}}$ is the set of utility functions.

We let players have finite sets of strategies denoted as PS_i (pure strategies) for the i-th player. Mixed strategies are probability distributions supported on a finite set PS_i, all of which constitute the set, i.e., simplex, $S_i := \Delta(PS_i)$

for the i-th player. Using the standard notation PS_{-i}, S_{-i} to denote the pure, resp. mixed, strategies of player i's opponents (all embodied within a single large vector), we let the utility functions u_i be vector-valued mappings from $S_i \times S_{-i}$ to $\mathbb{R}^d$, with $d \geq 1$ and the j-th coordinate in u_i be denoted as $u_i^{(j)} : S_i \times S_{-i} \to \mathbb{R}$. Accordingly, vectors will hereafter appear in bold lower-case letters, sets and random variables will be uppercase normal font letters. If the utilities are all scalar-valued ($d = 1$), we simply speak about a *game*, as opposed to a *multi-objective game* (MOG) having at least one player with at least two goals to optimize. In the case of vectors $u, v \in \mathbb{R}^d$, we write $u < v$ to mean $u_i < v_i$ for all $i = 1, 2, \ldots, d$. The complement relation $u \geq_1 v$ means the existence of at least one index i_0 for which $u_{i_0} \geq v_{i_0}$, no matter what the other components do. The usual Nash equilibrium condition, rephrased in terms of $\geq_1$ for minimizing players, then reads as: for each player i,

$$u_i(x, x_{-i}^*) \geq_1 u_i(x_i^*, x_{-i}^*) \quad \text{for all } x \in S_i. \tag{1}$$

As usual, this expresses that any unilateral deviation from the equilibrium x_i^* for the i-th player would cause a suboptimal payoff in at least one of its goals (by the $\geq_1$-relation), even though other payoffs may be improved (in the sense of decreased, since the player is minimizing). It is easy to see that (1) boils down to the standard condition if the payoff is scalar-valued. Any mixed strategy profile satisfying condition (1) is called a *Pareto-Nash equilibrium*.

For the sake of generality we shall consider games with a finite number of players yet allow each to have an infinitude (up to a compact continuum) of strategies. Nash's classical result has been extended towards this direction by I. Glicksberg [7]:

Theorem 1 (Glicksberg's theorem). *If for a game in normal form, the strategy spaces are nonempty compact subsets of a metric space, and the utility-functions are continuous w.r.t the metric, then at least one Nash equilibrium in mixed strategies exists.*

Remark 1. The requirement of continuous w.r.t the metric was later extended by Dasgupta and Maskin [11], who generalized Glicksberg's theorem to some classes of semi-continuous utility functions, where the discontinuities are restricted to occur only in subsets of the strategy space, in which all components of the (mixed) strategy vector of player i can be expressed via a finite number of *1-to-1 invertible functions* of a single component of another players strategy vector. Furthermore, the sum of utility functions of all players must be upper-semicontinuous and the individual utilities needs to be weakly-lower continuous over the set of discontinuities.

It is not difficult to lift Glicksberg's result to multi-goal equilibria, which will become relevant once we include disappointment as an explicit goal to minimize on its own:

Corollary 1. *Let Γ be a (MOG) that satisfies the hypothesis of Glicksberg's Theorem for each payoff function of each player. Then, Γ has a Pareto-Nash equilibrium in mixed strategies.*

Proof. Let $1 \leq i \leq n$ be an arbitrary among n maximizing players with $d_i \geq 1$ payoff functions $u_i^{(1)}, \ldots, u_i^{(d_i)}$. Let player i pick constants $\alpha_{i,1}, \ldots, \alpha_{i,d_i} > 0$, and define the (scalarized) function $f_i := \sum_j \alpha_{i,j} \cdot u_i^{(j)}$. Repeating this for each player, call the game with the payoff functions $f_1, \ldots, f_n$ game Γ_{sc}. So, Glicksberg's theorem gives an equilibrium $\boldsymbol{x}^* = (\boldsymbol{x}_1^*, \ldots, \boldsymbol{x}_n^*)$ in mixed strategies in Γ_{sc}. We show that this a Pareto-Nash equilibrium in the original game Γ: adopt an arbitrary player i's perspective and let it unilaterally deviate from $\boldsymbol{x}^*$ by playing an arbitrary mixed strategy $\boldsymbol{x}' = (\boldsymbol{x}_1^*, \boldsymbol{x}_2^*, \boldsymbol{x}_{i-1}^*, \boldsymbol{x}_i', \boldsymbol{x}_{i+1}^*, \ldots, \boldsymbol{x}_n^*) \neq \boldsymbol{x}^*$ Since $\boldsymbol{x}^*$ is an equilibrium in Γ_{sc}, we have $f_i(\boldsymbol{x}') \leq f_i(\boldsymbol{x}^*)$. Towards a contradiction, suppose that $\boldsymbol{x}'$ were chosen to outperform the strategy $\boldsymbol{x}^*$ in Γ, meaning that

$$u_i^{(j)}(\boldsymbol{x}') > u_i^{(j)}(\boldsymbol{x}^*) \quad \text{for all } j = 1, 2, \ldots, d_i. \tag{2}$$

Because the constants $\alpha_{i,j}$ are all by definition > 0, we have $f_i(\boldsymbol{x}') > f_i(\boldsymbol{x}^*)$, contradicting the fact that $\boldsymbol{x}^*$ is an equilibrium. Thus, (2) cannot hold and there must be an index j_0 for which $u_i^{(j_0)}(\boldsymbol{x}') \leq u_i^{(j)}(\boldsymbol{x}^*)$ and hence $\boldsymbol{u}_i(\boldsymbol{x}') \leq_1 \boldsymbol{u}_i(\boldsymbol{x}^*)$. Since i was arbitrary, $\boldsymbol{x}^*$ is, as an equilibrium, Pareto-optimal. $\square$

Remark 2. Some authors [10] additionally assume the constants to add up to 1. This has the geometric appeal of exhibiting parts of the convex hull's border as the Pareto front containing all optimal among the admissible strategies. Formally, the requirement merely amounts to a scaling of the scalarized payoffs by a positive factor, which just creates another strategically equivalent set of payoff functions.

Since the strategy spaces that our players use in the following are just stated to be compact (yet not necessarily discrete), we shall henceforth describe their mixed strategies as measures supported on a strategy space (which practically amount to certain distribution functions that help choosing a randomized action in the concrete game's instance). For the average (= expected) payoff $\boldsymbol{u}_i$ (possibly vector-valued) for the i-th player under a strategy profile $\boldsymbol{\mu} = (\mu_1, \ldots, \mu_n)$ for all players, we shall use the abbreviated notation

$$\mathrm{E}_{\boldsymbol{\mu}}(\boldsymbol{u}_i) = \int_{\prod_j S_j} \boldsymbol{u}_i d\boldsymbol{\mu},$$

where the integral is taken per coordinate function of $\boldsymbol{u}_i$. We shall write out the vector of measures more explicitly whenever it aids the explanation.

3   The Main Results

Let us consider a conventional static and repeated game as the simplest model to start with. Whenever there is an equilibrium in pure strategies, the payoff in the game will be constant over all repetitions. However, when the optimum exists in mixed strategies only, the equilibrium optimizes the long-run average over a hypothetical infinitude of independent instances of the game. This may create an unwanted side-effect for the player, such as temporary losses, since the actual payoff *per round* can be larger or lower than the average payoff that the equilibrium promises. Suppose that the player is minimizing, say, it strives for the least losses due to security breaches. Let $(\boldsymbol{x}^*,\ \boldsymbol{y}^*)$ be an equilibrium in the game, and let $u(X,Y)$ be the payoff (loss) obtained from the game upon a random choice $X \sim \boldsymbol{x}^*, Y \sim \boldsymbol{y}^*$.

Calling $Z = u(X,Y)$ the random variable describing the loss incurred by the game play, then a conventional equilibrium optimizes the first moment $\bar{z} = \mathrm{E}_{(\boldsymbol{x}^*,\boldsymbol{y}^*)}(Z) = (\boldsymbol{x}^*)^T \boldsymbol{A} \boldsymbol{y}^*$ only. This optimization, however, does not extend to higher moments (such as variance). Thus, among a sequence of repetitions of the game, amounting to a set of samples $z_1, z_2, z_3, \ldots$ from Z, we call the event $z_i > \bar{z}$ a *disappointing round*. We shall confine ourself to disappointment aversion hereafter, noting that the definitions and treatment based on the opposite event $z_i \leq \bar{z}$ follows mutatis mutandis.

Let us further confine our study to finite (matrix) games, so that $\bar{z} = (\boldsymbol{x})^T \cdot \boldsymbol{A} \cdot \boldsymbol{y}$ for randomized actions $\boldsymbol{x}, \boldsymbol{y}$.

Definition 1. *Let Γ be an n-person game and let $\mu = (\boldsymbol{x}_1^*, \ldots, \boldsymbol{x}_n^*)$ be an equilibrium. Depending on the nature of the i-th player we define the* disappointment rate *as*

$$d_i = \begin{cases} \mathrm{Pr}_\mu(Z > \mathrm{E}_\mu(Z)), \, \mathit{if\,player\,i\,is\,minimizing}; \\ \mathrm{Pr}_\mu(Z < \mathrm{E}_\mu(Z)), \, \mathit{if\,player\,i\,is\,maximizing}. \end{cases}$$

Remark 3. As mentioned in Sect. 1.1, there exist numerous definitions and concepts of disappointment. We chose this simple definition as an easy-to-understand example and stress the fact that the following results also apply for other disappointment concepts, such as [4–6,8].

From here onwards, and w.l.o.g., let us assume a finite two-person game and a minimizing first player whose perspective we are going to adopt (the upcoming results will be formulated to hold for more general games). It is straightforward to take the disappointment rate as a goal to optimize in the game, but obviously, this goal makes no sense by itself unless we combine it with at least one other goal. Otherwise, in case of a zero-sum game, we could just play towards maximal losses, in order to avoid being disappointed, but this is trivially against the purpose of the game at all.

As the nontrivial cases occur when the optimization is on multiple goals we shall coin the disappointment rate a *weak goal*, to express that the goal is not meaningful on its own. This is opposed to the "actual" goals in the game that we will call *strong*. The existence of goals whose optimization is only useful relative to other aims is not a new discovery, as the switching cost (i.e., the cost incurred when an instance of a mixed strategy is changed between repetitions of a game) [14] is another example of such a weak goal.

Definition 2 (Game with Disappointment Aversion). *Let any game Γ be given which optimizes one (or more) goals for the players. If we add the disappointment rate as an additional payoff to be minimized, we call the resulting game a* game *with disappointment aversion.*

Formally, let the primary payoff be described by a payoff matrix $\boldsymbol{A} = (a_{ij}) \in \mathbb{R}^{n \times m}$, whose average is $u_1(\boldsymbol{x}, \boldsymbol{y}) = \boldsymbol{x}^T \cdot \boldsymbol{A} \cdot \boldsymbol{y}$. The disappointment rate can, by the law of large numbers, be written as a long-run average of payoffs, where a loss given by u_1 is counted into the sum if and only if it exceeds the average loss u_1. Thus, the disappointment rate d_1 is

$$d_1(\boldsymbol{x}, \boldsymbol{y}) = \lim_{n \to \infty} \frac{1}{n} \sum_{k=1}^{n} \mathbb{I}(a_{rs} > \boldsymbol{x}^T \cdot \boldsymbol{A} \cdot \boldsymbol{y}) = \sum_{i=1}^{n} \sum_{j=1}^{m} x_i \cdot \mathbb{I}(a_{ij} > \boldsymbol{x}^T \cdot \boldsymbol{A} \cdot \boldsymbol{y}) \cdot y_j$$

where the random indices r, s are sampled from the distributions $\boldsymbol{x} = (x_1, \ldots, x_n)$, $\boldsymbol{y} = (y_1, \ldots, y_m)$, and $\mathbb{I}$ is the indicator function (returning 1 if and only if the inner condition is satisfied and 0 otherwise).

Remark 4. Obviously, yet not discussed in more depth hereafter, the magnitudes of the disappointment rate, being bounded within $[0, 1]$ should be relatively equal to the magnitudes of the other payoffs, in order to avoid the disappointment rate becoming a "negligible" loss or gain throughout the game play. We can assume this without loss of generality for any magnitude and number of payoffs, since it is a simple matter of scaling to equalize the magnitudes of all payoffs accordingly without strategically changing the game. For multi-objective games, this can be done along the scalarization algorithm as described in [10].

Thus, in a finite game with disappointment aversion the resulting utility for player 1 with disappointment aversion, denoted here as u_1^d, takes the form

$$u_1^d(\boldsymbol{x}, \boldsymbol{y}) = \alpha \cdot \boldsymbol{x}^T \cdot \boldsymbol{A} \cdot \boldsymbol{y} + (1 - \alpha) \cdot d_1(\boldsymbol{x}, \boldsymbol{y})$$
$$=: \boldsymbol{x}^T \cdot \boldsymbol{U}^d(\boldsymbol{x}, \boldsymbol{y}) \cdot \boldsymbol{y}$$

where $\boldsymbol{U}^d(\boldsymbol{x}, \boldsymbol{y}) = (u_{ij}^d(\boldsymbol{x}, \boldsymbol{y}))_{ij}$ with $u_{ij}^d(\boldsymbol{x}, \boldsymbol{y}) = \alpha \cdot a_{ij} + (1 - \alpha) \cdot \mathbb{I}(a_{ij} > \boldsymbol{x}^T \boldsymbol{A} \boldsymbol{y})$ and $\alpha > 0$ is a scalarization factor (for the multi-objective optimization).

Observe that the individual utility function u_1^d in a game with disappointment aversion need not be a continuous function, so neither Glicksberg's nor Nash's theorems are applicable to assure the existence of equilibria. As shown by an earlier example due to Sion and Wolfe [16], games with discontinuous payoff functions may in general even lack any equilibria at all. In addition, even though Dasgupta and Maskin have proven the existence of equilibria for some classes of discontinuous utility functions (see Sect. 2), u_1^d may not fall into this classes for several reasons: First, we observe that for given $\boldsymbol{y}$ the discontinuity set of $u_1(\boldsymbol{x}, \cdot)$ is in fact the set of all hyperplanes $a_{ij} = \boldsymbol{x}^T \cdot \boldsymbol{A} \cdot \boldsymbol{y}$ of dimension $n - 1$ (in $\boldsymbol{x}$). The set of discontinuities over $S_1 \times S_2$ is $\{(\boldsymbol{x}, \boldsymbol{y}), x_i, y_i \geq 0, \sum_{i \in \mathcal{I}_1} x_i = 1, \sum_{i \in \mathcal{I}_2} y_i = 1 \mid \exists i \in \mathcal{I}_1, \exists j \in \mathcal{I}_1 : a_{ij} = \boldsymbol{x}^T \cdot \boldsymbol{A} \cdot \boldsymbol{y}\}$. By definition of the disappointment rate, it is in general not possible to express the components of player 1's strategy vector $\boldsymbol{x}$ in the discontinuity set by a finite number of functions $f : \mathbb{R}^1 \to \mathbb{R}^1$ as Dasgupta and Maskin assume [11]. Second, even if it is possible to do so, u_1^d is by construction a piecewise continuous function, but it neither has to be upper semi-continuous, nor weakly lower continuous on the set of discontinuities. Therefore, disappointment averse games as in Definition 2, despite their decision theoretical value, are impractical and therefore ineffective in applications.

To fix the theoretical aspects and to ensure the existence of equilibria, we adopt Simon and Zame's concept of games with endogenous-sharing rules [15] that has also been used in [3]. In the following we will write S for $(S_i)_{i \in \mathcal{I}}$ to improve readability. We stress that the results of [15] applies to scalar-valued utility functions only, so, w.l.o.g., we assume our multi-criteria games to be scalarized (according to [10,12] or also Corollary 1) before computing equilibria. The resulting equilibria are then exactly the sought Pareto-Nash equilibria (optimizing the disappointment rate besides the primary utility).

Definition 3 (Game with endogenous-sharing). *A game with endogenous-sharing rule, or an endogenous-sharing game is any $\Gamma_s = (\mathcal{I}, S, U)$, where $\mathcal{I}, S$ are as in Sect. 2, and $U : S \twoheadrightarrow \mathbb{R}^n$ is a correspondence that specifies a set of utility payoff allocations for every combination of player's strategies.*

Thus, U is a multivalued function, and for any μ in S the correspondence U allocates a *set* of utility payoff allocations to each player. Thus, $U(\mu) = (U_i)_{i \in \mathcal{I}}$ where each $U_i(\mu) = \{u_i^1(\mu), u_i^2(\mu), \dots\} \subseteq \mathbb{R}$ is a (not necessarily countable) set of utilities for player i that could all occur, if strategy μ is chosen.

Definition 4 (Upper Hemicontinuity). *A correspondence $U : S \twoheadrightarrow \mathbb{R}^n$ with closed values[1] is upper hemicontinuous, if for all $\mu \in S$ and for all sequences $(\mu_n)_{n \in \mathbb{N}} \in S$ and for all $u \in U(S)$ and $(u_n)_{n \in \mathbb{N}}, u_n \in U(\mu_n)$ we have $\lim_{n \to \infty} \mu_n = \mu, \lim_{n \to \infty} u_n = u \implies u \in U(\mu)$.*

In other words, a correspondence U is upper hemicontinuous if the following holds: for every convergent sequence $(\mu_n)_{n \in \mathbb{N}}$ in S which maps to a sequence of sets $(U_n)_{n \in \mathbb{N}}$ in the range of U that contains a convergent sequence $(u_n)_{n \in \mathbb{N}}$, the image of limiting point in the domain must contain the limit of the sequence in the range. I.e. $U(\lim_{n \to \infty} (\mu_n)_{n \in \mathbb{N}}) \ni \lim_{n \to \infty} u_n$ whenever the limits of $(u_n)_{n \in \mathbb{N}}$ and $(\mu_n)_{n \in \mathbb{N}}$ exist.

Definition 5. *A correspondence U is bounded, if there exists a constant K such that for all strategies $\mu \in S$, for all $i \in \mathcal{I}$ and every $u_i^j(\mu) \in U_i(\mu)$ it holds: $|u_i^j(\mu)| < K$.*

Theorem 2 (Simon and Zame [15]). *Let Γ_s be an endogenous-sharing game as in Definition 3. Let S be a compact set within some metric space. Assume U is an upper-hemicontinuous and bounded correspondence. Furthermore, assume for each $\mu \in S$ the image $U(\mu)$ is a nonempty convex subset of $\mathbb{R}^n$. Then there exists some profile of utility functions $(\hat{u}_i(\mu))_{i \in \mathcal{I}} \in U(\mu)$ such that $\hat{u}_i$ is a measurable function for every μ and the resulting game has at least one Nash equilibrium in S.*

---

[1] A correspondence $U : S \twoheadrightarrow \mathbb{R}^n$ has *closed values*, if all $U(\mu) \ \mu \in S$ are closed subsets of $\mathbb{R}^n$.

Following this approach, we do not consider disappointment averse utility functions $u^d = (u_1^d, u_2^d)$, but we define a correspondence U, for which $U(\mu) = u^d(\mu)$ at points of continuity, and at the discontinuity points U maps μ to the convex hull of all limiting values of u^d. This can be interpreted as follows: in any discontinuity point μ we define the correspondence $U(\mu)$ as set of all limits of expected utility allocations that can be achieved by randomizing over strategy profiles which are arbitrarily close to μ. It can be shown that the resulting U is the coarsest upper hemicontinuous correspondence that only maps to convex sets [15]. We call this resulting mapping a *minimal correspondence*.

By Theorem 2 we can now ensure that there exists some profile of utility functions $\hat{u}$ such that u^d and only differs from $\hat{u}$ at points of discontinuity and an equilibrium of the resulting game $\hat{\Gamma} = (\mathcal{I}, S, (\hat{u}_i)_{i \in \mathcal{I}})$ exists.

Remark 5. At this point, it can easily be verified that the above results does not only apply disappointment as defined in Definition 1, but also to disappointment as defined in [4,8] or [5]. We can in fact use all kinds of disappointment functions as long as it can be ensured that a minimal correspondence U exists.

Another possibility to incorporate disappointment is to consider a smoothed version of $\hat{\Gamma} = (\mathcal{I}, S, (\hat{u}_i)_{i \in \mathcal{I}})$. Let $S_1, S_2, \ldots, S_n$ be the strategy sets of all players. W.l.o.g., let player 1 be minimizing its disappointment relative to a goal $u_1 : S_1 \times S_{-1} \to \mathbb{R}$. Let μ_1, μ_{-1} be the probability measures (practically represented by distribution or density functions if the latter exist) from which player 1 and its opponents choose their strategies, denoted as $X_1, \boldsymbol{X}_{-1}$. Recall the disappointment rate as

$$d_{(\mu_1, \mu_{-1})} = \mathrm{E}_{(\mu_1, \mu_{-1})} \mathbb{I} \left[u_1(X_1, \boldsymbol{X}_{-1}) - \mathrm{E}_{(\mu_1, \mu_{-1})}(u_1(X_1, \boldsymbol{X}_{-1})) \right]$$

Choose a mollifier $\delta_h : U^n \to \mathbb{R}$ of bandwidth $h > 0$ and so that $\delta_h \in C(\prod_i S_i)$, i.e., the function should be continuous w.r.t. the common metric of the host spaces covering the S_i's. Define $\tilde{d}_h := d * \delta_h$ and observe that $\tilde{d}_h$ is now a continuous payoff function. A simple admissible choice for a mollifier is the n-fold tensor product of a univariate mollifier such as $\delta_k(x) := \frac{k}{c} g(|kx|)$ with the C^∞-function

$$g(r) := \begin{cases} \exp\left(-\frac{1}{1-r^2}\right), & \text{for } r \in (-1, 1) \\ 0, & \text{otherwise.} \end{cases}$$

and the normalization constant $c := \int_\mathbb{R} g(|x|) dx$. The support of the tensor product $\delta_k(x_1, \ldots, x_n) = \prod_j \delta_k(x_j)$ is then the compact hypercube $[-1/k, 1/k]^n$.

Definition 6. *Let Γ be an n-person game, and let $\mu = (x_1^*, \ldots, x_n^*)$ be an equilibrium. Depending on the nature of the i-th player, the smooth disappointment rate with bandwidth h is defined as $\tilde{d}^i{}_h := d_i * \delta_h$.*

Analogously to 2 we can now define *games with smooth disappointment aversion* if we replace the disappointment rate by the smooth disappointment rate.

This corresponds to allowing not only a 0/1 formalism of disappointment but to specify some kind of degree of disappointment at points close to the expected value. This enables a more distinct perspective on disappointment and also helps in computing the equilibrium. It follows:

Theorem 3. *Let the game Γ have compact strategy sets within some metric space U, and let the initial payoff functions each be continuous let there be a player in Γ who is minimizing the smoothed disappointment rate w.r.t. at least one other goal. Then Γ has at least one Pareto-Nash equilibrium (in mixed strategies).*

Proof. Follows directly from Glicksbergs's Theorem via Corollary 1.   □

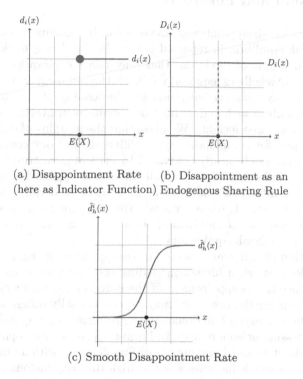

(a) Disappointment Rate   (b) Disappointment as an
(here as Indicator Function) Endogenous Sharing Rule

(c) Smooth Disappointment Rate

Fig. 1. Comparison of disappointment concepts

Figure 1 sums up the three concepts of disappointment discussed in this paper. Note that both (b) and (c) can be applied when dealing with games and display two different notions: When considering disappointment as an endogenous sharing rule (see (b)), we are disappointed whenever the utility exceeds the expected value, yet whenever it equals the mean we are – just like Schrödinger's cat – both disappointed and not. The smooth disappointment rate allows for a continuous view of disappointment. One may argue that smoothing may falsely incorporate some notion disappointment, even when the encountered loss does not exceed the expected damage, but is somewhat below it. Indeed, insurances naturally do not cover damages that are higher than the maximum liability amount, which causes disappointment. Yet, there always remains the risk of not receiving the full amount from an insurance company, but only partial compensation. The higher the damage, the more insurance companies try to lower the sum they have to come up for. Hence, smooth disappointment rates can incorporate this additional phenomenon. If this is not desired, we advice to shift the of the disappointment rate to the right, such that a positive disappointment value may only occur when the expected value is exceeded.

4 Conclusion and Future Work

We have shown that disappointment aversion can be accounted for in the computation of Nash equilibria in repeated games. In this being work in progress, we close with a couple of directions that may merit exploration along future work, including Stackelberg equilibria (where the problem is essentially one of optimizing a discontinuous functional for the leading player), or the difference between equilibria with and without disappointment aversion (in the latter regard, Remark 4 is a first insight). We stress that the meaning of disappointment for individuals and for companies may be different, and our concept of disappointment aversion was basically motivated by critical infrastructure protection applications. In a follow-up work, we shall explore an application of disappointment aversion to individual's decision making in more detail, specifically the lottery mentioned Sect. 1.1, where we study the disappointment aversion as one possible explanation for the empirically observed deviation of individuals from the prediction of the Nash equilibrium.

A combination of different concepts of disappointment, e.g., [5,6], may be interesting to look at when further modelling the insurance example from the introduction, since the disappointment of the individual (customer) and the disappointment event for the insurance may be conceptually different things, and thus lead to different payoff functionals in the resulting security games (then no longer being zero-sum or even repeated). From the insurance company's perspective, thinking about retained amounts, a disappointment with an insurance may occur if the bar for the deductibles is set so high that the customers would have to pay for most of the incidents. In turn, they will soon look for other insurances with better service. Conversely, if the bar is set too low, the insurance will not be profitable while the customer is never disappointed. The resulting game can thus be seen as one with disappointment aversion (on both sides even).

Acknowledgment. This work was done in the context of the project "Cross Sectoral Risk Management for Object Protection of Critical Infrastructures (CERBERUS)", supported by the Austrian Research Promotion Agency under grant no. 854766. We thank the anonymous reviewers for their valuable suggestions that helped to improve this work.

References

1. Al-Shaer, E., Duan, Q., Jafarian, J.H.: Random host mutation for moving target defense. In: Keromytis, A.D., Di Pietro, R. (eds.) SecureComm 2012. LNICSSITE, vol. 106, pp. 310–327. Springer, Heidelberg (2013). https://doi.org/10.1007/978-3-642-36883-7_19
2. Alpcan, T., Başar, T.: Network Security: A Decision and Game Theoretic Approach. Cambridge University Press, Cambridge (2010)
3. Balder, E.J.: An equilibrium closure result for discontinuous games. Econ. Theory **48**(1), 47–65 (2010)
4. Bell, D.E.: Disappointment in decision making under uncertainty. Oper. Res. **33**(1), 1–27 (1985)
5. Chauveau, T., Nalpas, N.: A theory of disappointment (2005)
6. Crandall, J.W.: Towards minimizing disappointment in repeated games. J. Artif. Int. Res. **49**(1), 111–142 (2014)
7. Glicksberg, I.L.: A further generalization of the kakutani fixed point theorem, with application to nash equilibrium points. Proc. Am. Math. Soc. **3**, 170–174 (1952)
8. Inman, J.J., Dyer, J.S., Jia, J.: A generalized utility model of disappointment and regret effects on post-choice valuation. Mark. Sci. **16**(2), 97–111 (1997)
9. Kahneman, D., Tversky, A.: Prospect theory: an analysis of decision under risk. Econometrica **47**, 263–291 (1979)
10. Lozovanu, D., Solomon, D., Zelikovsky, A.: Multiobjective games and determining pareto-nash equilibria. Buletinul Academiei de Stiinte a Republicii Moldova Matematica **3**(49), 115–122 (2005)
11. Maskin, E., Dasgupta, P.: The existence of equilibrium in discontinuous economic games, part i (theory). Rev. Econ. Stud. **53**(1), 1–26 (1986). Reprinted in K. Binmore and P. Dasgupta (eds.), Economic Organizations as Games, Oxford: Basil Blackwell, 1986, pp. 48–82
12. Rass, S.: On game-theoretic network security provisioning. Springer J. Netw. Syst. Manag. **21**(1), 47–64 (2013)
13. Rass, S., König, S., Schauer, S.: Defending against advanced persistent threats using game-theory. PLoS One **12**(1), e0168675 (2017)
14. Rass, S., König, S., Schauer, S.: On the cost of game playing: how to control the expenses in mixed strategies. In: Rass, S., An, B., Kiekintveld, C., Fang, F., Schauer, S. (eds.) GameSec 2017. LNCS, vol. 10575, pp. 494–505. Springer, Cham (2017). https://doi.org/10.1007/978-3-319-68711-7_26
15. Simon, L.K., Zame, W.R.: Discontinuous games and endogenous sharing rules. Econometrica **58**(4), 861–872 (1990)
16. Sion, M., Wolfe, P.: On a Game without a Value, pp. 299–306. Princeton University Press, Princeton (1957)
17. Voorneveld, M.: Pareto-optimal security strategies as minimax strategies of a standard matrix game. J. Optim. Theory Appl. **102**(1), 203–210 (1999)
18. Zhu, Q., Rass, S.: On multi-phase and multi-stage game-theoretic modeling of advanced persistent threats. IEEE Access **6**(1), 13958–13971 (2018)

Moving Target Defense for the Placement of Intrusion Detection Systems in the Cloud

Sailik Sengupta[1](✉), Ankur Chowdhary[2], Dijiang Huang[2],
and Subbarao Kambhampati[1]

[1] Yochan Lab, Arizona State Univeristy, Tempe, USA
{sailiks,rao}@asu.edu
[2] Secure Network and Computing Lab, Arizona State University, Tempe, USA
{achaud16,dijiang}@asu.edu

Abstract. A lot of software systems are deployed in the cloud. Owing to realistic demands for an early product launch, oftentimes there are vulnerabilities that are present in these deployed systems (or eventually found out). The cloud service provider can find and leverage this knowledge about known vulnerabilities and the underlying communication network topology of the system to position network and host-based Intrusion Detection Systems (IDS) that can effectively detect attacks. Unfortunately, deploying IDS on each host and network interface impacts the performance of the overall system. Thus, in this paper, we address the problem of placing a limited number of IDS by using the concept of Moving Target Defense (MTD). In essence, we propose an MTD system that allows a defender to shift the detection surfaces and strategically switch among the different IDS placement configurations in each round. To find a secure switching strategy, we (1) formulate the problem of placing a limited number of IDS systems in a large cloud network as a Stackelberg Game between the cloud administrator and an (external or stealthy) attacker, (2) design scalable methods to find the optimal strategies for switching IDS placements at the start of each round, and (3) formally define the problem of identifying the most critical vulnerability that should be fixed, and propose a solution for it. We compare the strategy generated by our method to other state-of-the-art strategies, showcasing the effectiveness and scalability of our method for real-world scenarios.

Keywords: Moving Target Defense · Intrusion Detection Systems
Stackelberg games

1 Introduction

System Administrators, oftentimes, use Intrusion Detection Systems (IDS) to detect on-going attacks on modern-day cyber-systems [34]. These IDS systems perform sophisticated operations – like signature-matching [3], anomaly detection [11,15], machine learning [1,17,21] etc. – to investigate either live traffic on

© Springer Nature Switzerland AG 2018
L. Bushnell et al. (Eds.): GameSec 2018, LNCS 11199, pp. 326–345, 2018.
https://doi.org/10.1007/978-3-030-01554-1_19

the wire (using Network-based IDS (NIDS) [2,33]), or monitor resources on a machine (using Host-based IDS (HIDS) [13,43]) to flag anomalous requests that might result in potential loss of confidentiality, integrity or availability. Cloud service providers, who host third parties on their platform, encounter non-trivial challenges when it comes to deploying these IDS that can identify vulnerabilities present in their system on account of legacy or operational constraints [12]. The foremost among these challenges is the placement of IDS on all nodes of a large network, which results in reduced performance [20,42] (also see Sect. 6.2). Moreover, third party users of the cloud platform, due to privacy and security reasons, have constraints about sharing their data with the cloud provider [6].

Thus, given a cloud service provider's performance constraints and their customer's privacy constraints, we look at the problem of placing a limited number of IDS systems in the various nodes of the cloud system. It is trivial to see that if we place IDS systems statically that only monitor certain attacks on specific nodes, an attacker (especially a *stealthy one*, i.e. one who resides inside a deployed systems and can attack a node anywhere in the network as opposed to having access to only hosts at the entry point) will eventually figure out our placement strategy [42]. At this point, a strategic attacker can always select attacks that circumvent the IDS placed, thus passing through our cloud network undetected [38]. To address this, we design a Moving Target Defense (MTD) approach for dynamic placement of IDS systems on cloud systems.

The placement mechanism for our cloud framework places both Network and Host-based IDS. We will use a NIDS called snort [32] for detecting malicious behavior over the network and a HIDS known as auditd on the hosts of our cloud system. The assumption is that NIDS is placed at the gateway of each tenant network and the HIDS is deployed on each individual VM. A dynamic switching (or MTD) strategy selectively turns on/off the different HIDS or NIDS systems that can be used to monitor requests or hosts, thereby shifting the detection surface at each round without the need to consider switching costs among configurations because on/off commands from a central server sent out only at the start of every round hardly impact performance.

The cyber-security community has mostly defined and used MTD, so far, to shift the attack surface of a system that takes away the advantage of reconnaissance that an attacker has [45]. In this work, we generalize this notion of MTD and introduce an MTD system that shifts the detection surface to keep an attacker from guessing about whether their next attack will be detected or not. In conjunction with that, the key contributions of this paper are,

- We formulate the problem of placing limited IDS systems in a large cloud-based network using MTD as a two-player Stackelberg Game between the defender and an attacker. The equilibrium of this game gives us the optimal movement strategy that the defender should use to switch between the various IDS placements.
- We obtain the utility values of the players in this game by combining (1) the Common Vulnerability Scoring System (CVSS) that has been previously used to represent the impact of attacks on the defender's system [23] and (2)

the centrality values of the nodes in which an IDS is deployed that lets us capture (i) the connectivity information and (ii) the impact on performance when an IDS is placed on that node [42].

- We design a scalable optimization problem to find the Stackelberg Equilibrium of our formulated game (Sect. 4). In this approach, we introduce an input parameter α that lets the defender balance between the security of the system and the impact on the performance of the system.
- We define the problem of finding the most critical vulnerability in a cloud environment with a strategic attacker and a multi-objective utility function and propose a method to solve it (Sect. 5).
- We demonstrate the effectiveness of our approach on a running example by comparing it to state-of-the-art deterministic, uniformly random and centrality based MTD switching strategies. We then provide experimental results in a real-world large-scale cloud-based environment that showcases the scalability of our approach (Sect. 6).

2   Related Work

Moving Target Defense [45] has been recently used to thwart a wide range of attacks against network-based [16,41] and cloud-based systems [7,9]. These methods mostly shift the attack surfaces that takes away the advantage of reconnaissance an attacker has. A stealthy and strategic adversary [5], who can reside deep within the network, can still render these methods ineffective.

For such cases, researchers have previously investigated the placement of detection systems in large network-based environments and designed both static [20] and dynamic [42] placement mechanisms based on graph-theoretic measures. Unfortunately, the former method cannot adapt its placement strategy when facing a stealthy adversary. On the other hand, the latter method, which does not incorporate the knowledge of known vulnerabilities, performs sub-optimally when facing a strategic and rational adversary.

A switching strategy for any dynamic placement method or MTD system needs to incorporate attacker modeling and thus, game theoretic reasoning for it to be effective [31,37,39]. Previously, authors in [22] have modeled an MTD system as a game called PLADD, based on FlipIt [40]. This work assumes that different agents control the server in different game rounds, which is an impractical setting for cloud environments. In [19], researchers assume known vulnerabilities and design a deception mechanism using a Stackelberg Model to introduce honeynets against a specific class of attackers. Authors in [36] and [35] formulate the switching between various web-stack configurations and classifiers in an ensemble respectively as a Stackelberg Game. Unfortunately, the methods to find the Stackelberg equilibrium in these cases become intractable as the number of defender strategies explodes combinatorially.

Researchers have shown that decomposition of the reward structure makes the problem of finding the Stackelberg Equilibrium computationally efficient [24]. We leverage this information and design the rewards for our game while ensuring that the Stackelberg equilibrium balances between two important metrics [23] – (1) the costs of placing IDSs (on performance, cost of countermeasure deployment etc.) and (2) the impacts on the security of our system.

Lastly, researchers have leveraged the attack graph information of a network and tried to come up with classical AI planning approaches [26] or MDP-style approaches [14,29] to find effective ways of finding critical attacks against a system. Unfortunately, these approaches cannot be easily applied in the case of dynamic systems like MTD and thus we develop an approach to find the most critical vulnerability that should be fixed in our system.

3   Game-Theoretic Modeling

In this section, we first define the threat model of our system, defining the players, their action/strategy sets using a small real-world scenario that we set up on an enterprise cloud (Fig. 1). We then describe how the rewards of this game are formulated leveraging the CVSS data and network topology information.

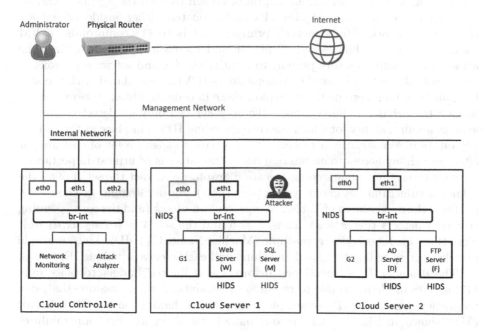

Fig. 1. Defender's system on the enterprise cloud that the attacker wants to attack.

Threat Model. In our attack model, we consider a multi-tenant cloud network. The controller node, shown in the Fig. 1, is used for network management and orchestration. The network administrator (or the defender) utilizes a management network to access controller nodes and cloud servers hosting VMs. We

Table 1. The different VMs in the defender's network, their betweenness centrality (c_b) in the graph, the known vulnerabilities in these nodes (VMs), and the corresponding Network/Host-based Intrusion Detection Systems (NIDS/HIDS) which can detect these attacks, also known as the Indicators of Compromise (IOC).

ID	VM	c_b	Vulnerability	CVE ID	IOC
a_1	G1	4	SSH Buffer Overflow	CVE-2016-6289	NIDS `sshAlert`
a_2	G2	7	`rlogin`	CVE-1999-0651	NIDS `rlogin`
a_3	W	0	Cross Side Scripting	CVE-2016-2163	HIDS `webAccess`
a_4	D	0	Weak Credentials	CVE-2001-0839	HIDS `fileIntegrity`
a_5	F	0	`vsftpd` backdoor	CVE-2015-1419	HIDS `ftpLogin`

consider two agents – the defender $\mathcal{D}$, who is trying to deploy IDS and an (external or stealthy) attacker $\mathcal{A}$, who is trying to remain undetected while attacking the system. As a running example, we will use the scenario deployed by $\mathcal{D}$ shown in Fig. 1. Furthermore, this system has a set of known vulnerabilities, that are yet to be fixed and as per our assumptions, known to both the agents $\mathcal{D}$ and $\mathcal{A}$.

We assume that the attacker $\mathcal{A}$ can be located either inside or outside the cloud network. The attacker's primary goal is to (1) compromise a VM using known vulnerabilities and (2) remain undetected while doing so. Since the attacker can utilize network probing to identify the OS and software versions, it will eventually get to know the vulnerabilities (CVEs) associated with the system, and can then systematically exploit these in order to obtain network access or elevated privileges. Furthermore, the attacker can only be detected when it attacks a vulnerability for which the corresponding IDS is in place at the time of exploitation. For stealthy attackers [5], who have to spend a lot of cost and/or effort in gaining access to an internal node, the latter is of utmost importance.

Now given the system's communication graph, we extract the set A of all the n known vulnerabilities in our system ($n = (|A|)$). For our system, we choose the a_i IDs in the first column of Table 1 to represent an *attack* (and the corresponding IDS that detects this attack). Thus, $n = 5$ and the set $A = \{a_1, a_2, a_3, a_4, a_5\}$. Note that this ID encodes a two-tuple $\langle$MachineName, CVE-ID$\rangle$. Thus, multiple attacks corresponding to a single machine will each receive a unique ID.

The defender $\mathcal{D}$, as mentioned before, has a limited budget to place only $k(< n)$ IDS mechanisms due to resource constraints. Also, we assume that, due to privacy constraints, $\mathcal{D}$ cannot place an IDS mechanism on the 'SQL Server (M)' (shown in Fig. 1). Thus, in our model, we disregard any vulnerabilities present on this node. (Note that although our system can detect a class of vulnerabilities that trigger NIDS alarms on the network interface G1 when they affect M, we exclude such vulnerabilities from our example). Now, $\mathcal{D}$ has $\binom{n}{k}$ ways in which it can deploy the k IDSs. This is the action set of $\mathcal{D}$. Formally, the defender's action set is denoted by the set $A_k = \{S \in A : |S| = k\}$. In the running example, we will assume that $k = 2$. Thus, the defender's action set is:

$$\{(a_1, a_2), (a_1, a_3), (a_1, a_4), (a_1, a_5), (a_2, a_3), (a_2, a_4), (a_2, a_5), (a_3, a_4), (a_3, a_5), (a_4, a_5)\}$$

Since, we assume a strong adversary who either knows or can find out all the attacks in our system, the action set of the attacker is the attack set $A = \{a_1, a_2, a_3, a_4, a_5\}$ itself.

In game theory, this action set is often referred to as the set of pure strategies, where each action (either a placement strategy or an attack) is a pure strategy (for $\mathcal{D}$ or $\mathcal{A}$ respectively). As stated earlier, if a defender chooses a pure strategy, i.e., any one out of the ten pure strategies shown, to deploy k IDS systems, the attacker, with reconnaissance on its side, will eventually figure out $\mathcal{D}$'s strategy and start choosing attacks that do not trigger these alarms. In order to address this limitation, the defender can play a mixed strategy, i.e. have a probability associated with playing each pure strategy and at the start of each round pick one by randomly sampling a pure strategy from the set of pure strategies. Note that this is similar to applying the concept of Moving Target Defense where the defender chooses to switch randomly among the different deployment configurations (i.e. by choosing one of the ten IDS placements in our case) at the start of each time period.

Common Vulnerability Scoring System (CVSS). The CVSS metric provides two quantitative scores for each CVE present in our system – (1) the Impact Score (IS) that represents the effect a particular attack has on the Confidentiality, Integrity, and Availability of a system and (2) the Exploitability Score (ES), which encodes the complexity of actually exploiting a particular vulnerability. The system defines a way to combine both of these scores to calculate a third score, known as the Base Score (BS) that tries to consider both the impact of an attack *vs.* the difficulty in exploiting it.

The CVSS scores thus leverage the knowledge of cybersecurity experts across the globe to provide a numerical value corresponding to each (known) vulnerability that reflects its severity and expertise necessary to exploit it. We, inspired by other research work before us [27,36,44], use the CVSS to calibrate the reward values of our game.

3.1 Stackelberg Games

Having defined the players and their action (or pure strategy) sets, there are additional real-world aspects that we want to incorporate in the formulation of our game. One such aspect is that the defender, who hosts the system that an attacker attacks, plays first. To accurately model this scenario, we use the concept of Stackelberg games in which one player ($\mathcal{D}$) acts before the other player ($\mathcal{A}$) plays and find the Stackelberg Equilibrium of these games, in which the leader's ($\mathcal{D}$) strategy is contingent upon the fact that the follower ($\mathcal{A}$) can observe D's strategy and play accordingly. Thus, in this adversarial leader-follower game, $\mathcal{D}$ can simulate $\mathcal{A}$ in their mind and decide on a mixed strategy that gives it the highest utility keeping in mind (that a rational) $\mathcal{A}$ will choose the best action ($\in A$), i.e. the action that maximizes A's reward, in response.

3.2 Utility Modeling

Having designed the action sets of both the players, we can now specify the utilities for both the players when each of them commits to a pure strategy. Note that just to enumerate all the utility values for our game we would have to specify $2 \cdot \binom{n}{k} \cdot n$ values corresponding to the reward values for each of the players $\mathcal{D}$ and $\mathcal{A}$ in the normal form game matrix. With this general reward structure, finding the mixed-strategy Stackelberg equilibrium of this game would be computationally inefficient, specifically $O(\binom{n}{k})$ [10]. Thus, we now devise a particular reward structure that captures all the aspects of our problem and lets us efficiently compute the equilibrium strategy.

For each attack $a \in A$, if $\mathcal{D}$ places an IDS to detect it, we will say that $\mathcal{D}$ *covers* it. Otherwise, we say that a is left *uncovered*. Since the defender can allocate only IDS resources to cover k elements in A, the remaining $n - k$ attacks will remain uncovered at any point in time. We will now decompose the reward structure of this game and define four types of utility values corresponding to each attack $a \in A$.

$$\langle U_{c,a}^{\mathcal{D}}, U_{u,a}^{\mathcal{D}}, U_{c,a}^{\mathcal{A}}, U_{u,a}^{\mathcal{A}} \rangle$$

where $U_{c,a}^{\mathcal{D}}$ and $U_{u,a}^{\mathcal{D}}$ denotes the utilities that a defender gets for covering or not covering an attack a respectively. Similarly, $U_{c,a}^{\mathcal{A}}$ and $U_{u,a}^{\mathcal{A}}$ represent the utility an attacker gets when they use an attack a that is covered (and thus gets detected) or not covered (and thus avoids detection) respectively. The values for these symbols are obtained by leveraging the knowledge of security experts as encoded in the Common Vulnerabilities Scoring System (CVSS) [28] and the realistic costs of deploying IDSs. For each attack a_i in the set of attack actions A, we will represent these scores as IS_{a_i}, ES_{a_i} and BS_{a_i} using CVSS metrics, previously discussed in Sect. 3.

Cost of Deploying IDS. We denote the cost of deploying an IDS corresponding to an attack $a \in A$ as $\hat{c}_a$. For our example, we assume the cost of deploying an IDS (shown in the IOC column of Table 1) to be proportional to the betweenness centrality of the VMs on which the IDS is deployed because a VM with high betweenness centrality will affect the latency of routing packets or the latency of processing a request. Also, the centrality values are normalized in the interval $[0, 10]$ to be comparable to the CVSS metrics IS_a, ES_a and BS_a as discussed in Sect. 3. Note that the model in this paper allows another user to define $\hat{c}_a$ in a different way.

We now leverage these defined metrics to design the following rewards for the four utilities associated with each attack a present in our system,

$$U_{c,a}^{\mathcal{D}} = -1 * \hat{c}_a \ , \ U_{u,a}^{\mathcal{D}} = -1 * IS_a$$
$$U_{c,a}^{\mathcal{A}} = -1 * ES_a \ , \ U_{u,a}^{\mathcal{A}} = +1 * BS_a$$

We now provide the rationale for modeling the rewards in this particular manner. The value of $U_{c,a}^{\mathcal{D}}$ is negative since even if it detected an attack, it incurred a cost in order to detect it and moreover there is no extra positive reward given to $\mathcal{D}$ for protecting their system, which is supposed to be the primary functionality. When $\mathcal{D}$ does not place an IDS for detecting the attack a, it incurs a negative utility $(U_{u,a}^{\mathcal{D}})$ equal to IS_a if the attacker uses attack a.

For the attacker $\mathcal{A}$, if it chooses an attack action a which the defender covers (i.e. can detect), it gets a negative utility $U_{c,a}^{\mathcal{A}}$ proportional to the time and cost it had to invest in doing it, which is (somewhat) measured by ES. Also, as $\mathcal{A}$ gains nothing by doing this attack (since the defender can deploy a countermeasure on detection [8]), no positive value is added to it. Lastly, when the attacker uses an attack for which the defender has not placed an IDS, we give a positive utility that (conceptually) adds the IS and subtracts the cost (ES) of performing the attack. Since BS already captures this trade-off, we use it directly.

4 Computing the Stackelberg Equilibrium

We need to solve for the Stackelberg Equilibrium of our game to obtain probability values for each configuration mentioned in A_k, where $A_k \subset A$ such that $|A_k| = k$. Unfortunately, since there are $\binom{n}{k}$ such probabilities (corresponding to each element in A_k), solving for all these variables at once will not yield an efficient solution. Instead, we will solve for the probabilities p_a which represents the probability that a certain attack $a \in A$ is covered by an IDS in a round.

To that extent, we first describe a method that can help in generating the marginal strategies for the defender by solving n ($= |A|$) Linear Programs. Note that the solution can be found in polynomial time in our case because of the particular reward structure our game has. Then, we shall propose an efficient Mixed Integer Quadratic Program (MIQP) method based on this method that helps us to obtain the same marginal strategy, but by solving just one optimization problem. We show that although this formulation, in the general case, is known to computationally hard to solve, in our case, by efficient use of the branch-and-cut mechanism, we can solve it in polynomial time.

4.1 Multiple LP Method

Let T denote the set of k *tokens* that the defender $\mathcal{D}$ can allocate to cover k of the n attacks. Allocating a token to an attack a means that $\mathcal{D}$ has placed the IDS that can detect the particular attack. Now, let the variables p_a represent the probability with which an attack a is covered by one of the k tokens and $p_{a,t}$ represent the probability with which a particular attack a is covered by a particular token $t \in T$. Having defined the probabilities p_a, the defender's expected utility for deploying an IDS to detect a particular attack a^* should be $U_{u,a^*}^{\mathcal{D}} * (1 - p_{a^*}) + U_{c,a^*}^{\mathcal{D}} * p_{a^*}$ [24,25]. Note that, for our scenario, this does not capture the cost $\mathcal{D}$ incurs in deploying the other $k - 1$ IDS mechanisms. Thus, we modify the defender's utility to $U_{u,a^*}^{\mathcal{D}} * (1 - p_{a^*}) + \frac{1}{k} \sum_{a \in A} U_{c,a}^{\mathcal{D}} * p_a$, where the second term denotes the average cost for a particular deployment configuration.

On the other hand, we can simply define the attacker's expected utility for using a particular attack a as $U_{c,a}^{A} * p_a + U_{u,a}^{A} * (1 - p_a)$. We now present the optimization problem that maximizes the defender's objective function and the attacker's utility given that an attacker chooses to use the attack a^*.

$$\max \quad \alpha \cdot \frac{1}{k} \sum_{a \in A} U_{c,a}^{D} p_a + (1 - \alpha) \cdot U_{u,a^*}^{D} (1 - p_{a^*}) \tag{1}$$

$$s.t. \quad p_a \in [0,1] \ \forall \, a \in A$$

$$p_{t,a} \in [0,1] \ \forall \, a \in A, t \in T$$

$$\sum_{a \in A} p_{t,a} = 1 \ \forall \, t \in T$$

$$\sum_{t \in T} p_{t,a} = p_a \ \forall \, a \in A$$

$$U_{c,a}^{A} p_a + U_{u,a}^{A} (1 - p_a) \leq U_{c,a^*}^{A} p_{a^*} + U_{u,a^*}^{A} (1 - p_{a^*})$$

where α is an input parameter that allows the defender to a trade the performance of the system with respect to the security of the system (and vice versa). In the extreme case when $\alpha = 0$, the defender optimizes only for security and completely ignores the fact that deploying k IDSs might affect the performance of the system. In this case, as shown in Sect. 6, $\mathcal{D}$ ends up randomizing more between the deployment configurations of the system. On the other hand, when $\alpha = 1$, the defender optimizes for performance, hardly placing an IDS on systems that affect performance even when it is detrimental to security. We discuss the effects of selecting various α-s in Sect. 6.

Before we dive into what the constraints mean, note that this is a Linear Program (LP) and thus, can be solved in polynomial time. The first two sets of constraints ensure that the optimization variables p_a and $p_{t,a}$ are valid probabilities. The third set of constraints ensures that all the tokens are utilized in covering the different attacks in A. The equality of this constraint is possible in our case since (1) all our tokens are homogeneous, i.e. any token $t \in T$ can be used to cover any attack $a \in A$ and (2) the number of tokens $k \ (= |T|)$ is less than the number of attacks $n \ (= |A|)$. Thus, we prune away solutions that do not fully utilize all the tokens. The fourth set of constraints ensure that the probabilities of allocating various tokens to cover an attack a add up to the probability that a is covered. The final set of constraints ensure that the attacker selecting a^* maximizes their utility. Lastly, note that given the values of $p_{t,a}$ one can easily obtain p_a using the fourth set of constraints.

To obtain the (globally) optimal solution (and thus find the optimal marginal strategy) for the defender, we can iterate over all the n attack choices made by the attacker and pick the solution that maximizes $\mathcal{D}$'s utility. Note that, here we enforce the attacker to select a pure strategy as opposed to a mixed strategy. This is not a limitation since for any mixed strategy the attacker can pick in this Stackelberg Game, there always exists a pure strategy in support of it [30].

As the number of VMs and vulnerabilities, i.e., n, increase, this solution method needs to solve a large number of LPs. Thus, we now propose an efficient

MIQP that finds the solution in one go and provides an efficient branch-and-cut algorithm for solving it in polynomial time.

4.2 Compiling Multiple LPs into an Efficient Mixed Integer Quadratic Program (MIQP)

Now, we first introduce n binary switch variables, one for each attack $a \in A$ and represent it as w_a. When the attacker exploits vulnerability a (i.e. uses the attack action a), $w_a = 1$. Otherwise, $w_a = 0$. We now propose the following optimization problem,

$$\max \quad \alpha \cdot \frac{1}{k} \sum_{a \in A} U_{c,a}^{D} p_a + (1 - \alpha) \cdot w_a * U_{u,a}^{D}(1 - p_a) \qquad (2)$$

$$s.t. \quad w_a \in \{0,1\} \ \forall \, a \in A$$

$$p_a \in [0,1] \ \forall \, a \in A$$

$$p_{t,a} \in [0,1] \ \forall \, a \in A, t \in T$$

$$\sum_{a \in A} w_a = 1$$

$$\sum_{a \in A} p_{t,a} = 1 \ \forall \, t \in T$$

$$\sum_{t \in T} p_{t,a} = p_a \ \forall \, a \in A$$

$$0 \le v_a - (U_{c,a}^{A} p_a + U_{u,a}^{A}(1 - p_a)) \le (1 - w_a) * M \ \forall \, a \in A$$

where M represents a large number with respect to the maximum reward the attacker can get, i.e. $M \gg 10$, and v_a is the utility value of the attacker at equilibrium. The first constraint ensures that the switch variables are binary. The fourth constraint enforces the attacker to select a pure strategy since the switch variable corresponding to only one attack can be turned on in a feasible solution. As mentioned in the previous section, this is not a limiting assumption. Lastly, the final set of constraints encodes the complementary slackness condition of the attacker's utility maximization problem [30].

As the defender plays first, it can reason about the attacker picking each attack and select the strategy which gives D the maximum reward. If the attacker responds to the defender's strategy with attack a^*, then $w_{a^*} = 1$. In that case, the RHS of the last constraint (with a^*) becomes zero and along with the LHS, equality holds. Thus, v_{a^*} is A's utility value. For all the other attacks $a(\neq a^*)$ that were not selected by A, both the inequalities can be trivially satisfied (as M is a large number) by selecting an appropriate value for v_a.

Theorem 1. *MIQP defined in Eq. 2 produces the same solution as the set of LPs described in Eq. 1.*

Proof. Let us say that when attacker selects an attack a_1, the defender gets the highest utility as per Eq. 1. Now, let us say that Eq. 2 decides that the defender's

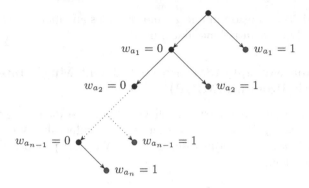

Fig. 2. Branch-and-cut tree for the proposed MIQP. (Color figure online)

Table 2. Player utilities for each vulnerability depending on whether (or not) an IDS is deployed to detect the attacks that exploit it.

Attack	a_1	a_2	a_3	a_4	a_5
$U_{c,a}^{\mathcal{D}}$	−5.7	−10.0	0.0	0.0	0.0
$U_{u,a}^{\mathcal{D}}$	−6.4	−6.4	−2.9	−6.4	−2.9
$U_{c,a}^{\mathcal{A}}$	−8.6	−10	−8.6	−10	−10
$U_{u,a}^{\mathcal{A}}$	6.8	7.5	4.3	7.5	5.0

Table 3. Probability of allocating a token (in order to deploy the corresponding IDS) for detecting each attack.

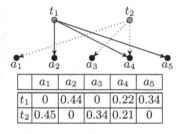

	a_1	a_2	a_3	a_4	a_5
t_1	0	0.44	0	0.22	0.34
t_2	0.45	0	0.34	0.21	0

utility is strictly better when attacker selects any another attack $a_2(\neq a_1)$, and thus, $w_{a_2} = 1$. Notice that if this is true, then the objective function value of LP when $a^* = a_2$ is strictly greater than the objective function value of the LP with $a^* = a_1$. But that is a contradiction. Hence, the MIQP defined in Eq. 2 must select a_1 for the attacker.

Similarly, we can prove the other way–that a solution that is optimal for the MIQP (Eq. 2) is also optimal for the LP case.   ■

Theorem 2. *MIQP defined in Eq. 2 can be solved in polynomial time with the branch-and-cut method.*

Proof. To prove this, we first represent the branch-and-cut tree for our MIQP in Fig. 2. In that, notice that the right children (shown in red) correspond to an LP problem (similar to the one defined in Eq. 1) where only a particular attack a_i is selected ($w_{a_i} = 1$) and other attacks are not used by the attacker. Since no children of any right child (red node) can generate another solution, the search tree below them can be pruned away. Now, the tree can have at most $n − 1$ left children which correspond to at most n right children, which in turn corresponds to at most n LP problems that need to be solved. Since each LP can be solved in polynomial time and we will solve no more than n LPs, this MIQP can be solved in polynomial time.   ■

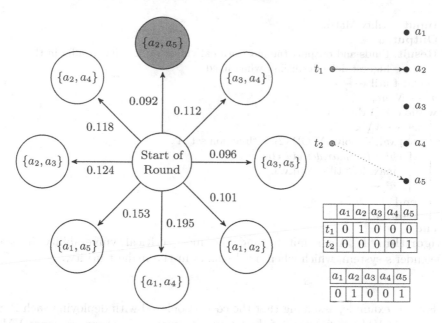

Fig. 3. Optimal mixed strategy of the defender for our scenario (when $\alpha = 0.1$). The probability values for picking up one of the eight IDS placements at the start of each round are written on the edges. For the strategy $\{a_2, a_5\}$ (colored in Pink), the allocation matrix is shown on the right. (Color figure online)

4.3 Obtaining Implementable Strategies

Although we have obtained the values p_a and $p_{t,a}$, there are no guarantees that we will be able to convert these marginal probabilities into $\binom{n}{k}$ probability values that correspond to a defender's deployment strategies, i.e. one that can be implemented in practice. In order to convert these into *implementable strategies*, we use the general version of the Birkhoff Von-Neumann Theorem as stated in [25]. We state this here for completeness.

Birkhoff Von-Neumann Theorem. *Consider an $k \times n$ matrix P with real numbers $p_{t,a} \in [0, 1]$, such that for each $1 \le t \le k$, $\sum_{a=1}^{n} p_{t,a} \le 1$, and for each $1 \le a \le n$, $\sum_{t=1}^{k} p_{t,a} \le 1$. Then, there exist matrices $P^1, P^2, \ldots, P^q$ and weights $w^1, w^2, \ldots, w^q \in (0, 1]$, such that (1) $\sum_{x=1}^{q} w^x = 1$; (2) $\sum_{x=1}^{q} w^x P^x = M$; (3) for each $1 \le x \le q$, the elements of M^x are $p_{t,a}^x \in \{0, 1\}$ and (4) for each $1 \le x \le q$, we have for each $1 \le t \le k$, $\sum_{a=1}^{n} p_{t,a}^x \le 1$ and for each $1 \le a \le n$, $\sum_{t=1}^{k} p_{t,a}^x \le 1$.*

This theorem guarantees that given the probability matrix $p_{t,a}$, we can always obtain the probabilities of the $\binom{n}{k}$ implementable strategies. The third and fourth equalities in the optimization problem in 1 ensure that the constraint structure imposed on P is a *bi-hierarchy*, which authors in [4] show as a sufficient condition for any marginal probability matrix P to be *implementable*.

Input: Utility Matrix
Output: a^*
Result: Finds and outputs the most critical vulnerability that results in the
highest defender utility when fixed
max_def_util $\leftarrow -\infty$;
$a^* \leftarrow None$;
while $a \in A$ **do**
    | $A' \leftarrow A \setminus a$;
    | obj_val, $\leftarrow$ solve MIQP (2) with action set A';
    | **if** $obj\_val > max\_def\_util$ **then**
    | | max_def_util $\leftarrow$ obj_val;
    | | $a^* \leftarrow a$;
    | **end**
    | return a^*
end

Algorithm 1. Algorithm to find the most critical vulnerability in the Defender's system, which when fixed results in the highest utility.

For our example, assuming that the cost associated with deploying each IDS on a certain VM is a function of the latency it creates. Furthermore, since VMs that are responsible for communication between other VMs would impact the latency the most when an IDS is placed on it. Thus, we assume time impact on the overall latency of the system is equal to the normalized and scaled betweenness centrality of the nodes in our network ($\in [0, 10]$). With that, the utility values for the attacker and defender are shown in Table 2. We first use these values to solve for the optimal marginal strategy (shown in Fig. 3) using the MIQP described in 2. We then use Theorem 1 to obtain the mixed strategies that the defender can actually use to deploy the IDS systems (shown in Fig. 3).

5   Identifying the Most Critical Vulnerability

In real-world scenarios, system administrators, who have a list of known vulnerabilities it should address, have limited developer resources to fix all of the known CVEs in their system at once. Thus, the question of which vulnerability they should fix in order to improve the security of the system is a critical one. In our case, since (1) the rewards of the formulated game are not zero-sum and (2) the defender wants to balance a multi-objective function (that tries to balance the security and usability metrics), figuring out the (critical) vulnerability that $\mathcal{D}$ needs to fix become even more difficult.

Given that we can find the utilities for the defender using Eq. 2, we can ask the question *which attack a* when removed would produce the maximum utility for $\mathcal{D}$. A simple algorithm would be to iterate over all the attacks, removing them one by one, reformulating the MIQP and selecting the attack that maximizes the defender's utility when removed. We describe this idea formally in Algorithm 1 and use it to find the most critical vulnerability of our system. The utilities obtained by removing one vulnerability at a time are shown below (for $\alpha = 0.1$).

$$\langle a_1 : -1.90; a_2 : -1.70; a_3 : -2.30; a_4 : -2.23; a_5 : -2.27 \rangle$$

Thus, in our system, a_2 is the most critical vulnerability since fixing a_2 will result in the highest (gain in) defender's utility.

6   Experiments

We present the results of two different experiments – (1) comparison of our placement strategy (Fig. 3) with existing approaches, and (2) implementation of the Stackelberg Game Strategy (SGS) on a large cloud network instance.

6.1   Comparison with Existing Strategies

In this section, we compare our approach to three other MTD strategies in the context of our running example where $n = 5$ and $k = 2$:

(1) Deterministic Pure Strategy (DPS). This strategy selects a single pure strategy out of the $\binom{5}{2}$ placement strategies. As per work by [20], for DPS, we place IDS to detect a_1 and a_2 (since G1 and G2 are the most critical VMs), which are on the critical paths for any attack flow. Note that, in the context of a stealthy attacker who can exploit any vulnerability in the system, the definition of a critical node, on which an IDS can be deployed, is not clear. Thus, DPS has an inherent disadvantage when compared to MTD strategies, which we now describe.

	a_1	a_2	a_3	a_4	a_5
URS	0.4	0.4	0.4	0.4	0.4
DPS	1	1	0	0	0
CBS	0.52	0.73	0.25	0.25	0.25

Fig. 4. Table showcasing the marginal probabilities with which IDS is places on a node for the different strategies.

(2) Uniform Random Strategy (URS). In this case, we select each of the $\binom{5}{2}$ placements or pure strategies with an equal probability of 0.1. In this case, each attack a is covered in four (out of the ten) pure strategies since having placed an IDS (or token which denotes an IDS was placed) for a, there are $\binom{4}{1} = 4$ ways of placing the other token. Thus, the marginal probabilities are $0.1 * 4 = 0.4$.

(3) Centrality Based Strategy (CBS). This strategy, motivated in the work by [42], has previously been shown to be effective for detecting stealthy bot-nets when PageRank is used as a centrality measure. Since our network is an undirected graph, we use the betweenness centrality measure for evaluation. Since only two of our nodes (G1 and G2) have non-zero values for betweenness centrality, we switch between seven of the ten configurations – three in which only a_1 is covered, three in which only a_2 is covered and one in which both a_1 and a_2 are covered. Since $G1$, on which a_1 is present has a lower centrality value in comparison to $G2$, on which a_2 is present, the first three configurations are less likely than the next three. The last configuration, in which both a_1 and a_2 are covered, is the most likely configuration. The marginal probabilities for covering each attack in the system, as per this strategy, is shown in Fig. 4.

Effectiveness of Our Approach. We plot the defender's utility value for our approach and compare it to all the other approaches. The results are shown in Fig. 5. When adversaries are strategic, i.e. can reason about defender strategies and act rationally to maximize their utility, our method clearly dominates the other methods (see the plots for CBS(min), URS(min) and DPS).

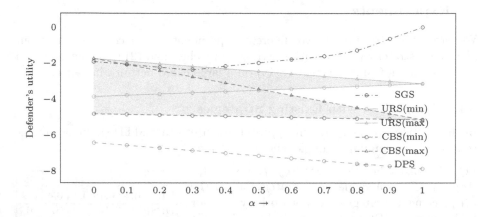

Fig. 5. Defender's utility for the various MTD strategies as the security-usability trade-off value (α) varies from zero to one.

On the other hand, if the attacker is irrational, i.e., selects attacks that do not maximize their profit, Stackelberg Equilibrium may not always be the best strategy. We plot the best case for the other MTD strategies (see URS(max) and CBS(max)) and it turns out that only URS is a little better when $\alpha \in (0, 0.37]$. In this range, our algorithm selects nodes with high centrality measure to improve security in the case of a strategic attacker. This increases the deployment cost and reduces the multi-objective function value, letting URS dominate. CBS on the other hand with no information about the known attacks or performance costs, switches only among the useless and performance expensive configurations, being strictly dominated by SGS. Note that none of the mechanisms we compare against adapt to the security and performance trade-off that is important to the defender. Thus, as the value of α changes, the marginal probabilities for selecting nodes using CBS, URS or DPS remain constant, resulting in straight line plots. On the other hand, SGS, our intelligent switching mechanism, solves the multi-objective optimization when coming up with its mixed strategy.

When α is low (i.e. $\in [0, 0.29]$), our method switches among eight out of the ten pure strategies. As α increases further and the costs start to matter, it places IDS systems more on nodes that impact performance the least. Beyond a certain value (when $\alpha > 0.76$) it realizes that the cost of placing IDS on G1 and G2 (for detecting $a1$ and $a2$) are extremely high on the performance of the system and sticks to only (three) strategies where neither G1 nor G2 is covered.

6.2   Testing on a Large Cloud Network

The setup comprised of 15 VMs and 42 CVEs distributed uniformly on a flat network 10.0.0.0/24, as shown in the Fig. 6. In this experiment, we will measure the throughput for the server (10.0.0.15) hosting an ssh application on port 5002 as the number of IDS systems placed increases. We now describe the different NIDS and HIDS agents pre-configured on the system with the known attack signatures to detect the intrusion attempts.

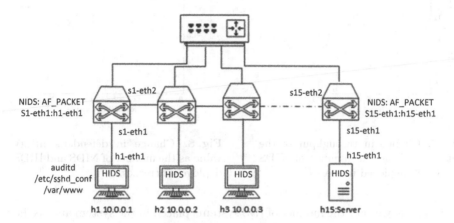

Fig. 6. Testing bandwidth on a flat network with 15 VMs and multiple Network and Host Intrusion Detection Systems (NIDS and HIDS).

Network-Based IDS. Snort [32] was configured to run in IDS (intrusion-detection) as well as IPS (intrusion-prevention) mode. For instance, the attack signature below checks the payload for shellcode targeting remote buffer overflow vulnerability on ssh service running on port 5022.

```
alert TCP any any -> 10.0.0.15 5002 (msg:"EXPLOIT ssh remote
    overflow"; content:"/bin/sh"; reference:Bugtraq,2347;
    reference:cve,2008-5161; sid:1324; rev:6;)
```

The AF packet, which is an IPS configuration, creates a bridge between inspected interfaces (e.g., h1-eth1:s1-eth1). This leads to increased packet processing latency since each packet on a particular bridge is inspected against all traffic patterns which are part of signatures.

Host-Based IDS. Auditd [18] was configured to monitor file integrity of configuration files such as /etc/sshd_conf and binary files for vulnerable services present on the network. A daemon was configured on each inspected host to generate an alert if there is a change in the hash value of inspected files.

The goal of this experiment was to measure the impact of the HIDS/NIDS deployment on the throughput of the service being accessed by normal users.

We show that as $\mathcal{D}$ places more IDSs (1 to 15), we observe a substantial drop in the throughput of the system from 18 Gbps to 6 Gbps (see Fig. 7). This shows that deployment of IDS without considering the impact on network latency can affect the Quality of Service (QoS) for legitimate users in a cloud network.

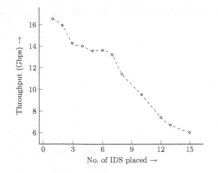
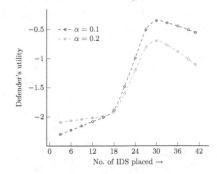

Fig. 7. Change in throughput of the flat network as the number of NIDS and HIDS deployed increases.

Fig. 8. Change in defender's utility value as the number of NIDS and HIDS deployed increases.

In Fig. 8, we vary the number of IDS systems placed in the system and see how the defender utilities vary. Initially, as the number of IDS increases from 2 to 17, the defender's utility increases at a slow rate since there are too few IDS systems to detect attacks on all the 42 vulnerabilities. As the number of IDS systems are increased beyond 18, the defender's utility starts to increase substantially in each step. At this point, if the attacker does not pick their attack strategically, it is detected with high probability. However, the placement of more IDSs beyond a certain point (30) as shown in the Fig. 8, results in a substantial decrease in throughput, outweighing the benefits of security provided by IDS. Lastly, the most critical vulnerability found in this system was CVE-2013-2207.

7   Conclusion and Future Work

In this paper, we addressed the problem of placing a fixed number of IDS systems in a large cloud environment by proposing a Moving Target Defense (MTD) approach for shifting the detection surface. We formulated this problem as a two-player general-sum Stackelberg Game between the cloud administrator (our defender) and an attacker. We then designed two scalable algorithms that can (1) find the Stackelberg Equilibrium of the formulated game, which lets the cloud service provided a balance between the security and usability of their system, and (2) find the most critical vulnerability in their system. We assumed that the attacker is rational, i.e. he will try to exploit the known vulnerabilities present of VMs in the cloud network by scanning the network. Also, a sophisticated attacker may perform reconnaissance over an extended period of time and use zero-day attacks that cannot be detected by IDS [38]. We plan to model these types of attackers in the future.

Acknowledgements. This research is supported in part by the AFOSR grant FA9550-18-1-0067, ONR grants N00014-16-1-2892, N00014-18-1-2442, N00014-18-12840, the NASA grant NNX17AD06G, the NRL N00173-15-G017, NSF Grants 1642031, 1528099, and 1723440, and NSFC Grants 61628201 and 61571375. The first author is also supported in part by the IBM Ph.D. Fellowship 2018-19.

References

1. Al-Jarrah, O., Arafat, A.: Network intrusion detection system using neural network classification of attack behavior. J. Adv. Inf. Technol. **6**(1), 1–6 (2015)
2. Bakshi, A., Dujodwala, Y.B.: Securing cloud from DDOS attacks using intrusion detection system in virtual machine. In: Second International Conference on Communication Software and Networks, ICCSN 2010, pp. 260–264. IEEE (2010)
3. Brown, D.J., Suckow, B., Wang, T.: A survey of intrusion detection systems. Department of Computer Science, University of California, San Diego (2002)
4. Budish, E., Che, Y.K., Kojima, F., Milgrom, P.: Designing random allocation mechanisms: theory and applications. Am. Econ. Rev. **103**(2), 585–623 (2013)
5. M. I. Center: APT1: Exposing One of Chinas Cyber Espionage Units. Mandian.com (2013)
6. Chen, D., Zhao, H.: Data security and privacy protection issues in cloud computing. In: 2012 International Conference on Computer Science and Electronics Engineering (ICCSEE), vol. 1, pp. 647–651. IEEE (2012)
7. Chowdhary, A., Alshamrani, A., Huang, D., Liang, H.: MTD analysis and evaluation framework in software defined network (MASON). In: Proceedings of the 2018 ACM International Workshop on Security in Software Defined Networks and Network Function Virtualization, pp. 43–48. ACM (2018)
8. Chowdhary, A., Pisharody, S., Huang, D.: SDN based scalable MTD solution in cloud network. In: Proceedings of the 2016 ACM Workshop on Moving Target Defense, pp. 27–36. ACM (2016)
9. Chung, C.J., Khatkar, P., Xing, T., Lee, J., Huang, D.: NICE: network intrusion detection and countermeasure selection in virtual network systems. IEEE Trans. Dependable Secure Comput. **10**(4), 198–211 (2013)
10. Conitzer, V., Sandholm, T.: Computing the optimal strategy to commit to. In: Proceedings of the 7th ACM Conference on Electronic Commerce, pp. 82–90. ACM (2006)
11. Dastjerdi, A.V., Bakar, K.A., Tabatabaei, S.G.H.: Distributed intrusion detection in clouds using mobile agents. In: Third International Conference on Advanced Engineering Computing and Applications in Sciences, ADVCOMP 2009, pp. 175–180. IEEE (2009)
12. Debar, H., Dacier, M., Wespi, A.: Towards a taxonomy of intrusion-detection systems. Comput. Netw. **31**(8), 805–822 (1999)
13. Deshpande, P., Sharma, S., Peddoju, S., Junaid, S.: HIDS: a host based intrusion detection system for cloud computing environment. Int. J. Syst. Assur. Eng. Manag. **9**, 1–10 (2014)
14. Durkota, K., Lisỳ, V., Bosanskỳ, B., Kiekintveld, C.: Optimal network security hardening using attack graph games. In: IJCAI, pp. 526–532 (2015)

15. Garfinkel, T., Rosenblum, M., et al.: A virtual machine introspection based architecture for intrusion detection. In: NDSS, vol. 3, pp. 191–206 (2003)
16. Hu, Z., Zhu, M., Liu, P.: Online algorithms for adaptive cyber defense on Bayesian attack graphs (2017)
17. Ibrahim, L.M.: Anomaly network intrusion detection system based on distributed time-delay neural network (DTDNN). J. Eng. Sci. Technol. **5**(4), 457–471 (2010)
18. Ilgun, K.: USTAT: a real-time intrusion detection system for UNIX. University of California Santa Barbara Master thesis (1992)
19. Jajodia, S., Park, N., Serra, E., Subrahmanian, V.: Share: a stackelberg honey-based adversarial reasoning engine. ACM Trans. Internet Technol. (TOIT) **18**(3), 30 (2018)
20. Jha, S., Sheyner, O., Wing, J.: Two formal analyses of attack graphs. In: Proceedings of 15th IEEE Computer Security Foundations Workshop, pp. 49–63. IEEE (2002)
21. Jo, S., Sung, H., Ahn, B.: A comparative study on the performance of intrusion detection using decision tree and artificial neural network models. J. Korea Soc. Digit. Ind. Inf. Manag. **11**(4), 33–45 (2015)
22. Jones, S., et al.: Evaluating moving target defense with PLADD. Technical report, Sandia National Labs-NM, Albuquerque (2015)
23. Kheir, N., Cuppens-Boulahia, N., Cuppens, F., Debar, H.: A service dependency model for cost-sensitive intrusion response. In: Gritzalis, D., Preneel, B., Theoharidou, M. (eds.) ESORICS 2010. LNCS, vol. 6345, pp. 626–642. Springer, Heidelberg (2010). https://doi.org/10.1007/978-3-642-15497-3_38
24. Kiekintveld, C., Jain, M., Tsai, J., Pita, J., Ordóñez, F., Tambe, M.: Computing optimal randomized resource allocations for massive security games. In: Proceedings of The 8th International Conference on Autonomous Agents and Multiagent Systems, vol. 1, pp. 689–696. International Foundation for Autonomous Agents and Multiagent Systems (2009)
25. Korzhyk, D., Conitzer, V., Parr, R.: Complexity of computing optimal stackelberg strategies in security resource allocation games. In: AAAI (2010)
26. Letchford, J., Vorobeychik, Y.: Optimal interdiction of attack plans. In: Proceedings of the 2013 International Conference on Autonomous Agents and Multi-agent Systems, pp. 199–206. International Foundation for Autonomous Agents and Multiagent Systems (2013)
27. Maleki, H., Valizadeh, S., Koch, W., Bestavros, A., van Dijk, M.: Markov modeling of moving target defense games. In: Proceedings of the 2016 ACM Workshop on Moving Target Defense, pp. 81–92. ACM (2016)
28. Mell, P., Scarfone, K., Romanosky, S.: Common vulnerability scoring system. IEEE Secur. Priv. **4**(6), 85–89 (2006)
29. Panda, S., Vorobeychik, Y.: Near-optimal interdiction of factored MDPs. In: Conference on Uncertainty in Artificial Intelligence (2017)
30. Paruchuri, P., Pearce, J.P., Marecki, J., Tambe, M., Ordonez, F., Kraus, S.: Playing games for security: an efficient exact algorithm for solving Bayesian stackelberg games. In: Proceedings of the 7th International Joint Conference on Autonomous agents and Multiagent Systems, vol. 2, pp. 895–902. International Foundation for Autonomous Agents and Multiagent Systems (2008)
31. Pita, J., et al.: Deployed armor protection: the application of a game theoretic model for security at the los angeles international airport. In: Proceedings of the 7th International Joint Conference on Autonomous Agents and Multiagent Systems: Industrial Track, pp. 125–132. AAMAS (2008)

32. Roesch, M., et al.: Snort: lightweight intrusion detection for networks. In: LISA 1999, pp. 229–238 (1999)
33. Roschke, S., Cheng, F., Meinel, C.: An extensible and virtualization-compatible ids management architecture. In: Fifth International Conference on Information Assurance and Security, IAS 2009, vol. 2, pp. 130–134. IEEE (2009)
34. Rowland, C.H.: Intrusion detection system. US Patent 6,405,318, 11 June 2002
35. Sengupta, S., Chakraborti, T., Kambhampati, S.: MTDeep: boosting the security of deep neural nets against adversarial attacks with moving target defense. arXiv preprint arXiv:1705.07213 (2017)
36. Sengupta, S., et al.: A game theoretic approach to strategy generation for moving target defense in web applications. In: Proceedings of the 16th Conference on Autonomous Agents and MultiAgent Systems, pp. 178–186. International Foundation for Autonomous Agents and Multiagent Systems (2017)
37. Sinha, A., Nguyen, T.H., Kar, D., Brown, M., Tambe, M., Jiang, A.X.: From physical security to cybersecurity. J. Cybersecur. 1(1), 19–35 (2015)
38. Tankard, C.: Advanced persistent threats and how to monitor and deter them. Netw. Secur. 2011(8), 16–19 (2011)
39. Vadlamudi, S.G., et al.: Moving target defense for web applications using Bayesian stackelberg games. In: Proceedings of the 2016 International Conference on Autonomous Agents and Multiagent Systems, pp. 1377–1378. International Foundation for Autonomous Agents and Multiagent Systems (2016)
40. Van Dijk, M., Juels, A., Oprea, A., Rivest, R.L.: Flipit: The game of "stealthy takeover". J. Cryptol. 26(4), 655–713 (2013)
41. Venkatesan, S., Albanese, M., Amin, K., Jajodia, S., Wright, M.: A moving target defense approach to mitigate DDOS attacks against proxy-based architectures. In: 2016 IEEE Conference on Communications and Network Security (CNS), pp. 198–206. IEEE (2016)
42. Venkatesan, S., Albanese, M., Cybenko, G., Jajodia, S.: A moving target defense approach to disrupting stealthy botnets. In: Proceedings of the 2016 ACM Workshop on Moving Target Defense, pp. 37–46. ACM (2016)
43. Vieira, K., Schulter, A., Westphall, C., Westphall, C.: Intrusion detection for grid and cloud computing. IT Prof. 12(4), 38–43 (2010)
44. Zhu, Q., Başar, T.: Game-theoretic approach to feedback-driven multi-stage moving target defense. In: Das, S.K., Nita-Rotaru, C., Kantarcioglu, M. (eds.) GameSec 2013. LNCS, vol. 8252, pp. 246–263. Springer, Cham (2013). https://doi.org/10.1007/978-3-319-02786-9_15
45. Zhuang, R., DeLoach, S.A., Ou, X.: Towards a theory of moving target defense. In: Proceedings of the First ACM Workshop on Moving Target Defense, pp. 31–40. ACM (2014)

Approximating Power Indices to Assess Cybersecurity Criticality

Daniel Clouse[1] and David Burke[2(✉)]

[1] Department of Defense, Fort Meade, MD, USA
djclouse@tycho.ncsc.mil
[2] Galois, Inc., Portland, OR, USA
davidb@galois.com

Abstract. This paper describes our work in developing approximation algorithms to calculate the Banzhaf Power Index (BPI) in a bicooperative game (that is, games with two coalitions) with large n for the number of players. Our motivation for this work is applying a cooperative game-theoretic framework to cybersecurity scenarios: our past experience with network defense made us receptive to the principle that differences in the criticality of players or network resources in a coalition setting is not always proportional to their differences in weighting or numbers of votes. Hence, calculating a game-theoretic power measure makes sense as a basis for both assessments and allocation decisions. The challenge is that for most real-world scenarios, the value of n is too high for an exact algorithm to solve in time to be actionable in a network defense scenario. We describe our approximation algorithm, and show empirical results that demonstrate that it produces solid estimates of the BPIs that would result from an exact calculation. Therefore, this approximation approach has utility in scenarios where it is imperative to deliver timely results and network membership can be dynamic.

1 Introduction

Cyber analysts require accurate assessments of their network's defensive posture in order to make effective decisions about resource allocations and next steps. One approach to this challenge would be to categorize each asset on the network as being in one of three states: secure, compromised, or indeterminate (where the latter state can be interpreted as an assessment of not being sure whether the asset is secure or compromised). The goal of the adversary is to alter the state of the secure assets, either compromising them, or at least putting them into an indeterminate state, or else moving indeterminate assets into the comprised camp. The defender's goal is the dual of the adversary. Each asset has a utility to both the defender and the attacker, so knowing the state of each asset can induce a score that captures the overall health of the network.

In order to make this approach more concrete, we recast this challenge in the language of cooperative game theory. Specifically, we consider our motivating scenario as being about coalition formation. The adversary is trying to create a

© Springer Nature Switzerland AG 2018
L. Bushnell et al. (Eds.): GameSec 2018, LNCS 11199, pp. 346–365, 2018.
https://doi.org/10.1007/978-3-030-01554-1_20

coalition of compromised assets on the network, and once this coalition is of sufficient strength, the adversary's objectives have been met. Similarly, the defender is attempting to harden the network in such a way as to create a sufficiently large coalition of secure assets. Each asset is assigned a weight describing its value to the defender in the secure state, and its value to the attacker in a comprised state (these weights can be distinct from each other). We can set a threshold for success for both attacker and defender (again, possibly distinct) such that if the sum of the value of secure assets is over the defender's success threshold, then the network is assessed as fundamentally secure, and likewise for the attacker. At any moment in time, attackers and defenders are trying to move assets into a coalition structure more favorable to them.

In cooperative game theory, a key insight is that the actual power of a player in a coalition is not equivalent to its weight, and this led to the formulation of two well-known measures of player power in a cooperative game: the Shapley value, and the Banzhaf power index. In the context of a network defense scenario, the **criticality** of an asset to an adversary is not simply its weight(s), but rather its power - its ability to turn a losing coalition into a winning coalition by *defecting*, that is, moving out of one state/coalition into another.

Traditional cooperative game theory deals with the formation of one coalition, with one associated threshold. Our use case involves two distinct attacker and defender perspectives and is known in the literature as a *bicooperative* game [1]. However, the fundamental drawback with the Shapley and Banzhaf power measures is that the naive versions of these algorithms are extremely inefficient - they are fundamentally exponential in their running time, which makes them less than useful as real-time algorithms applied to real-world network sizes, which can contain thousands of assets.

In this paper we first introduce the basic ideas behind coalition formation and cooperative game theory, focusing on the Banzhaf power measure. We next describe how the machinery of the cooperative setting can be extended to a bicooperative game. With this background, we then introduce the lattice theoretic ideas that provide the theoretical foundation for our approximation algorithms. We show the approximation is structure preserving, minimal and encodes all of the information of the non-approximate version and hence is likely less variance sensitive than other less principled approximations. We describe how our approximations work, and argue that their accuracy is sufficient in the context of network defense, where actionable decision-making is paramount. Finally, we draw some conclusions and sketch out some promising areas for future research and refinement.

2   Motivating Examples

We first motivate the subsequent discussion by presenting some representative scenarios where cooperative game theoretic modeling has something to offer. As a reminder, a loose description of cooperative game theory is that the field studies those situations in which agents/players can agree to cooperate with each other: they form coalitions, with potentially mutually binding agreements to enforce the coalition structure.

Both of our motivating examples are of *bicooperative* games, in particular, a voting game with two coalitions, each with a success threshold. In the first example, we use the bicooperative framework to model a network defense scenario, and in the second, a policymaking scenario. Even though the situations are superficially different, they both have similar underlying structures that can be captured by a bicooperative framework. One advantage to using this framework is that the richness of the coalition structure provides flexibility with respect to perspective - since both the attacker and defender (using the example of a network defense scenario) have separate asset weights and success thresholds. We can, for example, model situations in which the attacker and defender have reached their threshold, representing their separate perspectives - the defender believes the network is secure, and the attacker believes it to be compromised.

2.1   Network Defense Scenario

A network consists of n assets. These assets have a specific value to the defender, and a specific value to the adversary (and these values may be different). We can describe the current state of the network by assigning each of the n assets to one of three camps: the attacker, the defender, or 'undetermined'. Furthermore, for the purposes of network evaluation, we define thresholds for the attacker and defender coalitions, such that if either threshold is reached, we say that the network is either sufficiently compromised, or adequately protected, respectively, and if neither threshold is reached, then the state of the network is still under contention. Each network asset is assigned both an attacker and defender weighting: the number of votes, so to speak, that it contributes to either coalition. The overall state of the network (protected, compromised, indeterminate) can be dynamic, depending on whether assets are moving from one coalition to another as both attackers and defenders respond to each other.

2.2   Cyber Policy Scenario

Consider a scenario where the international community has developed a voting strategy for developing international order and rules in cyberspace through international governance mechanisms and platforms. In theory, all members of the international community should be entitled to equal participation in developing international order and rules in cyberspace. However, the investment realities of the impacts of international governance on the countries supporting and maintaining the majority of the infrastructure necessary for worldwide cyber support are also to be factored in. Hence, there is an argument for these countries at greater financial risk to have more approval power than those with little or no stake in the investments necessary. In order to balance this realization, it is decided that there is need of a mechanism for a majority number of these less vested countries to block a majority vote established by these more vested members so that developing countries will not be "held financially hostage" in the future. It is further recognized that countries, developing countries in particular, may not be adequately experienced in certain cyber matters or that parties may have a position on an issue but it might not be politically expedient to vote accordingly. Hence all members can place one of three votes, approve, block or abstain and that party votes would be weighted in a manner relevant to party's global investments in cyber affairs.

3 Bicooperative Games

We are casting the challenge of assessing the security or political posture of a network as an exercise in assessing the strength of coalitions on the network. By doing so, we can leverage existing work in cooperative game theory, which has extensively studied coalition formation. In particular, we use measures developed for understanding voting power. One of the most common game-theoretic power indices from cooperative game theory is called the Banzhaf Power Index (BPI), which is one way of measuring the amount of power held by each player in a coalition. The essential insight from Banzhaf is that a player's power in a coalition comes from that player's defection threat: given all the winning coalitions, how many of those coalitions would become losing coalitions if player p defects.

In this work, we will work with bicooperative games, an extension of cooperative games that offers a richer coalition structure. In this section, we follow the notation and definitions from Bilbao [1]. Specifically, instead of a player being in or out of the coalition, we have three states a player can be in: a player is either in the "for" coalition, the "against" coalition, or the "undecided" coalition. The set of players in the first coalition is denoted by S, and the set of players in the second coalition is denoted by T. Hence, any bicoalition is characterized by (S, T). As needed, we'll use $M = (S \cup T)^c$ to represent the 'middle', or 'undecided' coalition.

Given N players, we can define a ternary bicooperative game b over the 3^n possible player states where $b(S, T) \in \{-1, 0, 1\}$, and the following conditions hold:

$$b(\emptyset, N) = -1$$
$$b(\emptyset, \emptyset) = 0$$
$$b(N, \emptyset) = 1$$

The standard BPI is based on the concept of a defender swing; a swing occurs when the defection of player i turns a coalition from winning to losing. In the bicooperative case, there is a defender swing for player i if the game value changes from 1 when i moves out of set S and into set T. More formally, a defender swing for i exists if

$$b(S \cup i, T) = 1 \text{ and } b(S, T \cup i) \neq 1$$

Similarly, we can define a detractor swing for player i as taking place when

$$b(S, T \cup i) = -1 \text{ and } b(S \cup i, T) \neq -1$$

In the cooperative game case, the power of a player is related to their ability to be critical to the formation of a winning coalition. In the bicooperative case, each player can be critical by either participating in coalition S (the "for" coalition) or participating in coalition T (the "against" coalition). Hence, each player has two weights: their voting weight to "approve" a decision by joining coalition S and their voting weight to "block" a decision by joining coalition T. Not joining either S or T is akin to abstaining, or being undecided. There is both a quota for a winning defender coalition q_S, and a winning detractor coalition q_T.

The above definition of defender swing for player i is equivalent to one of the following conditions holding true:

1. Defender coalition S is no longer winning (that is, the sum of the player weights in coalition $S < q_S$)
2. Regardless of whether S is winning or not, detractor coalition $T \cup i$ is now winning (the sum of the player weights in coalition $T \geq q_S$).

These conditions for defender swing can also be described in the following way that will be useful in the sequel. Given player i, we write the term $S \to T$ to denote i's move from coalition S to T. As mentioned, both the S and T coalitions have thresholds associated with them. Since we have two thresholds, and each one can either be reached or not, we have four possible threshold states. For example, the state 10 refers to the state where the S threshold q_S is currently reached, while the T threshold q_T is not currently reached. The following diagram shows the $S \to T$ moves that lead to a state change.

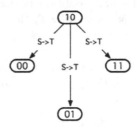

Fig. 1. Defender swing moves by the Bilbao definition

Detractor swing is the dual of defender swing, assessing moves by player i from T to S.

The naive algorithm to calculate BPI for a bicooperative game with n players is proportional to $\mathcal{O}(3^N * N)$, because we have 3^N states to evaluate, and each state has $\mathcal{O}(n)$ players to check for being either a defender or detractor swing. This inefficiency is our motivation for coming up with approximation algorithms for the BPI in a bicooperative context.

4   Lattice Theory and Problem Abstraction

4.1   The Plan

In this section we will expound upon the algebraic foundations for our approximation algorithm and why we believe it to be robust. Our approximation relies on identifying distinct states of the game as being equivalent, e.g. equivalence classes, and thereby reducing the complexity. We first establish the lattice theory foundations to facilitate this identification and Lemma 1 establishes the natural algebraic structure bicooperative games afford, referred to as core regular double Stone algebras, CRDSA [3]. This allows us to cite Lemma 2 which demonstrates the identification preserves CRDSA structure and is achieved in a minimal manner. Theorem 2 then shows the identification still encodes all the information necessary to reconstruct the original CRDSA. Hence the approximation is robust from the Universal Algebra perspective and likely less variance sensitive than other approximations derived from more random identifications.

Let J be any non-empty set of network nodes, not necessarily finite. We will consider all the nodes of the Universe, which subsumes our internal network, generically. Categorizing "types" of nodes can quickly become very complex, we wish to remain conceptually simple and computationally tractable and will define 3 classes of nodes. Our 3 node classes will be denoted 0 = "False", M = "Minus" Vote, and 1 = "True". From our defensive standpoint and drawing on familiar terminology, the nodes in 0, M, and 1 are the nodes that are "known bad", "indeterminate" and "known good", respectively, for our cause. Specific details on what factors are satisfactory for a node to be put into one of those classes are outside of our scope except for this important constraint:

1. Every node in the Universe must be in one and only one of these classes at any given time.

We note J = 1 is our minimal case and up to 2 of the 3 classes are allowed to be empty. Hence any given state of the network is a ternary node set partition, which we visualize as a "3-piece pie" while acknowledging potential "trivial slices". We define the node set bounded distributive lattice through the pairwise disjoint subsets of J with the well known binary operations of ternary set partitions. We then show the resultant bounded distributive lattice is isomorphic to C_3^J where C_3 is the 3 element chain CRDSA. From this result we use a result regarding factor congruences to derive an approximation algorithm for the Banzhaf Power Index of bi-cooperative game theory.

4.2   The C_3^J Construction

For the basic notation in lattice theory and universal algebra, see Burris and Sankappanavar [2]. We start with some definitions:

Definition 1. *Let J be a non-empty set of network nodes and let*
$L = \{(X_1, X_2) | X_1, X_2 \subseteq J \text{ such that } X_1 \cap X_2 = \emptyset\}.$
We define binary operations $\vee$ and $\wedge$ on L as follows:

$- (X_1, X_2) \vee (Y_1, Y_2) = (X_1 \cup Y_1, X_2 \cap Y_2)$ *and;*
$- (X_1, X_2) \wedge (Y_1, Y_2) = (X_1 \cap Y_1, X_2 \cup Y_2)$.

- *The fact that L is a bounded distributive lattice with bounds $(J, \emptyset)$ and $(\emptyset, J)$ is well known.*

We refer to the operations $\vee$, $\wedge$ as join, meet respectively, X_1 are the class 1 or "known good" nodes, X_2 are the class 0 or "known bad", and the nodes in $(X_1 \cup X_2)^c$ are of class M or "indeterminate". We call this lattice the "Node Set bounded distributive lattice" and denote it NS_J for a given node set J.

We note that if J is defined and X_1 and X_2 are understood, we make no mention of $(X_1 \cup X_2)^c$. We further note that in addition to $(J, \emptyset)$ and $(\emptyset, J)$, there is another very important element of NS_J and it is $k = (\emptyset, \emptyset)$. Lastly, it is very important to note that these binary operations coincide with the following partial ordering on L where $\leq$ denotes the familiar "less than or equal to" concept:

$- (X_1, X_2) \leq (Y_1, Y_2) \leftrightarrow X_1 \subseteq Y_1$ and $Y_2 \subseteq X_2$

So **"moving up" = "more known good" nodes and/or "less known bad" nodes** and conversely! Our minimal example, $J = \{1\}$ is evidently the 3 element chain denoted C_3 and Fig. 1. gives the Hasse diagrams of C_3 and also C_3^2 for $J = \{1, 2\}$. We find these diagrams useful, although we mention $J = \{1, 2, 3\}$ is the minumum case where at least one node can be in all 3 states X_1, X_2 and $(X_1 \cup X_2)^c$.

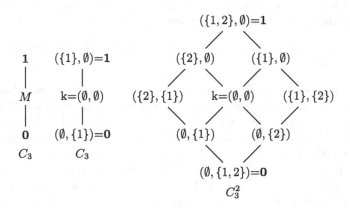

Fig. 2. Minimal examples, C_3 and C_3^2

Now we need to establish the CRDSA structure that will be the foundation of our approximation.

Definition 2. *A double Stone algebra, DSA, $<L, \wedge, \vee, *, +, 0, 1>$ is an algebra of type $<2, 2, 1, 1, 0, 0>$ such that:*

1. $<L, \vee, \wedge, 0, 1>$ is a bounded distributive lattice

2. x^* is the pseudocomplement of x i.e $y \leq x^* \leftrightarrow y \wedge x = 0$
3. x^+ is the dual pseudocomplement of x i.e $y \geq x^+ \leftrightarrow y \vee x = 1$
4. $x^* \vee x^{**} = 1$, $x^+ \wedge x^{++} = 0$, e.g. the Stone identities.

Definition 3. *Let L be a double Stone algebra. An element x of L is called a central element of L if $x^+ = x^*$. The center of L is denoted by $C(L) = \{x \in L | x^+ = x^*\}$.*

Definition 4. *A double Stone algebra L is called regular, RDSA, if it additionally satisfies*

- $x \wedge x^+ \leq y \vee y^*$
  • *this is equivalent to $x^+ = y^+$ and $x^* = y^* \rightarrow x = y$*

We will use the following result when we consider our approximation algorithm.

Theorem 1. *Let L be a regular double Stone algebra. Then $C(L)$ is a Boolean subalgebra of L with respect to the induced operations $\wedge$, $\vee$ and * [3].*

Our structure is even more rigid than that of RDSA and that is demonstrated through a very important element that is called the core element.

Definition 5. *Every element x of a RDSA with the property $x^* = 0$ (or equivalently, $x ** = 1$) is called dense. Every element of the form $x \vee x^*$ is dense and we denote the set of all dense elements of L, $D(L)$. Every element x with the property $x^+ = 1$ (or equivalently, $x^{++} = 0$) is called dually dense. Every element of the form $x \wedge x^+$ is dually dense and we denote the set of all dual dense elements of L, $\overline{D(L)}$.*

Definition 6. *The core of a double Stone algebra L is defined to be $K(L) = D(L) \cap \overline{D(L)}$ and we call a regular double Stone algebra with non-empty core a core regular double Stone algebra, CRDSA [3].*

For any CRDSA L, $|K(L)| = 1$ follows easily from regularity. Now we define the * and $^+$ operations for NS_J and C_3^J that are clearly the pseudocomplement and dual pseudocomplement for those respective structures and demonstrate that they are both double Stone algebras [4].

Definition 7. *Let $(X_1, X_2) \in NS_J$, then*

1. $(X_1, X_2)^* = (X_2, X_2^c)$ *and*
2. $(X_1, X_2)^+ = (X_1^c, X_1)$

define the pseudocomplement and dual pseudocomplement operations of NS_J. We define the following operations on C_3:

1. $^* : C_3 \rightarrow C_3$ *is defined by* $0 \rightarrow 1$, $M \rightarrow 0$ *and* $1 \rightarrow 0$;
2. $^+ : C_3 \rightarrow C_3$ *is defined by* $0 \rightarrow 1$, $M \rightarrow 1$ *and* $1 \rightarrow 0$;

The fact that the operations above extend to a (dual) pseudocomplement operation on C_3^J follows as operations are defined pointwise. Clearly both definitions of $*$ and $+$ demonstrate the Stone identities of Definition 2.

Corollary 1. NS_J and C_3^J are regular double Stone algebras.

Proof. We have already shown C_3^J to be a double Stone algebra. Let $x, y \in C_3^J$ and suppose $x^* = y^*$ and $x^+ = y^+$.

- $x_i = 1 \to y_i^* = 0 = y_i^+ \to y_i = 1$
- $x_i = M \to ((y_i^+ = 1 \to y_i = 0 \text{ or } M) \text{ and } (y_i^* = 0 \to y_i = M \text{ or } 1)) \to y_i = M$
- $x_i = 0 \to y_i^+ = 1 \to y_i = 0$.

So, we see that $x = y$ and C_3^J is regular. It is straightforward to see that NS_J is regular under its operations from Definition 7.

Note 1. We note that $k = (\emptyset, \emptyset) = D(L) \cap \overline{D(L)}$ is the only element of NS_J that is simultaneously dense and dually dense. Clearly C_3 and hence C_3^J is a CRDSA and from here forward we treat it as such. [4] exposites many properties indicating *nearly Boolean* nature of CRDSA including the fact that every CRDSA is a subdirect product of C_3. Now that we have established $NS_J \cong C_3^J$ as CRDSA, we are ready to show they're isomorphic.

Lemma 1. $NS_J \cong C_3^J$

Proof. We define $\alpha : NS_J \to C_3^J$ pointwise for $(X_1, X_2) \in NS_J$ by $\alpha(X_1, X_2) = (x_i)_{i \in J} =$

1. 1 if $i \in X_1$
2. M if $i \in (X_1 \cup X_2)^c$
3. 0 if $i \in X_2$.

Clearly α is bijective and to see that α and α^{-1} are order preserving follows from the partial order itself. Recall that $(X_1, X_2) \le (Y_1, Y_2) \leftrightarrow X_1 \subseteq Y_1$ and $Y_2 \subseteq X_2$, we consider α^{-1} and α below:

1. α^{-1}, suppose $(x_i) \le (y_i)$
   (a) $x_i = 1 \to y_i = 1$ and hence $X_1 \subseteq Y_1$.
   (b) $y_i = 0 \to x_i = 0$ and hence $Y_2 \subseteq X_2$.
2. α, suppose $(X_1, X_2) \le (Y_1, Y_2)$ and consider their images (x_i) and (y_i)
   (a) Suppose $x_i = 1$, then $X_1 \subseteq Y_1 \to y_i = 1$.
   (b) Suppose $x_i = M$, if $y_i = 0$ then $\exists i$ such that $i \in Y_2$ and $i \in (X_1 \cup X_2)^c$ yielding a contradiction with $Y_2 \subseteq X_2$.

The fact that it follows that α is a lattice isomorphism is well known, e.g. Theorem 2.3 of [2]. The fact that α preserves $*$ and $+$ follows from their definitions and the fact that they are extended point-wise from C_3 to C_3^J. Recall:

1. $* : L \to L$ is defined by $(X_1, X_2) \to (X_2, X_2^c)$ and;
2. $+ : L \to L$ is defined by $(X_1, X_2) \to (X_1^c, X_1)$ so that

(a) $* : C_3 \to C_3$ is defined by $0 \to 1$, $M \to 0$ and $1 \to 0$;
(b) $+ : C_3 \to C_3$ is defined by $0 \to 1$, $M \to 1$ and $1 \to 0$;

The fact that α preserves the constants $0 = (\emptyset, J)$ and $1 = (J, \emptyset)$ is clear and we note that it also preserves $k = (\emptyset, \emptyset)$.

Now that we have established $NS_J \cong C_3^J$ as a CRDSA, we are ready to cite some known results regarding its congruences we will use in our approximation algorithm. Recall that congruences are equivalence relations on an algebra that are compatible with its operations. They allow us to obtain quotient algebras by partitioning the elements of the algebra into equivalence classes given by the congruence relation. In the quotient algebra elements of the equivalence class are identified as one element and this will allow for the reduction in complexity of our approximation. Also, please recall that the set of congruences on an algebra L forms a lattice ordered by inclusion with smallest, greatest elements Δ, $L \times L$, respectively. We refer the reader to [2] for facts about congruences and take the following definition and Lemma directly from [3].

Definition 8. *Let θ be a congruence on an algebra L. Then θ is said to ba a factor congruence if there exists a congruence ψ on L such that*

1. *$\theta \wedge \psi = \Delta$ and,*
2. *$\theta \vee \psi = L \times L$.*

We note that when the above holds we refer to θ and ψ as a pair of factor congruences.

Lemma 2 [3]. *Let L be a core regular double Stone algebra and $x \in L$ and define $\theta_x = \{(p, q) \in L \times L | x \wedge p = x \wedge q\}$, then the following hold:*

1. *θ_x is a congruence on L if and only if $x \in C(L)$. Furthermore, θ_x is the smallest congruence containing $(x, 1)$.*
2. *θ is a factor congruence on L if and only if $\theta = \theta_x$ for some $x \in C(L)$.*

Note 2. So, if identifying $(x, 1)$ were desirable then θ_x would be the optimal congruence to do so in the sense that it identifies the smallest subset of C_3^J. In [3] it is shown that θ_x and θ_{x^*} are a pair of factor congruences for all $x \in C(L)$. Since $x \in C(L)$, $(X_1 \cup X_2)^c = \emptyset$ and this means that the roles of known good and known bad are being reversed in the two states represented by x and x^*. The following theorem is known.

Theorem 2 [2]. *Let θ_x and θ_{x^*} be be a pair of factor congruences on L, then $L \cong L/\theta_x \times L/\theta_{x^*}$.*

So as a pair θ_x and θ_{x^*} encode the information contained in L. It is evident from the definition in Lemma 2 and the fact that $x \in C(L)$ that when we consider the equivalence classes for θ_x and the related pairs (p, q) that p_i and q_i are free whenever $x_i = 0$ and $p_i = q_i$ whenever $x_i = 1$. Hence for finite J we can very easily determine $|L/\theta_x|$ based on the support of x. Evidently, if $sup(x) = K$ then $|L/\theta_x| = 3^K$ and the cosets are of cardinality 3^{J-K}. We finish this section by considering a small example, recall $J = \{1, 2, 3\}$ is the minumum case where at least one node can be in all 3 states. We choose $x = (100)$, hence $x^* = (011)$ and we will choose our coset representatives minimally.

Example 1. Let $x = (100)$ below we list the elements of L/θ_x and L/θ_{x^*}, we denote θ_x by θ and θ_{x^*} as θ^* as x is understood.

1. L/θ
   $(000)_\theta = \{(000), (00M), (001), (0M0), (0MM), (0M1), (010), (01M), (011)\}$
   $(M00)_\theta = \{(M00), (M0M), (M01), (MM0), (MMM), (MM1), (M10),$
   $(M1M), (M11)\}$
   $(100)_\theta = \{(100), (10M), (101), (1M0), (1MM), (1M1), (110), (11M), (111)\}$
2. L/θ^*
   $(000)_{\theta^*} = \{(000), (M00), (100)\}(00M)_{\theta^*} = \{(00M), (M0M), (10M)\}$
   $(001)_{\theta^*} = \{(001), (M01), (101)\}(0M0)_{\theta^*} = \{(0M0), (MM0), (1M0)\}$
   $(0MM)_{\theta^*} = \{(0MM), (MMM), (1MM)\}(0M1)_{\theta^*} = \{(0M1), (MM1), (1M1)\}$
   $(010)_{\theta^*} = \{(010), (M10), (110)\}(01M)_{\theta^*} = \{(01M), (M1M), (11M)\}$
   $(011)_{\theta^*} = \{(011), (M11), (111)\}.$

5   An Approximation Algorithm for Calculating BPI

We now discuss our approach to developing an algorithm for calculating an approximate *normalized BPI* [1], herein referred to as BPI, in a bicooperative game. Given a set S_n of n players we use the free variables in the coset representatives of factor congruences from Sect. 4 to decompose S_n into subsets $S_{k_1}, S_{k_2}, ...S_{k_i}$ where the size of each subset is small enough to be a tractable exact BPI calculation. At this point, though, the exact BPI calculations are only with respect to a particular subset; we still need to convert them to a BPI with respect to all n players. Our method for doing so has two steps:

1. **Aggregation.** After the BPIs have been calculated inside each subset, there are two ways to adjust them with respect to the group as a whole:
   (a) **Linear.** In a linear approach, we simply add up all of the weights of the players in a subgroup, and calculate the fraction of all n player weights that this is. This fraction becomes a normalizing coefficient that is applied to all of the weights in that subgroup.
   (b) **Banzhaf.** If we have enough subgroups (empirically, 4 or more), we can treat all the players in a subgroup as a "metaplayer", whose weights are the sums of the player weights in that subgroup. Then we do an exact Banzhaf calculation against all of the subgroup metaplayers - the resulting BPIs are then used as the normalizing factors to be applied to all the players in that subgroup.

2. **Expected Value.** The above step gives us one estimate of a player's overall BPI. This estimate may be skewed by "luck of the draw" - being put a subgroup that contains too many powerful players (or weak players), such that the BPI of the particular player measured against that subgroup may well fail to give an accurate representation of that player's power if it were to be compared to the complete set S_n. Therefore, the decomposition and aggregation steps are repeated many times, and we calculate the expected value of a particular player's power; the idea being that with a large enough number of iterations, the randomness of the subgroups will result in a good estimate for each player's BPI.

The potential savings for this approximation strategy are significant. In practice, we found that 10000 iterations was sufficient to get convergence on the estimates. Imagine that we have an n of 100, and we decompose this into ten subgroups of ten players each, and use a Banzhaf-style aggregation method. That means that we have a total of 11 exact BPI calculations to do, 10000 times each, which is a total of 110,000 exact BPI calculations with $n = 10$. Since the exact BPI calculation is of order $3^n * n$, we get a speedup of $(3^{100} * 100)/((3^{10} * 10) * 110,000) > 3^{88}$. This is turns a largely intractable problem into one with complexity less than 3^{23}, easily executed on most laptops.

Considering that for the applications we're considering, we're looking for solid estimates of the BPI for each player so as to inform decision-makers, not many decimal points of precision for precision's sake. If the approximation is sufficiently close, this is a worthwhile tradeoff.

For very large n, we recursively choose elements in the $C(L)$ from Definition 3 and the above algorithm, decomposing the group into subgroups and sub-subgroups, until we have decomposed the original player set into a tree structure where the leaves represent small enough groups to use the exact BPI algorithm. Then the aggregation steps collapse the tree starting at the leaves, calculating BPIs until we reach the root, which generates a full estimate of all n BPIs. Then we repeat this process, returning the expected values over the iterations.

6 Experiments

In this section, we provide examples of how our approximation algorithm works in practice, comparing its accuracy and performance to the exact algorithm.

6.1 Bilbao Example

The Bilbao paper presents an example of a ternary voting game based on the 19 autonomous communities of Spain. The game is defined by an approval vector

$$[501[178, 159, 136, 109, 60, 55, 47, 45, 44, 31, 29, 24, 23, 23, 13, 13, 7, 2, 2]]$$

and a blocking vector

$$[10; [1, 1, 1, 1, 1, 1, 1, 1, 1, 1, 1, 1, 1, 1, 1, 1, 1, 1, 1]]$$

With $n = 19$, a calculation of the exact BPI is tractable. Using the exact result as the baseline, we ran 10000 iterations where we split the 19 communities into two random **disjoint** groups, one with 9 players, and one with 10, e.g. states $x = (1111100000000001111)$ and $x^* = (0000011111111110000)$ etc., then we aggregated the results. Figure 2 below shows the typical results of an approximation run, where the players are listed from greatest power to least.

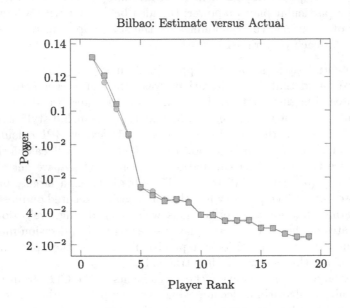

Fig. 3. Total Banzhaf power comparison for the Bilbao example

We can begin to characterize the quality of the estimate by pointing out that in doing numerous runs over 10000 iterations, in no case did we get an error larger than 3.3% between the value of the estimated and actual values of a specific community. The average RMS error across all 19 communities was less than 2% and the ranking was the same. This is accurate enough for, say, actionable resource allocation decision-making for cyber analysts, who generally work with much higher levels of uncertainty in their day-to-day estimations.

6.2   Stress Testing

The approximations to the Bilbao results were promising enough to follow up with further experimentation. In particular, we wanted to "stress test" the approximation algorithm by the following conditions:

1. Divide the n players into small-sized sets, where a specific player's power is likely to be overestimated compared to its power against the whole group (large voting weight), or underestimated (small voting weight). In all of our

testing, we never saw any power swings that were large enough such that the estimated power rankings would be different than the exact power rankings, but we were concerned with bounding any kind of estimation error due to a player with "superpower" compared to the others because of having an inordinate amount of votes.

2. Create wide variations in the order of magnitude of blocking and/or approval weights. And similarly, give some players wide discrepancies between their blocking and approval votes. Again, these "corner cases" looked more likely to generate discrepancies between estimated and exact values in our preliminary testing.

The following weight vectors is a representative experiment that we ran with ten players in order to stress the approximation algorithm as stated above. The approval weights are:

$$[2005, [1000, 1000, 1000, 1000, 2, 2, 2, 1, 1, 1]]$$

and a blocking weights are

$$[856, [1, 10, 100, 1000, 99, 100, 101, 99, 100, 101]].$$

Figure 4 shows a comparison of the total power for the exact value and approximated ones for each of the ten players, after running 10000 iterations. Note that the largest discrepancy occurs for player 4, which has the largest sum of approval and blocking weights (1000 in each case) - an example of how the approximation is more likely to overestimate players that have weights that are greater than most other players. Note this is unlikely to change the rank order.

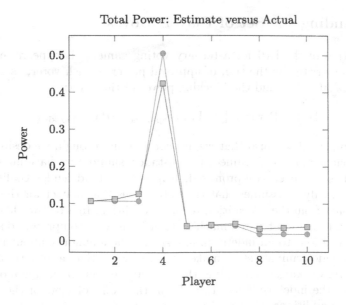

Fig. 4. Total power comparison for the stress test example

By separating out approval and blocking power, this approximation bias can be seen more clearly in Figs. 5 and 6. There are 3 other players with approval weights that are equal to player 4, and hence the approximation is closer in the approval case than in the blocking case (7.6% versus 19%).

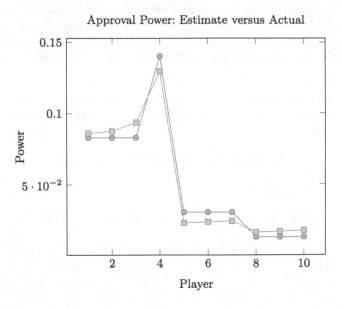

Fig. 5. Comparison of approval power for the stress test example

7 Extending the Set of Player Moves

The definition of the BPI for a ternary voting game as it appears in Bilbao's work can be written as the sum of approval power of each voter, as calculated by the Banzhaf index, and the blocking power of the voter:

$$\text{BPI} = \text{Power}_{\text{total}} = \text{Power}_{\text{approval}} + \text{Power}_{\text{blocking}}$$

In the practical scenario that we are considering, though, we desire a power measure that is more fine-grained. For instance, suppose we have an asset that we assess has not been compromised, hence is in the defender coalition. The Bilbao-style analysis assumes that the only moves that matter for the defender swing are ones from the S coalition to the T coalition. In a real-world situation, it matters not only if a trusted machine transitions to a compromised state, but also if it transitions to an indeterminate state. The ambiguity about its ground truth in the indeterminate state makes it of less value than a fully-trusted asset.

Therefore, we suggest extending the notion of power to include moves made to and from the indeterminate state. From the point of view of the defender, there are two additional classes of moves to consider:

Blocking Power: Estimate versus Actual

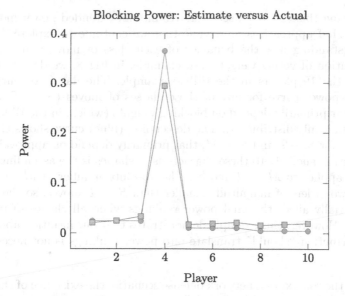

Fig. 6. Comparison of blocking power for the stress test example

1. $S \rightarrow M$ - an asset starting in the trusted state could move to the indeterminate state
2. $M \rightarrow T$ - an asset starting in the indeterminate state could move to the untrusted state.

The dual of these moves (reverse the arrows to get $M \rightarrow S$ and $T \rightarrow M$) completes the universe of possible swings. In Fig. 7, we depict the extended universe of moves that represent a loss for the defender: the existing Bilbao formulation only considers $S \rightarrow T$ moves, but additionally the $S \rightarrow M$ and $M \rightarrow T$ moves as ones that would reflect a change in the security posture of the network. The dual of this diagram would be the universe of moves that represent a loss for the attacker.

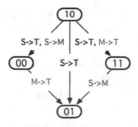

Fig. 7. Expanded defender swing move set

Translating this expanded set of moves into an extended power index based on the Banzhaf approach is an avenue that we continue to explore. In particular, understanding how the behavior of each class of move is dependent on the distribution of voting weights. For example, in Fig. 8, we depict the power indices for the 19 players in the Bilbao example. The flat (red) curve shows the typical power curve for any of these classes of moves ($S \to T$, $S \to M$, $M \to T$) that primarily depend on blocking weights (which, in the Bilbao example, were uniformly distributed). The descending (blue) curve shows the typical power curve for $S \to T$ and $S \to M$, that primarily depend on approval weights. The interesting anomaly to these characteristic shapes is the ascending (brown) curve that applies to $M \to T$ moves. The absolute number of $M \to T$ moves is almost two orders of magnitude smaller than $S \to T$ moves, so these swings don't materially affect the final power rankings when all classes of moves are aggregated. However, this example demonstrates that our intuition about how a voting distribution "should" translate into power rankings is not necessarily to be trusted.

Note 3. In the context of a network defense scenario, the existence of the ascending curve points out a **counterintuitive strategy** for an attacker, which is to concentrate on "flipping" low rank resources that are already in the indeterminate state, as opposed to investing resources in attacking trusted resources.

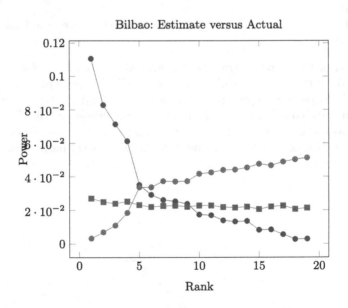

Fig. 8. Characteristic power curves for the Bilbao example (Color figure online)

8 Related Work

In the area of cybersecurity, most of the game-theoretic research has focused on non-cooperative games. Non-cooperative game models are prevalent: two representative examples (from a very extensive literature search) are calculating Nash equilibria for denial-of-service attacks [7] or solving Stackelberg games [6] for cyber-physical security. The animating idea behind non-cooperative games is a strategic interaction that is very often purely adversarial, which makes the non-cooperative model an obvious candidate for the domain of cybersecurity. Applications of cooperative game theory for cybersecurity are somewhat rarer: the underlying ideas behind cooperative game theory (building and maintaining coalitions) aren't necessarily an obvious mapping to adversarial scenario.

In cooperative game theory, the canonical problem has to do with the players assessing whether the value they receive from joining a coalition outweighs the costs of joining, which is a more natural fit for decision-making by self-interested, but not explicitly adversarial players. So, for example, in [5] we find cooperative game theory being applied to help model the decision-making that could take place in an institution carrying out security risk management, where various divisions of the organization need to make trade-offs between the vulnerabilities that exist in their division versus the cost of joining a coalition, and managing the inevitable friction between the goals and behavior of each division. In this cooperative game, new coalitions form only if the two sub-coalitions assess that they are under a friction threshold.

The above remarks notwithstanding, there exists cooperative game theoretic-research that is related to the work presented in this paper. First of all, Bilbao's work in bicooperative games has been fundamental in influencing the starting point for our research, especially his conceptualization of ternary voting games in [1]. In Sect. 7 we have extended his ideas of defender and detractor swings.

We're not the first to recognize the necessity of approximation algorithms to calculate power indices. In [8], the authors present an approximation to the Shapley value, a power index similar to the Banzhaf power index presented in this paper, offered as an improvement of early work by Owen [9]. The key insight of [8] is that there are two dimensions to a proposed approximation: the speed-up over the exact version, and the amount of approximation error. They show that as the number of players increases, average percentage error decreases.

9 Discussion and Future Work

9.1 Summary

Our work on this effort began as an exploration of how we could apply the Bilbao bicooperative voting game framework to cybersecurity scenarios (and later on, to other related domains, such as cyber policy). Our past experience with network defense made us receptive to the principle that differences in the criticality of players or network resources in a coalition setting is not always proportional to their differences in weighting or numbers of votes. Calculating a game-theoretic power measure made sense to us as the basis for both assessments and allocation decisions.

A bedrock principle of cyber security is that to be successful, it is critical to put yourself in the adversary's shoes. For this reason especially, the notion of an explicit bicooperative game with two sets of weights (characterized as approval or blocking) make sense. Instead of assuming that a particular player/resource is valued equally by you and your adversary, this framework discourages this kind of projection, and instead, forces you to get in the head of the adversary. This is a compelling reason for adopting the two-weight vector approach.

For most real-world scenarios, we are dealing with a value of n that is too high for an exact algorithm to solve in time to be actionable in a network defense scenario, which motivated us to investigate approximation algorithms for calculating the Banzhaf Power Index for bicooperative games. Our initial results have been promising: the lattice theoretic foundations, strategy of divide and aggregate, combined with randomness and the law of large numbers, gives us not only qualitative accuracy (ranking), but solid quantitative results (reliable estimates of power relative to the other players).

9.2   Future Work

Our investigations thus far suggest some natural extensions and follow-on work.

Efficiency of Resource Usage. One of the primary reasons for doing the kind of analysis we've been discussing in this paper is to decide which players or resources have the most power in a ternary voting game. This information should inform resource allocation decisions: in a cybersecurity scenario, which network assets to harden, or in a policy scenario, who to spend time with to influence. Given that there is always a finite investment limit when it comes to allocating those resources, what is the most efficient way to do this allocation?

Uncertainty in Coalition Moves. The coalition framework we've studied treats moves as deterministic, and only considers the moves of one player. It would be worthwhile to expand the analysis to account for probabilistic moves, as well as crowd behavior in policy scenarios. For example, one person's shift to another coalition may trigger a stampede of other players not wanting to be stuck in a losing coalition.

Uncertainty in Assessing Weights. Our algorithms are based on knowing the exact number of votes (both approval and blocking) for each player/resource. In practice, it often won't be possible to make such precise or accurate assessments. Instead, we may find ourselves doing rough estimates, or grouping a set of players and saying that they are perceived to have essentially the same voting weights. It is important, therefore, to assess how sensitive our analysis strategy and associated algorithms are to the precision of the weights, so as to establish what kinds of limitations exist in drawing precise and/or accurate conclusions.

Multiple Coalitions. We would like to extend our approach to encompass more than simply two explicit coalitions and thresholds. For example, the M coalition doesn't have a threshold. The challenge here is that the number of potential moves between coalitions goes up exponentially with the number of coalitions. Handling higher numbers of coalitions lets us model more nuanced scenarios, where a position isn't simply one of for, against, or undecided.

Coalition Neighborhoods. Our analysis approach is based on the assumption that for n players, all 3^n possible states are equally likely. We could save significant analysis time by only considering nearby states from the current state, assuming we have a decent estimate of what the current state is. This would give us power estimates that are conditional upon our assessment of the current coalition state, and this would aid in cybersecurity scenarios where real-time calculations are required.

Move Classes. As Fig. 8 depicted, our intuition about power curves for specific kinds of moves may be flawed; we'd like to be able to make general statements about voting distributions and power relative power rankings, by move class.

Scenario Development. We see our initial demonstrations as a useful technique to support scenario planning, where not only are the potential player weights and thresholds unknown, but we are trying to understand a set of possible or counterfactual futures, not simply predict power rankings over one future. We could be exploring sets of coalition neighborhoods, where these neighborhoods are potentially disparate, and reporting back not the expected value, but rather a vector of counterfactual outcomes.

References

1. Bilbao, J.M., Fernandez, J.R., Jimenez, N., Lopez, J.J.: The Banzhaf power index for ternary bicooperative games. Discret. Appl. Math. **158**(2010), 967–980 (2010)
2. Burris, S., Sankappanavar, H.: A course in universal algebra (2012). www.math.uwaterloo.ca/~snburris
3. Srikanth, A.R.J., Ravi Kumar, R.V.G.: Centre of core regular double stone algbera. Eur. J. Pure Appl. Math. **10**(4), 717–729 (2017)
4. Clouse, D.J.: The nearly boolean nature of core regular double stone algebras, CRDSA. Cornell arXiv preprint. https://arxiv.org/abs/1803.08313
5. Saad, W., Alpcan, T., Basar, T., Hjorungnes, A.: Coalitional game theory for security risk management. In: Proceedings of the 5th International Conference on Internet Monitoring and Protection, pp. 35–40 (2010)
6. Martinez, S.: Stackelberg-game analysis of correlated attacks in cyber-physical systems. In: Proceedings of the 2011 American Control Conference, pp. 4063–4068 (2011)
7. Spyridopoulos, T., Karanikas, G., Tryfonas, T., Oikonomou, G.: A game theoretic defence framework against DoS-DDoS cyber attacks. Comput. Secur. **38**, 39–50 (2013)
8. Fatima, S.S., Wooldridge, M., Jennings, N.R.: A linear approximation method for the Shapley value. Artif. Intell. **172**(2008), 1673–1699 (2008)
9. Owen, G.: Multilinear extensions of games. Manag. Sci. **18**(5), 64–79 (1972)

A Differentially Private and Truthful Incentive Mechanism for Traffic Offload to Public Transportation

Luyao Niu[✉] and Andrew Clark

Worcester Polytechnic Institute, Worcester, MA 01609, USA
{lniu,aclark}@wpi.edu

Abstract. Encouraging passengers to take public transportation reduces cost and enhances sustainability of urban ecosystems. However, the passengers incur some inconvenience cost due to potential delays and discomfort when switching from private to public transit service. In this paper, we propose a reverse auction-based mechanism so that the government can incentivize the passengers to take public transit system instead of private transit services. The proposed mechanism achieves individual rationality, truthfulness and near optimal social welfare. However, revealing passengers' truthful inconvenience cost raises privacy concerns. Hence, a truthful and privacy preserving auction mechanism is investigated in this paper. The mechanism design is formulated as a mixed integer program, which makes the VCG-like payment scheme computationally intractable. To mitigate the computation complexity, a heuristic algorithm is proposed as an approximation. We show that truthfulness, near optimal social welfare, individual rationality and differential privacy are preserved by the heuristic algorithm. The proposed approach is demonstrated using numerical case study.

Keywords: Urban transportation · Traffic offload · Auction theory · Differential privacy

1 Introduction

Rapid urban population growth around the world brings huge traffic demand and poses enormous burden on urban transportation system [27]. Due to the unbalance between the huge traffic demand caused by fast growing population and urban transportation infrastructure development, citizens are suffering from the worse and worse traffic condition, e.g., traffic congestion during rush hours in big cities such as New York City and Seattle [5].

Urban transit services are divided into two categories, denoted as *private transit services* such as taxis and ride-hailing services (e.g., Uber and Lyft) and *public transit services* such as buses and subways. Both services have their own

This work was supported by NSF grant CNS-1656981.

advantages and disadvantages. Private transit services intend to provide non-stop or few stop services which offer high quality of service (QoS). Thus the passengers incur higher operation cost. Moreover, private transit services can provide the passengers more flexibility in terms of route selection or destination selection. Public transit services intend to provide shared riding for a large number of passengers so that the operation cost is reduced while QoS is sacrificed. Thus the passengers incur less transit fare comparing to private transit services such as taxi. However, the passengers have less flexibility because the buses and subways follow fixed routes.

As a consequence of the popularity of private vehicles and passengers' higher budget, private transit systems are currently more popular, which introduces extra traffic congestion. To improve the urban transportation system's performance, policy makers have two choices. On one hand, they can improve the transportation infrastructure (e.g., widen the most often congested roads and build more roads). On the other hand, if the number of operating vehicles at the same time is reduced or balanced, the transportation condition is improved. Since the first choice is expensive and time consuming, we are motivated to focus on the second choice. Considering the natures of public transit services and private transit services, one way to implement the second choice is to offload the traffic to public transit services. However, when a passenger takes public instead of private transit services, it incurs more *inconvenience costs* due to several reasons such as delay, the fare charge, and the decrease of QoS. For example, the arrival time is delayed when taking buses comparing to taking taxi. Therefore, the passengers, who are rational and selfish, have no interest to change their transit habits, i.e., taking public instead of private transit services.

To incentivize the passengers' conversion from private to public transit services, in this paper we provide a reverse auction-based mechanism. The passengers first simultaneously bid the amount of traffic offload they can contribute and the associated inconvenience cost to the government. Then the government selects the passengers that should contribute to traffic offload and issue them the corresponding incentives. Three game-theoretic properties are satisfied: individual rationality (i.e., the passengers get non-negative utility), truthfulness (i.e., the passengers bid truthfully), and near optimal social welfare.

Although bidding truthfully is a desired property from the government's perspective, it raises privacy concerns from the passengers' perspectives. The bids submitted by the passengers normally contain private information such as transit behavior and region of interest that the passenger does not like to reveal to other passengers or public. Hence, a privacy sensitive passenger would intend not to bid truthfully, but rather introduce some noise into its bid and earn a suboptimal utility. Adopting the concept of differential privacy as the privacy measure [8,9], the mechanism is imposed an extra constraint that differential privacy should be achieved.

In this paper, we focus on the problem of designing a mechanism that guarantees individual rationality, truthfulness, approximate social welfare maximization, and differential privacy, we make the following contributions:

- We consider the problem of improving transportation system's performance by incentivizing the passengers to switch from private transit service to public transit service.
- We model the problem using a reverse auction, in which the government is the auctioneer and the passengers are the bidders. The mechanism achieves individual rationality, truthfulness, approximate social welfare maximization, and differential privacy.
- The problem we formulated is a mixed integer program, which makes the calculation of VCG-like payments infeasible. Therefore, we give an approximate algorithm to mitigate the computational complexity. The proposed algorithm is solvable in polynomial time, and it preserves the desired properties.
- We evaluate the proposed approach using a numerical case study. The results show that the proposed approach achieves positive social welfare, positive passenger utility and differential privacy.

The rest of this paper is organized as follows. Related works are reviewed in Sect. 2. The problem formulation is given in Sect. 3, and the proposed solution is presented in Sect. 4. A numerical case study is presented in Sect. 5 as a demonstration. We conclude the paper in Sect. 6.

2   Related Work

In this section, we review related works on improving transportation system's performance and works on mechanism design with differential privacy.

Traffic congestion pattern is analyzed in [4]. Motion planning problems on mobile systems have been investigated in [19,32], while distributed routing policies are investigated on dynamical networks [6,7]. Resource allocation based smart parking system is proposed in [11], and spatial temporal parking demand modelling is proposed in [10]. Recently, vehicle balancing approaches have been proposed. Various approaches on control of mobility-on-demand systems have been proposed in [29,34]. Balancing on bike sharing systems is investigated in [30]. The works in [25] aims to improve the transportation system performance by focusing on taxis. Robust vehicle balancing problem is solved in [24]. Dynamic taxi ride-share systems aiming to bring together travelers with similar itineraries and time schedules on short-notice utilizes optimization technology to match drivers and riders in real-time [17,20]. Different from previous works focusing on improving the transportation system's performance from either private transit service side or public transit service side, to the best of our knowledge, this is the first work that focusing on encouraging passengers to switch from private to public transit service.

Auction is one of the popular approaches for market resource allocations [18]. Among the efforts on auction-based mechanism design, Vickrey-Clarke-Groves (VCG) mechanism is widely adopted to preserve truthfulness [33]. Wide deployment of sensors and real-time sensing technology raised the concerns on confidentiality of the customers' data in different application domains including smart grid [22], smart transportation systems [14], smart buildings [1] and so on. To resolve the privacy issues, multiple efforts have been devoted from earlier ad hoc solutions [2,21,31] to recently more rigorous solutions such as information theoretic privacy [26] and differential privacy [8,9]. Various mechanisms have been designed to preserve differential privacy [13,23]. Motivated by the nice properties of exponential mechanism [15], we integrate reverse auction with differential privacy in this work. Due to the presence of inconvenience cost, the exponential mechanisms in [15,23] are not applicable to our problem. Moreover, how to efficiently select the winners and compute the VCG-like payments are not addressed in [15,23], and are studied in this paper.

3 Problem Formulation

In this section, we present the reverse auction model. We first give the models for the passengers and the government. Then we formulate the problem of traffic offload as a mixed integer program.

3.1 Passenger Model

In the auction model, the passengers act as the bidders. Denote the set of passengers as $\mathcal{N} = \{1, 2, \cdots, N\}$. Each passenger $i \in \mathcal{N}$ incurs some inconvenience cost $c_{i,s}$ if it switches from private transit service to public transit service for some road segment $s \in \mathcal{S}$ due to discomfort, time of arrival delays and so on. The inconvenience cost $c_{i,s}$ is private information and is only known to the passenger. Any passenger $j \neq i$ has no information about $c_{i,s}$. To participate in traffic offload, each passenger i needs to submit a bid $\mathbf{b}_i = [b_1, b_2, \cdots, b_S]$ to the government, where each bid $b_{i,s}$ is a pair $(h_{i,s}, \bar{c}_{i,s})$ implying the amount of traffic offload $h_{i,s}$ the passenger is willing to offer and the corresponding claimed inconvenience cost $\bar{c}_{i,s}$. Depending on the preference, the claimed cost $\bar{c}_{i,s}$ does not necessarily be the real cost $c_{i,s}$. The bids from all passengers are submitted simultaneously. By agreeing to switch from private transit service to public transit service, the passenger that is selected by the government will be reimbursed $r_{i,s}$ for the cost it incurred. Hence, the utility of each passenger i is computed as

$$U_i = r_i - \sum_{s \in \mathcal{S}} x_{i,s} c_{i,s}, \; \forall i \in \mathcal{N}, \tag{1}$$

where $x_{i,s} \in \{0, 1\}$ is a binary indicator computed by the government implying if passenger i is selected for road segment s. The passengers are assumed to be rational and selfish. Hence, the passengers always maximize (1) and never accept negative utilities.

3.2 Government Model

In the auction model, the government acts as the auctioneer. The government focus on a set of road segments $\mathcal{S} = \{1, 2, \cdots, S\}$ that require traffic offload, and it will incentivize the passengers nearby to participate in traffic offload. Based on the historical traffic information, the set of road segments $\mathcal{S}$ that will require traffic offload from passengers in the near future time horizon can be obtained. After receiving the bid profile $B = [\mathbf{b}_1, \mathbf{b}_2 \cdots, \mathbf{b}_N]^T$, i.e., the bids from all passengers $\mathcal{N}$, the government computes a selection profile $X = [\mathbf{x}_1, \mathbf{x}_2, \cdots, \mathbf{x}_N]^T \in \{0,1\}^{N \times S}$, with each element $x_{i,s} \in \{0,1\}$ defined as

$$
x_{i,s} = \begin{cases} 1 & \text{if passenger } i \text{ is selected for road segment } s; \\ 0 & \text{otherwise.} \end{cases} \tag{2}
$$

If passenger i is selected by the selection profile, i.e., $\sum_{s \in \mathcal{S}} x_{i,s} \geq 1$, the government issues passenger i an incentive r_i. In the meantime, the selected passengers switch from private to public transit service to contribute to the transportation system's performance improvement $h_{i,s}$. The utility obtained by the government is represented as

$$
V = \sum_{s \in \mathcal{S}} \sum_{i \in \mathcal{N}} x_{i,s}(\alpha h_{i,s}) - \sum_{i \in \mathcal{N}} r_i, \tag{3}
$$

where α is the parameter to transfer the amount of traffic offload into monetary utility. Without loss of generality, we assume $\alpha = 1$. Since a passenger can only contribute to one road segment s at each time, the government has the following constraint:

$$
\sum_{s \in \mathcal{S}} x_{i,s} \leq 1, \ \forall i \in \mathcal{N}. \tag{4}
$$

Finally, the public transit service has certain capacity Q_s at each road segment s. Hence we have

$$
\sum_{i \in \mathcal{N}} x_{i,s} \leq Q_s, \ \forall s \in \mathcal{S}. \tag{5}
$$

3.3 Social Welfare

Define the social welfare generated by incentivizing passengers to switch from private transit systems to public transit systems as the aggregated utilities of the government and passengers. Then the social welfare is represented as

$$
\Omega(X, B) = V + \sum_{i \in \mathcal{S}} U_i = \sum_{s \in \mathcal{S}} \sum_{i \in \mathcal{N}} x_{i,s}(h_{i,s} - c_{i,s}). \tag{6}
$$

Note that the reward $r_{i,s}$ in (1) and (3) get cancelled.

The objective of the government is to maximize the social welfare defined in (6). The optimization problem that the government intends to solve is as follows.

$$
\max_{X} \quad \sum_{s \in \mathcal{S}} \sum_{i \in \mathcal{N}} x_{i,s}(h_{i,s} - c_{i,s}) \tag{7}
$$

$$
\text{s.t.} \quad \sum_{s \in \mathcal{S}} x_{i,s} \leq 1, \ \forall i \in \mathcal{N}
$$

$$\sum_{i \in \mathcal{N}} x_{i,s} \leq Q_s, \ \forall s \in \mathcal{S}$$

$$x_{i,s} \in \{0,1\}, \ \forall i \in \mathcal{N}, \forall s \in \mathcal{S}$$

4   Reverse Auction Solution

In this section, we first introduce the properties that we want to satisfy. Motivated by exponential mechanism [15,23], we first give a modified exponential mechanism. To mitigate the computation complexity for VCG-like payment in exponential mechanism, we then present a solution approach that satisfies the admired properties.

4.1   Game-Theoretic Properties and Differential Privacy

Game-Theoretic Solution Concepts. The passengers are assumed to be rational. Therefore the utility obtained by each passenger should be non-negative, i.e.,

$$U_i = r_i - \sum_{s \in \mathcal{S}} x_{i,s} c_{i,s} \geq 0, \ \forall i \in \mathcal{N} \tag{8}$$

The government intends to reveal the truth inconvenience cost from the passengers, i.e., $\bar{c}_{i,s} = c_{i,s}$ for all $i \in \mathcal{N}$ and $s \in \mathcal{S}$. We characterize if the passengers tell the truth using the *truthfulness* property defined as

Definition 1. (Truthfulness): *An auction is truthful if and only if bidding the true inconvenience cost $c_{i,s}$ is the dominant strategy for any passenger $i \in \mathcal{N}$ regardless of the bids from the other passengers, i.e., given the bids from other passengers other than i, claiming $\bar{c}_{i,s} = c_{i,s}$ gives passenger i the maximum utility.*

Differential Privacy. Suppose a mechanism satisfies truthfulness property. Then by observing how passengers participate in traffic offload, other passengers or a third party player might be able to infer the private information that is encoded in the selected passengers' bids. For instance, a greedy and smart passenger might infer the inconvenience cost reported by the selected passengers to gain some advantage in future rounds of the auction. Therefore a concern of the passengers is that any other passenger can possibly infer the private information that is encoded in the bid profile. Taking the privacy concern into consideration, the passenger might not bid in a truthful manner. Hence, the government wishes that although the participation of passengers can be observed and publicly known, no one can compromise the privacy of each individual passenger. Differential privacy [8,9], which is emerging as one of the standard metrics of privacy measures, is used in this work to model the privacy concern of the passengers. Formally, it is defined as follows.

Definition 2 (ϵ-Differential Privacy). *Given $\epsilon \geq 0$, a mechanism M is said to be ϵ-differentially private if for any two input sets K_1 and K_2 that differ in a single element and for any set of outcomes $L \subseteq Range(M)$*

$$Pr(M(K_1) \in L) \leq \exp(\epsilon) \cdot Pr(M(K_2) \in L), \tag{9}$$

where $Range(M)$ is the set of all outcomes of computation P.

Parameter ϵ gives the level of privacy. A smaller ϵ value implies a higher level of privacy. A more relaxed and general definition of differential privacy is as follows.

Definition 3 ((ϵ, δ)-Differential Privacy). *Given $\epsilon \geq 0$ and $\delta \geq 0$, a mechanism M is said to be (ϵ, δ)-differentially private if for any two input sets K_1 and K_2 that differ in a single element and for any set of outcomes $L \subseteq Range(M)$*

$$Pr(M(K_1) \in L) \leq \exp(\epsilon) \cdot Pr(M(K_2) \in L) + \delta. \tag{10}$$

In particular, Definition 3 reduces to Definition 2 when $\delta = 0$.

Differential privacy satisfies composability property [23].

Lemma 1 (Composability [23]). *Suppose mechanisms M_1 and M_2 achieves ϵ_1-differential privacy and ϵ_2-differential privacy, respectively. Then a new mechanism $M = (M_1, M_2)$ achieves $\epsilon_1 + \epsilon_2$-differential privacy.*

Exponential mechanism provides us an approach to design a mechanism with differential privacy [15,23]. Let $q : K \times L \to \mathbb{R}$ be a score function mapping the input data set K and an outcome $l \in L$ to $\mathbb{R}$. Then an exponential mechanism EXP picks an outcome l with probability

$$Pr(EXP(K, L, q, \epsilon) = l) \propto \exp\left(\frac{\epsilon}{2\Delta}q(K, l)\right),$$

where Δ is the Lipschitz constant of the score function q. Given an exponential mechanism, we have the following theorem indicating that the probability of achieving a highly suboptimal solution is exponentially low.

Theorem 1 [12,23]. *The exponential mechanism is ϵ-differentially private and ensures that*

$$Pr\left(q(K, EXP(K, L, q, \epsilon)) < \max_l q(K, l) - \frac{\ln|L|}{\epsilon} - \frac{t}{\epsilon}\right) \leq \exp(-t). \tag{11}$$

4.2 Solution Approach

In this subsection, we leverage exponential mechanism to obtain a truthful and differentially private traffic offload mechanism for the government. The mechanism design can be accomplished applying Algorithm 1.

We remark that due to the passenger incur inconvenience cost when switching from private to public transit service, the payment schemes in [15,23] are not applicable to the problem we investigate since individual rationality and truthfulness cannot be preserved. To achieve all the game-theoretic properties discussed earlier, we propose the payment scheme (16). The payment (16) is still a VCG-like payment. However, it is determined by the social cost introduced by each passenger rather than the social welfare.

In the following, we characterize the game-theoretic properties and differential privacy of mechanism presented in Algorithm 1 following the analysis in [15]. We first characterize the social welfare obtained using the mechanism described in Algorithm 1 as follows.

Lemma 2. *The mechanism described in Algorithm 1 gives near optimal social welfare.*

Proof. Suppose the selection profile is subject to some probability distribution $\tilde{D}$. Then the expected social welfare can be rewritten as

$$
\begin{aligned}
& \underset{X \sim \tilde{D}}{\mathbb{E}} \{\Omega(X, B)\} \\
={} & \sum_X Pr_{X \sim \tilde{D}}(X) \sum_{s \in \mathcal{S}} \sum_{i \in \mathcal{N}} x_{i,s}(h_{i,s} - c_{i,s}) \\
={} & \frac{2\Delta}{\epsilon} \sum_X Pr_{X \sim \tilde{D}}(X) \sum_{s \in \mathcal{S}} \sum_{i \in \mathcal{N}} \frac{\epsilon}{2\Delta} x_{i,s}(h_{i,s} - c_{i,s}) \\
={} & \frac{2\Delta}{\epsilon} \sum_X Pr_{X \sim \tilde{D}}(X) \ln \left(\exp \left(\sum_{s \in \mathcal{S}} \sum_{i \in \mathcal{N}} \frac{\epsilon}{2\Delta} x_{i,s}(h_{i,s} - c_{i,s}) \right) \right) \\
={} & \frac{2\Delta}{\epsilon} \sum_X Pr_{X \sim \tilde{D}}(X) \ln \left(\frac{\exp \left(\sum_{s \in \mathcal{S}} \sum_{i \in \mathcal{N}} \frac{\epsilon}{2\Delta} x_{i,s}(h_{i,s} - c_{i,s}) \right)}{\sum_X \exp \left(\sum_{s \in \mathcal{S}} \sum_{i \in \mathcal{N}} \frac{\epsilon}{2\Delta} x_{i,s}(h_{i,s} - c_{i,s}) \right)} \right) \\
& + \frac{2\Delta}{\epsilon} \ln \left(\sum_X \exp \left(\frac{\epsilon}{2\Delta} \sum_{s \in \mathcal{S}} \sum_{i \in \mathcal{N}} x_{i,s}(h_{i,s} - c_{i,s}) \right) \right) \\
={} & \frac{2\Delta}{\epsilon} \sum_X Pr_{X \sim \tilde{D}}(X) \ln \left(Pr_{X \sim D}(X) \right) \\
& + \frac{2\Delta}{\epsilon} \ln \left(\sum_X \exp \left(\frac{\epsilon}{2\Delta} \sum_{s \in \mathcal{S}} \sum_{i \in \mathcal{N}} x_{i,s}(h_{i,s} - c_{i,s}) \right) \right),
\end{aligned} \tag{12}
$$

where the last equality follows from (15). Following [28], we introduce the concept of free social welfare defined as

$$
\tilde{\Omega}(X, B) = \underset{X \sim \tilde{D}}{\mathbb{E}} \{\Omega(X, B)\} + \frac{2}{\epsilon} E(\tilde{D}), \tag{13}
$$

where $E(\cdot)$ is the Shannon entropy. Substitute (12) into (13), the free social welfare can be rewritten as

$$\tilde{\Omega}(X,B) = \frac{2\Delta}{\epsilon} \sum_X Pr_{X\sim D}(X) \ln \left(\frac{Pr_{X\sim D}(X)}{Pr_{X\sim\tilde{D}}(X)} \right)$$

$$+ \frac{2\Delta}{\epsilon} \ln \left(\sum_X \exp \left(\frac{\epsilon}{2\Delta} \sum_{s\in S} \sum_{i\in N} x_{i,s}(h_{i,s} - c_{i,s}) \right) \right)$$

$$= \frac{2\Delta}{\epsilon} D_{KL}(D\|\tilde{D}) + \frac{2\Delta}{\epsilon} \ln \left(\sum_X \exp \left(\frac{\epsilon}{2\Delta} \sum_{s\in S} \sum_{i\in N} x_{i,s}(h_{i,s} - c_{i,s}) \right) \right).$$

$$(14)$$

where $D_{KL}(D\|\tilde{D})$ is the KL-divergence. Observing that the second term is independent of $\tilde{D}$, by the property of KL-divergence, we have (14) is maximized if $\tilde{D}$ is computed following (15).

By the definition of free social welfare (13), we have that the free social welfare is obtained by adding a term into the social welfare $\Omega(X,B)$. Hence we have that the mechanism described in Algorithm 1 gives near optimal social welfare.

Algorithm 1. Mechanism design for the government.

1: **procedure** MECHANISM(B)
2:     **Input:** Bid profile B
3:     **Output:** Selection profile X, incentives R
4:     Choose a selection profile X that is feasible for social welfare maximization problem (7) with probability

$$Pr(X) \propto \exp \left(\frac{\epsilon}{2\Delta} \Omega(X,B) \right).$$

$$(15)$$

5:     For each passenger that is selected, issue incentive r_i as

$$r_i = \mathop{\mathbb{E}}_{X\sim D(\mathbf{b}_i, B_{-i})} \left\{ \sum_j \sum_s x_{j,s} h_{j,s} - \sum_{j'\neq i} \sum_s x_{j',s} c_{j',s} \right\} + \frac{2\Delta}{\epsilon} E(D(\mathbf{b}_i, B_{-i}))$$

$$- \frac{2\Delta}{\epsilon} \ln \left(\sum_X \exp \left(\frac{\epsilon}{2\Delta} \Omega(X_{-i}, B_{-i}) \right) \right), \quad (16)$$

where Δ is the difference between the upper and lower bound of social welfare $\Omega(X,B)$, $E(\cdot)$ is the Shannon entropy, $D(\cdot)$ is the probability distribution over selection profile B, and X_{-i} and B_{-i} are the matrix obtained by removing the i-th row and i-th column in selection profile and bid profile, respectively.
6: **end procedure**

Next, we focus on the truthfulness of the mechanism.

Lemma 3. *The solution approach achieves truthfulness.*

Proof. Due to the space limit, we give a sketch of the proof. We prove truthfulness by showing for each player i, truth-telling is the dominant strategy. The difference between the utility of passenger i by bidding $\mathbf{b}_i$ and $\hat{\mathbf{b}}_i$ is represented as

$$
\left(r_i - \sum_s x_{i,s} c_{i,s} \right) - \left(\hat{r}_i - \sum_s \hat{x}_{i,s} c_{i,s} \right)
$$

$$
= \mathop{\mathbb{E}}_{X \sim D(\mathbf{b}_i, B_{-i})} \{ \Omega(X, (\mathbf{b}_i, B_{-i})) \} + \frac{2\Delta}{\epsilon} E(D(\mathbf{b}_i, B_{-i}))
$$

$$
- \mathop{\mathbb{E}}_{X \sim D(\hat{\mathbf{b}}_i, B_{-i})} \left\{ \Omega \left(X, (\hat{\mathbf{b}}_i, B_{-i}) \right) \right\} - \frac{2\Delta}{\epsilon} E(D(\hat{\mathbf{b}}_i, B_{-i}))
$$

$$
= \tilde{\Omega} \left(X, (\mathbf{b}_i, B_{-i}) \right) - \tilde{\Omega} \left(X, (\hat{\mathbf{b}}_i, B_{-i}) \right) \geq 0, \tag{17}
$$

where the last inequality holds by Lemma 2 which implies that the free social welfare is maximized when $X \sim D(\mathbf{b}_i, B_{-i})$.

To guarantee the participation from the passengers, the individual rationality is required for each passenger that is selected by X. Individual rationality property is stated in the following.

Lemma 4. *The mechanism described in Algorithm 1 achieves individual rationality.*

Proof. By Lemma 3, we have that the passengers always bid truthfully. In the following, we show that the passengers obtain non-negative utilities when bidding truthfully.

The utility of passenger i can be rewritten as

$$
U_i = r_i - \sum_s x_{i,s} c_{i,s}
$$

$$
= \mathop{\mathbb{E}}_{X \sim D(\mathbf{b}_i, B_{-i})} \left\{ \sum_j \sum_s x_{j,s} h_{j,s} - \sum_{j' \neq i} \sum_s x_{j',s} c_{j',s} \right\} + \frac{2\Delta}{\epsilon} E(D(\mathbf{b}_i, B_{-i}))
$$

$$
- \frac{2\Delta}{\epsilon} \ln \left(\sum_X \exp \left(\frac{\epsilon}{2\Delta} \Omega(X_{-i}, B_{-i}) \right) \right) - \sum_s x_{i,s} c_{i,s}
$$

$$
= \Omega(\tilde{X}, B) - \frac{2\Delta}{\epsilon} \ln \left(\sum_X \exp \left(\frac{\epsilon}{2\Delta} \Omega(X_{-i}, B_{-i}) \right) \right). \tag{18}
$$

By (14), we have the maximum free social welfare can be represented as

$$
\tilde{\Omega}(X, B) = \frac{2\Delta}{\epsilon} \ln \left(\sum_X \exp \left(\frac{\epsilon}{2\Delta} \sum_{s \in \mathcal{S}} \sum_{i \in \mathcal{N}} x_{i,s}(h_{i,s} - c_{i,s}) \right) \right).
$$

Hence, we have that (18) can be rewritten as

$$
U_i = \tilde{\Omega}(X, B) - \frac{2\Delta}{\epsilon} \ln \left(\sum_X \exp \left(\frac{\epsilon}{2\Delta} \Omega(X_{-i}, B_{-i}) \right) \right)
$$

$$
= \frac{2\Delta}{\epsilon} \ln \left(\sum_X \exp \left(\frac{\epsilon}{2\Delta} \sum_{s \in \mathcal{S}} \sum_{i \in \mathcal{N}} x_{i,s}(h_{i,s} - c_{i,s}) \right) \right)
$$

$$
- \frac{2\Delta}{\epsilon} \ln \left(\sum_X \exp \left(\frac{\epsilon}{2\Delta} \Omega(X_{-i}, B_{-i}) \right) \right)
$$

$$
\geq 0,
$$

where the inequality holds by the fact that the free social welfare is maximized.

Lemma 5. *The solution approach achieves ϵ-differential privacy.*

The proof follows from the analysis on exponential mechanism [23].

4.3 Efficient Algorithm

The social welfare maximization problem (7) is a mixed integer programming and hence is NP-hard, which makes the computation of VCG-like incentive design (16) intractable. In this subsection, we propose a polynomial time algorithm that guarantees the properties or the relaxed version of the properties stated in Lemmas 2 to 5.

First, we decompose the optimization problem (7) with respect to each road segment $s \in \mathcal{S}$. Then we have a set of optimization problems

$$
\max_{\mathbf{x}_s} \quad \sum_{i \in \mathcal{N}} x_{i,s}(h_{i,s} - c_{i,s}) \tag{19}
$$

$$
\text{s.t.} \quad \sum_{i \in \mathcal{N}} x_{i,s} \leq Q_s, \ \forall s \in \mathcal{S}
$$

$$
x_{i,s} \in \{0, 1\}, \ \forall i \in \mathcal{N}, \forall s \in \mathcal{S}.
$$

In real world implementation, such a decomposition is feasible since the passengers are geographically distributed and normally they are only willing to participate in traffic offload near them. Hence, except for the road segment near the passengers, the inconvenience cost submitted by the passengers can be extremely high for road segments that are far away. For the ease of presentation, we drop the index of s when the context is clear.

By observation, we have that the objective function (7) can be rewritten as

$$
\Omega(X, B) = \sum_{s \in \mathcal{S}} \Omega_s(\mathbf{x}_s, B),
$$

where $\Omega_s(\mathbf{x}_s, B)$ is the objective function (19). In the following, we give a heuristic algorithm that solves the decomposed problems (19) efficiently while guaranteeing the properties stated in Lemmas 2 to 5.

Denote the set of passengers that are selected by the government for road segment s as $\mathcal{W}_s$. The selected passenger set $\mathcal{W}_s$ is initialized as $\mathcal{W}_s = \emptyset$ for all $s \in \mathcal{S}$. Then $\mathcal{W}_s$ is updated iteratively. At each iteration k, the probability of choosing a passenger i who has not been selected is represented as

$$Pr\left(\mathcal{W}_s \leftarrow \mathcal{W}_s \cup \{i\}\right) \propto \begin{cases} \exp\left(\epsilon'(h_{i,s} - \bar{c}_{i,s})\right), & \text{if } i \text{ has not been selected;} \\ 0 & \text{otherwise,} \end{cases} \forall s \in \mathcal{S},$$

(20)

where $\epsilon' = \frac{\epsilon}{e \ln(e/\delta)}$. After a passenger i is selected, then i is removed from the passenger set for all sub-problems. By switching from private transit service to public transit service for road segment s, passenger i receives incentive

$$r_i = (h_{i,s} - \bar{c}_{i,s}) \exp\left(\epsilon'(h_{i,s} - \bar{c}_{i,s})\right) - \int_0^{h_{i,s} - \bar{c}_{i,s}} \exp(\epsilon' y) \mathrm{d}y.$$

(21)

We present the detailed algorithm to solve each sub-problem in Algorithm 2. Algorithm 2 takes $O(N)$ time to select the set of passengers for sub-problem (19).

Using Algorithm 2 as a subroutine, social welfare maximization problem 7 is solved following Algorithm 3. First, we make a copy of passengers $\mathcal{N}_s$ for each road segment s. Then we remove the passengers that provide negative social welfare. Then Algorithm 3 calls Algorithm 2 iteratively to solve the social welfare maximization problem 7. Using Algorithm 2, the government can computes the set of passengers in $O(SN)$ time, which provides us the potential of scalability.

Algorithm 2. Solution algorithm for decomposed problem (19).

1: **procedure** DECOMPOSE(B)
2:    **Input:** Bid profile B
3:    **Output:** Selection profile $\mathcal{W}_s$
4:    **Initialization:** Selected passenger set $\mathcal{W}_s \leftarrow \emptyset$, $\epsilon' \leftarrow \frac{\epsilon}{e \ln(e/\delta)}$
5:    **while** $|\mathcal{W}_s| \leq Q_s \wedge \mathcal{N} \neq \emptyset$ **do**
6:        **for** $i \in \mathcal{N}$ **do**
7:            Compute the probability of selecting passenger i as (20).
8:        **end for**
9:        **if** passenger i is chosen **then**
10:            $\mathcal{N} \leftarrow \mathcal{N} \setminus \{i\}$
11:       **end if**
12:   **end while**
13:   **return** $\mathcal{W}_s$
14: **end procedure**

We conclude this section by characterizing how the properties stated in Lemmas 2 to 5 are preserved by Algorithm 2.

First, we give a lower bound of the social welfare by using Algorithm 2 in the following theorem.

Algorithm 3. Solution algorithm for problem (7).

1: **procedure** SOCIAL_MAX(B)
2:    **Input:** Bid profile B
3:    **Output:** Selection profile X
4:    **Initialization:** $\mathcal{N}_s = \mathcal{N}$ for all s
5:    Remove all passengers that provide negative social welfare $B \leftarrow [(h_{i,s}, \bar{c}_{i,s}) :$ $h_{i,s}, \bar{c}_{i,s} \geq 0]$
6:    **for** $s \in \mathcal{S}$ **do**
7:        DECOMPOSE(B)
8:        $\mathcal{N}_s = \mathcal{N}_s \setminus \cup_{s'=1}^{s-1} \mathcal{W}_{s'}$
9:    **end for**
10:    **return** $X = \cup_{s \in \mathcal{S}} \mathcal{W}_s$
11: **end procedure**

Theorem 2. *By selecting the set of passengers given by Algorithm 2, the government achieves social welfare at least $\Omega_s^* - O(\ln Q_s)$ with at least probability $1 - \frac{1}{Q_s{}^{O(1)}}$, where Ω_s^* is the maximum social welfare that can be achieved by the government for sub-problem associated with road segment s.*

Proof. By Theorem 1, we have

$$Pr\left(\sum_i (h_{i,s} - c_{i,s}) < \Omega_s^* - \frac{\ln|L|}{\epsilon} - \frac{t}{\epsilon}\right) \leq \exp(-t),$$

where Ω_s^* is the optimal social welfare for sub-problem indexed s. Ignore the term $\frac{\ln|L|}{\epsilon}$ and let $t = \ln(Q_s)$. We have $Pr\left(\sum_i (h_{i,s} - c_{i,s}) < \Omega_s^* - \frac{O(\ln Q_s)}{\epsilon'}\right) \leq \frac{1}{Q_s{}^{O(1)}}$. Reversing the inequality, we then have that with probability of at least $1 - \frac{1}{Q_s{}^{O(1)}}$,

$$\sum_i (h_{i,s} - c_{i,s}) > \Omega_s^* - \frac{O(\ln Q_s)}{\epsilon'}. \tag{22}$$

Proposition 1. *Using Algorithm 3, the government achieves social welfare at least $\Omega^* - SO(\ln Q_s)$ with at least probability $1 - \frac{1}{Q^{*O(1)}}$, where Ω^* is the maximum social welfare that can be achieved by the government and $Q^* = \max_s Q_s$.*

Proof. Given Theorem 2, we sum over $s \in \mathcal{S}$ for (22). Then we have that with probability of at least $1 - \frac{1}{Q^{*O(1)}}$,

$$\sum_s \sum_i (h_{i,s} - c_{i,s}) > \sum_s \Omega_s^* - \sum_s \frac{O(\ln Q_s)}{\epsilon'}$$
$$\geq \Omega^* - SO(\ln Q^*),$$

where the second inequality follows from $\sum_s \Omega_s^* \geq \Omega^*$ and $Q^* \geq Q_s$. By observing LHS of the inequality above is the social welfare obtained using Algorithm 2, the theorem is proved.

Before analyzing the truthfulness property, we define a concept named virtual bid $\mathbf{b}_i^v$ for each passenger as $\mathbf{b}_i^v = \left[b_{i,1}^v, b_{i,2}^v, \cdots, b_{i,S}^v \right]$, where each entry $b_{i,s}^v = h_{i,s} - \bar{c}_{i,s}$. Then we characterize how truthfulness property is preserved when using Algorithm 2 in the following theorem.

Theorem 3. *The solution proposed in Algorithm 2 achieves truthfulness.*

Proof. Denote the set of passengers that are selected by the government as $\mathcal{W}_s$. Assume that $i \notin \mathcal{W}_s$. Then the probability that $\mathcal{W}_s$ is the selected by the government is represented as

$$Pr(i \notin \mathcal{W}_s) = (1 - \exp(\epsilon'(h_{i,s} - \bar{c}_{i,s})))^{|\mathcal{W}_s|}.$$

We observe that the probability of not selecting i is monotone decreasing with respect to the virtual bid $b_{i,s}^v$. As a consequence, the probability of selecting passenger i is monotone non-decreasing with respect to virtual bid $b_{i,s}^v$. By [3], we have that the solution proposed in Algorithm 2 is truthful in expectation. □

Next, we consider the individual rationality property.

Lemma 6. *Payment scheme (21) achieves individual rationality.*

Proof. By Algorithm 3, we have that only the passengers that can provide the government non-negative social welfare can be selected. Moreover, by Theorem 3, truthfulness is preserved using the proposed algorithm. Therefore we have $h_{i,s} - \bar{c}_{i,s} = h_{i,s} - c_{i,s} \geq 0$. By observing (21), we have that the first term models the size of a rectangle whose length is $h_{i,s} - \bar{c}_{i,s}$ and width is $\exp(\epsilon'(h_{i,s} - \bar{c}_{i,s}))$, while the second term models the size of the area below the curve $\exp(\epsilon'(h_{i,s} - \bar{c}_{i,s}))$. By the convexity of exponential function, we have that the payment scheme (21) is always non-negative. □

We finally prove that Algorithm 2 achieves differential privacy with respect to passengers' bids.

Theorem 4. *Algorithm 2 achieves $\left(\frac{\epsilon \Delta}{e(e-1)}, \delta \right)$-differential privacy.*

Proof. Consider two bid profiles B and $\hat{B}$ that differ in single entry for some road segment s. Denote the sets of passengers that are selected associated with B and $\hat{B}$ as $\mathcal{W}_s$ and $\hat{\mathcal{W}}_s$, respectively, where $\mathcal{W}_s = \hat{\mathcal{W}}_s = \{1, 2, \cdots, W\}$. Then the ratio of the probability of obtaining selection profile $\mathcal{W}_s$ and $\hat{\mathcal{W}}_s$ given bid profiles B and $\hat{B}$ is represented as

$$
\begin{aligned}
&\frac{Pr(\mathcal{W}_s)}{Pr(\hat{\mathcal{W}}_s)} \\
&= \prod_{i=1}^{W} \frac{\exp\left(\epsilon'(h_{i,s} - c_{i,s})\right) / \sum_{j \in \mathcal{N}_s^i} \exp\left(\epsilon'(h_{j,s} - c_{j,s})\right)}{\exp\left(\epsilon'(\hat{h}_{i,s} - \hat{c}_{i,s})\right) / \sum_{j \in \mathcal{N}_s^i} \exp\left(\epsilon'(\hat{h}_{j,s} - \hat{c}_{j,s})\right)} \\
&= \prod_{i=1}^{W} \frac{\exp\left(\epsilon'(h_{i,s} - c_{i,s})\right)}{\exp\left(\epsilon'(\hat{h}_{i,s} - \hat{c}_{i,s})\right)} \cdot \prod_{i=1}^{W} \frac{\sum_{j \in \mathcal{N}_s^i} \exp\left(\epsilon'(\hat{h}_{j,s} - \hat{c}_{j,s})\right)}{\sum_{j \in \mathcal{N}_s^i} \exp\left(\epsilon'(h_{j,s} - c_{j,s})\right)},
\end{aligned} \tag{23}
$$

where N_s^i is the set of passengers that have not been selected at iteration i.

In the following we consider the following two cases. Suppose $h_{i,s} - c_{i,s} > \hat{h}_{i,s} - \hat{c}_{i,s}$. Then (23) can be rewritten as

$$\prod_{i=1}^{W} \frac{\exp\left(\epsilon'(h_{i,s} - c_{i,s})\right)}{\exp\left(\epsilon'(\hat{h}_{i,s} - \hat{c}_{i,s})\right)} \cdot \prod_{i=1}^{W} \frac{\sum_{j \in N_s^i} \exp\left(\epsilon'(\hat{h}_{j,s} - \hat{c}_{j,s})\right)}{\sum_{j \in N_s^i} \exp\left(\epsilon'(h_{j,s} - c_{j,s})\right)}$$

$$\leq \prod_{i=1}^{W} \left(\exp\left(\epsilon'\left(h_{i,s} - c_{i,s} - \left(\hat{h}_{i,s} - \hat{c}_{i,s}\right)\right)\right)\right)$$

$$= \exp\left(\epsilon' \sum_{i=1}^{W} \left(h_{i,s} - c_{i,s} - \left(\hat{h}_{i,s} - \hat{c}_{i,s}\right)\right)\right)$$

$$= \exp(\epsilon' \Delta_s),$$

where Δ_s is the difference between the social welfare associated with B and $\hat{B}$ for s. The first inequality holds by the fact that the second term in (23) is upper bounded by one, and the last equality follows from definition (6).

Next, we suppose that $h_{i,s} - c_{i,s} < \hat{h}_{i,s} - \hat{c}_{i,s}$. Then (23) can be rewritten as

$$\prod_{i=1}^{W} \frac{\exp\left(\epsilon'(h_{i,s} - c_{i,s})\right)}{\exp\left(\epsilon'(\hat{h}_{i,s} - \hat{c}_{i,s})\right)} \cdot \prod_{i=1}^{W} \frac{\sum_{j \in N_s^i} \exp\left(\epsilon'(\hat{h}_{j,s} - \hat{c}_{j,s})\right)}{\sum_{j \in N_s^i} \exp\left(\epsilon'(h_{j,s} - c_{j,s})\right)}$$

$$\leq \prod_{i=1}^{W} \frac{\sum_{j \in N_s^i} \exp\left(\epsilon'(\hat{h}_{j,s} - \hat{c}_{j,s})\right)}{\sum_{j \in N_s^i} \exp\left(\epsilon'(h_{j,s} - c_{j,s})\right)}$$

$$= \prod_{i=1}^{W} \frac{\sum_{j \in N_s^i} \exp\left(\epsilon'\left(\hat{h}_{j,s} - \hat{c}_{j,s} - (h_{j,s} - c_{j,s})\right)\right) \exp\left(\epsilon'(h_{j,s} - c_{j,s})\right)}{\sum_{j \in N_s^i} \exp\left(\epsilon'(h_{j,s} - c_{j,s})\right)}$$

$$= \prod_{i=1}^{W} \mathbb{E}_{j \in N_s^i} \left\{\exp(\epsilon' \beta_{j,s})\right\},$$

where $\beta_{j,s} = \hat{h}_{j,s} - \hat{c}_{j,s} - (h_{j,s} - c_{j,s})$. The first inequality holds due to the first term in (23) is upper bounded by one. For all $\epsilon' \leq 1$ and $\beta_{j,s} \leq 1$ (which can be achieved by normalizing the social welfare), we have

$$\prod_{i=1}^{W} \mathbb{E}_{j \in N_s^i} \left\{\exp(\epsilon' \beta_{j,s})\right\} \leq \prod_{i=1}^{W} \mathbb{E}_{j \in N_s^i} \left\{1 + (e-1)\epsilon' \beta_{j,s}\right\}$$

$$\leq \exp\left((e-1)\epsilon' \sum_{i=1}^{W} \mathbb{E}_{j \in N_s^i} \{\beta_{j,s}\}\right),$$

where the first inequality holds due to for all $\beta \leq 1$, $\exp(\beta) \leq 1 + \beta(e-1)$. When $\mathbb{E}_{j \in \mathcal{N}_s^i}\{\beta_{j,s}\} \leq \Delta \ln(e/\delta)$, we have

$$\exp\left((e-1)\epsilon' \sum_{i=1}^{W} \mathbb{E}_{j \in \mathcal{N}_s^i}\{\beta_{j,s}\}\right) \leq \exp\left((e-1)\epsilon' \Delta \ln(e/\delta)\right) = \exp\left(\frac{\epsilon \Delta}{e(e-1)}\right).$$

By [12], the probability that $\mathbb{E}_{j \in \mathcal{N}_s^i}\{\beta_{j,s}\} > \Delta \ln(e/\delta)$ is at most δ. Hence, we have

$$Pr(\mathcal{W}_s) \leq \exp\left(\frac{\epsilon \Delta}{e(e-1)}\right) Pr(\hat{\mathcal{W}}_s) + \delta.$$

Proposition 2. *Algorithm 3 achieves* $\left(\frac{\epsilon \Delta S}{e(e-1)}, \delta S\right)$-*differential privacy.*

Proof. Given Theorem 4, Proposition 2 follows by applying Lemma 1 S times.

We finally remark that the result presented in Theorem 4 holds regardless of the order that the passengers are selected. If the passengers intend to protect the privacy against other passengers, then we can achieve $\left(\frac{\epsilon \Delta}{e(e-1)}, \delta\right)$-differential privacy since only the passengers that take the same transit service can observe the outcome, i.e., a passenger that is selected for road segment s' has no knowledge about the participation of road segment $s \neq s'$. However, when the passenger intends to protect the privacy against some third party that can observe the transit behaviors of all road segments, we achieve $\left(\frac{\epsilon \Delta S}{e(e-1)}, \delta S\right)$-differential privacy. In this case, the level of privacy is weakened.

5   Case Study

In this section, we demonstrate the proposed approach using a numerical case study.

5.1   Case Study Settings

In this case study, we focus on the transportation network near Boston, MA during rush hours (AM peak or PM peak). The government intends to improve the transportation performance between three road segments $\mathcal{S} = \{s_1, s_2, s_3\}$. The first road segment that the government is interested in is $s_1 = (South\ Station,\ Logan\ airport)$. Instead of driving, an alternative transit is to take Silver line (bus), which departs every 8 min during rush hours. Another two routes we consider are $s_2 = (Malden, Chinatown)$ and $s_3 = (Copley, North\ Station)$. Both routes can be accomplished by taking subway transit services, which depart every 6 min during rush hours. Due to lack of transit data from passengers, we use the five-minute electricity demand data [16] to simulate the pattern of traffic on road, which is further used to simulate the number of passengers for each road segment. The transportation capacity is assumed as $Q_{s_1} = 50$ and $Q_{s_i} = 150$ for all

$i \in \{1,2\}$. The transportation performance improvement induced by each passenger is generated as $h_{i,s} \sim \mathcal{N}(10, 0.5)$. Assume that the inconvenience cost is caused by the expected time delay and discomfort. Here we let the expected time delay be 0.8 times the departure time, and discomfort be generated following a Normal distribution with mean 2 and variance 0.1. Then the inconvenience cost is the l_2 norm of expected delay and discomfort. The detailed source-destination pairs and the associated private and public transit methods are listed in Table 1. The simulation is conducted with time scale 10 min.

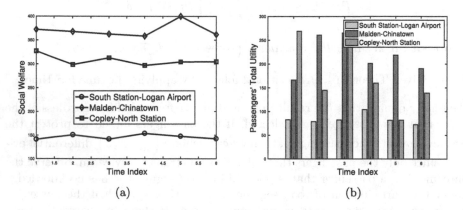

(a)   (b)

Fig. 1. The social welfare obtained from each route is presented in (a). The aggregated utilities of all selected passengers is presented in (b). The bars on the left denote the aggregated utility for s_1. The bars in the middle denote the aggregated utility for s_2. The bars on the right denote the aggregated utility for s_3. (Color figure online)

We evaluate the proposed approach using the metrics including social welfare, individual rationality, and privacy leakage. The privacy leakage is defined as follows.

Definition 4. *Given two bid profiles B and B' that differ in one entry. Let $Pr(X)$ and $Pr'(X)$ be the probability of obtaining selection profile X given bids B and B'. Then the privacy leakage is defined as $\max_X \ln\left(\frac{Pr(X)}{Pr'(X)}\right)$.*

Table 1. Source-Destination Pairs and corresponding transit approaches

Road segment	Private transit	Public transit
South Station-Logan Airport	Drive via I-90E	Silver Line
Malden-Chinatown	Drive via I-93S	Orange Line
Copley-North Station	Drive via MA-28N	Green Line

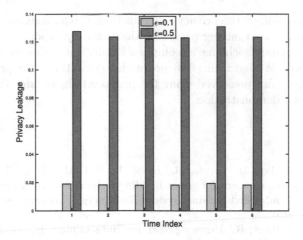

Fig. 2. Privacy leakage under different ϵ parameter. (Color figure online)

5.2 Performance Evaluation

In this subsection, we evaluate the proposed approach from the prospects of social welfare, passengers' utilities and privacy leakage.

We first show the social welfare obtained from each route listed in Table 1 at each time step in Fig. 1a. Due to the traffic demands and transit capacity, we have that the Silver Line obtains the minimum social welfare while the Orange Line obtains the highest social welfare. Also, we observe that the social welfare is positive, implying that traffic offload benefits the urban ecosystems. Next, we present the aggregated utilities from all selected passengers at each time step in Fig. 1b. We have that individual rationality is achieved using the proposed mechanism. Note that the difference between the values presented in Fig. 1a and the values presented in Fig. 1b is the utility obtained by the government, which is shown to be positive. Finally, the privacy leakage is presented in Fig. 2. In Fig. 2, we compare the privacy leakage under settings $\epsilon = 0.5$ (bars on the left) and $\epsilon = 0.1$ (bars on the right). Figure 2 implies that the proposed approach preserves privacy well. Privacy leakage under a higher level of privacy requirement ($\epsilon = 0.1$) is smaller. Consider the extreme case where no privacy concern is considered. The passengers' preferences are completely revealed and hence an intelligent and malicious passenger can always prohibit other passengers being selected by bidding in a smart way. Then the privacy leakage can be arbitrarily large.

6   Conclusion

In this paper, we propose a reverse auction-based mechanism to incentivize the passengers to convert from private to public transit services to improve the urban transportation performance. The mechanism preserves game-theoretic properties including truthfulness, individual rationality and social welfare maximization.

The model also considers the privacy concerns from the passengers. The problem is formulated as a mixed integer program. Motivated by exponential mechanism design, whose payment scheme is computationally infeasible in our problem, we given a heuristic algorithm. We prove the game-theoretic properties and differential privacy are preserved using the proposed algorithm. Numerical case study is used as a demonstration.

References

1. Agarwal, Y., Balaji, B., Gupta, R., Lyles, J., Wei, M., Weng, T.: Occupancy-driven energy management for smart building automation. In: Proceedings of the Workshop on Embedded Sensing Systems for Energy-Efficiency in Building, pp. 1–6. ACM (2010)
2. Agrawal, R., Srikant, R.: Privacy-preserving data mining. In: SIGMOD Record, vol. 29, pp. 439–450. ACM (2000)
3. Archer, A., Tardos, É.: Truthful mechanisms for one-parameter agents. In: Proceedings of the Symposium on Foundations of Computer Science, pp. 482–491. IEEE (2001)
4. Ben-Akiva, M., Cyna, M., De Palma, A.: Dynamic model of peak period congestion. Transp. Res. Part B: Methodol. 18(4), 339–355 (1984)
5. Brown, M.: Report: Seattle one of the worst U.S. cities for traffic congestion, tied with NYC. http://www.geekwire.com/2015/report-finds-seattle-is-one-of-the-worst-u-s-cities-for-traffic-congestion-tied-with-new-york/
6. Como, G., Savla, K., Acemoglu, D., Dahleh, M.A., Frazzoli, E.: Robust distributed routing in dynamical networks–part II: strong resilience, equilibrium selection and cascaded failures. Trans. Autom. Control 58(2), 333–348 (2013)
7. Como, G., Savla, K., Acemoglu, D., Dahleh, M.A., Frazzoli, E.: Robust distributed routing in dynamical networks–part I: locally responsive policies and weak resilience. Trans. Autom. Control 58(2), 317–332 (2013)
8. Dwork, C.: Differential privacy: a survey of results. In: Agrawal, M., Du, D., Duan, Z., Li, A. (eds.) TAMC 2008. LNCS, vol. 4978, pp. 1–19. Springer, Heidelberg (2008). https://doi.org/10.1007/978-3-540-79228-4_1
9. Dwork, C., McSherry, F., Nissim, K., Smith, A.: Calibrating noise to sensitivity in private data analysis. In: Halevi, S., Rabin, T. (eds.) TCC 2006. LNCS, vol. 3876, pp. 265–284. Springer, Heidelberg (2006). https://doi.org/10.1007/11681878_14
10. Fiez, T., Ratliff, L.J., Dowling, C., Zhang, B.: Data-driven spatio-temporal modeling of parking demand (2018)
11. Geng, Y., Cassandras, C.G.: New "smart parking" system based on resource allocation and reservations. Trans. Intell. Transp. Syst. 14(3), 1129–1139 (2013)
12. Gupta, A., Ligett, K., McSherry, F., Roth, A., Talwar, K.: Differentially private combinatorial optimization. In: Proceedings of the Symposium on Discrete Algorithms, pp. 1106–1125. SIAM (2010)
13. Han, S., Pappas, G.J.: Privacy in control and dynamical systems. Annu. Rev. Control Robot. Autonom. Syst. 1, 309–332 (2018)
14. Hoh, B., Gruteser, M., Xiong, H., Alrabady, A.: Enhancing security and privacy in traffic-monitoring systems. Pervasive Comput. 5(4), 38–46 (2006)
15. Huang, Z., Kannan, S.: The exponential mechanism for social welfare: private, truthful, and nearly optimal. In: Proceedings of the Symposium on Foundations of Computer Science, pp. 140–149. IEEE (2012)

16. ISO New England Inc.: Five minute system demand. https://www.iso-ne.com/isoexpress/web/reports/load-and-demand
17. Kleiner, A., Nebel, B., Ziparo, V.: A mechanism for dynamic ride sharing based on parallel auctions (2011)
18. Krishna, V.: Auction Theory. Academic Press, Cambridge (2009)
19. Lam, K., Krichene, W., Bayen, A.: On learning how players learn: estimation of learning dynamics in the routing game. In: Proceedings of the International Conference on Cyber-Physical Systems, pp. 1–10. IEEE (2016)
20. Ma, S., Zheng, Y., Wolfson, O.: T-share: a large-scale dynamic taxi ridesharing service. In: International Conference on Data Engineering, pp. 410–421. IEEE (2013)
21. Machanavajjhala, A., Gehrke, J., Kifer, D., Venkitasubramaniam, M.: L-diversity: privacy beyond k-anonymity. In: Proceedings of the International Conference on Data Engineering, p. 24. IEEE (2006)
22. McDaniel, P., McLaughlin, S.: Security and privacy challenges in the smart grid. Secur. Priv. **7**(3), 75–77 (2009)
23. McSherry, F., Talwar, K.: Mechanism design via differential privacy. In: Symposium on Foundations of Computer Science, pp. 94–103. IEEE (2007)
24. Miao, F., Han, S., Hendawi, A.M., Khalefa, M.E., Stankovic, J.A., Pappas, G.J.: Data-driven distributionally robust vehicle balancing using dynamic region partitions. In: Proceedings of the International Conference on Cyber-Physical Systems, pp. 261–271. ACM (2017)
25. Miao, F., et al.: Taxi dispatch with real-time sensing data in metropolitan areas: a receding horizon control approach. Trans. Autom. Sci. Eng. **13**(2), 463–478 (2016)
26. Moulin, P., O'Sullivan, J.A.: Information-theoretic analysis of information hiding. Trans. Inf. Theory **49**(3), 563–593 (2003)
27. Naphade, M., Banavar, G., Harrison, C., Paraszczak, J., Morris, R.: Smarter cities and their innovation challenges. Computer **44**(6), 32–39 (2011)
28. Nisan, N., Roughgarden, T., Tardos, E., Vazirani, V.V.: Algorithmic Game Theory. Cambridge University Press, Cambridge (2007)
29. Pavone, M., Smith, S.L., Frazzoli, E., Rus, D.: Robotic load balancing for mobility-on-demand systems. Int. J. Robot. Res. **31**(7), 839–854 (2012)
30. Schuijbroek, J., Hampshire, R.C., Van Hoeve, W.J.: Inventory rebalancing and vehicle routing in bike sharing systems. Eur. J. Oper. Res. **257**(3), 992–1004 (2017)
31. Sweeney, L.: k-anonymity: a model for protecting privacy. Int. J. Uncertain. Fuzziness Knowl.-Based Syst. **10**(05), 557–570 (2002)
32. Tumova, J., Karaman, S., Belta, C., Rus, D.: Least-violating planning in road networks from temporal logic specifications. In: Proceedings of the International Conference on Cyber-Physical Systems, p. 17. IEEE Press (2016)
33. Vickrey, W.: Counterspeculation, auctions, and competitive sealed tenders. J. Financ. **16**(1), 8–37 (1961)
34. Zhang, R., Rossi, F., Pavone, M.: Model predictive control of autonomous mobility-on-demand systems. In: Proceedings of the International Conference on Robotics and Automation, pp. 1382–1389. IEEE (2016)

Deep Learning Based Game-Theoretical Approach to Evade Jamming Attacks

Sandamal Weerasinghe[1(✉)], Tansu Alpcan[1], Sarah M. Erfani[1], Christopher Leckie[1], Peyam Pourbeik[2], and Jack Riddle[3]

[1] Melbourne School of Engineering, The University of Melbourne, Melbourne, Australia
pweerasinghe@student.unimelb.edu.au
[2] Defence Science and Technology Group, Canberra, Australia
[3] Northrop Grumman Corporation, Falls Church, USA

Abstract. Software-defined radios (SDRs) with substantial cognitive (computing) and networking capabilities provide an opportunity for malicious individuals to jam the communications of other legitimate users. Channel hopping is a well known anti-jamming tactic used in order to evade jamming attacks. We model the interaction between a transmitter, who uses chaotic pseudo-random patterns for channel hopping, and a sophisticated jammer, who uses advanced machine learning algorithms to predict the transmitter's frequency hopping patterns as a non-cooperative security game. We investigate the effectiveness of adversarial distortions in such a scenario to support the anti-jamming efforts by deceiving the jammer's learning algorithms. The optimal strategies in the formulated game indicate how adversarial distortions should be used by the players at every step of the game in order improve their outcomes. The studied jamming/anti-jamming scenario combines chaotic time series generators, game theory, and online deep learning.

Keywords: Jamming · Game theory · Adversarial learning

1 Introduction

Recent advances in software-defined radios (SDRs), cognitive networking technologies, and the increasing availability of low-cost hardware, have resulted in most applications becoming dependent on wireless networks for their regular operations. Inevitably, this has given adversaries new opportunities to conduct attacks and harm systems that rely on wireless networks. One of the most common forms of attacks in wireless networks is jamming attacks. Adversaries can utilize cheap and compact transmitters and receivers [8] to scan the transmission channels in a particular area and disrupt the communication between two or more legitimate parties by causing interference or collisions at the receiver side.

This work was supported in part by the Australian Research Council Discovery Project under Grant DP140100819 and by the Northrop Grumman Corporation.

© Springer Nature Switzerland AG 2018
L. Bushnell et al. (Eds.): GameSec 2018, LNCS 11199, pp. 386–397, 2018.
https://doi.org/10.1007/978-3-030-01554-1_22

This paper focuses on a particular scenario where stochastic channel hopping is utilized as an evasion strategy in the presence of a sophisticated jammer. Consider a unit immobilized in a contested environment with its location unknown to friendly search and rescue units in the area. Assume that the immobilized unit (T) still has the capability to transmit signals using its radio transmitter. Multiple friendly units in the area (receivers R) attempt to locate and rescue the immobilized unit (T) by using radio direction finding (RDF). In order to successfully triangulate the location of T, the search and rescue units need to establish communication with it via one of n pre-defined channels. All units are equipped with software defined radios (SDRs), which allows them to switch the transmission/receiver channels on the fly.

The problem of locating the transmitter T becomes challenging if an intelligent jammer J attempts to disrupt the communication through interference. Anti-jamming tactics for wireless networks have been an area of research for some time. For example, [13] propose channel surfing/hopping and spatial retreats as possible strategies for evading jamming attacks. In channel hopping, the signal transmitter would proactively switch the transmission channel according to some pattern (shared with the receiver).

In this paper, we propose a scheme in which the transmitter uses chaotic pseudo random patterns for frequency hopping and the jammer attempts to learn the underlying patterns by training a state of the art Recurrent Neural Network (RNN) in an online setting (i.e., updating the prediction model as new data becomes available). This allows the transmitter to deceive the jammer into learning a false representation of the generator functions by introducing adversarial distortions on top of the generated probability distributions. We apply a game theoretic approach to the interaction between a transmitter and a sophisticated jammer where the two players attempt to mislead each other by maliciously distorting data used by the other player to make decisions. The combination of games, pseudo-random generators and deep learning have not been used in jamming applications to the best of our knowledge.

The main contributions of the paper are highlighted as follows:

- A novel adversarial (deep) learning approach to jamming, where the transmitter and jammer attempt to mislead each other by maliciously distorting data used by the other player to make decisions.
- Integrated use of pseudo-random generators and online machine (deep) learning methods in the context of a frequency hopping scheme.
- An overarching security game modeling the decision making in the context of adversarial (deep) learning and deception by the transmitter and receiver.

2   Related Work

We focus on prior work that utilizes game theory for analyzing jamming problems. For example, the paper [3] uses a game-theoretical approach to analyze jamming/anti-jamming behavior between cognitive radio systems. The authors formulate the jamming problem as a fictitious play between the jammer and the transmitter. In [14], a non-cooperative game is formulated to model the interaction between wireless users and a malicious node that can act as a jammer and an eavesdropper. The authors also utilize a fictitious play based algorithm to find mixed strategy Nash equilibrium solutions. While machine learning techniques have been extensively used for intrusion detection, their usage in jamming applications is relatively recent. For example, [12] uses supervised learning to detect jamming attacks on IEEE 802.11 networks. They train a random forest classification model based on metrics collected from simulations and attempt to predict if a network is under a jamming attack.

In [2], the authors explore the use of chaotic systems to generate frequency hopping sequences. More recently, [6] proposes a pseudo-random sequence generator based on the Chen chaotic system. In order to make multi-step predictions on chaotic time series, [4] propose a variant of RNNs, which attempts to reduce the number of redundant connections between nodes prior to training. More recently, particular interest has been put into predicting chaotic time series using Long Short-Term Memory networks (LSTMs). A knowledge-based prediction modeled combined with a machine learning based prediction model is utilized by [11] to predict chaotic systems.

3   Problem Definition

We consider the interaction between a sophisticated jammer and a transmitter, where the transmitter T is attempting to establish communication with several receivers R while being interfered by the jammer J. At the network level, the only action available to T (J) is choosing a single channel out of the n available channels to transmit (cause interference on). The jammer may successfully disrupt the communication between the transmitter and the receivers by decreasing the *signal-to-interference-plus-noise* ratio (SINR) at the receivers. However, this would then give away the location of the jammer, which may be an unacceptable risk.

Instead of using just one specific channel to transmit signals over a specific time interval, the transmitter switches between the available channels according to some probability distribution p^T. If the transmitter chooses a static probability distribution p^T throughout, the jammer can approximate p^T by observing the channels used by T over a specific time period. To prevent the jammer from approximating p^T, and thereby successfully carry out jamming attacks, the transmitter should periodically change p^T. The manner in which $p^T(k)$ is changed over time cannot be purely random, as that would make it very difficult for the receivers to listen to the correct channel at any given time in order to successfully locate T. But if the changing mechanism is easily perceived, the jammer would learn the new $p^T(k)$ with minimal effort. Therefore, the transmitter utilizes a pseudo-random number generator function $g_i(k) : \mathbb{R} \rightarrow \mathbb{R}$ for each channel $c_i, i \in [1...n]$ in order to create probability distributions that change periodically. In this paper, we use chaotic pseudo-random number generators as a starting point, similar to [2,6]. Then, the probability of selecting channel c_i during the kth interval is given by

$$p_i^T(k) = \frac{g_i(k)}{\sum_{j=1}^n g_j(k)}. \tag{1}$$

Making the probability distribution over the n channels during the kth interval $p^T(k) = [p_1^T(k), p_2^T(k), \ldots, p_n^T(k)]$. Note that the transmitter T has the freedom to decide the duration of each time interval in which a particular $p^T(k)$ is used. If the interval duration changes with each $k \in \mathbb{Z}_{\geq 0}$, the jammer can use a *change point detection* algorithm to identify that the probability distribution has changed and react accordingly [7,9]. Therefore, without loss of generality, we assume that the time interval during which a particular probability distribution is used is fixed.

The jammer can observe the channel usage of the transmitter and approximate the probability distribution during the kth interval by creating a histogram $(\hat{p}^T(k))$. In order to successfully interrupt T's transmission, the jammer would have to know in advance the probability distribution T would use in the next time interval. Therefore, the jammer attempts to learn $g_i, i \in [1, n]$ by training prediction models for each g_i as new observations $\hat{p}^T(k)$ become available. For example, by using the observed $\hat{p}^T$ values from intervals 1 to $k - 1$, the jammer would be able to predict the possible $p^T(k)$ distribution.

The transmitter, who also has spectrum sensing capabilities, observes the channels utilized by the jammer during the kth interval and attempts to approximate the probability distribution J uses over the n-channels for jamming $(\hat{p}^J(k))$. If the observed $\hat{p}^J(k)$ does not diverge from $p^T(k)$ significantly (i.e., $\hat{p}^J(k) \approx p^T(k)$), it implies that the jammer has closely predicted $p^T(k)$ based on the transmitter's previous probability distributions. To hinder the online learners of the jammer, the transmitter T can mislead the jammer by introducing adversarial distortions to each $p_i^T(k)$. By adding adversarial distortions to each of the probabilities, the transmitter expects the jammer to learn a prediction model that is different from the actual generator functions used by the transmitter and predict a strategy $p^J(k)$ that is significantly different from $p^T(k)$. But the transmitter cannot greedily add significantly large distortions as the receivers who are attempting to locate the transmitter would be unaware of these distortion functions, and would continue to use the original pseudo-random generator functions to decide the channels they would listen to. As the transmitter's main objective is to be located without delay, adding adversarial distortions would have a detrimental effect.

If the jammer successfully predicts the p^T values over a period of time, the transmitter can react by either increasing the adversarial distortion intensity or by switching to different generator functions. If the transmitter switches the generator functions, the jammer would have to restart the learning processes. If the transmitter increases the adversarial distortions, it would make learning the true generator functions harder. Therefore, to prevent the transmitter from deviating from the usual generator patterns, the jammer could periodically add adversarial distortions to its own strategies p^J in order to mislead the transmitter into believing that the jammer has not learned the generator functions.

Therefore, the interaction between that jammer and transmitter has a two way obfuscation nature where both players attempt to confuse each other.

The following specific assumptions are made to reduce the complexity of the transmitter-jammer interaction as a starting point and formalize it as a game:

- The jammer and transmitter will only utilize a single channel at a time (with maximum power to maximize the range).
- The n channels are non-overlapping, therefore jamming on channel c_i would not cause interference on channel c_j where $i \neq j$.
- Jamming is modeled as a discrete event, it will either completely disrupt the communications or not.
- The transmitter has the flexibility of choosing different generators for each channel c_i. But once transmissions begin, the generator assignments are assumed to be fixed.
- While the transmitter can also decide the duration of the time interval to keep a particular probability distribution (i.e., $\Delta t \in [T_1, T_2], \Delta t \in \mathbb{Z}_{\geq 0}$), we assume the duration, in seconds, to be fixed for every time interval.

4   Methodology

The observations of the players, $\hat{p}^T$ and $\hat{p}^J$, are a combination of the other players' genuine probability distribution, p^J and p^T, and their respective adversarial distortions, d^T and d^J. As introducing adversarial distortions can lead to probability values becoming negative or greater than one, the resulting vector is projected onto the probability simplex as $\hat{p}_i^T(k) = [p_i^T(k) + d_i^T(k)]_P$, where $[.]_P$ is the projection onto the probability simplex Δ defined as

$$\Delta := \Big\{ p \in \mathbb{R}^n : \sum_{i=0}^{n} p_i = 1 \text{ and } 0 \leq p_i \leq 1, \ \forall i \Big\}. \tag{2}$$

4.1   Chaotic Time Series

While hardware based random number generators are available, especially for non-civilian usage, pseudo-random generators are essential in the above scenario for there needs to be a synchronization method (through pre-shared information) between the transmitter and the listeners. As a starting point [2,6], we select several chaotic time series, such as Rossler attractor, Lorenz attractor and Henon attractor as the generator functions for the transmitter. Even though chaotic time series appear to unpredictable and show divergent behavior, they are governed by well-defined nonlinear equations [1]. We will investigate alternative, cryptographic pseudo-random number generators and compare them to chaotic ones in our future work.

At every step of the game, we obtain the corresponding time series values from each generator function and derive the probability distribution of the transmitter by normalizing the values (1). Figure 1 shows the phase diagrams, where

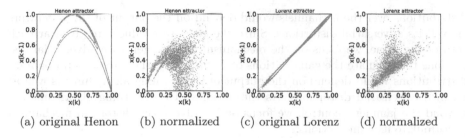

(a) original Henon   (b) normalized   (c) original Lorenz   (d) normalized

Fig. 1. The original phase graphs of the Henon and Lorenz attractors and the decorrelated graphs after combining with the other time series.

the times series value at time $k + 1$ is plotted against the time series value at time k, for Henon and Lorenz attractors. The phase diagrams indicate that the normalization process, which creates a dependency among the chaotic attractors, makes each time series decorrelated. Therefore each time series exhibits more "randomness". Due to this loss of correlation between adjacent time series values, the learning (prediction) task of the jammer becomes harder.

4.2 Learning Algorithm

Chaotic time series are generated by deterministic dynamical systems. Therefore, in order to predict future values, the jammer has to learn the underlying non-linear mappings of the time series. In the particular application scenario we are concerned, the time series have to be learned solely from the past observations, without prior knowledge of the dynamical system.

As the future values of a time series depend on its previous values, we choose RNNs as the learners for the jammer. Unlike traditional feed forward neural networks, RNNs have feed back connections within the layers. It is these feedback connections that allow past experience to be taken into account when predicting the subsequent steps in time series. We use Long Short Term Memory (LSTM) networks, a variant of RNNs that is not affected by the vanishing gradient problem as the jammer's learning algorithm [5].

5   Game Formulation

This section describes the transmitter-jammer interaction, modeled as a two-player static game between the jammer J and transmitter T, repeated over discrete time k. The myopic players interact over a sequence of steps (can be finite or infinite), and at each step they solve the static game and determine the actions they would play during that time step. Although the games at each time step are independent, the learner's of the jammer evolve with time, enabling more accurate predictions as time goes on.

Since both players are equipped with SDRs, the possible actions available to both players at the network layer can be defined by choosing one of the n transmission channels in order to maximize range. For the transmitter, the probability distributions over the n channels would depend on the output of the generators as well its adversarial distortions. Since the generator values are given at each step of the game, we focus on the mechanism used to generate adversarial distortions to formulate the game actions of T. Similarly, the jammer's probability distributions would depend on the output of the learning algorithms as well as its own adversarial distortions. As the outputs of the learning algorithms are beyond the jammer's control, we focus on its adversarial distortion mechanism to formulate its game actions.

5.1 Player Actions

Using adversarial distortions for deception of the other player comes with consequences. For the transmitter, adding adversarial distortions means using a probability distribution over the n channels that is different from what the listeners are using. This leads to unsuccessful radio transmissions (without the jammer's influence) as the listeners would be listening on different channels at a given time. For the jammer, it means using a probability distribution that is different from what the learning algorithm predicts, as a form of deception. Using a distorted probability distribution results in more unsuccessful jamming attempts as both players would be using different probabilities over the channels.

The action sets of both players are defined as different distortion severity values using an arbitrary uniform quantization:

– transmitter: $a^T = \{0.1, 0.2, \ldots, 0.9\}$
– jammer: $a^J = \{0, 0.1, 0.2, \ldots, 0.9\}$

The distortion severity value at the kth time step is used to determine the adversarial distortion vectors $d^T(k)$ and $d^J(k)$ for each player obtained by sampling from a uniform distribution with different support sets. For example, the jammer would decide $a^J(k)$ and create the adversarial distortion vector $d^J(k)$ by randomly sampling from a uniform distribution over the interval $[-a^J(k), a^J(k)]$.

Since $d^T(a^T(k), k)$ and $d^J(a^J(k), k)$ are functions of the players' actions, the distorted probability distributions, $\tilde{p}^T(a^T(k), k)$ and $\tilde{p}^J(a^J(k), k)$, also become dependent on the actions of the players.

Adversarial Deviation: Adversarial deviations are scalar values ($\phi^T(a^T(k), k)$ and $\phi^J(a^J(k), k)$) that indicate how much the originally intended probability distributions $p^T(k)$ and $p^J(k)$ deviate from the actually played distributions $\tilde{p}^T(a^T(k), k)$ and $\tilde{p}^J(a^J(k), k)$. As one possible metric, we choose root-mean-square error (RMSE) to measure the adversarial deviation caused by the distortions added during the kth time step:

$$\phi^T(a^T(k), k) = \left(\frac{1}{n} \sum_{i=1}^{n} \left(p_i^T(k) - \tilde{p}_i^T(a^T(k), k) \right)^2 \right)^{\frac{1}{2}}, \tag{3}$$

$$\phi^J(a^J(k), k) = \left(\frac{1}{n} \sum_{i=1}^{n} \left(p_i^J(k) - \tilde{p}_i^J(a^J(k), k) \right)^2 \right)^{\frac{1}{2}}. \tag{4}$$

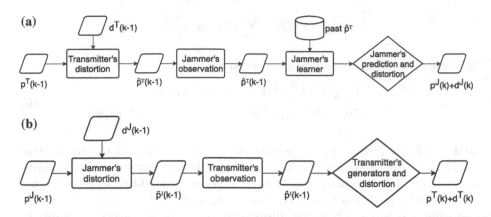

Fig. 2. (a) The decision making process of jammer based on transmitter's observed actions, (b) The decision making process of transmitter based on jammer's observed actions.

5.2 Utility Functions

At each step of the game, the players need to make two decisions (i) the probability distribution over the n channels, and (ii) the amount of adversarial distortions to introduce. As Figs. 2a and b depict, the two players use different approaches to address them. The transmitter obtains its undistorted probability distribution from the generator functions and uses the static game to decide the best adversarial distortion severity to use. The jammer observes the channel usage of the transmitter (i.e., $\hat{p}^T$) and trains n prediction models (as there is a unique generator function for each channel) to predict the next probability distribution the transmitter may use. Subsequently, similar to the transmitter, it decides on the severity of adversarial distortions based on the best response from the proposed game.

Note that the observed probabilities, $\hat{p}^T(k)$ and $\hat{p}^J(k)$, are obtained by counting the number of times each of the n channels is used by the other player during the kth time interval, i.e. creating a histogram. The observed probability distributions estimate the actually played probability distributions i.e., $\tilde{p}^T(a^T(k), k)$ and $\tilde{p}^J(a^J(k), k)$ closely as the length of the time interval increases. Since the observed probabilities depend on the distorted probability distributions, we define the observation function l as $\hat{p}(k) = l(p(k), a(k), k)$, making each $\hat{p}^T(k)$ and $\hat{p}^J(k)$ dependent on $a^T(k)$ and $a^J(k)$ respectively.

Utility of the Transmitter: For the transmitter to evade jamming, the jammer's estimation of transmitter's strategy $\hat{p}^T(k)$ should be significantly different from the actual generated strategy $p^T(k)$ during the kth interval. Since $\hat{p}^T(k)$ is merely the observation of $\tilde{p}^T(k)$, the transmitter can also calculate it. We use the Kullback-Leibler divergence to calculate the statistical distance between two probability distributions as:

$$D_{KL}(P||Q) = \sum_i P(i) \log \frac{P(i)}{Q(i)}. \tag{5}$$

The transmitter's utility function is defined as:

$$\begin{aligned} U^T(k) &= D_{KL}\big(\hat{p}^T(k)||p^T(k)\big) - \phi^T\big(a^T(k), k\big) \\ &= D_{KL}\big(l(p^T(k), a^T(k), k)||p^T(k)\big) - \phi^T\big(a^T(k), k\big). \end{aligned} \tag{6}$$

Utility of the Jammer: Large adversarial distortions from the transmitter would make the jammer's learning algorithms learn incorrect representations of the transmitter's generator functions. Therefore, by adding adversarial distortions to its predicted values, the jammer expects to deceive the transmitter into using less severe adversarial distortions. The jammer, hence, attempts to make $\tilde{p}^J(k)$ diverge from $\hat{p}^T(k)$ using its own adversarial distortions at a cost of jamming efficiency. The jammer's utility function is defined as:

$$U^J(k) = D_{KL}\big(\hat{p}^T(k)||\tilde{p}^J\big(a^T(k), k\big)\big) - \phi^J\big(a^J(k), k\big). \tag{7}$$

In the above formulations ϕ^T and ϕ^J are the adversarial deviations explained in Sect. 5.1 that penalize large adversarial distortions.

5.3   Nash Equilibrium Solution of the Game

A bi-matrix game is represented by two $(m \times n)$ matrices, $A = \{a_{i,j}\}$ and $B = \{b_{i,j}\}$ where each pair of entries $(a_{i,j}, b_{i,j})$ denotes the outcome of the game corresponding to a particular pair of decisions made by the players. These entries in the matrix are populated by the players' utility functions, U^J and U^T. A pair of strategies $(a_{i*,j*}, b_{i*,j*})$ is said to be a non-cooperative Nash equilibrium outcome of the bi-matrix game if there is no incentive for any unilateral deviation by any one of the players. While it is possible to have a scenario where there is no Nash equilibrium solution in pure strategies, there would always be a Nash equilibrium solution in mixed strategies [10].

   A player is said to use a mixed strategy when it chooses to randomize over a set of finite actions. Therefore, a mixed strategy can be defined as a probability distribution that gives each of the available actions a likelihood of being selected. At each step k of the game, the two players decide on their actions by computing the Nash equilibrium solutions in mixed strategies using their corresponding utility matrices. For example, Fig. 3 shows the combined utility matrix for the two players when $k = 60$. In this particular step of the game, the best responses of both players yield a pure strategy Nash equilibrium solution, which is $a^J = 0.2$ and $a^T = 0.1$.

6   Simulation Results

In the simulations, three time series are used to generate the probabilities for each of the channels from the transmitter's perspective. We use three popular

		transmitter - a^T			
		0.1	0.2	0.3	0.4
Jammer - a^J	0	(0.050,0.017)	(0.028,0.023)	(0.082,0.022)	(0.034,0.003)
	0.1	(0.038,0.005)	(0.019,0.001)	(0.073,0.016)	(0.009,0.011)
	0.2	**(0.096,0.049)**	(0.030,0.013)	(0.041,0.006)	(0.008,0.013)
	0.3	(0.048,0.083)	(0.091,0.012)	(0.062,0.000)	(0.004,0.005)
	0.4	(0.013,0.015)	(0.020,0.015)	(0.042,0.006)	(0.089,0.011)

Fig. 3. The utility matrix of the game depicting the outcomes. The jammer is the row player and the transmitter is the column player and payoffs are displayed as (jammer utility, transmitter utility).

chaotic time series, Rossler attractor, Lorenz attractor and Henon attractor as the generator functions (i.e., $g_i(k), i \in [1, 2, 3]$) for the three channels of the transmitter. At the start of the game (i.e., $k = 1$ and $k = 2$), where there are no prior observations, the jammer uses normalized probability distributions sampled from $\mathcal{U}(0, 1)$ to use over the n channels. Subsequently, after the learners commence the learning process, the predicted probability distributions $p^J(k)$ are used. During the initial stages of the game, where there are very few observations, the predictions of the online learning algorithms would not be accurate as machine learning based prediction models need sufficient data to learn the correct underlying patterns. After a certain threshold, the models are expected to stabilize and provide accurate predictions.

We train a four neuron LSTM model for each channel c_i using the observed probability distributions $\hat{p}^T$ as the training data. The performance of the LSTMs is compared against a baseline persistence algorithm which predicts the observation of the previous time step as the prediction for the current time step (i.e., $p^j(k) = \hat{p}^T(k - 1)$). Figure 4 shows the probability distributions used by the transmitter, the jammer and the baseline algorithm over the three channels under two conditions. The top row shows the probability distributions when the transmitter is not introducing distortions ($a^T(k) = 0, \forall k \in \mathbb{Z}_{\geq 0}$), and the bottom row shows the distributions when $a^T(k)$ is fixed at 0.4 for all time steps. Comparing the undistorted probability distributions with the distorted probability distributions show that by introducing adversarial distortions, the transmitter can make each time series behave more abruptly, deviating from the patterns governed by the underlying equations.

Figure 5 shows the root-mean-square error (RMSE) between the transmitter's distorted probability distribution ($\tilde{P}^T(k)$) and the jammer's predicted probability distribution ($p^J(k)$), and the baseline persistence algorithm under different adversarial distortion severities. As the LSTMs are trained online, during the early stages of the game they will not be able to make accurate predictions due to the lack of data. But as more data becomes available, the LSTMs are able to learn the underlying patterns of the data make more accurate predictions. Therefore, we show the RMSE values for the last 50% of the time series data as they reflect the true prediction capabilities of the LSTMs. We observe that

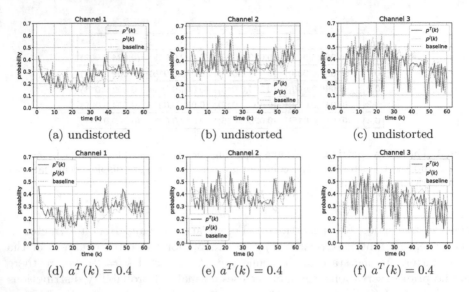

(a) undistorted   (b) undistorted   (c) undistorted

(d) $a^T(k) = 0.4$ (e) $a^T(k) = 0.4$ (f) $a^T(k) = 0.4$

Fig. 4. The probability distributions used by the transmitter, jammer with the deep learner and a jammer with the baseline algorithm on the three channels. The figures on the bottom row show the probability values when $a^T(k)$ is set to 0.4.

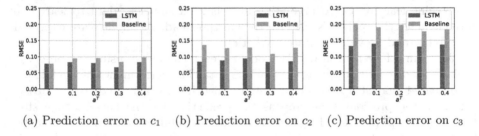

(a) Prediction error on c_1 (b) Prediction error on c_2 (c) Prediction error on c_3

Fig. 5. RMSE values of the LSTMs and the baseline algorithm for the probability distributions used on channels 1 to 3. The RMSE is calculated for the last 50% of each time series.

the performance of the LSTMs in predicting the time series are comparatively higher than the baseline persistence algorithm. The performance differences are quite significant on channels 2 and 3 where the two chaotic functions used appear more random compared to that of channel 1.

7   Conclusions and Future Work

This paper models the interaction between a sophisticated jammer and a transmitter in a search and rescue scenario as a stochastic game. The transmitter, who has a pre-shared key with the rescuers, uses stochastic channel hopping according to some pseudo-random generators as the anti-jamming mechanism.

The jammer attempts to learn the above pseudo-random generators by using online machine (deep) learning methods. In order to prevent the jammer from learning the pseudo-random generators, the transmitter introduces adversarial distortions. Similarly, to deceive the transmitter into thinking that the jammer has not been able to learn the underlying patterns, the jammer also distorts its jamming patterns on purpose. The empirical results suggest that transmitter can in fact hinder the learning capabilities of the jammer by using adversarial distortions.

Directions for future work include: comparing different (e.g. cryptographic) random number generating algorithms for the transmitters, and formulating different games, e.g. over a finite horizon or with additional solution concepts.

References

1. Boeing, G.: Visual analysis of nonlinear dynamical systems: chaos, fractals, self-similarity and the limits of prediction. Systems **4**(4), 37 (2016)
2. Cong, L., Songgeng, S.: Chaotic frequency hopping sequences. IEEE Trans. commun. **46**(11), 1433–1437 (1998)
3. Dabcevic, K., Betancourt, A., Marcenaro, L., Regazzoni, C.S.: Intelligent cognitive radio jamming - a game-theoretical approach. EURASIP J. Adv. Sig. Process. **2014**(1), 171 (2014)
4. Han, M., Xi, J., Xu, S., Yin, F.L.: Prediction of chaotic time series based on the recurrent predictor neural network. IEEE Trans. Sig. Process. **52**(12), 3409–3416 (2004)
5. Hochreiter, S., Schmidhuber, J.: Long short-term memory. Neural Comput. **9**(8), 1735–1780 (1997)
6. Hu, H., Liu, L., Ding, N.: Pseudorandom sequence generator based on the chen chaotic system. Comput. Phys. Commun. **184**(3), 765–768 (2013)
7. Kawahara, Y., Sugiyama, M.: Change-point detection in time-series data by direct density-ratio estimation. In: Proceedings of the 2009 SIAM International Conference on Data Mining, pp. 389–400. SIAM (2009)
8. Laufer, C.: The Hobbyist's Guide to the RTL-SDR: Really Cheap Software Defined Radio. CreateSpace Independent Publishing Platform (2015)
9. Liu, S., Yamada, M., Collier, N., Sugiyama, M.: Change-point detection in time-series data by relative density-ratio estimation. Neural Netw. **43**, 72–83 (2013)
10. Nash, J.: Non-cooperative games. Ann. Math. **54**, 286–295 (1951)
11. Pathak, J., et al.: Hybrid forecasting of chaotic processes: using machine learning in conjunction with a knowledge-based model. CoRR abs/1803.04779 (2018)
12. Pual, O., Akta, I., Schnelke, C.J., Abidin, G., Wehrle, K., Gross, J.: Machine learning-based jamming detection for IEEE 802.11: Design and experimental evaluation. In: Proceeding of IEEE International Symposium on a World of Wireless, Mobile and Multimedia Networks 2014, p. 110 (June 2014)
13. Xu, W., Wood, T., Trappe, W., Zhang, Y.: Channel surfing and spatial retreats: defenses against wireless denial of service. In: Proceedings of the 3rd ACM Workshop on Wireless Security, pp. 80–89. Wise 2004 (2004)
14. Zhu, Q., Saad, W., Han, Z., Poor, H.V., Başar, T.: Eavesdropping and jamming in next-generation wireless networks: a game-theoretic approach. In: Military Communications Conference, 2011-MILCOM 2011, pp. 119–124. IEEE (2011)

Towards Scientific Incident Response

Jonathan M. Spring[1](✉)(iD) and David Pym[1,2]

[1] University College London, Gower Street, London, UK
jspring@cs.ucl.ac.uk, d.pym@ucl.ac.uk
[2] Alan Turing Institute, 96 Euston Road, London, UK

Abstract. A scientific incident analysis is one with a methodical, justifiable approach to the human decision-making process. Incident analysis is a good target for additional rigor because it is the most human-intensive part of incident response. Our goal is to provide the tools necessary for specifying precisely the reasoning process in incident analysis. Such tools are lacking, and are a necessary (though not sufficient) component of a more scientific analysis process. To reach this goal, we adapt tools from program verification that can capture and test abductive reasoning. As Charles Peirce coined the term in 1900, "Abduction is the process of forming an explanatory hypothesis. It is the only logical operation which introduces any new idea." We reference canonical examples as paradigms of decision-making during analysis. With these examples in mind, we design a logic capable of expressing decision-making during incident analysis. The result is that we can express, in machine-readable and precise language, the abductive hypotheses than an analyst makes, and the results of evaluating them. This result is beneficial because it opens up the opportunity of genuinely comparing analyst processes without revealing sensitive system details, as well as opening an opportunity towards improved decision-support via limited automation.

Keywords: Incident response · Digital forensics
Science of security · Mathematical modelling
Logical modelling · Intrusion analysis

1 Introduction and Motivation

Incident analysis is the central feature of incident response and digital forensics. Incident response and digital forensics overlap largely in their modes of analysis. Otherwise, they have different goals, and are done by different sorts of organizations. One might take a broad view of digital forensics and say it includes incident response, but realistically the term "digital forensics" has too many law-enforcement connotations for this broad usage to quite work. We focus on incident analysis, which, as defined by [28], includes the evidence collection, analysis, and reporting phases of our topic, whether that topic is incident response or digital forensic investigation.

© Springer Nature Switzerland AG 2018
L. Bushnell et al. (Eds.): GameSec 2018, LNCS 11199, pp. 398–417, 2018.
https://doi.org/10.1007/978-3-030-01554-1_23

Incident analysis is part of the study of what has occurred on computers and computer networks. An incident is an event that violates some security policy [26]; that policy may be but is not necessarily a law. We treat incident analysis as akin to scientific investigation. The analyst has a hypothetical model about how the incident occurred, and tests it by gathering evidence and adjusting the model based on the results. This is not the naive binary hypothesis testing of a high-school science lab. Rather, it is building models for a purpose based on empirical, structured observations of the world—the conception of science of security argued for by [29].

We inform our logic development with examples as well as the incident response standards review by [28]. For example, we draw inspiration from [30]. Since [30] is a description of an incident analyst tracking foreign spies through computer networks, it is a rather obvious paradigmatic case. Another, less obvious, example of incident analysis is Assistant for Randomized Monitoring Over Routes (ARMOR) [31]. ARMOR represents a kind of ongoing incident analysis, though of physical security. One reason [31] is relevant is that it is deployed decision-making. Although the form of our model is different, deployability is a major consideration of our design choices. Our working definition of incident analysis, adapting from that of 'investigation' in [6, p. 244], is:

> *Incident analysis*: a process by an *agent* to build a *model* and *explanation* of the *phenomenon* responsible for a security violation. The process is forensic (as distinguished from engineering or design which are forward-looking, though results should inform engineering). The process will include collection of *evidence*; discovery of interrelated *mechanisms*; investigative heuristics and *methodology*; and *reporting* results. Different incident analyses may have different *goals*, such as fixing the impacted system, attributing the attack, or legal prosecution.

Italicized terms may need their own definitions in future work. However, we are not seeking an ontology, and shall not elaborate them here.

Incident analysis is a key aspect of incident response. In turn, incident response is a crucial aspect of information security broadly. One essential aspect of infosec is feedback from incidents to 'preparation' and 'protection' [1].

The National Institute of Standards and Technology (NIST) guide on forensics in incident response recommends analysts use "a methodical approach" [14, p. 3-8]. However, nowhere does NIST provide such a methodical approach. This is a general failing. A recent review of published incident response documents and standards found that the literature lacked this middle-level of description [28]. Fine-grained, type-this-on-the-keyboard advice is available. And high-level, do-these-management-practices advice is available. But published guidance on a methodical approach to incident analysis is lacking, despite the central importance of the topic to cyber security.

We will contribute towards a methodical approach to incident analysis by building a logical language for analysts to document their reasoning process precisely. This contribution advances towards scientific incident analysis because it improves interpretation of evidence. A logic improves interpretation because it enables communication and repetition of the interpretive process, allowing for iterative improvement and collaboration.

To make use of our logic for improved decision-making, we also need to understand human cognition and how we think about thinking. [11] makes progress on this topic, applying the approach by [10] for reducing the impact of cognitive biases in analysis to computer network incident analysis. Our goal is to combine these aspects and provide logical tools such that steps of interpretation can be made explicit and the gaps in our knowledge identified more easily.

The paper continues as follows. Section 2 develops a new logic as a tool to express reasoning patterns within incident analysis. Section 3 demonstrates how to apply the logic by an example construction to express and elaborate the kill chain model from [12]. Section 4 lays out benefits to decision-making in security and future work.

2 Logic Definitions

In this section, we build a logical system as a tool for expressing paradigmatic features of incident analysis. These features include abductive hypothesis generation, evidence-based evaluation of hypothetical explanations, and reasoning about technical events. Section 3 will use the tools we build here to further elaborate our logic through an example.

A necessary part of a logical system is its model. A model, in this logic sense, is a mathematical structure with which we can interpret a proposition, and then determine whether it is satisfied or not. This sense is quite far from a scientific model. However, as [22] argues, a logic will be most effective when its logic model aligns with the salient features of a scientific model of the represented phenomenon. Therefore, we develop logical tools with the purpose of incident analysis in mind at every step. The phenomena of interest are violations of security policy; that is, a resultant state of a computer system. We will represent these as histories, composed of series of states of the computer.

We make a variety of choices to adapt the logic to incident analysis. Some are simple: incident analysis is largely about past events, so we include both past-tense and future-tense temporal operators. Others are more subtle. For example, we define a separation of network, storage, and processor resources at a basic level because practitioners think about, monitor, and defend these things quite differently. We wanted the logic to reflect this reality deeply. And some of our choices have an eye towards pragmatics of usability and deployable decision-making. As [18] describes, the road from formal logic to operational implementation is long. However, we include the 'and, separately' operator in our logic, which supports composable reasoning and an eye towards scalability.

2.1   Expressions

Our definition of expressions is essentially the same as [13] and [4]. An expression can be an integer, an atom, or a variable.

$$
\begin{array}{rll}
E ::= & x & \text{Variable} \\
| & 37 & \text{Integer} \\
| & \texttt{nil} & \text{nil} \\
| & \texttt{a} & \text{atom} \\
| & \ldots &
\end{array}
$$

The open-ended definition of expressions allows for additional expressions so long as they can be interpreted in the semantic domain specified.

Our semantic domains are values, addresses, and content, analogous to and slightly more general than the values, stacks, and heaps used in [4]:

$$
Val = Int \cup Atoms \cup Loc \quad A = Var \rightharpoonup_{fin} Val \quad C = Loc \rightharpoonup_{fin} Val \times Val
$$

where $Loc = \{\ell, \ldots\}$ is an infinite set of locations, the term $Var = \{x, y, \ldots\}$ is a set of variables, $Atoms = \{\texttt{nil}, \texttt{a}, \ldots\}$ is the set of atoms, and finite partial functions are represented by $\rightharpoonup_{fin}$. Elements of addresses and content are $a \in A$ and $c \in C$, respectively. As is customary for stack variables, we do not provide an explicit operation for allocating address variables.

The domain of an element of addresses is $dom\,(a)$ for $a \in A$. Similarly, $dom\,(c)$ is the domain for an element of contents. Note that English grammar here may be confusing. An address a is a set of mappings from variables to values, not a singleton. Likewise, c is a set of content mappings, not a singleton.

Interpretation is independent of the particular computer being represented, analogous to heap-independent interpretations in [4]: $[\![E]\!]\,a \in Val$, where $dom\,(a)$ includes the free variables of E.

2.2   Basics and Syntax

We will make use of some familiar classical propositional connectives, some perhaps less-familiar temporal connectives, and a 'spatial' connective from a more recent logic. The familiar classical connectives are 'if, then', 'and', 'or', and 'not' and the familiar first-order quantifiers are 'there exists' and 'for all'.

Before marching on with definitions, we briefly describe the intention of the less common operators which we use. The operators 'until' and 'since' are both temporal, whose definition we take from [17]. 'Until' is about the future, and 'since' is about the past, but otherwise they are similar. We have 'ϕ until ψ' when the first formula ϕ is true now and into the future, for at least enough time such that the second formula becomes true at some time later. It is what one might expect when asking "Hold this cup until I get back." Though in our logic we will need to be explicit about the social assumption, in classical logic, of "If I return, then give me the cup." 'Since' is similar. We have 'ϕ since ψ' when at some point in the past ψ occurred, and ϕ has been occurring from then up through to the present. Again, as one might expect from "I have been sad since my cup broke."

The final less-familiar connective we use is $*$ for 'and, separately'. Usual, classical 'and' is collapsible. That is, "I have five coins and I have five coins" is, in classical logic, the same as "I have five coins." The connective 'and, separately' is not collapsible. We take this connective from O'Hearn and Pym's logic of bunched implications (BI) [8,19,23], a non-classical ('substructural') logic with a semantics that can be interpreted in terms of the composition and comparison of resources and which forms the basis for Separation Logic [13,24]. Separation Logic is a specific theory of BI for handling memory allocation—our direct starting point in this section. Readers may see [22] for an accessible introduction to Separation Logic.

Computers, like coins, are resources. We use Separation Logic because we want to be able to express "A computer is compromised and, separately, a computer is compromised" to be reasoned with as two computers are compromised, for example. The classical 'and' would lose this information that two computers are compromised, because the formula would collapse.

Following these intuitions, logical formulae are constructed inductively:

$$
\begin{array}{llll}
\phi, \psi ::= & \alpha & \text{Atomic formulae} \\
& | & \bot & \text{Falsity} \\
& | & \phi \Rightarrow \psi & \text{Material implication} \\
& | & \textbf{emp} & \text{Empty content} \\
& | & \exists x.\phi & \text{Existential quantification} \\
& | & \phi \mathcal{U} \psi & \text{Temporal Until} \\
& | & \phi \mathcal{S} \psi & \text{Temporal Since} \\
& | & \phi * \psi & \text{Spatial conjunction}
\end{array}
$$

Atomic formulae include equality and points-to relations, and predicates.

$$
\begin{array}{lll}
\alpha ::= & E = E' & \text{Equality} \\
& | \quad E \mapsto E_1, E_2 & \text{Points to} \\
& | \quad P\left((Val_1, E_1), (Val_2, E_2)\right) & \text{Relational predicate} \\
& | \quad \cdots
\end{array}
$$

In [13], points-to is defined as a three-place relation, $E \mapsto E_1, E_2$. [4] contains both a simple points-to relation, $E \mapsto E'$ and a higher-order concept of lists that treats the properties of lists as primary, rather than their contents. Our goal is not to analyze details of doubly-linked lists or higher-order lists. Our syntax does not treat lists directly. However, this three-place syntax provides a way to separate a large data element into arbitrary chunks while preserving their order. This works for memory, files on disk, and network packets. An example of why this is useful: we can represent malware analysis techniques, such as segment hashing, by representing properties of a connected series of expressions. However, our intention is not to be exhaustively faithful to the file-system representation. If the segments of a large file are not of interest, we may elide the details of the file system block size and the linked list that actually composes the file contents.

The usual classical and temporal symbols are defined from available formulae:

- negation; i.e., 'not', is $\neg\phi \overset{\text{def}}{=} \phi \Rightarrow \bot$
- truth is simply not false; i.e., $\top \overset{\text{def}}{=} \neg\bot$
- disjunction; i.e., 'or' is customarily $\phi \vee \psi \overset{\text{def}}{=} (\neg\phi) \Rightarrow \psi$
- conjunction; i.e., 'and' is thus $\phi \wedge \psi \overset{\text{def}}{=} \neg(\neg\phi \vee \neg\psi)$
- 'for all' is in terms of the existential, $\forall x.\phi \overset{\text{def}}{=} \neg\exists x.\neg\phi$
- 'at least once in the future' relates to until, $\Diamond\phi \overset{\text{def}}{=} \top\mathcal{U}\phi$
- 'henceforth' is $\Box\phi \overset{\text{def}}{=} \neg\Diamond\neg\phi$
- analogously, 'at least once in the past' is $\Diamondblack\phi \overset{\text{def}}{=} \top\mathcal{S}\phi$
- and 'has always been' is $\blacksquare\phi \overset{\text{def}}{=} \neg\Diamondblack\neg\phi$.

We follow [15], in that we do not have a simple 'next' temporal operator. For various reasons [15] lays out, and we feel a choice that is validated by how incident analysts reason in our case studies, we primarily care about observable changes, not the precise sequence that brings those changes about.

2.3 Model

Our model is designed to support incident response reasoning by embedding the most important objects of analysis as the basis of the model. We keep the three salient types of computing resources separate, and index by time. Each resource is a partial monoid with composition operator and unit.

$(R_M, \cdot_M, e_M)$ for processor and RAM (M for memory)
$(R_D, \cdot_D, e_D)$ for file storage (D for disk)
$(R_N, \cdot_N, e_N)$ for network bandwidth (N for network)

where, for $i \in \{M, D, N\}$, R_i is a set of resource elements of the given type, $\cdot_i : R_i \times R_i \rightharpoonup R_i$ is a partial function operating on resources of the given type, and e_i is the unit element of $\cdot_i$ such that for all $r \in R_i$ it is the case that $r \cdot_i e_i = r = e_i \cdot_i r$.

More concretely, each R_M, R_D, R_N is composed of (address, content) pairs analogous to (stack, heap) pairs. We define $\mathbf{m}::=s, h$ for $\mathbf{m} \in R_M$, $\mathbf{d}::=\delta, \beta$ for $\mathbf{d} \in R_D$, and $\mathbf{n}::=\kappa, \upsilon$ for $\mathbf{n} \in R_N$. These sub-parts of the resources are proper subsets of the address and content defined above. The fact that $s \in \mathsf{S}$ with $\mathsf{S} \subset A$ and $h \in \mathsf{H}$ with $\mathsf{H} \subset C$ makes the usual stack-heap model of separation logic somehow contained in our address-content model. Further, we define $\delta \in \mathsf{N}$ for $\mathsf{N} \subset A$ and $\beta \in \mathsf{B}$ for $\mathsf{B} \subset C$ (for inodes and file blocks). For network host addresses and data units (i.e., packets), $\kappa \in \mathsf{K}$ for $\mathsf{K} \subset A$ and $\upsilon \in \mathsf{U}$ for $\mathsf{U} \subset C$.

Formally, these three resource monoids could be considered as one monoid $\mathbf{R} = (R, \cdot, \mathbf{E})$ where $R = R_M \uplus R_D \uplus R_N$ (the disjoint union of the resources), composition $\cdot, \cdot : \mathbf{R} \times \mathbf{R} \to \mathbf{R}$ such that

$$\cdot(r_1, r_2) ::= \begin{cases} r_1 \cdot_i r_2 & \text{if } r_1, r_2 \in R_i \\ \text{undefined} & \text{otherwise} \end{cases}$$

and $\mathbf{E} = \{e_M, e_D, e_N\}$

where $\mathbf{E} \cdot r ::= \begin{cases} \bigcup_{e \in \mathbf{E}} r \cdot_i e = \{r\} = \bigcup_{e \in \mathbf{E}} e \cdot_i r & \text{if } r \in R_i \\ \text{undefined} & \text{otherwise} \end{cases}$

The definitions of $\cdot$ and a set of units are adapted from [3, Definition 2.3]. These definitions will be used to describe the state of a computer or a computer network at a given time as a composition of different programs, files, and network activity.

Incident analysis needs a notion of time and changes. Therefore, we adopt a linear time model composed of a sequence of states. Each state is represented by an element $r \in \mathbf{R}$. We define a history $H \in \mathcal{H}$ as a ordered finite set

$$H ::= \left\{ r^1, r^2, \ldots, r^t, \ldots, r^T \right\},$$

with $T \in \mathbb{N}$. (H, t) uniquely identifies the state $r^t \in \mathbf{R}$. The length of a history is $|H| = T$. There is no notion of absolute time or a "wall clock." The time T indicates a sequence without any claims about the time between transitions.

History Monoid. We define a monoid, $\mathbf{H} = (\mathcal{H}(\mathbf{R}), \circ, e)$ where $\mathcal{H}$ is the set of histories H (defined above) that can be constructed using a given resource monoid $\mathbf{R}$; $\circ : \mathcal{H} \times \mathcal{H} \to \mathcal{H}$; unit e to be the empty history with $|e| = 0$. More specifically, we define $\circ$ as:

$$(H_1 \circ H_2, t) ::= \begin{cases} (r_1^t \cdot r_2^t, t) \text{ for } r_1^t \in H_1 \text{ and } r_2^t \in H_2 & \text{if } |H_1| = |H_2| \\ (H_2, t) & \text{if } H_1 \prec H_2 \\ (H_1, t) & \text{if } H_2 \prec H_1 \\ \text{undefined} & \textit{otherwise} \end{cases}$$

Here $H_1 \prec H_2$ indicates that one history is contained in the other. We define four conditions that must all be met for this to hold. Specifically, $H_1 \prec H_2$ iff

1. $|H_1| < |H_2|$, where $|H_1| = T$, $|H_2| = T'$; and
2. for all $r_1^t \in H_1$, with $t \in T$, there exists some $r_2^{t'} \in H_2$ with $t' \in T'$ such that $r_1^t = r_2^{t'}$ and $t \leq t'$; and
3. for all $r_2^{t'} \in H_2$ and given any r_1^t, r_1^x in H_1 with $t, x \in T$, it is the case that $r_2^{t'} = r_1^t$ and $r_2^{t'} = r_1^x$ iff $t = x$; and
4. for all r_1^t, r_1^x in H_1 with $t, x \in T$ such that $t < x$, it is the case that, for $r_2^{t'}, r_2^{x'} \in H_2$ with $t', x' \in T'$, we have $r_1^t = r_2^{t'}$ and $r_1^x = r_2^{x'}$ iff $t' < x'$.

The intuition for these requirements as expressing the concept of "contained in" is as follows. A smaller history is contained in a larger one. All the events of the smaller history appear in the larger one, in the same relative ordering. The only change permitted is that new events are inserted into the larger history; such inserted events can be interleaved in any way.

The unit e as the empty history behaves as expected.

$$H \circ e = H = e \circ H$$

Proof of identity by cases. We have $|e| = 0$, so either

1. $|H| = 0$, that is H is e, thus we have to prove $e \circ e = e$
   (a) This is true. We follow $r^t ::= r^t_1 \cdot r^t_2$. However, $T = 0$ so there are no elements to compose. The result is the history of length 0, namely, e.
2. $|H| \geq 1$
   (a) Requirement 1 for $\prec$ holds $(0 < 1)$.
   (b) Requirement 2 holds vacuously (all $r^t_1 \in e$ is $\emptyset$).
   (c) Requirement 3 holds vacuously, without r^t_1, r^x_1 to compare.
   (d) Requirement 4 holds vacuously, without r^t_1, r^x_1 to compare.

One might think the unit for $\circ$ could be the history containing just the unit element $\mathbf{E}$ (recall $\mathbf{E} = \{e_M, e_D, e_N\}$). However, if defined thus, requirement 2 for $\prec$ might fail if there is no element of H in $H \circ e$ such that $(H, t) = \mathbf{E}$. Then $H \circ e$ could be undefined for $|H| > 1$, in which case $H \circ e = H = e \circ H$ would not hold as required. Every history could start with the unit element to make this true by construction, but that seems unnatural. Therefore the unit of $\circ$ should be the empty history $|e| = 0$.

A history will be used to represent a hypothesis for the series of events and changes to the resources of a computer system during the course of the incident. Combining histories can represent, for example, combining explanations of simultaneous events on two different locations on the network.

2.4 Semantics

The semantics of the atomic expressions are many-sorted operations. To unfold the truth value of an expression, recall $(H, t) \stackrel{\text{def}}{=} [(s^t, h^t), (\delta^t, \beta^t), (\kappa^t, \upsilon^t)]$.

$$[(s^t, h^t), (\delta^t, \beta^t), (\kappa^t, \upsilon^t)] \models E = E' \text{ iff } \begin{cases} [\![E]\!]\, s^t = [\![E']\!]\, s^t \\ [\![E]\!]\, \delta^t = [\![E']\!]\, \delta^t \\ [\![E]\!]\, \kappa^t = [\![E']\!]\, \kappa^t \end{cases}$$

We can abbreviate this as

$$H, t \models E = E' \text{ iff } [\![E]\!]\, a^t = [\![E']\!]\, a^t$$

Because these three resources are disjoint (namely $\mathsf{S} \subset A; \mathsf{N} \subset A; \mathsf{K} \subset A$ and $\mathsf{S} \cap \mathsf{N} = \mathsf{S} \cap \mathsf{K} = \mathsf{N} \cap \mathsf{K} = \emptyset$), only one of the three interpretations will be valid. Namely, only one of $[\![E]\!]\, s$ or $[\![E]\!]\, \delta$ or $[\![E]\!]\, \kappa$ can hold for any E, or they are equivalent. Only one exists because for $[\![E]\!]\, a$ to be interpretable, $dom(a)$ must include the free variables of E. The domains of s, δ, κ are disjoint by definition. If there are no free variables in E, then $[\![E]\!]\, s = [\![E]\!]\, \delta = [\![E]\!]\, \kappa$.

Similarly, points-to can be defined over the three disjoint parts of the model at a given time, and then abbreviated in terms of elements of A and C:

$$[(s^t, h^t), (\delta^t, \beta^t), (\kappa^t, \upsilon^t)] \models E \mapsto E_1, E_2$$
$$\text{iff } \begin{cases} h^t([\![E]\!]\, s^t) = \langle [\![E_1]\!]\, s^t, [\![E_2]\!]\, s^t \rangle & \{[\![E]\!]\, s^t\} = dom(h^t) \\ \beta^t([\![E]\!]\, \delta^t) = \langle [\![E_1]\!]\, \delta^t, [\![E_2]\!]\, \delta^t \rangle & \{[\![E]\!]\, \delta^t\} = dom(\beta^t) \\ \upsilon^t([\![E]\!]\, \kappa^t) = \langle [\![E_1]\!]\, \kappa^t, [\![E_2]\!]\, \kappa^t \rangle & \{[\![E]\!]\, \kappa^t\} = dom(\upsilon^t) \end{cases}$$

which we abbreviate as

$$H, t \models E \mapsto E_1, E_2 \text{iff} \left\{ \llbracket E \rrbracket a^t \right\} = dom\left(c^t\right) \text{ and } c^t\left(\llbracket E \rrbracket a^t\right) = \left\langle \llbracket E_1 \rrbracket a^t, \llbracket E_2 \rrbracket a^t \right\rangle$$

The element emp actually represents a set of three related elements: $\left\{ \overset{M}{\text{emp}}, \overset{D}{\text{emp}}, \overset{N}{\text{emp}} \right\}$. The semantics for emp is defined as

$$[(s^t, h^t), (\delta^t, \beta^t), (\kappa^t, v^t)] \models \overset{M}{\text{emp}} \text{ iff } h^t = []$$

$$[(s^t, h^t), (\delta^t, \beta^t), (\kappa^t, v^t)] \models \overset{D}{\text{emp}} \text{ iff } \beta^t = []$$

$$[(s^t, h^t), (\delta^t, \beta^t), (\kappa^t, v^t)] \models \overset{N}{\text{emp}} \text{ iff } v^t = []$$

$$H, t \models \text{emp iff } \overset{M}{\text{emp}} \text{ and } \overset{D}{\text{emp}} \text{ and } \overset{N}{\text{emp}}$$

Here, $h^t = []$, $\beta^t = []$, and $v^t = []$, represent the empty heap, empty file system, and empty network, respectively.

The semantics for a relational predicate, P, is given by

$$H, t \models P\left((Val_1, E_1), (Val_2, E_2)\right) \text{ iff } (H, t) \in \mathbb{V}\left[P\left((Val_1, E_1), (Val_2, E_2)\right)\right]$$

Here $\mathbb{V} : \mathbb{A} \to \mathcal{P}\left(States\right)$ is the valuation function from the set $\mathbb{A}$ of atoms of $P\left((Val_1, E_1), (Val_2, E_2)\right)$ to the powerset of possible states of the form (H, t).

The other semantic clauses are as follows:

$$
\begin{aligned}
H, t \models \phi \Rightarrow \psi \quad &\text{iff} \quad \text{if } H, t \models \phi \text{ then } H, t \models \psi \\
H, t \models \exists x.\phi \quad &\text{iff} \quad \text{for some } v \in Val. [a|x \mapsto v], c \models \phi \\
H, t \models \phi \mathcal{U} \psi \quad &\text{iff} \quad \text{for some } i \in T \text{ with } i \geq t \text{ and } (H, i) \models \psi \text{ such that} \\
&\qquad \text{for all } j \in T \text{ with } t \leq j < i \text{ it is the case } (H, j) \models \phi \\
H, t \models \phi \mathcal{S} \psi \quad &\text{iff} \quad \text{for some } i \in T \text{ with } i \leq t \text{ and } (H, i) \models \psi \text{ such that} \\
&\qquad \text{for all } j \in T \text{ with } i < j \leq t \text{ it is the case } (H, j) \models \phi \\
H, t \models \phi * \psi \quad &\text{iff} \quad \text{for some } H_1, H_2 \text{ such that } H_1 \# H_2 \text{ and } H_1 \circ H_2 = H \\
&\qquad \text{where } H_1, t \models \phi \text{ and } H_2, t \models \psi
\end{aligned}
$$

Here $H_1 \# H_2$ indicates the histories are pointwise disjoint. $H_1 \# H_2$ is true if and only if the following conditions hold:

1. $|H_1| = |H_2| = T$; and
2. For all $[(s_1^t, h_1^t), (\delta_1^t, \beta_1^t), (\kappa_1^t, v_1^t)] \in H_1$ and $[(s_2^t, h_2^t), (\delta_2^t, \beta_2^t), (\kappa_2^t, v_2^t)] \in H_2$ it is the case that, for all $t \in T$:
   (a) $dom\left(h_1^t\right) \cap dom\left(h_2^t\right) = \emptyset$ and
   (b) $dom\left(\beta_1^t\right) \cap dom\left(\beta_2^t\right) = \emptyset$ and
   (c) $dom\left(v_1^t\right) \cap dom\left(v_2^t\right) = \emptyset$.

2.5   Abduction

These tools will allow us to capture abduction. Abduction would naturally be grouped into a trio with deduction and induction. These terms have long, problematic histories of usage. Deduction requires a proof theory, and because one can justifiably define different proof theories for different purposes [21], 'deduction' is not just one thing. But generally 'deduction' captures the reasoning from premises to conclusions following explicit rules. We discuss proof theory briefly in Sect. 2.6. 'Induction' has received voluminous attention, since Hume in the 1740s [9]. It roughly means concluding that because something has been the case before, it will be again. A more fruitful discussion might be had under the topic of how we generalize from what we know. Generalization methods will generate the heuristics we need for the logic. However, we leave generalization aside for now; there are other discussions of effective methods (see, e.g., [29]).

Abduction is neither deduction nor induction. Abduction is the generation of an explanation, which can then be evaluated against available evidence [2, CP 5.171]. More formally, abduction asks what (minimal) formula needs to be added to a proposition such that it will be satisfied. As [4] demonstrates, abduction is automatable as long as the problem space is constrained, checking the validity of hypothetical additions is scalable, and human heuristics for generating additions can be encoded in the logic. Attack ontologies will serve as these heuristics for incident analysis. We will endeavor to represent one common attack ontology—the intrusion kill chain [12]—in our logic. We will also demonstrate that we can link existing knowledge bases, such as Snort rules, into this structure. Therefore, we are confident a system could be built that instrumented a computer network, ingested security-relevant information, and, given a security incident, used our logic to assist in the process of abducing explanations of how an adversary penetrated the network. Given this decision support, we would then imagine testing and improving different abduction rules in a scientific manner.

2.6   On the Metatheory of the Security Incident Analysis Logic

Generally, when setting up and explaining a system of logic, one gives a language (of propositions) and a semantics specified by a class of models together with a satisfaction relation which specifies which propositions are true in which parts of an arbitrary model. Typically, one also gives a proof system—that is, a collection of inference rules—which determines which propositions are provable. The first meta-theoretic challenge is then to establish that the provable things are also true in the models (soundness) and that there is model for which the notion of truth specified in the semantics coincides with the notion of provability specified by the inference rules (completeness). This, together with other metatheoretic analyses, is what assures us that a logic makes good sense.

In this section, we have described a logic for analysing security incidents. We have defined the logic by giving its propositional language together with a semantics given by a specific model together with a satisfaction relation which determines which propositions are true in which parts of the given model.

So, given that we haven't done all the usual work, why are we confident that the logic is a good one? Although the logic we have defined may look quite exotic, it is, in fact, based on a combination of some quite well-understood constructions together with a specific concrete model. In this respect, its definition

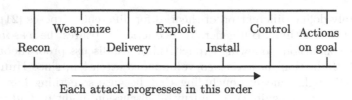

Each attack progresses in this order

Fig. 1. The intrusion kill chain, as explained by [12]. We will add more detail to this attack ontology by specifying certain aspects in our incident analysis logic.

somewhat resembles that of the logic from which it draws much inspiration, namely Separation Logic [4,23].

In short, for general mathematical reasons about how logics are constructed, we can be confident that the logic will work properly in the established senses.

3   A Worked Example

The "kill chain" was introduced by Lockheed Martin to explain an abstract pattern they observed in attacks targeting their organization [12]. It is a useful model of computer network attacks, because it helps inform the incident analyst about expected sorts of activities, against what sorts of entities, and their organization. The abstract nature of the kill chain makes it a good example to be expressed in our logic. It also models a useful unit of incident analysis – a single attack. Multiple attacks are almost always sequenced to achieve an adversary's overall goal during a campaign. Also, most attacks do not succeed, so usually many attacks occur in parallel. Therefore, modelling a single attack should be a fruitful example because we can compositionally build on it to analyze security incidents.

Figure 1 summarizes the steps in the kill chain. The mechanistic expression of the kill chain elaborated in [27] also guides the expression in our logic.

Our example is to turn this conceptual model of the kill chain into a set of logical statements of pre- and post-conditions that express useful abduction heuristics. However, we need to realign the components of the model. Our logic talks about observable computer activity, and as such the humans implicit in the kill chain have no place in our logic. Their interests are represented in the definition of our predicates. For example, the truth values of *compromised*() will depend on the security policy of the defender.

What counts as malware or an exploit is also dependent on the point of view of the agents. In our logic, we model only software instructions, computer systems, and bit-strings. These categories are intention-neutral. Malware is a subclass of software. Strictly, we do not discuss software (as this implies a complete product), but rather just instruction sets—a *computation*. But we shall not dictate how malware is classified as such. One benefit of our logic is to express precisely how an analyst determines how to differentiate malware from benign computations. Descriptions of what behaviors are indicative of malicious versions of those elements will be contingent.

To define our representation of a computation (i.e., software, functions, etc.), we adapt Hoare-Floyd logic. Hoare logic is a mainstay of program verification. It is primarily concerned with statements of the form $\{\phi\} \, C \, \{\psi\}$, where ϕ is pre-conditions, ψ is post-conditions, and C is some specific computation. The goal of Hoare logic is to verify that ψ can be guaranteed to be satisfied if C executes in an environment that satisfies ϕ.

The construction of Hoare logic is about the details of C and whether we can demonstrate post-conditions given pre-conditions. We are going to turn this on its head. The incident responder knows a post-condition, usually some security violation, and wants to understand more about the pre-conditions and software.

The computation C can be described in various levels of detail. This is an important benefit. Our logic, so defined, permits description of programmatic details. Malware reverse engineering tries to construct details of an unknown C. Incident analysis is primarily involved in a higher level task, merely constraining the observable traces in the system, not how some C made these changes. Therefore, while knowing malware details is helpful, because it narrows the potential pre- and post-conditions, we leave discussion of how C works in malware for future work. Practicing incident responders should reduce attention regards malicious logic as simply the Hoare triple $\{\phi\} \, C \, \{\psi\}$ where ϕ and ψ are known. This approach to knowledge is essentially the programming principle of encapsulation. If we know what goes in and what comes out, we do not need to know how it works to reason about impacts on our system.[1]

We represent a computer system as σ, taken from the systems known to the analyst. The full complement of systems is represented by **S**. At a given time t, the system is σ^t. The system σ^t is shorthand for a cluster of resources $[(s^t, h^t), (\delta^t, \beta^t), (\kappa^t, \upsilon^t)]$. Therefore, at any given time t, the state of the world (H, t) might be decomposed into one or more systems $\sigma_1^t \cdot \sigma_2^t \cdot ... \cdot \sigma_n^t$. The concept of system is therefore merely a shorthand for a cluster of resources that the incident analyst is interested to treat as a unit of analysis.

Our third and final entity, bit-strings are a type of expression E. Usually we represent strings in human-readable form. Human-readable strings can be represented as integers, so the syntax for E remains unchanged. We elide the details of local encodings (ASCII vs. unicode vs. hexadecimal, big- vs. little-endian, etc.) that complicate mapping between strings and integers. Notating strings as strings instead of expressions is merely a syntactic convenience.

Given computations and systems, we can define all the predicates we need:

- $compromised\,(\sigma^t)$
- $hostile\,(\sigma^t)$
- $malicious\,(C)$
- $trusts\left(\sigma_1^t, \sigma_2^{t'}\right)$ (often with $t = t'$)

- $match\,(string_1, string_2)$
- $vulnerable\,(\sigma^t, C)$
- $exploited\,(\sigma^t, C)$

---

[1] Any given $\{\phi\} \, C \, \{\psi\}$ for a program will be treated as a hypothesis, and one that given sufficient evidence might be overturned and modified.

Compromised, hostile, and malicious have the intuitive meanings. In our current set of definitions, these have binary truth values. We recognize analysts may be interested in intermediate values; however, we leave an extension of the logical definitions to a many-valued logic as future work.

Note that our intention here is that the compromised system is internal, under defender ownership, whereas a hostile system is on the Internet, not owned by the defender. Therefore, a different reasonable definition would be to define an ownership predicate, and define *compromised*() in terms of hostile and owned. That is, there are multiple compatible ways to represent relevant concepts. We select the above as a viable definition, not the only one.

The predicate $trusts\left(\sigma_1^t, \sigma_2^{t'}\right)$ is a relationship between two systems. Although it is an oversimplification, for the time being we reduce trust to the ability to communicate. More specifically, receive information. That is, given an address $a_1 \in A$ such that $a_1 \subset \sigma_1^t$ and address $a_2 \in A$ such that $a_2 \subset \sigma_2^t$ and any expression E, we have $trusts\left(\sigma_1^t, \sigma_2^{t'}\right)$ just in case that $(a_1 \mapsto E) \Rightarrow \Diamond(a_2 \mapsto E)$.

This is an abstract concept of communication. It just says that if some address in system one points to an expression, somehow eventually an address in system two comes to point to the same expression. The reason this is trust, and not chance, is that this relationship holds for any expression. This definition abstracts away from how that communication is executed. A real security policy may restrict which expressions are permitted or disallowed. We leave such definitions of a trust predicate as future work.

The predicate $match$() represents a common use case in incident analysis and computer network defense: pattern matching. Tools such as intrusion detection systems, firewall ACLs, and spam email detection all rely on matching incoming communications to known patterns of interest. These patterns are signatures or blacklists of malicious behavior.

We define the semantics of $match\left(string_1, string_2\right)$ such that:

$$\left[\left(s^t, h^t\right), \left(\delta^t, \beta^t\right), \left(\kappa^t, \upsilon^t\right)\right] \models match\left(string_1, string_2\right)$$

just in case

$$in\left(\left[\left(s^t, h^t\right), \left(\delta^t, \beta^t\right), \left(\kappa^t, \upsilon^t\right)\right], string_2\right) \wedge string_1 = string_2$$

The in() predicate holds just in case

$$\llbracket string_2 \rrbracket \in dom\left(s^t\right) \vee \llbracket string_2 \rrbracket \in dom\left(h^t\right) \vee$$
$$\llbracket string_2 \rrbracket \in dom\left(\delta^t\right) \vee \llbracket string_2 \rrbracket \in dom\left(\beta^t\right) \vee$$
$$\llbracket string_2 \rrbracket \in dom\left(\kappa^t\right) \vee \llbracket string_2 \rrbracket \in dom\left(\upsilon^t\right)$$

We may abbreviate this as $in\left(\sigma^t, string\right)$ or $in\left((H, t), string\right)$. If we wish to emphasize a certain type of string only occurs in the contents of files, for example, we may elide the other variables and write $in\left(\beta^t, string\right)$.

The equality operator is expression equality as defined in Sect. 2.4, since strings are expressions. Specifically, if strings are understood as integers, the expressions will have no free variables and so it becomes the usual integer equality.

We write $\sigma^t \models \{\phi\} \, \mathcal{C} \, \{\psi\}$ just in the case that there is some content $c \in C$ and $\sigma^t \models match\,(\mathcal{C}, c) \Rightarrow (\phi \Rightarrow \Diamond \psi)$. This assumes that the computation $\mathcal{C}$ terminates. But we are primarily concerned with malware that has successfully run, so this should not cause great trouble. Furthermore, we have defined time as finite, so termination can always be defined as the state at (H, t) when $t = T$.

We then propose to define $vulnerable\,(\sigma^t, \mathcal{C})$ to hold iff $\sigma^t \models (\{\phi\} \, \mathcal{C} \, \{\psi\}) \wedge \phi \wedge$ $malicious\,(\mathcal{C})$. The real-world impact if $vulnerable\,(\sigma^t, \mathcal{C})$ holds is a bad security situation. Such a system can be exploited at the will of the adversary.

To differentiate from the less severe situation where a system is vulnerable but exploit code is not present, we define $\sigma^t \models vul\,(\phi)$. This is a syntactic convenience; it means only that $\sigma^t \models \phi$ and that ϕ is the precondition for the execution of some malware.

Vulnerability is not the same as exploitation (in the traditional terminology of computer security). Exploit also requires access, which we can define in terms of trusting, execution, etc. However, simply the state of having been exploited, $exploited\,(\sigma^t, \mathcal{C})$, we can define as $\sigma^t \models \Diamond (\{\phi\} \, \mathcal{C} \, \{\psi\}) \wedge malicious\,(\mathcal{C}) \wedge \psi$.

3.1   A Logic of the Kill Chain

The kill chain provides the incident analyst with abduction heuristics for abducing the pre-conditions that lead to observed post-conditions. Thus, we can define pre- and post-conditions that we expect from each of the seven steps of the kill chain. If we observe the post-conditions of one, we can abduce its pre-conditions. We will use the kill chain to provide the basic structure of a single attack. Once this is complete, we will suggest how the logic can group attacks together into campaigns. Thirdly, we can specify more specific conditions for kill chain steps at a level of detail that is compatible with tools available to practicing incident analysts.

The last step in the kill chain is the first that an incident analyst is likely to observe. Thus our measure of time starts with $t = T$, the end of the history, and works backwards to $t = 0$. Because we have no absolute notion of time, each discrete phase moves back time one step. In this way, we will continue to step backwards through the attack from the end to the beginning:

- Action on Objectives, the final state: the system is under adversary control
  - *Post-condition* (observed): $H, t \models Compromised\,(\sigma_1^t)$ for $t = T$.
  - *Pre-condition*: C&C, defined as: there is some σ_2 such that $H, t \models trusts\,(\sigma_1^t, \sigma_2^t) \wedge hostile\,(\sigma_2^t)$ for $t = T - 1$.

This does not tell the analyst much, but it importantly identifies that there must be some hostile system that the defender's system has come to trust. Unwinding the next steps backwards would shed light on how.

- Command and control
  - *Post-condition* (observed): C&C, as defined above
  - *Pre-condition*: Installation of malware, that is

  $\sigma_1^t \models \Box\left(\left\{\widehat{\phi_{C_1}}\right\} C_1 \left\{\widehat{\psi_{C_1}}\right\} \wedge \widehat{\phi_{C_1}}\right)$, for $t = T - 2$. The $\Box$ indicates that the malware will be able to execute indefinitely into the future, not just once.

Where $\left\{\widehat{\phi_{C_1}}\right\} C_1 \left\{\widehat{\psi_{C_1}}\right\}$ as follows:

$\widehat{\psi_{C_1}}$ is a post-condition for the adversary's objectives, namely at minimum establishing a communication channel; i.e., $H, t \models trusts\left(\sigma_1^t, \sigma_2^t\right)$ for $t = T - 1$. Discovery of further unobserved objectives is likely one investigative goal.

$\widehat{\phi_{C_1}}$ is the pre-conditions for the malware to run. These may simply be the post-conditions of the installer (i.e., $\widehat{\psi_{C_2}}$, defined below), but may include what type of system the adversary can or wants to target.

A more flexible definition of the pre-conditions for command and control would be $\left(\left\{\widehat{\phi_{C_1}}\right\} C_1 \left\{\widehat{\psi_{C_1}}\right\}\right) \mathcal{U}\phi$, for some ϕ, instead of $\Box\left(\left\{\widehat{\phi_{C_1}}\right\} C_1 \left\{\widehat{\psi_{C_1}}\right\}\right)$.

- Installation of C_1 (the main malware) by C_2 (a downloader, installer, etc.)
  - *Post-condition* (observed): Installation, captured by

  $\sigma_1^t \models \left\{\widehat{\phi_{C_1}}\right\} C_1 \left\{\widehat{\psi_{C_1}}\right\} \wedge \widehat{\phi_{C_1}}$, for $t = T - 2$.
  - *Pre-condition*: Exploitation; i.e., $\sigma_1^t \models exploited\left(\sigma_1^t, C_2\right)$, for $t = T - 3$.

Note that the installation post-condition is weaker than the command and control pre-condition. The post-condition is what can be observed, but the pre-condition is abduced. In this context, the analyst should not assume the malware will stop, but rather that it will continue running indefinitely. Of course, like all abductions, this hypothesis might be changed by further observations.

Here $\left\{\widehat{\phi_{C_2}}\right\} C_2 \left\{\widehat{\psi_{C_2}}\right\}$ is as follows.

$\widehat{\psi_{C_2}}$ contains at least that $\sigma_1^t \models \left(\left\{\widehat{\phi_{C_1}}\right\} C_1 \left\{\widehat{\psi_{C_1}}\right\}\right) \wedge \widehat{\phi_{C_1}}$, for $t = T - 2$. I.e., system one both stores the malware and is configured such that it can run.

$\widehat{\phi_{C_2}}$ is a pre-condition containing at least the transfer of data necessary for the installation; i.e., there is some σ_3 such that $H, t \models trusts\left(\sigma_1^t, \sigma_3^t\right)$, for $t = T - 4$.

- Exploitation of system σ_1 by an exploit C_3.
  - *Post-condition* (observed): $\sigma_1^t \models \left\{\widehat{\phi_{C_2}}\right\} C_2 \left\{\widehat{\psi_{C_2}}\right\} \wedge \widehat{\psi_{C_2}}$, for $t = T - 3$.
  - *Pre-condition*: $\sigma_1^t \models vulnerable\left(\sigma_1^t, C_3\right)$, for $t = T - 5$.

Here $\left\{\widehat{\phi_{C_3}}\right\} C_3 \left\{\widehat{\psi_{C_3}}\right\}$ is as follows:

$\widehat{\psi_{C_3}}$ contains at least $\sigma_1^t \models \left(\left\{\widehat{\phi_{C_2}}\right\} C_2 \left\{\widehat{\psi_{C_2}}\right\}\right) \wedge \widehat{\phi_{C_2}}$, for $t = T - 4$. We say "at least" here because the exploit may or may not delete itself, for example, so in general additional traces on the system cannot be specified.

$\widehat{\phi_{C_3}}$ represents the exploited vulnerability and any targeting by the adversary.

- Delivery of an exploit
  - *Post-condition* (observed): There exists content $c, c' \in C$ such that it is the case $\sigma_1^t \models match\,(C_2, c) * match\,(C_3, c')$, for $t = T - 6$.
  - *Pre-condition*: There is σ_4 such that $(H, t) \models trusts\,(\sigma_1^t, \sigma_4^t)$, for $t = T - 7$.

The delivery phase does not assume the exploit runs, just that it reaches the defender's system from somewhere. We abduced the existence that system, σ_4.

- Weaponization against an observed vulnerability
  - *Post-condition* (explicitly unobserved): This is the creation of the malware. It also might include all the work the adversary did to discover the vulnerability, etc.
  - *Pre-condition*: The reconnaissance was successful and the adversary learns that the system $\sigma_1^t \models vul\,(\phi)$ for some ϕ, for $t = T - 8$.

Weaponization is an abduced step. Because it occurs local to the adversary, the defender almost never observes it, but knows that it must happen.

- Reconnaissance on target systems
  - *Post-condition*: Observable communication between σ_5 and σ_1. That is, $(H, t) \models trusts\,(\sigma_1^t, \sigma_5^t) \wedge \psi$, for $t = T - 9$, where ψ represents the information communicated. In some situations, it may be possible to learn what vulnerability is likely communicated, that is $\psi \Rightarrow vul\,(\phi)$.
  - *Pre-condition*: There exists σ_5 such that $(H, t) \models trusts\,(\sigma_1^t, \sigma_5^t)$, for $t = 0$. Depending on the communication, it may be possible to put constraints on what cluster of resources represent σ_5.

The adversary-controlled systems $\sigma_5, \sigma_4, \sigma_3, \sigma_2$ may or may not be the same real-world system, sharing some combination of resources.

3.2   Composition of Attacks into a Campaign

To model a campaign of many attacks, we would join attacks together by $*$. This is particularly important because the compromised system σ_1 might be used to conduct further attacks locally. The postconditions of one attack might be preconditions for other attacks. It's important that this is $*$ and not $\wedge$, to count compromised machines and attacks as individuals.

A logical description of botnet operations, such as Zeus, should be possible by composing aspects and instances of the kill chain. Indeed, [5] accomplish something similar by stitching together kill chain instances with Bayesian belief statements. Incorporating existing tools such as MulVal [20], which helps with vulnerability management by logical discovery of impactful attack graphs, are promising areas for synergy with the logic presented here. We leave a worked campaign example for future work.

3.3   Using More Granular Knowledge

[27] use the kill chain as an example of mechanistic explanation and demonstrate incorporating a lower (mechanistic) level of explanation via a type of exploitation: drive-by download. In our logic, we can similarly refine our expressions. For example, known exploits would put constraints on $\left\{ \widehat{\phi_{C_3}} \right\} C_3 \left\{ \widehat{\psi_{C_3}} \right\}$. We will demonstrate using a simpler example than drive-by downloads.

Integrating specific rules should enable automating the process of finding likely explanations. The incident analyst might have many thousands of potential specifications of various phases of the kill chain, derived from anti-virus signatures, blacklists, and so on. The logic mechanizes the inspection of which details are more likely to be at play in a given incident based on observations.

We will demonstrate how existing knowledge bases can be leveraged in this way via a Snort rule. An intrusion detection system (IDS) rule, such as Snort rules, is a structured statement of suspicious network activity. We consider an old, but representative, example rule from [25], which introduced Snort. Translations from anti-virus rules, etc., should be similarly easy.

```
alert tcp any any -> 192.168.1.0/24 143 (content:"|E8C0 FFFF
FF|/bin/sh"; msg:"IMAP Buffer Overflow detected!";)
```

This rule is a specification of the kill chain "Delivery" phase. Some parts are responses, such as "alert", which need not be represented in the logic. Similarly, annotation such as the "msg" field is useful, but would be implemented elsewhere.

This leaves essentially two elements of the rule. The header, which specifies the matching rules for packet headers, and the payload detection options (here, "content"). In this case, these aspects map to statements about the network, namely κ, ν. Specifically, header rules are about κ and content rules are about ν. This makes translation of such Snort rules relatively straightforward.

The network headers are simply communication between some external system, σ_4, and the defender's system σ_1. System σ_4 remains unconstrained, represented by **any any** for IP and port matches. However, we have two constraints on σ_1. Firstly, the system is 255 IP addresses, namely 192.168.1.0/24. We represent this as the claim that there exists some $\kappa \in A$ such that

$$\sigma_1^t \models dip\,(192.168.1.0, \kappa) \vee \ldots \vee dip\,(192.168.1.255, \kappa) \wedge dport\,(143, \kappa)$$

The predicates $dip\,()$ and $dport\,()$ use the $match\,()$ predicate, defined to match specific parts of an IP packet header (destination IP and port, respectively).

The content is a string-matching constraint on the communication between σ_4 and σ_1. We change the notation for hexadecimal content from $|FF|$, as Snort uses, to $\underline{FF}$. Then this half of the Snort rule is easily translated; we assert there exists some $\nu \in C$ such that

$$\sigma_1^t \models match\,(\underline{\texttt{E8C0FFFFFF}}/\texttt{bin}/\texttt{sh}, \nu)\,.$$

This matches with an exploit, represented as C_3 in our formulation. The Snort rule is the conjunction of these two statements.

Recall the broad statement of delivery in the kill chain. Transfer of data, including C_3, from some σ_4 to σ_1. We have demonstrated how one can specify greater detail of these aspects. Specifying the specifics of all such attacks is a huge undertaking. For that reason, we have chosen an example – Snort rules – where much of this undertaking has already been collected and curated in machine-readable form. Such existing data bases of attack patterns should be readily leveraged by our incident analysis logic.

We should also propagate specifics forward in the kill chain. This example finds an attack against email servers. Therefore, we know more accurate preconditions for C_3. Particularly, whether *vulnerable* (σ_1, C_3) holds. If σ_1 is not an email server, then it is not vulnerable. This sort of reasoning should allow the analyst to reduce the number of systems that need to be investigated as to whether the exploitation step was successful, for example.

4   Conclusions

One ambition for this logic is to represent the reasoning in [30]. This task requires a large – but finite – collection of observations, reasoning heuristics, hypothetical explanations, and deduced conclusions. We have not laid out these usage patterns in detail, but we are confident our tools would work similarly to Separation Logic, which has these features [4]. But the question may remain: why?

We envision three primary benefits to incident analysis (and perhaps cybersecurity broadly) from engaging with logical tools; namely, *communication, clarification,* and *decision-support potential.*

A logic such as the one we have sketched aids communication between analysts. In general, logical tools aid communication by reducing ambiguity. If one analyst describes their process in our logic, it will help other analysts understand and reproduce that process. Furthermore, one challenge in security is a justified secrecy among allies, which inhibits communication. A logic allows the analyst to abstract away from some sensitive system details.

Clarification of an analyst's own thinking is another benefit. Expressing one's reasoning in such a logical language forces an analyst to be precise. As [10] identifies, human cognitive biases often subtly insert themselves into analytic thinking. By specifying reasoning explicitly, we can examine the reasoning process for such instances of bias and work to reduce it.

Decision-support is an ultimate aim. We believe logics are a better tool for explanations than machine learning. And explanations are ultimately what scientists seek to make the unknown intelligible [7]. The components of a scientific explanation are outlined in [29]. Logical tools move us towards a scientific incident analysis in part because they can represent such explanations. The point of going through the pain of specifying a logic, rather than remaining in the realm of philosophy of science and natural language descriptions of incident analysis, is that logics are automatable. Automation is a clear prerequisite for any decision-support in a field like incident analysis, where data volumes are so large. At the same time, we have adapted logical tools that have demonstrated scalable reasoning in other contexts [16,22]. The design of our logic is not just tailored to incident analysis, but, insofar as is possible at this stage, tailored to a scalable automation of support for incident analysis.

Based on analyst accounts and case studies, we have developed logical tools for incident analysis. Our goal is both descriptive and prescriptive. We have sought a useful and accurate description of what analysts do. At the same time, analysts should emulate these descriptions and build on them, to express their process methodically. Of course, this process will be gradual. Logical tools provide a new paradigm which helps enable this gradual advancement, alongside existing incident management and forensics practices.

Our work begins an approach to decision support for incident analysts. What we have provided so far also serves to highlight where additional formal definitions are appropriate (e.g., see Sect. 2.6). And of course, as with Separation Logic, the devil will be in the details of implementing such formal definitions [18]. Although the core sense-making and goal-setting aspects likely will remain a distinctly human endeavor, our developments provide hope that logical tools tailored to incident analysis could reduce the analyst's workload.

Acknowledgements. Spring is supported by University College London's Overseas Research Scholarship and Graduate Research Scholarship. Thanks to Simon Docherty for discussion and constructive comments.

References

1. Alberts, C., Dorofee, A., Killcrece, G., Ruefle, R., Zajicek, M.: Defining incident management processes for CSIRTS: a work in progress. Technical report. CMU/SEI-2004-TR-015, Software Engineering Institute, CMU 2004 (2004)
2. Bergman, M., Paavola, S.: 'Abduction': Term in The Commens Dictionary: Peirce's Terms in His Own Words. New Edition, 14 July 2016. http://www.commens.org/dictionary/term/abduction
3. Brotherston, J., Villard, J.: Sub-classical Boolean bunched logics and the meaning of par. In: Proceedings of CSL, vol. 24, pp. 325–342. LIPIcs (2015)
4. Calcagno, C., Distefano, D., O'Hearn, P.W., Yang, H.: Compositional shape analysis by means of bi-abduction. J. ACM **58**(6), 26:1–26:66 (2011)
5. Caltagirone, S., Pendergast, A., Betz, C.: The diamond model of intrusion analysis. Technical report, Center for Cyber Intelligence Analysis and Threat Research (2013). http://www.threatconnect.com/methodology/diamond_model_of_intrusion_analysis
6. Casey, E.: Digital Evidence and Computer Crime: Forensic Science, Computers, and The Internet. Academic press, Cambridge (2000)
7. Dear, P.: The Intelligibility of Nature: How Science Makes Sense of the World. University of Chicago Press, Chicago (2006)
8. Galmiche, D., Méry, D., Pym, D.: The semantics of BI and resource tableaux. Math. Struct. Comp. Sci. **15**(06), 1033–1088 (2005)
9. Henderson, L.: The problem of induction. In: Zalta, E.N. (ed.) The Stanford Encyclopedia of Philosophy. Metaphysics Research Lab, Stanford University, Summer 2018 edn. (2018)

10. Heuer, R.J.: Psychology of Intelligence Analysis. US Central Intelligence Agency (1999)
11. Horneman, A.: How to think like an analyst, 17 July 2017. https://insights.sei.cmu.edu/sei_blog/2017/07/how-to-think-like-an-analyst.html
12. Hutchins, E.M., Cloppert, M.J., Amin, R.M.: Intelligence-driven computer network defense informed by analysis of adversary campaigns and intrusion kill chains. Lead. Issues Inform. Warfare Secur. Res. 1, 80 (2011)
13. Ishtiaq, S.S., O'Hearn, P.W.: BI as an assertion language for mutable data structures. In: Principles of Programming Languages, pp. 14–26. ACM, London (2001). https://doi.org/10.1145/360204.375719
14. Kent, K., Chevalier, S., Grance, T., Dang, H.: Guide to integrating forensic techniques into incident response. Technical report, SP 800-86, National Institute of Standards and Technology, August 2006
15. Lamport, L.: What good is temporal logic? In: Mason, R. (ed.) IFIP Congress, pp. 657–668. Elsevier (1983)
16. Lamport, L.: Specifying Systems: The TLA+ Language and Tools for Hardware and Software Engineers. Wesley, Boston (2002)
17. Manna, Z., Pnueli, A.: The Temporal Logic of Reactive and Concurrent Systems. Springer, New York (1992). https://doi.org/10.1007/978-1-4612-0931-7
18. O'Hearn, P.W.: From categorical logic to Facebook engineering. In: Logic in Computer Science (LICS), pp. 17–20. IEEE (2015)
19. O'Hearn, P.W., Pym, D.J.: The logic of bunched implications. Bull. Symbolic Logic 5(2), 215–244 (1999)
20. Ou, X., Govindavajhala, S., Appel, A.W.: MulVAL: a logic-based network security analyzer. In: USENIX Security Symposium, pp. 113–128 (2005)
21. von Plato, J.: The development of proof theory. In: Zalta, E.N. (ed.) The Stanford Encyclopedia of Philosophy. Metaphysics Research Lab, Stanford University, Winter 2016 edn. (2016)
22. Pym, D., Spring, J.M., O'Hearn, P.: Why separation logic works. Philosophy and Technology (2018). https://doi.org/10.1007/s13347-018-0312-8
23. Pym, D.J., O'Hearn, P.W., Yang, H.: Possible worlds and resources: the semantics of BI. Theor. Comput. Sci. 315(1), 257–305 (2004)
24. Reynolds, J.C.: Separation logic: a logic for shared mutable data structures. In: Logic in Computer Science, pp. 55–74. IEEE (2002)
25. Roesch, M.: Snort: lightweight intrusion detection for networks. In: Large Installation Systems Admin, pp. 229–238. USENIX, Seattle, November 1999
26. Shirey, R.: Internet Security Glossary, Version 2. RFC 4949, August 2007
27. Spring, J.M., Hatleback, E.: Thinking about intrusion kill chains as mechanisms. J. Cybersecur. 3(3), 185–197 (2017)
28. Spring, J.M., Illari, P.: Review of human decision-making during incident analysis. Under review (2018)
29. Spring, J.M., Moore, T., Pym, D.: Practicing a science of security: a philosophy of science perspective. In: New Security Paradigms Workshop, Santa Cruz, 1–4 October 2017
30. Stoll, C.: The Cuckoo's Egg: Tracking a Spy Through the Maze of Computer Espionage. Pan Books, London (1989)
31. Tambe, M.: Security and Game Theory: Algorithms, Deployed Systems, Lessons Learned. Cambridge University Press, Cambridge (2011)

Rational Trust Modeling

Mehrdad Nojoumian[(✉)]

Department of Computer & Electrical Engineering and Computer Science,
Florida Atlantic University, Boca Raton, FL 33431, USA
mnojoumian@fau.edu

Abstract. Trust models are widely used in various computer science disciplines. The primary purpose of a trust model is to continuously measure the trustworthiness of a set of entities based on their behaviors. In this article, the novel notion of *rational trust modeling* is introduced by bridging trust management and game theory. Note that trust models/reputation systems have been used in game theory (e.g., repeated games) for a long time, however, game theory has not been utilized in the process of trust model construction; this is the novelty of our approach. In our proposed setting, the designer of a trust model assumes that the players who intend to utilize the model are rational/selfish, i.e., they decide to become trustworthy or untrustworthy based on the utility that they can gain. In other words, the players are incentivized (or penalized) by the model itself to act properly. The problem of trust management can be then approached by game theoretical analyses and solution concepts such as Nash equilibrium. Although rationality might be built-in in some existing trust models, we intend to formalize the notion of rational trust modeling from the designer's perspective. This approach will result in two fascinating outcomes. First of all, the designer of a trust model can incentivize trustworthiness in the first place by incorporating proper parameters into the trust function, which can be later utilized among selfish players in strategic trust-based interactions (e.g., e-commerce scenarios). Furthermore, using a rational trust model, we can prevent many well-known attacks on trust models. These two prominent properties also help us to predict the behavior of the players in subsequent steps by game theoretical analyses.

Keywords: Trust management · Reputation system · Game theory
Rationality

1 Introduction

The primary purpose of a trust model is to continuously measure the trustworthiness of a set of entities (e.g., servers, sellers, agents, nodes, robots, players, etc.) based on their behaviors. Indeed, scientists across various disciplines have

---

This research was supported by the Department of Defense (DoD) Research and Education Program, grant 72498-RT-REP.

© Springer Nature Switzerland AG 2018
L. Bushnell et al. (Eds.): GameSec 2018, LNCS 11199, pp. 418–431, 2018.
https://doi.org/10.1007/978-3-030-01554-1_24

conducted research on trust over decades and produced fascinating discoveries, however, there is not only a huge gap among findings in these research communities but also these discoveries have not been properly formalized to have a better understanding of the notion of trust, and consequently, practical computational models of trust. We therefore intend to look at the problem of trust modeling from an interdisciplinary perspective that is more realistic and closer to human comprehension of trust.

From a social science perspective, *trust* is the willingness of a person to become vulnerable to the actions of another person irrespective of the ability to control those actions [7]. However, in the computer science community, *trust* is defined as a personal expectation that a player has with respect to the future behavior of another party, i.e., a personal quantity measured to help the players in their future dyadic encounters. On the other hand, *reputation* is the perception that a player has with respect to another player's intention, i.e., a social quantity computed based on the actions of a given player and observations made by other parties in an electronic community that consists of interacting parties such as people or businesses [9].

From another perspective [1], *trust* is made up of underlying beliefs and it is a function based on the values of these beliefs. Similarly, *reputation* is a social notion of trust. In our lives, we each maintain a set of reputation values for people we know. Furthermore, when we decide to establish an interaction with a new person, we may ask other people to provide recommendations regarding the new party. Based on the information we gather, we form an opinion about the reputation of the new person. This decentralized method of reputation measurement is called *referral chain*. Trust can be also created based on both local and/or social evidence. In the former case, trust is built through direct observations of a player whereas, in the latter case, it is built through information from other parties. It is worth mentioning that a player can gain or lose her reputation not only because of her cooperation/defection in a specific setting but also based on the ability to produce accurate referrals.

Generally speaking, the goal of reputation systems is to collect, distribute and aggregate feedback about participants' past behavior. These systems address the development of reputation by recording the behavior of the parties, e.g., in e-commerce, the model of reputation is constructed from a buying agent's positive or negative past experiences with the goal of predicting how satisfied a buying agent will be in future interactions with a selling agent. The ultimate goal is to help the players decide whom to trust and to detect dishonest or compromised parties in a system [17]. There exist many fascinating applications of trust models and reputation systems in various engineering and computer science disciplines.

In fact, trust models are widely used in scientific and engineering disciplines such as electronic commerce [4,12], computer security and rational cryptography [10,13–16], multiagent systems [18–20], game theory and economics [6,8], to name a few. To the best of our knowledge, there is no literature on *rational trust modeling*, that is, using game theory during the construction of a trust model.

Note that game theoretic models have been used for management and analyses of trust-based systems [2,3].

1.1 Our Motivation and Contribution

As our motivation, we intend to provide a new mechanism for trust modeling by which:

1. The trust model incentivizes trustworthiness in the first place, i.e., *self-enforcing*.
2. The model is naturally resistant to attacks on trust models, i.e., *resistant*.

We therefore introduce the novel notion of *rational trust modeling* by bridging trust management and game theory. We would like to emphasize that trust models have been used in game theory for a long time, for instance, in repeated games to incentivize the players to be cooperative and not to deviate from the game's protocol. However, game theory has not been utilized in the process of trust model construction; in fact, this is the novelty of our proposed approach.

In our setting, the designer of a trust model assumes that the players who intend to utilize the model are rational/selfish meaning that they cooperate to become trustworthy or defect otherwise based on the utility (to be defined by the trust model) that they can gain, which is a reasonable and standard assumption. In other words, the players are incentivized (or penalized) by the model itself to act properly. The problem of trust modeling can be then approached by strategic games among the players using utility functions and solution concepts such as Nash equilibrium.

Although rationality might be built-in in some existing trust models, we formalize the notion of rational trust modeling from the model designer's perspective. This approach results in two fascinating outcomes. First of all, the designer of a trust model can incentivize trustworthiness in the first place by incorporating proper parameters into the trust function, which can be later utilized among selfish players in strategic trust-based interactions (e.g., e-commerce scenarios between sellers and buyers). Furthermore, using a rational trust model, we can prevent many well-known attacks on trust models, as we describe later. These two prominent properties also help us to predict behavior of the players in subsequent steps by game theoretical analyses.

1.2 Our Approach in Nutshell

Suppose there exist two sample trust functions: The first function $f_1(\mathscr{T}_i^{p-1}, \alpha_i)$ receives the previous trust value $\mathscr{T}_i^{p-1}$ and the current action α_i of a seller S_i (i.e., cooperation or defection) as two inputs to compute the updated trust value $\mathscr{T}_i^p$ for the next round. However, the second function $f_2(\mathscr{T}_i^{p-1}, \alpha_i, \ell_i)$ has an extra input value known as the seller's lifetime denoted by ℓ_i. Using the second trust function, a seller with a longer lifetime will be rewarded (or penalized) more (or less) than a seller with a shorter lifetime assuming that the other two inputs (i.e., current trust value and the action) are the same. In this scenario, "reward" means gaining a higher trust value and becoming more trustworthy, and "penalty" means otherwise. In other words, if two sellers S_i and S_j both cooperate $\alpha_i = \alpha_j = \mathscr{C}$ and their current trust values are equal $\mathscr{T}_i^{p-1} = \mathscr{T}_j^{p-1}$ but their lifetime parameters are different, for instance, $\ell_i > \ell_j$, the seller with a higher lifetime parameter, gains a higher trust value for the next round, i.e., $\mathscr{T}_i^p > \mathscr{T}_j^p$. This may help S_i to sell more items and accumulate more revenue because buyers always prefer to buy from trustworthy sellers, i.e., sellers with a higher trust value.

Now consider a situation in which the sellers can sell defective versions of an item with more revenue or non-defective versions of the same item with less revenue. If we utilize the first sample trust function f_1, it might be tempting for a seller to sell defective items because he can gain more utility. Furthermore, the seller can return to the community with a new identity (a.k.a, re-entry attack) after selling defective items and accumulating a large revenue. However, if we use the second sample trust function f_2, it's no longer in a seller's best interest to sell defective items because if he returns to the community with a new identity, his lifetime parameter becomes zero and he loses all the credits that he has accumulated overtime. As a result, he loses his future customers and a huge potential revenue, i.e., buyers may prefer a seller with a longer lifetime over a seller who is a newcomer. The second trust function not only incentivizes trustworthiness but also prevents the re-entry attack.

Note that this is just an example of rational trust modeling for the sake of clarification. The second sample function here utilizes an extra parameter ℓ_i in order to incentivize trustworthiness and prevent the re-entry attack. In fact, different parameters can be incorporated into trust functions based on the context (whether it's a scenario in e-commerce or cybersecurity and so on), and consequently, different attacks can be prevented, as discussed in Sect. 3.

2   Rational Trust Modeling

We stress that our goal here is not to design specific trust models or construct certain utility functions. Our main objective is to illustrate the high-level idea of *rational trust modeling* through examples/analyses without loss of generality.

2.1   Trust Modeling: Construction and Evaluation

To construct a quantifiable model of trust, a mathematical function or model for trust measurement in a community of n players must be designed. First of all, a basic trust function is defined as follows:

Definition 1. *Let $\mathscr{T}_i^p$ denote trust value of player P_i in period p where $-1 \leq \mathscr{T}_i^p \leq +1$ and $\mathscr{T}_i^0 = 0$ for newcomers. A trust function is a mapping from $\mathbb{R} \times \mathbb{N}$ to $\mathbb{R}$ which is defined as follows: $(\mathscr{T}_i^{p-1}, \alpha_i) \mapsto \mathscr{T}_i^p$, where $\mathscr{T}_i^{p-1}$ denote the trust value of player P_i in period $p - 1$ and $\alpha_i \in \{0, 1\}$ denote whether P_i has cooperated, i.e., $\alpha_i = 1$, or defected, i.e., $\alpha_i = 0$, in period p.*

As an example, we can refer to the following mathematical model [11,12]. In this model, $\mathscr{T}_i^p = \mathscr{T}_i^{p-1} + \mu(x)$ or $\mathscr{T}_i^p = \mathscr{T}_i^{p-1} - \mu'(x)$ for $\alpha_i = 1$ or $\alpha_i = 0$ respectively, shown in Fig. 1. Parameters η, θ and κ are used to reward or penalize players based on their actions (for instance, as defined in [11], $\eta = 0.01$, $\theta = 0.05$ and $\kappa = 0.09$). Note that in $[1 - \epsilon, +1]$ and $[-1, \epsilon - 1]$, $\mu(x)$ and $\mu'(x)$ both converge to zero, as required by Definition 1, i.e., $-1 \leq \mathscr{T}_i^p \leq +1$.

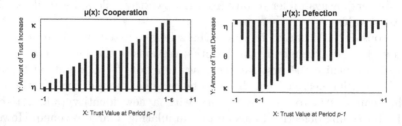

Fig. 1. Trust Adjustment by $\mu(x)$ and $\mu'(x)$

After designing a mathematical function, it must be assessed and validated from different perspectives for further improvement. We provide high-level descriptions of some validation procedures to be considered for evaluation of a trust model, that is, *behavioral*, *adversarial* and *operational* methodologies.

1. *Behavioral*: how the model performs among a sufficient number of players by running a number of standard tests, i.e., executing a sequence of "cooperation" and "defection" (or no-participation) for each player. For instance, how fast the model can detect defective behavior by creating a reasonable trust margin between cooperative and non-cooperative parties.
2. *Adversarial*: how vulnerable the trust model is to different attacks or any kinds of corruption by a player or a coalition of malicious parties. Seven well-known attacks on trust models are listed below. The first five attacks are known as *single-agent attacks* and the last two are known as *multi-agent* or *coalition attacks* [5].
   (a) **Sybil:** forging identities or creating multiple false accounts by one player.
   (b) **Lag:** cooperating for some time to gain a high trust value and then cheat.
   (c) **Re-Entry:** corrupted players return to the scheme using new identities.
   (d) **Imbalance:** cooperating on cheap transactions; defecting on expensive ones.
   (e) **Multi-Tactic:** any combination of attacks mentioned above.
   (f) **Ballot-Stuffing:** fake transactions among colluders to gain a high trust value.
   (g) **Bad-Mouthing:** submitting negative reviews to non-coalition members.
3. *Operational*: how well the future states of trust can be predicted with a relatively accurate approximation based on possible action(s) of the players (prediction can help us to prevent some well-known attacks), and how well the model can incentivize cooperation in the first place.

In the next section, we clarify what considerations should be taken into account by the designer in order to construct a proper trust model that resists against various attacks and also encourages trustworthiness in the first place.

2.2   Rational Trust Modeling Illustration: Seller's Dilemma

We now illustrate a dilemma between two sellers by considering two different trust functions. In this setting, each seller has defective and non-defective versions of an item for sale. We consider the following two possible actions:

1. *Cooperation*: selling the non-defective version of the item for \$3 to different buyers.
2. *Defection*: selling the defective version of the item for \$2 to different buyers.

Assuming that the buyers are not aware of the existence of the defective version of the item, they may prefer to buy from the seller who offers the lowest price. This is a pretty natural and standard assumption. As a result, the seller who offers the lowest price has the highest chance to sell the item, and consequently, he can gain more utility.

An appropriate payoff function can be designed for this seller's dilemma based on the probability of being selected by a buyer since there is a correlation between the offered price and this probability, as shown in Fig. 2. In other words, if they offer the same price, \$2 or \$3, they have an equal chance of being selected by a buyer, otherwise, the seller who offers a lower price (\$2) will be selected by the probability of 1.

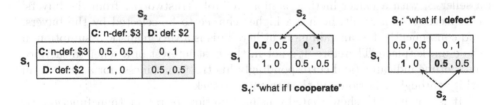

Fig. 2. Seller's Dilemma

Similar to the prisoner's dilemma, defection is Nash equilibrium meaning that it is in the best interest of each seller to maximize his utility by selling the defective version of the item. For instance, suppose S_1 cooperates by selling the non-defective item for \$3, S_2 will then offer the defective item for \$2 to have the highest chance to sell the item, and consequently, he can gain more utility. On the other hand, suppose S_1 defects by selling the defective item for \$2, S_2 will then offer the defective item for \$2 to compete with S_1. That is, regardless of whether seller S_1 cooperates or defects, seller S_2 will always defect, and since the payoff matrix is symmetric, defection (selling the defective item) is always Nash equilibrium.

Without loss of generality, we now show how a proper trust model can deal with this dilemma; note that this is just an example for the sake of clarification. We first consider two different trust functions, as we described earlier:

1. The first function $f_1 : (\mathscr{T}_i^{p-1}, \alpha_i) \mapsto \mathscr{T}_i^p$, where $\mathscr{T}_i^{p-1}$ denote the trust value of seller S_i in period $p-1$ and $\alpha_i \in \{0, 1\}$ denote whether seller S_i has cooperated or defected in the current period p.
2. The second function $f_2 : (\mathscr{T}_i^{p-1}, \alpha_i, \ell_i) \mapsto \mathscr{T}_i^p$, where $\mathscr{T}_i^{p-1}$ and $\alpha_i \in \{0, 1\}$ denote the same notions as of the previous function and $\ell_i \geq 0$ denote the lifetime of seller S_i as a new input in the trust function. This parameter defines how long a seller with a reasonable number of transactions has been in the market.

For the sake of simplicity, we didn't consider two different parameters for the lifetime and the number of transactions, however, two separate parameters can be simply incorporated into our trust function and we can still achieve the same game theoretical result. The main reason is because we want to make sure the sellers who have been in the market for a long time but have been inactive or have had a limited number of transactions cannot obtain a high trust value, which is a reasonable assumption.

Now considering the seller's dilemma that we illustrated in Fig. 2, the first function f_1 is significantly vulnerable to *re-entry* attack. That is, a seller S_i may defect on a sequence of transactions in the middle of his lifetime to gain substantial revenues (utility). He can then return to the market with a new identity as a newcomer.

However, the lifetime ℓ_i is part of the second trust function f_2 meaning that a seller S_i with a longer lifetime is more reliable/trustworthy from the buyers' perspective. As a result, he has a higher chance to be selected by the buyers, and consequently, he can gain more utility. This is a very realistic assumption in the e-marketplace. Therefore, it's not in the best interest of a seller to sacrifice his lifetime indicator (and correspondingly his trustworthiness) for a short term utility through defection and then re-entry attack.

It is not hard to show that, by using function f_2 rather than function f_1, "defection" is no longer Nash equilibrium in the seller's dilemma, as we illustrate in Sect. 2.3. When we assume the sellers are rational/selfish and they decide based on their utility functions, we can then design a proper trust function similar to f_2 to incentivize cooperation in the first place. Furthermore, we can deal with a wide range of attacks, as we mentioned earlier. Finally, at any point, the behavior of a seller can be predicted by estimation of his payoff through trust and utility functions.

2.3 Rational Trust Modeling: Design and Analysis

In our setting, the utility function $u_i : \mathscr{A} \times \mathscr{T}_i \mapsto \mathbb{R}$, which depends on the seller's action and his trust value. This function computes the utility that each S_i gains or loses by selecting a certain action. If we consider the 2nd trust function

$f_2 : (\mathcal{T}_i^{p-1}, \alpha_i, \ell_i) \mapsto \mathcal{T}_i^p$, the trust value then depends on the seller's lifetime ℓ_i as well. As a result, the lifetime of the seller directly affects the utility that the seller can gain or lose. Now consider the following simple utility function:

$$u_i = \Omega \times g(\mathcal{T}_i^p) \quad \text{where} \, 0 \leq g(\mathcal{T}_i^p) \leq 1, \Omega \, \text{is a constant} \tag{1}$$

As stated earlier, we first define the following parameters, where $-1 \leq \mathcal{T}_i^p \leq +1$ and $\alpha_i \in \{0, 1\}$ denote whether S_i has cooperated or defected in the previous period:

$$\tau_i = \mathcal{T}_i^p - \mathcal{T}_i^{p-1} \quad \text{where} \quad \frac{|\tau_i|}{\tau_i} = \begin{cases} +1 & \text{if} \, \alpha_i = 1 \\ -1 & \text{if} \, \alpha_i = 0 \end{cases} \tag{2}$$

In the following equations, the first function f_1 does not depend on the seller's lifetime ℓ_i, however, the second function f_2 has an extra factor that is defined by lifetime ℓ_i and constants ρ. We can assume that $\rho\ell_i$ is in the same range as of μ depending on the player's lifetime; that is why ℓ_i is multiplied by multiplicative factor ρ. Also, it's always positive meaning that no matter if a player cooperates or defects, he will always be rewarded by $\rho\ell_i$. We stress that parameter ℓ_i in function f_2 is just an examples of how a rational trust function can be designed. The designer can simply consider various parameters (that denote different concepts) as additive or multiplicative factors based on the context in which the trust model is supposed to be utilized. We discuss this issue later in Sect. 3 in detail.

$$f_1 : \mathcal{T}_i^p = \mathcal{T}_i^{p-1} + \frac{|\tau_i|}{\tau_i}\mu \tag{3}$$

$$f_2 : \mathcal{T}_i^p = \mathcal{T}_i^{p-1} + \frac{|\tau_i|}{\tau_i}\mu + \rho\ell_i \tag{4}$$

$-1 \leq \mathcal{T}_i^p \leq +1$, E.g.: $0 \leq \mu < 0.1$ is a unified function in f_1 and f_2

The first function f_1 rewards or penalizes the sellers based on their actions and independent of their lifetimes. This makes function f_1 vulnerable to different attacks such as the re-entry attack because a malicious seller can always come back to the scheme with a new identity, and then, starts re-building his reputation for another malicious activity. It is possible to make the sign-up procedure costly but it is out of the scope of this paper.

On the other hand, the second trust function f_2 has an extra term that is defined by the seller's lifetime ℓ_i. This term will be adjusted by ρ as an additional reward or punishment factor in the trust function. In other words, the seller's current lifetime ℓ_i in addition to a constant $\pm\beta$ (in the case of cooperation/defection) determine the extra reward/punishment factor. As a result, it is not in the best interest of a seller to reset his lifetime indicator ℓ_i to zero because of a short-term utility. This lifetime indicator can increase the seller's trustworthiness, and consequently, his long-term utility overtime.

Let assume our sample utility function is further extended as follows, where Ω is a constant, for instance, Ω can be \$100:

$$u_i = \Omega\left(\frac{\mathcal{T}_i^p + 1}{2}\right) \quad \text{where} \, 0 \leq \frac{\mathcal{T}_i^p + 1}{2} \leq 1, -1 \leq \mathcal{T}_i^p \leq +1 \tag{5}$$

The utility function simply indicates a seller with a higher trust value (which depends on his lifetime indicator as well) can gain more utility because he has a higher chance to be selected by the buyers. In other words, Eq. (5) maps the current trust value $\mathscr{T}_i^p$ to a value between zero and one, which can be also interpreted as the probability of being selected by the buyers. For the sake of simplicity, suppose $\mathscr{T}_i^{p-1}$ is canceled out in both f_1 and f_2 as a common factor. The overall utility $U_i^{f_1}$ is shown below when f_1 is used. Note that u_i computes the utility of a seller in the case of cooperation or defection whereas U_i also takes into account the *external utility* or *future loss* that a seller may gain or lose. For instance, more savings through selling the defective version of an item instead of its non-defective version.

$$
U_i^{f_1} = \Omega \times
\begin{cases}
\frac{+\mu+1}{2} & \text{using } f_1 \text{ when } \alpha_i = 1 \\
\frac{-\mu+1}{2} + \beta & \text{using } f_1 \text{ when } \alpha_i = 0 \text{ plus } \beta, \beta \text{ is the } external\ utility \\
& \text{that the seller obtains by selling the defective item}
\end{cases}
$$

As shown in $U_i^{f_1}$, function f_1 rewards/penalizes sellers in each period by factor $\pm\frac{\mu}{2}$. Accordingly, we can assume *external utility* β that the seller obtains by selling the defective item is slightly more than (as much as σ) the utility that the seller may lose because of defection; otherwise, the seller wouldn't defect, that is, $\beta = \frac{\mu}{2} + |-\frac{\mu}{2}| + \sigma = \mu + \sigma$ (note that the seller not only loses a potential reward $\frac{\mu}{2}$ but also he is penalized by factor $-\frac{\mu}{2}$ when he defects.) In other words, external utility β not only compensates for loss $\frac{\mu}{2} + |-\frac{\mu}{2}|$ but also provides additional gain σ.

As a result, $\frac{-\mu+1}{2} + \beta = \frac{-\mu+1}{2} + (\mu + \sigma) = \frac{\mu+1}{2} + \sigma$. Therefore, $\mathscr{D}$efection is always Nash Equilibrium when f_1 is used, as shown in Table 1. We can assume the seller cheats on δ rounds until he is labeled as an untrustworthy seller. At this point, he leaves and returns with a new identity with the same initial trust value of newcomers, i.e., re-entry attack. Our analysis remains the same even if cheating is repeated for δ rounds.

Table 1. Seller's Dilemma: $\mathscr{D}$efection is always Nash Equilibrium using f_1.

S_1 \ S_2	$\mathscr{C}$ooperation	$\mathscr{D}$efection
$\mathscr{C}$ooperation	$\frac{\mu+1}{2}, \frac{\mu+1}{2}$	$\frac{\mu+1}{2}, \frac{\mu+1}{2} + \sigma$
$\mathscr{D}$efection	$\frac{\mu+1}{2} + \sigma, +\frac{\mu+1}{2}$	$\frac{\mu+1}{2} + \sigma, \frac{\mu+1}{2} + \sigma$

Similarly, function f_2 rewards/penalizes sellers through $U_i^{f_2}$ in each period by factor $\pm\frac{\mu}{2}$. Furthermore, this function also has a positive reward (or forgiveness) factor $\frac{\rho\ell_i}{2}$ for cooperative (or non-cooperative) sellers, which is defined by their lifetime factors. Likewise, we can assume *external utility* β that the seller obtains by selling the defective item is slightly more than the utility that the seller may lose by defection ($\beta = \mu + \sigma$). The overall utility $U_i^{f_2}$ will be as follows when the f_2 is used:

$$U_i^{f_2} = \Omega \times \begin{cases} \frac{(+\mu+\rho\ell_i)+1}{2} & \text{using } f_1 \text{ when } \alpha_i = 1 \\ \frac{(-\mu+\rho\ell_i)+1}{2} + \beta - \gamma & \text{using } f_1 \text{ when } \alpha_i = 0 \text{ plus } \beta \text{ as before,} \\ & \text{where } \gamma \text{ is the } future\ loss \text{ due to the impact of } \ell_i \end{cases}$$

Without loss of generality, suppose the seller defects, leaves and then comes back with a new identity. As a result the lifetime index ℓ_i becomes zero. Let assume this index is increased by the following arithmetic progression to reach to where it was: $0, \frac{1}{5}\ell_i, \frac{2}{5}\ell_i, \frac{3}{5}\ell_i, \frac{4}{5}\ell_i, \ell_i$. In reality, it takes a while for a seller to accumulate this credit based on our definition, i.e., *years of existence* and *number of transactions*. Therefore,

$$\gamma \approx \frac{\rho}{2}\left((\ell_i - 0) + (\ell_i - \frac{1}{5}\ell_i) + (\ell_i - \frac{2}{5}\ell_i) + (\ell_i - \frac{3}{5}\ell_i) + (\ell_i - \frac{4}{5}\ell_i) + (\ell_i - \ell_i)\right)$$

$$= \frac{\rho}{2}(\ell_i + \frac{4}{5}\ell_i + \frac{3}{5}\ell_i + \frac{2}{5}\ell_i + \frac{1}{5}\ell_i + 0) = \frac{3}{2}\rho\ell_i$$

E.g., $(\ell_i - \frac{1}{5}\ell_i)$ denote the *lifetime* could be ℓ_i, or even more, but it's now $\frac{1}{5}\ell_i$ meaning that the seller is losing $\frac{4}{5}\ell_i$, and so on. We now simplify the $U_i^{f_2}$ when $\alpha_i = 0$ as follows:

$$U_i^{f_2} : \frac{(-\mu + \rho\ell_i) + 1}{2} + \beta - \gamma$$

$$= \frac{(-\mu + \rho\ell_i) + 1}{2} + \mu + \sigma - \frac{3}{2}\rho\ell_i = \overbrace{\frac{(+\mu + \rho\ell_i) + 1}{2}}^{\Psi} + \sigma - \frac{3}{2}\rho\ell_i$$

This is a simple but interesting result that shows, as long as $\frac{3}{2}\rho\ell_i > \sigma$, $\mathscr{C}$ooperation is always Nash Equilibrium when f_2 is used, Table 2. In other words, as long as future loss γ is greater than the short-term gain through defection, it's not in the best interest of the seller to cheat and commit to the re-entry attack, that is, the seller may gain a small *short-term* utility by cheating, however, he loses a larger *long-term* utility because it takes a while to reach to ℓ_i from 0. The analysis will be the same if the seller cheats on δ rounds before committing to the re-entry attack as long as the future loss is greater than the short-term gain. In fact, the role of parameter ℓ_i is to make the future loss costly.

3 Technical Discussion: An Important Message by the Authors

As stated earlier, we would like to emphasize that our intention here was not to design specific trust models, construct utility functions (which is hard in many cases), target a certain set of attacks, or focus on particular assumptions/games/dilemmas. Our main objective was to illustrate the high-level idea

Table 2. Seller's Dilemma: $\mathscr{C}$ooperation is always Nash Equilibrium using f_2 when $\frac{3}{2}\rho\ell_i > \sigma$.

S_2 $\backslash$ S_1	$\mathscr{C}$ooperation	$\mathscr{D}$efection
$\mathscr{C}$ooperation	Ψ , Ψ	$\Psi , \Psi + \sigma - \frac{3}{2}\rho\ell_i$
$\mathscr{D}$efection	$\Psi + \sigma - \frac{3}{2}\rho\ell_i , \Psi$	$\Psi + \sigma - \frac{3}{2}\rho\ell_i , \Psi + \sigma - \frac{3}{2}\rho\ell_i$

of *rational trust modeling* by some examples and analyses without loss of generality. The presented models, functions, dilemma scenarios, attack strategies, assumptions and parameters can be modified as long as the model designers utilize the technical approach and strategy of rational trust modeling.

Indeed, we are using game theory in the model construction from the perspective of the designer of the model. Our main objective is to emphasize that the designer of a trust model can incorporate appropriate mathematical parameters into the trust models as long as the players who utilize these models intend to maximize their utility regardless of where these models will be used and what the other parameters are. In other words, our main contribution is not to propose a specific trust model for a certain attack scenario. The main goal is to emphasize how the designers of trust models should *think* to construct a new class of trust models in which there is a direct correlation between *trust* and *profit* inside the model itself, i.e., self-rewarding or self-punishing.

As we illustrated, by designing a proper trust function and using a game-theoretical analysis, not only trustworthiness can be incentivized but also well-known attacks on trust functions can be prevented, such as re-entry attack in our example. Furthermore, *behavior of the players can be predicted* by estimating the utility that each player may gain. In this section, we further discuss on these issues while focusing on other types of attacks against trust models. As shown in Table 3, all single-agent attacks can be simply prevented if the designer of the model incorporates one or more extra parameters (in addition to the previous trust value $\mathscr{T}_i^{p-1}$ and the current action α_i) into the function.

For instance, to deal with the Sybil attack, we can consider a parameter that only reflects the total number of past transactions. In that case, it's not in the best interest of a player to create multiple accounts and divides his total number of transactions among different identities. For imbalance attack, we can consider a parameter for transaction cost, i.e., if the player defects on an expensive transaction, his trust value declines with much faster ratio. For other attacks and their corresponding parameters, see Table 3.

It is worth mentioning that when the trust value reaches to the saturated region, e.g., very close to $+1$, a player may not have any interest to accumulate more trust credits. However, in this situation, the *high expectancy* parameter (as shown in Table 3) can be simply utilized in the trust function to warn the fully trusted players that they can sustain this credibility as long as they remain

Table 3. Sample Parameters: to deal with single-agent attacks during rational trust modeling.

Attacks	Parameter	Description
Sybil	Total number of past transactions	Prevent the players to create multiple false accounts
Lag	High expectancy	Prevent the players to cheat after gaining a high trust value
Re-Entry	Lifetime of the player	Prevent the players to return with a new identity
Imbalance	Transaction cost	Prevent the players to cheat on expensive transactions
Multi tactic	Combination of parameters	Prevent the players to defect in various circumstances

reliable, and if they commit to defections, they will be negatively and significantly (more than others) affected due to high expectancy.

Similarly, we can consider more complicated parameters to incentivize the players not to collude, and consequently, deal with multi-agent/coalition attacks. It is also worth mentioning that consideration should be given to the context in which the trust model is supposed to be used. Some of these parameters are context-oriented and the designer of the model should take this fact into account when designing a rational trust function.

4   Concluding Remarks

In this paper, the novel notion of *rational trust modeling* was introduced by bridging trust management and game theory. In our proposed setting, the designer of a trust model assumes that the players who intend to utilize the model are rational/selfish, i.e., they decide to become trustworthy or untrustworthy based on the utility that they can gain. In other words, the players are incentivized (or penalized) by the model itself to act properly. The problem of trust management can be then approached by strategic games among the players using utility functions and solution concepts such as NE.

Our approach resulted in two fascinating outcomes. First of all, the designer of a trust model can incentivize trustworthiness in the first place by incorporating proper parameters into the trust function. Furthermore, using a rational trust model, we can prevent many well-known attacks on trust models. These prominent properties also help us to predict the behavior of the players in subsequent steps by game theoretical analyses. As our final remark, we would like to emphasize that our rational trust modeling approach can be extended to any mathematical modeling where some sorts of utility and/or rationality are involved.

References

1. Castelfranchi, C., Falcone, R.: Principles of trust for MAS: cognitive anatomy, social importance, and quantification. In: 3rd International Conference on Multi Agent Systems, pp. 72–79. IEEE (1998)
2. Feng, R., Che, S., Wang, X., Wan, J.: An incentive mechanism based on game theory for trust management. Secur. Commun. Netw. **7**(12), 2318–2325 (2014)
3. Harish, M., Mahalakshmi, G., Geetha, T.: Game theoretic model for P2P trust management. In: International Conference on Computational Intelligence and Multimedia Applications, vol. 1, pp. 564–566. IEEE (2007)
4. Jøsang, A., Ismail, R., Boyd, C.: A survey of trust and reputation systems for online service provision. Decis. Support Syst. **43**(2), 618–644 (2007)
5. Kerr, R.: Addressing the issues of coalitions & collusion in multiagent systems. Ph.D. thesis, UWaterloo (2013)
6. Mailath, G., Samuelson, L.: Repeated Games and Reputations: Long-Run Relationships. Oxford University Press, Oxford (2006)
7. Mayer, R.C., Davis, J.H., Schoorman, F.D.: An integrative model of organizational trust. Acad. Manag. Rev. **20**(3), 709–734 (1995)
8. Mui, L.: Computational models of trust and reputation: agents, evolutionary games, and social networks. Ph.D. thesis, Massachusetts Institute of Technology (2002)
9. Mui, L., Mohtashemi, M., Halberstadt, A.: Notions of reputation in multi-agents systems: a review. In: 1st ACM International Joint Conference on Autonomous Agents and Multiagent Systems, AAMAS 2002, pp. 280–287 (2002)
10. Nojoumian, M.: Novel secret sharing and commitment schemes for cryptographic applications. Ph.D. thesis, Department of Computer Science, UWaterloo, Canada (2012)
11. Nojoumian, M.: Trust, influence and reputation management based on human reasoning. In: 4th AAAI Workshop on Incentives and Trust in E-Communities, pp. 21–24 (2015)
12. Nojoumian, M., Lethbridge, T.C.: A new approach for the trust calculation in social networks. In: Filipe, J., Obaidat, M.S. (eds.) ICETE 2006. CCIS, vol. 9, pp. 64–77. Springer, Heidelberg (2008). https://doi.org/10.1007/978-3-540-70760-8_6
13. Nojoumian, M., Stinson, D.R.: Brief announcement: secret sharing based on the social behaviors of players. In: 29th ACM Symposium on Principles of Distributed Computing (PODC), pp. 239–240 (2010)
14. Nojoumian, M., Stinson, D.R.: Social secret sharing in cloud computing using a new trust function. In: 10th IEEE Annual International Conference on Privacy, Security and Trust (PST), pp. 161–167 (2012)
15. Nojoumian, M., Stinson, D.R.: Socio-rational secret sharing as a new direction in rational cryptography. In: Grossklags, J., Walrand, J. (eds.) GameSec 2012. LNCS, vol. 7638, pp. 18–37. Springer, Heidelberg (2012). https://doi.org/10.1007/978-3-642-34266-0_2
16. Nojoumian, M., Stinson, D.R., Grainger, M.: Unconditionally secure social secret sharing scheme. IET Inf. Secur. (IFS) Spec. Issue Multi-Agent Distrib. Inf. Secur. **4**(4), 202–211 (2010)
17. Resnick, P., Kuwabara, K., Zeckhauser, R., Friedman, E.: Reputation systems: facilitating trust in internet interactions. Comm. ACM **43**(12), 45–48 (2000)
18. Wang, Y., Singh, M.P.: Trust representation and aggregation in a distributed agent system. In: 21st National Conference on AI, AAAI 2006, pp. 1425–1430 (2006)

19. Wang, Y., Singh, M.P.: Formal trust model for multiagent systems. In: 20th International Joint Conference on Artificial Intelligence, IJCAI 2007, pp. 1551–1556 (2007)
20. Wang, Y., Singh, M.P.: Evidence-based trust: a mathematical model geared for multiagent systems. ACM Trans. Auto Adapt. Syst. 5(4), 1–28 (2010)

Scaling-Up Stackelberg Security Games Applications Using Approximations

Arunesh Sinha[1(✉)], Aaron Schlenker[2], Donnabell Dmello[2], and Milind Tambe[2]

[1] University of Michigan, Ann Arbor, USA
arunesh@umich.edu
[2] University of Southern California, Los Angeles, USA
{aschlenk,ddmello,tambe}@usc.edu

Abstract. Stackelberg Security Games (SSGs) have been adopted widely for modeling adversarial interactions, wherein scalability of equilibrium computation is an important research problem. While prior research has made progress with regards to scalability, many real world problems cannot be solved satisfactorily yet as per current requirements; these include the deployed federal air marshals (FAMS) application and the threat screening (TSG) problem at airports. We initiate a principled study of approximations in zero-sum SSGs. Our contribution includes the following: (1) a unified model of SSGs called adversarial randomized allocation (ARA) games, (2) hardness of approximation for zero-sum ARA, as well as for the FAMS and TSG sub-problems, (3) an approximation framework for zero-sum ARA with instantiations for FAMS and TSG using intelligent heuristics, and (4) experiments demonstrating the significant 1000x improvement in runtime with an acceptable loss.

1 Introduction

The Stackelberg Security Game (SSG) model has been widely adopted in literature and in practice to model the defender-adversary interaction in various domains [6,11,20]. Over time SSGs have been used to model increasingly large and complex real world problems, hence an important research area within SSG research is the study of scalable Strong Stackelberg Equilibrium (SSE) computation algorithms, both theoretically and empirically. The scalability challenge has led to the development of a number of novel algorithmic techniques that compute the SSE of SSGs (see related work).

However, scalability continues to remain a pertinent challenge across many SSG applications. There are real world problems that even the best known approaches fail to scale up to, such as threat screening games (TSGs) and the Federal Air Marshals (FAMS) domain. The TSG model is used to allocate screening resources to passengers at airports and solves the problem for every hour (24 times a day). Yet, recent state-of-the-art approach for airport threat screening [4] scales only up to 110 flights per hour whereas 220 flights can depart per hour from the Atlanta Airport [9]. The FAMS problem is to allocate federal air marshals to US based flights in order to protect against hijacking attacks. Again,

© Springer Nature Switzerland AG 2018
L. Bushnell et al. (Eds.): GameSec 2018, LNCS 11199, pp. 432–452, 2018.
https://doi.org/10.1007/978-3-030-01554-1_25

the best optimal solver for FAMS in literature [13] solves problems up to 200 flights (FAMS is a deployed application since 2011) and in our experiments a modified baseline approach scales up to 900 flights, whereas on average 3500 international flights depart from USA daily [22]. Further, the prior approaches are fundamentally limited by the hardness of computing the exact solution [23].

To overcome the computational hardness, and provide practical scalability we investigate approximation techniques for zero-sum SSGs. Towards that end, our *first contribution* is a *unified* model of SSGs that we name *adversarial randomized allocation* (ARA) games. ARA captures a large class of SSGs which we call linearizable SSGs (defined later) which includes TSGs and FAMS.

Our *second contribution* is a set of *hardness of approximation* results. For zero-sum ARAs, we show that the ARA equilibrium computation problem and the defender best response problem in the given ARA game have the same hardness of approximation property and in the worst case ARA is not approximable. Further, we show that subclasses of ARA problems given by FAMS and TSGs are hard to approximate to any sub-linear factor.

Our *third contribution* is a general *approximation framework* for finding the SSE of zero-sum ARAs. The approximation framework combines techniques from dependent sampling [21] with randomized rounding. However, the framework is not an out-of-the-box approach and requires specific insights for a successful application. As concrete instances, we instantiate the framework's for FAMS and TSGs family of problems by providing *intelligent heuristics*. We provide theoretical approximation bounds for both FAMS and TSGs.

Finally, as our *fourth contribution*, we demonstrate via experiments that we can solve FAMS problem up to 3500 flights and TSG problems up to 280 flights with runtime improvements up to 1000x over the current state of the art. Moreover, the loss for FAMS problems is less than 5% for 900 flights and the loss decreases with increasing flights. For TSGs, the loss is less than 1.5% across all cases upto the 110 flights that the state of the art could scale upto. Hence, our approach enables solving the real world FAMS and airport screening problem satisfactorily for a US wide deployment. All missing proofs are in the appendix.

2 Related Work

Two major approaches to scale up in SSGs include incremental strategy generation (ISG) and use of marginals. ISG uses a master slave decomposition, with the slave providing a defender or attacker best response [13]. All these approaches are limited by the NP hardness of finding an exact solution [15,23]. Use of marginals and directly sampling from marginals while faster suffers from the issue of non-implementable (invalid) marginal solutions [14,21]. Fixing the non-implementability again runs into complexity barriers [4]. Combination of marginals and ISG approaches has also been tried [3]. Our study stands in contrast to these approaches as we aim to approximate the SSE and not compute it exactly, providing a viable alternative to ISG and bypassing the non-implementability of marginals approach. Another line of work uses regret and endgame solving techniques [5,17] to approximately solve large scale sequential zero sum games. Our game does not have a sequential structure to exploit and the large action space precludes using a standard no-regret learning approach.

Our approximation is inspired by randomized rounding (RR) [18]. Previous work on RR with equality constraints address *only* equality constraints [10] or obtain an integral solution given an approximate fractional solution within a polyhedron with integral vertices [8]. However, our initial fractional solution may not lie within an integral polyhedron, and we have both equality and inequality constraints. Thus, we provide an approach that exploits the disjoint structure of equality constraints in TSGs and FAMS in order to use previous work on comb sampling [21] and then alters the output [2] to handle both equality and inequality constraints. Finally, our hardness of approximation results are the first such results for the classic FAMS and recent TSG problem.

3   Model and Notation

We present a general abstract model of *adversarial randomized allocation* (ARA). ARA captures all *linearizable* SSGs, which is defined as those in which the probability c_t of defending a target t is linear in the defender mixed strategy; these include TSGs and FAMS. The ARA game model is a Stackelberg game model in which the defender moves first by committing to a randomized allocation and the adversary best responds. We start by presenting the defender's action space. There are k defense assets that need to be allocated to n objects to be defended. In this model, assets and objects are abstract entities and do not represent actual resources and targets in a security games. We will instantiate this abstract model with concrete examples of FAMS and TSG in the following sub-sections.

Defender's Randomized Allocation of Resources: The allocation can be represented as a $k \times n$ matrix with the $(i,j)^{th}$ entry $x_{i,j}$ denoting the allocation of asset i to object j, and each $x_{i,j} \geq 0$. There is a set of *assignment constraints* on the entries of the matrix. Each assignment constraint is characterized by a set $S \subseteq \{1,\ldots,k\} \times \{1,\ldots,n\}$ of indexes of the matrix and the constraint is given by $n_s \leq \sum_{(i,j)\in S} x_{i,j} \leq N_S$, where n_s, N_S are non-negative integers. We will refer to each assignment constraint as S. Also for sake of brevity, we denote the vector of all the entries in the matrix as $\mathbf{x}$ and $\sum_{(i,j)\in S} x_{i,j}$ as $\mathbf{x}[S]$.

Pure strategies of the defender are *integral* allocations that respect the assignment constraints, i.e., *integral* $\mathbf{x}$'s such that $n_S \leq \mathbf{x}[S] \leq N_S$ for all assignment constraints S. See Fig. 1 for an illustrative example of the assignment constraints and a valid pure strategy. Let the set of pure strategies be P and we will refer to a single pure strategy as $\mathbf{P}$. On the other hand, the space of marginal strategies MgS are those $\mathbf{x}$'s that satisfy the assignment constraints $n_S \leq \mathbf{x}[S] \leq N_S$ for all S; note that marginal strategies need not be integral.

Mixed strategies are probability distributions over pure strategies, e.g., probabilities $a_1, \ldots, a_m$ ($\sum_m a_m = 1$) over pure strategies $\mathbf{P}_1, \ldots, \mathbf{P}_m$. An expected (marginal) representation of a mixed strategy is $\mathbf{x} = \sum_m a_m \mathbf{P}_m$. Thus, the space of mixed strategies is exactly the *convex hull* of P, denoted as $conv(P)$. Typically,

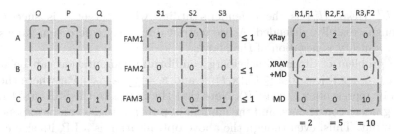

Fig. 1. Three illustrations: (a) ARA with assets A, B, C and objects O, P, Q with 3 example assignment constraints (shown as dashed lines) with upper bound 1 on the columns. Shown also is an assignment that satisfies these constraints. (b) FAMS problem with 2 flights, 3 schedules and 3 FAMS. S1 and S2 share one flight and so do S2 and S3. The two assignment constraints (for the two flights) with upper bound 1 are represented by the two dashed lines. Additional constraints are present on each row, shown on the right of the matrix. The attacker chooses a flight to attack, hence the dashed lines also show the index set T of targets. A sample pure strategy fills the matrix. (c) TSG with the two assignment constraints (resource capacity) with upper bound 7 for XRay and 15 for Metal Detector (MD) represented by the two dashed lines. Additional equality constraints denoting the number of passengers in each passenger category (R, F) are present on each column, shown on the bottom of the matrix. A passenger category (column) is made from risk and flight. An adversary of type $R1$ can only choose the first column $R1, F1$ and $R2$ can choose from the other two columns. Thus, the index set T for targets corresponds to columns. A sample pure strategy fills the matrix.

the space of marginal strategies is larger than $conv(P)$, i.e., $conv(P) \subset MgS$, hence every marginal strategies is not *implementable* as a mixed strategy. The conditions under which all marginal strategies are implementable (or not) has an easy interpretation in our model (see the implementability results in appendix).

Adversary's Action: The presence of an adversary sets our model (and SSGs) apart from a randomized allocation problem [7] and makes ARA a game problem. The attacker's action is to choose a target to attack. In our abstract formulation a target t is given by a set $T \subset \{1, \ldots, k\} \times \{1, \ldots, n\}$ of indexes of the allocation matrix. In order to capture linearizable SSGs, the probability of successfully defending an attack on target t is $c_t = \sum_{i,j \in T} w_{i,j} x_{i,j}$, which is linear in $x_{i,j}$'s as the $w_{i,j}$'s are constants such that $w_{i,j} \leq 1/\max_{\mathbf{x} \in conv(P)} \sum_{i,j \in T} x_{i,j}$. The constraint on $w_{i,j}$ ensures that $c_t \leq 1$. We assume that the total number of targets is polynomial in the size of the allocation matrix. Then, as is standard for SSGs, the defender expected utility given $\mathbf{x}$ and t is

$$U_d(\mathbf{x}, t) = c_t U_s^t + (1 - c_t) U_u^t$$

where U_s^t (resp. U_u^t) is the defender's utility when target t is successfully (resp. unsuccessfully) defended. As we restrict ourselves to zero-sum games, the attacker's utility is negation of the above.[1]

The problem of Strong Stackelberg equilibrium computation can be stated as: $\max_{\mathbf{x},z,a_i} z$ subject to $z \leq U_d(\mathbf{x},t)$ $\forall t$ and $\mathbf{x} = \sum_{i:\mathbf{P}_i \in P} a_i \mathbf{P}_i$, where the last constraint represents $\mathbf{x} \in conv(P)$. Note that the inputs to the SSE problem are the assignment constraints, and the number of pure strategies can be exponential in this input. Thus, even though the above optimization is a LP, its size can be exponential in the input to the SSE computation problem. However, using the marginal strategies MgS instead of the mixed strategies $conv(P)$ results in a polynomial sized $marginalLP$:

$$\max_{\mathbf{x},z,c_t} z$$
$$\text{subject to } z \leq U(\mathbf{x},t) \ \forall t \text{ and } n_s \leq \mathbf{x}[S] \leq N_S \ \forall S \text{ and } x_{i,j} \geq 0 \ \forall i,j$$

But, as stated earlier $conv(P) \subset MgS$, and hence the solution to the optimization above may not be implementable as a valid mixed strategy. In our approximation approach we will solve the above $marginalLP$ as the first step obtaining marginal solution $\mathbf{x}^m$.

Bayesian Extension[2]: We also consider the following simple extension where we consider types of adversary $\theta \in \Theta$ and each adversary type θ attacks a set of targets $\mathcal{T}_\theta$ such that $\mathcal{T}_\theta \cap \mathcal{T}_{\theta'} = \phi$ for all $\theta, \theta' \in \Theta$. The adversary is of type θ with probability p_θ ($\sum_\theta p_\theta = 1$). Then, the exact SSE optimization can be written as: $\max_{\mathbf{x},z_\theta,a_i} p_\theta z_\theta$ subject to $z_\theta \leq U_d(\mathbf{x},t)$ $\forall \theta \ \forall t \in \mathcal{T}_\theta$ and $\mathbf{x} = \sum_{i:\mathbf{P}_i \in P} a_i \mathbf{P}_i$. A corresponding $marginalLP$ can be defined in the same way as for original ARA.

Implementability: Viewing the defender's action space as a randomized allocation provides an easy way to characterize non-implementability of mixed strategies across a wide range of SSGs, in contrast to prior work that have identified non-implementability for specific cases [4,15,16]. The details of this interpretation can be found in the appendix.

3.1   FAMS

We model zero-sum FAMS in the ARA model. The FAMS problem is to allocate federal air marshal (FAMS) to flights to and from US in order to prevent hijacking attacks. The allocation is constrained by the number of FAMS available and the fact that each FAMS must be scheduled on round trips that take them back to their home airport. Thus, the main technical complication arises from the presence of schedules. A schedule is a subset of flights that has to be defended

---

[1] We remark that modeling-wise the extension to general-sum case, non-linearity in probabilities or exponentially many targets is straightforward; here we restrict the model as it suffices for the domains we consider.

[2] Typically player types denotes different utilities but as Harsanyi [12] originally formulated, types capture any incomplete information including, as for our case, lack of information about adversary action space. The game is still zero-sum.

together, e.g., flight f1 and f2 should be defended together as they form a round trip for the air marshal. Air marshals are allocated to schedules, no flight can have more than one air marshal and some schedules cannot be defended by some air marshals. The adversary attacks a flight.

Then, we capture the FAMS domain in the above model by mapping schedules in FAMS to objects (on columns) and air marshal in FAMS to assets (on rows). See Fig. 1 for an illustrative example. The assignment constraints include the constraint for each resource i: $\sum_j x_{i,j} \leq 1$, which states that every resource can be assigned at most once. If an air marshal i cannot be assigned to schedule j then add the constraint $x_{i,j} = 0$. A target t in the abstract model maps to a flight f in FAMS, and the set T are all the indexes for all schedules that include this flight: $\{(i,j) \mid \text{flight f is in schedule } j\}$. The constraint that a flight cannot have more than one air marshal is captured by adding the *target allocation constraint* $\mathbf{x}[T] \leq 1$. The probability of defending a target (flight) is $c_t = \mathbf{x}[T]$, hence the weights $w_{i,j}$'s in ARA are all ones.

3.2 TSG

We model TSGs using the Bayesian formulation of ARA. The TSG problem is how to allocate screening resources to screenees in order to screen optimally, which we elaborate in the context of airline passenger screening. In TSGs, different TSG resources such as X-Rays and Metal Detector act in teams to inspect an airline passenger. The possible teams are given. Passengers are further grouped into passenger categories with a given N_c number of passengers in each category c. The allocation is of resource teams to passenger categories. There are *resource capacity constraints* for each resource usage (not on teams but on each resource). Further, all passengers need to be screened. Each resource team i has an effectiveness $E_i < 1$ of catching the adversary. Observe that, unlike SSGs, the allocation in TSGs is not just binary $\{0,1\}$ but any positive integer within the constraints. The passenger category c is a tuple of risk level and flight (r, f); the adversary's action is to choose the flight f but he is probabilistically assigned his risk level.

Then, we capture the TSG domain in the above abstract model by mapping passenger categories in TSGs to objects (on columns) and resource teams in TSGs to assets (on rows). See Fig. 1 for an illustrative example. The capacity constraint for each resource r is captured by specifying the constraint $\mathbf{x}[S] \leq N_S$ which contains all indexes of teams that are formed using the given resource r: $S = \{(i,j) \mid \text{team } i \text{ is formed using resource } r\}$ with N_S equal to the resource capacity bound for resource r. For every passenger category j, the constraint $\sum_i x_{i,j} = N_j$ enforces that all passengers are screened. A target t in TSG is simply a passenger category j, thus, the set T is $\{(i,j) \mid j \text{ is given passenger category}\}$. The probability of detecting an adversary in category j is given by $\sum_{(i,j)\in T} E_i x_{i,j}/N_j$, hence the weights $w_{i,j}$ are E_i/N_j; since $E_i < 1$ it is easy to check that $\sum_{(i,j)\in T} w_{i,j}x_{i,j} \leq 1$ for any T. The adversary type is the risk level r, and each type r of adversary can choose a flight f, thus, choosing a target which is the passenger category (r, f). The probability of the adversary having a particular risk level is given.

4   Computation Complexity

In this section, we explore the *hardness of approximation* for ARAs, FAMS and TSGs. In prior work on computation complexity of SSGs, researchers [23] have focused on hardness of exact computation providing general results relating the hardness of defender best response (DBR) problem (defined below) to the hardness of exact SSE computation. In contrast, we relate the hardness of approximation of the DBR problem to hardness of approximation of ARAs. We also prove that special cases of ARA such as FAMS and TSGs are also hard to approximate.

First, we formally state the equilibrium computation problem in adversarial randomized allocation: given the assets, objects and assignment constraints of an adversarial randomized allocation problem as input, output the SSE utility and a set of pure strategies $P_1, \ldots, P_m$ and probabilities $p_1, \ldots, p_m$ that represents the SSE mixed strategy. We restrict m to be polynomial in the input size. This is natural, since a polynomial time algorithm cannot produce an exponential size output. Also, it is well known [23] that the size of the support set of any mixed strategy need not be more than $kn + 1$.

Next, as defined in prior literature [23], we state the DBR problem which aids in understanding the results. The DBR problem can be interpreted as the defender's best response to a given mixed strategy of the adversary. The DBR problem also shows up naturally as the slave problem in column generation based approaches to SSGs.

Definition 1. *The DBR problem is* $\max_{\mathbf{x} \in P} \mathbf{d} \cdot \mathbf{x}$ *where* $\mathbf{d}$ *is a vector of positive constants. DBR is a combinatorial problem that takes the assignment constraints as inputs, and not the set of pure strategies P.*

Next, we state the standard definition of approximation

Definition 2. *An algorithm for a maximization problem is r-approximate if it provides a feasible solution with value at least OPT/r, where OPT is the maximum.*

Note that lower r means better approximation. Depending on the best r possible, optimization problems are classified into various approximation complexity classes with increasing hardness of approximation in the following order PTAS, APX, log-APX, and poly-APX. We extensively use the well-known approximation preserving AP reduction between optimization problems for our results. AP reduction is analogous to reductions used for NP hardness but must also account for mapping of approximation ratios (and thus preserve hardness of approximation). AP reduction is among the strongest of all approximation preserving reductions as it preserves membership in most of the known approximation complexity classes. We do not delve into the formal definition of complexity classes or AP reduction here due to lack of space and these concepts being standard [1]. Our first result shows that the ARA's approximation complexity is same as that of the DBR problem and in the worst case cannot be approximated.

Theorem 1. *The following hardness of approximation hold for ARA problems: (1) ARA problems cannot be approximated by any bounded factor in poly time, unless $P = NP$; (2) if the DBR problem for given ARA problem lies in some given approximation class (APX, log-APX, etc.), then so does the ARA problem.*

Proof (Proof Sketch). The first result works by constructing a ARA from a NP hard unweighted ($d = 1$) DBR problem such that the feasibility of the constructed ARA solves the DBR problem, thereby ruling out any approximation. Such unweighted DBR problems exist (e.g., for FAMS). The second part of the proof works by constructing an ARA problem with one target and showing that the solution yields an approximate value for a relaxed DBR with $x \in conv(P)$. Moreover, this solution is an expectation over integral points (pure strategies), thus, at least one integral point in the support set output by ARA also provides an approximation for the corresponding combinatorial DBR.

As the above complexity result is a worst case analysis, one may wonder whether the above result holds for sub-classes of ARA problems. We show that strong versions of inapproximatibility also holds for FAMS and TSGs.

Theorem 2. *TSGs cannot be approximated to $O(n^{1-\epsilon})$ factor for any ϵ in poly time, unless $P = NP$.*

Proof (Proof Sketch). Using AP reduction from max independent set (MIS), the proof for TSG follows from an observation that a special case of the TSG problem is the MIS problem itself. MIS is known to be hard to approximate to any factor better than $n^{1-\epsilon}$ for any ϵ, unless $P = NP$.

Theorem 3. *FAMS problems cannot be approximated to $O(n^{1-\epsilon})$ factor for any ϵ in poly time, unless $P = NP$.*

Proof. We provide an AP reduction from max independent set (MIS). Given a MIS problem with vertices V and edges E construct the following FAMS problems, one for each k. Use $2n - k$ resources. All resources can be assigned to any schedule. Construct schedules $s_1, \ldots, s_n$ corresponding to the vertices $v_1, \ldots, v_n$. Construct target t_e corresponding to every edge $e = (u, v)$ such that $t_e \in s_u$ and $t_e \in s_v$. All t_e's have the same value for being defended or undefended and that value is $n+2$; thus, these targets do not need to covered but impose the constraint that s_u and s_v cannot be simultaneously defended. Thus, it is clear that any allocation of resources to $s_1, \ldots, s_n$ corresponds to an independent set. Next, consider additional $2n$ *valuable* targets and expand the set of targets of the schedules such that $t_i, t_{i+1} \in s_i$. Further, add $2n$ more singleton schedules $s_{n+1}, \ldots, s_{3n}$ with $t_i \in s_{n+i}$. All additional targets $t_1, \ldots, t_{2n}$ provide value k when defended and $k - 2n$ otherwise. Thus, the expected utility of defending a valuable target t given coverage c_t is $c_t(k) + (1 - c_t)(k - 2n) = 2n * c_t + k - 2n$.

For the given MIS problem, let the solution be k^*. Observe that for FAMS problems with resources $2n-k$ where $k \leq k^*$, all valuable (additional) targets can be covered by covering k^* schedules with $2k^*$ targets in $s_1, \ldots, s_n$ and using the remaining $\geq 2n - 2k^*$ resources to cover the remaining $2n - 2k^*$ valuable targets (via singleton schedules). This provides utility of k for the SSE. In particular, the utility with $2n - k^*$ resources is k^*. Also note that for every problem, there is always a trivial allocation of $2n - k$ resources to the $2n$ singleton schedules such that coverage of each target is $1 - k/2n$. This is deducible as the allocation to singleton schedules is unconstrained and can be implemented in poly time by Birkhoff-von Neumann result as provided in [15]. This trivial allocation provides an utility of 0.

Next, assume we have a poly time algorithm to approximately compute the SSE with approx factor r ($r > 1$). We will run this poly time algorithm with resources 2 to $2n - 1$ which is again a poly time overall, and also the overall output size is poly. We construct an approximation for the MIS problem.

Our construction relies on the following claim (proved in the next paragraph): given approximation factor r for the case with $2n - k^*$ resources then one of the pure strategy output for this case will have at least $k^* - l_{\min}$ schedules among $s_1, \ldots, s_n$ covered where $l_{\min} = \lfloor \text{argmin}_l \frac{k^*}{k^*-l} \geq r \rfloor$. Note that by definition of $l_{\min}$, $\frac{k^*}{k*-(l_{\min}+1)} > r$ and $\frac{k^*}{k*-l_{\min}} \leq r$. As k^* is the max size of independent sets we obtain an approximation ratio r' for the max independent set problem such that $r' = \frac{k^*}{k*-l_{\min}} \leq r$. Thus, we obtain an approximation r' for MIS as good as r approximation for the SSE. Thus, we have an AP reduction.

To prove the claim in last paragraph consider the contra-positive: suppose all pure strategies output cover at most $k^* - l_{\min} - 1$ schedules among $s_1, \ldots, s_n$, then in every pure strategy at least $l_{\min}+1$ valuable targets are not covered (since 2 valuable targets are covered for the $k^* - l_{\min} - 1$ schedules and rest of resources can cover only 1 valuable target). Then the coverage of the least covered target in the mixed strategy formed using such pure strategies is $\leq 1 - (l_{\min} + 1)/2n$ (this can be seen as sum of coverage of valuable targets must be at least $2n - l_{\min} - 1$, since that is true for every pure strategy). The utility for this least covered target is $\leq k^* - l_{\min} - 1$. The overall utility has to be lower than utility for any target, hence the utility is $\leq k^* - l_{\min} - 1$. The optimal utility is k^*. Thus, by definition of approximation ratio r we must have $k^* - l_{\min} - 1 \geq k^*/r$ or re-arranging $\frac{k^*}{k*-l_{\min}-1} \leq r$ but by definition of $l_{\min}$ we must have $\frac{k^*}{k*-l_{\min}-1} > r$ hence a contradiction.

5   Approximation Approach

Our approach to approximation first solves the *marginalLP*, which is quite fast in practice (see experiments) and provides an upper bound to the true value of the game. Then, we sample from the marginal solution, but unlike previous work [21], we alter the sampled value to ensure that the final pure strategy output is valid. We describe an abstract sampling and alteration approach for ARA in this part, which we instantiate for FAMS and TSGs in the subsequent sub-sections. Recall that a constraint is given by an index set S and the constraint is an equality if $n_S = N_S$. For our abstract approach we restrict our attention to ARAs with *partitioned equality assignment constraints*, which means the index set S for all equality constraints partitions the index set $\{1, \ldots, k\} \times \{1, \ldots, n\}$ of the allocation matrix. Further, for inequality constraints we assume $n_S = 0$. Call these problems as PE0-ARA; this class still includes FAMS and TSGs. For FAMS, which does not have equality constraints, we use dummy schedules s_i to get partitioned equalities $\sum_j x_{i,j} + s_i = 1$; $s_i = 1$ denotes that resource i is unallocated. Our abstract approximation approach for PE0-ARA is presented in Algorithm 1.

Algorithm 1. Abstract Approximation

Input: $\mathbf{x}^m$: the marginal solution
1 **forall the** $S \in EqualityConstraints$ **do**
2 $\quad \lfloor \mathbf{x} \leftarrow CombSample(\mathbf{x}^m, S)$

3 $\mathbf{x} \leftarrow FixViolatedInequalityConstraints(\mathbf{x})$
4 $\mathbf{x} \leftarrow FixEqualityConstraints(\mathbf{x})$

The Algorithm takes as input the marginal solution $\mathbf{x}^m$ from *marginalLP* and produces a pure strategy. The first for loop (lines 1–2) performs comb sampling for each equality constraint S to produce integral values for the variables involved in S. Comb sampling was introduced in an earlier paper [21]; it provides the guarantee that $x_{i,j}^m$ is rounded up or down for all $(i,j) \in S$, the sample $x_{i,j}$ has expected value $E(x_{i,j}) = x_{i,j}^m$ for all $(i,j) \in S$ and equality S is still satisfied after the sampling. See Fig. 2 for an example. Briefly, comb sampling works by creating Z buckets of length one each, where $Z = \sum_{(i,j) \in S} \{x_{i,j}^m\}$, where $\{.\}$ denotes fractional part. Each of the $\{x_{i,j}^m\}$ length fraction is packed into the bucket (in any order and some of the $\{x_{i,j}^m\}$ fraction may have to be split into two buckets), then a number between $[0, 1]$ is sampled randomly, say z, and for each bucket a mark is put at length z. Finally, the (i,j) whose $\{x_{i,j}^m\}$ fraction lies on the marker z for each bucket is chosen to be rounded up, and all other $x_{i,j}^m$ are rounded down.

Observe that in expectation the output of comb sampling matches the marginal solution, thus, providing the same expected utility as the marginal solution. Recall that this expected utility is an upper bound on the optimal utility. However, the samples from comb sampling may not be valid pure strategies. Thus, in case the output of comb sampling is not already valid, the two abstract methods in lines 3 and 4 modify the sample strategy by first decreasing the integral values to satisfy the violated inequalities and then increasing the integral values to satisfy the equalities. Such modification of the sampled strategy to obtain a valid strategy is guided by the *principle* that the change in defender utility between the sampled and the resultant valid strategy should be small, which ensures that change in expected utility from the marginal solution due to the modification is small. As the expected utility of the marginal solution is an upper bound on the optimal expected utility this marginal expected utility guided modification leads the output expected utility to be close to the optimal utility. Thus, the two methods on lines 3 and 4 need to be instantiated with carefully designed heuristics that aim to implement the principle of marginal

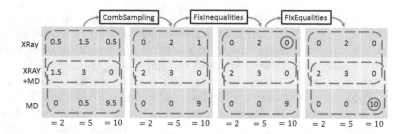

Fig. 2. (Left to right) Sample execution for the TSG example from Fig. 1. Recall that the resource capacity is 7 for XRay and 15 for MD. The marginal solution is the left matrix which after CombSampling on each column becomes integral, e.g., 0.5 in the left column is rounded down to 0 and 1.5 rounded up to 2. Note that the CombSampling output satisfies all equalities, but exceeds the resource capacity 7 for X-ray. Next, allocation values are lowered (shown as red circle) to satisfy the X-Ray capacity but the equality constraint on third column is violated. Next, allocation values are increased (again red circle) to fix the equality which produces a valid pure strategy. (Color figure online)

expected utility guided modification. Below, we show the instantiation for the TSG and FAMS family of problems. A sample execution for TSGs is shown in Fig. 2.

5.1   TSG

The heuristics for TSG are guided by three *observations*: (1) more effective resources are more constrained in their usage, (2) changing allocation for passenger categories with higher number of passengers changes the probability of detection of adversary by a smaller amount than changing allocation for category with fewer passengers and (3) higher risk passenger categories typically have lower number of passengers.

Algorithm 2 shows the heuristic for TSG. Recall that for TSGs the inequalities are resource capacity constraints. Thus, for fixing violated inequalities we need to decrease allocation which decreases utility; we wish to keep the utility decrease small as that ensures that the expected utility does not move much further away from the upper bound marginal expected utility. Our approach for such decrease in allocation has the following steps: (a) [Line 1] prioritize fixing inequality of most violated (negative slack) resources first and (b) [Lines 2–10] for each such inequality we attempt to lower allocation for passenger category with higher number of passengers. In light of the observations for TSG above this approach aims to keep the change in expected utility small. Specifically, observation 1 makes it likely that constraints for more effective resources are fixed in step a above. Observation 3 suggests that the changes in step b happens for lower risk passengers. Thus, step (a) aims to keep the allocation of effective resources for high risk passengers unchanged. This keeps the utility change

---

Algorithm 2. TSG Pure Strategy Generation

Input: x from Comb Sampling

1 $OrderedInequalityConstraints = Sort(InequalityConstraints, \mathbf{x})$ ascending by slack

2 **forall the** $R \in OrderedInequalityConstraints$ **do**

3     $\mathbf{X}_j^R \leftarrow$ variables corresponding to passenger category j in R (thus, $\mathbf{X}_j^R$ is a set of variables)

4     $\mathbf{X}^R \leftarrow Sort(\{\mathbf{X}_j^R\}_{j=1,..})$ descending by no. of passengers in category j.

5   **forall the** $\mathbf{X}_j^R$ in $\mathbf{X}^R$ **do**

6   **while** *any variable in* $\mathbf{X}_j^R$ *is* > 0 *AND R is violated* **do**

7           $x_{i,j} =$ Positive variable participating in the most inequality constraints among $\mathbf{X}_j^R$

8           $x_{i,j} = x_{i,j} - 1$

9   **if** *R is satisfied* **then**

10   **break**

11 $OrderedEqualityConstraints = Sort(EqualityConstraints, \mathbf{x})$ ascending by no. of passengers in the category corresponding to each equality constraint

12 **forall the** $C \in OrderedEqualityConstraints$ **do**

13    $\mathbf{X}_j \leftarrow$ variables in C (C corresponds to category j)

14    $\mathbf{X}_j^C \leftarrow Sort(\mathbf{X}_j)$ ascending by the min slack in the resource constraint of all resources that can inspect $x_{i,j} \in X_j$

15   **forall the** *component* $x_{i,j}$ *in* $\mathbf{X}_j^C$ **do**

16   **while** $x_{i,j} \neq 0$ *and C is violated* **do**

17          $x_{i,j} = x_{i,j} + 1$

18   **if** *C is satisfied* **then**

19   **break**

---

small as changing allocation for high risk passengers can change utility by a large amount. Next, by observation 2, step (b) aims to minimize the change in probability of detecting the adversary by a low amount so that expected utility change in small. For example in Fig. 2, the inequality fix reduces the allocation for the third passenger category (column) which also has the highest number of passengers (15). Also, observe that within each passenger category in step (b) we reduce those variables that participate in most resource capacity inequality constraints (Line 7) just to ensure that more constraints are fixed with fewer changes.

Next, the equalities in TSGs are the constraints for every passenger category. For fixing equalities we need to increase allocation which increases utility; we wish to keep this utility increase high as it brings the expected utility closer to the upper bound marginal expected utility. Here we aim to do so by (a) [Line 11] prioritizing increase of allocation for categories with fewer people and (b) [Lines 12–19] increasing allocation of those resources that have least slack in their resource capacity constraint (low slack means more utilized which could mean higher effectiveness). By Observation 1 low slack means that resource could be more effective and by Observation 2 fewer people means higher risk passengers. This ensures that higher risk passengers are screened more using more effective resources thereby raising the utility maximally. For example in Fig. 2, the equality for the third column is fixed by using the only available resource MD.

Recall that, unlike FAMS, the allocation for TSGs are non-binary. This offers an advantage for TSGs with respect to approximation, as small fractional changes do not change the overall allocation by much (0.5 to 1 is a 50% change, but 4.5 to 5 is less than 10%). Thus, we assume here that the changes due to Algorithm 1 do not reduce the probability of detecting an adversary in any passenger category (from the marginal solution) by more than $1/c$ factor, where $c > 1$ is a constant. This restriction is realistic as it is very unlikely that any passenger category will have few passengers and we aim to change the allocation for passenger categories with a higher number of passengers. Hence we prove

Theorem 4. *Assume that Algorithm 2 successfully outputs a pure strategy and the change in allocation from the marginal strategy does not change the probability of detecting an adversary by more than $1/c$ factor. Then, the approximation approach above with the heuristic provides a c-approximation for TSGs.*

As a remark, the above result does not violate the inapproximatability of TSGs since the above holds for a restricted set of TSG problems. Also, the approximation for TSGs may sometimes fail to yield a valid pure strategy as satisfying the equalities may become impossible after using certain sequences of decreasing allocation. In our experiments we observe that the failure of obtaining a pure strategy for TSG after Algorithm 2 is rare and easily handled by repeating the Algorithm 1 (sampling and adjusting runs in milli-secs).

5.2   FAMS

Recall that for FAMS the inequalities are the target allocation constraints: $\mathbf{x}[T] \leq 1$ and fixing violations for these involves decreasing allocation. Algorithm 3 shows the heuristic for TSG. Our heuristic is simple: we fix the most violated constraints first (Line 2), the variables $x_{i,j}$ are set to zero (i.e., decreased) starting from those schedules j that contain the most number of targets for which target allocation constraint is violated (Line 5) and do not contain any target for which the target allocation constraint is satisfied (Line 8). We are guaranteed to find a decrease in allocation that satisfies the constraint for T without changing the allocation for targets that already satisfy constraints in the cases when the target T with violated constraint (1) belongs to a schedule j that exclusively contains that target T ($x_{i,j}$ can be decreased without affecting any other constraint) or (2) T belongs to only one schedule (other targets in this schedule will violate their constraints). This approach ensures that we only work to fix the violated constraints and cause a minimal change in utility by leaving the satisfied constraints undisturbed. However, if in fixing a violated target allocation constraint for T it becomes necessary to reduce allocation for

---

Algorithm 3. FAMS Pure Strategy Generation

Input: **x** from Comb Sampling

1 $\mathbf{X}_j \leftarrow$ variables corresponding to schedule j
2 $OrderedInequalityConstraints = Sort(InequalityConstraints)$ ascending by slack
3 **forall the** $T \in OrderedInequalityConstraints$ **do**
4       $J \leftarrow$ schedules that T belongs to
5       $J \leftarrow Sort(J)$ descending by the number of violated target allocation (inequality) constraints for schedule j
6       $\mathbf{X}_J \leftarrow \cup_{j \in J} \mathbf{X}_j$
7   **while** *any variable in* $\mathbf{X}_J$ *is* > 0 *AND* T *is violated* **do**
8           $j \leftarrow 1stScheduleNoSatisifedTarget(J)$
9   **if** j *is -1* **then**
10              $j \leftarrow$ choose j randomly from J
11          $x_{i,j} \leftarrow$ any variable from $\mathbf{X}_j$
12          $x_{i,j} = x_{i,j} - 1$

---

another already satisfied target constraint, then sample uniformly from the ≥ 2 schedules that T belongs to in order to choose the $x_{i,j}$ allocation to reduce (Line 10) till all inequality constraints are satisfied.

Then, we do nothing to fix equality constraints since we have only decreased $x_{i,j}$ and if any equality $\sum_j x_{i,j} + s_i = 1$ is not satisfied we can always set the dummy s_i to be one. Also, observe that since we only always decrease allocations, we always find a pure strategy for any sample from Algorithm 3 (unlike TSGs). We prove:

Theorem 5. *Let* C_t *be the number of targets that share a schedule with any target* t, *and* $C = \max_t C_t$. *The approximation approach above with the heuristic provides a* $2^C k$-*approximation for FAMS.*

6   Experimental Results

Our experimental results reveal the average case loss of our approximation. **Baseline:** Our set of experiments provide a comprehensive analysis of our approximation approach, which we name RAND. We compare RAND to the best know solver for zero sum TSGs called MGA; MGA [4] has been previously shown to outperform column generation based approaches by a large margin. A more recent work [19], called GATE, approximates general sum TSGs using MGA in a branch and bound tree. However, this work suffers from loss of more than 11% for problems that are zero-sum (Fig. 7 in that paper) with runtime in 1000s of seconds compared to our loss of less than 1.5%. Moreover, the potential TSG application by Transport Security Administration (TSA) uses the zero-sum game version with MGA as the solver, which we confirmed through private communication with the authors of both these papers.

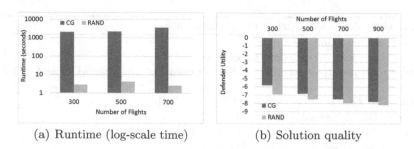

(a) Runtime (log-scale time)   (b) Solution quality

Fig. 3. CG and RAND comparison

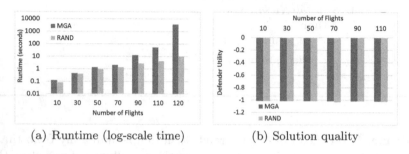

(a) Runtime (log-scale time)   (b) Solution quality

Fig. 4. MGA and RAND comparison

For the FAMS problem the best known solver in literature for the general sum case is ASPEN [13], which is a column generation based branch and price approach. Through private communication with the company (Avata Intelligence) managing the FAMS software, we know the FAMS problem is solved as a zero-sum problem for scalability using column generation. Even then the approach takes hours and is cut off without running to completion. On our end, for the zero-sum case we implemented a column generation (CG) solver for FAMS, since branch and price is an overkill for the zero sum case that we study.

All experimental results are averages over 30 randomly generated game instances. All game instances fix U_s^t to -1 and randomly select integral U_u^t between -2 and -10. The utility for RAND is computed by sampling 1000 pure strategies and taking their average as an estimate of the defender mixed strategy. All experiments were run with a Xeon 2.6 GHz processor and 4 GB RAM.

For FAMS, we vary the number of flights, keeping the number of resources fixed at 10 and number of schedules fixed at 1000 and 5 targets/schedule. The runtime *in log scale* is shown in Fig. 3. CG hits the 3600 s cut-off for 700 flights and the run time for RAND is much lower at only a few seconds. Next, we report the solution quality for RAND by comparing with the solution using CG. It can be seen that the solution gets better with increasing flights starting from 19% loss at 300 flights to 5% loss at 900 flights. An important point to note is that the approximation loss decreases with increasing number of flights, Thus, at 3500 flights (the number desired) we expect the loss percentage to be much lower, which we are unable to compare with CG as CG does not scale up. The numbers show that we obtain large speed-ups up to factor of 1000x and are still able to extract 95% utility for 900 flights beyond which CG does not scale.

For TSGs, we used six passenger risk levels, eight screening resource types and 20 screening team types. We vary the number of fights and we also randomly sample the team structure (how teams are formed from resources) for each of the 30 runs. The results in Fig. 4 show runtime (in log scale) and defender utility values varying with number of flights (on x-axis). As can be seen, MGA only scales up to 110 flights before hitting the cut-off of 3600 s, while RAND takes only 10 s for 110 flights. Also, the solution quality loss for RAND has a maximum averaged loss of 1.49%. Thus, we obtain at-least 360X speed-ups with very minor loss. We performed an additional experiment to show that the choices made by our heuristics are important. We change the heuristics in Algorithm 2 line 3 to sort ascending instead of descending and the modified RAND suffered 35% more loss over RAND for 110 flights. A figure showing the same with different number of flights is in the appendix.

Next, we test the scalability of RAND for FAMS and TSG, shown in Fig. 5. As can be seen, the runtime for RAND is low even with the highest number of flights we tested: 280 for TSG and 3500 for FAMS. The maximum runtime for FAMS was under 5 s; the maximum runtime for TSG was under 25 s.

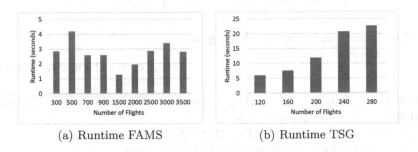

(a) Runtime FAMS   (b) Runtime TSG

Fig. 5. Scalability of RAND

7   Conclusion

We studied approximations in zero-sum SSGs both theoretically and practically. We provided approximation techniques to solve large scale zero-sum SSGs, which enables the application of already deployed application (FAMS) or applications under test (airport screening) at a national scale in USA. In fact, the number of international flights from USA was 2000 in 2010 [13] which has increased to 3500 [22] revealing the ever increasing trend. Our approach not only provide an avenue to solve the FAMS and airport screening problem for current problem sizes but is capable of scaling up to larger numbers in future.

Appendix

Implementability: Viewing SSGs as ARAs provides an easy way of determining implementability using results from randomized allocation [7]. First, we define *bi-hierarchical assignment constraints* as those that can be partitioned into two sets H_1, H_2 such that two constraints S, S' in the same partition (H_1 or H_2) it is the case that either $S \subseteq S'$ or $S' \subseteq S$ or $S \cap S' = \phi$. Further, as defined in [7], *canonical assignment constraints* are those that impose constraints on all rows and columns of the matrix. We obtain the following result

Proposition 1. *All marginal strategies are implementable, or more formally* $conv(P) = MgS$, *if the assignment constraints are bi-hierarchical. Given canonical assignment constraints, if all marginal strategies are implementable then the assignment constraints are bi-hierarchical.*

As Fig. 1 reveals, both FAMS and TSG have non-implementable marginals due to overlapping constraints. The proof of the proposition is straightforward applications of Theorems 1 and 2 in Budish et al. [7].

Modified Heuristic is Bad: The modified RAND approach is compared to RAND in Fig. 6. It can be seen that the loss increases a lot with almost 35% loss over RAND for 110 flights.

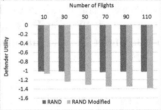

Proof of Theorem 1: First we define some problems related to the DB problem.

Fig. 6. RAND modified heuristic comparison

- DBR is the problem $\max_{\mathbf{x} \in P} \mathbf{d} \cdot \mathbf{x}$ where $\mathbf{d}$ is a vector of positive constants. DBR is a combinatorial problem.
- The continuous version of DBR is DBR-C: $\max_{\mathbf{x} \in conv(P)} \mathbf{d} \cdot \mathbf{x}$.
- The unweighted version of the DBR is DBR-U: $\max_{\mathbf{x} \in P} \mathbf{1} \cdot \mathbf{x}$.

Proof. For the first part, given a NP hard DBR-U instance (for the decision version of DBR-U), we construct an ARA instance such that the feasibility problem for that ARA instance solves the hard DBR-U decision problem. Thus, as the feasibility is NP Hard, there exists no approximation. First, since the ARA problem is so general there exists DBR-U problems that are NP Hard. For example, the DBR-U problem for FAMS has been shown to be NP Hard [23]. Given the hard DBR-U problem, form an ARA problem with by adding the constraint $\mathbf{1} \cdot \mathbf{x} = k$. Also, let there be only one target t in the problem, so that the objective becomes $U(\mathbf{x}, t)$ instead of z and all constraints in the optimization are just the marginal space constraints and $\mathbf{1} \cdot \mathbf{x} = k$. Now, the existence of any solution of the optimization gives a feasible point $\mathbf{x} = \sum_m a_m \mathbf{P_m}$, where $\mathbf{P_m} \in P$ is integral. Also, it must be that $\mathbf{1} \cdot \mathbf{P_j} \geq \mathbf{1} \cdot \mathbf{x} = k$ for some j. Then, $\mathbf{P_j}$ is a solution to the decision version of the DBR-U problem, i.e., does there exist a solution of the DBR-U optimization problem with value $\geq k$? Thus, since finding the existence of any solution for ARA is NP Hard, thus, no approximation exists in poly time.

For the second part, we present a AP approximation preserving reduction (with problem mapping that does not depend on approximation ratio); such a reduction preserves membership in PTAS, APX, log-APX, Poly-APX (see [1]). Given any DBR problem, we construct the ARA problem with one target such that $T = \{1, \ldots, k\} \times \{1, \ldots, n\}$. Choose the weights $w_{i,j}$'s such that $w_{i,j} \propto d_{i,j}$ and $w_{i,j} \leq 1/\max_{\mathbf{x} \in MgS} \sum_{i,j} x_{i,j}$. Observe that $\max_{\mathbf{x} \in MgS} \sum_{i,j} x_{i,j}$ is computable efficiently and $\max_{\mathbf{x} \in MgS} \sum_{i,j} x_{i,j} \geq \max_{\mathbf{x} \in conv(P)} \sum_{i,j} x_{i,j}$, thus, the ARA is well-defined. Thus, due to just one target, the ARA optimization is same as $\max_{\mathbf{x} \in conv(P)} \mathbf{w} \cdot \mathbf{x}$. Suppose we can solve this problem with r approximation with the solution mixed strategy being $\mathbf{x}^\epsilon = \sum_{i=1}^{m} a_i \mathbf{P_i}$ for some pure strategies $\mathbf{P_i}$. Now, since $w_{i,j} \propto d_{i,j}$ we also know that this solution also provides r approximation for DBR-C. Let the optimal solution for DBR-C be OPT; note that OPT is also the optimal solution for DBR. $\mathbf{x}^\epsilon$ provides a solution value $\mathbf{w} \cdot \mathbf{x}^\epsilon \geq OPT/r$. Further, as the objective is linear in $\mathbf{x}$ and $\mathbf{x}^\epsilon = \sum_{i=1}^{m} a_i \mathbf{P_i}$, it must be the case that there exists a $j \in \{1, \ldots, m\}$ such that $\mathbf{w} \cdot \mathbf{P_j} \geq \mathbf{w} \cdot \mathbf{x}^\epsilon \geq OPT/r$. Thus, since $\mathbf{P_j} \in P$, $\mathbf{P_j}$ provides r approximation for DBR. Since, m the number of the pure strategies in support of $\mathbf{x}^\epsilon$ is polynomial, $\mathbf{P_j}$ can be found in polynomial time by a linear search.

Proof of Theorem 2.

Proof. Given an independent set problem with V vertices, we construct a TSG with $\{1, \ldots, V+1\}$ team types, where each team type in $1, \ldots, V$ corresponds to a vertex. The $V + 1$ team is special in the sense that it does not correspond to any vertex and it is made up of just one resource with a very large resource capacity $2V$. Construct just one passenger category with passengers $N = V+1$. Since, there is just one passenger category (and target) we will use x_i as the matrix entries instead of $x_{i,j}$. Choose $U_s^t = V + 1$ and $U_u^t = 0$ and efficiencies $E_i = 1$ for all teams, except $E_{V+1} = 0$. Then, the objective of the integer LP is $\sum_{i=1}^{V} x_i = \mathbf{1}_V \cdot \mathbf{x}$ where $\mathbf{1}_V$ is a vector with first V components as 1 and last component as 0.

Next, have resources for every edge $(i, k) \in E$ with resource capacity 1. This provides the inequality $\sum_{(i,k) \in E} x_i + x_j \leq 1$. Also, we have $x_{V+1} \leq 2V$. Inspection of every passengers provides the constraints $\sum_{i=1}^{V+1} x_i = V+1$. Treating x_{V+1} as a slack, we can see that the constraint $x_{V+1} \leq 2V$ and $\sum_{i=1}^{V+1} x_i = V + 1$ are redundant. For the left over constraints $\sum_{(i,k) \in E} x_i + x_j \leq 1$, we can easily check that any valid integral assignment (pure strategy) is an independent set. Moreover, the objective $\sum_{i=1}^{V} x_i$ tries to maximize the independent set. The optimal value of this optimization over $conv(P)$ is an extreme point which is integral and equal to the maximum independent set OPT. Thus, suppose a solution $\mathbf{x}^\epsilon$ to the SSE problem with value $\geq OPT/r$. Further, as the objective is linear in $\mathbf{x}$ and $\mathbf{x}^\epsilon = \sum_{i=1}^{m} a_i \mathbf{P_i}$, it must be the case that there exists a $j \in \{1, \ldots, m\}$ such that $\mathbf{1}_V \cdot \mathbf{P_j} \geq \mathbf{1}_V \cdot \mathbf{x}^\epsilon \geq OPT/r$. Thus, since $\mathbf{P_j} \in P$, $\mathbf{P_j}$ provides r approximation for maximum independent set. Since, m the number of the pure strategies in support of $\mathbf{x}^\epsilon$ is polynomial, $\mathbf{P_j}$ can be found in poly time by a linear search.

Proof of Theorem 5.

Proof. Consider the event of a target t having an infeasible assignment after the comb sampling. Call this event E_t. Let $C_{t,i}$ be the event that resource i covers this target t. Then, $P(E_t) = \sum_i P(E_t|C_{t,i})P(C_{t,i})$. From the guarantees of comb sampling we know that $P(C_{t,i}) = \sum_{j:(i,j)\in T} x_{i,j}^m \leq 1$ and $P(x_{i,j} = 1) = x_{i,j}^m$. Also, by comb sampling if $x_{i,j} = 1$ then $x_{i,j'} = 0$ for any $j' \neq j$. Next, we know that $P(E_t|C_{t,i})$ is the probability that the any of the other $x_{i',j}$ is assigned a one, which is $1-$ the probability that all other $x_{i',j}$ are assigned 0. Thus,

$$P(E_t|C_{t,i}) = 1 - \prod_{i' \neq i}(1 - P(C_{t,i}))$$

Let $p_{t,i} = P(C_{t,i})$. Considering the fact that $\prod_i(1 - p_{t,i}) > 1 - \sum_i p_{t,i}$, we get

$$1 - \prod_{i' \neq i}(1 - P(C_{t,i})) \leq \sum_{(i',j):i' \neq i \wedge (i',j)\in T} x_{i',j}^m \leq 1 - \sum_j x_{i,j}^m$$

where the last inequality is due to the fact that $\sum_{(i,j)\in T} x_{i,j}^m \leq 1$.

Thus, $P(E_t) \leq \sum_i(1 - p_{t,i})p_{t,i} \leq \sum_i p_{t,i} - \sum_i (p_{t,i})^2$. Next, we know from standard sum of squares inequality that $\sum_i(p_i)^2 \geq (\sum_i p_i)^2/k$. Thus, we get $P(E_t) \leq (\sum_i p_i)(1 - \sum_i p_i/k)$ The RHS is maximized when $\sum_i p_i = 1$, thus, $P(E_t) \leq 1 - 1/k$. Also, then $P(\neg E_t) \geq 1/k$

Now consider the coverage of target t: $x_t^m = \sum_{(i,j)\in T} x_{i,j}^m$. According to our algorithm the allocation for target t continues to remain 1 with probability $(1/2)^C$ if its allocation is already feasible after comb sampling (and we always obtain a pure strategy). This is because this target shares schedules with C other targets and thus in the worst case may be reduced with $1/2$ probability for each of the C targets. We do a worst case analysis and assume that no resource is allocated to a target when the sampled allocation is infeasible for that target. Thus, let y_t denote the random variable denoting that target t is covered. Thus, $E(y_t) = P(y_t = 1) = P(y_t = 1|E_t)P(E_t) + P(y_t = 1|\neg E_t)P(\neg E_t)$. Now, $P(y_t = 1|\neg E_t)$ is same as $x_t^m/2^C$ and we assumed the worst case of $P(y_t = 1|E_t) = 0$. Thus, we have $E(y_t) \geq x_t^m/2^C k$. As the utilities are linear in y_t, we have the utility for t as $U_t \geq U_t^m/2^C k$, where U_t^m is the utility under the marginal $\mathbf{x}^m$. Thus, if t^* is the choice of adversary under the marginal $\mathbf{x}^m$ we know that $U_{t^*}^m$ is the lowest utility for the defender over all targets t. Hence, we can conclude that the utility with the approximation is at least $U_{t^*}^m/2^C k$

Proof of Theorem 4.

Proof. The main assumption in the proof is that the steps after comb sampling changes the probability of detecting an adversary in passenger category j by at most $1/c$. Also, by assumption of the theorem since Algorithm 1 does not fail ever, the change in utility for any passenger category j is at most a factor of $1/c$. By similar reasoning as for FAMS, we conclude that this provides a c-approximation.

References

1. Ausiello, G., Protasi, M., Marchetti-Spaccamela, A., Gambosi, G., Crescenzi, P., Kann, V.: Complexity and Approximation: Combinatorial Optimization Problems and Their Approximability Properties. Springer, Heidelberg (1999). https://doi.org/10.1007/978-3-642-58412-1
2. Bansal, N., Korula, N., Nagarajan, V., Srinivasan, A.: Solving packing integer programs via randomized rounding with alterations. Theory Comput. 8(1), 533–565 (2012)
3. Bošanský, B., Jiang, A.X., Tambe, M., Kiekintveld, C.: Combining compact representation and incremental generation in large games with sequential strategies. In: AAAI (2015)
4. Brown, M., Sinha, A., Schlenker, A., Tambe, M.: One size does not fit all: a game-theoretic approach for dynamically and effectively screening for threats. In: AAAI (2016)
5. Brown, N., Sandholm, T.: Safe and nested subgame solving for imperfect-information games. In: NIPS, pp. 689–699 (2017)
6. Bucarey, V., Casorrán, C., Figueroa, Ó., Rosas, K., Navarrete, H., Ordóñez, F.: Building real stackelberg security games for border patrols. In: Rass, S., An, B., Kiekintveld, C., Fang, F., Schauer, S. (eds.) GameSec 2017. LNCS, vol. 10575, pp. 193–212. Springer, Cham (2017). https://doi.org/10.1007/978-3-319-68711-7_11
7. Budish, E., Che, Y.K., Kojima, F., Milgrom, P.: Designing random allocation mechanisms: theory and applications. Am. Econ. Rev. 103(2), 585–623 (2013)
8. Chekuri, C., Vondrák, J., Zenklusen, R.: Dependent randomized rounding for matroid polytopes and applications. arXiv preprint arXiv:0909.4348 (2009)
9. FAA: Airport capacity profiles (2014). https://goo.gl/YZvzsU. Accessed 15 May 2018
10. Gandhi, R., Khuller, S., Parthasarathy, S., Srinivasan, A.: Dependent rounding and its applications to approximation algorithms. J. ACM (JACM) 53(3), 324–360 (2006)
11. Guo, Q., An, B., Vorobeychik, Y., Tran-Thanh, L., Gan, J., Miao, C.: Coalitional security games. In: AAMAS (2016)
12. Harsanyi, J.: Games with incomplete information played by Bayesian players, I-III part I. the basic model. Manag. Sci. 14(3) (1967)
13. Jain, M., Kardeş, E., Kiekintveld, C., Tambe, M., Ordóñez, F.: Security games with arbitrary schedules: a branch and price approach. In: AAAI, pp. 792–797 (2010)
14. Kiekintveld, C., Jain, M., Tsai, J., Pita, J., Ordóñez, F., Tambe, M.: Computing optimal randomized resource allocations for massive security games. In: AAMAS (2009)
15. Korzhyk, D., Conitzer, V., Parr, R.: Complexity of computing optimal Stackelberg strategies in security resource allocation games. In: AAAI (2010)
16. Letchford, J., Conitzer, V.: Solving security games on graphs via marginal probabilities. In: AAAI (2013)

17. Moravčík, M., et al.: Deepstack: expert-level artificial intelligence in heads-up no-limit poker. Science (2017)
18. Raghavan, P., Thompson, C.D.: Randomized rounding: a technique for provably good algorithms and algorithmic proofs. Combinatorica **7**(4), 365–374 (1987)
19. Schlenker, A., Brown, M., Sinha, A., Tambe, M., Mehta, R.: Get me to my gate on time: efficiently solving general-sum Bayesian threat screening games. In: ECAI, pp. 1476–1484 (2016)
20. Tambe, M.: Security and Game Theory: Algorithms, Deployed Systems, Lessons Learned. Cambridge University Press, New York (2011)
21. Tsai, J., Yin, Z., Kwak, J., Kempe, D., Kiekintveld, C., Tambe, M.: Urban security: game-theoretic resource allocation in networked physical domains. In: AAAI (2010)
22. USDOT: Bureau of transportation statistics (2016). https://goo.gl/Goz84L. Accessed 15 May 2018
23. Xu, H.: The mysteries of security games: equilibrium computation becomes combinatorial algorithm design. In: ACM-EC (2016)

A Learning and Masking Approach
to Secure Learning

Linh Nguyen, Sky Wang, and Arunesh Sinha[✉]

University of Michigan, Ann Arbor, USA
{lvngyuen,skywang,arunesh}@umich.edu

Abstract. Deep Neural Networks (DNNs) have been shown to be vulnerable against adversarial examples, which are data points cleverly constructed to fool the classifier. In this paper, we introduce a new perspective on the problem. We do so by first defining robustness of a classifier to adversarial exploitation. Further, we categorize attacks in literature into high and low perturbation attacks. Next, we show that the defense problem can be posed as a learning problem itself and find that this approach effective against high perturbation attacks. For low perturbation attacks, we present a classifier boundary masking method that uses noise to randomly shift the classifier boundary at runtime. We also show that both our learning and masking based defense can work simultaneously to protect against multiple attacks. We demonstrate the efficacy of our techniques by experimenting with the MNIST and CIFAR-10 datasets.

1 Introduction

Recent advances in deep learning have led to its wide adoption in various challenging tasks such as image classification. However, the current state of the art has been shown to be vulnerable to *adversarial examples*, small perturbations of the original inputs, often indistinguishable to a human, but carefully crafted to misguide the learning models into producing incorrect outputs. Recent results have shown that generating these adversarial examples are inexpensive [9]. Prior work has yielded a lot of attack methods that generate adversarial examples, and defense techniques that improve the accuracy on these examples (see related work). However, attacks and defenses have followed the cat-and-mouse game that is typical of many security settings. Further, traditional machine learning theory assumes a fixed stochastic environment hence accuracy in the traditional sense is not a meaningful measure of performance in the presence of an adversary.

In this paper, we pursue an approach informed by our *first contribution*: a definition of *robustness of classifiers* in the presence of an adversary. Towards the definition, we define an exploitable space by the adversary which includes data points already mis-classified (errors) by any given classifier and any data points that can be perturbed by the adversary to force mis-classifications. Robustness is defined as the probability measure of the exploitable space. We also analyze why accuracy fails to measure robustness. Using our formal set-up we categorize

© Springer Nature Switzerland AG 2018
L. Bushnell et al. (Eds.): GameSec 2018, LNCS 11199, pp. 453–464, 2018.
https://doi.org/10.1007/978-3-030-01554-1_26

known attacks into high and low perturbation attacks, and explain why defenses against one type of attacks does not work against the other type.

Our *second contribution* is a defense technique: *defense learning neural network* (DLN) against high perturbation attacks. A DLN D is a DNN that, given any classifier C attacked by an attack technique A, takes in an adversarial example $A(x)$ and aims to generate benign example $D(A(x))$ that *does not* lie in the mis-classified space of C. For non-adversarial inputs the DLN is encouraged to reproduce the input as well as make the classifier predict correctly. The DLN is *prepended* to the classifier C acting as a sanitizer for C. We show that DLN allows for attack and defense to be set up as a repeated competition leading to more robust classifiers. While DLN works efficiently for attacks that produces adversarial examples with high perturbation, such as fast gradient sign method [9] (FGSM), it is not practical for low perturbation attacks (illustrated in Fig. 3) such as Carlini-Wagner [5] (CW).

Our *third contribution* is a defense against low perturbation attacks that we call *noise augmented classifier* (NAC) which randomly shifts the classifier separator by injecting a very small noise at the last layer of the DNN classifier during runtime. The small noise *randomly* shifts the separator on each invocation, but not by much, thereby ensuring original accuracy is maintained, yet also fools low perturbation attacks. NAC alone defends against the low perturbation CW attack, but as expected fails against high perturbation FGSM attack.

Finally, we show that DLN and NAC can work together, thereby enabling simultaneous defense against both high and low perturbation attacks. We tested our approach on two datasets: MNIST and CIFAR-10, and the resultant classifier was robust to both FGSM and CW. All missing proofs are in the full version.

2 Model and Approach

Attack Model: First, we use *inference phase* of a classifier to mean the stage when the classifier is actually deployed as an application (after all training and testing is done). The attacker attacks *only* in the inference phase and can channel his attack *only* through the inputs. In particular, the attacker cannot change the classifier weights or inject any noise in the hidden layers or access any internal values when the DNN predicts in the inference phase. The attacker has access to the classifier weights, so that it can compute gradients, if required. The attacker's goal is to produce adversarial data points that get mis-classified by the classifier, and are not a garbage noisy image.

Notation: Let the function $C : X \to Y$ denote a classifier that takes input data points with feature values in X and outputs a label among the possible k labels $Y = \{1, \ldots, k\}$. Further, for DNNs we define $C_p : X \to \Delta Y$ as the function that takes in data and produces a probability distribution over labels. Thus, $C = \max\{C_p(x)\}$, where C is the maximum component of the vector $C_p(x)$. Let $H(p, q)$ denote the cross entropy $-\sum_i p_i \log(q_i)$. For this paper, we assume X is the set of legitimate images (and not garbage images or ambiguous images).

Given a label y, let $Cat(y)$ denote the categorical probability distribution with the component for y set to 1 and all else 0.

Robustness: We introduce some concepts from PAC learning [1], in order to present the formal results in this section. It is assumed that data points arise from a fixed but unknown distribution $\mathcal{P}$ over X. We denote the probability mass over a set $Z \subset X$ as $\mathcal{P}(Z)$. A loss function $l(y_x, C(x))$ captures the loss of predicting $C(x)$ when the true label for x is y_x. As we are focused on classification, we restrict ourselves to the ideal 0/1 loss, that is, 1 for mis-classification and 0 otherwise. A classifier C is chosen that minimizes the empirical loss over the n training data points $\sum_{i=1}^{n} l(y_{x_i}, x_i)$. Given enough data, PAC learning theory guarantees that C also minimizes the expected loss $\int_X l(y_x, C(x))\mathcal{P}(x)$. Given, 0/1 loss this quantity is just $\mathcal{P}(M_C(X))$, where $M_C(X) \subset X$ denote the region where the classifier C mis-classifies. Accuracy is then just $1 - \mathcal{P}(M_C(X))$. In this paper we assume that the amount of data is always enough to obtain low expected loss. Observe that a classifier can achieve high accuracy (low expected loss) even though its predictions in the low probability regions may be wrong [21]. All classifier families have a capacity that limits the complexity of separators that they can model; the capacity value is known only for simple classifiers [1]. Previous work [9] has conjectured that adversarial examples abound due to the low capacity of the classifier family used. See Fig. 2A.

Adversarial Exploitable Space: Define the adversarial exploitable space:

$$E_{C,\epsilon}(X) = M_C(X) \cup \{x \mid \overline{sim}(x, M_C(X)) \leq \epsilon\},$$

where $\overline{sim}$ is a *dissimilarity* measure that depends on the domain and $\overline{sim}(x, M_C(X))$ denotes the lowest dissimilarity of x with any data point in $M_C(X)$. For image classification $\overline{sim}$ can just be the l_2 (Euclidean) distance: $\sqrt{\sum_i (x_i - x_i')^2}$ where i indexes the pixels. $E_{C,\epsilon}(X)$ includes all points that are either mis-classified or can be mis-classified by a minor ϵ-perturbation. Observe that we posit that any already present mis-classifications of the classifier is exploitable by the adversary, e.g., if a stop sign image in a dataset is mis-classified then an adversary can simply use this image as is to fool a classifier.

Robustness Definition: Robustness is simply defined as $1 - \mathcal{P}(E_{C,\epsilon}(X))$. First, observe that robustness is a strictly stronger concept than accuracy, i.e., accuracy is always higher than robustness. We believe this property makes our definition more natural than other current definitions. Another readily inferable property is that a classifier C' with $M_{C'}(X) \subset M_C(X)$ has higher robustness than C in the same stochastic setting. We use this property later to justify our defense. Next, we elaborate on a number of subtle aspects of the definition.

First, a 100% robust classifier can still have $M_{C'}(X) \neq \phi$. This is because robustness is still defined w.r.t. the data distribution $\mathcal{P}$. For example, large compact regions R of zero probability with small sub-region of erroneous prediction far away from the boundary of R can still make robustness 100%. On the other hand, $M_{C'}(X) = \phi$ provides 100% robustness for any $\mathcal{P}$. Second, as shown in Fig. 2, low capacity classifiers cannot model complex separators, thus, large capacity is required to achieve robustness. A 100% robust classifier is practically impossible due to large data requirement of high capacity classifier family. On the other hand, large capacity but limited data causes over-fitting [1]. Thus, there is a delicate balance between capacity and amount of data, which is not well understood for DNNs. Third, robustness may appear to be computable by calculating the accuracy for the test set and for the adversarially perturbed test set, as done in all prior work. However, this relies on the assumption that the attack discovers *all* perturb-able points. An analysis of computing robustness is beyond the scope of this paper.

Lastly, compared to past work [8,24], our robustness has a clear relation to accuracy and not orthogonal to it. Also, we use the ideal 0/1 loss function rather than an approximate loss function l (often used in training due to smoothness) as used in other definitions [7,12,17]. We posit that the 0/1 loss measures robustness more precisely, as these other approaches specify the adversary goal as perturbing in order to produce the maximum loss within an ϵ ball $B(x, \epsilon)$ of any given point x, with the defender expected loss defined as $\int_X \max_{z \in B(x,\epsilon)} l(y_x, C(z)) \mathcal{P}(x)$, where l is the loss function used to train the classifier. For ease of optimization, typically, l is a smooth function approximation of the 0/1 loss. However, this means that even if the class is same throughout the ϵ ball, with a varying l the adversary still conducts a "supposed" attack and increases loss for the defender without flipping labels. For example, the well-known hinge loss varies rapidly within one of the classes and could overestimate the loss for defender and hence underestimate robustness.

Robustness vs Accuracy: Finally, we analyze the relation between accuracy and robustness. First, it is straightforward to check from definition that $1 - a$ robustness implies $1 - a$ accuracy. However, the converse is not true, and the example in Fig. 1 is a proof that the converse does not hold. In this example, assume the data is distributed uniformly over the 2d space and the true separator happens to be close to a large fraction of points in the given 2d space (an extreme example is where the separator is within ϵ of every point in the underlying space, in which case the separator is an ϵ-net). Then, the small misclassified parts (hence high accuracy) near the learned separator expands to produce

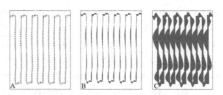

Fig. 1. Robustness vs Accuracy. (A) shows a piecewise linear classifier (solid line) is not able to exactly match the non-linear boundary (dashed line). (B) shows that the mis-classification space (red/shaded area) is small, hence accuracy is high. (C) shows that adversarial exploitable space (red/shaded area) is large, hence robustness is low. (Color figure online)

a large adversarial exploitable space (low robustness). Some defenses in literature [12] have tried to guarantee that the learned classifier does not change labels within an ϵ ball $B(x, \epsilon)$ of any (or most) given training data point x. This example (particularly, in the extreme case where the separator is an ϵ-net) shows that it may be the case the label changes legitimately in an ϵ ball around any data point x. Thus, the nature of the underlying ground truth is an important factor for robustness and its relation with accuracy. In the analysis in the next paragraph, we show that the data distribution is also another important factor.

Next, we analyze if accuracy is ever suitable to capture robustness. First, we make a few mild technical assumptions that there exists a density $p(x)$ for the data distribution $\mathcal{P}$ over X, X is a metric space with metric d and $vol(X) = 1$.

Theorem 1. $1 - a$ *accuracy implies at least* $1 - a - (\nu + K\epsilon/T)\mathcal{P}(E_{C,\epsilon}(X) \setminus M_C(X))$ *robustness for any output C if (1) For all $x \in X$, $\overline{sim}(x, x') \geq Td(x, x')$ for some $T > 0$, (2) $M_C(X)$ lies in a low density region, that is, for all $x \in M_C(X)$ we have $p(x) \leq \nu$ for some small ν, and (3) $p(x)$ is K-Lipschitz, that is, $|p(x) - p(x')| \leq Kd(x, x')$ for all $x, x' \in X$.*

The first two conditions above are quite natural. In simple words, these two conditions state that dissimilarity increases with distance (high T) and the regions where the classifier predicts badly has low amount of data in the data-set (low ν). However, the final condition may not be satisfied in many natural settings. This condition states that the data distribution must not change abruptly (low K). This is required as the natural behavior of most classifiers is to predict bad in a low data density region and if this region is near a high data density region, the adversary can successfully modify the data points in the high density region causing loss of robustness. But in high dimensional spaces, data distribution is quite likely to be not distributed smoothly with many pockets or sub-spaces of zero density as pointed out in a recent experimental work [22]. Thus, data distribution, especially in the region around the mis-classified space, has a huge effect on robustness.

Intuition Behind Attacks: *Any* adversarial example generation A can be seen as a distribution transformer F_A such that acting on the data distribution $\mathcal{P}$ the resultant distribution $F_A(\mathcal{P})$ has support mostly limited to $M_C(X)$. The support may not completely limited to $M_C(X)$ as the attacks are never 100% effective. Also, attacks typically aim to find points in $M_C(X)$ that are close to given images in the original dataset. See Fig. 2B for an illustration. As an example, a recent work [2] provides the adversarial transformation network (ATN) technique, which trains a DNN to produce adversarial examples. ATN is essentially a neural network representation of a distribution transformer function F. For other attack techniques like FGSM and CW, the function F is evaluated for each sample (data point) by solving an optimization problem, utilizing gradients of the classifier in case of FGSM.

High vs Low Perturbation: Lastly, we show in our experiments that FGSM produces adversarial examples whose perturbations are at least an order of magnitude higher than CW. We categorize FGSM as a high perturbation attack. On the other hand, the attack CW produces adversarial perturbation with very small perturbations; we call such attacks low perturbation attacks.

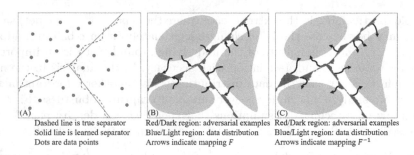

Dashed line is true separator   Red/Dark region: adversarial examples   Red/Dark region: adversarial examples
Solid line is learned separator   Blue/Light region: data distribution   Blue/Light region: data distribution
Dots are data points   Arrows indicate mapping F Arrows indicate mapping F^{-1}

Fig. 2. Intuition behind attacks and DLN. (A) shows a linear classifier (low capacity) is not able to accurately model a non-linear boundary. (B) shows attacks as the distribution mapping function F. (C) shows that DLN does the reverse mapping of attacks.

DLN: Our first defense approach is to insert a neural network DLN D between the input and classifier so that D sanitizes the input enabling the classifier to correctly classify the input. Each data point for training DLN has three parts: x' is the image to sanitize (input), x is the expected output and y_x is the correct label of x. The x's are always images from the provided dataset, and there are two possibilities for x': (1) $x' = x$ so that DLN attempts to satisfy $C(D(x)) = y_x$, even if $C(x) \neq y_x$, and (2) $x' = A(x)$ so that DLN undoes the attack and make the classifier C correctly classify $D(x')$. Thus, for training DLN, the original training set is attacked to produces $A(x)$'s and the training set for DLN is twice the original training set, with one half having $x' = x$ and another half having $x' = A(x)$. We formulate a loss function for DLN that has two terms: $\overline{sim}(x, D(x'))$ aims to produce output $D(x')$ close to x and $H(Cat(y_x), C_p(D(x')))$ aims to make the classifier output on $D(x')$ be the same as y_x. The loss function is

$$\overline{sim}(x, D(x')) + H(Cat(y_x), C_p(D(x'))) .$$

Note that the attack A is used as a black box here to generate training data and is not a part of the loss function. After training the DLN, our new classifier is C^1 which is C prepended by the DLN D, represented as $C^1 = \boxed{D \to C}$. The working of DLN can be interpreted as an inverse map F^{-1} for the mapping F induced by the attack A. See Fig. 2C for an illustration. For the image classification problem we use the l_2 distance for $\overline{sim}$.

Intuitively, as C^1 correctly classifies the adversarial examples in addition to correctly classifying more data points than C, it shrinks the mis-classification space of C^1 to within the mis-classifications of C. As argued when defining robustness, this leads to an increase in robustness for C^1 over C. See Fig. 3A for an illustration of how the mis-classification space of C^1 shrinks over that of C. Fig. 3(A and B) also motivate the repeated DLN below.

Repeated DLN: While the robustness of C^1 could be higher than C, unless the attack used discovers all potential exploitable data points of C, there may still be a lot of exploitable data points for C^1. This is why attacks on C^1 are still effective (see experiments). One approach to overcome this is to repeatedly attack and discover more of the exploitable space. DLN allows for efficient *modular retraining* (without retraining the classifier) of the DLN in rounds as follows: starting from $i = 0$, (A) attack the classifier $C^i = \boxed{D^{i-1} \to C}$ $(C^0 = C)$ at round i generating adversarial training data T_A from the original training data T; (B) (re)train the DLN with data T_i to get D^i, where T_i is formed by augmenting all the past data T_{i-1} $(T_0 = \phi)$ with T_A and T. Then, repeat step A with $i = i + 1$.

Observe that we add copies of original training data at each step i in order to prevent the adversarial data from swamping out the original training data. See Fig. 3 for an illustration of how repeated DLN works. Intuitively, in each round the exploitable space reduces providing less space for the attack to be successful. This makes the high perturbation attacks less effective within a few rounds.

In this attack-defense competition, in every round the dataset used to train the DLN grows. Practically, this requires DLN to have a large capacity in order to be effective; also depending on the capacity and the size of dataset over or under fitting problems could arise, which needs to be taken care of in practice. Also, the training becomes more expensive over rounds with increasing data size.

In particular, low perturbation attacks are not defeated within few rounds. We observed very small improvements with the low perturbation CW attack over rounds, as illustrated visually in Fig. 3 (C and D). The main reason, as shown in Fig. 3, is that low perturbation attacks only expose a very small volume of misclassified space, thus, fixing only a small part of the mis-classified space in every round of repeated DLN. Further, low perturbation attacks only need a small volume of misclassified space near the classifier boundary to be successful. It would require a huge number of rounds for repeated DLN to reduce the mis-classified space to such a small volume that cannot be

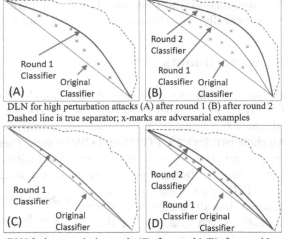

DLN for high perturbation attacks (A) after round 1 (B) after round 2 Dashed line is true separator; x-marks are adversarial examples

DLN for low perturbation attacks (C) after round 1 (D) after round 2

Fig. 3. Intuition behind working of repeated DLN against high and low perturbation attacks. (A), (B) shows a high perturbation attack causes a faster improvement in resultant classifier. Beyond some rounds the attack does not work as it can only find adversarial examples with high perturbation. (C), (D) shows a low perturbation attack causes a slow improvement in resultant classifier.

attacked. This motivates our next approach of noise augmented classifier.

NAC: Figure 3 provides a hint on how to overcome low perturbation attacks. Such attacks rely a lot on the knowledge about the exact classifier boundary in order to add a very small perturbation and yet change the label of input image. Thus, randomly shifting the classifier boundary may help against low perturbation attacks. We shift the boundary randomly by adding a small noise to the logits of the DNN (the last layer of the DNN that yields the class probabilities) C at *inference time only* calling the resultant classifier a noise augmented classifier (NAC) C^N. Through experimentation we chose a Gaussian noise with mean 0 and standard deviation 1. This noise is small enough that it does not affect the classification of original data points by much, but is able to mis-lead the low perturbation attack. Also, following our explanation, NAC should not provide any defense against high perturbation attacks, which we observe in our experiments.

As NAC defense is a inference time (runtime) technique, hence, NAC can be used in conjunction with any other training time defense, such as DLN. Further, according to our attack model, the adversary does not have access to the noise added to the logit layer. However, a natural idea to bypass the NAC defense is to take the average of multiple logit outputs for the same input image (to cancel the randomness) and then use the average logits for the CW attack. We show experimentally that this improved attack does not work effectively.

3 Experiments

All our experiments were conducted using the Keras framework on a NVIDIA K40 GPU. We consider two classifiers one for MNIST and one for CIFAR-10: we call them C_M and C_C. These classifiers are variants of well-known architectures. We show two attacks: FGSM and CW to show their categorization into high and low perturbation attacks. Attacks were used with default parameters. CW, while slow to run, has been referred to in the literature [25] as the best attack till date, while FGSM runs extremely fast. Observe that all these attacks work against a given classifier C, thus, we use the notation $A(C,.)$ to denote the attack A acting on an image x to produce the adversarial example $A(C, x)$ (A can be any of the three attacks). $A(C, Z)$ denotes

Table 1. Attacks on MNIST and CIFAR-10

Test data type	Accuracy	Distortion
FGSM(C_M, OTD)	0.72 %	14.99
CW(C_M, OTD)	0.03 %	1.51
FGSM(C_C, OTD)	4.21 %	10.03
CW(C_C, OTD)	0 %	0.18

the set of adversarial examples $\{A(C, x) \mid x \in Z\}$. We report accuracies on various test sets: (A) original test dataset (OTD): this is the original test set from the dataset under consideration, (B) $A(C, OTD)$ is the adversarially perturbed test data using attack A, for example, this could be FGSM(C_M, OTD). We also report distortion numbers as done in prior work [5]. Distortion is the average over all test images of the l_2 distance between the original and perturbed image.

Table 1 shows the result of attacks using FGSM and CW on MNIST and CIFAR-10. It can be seen that FGSM produces higher distortion than CW. For defense, we denote the new classifier using the DLN with i rounds of training as C_M^i (for MNIST) or C_C^i (for CIFAR); analogously for NAC we get C_M^N or C_C^N, and for both DLN and NAC we get $C_M^{i,N}$ or $C_C^{i,N}$. Also, we test accuracies on the adversarially perturbed test data against the newer classifiers, e.g., following our convention one such dataset would be denoted as $A(C_M^i, OTD)$.

DLN Defense Against Single Attack: Table 2 shows the results when DLN is trained to defend against FGSM or CW using MNIST dataset to yield a new classifier C_M^1. As expected, the accuracy on OTD drops slightly for all the cases. Moreover, when attacked again the new classifier C_M^1 is not resilient to attacks as shown by the low accuracies for FGSM(C_M^1, OTD) and CW(C_M^1, OTD). One number that stands out is the success of the new classifier C_M^1 in correctly classifying the adversarial examples CW(C_M, OTD) generated by CW (row 5). This supports our hypothesis that CW is sensitive to the exact classifier boundary, and a newer classifier C_M^1 with a slightly different boundary is able to correctly classify prior adversarial examples. Of course, CW is able to attack C_M^1 again successfully. For FGSM, we show next that the performance of the classifier greatly improves when DLN is repeatedly trained against FGSM.

Table 2. Performance of DLN prepended C_M^1 for MNIST

DLN Trained	Test data type	Accuracy	Distortion
FGSM	OTD	96.77%	–
FGSM	FGSM(C_M, OTD)	88.5%	4.55
FGSM	FGSM(C_M^1, OTD)	13.75%	6.98
CW	OTD	98.6%	–
CW	CW(C_M, OTD)	95.42%	5.77
CW	CW(C_M^1, OTD)	0.14%	3.5

Table 3. DLN trained repeatedly against FGSM for MNIST

Round	Acc. OTD	Acc. FGSM(C_M^i, OTD)	Distortion
0	99.36%	0.72%	14.99
1	97.70%	13.70%	13.63
2	97.61%	24.86%	14.58
3	97.95%	43.39%	14.73
4	97.79%	52.88%	14.57
5	97.77%	56.57%	14.52

Repeated DLN: Next, we run DLN repeatedly as described earlier. We cut off the experiments when a single round took more than 48 hours to solve. We show the results for MNIST in Table 3 showing a clearly increasing trend in accuracy on adversarial examples produced by FGSM attacking the newer

Table 4. Accuracy of NAC for MNIST and CIFAR-10

Attack	Test data type	Accuracy	Distortion
-	OTD(MNIST)	99.36%	-
CW	CW(C_M^N, OTD)	93.60%	1.49
FGSM	FGSM(C_M^N, OTD)	0.74%	14.99
-	OTD(CIFAR)	84.67%	-
CW	CW(C_C^N, OTD)	77.70%	0.17
FGSM	FGSM(C_C^N, OTD)	4.19%	10.04

classifier, revealing increasing robustness. For CIFAR, the approach becomes too computationally expensive within two rounds. Further, as stated earlier, DLN does not show much improvement against low perturbation attacks like CW. We tackle that next using the NAC defense.

NAC Defense: The NAC defense produces a new classifier C_M^N for MNIST and C_C^N for CIFAR. The second and fifth row in Table 4 shows that the NAC defense leads to a failure of the CW attack. Further, the new classifier's accuracy on the original test data-set is nearly unchanged. However, it can also be observed that the new classifier is not resilient to attack by FGSM, as shown by the third and sixth row, which follows from the intuition in Fig. 3.

Table 5. NAC classifier C_M^N against improved CW for MNIST

n	Adv. accuracy	Distortion
500	95.14 %	1.51
5000	82.07 %	1.51

As stated earlier, a natural idea to attack NAC would be to query an image n times and then average the logits before using it for the CW attack. This improved attack does make CW more effective but not by much. Table 5 shows that the accuracy on the adversarial example generated for C_M^N remains high. Moreover, more queries make it more difficult to conduct attacks in practice (e.g., query limited adversary), while also causing an increase (2% with 5000 samples) in the already high runtime of CW.

Defense Against Multiple Attacks: Finally, we show that DLN and NAC can work together. We show the accuracy on the adversarial example generated in each round of DLN repetition when the classifier C^i after each round is augmented with NAC $C^{i,N}$ and then attacked by FGSM and

Table 6. Classifier trained repeatedly against FGSM for MNIST and augmented with NAC in each round

Round	Acc. OTD	Acc. FGSM $(C_M^{i,N}, OTD)$	Acc. CW $(C_C^{i,N}, OTD)$
0	99.36 %	0.72 %	94.2
1	97.70 %	13.72 %	93.7
2	97.73 %	24.28 %	84.7
3	97.60 %	43.20 %	83.3
4	97.64 %	53.17 %	79
5	97.73 %	56.45 %	79.3

CW both. See Table 6. One observation is that NAC's performance decreases slightly over rounds stabilizing at 79%, while the accuracy for original test set and FGSM perturbed test set stays almost exactly same as Table 3.

4   Related Work and Summary

A thorough survey of security issues in machine learning, including types of attacks, is present in surveys [3,20,23] and some of the first results appeared in [16]. Here we discuss only the most closely related defense work.

Defense: Defense techniques can be roughly categorized into training time techniques that do (1) adversarial (re)training, which is adding back adversarial examples to the training data and retraining the classifier, often repeatedly [14], or modifying loss function to account for attacks [11,12]; (2) gradient masking, which targets that gradient based attacks by trying to make the gradient less informative [19]; (3) input modification, which are techniques that modify (typically lower the dimension) the feature space of the input data to make crafting adversarial examples difficult [25]; (4) game-theoretic formulation, which modifies the loss minimization to a constrained optimization with constraints provided by adversarial utility in performing perturbations [13], and (5) filtering and denoising [6,10,15,18], which aims to filter or de-noise adversarial examples.

Our DLN approach differs from the first four kinds of defense as our approach never modifies the classifier or its inputs but adds a sanitizer (DLN) before the classifier. Our approach, while similar in spirit to adversarial re-training, increases the capacity of the resultant classifier C^i, so that it can model more complex separators which is not achieved when the classifier family stays the same. Also, the re-training is not of the whole network but just the DLN module, which is faster than re-training large classifiers. Next, unlike the fifth kind of defense, our goal for DLN is targeted sanitization and not generic de-noising; we aim to reduce mis-classifications which means correctly classifiying adversarial examples as well as original mis-classifications. More significantly, attempts such as MagNet [18] reach a wrong conclusion that they defend against CW [4]. In contrast, we repeatedly attacked the new DLN classifier showing that a sanitizing approach like DLN cannot defend against low perturbation attacks.

As far as we know, NAC being a runtime technique, is novel and entirely different from training time approaches; moreover, NAC is compatible with any other training time approach. Interestingly, the DLN and NAC approaches can be used with any classifier that outputs class probabilities and not just DNNs.

Summary. We provided a new perspective of the adversarial examples defense problem with a formal intuition of how our approach works, using which we were able to defend simultaneously against multiple attacks including the potent CW attack. We identified two classes of attacks: high and low perturbation, and proposed the DLN technique to defend against high perturbation attacks and NAC to defender against low perturbation attacks. Extensions of our theory and tuning of the application framework provides rich content for future work.

References

1. Anthony, M., Bartlett, P.L.: Neural Network Learning: Theoretical Foundations, 1st edn. Cambridge University Press, New York (2009)
2. Baluja, S., Fischer, I.: Adversarial transformation networks: learning to generate adversarial examples. CoRR abs/1703.09387 (2017). http://arxiv.org/abs/1703.09387
3. Biggio, B., Roli, F.: Wild patterns: ten years after the rise of adversarial machine learning. arXiv preprint arXiv:1712.03141 (2017)
4. Carlini, N., Wagner, D.: Magnet and "efficient defenses against adversarial attacks" are not robust to adversarial examples. arXiv preprint arXiv:1711.08478 (2017)

5. Carlini, N., Wagner, D.: Towards evaluating the robustness of neural networks. In: 2017 IEEE Symposium on Security and Privacy (SP), pp. 39–57. IEEE (2017)
6. Chen, X., Li, B., Vorobeychik, Y.: Evaluation of defensive methods for DNNs against multiple adversarial evasion models (2016). https://openreview.net/forum?id=ByToKu9ll&noteId=ByToKu9ll
7. Cisse, M., Bojanowski, P., Grave, E., Dauphin, Y., Usunier, N.: Parseval networks: improving robustness to adversarial examples. arXiv preprint arXiv:1704.08847 (2017)
8. Fawzi, A., Fawzi, O., Frossard, P.: Fundamental limits on adversarial robustness. In: Proceedings of ICML, Workshop on Deep Learning (2015)
9. Goodfellow, I.J., Shlens, J., Szegedy, C.: Explaining and harnessing adversarial examples. CoRR abs/1412.6572 (2014). http://arxiv.org/abs/1412.6572
10. Grosse, K., Manoharan, P., Papernot, N., Backes, M., McDaniel, P.: On the (statistical) detection of adversarial examples. arXiv preprint arXiv:1702.06280 (2017)
11. Huang, R., Xu, B., Schuurmans, D., Szepesvári, C.: Learning with a strong adversary. arXiv preprint arXiv:1511.03034 (2015)
12. Kolter, J.Z., Wong, E.: Provable defenses against adversarial examples via the convex outer adversarial polytope. arXiv preprint arXiv:1711.00851 (2017)
13. Li, B., Vorobeychik, Y.: Feature cross-substitution in adversarial classification. In: Advances in Neural Information Processing Systems, pp. 2087–2095 (2014)
14. Li, B., Vorobeychik, Y., Chen, X.: A general retraining framework for scalable adversarial classification. arXiv preprint arXiv:1604.02606 (2016)
15. Li, X., Li, F.: Adversarial examples detection in deep networks with convolutional filter statistics. arXiv preprint arXiv:1612.07767 (2016)
16. Lowd, D., Meek, C.: Adversarial learning. In: ACM SIGKDD. ACM (2005)
17. Madry, A., Makelov, A., Schmidt, L., Tsipras, D., Vladu, A.: Towards deep learning models resistant to adversarial attacks. arXiv preprint arXiv:1706.06083 (2017)
18. Meng, D., Chen, H.: Magnet: a two-pronged defense against adversarial examples. In: ACM Conference on Computer and Communications Security (2017)
19. Papernot, N., McDaniel, P., Goodfellow, I., Jha, S., Celik, Z.B., Swami, A.: Practical black-box attacks against deep learning systems using adversarial examples. arXiv preprint arXiv:1602.02697 (2016)
20. Papernot, N., McDaniel, P., Sinha, A., Wellman, M.: Towards the science of security and privacy in machine learning. arXiv preprint arXiv:1611.03814 (2016)
21. Sinha, A., Kar, D., Tambe, M.: Learning adversary behavior in security games: a PAC model perspective. In: Conference on Autonomous Agents & Multiagent Systems (2016)
22. Tramèr, F., Papernot, N., Goodfellow, I., Boneh, D., McDaniel, P.: The space of transferable adversarial examples. arXiv preprint arXiv:1704.03453 (2017)
23. Tygar, J.: Adversarial machine learning. IEEE Internet Comput. 15(5), 4–6 (2011)
24. Wang, B., Gao, J., Qi, Y.: A theoretical framework for robustness of (deep) classifiers under adversarial noise. arXiv preprint arXiv:1612.00334 (2016)
25. Xu, W., Evans, D., Qi, Y.: Feature squeezing: detecting adversarial examples in deep neural networks. arXiv preprint arXiv:1704.01155 (2017)

Towards True Decentralization: A Blockchain Consensus Protocol Based on Game Theory and Randomness

Naif Alzahrani[✉] and Nirupama Bulusu

Portland State University, Portland, OR 97207, USA
{nalza2,nbulusu}@pdx.edu

Abstract. One of the fundamental characteristics of blockchain technology is the consensus protocol. Most of the current consensus protocols are PoW (Proof of Work) based, or fixed-validators based. Nevertheless, PoW requires massive computational effort, which results in high energy and computing resources consumption. Alternatively, fixed-validators protocols rely on fixed, static validators responsible for validating all newly proposed blocks, which opens the door for adversaries to launch several attacks on these validators such as DDoS and eclipse attacks. In this paper, we propose a truly decentralized consensus protocol that does not require PoW and randomly employs a different set of different size of validators on each block's proposal. Additionally, our protocol utilizes a game theoretical model to enforce the honest validators' behavior by rewarding honest validators and penalizing dishonest ones. We have analyzed our protocol and shown that it mitigates various attacks that current protocols suffer from.

Keywords: Blockchain · Consensus protocol · Game Theory
Randomness

1 Introduction

Over the last few years, blockchain technology has been an attractive solution for many different industries. The reasoning behind this is the transparency, security, quality assurance, global peer-to-peer transactions, and decentralization that blockchain technology provides [17]. Despite its potential to elevate security, as with all new technologies, security risks can be found beneath the hype [19]. Moreover, blockchain technology has introduced new kinds of attacks such as *block withholding* and *selfish mining* attacks. Such attacks occur for various incentives, mostly financial. To defend against such attacks and to strengthen blockchain security, *game theory* stands out as a potentially powerful means.

Fundamentally, a blockchain is a public, distributed ledger that contains chained blocks, each of which is made up of several transactions. These blocks are validated globally and transparently to guarantee security. This validation has

© Springer Nature Switzerland AG 2018
L. Bushnell et al. (Eds.): GameSec 2018, LNCS 11199, pp. 465–485, 2018.
https://doi.org/10.1007/978-3-030-01554-1_27

to be executed without the need for a central authority. Instead, the blocks are validated, shared and synchronized across nodes via a peer-to-peer, distributed, and decentralized consensus mechanism [15].

One of the fundamental characteristics of blockchain technology is the consensus protocol. In a blockchain, a consensus protocol ensures that all nodes in the blockchain network agree on the validity of a block to be included in the public ledger. It also guarantees that all nodes have the same order of blocks in their blockchains. This is of significance because blockchains are trustless distributed nodes which need a way to synchronize their copies of stored data. The nodes responsible for executing consensus protocols are the validators (or miners in some blockchains). There are a considerable number of existing consensus protocols. Nonetheless, not all of them guarantee the *true decentralization*, in which the blocks' validation is executed by anonymous, variable sets of validators to strengthen the protocol's robustness. Instead, they rely on fixed, known validators selected at the genesis state. This opens the door for various risk threats which will be discussed shortly. Besides, most of the current consensus protocols do not take the number of validators or how to select them into consideration, as will be discussed in Sect. 2. The number of validators in a blockchain network influences its security and efficiency substantially, especially in a fully decentralized blockchain, in which there are no special nodes, and all nodes are trustless.

In this paper, we mainly address the problem of validators' selection in terms of *how to select them* and *how many to select* to achieve a satisfiable trade-off between security and efficiency. Also, we study the incentives of malicious nodes to deviate from the consensus protocols, and we apply a game theoretical model to enforce honest behavior.

The first and most popular consensus protocol to secure and decentralize blockchains is the **Proof of Work (PoW)**. This protocol requires powerful nodes known as *miners* to validate the blocks. This consensus approach, however, demands massive computational effort from the miners, which ultimately results in high consumption in energy and computing resources. Additionally, the PoW protocol relies on a few mining pools (often just 2 or 3 mining pools), which raises doubt on the decentralization of PoW-based blockchains [7]. Furthermore, such blockchains frequently fork. As a result, the blockchain nodes are not able to rely on a new block as soon as it appears. Alternatively, they must wait until this block is deep enough in the chain, which results in very high latency [7].

An alternative approach that does not require the expensive PoW computation and, therefore, enhances *efficiency* is **Fixed-Validators Decentralization**. In this approach, a small fixed number of nodes are chosen to be validators. This approach ensures the integrity of the blockchain as long as the majority of the validators are honest. The validators are selected at the genesis state, and they are, usually, selected based on the stake they have. However, the efficiency of such protocols is influenced by the number of selected validators. This is because each validator performs some work to check the validity of a block and communicates with each other validator in the committee to reach a consensus. This incurs computation and communication overhead proportional to the committee size. The validators agree on a block to be included in the chain if the block is digitally signed by a majority of them.

Although the fixed-validators approach is efficient, it has several limitations. First, it relies on an extreme trust assumption that the majority of validators are honest; nevertheless, it is possible for a powerful adversary to corrupt or bribe most of them over time [6]. Second, a fixed committee of validators is vulnerable to adversarial attacks, since they are known and fixed. For example, an adversary can launch a DoS attack against the validators, preventing them from validating new blocks or receiving messages from each other. Third, although this approach is efficient, utilizing a relatively small number of validators in a large network with a massive number of transactions or blocks can bottleneck the performance.

The second alternative approach is **True Decentralization**, in which every node in the system can be chosen to be a member of the validators. In such an approach, a set of validators are selected randomly from the set of "all nodes" in each round of validation. In other words, it does not require a single set of validators to execute all rounds. As a result, the true decentralization approach distributes the validation work among all nodes and can withstand the powerful adversaries. Note that the fixed-validators approach is defined on the same group of validators and do not support validators' replaceability. In response to this, we propose a novel, truly decentralized consensus protocol that selects a different set of random validators on every block proposal.

Despite the security provided by the true decentralization, it does not guarantee that the validators are always honest and do not deviate from the protocol. For example, a dishonest validator might perform a block withholding attack (see Sect. 4) in favor of a malicious proposing node (i.e., the node which creates and proposes the new block). This attack can result in undermining the consensus process. To overcome such vulnerability, we integrate a game theoretical model into our consensus protocol to reward honest validators and to punish dishonest or lazy validators that do not adhere to the protocol. Additionally, the always-validation (i.e., validators always validate even if the risk likelihood of a block's proposer is low) is a performance shortcoming particularly found in blockchains with low hostility. Thus, utilizing a game theoretical model that enables validators to validate with some probability proportional to the proposers' risk likelihoods would significantly enhance the protocol efficiency.

The contribution of this paper is a *new consensus* protocol that deals with the problem of selecting validators and has the following advantages:

1. It achieves the true decentralization by selecting a *different set of validators* on every block proposal at random.
2. The *number of the selected validators* is dynamic and variable. Hence, instead of selecting a fixed static number of validators, our protocol utilizes game theory to select a different number of validators (on every block proposal) proportional to the *risk likelihood* of the proposing node.
3. The game theoretical approach exploited by our protocol accomplishes the following further benefits:

(a) It enforces the honest validators behavior by rewarding honest validators and penalizing dishonest ones.
(b) It enhances the efficiency by eliminating the *always-validation* mode. Thus, the validators validate with probability proportional to the *risk likelihood* of the proposing node.

2   Related Work

In this section, we will examine some related existing works. The related literature falls into two general camps: (1) current, widely-used consensus protocols, and (2) works that integrate blockchain and game theory.

2.1   Consensus Protocols

In this section, we present only the BFT (Byzantine Fault Tolerance) protocols, since they are more relevant to our proposed protocol.

Tendermint [3, 12] is a consensus BFT protocol that can work even if up to one-third of nodes in the network fail in arbitrary ways. It does not require the PoW mining, which overcomes the energy and resources consumption issues. Instead, it relies on a fixed, static set of validators (i.e., fixed-validators decentralization) selected at the genesis state to validate the new block and vote on them. In Tendermint, a proposer *proposes* a new block, then the validators *pre-vote* on the block and only proceed to *pre-commit* if they receive more than 2/3 of *pre-votes*. Validators only accept the block if more than 2/3 of *pre-commits* are received. Tendermint is notable for its simplicity, performance, and fork-accountability [13]. Our protocol is based on Tendermint and inherits all the features offered by Tendermint. However, it deals with the validators' selection issue by selecting a different random set of validators on each block proposal (i.e., true decentralization).

Hyperledger Fabric is a BFT consensus algorithm [9], which can tolerate up to one-third byzantine nodes in a blockchain network. In Fabric v0.6, there exists a fixed number of *validation peers* responsible for executing the consensus protocol. A proposer can submit a transaction to any of them. Then, the chosen peer broadcasts this transaction to the other peers. One of the validation peers is selected as a *leader*. When generating a block, the leader broadcasts it to all peers. When a validation peer receives this block, it hashes it, broadcasts the hash to all other peers, and begins counting their responses. If two-thirds of the responses were received with the same hash, it commits the new block to its local ledger. Hyperledger Fabric, like Tendermint, employs a fixed known number of validation peers.

In our previous work [2], we presented a protocol based on Tendermint and, hence, can tolerate up to one-third of Byzantine faulty nodes. This protocol overcomes the fixed set of validators that Tendermint suffers from and utilizes the randomness to select a different set of *log n* validators each time a new block is proposed (where n is the number of nodes in the network). This protocol outperformed Tendermint and achieved a remarkable performance with a satisfactory level of security. Nevertheless, this protocol is vulnerable to attacks such as block withholding. This paper aims to overcome the limitations presented in our previous work.

2.2 Blockchain and Game Theory

Although blockchain technology has gained considerable attention from the computer science and economics communities, the use of game theory methods in this technology is limited [16]. In this section, we present the most relevant and recent works that utilize game theory in blockchain technology.

Xu et al. [20] proposed a game theoretical approach to suppress the attack motivation on a blockchain that consists of mobile devices and edge servers. The game is formulated between a mobile device and an edge server, where the mobile device can send a request to the server to acquire a real-time service or launch an attack. On the other hand, the server chooses to either provide the service or to attack the mobile device. The authors introduced a punishment mechanism according to the action record to mitigate the attacks on the blockchain. They have concluded that both players tend to behave finely when the punishment weight is significant. The proposed approach was designed to deal with attacks like zero-day attack, DDOS attacks, and password-based attacks.

Johnson et al. [10] employed a game theoretical model to analyze the incentives for a mining pool to launch a DDoS attack against another mining pool. The players in the game are two competing mining pools, where each one may utilize additional computing resources to increase the chance of winning the mining race, or to trigger a DDoS attack to lower the expected success of the other competing mining pool.

Luu et al. [14] studied the block withholding attack on mining pools using a game theoretical approach by formulating the Bitcoin mining as a game. They analyzed the block withholding attack and concluded that the attack is profitable and well-incentivized in the long-term. The authors derived the game equilibrium state, which is a mixed strategy where all clients are incentivized to attack rather than participate honestly to maximize their payoffs. Finally, the authors concluded that the PoW protocol is vulnerable to such an attack.

In a paper entitled 'The Miner's Dilemma', Eyal [5] studies the scenario when pools attack each other. Open pools (i.e., pools of miners that allow any miner to join the mining work) are vulnerable to block withholding attacks performed by infiltrated miners from competing pools. This paper defines a game where pools recruit some of their participants to infiltrate other pools to diminish their mining capabilities. This game is called the miner's dilemma where players are two pools, and their strategies are whether or not to attack each other. The author observes that attacking is the dominant strategy for each player.

All the above works have introduced game theoretical approaches to the PoW mining protocol. As previously discussed in Sect. 1, PoW is not an attractive approach for blockchains that are efficient-sensitive due to its massive computation demands. In a more relevant work presented by Kiayias et al. [11], Ouroboros consensus protocol was proposed. Similar to our protocol, Ouroboros eliminates the need for an energy-hungry PoW protocol. Ouroboros is based on the Proof of Stake (PoS) protocol. It works by dividing the time into rounds called slots in which each slot is assigned to a leader. The leaders are picked based on the stake they have. A chosen leader is responsible for producing a block for its time slot. The authors utilized game theory to introduce a reward mechanism to incentivize the participants in the blockchain. By means of the game theoretical design, attacks such as selfish-mining and block withholding are mitigated. The rewarding mechanism works by awarding a positive payoff for participants who do not diverge from the protocol.

3   The Proposed Consensus Protocol

In this paper, we propose a new consensus protocol that exploits randomness and game theory to achieve true decentralization security with respect to efficiency. Our protocol is based on Tendermint and exploits its capability to overcome up to one-third of Byzantine faults. Unlike other protocols that rely on a fixed, static set of validators responsible for validating all proposed blocks, our protocol randomly selects a different set of different size of validators each time a new block is proposed. Thus, it improves the security, since the validators are not known before proposing the new block. Further, the number of validators employed in the consensus process is also unknown. These two factors make the job more difficult for an adversary to attack or bribe the set of validators. In respect to efficiency, our protocol distributes the validation work among nodes by selecting different sets of validators for different blocks instead of relying on the same static fixed set of validators for all proposed blocks. This is of significant concern, especially in a blockchain with a small number of validators and a massive number of transactions, or blocks. Additionally, the efficiency is enhanced, as not all selected validators upon proposing a new block will validate that block. Instead, a validator validates with a probability based on the outcomes of a game played between the proposing node and this validator. This saves a substantial computational cost, particular, in a low hostility blockchain environment.

Each node in the blockchain has a unique pair of keys (public pk and secret sk) and is identified by its public key. Moreover, each node has a public trust (reputation) value R where this value affect the selection of a node to be validator over time. There are four types of nodes in our protocol:

1. **Proposing (proposer):** This is the node which creates, proposes, and broadcasts to the network the new block.
2. **Validation-leader:** This is the node responsible for selecting the random set of validators for the proposing node.
3. **Validator:** This node is responsible for validating the newly proposed block. Moreover, validators communicate their votes on the block to reach consensus.

4. **Idle:** This node does nothing except wait for the decision to be made by validators on whether to accept or reject the block. All other nodes in the network are idle.

Our protocol works in two phases: the initialization phase, and the verification (validation) phase. The blockchain initiator executes the first phase at the genesis state, in which it randomly maps each proposer to its validation-leaders. In the second phase, each node becomes a proposer in a round-robin fashion. When a node is a proposer, it proposes a block, broadcasts it to all nodes, and its corresponding validation-leaders randomly select the validators to verify (validate) this block. In this phase, a two-stage attacker-defender game is proposed, where the proposer is the potential attacker (i.e., player x) in both stages. The defenders (i.e, player y) in the first-stage are the validation-leaders. The defenders in the second-stage are the validators (i.e., player z) that have been selected by the validation-leaders from the first-stage. Next two subsections present an in-depth description of how these two phases are executed.

3.1   Initialization Phase

This phase's main task is *mapping proposers to validation-leaders*. At the genesis state (i.e., when the genesis block is proposed), the blockchain initiator randomly maps four validation-leaders to each proposer in the network. The reasoning behind this choice is that four is the minimum number to provide tolerance to a single Byzantine fault [3]. This is because our protocol is based on Tendermint, and it is assumed that a Tendermint network has two-thirds of non-Byzantine nodes. A simple approach is to employ only one validation-leader per a proposer, however, to ensure safety and liveness of the consensus process, we need to utilize more. It is worth noting that this number (i.e., four) can be changed based on factors like the network's size and hostility, or the blockchain application that utilizes our protocol. Our approach works with any number of validation-leaders per proposer other than four, but we utilizes the minimum in favor of efficiency. Additionally, this number can be a random number to further increase robustness.

The mapping is executed randomly according to the nodes weights (reputations R). As shown in Algorithm 1, we use the Weighted Random Sampling (WRS) algorithm [4]. The weights in our algorithm are the nodes' reputation values. Furthermore, this mapping is done blindly; that is, no proposer knows its corresponding validation-leaders and no validation-leader knows its proposer until executing the consensus protocol. This way, we prevent a malicious proposer from corrupting or bribing its validation-leaders and vise versa.

To accomplish the anonymous mapping, the blockchain initiator, first, includes a secret S_1 in every node's genesis block, so it uses this secret when the node becomes a proposer. S_1 is a hash that includes the proposer's public key $pr.pk$, all the four selected the validation-leaders' public keys $[vl_1.pk - vl_4.pk]$, the blockchain ID $blockchainID$, and a random number $Rand_1$ as flows:

$$S_1 \leftarrow hash(pr.pk||vl_1.pk||vl_2.pk||vl_3.pk||vl_4.pk||blockcahinID||Rand_1)$$

Note that there is only one proposer secret S_1. Each proposer in the network has its own S_1. This secret is checked by each of the four validation-leaders.

Second, blockchain initiator generates a validation-leader's secret S_2. S_2 is a hash that includes the proposer's secret S_1, and a random number $Rand_2$ as flows:

$$S_2 \leftarrow hash(S_1 || Rand_2)$$

Here, we use different $Rand_2$ for each validation-leader to make S_2 different for each one of them. Note that $Rand_2$ is private and is only known to its particular validation-leader node.

To ensure that a validation-leader is *legitimate*, and that it has been elected by the blockchain initiator, we need to utilize a verifiable proof π. This proof is a digital signature signed by the initiator using its private key $in.sk$. The proof π includes the proposer's public key $pr.pk$, the validation-leader's public key $vl.pk$, and the blockchain ID $blockchainID$ as below.

$$\pi \leftarrow Sign_{in.sk}(pr.pk || vl_i.pk || blockcahinID)$$

The validation-leader must submit this proof to its elected validators so that each can verify π using the initiator's public key $in.pk$ prior to involving in the validation and consensus process. This protects against malicious nodes claiming that they are validation-leaders for a proposer.

As mentioned, for one proposer, there exists four leaders responsible for selecting the validators for the block proposed by this particular proposer. This arises a new problem of selection conflict, since each validation-leader selects the validators blindly without knowing its peer leaders. Consequently, the four leaders perform the validators' selection from the same pool of nodes without any communication or agreement between them. This can result in selecting a validator more than once by different leaders. Our protocol overcomes this problem by dividing the pool of nodes into four pools, each of which is assigned to a leader. Specifically, each validation-leader will have a range g to choose from determined at the genesis state. Note, we assume that all the nodes in the network have the same set of nodes in the same order. As shown in Algorithm 1, g is predetermined by the blockchain initiator and is defined as below:

$$g \leftarrow [((i-1).\frac{n}{4}) + 1, i.\frac{n}{4}]$$

where $1 \leq i \leq 4$ and is the index of a validation-leader among its peers.

In Algorithm 1, there are three lists. The first one (A) is a population of n nodes each of which has a reputation value R. The second list (B) is a temporary list for a proposer to hold the public keys for the selected validation-leaders. This list is flushed after selecting the validation-leaders and initializing their secrets and proofs. The last list (C) is for a validation-leader. There exists four corresponding proposers for each validation-leader. Thus, C stores four tuples, and each of them corresponds to one proposer. Each tuple includes the secret S_2, the random number $Rand_2$, the proof π, and the range g. By the end of executing

---

Algorithm 1. Proposers to leaders Mapping

    Input   : A population A of n nodes having reputation values

1 **foreach** $pr \in A$ **do**

2   **for** $k \leftarrow 1$ **to** 4 **do**

3   **Try:**

4          $p_i(k) \leftarrow \frac{R_i}{\Sigma_{s_j \in A - B} R_j}$

5   **Randomly** select vl_i **with** probability $p_i(k)$ **from** $A - B$

6   **if** $C_i.size > 4$ **then**

7 | Go to **Try**

8   **else**

9 | $B.add(vl_i.pk)$

10   **end**

11   **end**

12   **Randomly** generate $Rand_1$

13      $S_1 \leftarrow hash(pr.pk||vl_1.pk||vl_2.pk||vl_3.pk||vl_4.pk||blockcahinID||Rand_1)$

14   **Append** S_1 to the pr's genesis block

15   **foreach** $vl_i \in B$ **do**

16   **Randomly** generate $Rand_2$

17          $S_2 \leftarrow hash(S_1||Rand_2)$

18          $\pi \leftarrow Sign_{in.sk}(pr.pk||vl_i.pk||blockcahinID)$

19          $g \leftarrow [((i-1).\frac{n}{4}) + 1 \,, i.\frac{n}{4}]$

20          $C_i.add(S_2||Rand_2||\pi||g)$

21   **end**

22   **Flush** B

23 **end**

Algorithm 1, each node in the network will have exactly one proposer's secret S_1 used when the node becomes a proposing node, and a list C used whenever this node becomes a validation-leader for one of its four proposing nodes.

3.2 Verification (Validation) Phase

This phase is executed upon proposing a new block. It is carried out by three parties (proposer, validation-leaders, and validators). The main purpose of this phase to decide the validity of the newly proposed block and to reach a consensus on this decision.

When a node becomes a proposer, it broadcasts its secret S_1 to all nodes in the network. Every other node checks if it is a validation-leader for this proposer by looping through its list C and hashing the received S_1 and each private random number $Rand_2$ it has. If the resulting hash matches its secret S_2, then this node is a validation-leader for this proposer as shown in Algorithm 2.

After a node decides that it is a leader for the proposer, this leader plays the first-stage game with the proposer to decide how many validators (m) to select.

First-Stage Game. This game takes place between the proposer (i.e., player x) and each of its validation-leaders (i.e., player y). The validation-leader deter-

---

Algorithm 2. Validation-leader checking

Input   : The node's list C, and the received proposing node's secret S_1
Output: A decision of weather or not this node is a validation-leader
1 decision $\leftarrow$ false
2 **foreach** $tuple_i \in C$ **do**
3 | **if** $S_2^i = hash(S_1^i \| Rand_2^i)$ **then**
4 | | decision $\leftarrow$ True
5 | **end**
6 **end**
7 **Return** decision

---

mines the number of validators based on the outcome of the game. There are two strategies for the validation-leader from which to choose. The first one is to *UseMinimumValidators* where the minimum is four validators. The second strategy is to *AddMoreValidators* where the number of validators varies based on the outcome of the game, which is proportional to the risk likelihood of the proposer. The strategy profile for the second player (i.e., the proposer) is (a) *Cheat*, and (b) *NotCheat*. A proposer could be of two types: *malicious* or *regular*. Our game is considered to be a one-to-four game where each of the four leaders has no cooperation with the other leaders, so, we consider each game between a leader and the proposer as an independent event. Since the validation-leader do not know the type of player x (i.e., regular or malicious), we model our game as a Bayesian game. This is because the leader node (player y) in our model has incomplete information about the game. Player x, however, has this private information about its type known only to it.

Strategic Form of First-Stage Bayesian Game. First, we model our game as a strategic form as shown in Tables 2 and 3. Table 1 shows the notation used in our game theoretical approach. It is worth mentioning the importance of the proposer (β), and how it is obtained is not discussed in this paper due to space limitation. Table 2 shows the payoff matrix of the game when player x is of type *malicious*. For each cell in the payoff matrix, the first payoff is for player x and the second one is for player y. Table 3 shows the payoff matrix of the game when player x is of type *regular*. The goal of both players x and y is to maximize their payoffs. We assume that the players are rational.

Extensive Form of First-Stage Bayesian Game. The Bayesian game introduces a third player called Nature (denoted by N), which determines the type of player x by assigning a probability (μ) to player x of being *malicious*. Figure 1 represents the the Bayesian game extensive form. μ can be assigned according to the environment of the network, which can be learned dynamically by multi-stage games. A higher value of μ is given when the environment is hostile.

Bayesian Nash Equilibrium (BNE) Analysis

A. Game Pure-Strategy BNE: In this section, we analyze BNE assuming that player x knows player y's belief of μ. If player x plays his pure strategy

Table 1. The first-stage game notation.

Symbol	Definition
β	Importance of the proposer. We assume that some proposing nodes in the blockchain network have higher criticality than others
γ	A reward that player y can get if it maintains the performance of the consensus process under a cretin threshold by playing $UseMinimumValidators$. However, player y can loose γ (i.e. deducted from his gain g_y) if it plays $AddMoreValidators$ and the performance violates the specified threshold. We assume that player y will not win γ in case of a successful attack (i.e. player x plays $Cheat$ and player y plays $UseMinimumValidators$)
w_x	Work done by the proposing node (player x) to play $Cheat$
g_x	The gain for player x from a successful attack
c_x	The cost (risk) for player x if captured
w_y	Work done by the validation-leader (player y) to play $AddMoreValidators$
g_y	The gain for player y from capturing a cheater, in case the validation-leader employed more validators
c_y	The cost (risk) for player y if fails to capture a cheater
μ	The probability of player x being malicious
N	The nature node, which determines the type of player x

Table 2. Strategic form of the first-stage Bayesian game (player x is malicious)

Game matrix		Player y (validation-leader)	
		$AddMoreValidators$	$UseMinimumValidators$
Player x	$Cheat$	$(\beta.c_x) - w_x, [(\beta.g_y) - \gamma] - w_y$	$(\beta.g_x) - w_x, \beta.c_y$
	$NotCheat$	$0, -w_y - \gamma$	$0, \gamma$

Table 3. Strategic form of of the first-stage Bayesian game (player x is regular)

Game matrix		Player y (validation-leader)	
		$AddMoreValidators$	$UseMinimumValidators$
Player x	$NotCheat$	$0, -w_y - \gamma$	$0, \gamma$

($Cheat$ if malicious, $NotCheat$ if regular), then, the expected payoff of player y playing his pure strategy $AddMoreValidators$ is:

$$E\mu_y(AddMoreValidators) = \{\mu.[((\beta.g_y) - \gamma) - w_y]\} + \{(1 - \mu).(-w_y - \gamma)\}$$

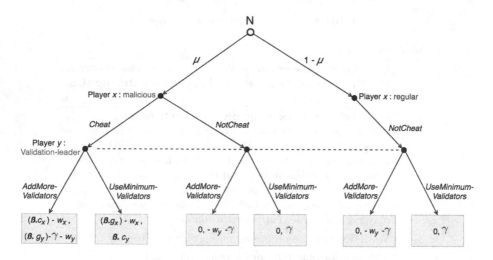

Fig. 1. Extensive form of first-stage Bayesian game.

Similarly, the expected payoff of player y playing his pure strategy *UseMinimumValidators* is:

$$E\mu_y(UseMinimumValidators) = [\mu.(\beta.c_y)] + [(1 - \mu).\gamma]$$

So, if $E\mu_y\,(AddMoreValidators) > E\mu_y\,(UseMinimumValidators)$ Or,

$$\{\mu.[((\beta.g_y) - \gamma) - w_y]\} + \{(1 - \mu).(-w_y - \gamma)\} > [\mu.(\beta.c_y)] + [(1 - \mu).\gamma]$$

Which can be simplified to:

$$\mu > \frac{w_y + 2\gamma}{\beta(g_y - c_y) + \gamma} \tag{1}$$

Then, the best response of player y is to play *AddMoreValidators*. Nevertheless, if player y chooses to play *AddMoreValidators*, *Cheat* will no longer is the best response for player x type *malicious* and, instead, will choose to play *NotCheat*. As a result, ((*Cheat* if malicious, *NotCheat* if regular), *AddMoreValidators*, μ) is not a Bayesian Nash Equilibrium (**BNE**). However, if $E\mu_y(AddMoreValidators) < E\mu_y\,(UseMinimumValidators)$ Or,

$$\mu < \frac{w_y + 2\gamma}{\beta(g_y - c_y) + \gamma} \tag{2}$$

Then, the best response for player y is to play *UseMinimumValidators* and thus ((*Cheat* if malicious, *NotCheat* if regular), *UseMinimumValidators*, μ) is a *pure-strategy* **BNE**.

If player x type *malicious* chooses to play the pure strategy *NotCheat*, player y's dominant strategy is *UseMinimumValidators*, regardless of μ. Nevertheless, if player y plays *UseMinimumValidators*, the best response for player x type *Malicious* is *Cheat*, which reduces to the above case. Hence, ((*NotCheat* if *Malicious*, *NotCheat* if *Regular*), *UseMinimumValidators*) is not a **BNE**.

B. Game Mixed-Strategy BNE: We previously showed that when Eq. 1 is true, there is no *pure-strategy* **BNE** exists. So, we have to find *mixed-strategy* **BNE**. Let p be the probability with that player x plays *Cheat*. Let q be the probability with player y plays *AddMoreValidators*. The expected payoff of player y playing *AddMoreValidators* is:

$$E\mu_y(AddMoreValidators) = \{p.\mu.[((\beta.g_y) - \gamma) - w_y]\} + \{(1 - p).\mu.(-w_y - \gamma)\}$$
$$+ \{(1 - \mu).(-w_y - \gamma)\}$$

The expected payoff of y playing *UseMinimumValidators* is.

$$E\mu_y(UseMinimumValidators) = \{p.\mu.(\beta.c_y)\} + \{(1 - p).\mu.\gamma\} + \{(1 - \mu).\gamma\}$$

So, player y plays *AddMoreValidators*, if $E\mu_y(AddMoreValidators) > E\mu_y(UseMinimumValidators)$. Or,

$$p > \frac{w_y + 2\gamma}{\mu\beta(g_y - c_y) + \mu\gamma} \tag{3}$$

Likewise, we calculate the expected payoffs player x. The expected payoff of x playing *Cheat* is:

$$E\mu_x(Cheat) = \{q.\mu.[(\beta.c_x) - w_x]\} + \{(1 - q).\mu.[(\beta.g_x) - w_x]\}$$

The expected payoff of x playing *NotCheat* is:

$$E\mu_x(NotCheat) = 0$$

As a result, player x plays *Cheat*, if $E\mu_x(Cheat) > E\mu_x(NotCheat)$, or:

$$q > \frac{w_x - (\beta g_x)}{\mu\beta(g_y - c_y)} \tag{4}$$

Now, we derive our game's mixed-strategy **BNE** as: ((q if malicious, *NotCheat* if regular), p, μ).

Thus far, we have obtained the above game's mixed-strategy **BNE**. However, this game is molded for one player x and one player y, and we have four defenders (validation-leaders) and player x knows this fact. Hence, ((q if malicious, *NotCheat* if regular), p, μ) is no longer a valid *mixed-strategy* **BNE**. Thus, we calculate a new *mixed-strategy* **BNE**. The events of validations are independent. We have four validation-leaders. Therefore, the likelihood that the four validators plays *AddMoreValidators* is $\hat{p}$ and is calculated as:

$$\hat{p} = (4.p) - p^4 \tag{5}$$

where, p is the probability that one validation-leader plays $AddMoreValidators$. Now, the attacker plays $Cheat$ with probability $\hat{q}$ defined as:

$$\hat{q} = q - (\hat{p} - p) \tag{6}$$

So, our new *mixed-strategy* **BNE** is: (($\hat{q}$ if malicious, $NotCheat$ if regular), p, μ).

Deciding the Number of Validators (M). After executing the first-stage game, each validation-leader decides its number of validators m, of which $m < n$ where n is the total number of nodes in the network. The m value can be: (a) four validators if the validation-leader chooses to play $UseMinimumVlaidators$, or (b) a fraction of n proportional to p it it plays $AddMoreValidators$.

p is the probability that the proposing node (player x) might attack (plays $Cheat$). In response to this probability, a validation-leader (player y) chooses the appropriate strategy that will maximize its payoff (i.e., whether or not to $AddMoreValidators$). Hence, we consider p as the *"risk likelihood"* of an attack. p is computed with the assumption that the validation-leader is 'risk-neutral,' that is in a fair game each player aims to maximize its expected payoff. In case if a validation-leader chooses to play $AddMoreValidators$, the number of validators (m) will be a random number bounded by the minimum number of validators (i.e. four) and a fraction of $\frac{n}{4}$ proportional to p (we choose $\frac{n}{4}$ because we have four validation-leaders). In other words, a validation-leader select a random number between 5 (the minimum number of validators plus one) and $\frac{p.(n-2)}{4}$ (excluding the proposing and the validation-leader nodes) as flows:

$$m = Random[5, \frac{p.(n-2)}{4}]$$

After a validation-leader decides its m, it selects its validators, instructs them, and broadcasts m to all nodes. When a node in the network receive all the ms from the validation-leaders, it calculate the overall number of the validators involving in the protocol (M) as flows:

$$M = \Sigma_{i=1}^{4} m_i$$

Note that our protocol inherits the Byzantine tolerance provided by Tendermint. In other words, the system can work with one faulty leader, of which M is the aggregation of only three ms. In case if more than one leader is faulty, each node in the network waits for a time period named *"leader − time − out"* and then switches to *"all − validate"* mode. In this mode, every node in the network votes on the received M to agree on it (details are not provided due to space limitation). This mode is costly but preserves the consensus liveness.

Selecting Validators. Each validation-leader selects its set of m validators. The four sets of selected validators will be responsible for validating the proposed block. Our protocol is based on Tendermint which involves two steps of voting (pre-vote and pre-commit). The validators are selected randomly, and each set

---

Algorithm 3. Validators' Selection

Input : A population V of $\frac{n-2}{4}$ nodes having reputation values, AND the risk
likelihood p

Output: A set of validators/pre-voters PV and a set of pre-committers PC of
size m

1 **if** *AddMoreValidators* **then**

2 $\quad |\quad m = Random[5, \frac{p \cdot (n-2)}{4}]$

3 **else**

4 $\quad |\quad m \leftarrow 4$

5 **end**

6 **for** $k \leftarrow 1$ **to** m **do**

7 $\quad |\quad p_i(k) \leftarrow \frac{R_i}{\Sigma_{v_j \in V - PV} R_j}$

8 $\quad |\quad$ **Randomly** select v_i **with** probability $p_i(k)$ **from** $V - PV$

9 $\quad |\quad PV.add(v_i)$

10 **end**

11 **for** $l \leftarrow 1$ **to** m_i **do**

12 $\quad |\quad p_i(l) \leftarrow \frac{R_i}{\Sigma_{c_j \in V - PC} R_j}$

13 $\quad |\quad$ **Randomly** select c_i **with** probability $p_i(l)$ **from** $V - PC$

14 $\quad |\quad PC.add(c_i)$

15 **end**

16 **Return** PV **AND** PC

---

of selected validators is only known to their validation-leader. A validator is only
known, to the other nodes in the network, when it contributes to one of the voting
steps. Therefore, an adversary can observe the validators after revealing their
identities in executing the first stage of voting (i.e., pre-voting). As a result, a
powerful adversary might be able to attack or corrupt a sufficient number of them
which can result in not executing the second step of voting (i.e., pre-committing).
In response to this issue, our protocol requires each validation-leader to select
two sets of nodes of size m. The first set is the validators/pre-voters, and the
second one is the pre-committers. The pre-voters are responsible for executing
the first step of voting, and the pre-committers execute the second step. As
a result, the adversary discovers a participating node in the voting only after
giving its vote, which is an unuseful knowledge. Algorithm 3 shows the process
of selecting the validators/pre-voters and pre-committers.

After selecting the validators and pre-committers nodes, each validation-
leader needs to include a proof of eligibility τ for each selected node to prove
that a legitimate validation-leader has selected this node. τ is a digital signature
signed by the validation-leader's private key $vl.sk$ and includes the validation-
leader's public key $vl.pk$, the selected node's public key ($pv.pk$ for a pre-voter
and $pc.pk$ for a pre-committer), and the validation-leader's proof π as flows:

$$\tau \leftarrow Sign_{vl.sk}(vl.pk \| pv.pk \| \pi)$$

A node which receives a vote accompanied by τ from a voting node (i.e, pre-voter or pre-committer) needs to perform two verifications. First, it needs to verify τ using the validation-leader's public key $vl.pk$. Second, after successful verification of τ, the node verifies π using the initiator's public key $in.pk$.

Second-Stage Game. After selecting the validators by their leaders, and after proposing and broadcasting the new block by the proposer, the second-stage game takes place between the proposer (player x) and each of the validators (player z). The strategy profile for a validator is (a) $Validate$, and (b) $NotValidate$. This game is modeled similarly to the first stage game. Tables 4 and 5 show the strategic form of the second-stage Bayesian game. The extensive form of this game is similar to the one in the first-stage game which was illustrated previously in Fig. 1. We use the same notations presented in Table 1 with following additional notations. w_z is the work done by the validator (player z) to play $Validate$. g_z is the gain for player z from capturing a cheater. c_z is the cost for player z if fails capturing a cheater.

Table 4. Strategic form of the second-stage Bayesian game (player x is malicious)

Game matrix		Player z (validator)	
		$Validate$	$NotValidate$
Player x	$Cheat$	$(\beta.c_x) - w_x, (\beta.g_z) - w_z$	$(\beta.g_x) - w_x, \beta.c_z$
	$NotCheat$	$0, -w_z$	$0, 0$

Table 5. Strategic form of of the second-stage Bayesian game (player x is regular)

Game matrix		Player z (validator)	
		$Validate$	$NotValidate$
Player x	$NotCheat$	$0, -w_z$	$0, 0$

A. Game Pure-Strategy BNE: We follow similar analysis that we presented in the first-stage game. If player x plays his pure strategy ($Cheat$ if malicious, $NotCheat$ if regular), then, the expected payoff of player z playing his pure strategy $Validate$ is:

$$E\mu_z(Validate) = \{\mu.[(\beta.g_z) - w_z]\} + \{(1 - \mu). - w_z\}$$

The expected payoff of player z playing his pure strategy $NotValidate$ is:

$$E\mu_z(NotValidate) = \mu.(\beta.c_z)$$

As a result if, $E\mu_z(Validate) > E\mu_z(NotValidate)$ Or,

$$\mu > \frac{w_z}{\beta(g_z - c_z)} \tag{7}$$

Then, the best response of player z is to play *Validate*. Therefore, ((*Cheat* if malicious, *NotCheat* if regular), *Validate*, μ) is not a (**BNE**). However, if $E\mu_z$ (*Validate*) $< E\mu_z$ (*NotValidate*) Or,

$$\mu < \frac{w_z}{\beta(g_z - c_z)} \tag{8}$$

Then, the best response for player z is to play *NotValidate* and thus ((*Cheat* if malicious, *NotCheat* if regular), *NotValidate*, μ) is a *pure-strategy* **BNE**. Nevertheless, similar to the first-stage game, ((*NotCheat* if *Malicious*, *NotCheat* if *Regular*), *NotValidate*) is not a **BNE**.

B. Game Mixed-Strategy BNE: Let p' be the probability with which player x plays *Cheat*. Let q' be the probability with player z plays *Validate*. The expected payoff of z playing *Validate* is:

$$E\mu_z(Validate) = \{p'.\mu.[(\beta.g_z) - w_z]\} + \{(1 - p').\mu. - w_z\} + \{(1 - \mu). - w_z\}$$

The expected payoff of z playing *NotValidate* is:

$$E\mu_y(NotValidate) = p'.\mu.(\beta.c_z)$$

So, the defender (player z) plays *Validate* when:

$$p' > \frac{w_z}{\mu\beta(g_z - c_z)} \tag{9}$$

Similarly, we acquire the expected payoffs the attacker (player x). The expected payoff of x playing *Cheat* is:

$$E\mu_x(Cheat) = \{q'.\mu.[(\beta.c_x) - w_x]\} + \{(1 - q').\mu.[(\beta.g_x) - w_x]\}$$

The expected payoff of x playing *NotCheat* is:

$$E\mu_x(NotCheat) = 0$$

As a result, the attacker (player x) plays *Cheat* when:

$$q' > \frac{w_x - (\beta g_x)}{\mu\beta(g_z - c_z)} \tag{10}$$

As in the first-stage game, this game is 1-to-M game, where M is the number of validators (player z). Hence, our new *mixed-strategy* **BNE** is: ((*q''* if malicious, *NotCheat* if regular), p', μ), where:

$$q'' = q' - (p'' - p') \tag{11}$$

And:

$$p'' = (M.p') - p'^M \tag{12}$$

Consensus Voting. We use Tendermint's voting mechanism, where there exists two steps of voting. The first one is 'pre-vote'. In this step, the validators/pre-voters validate the block and pre-vote on it. There are three types of pre-votes according to the outcome of the validation process: (a) *valid* if the block is valid, (b) *invalid* if it is not, and (c) *timed-out* if it is not received in a particular time window. Each validator validates with the probability p'. If a validator chooses to play *Validate*, then it contributes to the validation process; otherwise, it pre-votes *nil* and remains idle. The second step of voting is 'pre-commit'. A pre-committer advances to this step only if it receives more than two-thirds of M pre-votes (i.e., $> \frac{2.M}{3}$). The type of pre-commit (i.e., *valid, invalid,* or *timed-out*) depends on the type of the received pre-votes. Likewise, the block is committed or rejected if more than two-thirds of M pre-commits are received.

4   Security Analysis

In this section, we briefly present a threat model and demonstrate how our protocol protects against it. Utilizing the randomness and blind assignment protects from various attacks. Besides, exploiting game theory motivates the defenders in our protocol to adhere to the protocol, and disincentivizes malicious parties.

4.1   Randomness and Anonymity of Validators' Selection

As mentioned in Sect. 3, each proposer is blindly and randomly mapped to four leaders. Moreover, on each new block proposal, M number of validators are selected at random. The M value is also generated randomly proportional to the risk likelihood of the proposer. This selection approach protects against the following attacks:

DDoS Attacks: The DDoS attack is more likely to happen if the set of validators is known in advance. Such an attack can happen to undermine the blockchain and can be launched from inside or outside the network. Validators' replaceability and randomizing their selection can significantly mitigate this attack. This is because of the set of validators changes randomly, and their identities remain anonymous until they participate in the consensus voting. Besides, each step of voting has a different set of voters. Thus, launching a DDoS attack is almost impossible and require to attack all the nodes in the network to undermine the system. Similarly, attacking the validation-leaders is hard too since leaders are known only after completing their tasks (i.e., broadcasting the m value and instructing their selected validators/pre-voters and pre-commiters). Note that we only aim to protect the validation and consensus process form DDoS attacks.

Eclipse Attacks: This attack is presented by Heilman et al. [8] and allows an attacker who controls an adequate number of IP addresses to manage all connections to and from a victim node. As a result, the adversary can utilize the victim nodes for attacks on block validation and consensus system. As in the DDoS attack, an adversary mounting this attack needs to know the node participating in the validation and consensus process in advance. Introducing variable random validators on each block's proposal makes the adversary's job more difficult.

Validators' or Leaders' Bribing or Corruption: An example of this attack is when a malicious proposer bribes and convinces other leaders or voters to accept and vote for an invalid block. Performing such an attack requires knowing the identities of the targeted nodes. Our protocol anonymizes the interaction between the consensus and validation parties, which overcomes such an attack.

4.2 Game Theory

Utilizing game theory protects against several real attacks. We model the interaction between a proposer and leaders or validators as an attacker-defender game. This way the defenders will work hard to maximize the utility that each can gain as a reward for excellent work and avoid the punishment (cost) that might incur due to misbehaving or not obeying the protocol. Our theoretical game approach can protect against the following attacks:

Faulty or Lazy Validation-Leader: This attack happens when a validation-leader colludes with its corresponding malicious proposing node. It could result in many problems such as utilizing the minimum number of validators or colluding with other malicious nodes as validators. Another type of this attack is the lazy validation-leading, in which the validation-leader does not execute the protocol or does not obey its requirements. For example, it is possible for a validation-leader node to produce an assignment that is not truly random. Utilizing the reward and punishment payoffs provided by the proposed game mitigates the incentives of such an attack.

Block Withholding Attack. Rosenfeld [18]: In this attack, a dishonest validator does not participate in the validation process or does not reveal the result of the verification in favor of a malicious proposing node. The reward and punishment provided by our game incentivize the validators to avoid this attack.

4.3 Randomness and Game Theory

The main attack that we are defending against is the **adversary proposer (malicious proposed block).** This attack happens when a proposing node maliciously proposes an invalid new block. This attack occurs for various incentives; double spending is one of them. Integrating random and anonymous validators' selection with a game theoretical model contributes substantially in mitigating this attack. This is because a malicious proposer does not know the nodes that will validate its proposed block, which makes it hard to corrupt or bribe them to agree on its invalid block. Additionally, the punishment enforced by the game model could alleviate the attack motives.

5   Conclusion and Future Work

We have proposed a new true decentralized consensus protocol utilizing game theory and randomness. Our protocol randomly employs a different set of different size of validators each time a new block is proposed to protect against several real attacks mounted by powerful adversaries. Additionally, our protocol enjoys the feature offered by game theory to reward honest adhered parties and punish malicious ones.

This work, however, is in progress and has a few open problems. First, the probability μ that player x is of type *malicious* is static. To overcome this, μ can be determined dynamically, where the defenders y and z update their beliefs about μ at every stage of the game. Second, the proposers-leaders mapping guarantees the anonymous mapping only for one round of proposing. In other words, when a proposer proposes a block for the second time, its leaders' identities are revealed. This protocol was originally designed for a products' supply chain [1] where each node authenticates the product and proposes a block for it only once. Nevertheless, our protocol is suitable for many other blockchain applications, and we plan to make the proposers-leaders mapping dynamic in a way that preserves the anonymity. Third, the detailed evaluation of the protocol's safety and liveness nor the efficiency compared with other consensus protocols such as Ouroboros [11] are not presented in this paper.

References

1. Alzahrani, N., Bulusu, N.: Securing pharmaceutical and high-value products against tag reapplication attacks using nfc tags. In: 2016 IEEE International Conference on Smart Computing (SMARTCOMP). IEEE (2016)
2. Alzahrani, N., Bulusu, N.: Block-supply chain: a new anti-counterfeiting supply chain using NFC and blockchain. In: Proceedings of the 1st Workshop on Cryptocurrencies and Blockchains for Distributed Systems, pp. 30–35. ACM (2018)
3. Buchman, E.: Tendermint: byzantine fault tolerance in the age of blockchains. Ph.D. thesis (2016)
4. Efraimidis, P.S., Spirakis, P.G.: Weighted random sampling with a reservoir. Inf. Process. Lett. **97**(5), 181–185 (2006)
5. Eyal, I.: The miner's dilemma. In: 2015 IEEE Symposium on Security and Privacy (SP), pp. 89–103. IEEE (2015)
6. Gilad, Y., Hemo, R., Micali, S., Vlachos, G., Zeldovich, N.: Algorand: scaling byzantine agreements for cryptocurrencies. In: Proceedings of the 26th Symposium on Operating Systems Principles, pp. 51–68. ACM (2017)
7. Gorbunov, S.: Pure Proof-of-Stake Blockchains. https://medium.com/algorand
8. Heilman, E., Kendler, A., Zohar, A., Goldberg, S.: Eclipse attacks on bitcoin's peer-to-peer network. In: USENIX Security Symposium, pp. 129–144 (2015)
9. Hyperledger: hyperledger/fabric. https://github.com/hyperledger/fabric/tree/v0.6
10. Johnson, B., Laszka, A., Grossklags, J., Vasek, M., Moore, T.: Game-theoretic analysis of DDoS attacks against bitcoin mining pools. In: Böhme, R., Brenner, M., Moore, T., Smith, M. (eds.) FC 2014. LNCS, vol. 8438, pp. 72–86. Springer, Heidelberg (2014). https://doi.org/10.1007/978-3-662-44774-1_6

11. Kiayias, A., Russell, A., David, B., Oliynykov, R.: Ouroboros: a provably secure proof-of-stake blockchain protocol. In: Katz, J., Shacham, H. (eds.) CRYPTO 2017. LNCS, vol. 10401, pp. 357–388. Springer, Cham (2017). https://doi.org/10.1007/978-3-319-63688-7_12

12. Kwon, J.: Tendermint: Consensus without mining, 18 May 2014

13. Kwon, J., Buchman, E.: Cosmos: a network of distributed ledgers (2016)

14. Luu, L., Saha, R., Parameshwaran, I., Saxena, P., Hobor, A.: On power splitting games in distributed computation: the case of bitcoin pooled mining. In: 2015 IEEE 28th Computer Security Foundations Symposium (CSF), pp. 397–411. IEEE (2015)

15. Mackey, T.K., Nayyar, G.: A review of existing and emerging digital technologies to combat the global trade in fake medicines. Expert Opin. Drug Saf. **16**(5), 587–602 (2017)

16. Nojoumian, M., Golchubian, A., Njilla, L., Kwiat, K., Kamhoua, C.: Incentivizing blockchain miners to avoid dishonest mining strategies by a reputation-based paradigm. In: IEEE Computing Conference (CC). IEEE, London (2018)

17. Pilkington, M.: 11 blockchain technology: principles and applications. In: Research Handbook on Digital Transformations (2016)

18. Rosenfeld, M.: Analysis of bitcoin pooled mining reward systems. arXiv preprint arXiv:1112.4980 (2011)

19. Sheridan, K.: Blockchain All the Rage But Comes With Numerous Risks. https://www.darkreading.com/vulnerabilities--threats/blockchain-all-the-rage-but-comes-with-numerous-risks/d/d-id/1332038

20. Xu, D., Xiao, L., Sun, L., Lei, M.: Game theoretic study on blockchain based secure edge networks (2017)

A Game Theoretical Framework for Inter-process Adversarial Intervention Detection

Muhammed O. Sayin[1]([✉]), Hossein Hosseini[2], Radha Poovendran[2], and Tamer Başar[1]

[1] Department of Electrical and Computer Engineering,
University of Illinois at Urbana-Champaign, Urbana, IL 61801, USA
{sayin2,basar1}@illinois.edu
[2] Department of Electrical Engineering, University of Washington,
Seattle, WA 98195, USA
{hosseinh,rp3}@washington.edu

Abstract. In this paper, we propose and analyze a two-level game theoretical framework to detect advanced and persistent threats across processes. The two-level framework adapted facilitates abstraction of the complexity of process level interactions between defense mechanisms and adversaries from easier to interpret and more flexible system-level interaction. At the process-level, program anomaly detection algorithms have already been proposed to detect anomalous program behavior by comparing monitored activities with the predetermined expected behavior. This had led to significant detection performance initially until advanced adversaries modified the attacks to remain undetected. Therefore, we propose defense mechanisms that anticipate the reaction of advanced evaders and seek to maximize the complexity of undetectable attacks at the expense of additional false alarm rate. Furthermore, in the system-level, we propose defense mechanisms to detect adversarial intervention across processes through the assessment of all process activities together in a cohesive way so that the advanced adversaries need to craft their attacks further to remain undetected also at the system-level. This further increases the cost of complexity for the attacker, and correspondingly degrades the motivation to attack. We provide a game theoretical incentive analysis for both defenders and adversaries, and characterize pure and mixed strategy equilibria. We also analyze the coupling between the two levels of the game.

Keywords: Host-based intrusion detection · Mimicry attacks
Games-in-games · Anomaly detection · Process monitoring
Stackelberg games · Advanced persistent threats

M. O. Sayin—This research was supported by the U.S. Office of Naval Research (ONR) MURI grant N00014-16-1-2710.

L. Bushnell et al. (Eds.): GameSec 2018, LNCS 11199, pp. 486–507, 2018.
https://doi.org/10.1007/978-3-030-01554-1_28

1   Introduction

Recently, the arm race between defensive measures and adversaries for the security of digital systems has gained significant pace in favor of adversaries. Digitalization of our personal information and financial assets has made them vulnerable to threats throughout the world. It is no longer surprising to see news about data breach in world-wide organizations. Even though such organizations are expected to be secure against cyber threats by deploying the state-of-the-art defense mechanisms, attacks are becoming more and more sophisticated, more stealthy, and with far wider attack surfaces. Signature based defense mechanisms can no longer defend against such advanced threats effectively [20]. Unpredictable adaptation of attacks against existing defense measures or brand new attacks make it necessary to consider zero-day vulnerabilities in digital systems and to take precautions beyond signature based defenses.

Program anomaly detection inspired from human immune systems has achieved promising detection performance against any attack, whether it has earlier been encountered or not [8]. Particularly, monitored program activities are compared with its normal, i.e., benign, behavior. And deviation of the monitored behavior from the norm, according to a certain metric, indicates how anomalous the program activity is. Indeed, program anomaly detection mechanisms have initially achieved significant detection performance until they could no longer achieve it within the arm race between the defender and the attacker. As an example, mimicry attacks were first introduced by [19] to undermine n-gram based intrusion detection methods, e.g., [17]. Correspondingly, [7] has proposed anomaly detection using call stack information to detect such mimicry attacks. However, [12] has designed mimicry attacks that can undermine [7]. Therefore, any such attack-specific counter-measure is very likely to be undermined after a strategic modification. This leads to the Cohen impossibility result for cat-and-mouse-game-like interaction since broad deployment of defense measures enables attackers to inspect and study such (attack-specific) defenses before launching new attacks that can bypass the existing defenses [20]. Therefore, here we specifically focus on defenses against attacks that are strategically crafted to evade detection, and within a game theoretical framework.

Program anomaly detection has been studied extensively over the past decades. Interested reader can refer to [15] and [20] for detailed overviews of these studies. However, there still exist significant yet unsolved challenges, especially in terms of

(i) a game theoretical analysis to avoid cat-and-mouse-game-like interaction,
(ii) assessment of all the program activities together in a cohesive way.

A game theoretical framework enables us to exploit the trade-off faced by the attackers in terms of evasion and increased complexity of the attack, i.e., increased cost of complexity. Furthermore, cohesive consideration of all the program activities is essential, especially against advanced attacks that deploy modular structure with multiple components that are specialized on certain tasks [6]. Intuitively, strategic attackers would craft the attacks just until they can be assessed as benign, to keep the cost of complexity at minimum. However, if they infect multiple programs, and their behaviors are observed to be on the edge of classification as benign, that could imply the possibility of an advanced evasive attack. Therefore, cohesive consideration of program behaviors across whole system enables us to increase the complexity of undetectable attacks further and further.

Recently, [13] and [5] have studied adversarial intervention detection across all the system activities yet without considering evasive adaptability of strategic attackers. In [13], the authors have proposed an online algorithm to learn the structure of the interaction between programs across the system to detect anomalous ones through a graph based approach. In [5], the authors have proposed to use deep learning algorithms to compute the likelihood of current system activities given the previous ones. We re-emphasize that these studies have not considered inter-process adversarial intervention detection within a game theoretical framework.

Note that a software designer is not involved in designing how operating systems should execute the source code or how hardware level operations should take place in the physical world during that execution. This layered structure in technological infrastructure and systems has resulted in substantial enhancement within remarkable time by abstracting the complexity of lower levels from more flexible and easier to interpret higher levels. Correspondingly, a layered structure can facilitate analysis of complicated interaction between defense mechanisms and adversaries. To this end, in this paper, we propose a two-level game theoretical framework to detect advanced adversarial intervention across the processes. Note that a program is a collection of instructions while a process is the actual execution of these instructions in real time. We consider a defender seeking to detect adversarial intervention by monitoring and assessing process activities, and an attacker having a modular malware consisting of multiple malicious codes and seeking to inject them into the execution flow of benign processes after crafting them strategically to evade the defender.

In the process-level game, the defender deploys intrusion detection systems (IDSs) monitoring certain process activities and assigning scores indicating how anomalous the activities are, and the defender sets a threshold to detect adversarial intervention at the expense of false alarms, in which a benign process activity has been assessed adversarial. However, different from extensively studied program anomaly detection approaches, here the defender anticipates advanced evasive attackers' reaction to the threshold and sets it based on the trade-off between the complexity of an undetectable attack, i.e., a crafted attack that leads to scores under the threshold, and false alarm rates. On the other side, the attacker crafts his malicious code by adding redundant instructions such that the IDSs assign scores under the threshold at the expense of increased code complexity. In other words, the attacker seeks to keep the number of added instructions at a minimum. In the system-level game, the defender collects all the scores within certain time period from all the processes and assesses them together in a cohesive way to detect adversarial interventions across the processes. On the other side, the attacker seeks to remain undetected also at the system-level by setting virtual thresholds for the adversary induced scores.

We have analyzed the equilibria in both process and system level games, and analyzed the coupling between the levels. We can list our main contributions as follows:

- This is the first study to consider inter-process adversarial intervention detection within a game theoretical framework.
- We propose a two-level hierarchy for prompt response at the process-level with a theoretically grounded thorough incentive analysis at the system-level.
- We analyze the coupling between the process and system level games.

The paper is organized as follows: In Sect. 2, we provide preliminary information and motivating examples for the problem formulation. In Sect. 3, we provide the defense and threat models. In Sect. 4, we formulate the process and system level games between an attacker and a defender. In Sects. 5 and 6, we analyze the process-level and system-level games, respectively. We conclude the paper in Sect. 7 with several remarks and possible research directions.

The Notation Throughout the Paper: For a given set Σ, $\sigma^* = \sigma^1\sigma^2\sigma^3 \ldots$ denotes a string consisting of the elements of Σ with indefinite length, and Σ^* is the set of all corresponding strings, i.e., $\sigma^* \in \Sigma^*$. Further $\sigma^{(n)} = \sigma^1\sigma^2\ldots\sigma^n$ denotes a string consisting of n elements of Σ, and $\Sigma^{(n)}$ is the set of all corresponding strings, i.e., $\sigma^{(n)} \in \Sigma^{(n)}$. For a given string σ^*, $|\sigma^*|$ denotes the length of the string. We denote random variables with bold lower case letters, e.g., $\boldsymbol{\sigma}$.

2 Background

A computer system consists of various applications. An application (or program) is a collection of instructions and the actual execution of these instructions in real time is called a process [16]. A process can be considered consisting of a finite-state machine, a stack, and a random-access register, and they evolve with the temporal instructions, i.e., due to the execution of the source code by the central-processing unit (CPU) [15]. CPU instructions include both inner process activities related to the process's own assigned address space and *system-calls* directed to the kernel for hardware-related operations, e.g., reading a file in the disk or sending information to an external server through the ethernet card [16].

Note that there can be malware in the system intended to perform malicious behavior. Similar to other applications, malware also needs to conduct hardware related tasks. As an example, while exfiltrating data from the system, malware can read the files from the disk and send them to external servers by sending queries to the operating system. Major interactions between malware and hardware are conducted under the operating system's supervision unless the malware has root-access to the system [20]. This implies that interactions could leave a trace that can help detect and analyze attacks, if all such interactions between applications and OS are recorded [11,18,20].

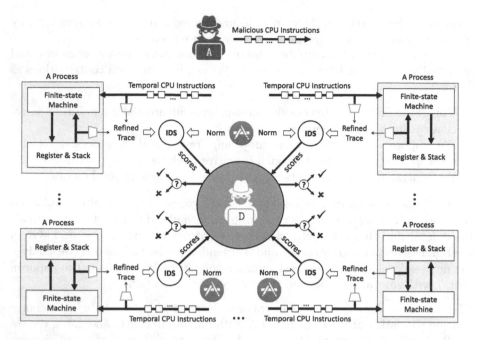

Fig. 1. A process is a system consisting of a finite-state machine, a random-access register and a stack. The state of the inner finite-state machine evolves according to the temporal CPU instructions, symbols in the stack, and the addresses in the registers. IDSs can monitor the process activities and assign scores to these traces by comparing with the norm. A seeks to inject his malicious code into the benign processes evasively while D seeks to detect A's attack based on all the collected scores across the processes.

Example 1. Consider a scenario where an attacker injects a malicious code into an email application in order to add a backdoor to a password file [19]. The infected *system-call* trace of the process could include a sub-trace as follows:

$$\texttt{open,write,close,socket,bind} \tag{1}$$

This sub-trace would be viewed as anomalous, since "normally" the email application would not open a file and then bind to a network socket in such immediate succession [19].

However, attackers can strategically modify the malware to bypass such defense mechanisms, e.g., by including redundant system-calls such that overall trace looks similar to the norm while fulfilling the malicious task. In the literature, such type of evasive attacks are studied as *mimicry attacks* and computation of the redundant calls with minimum length, i.e., complexity, is a combinatorial optimization problem [9,14,19]. Crafting long attack traces, including a lot of system-calls, to mimic the norm is a challenging problem for the attackers because of its combinatorial aspect. Furthermore, the length of the added redundancy, and correspondingly complexity, increases with the length of the attack trace substantially.

To this end, advanced cyber attacks can exploit modular design, i.e., malware with components that are specialized on certain tasks, to evade the detection easily [6]. Modules have relatively shorter traces, and correspondingly, crafting them to mimic the norm is easier than crafting the entire malware in a single trace. While individual process activities mimic the norm easily and evade detection, the combined activities of multiple processes will still be able to perform the malicious task. Hence, modularity enables the malware to evade the state-of-the-art defense mechanisms that focus on detecting anomalous behavior of individual processes [20]. Therefore, it is essential to consider the anomalous activities across the processes in a cohesive way.

3 System Model

Consider two agents: an attacker (A) and a defender (D). A seeks to fulfill certain adversarial objective in the host without being detected by D. To this end, A injects malicious codes into benign processes through various ways, e.g., dynamic-link library (DLL) injection, thread execution hijacking, etc. [2,6]. D deploys IDSs that can monitor process activities and assign scores by comparing them with the normal behaviors of the processes. She then uses these scores to detect A as shown in Fig. 1.

3.1 Defense Model

Let Δ denote certain quantization of the interval $[0, 1]$. For process i, corresponding IDS deploys a scoring metric $f_i : \Sigma^{(n)} \to \Delta$ to assign scores to sub-traces $\sigma^{(n)} \in \Sigma^{(n)}$ representing the likelihood that the behavior is anomalous. Let $\mathbf{P}_i$ denote the underlying distribution of the benign sub-traces of process i (with $n \gg 1$).

Assumption 1. Smoothness of Scoring Metrics. *Let $dist : \Sigma^{(n)} \times \Sigma^{(n)} \to [0, n]$ be a distance metric, e.g., edit distance, over $\Sigma^{(n)}$. Let $\sigma_1^{(n)}, \sigma_2^{(n)} \in \Sigma^{(n)}$ and $\sigma_1^{(n)} \neq \sigma_2^{(n)}$. We assume that there exists a constant $L \in [0, 1]$ such that*

$$\frac{|f_i(\sigma_1^{(n)}) - f_i(\sigma_2^{(n)})|}{dist(\sigma_1^{(m)}, \sigma_2^{(m)})} \leq L, \ \forall i. \tag{2}$$

D deploys two defense mechanisms at process-level and system-level. At process-level, she selects a fixed threshold

$$\lambda \in \Delta$$

for each application in the system and declares an anomaly if the scores of a process exceeds the threshold of the associated application. This approach can provide a prompt response against anomalous process behaviors. At system-level, she collects the normalized scores of all processes with respect to the associated threshold (projected onto Δ) periodically in order to make an assessment about whether there exists an adversarial intervention or not. Each period is called an epoch and D selects a detection rule for certain subsets of the processes being executed in an epoch since an advanced modular attacker can infect multiple processes. Let $\mathscr{K}$ denote the index set of these subsets and $n_k \in \mathbb{N}$ denote the number of scores in the kth subset. Then, D's detection rules are given by

$$d_k : \Delta^{n_k} \to \{0, 1\}, \tag{3}$$

for $k \in \mathscr{K}$, and $d_k(s) = 1$ implies that there is an adversarial intervention. We denote the set of all such detection rules by $\mathscr{D}_k$, i.e., $d_k \in \mathscr{D}_k$.

Remark 1. Note that $d_k(\cdot)$ can localize the infected processes within an epoch, which can be used in order to trigger further detailed investigation through, e.g., dynamic information-flow tracking techniques [11].

We provide the evasive attack model and formulate its complexity in the following subsection.

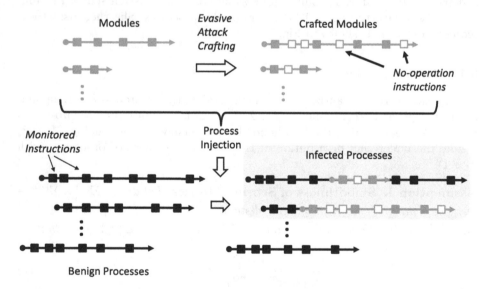

Fig. 2. One-direction arrows represent the execution flow of the processes over time, figuratively. A can craft the models by adding redundant instructions and inject them into benign processes to hide its presence while fulfilling the malicious objective.

3.2   Threat Model

A has a modular malware (e.g., $\{a_i^*\}_{i\in\Gamma}$, where Γ represents the index set of the modules), which is designed without considering D. Therefore, A seeks to modify the modules before injecting them to benign processes in order to evade D. To this end, A could include redundant instructions $r^* = r^1 r^2 r^3 \ldots$ into the trace of a module $a^* := a^1 a^2 a^3 \ldots$ such that the injected trace, e.g.,

$$\tilde{a}^* = a^1 r^1 r^2 a^2 r^3 a^3 \ldots \tag{4}$$

looks alike with the norm of that process as seen in Fig. 2.

For a successful attack, the feasibility constraint is to satisfy the adversarial objective, i.e., execution of all the modules, while evading D. A seeks to minimize the complexity of the attack, in line with Occam's razor. In other words, higher complexity of the crafted attack yields higher cost for A. Correspondingly, higher cost degrades the incentive to attack [3]. We can model the complexity of a given crafted attack as:

$$\sum_{i\in\Gamma} c(|a_i^*|, |r_i^*|), \tag{5}$$

where Γ denotes both the index set of the infected processes and that of the modules without loss of generality, and $a_i^* \in \Sigma^*$ denotes the original attack trace to be injected into process i while $r_i^* \in \Sigma^*$ denotes the corresponding trace of the redundantly added instructions. The injection cost $c : \mathbb{N}^2 \to [0, \infty]$ is increasing functions of $|a_i^*|$ and $|r_i^*|$.

Next, we formulate the two-level detection-evasion game between A and D.

4   Game Formulation

The attacker and the defender are seeking to achieve conflicting objectives. Therefore, their interaction can be analyzed within a game theoretical framework. Also, due to the weak coupling between the process and system level interaction between the players, and in order to reduce the complexity of the formulation, we can decompose the problem as a two-level game at process and system levels. In the following, we provide these game formulations.

4.1   Process-Level Game

At the process-level, A's objective for process i is to find undetectable attack trace with minimum complexity, which is given by[1]

$$L(a_i^*, \gamma_i) := \inf_{r_i^* \in \Sigma^*} c(|a_i^*|, |r_i^*|) \text{ subject to } f_i(\tilde{a}_{i,t}^{(n)}) \leq \gamma_{i,t}\lambda_i, \; \forall t, \tag{6}$$

---

[1] We have used infimum here since, the set of indefinite length strings, Σ^*, not being compact, there is no immediate guarantee of existence of a minimum.

where $\tilde{a}_{i,t}^{(n)} \in \Sigma^{(n)}$ denotes the sub-traces of the crafted attack (4). A selects the original attack trace $a_i^* \in \Sigma^*$, and the threshold multiplication factors $\gamma_i := \{\gamma_{i,t} \in [0,1]\}_t$ (such that the virtual thresholds $\lambda_{i,t}^v := \gamma_{i,t}\lambda_i \in \Delta$) according to the system-level game as explained in Subsect. 4.2 in detail. Note that there may not exist a solution to (6) for certain virtual thresholds.

While D does not know A's objective, she knows that the attack trace must be different from the normal behavior of the installed applications in the system. Therefore, D considers scenarios where a_i^* is drawn from the probability space $(\Omega^A, \mathscr{F}^A, \mathbf{P}_i^A)$, where Ω^A denotes the outcome space, $\mathscr{F}^A$ denotes the appropriate σ-algebra on Ω^A, and $\mathbf{P}_i^A$ denotes the probability distribution over Ω^A. D's objective is to maximize the complexity of evasive attacks *on average* (over Ω^A according to $\mathbf{P}_i^A$) with an added constraint incurred due to false alarms. Therefore, at the process-level, D's objective for process i is given by[2]

$$\max_{\lambda_i \in \Delta} \mathbb{E}_{a_i^*}\{g(c(|a_i^*|, |r_i^*(a_i^*)|))\} - c_{\text{FA}} \Pr(f_i(\sigma^{(n)}) > \lambda_i), \tag{7}$$

where $g : [0,\infty] \to [0,1]$ is a non-decreasing wrapping function for the attacker complexity and $c_{\text{FA}} \in [0,\infty)$ denotes the cost of false alarms.

In the process-level, we consider the scenario where there is a hierarchy between the players, i.e., a Stackelberg game, in which D leads the game by announcing her strategies, and correspondingly A selects his attack strategies by knowing her defense strategies [1]. In order to show this dependency explicitly, henceforth, we denote A's process-level reaction by $r_i^*(a_i^*)(\lambda_i)$. If a solution exists to (6) for a given threshold λ_i, we let $\Pi_i(a_i^*, \gamma_i)(\lambda_i) \subset \Sigma^*$ denote the reaction set of A, which is given by

$$\Pi_i(a_i^*, \{\gamma_{i,t}\}_t)(\lambda) := \underset{r^* \in \Sigma^*}{\operatorname{argmin}} \ c(|a_i^*|, |r^*(a_i^*)(\lambda)|) \ \text{s.t.} \ f_i(\tilde{a}_{i,t}^{(n)}) \leq \gamma_{i,t}\lambda \ \forall t,$$

which may not be a singleton; however, the following proposition shows that A's reaction is essentially unique.

Proposition 1. *Let $\sim$ denote an equivalence relation on Σ^* such that two traces σ_1^* and σ_2^* are equal if, and only if, $|\sigma_1^*| = |\sigma_2^*|$. Then, for given a_i^* and γ_i, the quotient set of the reaction set, i.e., $\Pi_i/\sim$, is a singleton.*

Proof. The proof follows from (6) and since $c(\cdot)$ is an increasing function of the length of added redundancy. Suppose $r_1^*, r_2^* \in \Pi_i(a_i^*, \{\gamma_{i,t}\}_t)(\lambda)$ while $|r_1^*| \neq |r_2^*|$. However, this would imply that $c(|a_i^*|, |r_1^*|) \neq c(|a_i^*|, |r_2^*|)$, which leads to a contradiction. Therefore, if $r_1^*, r_2^* \in \Pi_i(a_i^*, \{\gamma_{i,t}\}_t)(\lambda)$, then $r_1^* \sim r_2^*$ even though r_1^* and r_2^* may not be the same. $\square$

To summarize the process-level interaction, we define the following game:

---

[2] With abuse of notation, we denote r_i^* as a function of a_i^* in order to show the dependence explicitly.

Definition 1. Process-level Game $\mathscr{G}_P^i$: *For process-i, the process-level game*

$$\mathscr{G}_P^i := \left(\Delta, \Sigma^*, \mathbf{P}_i^A, \mathbf{P}_i, c(\cdot), g(\cdot), f_i(\cdot), a_i^*, c_{FA}, \{\gamma_{i,t}\}_t \right)$$

is a Bayesian Stackelberg game between A *and* D, *where* D *is the leader, who announces her strategies beforehand.* A*'s type is drawn from* $\mathbf{P}_i^A$ *and his strategy space is* Σ^* *while* D *has a single type and her strategy space is* Δ. *Objectives of* A *and* D *are given by* (6) *and* (7), *respectively, with parameters:*

- $\mathbf{P}_i$: *probability distribution of the benign sub-traces;*
- $c(\cdot) : \mathbb{N}^2 \to [0, \infty]$: *complexity of the evasive attacks;*
- $g(\cdot) : [0, \infty] \to [0, 1]$: *complexity wrapping function;*
- $f_i : \Sigma^* \to \Delta$: *scoring function;*
- $a_i^* \in \Omega^A$: *type of* A, *i.e., original attack trace (private to* A*);*
- $c_{FA} \in [0, \infty)$: *cost of false alarm;*
- $\gamma_{i,t} \in [0, 1]$: *multiplication factor set by* A *at the system-level game (private to* A*).*

Furthermore, the pair of strategies: $[\lambda_i; r_i^*(a_i^*), a_i^* \sim \mathbf{P}_i^A]$ *attains the Bayesian Stackelberg equilibrium provided that a solution exists for* a_i^* *and* $\gamma_{i,t}\lambda$ *in* (6), *and*

$$\lambda_i = \underset{\lambda \in \Delta}{\operatorname{argmax}}\ \mathbb{E}_{a_i^*}\{g(c(|a_i^*|, |r_i^*(a_i^*)(\lambda)|))\} - c_{FA}\Pr(f_i(\sigma^{(n)}) > \lambda), \qquad (8a)$$

$$r_i^*(a_i^*)(\lambda) = \underset{r^* \in \Sigma^*}{\operatorname{argmin}}\ c(|a_i^*|, |r^*(a_i^*)(\lambda)|)\ \text{s.t.}\ f_i(\tilde{a}_{i,t}) \le \gamma_{i,t}\lambda\ \forall t. \qquad (8b)$$

If a solution does not exist for a_i^* *and* $\gamma_{i,t}\lambda$ *in* (6), *then* A*'s complexity* $c(\cdot) = \infty$ *and correspondingly* $g(\cdot) = 1$.

4.2 System-Level Game

At the process-level, A's objective (6) is to execute the original attack trace with minimum complexity. Correspondingly, the following proposition shows that the scores of the infected processes lie near the edge of the threshold if the multiplication factor $\gamma_{i,t} = 1$ for all t.

Proposition 2. *Let the multiplication factors* $\gamma_{i,t} = 1\ \forall t$. *Suppose* $r_i^* \in \Pi_i(a_i^*, \{\gamma_{i,t}\}_t)(\lambda_i)$ *and* $|r_i^*| > 0$. *Let* $\{s_{i,t}\}_t$ *denote the scores obtained by the sub-traces of the crafted attack, i.e.,* $\tilde{a}_i^* = \{\tilde{a}_{i,t}^{(n)}\}_t$. *Then, we have* $\lambda_i - L < \max_t s_{i,t} \le \lambda_i$.

Proof. Suppose that $\max_t s_{i,t} \le \lambda_i - L$. Then, there exists an $r^* \in \Sigma^*$ obtained by removing a redundant instruction from r_i^*, i.e., $|r^*| = |r_i^*| - 1$. Let $\{s'_{i,t}\}_t$ denote the scores for the modified attack trace. Then, we obtain $\max_t s'_{i,t} \le \lambda_i$, which leads to a contradiction since r^* yields lower complexity (since the complexity $c(\cdot)$ is an increasing function of the length of the added redundancy) while r_i^* is the best reaction. $\qquad \square$

Based on Proposition 2, the scores of the infected processes are expected to be at the edge of the threshold. Therefore, too many scores just at the edge of the thresholds (even though they might be coming from different processes) could imply adversarial intervention. Therefore, at the system-level, D selects a detection rule for the collected scores while A selects which process to infect and threshold multiplication factors $\gamma_{i,t} \in [0,1]$ so that the scores due to adversarial intervention always remain under the virtual threshold $\lambda^v_{i,t} := \gamma_{i,t}\lambda_i$ at the infected processes.

Remark 2. We emphasize that D does not simply design a heuristic detection rule, e.g., setting a threshold over the (weighted) sum of scores, at the system-level.

Remark 3. A's modular malware, i.e., $\{a^*_i\}_{i \in \Gamma}$, is private to D and this seemingly disadvantageous uncertainty enables D to design the defense by handling A's ability to select infected processes, implicitly, within a stochastic framework.

To this end, for each $k \in \mathcal{K}$, we consider the scenarios where there can be an adversarial intervention at that subset with probability $p_k \in [0,1]$ (i.e., $\sum_{k \in \mathcal{K}} p_k = 1$) and if there is an intervention, then A has a type drawn from the type space Ω according to a distribution $\mathbf{P}^\omega$ and his type determines which modules are injected into which processes in that subset. Then, for type ω attacker, in subset k, the complexity due to the threshold multiplication factors is given by

$$C_{\omega,k}(\gamma) := g\left(\sum_i L_i(a^*_i, \gamma_i)\right), \tag{9}$$

where $L_i(\cdot)$ is defined in (6) and $\gamma := \{\gamma_i\}_i$. Note that the range of $C_{\omega,k}$ is discrete since its domain Δ^{n_k} is discrete.

Let $\mathbf{P}^s_k$ denote the joint distribution of the normalized scores (with respect to the threshold selected at the process-level) collected within an epoch for subset $k \in \mathcal{K}$ when there is no adversarial intervention, which may be computed based on $\mathbf{P}_i$'s and $f_i(\cdot)$'s, i.e., the collected scores $s \sim \mathbf{P}^s_k$. Then, for each $k \in \mathcal{K}$, A and D's cost functions are given by

$$J^A_{\omega,k}(\gamma_\omega; d_k) := C_{\omega,k}(\gamma_\omega) + C_D \mathbf{1}_{\{d_k(\gamma_\omega)=1\}}, \tag{10}$$

$$J^D_k(\gamma_\omega, \omega \sim \mathbf{P}^\omega; d_k) := -p_k \mathbb{E}_\omega\left\{J^A_{\omega,k}(\gamma_\omega; d_k)\right\} + (1 - p_k)C_{FA} \Pr(d_k(s) = 1) \tag{11}$$

where $C_D \in [0, \infty)$ denotes the cost of detection for A while $C_{FA} \in [0, \infty)$ denotes the cost for false alarms in the system-level.

To summarize the system-level interaction, we define the following game:

Definition 2. System-level Game $\mathcal{G}^k_S$: *For $k \in \mathcal{K}$, the system-level game*

$$\mathcal{G}^k_S := (\mathcal{D}_k, \Delta^{n_k}, \mathbf{P}^\omega, \mathbf{P}^s_k, C_{\omega,k}(\cdot), C_D, C_{FA}, p_k)$$

is a Bayesian non-zero sum game between A and D. A's type is drawn from Ω according to $\mathbf{P}^\omega$ and his strategy space is Δ^{n_k} while D has a single type and her strategy space is $\mathcal{D}_k$. Therefore, the players A and D seek to minimize their cost functions (10) and (11), respectively, with parameters:

- $\mathbf{P}_k^o$: *distribution of the collected scores when there is no adversarial intervention;*
- $C_{\omega,k} : \Delta^{n_k} \to [0,1]$: *complexity due to the virtual thresholds;*
- $C_D \in [0,\infty)$: *cost of detection for* A;
- $C_{FA} \in [0,\infty)$: *cost of false alarms in the system-level;*
- $p_k \in [0,1]$: *probability that there can be an adversarial intervention at subset k.*

Furthermore, the pair of strategies: $[d_k; \gamma_\omega, \omega \sim \mathbf{P}^\omega]$ *attains the Bayesian Nash equilibrium provided that*

$$\gamma_\omega = \underset{\gamma \in \Delta^{n_k}}{\mathrm{argmin}} \; C_{\omega,k}(\gamma) + C_D \mathbf{1}_{\{d_k(\gamma)=1\}}, \tag{12a}$$

$$d_k = \underset{d \in \mathscr{D}_k}{\mathrm{argmin}} \; -p_k \mathbb{E}_\omega \left\{ J_{\omega,k}^A(\gamma_\omega; d) \right\} + (1-p_k) C_{FA} \Pr(d(\boldsymbol{s}) = 1). \tag{12b}$$

Note that whether there will be an adversarial intervention at subset k or not is A's strategic decision; however, the detection rules that are selected according to (11) depend on the probability p_k. Correspondingly, D can consider the scenarios where

$$\{p_k\}_{k \in \mathscr{K}} = \underset{p_k', k \in \mathscr{K}}{\mathrm{argmax}} \sum_{k \in \mathscr{K}} -p_k' \mathbb{E}_\omega \left\{ J_{\omega,k}^A(\gamma_\omega; d_k) \right\} + (1 - p_k') C_{FA} \Pr(d_k(\boldsymbol{s}) = 1).$$

Remark 4. We re-emphasize that this two-level approach decouples the analysis of program anomaly detection from information flow across the processes for *prompt* response to an adversarial intervention. Furthermore, the inter-process analysis can detect the adversaries that can bypass the individual IDSs via modularity. Therefore, the attacker needs to increase the complexity further and further in order to bypass the detection at both levels.

This could also have been considered within a single big-game formulation. However, we seek to provide a neat solution through a hierarchical approach instead of complicating the analysis of this complex problem with a big-game formulation. Note that there is a coupling between the games, e.g., due to the virtual thresholds, which could imply that there can be room for D to increase the process-level thresholds to reduce the expected false alarm rate in the joint consideration of the game. In Sect. 6, we will analyze the couplings between the games in detail.

Remark 5. Note that, here we have only considered a single-stage game formulation, where the defender seeks to optimize the expected objective with fixed defense strategies without any adaptation. A multi-stage dynamic game formulation, where the defender selects dynamic defense strategies, could be an interesting future research direction.

5 Process-Level Game: Optimal Threshold for IDSs Against Evasive Attacks

We consider the scenarios where all the threshold multiplication factors are 1 as if there is no system-level defense across the processes due to the decomposition of the process and system level interaction between the players. Then, for given original attack trace a_i^* and threshold λ, A's objective is given by

$$\inf_{r_i^* \in \Sigma^*} c(|a_i^*|, |r_i^*|) \text{ s.t. } f_i(\tilde{a}_{i,t}^{(n)}) \leq \lambda. \tag{13}$$

Following the same lines as in [19], let $\mathscr{B}_\lambda$ denote all the acceptable traces for threshold λ, and $\mathscr{A}_{a_i^*}$ denote all the possible crafted attack traces for original attack trace a_i^*. Then, A can compute the optimal redundancy through a breath-first search over the product automaton $\mathscr{B}_\lambda \times \mathscr{A}_{a_i^*}$ starting from a_i^* as the initial state.

In order to anticipate A's reaction to any selected threshold, D can compute the expected minimum complexity for a given threshold λ through a Monte Carlo approach. To this end, D can randomly draw sample original attack traces from Ω^A according to $\mathbf{P}_i^A$ and compute the optimal redundancy, which leads to a collection of minimum complexity. Therefore, for given threshold λ, D can learn the distribution for the minimum complexity $c(|a_i^*|, |r_i^*(a_i^*)|)$ based on this collection and furthermore can compute the expected minimum complexity wrapped by $g(\cdot)$. The following lemma characterizes the relation between threshold and the corresponding expected minimum complexity.

Lemma 1. *Expected minimum complexity*

$$\bar{c}_i(\lambda) := \mathbb{E}_{\boldsymbol{a}_i^*} \left\{ \min_{\tilde{a}_i^* \in \mathscr{B}_\lambda \cap \mathscr{A}_{\boldsymbol{a}_i^*}} g(c(|\boldsymbol{a}_i^*|, |r_i^*(\boldsymbol{a}_i^*)|)) \right\} \tag{14}$$

is a non-increasing function of the threshold.

Proof. The proof follows from the assumptions that the wrapping function $g(\cdot)$ is non-decreasing, and the complexity $c(\cdot)$ is an increasing function of the length of the redundancy for given original attack trace a_i^* and threshold λ. Suppose $\bar{c}_i(\lambda_1) < \bar{c}_i(\lambda_2)$ while $\lambda_1 < \lambda_2$, which implies

$$\mathbb{E}_{\boldsymbol{a}_i^*} \left\{ \min_{\tilde{a}_i^* \in \mathscr{B}_{\lambda_1} \cap \mathscr{A}_{\boldsymbol{a}_i^*}} g(c(|\boldsymbol{a}_i^*|, |r_i^*(\boldsymbol{a}_i^*)|)) \right\} < \mathbb{E}_{\boldsymbol{a}_i^*} \left\{ \min_{\tilde{a}_i^* \in \mathscr{B}_{\lambda_2} \cap \mathscr{A}_{\boldsymbol{a}_i^*}} g(c(|\boldsymbol{a}_i^*|, |r_i^*(\boldsymbol{a}_i^*)|)) \right\}. \tag{15}$$

However, since $\lambda_1 < \lambda_2$, we have $\mathscr{B}_{\lambda_1} \subset \mathscr{B}_{\lambda_2}$. And we obtain

$$\mathbb{E}_{\boldsymbol{a}_i^*} \left\{ \min_{\tilde{a}_i^* \in \mathscr{B}_{\lambda_2} \cap \mathscr{A}_{\boldsymbol{a}_i^*}} g(c(|\boldsymbol{a}_i^*|, |r_i^*(\boldsymbol{a}_i^*)|)) \right\} \leq \mathbb{E}_{\boldsymbol{a}_i^*} \left\{ \min_{\tilde{a}_i^* \in \mathscr{B}_{\lambda_1} \cap \mathscr{A}_{\boldsymbol{a}_i^*}} g(c(|\boldsymbol{a}_i^*|, |r_i^*(\boldsymbol{a}_i^*)|)) \right\} \tag{16}$$

which constradicts with (15).   □

Furthermore, the second term in D's objective function (7), i.e., $-c_{\text{FA}} \Pr(f_i(\boldsymbol{\sigma}^{(n)}) > \lambda_i)$, is a non-decreasing function of threshold since

$$\left\{ \sigma^{(n)} \in \Sigma^{(n)} \mid f_i(\sigma^{(n)}) > \lambda_1 \right\} \subset \left\{ \sigma^{(n)} \in \Sigma^{(n)} \mid f_i(\sigma^{(n)}) > \lambda_2 \right\} \tag{17}$$

when $\lambda_1 > \lambda_2$. Therefore, D's objective function (7) is a linear combination of non-increasing and non-decreasing functions of the threshold while D seeks to maximize this objective function through the threshold $\lambda \in \Delta$. However, this yields that the objective function could be a non-convex function of the threshold and there can be many local minima. Correspondingly, gradient-based iterative approaches are likely to get stuck at such local minima. Hence, D can compute the optimal threshold through exhaustive, e.g., linear, search over Δ as in [10]. Note that we can also prune out the search based on the monotonic characterization of the terms in the objective function. Let $\lambda_{min}, \lambda_{max} \in \Delta$ denote, respectively, the smallest and largest scores in Δ. Then, we have

$$\bar{c}_i(\lambda_o) - c_{FA} \Pr(f_i(\boldsymbol{\sigma}^{(n)}) > \lambda_{max}) \geq \bar{c}_i(\lambda) - c_{FA} \Pr(f_i(\boldsymbol{\sigma}^{(n)}) > \lambda) \; \forall \lambda > \lambda_o, \quad (18)$$

$$\bar{c}_i(\lambda_{min}) - c_{FA} \Pr(f_i(\boldsymbol{\sigma}^{(n)}) > \lambda_o) \geq \bar{c}_i(\lambda) - c_{FA} \Pr(f_i(\boldsymbol{\sigma}^{(n)}) > \lambda) \; \forall \lambda < \lambda_o. \quad (19)$$

This implies that in linear search over Δ from λ_{min} to λ_{max}, D can prune out $\lambda > \lambda_o$ if

$$\max_{\lambda < \lambda_o} \left\{ \bar{c}_i(\lambda) - c_{FA} \Pr(f_i(\boldsymbol{\sigma}^{(n)}) > \lambda) \right\} \geq \bar{c}_i(\lambda_o) - c_{FA} \Pr(f_i(\boldsymbol{\sigma}^{(n)}) > \lambda_{max}). \quad (20)$$

A detailed description of the proposed algorithm is provided in Table 1.

Table 1. A description to compute equilibrium achieving defense policies for process i at process-level.

Algorithm 1: Algorithm for Optimal Threshold in Process-level

---

1: **Inputs:** $\mathbf{P}_i^A, \mathbf{P}_i, g(c(\cdot)), f_i(\cdot), c_{FA}$, and N.

2: *Initialize* $\lambda_o \leftarrow \lambda_{min}, M \leftarrow 0$

3: **for** λ **in** Δ:

4:     **Initialize** $\bar{c}_i \leftarrow 0$

5:     **for** n **in range** (N):

6:         *Draw a sample a_i^* from* $\mathbf{P}_i^A$

7:         *Compute optimal r_i^* and $c(|a_i^*|, |r_i^*|)$*

8:         $\bar{c}_i \leftarrow \bar{c}_i + g(c(|a_i^*|, |r_i^*|))$

9:     $\bar{c}_i \leftarrow \bar{c}_i / N$

10:    **if** $M \leq \bar{c}_i - c_{FA} \Pr(f_i(\boldsymbol{\sigma}^{(n)}) > \lambda)$ **then**

11:        $M \leftarrow \bar{c}_i - c_{FA} \Pr(f_i(\boldsymbol{\sigma}^{(n)}) > \lambda)$

12:        $\lambda_o \leftarrow \lambda$

13:    **if** $M \geq \bar{c}_i - c_{FA} \Pr(f_i(\boldsymbol{\sigma}^{(n)}) > \lambda_{max})$ **then**

14:        **break**

15: **return** λ_o

Remark 6. Computing the optimal threshold can be demanding because of the breath-first search, Monte Carlo simulation, and exhaustive search steps. We note, however, the optimal threshold is computed off-line before deploying the defense mechanism.

6   System-Level Game: Optimal Inter-process Adversarial Intervention Detection

At the system-level, the players A and D can select mixed strategies over their strategy spaces $\Gamma_k := \Delta^{n_k}$ and $\mathscr{D}_k$, respectively. Let $\alpha_\omega := \{\alpha_\omega^\gamma\}_{\gamma \in \Gamma_k}$ denote type-ω A's mixed strategy[3] over Γ_k and $\beta_k := \{\beta_k^d\}_{d \in \mathscr{D}_k}$ denote D's mixed strategy over $\mathscr{D}_k$. Then, the objectives of the players can be written as

$$J_{\omega,k}^{\mathsf{A}}(\alpha_\omega; \beta_k) = \sum_{\gamma \in \Gamma_k} \left(\alpha_\omega^\gamma C_{\omega,k}(\gamma) + \alpha_\omega^\gamma C_{\mathsf{D}} \sum_{d \in \mathscr{D}_k} \beta_k^d \mathbf{1}_{\{d(\gamma)=1\}} \right)$$

$$J_k^{\mathsf{D}}(\alpha_\omega, \omega \sim \mathbf{P}^\omega; \beta_k) = -p_k \mathbb{E}_\omega \{ J_{\omega,k}^{\mathsf{A}}(\alpha_\omega, \beta_k) \} + (1-p_k) C_{\mathrm{FA}} \mathbb{E}_s \left\{ \sum_{d \in \mathscr{D}_k} \beta_k^d \mathbf{1}_{\{d(s)=1\}} \right\}.$$

Note that cost functions of the players depend on D's mixed strategy β_k only through the probability of detection function $\pi_{\mathsf{D}}^{\beta_k} : \Delta^{n_k} \to [0,1]$, defined as follows:

$$\pi_{\mathsf{D}}^{\beta_k}(s) := \sum_{d \in \mathscr{D}_k} \beta_k^d \mathbf{1}_{\{d(s)=1\}}. \tag{21}$$

Therefore, the objectives of the players can also be written as

$$J_{\omega,k}^{\mathsf{A}}(\alpha_\omega; \beta_k) = \sum_{\gamma \in \Gamma_k} \left(\alpha_\omega^\gamma C_{\omega,k}(\gamma) + \alpha_\omega^\gamma C_{\mathsf{D}} \pi_{\mathsf{D}}^{\beta_k}(\gamma) \right) \tag{22}$$

$$J_k^{\mathsf{D}}(\alpha_\omega, \omega \sim \mathbf{P}^\omega; \beta_k) = -p_k \mathbb{E}_\omega \{ J_{\omega,k}^{\mathsf{A}}(\alpha_\omega, \beta_k) \} + (1-p_k) C_{\mathrm{FA}} \mathbb{E}_s \left\{ \pi_{\mathsf{D}}^{\beta_k}(s) \right\}. \tag{23}$$

Assumption 2. Uniformly Favorable Infection. For all $\omega, \omega' \in \Omega$, we have

$$C_{\omega,k}(\gamma) \geq C_{\omega,k}(\gamma') \Rightarrow C_{\omega',k}(\gamma) \geq C_{\omega',k}(\gamma'). \tag{24}$$

In other words, any infected process is not exclusively favorable for a specific type of attacker among his infected processes, since all types of attackers select which processes to infect strategically.

The following lemma shows that at mixed strategy equilibria of the game $\mathscr{G}_S^k$ if all types of attackers assign zero probability to $\gamma \in \Gamma_k$ in their mixed strategies, then D must have always classified it as benign if it is in the support of benign score distribution $\mathbf{P}_k^s$.

---

[3] For notational simplicity, we do not represent α_ω's dependence on subset k explicitly.

Lemma 2. *Let the pair $[\beta_k; \alpha_\omega, \omega \sim \mathbf{P}^\omega]$ attain mixed strategy equilibrium for the game $\mathscr{G}_S^k$. If $\alpha_\omega^\gamma = 0$ for all $\omega \in \Omega$ for some $\gamma \in \Gamma_k$, $\mathbf{P}_k^s(\gamma) > 0$ and $p_k > 0$, then we have $\pi_D^{\beta_k}(\gamma) = 0$.*

Proof. Suppose there exists $\gamma_o \in \Gamma_k$ such that $\alpha_\omega^{\gamma_o} = 0$ for all $\omega \in \Omega$ yet $\pi_D^{\beta_k}(\gamma_o) > 0$ while $\mathbf{P}_k^s(\gamma_o) > 0$. Let $\hat{\beta}$ be a mixed strategy over $\mathscr{D}_k$ such that $\pi_D^{\hat{\beta}}(\gamma_o) = 0$ and $\pi_D^{\hat{\beta}}(\gamma) = \pi_D^{\beta_k}(\gamma)$ for all $\gamma \neq \gamma_o$. Note that there exists such a mixed strategy $\hat{\beta}$ since any function, e.g., $\mu : \Delta^{n_k} \to [0,1]$, can be expressed by a mixed strategy β over $\mathscr{D}_k$ such that $\mu(s) = \pi_D^\beta(s)$ for all $s \in \Delta^{n_k}$ as shown in Lemma 2 of [4]. Then, we obtain

$$J_k^D(\alpha_\omega, \omega \sim \mathbf{P}^\omega; \hat{\beta}) = J_k^D(\alpha_\omega, \omega \sim \mathbf{P}^\omega; \beta_k) - (1 - p_k) C_{FA} \mathbf{P}_k^s(\gamma_o) \pi_D^{\beta_k}(\gamma_o)$$
$$< J_k^D(\alpha_\omega, \omega \sim \mathbf{P}^\omega; \beta_k), \tag{25}$$

which leads to a contradiction to the definition of equilibrium (12). □

Based on Lemma 2 and Assumption 2, the following lemma shows that the probability of detection (21) is a non-decreasing function of the attacker complexities.

Lemma 3. *If $C_{\omega,k}(\gamma) \leq C_{\omega,k}(\gamma')$ for $\omega \in \Omega$ and any $\gamma, \gamma' \in \Gamma_k$ in the support of $\mathbf{P}_k^s$, then at a mixed strategy Nash equilibrium, D's mixed strategy β_k satisfies $\pi_D^{\beta_k}(\gamma) \geq \pi_D^{\beta_k}(\gamma')$.*

Proof. The proof follows from Assumption 2 and [4]. Let the pair $[\beta_k; \alpha_\omega, \omega \sim \mathbf{P}^\omega]$ attain mixed strategy equilibrium for the game $\mathscr{G}_S^k$. Suppose there exist $\gamma_1, \gamma_2 \in \Gamma_k$ such that $C_{\omega,k}(\gamma_1) \leq C_{\omega,k}(\gamma_2)$ for some $\omega \in \Omega$, yet $\pi_D^{\beta_k}(\gamma_1) < \pi_D^{\beta_k}(\gamma_2)$. Then, for any $\gamma_1, \gamma_2 \in \Gamma_k$, we have the following cases:

Case 1. A selects γ_2 with non-zero probability in α_ω, i.e., $\alpha_\omega^{\gamma_1} \geq 0$ and $\alpha_\omega^{\gamma_2} > 0$. Then we have

$$C_{\omega,k}(\gamma_1) + C_D \pi_D^{\beta_k}(\gamma_1) \geq C_{\omega,k}(\gamma_2) + C_D \pi_D^{\beta_k}(\gamma_2), \tag{26}$$

while $C_{\omega,k}(\gamma_1) \leq C_{\omega,k}(\gamma_2)$, which leads to a contradiction to $\pi_D^{\beta_k}(\gamma_1) \geq \pi_D^{\beta_k}(\gamma_2)$.

Case 2. A does not select γ_2 with non-zero probability in α_ω, i.e., $\alpha_\omega^{\gamma_1} \geq 0$ and $\alpha_\omega^{\gamma_2} = 0$. Then we have

$$C_{\omega,k}(\gamma_1) + C_D \pi_D^{\beta_k}(\gamma_1) \leq C_{\omega,k}(\gamma_2) + C_D \pi_D^{\beta_k}(\gamma_2), \tag{27}$$

which does not lead to any contradiction. However, $\pi_D^{\beta_k}(\gamma_2) > \pi_D^{\beta_k}(\gamma_1) \geq 0$ implies $\pi_D^{\beta_k}(\gamma_2) > 0$ and Lemma 2 yields that there exists $\omega' \in \Omega$ such that $\alpha_{\omega'}^{\gamma_2} > 0$. Then, by the definition of equilibrium (12), we obtain

$$C_{\omega',k}(\gamma_1) + C_D \pi_D^{\beta_k}(\gamma_1) \geq C_{\omega',k}(\gamma_2) + C_D \pi_D^{\beta_k}(\gamma_2) \tag{28}$$

while $C_{\omega',k}(\gamma_1) \leq C_{\omega',k}(\gamma_2)$ by Assumption 2 and condition $C_{\omega,k}(\gamma_1) \leq C_{\omega,k}(\gamma_2)$. This leads to a contradiction to $\pi_D^{\beta_k}(\gamma_1) \geq \pi_D^{\beta_k}(\gamma_2)$.

This concludes the proof. □

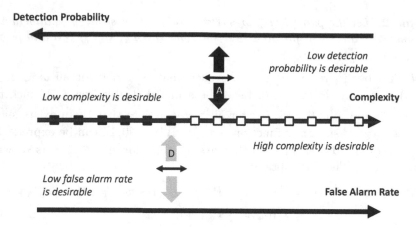

Fig. 3. At any mixed-Nash equilibria, A selects a mixed strategy over the multiplication factors leading to discrete complexities while D selects a mixed strategy over all the detection rules setting a threshold on A's complexity. Therefore, A can be detected with some probability based on the selected mixed strategies, and the players A and D select the mixed strategies with respect to the trade-off between low detection probability versus high complexity, and high false alarm rate versus high complexity, respectively.

Recall that there exists a mixed strategy Nash equilibrium because of the finiteness of the strategy spaces [1]. Based on Lemma 3 and [4], the following theorem characterizes the equilibrium achieving strategy pairs.

Theorem 1. *For system-level game $\mathcal{G}_S^k$, D can attain any mixed strategy equilibrium via mixed strategies over the detection rules that set threshold for the attacker complexity. Correspondingly, A can attain any mixed strategy equilibrium via mixed strategies over quotient space of the multiplication factors, where the equivalence relation is defined with respect to the associated complexity, i.e., $\gamma \sim \gamma'$ if, and only if, $C_{\omega,k}(\gamma) = C_{\omega,k}(\gamma')$.*

Proof. The proof follows directly from Theorem 1 in [4] and Lemma 3 since probability of detection is non-decreasing function of the attacker complexity for all $\gamma \in \Gamma_k$, i.e., in or out of $\mathbf{P}_k^s$'s support. We emphasize that if A selects a pure strategy $\gamma_o \in \Gamma_k$ that is out of $\mathbf{P}_k^s$'s support, then D's detection rule must have detected it with probability 1, i.e., $\pi_D^{\beta_k}(\gamma_o) = 1$, since there is no trade-off due to an associated false alarm. Therefore, A could select a pure strategy γ_o that is out of $\mathbf{P}_k^s$'s support with a non-zero probability if, and only if, γ_o attains the minimum possible complexity, i.e., $C_{\omega,k}(\gamma_o) = \min_{\gamma \in \Gamma_k} C_{\omega,k}(\gamma)$, and

$$C_{\omega,k}(\gamma_o) + C_D \leq C_{\omega,k}(\gamma') + C_D \pi_D^{\beta_k}(\gamma') \ \forall \gamma'. \tag{29}$$

We obtain $C_{\omega,k}(\gamma_o) \leq C_{\omega,k}(\gamma')$ and $\pi_D^{\beta_k}(\gamma_o) = 1 \geq \pi_D^{\beta_k}(\gamma')$. Therefore, $\pi_D^{\beta_k}(\cdot)$ is a non-increasing function of the complexity function $C_\omega(\gamma)$ over all Γ_k. This concludes the proof. $\square$

Theorem 1 reduces the system-level game into one-dimension, where A mixes over the complexities while D mixes over the thresholds for these complexities as seen in Fig. 3. Note also that a pure strategy is also a degenerate mixed strategy. However, there may not exist a pure strategy equilibrium in general [1]. Furthermore, Theorem 1 does *not* imply that if a pure strategy equilibrium exists, then D can attain the pure strategy equilibrium via a detection rule setting threshold for the attacker complexity. In the following, we characterize pure strategy equilibria when D *restricts* herself only to such threshold based detection rules and A selects the complexity through the multiplication factors.

Let $\Xi_k \subset [0, \infty)$ denote the finite range of $C_{\omega,k}$ while $C_{\min}$ and $C_{\max}$ denote the minimum and maximum complexities, respectively. As an example, $C_{\min} \in \Xi_k$ could be obtained when $\gamma = 1$ while $C_{\max} \in \Xi_k$ could be obtained when $\gamma = 0$. Furthermore, by Assumption 2, if D selects a threshold $\xi_\omega \in \Xi_k$ for $C_{\omega,k}$ then for any $\omega' \in \Omega$, there exists certain $\xi_{\omega'} \in \Xi_k$ such that for all $\gamma \in \Gamma_k$, we have

$$C_{\omega,k}(\gamma) \le \xi_\omega \Leftrightarrow C_{\omega',k}(\gamma) \le \xi_{\omega'}. \tag{30}$$

Therefore, D indeed only selects a single threshold. Let

$$\Lambda_k := \{\{\xi_\omega \in \Xi_k\}_\omega | \xi_\omega \text{ and } \xi_{\omega'} \text{ satisfy } (30) \; \forall \omega, \omega' \in \Omega\}$$

denote all such thresholds for different type attacker complexities. Note that Λ_k is a totally ordered set. Correspondingly, let $FA : \Lambda_k \to [0,1]$ denote the false alarm rate for the threshold $\xi \in \Lambda_k$. Then, $FA(\cdot)$ is a non-decreasing function of the threshold ξ.

The following theorem characterizes the pure strategy equilibrium for the scenarios where the strategy spaces of the players are restricted as such.

Theorem 2. *Suppose type ω attacker selects[4] $C_\omega \in \Xi$ while D selects $\xi \in \Lambda$ such that the attacker is detected if $\xi_\omega \ge C_\omega$. Suppose also that cost of detection for A is sufficiently large, i.e., C_D is larger than any unit decrease in complexity cost. Let $\mathscr{E} \subset \Omega$ denote the type indices of the evasive attackers, i.e., $\mathscr{E} := \{\omega \in \Omega | C_\omega \le \xi_\omega\}$. Then, a pure strategy equilibrium $[\xi; C_\omega, \omega \sim \mathbf{P}^\omega]$ satisfies*

$$C_\omega = \begin{cases} C_{\min} & \text{if } \omega \in \Omega \backslash \mathscr{E} \\ \xi_\omega^+ & \text{else} \end{cases} \quad \text{and} \quad \begin{array}{l} i) \;\; FA(\xi) = FA_{\min} \\ ii) \;\; \xi_\omega^+ \ge C_{\min} + C_D \text{ for } \omega \in \Omega \backslash \mathscr{E} \\ iii) \;\; p_k \Pr(\omega \in \mathscr{E}) \le \frac{(1-p_k)C_{FA}}{C_D}(FA(\xi^+) - FA(\xi)) \end{array}$$
$$\tag{31}$$

where $FA_{\min} \in [0,1]$ denotes the minimum possible false alarm rate, e.g., $FA_{\min} = 0$, and ξ^+ denotes the element next to ξ in the totally ordered set Λ.

Proof. Given $[\xi; C_\omega, \omega \sim \mathbf{P}^\omega]$, suppose we have

$$\omega_1 := \operatorname{argmax}\{\omega \in \Omega | C_\omega \le \xi_\omega\} \tag{32}$$

$$\omega_2 := \operatorname{argmin}\{\omega \in \Omega | C_\omega > \xi_\omega\} \tag{33}$$

---

[4] For notational simplicity, we have dropped the subset index k.

and $\xi_1 \in \Lambda$ leads to $C_{\omega_1} = \xi_{1,\omega_1}$ while $\xi_2 \in \Lambda$ leads to $C_{\omega_2} = \xi_{2,\omega_2}$.

Type ω_1 attacker, which is detected by D, has incentive to decrease the complexity unless $C_{\omega_1} = C_{\min}$ since he will still be detected yet at least with minimum complexity. He has incentive to increase the complexity if he can be evasive with a cost that is less than the current one, i.e., if $C_{\omega_1} + C_D > \xi_{\omega_1}^+$. On the other side, D would have incentive to decrease the threshold unless a decrease in threshold does not lead to a decrease in false alarm rate, i.e., if $FA(\xi) = FA_{\min}$, or a change the decrease in threshold leads to a change in the detection of an attacker.

Type ω_2 attacker, which is not detected by D, has incentive to decrease the complexity as long as $C_{\omega_2} \geq \xi_{\omega_2}^+$, i.e., as long as he remains undetectable. On the other side, D can have incentive to decrease the threshold in order to decrease the false alarm rate. Or D can have incentive to increase the threshold unless the increase in the false alarm rate is less than the benefit of detecting type ω_2 attacker, i.e., if

$$p_k C_D \Pr(\boldsymbol{\omega} = \omega_2) > (1 - p_k) C_{FA} (FA(\xi_2) - FA(\xi)). \tag{34}$$

Therefore, a pure strategy equilibrium exists if, and only if, (31) is satisfied. □

Remark 7. Due to the restrictive conditions in (31), Theorem 2 yields that pure strategy equilibrium may not exist in general.

The following lemma shows that an increase in the multiplication factor leads to a decrease in the complexity, and correspondingly, leads to an increase in probability of detection.

Lemma 4. *Let "$\prec$" denote a partial order over Γ_k such that for $\gamma := \{\gamma_i\}_i, \gamma' := \{\gamma_i'\}_i \in \Gamma_k$, we say $\gamma \prec \gamma'$ if $\gamma_i < \gamma_i'$ for all i. Then, at any mixed-strategy Nash equilibrium of $\mathscr{G}_S^k$, i.e., $[\beta_k; \alpha_{\boldsymbol{\omega}}, \boldsymbol{\omega} \sim \mathbf{P}^{\omega}]$, if $\gamma \prec \gamma'$, then we have $C_{\omega,k}(\gamma) \geq C_{\omega,k}(\gamma') \forall \omega \in \Omega$, and correspondingly $\pi_D^{\beta_k}(\gamma) \leq \pi_D^{\beta_k}(\gamma')$.*

Proof. By Lemma 3 and (29), whether γ and γ' are in the support of $\mathbf{P}_i^s$ or not, we have $\pi_D^{\beta_k}(\gamma) \leq \pi_D^{\beta_k}(\gamma')$ if $C_{\omega,k}(\gamma) \geq C_{\omega,k}(\gamma')$. Suppose $\gamma \prec \gamma'$ yet $C_{\omega,k}(\gamma) < C_{\omega,k}(\gamma')$. Then, by (6) and (9), $C_{\omega,k}(\gamma) < C_{\omega,k}(\gamma')$ can be written as

$$g\left(\sum_i \inf_{r_i^* \in \mathscr{W}_i} c(|a_i^*|, |r_i^*|)\right) < g\left(\sum_i \inf_{r_i^* \in \mathscr{W}_i'} c(|a_i^*|, |r_i^*|)\right), \tag{35}$$

where the constraint sets on the redundant instructions are defined by $\mathscr{W}_i := \{r_i^* \in \Sigma^* | f_i(\tilde{a}_{i,t}^{(n)}) \leq \gamma_{i,t} \lambda_i\}$ and $\mathscr{W}_i' := \{r_i^* \in \Sigma^* | f_i(\tilde{a}_{i,t}^{(n)}) \leq \gamma_{i,t}' \lambda_i\}$. Since $\gamma \prec \gamma'$, we obtain $\gamma_{i,t} < \gamma_{i,t}'$ for all i and t, which implies $\mathscr{W}_i \subset \mathscr{W}_i'$ for all i. However, this relation between the constraint sets leads to a contradiction to $C_{\omega,k}(\gamma) \geq C_{\omega,k}(\gamma')$. □

Based on Lemma 4, the following lemma analyzes the coupling between process and system level games. The lemma implies that at any mixed strategy equilibrium, A assigns non-zero probabilities to the multiplication factors close to 1. Therefore, if D increases the threshold at the process level, then A would also give non-zero probabilities to the multiplication factors leading to larger scores, and correspondingly, lower complexities.

Lemma 5. *Suppose* $[\beta_k; \alpha_\omega, \omega \sim \mathbf{P}^\omega]$ *has attained a mixed strategy equilibrium in subset* k. *If there exists* $\gamma_o \in \Delta$ *such that* $\alpha_\omega^\gamma = 0$ *for* $\gamma_o \prec \gamma$ *for all* $\omega \in \Omega$, *then* $\gamma_o = 1$ *unless* $\pi_D^{\beta_k}(\gamma) = 0$ *for all* $\gamma \in \Gamma_k$, *i.e., if* D *assesses every score as benign.*

Proof. Suppose there exists $\gamma_o \in \Delta$ such that $\alpha_\omega^\gamma = 0$ for $\gamma_o \prec \gamma$ for all $\omega \in \Omega$ and $\gamma_o \neq 1$. Then, Lemma 2 implies that $\pi_D^{\beta_k}(\gamma) = 0$ for $\gamma_o \prec \gamma$. However, we have $\gamma_o \prec 1$ and this yields that $\pi_D^{\beta_k}(1) = 0$. Correspondingly, Lemma 4 implies that $\pi_D^{\beta_k}(\gamma) \leq \pi_D^{\beta_k}(1) = 0$ for all $\gamma \prec 1$, i.e., $\pi_D^{\beta_k}(\gamma) = 0$ for all $\gamma \in \Gamma_k$. Note that if $\gamma_o = 1$, we have $\{1 \prec \gamma\} = \varnothing$. This concludes the proof. □

7   Concluding Remarks

We have provided a two-level game theoretical framework for inter-process advanced and evasive adversarial intervention detection. This two-level framework has facilitated abstraction of the complicated process-level interaction between IDSs and evasively crafted malicious codes from more flexible and easier to interpret system-level interaction across the processes. Within a game theoretical framework, we have analyzed the incentives of the players while selecting their strategies. We have also highlighted the significance of anticipating the reaction of the advanced evasive adversaries to the selected defense mechanisms. Finally, we have analyzed the coupling between process and system level games.

Some future directions of research on this topic include:

- A *provenance graph* $\mathscr{P} = (\mathscr{V}, \mathscr{E})$ is a directed graph, where $\mathscr{V}$ denotes the set of vertices representing the objects, i.e., processes or files or external hosts, and $\mathscr{E}$ denotes the set of edges representing the information-flow among the objects, e.g., due to system-calls [11]. Inter-process information flow can be captured via a provenance graph. Incorporating the provenance graph into the system-level game can enable more effective defense measures.
- Empirical evalution of the proposed defense measures in real life cyber attack scenarios is left as a future work.
- Here, we have only considered single-shot games. This formulation can also be extended to multi-stage games in dynamic environments as in [21].
- We haved considered here the scenarios where IDSs provide discrete scores for the sub-traces while its extension to continuum is left as a future work.

References

1. Başar, T., Olsder, G.: Dynamic Noncooperative Game Theory. Society for Industrial Mathematics (SIAM) Series in Classics, Applied Mathematics (1999)
2. Barabosch, T., Gerhards-Padilla, E.: Host-based code injection attacks: a popular technique used by malware. In: The 9th International Conference on Malicious and Unwanted Software: The Americas (MALWARE) (2014)
3. Brangetto, P., Aubyn, M.K.-S.: Economic aspects of national cyber security strategies. Technical report, NATO Cooperative Cyber Defense Centre of Excellence Tallinn, Estonia (2015)
4. Dritsoula, L., Loiseau, P., Musacchio, J.: A game-theoretic analysis of adversarial classification. IEEE Trans. Inf. Forensics Secur. **12**(12), 3094–3109 (2017)
5. Du, M., Li, F., Zheng, G., Srikumar, V.: DeepLog: anomaly detection and diagnosis from system logs through deep learning. In: Proceedings of the 24th ACM Conference on Computer and Communications Security (2017)
6. Elisan, C.C.: Malware, Rootkits and Botnets: A Beginner's Guide. McGraw-Hill, New York (2013)
7. Feng, H.H., Kolesnikov, O.M., Fogla, P., Lee, W., Gong, W.: Anomaly detection using call stack information. In: Proceedings of the IEEE Security and Privacy (2003)
8. Forrest, S., Hofmeyr, S.A., Somayaji, A., Longstaff, T.A.: A sense of self for Unix processes. In: Proceedings of IEEE Symposium on Security and Privacy (1996)
9. Gao, D., Reiter, M.K., Song, D.: On gray-box program tracking for anomaly detection. In: Proceedings of the 13th Conference on USENIX Security Symposium (2004)
10. Ghafouri, A., Abbas, W., Laszka, A., Vorobeychik, Y., Koutsoukos, X.: Optimal thresholds for anomaly-based intrusion detection in dynamical environments. In: Zhu, Q., Alpcan, T., Panaousis, E., Tambe, M., Casey, W. (eds.) GameSec 2016. LNCS, vol. 9996, pp. 415–434. Springer, Cham (2016). https://doi.org/10.1007/978-3-319-47413-7_24
11. Ji, Y., et al.: RAIN: refinable attack investigation with on-demand inter-process information flow tracking. In: Proceedings of the 24th ACM Conference on Computer and Communications Security (2017)
12. Kruegel, C., Kirda, E., Mutz, D., Robertson, W., Vigna, G.: Automating mimicry attacks using static binary analysis. In: Proceedings of the 14th USENIX Security Symposium (2005)
13. Manzoor, E., Milajerdi, S.M., Akoglu, L.: Fast memory-efficient anomaly detection in streaming heterogeneous graphs. In: Proceedings of the 22nd ACM SIGKDD International Conference on Knowledge Discovery and Data Mining (2016)
14. Parampalli, C., Sekar, R., Johanson, R.: A practical mimicry attack against powerful system-call monitors. In: Proceedings of the 2008 ACM Symposium on Information, Computer and Communications Security (2008)
15. Shu, X., Yao, D.D., Ryder, B.G.: A formal framework for program anomaly detection. In: Bos, H., Monrose, F., Blanc, G. (eds.) RAID 2015. LNCS, vol. 9404, pp. 270–292. Springer, Cham (2015). https://doi.org/10.1007/978-3-319-26362-5_13
16. Silberschatz, A., Galvin, P.B., Gagne, G.: Operating System Concepts. Wiley, Hoboken (2013)
17. Somayaji, A., Forest, S.: Automated response using system-call delays. In: Proceedings of the 9th USENIX Security Symposium (2000)

18. Wagner, D., Dean, D.: Intrusion detection via static analysis. In: Proceedings of the Symposium on Security and Privacy (2001)
19. Wagner, D., Soto, P.: Mimicry attacks on host-based intrusion detection systems. In: Proceedings of the 9th ACM Conference on Computer and Communications Security (2002)
20. Yao, D., Shu, X., Cheng, L., Stolfo, S.J.: Anomaly Detection as a Service: Challenges, Advances, and Opportunities. Synthesis Lectures on Information Security, Privacy, and Thrust #22, Morgan & Claypool Publishers (2017)
21. Zhu, Q., Başar, T.: Game-theoretic methods for robustness, security, and resiliency of cyberphysical control systems: games-in-games principle for cross-layer resilient control systems. IEEE Control Syst. Mag. **35**(1), 46–65 (2015)

Cyber-Insurance as a Signaling Game: Self-reporting and External Security Audits

Aron Laszka[1], Emmanouil Panaousis[2(✉)], and Jens Grossklags[3]

[1] Department of Computer Science, University of Houston, Houston, USA
[2] Surrey Centre for Cyber Security, University of Surrey, Guildford, UK
`e.panaousis@surrey.ac.uk`
[3] Department of Informatics, Technical University of Munich, Munich, Germany

Abstract. An insurer has to know the risks faced by a potential client to accurately determine an insurance premium offer. However, while the potential client might have a good understanding of its own security practices, it may also have an incentive not to disclose them honestly since the resulting information asymmetry could work in its favor. This information asymmetry engenders adverse selection, which can result in *unfair premiums* and *reduced adoption of cyber-insurance*. To overcome information asymmetry, insurers often require potential clients to self-report their risks. Still, clients do not have any incentive to perform thorough self-audits or to provide comprehensive reports. As a result, insurers have to complement self-reporting with external security audits to verify the clients' reports. Since these audits can be very expensive, a key problem faced by insurers is to devise an auditing strategy that deters clients from dishonest reporting using a minimal number of audits. To solve this problem, we model the interactions between a potential client and an insurer as a two-player signaling game. One player represents the client, who knows its actual security-investment level, but may report any level to the insurer. The other player represents the insurer, who knows only the random distribution from which the security level was drawn, but may discover the actual level using an expensive audit. We study the players' equilibrium strategies and provide numerical illustrations.

1 Introduction

Technological innovations, such as artificial intelligence and ubiquitous computing, are becoming integral parts of our lives, and providing us with many benefits. But these developments also bring new threats, and the insurance industry is playing catch-up to keep pace with the rapid rise of cyber-risks. Cyber-threat remains one of the most significant—and growing—risks facing businesses. For example, a UK government survey estimated that in 2014, 81% of large corporations and 60% of small businesses have suffered a security breach. The average cost of breaches, in the UK, was between £600,000 and £1.15 million for large businesses and between £65,000 and £115,000 for small businesses [1]. Further,

L. Bushnell et al. (Eds.): GameSec 2018, LNCS 11199, pp. 508–520, 2018.
https://doi.org/10.1007/978-3-030-01554-1_29

in 2016, more than 1.1 billion identities were stolen in data breaches, almost double the number stolen in 2015 [23]. In aggregate, Forbes reports that cyber-crime losses will be more than US$2.1 trillion by 2019 [9].

Unfortunately, even with the strongest cyber-security controls purchased and implemented, an organization is at risk of being compromised. As such, apart from security measures, responses to cyber-security risk include outsourcing it by purchasing cyber-insurance coverage. However, 60% of Fortune 500 companies still lack any insurance against cyber-incidents, primarily due to a lack of cover currently available for many types of cyber-risk [14].

Cyber-insurance, as any other field of insurance, faces a number of challenges [6,15,16]. In particular, *asymmetry of information* and the resulting *adverse selection* caused by organizations being reluctant to share their actual levels of cyber-risk may present significant premium pricing obstacles to insurers. It is, therefore, perhaps unsurprising that insurers tend to offer a pricing structure that charges companies similar rates regardless of the underlying actual risks [18]. However, if a cyber-insurer cannot differentiate between clients based on their security level and therefore cannot offer differentiated premiums, the insurer will not be able to sustain a profitable business [3].

Typically, insurers require organizations to self-report on their security level in order to determine premiums. Prior to setting the premium, the insurer must then decide whether the security level reported by the client must be confirmed by undertaking some audit (e.g., penetration testing). Although it is beneficial for the insurer to know the exact security level of its potential client so that it can ask for a *fair* premium, there is a cost associated with conducting an audit.[1] The insurer has two options: (i) to trust that the security level the client reported is true and compute the premium based on this level, thereby saving audit costs; or (ii) not to trust the reported security level and perform an audit to reveal the real security level despite having to pay for an audit to take place.

After the insurer offers a premium, the client must decide whether it will accept the offer and be underwritten, or whether it will not use cyber-insurance at all. This is an important decision to be made, and it has been noticed that many organizations, especially small-to-medium enterprises, decide not to purchase cyber-insurance due to the incurred financial costs [11].

Contributions: The aim of this research is to introduce a new model to study optimal strategies for self-reporting security levels (for organizations) and undertaking audits (for insurers). The insurers' strategy aims to ensure that the actual security levels of their clients have been elicited and therefore "fair" contracts (coverage, premium) are put in place.

More concretely, we model the interactions between a potential client and an insurer as a two-player signaling game, where the organization plays the role of the sender, while the insurer plays the role of the receiver. We assess our game model using numeric simulations to derive the probability of reporting each type,

---

[1] In fact, the cost of penetration testing, cyber-security risk assessment and related services is non-trivial and quickly increases with the size of an organization. See, for example, the pricing examples at: https://www.trustnetinc.com/pricing/.

the audit probabilities, and the insurance premiums for various audit cost values. The proposed game-theoretic model can form the basis of a framework that can further accelerate the adoption of cyber-insurance.

2 Model

We model the interactions between an *insurer* and a potential client, whom we will call the *organization*, as a two-player single-shot game. For a list of symbols that are used in our model, see Table 1. We assume that the organization has a type $t \in S$, where S is a finite set of types. Type t models the level of security investments and the combination of security measures that the organization implements. For simplicity, we let type t be equal to the estimated probability of the organization not suffering a cyber-incident.

Table 1. List of symbols

Symbol	Description
S	Set of organization types (i.e., security levels)
P_t	Probability of the organization's type being t
t, T	Organization's real type (realization, random variable)
r, R	Organization's reported type (realization, random variable)
p	Cyber-insurance premium
ρ^t	Reporting strategy of organization with real type t
a	Insurer's strategy for auditing the organization
p^A	Insurer's strategy for premium selection after auditing
p^N	Insurer's strategy for premium selection without auditing
W	Organization's initial wealth
L	Organization's loss in case of a cyber-incident
U	Organization's utility function
C	Insurer's cost for auditing the organization

The organization applies for insurance coverage and the insurer determines the premium as follows (Fig. 1):

- First, the organization's type t is drawn randomly from the set of types S according to a known distribution[2]. We let T denote the random variable taking the value of the organization's type, and we let P_t denote the probability that the organization's type is t (i.e., $P_t = \Pr[T = t]$).

---

[2] Randomness models the insurer's a priori uncertainty regarding what type of organization it faces.

- Second, the organization chooses a type $r \in S$ that it reports to the insurer. The organization's choice may be randomized based on a mixed strategy. We let R denote the random variable taking the value of the reported type.
- Based on the reported type r, the insurer decides whether to audit the organization or not. If the insurer chooses to audit the organization, then the true type t is revealed, but the insurer incurs a constant auditing cost C.
- Finally, based on the type t or r (depending on whether the organization has been audited), the insurer chooses a premium p that is asked from the organization in exchange for insurance coverage. The organization rejects the coverage if doing so increases its utility; otherwise, it accepts the coverage and pays the premium.

2.1 Strategies

An organization's strategic choice is to select what type to report to the insurer. We let ρ^t denote the mixed strategy of an organization with real type t, where ρ_r^t is the probability that the organization reports type r (i.e., $\rho_r^t = \Pr[R = r \mid T = t]$). Note that we assume that the organization's strategic choice does not include coverage acceptance or rejection (i.e., we assume that coverage is rejected if and only if it is not worth purchasing). This is similar to assuming that the organization makes coverage decisions but restricting the solutions to subgame perfect equilibria (i.e., prohibiting non-credible threats of not purchasing insurance).

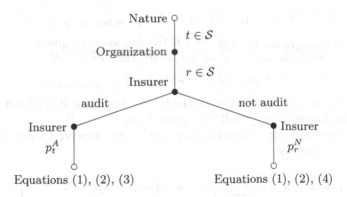

Fig. 1. Tree representation of the game. The players' payoffs are given by Eqs. (1), (2), (3), and (4).

The insurer's first strategic choice is to decide whether to audit the organization or not. Before auditing, the insurer does not know the organization's real type t, but it does know the exogenous parameter values of the model[3], which include the distribution from which the type was drawn (i.e., it knows the

---

[3] These may be learned from statistics that are available to the insurer.

probabilities P_t), as well as the organization's reporting strategies $\boldsymbol{\rho}$. We let $\boldsymbol{a}$ denote the insurer's strategy, where a_r is the probability that the insurer audits an organization with reported type r. The insurer's second strategic choice is to choose a premium p. First, we let $\boldsymbol{p}^N$ denote the insurer's strategy given that it has not performed an audit, where p_r^N is the premium asked from an organization with reported type r. Second, we let $\boldsymbol{p}^A$ denote the insurer's strategy given that it has performed an audit, where p_t^A is the premium asked from an organization with real type t.

2.2   Payoffs

Now, we define the players' payoffs in the various outcomes of our game. As it is standard in the cyber-insurance literature, we capture the risk aversion of clients using a concave utility function, initial wealth, and potential losses. First, the organization's payoff (i.e., utility), if it accepts coverage is

$$\mathcal{U}_t^{org,acc}(p) = U(W - p), \tag{1}$$

where W is the organization's initial wealth, and U is its utility function, which we assume to be continuous, monotonically increasing, and concave.

Second, the organization's payoff if it rejects coverage is

$$\mathcal{U}_t^{org,rej} = (1 - t) \cdot U(W - L) + t \cdot U(W), \tag{2}$$

where L is its loss in case of a cyber-incident. The two terms correspond to the cases of suffering a cyber-incident and not suffering one, respectively.

If the insurer audits the organization, its payoff (i.e., profit) is

$$\mathcal{U}^{ins,aud}(t,p) = (p - (1 - t) \cdot L) \cdot 1_{\{\text{insurance accepted}\}} - C, \tag{3}$$

where $1_{\{\text{insurance accepted}\}}$ is equal to 1 if the organization purchases insurance, and 0 otherwise. If the insurer does not audit, then its payoff is

$$\mathcal{U}^{ins,noaud}(t,p) = (p - (1 - t) \cdot L) \cdot 1_{\{\text{insurance accepted}\}}. \tag{4}$$

Note that the insurer does not learn the true value of t if it does not audit the organization; however, its payoff still depends on t.

Given mixed-strategy profile $(\boldsymbol{\rho}, (\boldsymbol{a}, \boldsymbol{p}^N, \boldsymbol{p}^A))$, the expected utility of an organization with type t is

$$\mathbb{E}\left[\mathcal{U}_t^{org}\right](\boldsymbol{\rho}, \boldsymbol{a}, \boldsymbol{p}^N, \boldsymbol{p}^A) = \sum_{r \in \mathcal{S}} \rho_r^t \left[a_r \cdot \max\left\{\mathcal{U}_t^{org,acc}(p_t^A),\ \mathcal{U}_t^{org,rej}\right\} \right.$$

$$\left. + (1 - a_r) \cdot \max\left\{\mathcal{U}_t^{org,acc}(p_r^N),\ \mathcal{U}_t^{org,rej}\right\}\right],$$

while the insurer's expected utility is

$$\mathbb{E}\left[\mathcal{U}^{ins}\right](\boldsymbol{\rho}, \boldsymbol{a}, \boldsymbol{p}^N, \boldsymbol{p}^A) =$$

$$\sum_{t \in \mathcal{S}} P_t \sum_{r \in \mathcal{S}} \rho_r^t \left[a_r \cdot \mathcal{U}^{ins,aud}(t, p_t^A) + (1 - a_r) \cdot \mathcal{U}^{ins,noaud}(t, p_r^N)\right].$$

2.3   Solution Concept

We are interested in finding an equilibrium of our game, which can capture the long-term insurance market equilibrium. Since our model is essentially a signalling game, we use *perfect Bayesian Nash equilibrium* as the solution concept.

After receiving the reported level r, the insurer's belief regarding the potential client's real type can be expressed using Bayes' rule as

$$\Pr[T = t \mid R = r] = \frac{\Pr[T = t, R = r]}{\Pr[R = r]} = \frac{P_t \cdot \rho_r^t}{\sum_{t' \in \mathcal{S}} P_{t'} \cdot \rho_r^{t'}}.$$

A mixed-strategy profile $(\rho^*, (a^*, p^{N*}, p^{A*}))$ is an equilibrium if

- for each security level $t \in \mathcal{S}$, the strategy ρ^{t*} maximizes the expected utility of an organization with level t given the insurer's strategy (a^*, p^{N*}, p^{A*}):

$$\rho^{t*} \in \operatorname{argmax}_{\rho^t} \mathbb{E}\left[\mathcal{U}_t^{org}\right] \left(\rho^t, a, p^N, p^A\right);$$

- for each reported security level $r \in S$, the strategy (a^*, p^{N*}, p^{A*}) maximizes the expected utility of the insurer given its belief regarding the potential client's real type t:

$$(a^*, p^{N*}, p^{A*}) \in \operatorname{argmax}_{(a, p^N, p^A)} \sum_{t \in \mathcal{S}} \Pr[T = t \mid R = r] \Big[a_r \cdot \mathcal{U}^{ins, aud}(t, p_t^A)$$

$$+ (1 - a_r) \cdot \mathcal{U}^{ins, noaud}(t, p_r^N)\Big].$$

3   Preliminary Analysis

Next, we provide some necessary conditions on the players' best responses.

Lemma 1. *An organization of type t accepts insurance coverage for premium p if and only if $p \leq \hat{p}_t$, where*

$$\hat{p}_t = W - U^{-1}\left((1 - t) \cdot U(W - L) + t \cdot U(W)\right). \tag{5}$$

Proof. By definition, an organization with type t accepts coverage for premium p if and only if

$$\mathcal{U}_t^{org, acc}(p) \geq \mathcal{U}_t^{org, rej}$$
$$U(W - p) \geq (1 - t) \cdot U(W - L) + t \cdot U(W)$$
$$W - p \geq U^{-1}\left((1 - t) \cdot U(W - L) + t \cdot U(W)\right)$$
$$p \leq W - U^{-1}\left((1 - t) \cdot U(W - L) + t \cdot U(W)\right) := \hat{p}_t.$$

$\square$

Lemma 2. *In an equilibrium, the premium $p_t^{A^*}$ that an insurer requests from an organization with type t after an audit is $p_t^{A^*} = \hat{p}_t$ if $\hat{p}_t \geq (1-t) \cdot L$. Otherwise, the insurer asks for some premium $p_t^{A^*} > p_t^*$, which will always be rejected by the organization.*

Proof. If the insurer has audited an organization and found its type to be t, then its payoff for premium p will be

$$\mathcal{U}^{ins,aud}(t,p) = (p - (1-t) \cdot L) \cdot 1_{\{\text{insurance accepted}\}} - C \qquad (6)$$

$$= (p - (1-t) \cdot L) \cdot 1_{\{p \leq \hat{p}_t\}} - C. \qquad (7)$$

When $p \leq \hat{p}_t$, the first derivative of the payoff $\mathcal{U}^{ins,aud}(t,p)$ is

$$\frac{\partial \mathcal{U}^{ins,aud}(t,p)}{\partial p} = 1; \qquad (8)$$

hence, the maximum on interval $(-\infty, \hat{p}_t]$ is attained at $\hat{p}_t$, and the maximum payoff is $\hat{p}_t - (1-t) \cdot L - C$. When $p > \hat{p}_t$, the payoff is always $-C$ since the organization rejects coverage. Hence, $\hat{p}_t$ is an optimal premium $p_t^{A^*}$ if and only if

$$\hat{p}_t - (1-t) \cdot L - C \geq -C \qquad (9)$$

$$\hat{p}_t \geq (1-t) \cdot L; \qquad (10)$$

otherwise, premiums greater than $\hat{p}_t$ are optimal, which will be rejected.   □

Lemma 3. *In an equilibrium, the premium $p_r^{N^*}$ that an insurer requests without an audit from an organization with reported type r is either $p_r^{N^*} \in \{\hat{p}_t \mid t \in \mathcal{S}\}$, which may be accepted by some organizations, or $p_r^{N^*} > \max \{\hat{p}_t \mid t \in \mathcal{S}\}$, which will be rejected by any organization.*

Proof. If the insurer has not audited an organization that reported type r, then its payoff for premium p will be

$$\sum_{t \in \mathcal{S}} \Pr[T = t | R = r] \mathcal{U}^{ins,noaud}(t,p) \qquad (11)$$

$$= \sum_{t \in \mathcal{S}} \Pr[T = t | R = r] (p - (1-t) \cdot L) \cdot 1_{\{\text{insurance accepted}\}} \qquad (12)$$

$$= \sum_{t \in \mathcal{S}} \Pr[T = t | R = r] (p - (1-t) \cdot L) \cdot 1_{\{p \leq \hat{p}_t\}}. \qquad (13)$$

The values $\{\hat{p}_t \mid t \in \mathcal{S}\}$ divide the set of possible premium values $[0, \infty)$ into $|\mathcal{S}|+1$ contiguous intervals, the last one being $(\max \{\hat{p}_t \mid t \in \mathcal{S}\}, \infty)$. The payoff is strictly increasing on each interval, except for the last one. On the last interval, $(\max \{\hat{p}_t \mid t \in \mathcal{S}\}, \infty)$, the payoff is always zero. Therefore, the optimal premium $p_r^{N^*}$ is either one of the values $\{\hat{p}_t \mid t \in \mathcal{S}\}$ or any value $p_r^{N^*} > \max \{\hat{p}_t \mid t \in \mathcal{S}\}$, which will be rejected by any organization.   □

4   Numerical Illustrations

In this section, we present numerical illustrations of our model. We let $\mathcal{S} = \{0.5, 0.65, 0.8, 0.95\}$, $W = 10$, $L = 5$, the utility function U be the natural logarithm function, and the organization's type t be drawn according to $P_{0.5} = 0.125$, $P_{0.65} = 0.375$, $P_{0.8} = 0.375$, and $P_{0.95} = 0.125$; we used numerical search to find equilibria for various audit costs C.

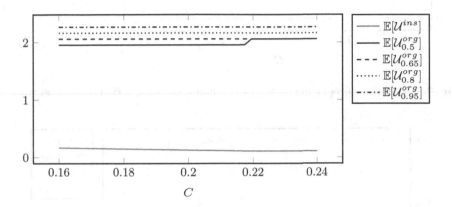

Fig. 2. Players' payoffs in equilibrium with various audit cost values.

Figure 2 shows the organization's and the insurer's expected payoffs in equilibrium as functions of the audit cost C. The organization's expected payoff remains steady if it is secure and has little incentive to misreport. But in the case of an organization with security level 0.5, the payoff increases when the auditing cost reaches the value of 0.22. On the other hand, the insurer's expected payoff decreases with the auditing cost, but the rate of reduction is fairly small.

Figure 3 shows the probabilities $\Pr[T = t]$ of reporting various types as functions of the audit cost C. We observe rampant misreporting since the organization's security level is either $t = 0.5$ or $t = 0.65$ with probability $0.5 = P_{0.5} + P_{0.65}$, but it *never* reports these low levels (i.e., $\Pr[R = 0.5] = 0$ and $\Pr[R = 0.65] = 0$). We also see that the probability $\Pr[R = 0.95]$ of misreporting a higher, "more suspicious" level increases as audits become more expensive.

Figure 4 shows the equilibrium auditing probabilities $\boldsymbol{a}^*$ as functions of the audit cost C. Interestingly, the results show that in an equilibrium, the insurer does not conduct audits for reported security levels equal to or less than 0.8. For reported level 0.95, we observe a sharp threshold: the insurer always audits if the cost of the audit is less than 0.22, but never audits if it is greater.

Figure 5 shows the equilibrium premiums without audit $\boldsymbol{p}^{N^*}$ as functions of the audit cost C. We notice that for the lowest security level assessed, 0.5, the premium is the highest one and remains steady for the entire range of audit costs. Such a security level means having a 50% chance of getting compromised

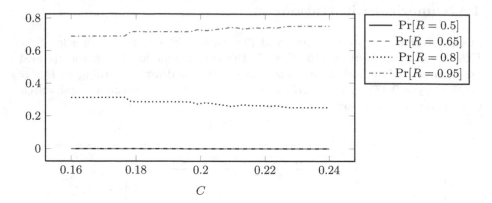

Fig. 3. Probability of reporting each type in equilibrium with various audit cost values.

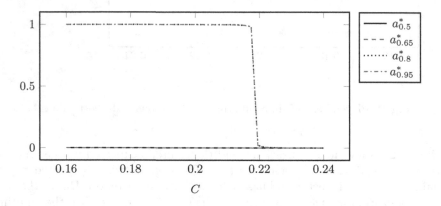

Fig. 4. Audit probabilities in equilibrium with various audit cost values.

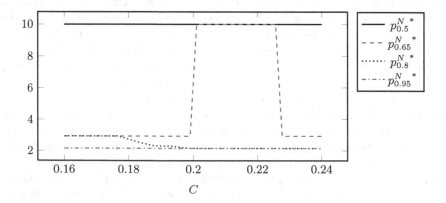

Fig. 5. Premiums (without audit) in equilibrium with various audit cost values.

and therefore the insurer must ask for a sizable premium. For security levels 0.8 and 0.95, when audit costs are higher than 0.2, the equilibrium premiums are identical and lower than for the other two security levels, 0.5 and 0.65. In future work, we will conduct further experiments to understand the behaviour of the insurer's strategy in terms of premiums in the equilibrium, considering both the audited and non-audited cases.

5   Related Work

We discuss two classes of related work: literature on cyber-insurance—more specifically on adverse selection, moral hazard, and information asymmetries— and literature on security audits.

Cyber-Insurance and Information Asymmetry: Some of the main factors that hinder cyber-risk management via cyber-insurance are *risk correlations*, *interdependence*, and *information asymmetries* [8]. Among these, we focus on information asymmetries, which are taken into account by many articles in the field of security economics and cyber-insurance [4,12,17,20].

Shetty et al. [21,22] prove a proposition providing a condition, which when satisfied, states that any insurance contract with security levels unobservable by the insurers strictly decreases the utility of the users, leading to a missing insurance market. Yet, with insurers present, and security levels contractible, in any equilibrium, full client coverage is offered.

Schwartz et al. [19] investigate the occurrence of a "lemon market" [2] when insurers cannot differentiate between different risk behaviors of clients. Lack of rich information about user choices and activities, leads to information asymmetry, which worsens the usual insurers' problems of moral hazard and adverse selection. They prove that no matter how small the fraction of malicious users is, an equilibrium does not exist, and therefore the cyber-insurance market is missing. In addition, they claim that due to adverse selection, cyber-insurers would not underwrite contracts conditioning user premiums on their security.

Bandyopadhyay et al. [5] build an economic model describing an optimal cyber-insurance contract and the optimal claim strategy for the insured firm. They show that insured firms optimally transfer more risk through insurance contracts under information symmetry than otherwise. They also present a circle of steps going from information symmetry for the cyber-insurance market to information asymmetry when the client first realizes the effect of IT risks, to end up back in information symmetry when the insurer finds out about the altered claiming and buying behavior as well as the underlying reasons.

Security Audits for Cyber-Insurance Underwriting: In [3], Baer and Parkinson suggest that both insurers and clients are sophisticated in dealing with security assessments regarding cyber-insurance coverage decisions. Cyber-insurers demand audits by independent consultants on a case-by-case basis, depending on the risks to be insured and the client requirements with regards to policy limits [10]. For example, the largest cyber-insurance underwriter, called AIG, asks prospective clients to complete an "Information Security Self Assessment" online. The results of such self-assessments determine whether the insurer will undertake a security audit on client's premises to bind coverage.

Böhme [7] argues that security audits can generate positive utility overcoming information asymmetries in a scenario focused on "solving coordination problems." According to this, the players themselves decide about their own security investment and whether or not to give away information about the resulting security level. Security audits are a tangible way to derive such security levels. The author states that it is difficult to measure the security level of products due to: (i) the difficulty of specifying all security requirements; and (ii) attacks neither occur deterministically nor is their occurrence observable in real time. The hardness of measurement implies significant effort to undertake a meaningful audit and requires special knowledge and experience. The difficulty of the audit increases disproportionately to the complexity of the system due to the non-linear growth of interdependencies among different assets.

Khalili et al. [13] suggest that recent advances in Internet measurement combined with machine learning techniques enable accurate quantitative assessments of security posture at a firm level. They claim that this can be used as a tool to perform an initial security audit, or pre-screening, of a prospective client to better enable premium discrimination and the design of customized policies.

6   Conclusions

Cyber-insurers face the challenge of devising a policy that is "reasonable" for the client to purchase but profitable for the insurer as well. To elicit risk levels for premium calculations, the insurer either asks the organization to conduct some self-assessment and report it, or it undertakes an audit to identify the real security level with certainty. Further, the possibility of being audited by the insurer may incentivize the organization to report truthfully. However, such an audit introduces costs for the insurer, which may be relatively high.

We introduced a new model to study optimal strategies for self-reporting security levels (for organizations) and undertaking expensive audits (for insurers). The insurers' strategy aims to ensure that the actual security levels of their clients have been elicited and therefore "fair" contracts (coverage, premium) are put in place. More concretely, we modeled the interactions between a potential client and an insurer as a two-player signaling game, where the organization plays the role of the sender, while the insurer plays the role of the receiver. To the best of our knowledge, this paper is the first to attempt studying incentives for auditing potential clients before cyber-insurance premium calculations. The proposed model may form the basis of a framework that can further accelerate the adoption of cyber-insurance.

Our model and analyses do have certain limitations, which we intend to improve upon in future work. First, future work may allow the insurer to offer multiple levels of coverage (for different premiums) to an organization; i.e., when the insurer computes premiums, it also associates these premiums with certain degrees of loss recovery. Secondly, future work may allow the insurer to perform cyber-forensics when a claim is filed in order to reveal whether the organization was honest when reporting its security level. In this case, the insurer avoids auditing costs, but may still be able to deter clients from misreporting. We shall investigate the trade-offs between forensics and auditing costs. Furthermore, we will consider penalties for untruthful organizations. Punishment of such behavior may be realized in the form of increased premiums or reduction of some reputation metric that affects any future cyber-insurance contract of the organization. More ambitiously, our plan is to work with cyber-insurers to acquire realistic data as part of a recently funded research project.

Acknowledgement. We thank the anonymous reviewers for their comments. The research activities of Jens Grossklags are supported by DIVSI. Emmanouil Panaousis' work is supported by the H2020-MSCA-RISE-2018 SECONDO project.

References

1. ABI: Cyber Risk Insurance. https://www.abi.org.uk/products-and-issues/products/business-insurance/cyber-risk-insurance/. Accessed 19 June 2017
2. Akerlof, G.: The market for "lemons": quality uncertainty and the market mechanism. Q. J. Econ. **84**, 488–500 (1970)
3. Baer, W., Parkinson, A.: Cyberinsurance in IT security management. IEEE Secur. Priv. **5**(3), 50–56 (2007)
4. Bandyopadhyay, T., Mookerjee, V., Rao, R.: Why IT managers don't go for cyber-insurance products. Commun. ACM **52**(11), 68–73 (2009)
5. Bandyopadhyay, T., Mookerjee, V., Rao, R.: A model to analyze the unfulfilled promise of cyber insurance: the impact of secondary loss. Technical report, University of Texas at Dallas (2010)
6. Böhme, R.: Cyber-insurance revisited. In: Workshop on the Economics of Information Security (WEIS) (2005)
7. Böhme, R.: Security audits revisited. In: Keromytis, A.D. (ed.) FC 2012. LNCS, vol. 7397, pp. 129–147. Springer, Heidelberg (2012). https://doi.org/10.1007/978-3-642-32946-3_11
8. Böhme, R., Schwartz, G.: Modeling cyber-insurance: towards a unifying framework. In: Workshop on the Economics of Information Security (WEIS) (2010)
9. Forbes: Worldwide cybersecurity spending increasing to $170 billion by 2020. https://www.forbes.com/sites/stevemorgan/2016/03/09/worldwide-cybersecurity-spending-increasing-to-170-billion-by-2020/#5804298e6832. Accessed Mar 2016
10. Gordon, L., Loeb, M., Sohail, T.: A framework for using insurance for cyber-risk management. Commun. ACM **46**(3), 81–85 (2003)
11. HM-Government: UK cyber security: the role of insurance in managing and mitigating the risk. https://www.gov.uk/government/uploads/system/uploads/attachment_data/file/415354/UK_Cyber_Security_Report_Final.pdf. Accessed June 2015

12. Hofmann, A.: Internalizing externalities of loss prevention through insurance monopoly: an analysis of interdependent risks. Geneva Risk Insur. Rev. **32**(1), 91–111 (2007)
13. Khalili, M.M., Naghizadeh, P., Liu, M.: Designing cyber insurance policies: the role of pre-screening and security interdependence. IEEE Trans. Inf. Forensics Secur. **13**(9), 2226–2239 (2018)
14. KPMG: Seizing the cyber insurance opportunity. https://assets.kpmg.com/content/dam/kpmg/xx/pdf/2017/07/cyber-insurance-report.pdf. Accessed July 2017
15. Laszka, A., Grossklags, J.: Should cyber-insurance providers invest in software security? In: Pernul, G., Ryan, P.Y.A., Weippl, E. (eds.) ESORICS 2015. LNCS, vol. 9326, pp. 483–502. Springer, Cham (2015). https://doi.org/10.1007/978-3-319-24174-6_25
16. Laszka, A., Johnson, B., Grossklags, J., Felegyhazi, M.: Estimating systematic risk in real-world networks. In: Christin, N., Safavi-Naini, R. (eds.) FC 2014. LNCS, vol. 8437, pp. 417–435. Springer, Heidelberg (2014). https://doi.org/10.1007/978-3-662-45472-5_27
17. Lelarge, M., Bolot, J.: Economic incentives to increase security in the internet: the case for insurance. In: Proceedings of the 28th IEEE International Conference on Computer Communications (INFOCOM), pp. 1494–1502. IEEE (2009)
18. Low, P.: Insuring against cyber-attacks. Comput. Fraud Secur. **2017**(4), 18–20 (2017)
19. Schwartz, G., Shetty, N., Walrand, J.: Cyber-insurance: missing market driven by user heterogeneity. Technical report, UC Berkeley (2010)
20. Schwartz, G., Shetty, N., Walrand, J.: Why cyber-insurance contracts fail to reflect cyber-risks. In: Proceedings of the 51st Annual Allerton Conference on Communication, Control, and Computing (Allerton), pp. 781–787. IEEE (2013)
21. Shetty, N., Schwartz, G., Felegyhazi, M., Walrand, J.: Competitive cyber-insurance and internet security. In: Moore, T., Pym, D., Ioannidis, C. (eds.) Economics of Information Security and Privacy. Springer, Boston (2010). https://doi.org/10.1007/978-1-4419-6967-5_12
22. Shetty, N., Schwartz, G., Walrand, J.: Can competitive insurers improve network security? In: Acquisti, A., Smith, S.W., Sadeghi, A.-R. (eds.) Trust 2010. LNCS, vol. 6101, pp. 308–322. Springer, Heidelberg (2010). https://doi.org/10.1007/978-3-642-13869-0_23
23. Symantec: ISTR: Internet security threat report. https://www.symantec.com/security-center/threat-report. Accessed Apr 2017

A Bayesian Multi-armed Bandit Approach for Identifying Human Vulnerabilities

Erik Miehling[1(✉)], Baicen Xiao[2], Radha Poovendran[2], and Tamer Başar[1]

[1] Coordinated Science Lab, University of Illinois at Urbana–Champaign,
Urbana, IL 61801, USA
miehling@illinois.edu
[2] Department of Electrical Engineering, University of Washington,
Seattle, WA 98195, USA

Abstract. We consider the problem of identifying the set of users in an organization's network that are most susceptible to falling victim to social engineering attacks. To achieve this goal, we propose a testing strategy, based on the theory of multi-armed bandits, that involves a system administrator sending fake malicious messages to users in a sequence of unannounced tests and recording their responses. To accurately model the administrator's testing problem, we propose a new bandit setting, termed the structured combinatorial multi-bandit model, that allows one to impose combinatorial constraints on the space of allowable queries. The model captures the diversity in attack types and user responses by considering multiple multi-armed bandits, where each bandit problem represents an attack (message) type and each arm represents a user. Users respond to test messages according to a response model with unknown statistics. The response model associates a Bernoulli distribution with an unknown mean with each message-user pair, dictating the likelihood that a user will respond to a given message. The administrator's problem of identifying the most susceptible users can then be expressed as identifying the set of message-user pairs with means that exceed a given threshold. We adopt a Bayesian approach to solving the problem, associating a (beta) prior distribution with each unknown mean. In a given trial, the system administrator queries a selection of users with test messages, generating query responses which are then used to update posterior distributions on the means. By defining a state as the parameters of the posteriors, we show that the optimal testing strategy can be characterized as the solution of a Markov decision process (MDP). Unfortunately, solving the MDP is computationally intractable. As a result, we propose a heuristic testing strategy, based on Thompson sampling, that focuses queries on message-user pairs that are estimated to have means close to the threshold. The heuristic testing strategy is shown to yield accurate identifications.

This research was supported by the U.S. Office of Naval Research (ONR) MURI grant N00014-16-1-2710.

L. Bushnell et al. (Eds.): GameSec 2018, LNCS 11199, pp. 521–539, 2018.
https://doi.org/10.1007/978-3-030-01554-1_30

Keywords: Sociotechnical systems · Social engineering attacks
Multi-armed bandits · Dynamic programming · Thompson sampling

1 Introduction

Social engineering attacks represent an emerging threat that involve the persuasion of a user into unknowingly aiding the attacker, whether it be through divulging sensitive information or opening a backdoor to the system. Such attacks (also referred to as *semantic attacks* [30]) involve adversaries sending malicious messages to users with the intent of making them believe that the message is actually legitimate. Some prominent types of social engineering attacks include *email and voice phishing*, in which a user is presented with seemingly legitimate emails or phone calls asking them to provide information, access a website, or open an attachment, *file/application masquerading*, where a user is presented with a malware-infected document or program, and *malvertisement*, where an adversary injects malicious advertisements into websites in the hope that a user will click [15, 27]. While successful social engineering attacks can have damaging consequences for an individual user, such as revealing one's login credentials or personal information, the consequences of a successful attack can be dire if the targeted user resides within an organization's enterprise network. For example, preliminary investigations into the Target breach of 2013 revealed that the initial intrusion into its network was facilitated by theft of credentials, via phishing emails, from one of its contractor companies [20]. The resulting breach exposed more than 40 million credit and debit card accounts. More recently, the Ukrainian power grid hack of 2015 involved attackers sending operators phishing emails that contained a malicious Word document [33]. Upon opening the file, malware was installed on their computers allowing a backdoor to be opened. The attackers later used this backdoor to gather workers' credentials and subsequently access the system, carrying out actions that left nearly a quarter million people without power.

Social engineering attacks highlight the fact that no matter how secure we make our systems, an unaware user can inadvertently render advanced defenses completely ineffective. Making our systems more robust to these *human vulnerabilities* involves first understanding how social engineering attacks succeed. Doing so is complicated by the fact that such attacks target users, rather than the system directly, making them very difficult to detect [15]. Furthermore, the diversity of social engineering attacks, coupled with an even more diverse range of user behavior, presents significant difficulties in modeling how users respond to attacks. As a result, quantification of the security of the system will require the development of accurate behavioral models for how humans respond to such adversarial attacks.

In this paper, we propose a formal testing procedure, based on the theory of *multi-armed bandits* [28], for identifying the set of users in an organization that are most susceptible to social engineering attacks. The testing procedure involves a system administrator carrying out a sequence of unannounced tests where users are queried with fake malicious messages, designed to mimic true social engineering attacks, with the goal of identifying the set of users that pose the highest security risk, *i.e.* the users that are most likely to respond to a true attack. Given a limited amount of testing resources (specifically a fixed number of testing trials), the system administrator must determine which users to query with which messages, in each trial, in order to obtain the best possible estimate of the high-risk users at the end of the testing horizon. To accurately model the testing environment, we propose a new bandit setting, termed the *structured combinatorial multi-bandit model*. By categorizing various attack messages into a finite set of *message types* and associating each message type with its own distinct multi-armed bandit (with arms representing users), querying a specific user with a message of a given type corresponds to pulling a bandit-arm pair. In each testing trial, the system administrator selects a collection of users to query with various message types (a collection of bandit-arm pairs), in what is termed a *query set*, where the space of allowable query sets is constrained by practical considerations, *e.g.* in each trial, no user should be tested more than once and no more than a fixed proportion of the users should be tested. The selected query set generates responses from the corresponding users according to a *response model* with unknown statistics. Specifically, each user's response to each message type is characterized by a Bernoulli distribution with an unknown mean. Under this setting, the administrator's problem of identifying the high-risk users corresponds to identifying the set of message-user pairs with means above a given threshold, termed a thresholding criterion in the bandit literature. The administrator's goal is to determine an optimal *testing strategy*, defined by a sequence of query sets, selected as a function of user feedback, and a prescription of an *identification set* of the means exceeding the threshold, in order to ensure that the terminal estimate is as accurate as possible.

To solve for an optimal testing strategy, we adopt a Bayesian approach involving maintaining probability distributions over the unknown means of the response model. By assuming a structured prior, specifically a beta distribution, the Bernoulli responses of the users to the test messages ensures that the updated posterior distributions are also beta-distributed [13]. Through appropriate definition of an information state, specifically the parameters of the posteriors, the optimal testing strategy can be characterized as the solution to a type of sequential decision process termed a *Markov decision process* (MDP) [26]. Unfortunately, due to the scale of the resulting MDP, we cannot solve it exactly. As a result, we propose a heuristic strategy, based on the top-two Thompson sampling algorithm of [29], that involves selecting queries in such a way as to focus samples on message-user pairs with means that are believed to be close to the threshold. As shown through numerical experiments in a variety of settings, the heuristic testing strategy yields accurate identifications, performing especially well in domains with a large number of users and message types.

1.1   Relevant Literature

The nature of our modern information systems – specifically, the increased use of social networks, cloud storage, and digital communications – has made them especially vulnerable to social engineering attacks. In response, researchers have studied the wide-range of possible attacks, classifying them into taxonomies [15, 21] and aiding our understanding of how they unfold. Since social engineering attacks inherently involve the user, much of the research in the security literature draws from ideas introduced in behavioral psychology. In particular, the emerging field of *behavioral information security* [9] addresses how the behavior of the user impacts the security of the system, helping to describe security policy compliance, employee behavior, and even attack motives. Additional research has investigated how the *principles of persuasion* [8] influence a user's likelihood of falling victim to social engineering attacks [6]. While education and training for social engineering attacks has been shown to be an effective method for improving security awareness [22], there has been limited work in regard to evaluating how these testing resources should be allocated. One of the few examples is the work of Dodge *et al.* [10] in which a survey is developed where users are sent phishing emails in order to evaluate their likelihood of responding. While interesting, the approach is empirical and does not leverage any formal theory.

Multi-armed bandits offer a principled approach for the design of experiments, and form the basis of our testing problem. First introduced in the 1930s by Thompson [31] for the design of medical trials, and later formalized by Robbins [28], multi-armed bandits have found applications in a wide variety of areas, most recently in sequential decision-making [19] and recommendation systems [24]. The classical bandit setting is a sequential decision problem where, in each trial, an agent samples (termed a *pull*) one of a finite set of unknown reward distributions (termed *arms*), in order to minimize the difference between the sum of sampled rewards and the highest possible reward (termed the cumulative *regret*). Inherent to the problem is the trade-off between *exploitation*, pulling arms that are believed to give a high reward, and *exploration*, pulling other arms in order to rule out better alternatives. The problem has been well-studied, generating results under both *frequentist* [3, 23] and *Bayesian* [13] viewpoints.

Departing from the traditional exploration-exploitation setting, Bubeck *et al.* [4] introduced a new paradigm, termed *pure exploration*. Unlike in the classical bandit setting where exploration and exploitation are interleaved, the pure exploration setting instead concerns how one can make best use of a limited amount of resources (for example, the total number of trial periods) in order to ensure that some terminal estimate is as accurate as possible. The problem has primarily been investigated under the frequentist setting, where a wide-variety of criteria have been considered, including top arm identification [2, 4], top m arm identification [5], top subset identification [7], and thresholding set identification [25]. Other work [12] has considered more general settings that consist of a collection of multi-armed bandits, termed a *multi-bandit*, with the motivating context of designing clinical trials for multiple subpopulations of patients. More recently, others have explored more general action spaces, where the agent can pull more than a single arm in each trial, *e.g.* batch pulls [32] and combinatorial (probe) pulls [17]. Compared to frequentist approaches, investigation into pure exploration problems from a Bayesian perspective have received less attention in the literature. We are aware of two approaches in the bandit literature, both that aim to solve the top arm identification problem. In the first approach [16], the authors study a top arm identification problem (under a finite query budget) where the reward distributions of arms are assumed to be correlated. The second approach [29] proposes three heuristic algorithms for the top arm identification problem and presents theoretical guarantees on their performance. A similar problem has also been investigated outside of the bandit literature, termed the *ranking and selection* problem [11].

1.2 Contribution

While social engineering attacks have received much attention in the security literature in recent years, our paper is the first to present a formal approach for evaluating users' likelihoods of responding to attacks. Our paper has a similar objective as that of [10], namely of aiming to identify high-risk users; however, the approach of [10] is strictly empirical. As outlined in [9], one of the key difficulties in the security of sociotechnical systems is the challenge in "observing and collecting actual user behavior data." Our proposed testing strategy provides a principled framework for extracting data from users and formally describes how it can be used to learn how they may respond to real-world attacks. Knowledge of the users' behavioral model is a critical first step in ensuring system robustness to social engineering attacks, *e.g.* by allowing for more targeted educational and training resources.

To place our work within the bandit literature, our paper lies at the intersection of pure exploration and Bayesian analysis. Other Bayesian approaches to pure exploration problems, namely [11,16], and [29], aim to identify the best alternative (top arm). Our paper is the first to investigate the thresholding criterion from a Bayesian pure exploration viewpoint. Due to the practical requirements imposed by our problem, we develop a new bandit setting, termed the *structured combinatorial bandit model*, that allows one to impose constraints on the form of allowable queries (pulls), generalizing existing models, *e.g.* [17]. Our proposed algorithm, based on the top-two Thompson sampling algorithm of [29], is able to take into account these constrained queries and accurately identify all means that are above a given threshold.

2 The Testing Environment

The testing environment consists of an organization, operated by a single system administrator, and a collection of K users that are subject to social engineering attacks from the external network. The various attack types are categorized into a finite set of M message types. Diversity in individual user responses to different attacks is achieved by defining a response model that is a function of message-user pairs, allowing for a given user to have different response characteristics across message types. In a given testing trial, the system administrator selects a subset of users to query with a collection of message types, as seen in Fig. 1, where the query sets available to the administrator are constrained by practical considerations (per-trial limits are imposed on the number of times a user can be tested, as well as on the number of tested users). The users' responses are received by the system administrator and used to compute a new query set.

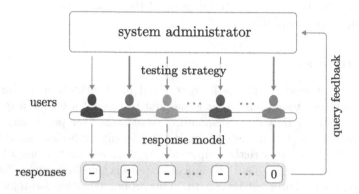

Fig. 1. *The testing model.* The system administrator sends test messages to a subset of the users according to a *testing strategy.* Queried users respond according to a *response model* whose statistics are unknown to the system administrator. Responses to the test messages are recorded and used by the testing strategy to determine the next set of queries.

The requirements of our problem necessitate a richer bandit model than can be found in the literature. As a result, we introduce a new setting, termed the structured combinatorial multi-bandit model, which consists of a set of multi-armed bandits where pulls take the form of constrained *collections* of bandit-arm pairs. After we present the general model, we explain how it can be used to formulate the testing problem.

2.1   The Structured Combinatorial Multi-bandit Model

The general model consists of M multi-armed bandits, denoted by the set $\mathcal{M}$, with each bandit $m \in \mathcal{M}$ consisting of K_m arms, denoted by the set $\mathcal{K}_m$. For a given bandit m, each arm k is characterized by an unknown distribution ν_{mk}. In a given trial, samples are drawn from the distributions by selecting a *query set* from the space of feasible queries $\mathcal{Q}$, defined as

$$\mathcal{Q} = \left\{ Q \subseteq \mathcal{P} \,\middle|\, \underline{c}_i \leq |Q \cap C_i| \leq \bar{c}_i, \, i = 1, \ldots, R \right\} \tag{1}$$

where $\mathcal{P} = \{(m, k) : m \in \mathcal{M}, k \in \mathcal{K}_m\}$ represents the set of all bandit-arm pairs. Each feasible query $Q \in \mathcal{Q}$ takes the form of a set of bandit-arm pairs $(m, k) \in \mathcal{M} \times \mathcal{K}_m$ that must satisfy R (per-trial) constraints described by the sets $C_i \subseteq \mathcal{P}$ and corresponding cardinality bounds $\underline{c}_i, \bar{c}_i \in \mathbb{N}$. Each C_i, termed a constraint set, is a collection of bandit-arm indices that allows one to impose a structure on the form of query sets. Through appropriate definition of each C_i and $\underline{c}_i, \bar{c}_i$, $i = 1, \ldots, R$, the set $\mathcal{Q}$ can describe a wide range of action spaces. For example, the single-play multi-bandit setting of [12] can be described by considering a single constraint set ($R = 1$) of the form $C = \mathcal{M} \times \mathcal{K}$ with cardinality bounds $\underline{c} = \bar{c} = 1$. The single-bandit, multiple-play setting of [1] is captured by considering a singleton $\mathcal{M}$ and defining $C = \mathcal{K}$ and $\underline{c} = \bar{c} = b$ such that $|Q \cap \mathcal{K}| = b$ (all subsets of $\mathcal{K}$ of size b).

In a given trial t, a feasible query set $Q_t \in \mathcal{Q}$ is selected, generating samples $X(t) = (X_{mk}(t))_{(m,k) \in Q_t}$ from the corresponding distributions. It is assumed that each sample, $X_{mk} \sim \nu_{mk}$, is independent of all other samples, $\{X_{mk}\}_{(m,k) \in \mathcal{P}}$. The samples collected from a given query are used to update the empirical estimates of the means of each of the sampled bandit-arm pairs, denoted by $\hat{\mu}_{mk}(t) = \frac{1}{T_{mk}(t)} \sum_{s=1}^{T_{mk}(t)} X_{mk}(s)$, $(m, k) \in Q_t$, where $T_{mk}(t)$ denotes the number of times that bandit-arm pair (m, k) has been sampled by trial t. In the subsequent trials, query sets are sequentially selected and samples are received until a predetermined stopping condition is satisfied. The algorithm dictating the query selection strategy, termed the testing strategy, is determined based on the intended goal, which is in turn dictated by the specific application at hand.

2.2 Statement of the Testing Problem

The structured combinatorial multi-bandit model provides a natural setting for the testing problem. In particular, associating each bandit m with a message type and each arm k with a user (as seen in Fig. 2), the selection of a query set corresponds to the system administrator sending a collection of test messages to a set of users, termed message-user queries. Since feedback for a given message-user query is binary (a user either responds or does not respond to a message), each ν_{mk} is modeled as a Bernoulli distribution characterized by an unknown mean θ_{mk}, that is $\nu_{mk} = \text{Bern}(\theta_{mk})$, where each θ_{mk} specifies the probability that user k will respond to message type m.

Practical considerations in our problem, such as constraints on the number of times a user can be queried in each trial, as well as the number of users queried in each trial, are captured by appropriate selection of constraint sets and cardinality bounds. In particular, we impose the following restrictions: (i) each user k can be queried at most once per trial, and (ii) exactly b users are queried in each trial. In the context of the general model of Sect. 2.1, the first restriction is captured by defining constraint sets $C_k = \{(1, k), \ldots, (M, k)\}$ and cardinality bounds $\underline{c}_k = 0$ and $\bar{c}_k = 1$ for all $k \in \mathcal{K}$, whereas the second restriction is described by $C' = \mathcal{M} \times \mathcal{K}$ with bound $\underline{c}' = \bar{c}' = b$. In summary, the system

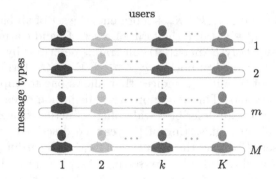

Fig. 2. *The interpretation of bandit-arm pairs in the testing problem.* Each bandit m corresponds to a message type and consists of the complete set of K arms (users), that is, $\mathcal{K}_m = \mathcal{K}$. A given user is assigned the same index across bandits, that is, for distinct bandits m, m' index k always corresponds to user k.

administrator is restricted to selecting its message-user queries from query space $\mathcal{Q}_{sa}$, defined as

$$\mathcal{Q}_{sa} = \left\{ Q \subseteq \mathcal{P} \,\middle|\, |Q \cap \{(1, k), \ldots, (M, k)\}| \leq 1 \text{ for all } k \in \mathcal{K}, \right.$$
$$\left. |Q \cap (\mathcal{M} \times \mathcal{K})| = b \right\} \tag{2}$$

where $\mathcal{P}$ simplifies to $\mathcal{P} = \mathcal{M} \times \mathcal{K}$ in the testing problem.

The goal of the system administrator is to identify the users that pose the highest risk to the security of the system. In particular, given a threshold probability τ, the system administrator wishes to identify, as accurately as possible, all users that will (on average) respond to a message with probability of at least τ, for each of the M message types. Formally, the administrator's objective is to identify the set of users with means above the threshold, given by the set

$$\mathcal{K}_{m,\tau}^* = \{ k \in \mathcal{K} \mid \theta_{mk} \geq \tau \} \tag{3}$$

for each message type m.[1] It is assumed that the system administrator must perform this identification after a fixed number of testing trials n (referred to as a *fixed budget* in the bandit literature). Through sequential selection of query sets $Q_t \in \mathcal{Q}_{sa}$, and recording of user responses, $X_{mk}(t) \sim \text{Bern}(\theta_{mk})$, $(m, k) \in Q_t$, the administrator constructs empirical estimates over time, eventually obtaining terminal estimates $\hat{\theta}_{mk}(n) = \frac{1}{T_{mk}(n)} \sum_{s=1}^{T_{mk}(n)} X_{mk}(s)$, $(m, k) \in \mathcal{P}$, after n trials. From this, the administrator provides the estimates

$$\mathcal{K}_{m,\tau}(n) = \{ k \in \mathcal{K} \mid \hat{\theta}_{mk}(n) \geq \tau \} \tag{4}$$

---

[1] Note that thresholds can depend on the specific message-user pair (m, k); however, for ease of presentation, we assume identical thresholds τ across all (m, k).

of the sets $\mathcal{K}_{m,\tau}^{*}$ for each m. The quality of the resulting estimates crucially depends on the samples that are collected and, in turn, on the querying procedure of the system administrator. The focus of the following section is to determine this querying procedure, termed a testing strategy, in order to obtain the best possible estimates.

3   The Testing Strategy

Formally, a testing strategy is a sequence of $n + 1$ functions, $\pi = \{\pi_0, \ldots, \pi_{n-1}, \pi_n\}$, where $\{\pi_0, \ldots, \pi_{n-1}\}$ map estimates of the message-user means into a prescription of query sets and π_n maps estimates into an identification of the set of message-user means above the threshold probability. The goal of the system administrator is to find a testing strategy π that results in an identification set $P \subseteq \mathcal{P}$ that maximizes

$$J(\theta, P; \tau) = \mathbb{1}\left(\bigcap_{(m,k) \in P} \{\theta_{mk} > \tau\}\right) \cdot \mathbb{1}\left(\bigcap_{(m,k) \in \bar{P}} \{\theta_{mk} \leq \tau\}\right) \qquad (5)$$

where $\bar{P} = \mathcal{P} \setminus P$. Notice that the reward function $J(\theta, P; \tau)$ is equal to one only for the subset of message-user pairs $P^* \subseteq \mathcal{P}$ that have means above the threshold τ. The sets $\mathcal{K}_{m,\tau}^{*}$ in Eq. (3) are recovered from P^* via $\mathcal{K}_{m,\tau}^{*} = \{k \in \mathcal{K} \mid (m,k) \in P^*\}$ for each m.

Similar to an argument from the identification problem addressed in [11], if we knew the true means, then the expected reward under testing strategy π would simply be $\mathbb{E}^{\pi}[J(\Theta, P; \tau) \mid \Theta = \theta]$. While we do not know the true means, by assuming a prior f_0 we can write $\mathbb{E}[\mathbb{E}^{\pi}[J(\Theta, P; \tau) \mid \Theta = \theta] \mid \Theta \sim f_0] = \mathbb{E}^{\pi}[J(\Theta, P; \tau) \mid \Theta \sim f_0] =: \mathbb{E}_0^{\pi}[J(\Theta, P; \tau)]$. In each trial $t = 0, \ldots, n - 1$, the selection of a query set $Q_t \in \mathcal{Q}_{sa}$ results in responses from users that are distributed according to Bernoulli distributions with unknown means (recall the response model of Sect. 2.2). Given that likelihoods are Bernoulli, a natural choice for a prior on the unknown means is the beta distribution. Such a choice ensures that the posterior at any given time is also beta-distributed [13]. Explicitly, we assume a beta prior $\Theta_{mk} \sim f_0(\theta_{mk}) = \mathrm{Beta}(\alpha_{mk,0}, \beta_{mk,0})$, where parameters $\alpha_{mk,0}$ and $\beta_{mk,0}$ represent initial counts of responses and non-responses, respectively, for each $(m, k) \in \mathcal{P}$ (each initialized to one for the testing problem). The posterior of mean Θ_{mk} at any trial t can then be written as $f_t(\theta_{mk}) = \mathrm{Beta}(\alpha_{mk,t}, \beta_{mk,t})$, where $\alpha_{mk,t} = \alpha_{mk,0} + \sum_{s \leq t} \mathbb{1}_{Q_s}((m, k)) x_{mk,s}$, $\beta_{mk,t} = \beta_{mk,0} + \sum_{s \leq t} \mathbb{1}_{Q_s}((m, k))(1 - x_{mk,s})$, and $x_{mk,s}$ denotes the realized sample of $X_{mk,s}$. In particular, at trial n, each mean Θ_{mk} is distributed according to posterior $f_n(\theta_{mk})$. Consequently, the system administrator's objective can be represented in terms of the parameters of this posterior, as characterized by Lemma 1.

Lemma 1. *The system administrator's objective can be written as* $\mathbb{E}_0^\pi[J^\pi(P;\tau)]$, *where*

$$J^\pi(P;\tau) = \prod_{(m,k)\in P^\pi} I_{1-\tau}(\beta_{mk,n}, \alpha_{mk,n}) \prod_{(m,k)\in \bar{P}^\pi} I_\tau(\alpha_{mk,n}, \beta_{mk,n}) \qquad (6)$$

and $I_\tau(\alpha, \beta)$ *is the normalized incomplete beta function.*

Proof. See Appendix A.

In summary, the system administrator wishes to find a testing strategy $\pi = \{\pi_0, \ldots, \pi_{n-1}, \pi_n\}$ that solves the following problem

$$\sup_{\pi \in \Pi} \mathbb{E}_0^\pi \big[J^\pi(P;\tau) \big] \qquad (7)$$

where Π represents the space of admissible testing strategies. A testing strategy π that solves (7) is termed an optimal testing strategy and is denoted by $\pi^* = \{\pi_0^*, \ldots, \pi_{n-1}^*, \pi_n^*\}$. The problem of determining π^* can be cast as a type of sequential decision problem, termed a Markov decision process (MDP), as outlined in the following section.

3.1   An Optimal Testing Strategy

Through appropriate definition of a state process and decision variables, the problem of determining an optimal testing strategy can be cast as an MDP. In particular, we define the state in testing trial t, denoted by s_t, as the current trial index and the collection of current counts of responses and non-responses across all message-user pairs, that is,

$$s_t = (t, \alpha_t, \beta_t) \in \mathcal{S}$$

where $\alpha_t = \{\alpha_{mk,t}\}_{(m,k)\in\mathcal{P}}$ and $\beta_t = \{\beta_{mk,t}\}_{(m,k)\in\mathcal{P}}$. Note that the set of all feasible states, $\mathcal{S}$, depends on the structure of the query space $\mathcal{Q}_{sa}$ and the number of testing trials n. The evolution of the state is dictated by the information that the system administrator gathers over time. In particular, in a given state $s_t = (t, \alpha_t, \beta_t)$, selection of a query set $Q_t = Q$ generates a collection of samples from the queried message-user pairs that results in the update

$$s_{t+1} = (t+1, \alpha_{t+1}, \beta_{t+1}) = \big(t+1, f(\alpha_t, x), g(\beta_t, x)\big)$$

where x represents the realized query feedback under Q, that is, $x \in \Omega(Q)$, where $\Omega(Q)$ represents all possible (binary) realizations of query responses under query set Q. Update functions f and g are defined element-wise as

$$\alpha_{mk,t+1} = f_{mk}(\alpha_{mk,t}, x_{mk}) = x_{mk} + \alpha_{mk,t}$$
$$\beta_{mk,t+1} = g_{mk}(\beta_{mk,t}, x_{mk}) = 1 - x_{mk} + \beta_{mk,t}$$

for all $(m,k) \in \mathcal{P}$.

Considering query sets $Q_t \in \mathcal{Q}_{sa}$, for each trial $t = 0, \ldots, n-1$, and an identification set $P \subseteq \mathcal{P}$, for the final trial n, as the decision variables of the problem, an optimal testing strategy can be characterized recursively via the following dynamic programming equations. From the reward function defined in Eq. (6), the value function at the final trial, $t = n$, is defined as

$$V_n(s_n) = \max_{P \subseteq \mathcal{P}} \prod_{(m,k) \in P} I_{1-\tau}(\beta_{mk,n}, \alpha_{mk,n}) \prod_{(m,k) \in \bar{P}} I_\tau(\alpha_{mk,n}, \beta_{mk,n}). \tag{8}$$

The value functions at all previous trials $t = 0, \ldots, n-1$ are defined as

$$V_t(s_t) = \max_{Q \in \mathcal{Q}_{sa}} \left\{ \mathbb{E}\left[V_{t+1}(s_{t+1}) \,\middle|\, Q_t^* = Q, s_t = (t, \alpha_t, \beta_t) \right] \right\}$$

$$= \max_{Q \in \mathcal{Q}_{sa}} \left\{ \sum_{x \in \Omega(Q)} \sigma(s_t, x) V_{t+1}\big((t+1, f(\alpha_t, x), g(\beta_t, x))\big) \right\} \tag{9}$$

where $\sigma(s_t, x) = \prod_{\{x_{mk} \,:\, x_{mk}=1\}} \tilde{\theta}_{mk}(s_t) \prod_{\{x_{mk} \,:\, x_{mk}=0\}} \big(1 - \tilde{\theta}_{mk}(s_t)\big)$, $\tilde{\theta}_{mk}(s_t) = \frac{\alpha_{mk,t}}{\alpha_{mk,t} + \beta_{mk,t}}$. The maximizer of Eq. (8) is the optimal identification set, denoted by $P^* = \pi_n^*(s_n)$, whereas the maximizers of each of the functions in Eq. (9) are the optimal query sets, denoted by $Q_t^* = \pi_t^*(s_t)$.

In principle, Eqs. (8) and (9) could be solved via backward induction to yield an optimal testing strategy $\pi^* = \{\pi_0^*, \ldots, \pi_{n-1}^*, \pi_n^*\}$. Unfortunately due to the scale of the state space $\mathcal{S}$, one cannot possibly enumerate over all possible states to obtain a solution, even for a moderate testing horizon n and query space dimension $|\mathcal{Q}_{sa}|$. In the following section, we develop a heuristic that yields an approximation to the optimal testing strategy π^*.

3.2   A Heuristic Testing Strategy

To avoid solving the dynamic programming equations, we propose a simple heuristic algorithm that yields a heuristic testing strategy. The proposed algorithm, based on the top-two Thompson sampling algorithm developed in [29] for the top-arm identification problem, is an online algorithm that adapts its selection of query sets based on user feedback from previous queries. By encouraging exploration of means that are estimated to be close to the threshold, the proposed algorithm allows for efficient estimation of the identification set.

The general idea of the heuristic testing strategy is as follows. In each testing trial t, samples are drawn from each of the $f_t(\theta_{mk})$, $(m, k) \in \mathcal{P}$, posterior distributions. The resulting samples are then used to define a subset $P_\tau \subseteq \mathcal{P}$ of the message-user pairs with sampled means that exceed the threshold τ. A resampling step is then performed where a second set of samples are drawn from the posteriors, with corresponding set P_τ'. Resampling is performed until P_τ' differs from P_τ by at least one element. To enforce exploration of message-user pairs with means closer to the threshold, the symmetric difference of P_τ and P_τ', denoted by $P_\tau \triangle P_\tau'$, is computed. Since the elements of $P_\tau \triangle P_\tau'$ represent the set of message-user pairs with samples that exceed the threshold in either P_τ or P'_τ, but not both, message-user pairs with posterior distributions far above the threshold are more likely to appear in both sets. Based on the message-user pairs present in $P_\tau \triangle P'_\tau$, a feasible query set $Q \in \mathcal{Q}_{sa}$ is selected. Since the query set is drawn from the symmetric difference, message-user pairs that are closer to the threshold are explored more frequently. Posteriors are updated based on the query responses, the trial index is incremented, and the process repeats. The pseudo-code of the proposed algorithm is presented in Algorithm 1.

Algorithm 1. The Heuristic Testing Strategy

---

function ESTIMATETHRESHOLDSET$(\mathcal{Q}, \mathcal{P}, \alpha_0, \beta_0, n, \tau)$
   $f_0(\theta_{mk}) = \text{Beta}(\alpha_{mk,0}, \beta_{mk,0}), (m,k) \in \mathcal{P}$
   for $t = 0, \ldots, n-1$ **do**
      $P \leftarrow$ SAMPLESECONDARYSET$(f_t, \mathcal{P}, \tau)$
      $Q \in \mathcal{O}(\mathcal{Q}, P)$
      $x_{mk,t} \sim f_t(\theta_{mk}), (m,k) \in Q$
      $\alpha_{mk,t+1} \leftarrow \alpha_{mk,t} + \mathbb{1}_Q\big((m,k)\big)x_{mk,t}, (m,k) \in \mathcal{P}$
      $\beta_{mk,t+1} \leftarrow \beta_{mk,t} + \mathbb{1}_Q\big((m,k)\big)(1 - x_{mk,t}), (m,k) \in \mathcal{P}$
      $f_{t+1}(\theta_{mk}) \leftarrow \text{Beta}(\alpha_{mk,t+1}, \beta_{mk,t+1})$
   end for
   $\vartheta_{mk} \sim f_n(\theta_{mk})$
   return $\underset{P \subseteq \mathcal{P}}{\text{argmax}}\ J(\vartheta, P; \tau)$
end function

function SAMPLESECONDARYSET$(f, \mathcal{P}, \tau)$ **function** SAMPLESET$(f, \mathcal{P}, \tau)$
   $P_\tau \leftarrow$ SAMPLESET$(f, \mathcal{P}, \tau)$ **for** $(m,k) \in \mathcal{P}$ **do**
   $P'_\tau \leftarrow P_\tau$ $\vartheta_{mk} \sim f(\theta_{mk})$
   while $P_\tau \triangle P'_\tau = \varnothing$ **do**   **end for**
      $P'_\tau \leftarrow$ SAMPLESET$(f, \mathcal{P}, \tau)$ **return** $\underset{P \subseteq \mathcal{P}}{\text{argmax}}\ J(\vartheta, P; \tau)$
   end while   **end function**
   return $P_\tau \triangle P'_\tau$
end function

The oracle function $\mathcal{O} : \mathcal{Q} \times \mathcal{P} \to \mathcal{Q}$ selects a feasible query set from the symmetric difference set $P_\tau \triangle P'_\tau$. If $P_\tau \triangle P'_\tau$ contains enough elements to satisfy the constraints in $\mathcal{Q}$, then a feasible query set Q is simply drawn from the set at random. If there are not enough elements to satisfy the constraints, then the query set is constructed to contain as many elements of $P_\tau \triangle P'_\tau$ as possible without violating feasibility, with the remaining elements selected uniformly at random to ensure the resulting set remains feasible. In the context of our testing problem, since we have a constraint that no user is to be queried more than once per trial, the oracle simply searches $P_\tau \triangle P'_\tau$ for the number of message-user pairs with distinct users. If the number of distinct users exceeds b (the bound on the number of distinct users queried per trial), then a random feasible query set is selected from the elements of $P_\tau \triangle P'_\tau$. If $P_\tau \triangle P'_\tau$ does not contain at least b

distinct users, then the remaining message-user pairs are drawn at random until b distinct users are sampled.

4   Numerical Experiments

A collection of experiments are studied to illustrate the behavior and accuracy of the heuristic testing strategy. In particular, we consider the following four settings:

Experiment 1: $M = 2$, $K = 4$, $b = 2$, $\tau = 0.5$, and true means

$$\theta_1 := (\theta_{11}, \theta_{12}, \theta_{13}, \theta_{14}) = (0.80, 0.60, 0.40, 0.35)$$
$$\theta_2 := (\theta_{21}, \theta_{22}, \theta_{23}, \theta_{24}) = (0.55, 0.45, 0.30, 0.20)$$

Experiment 2: $M = 2$, $K = 4$, $b = 2$, $\tau = 0.5$, and

$$\theta_1 = (0.60, 0.55, 0.45, 0.50)$$
$$\theta_2 = (0.50, 0.48, 0.45, 0.55)$$

Experiment 3: $M = 5$, $K = 12$, $b = 4$, $\tau = 0.5$, and

$$\theta_1 = (0.22, 0.10, 0.34, 0.45, 0.55, 0.23, 0.05, 0.21, 0.74, 0.60, 0.09, 0.65)$$
$$\theta_2 = (0.41, 0.65, 0.12, 0.76, 0.53, 0.79, 0.23, 0.35, 0.67, 0.69, 0.03, 0.34)$$
$$\theta_3 = (0.05, 0.21, 0.67, 0.12, 0.13, 0.25, 0.43, 0.63, 0.32, 0.54, 0.11, 0.27)$$
$$\theta_4 = (0.32, 0.35, 0.46, 0.41, 0.24, 0.30, 0.11, 0.12, 0.15, 0.10, 0.18, 0.29)$$
$$\theta_5 = (0.10, 0.75, 0.12, 0.57, 0.86, 0.26, 0.28, 0.89, 0.85, 0.23, 0.45, 0.41)$$

Experiment 4: $M = 8$, $K = 50$, $b = 10$, $\tau = 0.5$, with each θ_{mk} randomly initialized in $[0, 1]$.

We first illustrate the behavior of the heuristic testing strategy, in the context of experiment 1, by studying how query sets are selected as a function of the posterior distributions. As shown in Fig. 3, the distributions are initially uncertain. As dictated by the testing strategy, successive query sets are selected in order to sufficiently explore all message-user pairs. This explorative nature of the testing strategy is evident from the plots in Fig. 3 – in trial $t = 300$, the testing strategy queries message-user pairs that have estimated means close to the threshold whereas in trial $t = 400$, queries are allocated to message-user pairs with estimated means far from the threshold. As seen in later testing trials ($t = 600$), posterior distributions that have means closer to the threshold are the most certain, illustrating that the heuristic testing strategy allocates more samples to message-user pairs that are more difficult to identify.

The estimation error of the heuristic testing strategy as a function of the number of testing trials is now investigated. To quantify the accuracy, we define

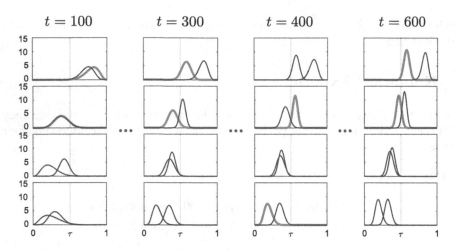

Fig. 3. *The evolution of posterior distributions for a given sample path of queries in experiment 1.* For each trial, each plot represents the posterior distributions of the means of given user for the two message types (users 1 through 4, from top to bottom). The red (bold) distributions in each trial represent the queried distributions.

a multi-bandit generalization of the single-bandit loss function of [25] as $l_\varepsilon(n) = \max_{m \in \mathcal{M}} l_{m,\varepsilon}(n)$, where

$$l_{m,\varepsilon}(n) = \mathbb{P}\left(\{\mathcal{K}^*_{m,\tau+\varepsilon} \cap \bar{\mathcal{K}}_{m,\tau}(n) \neq \varnothing\} \cup \{\bar{\mathcal{K}}^*_{m,\tau-\varepsilon} \cap \mathcal{K}_{m,\tau}(n) \neq \varnothing\}\right). \quad (10)$$

The term $\{\mathcal{K}^*_{m,\tau+\varepsilon} \cap \bar{\mathcal{K}}_{m,\tau}(n) \neq \varnothing\}$ represents an underestimation error (incorrectly designating that at least one user had a mean below the threshold) whereas $\{\bar{\mathcal{K}}^*_{m,\tau-\varepsilon} \cap \mathcal{K}_{m,\tau}(n) \neq \varnothing\}$ represents an overestimation error. The additive ε term allows for one to specify a reasonable margin of error – if the distance between the true mean and the threshold is less than ε, then no loss should be incurred for a misidentification. For each experiment, the accuracy of the heuristic testing strategy is compared to a *uniform strategy* that involves uniformly drawing a query set from the query space $\mathcal{Q}_{sa}$ in each testing trial. Figure 4 shows the accuracy of both the heuristic testing strategy and the uniform strategy, as a function of n, for each experiment.

As evidenced by the plots in Fig. 4, the heuristic testing strategy results in more accurate estimates than the uniform strategy for any testing horizon n. The gain in accuracy over the uniform strategy is especially evident in larger domains, as shown in Figs. 4c and d. The reason for the increased gap in accuracy is due to the fact that, in larger domains, the uniform strategy spreads queries out over a larger query space $\mathcal{Q}_{sa}$, resulting in slow convergence of individual estimates. The heuristic testing strategy, on the other hand, takes into account the query feedback received so far to allocate more queries to message-user pairs that are estimated to be closer to the threshold. Indeed, as shown in Fig. 5, this intuition is reinforced by analyzing the frequency of queries across message-user pairs for a given testing horizon. Figure 4 provides an additional observation, namely that

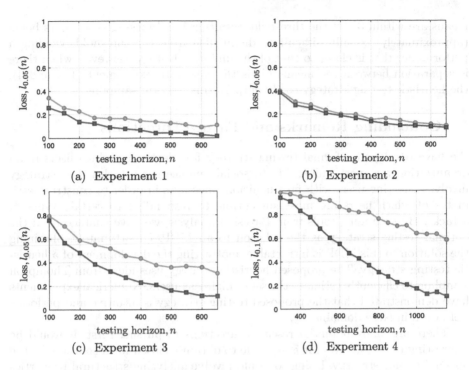

Fig. 4. *Averaged loss curves for each experiment.* The red curves (circular markers) represent the average loss of the uniform sampling strategy, whereas the blue curves (square markers) represent the average loss of the heuristic testing strategy. All simulations are averaged over 1000 runs.

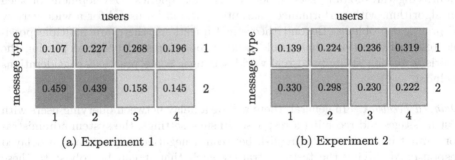

Fig. 5. *Averaged relative frequency of queries for experiments 1 and 2.* Under the heuristic testing strategy, means that are closer to the threshold are allocated more pulls, as evidenced by the heatmaps in (a) and (b) above. Frequencies are averaged over 1000 runs.

the accuracy of the heuristic testing strategy also depends on the spread of the means across message-user pairs. By observing the difference in the true means in experiments 1 and 2, we can see that some means in experiment 1 are closer to the threshold, namely θ_{21} and θ_{22}, than others, θ_{11} and θ_{24}. In experiment 2, all means are within 0.1 of the threshold, resulting in all message-user pairs being (approximately) equally difficult to distinguish from the threshold, yielding a performance that is closer to that of the uniform strategy. However, when there is separation between the means (as is the case with experiments 1,3, and 4), the heuristic testing strategy easily outperforms uniform sampling.

5   Concluding Remarks and Future Directions

We have developed a formal testing strategy for identifying which users in an organization are most vulnerable to social engineering attacks. The strategy involves querying users with fake malicious messages in order to construct estimates of which users are most susceptible to responding to certain types of attacks. By leveraging tools from Bayesian analysis, we have characterized the optimal testing strategy as the solution to an MDP. Unfortunately, obtaining the solution to this MDP is intractable, motivating the development of a heuristic testing strategy. The proposed heuristic strategy uses ideas from Thompson sampling to efficiently estimate the set of high-risk users. Numerical experiments have demonstrated that the proposed testing strategy is intuitive and performs well, even in large domains.

There are many potential research directions to pursue. First, it would be interesting to investigate if it is possible to obtain a closed-form solution for the optimal testing strategy. Doing so would involve analyzing structural properties of the dynamic programming equations (recently discovered properties of the normalized incomplete beta function may be useful [18]). Second, the proposed heuristic testing strategy hints at the form of a general purpose algorithm for identifying thresholding sets under constrained queries. Development of such an algorithm, with performance guarantees, would be useful for a wide variety of practical problems. Beyond theoretical questions, there are multiple possible research directions that would need to be addressed before deploying the heuristic testing strategy to real-world settings. Some practical considerations include:

Delayed Feedback – In general, there will be a delay between querying users with test messages and receiving a response. In such settings, the system administrator cannot immediately distinguish between a negative response and a delayed response. Modifying the testing strategy such that it can be robust to these delays is necessary for deployment in real-world systems.

Correlated Responses – The proposed model assumes independence of the means; this can be relaxed in two directions. First, a given user's responses could be correlated across message types, modeling the fact that if a user is likely to fall victim to one type of attack, they may also be likely to fall victim to another type. Second, users' responses may be correlated with other users due to the possibility of side communication/verification with other users. In either case, one could learn the correlation in order to improve the efficiency of the algorithm (the result of one query can be informative for another query).

Construction of Message Database   One obstacle to deployment in real-world settings is the need for a large collection of carefully constructed and believable test messages. We believe that modern machine learning techniques can be useful in building such a database, *e.g.* via *generative adversarial networks* (GANs) [14].

A   Proof of Lemma 1

Denoting $\mathbb{E}_n^\pi[J(\Theta, P; \tau)] := E_{\Theta \sim f_n(\theta_{mk})}[J(\Theta, P; \tau) \mid P = P^\pi]$ as the expectation of the reward with respect to the posteriors $f_n(\theta_{mk})$, application of the law of iterated expectations allows one to write the expected reward as $\mathbb{E}_0^\pi[J(\Theta, P; \tau)] = \mathbb{E}_0^\pi[\mathbb{E}_n^\pi[J(\Theta, P; \tau)]]$, where

$$
\mathbb{E}_n^\pi[J(\Theta, P; \tau)] = \mathbb{P}_n \left(\bigcap_{(m,k) \in P^\pi} \{\Theta_{mk} > \tau\} \cap \bigcap_{(m,k) \in \bar{P}^\pi} \{\Theta_{mk} \leq \tau\} \right)
$$

$$
= \prod_{(m,k) \in P^\pi} \mathbb{P}_n(\{\Theta_{mk} > \tau\}) \prod_{(m,k) \in \bar{P}^\pi} \mathbb{P}_n(\{\Theta_{mk} \leq \tau\})
$$

$$
= \prod_{(m,k) \in P^\pi} I_{1-\tau}(\beta_{mk,n}, \alpha_{mk,n}) \prod_{(m,k) \in \bar{P}^\pi} I_\tau(\alpha_{mk,n}, \beta_{mk,n}) =: J^\pi(P; \tau)
$$

where $I_\tau(\alpha, \beta)$ is the normalized incomplete beta function (we have used the identity $1 - I_\tau(\alpha, \beta) \equiv I_{1-\tau}(\beta, \alpha)$). The dependency of the identification set P on the testing strategy π is made explicit by writing P^π.

References

1. Anantharam, V., Varaiya, P., Walrand, J.: Asymptotically efficient allocation rules for the multiarmed bandit problem with multiple plays - Part I: IID rewards. IEEE Trans. Autom. Control **32**(11), 968–976 (1987)
2. Audibert, J.Y., Bubeck, S., Munos, R.: Best arm identification in multi-armed bandits. In: Proceedings of the 23rd Annual Conference on Learning Theory, pp. 41–53 (2010)
3. Auer, P., Cesa-Bianchi, N., Fischer, P.: Finite-time analysis of the multiarmed bandit problem. Mach. Learn. **47**(2–3), 235–256 (2002)
4. Bubeck, S., Munos, R., Stoltz, G.: Pure exploration in multi-armed bandits problems. In: Gavaldà, R., Lugosi, G., Zeugmann, T., Zilles, S. (eds.) ALT 2009. LNCS (LNAI), vol. 5809, pp. 23–37. Springer, Heidelberg (2009). https://doi.org/10.1007/978-3-642-04414-4_7
5. Bubeck, S., Wang, T., Viswanathan, N.: Multiple identifications in multi-armed bandits. In: Proceedings of the 30th International Conference on International Conference on Machine Learning, pp. 258–265 (2013)
6. Bullée, J.W.H., Montoya, L., Pieters, W., Junger, M., Hartel, P.H.: The persuasion and security awareness experiment: reducing the success of social engineering attacks. J. Exp. Criminol. **11**(1), 97–115 (2015)
7. Chen, S., Lin, T., King, I., Lyu, M.R., Chen, W.: Combinatorial pure exploration of multi-armed bandits. In: Advances in Neural Information Processing Systems, pp. 379–387 (2014)

8. Cialdini, R.B.: Influence: Science and Practice, vol. 4. Pearson Education, Boston (2009)
9. Crossler, R.E., et al.: Future directions for behavioral information security research. Comput. Secur. **32**, 90–101 (2013)
10. Dodge Jr., R.C., Carver, C., Ferguson, A.J.: Phishing for user security awareness. Comput. Secur. **26**(1), 73–80 (2007)
11. Frazier, P.I.: Learning with dynamic programming. In: Wiley Encyclopedia of Operations Research and Management Science, pp. 1–13. Wiley, New York (2010)
12. Gabillon, V., Ghavamzadeh, M., Lazaric, A., Bubeck, S.: Multi-bandit best arm identification. In: Advances in Neural Information Processing Systems, pp. 2222–2230 (2011)
13. Gittins, J., Glazebrook, K., Weber, R.: Multi-Armed Bandit Allocation Indices. Wiley, Hoboken (2011)
14. Goodfellow, I., et al.: Generative adversarial nets. In: Advances in Neural Information Processing Systems, pp. 2672–2680 (2014)
15. Heartfield, R., Loukas, G.: A taxonomy of attacks and a survey of defence mechanisms for semantic social engineering attacks. ACM Comput. Surv. **48**(3), 37:1–37:39 (2016)
16. Hoffman, M., Shahriari, B., Freitas, N.: On correlation and budget constraints in model-based bandit optimization with application to automatic machine learning. In: Artificial Intelligence and Statistics, pp. 365–374 (2014)
17. Jun, K.S., Jamieson, K.G., Nowak, R.D., Zhu, X.: Top arm identification in multi-armed bandits with batch arm pulls. In: Proceedings of the 19th International Conference on Artificial Intelligence and Statistics, pp. 139–148 (2016)
18. Karp, D.B.: Normalized incomplete beta function: log-concavity in parameters and other properties. J. Math. Sci. **217**(1), 91–107 (2016)
19. Kocsis, L., Szepesvári, C.: Bandit based monte-carlo planning. In: Fürnkranz, J., Scheffer, T., Spiliopoulou, M. (eds.) ECML 2006. LNCS (LNAI), vol. 4212, pp. 282–293. Springer, Heidelberg (2006). https://doi.org/10.1007/11871842_29
20. Krebs, B.: Target hackers broke in via HVAC company. https://krebsonsecurity.com/2014/02/target-hackers-broke-in-via-hvac-company/. Accessed 05 Feb 2014
21. Krombholz, K., Hobel, H., Huber, M., Weippl, E.: Advanced social engineering attacks. J. Inf. Secur. Appl. **22**, 113–122 (2015)
22. Kumaraguru, P., Sheng, S., Acquisti, A., Cranor, L.F., Hong, J.: Teaching Johnny not to fall for phish. ACM Trans. Internet Technol. **10**(2), 7 (2010)
23. Lai, T.L., Robbins, H.: Asymptotically efficient adaptive allocation rules. Adv. Appl. Math. **6**(1), 4–22 (1985)
24. Li, L., Chu, W., Langford, J., Schapire, R.E.: A contextual-bandit approach to personalized news article recommendation. In: Proceedings of the 19th International Conference on World Wide Web, pp. 661–670. ACM (2010)
25. Locatelli, A., Gutzeit, M., Carpentier, A.: An optimal algorithm for the thresholding bandit problem. Proceedings of The 33rd International Conference on Machine Learning, pp. 1690–1698 (2016)
26. Puterman, M.L.: Markov Decision Processes: Discrete Stochastic Dynamic Programming. Wiley, New York (1994)
27. Reeves, J.: Yes, it's bad. Robocalls, and their scams, are surging. https://www.nytimes.com/2018/05/06/your-money/robocalls-rise-illegal.html. Accessed 20 May 2018
28. Robbins, H.: Some aspects of the sequential design of experiments. Bull. Am. Math. Soc. **58**(5), 527–535 (1952)

29. Russo, D.: Simple Bayesian algorithms for best arm identification. In: Conference on Learning Theory, pp. 1417–1418 (2016)
30. Schneier, B.: Inside risks: semantic network attacks. Commun. ACM **43**(12), 168–168 (2000)
31. Thompson, W.R.: On the likelihood that one unknown probability exceeds another in view of the evidence of two samples. Biometrika **25**(3/4), 285–294 (1933)
32. Wu, Y., Gyorgy, A., Szepesvári, C.: On identifying good options under combinatorially structured feedback in finite noisy environments. In: International Conference on Machine Learning, pp. 1283–1291 (2015)
33. Zetter, K.: Inside the cunning, unprecedented hack of Ukraine's power grid. https://www.wired.com/2016/03/inside-cunning-unprecedented-hack-ukraines-power-grid/. Accessed 03 Mar 2016

Hypothesis Testing Game
for Cyber Deception

Tao Zhang$^{(\boxtimes)}$ and Quanyan Zhu

Department of Electrical and Computer Engineering, Tandon School of Engineering,
New York University, Brooklyn, NY 11201, USA
{tz636,qz494}@nyu.edu

Abstract. Deception is a technique to mislead human or computer systems by manipulating beliefs and information. Successful deception is characterized by the information-asymmetric, dynamic, and strategic behaviors of the deceiver and the deceivee. This paper proposes a game-theoretic framework to capture these features of deception in which the deceiver sends the strategically manipulated information to the deceivee while the deceivee makes the best-effort decisions based on the information received and his belief. In particular, we consider the case when the deceivee adopts hypothesis testing to make binary decisions and the asymmetric information is modeled using a signaling game where the deceiver is a privately-informed player called sender and the deceivee is an uninformed player called receiver. We characterize perfect Bayesian Nash equilibrium (PBNE) solution of the game and study the deceivability of the game. Our results show that the hypothesis testing game admits pooling and partially-separating-pooling equilibria. In pooling equilibria, the deceivability depends on the true types, while in partially-separating-pooling equilibria, the deceivability depends on the cost of the deceiver. We introduce the receiver operating characteristic curve to visualize the equilibrium behavior of the deceiver and the performance of the decision making, thereby characterizing the deceivability of the hypothesis testing game.

Keywords: Game theory · Cyber deception · Signaling game
Hypothesis testing · Cybersecurity

1 Introduction

Deception is a technique used to cause animals [3], human [7,16] or computer systems [1] to have false beliefs. The purpose of deception is to mislead the deceivees to behave in a way that is favorable to the deceiver, while keeping the true intensions of the deceiver undetected. This is often accomplished by instilling deceptive information into the target deceivee. As information carried in cyber systems can be easily crafted, the proliferation of information technology creates particular opportunities for deception on cyber domain, making it more

© Springer Nature Switzerland AG 2018
L. Bushnell et al. (Eds.): GameSec 2018, LNCS 11199, pp. 540–555, 2018.
https://doi.org/10.1007/978-3-030-01554-1_31

difficult to infer the intention and gauge the reliability of information sources. Moreover, the challenge of identifying participants in the cyber domain also makes the accountability difficult in the cyber domain [10]. Deceivers can take advantage of such features to launch cyber deceptive activities.

Cyber deceptions can be viewed as an approach for attacks as well as defense. For example, honeyfile is a common deception tool for defense that creates a fake file directory that behaves like a normal file system of an active user to detect intrusions or malicious insiders. Attacks can hide their activities by imitating normal users in the lateral movement during an advanced persistent threat (APT) attack. Similarly, defenders can place a piece of software in a honeypot to allure attackers to download, which can report the attackers' identity information to authorities when escaping from the system. Attackers could create a website with fake promotions to attract target deceivees to reveal their personal data such as credit card information and social security number.

Successful deception fundamentally depends on the information asymmetry between the deceiver and the deceivee. Deceivees need to obtain information that is indirect and difficult to verify for decision-making. Deceivers can take advantage of this by pretending to be a trustworthy information provider. Successful deceptions require the deceivers to have the ability to acquire information and accurately understand the goals of the deceivees. The process of deceptions can be one-shot static or sequentially dynamic. The dynamic deception can engage the target in long term, create a chain of uncertainties, and achieve a higher level of believability compared to its static counterpart [9]. The deceivers strategically manipulate the private information to suit their own self-interests. The manipulated information is then revealed to the deceivees.

The deceivees, on the other hand, make decisions about the information received. This paper focuses on the case when decisions are made based on observations and beliefs. Hypothesis testing provides a fundamental framework for such decision makers who observe a signal or measurement and make decisions. Hypothesis testing is based on the statistical inference that evaluates mutually exclusive hypothesis about the nature to determine which hypothesis is best supported by realizations or samples of the nature. Decision-maker using the classical hypothesis testing approach can be easily deceived because the model presumes that the decision making completely trust the received information and hence their decisions can be manipulated by a tampered source of information. Therefore, it is important for the deceivee to form correct beliefs based on past observations, take into account the potential damage caused by deception, and strategically use the observed signal for decision-making.

Holistic quantitative frameworks are pivotal to model such strategic behaviors of the attacker and the defender and construct strategies for both attacks and defenses. Non-cooperative game theory provides befitting tools to model the competitive interactions between the deceiver and the deceivee. In particular, signaling games is a class of games that naturally capture the information-asymmetric, dynamic, and strategic behaviors of deceptions by modeling the deceiver as a privately-informed player called sender and the deceivee as an uninformed player called receiver. The sender strategically sends a message to the receiver, who takes an action upon receiving the message. Based on the private information of the sender and strategies of both players, they obtain rewards or suffer costs, which characterize the conflicting goals and preferences of the sender and the receiver.

In this paper, we study the deception game in which the receiver adopts hypothesis testing [12] to determine the binary nature of the system while the sender can strategically manipulate the signal or message that is sent to the receiver. In particular, we study the impact of deceiver's manipulation of the decision maker's beliefs on the information received. We characterize the perfect Bayesian Nash equilibrium (PBNE) to our game and analyze the *deceivability* of the game. Our results show that the deception game admits pooling and partially-separating-pooling equilibria. In pooling equilibria, the deceivability depends on the true types, while in partially-separating-pooling equilibria, the deceivability depends on the cost of the deceiver.

We characterize the receiver operating characteristic (ROC) for the decision making using hypothesis testing. By introducing the true positive rate (TPR) and the false positive rate (FPR), the performance of the decision function of the deceivee is determined by the strategy of the deceiver. The ROC curve graphically illustrates the equilibrium behavior of the deceiver and the performance of the decision making of the deceivee, thereby characterizing the deceivability of the hypothesis testing game.

1.1 Related Work

The proposed hypothesis testing game is established based on the cheap-talk signaling game model presented in Crawford and Sobel [4]. In cheap-talk games, lying of private information is as inexpensive as truthfully revealing it. Kartik has studied a signaling game model with lying cost where the sender suffers cost for misrepresenting the private information in [11]. Cost lying allows more information to be transmitted in equilibria. Other game models (e.g., [13]) have explored the truthful partial-disclosure of the private information instead of lying. For example, in the work of Grossman [8], the privately-informed agent truthfully discloses information to the uninformed agent.

Our model is also related to a class of security games of incomplete information. For example, Powell in [15] has considered a game between an attacker and a defender, where the defender has private information about the vulnerability of their targets under protection. Powell models the information asymmetric interactions between players by a signaling game, and finds a pooling equilibrium where the defender chooses to pool, i.e., allocate resources in the same way for all targets of different vulnerabilities, and the attacker cannot know the true level of vulnerability of all targets. Brown et al. [2] have studied a zero-sum game between an attacker and a defender in the scenario of ballistic missile positioning. They have introduced the incomplete information to investigate the value of secrecy by restricting the players' access to information.

Previous literature has also considered deception in a variety of scenarios. Pawlick et al., [14] have considered a class of deception for network security and extended the formulation of signaling game [4] by including a detector that provides probabilistic evidence of deception. They have analyzed the deceivability in pooling and partially-separating equilibria of the game. Zhang et al., [17] have proposed an equilibrium approach to analyze the GPS spoofing in a model of signaling game with continuous type space. They have found a PBNE with pooling in low types and separating in high types, and provided an equilibrium analysis of spoofing. The model proposed in Ettinger et al. [5] have used an equilibrium approach to belief deception in bargaining problems when the agents only have coarse information about their opponent's strategy.

This work presents a hypothesis testing game that bridges the frameworks of hypothesis testing and a cheap-talk signaling game framework to model the deception. It yields a fundamental framework to understand the strategic behaviors of the players and their outcomes.

1.2 Organization

This rest of the paper is organized as follows. Section 2 presents the problem statement and describes the hypothesis-testing-based decision making process. Section 3 develops the hypothesis testing game model and defines the PBNE. In Sect. 4, we provide the equilibrium analysis of the game, and analyze the performance of decision making under deception in equilibria through ROC. Finally, Sect. 5 concludes the paper.

Notations and Conventions. Any function defined on a measurable set is assumed to be measurable. The tilde symbol distinguishes between a random

Table 1. Summary of notation

Notation	Meaning
S, R	Deceiver and deceivee
$H_i \in H = \{H_i\}_{i=0}^1$	Type/hypothesis
$\pi_i = p(H_i)$, $\forall i \in \{0, 1\}$	Prior probability of H_i
$\theta \in \Theta$, $m \in M$	Signal, message
$\delta(\cdot) = 0, 1$	Decision function of hypothesis testing
$a \in A = \{0, 1\}$	Action of R
c_{ij}, $i, j \in \{0, 1\}$	Cost of deciding H_i when H_j holds
$\sigma^S(m \vert H_i)$, $\forall i \in \{0, 1\}$	Mixed strategy of S
$\sigma^R(a \vert m)$, $\forall i \in \{0, 1\}$	Pure strategy of R
$C^X(\cdot)$	Cost function of player $X \in \{S, R\}$
$\bar{C}^X(\cdot)$	Expected cost function of player $X \in \{S, R\}$
$\mu(H_i \vert m)$, $\forall i \in \{0, 1\}$	(Posterior) belief of R that S is of type H_i

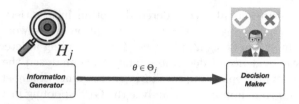

Fig. 1. Decision making based on binary hypothesis testing for hypothesis H_j, observation $\theta \in \Theta$, $\forall j \in \{0,1\}$.

variable from its realizations, for example, if $\tilde{\theta}$ is a random variable, then $\theta \in \Theta$ denotes a realization of $\tilde{\theta}$, where Θ is the support of $\tilde{\theta}$. Table 1 summarizes the notation.

2   Problem Formulation

With reference to Fig. 1, consider that there exists an information generator (IG) that provides observations of the true state of nature (e.g., diagnosis of a disease, decision of increasing interest rate). We consider a case when there are two states of nature, denoted by H_0 and H_1. The observations (e.g., symptom, inflation level) can be used to determine the occurrence of the state. Let the discrete random vector $\tilde{\theta}$ denote the observation of the event. Assume the states H_0 and H_1 admit a-prior probabilities

$$\pi_0 = P(H_0), \qquad \pi_1 = P(H_1), \tag{1}$$

with $\pi_0 + \pi_1 = 1$, and the observation $\tilde{\theta}$ admits the probability mass distribution functions $P(\tilde{\theta} = \theta | H_i)$ condition on the state H_i, $\forall i \in \{0,1\}$. Let $p(\cdot)$ be the short hand notation of $P(\cdot)$.

Suppose the information generator provides an observation $\theta \in \Theta$. A decision maker (DM) uses (binary) hypothesis testing to decide the occurrence of H_0 or H_1. In the context of hypothesis testing, H_0 and H_1 act as two hypotheses described as follows:

$$H_0 : \tilde{\theta} \in \Theta_0, \text{ with } p(\theta | H_0) = P(\tilde{\theta} = \theta | H_0),$$

$$H_1 : \tilde{\theta} \in \Theta_1, \text{ with } p(\theta | H_1) = P(\tilde{\theta} = \theta | H_1),$$

where $\Theta_i = \{\theta : p(\theta | H_i) > 0\}$, $\forall i \in \{0,1\}$ with $\Theta_0 \cup \Theta_1 = \Theta$ and $\Theta = \Theta_0 \cap \Theta_1 = \emptyset$. The goal of the DM is to decide between H_0 and H_1 based on the observation θ by choosing a decision function $\delta(\cdot) : \Theta \rightarrow \{0,1\}$ such that $i = \delta(\theta)$ indicates the decision that H_i holds, $\forall i \in \{0,1\}$. Therefore, δ partitions the observation space Θ into two disjoint sets $\bar{\Theta}_0$ and $\bar{\Theta}_1$, where $\bar{\Theta}_i = \{\theta \in \Theta : \delta(\theta) = i\}$.

Now we consider the scenario when the information transmission from the IG to the DM is not directly established but through an intermediary (e.g., medical instrument, government agency). As shown in Fig. 2, the intermediary

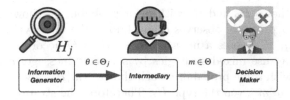

Fig. 2. Decision making based on binary hypothesis through communication with an intermediary.

privately possesses the observation θ and generates a message $m \in \Theta$ to the DM. The message m is chosen from the observation space Θ and we assume each m is a realization of a random vector $\tilde{m}$. Suppose nature chooses H_i, $i \in \{0,1\}$. We say that the intermediary is trustworthy if $\delta(m) = H_i$. After observing a message m, the DM applies hypothesis testing based on the message m and the corresponding conditional probability mass distribution functions

$$q(m|H_i) = Q(\tilde{m} = m|H_i), \quad \forall i \in \{0,1\}, \tag{2}$$

which is determined by the intermediary.

The DM selects the decision function δ by solving an optimization problem based on a Bayesian formulation [12]. Let $c_{ij} \geq 0$ denote the cost with $i,j \in \{0,1\}$ such that c_{ij} represents the cost of deciding that H_i is true when H_j holds. When $i \neq j$, c_{ij} represents the cost of incorrect decision making. For example, in cyber domain, wrong decision may allow a malicious user into the system, and c_{ij} may include the cost of recovering the damage caused by malicious activities. We have the following assumptions about the cost c_{ij}.

Assumption 1: $c_{01} > c_{11} = 0$ and $c_{10} > c_{00} = 0$.

Lemma 1 is based on [12].

Lemma 1. *Under Assumption 1, the optimal decision function can be written as*

$$\delta^*(m) = \begin{cases} 1, & if \quad \frac{q(m|H_1)}{q(m|H_0)} \geq \frac{c_{10}}{c_{01}} \frac{\pi_0}{\pi_1}, \\ 0, & if \quad otherwise. \end{cases} \tag{3}$$

Proof. The result directly follows from the proof of Lemma 2.

In this paper, we focus on the case when the intermediary is a deceiver, who aims to deceive the DM by sending the strategically selected message m. We model the strategically deceptive interaction between the DM and the intermediary by a signaling game framework.

3   Hypothesis Testing Game Model

Our game has two players: a deceiver (sender, he, S) and a decision maker (receiver, she, R). In our hypothesis model, the private information (i.e., type) is the true hypotheses H_0 and H_1 with prior probabilities shown in Eq. (1). As shown in Fig. 3 S privately observes θ and knows the true hypothesis $H_i : \theta \in \Theta_i$. Based on H_i, S chooses a message $m \in M = \Theta$ according to a strategy $\sigma^S \in \Omega^S$. He may use mixed strategies by selecting message m from each set $\Theta_i, \forall i \in \{0, 1\}$, with some probability such that $\sigma^S(m|H_i)$ gives the probability of sending message m given the type H_i. Therefore, the strategy space satisfies

$$\Omega^S = \{\sigma^S : \forall i \in \{0, 1\}, \sum_{m \in M} \sigma^S(m|H_i) = 1; \forall i \in \{0, 1\}, m, \sigma^S(m|H_i) \geq 0\}.$$

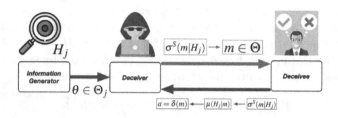

Fig. 3. The hypothesis testing game with strategic interaction between the deceiver and the deceivee.

After receiving the message m, R chooses an action $a \in A = \{0, 1\}$ according to a decision function δ based on hypothesis testing. In our game model, the decision function δ is the pure strategy of R, i.e., $\sigma^R \equiv \delta$. Based on m, R forms a posterior belief about the true type H_i. Define the belief as $\mu : H \to [0, 1]$ such that for all $i \in \{0, 1\}$ and m, $\mu(H_i|m)$ shows the probability with which R infers that the true type is H_i. The belief μ is used to find the optimal strategy for R.

The optimal strategy of R depends on her belief $\mu(H_i|m)$ about the type H_i, $\forall i \in \{0, 1\}$, such that $\mu(H_i|m)$ gives the probability with which R believes that the type is H_i given the message m. The action a is determined based on the belief μ.

3.1 Cost Functions

Let $C^R(H_i, m, a) : H \times M \times A \to \mathbb{R}$ be the cost that R suffers when she takes action a, the message is m, and the type is H_i. Basically, $C^R(H_i, m, a)$ coincides with the costs in hypothesis testing, i.e.,

$$C^R(H_i, m, a) = c_{ai}, \tag{4}$$

which satisfies Assumption 1. As mentioned in Sect. 2, the hypothesis testing requires the knowledge of the conditional probability mass distribution function, i.e., $q(m|H_i)$ shown in Eq. (2). Clearly, $q(m|H_i)$ can be taken as $\sigma^S(m|H_i)$ in our signaling game. However, R does not directly observe the $\sigma^S(m|H_i)$ but the message m chosen by $\sigma^S(m|H_i)$; therefore, we can assume that she has a conjecture $\hat{\sigma}^S(\cdot|H_i)$, $\forall i \in \{0,1\}$, about the strategy of S. R attempts to make inference using $\hat{\sigma}^S(\cdot|H_i)$. In the equilibrium, the conjecture $\hat{\sigma}^S$ coincides with the actual strategy σ^S of S. In this paper, we focus on the equilibrium behaviors of the players, and analyze the strategic interactions between R and S when σ^S is common knowledge, but the state of the truth is unknown to R.

Similarly, let $C^S : H \times \Theta \times A \rightarrow \mathbb{R}$ denote the cost function of R so that $C^S(H_i, m, a)$, $\forall i \in \{0,1\}$ gives the cost that S suffers when type is H_i, he sends message m, and R takes action a. We have the following assumption about C^S that reflects the deceptive nature of S. Specifically, S always suffers more cost if R infers the true type than otherwise.

Assumption 2: $C^S(0, m, 0) > C(0, m, 1)$ and $C^S(1, m, 1) > C^S(1, m, 0)$.

Together, Assumptions 1–2 show that our hypothesis testing game is a cheap-talk signaling game. Given the strategy σ^S, we can define the expected cost functions for both S and R. Let $\bar{C}^S : \Omega^R \times \Omega^S$ denote the expected cost for S defined as

$$\bar{C}^S(H_i, \sigma^S, \sigma^R) = \sum_{a \in A} \sum_{m' \in \Theta} \sigma^S(m'|H_i) C^S(H_i, m', a), \tag{5}$$

such that $\bar{C}^S(H_i, \sigma^S, \sigma^R)$ gives the expected cost when S plays σ^S, and the type is H_i.

The decision function δ of R partitions the message space M into two disjoint sets M_0 and M_1 with $M_0 \cup M_1$. The Bayes risk of R choosing δ when the type is H_j and S plays σ^S is defined as

$$\lambda(\delta|H_j, \sigma^S) = \sum_{i=0}^{1} \sum_{m' \in M_i} c_{ij} \sigma^S(m'|H_j). \tag{6}$$

Given a message m, R uses the belief $\mu(H_j|m)$ to formulate the total Bayes risk for δ is defined as

$$\bar{C}^R(\delta|m, \sigma^S, \mu) = \sum_{j=0}^{1} \lambda(\delta|H_j, \sigma^S) \mu(H_j|m), \tag{7}$$

such that $\bar{C}^R(\delta|m)$ gives the Bayes risk when R plays $\sigma^R = \delta$, S sends message m.

3.2 Equilibrium

We consider the perfect bayesian Nash equilibrium (PBNE) [6] as the solution concept of our hypothesis testing game. PBNE captures the information asymmetry between two players and asynchronous optimizations of two players. Also, PBNE characterizes the Bayesian belief for our hypothesis testing model. Definition 1 modifies the PBNE for the hypothesis testing game model.

Definition 1 *(Perfect Bayesian Nash Equilibrium). A PBNE of the hypothesis testing game is a strategy profile $(\sigma^{S*}, \sigma^{R*})$ and posterior beliefs $\mu(H_i|m)$ that satisfies the following conditions:*

1. *(Deceiver's Sequential rationality) S minimizes his expected cost given R's strategy σ^R: For $i = 0, 1$:*

$$\sigma^{S*} \in \arg\min_{\sigma^S \in \Omega^S} \bar{C}^S(H_i, \sigma^S, \sigma^R). \tag{8}$$

2. *(Deceivee's Sequential rationality) R minimizes the total Bayes risk for the pure strategy $\sigma^R \equiv \delta$ given the sender's strategy σ^{S*}, the message m, and the system of beliefs μ, i.e.,*

$$\sigma^R \equiv \delta^* = \arg\min_{\delta} \bar{C}^R(\delta|m, \sigma^{S*}, \mu) \tag{9}$$

The optimal action is obtained as

$$a^* = \delta^*(m). \tag{10}$$

3. *(Consistent belief) $\forall m \in M$, $i = 0, 1$:*

$$\mu(H_i|m) = \begin{cases} \dfrac{\sigma^{S*}(m|H_i)\pi_i}{\sum_{j=0}^{1}\sigma^{S*}(m|H_j)\pi_j}, & \text{if } \sum_{j=0}^{1}\sigma^{S*}(m|H_j)\pi_j > 0, \\ any\ distribution, & otherwise. \end{cases} \tag{11}$$

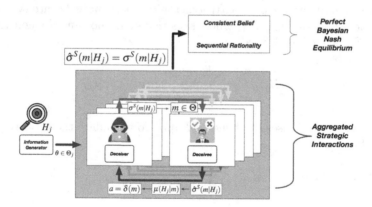

Fig. 4. Illustration of hypothesis testing game based on a signaling game model. The deceiver privately observes the observation θ and knows the type H_j. Then, S sends a message m to the deceivee according to the strategy $\sigma^S(m|H_j)$. After receiving m, R updates her conjecture about σ^S and then updates the posterior belief $\mu(H_j|m)$. R takes an action a based on the outcome of the decision function δ from hypothesis testing. The action a influence the cost of the deceiver. At PBNE, the conjecture $\hat{\sigma}^S$ coincides with σ^S.

Figure 4 illustrates the procedures of the hypothesis testing based on a signaling game model. Lemma 2 shows the optimum decision function for R in PBNE.

Lemma 2. *Under Assumption 1, the optimum decision function at PBNE can be written as*

$$\delta^*(m) = \begin{cases} 1, & if \quad \frac{\sigma^{S*}(m|H_1)}{\sigma^{S*}(m|H_0)} \geq \frac{c_{10}}{c_{01}} \frac{\mu(H_0|m)}{\mu(H_1|m)}, \\ 0, & otherwise. \end{cases} \quad (12)$$

Proof. See Appendix A.

Based on the strategy of S, PBNE can be categorized into three classes: *separating*, *pooling*, and *partially-separating-pooling*. In separating PBNE, S selects message m from opposite message spaces for two types, i.e., choosing $m \in \Theta_i$ and $m \in \Theta_j$ respectively for H_k and H_ℓ, for $i \neq j \in \{0,1\}$ and $k \neq \ell \in \{0,1\}$. Separating PBNE is also called revealing PBNE because R is able to infer the true type. In pooling PBNE, however, S selects message m from either message space with equal probability, i.e., $\forall m \in \Theta_k$, $\sigma^S(m|H_i) = \sigma^S(m|H_j)$, $\forall i \neq j \in \{0,1\}$. From Eqs. (2) and (11), the optimum decision δ^* depends only on the prior belief π_i and cost c_{ij}, $\forall i,j \in \{0,1\}$, i.e.,

$$\delta^*(m) = \begin{cases} 1, & if \quad 1 \geq \frac{c_{10}}{c_{01}} \frac{\pi_0}{\pi_1}, \\ 0, & otherwise. \end{cases} \quad (13)$$

In partially-separating-pooling, however, S selects message m for type H_0 and H_1 respectively according to $\sigma^S(m|H_0)$ and $\sigma^S(m|H_1)$, with $\sigma^S(m|H_0) \neq \sigma^S(m|H_1)$ and $\sigma^S(m|H_0) \neq 1 - \sigma^S(m|H_1)$.

4   Equilibrium Results

In this section, we determine the PBNE of the hypothesis testing game. First, we summarize in Lemma 3 that our model does not support (pure) separating PBNE.

Lemma 3. *Under Assumptions 1 and 2, the hypothesis testing game admits no separating PBNE.*

Remark 1. Lemma 3 results from the opposite incentives of S and R, i.e., S wants to deceive R and R wants to make the accurate decision. This is reflected in the costs of S and R as shown in Assumptions 1 and 2. As a result, there is no incentive for S to choose a separating strategy to reveal the true type.   △

Lemma 4 states the pooling PBNE.

Lemma 4. *In pooling PBNE, S uses the strategies satisfying $\sigma^{S*}(m|H_0) = \sigma^{S*}(m|H_0)$, $\forall m \in \Theta$. The optimal decision function (optimum strategy σ^{R*}) of R is shown in Eq. (13).*

Remark 2. In pooling PBNE, the optimum action taken by R only depends on the deterministic value of $\frac{c_{10}}{c_{01}} \frac{\pi_0}{\pi_1}$. Suppose $\frac{c_{10}}{c_{01}} \frac{\pi_0}{\pi_1} \leq 1$, then R always infers the type as H_1 no matter what message m is sent.   △

Theorem 1 shows the deceivability of the pooling strategies of S.

Theorem 1. *The deceivability of σ^S in pooling PBNE is shown as follows.*

1: *If $\frac{c_{10}}{c_{01}} \frac{\pi_0}{\pi_1} \leq 1$, then R always chooses $\delta^*(m) = 1$, $\forall m \in \Theta$. Then the probability of successful deception is π_0.*

2: *If $\frac{c_{10}}{c_{01}} \frac{\pi_0}{\pi_1} > 1$, then R always chooses $\delta^*(m) = 0$, $\forall m \in \Theta$. Then the probability of successful deception is π_1.*

Remark 3. If R always infers $\delta^*(m) = i$, $\forall m \in \Theta$, $i = 0$ or 1, then S is successful if the true type is H_j, $i \neq j \in \{0, 1\}$. In other words, the successful deception of S using pooling strategies only depends on the true type H_j. Then the probability of the occurrence of H_j is the probability of successful deception.   △

Next, we look for partially-separating-pooling PBNE. In our game model, R always chooses pure strategy, i.e., the optimum decision function shown in Eq. (2). In other words, R is a passive decision maker in our game. In these PBNE, S plays mixed strategy σ^S. Theorem 2 gives the results.

Theorem 2. *In partially-separating-pooling PBNE, there are three cases as follows.*

1. $C^S(H_0, m, 1) < C^S(H_1, m, 0)$:
   S *chooses $\sigma^{S*}(m|H_0)$ and $\sigma^{S*}(m|H_1)$ satisfying*

$$\sigma^{S*}(m|H_0) \leq \sigma^{S*}(m|H_1)\sqrt{\frac{c_{01}}{c_{10}} \frac{\pi_1}{\pi_0}}.$$

   R *chooses $a = \delta^*(m) = 1$, $\forall m \in \Theta$. The rate of successful deception is π_0.*

2. $C^S(H_0, m, 1) > C^S(H_1, m, 0)$:
   S *chooses $\sigma^{S*}(m|H_0)$ and $\sigma^{S*}(m|H_1)$ satisfying*

$$\sigma^{S*}(m|H_1) < \sigma^S(m|H_0)\sqrt{\frac{c_{10}}{c_{01}} \frac{\pi_0}{\pi_1}}.$$

   R *chooses $a = \delta^*(m) = 0$, $\forall m \in \Theta$. The rate of successful deception is π_1.*

3. $C^S(H_0, m, 1) = C^S(H_1, m, 0)$:
   S *uses pooling strategy as in Theorem 1.*

Proof. See Appendix B.

4.1   Performance Analysis

In this section, we characterize the receiver operating characteristic (ROC) for the equilibria of the hypothesis testing game.

As mentioned earlier, the decision function δ partitions the space Θ into two disjoint sets M_0 and M_1 over which R decides that H_0 and H_1 hold, respectively. Without loss of generality, suppose H_0 is the null hypothesis for the decision

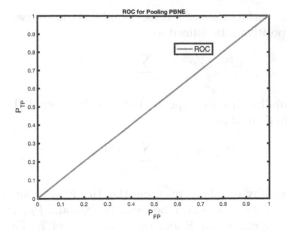

Fig. 5. ROC for pooling PBNE. Since $P_{TP}(\delta) = P_{FP}(\delta)$ for all possible δ, the ROC curve is the blue diagonal line. (Color figure online)

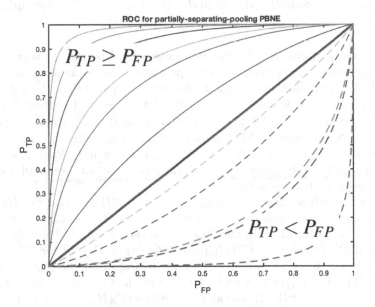

Fig. 6. ROC for partially-separating-pooling PBNE. The upper-left half (including the solid diagonal line) is the region formed by all possible ROC curves when $C^S(H_0, m, 1) < C^S(H_1, m, 0)$. The lower-right half is the region formed by all possible ROC curves when $C^S(H_0, m, 1) > C^S(H_1, m, 0)$. The solid and dashed lines are the examples of the case $P_{TP} \geq P_{FP}$ and the case $P_{TP} < P_{FP}$, respectively.

making of R. The performance of δ is measured in terms of two quantities. The first one is true positive rate defined as

$$P_{TP}(\delta|\sigma^S) = \sum_{m \in M_1} \sigma^S(m|H_1). \tag{14}$$

P_{TP} is the probability that the type H_1 is correctly inferred. The second is the false positive rate defined as

$$P_{FP}(\delta|\sigma^S) = \sum_{m \in M_1} \sigma^S(m|H_0). \tag{15}$$

P_{FP} is the probability of falsely rejecting the H_0. Except for some numerical coincidences, $P_{TP} \neq 1 - P_{FP}$. As can be seen, the P_{TP} and P_{FP} are characterized entirely by the strategy σ^S of S and the strategy δ of R. From [12], we can parameterize the cost in Eq. (7) by P_{TP} and P_{FP} as

$$\begin{aligned} \bar{C}^R(\delta|m, \sigma^S, \mu) =& c_{00}\mu(H_0|m) + c_{01}\mu(H_1|m) + (c_{10} - c_{00})P_{FP}(\delta|\sigma^S)\mu(H_0|m) \\ &+ (c_{11} - c_{01})P_{TP}\mu(H_1|m). \end{aligned} \tag{16}$$

Therefore, the performance of δ can be characterized by the strategy σ^S. The receiver operating characteristic (ROC) provides tools to analyze all possible P_{TP} and P_{FP}, and characterize the achievable test pair (P_{TP}, P_{FP}) given the strategy σ^S of S. To simplify the analysis, let $\frac{c_{10}}{c_{01}}\frac{\pi_0}{\pi_1} = 1$. When S chooses the pooling strategy $\sigma^S(m|H_0) = \sigma^S(m|H_1)$, $P_{TP}(\delta) = P_{FP}(\delta)$. As shown in Fig. 5, the ROC of poolin PBNE is a diagonal line connecting the point $(P_{TP} = 0, P_{FP} = 0)$ and $(P_{TP} = 1, P_{FP} = 1)$. From Theorem 1, R always chooses $\delta^*(m) = 1$ for all $m \in \Theta$. Since $\frac{c_{10}}{c_{01}}\frac{\pi_0}{\pi_1} = 1$, the probability of successful deception using the pooling strategy is π_0.

For the partially-separating-pooling PBNE, if $C^S(H_0, m, 1) < C^S(H_1, m, 0)$, S chooses strategy σ^S such that $\sigma^S(m|H_0) \leq \sigma^S(m|H_1)$ for all $m \in \Theta$. Then, $P_{TP}(\delta) \geq P_{FP}(\delta)$ for all δ. In this case, R chooses $\delta^*(m) = 1$ for all $m \in \Theta$. Similarly, if $C^S(H_0, m, 1) > C^S(H_1, m, 0)$, $P_{TP}(\delta) < P_{FP}(\delta)$ for all δ, and R chooses $\delta^*(m) = 0$ for all $m \in \Theta$. As shown in Fig. 6, all the ROC curves for $C^S(H_0, m, 1) \leq C^S(H_1, m, 0)$ forms the upper-left half region including the blue diagonal line (pooling PBNE), and all the ROC for $C^S(H_0, m, 1) > C^S(H_1, m, 0)$ forms the lower-right half region.

5   Conclusion

In this paper, we have modeled the cyber deception as a signaling game in which the deceivee uses hypothesis testing to make his best-effort decision while the deceiver strategically manipulates the message or observation to mislead the deceivee. We have studied the solution concept of perfect Bayesian Nash equilibrium (PBNE) to analyze the outcome of the deception game and characterize the deceivability of the game. We have shown that the hypothesis testing game does not admit separating equilibria and have obtained all the pure equilibria. Our results have shown that in the pooling equilibria the deceivability depends on the deceivee's cost and the prior belief of the type, and in the partially-separating-pooling equilibria, the deceivability depends on the cost of the deceiver. Future works would extend the proposed framework by considering an additional deception cost induced by the distance between the message and the observation. This scenario leads to a class of non-cheap-talk signaling games. Another possible direction would be to consider the leaky deception. Specifically, side-channel information can be used as additional evidence for the decision maker to improve the accuracy of decision functions.

A   Appendix A: Proof of Lemma 2

Expand the total Bayes risk in Eq. 7 as follow,

$$
\bar{C}^R(\delta|m,\sigma^S,\mu) = \sum_{j=0}^{1} \lambda(\delta|H_j,\sigma^S)\mu(H_j|m)
$$
$$
= \sum_{j=0}^{1}\sum_{i=0}^{1}\sum_{m'\in M_i} c_{ij}\sigma^S(m'|H_j)\mu(H_j|m). \tag{17}
$$

Let $\Xi(M_i|H_j)$ be defined as

$$
\Xi(M_i|H_j) = \sum_{m\in M_i} p(m|H_j).
$$

Then, we have $\Xi(M_i|H_0) + \Xi(M_i|H_1) = 1 \ \forall j \in \{0,1\}$. Thus, Eq. 17 can be written as

$$
\bar{C}^R(\delta|m,\sigma^S,\mu) = \sum_{j=0}^{1} c_{0j}\mu(H_j|m) + \sum_{j=0}^{1}(c_{1j} - c_{0j})\Xi(M_1|H_j)\mu(H_j|m)
$$
$$
= \sum_{j=0}^{1} c_{0j}\mu(H_j|m) + \sum_{m'\in M_1} \left(\sum_{j=0}^{1}(c_{1j} - c_{0j})\sigma^S(m'|H_j)\mu(H_j|m)\right). \tag{18}
$$

Therefore, a decision function δ^* is optimum if it can partition Θ into M_0 and M_1 such that M_1 satisfies

$$
M_1 = \{m \in \theta : \sum_{j=0}^{1}(c_{1j} - c_{0j})\sigma^S(m'|H_j)\mu(H_j|m) \le 0\}.
$$

Under Assumption 1, we have

$$
c_{10}\sigma^S(m|H_0)\mu(H_0|m) - c_{01}\sigma^S(m|H_1)\mu(H_1|m) \le 0.
$$

Therefore, H_1 is selected, i.e., $\delta^*(m) = 1$ if the following inequality holds,

$$\frac{\sigma^S(m|H_1)}{\sigma^S(m|H_0)} \geq \frac{c_{10}}{c_{01}} \frac{\mu(H_0|m)}{\mu(H_1|m)}.$$

Similarly, we can find the condition for H_0. $\triangle$

B   Appendix B: Proof of Theorem 2

Suppose the true type is H_0. S wants R to believe the type is H_1, i.e., $\delta^*(m) = 1$. This requires the strategy σ^{S*} of S to satisfy

$$\frac{\sigma^{S*}(m|H_1)}{\sigma^{S*}(m|H_0)} \geq \frac{c_{10}}{c_{01}} \frac{\mu(H_0|m)}{\mu(H_1|m)}. \tag{19}$$

Given R's action a, the corresponding costs are $C^S(H_0, m, a = 0)$ and $C^S(H_0, m, a = 1)$.

Similarly, if the true type is H_1, the successful deception requires σ^{S*} to satisfy

$$\frac{\sigma^{S*}(m|H_1)}{\sigma^{S*}(m|H_0)} < \frac{c_{10}}{c_{01}} \frac{\mu(H_0|m)}{\mu(H_1|m)}. \tag{20}$$

Given R's action a, the corresponding costs are $C^S(H_1, m, a = 0)$ and $C^S(H_1, m, a = 1)$.

Clearly, (19) and (20) cannot hold at the same time. Therefore, S has to decide between (19) and (20) such that the cost is minimized given the true type H_j, $\forall j \in \{0, 1\}$. Therefore, if $C^S(H_0, m, 1) < C^S(H_1, m, 0)$, S chooses the strategy σ^{S*} that satisfies (19); if $C^S(H_0, m, 1) > C^S(H_1, m, 0)$

S chooses the strategy σ^{S*} that satisfies (19) if $C^S(H_0, m, 1) < C^S(H_1, m, 0)$. In this case, R is deceivable if H_0 holds and is not deceivable if H_1 holds. The corresponding rate of successful deception is the probability of occurrence of H_0, i.e., π_0. If $C^S(H_0, m, 1) > C^S(H_1, m, 0)$, S chooses σ^{S*} satisfying (19). In this case, S can deceive R if H_1 holds and cannot deceive her if H_0 holds. The rate of successful deception is π_1. If $C^S(H_0, m, 1) = C^S(H_1, m, 0)$, and chooses σ^{S*}, S is indifferent between (19) and (20), and he can choose either strategy. $\triangle$

References

1. Bodmer, S., Kilger, M., Carpenter, G., Jones, J.: Reverse Deception: Organized Cyber Threat Counter-Exploitation. McGraw Hill Professional, New York (2012)
2. Brown, G., Carlyle, M., Diehl, D., Kline, J., Wood, K.: A two-sided optimization for theater ballistic missile defense. Oper. Res. **53**(5), 745–763 (2005)
3. Cott, H.B.: Adaptive Coloration in Animals. Methuen, London (1940)
4. Crawford, V.P., Sobel, J.: Strategic information transmission. Econom. J. Econometric Soc. **50**(6), 1431–1451 (1982)
5. Ettinger, D., Jehiel, P.: A theory of deception. Am. Econ. J. Microecon. **2**(1), 1–20 (2010)

6. Fudenberg, D., Tirole, J.: Game Theory (1991). Cambridge, Massachusetts **393**(12), 80 (1991)
7. Gneezy, U.: Deception: the role of consequences. Am. Econ. Rev. **95**(1), 384–394 (2005)
8. Grossman, S.J.: The informational role of warranties and private disclosure about product quality. J. Law Econ. **24**(3), 461–483 (1981)
9. Jajodia, S., Subrahmanian, V.S.S., Swarup, V., Wang, C. (eds.): Cyber Deception. Springer, Cham (2016). https://doi.org/10.1007/978-3-319-32699-3
10. Janczewski, L., Colarik, A.: Cyber warfare and cyber terrorism (2008)
11. Kartik, N.: Strategic communication with lying costs. Rev. Econ. Stud. **76**(4), 1359–1395 (2009)
12. Levy, B.C.: Principles of Signal Detection and Parameter Estimation. Springer Science & Business Media, Boston (2008). https://doi.org/10.1007/978-0-387-76544-0
13. Milgrom, P.R.: Good news and bad news: representation theorems and applications. Bell J. Econ. **12**(2), 380–391 (1981)
14. Pawlick, J., Colbert, E., Zhu, Q.: Analysis of leaky deception for network security using signaling games with evidence
15. Powell, R.: Allocating defensive resources with private information about vulnerability. Am. Polit. Sci. Rev. **101**(4), 799–809 (2007)
16. Vrij, A., Mann, S.A., Fisher, R.P., Leal, S., Milne, R., Bull, R.: Increasing cognitive load to facilitate lie detection: the benefit of recalling an event in reverse order. Law Hum. Behav. **32**(3), 253–265 (2008)
17. Zhang, T., Zhu, Q.: Strategic defense against deceptive civilian GPS spoofing of unmanned aerial vehicles. In: Rass, S., An, B., Kiekintveld, C., Fang, F., Schauer, S. (eds.) GameSec 2017. LNCS, vol. 10575, pp. 213–233. Springer, Cham (2017). https://doi.org/10.1007/978-3-319-68711-7_12

Algorithms for Subgame Abstraction with Applications to Cyber Defense

Anjon Basak$^{(\boxtimes)}$ⓘ, Marcus Gutierrezⓘ, and Christopher Kiekintveldⓘ

The University of Texas at El Paso, 500 W University Ave, El Paso, TX 79968, USA
{abasak,mgutierrez22}@miners.utep.edu, cdkiekintveld@utep.edu

Abstract. It is typically infeasible to use automated intrusion detection systems to scan every single host in a network with high sensitivity and frequency due to high costs and large network sizes. We present a game-theoretic model between a network administrator and a worm using normal form games with a particular structure where the network admin wants to maximize the security of the network using limited resources, and the attacker wants to infect the network without getting caught. However, a large number of hosts in a network can result in a massive game, making it problematic to compute standard solutions like Nash equilibrium. We propose an abstraction approach for solving large games that have a subgame structure and show that it can be used to solve much larger instances of this cybersecurity scenario than standard algorithms.

Keywords: Cybersecurity · Game theory · Abstraction
Nash Equilibrium · Solution quality

1 Introduction

Most real-world networks are divided into subnets to increase performance and security, but there are limited resources to inspect/harden devices against attacks. Automated Intrusion Detection Systems (IDS) [13,17] are an essential defense, but it may not be possible to use a costly IDS on every network host [1]. In a network, botnets often spread easily within a subnet using worms that exploit open ports and unpatched vulnerabilities. However, spreading between subnets requires moving through more secure and highly monitored routers that limit connectivity. This locality leads a game model with a particular structure in a Normal Form Game (NFG). We present a game-theoretic model based on this cyberdefense scenario using an NFG for stopping the spread of an attacker (e.g., a botnet) through a network that has a subnet architecture. In this game model, the network administrator acts as the defender and a worm acts as the attacker. The network administrator wants to use his defense mechanism to stop the spread of a botnet by hardening the security in one or more hosts.

While NFG is a very general representation, it is often problematic to solve an NFG for real-world scenarios because enumerating all possible strategies results

© Springer Nature Switzerland AG 2018
L. Bushnell et al. (Eds.): GameSec 2018, LNCS 11199, pp. 556–568, 2018.
https://doi.org/10.1007/978-3-030-01554-1_32

in an extremely large game. For example, in an enterprise network the large number of hosts and interconnections can lead to intractable NFG models. Solving an NFG is known to be a computationally hard problem [6], and most existing algorithms (e.g., implemented in Gambit [14]) do not scale well in practice. An increasingly common approach is to apply some form of automated abstraction to simplify the game. The simplified game is then analyzed using an available solver, and the solution is mapped back into the original game. If the reduced game can retain the vital strategic features of the original game, then in principle the solution of the simpler game may be a reasonable approximation of the solution to the original game.

This general approach has been successful in developing computer poker agents (e.g., [8–11,18]). Brown et al. used CFR [18] and imperfect recall abstraction with earth mover's distance [7] for a hierarchical abstraction [4] technique. Another widespread approach to handle massive games is Double Oracle (DO) Algorithm [3,15] which relies on the concept of column/constraint generation techniques.

Two works very closely related to an NFG reduction are one by Conitzer et al. [5] and another one by Bard et al. [2]. In the former paper, the authors gave an abstraction technique which can be used in a class of NFGs called *Any Lower Action Gives Identical Utility* (ALAGIU). The authors show that their technique can be applied recursively in ALAGIU games to abstract the game and find approximate Nash equilibrium. Motivated by the approach, we introduce an abstraction technique we call Iterative Subgame Abstraction and Solution Concept (ISASC). To evaluate this technique, we use a class of NFGs where some actions give identical utility that we call *Approximately Identical Outside Subgames* (AIOS). We also introduce a Pure Strategy Nash Equilibrium solution concept called *Minimum Epsilon Bound* (MEB).

Our main contributions are as follows: (1) we model a cyberdefense scenario using NFG that naturally leads to games with AIOS structure, (2) we offer sophisticated non-iterative and iterative algorithms for solving games using abstraction with both exact and noisy AIOS structure, (3) we present experimental evaluation of our algorithms on both generic games and games based on a cyberdefense scenario, showing that our algorithms substantially improve scalability over baseline equilibrium solution algorithms.

2   Games with AIOS Structure

A *Normal Form Game* (NFG) is a standard representation in game theory in which the outcomes of all possible combinations of strategies are represented using a payoff matrix. The tuple (N, A, u) represents a finite N-player NFG [16], where each player is indexed by i. The set of actions (pure strategies) is given by $A = A_1 \times ... \times A_N$, where A_i is the set of actions for player i. Each vector $a = (a_1, ..., a_N) \in A$ is an action profile. An action (kth) for player i is represented by $a_{i,k}$. We extend to mixed strategies $s_i \in S_i$, and use the notation $\pi^i(a_i)$ to refer to the probability of playing action a_i for player i. Each player has a real-valued utility (payoff) function $u = (u_1, ..., u_N)$ where $u_i : A^N \to \mathbb{R}$, extended to mixed strategies as usual by using expected utility.

We will consider abstracted games represented as (simpler) NFGs. For these games, we use the same notation but with a hat to denote that it is an abstracted game, $(\hat{N}, \hat{A}, \hat{u})$. We also use $A_i(O)$ to refer to the set of available actions for player i in NFG O. The set of clusters for player i is denoted using $c_i = \{c_{i,1}, ..., c_{i,m}\}$, where $c_{i,m} \subset A_i$ and $c_{i,m}$ is the mth cluster for player i, and $c_{i,m} = \{a_{i,1}, ..., a_{i,k}\}$. Every action belongs to exactly one cluster, so $c_{i,1} \cap c_{i,2} \cap ... \cap c_{i,k} = \emptyset$.

We now introduce a game structure based on the idea of forming subgames with strong interactions within a subgame, but weak interactions outside of the subgame. We call this *Approximately Identical Outside Subgames* (AIOS), as shown in Fig. 1. The fundamental idea is to create clusters of strategies for both players that form subgames. Within a subgame, the strate-

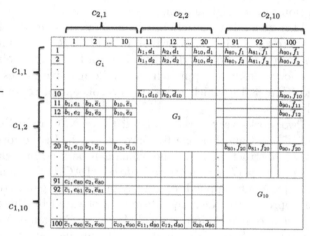

Fig. 1. AIOS Structure in an NFG

gies and payoffs can vary arbitrarily. However, outside of the subgame, the strategies for each player should have payoffs as similar as possible for playing against any opponent strategy, not in the subgame. Games with exact AIOS have identical payoffs outside the subgame, while games with noisy AIOS weaken this to allow some variation in the payoffs outside the subgames.

In Fig. 1, suppose the row player is player 1 and column player is player 2. If player 1 decides to play any strategy from $\{1 - 10\} \in c_{1,1}$, he needs to worry only about the probabilities assigned by player 2 to strategies $\{1 - 10\} \in c_{2,1}$. Intuitively this is because if player 2 plays from strategies outside of $c_{2,1}$ the payoff is the same for the row player no matter which action he chooses among $\{1 - 10\} \in c_{1,1}$. The subgame G_1 is formed by considering only actions in $c_{1,1}$ and $c_{2,1}$.

3   A Cyber Defense Game with AIOS

We now present a cybersecurity scenario for a *botnet* attack where the AIOS (Sect. 2) structure arises naturally. Figure 2 shows an example with 2 subnets containing 3 nodes each. A network is a collection of nodes that belong to exactly 1 subnet η_k. Every host has a value v_i. $t_{i,j}$ represents the *intra-transmission probability* for the botnet to propagate from node i to j within the same subnetwork

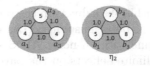

Fig. 2. Example network with $t_{i,j} = 1$ and $T(\eta_k, \eta_l) = 0$

η_k. The *inter-transmission probabilities*, represented by $T(\eta_k, \eta_l)$, is for the botnet propagating from subnet η_k to η_l. The botnet spreads on a new subnet η_l from current subnet η_k and infects the nodes of subnet η_l like a worm maintaining the intra-transmission probabilities. We model a one-shot game where the Defender selects a node i to *defend* (e.g., closing ports, patching vulnerabilities, increasing monitoring). The defend action reduces the transmission probabilities for all edges connected to i and stops any attack that spreads to node i. The attacker selects an initial node to attack, which spreads according to the transmission probabilities (which can be estimated using simulation).

If the botnet spreads to a defended node and is detected, the Defender pays a cost equal to the total value of the infected nodes (to clean up the attack), but the attacker receives a payoff of zero. If the attack does not interact with a defended node, the attacker receives the sum of the values of all the infected nodes. We estimate the payoff matrix for a particular game using Monte Carlo simulation to estimate the spread of the infection for each pair of strategies.

				Attacker		
	a_1	a_2	a_3	b_1	b_2	b_3
a_1	-4.0, 0.0	-7.01, 2.27	-6.47, 2.24	-20.0, 20.0	-20.0, 20.0	-20.0, 20.0
a_2	-5.97, 1.97	-5.0, 0.0	-8.0, 2.02	-20.0, 20.0	-20.0, 20.0	-20.0, 20.0
a_3	-9.0, 2.19	-9.0, 2.29	-4.0, 0.0	-20.0, 20.0	-20.0, 20.0	-20.0, 20.0
b_1	-13.0, 13.0	-13.0, 13.0	-13.0, 13.0	-5.0, 0.0	-10.99, 3.75	-11.46, 3.69
b_2	-13.0, 13.0	-13.0, 13.0	-13.0, 13.0	-8.97, 3.18	-7.0, 0.0	-13.0, 3.2
b_3	-13.0, 13.0	-13.0, 13.0	-13.0, 13.0	-12.0, 2.99	-12.0, 3.08	-8.0, 0.0

(a)

				Attacker		
	a_1	a_2	a_3	b_1	b_2	b_3
a_1	-4.0, 0.0	-7.62, 3.09	-7.12, 3.04	-20.7, 18.58	-20.69, 18.53	-20.7, 18.44
a_2	-6.83, 2.97	-5.0, 0.0	-8.82, 2.93	-20.88, 18.48	-20.84, 18.45	-20.89, 18.44
a_3	-8.6, 2.38	-8.66, 2.33	-4.0, 0.0	-19.89, 18.66	-19.93, 18.77	-19.91, 18.79
b_1	-12.97, 12.17	-12.96, 12.15	-12.96, 12.18	-5.0, 0.0	-10.64, 3.96	-11.28, 4.01
b_2	-14.01, 12.36	-14.02, 12.34	-14.03, 12.38	-9.39, 4.09	-7.0, 0.0	-13.14, 4.06
b_3	-14.41, 12.33	-14.45, 12.26	-14.44, 12.3	-12.39, 3.86	-12.41, 4.08	-8.0, 0.0

(b)

Fig. 3. (a) Game for Fig. 2 with $t_{i,j} = 1$ and $T(\eta_k, \eta_l) = 0$. (b) Game for Fig. 2 with $t_{i,j} = [0.85, 1.0]$ and $T(\eta_k, \eta_l) = 0.10$

Figure 3(a) shows the NFG representation for the example in Fig. 2 assuming $t_{i,j} = 1$ and no edges exist between subnets. In this case, the game has an exact AIOS structure. When the two players play on the same subnet, there is a strategically interesting game. However, when the two players play outside of the same subnets, there is no interaction. Intuitively, this is because the Defender will never be able to detect the Attacker's botnet because no connection exists between subnets. Figure 3(b) shows the network seen in Fig. 2 with a low inter-transmission probability between subnets where $T(\eta_k, \eta_l) = 0.10$ and transmission probabilities within the subnets in the range $t_{i,j} = [0.85, 1.0]$. When we add these weak interactions between subnets (i.e., relatively low transmission probabilities), we have a game with an noisy AIOS structure where actions in different subnets have only limited effects on the payoffs.

4   Hierarchical Solution Method

We now describe a solution approach that constructs subgames based on strategy clusters and uses the solutions to these subgames to create a more accurate abstracted game. When games have exact AIOS structure, this will result in finding an exact solution to the original game by composing the results of the subgame solutions. In cases where games have noisy AIOS structure, we propose an iterative solution method that improves solution quality by taking into account error from outside of the subgames.

4.1   Subgames

Consider the AIOS example shown in Fig. 1. Ten subgames correspond to ten pairs of clusters of actions for the players. For example, G_1 is played using clusters $c_{1,1}$ and $c_{2,1}$. Now we consider building an abstracted game by first solving each of the subgames G_1 to G_{10} utilizing any solution concept to get a mixed strategy for each player in each game. The abstracted game will have one action for each

	$c_{2,1}$	...	$c_{2,10}$
$c_{1,1}$	$G_{1,1}, G_{1,2}$	...	
.	.		.
.	.	...	.
.	.		.
$c_{1,10}$	...	...	$G_{10,1}, G_{10,2}$

Fig. 4. Abstracted (hierarchical) Game R

player corresponding to each cluster (10 in the example). To fill in the payoffs for each pair of clusters (a 10×10 matrix), we compute the expected payoffs using the mixed strategies for the corresponding clusters (for the subgames, this is the expected payoff from the solution to the game). Figure 4 shows the resulting abstracted game R. Next, we solve R using any solution concepts mentioned in Sect. 4.3. To get the reverse mapping here we must distribute the probabilities of $c_{1,1}, c_{1,2}, ..., c_{1,10}$ over all the actions in $c_{1,1}, c_{1,2}, ..., c_{1,10}$ for player 1 to get the strategy for the original game (resp. for player 2). Equation 1 gives this reverse mapping, where $i \in N, \forall a_{i,k} \in c_{i,m}$. In Eq. 1 the probabilities $\pi^i(a_{i,k})$ on the right-hand side are the mixed strategies for the subgames. We call this approach Subgame Abstraction and Solution Concept (SASC).

$$\pi^i(a_{i,k}) = \pi^i(c_{i,m}) \times \pi^i(a_{i,k}) \tag{1}$$

4.2   Noisy AIOS Games

The AIOS structure is strict if we require identical payoffs outside of the subgames. However, it is much more plausible to find approximate forms of this structure. For example, in Sect. 3 we saw how low transmission probabilities between subnets lead to an noisy AIOS game. For a noisy version of AIOS, we define the *delta* (δ) parameter to specify how much variation in the payoffs is allowed outside of the subgames. Let $\delta_{i,k}$ be the maximum payoff difference for any pair of actions in cluster k for player i for any strategy of the of the opponent that is not in the same subgame. δ_i is the maximum of $\delta_{i,k}$ for player i, where k can be from 1 to a number of clusters. Equation 2 picks the maximum δ considering all of the clusters and players. Equation 3, where $(i, j) \in N, i \neq j$, calculates δ for one cluster $c_{i,k}$ for a player i.

$$\delta = max_{i \in N}(max(\delta_{i,k})), \qquad k = 1, ..., |\hat{A}_i(R)| \tag{2}$$

$$\delta_{i,k} = max(u_i(a_{i,m}, a_{j,t}) - u_i(a_{i,n}, a_{j,t})) \tag{3}$$

4.3   Solving Games

We consider several solution methods for solving games. We consider both pure and mixed-strategy Nash equilibrium, as well as a different concept that directly minimizes the bound on the approximation quality in the original game.

Approximate Pure Strategy Nash Equilibrium. In a Pure-Strategy Nash Equilibrium (PSNE) all players play pure strategies that are mutual best-responses. However, PSNE is not guaranteed to exist. Therefore, we instead look for the pure-strategy outcome that is the best approximate equilibrium. We first calculate the values of deviations for each action a_i and then select the action profile that minimizes the maximum benefit to deviating.

Mixed Strategy Nash Equilibrium. We also calculate a version of mixed-strategy Nash equilibrium using the software package Gambit [14]. There are several different solvers for finding Nash equilibria in this toolkit. We used one based on Quantal response equilibrium (QRE) [12].

Minimum Epsilon Bounded Equilibrium. When solving an abstracted game, the best analysis may not be finding a Nash Equilibrium, since this may not be an equilibrium of the original game. As an alternative, we introduce *Minimum Epsilon (ε) Bounded* equilibrium (MEB). Instead of considering deviations to clusters of actions (and the average payoff of the cluster), we use the maximum expected payoff for any of the actions in the original game. This heuristic allows for a better estimate of how close the outcome will be to an equilibrium in the original game. The difference in comparison with PSNE is in the calculation of $\varepsilon(\hat{a}_i^*)$. Equation 4 is used to compute the ε for MEB.

$$\varepsilon(\hat{a}_i^*) = max_{\forall \hat{a}_i \in \hat{A}_i, \hat{a}_j \in \hat{A}_j}[\overline{u}_i(\hat{a}_i, \hat{a}_j) - \hat{u}_i(\hat{a}_i^*, \hat{a}_j)] \tag{4}$$

In the above equation $\overline{u}_i(\hat{a}_i, \hat{a}_j)$ returns a payoff from an upper bound game $\overline{R}$. Payoffs for the upper-bounded game $\overline{R}$ are computed using Eq. 5. Equation 5 calculates the maximum expected payoff for an abstracted action by reverse mapping to the original actions and calculating the expected payoff for every original action, selecting the maximum one. Next, where $\forall \hat{a}_i \in \hat{A}_i(R), \forall \hat{a}_j \in \hat{A}_j(R), (i,j) \in N, i \neq j$, the equation iterates over all the actions for every player and calculates the payoffs for the upper-bounded game $\overline{R}$. Equation 4 cannot be used in the original game because we need an upper-bounded game where we use reverse mapping. Unless we have an abstracted game, it is not possible to compute an upper-bounded game.

$$\overline{u_i}(\hat{a}_i, \hat{a}_j) = max_{\forall a_{i,k} \in g(\hat{a}_i)} \frac{\sum_{\forall a_{j,l} \in g(\hat{a}_j)} u_i(a_{i,k}, a_{j,l})}{|g(\hat{a}_j)|} \tag{5}$$

Double Oracle Algorithm. The Double Oracle (DO) is not a solution concept. It is a technique used to handle massive games. Double Oracle Algorithms [3,15] utilize the method of column/constraint generation. The idea is to restrict the strategies of all the players and solve the restricted game exactly using the LP [16] for solving an NFG. We used the QRE [12,14] to solve the restricted general-sum NFG. The QRE gives an approximate Nash Equilibrium.

Counter Factual Regret. Counterfactual Regret Minimization (CFR) [18] is an iterative algorithm to find approximate Nash Equilibrium. In every iteration, it updates the strategies of the players to minimize a weighted sum of regret at each decision. The average strategies then approach NE.

4.4   Iterative Solution Algorithm

For games with noisy AIOS structure, simply composing (as above) the solutions of the subgames may not be an equilibrium of the original game. The solution may occasionally play in quadrants of the game that are *not* one of the subgames solved explicitly, which results in an error when the payoffs do not match identically. We now introduce an iterative solution technique that (partially) accounts for this error. After solving the subgames and abstracted game as previously, we now calculate the expected payoff for each strategy outside its subgame. Then, we modify the subgames using this error term added to the payoffs in the subgame and solve them again, and then recalculate the abstracted game and solve it again. This process results in a sequence of modified solutions that account for the differences in payoffs outside of the subgames from the previous iteration. We call this algorithm the Iterative Subgame Abstraction and Solution Concept (ISASC).

Consider the subgame G_1 in Fig. 1. We want to internalize the noise outside of the subgame into the payoffs of the subgame. So, before solving G_1, we update the payoffs for both player 1 and player 2. For action $\{1-10\} \in c_{1,1}$, we calculate the expected utility when player 2 does not play the actions in the subgame. That means that when player 1 plays $\{1-10\}$, we calculate the expected utility of $\{1-10\}$, denoted Ω_i, by considering the probabilities of player 2 playing $\{11-100\}$ from the strategy on the previous iteration. Then we update the payoffs of G_1 for player 1 for action $\{1-10\} \in c_{1,1}$ for every $\{1-10\} \in c_{2,1}$ by adding the Ω_i. This process repeats for all strategies in the game.

Pseudocode for updating the subgames is shown in Algorithm 1. Subgames are updated using $[u_i(a_i, a_j) = u_i(a_i, a_j) + \Omega_i(a_i)]$, where $\forall a_i \in A_i(G), \forall a_j \in A_j(G), \forall (i,j) \in N, i \neq j$, line 4–12. Lines 5–7 are used to compute the expected payoff Ω_i, for an action of player i, when player j plays outside of the subgame G. The action set for player i in game G is $A_i(G)$. The probability of action a_j from the mixed strategy for iteration $T-1$ is $\pi_{T-1}(a_j)$.

5 Experiments

In the experiment section, we used two criteria to measure the performance of our proposed algorithm: (a) runtime (b) epsilon (ϵ). ϵ measures whether there is an incentive for a player to switch to another pure strategy from the current Nash Equilibrium strategy (which can be either a mixed strategy Nash Equilibrium using QRE or a pure strategy Nash Equilibrium using PSNE, MEB). To compute ϵ of an approximate Nash Equilibrium strategy for player i first we calculate the expected payoff of player i given the approximate Nash Equilibrium strategy of the players. Next, we check whether there is an incentive for player i to switch to a pure strategy from the current approximate Nash Equilibrium strategy (which can be either pure or a mixed strategy Nash Equilibrium). Finally, we take the maximum of all the players' ϵ which gives us the ϵ for an approximate Nash Equilibrium. In a Nash Equilibrium, there is no incentive to switch to a pure strategy for all the participating players ($\epsilon = 0$).

For our first experiment we considered 2-player games of different sizes ($\#Actions = 25, 36, 64, 81, 100$) with a fixed $\delta = 10$. For each size, we created 20 different games. For each size, the strategies for each player are partitioned into $5, 6, 8, 9, 10$ clusters with $5, 6, 8, 9, 10$ actions respectively. The subgames are completely random games with payoffs generated uniformly between 0 and 100. The payoffs outside of the subgames are generated randomly with the constraint

---

Algorithm 1. Update Subgame Algorithm

Input: Subgame G', original game G, player i
1: Subgame actions o' = Actions(G', i)
2: Opponent actions in G', p = Actions(G, G', i_{op})
3: Opponent actions outside G', p' = OutActions(G, G', i_{op})
4: **for** $j \leftarrow 1, o'$ **do**   ▷ for every action of player i in G'
5:     **for** $k \leftarrow 1, p'$ **do**   ▷ for every action of opponent $\notin$ G'
6:         $\omega = \omega + $ PayOff(j,k,G) $\times \pi(k)$
7:     **end for**
8:     **for** $l \leftarrow 1, p$ **do**   ▷ for every action of opponent in G'
9:         Outcome o = [j, l]
10:         G'(o,i) = PayOff(G, o) $+ \omega$ ▷ update the payoff in G'
11:     **end for**
12: **end for**

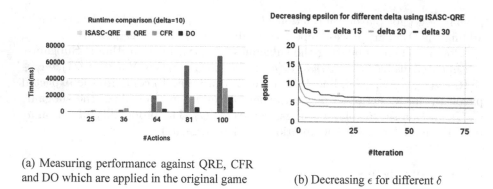

(a) Measuring performance against QRE, CFR
and DO which are applied in the original game

(b) Decreasing ϵ for different δ

Fig. 5. Measuring performance of ISASC-QRE

that in every cluster the maximum payoff difference between the payoffs for the actions is δ for all actions of the opponent that are not part of the subgame (i.e., for every action outside the subgames we add noise).

We begin by showing that ISASC has benefits when there are limited resources available since ISASC can solve a large game using fewer resources and much more quickly. We compare the runtime performance of ISASC-QRE (ISASC-QRE means we used the ISASC algorithm to solve games where QRE is used to solve the subgames and the hierarchical games) against different solution methods: QRE, CFR and DO, when these different methods are applied to the original game without the use of any abstraction as shown in Fig. 5a. The results clearly show that ISASC-QRE was able to solve games faster than QRE, CFR and DO by considerable margins.

Our next experiment focuses on showing that the iteration scheme in ISASC-QRE is effective at improving solution quality. For this experiment we created 20 2-player games for each $\delta = \{5, 15, 20, 30\}$ where 100 actions were available for each player. In Fig. 5b we show the error (quantified by the ϵ in the original game) for different levels of δ as we increase the number of iterations. We can see a clear improvement in solution quality with increasing iterations. We also note that the biggest improvements come in the cases with the largest values of δ.

The next experiment compares the solution quality of iterative (ISASC) and non-iterative (SASC) subgame abstraction techniques: ISASC-QRE, SASC-PSNE, SASC-QRE, SASC-MEB. For each algorithm, we explicitly mentioned which solution concept is used to solve the subgames and hierarchical games. For example, in SASC-QRE, we used the QRE to solve the subgames and the hierarchical games. The only exception is SASC-MEB, where we used QRE to solve the subgames since MEB can only be used to solve a hierarchical/abstract game. For this experiment, we created 20 2-player games for each $\delta = \{0, 1, 2, 3, 5, 7, 10, 15, 20, 30\}$ where 100 actions were available for each player. The strategies for each player are partitioned into 10 clusters with 10 actions for each: $|c_1| = |c_2| = 10$, $|c_{1,m}| = 10$, $m = 1, 2, ..., 10$. For this experiment, we assumed

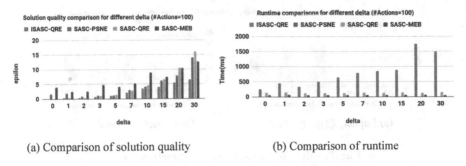

(a) Comparison of solution quality   (b) Comparison of runtime

Fig. 6. Performance comparisons for ISASC and SASC algorithms

that the subgames are known to ISASC and SASC algorithms. Figure 6a and b shows the results. ISASC-QRE and SASC-QRE does very well in cases with low δ, as expected. However, ISASC-QRE continues to perform better when the values of δ are much more significant. Figure 6a and b also show that there is a tradeoff between solution quality and runtime. ISASC-QRE produces the better results but requires more time than SASC-QRE.

Table 1. Network settings

Parameter	Value range
$t_{i,j} = t_{j,i}$	$[70, 100]$
$T(\eta_i, \eta_j)$	$[10, 30]$
v_i	$[6, 10]$
$c^d(v_i)$	$[1, 3]$
$c^a(v_i)$	$[1, 3]$
$|e_{\eta_k}, e_{\eta_l}|$	1
$|e_{\eta_k}|$	$|e_{min}, e_{max}|$

We now consider the more realistic cyber defense games described in Sect. 3. We compared our ISASC and SASC algorithms. We generated 20 games using the parameter settings shown in Table 1. Each parameter is drawn uniformly from the given range. The number of edges in subnet η_l is $|e_{\eta_l}|$ in the range $|e_{min}, e_{max}|$ where e_{min} and e_{max} are the minimum and maximum number of edges respectively. All networks are connected, and the parameters $T(\eta_k, \eta_l)$ and $t_{i,j}$, where $t_{i,j} \gg T(\eta_k, \eta_l)$ control worm propagation. We use Monte Carlo simulation for $10,000$ iterations to estimate the payoffs based on the propagation of the attack. Each subnet forms a cluster of actions for our solution methods. Since we already know the subnets for this cyber defense scenario, and thus the subgames, we assumed that the subgames are already known.

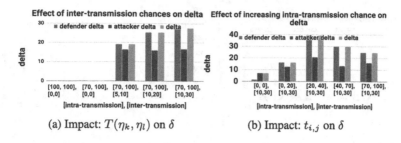

(a) Impact: $T(\eta_k, \eta_l)$ on δ (b) Impact: $t_{i,j}$ on δ

Fig. 7. Effect of transmission parameters on δ

Our first experiment shows how δ varies as we vary the *inter* and *intra-transmission probability* in Fig. 7a, b. We used games with 50 nodes and 5 subnets with the same number of nodes. We can see in Fig. 7a that when $t_{i,j} = [100, 100]$ and $T(\eta_k, \eta_l) = 0$ so the subnets are totally disconnected from each other $\delta = 0$. In this case, we can find an exact equilibrium by composing subgame solutions. However, when $T(\eta_k, \eta_l)$ starts to increase δ increases. In both Fig. 7a and b, we see that δ reaches a maximum when $T(\eta_k, \eta_l) \approx t_{i,j}$ as the spreading of botnet becomes random across the entire network, losing the AIOS structure.

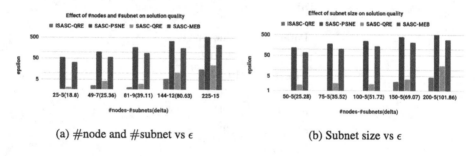

(a) #node and #subnet vs ϵ (b) Subnet size vs ϵ

Fig. 8. Performance of ISASC-QRE

Next, we show how δ and ϵ change when we vary both network size and subnet size. In Fig. 8a we can see that ISASC-QRE performs favorably compared to the other solution algorithms. Next, we increase subnet size but keep the number of subnets fixed. Figure 8b shows that as the subnet size increases δ increases. However, the ISASC algorithm continues to provide better solution quality with very low ϵ for higher δ. In all of the experiments, ISASC gives very high solution quality compared to other algorithms.

6   Conclusion

Defending a network against malicious worm requires sophisticated defense mechanism. However, due to large network size and limited resources, it's difficult for a network administrator to harden the security in every host of the network. Solving the game becomes harder due to large action space of the game model. We propose a new class of abstraction methods for NFG based on the AIOS structure. We show that there exist several abstraction-based solution methods that can take advantage of this structure to quickly find solutions to huge games by decomposing them into subgames. For games with only noisy AIOS structure, we show that iterative solution methods can give us very high-quality approximations to the solution of the original game.

Acknowledgement. This research was sponsored by the Army Research Laboratory and was accomplished under Cooperative Agreement Number W911NF-13-2-0045 (ARL Cyber Security CRA). The views and conclusions contained in this document are those of the authors and should not be interpreted as representing the official policies, either expressed or implied, of the Army Research Laboratory or the U.S. Government. The U.S. Government is authorized to reproduce and distribute reprints for Government purposes not with standing any copyright notation here on.

References

1. Alpcan, T., Basar, T.: An intrusion detection game with limited observations. In: 12th International Symposium on Dynamic Games and Applications, Sophia Antipolis, France, vol. 26 (2006)
2. Bard, N., Nicholas, D., Szepesvári, C., Bowling, M.: Decision-theoretic clustering of strategies. In: AAMAS (2015)
3. Bosansky, B., Kiekintveld, C., Lisy, V., Pechoucek, M.: An exact double-oracle algorithm for zero-sum extensive-form games with imperfect information. J. Artif. Intell. Res. **51**, 829–866 (2014)
4. Brown, N., Ganzfried, S., Sandholm, T.: Hierarchical abstraction, distributed equilibrium computation, and post-processing, with application to a champion no-limit Texas Hold'em agent, Technical report (2014)
5. Conitzer, V., Sandholm, T.: A technique for reducing normal-form games to compute a nash equilibrium. In: AAMAS, pp. 537–544 (2006)
6. Fabrikant, A., Papadimitriou, C., Talwar, K.: The complexity of pure nash equilibria. In: Proceedings of the Thirty-sixth Annual ACM Symposium on the Theory of Computing, pp. 604–612 (2004)
7. Ganzfried, S., Sandholm, T.: Potential-aware imperfect-recall abstraction with earth mover's distance in imperfect-information games. In: Conference on Artificial Intelligence (AAAI) (2014)
8. Gilpin, A., Sandholm, T.: A competitive Texas Hold'em poker player via automated abstraction and real-time equilibrium computation. In: Proceedings of the National Conference on Artificial Intelligence (AAAI), vol. 21, p. 1007 (2006)
9. Gilpin, A., Sandholm, T.: Better automated abstraction techniques for imperfect information games, with application to Texas Hold'em poker. In: AAMAS, p. 192 (2007)
10. Gilpin, A., Sandholm, T., Sørensen, T.B.: Potential-aware automated abstraction of sequential games, and holistic equilibrium analysis of Texas Hold'em poker. In: Proceedings of the Conference on Artificial Intelligence (AAAI), vol. 22, p. 50 (2007)

11. Gilpin, A., Sandholm, T., Sørensen, T.B.: A heads-up no-limit Texas Hold'em poker player: discretized betting models and automatically generated equilibrium-finding programs. In: AAMAS, pp. 911–918 (2008)
12. Goeree, J.K., Holt, C.A., Palfrey, T.R.: Quantal response equilibrium. In: The New Palgrave Dictionary of Economics. Palgrave Macmillan, Basingstoke (2008)
13. Matta, V., Di Mauro, M., Longo, M.: DDoS attacks with randomized traffic innovation: Botnet identification challenges and strategies. IEEE Trans. Inf. Forensics Secur. 12(8), 1844–1859 (2017)
14. McKelvey, R.D., McLennan, A.M., Turocy, T.L.: Gambit: software tools for game theory (2006)
15. McMahan, H.B., Gordon, G.J., Blum, A.: Planning in the presence of cost functions controlled by an adversary. In: Proceedings of the 20th International Conference on Machine Learning (ICML-03), pp. 536–543 (2003)
16. Shoham, Y., Leyton-Brown, K.: Multiagent Systems: Algorithmic, Game-theoretic, and Logical Foundations. Cambridge University Press, Cambridge (2008)
17. Venkatesan, S., Albanese, M., Shah, A., Ganesan, R., Jajodia, S.: Detecting stealthy Botnets in a resource-constrained environment using reinforcement learning. In: Proceedings of the 2017 Workshop on Moving Target Defense, pp. 75–85. ACM (2017)
18. Zinkevich, M., Johanson, M., Bowling, M., Piccione, C.: Regret minimization in games with incomplete information. In: Advances in neural information processing systems, pp. 1729–1736 (2008)

A Two-Stage Deception Game
for Network Defense

Wei Wang and Bo Zeng[(⊠)]

University of Pittsburgh, Pittsburgh, PA, USA
{w.wei,bzeng}@pitt.edu

Abstract. Computer network is always under the threat of adversaries. Before launching any real attacks, adversaries may scan and probe the systems to gain some key information. In this paper, we build a two-stage deception game to determine how to answer attackers' scan and probe queries to minimize defender's expected loss. To achieve optimal defense strategy, a sophisticated mixed integer program is formulated. To support fast computation in reality, a two-stage heuristic method is also developed based on the problem's structural properties. Computational experiment shows that after scanning the whole network, adversary's probe against some hosts and how such probe is responded have significant influences on defender's expected loss. Our heuristic method is able to produce high quality solutions with a drastically improved computational performance.

Keywords: Two-stage security game · Game theory · Cyber security
Network security · Deception

1 Introduction

During the past decades, the development of computer and network technology has profoundly changed our society. On one hand, by penetrating to almost every area of our modern world with strong computing and communication powers, it provides us with great convenience. On the other hand, the drastically intensified dependence on information science and network technology raises many security challenges and concerns. It has been well recognized that adversaries may launch malicious attacks in the cyber layer to disrupt systems' regular services or steal classified information, which has become a critical threat that every enterprise and organization must deal with. In particular, as more and more people are heavily involved in various online activities, such attacks can be launched with little difficulties but cause much deeper negative influences. For example, in 2016, a large amount of leaked confidential documents from a law firm in Panama exposed "how some of the world's most powerful people may have used offshore bank accounts and shell companies to conceal their wealth or avoid taxes" [23]. In the same year, Yahoo! reported that more than 500 million of its users' account information were stolen [19]. Later in 2017, Yahoo! affirmed that the number of

© Springer Nature Switzerland AG 2018
L. Bushnell et al. (Eds.): GameSec 2018, LNCS 11199, pp. 569–582, 2018.
https://doi.org/10.1007/978-3-030-01554-1_33

influenced users is actually 3 billion [18]. Another case happened in 2017 is the Equifax data breach, which caused the leakage of 143 million people's personal data, almost half the population of the United States, including their names, dates of birth, social security numbers and addresses [17]. Cyber security has become one of the most significant issues in the world.

Deception has been widely used in two player games. Among sending false signals about their real situations and plans [12], hiding some private information [5], and making credible and not credible retaliation threats [22], we note that the key idea is to take advantage of asymmetric information to influence opponent's behavior.

Before launching any real attack, adversaries need to collect sufficient information to build a sound understanding on the target network, such as the types of the hosts, the operating systems and their versions. Equipped with these information, adversaries can not only maximize the probability of success attacks, but also increase their gains, after their more intelligent attacks. During this stage, scan tools, like NMap [16] and SinFP [3], might be used. If such scan queries are all honestly answered, attackers are able to identify the vulnerability of the systems and prepare appropriate hacking methods easily, and the defender loses her asymmetric information advantage. On the contrary, if the responses to adversaries' scan queries are intensionally controlled, then either adversaries have to devote more efforts during reconnaissance stage or their attack cannot achieve intended goals.

Given that, many studies have been focused on dealing with attackers' scan queries. One type of techniques is to dynamically change some aspects of systems' configuration [13]. By doing this, even if adversaries have collected enough information about the systems, it probably has already changed when they launch attacks. Since changing the systems' configuration is quite resource consuming, this method may significantly increase the defender's cost. Another approach is to manipulate the outgoing traffic without actually changing systems' configuration [1,2]. Then, based on inaccurate scan results, the attackers may make incorrect inferences about the systems, especially the flaws that can be used. In addition, if such deceptive scan responses are elaborately designed, adversaries might be misled to concentrate on low value hosts, which can significantly decrease damages caused by attackers or help defenders earn additional time for defense [14,21].

In network defense, honeypots are also widely used. Honeypots are fake hosts camouflaged with high values to attract attackers' attention. Once attacked, they not only consume adversaries' time and resources, but also record attackers' behavior for further analysis and system's security improvement [15,25]. Honeypots are very powerful but expensive defense resources. Therefore they should be delicately designed in order to increase the chance they are attacked [10]. What makes the situation subtle is that the utilization of honeypots is not a secret. On one hand, since adversaries know honeypots may be deployed, high value real hosts can avoid being attacked by disguising as honeypots [7]. On the other hand, attackers may implement advanced methods to detect and disable honeypots [8]. Hence, both the protection of honeypots [6,24] and influence of being probed [20] should be considered when designing defense strategies.

In this paper, we consider a two-stage deception game for network protection. In the first stage, the adversary scans the whole network and the defender decides how to answer such queries to distract the attacker from high value hosts. In the second stage, the adversary can probe some specific hosts that he is interested in getting more information before launching any real attacks and the defender decides how to respond to such probes.

The remainder of this paper is organized as follow. In Sect. 2, we give a detailed description of the game, notations we used and a mixed integer programming formulation. To solve this problem efficiently, heuristic algorithms are developed in Sect. 3. Computational experiments are presented in Sect. 4. Finally, Sect. 5 concludes the paper.

2   Two-Stage Deception Game for Cyber Security

Our *two-stage deception game* (TSDG) contains two players, i.e., a defender who maintains a network system and an adversary who tries to cause damage to the system or to acquire secretary data. Before launching any real attacks, the adversary can first scan the whole network and then probe some specific hosts to gather information. The defender decides how to answer such scan and probe queries, which is predetermined. She is allowed to lie at some cost. The TSDG is not a zero-sum game. On the contrary, each host has a specific value to the defender and the attacker has a preference over them based on his scan and probe results, i.e., how such scan and probes are answered.

2.1   Game Description and Notation

Let $N = \{1, 2, \cdots, n\}$ be the set of all hosts in the network that need to be protected. Each of them has value u_i for $i \in N$ to the defender, representing the loss of her if host i is attacked. If host i is a honeypot, u_i will be a negative value representing a profit if it is attacked. By scanning the network, the adversary gains some information about the hosts, based on which he can divide them into several types. Each type could be a specific configuration, like a database running Red Hat Linux 7 or just a rough class as the attacker may not be able to collect enough detailed information. The set of all possible types is $T = \{1, 2, \cdots, m\}$. If the attacker cannot tell the difference between two hosts, then he views them as the same type. Scan result, i.e., the categorization that assigns hosts to types, is determined by both the hosts' own nature and the defender. The defender can honestly answer scan queries or lie at some cost.

According to the adversary's preference on all types, he will choose one for further reconnaissance. For the selected type, he can probe one or more hosts to gather more information about them. With more knowledge about the probed hosts, he is able to tell whether they are more or less valuable to him. If some of the probed hosts are more valuable, he randomly picks hosts from them to attack. If all probed hosts are less valuable, he randomly picks hosts from the rest of this type to attack. We assume the attacker will concentrate on one type once he probes it, as he has no reason to give up the information he acquired through probing. Again, the probe result is determined by both the hosts' own nature and the defender. The defender can honestly answer probes or lie at some cost.

As scan queries and probes are responded in real time, the defender's defense strategy, including the answers to both scans and probes, should be determined before the adversary's reconnaissance starts. Because the defender knows what information the attacker will acquire, she can infer how hosts will be classified and which one or some types are more attractive to the adversary. Therefore, she is able to calculate her expected loss if some hosts of type $j \in T$ are probed and then attacked. What she needs to do is to find a defense strategy such that her expected loss is minimized.

Let $\mathbf{X}$ be all possible defense decisions that the defender can make and $N_j(\mathbf{x})$ be the set of all hosts of type $j \in T$ under defense strategy $\mathbf{x} \in \mathbf{X}$. Let $R_j(\mathbf{x}, m, n)$ represent the expected loss to the defender if the adversary picks type $j \in T$, probes m and then attacks n hosts. When $\hat{T} \subseteq T$ is the set of all possible selected types by the attacker, the highest expected loss is $\hat{R} = \max\{R_j(\mathbf{x}, m, n) | j \in \hat{T}\}$. What the defender needs to do is to choose a defense strategy $\mathbf{x} \in \mathbf{X}$ such that $\hat{R}$ is minimized.

2.2   Mixed Integer Programming Formulation

We give a mixed integer programming(MIP) formulation for $m = 1$ and $n = 1$, i.e., the adversary will probe one host and attack one according to his scan and probe result, to show how our game model works. For simplicity, in the rest of this section, we use R_j to represent $R_j(\mathbf{x}, 1, 1)$.

Let x_{ij_+} be binary variables that equal 1 when host i is classified into type j after adversary's scanning and will be viewed more valuable if probed. Similarly, x_{ij_-} are binary variables that equal 1 when host i is classified into type j after adversary's scanning and will be viewed less valuable if probed. Constants c_{ij_+} and c_{ij_-} are corresponding costs, respectively. Therefore, for defense decision $\mathbf{x}$, the attacker will find $\sum_{i \in N}(x_{ij_+} + x_{ij_-})$ hosts of type j after his scanning.

Let $j \in \hat{T}$ be a type that the adversary chooses to probe and attack. Then for any host $k \in N$, the probability that it is probed is $(x_{kj_+} + x_{kj_-})/\sum_{i \in N}(x_{ij_+} + x_{ij_-})$. If $x_{kj_+} = 1$, after probing host k, the adversary will attack this host and the defender's expected loss is u_k. If $x_{kj_-} = 1$, after probing host k, he will not attack it. As in this example we only allow him to probe one host, he will attack any rest hosts of type j with equal probability and the defender's expected loss is $(\sum_{i \in N}(u_i x_{ij_+} + u_i x_{ij_-}) - u_k)/(\sum_{i \in N}(x_{ij_+} + x_{ij_-}) - 1)$. Therefore, for type j, the total expected loss is

$$R_j = \sum_{k \in N} x_{kj_-} \frac{\sum_{i \in N}(u_i x_{ij_+} + u_i x_{ij_-}) - u_k}{\sum_{i \in N}(x_{ij_+} + x_{ij_-}) - 1} \cdot \frac{1}{\sum_{i \in N}(x_{ij_+} + x_{ij_-})}$$
$$+ \sum_{k \in N} x_{kj_+} \frac{u_k}{\sum_{i \in N}(x_{ij_+} + x_{ij_-})} \tag{1}$$

Let $M = \max\{|u_i| \, \| i \in N\}$ and η be the highest expected loss over all types in $\hat{T}$ that may be probed and then attacked. When the defender has a total budget D, our TSDG for network security with $m = n = 1$ can be modeled as the following optimization problem

TG   min η $\hspace{8cm}$ (2)

s.t. $\left(\sum_{i \in N}(x_{ij_+} + x_{ij_-}) - 1 \right) \sum_{i \in N}(x_{ij_+} + x_{ij_-})\eta$

$$\geq \sum_{k \in N} \left[x_{kj_-} \left(\sum_{i \in N}(u_i x_{ij_+} + u_i x_{ij_-}) - u_k \right) \right]$$

$$+ \sum_{k \in N} u_k x_{kj_+} \left(\sum_{i \in N}(x_{ij_+} + x_{ij_-}) - 1 \right) \quad \forall j \in \hat{T} \tag{3}$$

$$\sum_{i \in N}(x_{ij_+} + x_{ij_-})\eta \geq \sum_{i \in N}(x_{ij_+} + x_{ij_-})\left(1 - \sum_{i \in N}(x_{ij_+} + x_{ij_-}) \right) M$$

$$+ (x_{kj_+} + x_{kj_-})u_k \quad \forall k \in N, j \in \hat{T} \tag{4}$$

$$\sum_{j \in T}(x_{ij_+} + x_{ij_-}) = 1 \quad \forall i \in N \tag{5}$$

$$\sum_{i \in N}\sum_{j \in T}(c_{ij_+} x_{ij_+} + c_{ij_-} x_{ij_-}) \leq D \tag{6}$$

$$(x_{ij_+}, x_{ij_-}) \in \mathbf{X} \subseteq \{0,1\}^{2mn}.$$

In this model, we are trying to minimize the highest expected loss η. Constraint (3) is a reformulation of $\eta \geq R_j \, \forall j \in \hat{T}$ in case there is no or only one host in type j, making the denominators in Eq. (1) zero. When $\sum_{i \in N}(x_{ij_+} + x_{ij_-}) = 0$ or 1, both sides of constraint (3) are zeros and η is not restricted. A special case is $\sum_{i \in N}(x_{ij_+} + x_{ij_-}) = 1$, i.e., there is only one host belonging to type j. In this situation, we assume the adversary will attack this host regardless his probe result (or he may even not need any probe). Then constraint (4) guarantees η is at least the value of this host. When $\sum_{i \in N}(x_{ij_+} + x_{ij_-}) = 0$ or ≥ 2, constraint (4) is relaxed. Constraint (5) guarantees each host can only belong to one type and have one probe result. Defender's total cost is limited under budget by constraint (6). At last, variable $\mathbf{x}$ should represent a feasible defense decision.

Note that there are products of continuous and binary variables in the model, which can be linearized by widely adopted methods. This problem can be converted to an MIP problem and solved by solvers like CPLEX and Gurobi directly.

3   Heuristic Algorithms

Even though the MIP problem **TG** in Sect. 2.2 can be solved by solvers directly, it may be quite time consuming when the network consist a large number of hosts. Under such situations, suboptimal but fast obtained heuristic solutions could be a better option than time consuming optimal solutions. Considering the two-stage frame of our model, a natural way is to divide the problem into two distinct sequential problems, each of which determines one stage decision making.

3.1   Deceiving Adversary's Scan Queries

The first decision the defender needs to make is how to answer the adversary's scan queries, i.e., which type should each host to be without considering attacker's probe. This part is similar to the research in [21]. The powerful and naive adversaries in [21] can be viewed as two special cases with $\hat{T} = T$ and $|\hat{T}| = 1$ in our problem, respectively. It has been shown in [21] that these two cases could be NP-hard problems. However, thank to today's powerful MIP solvers, the MIP formulation of this problem is not very hard to solve, especially compared to the MIP formulation of our original two-stage problem **TG**.

Let $c_{ij} = \min\{c_{ij_+}, c_{ij_-}\}$ and D_1 be the defender's first stage budget, i.e., the budget for deceiving adversary's scan queries. The first stage problem is formulated as below

$$\textbf{ST1} \quad \min \quad \eta \tag{7}$$

$$\text{s.t.} \quad \sum_{i \in N} x_{ij} \eta \geq \sum_{i \in N} u_i x_{ij} \quad \forall j \in \hat{T} \tag{8}$$

$$\sum_{j \in T} x_{ij} = 1 \quad \forall i \in N \tag{9}$$

$$\sum_{i \in N} \sum_{j \in T} c_{ij} x_{ij} \leq D_1 \tag{10}$$

$$\mathbf{x} \in \mathbf{X} \cap \{0, 1\}^{mn}$$

Here, the decision variable x_{ij} takes one if host i is covered by type j. The objective function and constraints are similar to problem **TG**.

3.2   Deceiving Adversary's Probe

By scanning defender's network, the adversary will have a brief understanding about the systems in it. According to his scan result, the hosts will be divided into several types and one or more may be attractive to him. If he picks one type and attacks one host randomly, the defender's expected loss is the average value of all hosts in this type. By probing the hosts, the adversary can gain more information therefore possibly cause larger damage to the network. However, if the defender can lie to the attacker's probe queries, incorrect information can lower the loss the defender will suffer.

Let $j \in \hat{T}$ be a type that the adversary may pick to probe and attack. Then $\overline{R}_j = \sum_{i \in N}(u_i x_{ij_+} + u_i x_{ij_-})/\sum_{i \in N}(x_{ij_+} + x_{ij_-})$ is the average value of all hosts of this type and $R_j^+ = \sum_{i \in N} u_i x_{ij_+}/\sum_{i \in N} x_{ij_+}$ and $R_j^- = \sum_{i \in N} u_i x_{ij_-}/\sum_{i \in N} x_{ij_-}$ are average values of the hosts that are more and less attractive to the attacker after his probe, respectively. When $m = n = 1$, we have the following insightful proposition.

Proposition 1. *When $\sum_{i \in N} x_{ij_+} \geq 1$ and $\sum_{i \in N} x_{ij_-} \geq 1$, we have $R_j < \overline{R}_j$ if and only if $R_j^+ < R_j^-$.*

Proof. It is easy to check that they have the following relationship and the result holds.

$$R_j - \overline{R}_j = \frac{1}{\sum_{i \in N}(x_{ij_+} + x_{ij_-})} \cdot \frac{1}{\sum_{i \in N}(x_{ij_+} + x_{ij_-} - 1)}$$
$$\cdot \frac{1}{\sum_{i \in N} x_{ij_+} \sum_{i \in N} x_{ij_-}}(R_j^+ - R_j^-) \tag{11}$$

$\square$

If the adversary can always receive correct information through probing, he must have $R_j^+ > R_j^-$ as high value hosts are more attractive to him. Then the expected damage he can make will be larger than that of random attack. On the contrary, by lying to his probe queries, the defender can make $R_j^+ < R_j^-$, then her expected loss will be decreased. Given a first stage decision x_{ij} for $i \in N$, $j \in T$, based on Proposition 1, we develop Algorithm 1 to decide the answers for attacker's probe queries when the defender's budget is sufficiently large.

The algorithm starts by sorting the hosts descendingly according to their values u_i. In line 2, $\mathbf{x}^*$ and $\hat{\mathbf{x}}$ are initialized to all zero $|N| \times |T|$ matrices used for storing final and temporal defense strategies, respectively and $\mathbf{U}^*$ is a $|T|$ dimensional vector initialized with very large values used for storing expected loss if corresponding type is selected by the attacker. For each possible selected type $j \in \hat{T}$, the number of hosts of this type, i.e., Q, is first calculated in line 4. When $Q = 0$ or 1, it is trivial (line 5 to 15). When $Q \geq 2$, we divide the hosts into two groups, one has q hosts with the highest values and another has $Q - q$ with the lowest values. A temporal strategy is to deceive the adversary that the $Q - q$ hosts with low values are important (line 20 to 22) but the q hosts in another group are not important (line 23 to 26). Then the expected loss under this strategy if type j is picked is calculated (line 27). Iterating over all possible ways for dividing the hosts (line 17) and picking the one with lowest expected loss (line 28 to 30) gives the best deceiving strategy. At last, as types not in $\hat{T}$ are not attractive to the attacker, it does not matter how those hosts look like. We can assign them scan and probe results with the lowest cost (line 36).

Proposition 2. *For $m = n = 1$, Algorithm 1 derives an optimal second stage defense strategy in $O(|T||N|^2)$ iterations when the defender has a sufficiently large budget.*

Algorithm 1. Unlimited Budget Probe Deception

1: relabel the hosts in N descendingly by u_i
2: **initialize** $\mathbf{x}^*$, $\hat{\mathbf{x}}$, $\mathbf{U}^*$
3: **for** $j = 1$ to $|\hat{T}|$ **do**
4:     $Q \leftarrow \sum_{i \in N} x_{ij}$
5:     **if** $Q == 0$ **then**
6:         $U_j^* \leftarrow 0$
7:     **end if**
8:     **if** $Q == 1$ **then**
9:         **for** $i = 1$ to $|N|$ **do**
10:             **if** $x_{ij} == 1$ **then**
11:                 $x_{ij_+}^* \leftarrow 1$ or $x_{ij_-}^* \leftarrow 1$
12:                 $U_j^* \leftarrow u_i$
13:             **end if**
14:         **end for**
15:     **end if**
16:     **if** $Q > 1$ **then**
17:         **for** $q = 0$ to Q **do**
18:             $p \leftarrow q$
19:             **for** $i = 1$ to $|N|$ **do**
20:                 **if** $x_{ij} == 1 \& p == 0$ **then**
21:                     $\hat{x}_{ij_+} \leftarrow 1$
22:                 **end if**
23:                 **if** $x_{ij} == 1 \& p > 0$ **then**
24:                     $\hat{x}_{ij_-} \leftarrow 1$
25:                     $p \leftarrow p - 1$
26:                 **end if**
27:                 calculate R_j according to $\hat{x}_{.j}$
28:                 **if** $U_j^* > R_j$ **then**
29:                     $U_j^* \leftarrow R_j$, $x_{.j}^* \leftarrow \hat{x}_{.j}$
30:                 **end if**
31:             **end for**
32:         **end for**
33:     **end if**
34: **end for**
35: **for** $j = |\hat{T}| + 1$ to $|T|$ **do**
36:     assign $x_{.j}^*$ according to their cost
37: **end for**

Proof. For a given first stage strategy, $\overline{R}_j$ is a constant, therefore minimum R_j can be achieved by minimizing the right hand side of Eq. (11). For fixed numbers of attractive and unattractive hosts, we only need to assign high value hosts as unattractive ones and make low value hosts attractive ones. Since all possible ways for dividing hosts into two groups are enumerated, the result is guaranteed to be optimal. The complexity of this algorithm follows easily.   □

In real situations, defenders always need to balance the tradeoff between the resources they devote and the benefit they can derive. Usually their budget should be limited, which will make the decision more difficult to make. For such problems, we give Algorithm 2 to derive heuristic solutions.

Algorithm 2. Limited Budget Probe Deception

1: **for** $i = 1$ to $|N|$ **do**
2:     **for** $j = 1$ to $|T|$ **do**
3:         **if** $x_{ij} == 1 \& c_{ij_+} > c_{ij_-}$ **then**
4:             $x^*_{ij_-} \leftarrow 1$
5:         **end if**
6:         **if** $x_{ij} == 1 \& c_{ij_+} \leq c_{ij_-}$ **then**
7:             $x^*_{ij_+} \leftarrow 1$
8:         **end if**
9:     **end for**
10: **end for**
11: **update** $\hat{x}$, U^*, D_2
12: $j^* \leftarrow \arg\max_{j \in \hat{T}}\{U^*_j\}$
13: **for** $i = 1$ to $|N|$ **do**
14:     **if** $\hat{x}_{ij^*_+} == 1 \& c_{ij^*_-} - c_{ij^*_+} \leq D_2$ **then**
15:         $\hat{x}_{ij^*_+} \leftarrow 0$, $\hat{x}_{ij^*_-} \leftarrow 1$
16:         calculate R_{j^*} according to $\hat{x}_{.j^*}$
17:         **if** $R_{j^*} < U^*_{j^*}$ **then**
18:             $x^*_{ij^*_+} \leftarrow 0$, $x^*_{ij^*_-} \leftarrow 1$, **go to** line 11
19:         **else**
20:             $\hat{x}_{ij^*_+} \leftarrow 1$, $\hat{x}_{ij^*_-} \leftarrow 0$
21:         **end if**
22:     **end if**
23:     **if** $\hat{x}_{ij^*_-} == 1 \& c_{ij^*_+} - c_{ij^*_-} \leq D_2$ **then**
24:         $\hat{x}_{ij^*_-} \leftarrow 0$, $\hat{x}_{ij^*_+} \leftarrow 1$
25:         calculate R_{j^*} according to $\hat{x}_{.j^*}$
26:         **if** $R_{j^*} < U^*_{j^*}$ **then**
27:             $x^*_{ij^*_-} \leftarrow 0$, $x^*_{ij^*_+} \leftarrow 1$, **go to** line 11
28:         **else**
29:             $\hat{x}_{ij^*_-} \leftarrow 1$, $\hat{x}_{ij^*_+} \leftarrow 0$
30:         **end if**
31:     **end if**
32: **end for**

Given a first stage defense strategy, the algorithm starts by building a defense strategy with the lowest cost (line 1 to 10). This is always feasible if the first stage decision is made by solving problem **ST1** in Sect. 3.1. In line 11, temporal strategy $\hat{x}$ is set to the same as current strategy x^*. Expected loss of each type U^* and available budget D_2 are calculated. Then the type with the highest expected loss is picked in line 12. In the following loop, if the expected loss can be decreased by changing a host's probe answer, then do it. Otherwise, we are done.

When we are considering two stages together, we can first solve the problem **ST1** with all or part budget, then run Algorithm 2 with what remains. Network

Table 1. Host's value and camouflage cost

Host	Value	1+	1−	2+	2−	3+	3−	4+	4−	5+	5−
1	100	0	60	NA	NA	NA	NA	NA	NA	NA	NA
2	80	0	40	60	80	80	100	NA	NA	NA	NA
3	80	0	40	60	80	80	100	NA	NA	NA	NA
4	70	30	20	0	40	30	60	60	80	NA	NA
5	70	30	20	0	40	30	60	60	80	NA	NA
6	70	30	20	0	40	30	60	60	80	NA	NA
7	50	60	40	50	20	0	30	20	40	NA	NA
8	50	60	40	50	20	0	30	20	40	NA	NA
9	50	60	40	50	20	0	30	20	40	NA	NA
10	30	90	70	60	50	40	20	0	20	10	30
11	30	90	70	60	50	40	20	0	20	10	30
12	30	90	70	60	50	40	20	0	20	10	30
13	20	100	80	70	60	50	40	20	0	0	20
14	20	100	80	70	60	50	40	20	0	0	20
15	20	100	80	70	60	50	40	20	0	0	20
16	5	NA	NA	NA	NA	80	60	40	30	20	0
17	5	NA	NA	NA	NA	80	60	40	30	20	0
18	5	NA	NA	NA	NA	80	60	40	30	20	0
19	5	NA	NA	NA	NA	80	60	40	30	20	0
20	5	NA	NA	NA	NA	80	60	40	30	20	0

operators can try several approaches to partition their budget for each stage then pick the one with the lowest expected loss.

4   Computation Results

To evaluate our model and solution methods, we build an experimental instance for computational test. We use programming language `Julia` [4] to run our algorithms. All optimization problems are modeled by the package `JuMP` [9] and then solved by calling `Gurobi 7.5` [11].

The instance we generate has 20 hosts and 5 possible types. The value of each host and the cost to camouflage them are shown in Table 1. In the first row, the number means which type will the host be classified after the attacker's scanning. The signs + and − represent whether the host will appear more or less attractive to the adversary after his probe. In the cost values, "NA" means the host cannot be camouflaged to that type no matter how much resources are devoted. We assume the adversary can probe and attack one host after his scanning.

4.1   Unlimited Budget

We first consider the case when the defender has an unlimited defense budget. Defender's worst expected loss with different adversary's interesting set $\hat{T}$ is shown in Table 2. The column MIP is derived by directly solving problem **TG**. In the other columns, problem **ST1** is first solved. In column NoDeNoPb, the adversary picks one type in the set $\hat{T}$ then randomly attacks one host without any probe. In column NoDePb, the adversary probes but the defender answers his probe queries honestly. In the last column DePb, the adversary probes and the defender can manipulate his probe result.

Table 2. Defender's loss under unlimited defense budgets

	MIP	NoDeNoPb	NoDePb	DePb
$\hat{T} = \{1\}$	20	35.7	46.4	25
$\hat{T} = \{1, 2\}$	20	35.7	46.4	25
$\hat{T} = \{1, 2, 3\}$	20	35.7	57.5	25
$\hat{T} = \{1, 2, 3, 4\}$	20	40	58.7	32.5

From the result we can see, by considering the two stages together, our MIP model **TG** gives the best defense strategy. Without probing, the adversary can only attack a host randomly, so the defender's expected loss is the average value of the hosts in the picked type. If the adversary can derive correct probe result, he can increase his profit significantly. On the contrary, with incorrect probe result, the attacker's profit is even lower than random attack. This is consistent with our analysis of Proposition 1.

However, this may cause a new problem. Table 3 shows the optimal defense strategy achieved by solving the MIP model **TG** when $\hat{T} = \{1, 2, 3, 4\}$. Each row shows which hosts are assigned to that type and how to answer attacker's probe. For example, in the row type 1, 1− means host 1 will be classified into this type after adversary's scanning and become less attractive after his probe (similarly, + means more attractive after probe). As attacker's probe queries are not honestly answered, defender's expected loss are the values in the column R_j if corresponding type is selected. But, if the attacker realizes his probe is cheated, he may ignore all probe results and attack randomly. Then the defender's expected loss would be the column $\overline{R}_j$, which is much higher than the previous one. The worst case loss is even greater than answering attacker's probe honestly, making the defender at very high risk.

Two approaches can be adopted to deal with this situation. One is to use the two-stage method, since problem **ST1** gives optimal solution against random attack, then for given first stage decision, Algorithm 1 gives optimal solution against adversary's probe queries. This results in the column DePd in Table 2, which is not guaranteed to be optimal but can be calculated easily. The other method is adding additional constraint $\sum_{i \in N}(x_{ij_+} + x_{ij_-})\eta \geq \sum_{i \in N} u_i(x_{ij_+} + x_{ij_-})$ to the MIP formulation. By adding this constraint, defender's loss through adversary's random attack is also considered in this optimization problem. The solution is guaranteed to be optimal but the resulting problem might be difficult to solve.

Table 3. Optimal defense strategy and expected loss of each type

	Hosts	R_j	$\overline{R}_j$
Type 1	1−, 14+	20	60
Type 2	3−, 15+	20	50
Type 3	2−, 13+	20	50
Type 4	4−, 5−, 6−, 7−, 8−, 9−, 16+, 17+, 18+, 19+, 20+	20	35
Type 5	10+, 11+, 12+	30	30

Table 4. Worst expected loss under different methods with limited budgets

	1000	900	800	700	600	500
MIP	38	40	45	46.7	50	53.3
Heu100	48	57.5	60	63	73.3	65
Heu80	40	43.8	47.5	48	58	58
Heu60	46.7	48.3	50	52	53.3	59.5

Table 5. Calculation time (in seconds) of different methods with limited budgets

	1000	900	800	700	600	500
MIP	18	25	93	78	119	104
Heu100	0.6	0.1	0.04	0.1	0.1	0.1
Heu80	0.5	0.1	0.1	0.1	0.2	0.1
Heu60	0.6	0.1	0.2	0.1	0.1	0.1

4.2 Limited Budget

We also test our model and heuristic algorithms with a limited defense budget. Table 4 shows the worst expected loss of the defender under different methods with limit budgets. Table 5 shows the corresponding calculation time (in seconds). We set $\hat{T} = \{1, 2, 3\}$ and the budget ranges from 1000 to 500. The row MIP solves the problem **TG**. For more reliable results, the additional constraint we mentioned in Sect. 4.1 is added. Therefore both adversaries with or without probe are considered. The other three rows use two-stage heuristic to solve the problem. First, problem **ST1** is solved with 100%, 80% and 60% of the total budget, respectively. By doing this, the answers to the adversary's scan queries are determined. Then we run Algorithm 2 with the remaining budget to decide how to reply to his probe. We take the worst result of these two stages as we want to defend attackers with or without probe at the same time.

Unsurprisingly, the row MIP gives the best, which is also the optimal, defense strategy since both stages are considered together. However, the MIP model may take up to two minutes to solve. On the contrary, all heuristics are finished within only one second. Indeed, the row Heu80 gives results quite close to the optimal solutions of MIP formulation. Overall, our two-stage heuristic method can achieve high quality defense strategy within reasonable time.

5 Conclusion

In this paper, we consider a network security problem where the adversary will scan then probe the systems before launching any real attacks. We build a two-stage game model to determine how such scan and probe queries should be answered to minimize the defender's expected loss. The game is formulated as a mixed integer program, by solving which the optimal defense strategy can be derived. Based on the problem's structural properties, a fast two-stage heuristic method is also developed to support real applications. Computational experiment shows that after scanning the whole network, adversary's probe against some hosts and how such probe is responded have significant influences on defender's expected loss. Our heuristic method is also able to produce high quality solutions with a drastically improved computational performance.

References

1. Albanese, M., Battista, E., Jajodia, S.: A deception based approach for defeating OS and service fingerprinting. In: 2015 IEEE Conference on Communications and Network Security (CNS) pp. 317–325. IEEE (2015)
2. Albanese, M., Battista, E., Jajodia, S.: Deceiving attackers by creating a virtual attack surface. In: Jajodia, S., Subrahmanian, V.S.S., Swarup, V., Wang, C. (eds.) Cyber Deception, pp. 169–201. Springer, Cham (2016). https://doi.org/10.1007/978-3-319-32699-3_8
3. Auffret, P.: SinFP, unification of active and passive operating system fingerprinting. J. Comput. Virol. **6**(3), 197–205 (2010)
4. Bezanson, J., Edelman, A., Karpinski, S., Shah, V.B.: Julia: a fresh approach to numerical computing. SIAM Rev. **59**(1), 65–98 (2017)
5. Brown, G., Carlyle, M., Diehl, D., Kline, J., Wood, K.: A two-sided optimization for theater ballistic missile defense. Oper. Res. **53**(5), 745–763 (2005)
6. Cai, J.-Y., Yegneswaran, V., Alfeld, C., Barford, P.: An attacker-defender game for honeynets. In: Ngo, H.Q. (ed.) COCOON 2009. LNCS, vol. 5609, pp. 7–16. Springer, Heidelberg (2009). https://doi.org/10.1007/978-3-642-02882-3_2

7. Carroll, T.E., Grosu, D.: A game theoretic investigation of deception in network security. Secur. Commun. Netw. **4**(10), 1162–1172 (2011)
8. Dornseif, M., Holz, T., Klein, C.N.: Nosebreak-attacking honeynets. In: Proceedings from the Fifth Annual IEEE SMC Information Assurance Workshop 2004, pp. 123–129. IEEE (2004)
9. Dunning, I., Huchette, J., Lubin, M.: Jump: a modeling language for mathematical optimization. SIAM Rev. **59**(2), 295–320 (2017)
10. Garg, N., Grosu, D.: Deception in honeynets: a game-theoretic analysis. In: Information Assurance and Security Workshop 2007. IAW 2007. IEEE SMC, pp. 107–113. IEEE (2007)
11. Gurobi Optimization, I.: Gurobi optimizer reference manual (2016). http://www.gurobi.com
12. Hendricks, K., McAfee, R.P.: Feints. J. Econ. Manag. Strat. **15**(2), 431–456 (2006)
13. Jajodia, S., Ghosh, A.K., Swarup, V., Wang, C., Wang, X.S.: Moving Target Defense: Creating Asymmetric Uncertainty for Cyber Threats, vol. 54. Springer, Heidelberg (2011). https://doi.org/10.1007/978-1-4614-0977-9
14. Jajodia, S., et al.: A probabilistic logic of cyber deception. IEEE Trans. Inf. Forensics Secur. **12**(11), 2532–2544 (2017)
15. Kuwatly, I., Sraj, M., Al Masri, Z., Artail, H.: A dynamic honeypot design for intrusion detection. In: IEEE/ACS International Conference on Pervasive Services, 2004. ICPS 2004,, pp. 95–104. IEEE (2004)
16. Lyon, G.F.: Nmap Network Scanning: The Official Nmap Project Guide to Network Discovery and Security Scanning. Insecure (2009)
17. Mathews, L.: Equifax data breach impacts 143 million americans, 7 September 2017. https://www.forbes.com/sites/leemathews/2017/09/07/equifax-data-breach-impacts-143-million-americans/#5a924209356f
18. McMillan, R., Knutson, R.: Yahoo triples estimate of breached accounts to 3 billion, 3 October 2017. https://www.wsj.com/articles/yahoo-triples-estimate-of-breached-accounts-to-3-billion-1507062804
19. Perlroth, N.: Yahoo says hackers stole data on 500 million users in 2014, 22 September 2016. https://www.nytimes.com/2016/09/23/technology/yahoo-hackers.html
20. Píbil, R., Lisý, V., Kiekintveld, C., Bošanský, B., Pěchouček, M.: Game theoretic model of strategic honeypot selection in computer networks. In: Grossklags, J., Walrand, J. (eds.) GameSec 2012. LNCS, vol. 7638, pp. 201–220. Springer, Heidelberg (2012). https://doi.org/10.1007/978-3-642-34266-0_12
21. Schlenker, A., et al.: Deceiving cyber adversaries: a game theoretic approach. In: International Conference on Autonomous Agents and Multiagent Systems (2018)
22. Shan, X., Zhuang, J.: Modeling credible retaliation threats in deterring the smuggling of nuclear weapons using partial inspection'a three-stage game. Decis. Anal. **11**(1), 43–62 (2014)
23. Times, T.N.Y.: What are the panama papers? 4 April 2016. https://www.nytimes.com/2016/04/05/world/panama-papers-explainer.html
24. Yegneswaran, V., Alfeld, C., Barford, P., Cai, J.Y.: Camouflaging honeynets. In: IEEE Global Internet Symposium, 2007, pp. 49–54. IEEE (2007)
25. Zhang, F., Zhou, S., Qin, Z., Liu, J.: Honeypot: a supplemented active defense system for network security. In: Proceedings of the Fourth International Conference on Parallel and Distributed Computing, Applications and Technologies, 2003. PDCAT 2003, pp. 231–235. IEEE (2003)

Imbalanced Collusive Security Games

Han-Ching Ou[✉], Milind Tambe, Bistra Dilkina, and Phebe Vayanos

Computer Science Department, University of Southern California, Los Angeles, USA
{hanchino,tambe,dilkina,phebe.vayanos}@usc.edu

Abstract. Colluding adversaries is a crucial challenge for defenders in many real-world applications. Previous literature has provided Collusive Security Games (COSG) to model colluding adversaries, and provided models and algorithms to generate defender strategies to counter colluding adversaries, often by devising strategies that inhibit collusion [6]. Unfortunately, this previous work focused exclusively on situations with perfectly matched adversaries, i.e., where their rewards were symmetrically distributed. In the real world, however, defenders often face adversaries where their rewards are asymmetrically distributed. Such inherent asymmetry raises a question as to whether human adversaries would attempt to collude in such situations, and whether defender strategies to counter such collusion should focus on inhibiting collusion. To address these open questions, this paper: (i) explores and theoretically analyzes Imbalanced Collusive Security Games (ICOSG) where defenders face adversaries with asymmetrically distributed rewards; (ii) conducts extensive experiments of three different adversary models involving 1800 real human subjects and (iii) derives novel analysis of the reason behind why bounded rational attackers models outperform perfectly rational attackers models. The key principle discovered as the result of our experiments is that: careful modeling of human bounded rationality reveals a key difference (when compared to a model using perfect rationality) in defender strategies for handling colluding adversaries which face symmetric vs asymmetric rewards. Whereas a model based on perfect rationality always attempts to break collusion among adversaries, a bounded rationality model acknowledges the inherent difficulty of breaking such collusion in symmetric situations and focuses only on breaking collusion in asymmetric situation, and only on damage control from collusion in the symmetric situation.

Keywords: Stackelberg security game · Collusion
Human behavior model · Amazon mechanical turk

1 Introduction

Motivated by threats on human and cyber-physical systems, game theoretic approaches have been devised to help solve real-life security problems in many domains. [1,13,19] In these applications, Stackelberg security game based models

© Springer Nature Switzerland AG 2018
L. Bushnell et al. (Eds.): GameSec 2018, LNCS 11199, pp. 583–602, 2018.
https://doi.org/10.1007/978-3-030-01554-1_34

have proved to be both practical and effective in many scenarios, e.g., to protect airports [17,19], train stations [22], and even wildlife [4,5,21].

In order to advance these applications, collusion among adversaries in security games is a vital issue that needs to be addressed. Instead of working alone, adversaries colluding with one another often attack targets more effectively. For example, smugglers in Colombia have developed from small criminal groups to huge drug cartels by working closely since the 1950s [18]. Terrorists received material support from criminal groups and carried out more severe violent actions in the US [8]. These examples show that if we do not break the collusion in an early stage, the attackers might collude to become a stronger threat to defenders.

Previous literature has provided Collusive Security Games (COSG) to model colluding adversaries [6]. It has provided algorithms to generate defender strategies to counter the colluding adversaries in such a model. However, this previous work focused exclusively on situations with perfectly matched adversaries, i.e., where their rewards were symmetrically distributed. In the real world, however, defenders often face adversaries where rewards are asymmetrically distributed [3].

Such inherent asymmetry raises a question as to whether human adversaries would attempt to collude in such situations, and whether defender strategies to counter such collusion should focus on inhibiting such collusion. To address these open questions, this paper: (i) explores and theoretically analyzes Imbalanced Collusive Security Games (ICOSG) expand from COSG where defenders face adversaries with asymmetrically distributed rewards; (ii) conducts extensive experiments involving 1800 real human subjects of three different adversary models and (iii) derives novel analysis of the reason behind why bounded rational attackers models outperform perfectly rational attackers models. The key principle discovered as the result of our experiments is that: Careful modeling of human bounded rationality reveals a key difference (when compared to a model using perfect rationality) in defender strategies for handling colluding adversaries which face symmetric vs asymmetric rewards. Whereas a model based on perfect rationality always attempts to break collusion among adversaries, a bounded rationality model acknowledges the inherent difficulty of breaking such collusion in symmetric situations and focuses only on breaking collusion in asymmetric situation, and only on damage control from collusion in the symmetric situation.

2   Imbalanced Collusive Security Games

The Stackelberg Security Game model is widely used in both literature and security applications. [2,11,15,19] Models based on it usually consist of two stages, the defender decides her strategy in the first stage. After observing the defender strategy, the attacker chooses a strategy as the best response to it in the second stage. The objective of the defender is to use a limited number m of resources to protect several targets in a set T, with each target having a different value. The attacker on the other hand seeks to attack the target that gives him the highest utility while avoiding being caught by the defender. Knowing the attacker will observe her strategy[1], the best choice for the defender is to deploy a mixed strategy that defends each target stochastically (rather than using pure strategies to always defend the same set of targets). This mixed strategy can be viewed as a probability distribution over pure strategies. We can equivalently represent such strategy with a vector c with elements $c_t \in [0,1]$ ($\sum_t c_t = 1$) [11] denoting the probability of target t being covered. As for the attacker, after observing the defender strategy, his strategy consists of choosing a particular target to attack. We express the attacker's choice using a vector α with element $\alpha_t \in \{0,1\}$, $t \in T$, equal to 1 iff target t is chosen.

For each target, we denote the utility that the defender receives when she successfully defends the target by $U_\Theta^S(t)$. The defender commits to a strategy and the adversary observes this strategy and each select a target to attack; accordingly, if she fails to protect the target, she receives the utility $U_\Theta^F(t)$. We also denote the utility of the attacker when he successfully attacks a target (without being caught) as $U_\Psi^S(t)$; accordingly, if he gets caught attacking a target, he receives the utility $U_\Psi^F(t)$.

The expected utilities of the defender and the attacker for a given defense strategy c and attack vector α can be respectively expressed as

$$U_\Theta(c,\alpha) = \sum_{t \in T} \alpha_t \left(c_t U_\Theta^S(t) + (1 - c_t)U_\Theta^F(t) \right) \tag{1}$$

$$U_\Psi(c,\alpha) = \sum_{t \in T} \alpha_t \left(c_t U_\Psi^F(t) + (1 - c_t)U_\Psi^S(t) \right). \tag{2}$$

The solution concept, known as Strong Stackelberg Equilibrium (SSE), assumes that the attackers maximize their own expected utility and break ties in favor of the defender [10,19]. In such equilibrium, the defender plays the strategy that is the best response to the attacker's strategy $\overline{c}(\overline{\alpha})$ and the attacker plays the strategy that is best response the the defender strategy $\overline{\alpha}(\overline{c})$ such that $U_\Theta(\overline{c},\overline{\alpha}) \geq U_\Theta(c,\overline{\alpha}) \ \forall \ c$ and $U_\Psi(\overline{c},\overline{\alpha}) \geq U_\Psi(\overline{c},\alpha) \ \forall \ \alpha$.

Numerous security problems from the real world have been cast in the Stackelberg Security Game framework. For example, [12,23] provide a model where the attacker has the ability to attack multiple targets, [7] models the cooperation methods between multiple attackers and finally, [6] models the possibility of collusion between identical individual attackers. In this paper, we exploit and expand the work from [6].

In [6], the authors defined a model called Collusive Security Games (COSG) in which each attacker needs to make an extra decision of whether or not to collude with each other besides choosing which target to attack. They have introduced a new solution for COSG, termed Collusive Security Equilibrium (CSE), which generalizes the SSE. This solution concept eliminates weak equilibria while preserving properties of SSE. In CSE, the defender and attackers

---

[1] By convention in the security game literature, we refer to the defender as a "she" and the adversary as a "he".

form a Nash equilibrium that the attackers will both choose to collude if and only if they both receive strictly higher expected utility. In addition, the attacker breaks ties between equilibria of the colluding decision in favor of the defender. Next, we expand this concept to the Imbalanced Collusive Security Games model (ICOSG), which captures the imbalance in wealth of the attackers in COSG.

2.1   Problem Formulation

In this paper, we consider a problem similar to the classic Stackelberg Security Games [19], where the defender plays as the leader of the two-stage game and needs to deploy a defense strategy before knowing the action of the attacker.

In contrast to most works in this setting, our game consist of 1 defender Θ and N attackers $\Psi_1 \ldots \Psi_N$. Given a set of target $T = \{t_1, t_2, \ldots t_n\}$ that consist of N disjoint sets $T_1, \ldots, T_N$, each attacker Ψ_i is restricted to choosing one target within his own set T_i. By choosing and successfully attacking target t without being captured, the attacker Ψ_i will receive utility $U_{\Psi_i}^S(t)$, and penalty of being capture $U_{\Psi_i}^F(t)$ otherwise. Similarly for the defender Θ, if attacker Ψ_i choose to attack target t, she receives certain utility when successfully capturing the attacker of $U_{\Theta}^S(t)$ and otherwise $U_{\Theta}^F(t)$ as the penalty of failure to protect it. Both the defender and the attacker receive zero utilities from non-attacked targets.

We introduce the notion of a *wealth index*, which captures the relative wealth of each attacker mentioned above by evaluating the portion of total utility he could earn. The wealth index of attacker i is defined as

$$\lambda_i := \frac{\sum_{t \in T_i} U_{\Psi_i}^S(t)}{\sum_{k=1}^N \sum_{t \in T_k} U_{\Psi_k}^S(t)} \tag{3}$$

For the following paper, to streamline the presentation, we henceforth focus on ICOGS with a single defender and two attackers with zero-sum game structures. Without loss of generality we also assume $\lambda_1 \in [0.5, 1]$ and $\lambda_2 = 1 - \lambda_1 \in [0, 0.5]$ so that the first attacker is more "powerful" (has higher relative wealth). We define the utility that the defender will receive in each case as $U_{\Theta}^F(t) = -U_{\Psi_i}^S(t) := -R(t) \leq 0$ and $U_{\Theta}^S(t) = -U_{\Psi_i}^F(t) := -P \geq 0$ of constant P for all targets t.

After deciding which target to attack, each attacker can choose if he wants to offer collusion or not. The collusion (which can be thought of as an alliance) will only be established if both attackers agree to collude. If the collusion is established, they will receive some collusion bonus δ for each successful attack, which captures the extra benefit they gain through collusion. However, they will split their total reward based on their relative wealth.

Given that the collusion between attackers may result in a higher loss, the defender's strategy is no longer simply to defend the high-risk target with more resources. For example, the defender may benefit by allocating resources in a way that breaks the willingness of the adversaries to collude by allowing them to have a higher utility from working alone while still maintaining some level of defense against these attackers.

For defender strategy, due to the same reasons as SSG, we consider only mixed defender strategies and define them as coverage vectors c. As for attacker strategies, there is always an equilibrium in which all of them play only pure strategies after observing the defender's mixed strategy [10]. We represent the attack decision over the N target sets $T_1 \ldots T_N$ of the N attackers as N vectors $\alpha_1, \ldots, \alpha_N$ of different length $|T_i|$, where $\alpha_i \in \{0,1\}^{|T_i|}$ with its tth element equal to 1 iff attacker i chooses to attack target t. We also encapsulate their decision about offering collusion as β, of which $\beta_i = 1$ if Ψ_i offers collude and 0 otherwise. Finally, we can represent the strategy of each attacker Ψ_i as the Cartesian product of the two decision vector $g_i = \alpha_i \times \beta_i \in \{0,1\}^{|T_i|} \times \{0,1\}$ or $G = \alpha \times \beta \in \{0,1\}^{|T|} \times \{0,1\}^N$ that encapsulate strategies of all the attackers as $\alpha = [\alpha_1^T, \alpha_2^T \ldots \alpha_N^T]^T$ and $\beta = [\beta_1, \beta_2 \ldots \beta_N]^T$. For the sake of easier expression, we represent U_Θ^S and U_Θ^F as vectors of length $|T|$ with their tth element as $U_\Theta^S(t)$ and $U_\Theta^F(t)$ respectively. Given the strategies of the defender and attackers, the expected utility of defender can be expressed as:

$$U_\Theta(c, G) = \alpha^T(c \circ U_\Theta^S + (1_{|T|} - c) \circ U_\Theta^F) - (N - \alpha^T c)\delta \prod_{i=1}^N \beta_i \qquad (4)$$

where $\circ$ denotes element wise product (Hadamard product) of same length vectors and $1_{|T|}$ is the element vector of length $|T|$.

As for attacker reward calculation, if any of the players refuse to collude with others, the expected utilities they received, defined as $U_{\Psi_1}, U_{\Psi_2} \ldots U_{\Psi_N}$, are expressed as

$$U_{\Psi_i}(c, g_i) = \sum_{t \in T_i} \alpha_i(t) \left((1 - c_t) U_{\Psi_i}^S(t) + c_t U_{\Psi_i}^F(t) \right) \qquad (5)$$

If all the players choose to collude ($\beta_i = 1 \ \forall i$), the total reward they receive is calculated as

$$U_\Psi^*(c, G) = \sum_{i=1}^N \sum_{t \in T_i} \alpha_i(t) \left((1 - c_t) U_{\Psi_t}^{*S}(t) + c_t U_{\Psi_i}^{*F}(t) \right) \qquad (6)$$

where $U_{\Psi_i}^{*S}(t) = U_{\Psi_i}^S(t) + \delta$ and $U_{\Psi_i}^{*F}(t) = U_{\Psi_i}^F(t)$. The final reward each attacker receives depends on their wealth index.

$$U_{\Psi_i}^* = \lambda_i U_\Psi^* \qquad (7)$$

Also noted that in zero-sum reward structure settings, the above equation yields to $U_\Theta = -U_\Psi^*$ for $\prod \beta_i = 1$ and $U_\Theta = -U_\Psi$ for $\prod \beta_i = 0$ in the respective colluding and non-colluding cases.

The goal is to find the optimal strategy c to maximize the expected defender utility U_Θ by breaking the collusion of the attackers while maintaining good defense. However, such strategy diverges for different attacker behavior assumptions, which will be elaborated in the following section.

2.2   Defender Strategies

Perfectly Rational Model (PRM). By assuming each attacker to be perfectly rational, we assume each of them selects the strategy to maximize their expected utility U_{Ψ_i}. We applied the solution concept of Collusive Security Equilibrium (CSE) used in [6]. CSE requires that (i) the defender's strategy is a best response to each attacker's strategy, (ii) the attacker strategies form a Nash Equilibrium in their game, (iii) both attackers play collude if they obtain strictly greater utility in a (collude, collude) equilibrium than (not collude, not collude) equilibrium, and (iv) the attackers break ties between equilibria which satisfy (i)-(iii) in favor of the defender.

In addition, the CSE of our problem can also be calculated by modifying the mixed integer linear program (MILP) in [6]. The MILP set is based on the ERASER formulation introduced by Kiekintveld et al. [10] that solves the equilibrium of traditional SSGs. More details can be found in [6].

This algorithm can return the CSE of any reward structure and gives us the equilibrium strategies of the defender $\overline{c}(\overline{g}_1, \overline{g}_2)$ and attackers $\overline{g}_1(\overline{c}, \overline{g}_2)$ and $\overline{g}_2(\overline{c}, \overline{g}_1)$. If the attackers select their strategies in a perfectly rational way, this method generates the optimal strategy for the defender.

Bounded Rational Model (BRM). In contrast to perfectly rational model, BRM assumes players perceive the utility in a bounded rational way. Instead of strictly maximizing their expected utility, it is often more effective to assume human adversaries choose strategies (i) *which grid to attack* (ii) *collude with another player or not* stochastically based on their perceived utility [14]. The features we applied to model the bounded rationality of human subjects, which were used and proven to be effective in [6] are:

1. SUQR model [16]
2. Prospect Theory [9,20].

For the first feature, SUQR is an extension of Quantal Response (QR). Instead of expected utility, SUQR assumes humans make decisions stochastically based on their perceived utility, which is a weighted function of different factors. In addition, the bounded rationality of how people perceive probabilities is also considered using Prospect Theory (PT). PT proposes that individuals perceive the probability of success and failure in a non-linear way. Such nonlinearity can be captured by various functional forms [9,20].

What follows are the details of how we construct and learn our BRM model. Given the defender strategy (c), reward $(U_{\Psi_i}^S)$ and penalty $(U_{\Psi_i}^F)$ for each target $t \in T_i$, the perceived utility of attacking it for attacker Ψ_i is defined as

$$\hat{U}_{\Psi_i}^\alpha(t, c) = \omega_c^\alpha \cdot \hat{c}_t(c) + \omega_R^\alpha \cdot U_{\Psi_i}^S(t) + \omega_P^\alpha \cdot U_{\Psi_i}^F(t) \tag{8}$$

where $\hat{c}_{t_j}$ is the Prospect Theory modified perceived probability of the original probability c_{t_j}, defined as

$$\hat{c}_t = \frac{\eta c_t^{\gamma}}{\eta c_t^{\gamma} + (1 - c_t)^{\gamma}} \tag{9}$$

From the SUQR model, the probability of that the adversary Ψ_i will attack target $t \in T_i$ is given by:

$$\hat{\alpha}_i(t, c) = \frac{e^{\hat{U}_{\Psi_i}^{\alpha}(t, \hat{c})}}{\sum\limits_{t \in T_i} e^{\hat{U}_{\Psi_i}^{\alpha}(t, \hat{c})}} \tag{10}$$

Another decision of the bounded rational attacker we need to model is the probability of collusion. Similar to attack probability, we define the perceived utility of colluding and not colluding as

$$\hat{U}_{\Psi_i}^{*\beta}(c) = \lambda_i \sum_{j=1}^{N} \frac{\omega_c^{\beta} \cdot \sum_{t \in T_j} c_t + \omega_R^{\beta} \cdot \sum_{t \in T_j} U_{\Psi_j}^{*S}(t) + \omega_P^{\beta} \cdot \sum_{t \in T_j} U_{\Psi_j}^{*F}(t)}{|T_j|} \tag{11}$$

$$\hat{U}_{\Psi_i}^{\beta}(c) = \frac{\omega_c^{\beta} \cdot \sum_{t \in T_i} c_t + \omega_R^{\beta} \cdot \sum_{t \in T_i} U_{\Psi_i}^{S}(t) + \omega_P^{\beta} \cdot \sum_{t \in T_i} U_{\Psi_i}^{F}(t)}{|T_i|} \tag{12}$$

Again, from the SUQR model, the probability adversary Ψ_i will offer collusion is given by

$$\hat{\beta}_i(c) = \frac{e^{\hat{U}_{\Psi_i}^{*\beta}(t_j, c)}}{e^{\hat{U}_{\Psi_i}^{*\beta}(t_j, c)} + e^{\hat{U}_{\Psi_i}^{\beta}(t_j, c)}} \tag{13}$$

There are a total of 5 parameters for attack probability and 3 parameters for collusion probability to be determined, which are $(\omega_c^{\alpha}, \omega_R^{\alpha}, \omega_P^{\alpha}, \eta, \gamma)$ and $(\omega_c^{\beta}, \omega_R^{\beta}, \omega_P^{\beta})$ respectively. These parameters are estimated via Maximum Likelihood Estimation (MLE) using data collected from the human subject experiments of PRM strategy.

Note that in the bounded rational model applied for identical powerful adversaries in the previous work [6], it is assumed the grid attacking probabilities of an attacker are conditional probabilities of given his decision to collude or not and given which attacker he is. Thus it has a total number of 4×5 (4 condition of 5 parameters to model attack probabilities)+3 (parameters to model collusion probabilities)= 23 parameters to learn for each game. By assuming the $\hat{\alpha}$ and $\hat{\beta}$ to be independent, the modified model is able to reduce the number of parameters and still be applicable when either type of decision making data is missing for certain data points.

Given a learned parameter set and a defender strategy as input, BRM can generate the response "strategy" of a bounded rational attacker for each attacker

Ψ_i, which can be expressed as the Cartesian product of the two decision probability vector of length $|T_i|$ and 1 as $\hat{g}_i = \hat{\alpha}_i \times \beta_i$ or $\hat{G} = \hat{\alpha} \times \hat{\beta}$ that encapsulate probabilities of all the attackers decisions as $\hat{\alpha} = \left[\hat{\alpha}_1^T, \hat{\alpha}_2^T \ldots \hat{\alpha}_N^T\right]^T$ and $\hat{\beta} = \left[\hat{\beta}_1, \hat{\beta}_2 \ldots \hat{\beta}_N\right]^T$. Given C as the feasible solution space of defender's coverage vector c, by replacing G with $\hat{G}$, we want to find $c = \underset{c \in C}{\arg\max}\left(U_\Theta(c, \hat{G}(c))\right)$ in Eq. 4, which we approximate by multiple runs of fmincon optimizer.

Simulations. Figure 1 shows the simulation of the probabilities that collusion between two attackers is actually established. The number of defender resources is set to be $m = 3$. Along the rows are different wealth index combinations; along the columns are different values of delta, which gives the collusion bonus.

δ λ_1-λ_2	1	2	3	4	5	6
0.8-0.2	0	0	0	0	0	0
0.6-0.4	0	0	0	0	0	1
0.5-0.5	0	0	0	0	1	1

(a) Perfectly rational attackers

δ λ_1-λ_2	1	2	3	4	5	6
0.8-0.2	0.645674	0.833459	0.907055	0.946411	0.9693	0.9826
0.6-0.4	0.64303	0.876889	0.962063	0.98841	0.9994	0.9989
0.5-0.5	0.636445	0.889326	0.972065	0.993309	0.99381	0.9986

(b) Bounded rational attackers

Fig. 1. Simulation of actual collusion probability (attacker 1 collusion offering probability $\times$ attacker 2 collusion offering probability) with different collusion bonuses (δ) and wealth indexes (λ_1 and λ_2) of the two attackers. Larger bonuses and closer wealth indexes yield higher probabilities of collusion.

One interesting observation is that it is easier to break the collusion for higher wealth imbalance in both PRM and BRM simulations. In fact in PRM, there is a transition λ that determines if the collusion is breakable or not in the CSE for some given structure, which we will elaborate on the next section.

Another interesting observation is that in the simulations, PRM always breaks the collusion between perfectly rational attackers when the collusion bonus is low, whereas BRM predicts that even with low collusion bonuses, the bounded rational attackers are still going to collude with high probability.

Our experiment focused on the first column of the simulation, which is collusion bonus $\delta = 1$ for different wealth imbalance. The bonus value is far from the value that PRM starts to give up on breaking the collusion ($\delta \geq 5$). If the human subjects are perfectly rational, PRM strategy should be able to break the collusion completely.

3   Effect of Imbalance

In this section, we provide an analysis of the effect of imbalance, and use the perfectly rational model for simplicity. For N player ICOSGs, the expected utility of the defender and each attacker can be expressed as Eqs. 4–7. By using a MILP, we can solve the equilibrium strategy of the defender. However, it is complicated to analyze the effect of the parameters due to the complexity of reward structure, as the general structure does not have a closed form of utility gain.

To analyze the effect of imbalance degree λ, we start with a more straightforward case. We denote the total value of targets as $\sum_t U_\Theta^F(t) = -R_\Theta$ and $\sum_i \sum_t U_{\Psi_i}^S(t) = R_\Psi$, the reward/penalty of catching/being caught as $U_\Theta^S(t) = P_\Theta$ and $U_{\Psi_i}^F(t) = -P_\Psi \; \forall t \in T$ for the defender and attackers respectively. All of the parameters above (R_Θ, R_Ψ, P_Θ and P_Ψ) are non-negative number to avoid confusion. For zero-sum game, $R_\Theta = R_\Psi$ and $P_\Theta = P_\Psi$. The total number of defender resources is set to be m.

3.1   Uniform Distribution Reward Structure

Assume we have a uniform distribution of value allocated on each target set T_i with density $U_{\Psi_1}^S(t) = \lambda R_\Psi \; \forall t \in T_1$ and $U_{\Psi_2}^S(t) = (1-\lambda)R_\Psi \; \forall t \in T_2$. We simplify each field to a single target as they all have the same utility.

Since the structure is simplified, the only decision that the attackers have to make is to collude or not. The only decision the defender has to make is how many resources to allocate to each attacker, denote as m_i. We separate the colluding (U_Θ^* and $U_{\Psi_i}^*$) and non-colluding (U_Θ and U_{Ψ_i}) case and rewrite the expected utility in Eqs. 4–7 as:

$$U_\Theta^*(c) = - \sum_{i=1}^N (1 - m_i)\lambda_i R_\Theta + mP_\Theta - (N - m)\delta \qquad (14)$$

$$U_\Theta(c) = - \sum_{i=1}^N (1 - m_i)\lambda_i R_\Theta + mP_\Theta \qquad (15)$$

$$U_{\Psi_i}^*(c) = \lambda_i \left(\sum_{j=1}^N (1 - m_j)\lambda_j R_\Psi - mP_\Psi + (N - m)\delta \right) \qquad (16)$$

$$U_{\Psi_i}(c) = (1 - m_i)\lambda_i R_\Psi - m_i P_\Psi \qquad (17)$$

Proposition 1. *In two attackers imbalanced COSGs with uniform reward distribution and negligibly small penalties of failing the attack, the best defender strategy is to allocate all its resources to the attacker with the largest wealth index λ, regardless of other parameters.*

Proof. Suppose the optimal defender strategy is c^* in the CSE and the defender resources it deployed on Ψ_1 and Ψ_2 are m_1^* and m_2^* respectively. Without loss of generality, assume $\lambda_1 > 0.5 > \lambda_2$. We prove the proposition by showing $m_1^* \geq m_2^*$ first. Then we show that if $m_1^* \geq m_2^*$, allocating more resources to m_1^* always results in higher defender utility until Ψ_1 is fully covered.

First, we prove that $m_1^* \geq m_2^*$. Suppose $m_1^* < m_2^*$, consider another defender strategy $\bar{c}$ such that $\overline{m}_1 = m_2^*$ and $\overline{m}_2 = m_1^*$. We prove that this alternate defender strategy returns higher defender utility thus $m_1^* < m_2^*$ can not be optimal. To be clear, attacker strategy *collude* means both attackers choose to collude ($\beta_1\beta_2 = 1$) and attacker strategy *not collude* means at least one of the attackers refuse to collude ($\beta_1\beta_2 = 0$). If the attacker strategies against the two defender strategies (c^* and $\bar{c}$) are both *collude*, both *not collude* or *collude* against c^* and *not collude* against $\bar{c}$, the new strategy $\bar{c}$ returns higher defender utility in all three cases thus c^* can not be the optimal strategy. Since $U_\Theta^*(c^*) < U_\Theta^*(\bar{c})$, $U_\Theta^*(c^*) < U_\Theta(\bar{c})$ and $U_\Theta(c^*) < U_\Theta(\bar{c})$ for $\lambda_1 > \lambda_2$ and $-(N-m)\delta < 0$ in Eqs. (14) and (15).

As for the last case, the attackers playing *not collude* against c^* and *collude* against $\bar{c}$, we prove that such a scenario is not possible. The condition of breaking the collusion is $U_{\Psi_i} \geq U_{\Psi_i}^*$ for any i. In the two attackers case, since P_Ψ is negligibly small, it can be derived from Eqs. 16 and 17 that the condition of breaking the collusion is to satisfy one of the following two inequalities:

$$m_2 \leq \frac{m\lambda_1\lambda_2 R_\Psi + m\lambda_2 P_\Psi - (2-m)\lambda_2\delta}{2\lambda_1\lambda_2 R_\Psi + P_\Psi} \sim \frac{m}{2} - \frac{(2-m)\delta}{2\lambda_1 R_\Psi} \tag{18}$$

$$m_1 \leq \frac{m\lambda_1\lambda_2 R_\Psi + m\lambda_1 P_\Psi - (2-m)\lambda_1\delta}{2\lambda_1\lambda_2 R_\Psi + P_\Psi} \sim \frac{m}{2} - \frac{(2-m)\delta}{2\lambda_2 R_\Psi} \tag{19}$$

Note that these two equations cannot be satisfied simultaneously since $m_1+m_2 = m$ and only one of them can be less than $m/2$. This suggests that at least one of the attackers is willing to offer the collusion when the penalties are negligibly small. If $m_1^* < m_2^*$ in c^* and the two attackers are not colluding, c^* must satisfy Eq. 19. However, since $\overline{m}_2 = m_1^*$ and $\lambda_1 > \lambda_2$, we have

$$\overline{m}_2 = m_1^* \leq \frac{m}{2} - \frac{(2-m)\delta}{\lambda_2 R_\Psi} < \frac{m}{2} - \frac{(2-m)\delta}{\lambda_1 R_\Psi}$$

thus for defender strategy $\bar{c}$ satisfy Eq. 18 and the collusion will be break as well.

Second, we prove that for $m_1 \geq m_2$, allocating more resources on attacker 1 before it is fully covered will result in higher defender utility. Similar to the first part of proof, suppose the optimal defender strategy is c^* and $1 > m_1^* \geq m_2^* > 0$, consider another defender strategy $\bar{c}$ such that $\overline{m}_1 = m_1^* + \epsilon$ and $\overline{m}_2 = m_2^* - \epsilon$. If c^* breaks the collusion, c^* must satisfy Eq. 18 as $m_1^* > m_2^*$ in the optimal strategy. Since $\overline{m}_2 < m_2^*$, the new strategy $\bar{c}$ must break the collusion as well. Again, from Eqs. 14 and 15, $\bar{c}$ always returns higher defender utility in the other three possible cases. Thus we have proven the proposition.

Proposition 2. *Define the transition threshold λ^* as the two attackers will not collude in the equilibrium if and only if $\lambda \geq max(\lambda^*, 0.5)$ for fixed total R_Ψ. In two attackers ICOSGs with uniform distribution, assuming none of the attackers is fully covered, the transition threshold is*

$$\lambda^* = \frac{(2-m)\delta}{mR_\Psi} - \frac{P_\Psi}{R_\Psi} \tag{20}$$

Proof. By Proposition 1, we can replace m_2 with 0 and m_1 with m for $m \leq 1$ in Eq. 18 and derive the above transition threshold.

This equation indicates whether the collusion is breakable or not in the uniform distribution game for a specific parameter set. The collusion becomes harder to break when collusion bonus δ is higher and easier to break when defender resource m, penalty P_Ψ and the wealth index of stronger attacker λ is higher. In other words, when other conditions are the same, higher wealth imbalance makes the collusion easier to break.

Unfortunately, the transition threshold λ^* does not have a closed form in general structure game. However, it is still obtainable using numerical approach.

3.2 Uniform Scale Affine Transformation Reward Structure

It is difficult to derive closed-form analysis for the reward structure of the general distribution. However, one class of distribution; which is what we used in the latter experiments as the example Fig. 3 shows, have some nice properties to be explored.

Definition 1. *Uniform Scale Affine Transformation Reward Structure*

Given a base reward structure with $|T|/N$ targets $t_1...t_{|T|/N}$ of a general distribution define as U_Ψ^S such that $\sum_t U_\Psi^S(t) = R_\Psi$. Each attacker has the same number of targets to choose from $(|T_i| = |T|/N| \forall i)$. The reward structure of each attacker is the uniform scale affine transformation of the base reward structure, in which the scale is given by $U_{\Psi_i}^S(t_j) = \lambda_i U_\Psi^S(t_j)$ for $j = 1 \cdots |T_i|$ and the penalty $U_{\Psi_i}^F(t_j) = P$ is an ignorable small constant for all targets.

Define $\Lambda = (\lambda_1, \lambda_2, ... \lambda_N)$ as a set of wealth indexes. For the same base reward structure, we define $U_{(\Theta,\Lambda)}(c, G)$ as the defender utility in game with wealth index set Λ. We decompose the first term of the right hand side in Eq. 4 and rewrite the equation as $U_{(\Theta,\Lambda)}(\bar{c}_\Lambda, G) = \sum_{i=1}^N E_\Theta(\Psi_i, \lambda_i, \bar{c}_\Lambda) - (N - \alpha^T \bar{c}_\Lambda) \delta \prod_{i=1}^N \beta_i$. The term $E_\Theta(\Psi_i, \lambda_i, \bar{c}_\Lambda)$ represents the expected utility of defender gain from defending attacker Ψ_i and $\bar{c}_\Lambda$ represent the best response of the defender for game with wealth index set Λ. This term has the following three properties

1. $E_\Theta(\Psi_i, \frac{1}{N}, \bar{c}_\Lambda) \geq E_\Theta(\Psi_j, \frac{1}{N}, \bar{c}_\Lambda)$ for $m_i \geq m_j$
2. $E_\Theta(\Psi_i, \hat{\lambda}, \bar{c}_\Lambda) = \frac{\hat{\lambda}}{\lambda} E_\Theta(\Psi_i, \lambda, \bar{c}_\Lambda)$ for any $\hat{\lambda}, \lambda > 0$
3. $m_i \geq m_j$ in $\bar{c}_\Lambda$ for $\lambda_i \geq \lambda_j$

The proof of the first property is straightforward. In game with identical wealth index attackers, the more resources the defender allocate to the attacker, the more expected utility she will gain from him. As for the second term, since we have the same reward distribution and same strategy, the reward on every target is proportional to λ and yields to the expected reward proportional to λ. Finally, term 3 can be proved using the same method in the first part of Proposition 1. Based on the above properties, we are now able to prove Proposition 3.

Proposition 3. *In two attackers ICOSGs with uniform or zero-sum uniform scale affine transformation reward structure, a larger wealth imbalance results in a smaller defender loss.*

Proof. The uniform distribution part is straightforward, as it can be inferred that the defender in the game with larger wealth imbalance could always break the collusion if the defender in the game with lower wealth could break the collusion from Proposition 2 thus its utility is higher from Eqs. 14, 15 and Proposition 1.

As for zero-sum uniform scale affine transformation reward structure, assume $\Lambda = (\lambda, (1 - \lambda))$ and $\lambda \geq 0.5$, we want to prove that $U_{(\Theta, \hat{\Lambda})} > U_{(\Theta, \Lambda)}$ for any $\hat{\Lambda} = (\hat{\lambda}, (1 - \hat{\lambda})), \hat{\lambda} > \lambda$. From above properties and the fact that the defender gain higher utilities when playing the best response, assume $\beta_1 \beta_2 = 0$ in both games, we have:

$$
\begin{aligned}
U_{(\Theta, \Lambda)} &= E_\Theta(\Psi_1, \lambda, \overline{c}_\Lambda) + E_\Theta(\Psi_2, (1 - \lambda), \overline{c}_\Lambda) \\
&= 2\lambda E_\Theta(\Psi_1, \frac{1}{2}, \overline{c}_\Lambda) + 2(1 - \lambda) E_\Theta(\Psi_2, \frac{1}{2}, \overline{c}_\Lambda) \\
&< 2\hat{\lambda} E_\Theta(\Psi_1, \frac{1}{2}, \overline{c}_\Lambda) + 2(1 - \hat{\lambda}) E_\Theta(\Psi_2, \frac{1}{2}, \overline{c}_\Lambda) \\
&= E_\Theta(\Psi_1, \hat{\lambda}, \overline{c}_\Lambda) + E_\Theta(\Psi_2, (1 - \hat{\lambda}), \overline{c}_\Lambda) \\
&\leq E_\Theta(\Psi_1, \hat{\lambda}, \overline{c}_{\hat{\Lambda}}) + E_\Theta(\Psi_2, (1 - \hat{\lambda}), \overline{c}_{\hat{\Lambda}}) \\
&= U_{(\Theta, \hat{\Lambda})}
\end{aligned}
$$

Since $\lambda < \hat{\lambda}$, for some transition threshold λ^*, the only possible relations of the three parameters are either $\lambda \leq \hat{\lambda} \leq \lambda^*$ ($\beta_1 \beta_2 = 1$ for both game), ($\lambda \leq \lambda^* \leq \hat{\lambda}$)($\beta_1 \beta_2 = 1$ for Λ and $\beta_1 \beta_2 = 0$ for $\hat{\Lambda}$) or ($\lambda^* \leq \lambda \leq \hat{\lambda}$)($\beta_1 \beta_2 = 0$ for both game). Similar inequalities can be derived for remaining two cases by adding the collusion bonus term. Thus we have proved Proposition 3.

4   Empirical Investigation Using Human Subjects

4.1   Imbalanced Wildlife Poaching Game

To investigate imbalance in COSG, we developed the imbalanced wildlife poaching game and asked human subjects to play the role of poachers in a national park of Africa. We recruited 1800 unique participants from Amazon Mechanical Turk (AMT) and offered them bonus rewards as an incentive for them to perform well. Figure 2 shows the interface of the game used in our human subject experiments. We will elaborate the detail of experiment design in the following section.

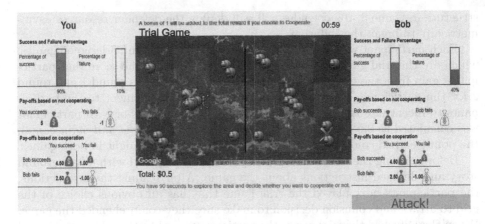

Fig. 2. Imbalanced wildlife poaching game: the human subject is assigned to the left side of the park. His partner attacker is assigned to the right side. The probabilities of being caught can be observed by human subject through interacting with the game.

4.2 Human Subject Experiments

Our wildlife poaching game is a three-player security game with $|T_1| = |T_2| = 9$ targets available to each adversary. There are a total of $|T| = 18$ grids that contains some fixed number of animals. Each attacker is able to attack 9 targets in a 3×3 reward distribution. A total of two reward structures of three different wealth imbalance has been deployed on AMT as Fig. 3 shows. The penalty of the attacker getting caught is set to be $P = -1$. The total number of rangers is set to be $m = 3$, and the collusion bonus is set to be $\delta = 1$.

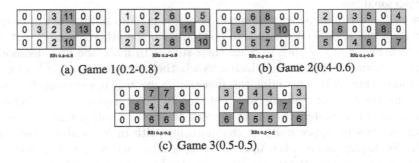

(a) Game 1(0.2-0.8)   (b) Game 2(0.4-0.6)

(c) Game 3(0.5-0.5)

Fig. 3. Reward (animal density) structures of different wealth imbalance (λ_1-λ_2) deployed on AMT.

For each wave of the experiment, we deployed different defender mixed strategies against human adversaries played as each side of Game 1, Game 2 and Game 3 of both reward structures. Note that although we have a symmetric reward structure in Game 3, the defender will still deploy the defender resources asymmetrically to break the collusion.

Each participant was asked to play three rounds of carefully designed games, which are the trial game, test game, and the main game. The score that participants gain from the test game and main game (displayed as round 1 and round 2 for the participants) were accumulated as the bonus payment to the participants to incentivize the players to perform well. The bonus of each participant was calculated as $0.5 + 0.05 \times$ (*points earned in the test game and main game*), the points earned could be negative if the participant got caught in both games.

Before playing the trial game, participants were provided with a background story and detailed instructions about the game. After reading the instructions, the participants next played the trial game that has an obvious choice of the grid to attack and collusion decision to make sure they comprehended the game. When they finished the trial game, the participants could either choose to reread the instructions or begin to play the round 1 game (test game) and earn points. The test game, acts as a validation game, having an apparent yet opposite choice for the collusion decision to the test game to avoid any bias.

The test game serves two purposes. The first purpose is for us to validate if the participants understand the game or not. The data of the participant was excluded if it does not meet certain criteria in the test game. The second purpose is to balance the total reward payment of different settings in the main game. For example, the participant played as 0.2 side of game 3 has a limit potential to earn points in round 2 (the main game). Thus he/she will be assigned to a higher potential reward in round 1 (test game) to be fair and avoid bias as much as possible.

Finally, the second round game that participants played was the main game that we used to collect data of their decision making. After the game, the participants were asked to take a survey about their experience of the game and their personalities.

In each individual game, the human player is given a set amount of time to make decisions about: (i) whether to collude with the other player or not and (ii) which region of the park to place their snare. To make the first decision, a question appears on the screen which asks whether the human player is inclined to collude or not. After answering this question, a message appears on the screen that indicates whether collusion was preferred by both players or not. Collusion occurs only if it is preferred by both players. It is worth noting that the human participant has no opportunity to communicate with or learn about the other player. Next, players are asked to choose a target in their own region to attack. As before, players cannot communicate about which target to attack.

Note that whereas the human player plays as one of the adversaries, we designed a computer agent with rational behavior to play as the second adversary; thus there is an algorithm generating defender strategies, and two adversaries (one a human and one a computer agent). Choosing a computer agent as a second player let us to avoid requiring coordination between two human players in the experiments. While the other player is a computer, it is suggested to the human player that they are actually another human. The computer agent rationally chooses its decision to collude. To simplify the analysis, we assume that the second stage of decision making (where each adversary chooses a target to attack) depends on his own inclination for collusion and does not depend on the attitude of the other adversary.

There are total of 50 participants for each game set. For each strategy, 12 sets of games ({Game Structure| RS1, RS2} $\times$ {λ_1|0.2, 0.4, 0.5A, 0.5DA, 0.6, 0.8}) were deployed, in which RS1 represent reward structure 1, RS2 represent reward structure 2, 0.5A represents human player playing the side with less coverage in the symmetric game ($\lambda_1 = \lambda_2 = 0.5$) and 0.5$DA$ represents otherwise for the sake of distinguishing. Thus, a total of 600 human players participated in the experiments for each strategy, and we deployed three strategies in total. We show and analyze our results in the following section.

4.3   Numerical Results

Three waves of experiments have been conducted. In the first wave, we deployed the optimal strategy acquired from PRM and asked human subjects to play the security poaching game described above. We collected the human decision data of the attacking decision α and the collusion decision β on these 12 sets of games.

Two models that assume the attackers are bounded rational have been learned using the data collected in the first wave. For the first BRM strategy, we used maximum likelihood estimation on all the data collected and learned the 8 parameters required to generate the strategy, which are $(\omega_C^\alpha, \omega_R^\alpha, \omega_P^\alpha, \eta, \gamma)$ and $(\omega_C^\beta, \omega_R^\beta, \omega_P^\beta)$. The model is named "BRM" in the figure below.

As for the second BRM strategy (called BRM05), we only used data collected from symmetric case in the first wave ({Game Structure| RS1, RS2} $\times$ {λ_1|0.5A, 0.5DA}) and learned the 8 parameters that generate the third strategy.

Next, two waves of experiments were deployed, one using BRM strategy and one using BRM05 strategy. Each wave involved another 600 human subjects playing the 12 sets of games. To analyze which model is the more effective one, we looked at two perspective accuracy and performance.

Accuracy. The human decision data from the wave 1 experiment acts as the training data for the BRM and BRM05 models. To be fair, we compare the prediction accuracy of the three models on wave 2 human decision data, which has not been used for the training of any of the models. In Fig. 4, we vary the wealth imbalance($\lambda_1 - \lambda_2$) along the x-axis and shows the prediction of each model versus the actual defender loss along y-axis in the wave 2 games we conducted. The loss here refers to the total reward the defender faces due to collusion and target choices of the attackers. Note that in this game, the penalty is constant and low; and hence the defender usually faces a loss and must reduce it as much as possible. This is intentionally designed to be consistent with real world situation involving poaching in national parks.

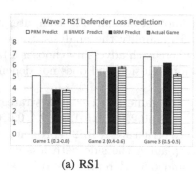 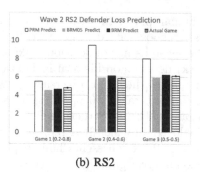

(a) RS1   (b) RS2

Fig. 4. Prediction of the defender loss by each model and the actual defender loss in wave 2 experiments. The error bars of the actual defender loss are small due to large sample size.

In terms of accuracy, both BRM models outperforms the PRM model. The inaccuracy of PRM model comes from two reasons, overestimating the defender loss from the attacker target choice α and underestimating the defender loss from collusion offering probability β. While the latter factor sometimes helps in reducing the error, overall its performance suffers compared to the BRM models.

The reason PRM overestimates the defender loss from the attacker target choice is because it assumed the attackers to be perfectly rational and always choose the grid with highest expected value to attack. However, in the experiments, we observe that human subjects avoids high-risk high-reward grid cells and choose some safer yet lower expected reward grid with high probability. The two BRM models are able to capture and exploit this along with other bounded rational behavior as explained in Sect. 2.2 and thus leads to a relatively more accurate prediction on α.

The two BRM models also perform better than PRM in predicting the probability of collusion. In Fig. 5, we vary the wealth index of the attacker along the x-axis and show the prediction of collusion offering probabilities of players versus actual collusion offering probability in the wave 2 experiments along the y-axis.

In RS1, PRM predicts the strategy applied in wave 2 can always break the collusion (for situations shown in Fig. 5(a)) by making the weaker attacker collude with probability 0. In the real experiments, however, human subjects still offer collusion with high probability, even if collusion results in a lower expected utility.

Given the prediction toward wave 2 experiments as an example, BRM are better than PRM at predicting attacker strategy. We now look into the performance of the strategy they generated in the actual experiments.

Performance. In each wave, games with two reward structures of three wealth imbalance with multiple human subjects playing as both the weaker and stronger sides have been conducted with the three strategies. Figure 6 shows the performance of the three strategies in the experiments against real human attackers.

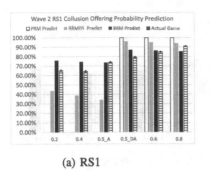
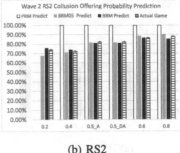

(a) RS1   (b) RS2

Fig. 5. Prediction of the collusion offering probabilities by each model and the actual collusion offering probabilities. PRM predicts 0 collusion offering probability of adversaries with wealth index 0.2, 0.4 and 0.5A in RS1 hence no bar is shown. Same for adversaries with wealth index 0.2 in RS2.

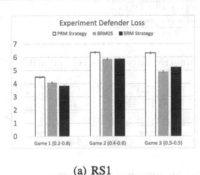
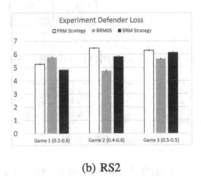

(a) RS1   (b) RS2

Fig. 6. Average defender loss from experiments with 100 participants (50 on each side) in each game per strategy (each bar). Error bars are small due to large sample size.

The BRM strategy outperforms PRM strategy in every game with different wealth imbalance of both reward structures. The error bars shown in the graph are small due to large sample size. The BRM05 however, is more unstable. It outperforms the other two strategies in some games with lower wealth imbalance. However, it performs poorly for high wealth imbalance and even lost to PRM in RS2. This fact suggests that it could not capture some properties about the attacker behavior of the high imbalance game.

Another phenomenon worth noticing is that the defender loss did decrease as the wealth imbalance increases as Proposition 3 suggested for both PRM and BRM in asymmetric games. Interestingly, BRM deployed some surprisingly different strategies when dealing with symmetrically powerful adversaries, which will be analyzed in the next section.

Strategy Difference. Other than better prediction and the exploitation of bounded rational behavior when choosing grids to attack, there is another

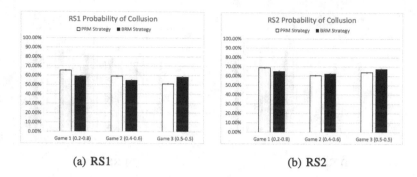

(a) RS1   (b) RS2

Fig. 7. Comparison of the actual collusion probabilities between the PRM and BRM defender strategies.

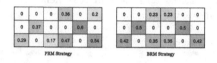

Fig. 8. Strategies of PRM and BRM for symmetric adversaries (Game 3(0.5–0.5)).

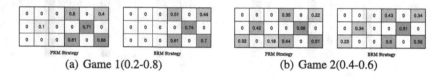

(a) Game 1(0.2-0.8)   (b) Game 2(0.4-0.6)

Fig. 9. Strategies of PRM and BRM for asymmetric adversaries.

crucial reason for the BRM to perform well. Figure 7 shows the actual collusion probability of PRM and BRM strategy in real experiment.

In asymmetric games, BRM is able to break the collusion with higher probabilities than PRM. Surprisingly, in the symmetric game(game 3), BRM did not break more collusion than PRM. To investigate this, we compare the strategy deployed in PRM and BRM for such game in Fig. 8. It can be observed that BRM did not try to break the collusion at all by defending both side symmetrically. By accepting the fact that human adversaries are still going to collude and the resources it has are too little to spare, BRM is able to keep the collusion probability within an acceptable amount without sacrificing one side too much.

As for asymmetric adversaries, Fig. 9 shows the difference between the strategies PRM and BRM deployed. The first thing to notice is that although the reward structure is not uniformly distributed on each side, both PRM and BRM agrees that more defender resources should be deployed on the attacker with more wealth as Proposition 1. In these games, BRM tries to break the collusion harder than PRM by deploying more defender resources on stronger attacker than PRM.

5 Conclusions

This paper modeled and addressed a security game problem that focused on breaking the collusion between asymmetric adversaries, which is often the case in the real world. Questions as to whether human adversaries would attempt to collude in such situations, and whether defender strategy to counter such collusion should focus on inhibiting such collusion were addressed in this paper by: (i) theoretically analyzing Imbalanced Collusive Security Games (ICOSG) where defenders face adversaries with asymmetrically distributed rewards; (ii) conducting extensive experiments of three different adversary models involving 1800 real human subjects and (iii) deriving novel analysis of the reason behind why bounded rational attacker models outperform perfectly rational attacker models. (iv) analyze the essential difference between balanced and imbalanced adversaries game. The key principle we found is that: Careful modeling of human bounded rationality reveals a key difference (when compared to a model using perfect rationality) in defender strategies for handling colluding adversaries which face symmetric vs asymmetric rewards. Whereas a model based on perfect rationality always attempts to break collusion among adversaries, a bounded rationality model acknowledges the inherent difficulty of breaking such collusion in symmetric situations and focuses only on breaking collusion in asymmetric situation, and only on damage control from collusion in the symmetric situation.

Acknowledgments. We gratefully acknowledge DARPA contract grant FA8650-15-D-6583, and subcontract from Lockheed Martin supported this research.

References

1. Basilico, N., Gatti, N., Amigoni, F.: Leader-follower strategies for robotic patrolling in environments with arbitrary topologies. In: Proceedings of The 8th International Conference on Autonomous Agents and Multiagent Systems-Volume 1, pp. 57–64. International Foundation for Autonomous Agents and Multiagent Systems (2009)
2. Bucarey, V., Casorrán, C., Figueroa, Ó., Rosas, K., Navarrete, H., Ordóñez, F.: Building real stackelberg security games for border patrols. In: Rass, S., An, B., Kiekintveld, C., Fang, F., Schauer, S. (eds.) GameSec 2017. LNCS, pp. 193–212. Springer, Heidelberg (2017). https://doi.org/10.1007/978-3-319-68711-7_11
3. Clark, R., Houde, J.F.: Collusion with asymmetric retailers: evidence from a gasoline price-fixing case. Am. Econ. J.: Microecon. **5**(3), 97–123 (2013)
4. Fang, F., et al.: Deploying paws: field optimization of the protection assistant for wildlife security. In: AAAI, pp. 3966–3973 (2016)
5. Fang, F., Stone, P., Tambe, M.: When security games go green: designing defender strategies to prevent poaching and illegal fishing. In: IJCAI (2015)
6. Gholami, S., Wilder, B., Brown, M., Thomas, D., Sintov, N., Tambe, M.: Divide to defend: collusive security games. In: Zhu, Q., Alpcan, T., Panaousis, E., Tambe, M., Casey, W. (eds.) GameSec 2016. LNCS, vol. 9996, pp. 272–293. Springer, Cham (2016). https://doi.org/10.1007/978-3-319-47413-7_16
7. Guo, Q., An, B., Vorobeychik, Y., Tran-Thanh, L., Gan, J., Miao, C.: Coalitional security games. In: Proceedings of AAMAS, pp. 159–167 (2016)

8. Harms, J.: The war on terror and accomplices: an exploratory study of individuals who provide material support to terrorists. Secur. J. **30**(2), 417–436 (2017)
9. Kahneman, D., Tversky, A.: Prospect theory: an analysis of decision under risk. Econometrica **47**, 263–291 (1979)
10. Kiekintveld, C., Jain, M., Tsai, J., Pita, J., Ordóñez, F., Tambe, M.: Computing optimal randomized resource allocations for massive security games. In: AAMAS (2009)
11. Korzhyk, D., Conitzer, V., Parr, R.: Complexity of computing optimal stackelberg strategies in security resource allocation games. In: AAAI (2010)
12. Korzhyk, D., Conitzer, V., Parr, R.: Security games with multiple attacker resources. In: IJCAI Proceedings, vol. 22, p. 273 (2011)
13. Letchford, J., Vorobeychik, Y.: Computing randomized security strategies in networked domains. Appl. Advers. Reason. Risk Model. **11**, 06 (2011)
14. McFadden, D.L.: Quantal choice analysis: a survey. In: Annals of Economic and Social Measurement, vol. 5, no. 4, pp. 363–390. NBER (1976)
15. Nguyen, T.H., Kar, D., Brown, M., Sinha, A., Tambe, M., Jiang, A.X.: Towards a science of security games. In: Toni, B. (ed.) New Frontiers of Multi-disciplinary Research in STEAM-H, vol. 157, pp. 347–381. Springer, Heidelberg (2015). https://doi.org/10.1007/978-3-319-31323-8_16
16. Nguyen, T.H., Yang, R., Azaria, A., Kraus, S., Tambe, M.: Analyzing the effectiveness of adversary modeling in security games. In: AAAI (2013)
17. Pita, J., et al.: Deployed armor protection: the application of a game theoretic model for security at the los angeles international airport. In: Proceedings of the 7th International Joint Conference on Autonomous Agents and Multiagent Systems: Industrial Track, pp. 125–132. International Foundation for Autonomous Agents and Multiagent Systems (2008)
18. Restrepo, A.L., Guizado, Á.C.: From smugglers to warlords: twentieth century colombian drug traffickers. Can. J. Lat. Am. Caribb. Stud. **28**(55–56), 249–275 (2003)
19. Tambe, M.: Security and Game Theory: Algorithms, Deployed Systems, Lessons Learned. Cambridge University Press, Cambridge (2011)
20. Tversky, A., Kahneman, D.: Advances in prospect theory: cumulative representation of uncertainty. J. Risk Uncertain. **5**(4), 297–323 (1992)
21. Yang, R., Ford, B., Tambe, M., Lemieux, A.: Adaptive resource allocation for wildlife protection against illegal poachers. In: Proceedings of the 2014 International Conference on Autonomous Agents and Multi-agent Systems, pp. 453–460. International Foundation for Autonomous Agents and Multiagent Systems (2014)
22. Yin, Z., et al.: Trusts: scheduling randomized patrols for fare inspection in transit systems. In: IAAI (2012)
23. Yin, Z., Korzhyk, D., Kiekintveld, C., Conitzer, V., Tambe, M.: Stackelberg vs. Nash in security games: interchangeability, equivalence, and uniqueness. In: AAMAS (2010)

A Robust Optimization Approach
to Designing Near-Optimal Strategies
for Constant-Sum Monitoring Games

Aida Rahmattalabi[✉], Phebe Vayanos, and Milind Tambe

University of Southern California, Los Angeles, USA
{rahmatta,vayanos,tambe}@usc.edu

Abstract. We consider the problem of monitoring a set of targets, using scarce monitoring resources (e.g., sensors) that are subject to adversarial attacks. In particular, we propose a constant-sum Stackelberg game in which a defender (leader) chooses among possible monitoring locations, each covering a subset of targets, while taking into account the monitor failures induced by a resource-constrained attacker (follower). In contrast to the previous Stackelberg security models in which the defender uses mixed strategies, here, the defender must commit to pure strategies. This problem is highly intractable as both players' strategy sets are exponentially large. Thus, we propose a solution methodology that automatically partitions the set of adversary's strategies and maps each subset to a *coverage policy*. These policies are such that they do not overestimate the defender's payoff. We show that the partitioning problem can be reformulated *exactly* as a mixed-integer linear program (MILP) of moderate size which can be solved with off-the-shelf solvers. We demonstrate the effectiveness of our proposed approach in various settings. In particular, we illustrate that even with few policies, we are able to closely approximate the optimal solution and outperform the heuristic solutions.

1 Introduction

Protection[1] of important targets is a critical security problem with a wide range of applications including environmental surveillance, and infrastructure security. One of the strategies is to monitor the targets by allocating resources, such as inspection posts, sensor devices, etc. However, this allocation task can become extremely challenging if one considers the possibility of malicious attacks [9]. Such adversarial actions will increase the vulnerability of targets; therefore, more strategic monitoring policies should be implemented in order to ensure a high level of robustness against potential adversarial attacks.

Game theory, and in particular, Stackelberg games have been used to model complex security problems, in which a defender first commits to a strategy and an attacker who can surveil the defender's strategy acts next to maximize the harm.

---

[1] Throughout the paper, we will use the terms "cover", "monitor", "protect" interchangeably.

© Springer Nature Switzerland AG 2018
L. Bushnell et al. (Eds.): GameSec 2018, LNCS 11199, pp. 603–622, 2018.
https://doi.org/10.1007/978-3-030-01554-1_35

Some of the important applications of these models can be found in [15,16]. In Stackelberg security games, it is often assumed that the defender commits to a randomized strategy. While in many applications, the randomness is advantageous to the defender by making the action less predictable, there are also many security domains for which a randomized solution is not feasible, e.g., static sensor placement for monitoring. Also, most of the previous work has focused on models in which the targets are subject to attacks, whereas it is also possible for an adversary to attack the defender's resources.

In this paper, we introduce the "strategic monitoring problem", in which a defender aims to maximize the total value of the targets it protects by placing a limited number of monitors. An adversary who aims to make the targets vulnerable, attacks some of the monitors such that the value of the unprotected targets is maximized. We view this problem as a two-player Stackelberg game.

In our model, we assume that all of the targets are at risk and important to be protected; therefore, the defender obtains a positive payoff equal to the total value of protected targets, whereas the attacker's reward is evaluated based on the accumulative value of the targets that are unprotected. As a result, the sum of both players' payoff is equal to the total value of the targets. Our goal is to find a minimax pure strategy for the defender, that is, a strategy that maximizes the minimum payoff that the defender can obtain.

In terms of modeling, our model extends the existing literature of Stackelberg security games by considering a more general attack model, which allows the adversary to attack the resources. In addition, we solve for pure strategies for the defender. Our commitment to pure strategies is due to the assumption that the monitors are fixed and as a result randomized solutions are not applicable. Furthermore, our model is general as it can accommodate for heterogeneous targets (with arbitrary values) and monitors (with different monitoring powers). We will elaborate on this in the formal problem description.

In terms of technical contributions, the strategic monitoring problem that we study is highly intractable as both players' strategy set is exponentially large. In order to tackle this problem, we propose a novel max-min-max binary optimization model, which allows us to leverage techniques from robust optimization literature. In particular, we extend the K-adaptability idea from two-stage robust optimization literature, based on which first the desired set of monitors together with K candidate coverage policies are selected. This is equivalent to partitioning adversary actions into K subsets, such that each subset is mapped to a particular coverage policy. The coverage policies are such that the value of the covered targets is not overestimated, but as high as possible. We extend the work of Hanasusanto et al. [11] by generalizing their approach to the case of discrete adversary actions by exploiting the specific structure of our problem. We show that, in contrast to their formulation, we can reformulate the K-adaptability problem as an MILP that is exact. The significance of the MILP formulation is that it is polynomial in all problem inputs; thus, it circumvents the exponentiality of the attacker's action. Furthermore, our approach bridges the gap between the suboptimal heuristic solutions and the fully optimal, yet intractable exact approach, where the trade-off between complexity and optimality can be tuned using a single design parameter K.

In the remainder of this paper, we first give an overview of the related work. Next, in Sect. 3 we formally define the strategic monitoring problem as a constant-sum Stackelberg game and we show that it can be equivalently modeled as a two-stage robust optimization problem. Following that, we introduce the K-adaptability counterpart problem and we prove it can be reformulated exactly as a single optimization problem of moderate size. Finally, in Sect. 4 we present results that demonstrate how the presented approach performs across different criteria. The paper concludes with a summary of contributions.

2 Related Work

The strategic monitoring problem falls under the category of *large scale constant-sum games* with exponential strategy space. Mainly, there are two approaches to tackle large scale games: One approach is based on iterative strategy generations used by double-oracle algorithms [8,12] for which there is no guaranteed polynomial run-time. The other approach focuses on using compact representations of the games, where a common approach is based on clustering strategies to solve simpler games. In this regard, Bard et al. [1] propose a greedy-based clustering approach. Also, in [2] authors use k-means clustering to construct the abstract games. What we propose in this work can be viewed as an automatic generation of a partition of adversary's strategy set, which is not reliant on any metric such as the ones used in the clustering algorithms. In fact, the partitioning is performed implicitly by choosing limited number of coverage policies.

This problem is also related to *robust sub-modular optimization*. In this regard, Krause et al. [13] formalized a general max-min problem, and they proposed an approximation algorithm to maximize the worst-case performance of a sub-modular function against a set of possible failure scenarios but their algorithm is only efficient for moderately-sized set of scenarios. Later, Orlin et al. [14] studied a problem, in which one chooses a set of up to I items, and nature counteracts by eliminating at most J of the selected items. The objective to maximize a monotone sub-modular set function. The authors propose a greedy-based algorithm with a constant (0.387) factor approximation result, valid for $J = o(\sqrt{I})$. This work was followed by [7], in which they show the same approximation factor for $J = o(I)$. In [17], the authors propose another greedy-based algorithm and provide a bound using the curvature of the sub-modular function. Although these greedy algorithms are computationally efficient, the approximation guarantees are quite loose, whereas in some applications, such as monitoring, it is more desirable to spend more time in the decision making phase, since once the monitoring locations are chosen, they will be in use for a long duration.

Finally, our solution approach draws from *robust optimization* (RO) literature. RO models concern decision making problems affected by uncertainty, in which the uncertainty is modeled as a set, also referred to as uncertainty set. This class of problems are modeled as max-min optimization problems and can also be considered as a zero-sum game against "nature" which acts as an adversary by choosing the worst setting of the uncertain parameters. For further reading one can refer to [3,5]. *Two-stage robust optimization* is an extension of the single-stage RO problems in which the decision maker chooses a secondary action upon observing nature's choice.

This class of problems are intractable in general [4], specially if the second-stage actions are binary. However, there exists efficient approximation schemes which have been proven to perform well in practice. In particular, finite adaptability has been proposed [6], in which the nature's action set, is partitioned and a second-stage decision is determined for each partition. These partitions can be either fixed by the modeler [18] or decided in the optimization [6,11] process. In the present work, we propose a novel two-stage optimization model for the strategic monitoring problem and we build on the work of [11] which proposes a methodology for obtaining K partitions, also known as K-adaptability. In [11], the authors show that for polyhedron (convex) uncertainty sets, a two-stage robust optimization can be approximately reformulated as an MILP. We generalize their result to the case of discrete sets, and we provide an MILP reformulation that is exact.

3   Strategic Monitoring Problem

We are given a set of monitoring locations $\mathcal{N} := \{1, \ldots, N\}$, and a set of targets $\mathcal{T} := \{1, \ldots, T\}$. Each target n has a (normalized) value $U_n \in [0,1]$ which indicates the importance of that target. Further, each monitor $n' \in \mathcal{N}$ can cover a subset of the targets. We represent the target coverage via a bipartite graph $G = (\mathcal{N}, \mathcal{T}, \mathcal{E})$, where $\mathcal{E}$ is the set of edges between $\mathcal{N}$ and $\mathcal{T}$. An edge from $n' \in \mathcal{N}$ to $n \in \mathcal{T}$, denoted by (n', n), exists if n can be monitored by n' (e.g., n is within the observable range of n'). For each target n, we define $\delta(n) := \{n' \in \mathcal{N} : (n', n) \in \mathcal{E}\}$ which is the set of nodes that can monitor n. Fig. 1 depicts an example graph, in which the circles are the monitoring locations, and the squares are the targets that need to be protected. We consider a constant-sum Stackelberg game as:

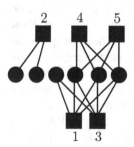

Fig. 1. An example input of the strategic monitoring problem. In this figure the circles represent targets, and squares are the monitoring locations.

$$\max_{\substack{\mathcal{X} \subseteq \mathcal{N} \\ |\mathcal{X}| \leq I}} \min_{\substack{\mathcal{Z} \subseteq \mathcal{X} \\ |\mathcal{Z}| \leq J}} F(\mathcal{X} \backslash \mathcal{Z}), \tag{1}$$

in which a defender aims to select a set of nodes $\mathcal{X} \subseteq \mathcal{N}$ of cardinality at most I as monitors such that it maximizes the coverage of the targets after an adversary eliminates subset $\mathcal{Z} \subseteq \mathcal{X}$ of the chosen monitors. The payoff function $F(\cdot)$ evaluates the targets that are covered, given the defender and attacker's strategies, and it is defined precisely as follows:

$$F(\mathcal{Y}) := \sum_{n \in \mathcal{T}} U_n \mathcal{I} \left(\exists n' \in \mathcal{Y} : n' \in \delta(n) \right), \tag{2}$$

where $\mathcal{I}(\cdot)$ is the indicator function defined as:

$$\mathcal{I}(P) = \begin{cases} 0 & \text{if } P \equiv \textbf{FALSE} \\ 1 & \text{if } P \equiv \textbf{TRUE} \end{cases}. \tag{3}$$

According to this definition, a target is covered iff at least one its neighbors is chosen as a monitor and has not been attacked by the adversary.

In the following proposition, we show the importance of modeling the adversary. We prove that the optimal solution of the problem that ignores the existence of an adversary can be quite sub-optimal in the presence of adversary.

Observation 1. *The optimal solution of a problem that ignores the possibility of adversarial attacks can be sub-optimal in Problem* (1) *with optimality gap in the order* $\mathcal{O}(T)$.

Proof. We prove this by means of an example. Consider an instance of Problem (1) on the network depicted in Fig. 1, with input given as $N = 5$, $T = 6$, $I = 2$, $J = 1$. We also assume that all of the targets have a value equal to 1. In the absence of an adversary, (or if we ignore the adversary), an optimal solution is to choose nodes 1 and 2 which will cover all of the targets. If an adversary exists, however, this decision can be highly sub-optimal as in this case if node 1 is attacked, only 2 targets will be covered. By optimizing against an adversary, the optimal decision is to select nodes 1, and 3. This solution obtains a coverage of 4.

In this particular example, we observed an optimality gap of $2 (= 4 - 2)$. Now, consider the same network structure with T targets, in which nodes 1, and 3 are connected to $T - 2$ targets and node 2 covers the remaining 2 targets. The optimality gap in this case is $T - 4$ which increases linearly with the number of targets. Therefore, we can conclude that in the worst-case this gap is $\mathcal{O}(T)$. □

In the description of Problem (1), the adversary's choice is *dependent* on the decision maker's choice $\mathcal{X}$. We propose an alternative formulation in which the dependence on $\mathcal{X}$ is removed, and the adversary can choose from the ground set $\mathcal{N}$ (instead of $\mathcal{X}$). We show that the two problems are equivalent.

Proposition 1. *Stackelberg game model* (1) *is equivalent to:*

$$\max_{\substack{\mathcal{X} \subseteq \mathcal{N} \\ |\mathcal{X}| \leq I}} \min_{\substack{\mathcal{Z} \subseteq \mathcal{N} \\ |\mathcal{Z}| \leq J}} F(\mathcal{X} \backslash \mathcal{Z}), \tag{4}$$

in which the adversary can choose among the set $\mathcal{N}$.

Proof. This proof is based on the intuition that a rational adversary will always choose among the selected monitors by the defender, even if it is given the option to attack other nodes. The formal proof is given below.

Fix an arbitrary $\mathcal{X} \subseteq \mathcal{N}$ and let z and w denote the optimal objective values of the inner minimization problems in (1) and (4), respectively. We will show that $w = z$, which given the choice of $\mathcal{X}$ is arbitrary, results in the equivalence of the two problems. Since $X \subseteq \mathcal{N}$, it follows that $w \leq z$. We show that the converse is also true. Let $\mathcal{Z}^*$ be optimal decision for the inner minimization problem in (4). We show that one can construct a solution $\overline{\mathcal{Z}} \subseteq \mathcal{X}$ feasible in the inner minimization problem of (1) such that $F(\mathcal{X} \backslash \overline{\mathcal{Z}}) = F(\mathcal{X} \backslash \mathcal{Z}^*)$, implying that $z \leq w$. If $\mathcal{Z}^* \subseteq \mathcal{X}$, we can define $\overline{\mathcal{Z}} = \mathcal{Z}^*$ and the claim follows. Else, let $z \in \mathcal{Z}^* \backslash \mathcal{X}$ and define $\overline{\mathcal{Z}} := \mathcal{Z}^* \backslash \{z\}$. Then $\mathcal{X} \backslash \overline{\mathcal{Z}} = \mathcal{X} \backslash \{\mathcal{Z}^* \backslash \{z\}\} = \mathcal{X} \backslash \mathcal{Z}^*$ and thus $F(\mathcal{X} \backslash \overline{\mathcal{Z}}) = F(\mathcal{X} \backslash \mathcal{Z}^*)$. As the choice of $\mathcal{X}$ was arbitrary, the proof is complete. □

3.1   Reformulation as a Two-Stage Robust Binary Program

In this section, we show that the strategic monitoring problem can be reformulated as a two-stage binary program. Since the two Problems (1) and (4) are equivalent, we will focus on the latter. Indeed, as it will become apparent later on, this simplification will enable us to reformulate Problem (1) exactly as an MILP. The two-stage binary program is as follows:

$$\max_{\boldsymbol{x} \in \mathcal{U}} \min_{\boldsymbol{\xi} \in \Xi} \max_{\boldsymbol{y} \in \{0,1\}^T} \left\{ \sum_{n \in \mathcal{T}} U_n y_n : \sum_{n' \in \delta(n)} \xi_{n'} x_{n'} \geq y_n, \forall n \in \mathcal{T} \right\}. \tag{5}$$

In this formulation, $\boldsymbol{x}$ is a binary vector and $x_n = 1$ iff node n is chosen to place a monitor. Binary vector $\boldsymbol{\xi}$ encodes whether a node is not attacked, where $\xi_n = 0$ iff node n is attacked by the adversary. Also, binary vector $\boldsymbol{y}$ indicates which targets are monitored. Note that the value of $\boldsymbol{y}$ can be determined after the adversary's action is revealed, which forces the introduction of the second-stage counting stage. Set $\mathcal{U} = \{\boldsymbol{x} : \sum_{n \in \mathcal{N}} x_n \leq I\}$ is the set of all feasible monitor selections. Also, Ξ is the set of feasible actions of the adversary and it is defined as:

$$\Xi := \left\{ \boldsymbol{\xi} \in \{0,1\}^{|\mathcal{N}|} : \sum_{n \in \mathcal{N}} (1 - \xi_n) \leq J \right\}. \tag{6}$$

This set expresses that at most J nodes can be attacked by the adversary, which is equivalent to the definition used in Problem (4). The first maximization problem determines the value of x, i.e., the set of monitoring locations. In the inner minimization problem, the adversary chooses which monitors to attack. Finally, the innermost maximization problem determines the covered targets i.e., the problem $\max_{y \in \{0,1\}^T} \left\{ \sum_{n \in T} U_n y_n : \sum_{n' \in \delta(n)} \xi_{n'} x_{n'} \geq y_n, n \in T \right\}$ models the payoff function $F(\cdot)$ introduced in Problem (1). The constraints of this problem stipulate that a target node is monitored if there is at least a monitor among its neighbors, which is not attacked.

Remark 1. In Problem (5), set $\mathcal{U}$ can be defined by any arbitrary linear constraints, and our solution approach remains valid. However, we are only considering cardinality constraints in the definition of $\mathcal{U}$.

Proposition 2. *Problem (4) is equivalent to the two-stage robust monitoring Problem (5).*

Proof. Problem (4) is equivalent to:

$$
\max_{\substack{\mathcal{X} \subseteq \mathcal{N} \\ |\mathcal{X}| \leq I}} \min_{\substack{\mathcal{Z} \subseteq \mathcal{N} \\ |\mathcal{Z}| \leq J}} F(\mathcal{X} \setminus \mathcal{Z}) = \max_{x \in \mathcal{U}} \min_{\xi \in \Xi} F(\{n \in \mathcal{N} : x_n = 1\} \setminus \{\xi \in \Xi : \xi_n = 0\}),
$$

thus, it suffices to show that for any x, and ξ:

$$
F(\{n \in \mathcal{N} : x_n = 1\} \setminus \{\xi \in \Xi : \xi_n = 0\}) =
$$
$$
\max_{y \in \{0,1\}^T} \left\{ \sum_{n \in T} U_n y_n : \sum_{n' \in \delta(n)} \xi_{n'} x_{n'} \geq y_n, \forall n \in T \right\}. \tag{7}
$$

Let y^* be the optimal solution of the maximization problem:

$$
\forall n \in T : y_n^* = 1 \Rightarrow \sum_{n' \in \delta(n)} \xi_{n'} x_{n'} \geq 1.
$$

Also, we note that the opposite direction holds true, meaning that:

$$
\sum_{n' \in \delta(n)} \xi_{n'} x_{n'} \geq 1 \Rightarrow y_n^* = 1,
$$

otherwise, we can construct a new solution $\tilde{y}$ with higher objective which contradicts the optimality of y^*. As a result,

$$
y_n^* = 1 \Leftrightarrow \exists n' \in \delta(n) : \xi_{n'} = 1, \ x_{n'} = 1,
$$

or equivalently:

$$
y_n^* = \mathcal{I}(\exists n' \in \delta(n) : \xi_{n'} = 1, \ x_{n'} = 1).
$$

By summing over all $n \in T$:

$$
\sum_{n \in T} U_n y_n^* = \sum_{n \in T} U_n \mathcal{I}(\exists n' \in \delta(n) : \xi_{n'} = 1, \ x_{n'} = 1)
$$
$$
= F(\{n \in \mathcal{N} : x_n = 1\} \setminus \{\xi \in \Xi : \xi_n = 0\}), \tag{8}
$$

where the last equality follows by the definition of the coverage function $F(\cdot)$. $\square$

3.2 K-Adaptability

K-Adaptability has been proposed to approximate the solution to the two-stage robust optimization problems with integer recourse decisions. In K-adaptability, K non-adjustable second-stage policies $\boldsymbol{y}^k, k \in \{1, \cdots, K\}$ are chosen in the first stage, that is before the adversary takes an action. Upon observing the adversary's action, the best policy among the feasible ones will be output as the solution. This is equivalent to automatically partitioning the adversary actions into K subsets, such that each subset is mapped to particular covering policy. The covering policies are such that the number of covered nodes is not overestimated, but is as high as possible. In the strategic monitoring game, the second-stage variables are in fact indicator functions that indicate, for each node, whether it is covered or not. In K-adaptability, we approximate this indicator function, where we limit ourselves to a small number (K) of counting policies. The payoff will be then evaluated based on the indicator function, thus, K-adaptability serves as an approximation scheme of the payoff function.

K-Adaptability in Strategic Monitoring Problem

The K-adaptability counterpart of Problem (5) can be expressed as:

$$\max_{\substack{\boldsymbol{x} \in \mathcal{U} \\ \boldsymbol{y}^k \in \{0,1\}^T}} \min_{\boldsymbol{\xi} \in \Xi} \max_{k \in \mathcal{K}} \Big\{ \sum_{n \in \mathcal{N}} U_n y_n^k : y_n^k \leq \sum_{n' \in \delta(n)} \xi_{n'} x_{n'}, \forall n \in \mathcal{T} \Big\}. \tag{9}$$

In Formulation (9), $\boldsymbol{x}$ encodes which nodes are chosen as monitors. Variables $\boldsymbol{y}^k$ are the K covering policies, where each policy $\boldsymbol{y}^k$ indicates which target nodes are covered. In other words, $y_n^k = 1$ means that according to the kth policy, node n is monitored. These policies are chosen in the first stage, before observing the adversary's action. In addition, $\boldsymbol{\xi}$ denotes the adversary's action which lies in the set of adversary's pure strategies Ξ. This set is defined in Eq. (6). Also, set $\mathcal{K} := \{1, \cdots, K\}$.

In the first maximization problem, the defender chooses both the monitoring nodes, and K covering policies. If $y_n^k = 1$, it means that according to policy k, node n is monitored. In the minimization problem, the adversary counteracts by choosing which nodes to attack. After observing which monitoring nodes are not attacked, the best feasible policy is chosen in the inner-most maximization problem. Policy k is feasible if it satisfies the constraints in the innermost maximization problem. The chosen policy is an approximation to the true payoff that the defender receives.

These policies approximate the true coverage, meaning that instead of enumerating all defender-attacker pairs of actions and evaluating the corresponding payoffs, one approximates the payoff, using K covering policies. This function is determined simultaneously with the defender's optimal strategy, in the formulation presented. We will illustrate the K-adaptability via an example.

Example 1. Consider an instance of the problem on a graph depicted in Fig. 2, where all of the targets have equal values. We consider a setting with $I = 3$, and

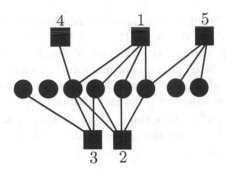

Fig. 2. Companion figure to Example 1. An example to illustrate the K-adaptability

$J = 1$. For $K = 1$, an optimal solution to the 1-adaptability problem is $\boldsymbol{x} = [1, 1, 0, 0, 1]$, with the policy $\boldsymbol{y}^1 = [0, 0, 1, 1, 1, 1, 0, 0]$. According to this solution, the defender chooses nodes 1, 2, and 5 as monitors. In this case, the adversary's best response is to attack node 5 which results in the coverage of only 4 target nodes (those covered by 1, and 2) and this is captured by policy $\boldsymbol{y}^1$. Note that the policy y^1 is feasible under any other attacker's response. This means that even if the adversary chooses nodes 1 or 2 to attack, the same 4 targets would be covered. In fact, under these scenarios more targets are covered, but the policy under-counts those covered targets by setting their coverage value to 0 in order to ensure feasibility for the case that node 5 is attacked. As a result, we obtain a conservative approximation of the problem.

Now, let us compare this solution to the solution to the 2-adaptability problem. With $K = 2$, the payoff function is described approximately via two policies. In this case, the optimal defender strategy is $\boldsymbol{x} = [1, 0, 1, 0, 1]$ and the two policies are equal to: $\boldsymbol{y}^1 = [1, 0, 1, 1, 1, 1, 0, 0]$, and $\boldsymbol{y}^2 = [0, 0, 1, 1, 0, 1, 1, 1]$. If the attacker chooses to attack either node 1 or 3, policy y^2 will be feasible, which indicates that 5 nodes will be always covered (in either of the scenarios). If the attacker chooses node 5, policy y^1 is feasible which covers another set of 5 nodes. Comparing to the $K = 1$ case, the coverage is increased by 1.

This example also gives insights on how our approach allows an adjustable approximation to the true optimal solution with a single parameter K. In fact, in this example, the solution of $K = 1$ is the same as the greedy algorithms proposed in [7,10,14]. By increasing K, the optimal objective value of the K-adaptability problem approaches the optimal solution of the original problem. Also, in this example, the solution of the 2-adaptability problem is optimal as it yields the optimal coverage of 5.

Proposition 3. Value of K in order to recover an optimal solution to Problem (5) is upper-bounded by $\binom{I}{J}$. Moreover, there are instances of Problem (5) for which this bound is tight, in the sense that exactly $K = \binom{I}{J}$ policies are needed in order to obtain the optimal coverage.

Proof. We note that Problem (5) is always solvable since given any fixed value of K, $\boldsymbol{x} = \boldsymbol{0}$ and $\boldsymbol{y}^k = \boldsymbol{0}$, $\forall k \in \{1, \cdots, K\}$ is always a feasible solution. Also, observe that the cardinality of the set of feasible second stage actions is $|\{0,1\}^T| = 2^T$. Thus, there exists an optimal solution with 2^T policies. Given an optimal solution $(\boldsymbol{x}^\star, \boldsymbol{y}^{1^\star}, \ldots, \boldsymbol{y}^{K^\star})$, we show that we can construct an optimal solution with the same objective value and with only $K' = \binom{I}{J}$ policies.

Since $(\boldsymbol{x}^\star, \boldsymbol{y}^{1^\star}, \ldots, \boldsymbol{y}^{K^\star})$ is optimal, there exists a partition of Ξ into K disjoint subsets $\{E^{(k)}\}_{k=1}^K$ such that $\boldsymbol{y}^k$ is feasible and optimal, for all $\boldsymbol{\xi} \in \Xi^{(k)}$. Specifically, we can define:

$$
\Xi^{(k)} = \left\{ \boldsymbol{\xi} \in \Xi : k = \min \left\{ k' : k' \in \underset{k \in \{1, \cdots, K\}}{\arg\max} \left\{ \sum_{n \in T} U_n y^{k^\star}_n : \sum_{n' \in \delta(n)} \xi^k_{n'} x^\star_{n'} \geq y^{k^\star}_n, \forall n \right\} \right\} \right\}.
$$

Also, it follows directly from the definition of $\{\Xi^{(k)}\}_{k=1}^K$ that:

$$
\boldsymbol{\xi} \in \Xi^{(k)} \Rightarrow \boldsymbol{\xi}' \in \Xi^{(k)} : \boldsymbol{\xi}' \circ \boldsymbol{x} = \boldsymbol{\xi} \circ \boldsymbol{x},
$$

where $(\circ)$ indicates the Hadamard product. This implies that for any K such that $\Xi^{(k)}$ is non-empty, $\boldsymbol{\xi}' \circ \boldsymbol{x}$ has a unique value for the $\boldsymbol{\xi} \in \Xi^{(k)}$. Finally, we note that, for any $\boldsymbol{x}$, there are only $\binom{I}{J}$ uniques values for $\boldsymbol{\xi} \in \Xi^{(k)}$, it follows that the maximal number of subsets that are non-empty is at most $\binom{I}{J}$. Since at most $\binom{I}{J}$ subsets are non-empty, we can eliminate all policies associated with empty subsets, and maintain an optimal solution.

Now we prove, via an example, that there exist instances where exactly $K = \binom{I}{J}$ is needed in order to obtain the optimal solution. Consider the example network in Fig. 3. Let us assume the values $I = N$, and $J = 1$. For simplicity, we assume all targets have equal values. Here, the defender will choose all the monitoring nodes and the optimal coverage value is $N - 1$.

In the K-adaptability problem, an example policy (feasible for the case that node 1 is attacked) will be equal to $[0, 1, \cdots, 1]$, which gives the $N - 1$ coverage. However, this policy is not feasible under other attack scenarios. In general if node n is attacked, a feasible policy would be a vector whose entries are equal to 1, except for the nth entry, which is equal to 0. Since the total number of scenarios is N, we can only obtain the optimal coverage of $N - 1$ with $K = \binom{N}{1}$ policies. □

Remark 2. This result is stronger than what authors in [11] propose. Their upper bound on the number of policies needed in order to obtain an optimal solution to the Problem (5) is $K = 2^T$ (remember T is the number of targets). Here, we showed that this bound can be improved to $K = \binom{I}{J}$.

The following proposition provides the lower bound on the value of K in order to ensure that the K-adaptability problem yields a non-zero solution.

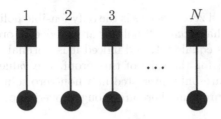

Fig. 3. Companion figure of Propositions 3 and 4.

Proposition 4. *Let $\Delta^{(t)}$ be the tth highest degree in the network (e.g. $\Delta^{(1)}$ is the maximum degree and $\Delta^{(N)}$ is the minimum degree). For any $K \geq \min\{T : \min(I, \sum_{t=1}^{T} \Delta^{(t)}) \geq J+1\}$, at least one node will be covered. Moreover, this bound is tight in the sense that there are instances for which exactly $K = \min\{T : \min(I, \sum_{t=1}^{T} \Delta^{(t)}) \geq J+1\}$ is needed to have a non-zero coverage.*

Proof. We first show a way to construct a solution x to the Problem (9), which requires the minimum number of policies (value of K) and obtains a non-zero coverage.

The intuition is that if we require that at least one node is covered, that node had better have the maximum number of neighbors, because this will increase the likelihood that the node will be covered. As a result, we rank and rename all the nodes in descending order of their degree. Let us use $\Delta^{(t)}$ to denote the tth highest degree node in the network, meaning that $\Delta^{(1)} \geq \Delta^{(2)} \geq \cdots \geq \Delta^{(N)}$.

We start from the first node in this order, and we select all of its neighbors. We continue until either we exceed the budget I, or we have chosen all the neighbors. Next, we check whether $\min(I, \sum_{t=1}^{T} \Delta^{(t)}) \leq J$, in which T is the current node's index, i.e., T^{th} highest-degree node. This condition determines if the number of chosen nodes is less than the number of nodes that can be attacked. If this condition holds, we move to the next highest-degree node and repeat the steps.

At termination, there are $T^\star$ nodes which have neighbor nodes that are chosen. The condition $J < \min(I, \sum_{t=1}^{T^\star} \Delta^{(t)})$ also suggest that *at least one* of these $T^\star$ nodes will be covered since the total number of chosen nodes exceeds the number of nodes that are unavailable. We do not know a priori which of these $T^\star$ node will be covered. Therefore, we define $T^\star$ policies, where policy $y^k := e^k$ (e^k is a all-zeros vector with 1 in k^{th} entry), $\forall k \in \{1, \cdots, T^\star\}$. These policies are feasible in Problem (9), as for each possible adversary's action, one of the above policies will be a feasible coverage. Also, the worst-case coverage is 1.

So far, we have constructed a solution which ensures a worst-case coverage of 1. In other words, $T^\star$ is an upper bound on K. Next, we prove that there are network structures for which this bound is tight, meaning that exactly $K = T^\star$ is needed in order to obtain a non-zero objective. Consider a network structure such as the one depicted in Fig. 3. For $I = 2$ and $J = 1$, a solution is to choose nodes 1, and 2 and $T^\star = 2$. We can observe that with fewer policies, i.e., $K = 1$, the covering policy is all zeros, as this is the only feasible policy for all adversarial actions. This means that *exactly* 2 policies are needed in order to obtain a non-zero coverage which is equal to 1, and indeed it is optimal.

Finally, note that, for the sake of this proof, the values of the targets are not important as we are only interested in a non-zero solution and this will be achieved by making sure that there are enough covering policies.   □

3.3   Reformulation as an MILP

In this section, we derive an exact formulation for the K-adaptability counterpart of the strategic monitoring problem. Our approach is inspired by work of Hanasusanto et al. [11] who show that the K-adaptability problem of a two-stage robust optimization problem with binary second-stage actions can be approximately reformulated, as an MILP, for $\varXi$ defined as a non-empty polyhedron. In this section, we show a stronger result by proving that we can provide an MILP formulation that is exact, and it extends to the discrete set $\varXi$.

The constraints in the inner maximization problem make Problem (9) less well-behaved. An alternative formulation is:

$$\max_{\substack{x \in \mathcal{U} \\ y^k \in \{0,1\}^T}} \min_{l \in \mathcal{L}} \min_{\xi \in \varXi(x,y^{\mathcal{K}},l)} \max_{k \in \mathcal{K},\, l_k = 0} \sum_{n \in \mathcal{T}} U_n y_n^k, \tag{10}$$

in which, $\mathcal{L} = \{0, \dots, T\}^K$. Also, set $\varXi(x, y^{\mathcal{K}}, l)$ is a subset of the set $\varXi$, dependent on x, $y^{\mathcal{K}} := \{y^1, \cdots, y^K\}$, and l and is defined as:

$$\varXi(x, y^{\mathcal{K}}, l) = \left\{ \xi \in \varXi : \begin{array}{ll} y_{l_k}^k > \sum_{n' \in \delta(l_k)} \xi_{n'} x_{n'}, & \text{if } \forall k \in \mathcal{K} : l_k > 0 \\[4mm] y_n^k \leq \sum_{n' \in \delta(n)} \xi_{n'} x_{n'}, \ \forall n \in \mathcal{T}, & \text{if } \forall k \in \mathcal{K} : l_k = 0 \end{array} \right\}, \tag{11}$$

In the above definition, vector l encodes which of the K second-stage policies are feasible. If $l_k = 0$, it means that policy k is feasible; therefore, all the constraints must be satisfied, i.e., all the coverage constraints for all of the targets. Note that the inner-most maximization problem chooses the best feasible policy ($l_k = 0$). On the other hand, if $l_k > 0$, it indicates that there is at least one constraint that is violated by policy k, and the value of l_k indicates which constraint. In this definition, and according to the first constraint for $l_k > 0$, policy k violates the constraint corresponding to node l_k, whereas if $l_k = 0$, it means that policy k must satisfy all the constraints, thus the constraints are imposed for all $n \in \mathcal{T}$. As a result, by introducing l, the constraints of the inner maximization problem are absorbed by decision l, and parameterized sets $\varXi(x, y^{\mathcal{K}}, l)$.

Remark 3. In the above definition of vector l, it is sufficient to find at least one constraint violation in order for policy k to be infeasible, and l_k records the index of that constraint (equivalently, the node for which the coverage constraint is violated).

While the discrete nature of set Ξ prohibits any attempts to use duality theory in the reformulation as an MILP, in the following proposition, we show that using certain structure of sets defined by Eq. (11), we can disregard the intergality constraints and obtain a convex set.

Proposition 5. *Problem* (10) *remains unchanged if we replace the set Ξ with the following:*

$$\Xi := \left\{ \boldsymbol{\xi} \in [0,1]^{|\mathcal{N}|} : \sum_{n \in \mathcal{N}} (1 - \xi_n) \leq J \right\}. \tag{12}$$

in which the integrality constraint on $\boldsymbol{\xi}$ is relaxed.

Proof. Throughout this proof we use Ξ^{convex} and Ξ to refer to the convex, and discrete sets, respectively. In order to show that the optimal objective value of Problem (10) does not change under the set Ξ^{convex}, first, note that the payoff function is only dependent on the $\sum_{n \in \mathcal{T}} y_n^k, \forall k \in \mathcal{K}$ and not the values of $\boldsymbol{\xi}$. As a result, we only need to prove, for any arbitrary $(\boldsymbol{x}, \boldsymbol{y}^{\mathcal{K}}, \boldsymbol{l})$:

$$\text{if } \Xi^{\mathrm{convex}}(\boldsymbol{x}, \boldsymbol{y}^{\mathcal{K}}, \boldsymbol{l}) \neq \emptyset \Rightarrow \Xi(\boldsymbol{x}, \boldsymbol{y}^{\mathcal{K}}, \boldsymbol{l}) \neq \emptyset.$$

This follows since for cases when both sets are non-empty, for any fix $(\boldsymbol{x}, \boldsymbol{y}^{\mathcal{K}}, \boldsymbol{l})$, the objective values of both problems are equal. Let us choose an arbitrary $(\boldsymbol{x}, \boldsymbol{y}^{\mathcal{K}}, \boldsymbol{l})$. For the sake of conciseness, we drop the dependence on $\boldsymbol{x}$, and $\boldsymbol{y}^{\mathcal{K}}$.

Now, suppose $\tilde{\boldsymbol{\xi}} \in \Xi^{\mathrm{convex}}(\boldsymbol{l})$:

$$y_{l_k}^k > \sum_{n' \in \delta(l_k)} \tilde{\xi}_{n'} x_{n'}, \qquad\qquad \text{if } \forall k \in \mathcal{K} : l_k > 0, \tag{13}$$

$$y_n^k \leq \sum_{n' \in \delta(n)} \tilde{\xi}_{n'} x_{n'}, \forall n \in \mathcal{T}, \qquad \text{if } \forall k \in \mathcal{K} : l_k = 0, \tag{14}$$

According to Eq. (13), and since $\boldsymbol{x} \geq \boldsymbol{0}$, $\tilde{\boldsymbol{\xi}} \geq \boldsymbol{0}$ and $\boldsymbol{y} \leq \boldsymbol{1}$:

$$l_k > 0 \Rightarrow y_{l_k} = 1, \ \xi_{n'} x_{n'} = 0, \ \forall n' \in \delta(l_k) \Rightarrow$$
$$\xi_{n'} = 0, \ \forall n' \in \delta(l_k) : x_{n'} = 1.$$

Now, we define $\hat{\xi}_n := \lceil \tilde{\xi}_n \rceil, \forall n \in \mathcal{N}$, and we show that $\hat{\xi}_n \in \Xi(\boldsymbol{l})$. In order for $\hat{\xi}_n$ to be in $\Xi(\boldsymbol{l})$, it must satisfy the constraints that define the set $\Xi(\boldsymbol{l})$.

$$\forall k : l_k > 0 \sum_{n' \in \delta(l_k)} \hat{\xi}_{n'} x_{n'} = \sum_{n' \in \delta(l_k): x_{n'}=1} \hat{\xi}_{n'} x_{n'} = \sum_{n' \in \delta(l_k): x_{n'}=1} \lceil \tilde{\xi}_n \rceil x_{n'} = 0 \leq y_{l_k}^k.$$

$$\tag{15}$$

Also,

$$\forall k : l_k = 0 \sum_{n' \in \delta(n)} \hat{\xi}_{n'} x_{n'} \geq \sum_{n' \in \delta(n)} \tilde{\xi}_{n'} x_{n'} \geq y_n^k, \forall n \in \mathcal{T}. \tag{16}$$

The proof is complete, as we showed $\hat{\boldsymbol{\xi}} \in \Xi(\boldsymbol{l})$. $\qquad\qquad\square$

Before reformulating the problem as an MILP, we note that the set described by Eq. (11) is not closed. We propose to substitute this set with the following set:

$$
\Xi_c(\boldsymbol{x}, \boldsymbol{y}^{\mathcal{K}}, \boldsymbol{l}) = \left\{ \boldsymbol{\xi} \in \Xi : \begin{array}{ll} y_{l_k}^k \geq \sum\limits_{n' \in \delta(l_k)} \xi_{n'} x_{n'} + 1, & \text{if } l_k > 0, \ \forall k \in \mathcal{K} \\[2ex] y_n^k \leq \sum\limits_{n' \in \delta(n)} \xi_{n'} x_{n'}, & \forall n \in \mathcal{T}, \text{ if } l_k = 0, \ \forall k \in \mathcal{K} \end{array} \right\}. \tag{17}
$$

Proposition 6. *Sets* $\Xi_c(\boldsymbol{x}, \boldsymbol{y}, \boldsymbol{l})$ *and* $\Xi(\boldsymbol{x}, \boldsymbol{y}, \boldsymbol{l})$ *are equal.*

Proof. It suffices to show that if $l_k > 0$:

$$
y_{l_k}^k > \sum_{n' \in \delta(l_k)} \xi_{n'} x_{n'} \Leftrightarrow y_{l_k}^k \geq \sum_{n' \in \delta(l_k)} \xi_{n'} x_{n'} + 1.
$$

For a given $(\boldsymbol{x}, \boldsymbol{y}, \boldsymbol{l})$, $\boldsymbol{\xi}$ satisfies the constraint $\left(y_{l_k}^k > \sum_{n' \in \delta(l_k)} \xi_{n'} x_{n'} \right)$ only if $\left(\sum_{n' \in \delta(l_k)} \xi_{n'} x_{n'} = 0 \right)$.

The same is true for $\boldsymbol{\xi}$ satisfying the constraint $\left(y_{l_k}^k \geq \sum_{n' \in \delta(l_k)} \xi_{n'} x_{n'} + 1 \right)$. Therefore, the two sets are equal. □

Remark 4. This result is stronger than [11] as we are able to obtain an exact reformulation rather than an approximate formulation.

Next, we present the MILP reformulation of Problem (9).

Theorem 1. *Problem* (9) *can be exactly reformulated as the following MILP:*

$$
\max \ \tau
$$
s.t. $\boldsymbol{x} \in \mathcal{U}, \ \boldsymbol{y}^k \in \{0,1\}^N, \ k \in \mathcal{K}, \ \tau \in \mathbb{R}$

$$
\left. \begin{array}{l}
\lambda(l) \in \Delta_K(l), \ \alpha(l) \in \mathbb{R}_+^{N+2}, \ \beta^k(l) \in \mathbb{R}_+^N, \ \forall k \in \mathcal{K}, \ \nu(l) \in \mathbb{R}_+^K \\[1ex]
\tau \leq \sum\limits_{n \in \mathcal{N}} -\alpha_n(l) + (N-J)\alpha_{N+1}(l) - \sum\limits_{\substack{k \in \mathcal{K} \\ l_k \neq 0}} (y_{l_k}^k - 1)\nu_k(l) + \cdots \\[2ex]
\cdots \sum\limits_{\substack{k \in \mathcal{K} \\ l_k = 0}} \sum\limits_{n \in \mathcal{T}} y_n^k \beta_n^k(l) + \sum\limits_{k \in \mathcal{K}} \lambda_k(l) \sum\limits_{n \in \mathcal{T}} U_n y_n^k, \\[2ex]
-\alpha_n(l) + \alpha_{N+1}(l) - \sum\limits_{\substack{k \in \mathcal{K} \\ l_k \neq 0}} \sum\limits_{n' \in \delta(l_k)} x_{n'} \nu_k(l) + \sum\limits_{\substack{k \in \mathcal{K} \\ l_k = 0}} \sum\limits_{n' \in \delta(n)} x_{n'} \beta_n^k(l) \leq 0, \forall n \in \mathcal{N},
\end{array} \right\} , \ \forall l \in \partial \mathcal{L}
\tag{18}
$$

$$
\left. \begin{array}{l}
\alpha(l) \in \mathbb{R}_+^{N+1}, \ \nu(l) \in R_+^K \\[1ex]
\sum\limits_{n \in \mathcal{N}} -\alpha_n(l) + (N-J)\alpha_{N+1}(l) - \sum\limits_{\substack{k \in \mathcal{K} \\ l_k \neq 0}} (y_{l_k}^k - 1)\nu_k(l) \geq 1 \\[2ex]
-\alpha_n(l) + \alpha_{N+1}(l) - \sum\limits_{\substack{k \in \mathcal{K} \\ l_k \neq 0}} \sum\limits_{n' \in \delta(l_k)} x_{n'} \nu_k(l) = 0, \ \forall n \in \mathcal{N}
\end{array} \right\} , \ \forall l \in \mathcal{L}_+
$$

Proof. This result follows from Propositions 5 and 6 and derivation in [11]. In order to make the paper self-contained, we will provide the full derivation in Appendix B. □

Remark 5. For a fixed K, the size of the above MILP is polynomial in all problem inputs, thus, it circumvents the exponentiality of the attacker's action set.

4 Results

In this section, we present different numerical results that demonstrate the performance of K-adaptability, in terms of both computation effort and approximation quality. We use randomly generated graphs, where an edge between a monitor and a target exists with probability $P = 0.2$. Our results are averaged over 20 sample networks. In all experiments, there is a time limit of 60 min. Also, all the targets are assumed to have equal value. This assumption is to facilitate the interpretation of the results.

In our experiments, we compare our approach against an exact scenario-based MILP solution, which explicitly enumerates the adversary's actions and solves for the best defender strategy against the worst-case attacker action. The formulation for the scenario-based problem is presented in Appendix A. We also compare our approach to the greedy-based algorithm by Tzoumas et.al [17].

Optimal Coverage vs. K [N $= 20$, T $= 5$, I $= 8$, J $= 5$]: The first experiment compares the optimal solution of the K-adaptability problem, for various values of K, with the exact solution. Both problems use greedy solution as warm-start. In Fig. 4, the vertical axis shows the normalized coverage (optimal coverage divided by the total number of targets). The first three bars in this plot are the optimal coverage results from 1-, 2-, and 3-adaptability problems, and the last bar corresponds to the exact solution. Here, we can observe that by increasing K from 1 to 2 and 3, the optimality gap monotonically decreases, where for $K = 3$, this gap is less that 10%.

Coverage/Solver Time vs. Number of Attacks [N $= 30$, T $= 8$, I $= 12$, K $= 2$]: We now investigate how our approach performs, both in terms of solver-time and solution quality, compared to the exact approach. Figure 5(a) shows the normalized coverage, plotted versus different numbers of adversarial attacks (J). The blue and yellow bars are the results of the 2-adaptability and exact problems, respectively. We observe that as J increases, the coverage decreases, until $J = 8$ for which the exact formulation could not find a feasible solution within the time-budget. This is because, going beyond $J = 7$, the number of attack scenarios, i.e., the number of constraints, becomes very large. For example, for ($J = 8$),

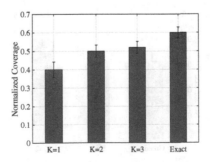

Fig. 4. Coverage vs. K

there were $\binom{30}{8} \approx 6 \times 10^6$ constraints and the solver did not obtain a feasible solution within the 1-h time budget. However, we observe that the 2-adaptability solution does not suffer from this issue, as it is able to solve for such cases. Also, for $(J < 8)$, it closely approximates the exact solution.

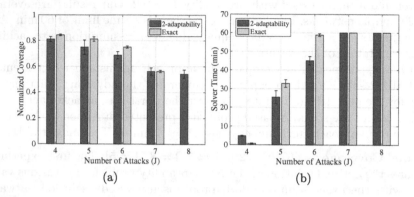

Fig. 5. Comparing solver time and coverage for exact and 2-adaptability problems

Figure 5(b) compares the solver time of the 2-adaptability and exact solution. We observe that the exact solution quickly becomes intractable as J increases. For larger J, both problems reach the time limit, however, as Fig. 5(a) suggests, for $(J > 7)$ the exact approach fails to provide a solution within the time limit, whereas the 2-adaptability problem yields a high quality solution.

K-**Adaptability vs. Greedy** $[\mathbf{N = 20, \ T = 5, \ I = 8, \ J = 4, \ K = 2}]$: In this experiment, we test our approach on harder graph instances, graphs with solutions that are hard for heuristic algorithms to find, and we average over 10 such graphs. For instance, see Fig. 2. In our comparison, we use the greedy algorithm proposed in [17] as the baseline. There are several works on greedy solutions, however, most of them are limited in terms of allowable ranges for J [7,14]. Thus, we compare our solution to the work of [17], since it applies to all regimes

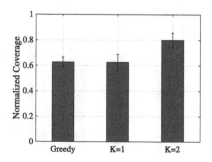

Fig. 6. Comparing greedy solution with 1- and 2-adaptability problems

of J. Figure 6 shows the normalized coverage, for greedy, 1- and 2-adaptability problems. This result indicates that by K as low as 1, on average we are able to recover the greedy solution, where the 2-adaptability significantly outperforms the greedy solution. As a result, this experiment illustrates that on hard graph instances that greedy does not perform well, K-adaptability can outperform, using only small values of K.

5 Conclusion

This work studies a Stackelberg game model for the strategic monitoring problem. This problem is highly intractable. Thus, we provide a tractable approximation scheme based on K-adaptability formulation. Our solution methodology automatically partitions the set of adversary's strategies and maps each subset to a coverage policy. These policies are such that they do not overestimate the defender's payoff. We show that there exists an exact MILP reformulation of the K-adaptability problem whose size grows polynomially in the description of the problem input. We empirically show, the shortcomings of both the heuristic and exact approaches and that K-adaptability can remedy those issues. In particular, our experiments indicate that with even with small values of K, ranging from 1, to 3, K-adaptability recovers both the greedy and exact solutions.

Acknowledgement. This work was supported by the Army Research Office (W911NF-17-1-0370, W911NF-15-1-0515, W911NF-16-1-0069), National Science Foundation (CNS-1640624, IIS-1649972, and IIS-1526860), Office of Naval Research (N00014-15-1-2621), and the USC Office of the Provost and USC Viterbi School of Engineering.

A   Exact Scenario-Based MILP

In Problem (5), the optimal pure strategy for the defender can be obtained from the solution of the following deterministic MILP problem which enumerates all the attacker pure strategies. This reformulation is exact, however, it requires a number of variables and constraints which is exponential in N. In this formulation $y_{\xi,n}$ is a binary variable and it is equal to 1 iff under attack scenario ξ, target n is covered.

$$\max_{\substack{x \in \mathcal{U} \\ y \in \{0,1\}^{|\Xi| \times N}}} \tau$$

$$\text{s.t.} \quad y_{\xi,n} \leq \sum_{n' \in \delta(n)} \xi_{n'} x_{n'}, \ \forall n \in \mathcal{N}, \ \forall \xi \in \Xi \tag{19}$$

$$\tau \leq \sum_{n \in \mathcal{N}} y_{\xi,n}, \ \forall \xi \in \Xi$$

B   Exact MILP Formulation of the K-Adaptability

The following reformulation is based on [11]. The objective function of the Problem (10) is identical to:

$$\min_{l \in \mathcal{L}} \min_{\xi \in \Xi_c(x,y,l)} \left[\max_{\lambda \in \Delta_K(l)} \sum_{k \in \mathcal{K}} \lambda_k \sum_{n \in \mathcal{T}} U_n y_n^k \right], \tag{20}$$

where $\Delta_K(l) = \{\lambda \in \mathbb{R}_+ : e^\top \lambda = 1, \lambda_k = 0, \forall k \in \mathcal{K} : l_k \neq 0\}$. We define $\partial\mathcal{L} := \{l \in \mathcal{L} : l \not> 0\}$, and $\mathcal{L}_+ := \{l \in \mathcal{L} > 0\}$. Note that $\Delta_K(l) = \emptyset$ if and only if $l > 0$. If $\Xi_c(x,y,l) = \emptyset$ for all $l \in \mathcal{L}_+$, then the problem is equivalent to:

$$\min_{l \in \partial\mathcal{L}} \min_{\xi \in \Xi_c(x,y,l)} \left[\max_{\lambda \in \Delta_K(l)} \sum_{k \in \mathcal{K}} \lambda_k \sum_{n \in \mathcal{T}} U_n y_n^k \right]. \tag{21}$$

By applying the classical min-max theorem:

$$\min_{l \in \partial\mathcal{L}} \max_{\substack{\lambda \in \Delta_K(l) \\ l \in \partial\mathcal{L}}} \min_{\xi \in \Xi_c(x,y,l)} \sum_{k \in \mathcal{K}} \lambda_k \sum_{n \in \mathcal{T}} U_n y_n^k. \tag{22}$$

This problem is also equivalent to:

$$\max_{\substack{\lambda(l) \in \Delta_K(l) \\ l \in \partial\mathcal{L}}} \min_{l \in \partial\mathcal{L}} \min_{\xi \in \Xi_c(x,y,l)} \sum_{k \in \mathcal{K}} \lambda_k(l) \sum_{n \in \mathcal{T}} U_n y_n^k. \tag{23}$$

We note that if $\Xi_c(x,y,l) \neq \emptyset$, for some $l \in \mathcal{L}_+$ the objective of Problem (10) evaluates to $-\infty$. Using the epigraph form, Problem (10) is equivalent to:

$$\begin{aligned}
\max \ & \tau \\
\text{s.t.} \ & x \in \mathcal{U}, y^k \in \{0,1\}^N, k \in \mathcal{K} \\
& \tau \in \mathbb{R}, \ \lambda(l) \in \Delta_K(l), \ l \in \partial\mathcal{L} \\
& \tau \leq \sum_{k \in \mathcal{K}} \lambda_k(l) \sum_{n \in \mathcal{T}} U_n y_n^k, \qquad \forall l \in \partial\mathcal{L}, \ \xi \in \Xi_c(x,y,l) \\
& \Xi_c(x,y,l) = \emptyset, \qquad \forall l \in \mathcal{L}_+.
\end{aligned} \tag{24}$$

The semi-infinite constraint associated with $l \in \partial\mathcal{L}$ is satisfied if and only if:

$$\begin{aligned}
\min \ & \sum_{k \in \mathcal{K}} \lambda_k(l) \sum_{n \in \mathcal{T}} U_n y_n^k \\
\text{s.t.} \ & 0 \leq \xi_{n'} \leq 1, \ \forall n' \in \mathcal{N} \\
& \sum_{n' \in \mathcal{N}} \xi_{n'} \geq N - J \\
& y_{l_k}^k \geq \sum_{n' \in \delta(l_k)} \xi_{n'} x_{n'} + 1, \qquad \text{if } l_k > 0, \ \forall k \in \mathcal{K} \\
& y_n^k \leq \sum_{n' \in \delta(n)} \xi_{n'} x_{n'}, \ \forall n \in \mathcal{T}, \ \text{if } l_k = 0, \ \forall k \in \mathcal{K}
\end{aligned} \tag{25}$$

is greater than τ.

In order to obtain the dual formulation, we introduce an auxiliary variable $\xi_{T+1} = 1$, and we rewrite the objective as: $\left(\sum_{k\in\mathcal{K}} \lambda_k(l) \sum_{n\in\mathcal{T}} U_n y_n^k\right) \xi_{T+1}$. Using strong linear programming duality:

$$\max \sum_{n\in\mathcal{N}} -\alpha_n(l) + (N-J)\alpha_{N+1}(l) - \sum_{\substack{k\in\mathcal{K}\\ l_k\neq 0}} (y_{l_k}^k - 1)\nu_k(l) + \sum_{\substack{k\in\mathcal{K}\\ l_k=0}}\sum_{n\in\mathcal{T}} y_n^k \beta_n^k(l) + \alpha_{N+2}(l)$$

$$\text{s.t. } \alpha_n(l) \geq 0, n \in \{1,\dots,N+1\}, \; \beta^k(l) \in \mathbb{R}_+^N, \; \forall k \in \mathcal{K}, \; \nu(l) \in \mathbb{R}_+^K$$

$$-\alpha_n(l) + \alpha_{N+1}(l) - \sum_{\substack{k\in\mathcal{K}\\ l_k\neq 0}}\sum_{n'\in\delta(l_k)} x_{n'}\nu_k(l) + \sum_{\substack{k\in\mathcal{K}\\ l_k=0}}\sum_{n'\in\delta(n)} x_{n'}\beta_n^k(l) \leq 0, \forall n \in \mathcal{T}, \quad (26)$$

$$\alpha_{N+2}(l) = \sum_{k\in\mathcal{K}} \lambda_k(l) \sum_{n\in\mathcal{T}} U_n y_n^k.$$

Also, the last constraint in formulation (24) is satisfied if the following linear program is infeasible:

$$\min 0$$
$$\text{s.t. } 0 \leq \xi_n \leq 1, \qquad\qquad \forall n \in \mathcal{N}$$
$$\sum_{n\in\mathcal{N}} \xi_n \geq N - J \qquad\qquad\qquad (27)$$
$$y_{l_k}^k \geq \sum_{n'\in\delta(l_k)} \xi_{n'} x_{n'} + 1, \forall k \in \mathcal{K}, \; l_k \neq 0.$$

Using strong duality, this occurs if the dual problem is unbounded. Since the feasible region of the dual problem constitutes a cone, the dual problem is unbounded if and only if there is a feasible solution with an objective value of 1 or more. The dual problem is as below:

$$\max \sum_{n\in\mathcal{N}} -\alpha_n(l) + (N-J)\alpha_{N+1}(l) - \sum_{\substack{k\in\mathcal{K}\\ l_k\neq 0}} (y_{l_k}^k - 1)\nu_k(l)$$

$$\text{s.t. } \alpha(l) \in \mathbb{R}_+^{N+1}, \; \nu(l) \in \mathbb{R}_+^K$$
$$-\alpha_n(l) + \alpha_{N+1}(l) - \sum_{\substack{k\in\mathcal{K}\\ l_k\neq 0}}\sum_{n'\in\delta(l_k)} x_{n'}\nu_k(l) = 0, \; \forall n \in \mathcal{N} \qquad (28)$$

References

1. Bard, N., Nicholas, D., Szepesvaári, C., Bowling, M.: Decision-theoretic clustering of strategies. In: Proceedings of the 2015 International Conference on Autonomous Agents and Multiagent Systems, pp. 17–25. International Foundation for Autonomous Agents and Multiagent Systems (2015)
2. Basak, A.: Abstraction using analysis of subgames. In: Proceedings of the Thirtieth AAAI Conference on Artificial Intelligence, pp. 4196–4197. AAAI Press (2016)
3. Ben-Tal, A., El Ghaoui, L., Nemirovski, A.: Robust Optimization. Princeton University Press, Princeton (2009)
4. Ben-Tal, A., Goryashko, A., Guslitzer, E., Nemirovski, A.: Adjustable robust solutions of uncertain linear programs. Math. Program. **99**(2), 351–376 (2004)

5. Bertsimas, D., Brown, D.B., Caramanis, C.: Theory and applications of robust optimization. SIAM Rev. **53**(3), 464–501 (2011)
6. Bertsimas, D., Caramanis, C.: Finite adaptability in multistage linear optimization. IEEE Trans. Autom. Control **55**(12), 2751–2766 (2010)
7. Bogunovic, I., Mitrović, S., Scarlett, J., Cevher, V.: Robust submodular maximization: a non-uniform partitioning approach. arXiv preprint arXiv:1706.04918 (2017)
8. Bošanský, B., Jiang, A.X., Tambe, M., Kiekintveld, C.: Combining compact representation and incremental generation in large games with sequential strategies. In: Proceedings of the Twenty-Ninth AAAI Conference on Artificial Intelligence, pp. 812–818. AAAI Press (2015)
9. Brown, G., Carlyle, M., Salmerón, J., Wood, K.: Defending critical infrastructure. Interfaces **36**(6), 530–544 (2006)
10. Dahan, M., Sela, L., Amin, S.: Network monitoring under strategic disruptions. arXiv preprint arXiv:1705.00349 (2017)
11. Hanasusanto, G.A., Kuhn, D., Wiesemann, W.: K-adaptability in two-stage robust binary programming. Oper. Res. **63**(4), 877–891 (2015)
12. Jain, M., Korzhyk, D., Vaněk, O., Conitzer, V., Pěchouček, M., Tambe, M.: A double oracle algorithm for zero-sum security games on graphs. In: 10th International Conference on Autonomous Agents and Multiagent Systems, vol. 1, pp. 327–334 (2011)
13. Krause, A., McMahan, H.B., Guestrin, C., Gupta, A.: Robust submodular observation selection. J. Mach. Learn. Res. **9**(Dec), 2761–2801 (2008)
14. Orlin, J.B., Schulz, A.S., Udwani, R.: Robust monotone submodular function maximization. In: Louveaux, Q., Skutella, M. (eds.) IPCO 2016. LNCS, vol. 9682, pp. 312–324. Springer, Cham (2016). https://doi.org/10.1007/978-3-319-33461-5_26
15. Pita, J., Tambe, M., Kiekintveld, C., Cullen, S., Steigerwald, E.: GUARDS: game theoretic security allocation on a national scale. In: 10th International Conference on Autonomous Agents and Multiagent Systems, vol. 1, pp. 37–44. International Foundation for Autonomous Agents and Multiagent Systems (2011)
16. Tsai, J., Kiekintveld, C., Ordonez, F., Tambe, M., Rathi, S.: IRIS-a tool for strategic security allocation in transportation networks (2009)
17. Tzoumas, V., Gatsis, K., Jadbabaie, A., Pappas, G.J.: Resilient monotone submodular function maximization. arXiv preprint arXiv:1703.07280 (2017)
18. Vayanos, P., Kuhn, D., Rustem, B.: Decision rules for information discovery in multi-stage stochastic programming. In: 2011 50th IEEE Conference on Decision and Control and European Control Conference (CDC-ECC), pp. 7368–7373. IEEE (2011)

An Initial Study of Targeted Personality Models in the FlipIt Game

Anjon Basak[1]([⊠]) [iD], Jakub Černý[2] [iD], Marcus Gutierrez[1] [iD], Shelby Curtis[1] [iD],
Charles Kamhoua[3] [iD], Daniel Jones[1] [iD], Branislav Bošanský[2] [iD],
and Christopher Kiekintveld[1] [iD]

[1] The University of Texas at El Paso, 500 W University Ave,
El Paso, TX 79968, USA
{abasak,mgutierrez22,srcurtis}@miners.utep.edu, jonesdn@gmail.com,
cdkiekintveld@utep.edu
[2] Czech Technical University in Prague,
Technicka 2, 166 27 Prague 6, Czech Republic
{jakub.cerny,branislav.bosansky}@agents.fel.cvut.cz
[3] Army Research Laboratory, 2800 Powder Mill Rd, Adelphi, MD 20783, USA
charles.a.kamhoua.civ@mail.mil

Abstract. Game theory typically assumes rational behavior for solution concepts such as Nash equilibrium. However, this assumption is often violated when human agents are interacting in real-world scenarios, such as cybersecurity. There are different human factors that drive human decision making, and these also vary significantly across individuals leading to substantial individual differences in behavior. Predicting these differences in behavior can help a defender to predict actions of different attacker types to provide better defender strategy tailored towards different attacker types. We conducted an initial study of this idea using a behavioral version of the FlipIt game. We show that there are identifiable differences in behavior among different groups (e.g., individuals with different Dark Triad personality scores), but our initial attempts at capturing these differences using simple known behavioral models does not lead to significantly improved defender strategies. This suggests that richer behavioral models are needed to effectively predict and target strategies in these more complex cybersecurity game.

Keywords: Game theory · Cybersecurity · Extensive-form game
Agent Quantal Response Equilibrium · Dark Triad personality

1 Introduction

Game theory has a growing number of uses in cybersecurity, such as the strategic allocation of honeypots [12,20] to learn more about the attacker or to slow the progress of the attacker. There are other examples [5,22] where the game is dynamic (stochastic or in the extensive form). A common assumption in standard game models is that players are rational and the goal is to seek an optimal

© Springer Nature Switzerland AG 2018
L. Bushnell et al. (Eds.): GameSec 2018, LNCS 11199, pp. 623–636, 2018.
https://doi.org/10.1007/978-3-030-01554-1_36

strategy in a form of a Nash Equilibrium [16]. However, in many cases, we deploy game strategies against humans or other types of opponents with limited rationality. The literature on behavioral game theory has started to address the question of developing more predictive models of human behavior, but much of the work to date focuses on very simple games, and it typically ignores the substantial individual differences among humans. In addition, most of this work is not in the context of cybersecurity.

We take a first step towards developing targeted behavioral models that make specific predictions for different groups of human players. This is motivated in part by a long history of work in personality psychology that identifies different dimensions of personality in humans that lead to different behavioral predictions, such as the "Dark Triad" [19] that focuses on malicious behavior types. However, the general idea of developing targeted behavior models can extend beyond personality factors to many other aspects that might influence behavior. We investigate this idea in the context of cybersecurity, conducting a behavioral study for a variant of the FlipIt game.

There are some previous works that consider behavioral modeling of attackers. An initial study on the FlipIt game was done by Nochenson and Grossklags [18] to analyze the impact of participants' age and gender on performance. The authors built a regression model to predict the behavior of the users. Another work by Reitter et al. [21] did analysis on risk propensity and performance of the participants in the FlipIt game and found that high risk affects decision making. The authors also built a cognitive model based on ACT-R [2] which models an individual's risk propensity and decision making strategy.

Another approach is to use Instance Based Learning (IBL) [1] to model the attacker or to support the network administrator by modeling the defender. Another notable line of work is in Stackelberg Security Games (SSGs) where different behavioral models including Prospect Theory (PT) [10], Quantal Response (QR) [15] and Subjective Utility Quantal Response (SUQR) model [17], are used to model the attacker [17,24,25]. However, in these works, the game model is a repeated Stackelberg game where the dynamic nature of the real world interaction between an attacker and a defender is not represented in full generality. The attacker model parameters are estimated by considering repeated games where the defender is committed to a mixed strategy in a round rather than committing to a pure strategy. A Bayesian SUQR model has also been proposed where the parameters were fitted for every attack [24]. Kar et al. considered the attacker's attack history to improve the attacker model [11]. The main difference in our work is that we consider consider *targeted* models for different groups of attackers with distinctive behavior patterns.

We consider Extensive Form Games (EFG), a richer representation of the multi-agent interaction than repeated Stackelberg games. The defender and attacker mixed strategy can change in every round depending on previous actions of the players and, as a result, the dynamic nature of the attacker and defender interactions are fully represented. We introduce a variant of an EFG we call a Type-revealing game and a standard Bayesian Game to model dynamic interactions with bounded rational players in cybersecurity settings. Using this model, we evaluated the quality of defender strategies depending on different attacker groups based on different grouping techniques.

We created an online game called *StrataFlip* [3]. We recruited users from Amazon Mechanical Turk (AMT) to play the game as the attacker against the defender, including an equlibrium "strategic" defender. We used the QR behavioral model to fit parameters to the attackers' behavior using Maximum Likelihood Estimation (MLE), and then we used this model in a variant of an EFG and in a Bayesian Game. To differentiate between different attacker types we used the gameplay of the AMT participants in the StrataFlip game. We also considered the personality of the AMT participants. We studied three personality traits that have been linked to deception and interpersonal harm (Machiavellianism, and subclinical versions of psychopathy and narcissism), which is called the "Dark Triad" [19]. Our initial results show that while there are behavioral differences between the groups, the simple one-parameter QR model appears not to capture them well enough for the defender to effectively target the different groups, so we will need to consider richer behavioral models (such as SUQR) in future work.

2   Background

First, we describe a model of EFGs, a representation of sequential interactions between players. EFGs is a rich representation that is able to represent partial knowledge of the players. Formally, a two-player EFG is defined as a tuple $G = (\mathcal{N}, \mathcal{H}, \mathcal{Z}, \mathcal{A}, u, \mathcal{I})$: $\mathcal{N} = \{d, a\}$ is a set of players, the defender and the attacker. We use i to refer to one of the players, and $-i$ to refer to his opponent. $\mathcal{H}$ denotes a finite set of *nodes* in the game tree. Each node corresponds to a unique *history* of actions taken by all players and chance from the root of the game; hence, we use the term history and node interchangeably. $\mathcal{A}$ denotes the set of all actions. $\mathcal{Z} \subseteq \mathcal{H}$ is the set of all *terminal nodes* of the game. For each $z \in \mathcal{Z}$ we define a *utility function* for each player i ($u_i : \mathcal{Z} \to \mathbb{R}$). In this work we consider only zero-sum EFGs, for which $u_d = -u_a$.

The imperfect observation of player i is modeled via *information sets* $\mathcal{I}_i$ that form a partition over $h \in \mathcal{H}$ where i chooses an action. We use $A(I_i)$ to denote possible actions available in each node from an information set $I_i \in \mathcal{I}_i$. We assume *perfect recall*, which means that players remember the history of their own. As a consequence, all nodes in any information set I_i have the same history of actions for player i.

Pure strategies Π_i assign one action for each $I \in \mathcal{I}_i$. A *mixed strategy* $\delta_i \in \Delta_i$ is a probability distribution over Π_i. A *best response* of player i to the opponent's strategy δ_{-i} is a strategy $\delta_i^{BR} \in BR_i(\delta_{-i})$, such that δ_i^{BR} is optimal against δ_{-i} according to a given criterion (see Sect. 3). Strategies in EFGs with perfect recall can be compactly represented by using the sequence form [13]. A *sequence* $\sigma_i \in \Sigma_i$ is an ordered list of actions taken by a single player i in history h. We use $seq_i(I_i)$ and $seq_i(h)$ to denote the sequence of i leading to I_i and h, respectively. A mixed strategy of a player can now be represented as a *realization plan* $(r_i : \Sigma_i \to \mathbb{R})$. A realization plan for a sequence σ_i is the probability that player i will play σ_i under the assumption that the opponent plays to allow the actions specified in σ_i to be played.

Solution Concepts in EFGs. We provide a formal definition of Nash Equilibrium (NE) and its extension into games with subrational players. We say that a strategy profile $\delta_{NE} = (\delta_1, ..., \delta_n) \in \Delta$ is a *Nash equilibrium* if and only if for each player i it holds that δ_i is a best response to δ_{-i}. NE assumes that the structure of the game is always common knowledge among the players. Now we explain a concept introducing uncertainty in the game being played. The uncertainty is expressed as a probability distribution over the set of possible opponents the player can face. We consider a simplified scenario in which the defender is of a given type, but there might be several types of the attackers: a *Type-revealing game* based on EFG G is a tuple $B_G = (G, n, \overline{p}, \overline{BR}, \overline{u},)$, such that $\overline{p_k}$ is the probability that a defender plays a modified game G with the attacker's utility function $\overline{u_k}$ and best-response function $\overline{BR_k} : \Delta_d \to \Delta_a$, $k \in \{1, \ldots, n\}$.

In the Type-revealing game, the type of the attacker is revealed to the defender after the game begins. In contrast, in a standard *Bayesian game* [7] the type of the attacker is not revealed. An example of a Bayesian game is depicted in Fig. 1. The attacker is one of the two possible types: the defender faces the first type with probability 0.7 and the second type with probability 0.3. Since he cannot distinguish the individual types, the former singleton game states are now grouped into information sets. Both types of attackers are purely rational utility maximizing players, but with different utilities. For example, in case the defender decides to play action b_3, the best response of the first type is to play b_8, while the best-response of the second types is b_7.

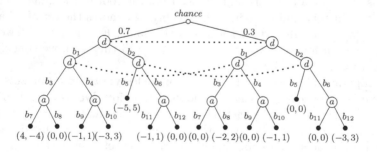

Fig. 1. A Bayesian extension game. Each internal node is labeled by a player who acts in this node. Under every terminal node is a tuple of utilities obtained by the defender and the attacker, respectively. Nodes in the same information set are connected by a dashed line.

Computing Solution Concepts. The baseline approach for computing an exact NE in zero-sum games with imperfect information is via mathematical programming [4,13]. For computing strategies in large EFGs we use a state-of-the-art algorithm for approximating NE called *Counterfactual Regret Minimization (CFR)* [26]. CFR is an iterative algorithm, which in every iteration updates the strategies of the players in order to minimize a weighted sum of regret at each decision. The average strategies then approach NE. Because the individual attackers choose their strategies according to a specific best-response method, we use a variant of CFR called CFR-BR [8]. In this algorithm, one player updates his strategy using CFR (the defender), while the second player (the attacker) computes his best response against this strategy. The algorithm can be modified for a Type-revealing or Bayesian game by considering a game tree as in Fig. 1. It can consider several methods for computing response functions, so that each attacker type can behave according to a different behavioral model.

3 Game Model

The domain we use in this work is a variant of the "FlipIt" game [23]. This game is motivated by a cybersecurity scenario where an attacker can perform a stealthy attack to gain control of a resource (e.g., install malware on a host or steal a password) that may not be immediately detected by the defender. However, the defender can take actions to restore control to the defender (e.g., performing a virus scan or resetting a password).

A two-player FlipIt game is defined as a tuple $F = (V, t, \rho, \gamma)$. The game is played by a defender and an attacker on an empty graph with nodes V for a finite number of simultaneous rounds t. There is a positive reward $\rho : V \to \mathbb{R}^+$ and a positive cost $\gamma : V \to \mathbb{R}^+$ associated with each node $v \in V$. At the beginning of the game, the defender controls all nodes. In each round, each player selects one node to flip, i.e. to attempt to gain control of. The flipping action is successful when the current owner of the node does not also flip it. For every flipping action, the players pay the cost assigned to the node. At the end of every round the players collect the total rewards from all nodes they control. After t rounds the game ends and the final utilities are the sum of the rewards collected in the individual rounds. We consider the version of the game when after every round the players are provided with the action of the other player. To represent the FlipIt game, we use the EFG formalism. For example, a representation of a FlipIt game with 2 nodes: N_0 and N_1, played for 1 round is depicted in Fig. 2.

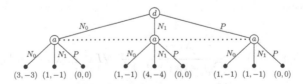

Fig. 2. An example of EFG representation of a FlipIt game with 2 nodes (N_0 and N_1) played for 1 round. The game also contains a pass action (P). The figure follows a standard denotation of an extensive-form game.

We assume $\rho(N_0) = 2, \gamma(N_0) = 3, \rho(N_1) = 3$ and $\gamma(N_1) = 4$. Then we define both a Type-revealing and a Bayesian game based on this game with multiple attacker types. Each types is described by its behavioral model (see the next section). A NE in these games are computed using CFR-BR.

4   Models for Attacker Behavior Prediction

The existing attacker models (QR, SUQR, PT) for SSGs consider only one-shot or repeated SSGs with only one generic type of attacker or as many attackers as the number of attacks. However, these assumptions may cause the defender to adopt a suboptimal strategy if the correct model is not used for the attacker. In this work, we model the interaction between a defender and an attacker using a Type-revealing game and a Bayesian game models. We solve the game with CFR-BR where the BR is provided by the attacker. Next, we present a behavioral game theoretic model for modeling attacker behavior to provide best responses (BR) against defender strategy using CFR in our behavioral game based on the EFG model where the defender knows which type of attacker he is facing.

Agent Quantal Response Model. In this work we consider the Agent Quantal Response Equilibrium (AQRE) [15] which is compatible with the behavioral strategy representation to support the sequential interaction between the attacker and the defender. Agent Quantal Response (AQR) model in an EFG assumes that different information sets of a player are played by different agents. Each agent of each player has an additive payoff disturbance that is added to the continuation payoff for each possible action at that agent's information set. All the agents share the same payoff function. In the model each agent, i simply chooses the maximum of $\hat{u}_{a,I}$ at information set $I \in \mathcal{I}_a$ and acts independently of the other agents of the same player.

For the AQR model there is only one parameter, λ, which has a value from 0 to ∞. When $\lambda = 0$ the model behaves like a pure random agent, and when $\lambda = \infty$ the AQR model converges to the rational best response model. A logit-AQRE is any solution to the set of k equations: one equation for each action in each information set of each agent. In Eq. 1, Agent Quantal Best Response $AQBR(r_d, a)$ gives the probability for playing action a for the attacker in information set $I \in \mathcal{I}_a$. Equations 2, 3, and 4 define how to compute attacker's expected utility u_a using defender's realization plan r_d in case h is an inner node. Otherwise, the leaf utility is used.

$$AQBR(\lambda|a, I, r_d) = \frac{e^{\lambda \hat{u}(r_d, a)}}{\sum_{a' \in A(I)} e^{\lambda \hat{u}(r_d, a')}} \quad \forall I \in \mathcal{I}_a, \forall a \in A(I) \tag{1}$$

$$\hat{u}(r_d, a) = \frac{\sum_{h \in I} r_d(seq_d(h)) u_a(h, a)}{\sum_{h \in I} r_d(seq_d(h))} \quad \forall I \in \mathcal{I}_a, \forall a \in A(I) \tag{2}$$

$$u_a(h, a) = \sum_{\substack{I' \in \mathcal{I}_a, h' \in I' \\ seq_a(h') = seq_a(h)a}} \frac{u_a(h')r_d(seq_d(h'))}{r_d(seq_d(h))}$$

$$\forall I \in \mathcal{I}_a, \forall h \in I, \forall a \in A(I) \tag{3}$$

$$u_a(h) = \sum_{a \in A(h)} u_i(h, a)AQBR(r_d, a) \quad \forall I \in \mathcal{I}_a, \forall h \in I \tag{4}$$

5   Parameter Estimation

We now describe how we collected data from the AMT participants using the StrataFlip game so that we can analyze different attacker behavior and fit the parameters of the QR model according to different attacker groups.

StrataFlip Game. The StrataFlip game is based on the description provided in Sect. 3. In this game, two players compete over a network with multiple nodes. A node can be any machine in the network. In our experiment we used six nodes: Node A(10/8), Node B(10/2), Node C(4/2), Node D(4/8), Node E(10/5), Node F(0/0). Each node has a reward (ρ) and a cost (γ). For example, Node A has reward 10 and cost 8. The defender/attacker has to pay the cost each time he wants to defend/capture a node. Each node can be either captured by the attacker (red) or not (blue) as shown in Fig. 3.

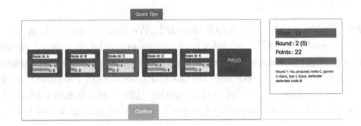

Fig. 3. Game interface of the StrataFlip game

The game has five rounds. Initially, the defender has control over all of the nodes. The purpose of the attacker/participant is to take over control from the defender by attacking nodes. In each round, the defender defends a node and the attacker attacks a node. If the attacker or defender chooses to attack/defend a node he/she has to pay the cost associated with that node. If the defender and attacker do not make the same move then the attacker takes control of the node and receives the reward associated with that node and pays the cost. If both players make the same move then the previous controller of the resource retains the control and attacker and defender both pay the cost. In each round, the user interface shows the following information: total points, current round, time, action history (log), and who currently controls each node. After each round the attacker receives points for all the nodes he controls. Red and blue mean the attacker or the defender controls a node, respectively. The attacker is able to observe the effect of the defender action in the next round. Each player tries to maximize their utility by controlling the nodes. The defender uses a pre-computed Nash Equilibrium strategy by formulating the StrataFlip game as a zero-sum EFG (strategic defender) and a random strategy where the actions played by the defender were completely random (random defender). The attackers are the AMT participants. In the next section, we describe how we collected data from AMT using the StrataFlip game to analyze attacker behavior.

AMT Experiment. We recruited 155 participants using AMT. After agreeing to participate the participants filled out the Short Dark Triad (SD3) [9,14] scale. The participants were given instructions on how to play the StrataFlip game. Next, they answered some comprehension check questions. The participants were not allowed to go ahead until they answered correctly. If they answered incorrectly, proper instructions were given on why the answer is wrong. Then they played a practice game where the participants could make themselves familiar with the StrataFlip game.

Each participant played six StrataFlip games: three against the strategic defender and three against the random defender. Fifty percent of all the participants played against the strategic defender first and later against the random defender and the other fifty percent played the random defender first and then the strategic defender. We collected all the participant's gameplay in each round including temporal data.

Parameter Estimation for AQR Model. We now describe how we estimate the λ parameter of the AQR model which represents the degree of rationality of a player in a certain sense. As λ reaches ∞ the response of the player approaches perfectly rational behavior. We use Maximum Likelihood Estimation (MLE) [6] to estimate the parameter of the AQR model. The idea behind MLE is to find parameter estimates that maximize the probability of seeing what is observed in the data.

Given the defender's realization plan r_d and M samples of the players' choices, the following equation defines the log-likelihood function for a given λ:

$$\log(L(\lambda|r_d)) = \sum_{I \in \mathcal{I}_a} \sum_{a \in A(I_k)} M_a(I) \log(AQBR(\lambda|a, I, r_d)), \qquad (5)$$

where $AQBR(\tau_j, I, r_d)$ is the probability of playing action τ_j in sample j in information set $I \in \mathcal{I}_a$ for attacker, and $M_a(I)$ is the number of samples taking action a in information set I. An optimal $\hat{\lambda}$ is then selected as λ maximizing the loglikelihood function. For the computation we used a modified binary search.

5.1   Attacker Grouping

The AQR model described above is used to model different attacker types depending on the parameter values that can be fitted to different attacker types. For example the parameter λ_P in the AQR model can either be fitted to one generic group with the full attacker population P, or we can have $\{\lambda_{p_1}, \lambda_{p_2}, ..., \lambda_{p_q}\}$ fitted to different subgroups where $P = \{p_1, p_2, ...p_q\}$. Detecting the attacker groups can be done in many ways. Next we present how we detect different attacker groups $\{p_1, p_2, ...p_q\}$ among the attacker population P.

Clustering Using Attacker Behaviors (c_{bhv}). Clustering using attacker behaviors (c_{bhv}) is based on the actions played by the AMT participants in the online StrataFlip experiment. For features we used the node value, node cost, and points received for the node attacked in each round. We used k-means and density based clustering to detect the best groupings of attackers $\{p_1, p_2, ...p_q\}$. The best number of possible groups we could find is three ($k = 3$).

Clustering Using DT Scores (c_{DT}). Clustering using DT scores (c_{DT}) is based on the three personality scores, Machiavellian score (s_m), Narcissist score (s_n) and Psychopath score (s_p), computed from the Dark Triad survey given to the AMT participants at the beginning of the AMT experiment. There is no straightforward way to differentiate these three personalities since there is no pure Machiavellian or no pure Narcissist or no pure Psychopath. We tried density-based clustering and k-means clustering with $k = 2, 3$ using the three personalities scores as features. We found the best clustering when $k = 3$.

Grouping Using DT Maximum Score (c_{DTM}). Another way we can find different groups inside a generic group is to use the individual maximum DT score among the three scores: s_m, s_n, s_p. So, we can have three groupings where each group represent each personality. An individual is assigned to a group for which he has the maximum DT score.

6   Experiments

We now show that differences in opponent models and differences in the ways in which these models are integrated into the game model can significantly impact the quality of the strategy of the defender. We consider three cases: a generic subrational attacker population P in an EFG model, different attacker groups (p_1, p_2, p_3) in a Type-revealing game model and also in a Bayesian game model. We also show the rationality and strategic differences between different attacker groups after separating them using different grouping techniques.

Game Values. In our first experiment, we show defender game values considering different variations of attacker groups using different game models. Game value is the expected utility of a player when following an optimal strategy.

The left and the middle graphs in the Fig. 4 show the results. In the first column the defender considers a rational attacker, but actually, he faces a subrational attacker (*r-sr* scenario). We assumed λ_P for population P for the actual attacker. In the second column, we show the game value when the defender knows the actual attacker with λ_P for population P (*sr-sr* scenario). The next three columns show game values when the defender considers different groups of attacker (p_1, p_2, p_3) in the variant of EFG model (where he knows the attacker types) and in the Bayesian Game model. We consider three different grouping techniques: c_{bhv}, c_{DT} and c_{DTM}. In Fig. 4 (ignore the legends for the first two graphs) we see that the game value is noticeably higher when the defender models a subrational attacker than when he models a rational attacker. That means the defender was able to exploit the attacker strategies rather than being too conservative.

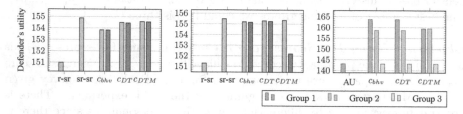

Fig. 4. Apply legends to the rightmost graph only. Defender's expected utility when attacker faced (Left) a strategic defender and (Middle) a random defender in the former EFG (first two columns), in the Type-revealing game (last three results in lime) and in the Bayesian game (last three results in cyan). (Right) Defender's expected utility against different attacker's empirical strategy including the generic attacker (AU) against a strategic defender.

To be sure that different attacker groups have significant strategical differences, we computed the defender's utility against the empirical strategies of different attacker groups. In Fig. 4 (rightmost graph), where the defender considered the attackers separately in separate EFGs, we can see that there are significant differences between the defender's expected utilities. That means that the defender can potentially exploit the strategical differences of different attacker groups by using tailored strategies targeted towards specific attacker subgroups. Overall, the results confirm that the defender can explicitly exploit a single subrational opponent. However, such a strategy can be exploitable by the attacker if the model is not precise. When facing a group of several types of the attackers, the strategy of the defender is more conservative since there is a more rational attacker present in the group. The overall quality of the strategy (in terms the expected utility of the defender) in the settings with groups of models of the attackers, however, is comparable to the setting with just a single model of the attacker. This may present a way of exploiting weak attackers while still being able to defend against more rational ones.

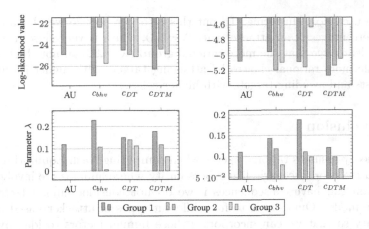

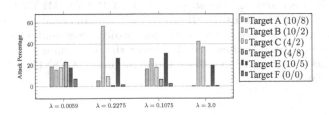

Fig. 5. (Up) Log-likelihood values and (Down) λ parameter values for different grouping techniques compared to one generic group (AU) when attacker faced (Left) a strategic defender and (Right) a random defender.

The MLE technique fits parameters when the Log-Likelihood Value (LLV) is maximized or the negative of the LLV is minimized. In our experiment, we fit the parameter by maximizing the LLV. As we can see in Fig. 5, for each of the game instances Log-likelihood value is almost same when we used different grouping techniques instead of considering only one generic group P.

Targeted λ Value. In our next experiment, we show more targeted values of the the AQR model parameter considering different grouping techniques. Figure 5 shows the λ value we found for all the users against the strategic and random defender. The results show that dividing the users into different subgroups highlight differences between their level of rationality (different values of their λ). We found that the error percentage of the MLE to estimate λ is about 6.7%. However, this may vary depending on the number of data points available.

Fig. 6. Attack pattern by different groups of attackers on different targets for c_{bhv}.

Attack Pattern. Next, we present Fig. 6, which shows the percentage of attacks on different targets by different groups of attackers against a strategic defender when we used c_{bhv} clustering. To put this into perspective we also added the attack percentages of an attacker with $\lambda = 3.0$, which is very close to rational. We can clearly see that the more rational group ($\lambda = .2275$), not the simulated one, made more rational choices by attacking targets with higher rewards and lower costs and avoiding targets with higher costs.

7   Conclusion

Game theory assumes rational agents when computing Nash Equilibrium. However, in a real-world scenario like cybersecurity where humans are involved, this assumption can have consequences if we do not consider human factors into the game model. Our goal is to find different types of attacker based on their personality so that we can incorporate those human factors to identify different attack types and predict their actions to provide better defender strategy against different types of attackers. We show that there are strategic differences between different groups of attackers and the defender can benefit by modeling sub-rational attackers. In our initial analysis we have considered only the quantal-response model, which is well established in the behavioral game theory literature. While this model does capture at least some of the limited rationality of the human players, it appears to be too simple with a single parameter to allow the defender to effectively target different groups of attackers. In future work we plan to investigate other models that allow for more fine-grained predictions such as SUQR. In addition, we plan to investigate ways that a defender can safely exploit (uncertain) knowledge of the type of opponent he is facing when using such behavioral models.

Acknowledgment. This research was sponsored by the Army Research Laboratory and was accomplished under Cooperative Agreement Number W911NF-13-2-0045 (ARL Cyber Security CRA). The views and conclusions contained in this document are those of the authors and should not be interpreted as representing the official policies, either expressed or implied, of the Army Research Laboratory or the U.S. Government. The U.S. Government is authorized to reproduce and distribute reprints for Government purposes not with standing any copyright notation here on. The authors also acknowledge the support of the OP VVV MEYS funded project CZ.02.1.01/0.0/0.0/16_019/000 0765 "Research Center for Informatics". Access to computing and storage facilities owned by parties and projects contributing to the National Grid Infrastructure MetaCentrum provided under the programme "Projects of Large Research, Development, and Innovations Infrastructures" (CESNET LM2015042), is greatly appreciated.

References

1. Abbasi, Y.D., Short, M., Sinha, A., Sintov, N., Zhang, C., Tambe, M.: Human adversaries in opportunistic crime security games: evaluating competing bounded rationality models. In: Proceedings of the Third Annual Conference on Advances in Cognitive Systems ACS, p. 2 (2015)

2. Anderson, J.R.: ACT: a simple theory of complex cognition. Am. Psychol. **51**(4), 355 (1996)
3. Basak, A., Shelby, C., Gutierrez, M., Černý, J.: StrataFlip Game. http://iasrl1.cs.utep.edu/ (2017)
4. Bosansky, B., Kiekintveld, C., Lisy, V., Pechoucek, M.: An exact double-oracle algorithm for zero-sum extensive-form games with imperfect information. J. Artif. Intell. Res. **51**, 829–866 (2014)
5. Durkota, K., Lisý, V., Kiekintveld, C., Horák, K., Bošanský, B., Pevný, T.: Optimal strategies for detecting data exfiltration by internal and external attackers. In: Rass, S., Kiekintveld, C., Fang, F., Schauer, S. (eds.) GameSec 2017. LNCS, vol. 10575, pp. 171–192. Springer, Cham (2017). https://doi.org/10.1007/978-3-319-68711-7_10
6. Friedman, J., Hastie, T., Tibshirani, R.: The Elements of Statistical Learning. Springer series in statistics, vol. 1. Springer, New York (2001). https://doi.org/10.1007/978-0-387-84858-7
7. Harsanyi, J.C.: Games with incomplete information played by "bayesian" players, i-iii part i. The basic model. Manag. Sci. **14**(3), 159–182 (1967)
8. Johanson, M., Bard, N., Burch, N., Bowling, M.: Finding optimal abstract strategies in extensive-form games. In: AAAI (2012)
9. Jones, D.N., Paulhus, D.L.: Introducing the short dark triad (SD3) a brief measure of dark personality traits. Assessment **21**(1), 28–41 (2014)
10. Kahneman, D., Tversky, A.: Prospect theory: an analysis of decision under risk. In: Handbook of the Fundamentals of Financial Decision Making: Part I, pp. 99–127. World Scientific (2013)
11. Kar, D., Fang, F., Delle Fave, F., Sintov, N., Tambe, M.: A game of thrones: when human behavior models compete in repeated stackelberg security games. In: Proceedings of the 2015 International Conference on Autonomous Agents and Multiagent Systems, pp. 1381–1390. IFAAMAS (2015)
12. Kiekintveld, C., Lisý, V., Píbil, R.: Game-theoretic foundations for the strategic use of honeypots in network security. In: Jajodia, S., Shakarian, P., Subrahmanian, V.S., Swarup, V., Wang, C. (eds.) Cyber Warfare. AIS, vol. 56, pp. 81–101. Springer, Cham (2015). https://doi.org/10.1007/978-3-319-14039-1_5
13. Koller, D., Megiddo, N., von Stengel, B.: Efficient computation of equilibria for extensive two-person games. Games Econ. Behav. **14**, 247–259 (1996)
14. Maples, J.L., Lamkin, J., Miller, J.D.: A test of two brief measures of the dark triad: the dirty dozen and short dark triad. Psychol. Assess. **26**(1), 326 (2014)
15. McKelvey, R.D., Palfrey, T.R.: Quantal response equilibria for extensive form games. Exp. Econ. **1**(1), 9–41 (1998)
16. Nash, J.: Non-cooperative games. Ann. Math., 286–295 (1951)
17. Nguyen, T.H., Yang, R., Azaria, A., Kraus, S., Tambe, M.: Analyzing the effectiveness of adversary modeling in security games. In: AAAI (2013)
18. Nochenson, A., Grossklags, J., et al.: A behavioral investigation of the Flipit game. In: Proceedings of the 12th Workshop on the Economics of Information Security (WEIS) (2013)
19. Paulhus, D.L., Williams, K.M.: The dark triad of personality: narcissism, machiavellianism, and psychopathy. J. Res. Pers. **36**(6), 556–563 (2002)
20. Píbil, R., Lisý, V., Kiekintveld, C., Bošanský, B., Pěchouček, M.: Game theoretic model of strategic honeypot selection in computer networks. In: Grossklags, J., Walrand, J. (eds.) GameSec 2012. LNCS, vol. 7638, pp. 201–220. Springer, Heidelberg (2012). https://doi.org/10.1007/978-3-642-34266-0_12

21. Reitter, D., Grossklags, J., Nochenson, A.: Risk-seeking in a continuous game of timing. In: Proceedings of the 13th International Conference on Cognitive Modeling (ICCM), pp. 397–403 (2013)
22. Shiva, S., Roy, S., Dasgupta, D.: Game theory for cyber security. In: Proceedings of the Sixth Annual Workshop on Cyber Security and Information Intelligence Research, p. 34. ACM (2010)
23. Van Dijk, M., Juels, A., Oprea, A., Rivest, R.L.: Flipit: the game of "stealthy takeover". J. Cryptol. **26**(4), 655–713 (2013)
24. Yang, R., Ford, B., Tambe, M., Lemieux, A.: Adaptive resource allocation for wildlife protection against illegal poachers. In: Proceedings of the 2014 International Conference on Autonomous Agents and Multi-agent Systems, pp. 453–460. IFAAMAS (2014)
25. Yang, R., Kiekintveld, C., Ordonez, F., Tambe, M., John, R.: Improving resource allocation strategy against human adversaries in security games. In: IJCAI Proceedings-International Joint Conference on Artificial Intelligence, vol. 22, p. 458 (2011)
26. Zinkevich, M., Johanson, M., Bowling, M., Piccione, C.: Regret minimization in games with incomplete information. In: Platt, J., Koller, D., Singer, Y., Roweis, S. (eds.) Advances in Neural Information Processing Systems 20 (NIPS), pp. 1729–1736. MIT Press, Cambridge (2008)

Author Index